KINGDOMS OF EUROPE

Other Books by Gene Gurney

THE AIR FORCE MUSEUM

AMERICAN HISTORY IN WAX MUSEUMS

AMERICANS INTO ORBIT

AMERICANS TO THE MOON

ARLINGTON NATIONAL CEMETERY

BEAUTIFUL WASHINGTON, D.C.

THE B-29 STORY

CHRONOLOGY OF WORLD AVIATION

COSMONAUTS IN ORBIT

FIVE DOWN AND GLORY

FLYING ACES OF WORLD WAR I

FLYING MINUTEMEN - THE STORY OF THE CIVIL AIR PATROL

GREAT AIR BATTLES

HIGHER, FASTER AND FARTHER

HOW TO SAVE YOUR LIFE ON THE NATION'S HIGHWAYS AND BYWAYS

JOURNEY OF THE GIANTS

THE LIBRARY OF CONGRESS

MARYLAND

MONTICELLO

MOUNT VERNON

NORTH AND SOUTH KOREA

THE PENTAGON

THE PICTORIAL HISTORY OF THE U.S. ARMY

PRIVATE PILOT'S HANDBOOK OF NAVIGATION

PRIVATE PILOT'S HANDBOOK OF WEATHER

THE P-38 LIGHTNING

ROCKET AND MISSILE TECHNOLOGY

THE SMITHSONIAN INSTITUTION

TEST PILOTS

UNIDENTIFIED FLYING OBJECTS

THE UNITED STATES COAST GUARD

WALK IN SPACE - THE STORY OF PROJECT GEMINI

THE WAR IN THE AIR

WOMEN ON THE MARCH

KINGDOMS OF EUROPE

An Illustrated Encyclopedia
of Ruling Monarchs
from Ancient Times
to the Present

Gene Gurney

Crown Publishers, Inc. • New York

Inquiries should be addressed to Crown Publishers, Inc., 225 Park
Avenue South, New York, New York 10003
and represented in Canada by the Canadian MANDA Group
Manufactured in the United States of America
Library of Congress Cataloging-in-Publication Data
Gurney, Gene.
Kingdoms of Europe. 1. Kings and rulers—Biography. 2. World
politics—Dictionaries. I. Title.
D107.G85 1982   909   81-579
ISBN 0-517-54395-8   AACR2

Book design by Deborah and Richard Waxberg

10 9 8 7 6

Contents

Acknowledgments

The text for this book was mainly derived from three sources: the U.S. Army *Area Handbooks,* Francis R. Niglutsch's publications *The Story of the Greatest Nations,* and the U.S. Department of State's *Background Notes* publications on the countries of the world. The first, started by the War Department in World War II, were published by Alfred A. Knopf and served as a definitive study of the various foreign nations with which we were engaged in that war. Later, the research, writing, and publication was taken over for the Department of the Army by the Foreign Area Studies of the American University in Washington, D.C. The individual publications for the foreign countries were then called *Area Handbooks* and were made available to all armed forces and government personnel concerned with obtaining the best possible information about nations around the world. *The Story of the Greatest Nations* is probably the most comprehensive history about foreign nations ever written in the United States. (Additional important works I consulted were: Ridpath's *History of the World,* Henry Smith Williams's *Historians' History of the World,* and Henry Cabot Lodge's twenty-five volumes of *History of Nations.*) The third primary source was the U.S. State Department's *Background Notes,* which are published—and updated frequently—as a political science and historical aid for its personnel around the world.

The lists of the thousands of royal sovereigns covered in this book were compiled from various sources, mainly, *Kings, Rulers and Statesmen* by L. F. Egan, *Rulers and Governments of the World* by Bertold Spuler, and Burke's *Royal Families of the World.* Where my lists differ from these three are in the spellings, dates, and so forth, where the individual country's embassy or government's historical records showed better evidence of the information.

For the photographs and illustrations, I have deep-felt gratitude toward the many sources who helped me acquire the "pictures" for the book. Bibliothèque nationale, Paris, has, in my estimation, the greatest collection of royalty illustrations in the entire world. Also, the two special collections at the New York Public Library and the Newark (New Jersey) Public Library are quite extensive. My thanks to all three. The next category would be the individual foreign embassies in Washington, D.C., who were an endless source for acquiring from their countries, all of the photographs that I needed to illustrate this book. In particular, may I thank the Swedish Institute in Stockholm. And, last but not least, the United Nations Information Service-Photo Section in New York City.

I welcome any comments or questions and hope to incorporate them into the next edition of the book. Also, my personal thanks to Billy B. Shaddix for supplying photographs of the President and the First Lady with visiting royalty. Thank you one and all for making this volume possible.

GENE GURNEY

KINGDOMS
OF
EUROPE

I
The Roman Empire and Italy

Italian civilization is ancient—a product of the Roman Empire and the source of the Renaissance—but Italy as a nation-state is relatively young, emerging only in 1861 as a political entity. The name Italy is one of great antiquity, used for nearly three thousand years to identify the boot-shaped peninsula that juts from the Alps and the Po Valley into the Mediterranean Sea. It was the Greeks who coined the term *Italy* to describe a spacious country good for grazing cattle. Poets and patriots, ancient and modern, have heard in it the name of their homeland. The Roman political reformer of the second century B.C., Tiberius Gracchus, understood this when at the end of the Punic Wars he protested, "The wild beasts of Italy have their dens and holes and hiding places, while they who fight and die in defense of Italy enjoy indeed the air and light, but nothing more." Vergil wrote of the exiled Aeneas that he was "the first to sail from the land of Troy and reach Italy." Dante, Petrarch, and Machiavelli all understood that Italy had cultural if not political boundaries that set it apart from the rest of Europe. Nineteenth-century European statesmen dismissed a politically disunited Italy as a mere geographical expression. Italy's cultural, emotional, physical, and political boundaries have historically seldom coincided, but that an Italy and an Italian people have existed from antiquity has been recognized by Italians—although they may have called themselves Venetians and Florentines—and by foreigners alike.

Three wars with Austria and an open breach with the papacy were the price paid to complete the long process of Italian unification, known as the *Risorgimento* (Revival), and to establish a national monarchy under the House of Savoy in the late nineteenth century. As one of the victorious powers in World War I, Italy annexed additional territory. Parliamentary institutions broke down, however, in the atmosphere of depression, disillusionment, and fear that gripped the country in the aftermath of the war, and the country succumbed to Benito Mussolini's Fascist dictatorship. Mussolini led Italy to defeat as the ally of Nazi Germany in World War II. Elements of the Italian army and the anti-Fascist partisan movement participated, however, in the liberation of Italy after Mussolini's ouster in 1943. The monarchy was abolished after a plebiscite in 1946 and a republic established.

EARLY INHABITANTS

The Latins and other Italic tribes, speakers of Indo-European languages who had settled in Italy by 2000 B.C., provided the basic genetic stock. There was a disparity in the levels of civilization achieved by early Italic cultures, which were usually intensely local in their expression. These tribal groups consolidated unsuccessfully in common defense against the intrusion of the Etruscans, who appeared in Italy about 1200 B.C. The origin of the Etruscans, whose influence and civilization in Italy were not surpassed until the emergence of Latin Rome as an independent power, is a mystery that has confounded scholars for centuries. Archaeological evidence of their civilization, though plentiful, is subject to contradictory interpretations. Their language, its alphabet derived from Greek, had no known affinities with other languages and is undecipherable. The explanation put forward by Herodotus that the Etruscans had migrated from Asia Minor has remained a popular speculation. Although their origin is obscure, much is known of their politics and art. It was the Etruscans who introduced the city-state as a form of political organization to Italy. Although politically disunited and often hostile, the city-states of Etruria were linked in a religious confederation and were capable of concerted action against common enemies. Rivals of the Greeks, they nonetheless assimilated Hellenic culture and transmitted it to the Italic peoples whom they had subdued.

In the second millennium B.C. lines of trade extended from the Aegean Islands into Italy, the depot for amber

1

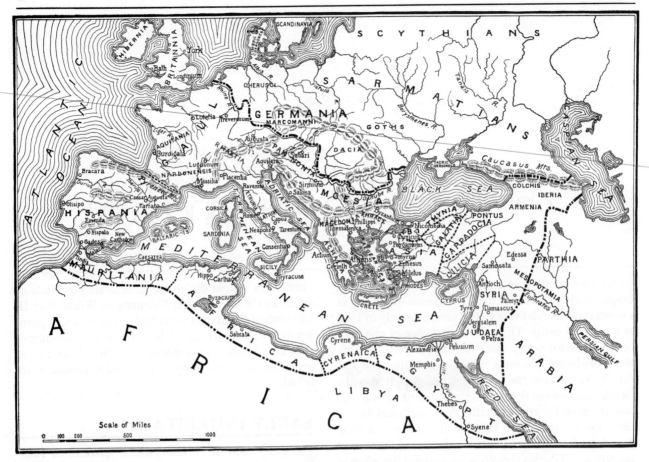

The Roman Empire

and copper brought from beyond the Alps. The first Greek colonies were planted in southern Italy in the eighth century B.C. Politically and economically independent of their mother cities, the colonies in Magna Graecia (Greater Greece)—as Sicily, Catania, Apulia, and Lucania were called in antiquity—remained an integral part of the Hellenic world. Some of the city-states of Magna Graecia—for example, Syracuse on Sicily—were powerful and prosperous and played a part in the political life of Greece and the Aegean. In Italy the Greeks also manifested their suicidal tendency for warring among themselves. The Greeks were challenged by the Phoenician colony of Carthage, which in its drive for hegemony in the western Mediterranean settled enclaves in Sicily and Sardinia in the sixth century B.C. and made allies of the Etruscans. The Etruscans, in their turn, were pressed by waves of Celts who crossed the Alps and settled in the northern plains.

ROME

The origins of Rome are the stuff of myth, not history. It is probable that in the eighth century B.C. (756 B.C. is the traditional date) Latin villagers and refugees from a countryside harassed by hill tribes sought safety behind the wooden palisades constructed on the Palatine Hill overlooking a crossing on the Tiber River. Legend re-

lates that these outcasts took as their first king Romulus, descendant of Aeneas the Trojan, and that he gave his name to the city. The families, clans, and tribes to which all citizens claimed ties by blood or adoption were the basis of the city-states' social structure and military and political organization. A hereditary Etruscan monarchy was overthrown and a republic established in 510 B.C. The Etruscans, however, left their imprint on Roman institutions, particularly in the identification of religion and the state. The proverbial Roman habits of austerity are also thought to have been a reaction to the hedonism of their Etruscan overlords, but both tendencies remained as strains in Roman and later, Italian, thought. The political history of the Roman Republic, governed by a patrician oligarchy, was marked even in its early stages by the persistent and ultimately successful struggle of the plebeians—as a class—to gain an effective voice in government and to improve their social and economic status.

The building of the Roman Empire was begun with the slow subjugation of Italy and the gradual assimilation of its diverse peoples into the Roman state system. The poet Vergil eulogized the toil it took to make the Roman state, but Roman expansion in Italy was not deliberate or the result of a preconceived strategy. It developed haphazardly from commitments made to

The story of the finding of the two lost children of Rome, Romulus and Remus, is to this day told by the mothers of Italy to their children. The twin brothers were put in a basket and set afloat in the Tiber River by a cruel uncle who was acting as the king of Alba Longa, a throne that rightfully belonged to Romulus and Remus. They were found by a shepherd, Faustulus, on the river's edge, being nursed by a she-wolf. This scene is a national emblem of Italy and appears on its coins and stamps. Here we see Romulus being handed to the shepherd's wife.

Aeneas the Trojan on his travels goes to Carthage and meets Dido, its founder.

other Latin towns and from intervention into the political squabbles of the Greek cities that took Rome step by step from conquest to conquest. Victories in the Punic Wars against Carthage gave Rome mastery of the Mediterranean and put Italy at the center of an empire that would stretch from the British Isles to the Euphrates River at its height in the first century A.D.

During his dictatorship Julius Caesar pledged to return the Republic to the people but, while preserving the name *republic,* the state evolved toward a monarchical system. His statue was erected in the Capitol, and another bore the fulsome inscription, "Caesar the demigod." His image was to be carried in the procession of the gods, and a golden chair was provided for him in the Senate house. The month Quintilis had its name changed to Julius, which we still retain as July. While he was not king in name he was in substance, for no monarch could have been more absolute. He was made dictator for ten years, which was soon changed to perpetual dictator, and he was hailed as imperator for life. This title was one

Julius Caesar, the greatest Roman general of all time

In his conquests to the north, Caesar defeats the Gauls. Here their king, Vercingetorix, is seen surrendering to Caesar.

that was given under the Republic to a victorious general (for the word means "commander"), but it was always laid aside at the close of the military command. By clipping the word *imperator,* it will be seen that it readily becomes *emperor.*

He had obtained power by overriding the laws, but such is the necessity of all revolutions, and having secured that power, he was determined to use it for the good of the people. He laid the foundations broad and strong. He promoted distinguished and trustworthy foreigners to places of dignity in the city; Gauls and others were introduced into the Senate; whole classes of useful subjects, such as those of the medical profession, were admitted to the franchise, and colonies were planted at Carthage and Corinth. An elaborate geographical survey was made of the immense regions in his dominion, and a most important project undertaken was the condensation and arrangement into a compact code of the thousands of fragments of the old Roman laws. This work had been dreamed of by Cicero and others, who were forced to believe it an impossible task, but Caesar set about it with such practical sense and system that it assuredly would have been completed, had his life been

spared to the usual limit. As it was, six centuries had to elapse before the glory of the work was earned by Justinian, the imperial legislator.

One notable achievement was the reform of the calendar. The Roman year had been calculated on the basis of 354 days, with the intercalation or insertion every second year of a month of twenty-two and twenty-three days respectively; but another day had been added to the 354, so as to secure an odd or fortunate number, to meet which an intricate process, that only the scholars understood, was brought into use. The jumble became intolerable. Caesar was a good astronomer, and with the aid of Sosigenes, the most eminent in the science, the Julian calendar was devised. This is still known by that name, and makes each year to consist of 365 days, with an additional day added to every fourth or leap year. Even this is not mathematically exact; and the slight error, in the course of centuries, grew into an importance which required the correction made by Pope Gregory XIII, and put into effect in Rome, October 5–15, 1582. By this Gregorian calendar leap year is omitted at the close of each century whose figures are not divisible by four hundred.

Spain, Portugal, and a part of Italy adopted the Gregorian calendar with Rome; France, in December 1582, and the Catholic states of Germany in 1583. In Scotland it was adopted on January 1, 1600; and in the Protestant states of Germany in 1700. England and Ireland and the English colonies, however, kept the Julian calendar until 1752, when the change was made. Russia alone had retained the Julian system, its dates being thirteen days behind the rest of the world for a considerable period of time.

Julius Caesar was undoubtedly one of the greatest geniuses that ever lived. No general ever surpassed him in ability; he was a statesman, an orator, a mathematician, a historian, an architect, a jurist, and was preeminent in each capacity. His personality was impressive. Tall and dignified of presence, with a fair complexion and keen, expressive black eyes, he never wore a beard, and, as he grew bald, he showed that care for his looks which was almost a passion with him from youth. He wore a laurel chaplet, which hid his baldness and was at the same time a badge of his military greatness.

Having heard of civil unrest in Rome, Caesar crosses the Italian frontier at the Rubicon River. Knowing full well that he is in rebellion of standing orders to do so, he hesitated for a number of hours on the northern side. Once on the other side, he told his soldiers, "The die is cast."

CAESAR'S RULE AND DEATH

Many of the designs of this remarkable genius were never carried to completion, for the reason that his life was cut off in its prime and before he had time to do more than form the far-reaching plans. His scheme of changing the course of the Tiber, so as to enlarge the Campus Martius, was never followed out, nor did he cut through the Isthmus of Corinth.

He shone as a leader among the intellectual men of his time. While he was modest and affable in his intercourse, none talked or wrote better than he. His "Commentaries," despite the great length of some of the sentences,

Caesar invades Britain at the head of his legions (a legion of soldiers usually numbered about 4,200).

remains as a monument of his extraordinary skill as a historian and writer. He was abstemious among the free livers, and Cato has said of him that, of all the revolutionists of his day, he alone took up his task with perfect soberness at all times. In this respect he was a marked contrast to Alexander.

Moreover, it is impossible to study the character of the man without giving him credit for nobility of purpose. He judged rightly, when he felt that the only safety of Rome lay in its government by a wise, firm, and discreet ruler, and certainly there was none in that age who so fully met the requirements of the position as himself. The blot upon the character of Caesar is that he accepted the blind, sacrilegious idolatry of his people without protest, and that his private life was scandalous. He openly declared his unbelief in immortality, and lived defiantly with Cleopatra as his wife, though he never made her such.

He became haughty and capricious and, like Napoleon at St. Helena, dreamed of the glories of his past campaigns and longed to engage in more. Brooding over all this, he formed the plan of crushing the Parthians, conquering the barbarians of the North, and then attacking the Germans in the rear. In the closing months of the year 45 B.C., he ordered his legions to cross the Adriatic and meet at Illyricum, where he would speedily join them. He expected to be absent for a long time from Rome, and arranged for the succession of chief magistrates for the following two years. He entered on his fifth consulship on the first of January 44 B.C., Marcus Antonius being his colleague.

At that time, Gaius Octavius, the eighteen-year-old son of Caesar's sister, was in camp at Apollonia, receiving instructions in war from the ablest teachers. He showed great ability, but was of delicate health. Caesar let it be known that he intended to make Octavius his son by adoption, and to bequeath to him all those dignities which the Senate had declared hereditary in his family.

Human nature has been the same in all ages, and no man can rise to exalted position without incurring the deadly envy of those who have failed to keep pace with him. There were many such in Rome. They met in secret, whispered and plotted, and finally formed a conspiracy for taking the life of the imperator. The persons concerned in this hideous crime were sixty or eighty in number, and among them were many who had received marked favors at the hands of Caesar and professed the warmest devotion to him. The leader was Gaius Longinus Cassius, who had lately been appointed praetor. At the breaking out of the civil war, he had sided with Pompey, but was pardoned by Caesar, and besides being made praetor was promised the governorship of Syria in the following year. The more favors he received, the more malignant he seemed to become in his hatred of the benefactor. Associated with him were Decimus Brutus, Trebonius, Casca, Cimber, and more, all of whom were

Cleopatra, secreted in a rolled-up rug, is unveiled in the presence of Caesar.

Caesar in Egypt visits the grave site of Alexander the Great and views a waxen figure of the great conqueror.

Mark Antony offers to crown Caesar king of the Roman Empire, but Caesar refuses, saying, "I am no king, but Caesar. The Romans have no king but Jupiter." He knew full well that the people hated the title king ever since they overthrew their last one in 510 B.C.—Tarquinius the Proud and the Haughty. But Caesar, in fact, served as emperor until his assassination on March 15, 44 B.C. a day which is marked in infamy forever as "beware the Ides of March."

The Roman senators urge Pompey to bear arms and join them in a conspiracy to eliminate Caesar from control.

under deep obligations to Caesar for numerous favors.

These men knew they were taking frightful risks, for the crime they contemplated would shake Rome to its center and resound through the coming ages. They needed a strong name to help them through, and fixed upon Marcus Junius Brutus, who had also been a partisan of Pompey, but made his submission to Caesar after the battle of Pharsalia, and in the following year was appointed governor of Cisalpine Gaul. Brutus was a nephew of Cato, and claimed to trace his descent from a son of the famous Brutus who had founded the Republic, and whose other sons had perished by the axe of the executioner. His descendant was now made vain by the many favors shown him by Caesar, who one day remarked that, of all Romans, Brutus was the most worthy to succeed him. Brutus accepted this as earnest, and it was easy for the conspirators, by appealing to this, to procure his consent to become their leader in the dark counsels they often held together.

Caesar received hints of what was going on. He had dismissed the guard appointed for him, and was, therefore, continually exposed to treacherous attack. When his friends remonstrated because of the fearless way in which he walked through the streets, he replied that it was better to die and have done with it than to live in continual fear of dying. He scorned to take the least precautions, and since he had almost completed his preparations for leaving on his campaigns, his enemies determined to wait no longer. The Senate was convened for the Ides of March, the fifteenth day of the month, and it was agreed that on that day he should be struck down as he entered the Curia.

Caesar is said to have shown some hesitation, due to the many warnings he had received, but he naturally shrank from appearing timid. He determined to go. On the way along the Forum to the theater of Pompey, in the Campus, several persons pressed near to warn him of his peril. One man hastily shoved a paper into his hand and begged him to read it without an instant's delay. He paid no heed, but held the roll, when he reached the Senate house, remarking with a smile to the augur Spurinna, "The Ides of March have come." "Yes," replied the other, "but they are not yet passed."

As he entered the hall, his enemies kept near him so as to hold his friends at a distance. Caesar advanced to his seat, when Cimber immediately approached with a petition for the pardon of his brother. The others, as agreed upon, joined in the prayer with much importunity, seizing his hands and even attempting to embrace him. Caesar gently repelled their attentions, but they persisted, and Cimber caught hold of his toga with both hands and snatched it over his arms. Then Casca, who was behind him, drew a dagger from under his cloak and reaching forward struck at Caesar, but in the flurry merely grazed his shoulder. Caesar saw the blow, and tried to seize the hilt of the dagger with one hand. Then Casca uttered the signal that had been agreed upon. This was the cry "Help!" Immediately the others swarmed forward, pushing and striving to get closer to their victim, and all striking vicious blows, even though a number were not within reach of him. Caesar defended himself as best he could, and wounded one of his assailants with his stylus; but when he recognized the gleaming face of Brutus among the panting countenances and saw the upraised steel in his hand, as he fought to get near enough to strike, he exclaimed, "What! Thou too, Brutus!" (*Et tu, Brute!*), and, drawing his robe over his face, made no further resistance. The assassins plunged their weapons into his body again and again, until at last, bleeding from twenty-three wounds, he sank down and breathed out his life at the feet of the statue of Pompey.

The awful crime was completed, and the assassins, flinging their gowns over their left arms, as shields, and brandishing aloft their dripping daggers in their right hands, marched out of the Curia to the Forum, calling aloud that they had killed a tyrant, and displaying a

The murderers strike twenty-three dagger blows into Caesar's body.

Marcus Junius Brutus, a former friend of Caesar, participated in the assassination. Caesar, upon identifying him, said, "Et tu, Brute!" (Thou, too, Brutus!).

liberty cap on the head of a spear. The multitude were dazed and stupefied for the moment, but the signs were so ominous that the conspirators hunted out a place of refuge in the temple of Jupiter, on the Capitol.

In this place they were joined by others, and among them Cicero, who, though he had nothing to do with the conspiracy, did not condemn it, and advised that the Senate should be called together at once. Brutus was distrustful and determined to make another appeal to the populace. He entered the Forum the next day, and his speech was listened to coldly, even if with respect. When, however, others followed in the same strain, the hearers broke out with such violence that the Republicans were driven back to their quarters.

Meanwhile the consul Antonius had been active. He communicated secretly with Calpurnia, the widow of Caesar, who seems to have been a woman of little force of character, and secured possession of her husband's immense treasures and also his will. Assisted by his two brothers—one of whom was a tribune and the other a praetor—Antonius opened, as consul, the national coffers in the temple of Ops, and drawing a large sum, secured the promise of support from Lepidus, who had been leader of the army during Caesar's absence in Spain, and was his colleague in the consulate, 46 B.C. Lepidus was weak of character, lacking both military ability and statesmanship.

Antonius, as the minister and favorite of Caesar, was looked upon by many as his natural successor. Cicero alone opposed the conspirators' negotiations with him, for, though a brave man, Antonius was dissipated to the last degree. He was agreed upon as the proper man to act, and it was arranged that he should convene the Senate on March 17. He selected as a place for the meeting the temple of Tellus, near the Forum, and filled it with armed soldiers. Since the assassins were afraid to leave the Capitol, the discussion took place in their absence. The majority favored declaring Caesar a tyrant, but Antonius pointed out that this would invalidate all his acts and appointments. While the discussion was going on, Antonius went out and entered the Forum. He was received with acclamations, and Cicero showed that the only dignified course that could relieve them from their embarrassment was an amnesty which should confirm every acquired right and leave the deed of the conspirators to the judgment of posterity.

Cicero carried his point, and by his eloquence the next day he calmed the populace, who invited the conspirators to descend from the Capitol, Lepidus and Antonius sending their children as hostages, and one entertained Brutus and the other Cassius at supper. The following morning all parties met in the Curia, and Caesar's assignment of provinces was confirmed. To Trebonius went Asia, to Cimber Bithynia, and to Decimus the Cisalpine, while Macedonia was to go to Brutus, and Syria to Cassius, when their terms of office at home expired.

Caesar was dead but not buried. Inasmuch as his acts were valid, his will had to be accepted and his remains honored with a public funeral. Antony read to the people the last testament of their idol, by which it appeared that the youthful Octavius had been adopted as his son; that the Roman people had been endowed with his gardens on the bank of the Tiber, and he had bequeathed some twelve dollars to every citizen.

This liberality roused all to fury, which was kindled to the ungovernable point by the funeral oration of Mark

Mark Antony, a true friend of Caesar's, who was also marked for death but escaped, delivers the final public words over Caesar's body.

Antony. The body was laid out on a couch of gold and ivory, on a shrine gleaming with gold and erected before the rostra. At the head was hung the toga in which Caesar had been slain, showing the rents made by the daggers of the assassins. The mangled remains were concealed, but in their place was displayed a waxen figure, which faithfully showed every one of the three-and-twenty wounds.

When the people were swept by grief and indignation, Mark Antony stepped forward, as the chief magistrate of the Republic. He did this with marvelous dramatic power. Then pointing to the bleeding corpse, and striding toward the Capitol, he proclaimed in a thrilling voice: "I at least am prepared to keep my vow to avenge the victim I could not save!"

The people were now beyond restraint, as the orator intended they should be. They would not allow the body to be carried outside of the city, but insisted that it should be burned within the walls. Benches, tables, and chairs were torn up and heaped before the pontiff's dwelling in the Forum, and the body placed upon it. The torch was applied by two youths, girt with swords and javelin in hand, while the people flung on more fuel, wherever it could be gathered, the veterans adding their arms, the matrons their ornaments, and the children their trinkets. It was a touching fact that among the most grief-stricken of the mourners were Gauls, Iberians, Africans, and Orientals, all of whom had loved Caesar with no less fervency than did his own countrymen.

Caesar had been the friend and champion of the common people. Attacking him unawares, his enemies had struck the fragile, human life from his body. Yet so great had been the spirit of the man, so enormous his influence, that even that dead body was sufficient to defeat the conspirators. The sudden, unquenchable rebellion that sprang up around his corpse was Caesar's last and greatest triumph.

ANTONY AND OCTAVIUS— ROME BECOMES AN EMPIRE

No orator had ever attained more perfect success than did Mark Antony in that celebrated speech over Caesar's body. The frenzied people rushed like madmen through the streets, with blazing brands, determined to set fire to the houses of the conspirators and slay the inmates. The blind attacks were repulsed for the time, but Brutus and Cassius and their associates made haste to get out of the city. Had the incensed populace been able to lay hands upon them, they would have been torn limb from limb.

Ah, but Mark Antony was sly! He interfered and stopped the disorder, and then set himself to win the goodwill of the Senate, which was needed to carry out his plans. He secured the passage of a resolution abolishing the office of dictator, and it was never revived; and then,

with a stern hand, he put down the rioting which broke out in many quarters. He even visited Brutus and Cassius in their hiding, and offered to guarantee their safety, but they wisely declined to enter the city. Their praetorial office required them to reside in Rome, but he obtained for the two a charge for supplying provisions which would justify their absence. In return, Antony asked one small favor: since he, too, was in danger, he asked the Senate to grant him an armed bodyguard. The Senate promptly did so, and he as promptly raised it to six thousand men and thus made himself safe.

Antony was for the moment as much dictator as Caesar had ever been. He secured the sanction of the Senate, not only for all the imperator had done, but for all that he might have planned to do. Having won over the secretary of the deceased and secured all his papers, Antony carried out what schemes he liked, and when he lacked authority for them, he, with the help of the secretary forged Caesar's authority. It is unnecessary to say that with such boundless facilities at command, he did not neglect to "feather his own nest," and to secure enough funds to bribe senators, officers, and tributary provinces. He did not hesitate to break the engagements he had made with the conspirators, by taking from Brutus and Cassius the governments that had been promised them, and seizing Macedonia with the legions Caesar had ordered to assemble at Apollonia. Beholding all this, Cicero sadly murmured: "The tyrant is dead, but the tyranny still lives."

Now, you will remember that Octavius, the young nephew of Caesar, was at Apollonia preparing himself for the campaign in which he had expected to take part. When he learned the particulars of his uncle's assassination, and the letters from his mother made known that he was the heir to all that had been left, he was thrilled by the ambition that sprang to life within him, and determined to return to Rome in the face of every danger. His friends tried to dissuade him, but he had the fervent devotion of the soldiers, who burned to avenge the murder of their idolized chief. Nothing could restrain the young man's resolution and, when he landed on the coast of Apulia, copies of the will and decrees of the Senate were shown to him. He immediately assumed the title of Gaius Julius Caesar Octavianus, and offered himself before the troops at Prundisium as the adopted son of the great imperator. He was received with the wildest demonstrations, and the veterans who crowded around drew their swords and clamored to be led against all who dared to oppose the will of him who, being dead, yet spoke in the same trumpet tones as of yore.

Octavius, in spite of his years, was prudent, even while impetuous. Instead of appealing to force he addressed the Senate in temperate language, claiming that, as a private citizen, he had the right to the inheritance left him by Caesar. On his way to Rome, he visited the despondent Cicero, who was staying near Cumae, and succeeded in convincing the orator of his loyal and wise views.

Octavius entered Rome in April and, despite the remonstrance of his mother and stepfather, went before the praetor and declared himself the son and heir of the dictator. Mounting the tribune, he addressed the people, pledging to pay the sums bequeathed to them by his illustrious parent. He made many friends and won over a large number of enemies. Antony had no fear at first of this stripling, but the news that reached him led him to return to Rome about the middle of May. When he and Octavius met, the latter professed friendship for him, but at the same time upbraided the consul for his failure to punish the assassins. The Second Triumvirate, formed in 43 B.C., divided among its members the provinces around Italy. Antony was to have the two Gauls; Lepidus the Spains, with the Narbonensis; while Octavius secured Africa and the islands. Italy, the heart of empire, they were to retain in common, while the division of the eastern provinces was postponed until after Brutus and Cassius should be driven out of them. Octavius and Antony, with twenty legions each, were to take charge of the conduct of the war, while Lepidus remained to protect their interests in Rome.

Having formed their far-reaching scheme, the three agreed that the first necessary precaution was to leave no enemies in their rear. All from whom danger threatened must be crushed beyond the possibility of doing harm. Octavius, Antony, and Lepidus entered the city on three successive days, each at the head of a single legion. The troops occupied the temples and towers and their banners waved from the Forum. The farce of a plebiscitum was gone through, and on November 28 the Triumvirate was proclaimed. They decreed a formal proscription. Each man had his list of chief citizens before him and, sitting down, picked out the names of those whose deaths would give him special happiness.

Now, since everyone was certain to want the sacrifice of the relatives of the others, they made a ghastly agreement among themselves to the effect that each, by giving up a relative, would be entitled to proscribe a kinsman of his colleagues. As a result, among the first names on the fatal list were a brother of Lepidus, an uncle of Antony, and a cousin of Octavius. Three hundred senators, two thousand knights, and many thousands of citizens were put to death. Many escaped by fleeing to Macedonia and others to Africa, while more found refuge on the vessels of Sextus Pompeius that were cruising off Africa. Some bought their lives with bribes.

Antony demanded the death of Cicero, whose blistering philippics still rankled in his memory, and Octavius, to his eternal shame, consented. Cicero was staying at the time with his brother at his Tusculan villa. As soon as they heard of the proscription, they fled to Astura, another villa, on a small island off the coast of Antium, whither they intended to embark for Macedonia. In the pursuit the brother was overtaken and killed, but Cicero gained the sea, set sail, and landed several times, distressed in body and mind and caring little what became of him. The last time he went ashore near Formiae, he was warned of the danger of delay. "Let me die here, in my fatherland," he said mournfully, but his slaves placed the man, who was suffering great bodily pain, upon a litter, and moved as rapidly as they could toward the seacoast.

Hardly had they left the house, when an officer, whose life Cicero had once saved, appeared and pounded on the door. A man pointed out the course taken by the fugitives, and he and his small force ran after them. Cicero saw them coming up and noted that they were in less number than his own party, who prepared to defend him.

But he would not permit it. He ordered the slaves to set down the litter and, fixing his eyes calmly on his enemies, he bared his throat to their swords. Many of the spectators covered their faces with their hands, and the leader hesitated and bungled, until at last he pulled himself together and then all was quickly over. The head of the orator was sent as a gracious present to Antony, whose wife, Fulvia, remembering how nearly she and her husband had been overthrown by that bitter tongue, thrust long pins through it, taunting the dead man and crying that she had given the final answer to his orations.

The Second Triumvirate had crushed its enemies at home; it had still to destroy the Republican forces. Brutus and Cassius, knowing they could not sustain themselves in Italy, had retired to the East. When Brutus appeared before Athens, the citizens erected his statue by the side of those of Harmodius and Aristogiton, and many of the younger men enlisted in his ranks. Horace, the future poet, was made a tribune, and numerous veterans also joined the patriot forces. The kings and rulers of Macedonia were quick to declare themselves on the same side, one of the adherents being a brother of Antony.

Cassius had gone to his promised government of Syria, where he was held in high esteem because of the courage he had displayed in the conquest of the Parthians, after the fall of Crassus. He devastated the country and then prepared to pass over into Macedonia. The legend is that Brutus, watching in his tent at night, saw a fearful apparition, which being addressed replied: "I am thy evil spirit; thou shalt see me again at Philippi." When he and Cassius encamped on an eminence, twelve miles east of Philippi, their forces numbered probably one hundred thousand men. Those which Octavius and Antony brought against them were fewer, but in a better state of discipline. In the battle Brutus opposed Octavius; Cassius, Antony. Octavius was ill, and at the first shock his division yielded, but Antony was successful. Cassius fell back, and was left almost alone and unaware of the success of his colleague. Observing a body of horsemen approaching, he was panic-stricken, and, believing them

Brutus takes his life when his luck turns and he is about to be killed in battle.

the enemy, threw himself on the sword of a freedman and died. The messenger sent by Brutus with news of his triumph arrived just a moment too late. It was a drawn battle, and each side withdrew, glad of a respite.

Brutus found it difficult to hold his legions in hand and, yielding to his impatience, he renewed the battle twenty days later on the same field. The fight was well contested, but the Caesareans under Octavius broke the ranks of their enemies, and attacked them in their camp. Brutus held an anxious position throughout the night on a neighboring hill. When daylight came, his remaining men refused to renew the fight, and in despair he ended his life with his own sword. The remnant of the shattered Republican armies was carried off by the fleet that had attended their movements.

The decisive victory having been gained, the victors made a new partition of the spoils. Octavius took Spain and Numidia; Antony, Gaul beyond the Alps; and Lepidus the province of Africa. But the division was hardly made when the possessors began to quarrel over it. Lepidus was feeble, and of such insignificance that his share was soon taken from him, after which nothing was more certain than that Octavius and Antony would soon come to strife over their portions and each would intrigue against the other. Octavius was still suffering in health, and chose to seek repose by returning to the balmy climate of Italy, and undertaking the task of placing the veterans on the estates of the natives. The gross Antony stayed in the East, indulging in the lowest dissipation.

He ordered Cleopatra to meet him at Cilicia, on a charge of intrigue with his enemy Cassius. It is said that the wit and piquancy of this remarkable woman were more effective than her dazzling beauty, and none knew better how to use her gifts than she. Sailing for Tarsus, she glided up the Cydnus in a gilded vessel, with purple sails and silver oars, to the sound of flutes and pipes. Under an awning, spangled with gold, she reclined in the garb of Venus, surrounded by Cupids, Graces, and Nereids, while Antony appeared in the character of Bacchus. Impressed by her splendid equipage, he invited her

to land and sit at his banquet, but with the air of a queen she summoned him to attend her.

That meeting sealed his fate. He was utterly enthralled. Under the spell of the arch temptress, he forgot wife, Rome, and every duty, and only asked the bliss of becoming her slave and adorer; and, inasmuch as that was the object for which she played from the beginning, she made sure of retaining her sway over him.

In the middle of the summer of 36 B.C., Antony had gathered one hundred thousand men on the Euphrates with the intention of completing the conquest of the Parthians. His alliance with Cleopatra had delayed him so long that he advanced too rapidly and, on reaching Praaspa, three hundred miles beyond the Tigris, he found himself without any artillery with which to conduct a siege. He therefore settled for an attempt at the reduction of the city by blockade, but the Parthian horsemen cut off his supplies and a number of his Armenian allies deserted. This compelled him to retreat, and for twenty-seven days his men were subjected to incredible sufferings. Not until they had crossed the Araxes did the Parthians cease their attacks. Antony still hurried his wearied soldiers, intent only on rejoining Cleopatra at the earliest moment. She had come to Syria to meet him and, caring nothing for honor or duty, he returned with her to the dissipations of the Egyptian capital, not hesitating in his shamelessness to announce his recent campaign as a victory. It suited Octavius to maintain the appearance at least of friendship, and he did not dispute the claim.

Antony's second wife, the faithful Octavia, hoping to save her husband from the thralldom of Cleopatra, obtained the consent of her brother Octavius to rejoin Antony. He had returned to Syria, and was preparing for a new expedition when he learned that his wife had arrived in Athens. He sent her orders to come no farther. She could not mistake the meaning of the message, but asked leave to send forward the presents she brought with her,

The first meeting of Mark Antony and Cleopatra in Egypt. The queen soon became his fifth wife, replacing Octavia, Caesar's sister, and they also joined military forces against the Romans under Octavius.

which consisted of clothing for the soldiers, money, and equipments, including two thousand picked men as a bodyguard for the imperator. Then the "Serpent of the Nile" exerted all her devilish arts, and the fool Antony fled with her to Alexandria. Octavia, with the serene dignity of wounded womanhood, resigned her unworthy husband to the fate he richly deserved.

Some modern courts have illustrated the depths of debauchery of which men and women are capable, but none have surpassed the court of Cleopatra, whose dominion over Mark Antony was so complete that he seemed unable to live except in her presence. It was as if Nature had displayed the utmost achievements of which she is capable in the creation of this woman. While her portraits do not show a superlative degree of beauty, she must have possessed it to a remarkable extent, and her magnetism of manner was resistless. She was a fascinating singer and musician, spoke several languages, and was past mistress in all the arts and artifices of her sex. None knew better how to capture and retain her dominion over such a coarse wretch as Antony. What strange stories have come down to us of that extraordinary couple! When he dropped a line into the water, trained divers by her orders slipped unperceived underneath and fastened live fish to the hook; she dissolved a pearl of princely value in a cup of vinegar, and drank it to his health.

The rumors of these orgies caused resentment in Rome, where the tact and wisdom of Octavius steadily added to his popularity. One of the chief supporters of Antony became so nauseated that he appeared in the Senate and openly declared his abhorrence of his late master. Then he went to Octavius and revealed the testament of Antony, which reeked with treason. It declared the child of Cleopatra and Caesar the heir of the dictator, and ratified Antony's drunken gifts of provinces to favorites, finally directing that his body should be entombed with Cleopatra's in the mausoleum of the Ptolemies. All this hideous wickedness being known, everyone was ready to believe the story that Antony when drunk had given his pledge to Cleopatra to sacrifice the West to her ambition and to remove to Alexandria the government of the world.

Octavius, while refraining from declaring Antony a public enemy, proclaimed war against Egypt, and did not renew the terms of the Triumvirate, which had expired, but directed the Senate to annul the appointment of Antony as consul, assuming it himself at the opening of 31 B.C.

Antony still had friends, and they now begged him to wrench himself free from Cleopatra. He replied by divorcing his legitimate wife, thus breaking the last legal tie that bound him to his country. He could not wholly close his eyes to his peril, however, and showed some of his old-time vigor in preparing to resist Octavius, who was equally energetic in preparations against him.

The forces of Antony are given at one hundred thousand infantry and twelve thousand horses, while his fleet numbered five hundred large war galleys. Octavius had twenty thousand less, and only one hundred fifty smaller vessels, which on that account were more manageable. The desertion of many of his troops awakened distrust in the mind of Antony, who became suspicious of Cleopatra herself and compelled her to taste all viands before he partook of them. At last the two great armies gathered in front of each other on the shores of the Gulf of Ambracia, the narrow channel between being occupied by the fleet of Antony.

This field of war was ill-chosen, for it was confined and unhealthful, and Antony wished to remove his forces to the plains of Thessaly; but Cleopatra, fearing for her own way of retreat, dissuaded him. Distrusting the issue of the battle, he secretly prepared to lead his fleet into the open waters of the Leucadian bay, so as to break through the enemy's line, and escape to Egypt, leaving the army to do the best it could to retreat into Asia.

The wind was so high for several days that the rough waters would not permit the ships of either side to move; but it fell, and, on September 2, 31 B.C., at noon, while the galleys of Antony lay becalmed at the entrance to the strait, a gentle breeze sprang up, so that the immense armament moved out to sea.

It immediately became apparent that the ships were greatly handicapped by their bulkiness, which held them from moving with the nimbleness of their opponents. They hurled huge stones from their wooden towers and reached out enormous iron claws to grapple their assailants, who dodged and eluded them like a party of hounds in front of a wounded bear. How curiously the account of this naval battle reads when compared with one of our modern contests on the water! The Caesarean rowers shot forward and backed with great agility, or swept away the banks of the enemy's oars, under cover of showers of arrows, circling about the awkward masses and helping one another against boarding or grappling. It was a school of whales fighting sharks, but the result was indecisive, for although the whales were wounded, the sharks did not disable them.

Then suddenly took place a shameful thing. Cleopatra's galley, anchored in the rear, hoisted its sails and sped away, followed by the Egyptian squadron of sixty barks. Antony caught sight of the signal and, leaping into a boat, was rowed rapidly in their wake. Many of the crews, enraged at the desertion, tore down their turrets, flung them into the sea to lighten their craft, and hastened after him, but enough remained to put up a brave fight. Then the Caesareans, unable otherwise to destroy them, hurled blazing torches among the ships, which, catching fire, burned to the water's edge, and sank one after the other. Thus ended the great sea fight of Actium. Three hundred galleys fell into the victor's hands, but the army on shore was still unharmed. It was not until its commander abandoned it and sought the camp of Octavius, that the legions surrendered.

Antony and Cleopatra had fled in the same vessel. Proceeding direct to Alexandria, she sailed into the harbor, her galley decked with laurels through fear of a revolt of the people. Antony had remained at Paraetonium to demand the surrender of the small Roman garrison stationed there, but was repulsed, and learned of the fate of his army at Actium. In his despair, he was ready to kill himself, but his attendants prevented and took him to Alexandria, where he found Cleopatra preparing for defense. Defections broke out on every hand, and she proposed to fly into far-away Arabia. She commenced the transport of her galleys from the Nile to the Red Sea, but some were destroyed by the barbarians on the coast, and she abandoned the project. Then the distracted woman thought she could seek a refuge in Spain and raise a revolt against Octavius. This wild scheme was also given up, and Antony shut himself up in a tower on the seacoast; but Cleopatra was not ready to yield, and showed herself dressed as a man to the people that they might feel they were governed by him and not by a woman.

Still hopelessly captivated, Antony sneaked back to his royal mistress, and the two plunged into reckless orgies till the moment should come for both to die together. It is said that at this time the woman made many careful experiments of the different kinds of poison on slaves and criminals, and was finally convinced that the bite of an asp afforded the most painless method of taking one's departure from life.

Meanwhile, she and Antony applied to Octavius for clemency. He disdained to make any answer to Antony, but told Cleopatra that if she would kill or drive away her paramour, he would grant her reasonable terms. Octavius was playing with his victims like a cat with mice. He meant to have her kingdom, but was determined to carry the detested woman herself to Rome and exhibit her in his triumph. Cunning agents of his suggested to her that Octavius was still a young man, and she no doubt could exert the same power over him that had taken Antony captive. It was not strange that she should believe this, for her past experience warranted such belief. She encouraged Antony to prepare for the last struggle, and all the time was secretly contriving to disarm and betray him. The forces of Octavius drew nearer. Pelusium was captured, but Antony gained the advantage in a skirmish before the walls of Alexandria, and was on the point of seizing the moment for a flight to sea when he saw his own vessels, won away by Cleopatra, pass over to the enemy. Almost at the same moment, his cohorts, seduced by the same treachery, deserted him.

Cleopatra had shut herself up in a tower, built for her mausoleum, but fearing that the man whom she had ruined would do her violence, had word sent to him that she had committed suicide. This was the final blow to Antony, who with the aid of his freedman Eros inflicted a mortal wound upon himself. Immediately after, he learned that he had been tricked, and that the queen was unharmed. He caused himself to be carried to the foot of the tower, where, with the assistance of two women, her only attendants, he was drawn up, and breathed his last in her arms.

By this time, Octavius had entered Alexandria and sent an officer to bring Cleopatra to him. She refused to admit the messenger, but he scaled the tower undiscovered and entered. She snatched up a poniard to strike herself, but the man caught her arm and assured her that his master would treat her kindly. She listened for some minutes, and then allowed herself to be led to the palace, where she resumed her state, and was recognized as a sovereign by her victor.

Then Octavius called upon her. Never in all her wonderful experience did she so exert herself to capture one of the sterner sex; but Octavius had nerved himself for the meeting, and for the first time the charmer found she had no power to charm. He talked with coolness and self-possession, demanded that she should give him a list of her treasures, and then, bidding her to be of good heart, left her.

Cleopatra was chagrined at her failure, but she did not despair, till she learned that Octavius was determined to take her as a captive to Rome. She then retired to the mausoleum where the body of Antony still lay, crowned the tomb with flowers, and was found the next morning dead on her couch, her two women attendants expiring at her side. Although the common account makes Cleopatra die of the bite of an asp, brought to her in a basket of figs, the truth concerning her end will never be known with certainty. As we have learned in Egypt's story, there were no wounds discovered on her body, and it may be that she perished from some self-administered subtle poison. At the triumph of Octavius, her image was carried on a bier, the arms encircled by two serpents, and

Octavius defeated Antony and Cleopatra's forces and with Antony already a suicide, Octavius proposed to return Cleopatra to parade her in the streets of Rome as a trophy. The queen tried her wiles on him in a private interview but failed. Suicide was the only remaining choice.

this aided the popular rumor as to the means of her death. The child which she had borne to Julius Caesar was put to death by Octavius, who could brook the existence of no such dangerous rival, but the children of Antony were spared, though deprived of the royal succession. The dynasty of the Ptolemies ended, and Egypt became a Roman province (30 B.C.).

The death of Antony closes the period of civil strife. The commonwealth was exhausted and Octavius was supreme. With masterly ability, he regulated his new province, and then made his tour through the eastern dominions, dispossessing his enemies and rewarding his allies and friends. When everything was settled, he went to Samos, where he spent the winter in pleasant retirement. He reached Rome in the middle of the summer of 29 B.C., and was received with acclamations of joy. With a wisdom worthy of his adopted father, he recognized the authority of the Senate and claimed to have wielded delegated powers only. He had laid aside the functions of the Triumvirate, and it was as a simple consul, commissioned by the state, that he had conquered at Actium and won the province of Egypt, while his achievements in Greece and Asia still awaited confirmation by the Senate. So modest and loyal did his conduct appear, that his popularity was like that of the great imperator whose name he inherited.

To him was awarded the glory of a triple triumph, at the conclusion of which, according to the laws of the free state, he as imperator must disband his army, but he overcame the necessity by allowing the subservient Senate to give him the permanent title of imperator, as it had been conferred upon Julius Caesar, and to prefix it to his name. He was thus made lifelong commander of the national forces. This accomplished the all-important result of securing to him the support of the army, which was the real strength of the country. He acknowledged the Senate as the representative of the public will, but caused himself to be vested with the powers of the censorship, which, you will remember, gave him authority to revise the list of senators. This right he exercised with discretion and wisdom. It will be recalled that Julius Caesar degraded the body by adding to it many men of low degree, including obnoxious foreigners. Octavius restored the old number of six hundred, and kept strictly to the requirement of property qualification. He placed himself at the head as *princeps,* which, while it implied no substantial power, was looked upon as the highest honorary office. This civic dignity was always held for life.

While he was thus gathering these powers to himself, he prudently waived all formal recognition of his sovereign status. He refrained from reviving the dictatorship, and permitted no one to hail him with the title of king. Still he craved a title, and consulted with his trusted friends. Some suggested the name of Quirinus or Romulus, but the one was a god and the other had perhaps

been slain as a tyrant. Finally the name Augustus was proposed, and it seemed to "fit" the requirements exactly. It had not been borne by a previous ruler, but as an adjective it possessed a noble meaning. The rites of the temples and their gods were "august," and the word itself came from *auguries* by which the divine will was revealed. And so the name of Octavius was dropped, and the lord of Rome stood forth as Augustus Caesar.

This man was thirty-six years old when he became master of the Roman world, though there was no open establishment of a monarchical government. He aimed to maintain, so far as possible, the old law, to defend his country from foreign aggressions, and to make it as truly great as was within the compass of human endeavor. The example of Julius Caesar was ever before him, and, since the first Caesar had been assassinated for grasping at the name of king, the second avoided his error. Remembering, too, that the great imperator lightly regarded religion, Augustus strove to revive the faith of Rome. The decaying temples were repaired, the priesthoods renewed, and the earlier usages of the Republic restored. Augustus did not allow his impulses to lead him astray. He saw with vivid clearness, and the grandest political work ever accomplished by a single man was his, in the establishment of the Roman Empire.

In reflecting upon the ease with which the Romans "passed under the yoke," as may be said, it must be remembered that they had been carried close to the verge of exhaustion by the century of civil strife. Many of the nobler families of Rome had been nearly or quite wiped out, and the survivors were weary of the seemingly endless warring of factions. So many mongrels had mixed their blood with that of the Romans that the pure strain was vitiated. In short, the people were in just the mood, and just the condition, just the epoch had arrived when they needed a single, stern ruler. And since that must be, it was surely fortunate that their sovereign should be Augustus.

He is described as a model in his personal traits and habits. He avoided the personal familiarity with which Julius Caesar was accustomed to address his legionaries. The elder loved to speak of his soldiers as "comrades," the younger referred to them as his "soldiers" only. While he encouraged the magnificence of his nobles, his own life was of striking simplicity. His home on the Palatine Hill was modest in size and in ornament. While his dress was that of a plain senator, he took no little pride in calling attention to the fact that it was woven by his wife and the maidens in her apartment. When he walked the streets, it was as a private citizen, with only the ordinary retinue of attendants. If he met an acquaintance, he saluted him courteously, taking him by the hand or leaning on his shoulder, in a way that was pleasing to everyone to whom he showed the delicate attention.

One striking fact regarding the reign of Augustus was

the friendship which he secured from the poets. It was Horace who taught others to accept the new order of things with contentment, while Vergil wreathed the empire of the Caesars in the halo of a legendary but glorious antiquity. The *Aeneid* proved that Octavius was a direct descendant of the goddess Venus and a worthy rival of Hercules. Thus spoke the giants among the poets, but there were minor singers as well, who called upon their countrymen to remember in their prayers he who had restored order and brought universal felicity. The citizens were urged in the temples and in their own homes to thank the gods for all their prosperity, and to join with the gods themselves the hallowed name of Aeneas, the patron of the Julian race. Then, too, when they rose from their evening meal, the last duty of the day was to call with a libation for a blessing on themselves and on Augustus, whom they called the father of his country.

No prouder title than this could be conferred upon any Roman. It had been associated in private with their hero, and finally the Senate, echoing the voice of the nation, conferred it on him publicly and with all solemnity. That he was deeply touched was shown in his tremulous response:

"Conscript fathers, my wishes are now fulfilled, my vows are accomplished. I have nothing more to ask of the Immortals, but that I may retain to my dying day the unanimous approval you now bestow upon me."

Caesar's nephew concentrated all power in his hands and, having been named *princeps* (first citizen) and given the title Augustus by the Senate, began the reign of the Roman emperors in 27 B.C.

THE EMPERORS' PERIOD OF POWER

The most impressive event of the reign of Augustus was the birth of Christ at the little village of Bethlehem, in Judea—an event that marked the most momentous crisis in the spiritual history of the world. This human appearance of Christ took place at the time when there was general peace throughout the earth, and was, therefore, in accordance with Scripture prophecy. The government of Augustus was tranquil, and there were no civil wars, though there may have been some unrest on the frontiers.

There was, indeed, only one serious war during the forty years of Augustus's supreme power. This was with the Germans, the wild tribes which Caesar had defeated. They had never been fully subdued, and in the year 9 B.C. they rose in sudden rebellion under their chief Hermann, or, as the Romans called him, Arminius. The three Roman legions along the Rhine were commanded by Varus, who proved both reckless and incompetent. He marched his entire force into the wild German forests where they were surrounded by the rebels and, after three days of savage fighting, exterminated. Great was

The Christ, ĬNRI (Jesus of Nazareth—king of the Jews), was the founder of Christianity. From the most famous painting of Him—by Correggio in the Dresden (Germany) Art Gallery.

the consternation at Rome. Augustus beat his head against the wall, crying, "Varus, Varus, give me back my legions." The people feared the Germans would imitate the ancient Gauls and make a terrible raid upon Rome. But the Germans were busy quarreling among themselves; fresh legions were hastily raised, and the danger passed away.

Augustus died in A.D. 14, and was succeeded by his stepson Tiberius Claudius Nero, known as Tiberius, who was born 42 B.C. Jesus Christ was crucified in the nineteenth year of this reign. It was at Antioch, in Syria, where Saul and Barnabas taught the faith, that the believers first received the name of Christians. Then began those wonderful missionary journeys of the Apostles, which carried the gospel through Asia Minor, Greece, and Italy, and Rome became the capital of Christendom. Silently but irresistibly the true faith spread, first among the Jews, then among the Greeks, or eastern, and the Latin, or western, Gentiles, until it became the one true and accepted religion throughout the civilized world.

When Tiberius ascended the throne, his manliness and moderation gave promise of a prosperous reign, but he was jealous from the first of his popular nephew Germanicus, who was entrusted with important commands in Dalmatia and Pannonia, and raised to the consulate before he was thirty years of age. Two years later he repressed a terrible revolt of the Germanic legions, who wished to salute him as emperor. In a campaign against the Germans, he ousted Hermann, their chief, in A.D. 16, recaptured the eagles lost by Varus, and earned for himself the surname of Germanicus. Tiberius summoned him home, and he returned as a victorious general. The Senate awarded him a magnificent triumph, in which Thusnelda, wife of Arminius, preceded his carriage with her children. Germanicus died in A.D. 19, from poison,

Tiberius relaxing at his residence on the Isle of Capri

Early rulers of the Roman Empire. Top, left to right: Nero, the sixth Caesar of twelve, started the fire that burned Rome to divert suspicion of his prosecution of the Christians and then blamed them for it, ordered the assassination of his mother, ruled from A.D. 54 to 68—when he committed suicide. Claudius I, the fifth Caesar, who reigned from 41 to 54, was the stepfather of Nero. And Agrippina, Claudius's wife, poisoned him so that Nero, her son by a previous marriage, might become emperor. Center, left to right: Tiberius, the third Caesar, adopted son of Augustus, reigned from A.D. 14 to 37, put his nephew Germanicus to death. Augustus Caesar, the "father of his country," was the first Roman emperor, its second Caesar, and was the victor over Cleopatra and Antony at the Battle of Actium in 31 B.C. Bottom, left to right: Vespasian, the tenth Caesar, ruled from A.D. 69 to 79, was noted for the expansion into the Austro-Hungarian territory. Titus, the eleventh Caesar, ruled from A.D. 79 to 81, was the besieger of Jerusalem. And Caligula, the fourth Caesar of the empire, reigned from A.D. 37 to 41 and is remembered as the emperor who replaced the image of God in the temples of Jerusalem with his own.

as he had predicted. Tiberius then revealed himself as moody and irresolute, with scarcely a trace of affection or sympathy. He became a tyrant. The number and amount of taxes were increased, all power was taken from the people and Senate. Prosecutions for high treason were based on mere words or even looks that gave displeasure to the emperor, who found thus a convenient method of ridding himself of those who displeased him. As years advanced, he abandoned the real government of the empire to Aelius Sejanus, commander of the Prae-

torian Guards, and wallowed in licentious excesses at his villa in Capri until, worn out by debauchery, he ended his infamous life in the year A.D. 37, his death being hastened either by poison or suffocation.

There were many Roman emperors whose history is not worth the telling. Some held the throne but a short time, and others played an insignificant part in the annals of the empire.

Gaius Caesar, or Caligula, as he is more generally known, was in his twenty-fifth year when he became emperor. He was suspected of helping the death of Tiberius, who had appointed him his heir. He was another of the diabolical miscreants produced by licentiousness and debauchery. It took him just one year to expend the $3 million left by Tiberius, and he confiscated and murdered and banished until it is only charitable to believe he was afflicted with insanity. He enlivened his feasts by having those whom he disliked tortured in his presence, and once expressed the wish that all the Roman people had but one neck that he might decapitate Rome at a single blow. He stabled his favorite horse in the palace, fed him at a marble manger with gilded oats, and afterward raised him to the consulship. As a climax to his foolery, he declared himself a god and had temples erected and sacrifices offered to his family. The people stood all this and much more with incredible patience, but finally formed a conspiracy and removed him by assassination from the earth which he had cumbered too long.

Claudius I, fortunately for himself, was suspected of imbecility, or else Caligula would have "removed" him. As it was, he might have done well had he not, in A.D. 42, when terrified by hearing of a conspiracy against his life, abandoned himself wholly to the will of his ferocious wife Messalina, who robbed and slew with a mercilessness worthy of the former emperor. Abroad, however, the Roman armies were victorious. Mauritania became a Roman province, progress was made in Germany, and the conquest of Britain was begun. The experience of Claudius in the matrimonial line was discouraging. Messalina was executed for her crimes, after which he married Agrippina, who poisoned him in 54, so as to make sure of the succession of her son Nero. After the death of Claudius, he was deified, though the sacrilege surely could not have benefited him much.

And now comes another of those infamous persons in history. This was Nero, whose full name was Nero Claudius Caesar Drusus Germanicus. He began his reign well, and but for the baleful influence of his mother Agrippina, might have continued in the good way, under the tutelage of Seneca the philosopher. He soon yielded, however, to temptation or to his natural inclinations, and plunged headlong into tyranny, extravagance, and every species of debauchery that human ingenuity could devise. Falling out with his mother, he caused her to be assassinated to please one of his mistresses, the wife of Otho, afterward emperor. To marry this woman Nero had put to death his own wife; now his mother followed, and the servile Senate actually issued an address congratulating the matricide on her death.

The rebellion which broke out in Britain under Queen Boadicea was suppressed in 61, but the war against the Parthians the next year was unsuccessful. In July 64 occurred the great conflagration in Rome, by which two-thirds of the city was reduced to ashes. It is recorded that while the conflagration was raging, Nero watched it from a turret in his palace, singing verses to the music of his lyre, and it is the general belief that it was his hand that kindled the flames. Sated with every known indulgence, he had set out to discover some new kind of enjoyment.

Could his guilt have been established, the populace would have wreaked quick vengeance upon him. The cowardly miscreant was scared, and strove to turn aside the suspicion whose whispers had reached his ears. He traversed the stricken streets with hypocritical expressions of sympathy, and gave away all the money he could steal to help the sufferers; but seeing the necessity of directing distrust toward someone, he cunningly chose the new sect known as Christians, who had become numerous and active in Rome. Scores were arrested, and he condemned them to be burned. Many were wrapped in pitched cloth and set up in his own gardens, which were illuminated by the awful human "torches." It was not the emperor's pity, but that of the refuse of the city, which finally brought the horrible spectacles to an end. Among the victims of these tortures were Saint Paul, Saint Peter, and Seneca.

Nero was guilty of atrocities that cannot even be hinted at. Suspecting Seneca and the poet Lucian of conspiring against him, he took the lives of both. One day, because he felt out of sorts, he kicked his wife to death. Being refused by another lady, he had her slain by

Claudius acting the part of the idiot when the Praetorians sought him out to be emperor, for he believed the Caesars did not live long on the throne. But he was only half right—he reigned thirteen years, and it has been considered an unlucky number ever since.

Messalina, consort of Claudius

Nero "fiddled" a harp while Rome burned.

Nero watching the Christians being burned at the stake

Galba, the seventh Caesar, reigned from A.D. 68 to 69.

Otho, the eighth Caesar, ruled in a tri-reign in the year A.D. 69 with Galba and Vitellius

The death of Nero

Vespasian planning the Colosseum open air auditorium for Rome

way of teaching her a lesson, and then secured another wife by killing an obstinate husband.

The blow which brought Nero low came from an unexpected quarter. In the year 68, the Gallic and Spanish legions revolted, and the Praetorian Guards followed, all animated by the purpose of making Galba, one of their commanders, emperor. Their approach to the city heartened the Senate and terrified Nero, whose frame shivered and whose teeth rattled with terror. He fled at night to the villa of one of his freedmen, having learned the Senate had proclaimed him a public enemy. Being warned that his death by torture had been ordered, and hearing the sound of the approaching hoof beats of the guards, he at last mustered enough courage to place a sword to his breast and order his slave to drive it home.

Galba entered Rome on January 1, 69, and was accepted as emperor with the right to assume the title of Caesar. He was a simple soldier and nothing more. Among those who accompanied him was Otho, whom Nero had robbed of his wife. He found the troops discontented with Galba's parsimony and strict discipline, and succeeded in working them up to the point of revolt, when Galba was slain and Otho succeeded him.

His reign, however, was to be brief, for Vitellius had been proclaimed emperor by his troops almost on the same day that Galba reached Rome. This was in Gaul, and came about because, through his liberality, he had made himself extremely popular with the soldiers. He was drunk all the way to Rome, whither most of his military supporters had preceded him. When he arrived there, having routed the forces of Otho on the road, his first act was to deify Nero. After that sacrilege, there was nothing too base for him, and he became such a vile debauchee that he was unable even to act the tyrant. The administration was mostly in the hands of the freedman Asiaticus, though P. Sabinus, brother of Vespasian, was high in authority. Their government was marked by moderation. The legions of Pannonia and Illyricum proclaimed Vespasian emperor, and advanced into Italy under Antonius Primus. Several battles were fought, and Rome was desolated by violence and bloodshed, till the troops of Primus entered the city. Vitellius was found wandering about his palace in a state of drunken terror, and when he appeared on the streets was pounded to death by the angry mob. His head was carried around Rome, and his body thrown into the Tiber.

Vespasian had left his ton Titus to prosecute the siege of Jerusalem, and was joyfully received in Rome, where he set vigorously to work in restoring order. He was a fine soldier, held the troops under firm discipline, improved the finances, cooperated with the Senate and, best of all, set a good example by his own conduct to his subjects. He was simple in his habits, indifferent to flattery, good-humored, and easy of access. Although parsimonious in his private life, he was lavish in embellishing the city with public works, and was a liberal patron of the arts and sciences. He reigned ten years, and died in the sixty-ninth year of his age.

Titus was the eldest son of Vespasian, and through his careful training had become an accomplished scholar and an adept in manly exercises. He was an admirable soldier, and the task that his father left him, of prosecuting the siege of Jerusalem, had been carried through with success. His victory caused the utmost joy in Rome, when the news reached the city. He laid the trophies of victory at his father's feet, and the two were given the honor (in 71) of a joint triumph. Becoming the colleague of his parent in the empire, Titus made an unfavorable impression by his immoral and cruel conduct. He caused persons whom he suspected of enmity to be put to death, and his liaison with Berenice, daughter of Herod Agrippa, gave great offense to the Romans.

When, however, Titus became emperor, he agreeably disappointed everyone. He immediately stopped all persecutions for treasonable words and looks; repaired the ancient and venerated structures of Rome; built new ones, among them the Colosseum and the baths which bear his name, and delighted the populace by games which lasted one hundred days. The splendid beneficence of his reign was sorely needed, for in 79 occurred the appalling eruption of Vesuvius which destroyed Herculaneum and Pompeii and many other towns and villages. Herculaneum stood in the Campagna, close to the Bay of Naples. It is not known when it was founded, but its inhabitants took an active part in the social and civil wars of Rome. It was completely buried under a shower of ashes, over which a stream of lava flowed and afterward hardened. The configuration of the coast was so

changed that the city was entirely lost for sixteen centuries, when an accident led to the discovery of its ruins in 1713. Twenty-five years later a systematic course of excavation was begun. The interesting relics of antiquity, so far as they were capable of removal, were taken to Naples, and are now deposited, along with other relics from Pompeii, in a large museum attached to the royal palace. They include not only frescoes, statues, and works of art, but articles of household furniture, such as tripods, lamps, chandeliers, basins, mirrors, musical or surgical instruments, and even cooking utensils. Excavations have been resumed in recent years with the most interesting results.

Pompeii was about twelve miles southeast from Naples, in the plain at the foot of Mount Vesuvius, and was one of the fashionable provincial cities of the Roman Empire. Though most of the citizens escaped during the incessant bombardment of lava stones, a large number must have perished, as is proved by the finding of the skeletons of soldiers on guard, and citizens apparently overtaken by death in the midst of their usual employments. As in the case of Herculaneum, the discovery of Pompeii in 1750 was accidental, but the excavations have brought to light a living picture of a Roman city more than eighteen hundred years ago, with all its departments of domestic and public life, the worship of the gods, the shows of the arena, architecture, painting, and sculpture, and in short all the appliances of comfort and luxury as they existed in a wealthy community of those remote days.

The year following the destruction of these cities, a three-day fire in Rome reduced to ashes the Capitol, Augustus's library, Pompey's theater, and numerous houses, while on the heels of the conflagration came a dreadful pestilence. Titus did everything in his power for the homeless sufferers, even to the despoiling of his palaces of their ornaments to obtain money, and he schemed

The death of Vitellius by the people in the year A.D. 69

Aulus Vitellius reigned from A.D. 69 to 79 and was the ninth Caesar. (From a coin of the time)

Domitian, the twelfth and the last of the reigning Caesars, who ruled (from A.D. 81 to 96) before the advent of the Antonine Dynasty beginning with Nerva in 96

and planned to find occupation for them. He became the idol of his subjects, the "love and delight of the human race," but at the beginning of the third year of his reign, September 13, 81, he suddenly fell ill and died, his younger brother Domitian being suspected by some of having poisoned him.

Be that as it may, Domitian came to the throne in 81, and ruled till 96. At first, he passed many good laws, governed the provinces carefully, and administered justice, but the failure of his campaigns against the Dacians and the Marcomanni (in 87) soured his whole nature. He became ferocious in his suspicions, jealousy, and hatred; and through murder and banishment, it is said, deprived Rome of nearly all of the citizens conspicuous for their learning, talent, or wealth. He held the army to him by greatly increasing its pay, and won the favor of the people by extravagant gifts and gladiatorial games and shows, in some of which he took part. His cruelties finally became so intolerable that his wife Domitia joined in a conspiracy against him, and he perished from the dagger on September 18, 96.

The Senate immediately elected M. Nerva as his successor, though he was past three-score years of age. He had twice held the honor of the consulship before his election, and displayed great wisdom and moderation. The taxes were lessened, and the administration of justice improved, but his advanced age rendered him unable to repress the insolence of the Praetorian Guards, and he adopted M. Ulpius Trajanus, known as Trajan, who succeeded him on his death, January 27, 98.

Trajan began his administration by the usual largess to the soldiers, extending the same to the Roman citizens and their families, and he made large provision out of the imperial treasury for the upbringing of the children of poor freemen in Rome and other Italian towns. It was in the year 101 that Rome beheld, for the first time, its

emperor leading forth its legions in person upon their career of conquest. Trajan then set out on his first campaign against the Dacians, who had compelled Rome since the time of Domitian to pay them tribute. The struggle was long and severe, but was completely successful (104–105), and Dacia became a royal province. This was the first conquest since the death of Augustus, and was celebrated on Trajan's return to Rome by a triumph and splendid games which lasted for four months.

Trajan's appetite for foreign conquest was whetted by his success, and in 106 he again set out for the East. Landing in Syria, he moved northward, receiving the submission of numerous princes on the way, and occupying Armenia, which he made a province of the empire. Though he was busy for the succeeding seven years, we have no clear record of what he did. Once more he went to Syria in 115, his objective point being the Parthian Empire. Its capital hardly offered the semblance of resistance, and he descended the Tigris, subduing the tribes on both banks and being the first and only Roman general to navigate the Persian Gulf. When he returned, he found it necessary to reconquer Mesopotamia, north Syria, and Arabia, and he did it more thoroughly than before. By this time he was in a sad bodily condition from dropsy and paralysis and, while on the return to Italy, died at Selinus, in Cilicia, in August 117.

Although so much of Trajan's reign was taken up with his military campaigns, his administration of civil affairs was admirable. Equal justice was secured for all; the imperial finances were greatly improved, and peculation on the part of public officers was severely punished. One of the fads of the Roman emperors was the improvement and beautifying of Rome, and none did more through work in that respect than Trajan. The empire was traversed in all directions by military routes; canals and bridges were built, new towns arose, the Via Appia was restored, the Pontine Marshes partially drained, the "Forum Trajani" erected, and the harbor of Civita Vecchia constructed. A striking proof of the sincerity of this emperor's labors to improve the condition of his subjects was shown in the wish, which it became the fashion formally to utter, on the accession of each of his

The Trajan Arch in Rome erected in honor of the emperor

successors: "May he be happier than Augustus, better than Trajan."

Trajan died childless, and his successor was P. Aelius Hadrianus, or Hadrian, the son of Trajan's cousin. He had not only displayed great ability in the various high offices he filled, but he was a favorite of the empress. Trajan had the right to name his heir, and when the empress announced that it was Hadrian, the citizens and Senate accepted him without murmur.

The empire at this time was in a critical condition. There were insurrections in Egypt, Palestine, and Syria; the barbarian hordes were swarming into Moesia in the East and Mauritania in the West, and the turbulent Parthians had once more asserted their independence and administered several defeats to the imperial forces.

Looking calmly at the situation which confronted him, Hadrian was convinced that a peaceful policy was the true one. He decided to limit the Roman boundaries in the East, and concluded a peace with the Parthians by which he surrendered all the country beyond the Euphrates to them. Returning to Rome in 118, he treated the people liberally, but suppressed with relentless severity a patrician conspiracy against his life. He then, by means of large gifts, induced the Roxolani, who are the modern Russians, to retire from Moesia, which they had invaded.

The year 119 saw the beginning of Hadrian's remarkable journey, most of which he is said to have performed on foot. He visited Gaul, Germany, Britain, Spain, Mauritania, Egypt, Greece, and Asia Minor. In Britain, he built the wall which extends from the Solway to the Tyne, and did not return to Rome until seven years later, when he received the title of *Pater Patriae.* He was so fond of the city of Athens that he spent the years 132 and 133 there. Making another visit to Syria, he came back to Italy, and passed the remainder of his life around Rome, dying July 10, 138, at Baiae.

The vigor and thoroughness with which Hadrian reorganized and disciplined the army remove all thought that his peaceful policy was attributable to fear or weakness. He did more than any emperor to consolidate the monarchical system of Rome. He divided Italy into four parts, each under a consul, to whom was entrusted the administration of justice. Among the numerous splendid edifices he erected was the mausoleum called the *Moles Hadriani,* the Aelian bridge leading to it, and the splendid villa at Tibur. He also laid the foundation of several cities, the most important of which was Adrianopolis. He placed a high value on Greek literature, and was a lover and patron of the fine arts.

Hadrian adopted as his heir T. Aurelius Antoninus, of excellent abilities and in middle life. Him Hadrian required to select two heirs, M. Annius, his own sister's son, and Lucius Verus, the child of his late comrade. Antoninus Pius (the Senate having added the latter name) had served Hadrian as proconsul in Asia, where

Later Roman emperors. Top, left to right: *Caracalla, son of Septimius Severus, who reigned from 211 to 217, was credited with giving all free inhabitants of the Roman Empire citizenship; Domitian, emperor from 81 to 96, left no particular mark in history; Trajan, who reigned from 98 to 117, conquered Dacia (Romania); and Diocletian (284–305) organized the empire into 101 provinces, which was a creditable reorganization, and the remnants of it remain until this day.* Center, left to right: *Constantine the Great, who ruled from 307 to 337, came to terms with Licinius, the Augustus of the East, and defeated Augustus of the West at the gates of Rome in 312 in the Battle of Milvian Bridge. It was at the conclusion of the battle that the soldiers saw the Christian Cross in the sky, giving rise to the legend that this vision was the symbol of victory; he allowed the Christians freedom of worship and moved the capital of the empire to Byzantium, which was renamed Constantinople in his honor. Septimius Severus (193–211) was another emperor who left no historical mark.* Bottom, left to right: *Antonius Pius, who reigned from 138 to 161, was the actual founder of the Antonine Dynasty; Commodus (180–92), did little to advance the empire; Julianus (the Apostate) was named emperor at Lutetia (Paris) at twenty-nine years of age and upon the death of Constantius II, his father, in 361, he was left the legitimate emperor, tried to bring back paganism to the world but died in a battle with the Persians in 363 before he could make much progress. His papers are still read and accepted today on Neoplatonist philosophy. And Hadrian, emperor from 117 to 138, is most famous today for his Hadrian Wall in Britain, a part of his efforts to keep the territory his predecessors had conquered.*

Marcus Aurelius

the gentle wisdom of his rule gave him a higher reputation than any of his predecessors. He inherited great wealth and made one of the best emperors who ever ruled imperial Rome. He was simple, temperate, and kind, his highest object being that of benefiting his people, who looked up to him in the truest sense as the father of his country. His mild hand partly stayed the persecution of the Christians, which was continued during his reign. Fond of peace, the only important war in which he engaged was against Britain, where the Roman power was extended. He also built a wall between the Forth and the Clyde, as a check against the predatory tribes of the North. He was so widely known for his integrity and justice that he was often employed to arbitrate in the affairs of foreign states. To his wisdom, kindness, and unvarying courtesy was due the freedom of his vast empire from insurrections, violence, conspiracies, and bloodshed. It may be said, in brief, that he furnished a model for those who came after him, though, sad to say, few were able to measure up to his splendid standard. He died in 161, and was succeeded by Marcus Annius, called Aurelius, who, as we have learned, had been selected as heir at the command of Hadrian.

Aurelius had been made consul in 140, and, up to his accession to the throne, he discharged the duties with faithfulness and ability. He and the emperor had been the closest of friends. Aurelius, on becoming emperor, showed his chivalry of character by voluntarily sharing the government with young Lucius Verus, who from that time bore the title of Lucius Aurelius Verus. Such a ruler as Aurelius was sure to win the respect and love of his subjects, but Lucius, when sent to take part in the Parthian War, remained in Antioch, sunk in debasing pleasures, leaving his officers to prosecute the struggle, and at the close he returned home and enjoyed the triumph to which he had no claim. The troops brought a pestilence, which, together with appalling inundations and earthquakes, laid much of the city in ruins, and destroyed the granaries where the supplies of corn were

kept. A formidable insurrection had long been fomenting in the German provinces; the Britons were on the point of revolt, and the Catti (the Suevi of Julius Caesar, who lived in the country nearly corresponding to the present Hesse) were ready to devastate the Rhenish provinces.

The manifold calamities that had fallen and still threatened to fall so terrified the Romans that, to allay them, Marcus determined to go forth to war himself. For a time Marcus and Lucius were completely successful. The Marcomanni and the other rebellious tribes, living between Illyria and the sources of the Danube, were compelled to sue for peace in 168, the year preceding the death of Lucius. The contest was renewed in 170 and, with little intermission, lasted throughout the life of the emperor. Marcus carried on the campaign with amazing vigor and skill, and nearly annihilated the Marcomanni and the Jazyges.

Connected with this war was a victory so unprecedented that some historians accept it as a miracle. The Romans were perishing of thirst and heat, on a summer day in 174, when, without warning, the flaming sky was darkened by a black cloud from which the cooling rain descended in torrents. The feverish soldiers abandoned themselves to the lifegiving drafts, when the barbarians assailed them with furious energy, and assuredly would have annihilated them, had not a storm of hail and fire descended upon the assailants alone, and scattered them in headlong terror. So profound indeed was the dread inspired that the Germanic tribes hastened from all directions to beg for mercy.

This astounding occurrence could hardly be believed were it not established by every soldier of a large army, and by Aurelius himself, who was incapable of falsehood. It certainly was one of the strangest incidents in history.

At this juncture, a new outbreak occurred in the East, brought about by the shocking treachery of the emperor's own wife. This wicked woman urged rebellion by Governor Avidius Cassius, a descendant of the Cassius who had slain Caesar. The emperor, though in poor health, was obliged to leave Pannonia with the least possible delay. Cassius seized the whole of Asia Minor, but was slain by his own soldiers. Marcus Aurelius expressed his sorrow that the fates had thus deprived him of the happiness of pardoning the man who had conspired against his happiness. He exhibited the same magnanimity on his arrival in the East, where he refused to read the papers of Cassius, and ordered them to be burned, so that he might not be led to suspect anyone of being a traitor. He treated the provinces with such gentleness that he won their love and disarmed them of all enmity. While he was thus engaged, his disloyal wife died in an obscure village, and the husband paid her every honor.

On his way back to Rome, he visited Lower Egypt and Greece, and by his noble efforts in behalf of his subjects won their profound gratitude. In Athens he founded chairs of philosophy for each of the four chief sects—Platonic, Stoic, Peripatetic, and Epicurean. Reaching Italy, he celebrated his bloodless triumph on December 23, 176. Fresh disturbances having broken out in Germany, he went thither in the following autumn and was again successful. But his weak constitution by this time was shattered by the hardships, sufferings, and anxiety he had borne so long. He died in Vienna on March 17, 180.

THE GROWTH OF CHRISTIANITY

With all that has been said of that extraordinary man and emperor, Marcus Aurelius, justice requires mention of a feature of his character that the reader probably has not suspected—his hostility to Christianity. He was a persecutor of the new religion, and must have known of the cruelties perpetrated upon the believers. There have been many explanations of his course, the generally accepted one being that he was led astray by evil counselors, but the more probable cause is that he was actuated by his earnestness in the heathen faith of his ancestors, and the belief that the new doctrine threatened to undermine the empire itself. He did not comprehend the religion of gentleness and love, and thought it his duty to extirpate the dangerous sect.

The most important facts connected with the history of the Roman Empire is the spread of Christianity within its confines. The variety of peoples had a variety of religions, but all, with the exception of the Jews, were pagans and polytheists, or believers in many gods. Such was the spiritual state of the myriads of human beings, when Christ was born in an obscure corner of the dominion of Augustus, and when the seed was sown whose harvest no man could foresee or dream of in his wildest imaginings.

The propagation of the new faith was marked by ferocious persecutions. We have learned of the first one, which was that by the fiendish Nero, who aimed to turn suspicion against the Christians as the incendiaries of Rome, in order to hide his own guilt. Tacitus, the great Roman historian, who was born under Nero, says of this diabolical infamy: "Some were nailed on crosses, others sewn up in the skins of wild beasts and exposed to the fury of dogs; others again smeared over with combustible materials were used as torches to illuminate the darkness of the night. The gardens of Nero were destined for the melancholy spectacle, which was accompanied with a horse-race, and honored with the presence of the Emperor, who mingled with the populace in the dress and attitude of a charioteer."

Now it may be asked why the Romans, who permitted innumerable religions to flourish within their empire, concentrated their furious persecutions upon the Christians. The main cause was the proselyting ardor of the Christians themselves. The believer in that faith was taught as one of his basic duties that he must not selfishly absorb it unto himself, but do all he could to persuade his brethren to share it with him. Its very nature, therefore, made it aggressive, while the numerous pagan faiths were passive. Christianity did what no other faith did. It boldly taught that all the gods of the Romans were false, and that it was a sin to bow down to them. Not only that, but it did its utmost to lead all others to think the same. The early Christians held their meetings secretly and at night, and this was looked upon with disfavor by the authorities, who saw the germs of danger in the practice. But, as has been said, the blood of the martyrs was the seed of the church, and as we progress in the history of the Roman Empire, this truth will manifest itself again and again.

The reader has gone sufficiently far through these pages to note another fact: the real power of empire lay in the soldiery who stood behind the throne. We have learned of the insolence of the Praetorian Guards, who dared to insult an emperor to his face, and who did not hesitate to make and unmake sovereigns at will, with the Senate always ready to record and accept the decree of the soldiers. Inasmuch as each new ruler signalized his accession to the throne by distributing largesses, it followed that the more emperors there were, the greater would be the gifts distributed. So the troops became addicted to deposing emperors and selecting new ones. The man fixed upon for the purple was usually a favorite general, and as there were plenty of them, it followed that Rome sometimes had several emperors at the same time. No man dared aspire to the crown without the backing of the soldiers.

The only accession of territory by Rome during the first century of the Christian Era was Britain. In the words of Edward Gibbon, the outstanding English historian of the eighteenth century: "After a war of about forty years, undertaken by the most stupid (Claudius), maintained by the most dissolute (Nero), and terminated by the most timid (Domitian) of all the emperors, the greater part of the island of Britain submitted to the Roman yoke." We remember the addition of the province of Dacia by Trajan in the early part of the second century.

One cruel amusement of the Romans was their gladiatorial fights, which date from their earliest history. The popularity of these increased, till the time came when magistrates, public officers, and candidates for the popular suffrage gave shows to the people, which consisted mainly of the bloody and generally fatal encounters; but no earlier leaders equaled the emperors in providing the people with the fearful exhibitions. In one given by Julius Caesar, 320 couples engaged in combat. In the terrific display offered by Trajan, lasting 123 days, ten thousand gladiators were exhibited at once, and two thousand fought with and killed one another, or contended with wild beasts for the amusement of the seventy thousand spectators in the Colosseum, who included every grade of society from the highest to the lowest.

Sinewy, athletic slaves were brought from all parts of the dominions and trained for the combats, as horses have been trained in later times for races. There were so many gladiators during the conspiracy of Catiline that they were deemed dangerous to the public safety, and the proposal was made to distribute them among the different garrisons. The exhibitions became so numerous that efforts were made to limit the number of gladiators. Cicero advocated a law forbidding anyone giving a show for one or two years before becoming a candidate for public office, and Augustus prohibited more than two shows a year, or the giving of one by a person worth less than twenty thousand dollars; but the passion was so strong that it was impossible to keep the terrible exhibitions within moderate limits.

A gladiatorial show was announced by pictures and show bills, after the fashion of modern theatrical plays. All the trained contestants were sworn to fight to the death, and the display of cowardice was followed by fatal tortures. The fighting at first was with wooden swords, which soon gave way to steel weapons. When one of the combatants had disarmed his opponent, he placed his foot on his body, and looked at the emperor, if present, or to the people, for the signal of life or death. If they raised their thumbs, he was spared; if they turned them down, he was slain. The gladiator who conquered was rewarded with a palm and in some cases with his freedom. At first the gladiators were slaves, but afterward freemen and even knights entered the arena. In the time of Nero senators and knights fought, and under Domitian women appeared as combatants. The gladiatorial contests were prohibited by Constantine in 325, but it was not till nearly two centuries later, under Theodoric, that they were finally abolished.

The decline of the mighty empire was thus begun through the sapping of Roman manliness; the process continued to the final crash. Commodus (180–92) was the legitimate son and heir of Marcus Aurelius, and

The death of Emperor Commodus

under him the worst days of Caligula and Nero were revived. He brought the Macedonian War, inherited from his father, to an end by a dishonorable peace, and abandoned himself to the most degrading debauchery. Seven hundred and fifty times he posed as a gladiator in the arena. He had arranged to enter a specially splendid festival as a gladiator on the first of January 193, but was murdered the night preceding, and the Senate by resolution declared his memory dishonored. The honorable and vigorous Senator P. Helvidius Pertinax spent three months in bringing order out of chaos. His ability made him feared by the Praetorians, and they murdered him. They then openly offered the empire to the highest bidder, and set a pretender on the throne. At the same time three other claimants were advanced by three other bodies of troops.

L. Septimius Severus (193–211), commander on the Danube, was the first to enter Rome, where by his energy and address he won over the Senate. It required four years of vigorous fighting to dispose of his competitors, and he then became supreme. The Parthians having supported one of his opponents, he waged successful war against them and succeeded even in gaining a new province in Mesopotamia. He was finally compelled to take the field against the turbulent tribes of Britain, and died at the present city of York in February 211.

M. Aurelius Antoninus Caracalla (211–17), son of Severus, was another miscreant, who, impatient to obtain the throne, made an attempt on his father's life. He lost no time in killing his brother and fellow emperor Geta, with all who supported him, twenty thousand in number. He found means for his extravagance and excesses, in robbing his subjects. A monument of his lavishness as a builder is the immense ruins of the famous Baths of Caracalla, in Rome. An important political act of his reign was the bestowment of Roman citizenship on all municipalities of the empire—a step necessary in order to obtain new taxes for filling his treasury. He showed feebleness in his wars on the frontiers of the Rhine and the Danube, and against the Parthians. He showed his savage cruelty at Alexandria in Egypt. He had entered that city in triumphal procession; but in the midst of all the pomp the "Emperor of the World" fell back in his chariot and slumbered in drunken stupor. The young men of the city laughed and made a jest of this, whereon Caracalla sent his troops out through the streets for six successive days on a general massacre.

While engaged in a last campaign against Parthia, he was murdered by order of Macrinus, his prefect of the guard, who wore the purple for a brief while, until the Syrian troops raised to the throne Heliogabalus (Elagabalus), who was a distant relative of the house of Severus, and only fourteen years old. The soldiers endured this degenerate youth for nearly four years, and then murdered him and his mother.

Alexander Severus (222–35), a cousin of the wretch

who had been murdered, was too young to carry on the government alone, and it remained for the time in the hands of his grandmother Maesa. The young emperor meant well, but was too weak by nature to impress himself upon those troublous times. His wars brought no credit to the Roman Empire, and he vainly combated the assaults on the Roman possessions in Asia made by the new Persian Empire. Equally fruitless were his campaigns against the Germans, which he next undertook. His attempts at discipline angered the legions, and when Maximinus, a popular general, presented himself as a rival emperor, the soldiers slew Alexander and went over to Maximinus in a body.

Thus passed away the last of the descendants of Severus, and the decline of the empire grew more rapid. Rome became the scene of anarchy, violence, and bloodshed, for the struggle was fierce and continuous among those bitten with the madness of ruthless ambition. Our list contains the names of all these imperators, some of whom held their power for only a few weeks or months. Gordianus III (238–44) prosecuted a successful campaign against the Persians, and compelled them to give back Mesopotamia, but he was slain before the close of the war by his prefect of the guards, Philippus (244–49), who fell in battle with a rival, Decius.

Valerian (253–60) braced all his energies against the tide that was sweeping everything to destruction, but was unable to stay it, and was carried with the resistless current. The territory between the Limes and Rhine was lost; the Saxons plundered the coasts; the Goths were edging into Greece; the Franks and Alemanni tramped through Gaul, and Valerian himself was taken prisoner by the Persians and died in captivity. Claudius II (268–70) started well, but had only fairly done so when he died.

Aurelian (270–75), a famous general, roused the hope of his countrymen by his skill and patriotism. He repelled the Alemanni and Goths, and restored for a brief while the unity of the empire. He conquered a Gallic usurper and destroyed Zenobia's kingdom of Palmyra. Zenobia was a beautiful Arab queen. Her husband founded an empire in the Asian deserts, and defeated both the Persians and the Romans. After his death Zenobia maintained and even increased the power of her empire. Great men rallied round her, and for a moment it seemed that Rome had found a rival. Aurelian, however, besieged and mastered her capital after a struggle heroic on both sides; and the proud and beautiful queen was led as his captive in a Roman triumph. Aurelian's home government was firm and wise, and the circumvallation of Rome, still largely preserved, is a monument to his public spirit and enterprise. While fighting against the Persians, he was murdered near Byzantium in 275.

Probus (276–82) was, like Aurelian, of Illyrian descent, and was commander of the Syrian troops. He displayed brilliant ability in driving back the Germans, and restored the old frontier of the Limes. He was wise in inducing thousands of Germans to settle on Roman soil, where they were encouraged in vine growing and the tillage of the land. He also took many of them into the army, and treated the Senate with consideration, but he was doomed to share the fate of so many of his predecessors, for the soldiers, angered by his goodness and strictness, put him to death. From the swirl of strife and bloodshed finally emerged Diocletian (284–305), who introduced a new era in the history of the monarchy.

The first years of his administration were so disturbed by the aggressions of the barbarians that he took a colleague, Maximian, who, under the title of Augustus, became joint emperor in 286. Diocletian retained for himself the government of the eastern empire and gave the western to Maximian, but the attacks became more threatening and Diocletian divided the kingdom again. In 292, Constantius Chlorus and Galerius were proclaimed as caesars, and the fourfold partition was appropriated as follows: Diocletian the East, with Nicomedia as his seat of government; Maximian, Italy and Africa, with Milan as his residence; Constantius, Britain, Gaul, and Spain, with Treves as his capital; Galerius, Illyricum and the valley of the Danube, with Sirmium as his headquarters. Diocletian seldom took the field, so that most of the fighting fell to his colleagues. Among the reconquests was that of Britain, which in 296 was restored to the empire. In addition, the Persians were defeated and compelled to submit in 298, and the northern barbarians were driven beyond the frontiers. Diocletian's tempestuous rule lasted for twenty-one years, when he abdicated his throne, forcing his colleague Maximian, much against his will, to do the same at Milan. Two years before his abdication, he was instigated by his colleague Galerius, his son-in-law, to that bloody persecution of the Christians which has made his rule memorable in history.

The emperor issued an edict commanding all Christian churches to be demolished, all copies of the sacred

Diocletian tried to destroy Christianity but gave up and resigned. He built the greatest palace ever erected by a sovereign. It was an entire town and parts of it still stand today in Spalato on the Dalmatia coast.

When Diocletian gave up his throne in 305, Constantine the Great, a very religious person, took over the empire soon afterward. He is seen here in an allegorical painting showing the Christian Cross in a vision over his soldiers, and himself.

Scriptures to be burned, and every Christian to be degraded from honor and rank. Hardly had this proclamation been posted up, when a Christian noble stepped forward and tore it down. He made no attempt to conceal his act, and being arrested was roasted to death. A fire broke out in the palace, but, since it was quickly extinguished, there is cause for belief that it was kindled to furnish a pretext for persecuting the Christians. They suffered every conceivable torture, and the flames of persecution raged everywhere in the empire except in Gaul, Britain, and Spain, where Constantius ruled. Diocletian and Maximian abdicating as we have shown, Galerius gave unrestrained indulgence to his infernal hatred of the Christians. "With little rest, for eight years," says a writer, "the whip and the rack, the tigers, the hooks of steel, and the red-hot beds continued to do their deadly work. And then in 311, when life was fading from his dying eye, Galerius published an edict permitting Christians to worship God in their own way."

Christianity from its divine nature is deathless, and no persecution or human enmity can stay its advances. Galerius, its fiendish foe, was dead, and now came the wonderful occurrence of a Roman emperor professing Christianity. While Constantius Chlorus was fighting in Britain, he died, and the soldiers proclaimed his son Constantine emperor. This was easy enough, and in accordance with the usual fashion, but the first step the new emperor had to take by way of self-preservation was to overcome five rivals.

In the prosecution of this stupendous task, he was on his way in 312 to attack his rival Maxentius near Rome, when, so he declared, he saw with his own eyes the form of a flaming cross in the heavens, standing out above the sun and inscribed with the words: *"In hoc vince"* (By this conquer). In the battle which shortly followed, Maxentius was overthrown, and, like Saul of Tarsus, who saw the great light on the way to Damascus, Constantine resolved to accept the new faith and become a Christian.

It is said by the early church historians that on the night following this vision, the Savior appeared to Constantine in a dream, and commanded him to frame a similar standard, and to march under it with the assurance of victory. Thus originated the famous *labarum,* or standard of the cross, displayed by the Christian emperors in their campaigns. The *X* in the top of the labarum represents the cross, and is the initial of the Greek word for Christ.

While the personal conduct of Constantine in many instances was shockingly contrary to the spirit of Christianity, for he was cruel and licentious, it cannot be denied that he dealt prodigious blows in favor of the new faith. His first act was the issuance of the Edict of Milan, which brought peace to the sorely harried Christian church. In 324, he defeated the last of his rivals, and made Christianity the religion of the state. He sent out circular letters to his subjects, whom he exhorted to embrace the divine truth of Christianity. His example could not fail to have tremendous influence, and thousands did as he asked them. It is estimated that during his reign a twentieth part of the population were professing Christians. Instead of persecuting paganism in its turn, Constantine assailed it with ridicule and neglect. With the public money he repaired the old churches and built new ones, so that it came about that in all the leading cities the strange sight was presented of the pagan temples being surpassed in splendor by the new places of worship. The Christian clergy were no longer required to pay taxes, and Sunday was proclaimed a day of rest. Finally, Constantine removed the seat of government to Byzantium, which henceforth became known as Constantinople, in his honor, and was essentially a Christian city.

Now, while Constantine professed Christianity, it is impossible to believe that his heart was touched by its gentle teachings, for his private conduct was ferocious. He must have been controlled largely by political and selfish motives. He and Licinius, through the famous edicts of Milan and Nicomedia, simply declared the equality of Christianity with the old state religion. The path of Constantine was crimsoned with blood, for he shrank from no crime against even his nearest relatives, in order that he might accomplish his aims. His father-in-law Maximinus, his brother-in-law Licinius, and the latter's son, fell before him in the struggle for the monarchy, and finally his own son by his first marriage, the worthy Caesar Crispus, because of his popularity, aroused the fatal jealousy of Constantine. This emperor died, May 22, 337, while making his preparations for a Persian war in Nicomedia.

THE BARBARIANS DESTROY THE EMPIRE

Constantine had shifted his capital to Constantinople. In the vigor of his career, he had appointed his three sons by his second marriage to be caesars, and at his death the empire was apportioned among them. Constantine II received the West; Constantius, Asia with Egypt; and Constans, Italy and Africa. Almost from the first a furious quarreling raged among them. Constantine was defeated by Constans and killed at Aquileia in 340. This gave the latter dominance in the empire, and he gained some creditable successes over the Germans, but he made himself so odious by his arbitrary conduct that his troops slew him and proclaimed as emperor one of his generals, Magnentius, a Frank by birth (350). Magnentius suffered defeat at the hands of Constantius, and in despair slew himself. Thus Constantius became sole monarch in 353, and reigned until 360. Before leaving the East, he had appointed his cousin Gallus as caesar, but, suspecting his infidelity, caused him to be murdered in 354. There was urgent need of the presence of the emperor in the East, and the inroads of the Germans into Gaul demanded a strong commander in the West. Constantius, therefore, sent his cousin Julianus, brother of the murdered Gallus, into Gaul as caesar.

This was the man of whom we have already learned something, and who figures in history as Julian the Apostate. He was successful against the Alemanni and Franks, and checked the tide of German invasion for several years. Constantius did not do so well in the territory of the Danube and, becoming jealous of Julianus, ordered him to send him a part of his troops to help in an impending Persian war. These soldiers refused to leave Julianus, and proclaimed him emperor in Paris. Before Constantius could march to the attack, he died at Cilicia, and Julianus became sole emperor (361–63).

He gained the name of the Apostate through his efforts to supplant Christianity with paganism. He had been brought up in the former belief, but he abandoned it; and it is not unlikely that the bloody quarrels of Constantine and other professing Christian leaders had much to do with his contempt for the faith they claimed to follow. How far Julianus would have succeeded in his purpose

it is impossible to say, had his life been spared, but all his plans came to naught through his death in June 363.

Jovian was the nominee of the army, and, having made a disgraceful peace with the Germans, he retreated and then died in February 364, whereupon Valentinian I was elected emperor and, at the request of the army, took his brother Flavius Valens to share the throne with him. Valentinian had charge of the West, and reigned from 364 to 375, while Valens, beginning in the same year, held power till 378.

Valentinian fought with success against the Alemanni and Sarmatians, and his distinguished general, Theodosius, father of the later emperor of that name, held Britain and Africa. Valentinian, dying in the year named, was followed by his two sons Gratian and Valentinian II, the latter still a minor. The former was persuaded by Ambrose, the famous Bishop of Milan, to deprive the pagan worship of the support hitherto received from the state.

The reader has not failed to note the great change through which the Roman Empire had been passing for a long time. The "pangs of transformation" were protracted through centuries, but they were complete. The empire consisted of Italy and the provinces, and for a time their respective governments were on a different footing. The inhabitants of Italy were Roman citizens, with the provincials under the rule of Roman officials. But there began the formation of a nation of Romans in the provinces through the expedient of introducing colonies and of admitting the most deserving of the provin-

Valentinian I, the last emperor of the Roman Empire, divided his domain with his brother Valens, who became the emperor of the East in 364. The two empires remained separate until 476.

The death of Julian the Apostate

Theodosius I (the Great), considered a great general, had some early conflict with the Church and is seen here being refused admission to the church by Saint Ambrose, the bishop of Milan. Theodosius soon accepted Christianity in its fullest terms. Upon his death, in 395, he was the emperor of both the East and the West empires and they were split up between his sons, Arcadius taking the East and Honorius the West.

A gold medal issued by Theodosius

cials to the freedom of Rome. Under Caracalla (211–17), the distinction between Romans and provincials was wiped out, and Roman citizenship was given to all the free inhabitants of the empire. By this time, the inhabitants of Gaul, Spain, North Africa, and Illyria had become thorough Romans, a proof of which is that several of the later emperors were provincials, as they would have been called at an earlier date.

It inevitably followed that when all distinction ceased between Italy and the rest of the Roman Empire, Rome lost its importance as the center of imperial dominion. You recall the division of the empire under Diocletian, and the removal of the capital to Byzantium (Constantinople) by Constantine. The pulsations of the great heart at Rome had sent all the blood through the arteries into the provinces, where it remained.

Theodosius I (379–95) was the last emperor who ruled over the whole Roman Empire. He was a great man and a zealous friend of the Christian religion. You have been told of the meekness with which he submitted to the repulse by Ambrose, Bishop of Milan, because of the massacre in Thessalonica. His reign, however, was very brief, for he died in January 395 at Milan. He left the empire to his two sons, Honorius ruling in the West, which was the Latin Empire, while Arcadius held sway over the East, which was the Greek, or Byzantine, Empire. This division was in reality only the continuance or, rather, completion of what had been done by preceding emperors.

There could be no mistaking the signs which foretold the fall of Rome. It has been shown that the Romans had ceased to be a *nation,* because the nation was absorbed by the *empire.* There had been a steady mixture of foreign bloods, until only a mongrel race remained in the ancient city. The sturdy ancient Roman—the perfection of manly vigor and strength—was gone, and in his place remained a debauched, effeminate, luxury-loving people, wholly abandoned to self-indulgence. If a few exceptions rose here and there, like towering oaks in a decaying forest, the majority were rotten to the core. The emperors and wealthy classes lived for animal pleasure alone.

The lusty Teutonic or German tribes had lived for centuries among the forests of the North, and gave more than one Roman emperor all he could do to shove them back over the boundaries they persisted in crossing. In time the question arose whether it was not a wise step to permit these barbarians to come into the country and mix with the Romans, who could not fail to be improved by the infusion of so superb a strain. Moreover, these massive neighbors had heard of the new faith—Christianity—and in a crude way accepted its truths. Finally, in the latter half of the fourth century, under the Roman emperor Valens, a large body of Teutons were permitted to make their homes within the limits of the empire. Their dwelling place north of the Danube is now called Moldavia and Wallachia, and had been the province of Dacia in the time of Trajan, but it was abandoned by the Romans under Aurelian. These Goths accepted Christianity in the Arian form (Arius held Christ to be inferior to God the Father in dignity and nature), from Bishop Ulfilas, whose translation of the Scriptures into the Gothic tongue is the oldest Teutonic writing of which we have knowledge.

Valens, the first emperor of the East

In the latter part of the fourth century, the Goths became restless under the pressure of the shaggy Huns —Tartars, or Kalmucks—who, yielding to that strange impulse known as the "wanderings of nations," were come out of eastern Asia, and were pushing their way into Europe. Helpless to hold their own against them, the Goths appealed to the emperor Valens, then ruling over the East, to allow them to cross to the south side of the Danube, and thus place that river as a barrier between them and their ferocious enemies. The emperor was suspicious of the fealty of the Goths, and consented only on condition that they should surrender their children and weapons. This hard proposal was accepted, and the Romans furnished the boats, which for days and nights were rowed back and forth, carrying their loads of innocent ones. Then having given them up, the Goths bribed the Roman officers to allow them to keep their arms. Thus, in 376, a million men, women, and slaves crossed one of the natural frontiers of the empire and settled within its borders.

But the Romans counted unwisely upon the forbearance of the Goths, when they treated them with great brutality and left them with no means against starvation. In their desperation, the Goths marshaled their fierce warriors and marched against Constantinople. The angered Roman army met them near Adrianople, and were disastrously defeated, the emperor losing his life in the battle, which was fought in 378. Then the horde overran the fertile region westward to the borders of Italy and the Adriatic Sea.

Theodosius, who well deserved the name of the Great, compelled the Goths to submit and settle down quietly, many of them taking service in the Roman armies. But this did not last long. The sons of Theodosius were weaklings, and, when they divided the Roman Empire between them, the Visigoths, or Western Goths, rebelled, and elevated their chief Alaric upon their shields, which was their national mode of electing a king. Alaric spread desolation through Greece, conquered the Roman armies there, and sacked their cities. Then he and his Goths hurled themselves upon Italy. They captured and sacked Rome in 410. It was what Pyrrhus and Hannibal, the Greek and the Carthaginian, had failed to do. Until Alaric entered, Rome had not seen a foreign master within her gates since the time of Brennus, eight hundred years before.

After six days of pillage Alaric withdrew from Rome and ravaged southern Italy. His adoring followers looked on him almost as a god. When he died they turned aside the waters of the river Busentinus and buried him on horseback within its depths. Then the waters were allowed to flow back over the grave, and all the slaves who knew where it lay were slain, so that he might rest forever undisturbed.

The Western Empire was fast crumbling to pieces. Britain was abandoned by the Romans and was soon inundated by the German tribes known as Angles and Saxons. The different Teutonic clans invaded Gaul and from Gaul passed into Spain, which was conquered by Vandals, Sueves, and other German races; while Gaul was overrun by Franks, Burgundians, and Goths, all members of the Teutonic family. Then a host of Vandals under Geiseric crossed from Spain into Africa. Carthage was captured in 439. Thus the most vigorous limbs were lopped off from the decaying trunk.

Meanwhile, a hideous creature, squat of form, with huge head, broad shoulders, gleaming deep-set eyes, emerged from his log hut on the plains of Hungary, and set out on his career of conquest and desolation. He was Attila, the Hun, who had murdered his brother rather than permit him to share in his sovereignty over the prodigious hordes of savages scattered through the north of Asia and Europe. Christendom called him the Scourge of God, and his superstitious followers believed he carried a supernatural sword. Under his bloody banner fought the Vandals, Ostrogoths, Gepidae, and many of the Franks. In a short time, he forced his dominion over the people of Germany and Scythia. He ruled from the frontiers of Gaul to those of China. His campaign in 447

Alaric, king of the Visigoths, in his second attempt at the gates of Rome in 408, conquered and occupied the city.

in Persia and Armenia was unsuccessful, but afterward he swept through Illyria and destroyed the countries between the Black Sea and the Mediterranean. At his approach cities were left desolate; the unhappy people fled to crouch in caverns among the woods and cliffs. Starvation was less cruel than the Hun. He gave to all only the choice of annihilation or of following in his train. Theodosius fought three terrific battles with him and was beaten in all. Constantinople escaped because the shaggy demons did not know how to besiege the strong fortifications; but Attila wrought his ferocious will in Thrace, Macedon, and Greece, where seventy cities were desolated. Theodosius, after treacherously trying to murder his conqueror, was compelled to cede to him a portion of his territory south of the Danube and to pay him an immense tribute.

In 451, the Scourge wheeled his horse westward to invade Gaul, but was confronted by Aëtius, leader of the Romans, and Theodoric, king of the Visigoths. There Tartar despotism and Aryan civilization met in the life-and-death struggle, and the latter triumphed. The Huns were routed on every side, Attila himself narrowly escaping capture or death. If we can trust the older historians, this was the bloodiest battle ever fought in Europe. It took place near the site of the present city of Châlons-sur-Marne, and it is said that the dead left on the field numbered from 250,000 to 300,000.

Attila was in despair and, having retired to his camp, collected all the wooden shields, saddles, and other baggage into an immense funeral pile, determined to die in the flames rather than surrender; but through the advice of Aëtius, the Roman commander, the Huns were allowed to retreat in safety, lest they should gain from despair the strength to conquer.

The Scourge recovered his strength in the following year, and again invaded Italy, devastating Aquileia, Milan, Padua, and other cities, and driving the panic-stricken people into the Alps, the Apennines, and the lagoons of the Adriatic, where they founded the city of Venice. Rome was utterly helpless, but was saved through Pope Leo I, who boldly visited the terrible barbarian and by his majestic mien and apostolic mission terrified him into sparing the city. Attila returned to Hungary, but two years later regained his ruthless courage, and was making preparations for another invasion of Italy when he burst a blood vessel and died. What a grim comment on the folly of puny man in arraying himself against the cause of truth and justice! Attila boasted that the grass never grew on the spot trodden by the hoof of his horse, but the prick of a pin or the most trifling occurrence has been sufficient many a time to bring the proudest wretch to the dust. The immense empire of the Scourge of God immediately crumbled to fragments.

Attila had hardly shrunk away from Rome before the imprecations of the Pope, when Geiseric, the Vandal chief of Africa, sailed with his fleet from Carthage and anchored at the mouth of the Tiber. This time Leo could not turn aside the fury of the barbarians. Rome was captured (455), and for two weeks the Vandals and Moors plundered and pillaged and looted, without a gleam of mercy. Scores of ships were laden with captives and treasures, and sailed across the sea to Carthage.

The emperors of the West still came and went like a procession of phantoms. Scan the list and you will find their names, but they were no more than so many figments of sleep, so far as their power went to stay the rush of the empire to destruction. Finally, the Roman Senate declared that one emperor was enough, and that he should be the Eastern emperor Zeno, but the government of Italy was to be trusted to Odoacer, who took the title of Patrician of Italy. This Odoacer had been a bandit among the Noric Alps and, entering the Roman service, rapidly rose to eminence. He aided Orestes, in 475, in driving the emperor Julius Nepos from the throne, and conferred on his son Romulus the title of Augustus, which the people in ridicule changed to Augustulus. This feeble youth, who, by a strange sarcasm of destiny, bore the names of the founder of Rome and of the empire, was pensioned off, and, when Odoacer became king, the Senate sent back to Constantinople the tiara and purple, for the Western Empire had passed away forever.

The western or Latin provinces of the Roman Empire having dissolved before the onrush of the barbarians, let us now glance at the history of the Eastern Empire, which survived the general wreck for a thousand years, though steadily decaying and going to ruin. The Greek or Byzantine Empire reached its zenith in the sixth century, under Justinian, who reigned from 527 to 565.

The last of the emperors of the West, Romulus Augustulus (475–76)

Odoacer, a leading Italian chieftain, defeats Augustulus and becomes the first king of Italy. This action ended the empire of the West. He reigned from 476 to 493. The period of reign by kings of Italy was subject to the Eastern Empire and lasted until the Lombard king Alboin took control in 568.

A gold medallion issued by Justinian

Justinian the Great, emperor of the East from 527 to 565. Under his rule Roman law was revised, and he published the Code, Pandects, and Institutes of Justinian. He also made new laws called Novellae, which are a foundation for such laws today.

Although of little military capacity, he had the wisdom to select the ablest generals of the last days of Roman ascendancy, and under their direction, especially that of the distinguished Narses and Belisarius, the empire was restored, at least so far as outward appearance went, to its ancient limits, and the East and West were reunited under a single rule. His first war, that with Persia, had scarcely been brought to a half-successful conclusion when a revolt took place against him. A rival emperor was elected, and Justinian was so frightened that he would have fled but for the vigor and resolution of his wife, Theodora. Narses repressed the rising with merciless severity, and it is said that thirty thousand of the insurgents were slain in one day.

Belisarius by the force of arms reannexed the Vandal kingdom of Africa to the empire; and he and Narses restored the imperial authority in Rome, in northern Italy, and in a large portion of Spain. One of the remarkable works of Justinian was the renewing and strengthening of the immense line of fortifications along the eastern and southeastern frontier of the empire. These works of defense and many public buildings in Rome and other cities involved enormous expenditures, but they were ably and honestly carried out. The most famous of his buildings is the great church of Saint Sophia in Constantinople.

But the chief renown of Justinian rests upon his work as a legislator. Directly on his accession, he set to work to collect the vast mass of previous legislative enactments which were still in force; and, to make this thorough, he first compiled a code comprising all the constitutions of his predecessors (527–29). His most important legal undertaking was the composition of a systematic treatise on the law for the guidance of students and lawyers, which was published shortly before the Digest, under the title of *Institutiones* (Institutes). They were originally written in Latin, while the later treatises which Justinian caused to be prepared were in Greek, and bore the name *Novellae* (New Works). This complete system, known as the *Civil Law* (*Corpus juris civilis*), formed the groundwork of the law of nearly all of the nations of Europe, England being the most notable exception.

After the fall of Rome and the collapse of the Western Empire, Odoacer, the Visigothic chief, continued governing, claiming to do so by authority of the emperor of the East, but he paid little attention to the Byzantine court at Constantinople. Meanwhile, the Ostrogoths, or Eastern Goths, had established a kingdom between the Black Sea and the Adriatic, under the rule of their own hero, Theodoric. The emperor Zeno commissioned Theodoric to invade Italy and bring that country back into the empire. With Theodoric went all his people, including women and children and aged men, so that it was another migration of a nation. The campaign against Odoacer lasted for three years, but in 493 he was compelled to come to terms, and soon after was assassinated by his rival. Theodoric distributed one-third of the conquered territory among his soldiers in military tenures, and ordered his men to be kind to the people and to obey the laws. The wise rule of Theodoric brought peace and prosperity to Italy, which continued till his death in 526.

Then came turmoil, confusion, bloodshed, and lasting anarchy. It was at this time that Justinian, emperor of the East, interfered, and the imperial forces under Belisarius captured Rome. Narses, his successor, overthrew the Ostrogothic power in Italy in 553, in a great battle on the slopes of Mount Vesuvius. The last king of

Theodoric the Great, the second king of Italy (493–526). He is shown here in an ivory carving with his son Athalaric on his right and his daughter Amalasuntha to his left. Athalaric replaced him as king in 526.

King Alboin

Alboin conquered northern Italy and became the first Lombard king of Italy. He is seen here entering Pavia. His reign was from 568 to 573.

This iron crown of Lombardy was made for the fourth Lombard king, Agilulf, who used it in his coronation in 591, and it was used by all future kings of Lombard and Holy Roman emperors, who were also kings of Lombardy. This crown is unique among crowns because the interior of it was hammered from a nail of the cross of crucifixion of Christ. The jeweled exterior was added in 1100.

culture of postclassical Greece, which in time permeated every aspect of Roman thought, religion, and art. Skilled at integrating conquered peoples, imperial Rome was a melting pot of cultures. In turn, Roman law, institutions, and ideals and the use of the Latin language radiated like its roads out from the city and across the empire, survived its decline, and provided the basis for a new European civilization.

From a military perspective the empire went on the defensive in the first century A.D. By the third century it was in full retreat, although Italy remained secure from invasion for another century. There was no one reason for Rome's decline. Its security system was tested beyond its capacity to defend the empire's frontiers, and its natural leaders withdrew gradually from state service. In simple terms the Roman state suffered ultimately from a loss of will to survive. By the end of the third century the empire had been divided for administrative purposes, and the city of Rome had lost its status as a capital. Although remaining the symbol of Roman unity, the city was an unproductive consumer of wealth too distant from the military frontiers to provide leadership.

Sacked by the Visigoths in 410, Rome was prey thereafter to attacks by marauding Germans. The imperial government encouraged the settlement of some Germanic tribes as allies on Italian land, however, and Germans increasingly made careers in the army and in the administration of the empire. In 476 a palace coup forced the abdication of the last Western emperor, a puppet of his German advisers. In 488 Theodoric, king of the Goths but also a Roman patrician, set about to restore Italy and rebuild Rome. Defending Italy with his Gothic

the Goths, Teias, was slain; and his warriors asked permission of the Romans to depart in peace, bearing with them the body of their leader. Narses gladly consented, and the whole nation of Goths marched in a body out of Italy forever. It became a Byzantine province, governed by rulers appointed from Constantinople, with the title of Exarchs of Ravenna.

Justinian had been dead only three years, when Italy, still governed by an exarch living at Ravenna, was overrun by the third and last of the Teutonic invasions. The Lombards or Longobardi, thus named perhaps from their long beards, came from central Europe, swarmed through the Alps and, sweeping into the valley of the Po, occupied the extensive district still known as Lombardy, with Pavia as its capital.

Through their early history Romans displayed a natural conservatism that opposed acceptance of alien ideas. Not without a struggle from the puritans in their midst, they became deeply affected, however, by the Hellenistic

King Cleph

The last of the Lombard kings, King Desiderius, in his battle "coat of mail"

army, he ruled it as a Roman official. In 526 Justinian, the Eastern Roman (Byzantine) emperor, turned on the Goths and revived direct imperial control over Italy. Justinian introduced into Italy the *Corpus juris civilis,* the compilation of Roman law, which was passed five hundred years later from Italy to the rest of western Europe. In removing his Gothic allies, however, Justinian left Italy open to invasion by the Germanic Lombards who, although few in number, established kingdoms throughout the peninsula. Other portions of Italy including Rome remained in Byzantine hands, but with the creation of the Lombard kingdoms an end was put to the political unity of Italy for the next fourteen hundred years.

PAPACY AND EMPIRE

Christianity was brought to the Greek-speaking Jewish communities of the cities and towns in Italy in the first century. As one of a number of Oriental mystery religions that gained in popularity among native Italians as traditional ethics and morality lost their relevance, Christianity survived persecution and was granted recognition by Constantine, the first Christian emperor, in 315. Christianity had been accepted throughout Italy by the time that it was adopted as the official religion of the Roman Empire late in the fourth century. Heir to the empire's institutions, the church adapted Roman law for ecclesiastical uses.

By the fourth century the Christian bishops of Rome, who claimed succession from Saint Peter, had assumed a position of primacy in the Western, or Latin, church and bore the title Pope. With the transfer of the imperial capital to Constantinople, temporal jurisdiction over the city of Rome was passed to the pope, and estates were conferred on the holder of the office to provide him revenue as an imperial agent. The papacy grew more independent of the distant imperial authority, and theories grounded on tradition were introduced to define the sometimes ambiguous relationship between secular and spiritual jurisdictions, between empire and church, whose interests overlapped in many areas. Papal theorists explained that, whereas civil and ecclesiastical jurisdictions were distinct, only the papacy possessed a *plentitudo protestatis* (fullness of power) and that the authority exercised by civil authorities was merely a reflection of the power of the church. The argument continued that Constantine had made a free gift of Rome to the pope, to whom he and his successors owed their imperial titles. Whatever the theoretical underpinning for his position, the pope was called on in the absence of other authorities to assume a wide range of civil, diplomatic, and even military responsibilities in Italy albeit in the emperor's name, as Byzantine power contracted under pressure from the Lombards.

Because imperial Italy had been left to its own devices,

This coin is considered by experts to have the best likeness of Charlemagne in existence. It was issued in the last year of his reign, 814.

On Christmas Day, 800, Charlemagne was crowned in St. Peter's Church in Rome by Pope Leo III, as the Holy Roman emperor. He had defeated King Desiderius of Lombard in 774, which ended the rule of the Lombard kings over Italy. This mosaic shows Leo III and Charlemagne at the feet of Saint Peter.

Rome came to resent imperial interference in Italian affairs, a situation exacerbated by religious differences that had developed between the Latin and Greek churches. In 754 the pope called on Pepin, king of the Franks and strongest of the Germanic warlords, to expel the troublesome Lombards from Roman territory, which Pepin restored to the pope rather than to the Byzantine emperor, thus establishing the basis of what became the Papal States.

In 800 Pope Leo II re-created the Western Roman Empire by conferring an imperial crown on the Frankish king, Charlemagne. The practical effect on Italy of the reestablishment of the Western Empire—including areas that were never part of the old empire—under a Germanic king was to link Italy's political future to the emerging states of northern Europe rather than to the Byzantine Empire. The Holy Roman Empire stood for one thousand years as the visible sign of the unfulfilled ideal of European unity and of the cooperation between the civil and ecclesiastical order. The authority of the Western emperors in northern and central Italy was nominal, but periodic intervention on their part was required to restore order in Rome, where in the tenth century the papacy had become the pawn of rival Roman aristocratic factions.

By tradition emperors of the Holy Roman Empire were elected by German princes and traveled to Rome for their coronations. Some emperors, such as Otto III, found residence in Italy more congenial than in Germany, but the concentration of imperial power in either one of the two parts of the empire always implied neglect of the other and a decline of imperial influence there.

The eleventh-century reform movement within the church aimed at disciplining the ecclesiastical hierarchy by curbing lay investiture of bishops, that is, the control of ecclesiastical appointments by secular rulers. Bishops were seen to owe not only their temporalities but also their spiritual offices to the emperor. There was a complementary effort to forge a chain of command that tied bishops directly to the pope through a centralized ecclesiastical administrative system. Concurrently the selection of the pope was removed from the Roman nobility to an electoral college of eminent churchmen—the cardinals.

The moving spirit in this medieval reformation was Pope Gregory VII, himself a Roman nobleman, who waged a running battle with Henry IV in Italy and Germany. When moral sanctions failed to bring the emperor to heel, the pope stirred rebellion against him among the Italian towns that were anxious to diminish imperial power over them. Henry IV's abject submission at Canossa in 1077 was a fleeting triumph for the pope. Gregory ultimately failed in his struggle with the emperor, who drove him from Rome and set up an antipope in his stead. But Gregory's long-range goals, separating the spiritual credentials of bishops from their temporal positions as imperial agents, were vindicated by his successors, adding to the strength and prestige of the papacy in the twelfth and thirteenth centuries and freeing it to play a vigorously independent role in the political development of Italy. Nevertheless, conflict between the spiritual and the temporal remained the recurrent theme of medieval history, and nowhere was it more apparent than in Italy.

Although there were acute shifts in papal foreign policy, a single principle dominated the papacy's relations with foreign rulers and its dealings in Italian affairs. Experience had proved that, in order for the church to fulfill its spiritual mission unimpeded by secular authorities, the pope had to have temporal sovereignty in his own right in the Papal States and, as a corollary to the principle, southern Italy had to be kept independent of imperial control and its ruler tied to the papacy.

Sicily and the South remained in Byzantine hands after reestablishment of the Western Empire, although the Byzantine hold on them was weak. Early in the eleventh century landless Norman knights, employed by the Greeks as mercenaries, seized the southern provinces and staked out their individual claims. In 1053 Robert Guiscard united the Norman territories in southern Italy. He and his dynasty created a centralized feudal kingdom in which all land tenure was granted by the king to whom all his subjects owed their primary allegiance. In Italy as elsewhere the Normans combined ambition and a genius for organization and administration. At first resisted by the papacy, Robert Guiscard's claim to a portion of the Byzantine Empire was legitimated by the pope, who accepted the Normans as his vassals, using them many times as a weapon to hold the Western emperor at bay in Italy and to defend the Papal States. In 1130 the Normans added Sicily, conquered in the ninth century by the Saracens, to their domains.

Twelfth-century Italy

MEDIEVAL COMMUNES

Towns, although diminished in size and activity, had survived from antiquity in northern and central Italy. Although nominally subjects of the emperor, the city-republics or communes won greater autonomy in the eleventh century during the investiture controversy at the expense of their bishops, who had governed them as imperial vicars. The maritime republics—Venice, Genoa, and Pisa—had a longer tradition of independence.

Greater political freedom in the communes coincided with improved security in the countryside and on the land and sea trade routes. Italian nobles and townsmen, the first in Europe to understand the use of money and to master business procedure, invested a slowly accumulated surplus of wealth in increasing agricultural output. Surplus food production made it possible to support an urban population of craftsmen and workers and to create the marketplaces around which industry and commerce grew. Northern Italy was medieval Europe's first industrial center, and in its countinghouses, warehouses, and workshops capitalism originated.

The life of the communes engendered the fierce local patriotism and competitiveness that fueled incessant warfare among them. Strong class feeling and intense family rivalries also bedeviled the communes with political and social turmoil. Having secured recognition of their autonomy within their walls, the communes forced the submission of the landed nobility and annexed the surrounding countryside. Many of the old nobility retained their influence but only by joining the guilds and entering the full life of the communes on the same basis as the merchants and manufacturers. Attempts by the guilds—on which representation in communal governments was based—to regulate economic life varied in effectiveness, but a tension existed between corporations and individuals that was the basis of much of the social discontent within the communes that spilled over into their political life.

Although political institutions developed differently in each commune, patterns common to each are discernible. Oligarchies composed of merchant families dominated political life through the more important guilds. The members of the unrepresented lesser guilds struggled to win recognition and a voice in communal affairs. The internal politics of the communes was so turbulent that foreigners—anyone from outside the commune—were employed to serve as chief executives (podestas) to arbitrate among the factions.

Urged on by Italian nobles to curb the radicalism of the communes, the emperor, Frederick of Hohenstaufen (called Barbarossa in Italy), insisted on their membership in a federation under imperial supervision. Putting aside their rivalries, the communes of Lombardy united for their collective security under the pope, and at Legnano in 1176 the Lombard League defeated the emperor's forces and won Barbarossa's grudging confirmation of their liberties. But the question of their independence was not settled. Emperor Frederick II, Bar-

Pope Innocent III, a scion of the noble Italian house of Conti, became pope before his fortieth birthday and held his office from 1198 to 1215. He had nearly absolute control over the monarchs of Europe. The strongest politically set pope to date, he compelled Philip Augustus of France to restore his wife to her position by putting France under an interdict; he excommunicated and dethroned Otho, emperor of Germany, and gave the throne to Frederick of Sicily. Also, he put John of England under interdict and ordered him to be deposed, and told Philip Augustus to carry it out. John submitted and signed a treaty by which England and Ireland became fiefs of Rome.

barossa's grandson, inherited the crowns of Naples and Sicily through his Norman mother, allowing the Hohenstaufens to outflank the Papal States. Called *Stupor Mundi* (Wonder of the World), Frederick II considered himself an Italian prince and kept a brilliant, polyglot court at Palermo, from which he ruled a kingdom that was prosperous and possessed the strongest government known in the Middle Ages. His attempts to subdue the communes of Lombardy and Tuscany came to nothing, however, and in the effort he exhausted the resources of the southern kingdom, which his heirs were unable to hold. Naples and Sicily passed under papal patronage to the French House of Anjou, a move intended to counter imperial influence in Italy. Angevin claims in the South were in time contested by the kings of Aragon, and the seed was planted for the centuries-long competition between France and Spain for control of Italy.

Italians were by no means unanimous in their opposition to the Hohenstaufen scheme for an imperial federation, and the struggle between the emperor and the communes for control of the city-states intensified party strife under the titles of the pro- and anti-imperial parties in Germany. The Ghibellines favored federalism and an imperial presence in Italy. The Guelfs, who stood for particularism (the independence of the communes and the primacy of local interests), looked to the pope as their nominal leader, not as an alternative to the emperor but as the steadiest representative of resistance to imperial claims to overlordship in Italy.

There existed a distinction, not always easy to maintain, between the pope as temporal ruler of the Papal States and as head of the church. In the context of Italian politics, he was but one of several princes, and on that level, rather than as a spiritual leader, relations with him were conducted by other states. However, the powerful thirteenth-century papacy increasingly employed moral sanctions—part of its spiritual arsenal—as political weapons, ultimately to the detriment of both the church and Italy. The pope's responsibility to intervene in questions affecting morality was universally understood, but Dante Alighieri in the *Divina Commedia* (Divine Comedy) and other works berated the papacy for having usurped the function of empire, weakened secular authority, and thus sown the seeds of human discord.

The fourteenth century—a time of war, famine, plague, and doubt, contrasting sharply with the relative stability of the previous century—witnessed the transformation of many city-republics into lordships (seigniories). The intense, disruptive activity of the political factions encouraged a demand for the arrogation of constitutional authority in the communes to a single ruler, above party, who could restore order. Having popular support, the despots needed not tolerate any check on their authority. The courts of the dynasties that ruled the Italian city-states—the Visconti of Milan, the Gonzagas of Mantua, the d'Este of Ferrara, the Scaligeri of Verona

Cosimo de' Medici

—ranked in their time as the equal in magnificence of those of the royal houses of Europe. Often men of intelligence and usually of refined taste, the seigniors attracted to their courts the genius of Italy—scholars, poets, artists—and created the atmosphere in which a great epoch in civilization, the Renaissance, flourished.

The political history of Renaissance Italy is that of the interaction of five Italian states—Naples, the Papal States, Venice, Milan, and Florence—which had drawn many of the smaller states within the orbit of their influence. These states, all fully sovereign by the end of the fourteenth century, took on the characteristics of nation-states and devised systems of alliances within which they acted out in Italy the balance-of-power diplomacy that the great kingdoms of Europe adopted in their practice of statecraft.

The Italian League, a formal alliance agreed to in 1455 at the pope's prompting, was designed to keep the peace among the Italian states and to prevent foreign intervention in Italian affairs. A succession of particularly able statesmen-popes, who possessed the political and diplomatic skills demanded by the times, constructively contributed to the success of the league, which endured for forty years and coincided with the period of the finest cultural and intellectual achievements of the Renaissance.

It was Florence, a city of wool and banks, that was the linchpin in the alliance system. Its politics were dominated by the remarkable Medici family, whose banking house operated branches in Europe's most important commercial centers. Cosimo de' Medici was in every sense a seignior, although he took no title and seldom held public office. He controlled the commune through the manipulation of elections and, not the least, because of public confidence in his ability to provide for the welfare of Florence. Under his grandson, Lorenzo the Magnificent, the Medici seigniory assumed princely proportions but always within the limits of the commune's republican institutions. His taste, good judgment, and generous patronage confirmed the artistic and intellectual preeminence of Florence in Italy and in Europe.

CENTURIES OF FOREIGN DOMINATION

The Italian allies fell out after the collapse of the Medici seigniory, and in 1494 France took advantage of the breach to put forward long-standing claims to Milan and Naples. When Spain intervened on Naples' behalf, divided Italian states chose sides between the two foreign powers, and Italy was made a battleground for the protracted rivalry between France and the Habsburgs. Charles V, Holy Roman emperor and king of Spain, subsequently forged a defensive arc—sweeping from Spain through Italy to Germany and the Low Countries—to contain France, ensuring Spanish Habsburg dominance in Italy for nearly two hundred years. Milan and Naples became part of the Spanish crown and other Italian states its satellites.

It was in this environment that the Florentine, Niccolò Machiavelli, a politician possessed of extraordinary insight into the dynamics of politics, wrote *Il Principe* (The Prince). Infuriated by Italy's weakness, which had invited its domination by foreigners, Machiavelli searched—as Dante had—for a liberator, suggesting in his treatise the qualities needed in a strong man by describing the tactics of the most successful princes. Reviewing the so-called dwarfing of Italy with remarkable detachment, Machiavelli's contemporary, Francesco Guicciardini, acknowledged that states like men were mortal but nevertheless deplored "the infelicity of being born at such a time when his country has to fulfill its doom."

After the conclusion of the War of the Spanish Succession (1701–14), Austria replaced Spain as the dominant foreign power in northern Italy. A Bourbon king was put on the Neapolitan throne, but Lombardy (Milan) was retained in the Habsburg dominions. The kingdom of the Two Sicilies, as Naples-Sicily was styled, entered into a family compact with France and Spain, and, to keep the influence of the Bourbon and Habsburg rivals in balance in Italy, Sardinia was awarded to Piedmont, carying with it a royal title for its reigning House of Savoy. Italy was the outcast of Europe in the eighteenth century, but the despots imposed by foreign rulers, especially in the smaller states of central Italy, were often benevolent and reform minded, providing enlightened and frequently progressive government. Tuscany in particular, ruled by

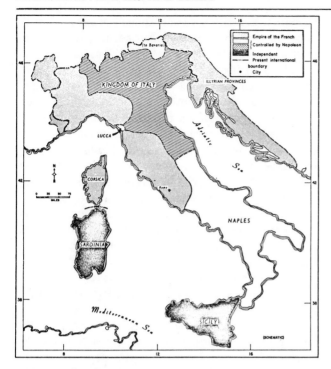

Italy under Napoleon, 1812

the Habsburg-related House of Lorraine, gained a reputation as one of the most liberal states in Europe.

News of the French Revolution was given a sympathetic reception in Italy only among small groups of middle-class liberals. The old regimes busied themselves rounding up local subversives but—except for Austrian Lombardy—took few precautions against the possibility of France's exporting its revolution by force. Napoleon Bonaparte's spectacular Italian campaigns in 1797 and 1799 shattered Austrian hegemony, drove the Bourbon king of the Two Sicilies from the mainland, and ended the twelve-hundred-year history of the Venetian Republic. By 1806 Napoleon—now emperor—had annexed large portions of Italy, including Rome, Piedmont, and Venetian possessions in Dalmatia, to France; deeded Naples to his brother-in-law, Marshal Joachim Murat; and created the kingdom of Italy in northern and central Italy, naming himself its king. The Napoleonic period was crucial for the development of modern Italy, and the changes wrought by the French occupation had a lasting impact on the laws and institutions of the country. The most effective opposition came on a regional basis from small groups of patriots organized in underground secret societies. They had no regard for the old regimes but were inspired by a deep desire to rid Italy of all foreigners and to establish independent, constitutional governments in their respective regions.

RISORGIMENTO

The Risorgimento was the movement for political unity in Italy in the nineteenth century. It was not a mass movement, and until its last years it did not engage the imagination and support of a broad range of Italians. It was, from the first, promoted chiefly by an elite of middle-class liberals and the intelligentsia and entailed a running civil war between the old and the emerging Italian ruling classes. Violent revolution and gradual reform, republicanism and national monarchy, federalism and the unitary state were all proposed as solutions for Italian disunity and subservience. The Nationalist movement was organized during the French occupation around a core of secret societies. Later in the century three figures—Giuseppe Mazzini, Giuseppe Garibaldi, and Camillo di Cavour—emerged, often in competition, as leaders of the Risorgimento.

In the reactionary atmosphere that attended Napoleon's defeat, nationalism seemed a dangerous corollary of the French Revolution. Governments represented at the Congress of Vienna (1815) were intent on reviving the prerevolutionary equilibrium of a Europe torn by a generation of war. Old boundaries and old rulers were restored and their security guaranteed by the great powers. Lombardy-Venetia was returned to Austria, which also counted the satellite states—Tuscany, Modena, and Parma—within its sphere of influence. The Bourbons were restored to Naples and the pope to Rome. Only

Giuseppe Mazzini

Count di Cavour

Giuseppe Garibaldi

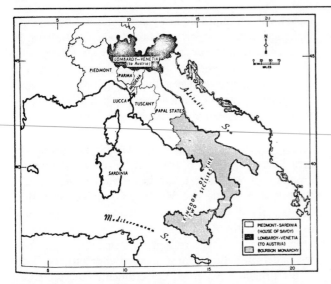

Italy after the Congress of Vienna, 1815

Piedmont stood outside the circle of foreign control or influence; yet there, as elsewhere in Italy, efficient, well-organized repression quashed the petty rebellions stirred by the secret societies.

After 1830 direction of the Risorgimento was pre-empted by Mazzini's Young Italy movement. Mazzini, an ascetic who brought a quasireligious element to the struggle for independence, demanded that his followers make themselves morally worthy to lead Italy to the destiny that history had appointed for it. Mazzini contended that only by violent revolution could Italy be freed and unified and that the struggle itself would have a purifying effect on Italians. Mazzini's goal was a unitary state—eliminating the regionalism that had divided Italians throughout their history—under a republican government with its capital in Rome. From exile he and his followers organized expeditions and conspiracies that touched every part of Italy.

The shock wave of the Paris revolution in 1848 was quickly felt in Italy, sparking rebellions in Lombardy and driving Pope Pius IX from Rome, where Mazzini set up a short-lived republic. Piedmont, joined by other Italian states, took advantage of political unrest in Austria to invade Lombardy, but the campaign—referred to as the First War of Independence—ended in their decisive defeat. Mazzini's revolutionary government in Rome fled before the French troops dispatched by Louis Napoleon (Napoleon III), newly elected president of the Second Republic in France. A permanent garrison was left behind to guard the pope. In its long-range effects, however, the most significant event in Italy in 1848 was the promulgation of a liberal constitution in Piedmont, which transformed the state into a limited monarchy with a strong parliamentary government.

Piedmont was a relatively old state that had been kept outside the mainstream of Italian political development. Traditionally oriented toward France and the only Ital-ian state with a military establishment of any size, Piedmont was set apart by its independence from foreign control or entanglements with foreign dynasties. Despite its setback in the brief war against Austria, Piedmont was recognized after 1848 as the only Italian state capable of giving concerted leadership to the Risorgimento.

Cavour, prime minister of Piedmont, set himself the task of building an efficiently functioning parliamentary government. His territorial aims were limited to creating an enlarged kingdom in northern Italy under the House of Savoy. Conspiring with Napoleon III, Cavour's government entered into a secret agreement guaranteeing French assistance in taking Lombardy-Venetia. Piedmont's rejection of an Austrian ultimatum provided the pretext for an invasion of Lombardy in 1859. Austrian forces were defeated, but the cost of the fighting was greater than Napoleon III had bargained for, and the Piedmontese were forced to accept a peace less advantageous than Cavour had been promised. Under the provisions of the treaty of Villafranca, negotiated by the French and Austrians, Lombardy was surrendered to France, which re-ceded it to Piedmont in return for Savoy and Nice; Venetia remained in Austrian hands; and, more humiliating, a federation of northern Italian states, with Habsburg interests intact, was proposed in place of the unified kingdom envisioned by Cavour.

The war with Austria had, however, stirred successful rebellions in the satellite states and in Romagna (in the Papal States), from which appeals came for union with Piedmont. Commissioners were dispatched to hold these areas for King Vittorio Emanuele II, and, disregarding the peace treaty, Cavour called for plebiscites to approve the annexation of each region into a unitary state. At that point he braked the momentum of the Risorgimento, and Mazzini condemned Cavour as a traitor for not moving to annex Rome and Naples. It was Garibaldi, a follower of Mazzini, who forced Cavour's hand and brought the south into the kingdom of Italy.

Garibaldi welcoming Vittorio Emanuele II as the king of Italy

The young King Vittorio Emanuele II

King Vittorio Emanuele II as he appeared in later years

Garibaldi launched his red-shirted "Thousand" on a triumphal procession through Sicily and Naples, deposed the Bourbon monarchy, and proclaimed a dictatorship in the name of Vittorio Emanuele II. His conquest was as rapid as it was complete, and Garibaldi turned his attention to Rome. Cavour feared the international repercussions of an assault on Rome, defended by its French garrison; and a Piedmontese army, the king at its head, was sent to block Garibaldi's advance. The two forces confronted one another south of Rome, and in a dramatic gesture, typical of the man, Garibaldi turned over Naples and Sicily to Vittorio Emanuele II. Venetia was acquired in 1866 after a third war with Austria. Only Rome remained outside a united Italy.

Cavour called a national Parliament in 1861 to proclaim Vittorio Emanuele II king of Italy. The Piedmontese constitution, providing for representative institutions, became the basic law of the new kingdom. The euphoria of unification soon wore thin and was replaced by misgivings, especially pronounced in the South, about

Piedmontese influence in the national government—a highly centralized administration distant from the people—and its lack of sympathy for local institutions. Each region had its own history, unique culture, and social and economic structures, and there was no tradition of practical cooperation among them. Only Piedmont was experienced in parliamentary government. Mazzini's followers complained that political unification had not been accompanied by social revolution, something Cavour had not intended it should. Catholics protested the seizure of the Papal States and the confiscation of church property by the new anticlerical government. Italy was united, but the Italians were not, and Cavour died in 1862 leaving his successors with the problem of making a nation out of the new kingdom.

KINGDOM OF ITALY

The Roman Question, that is, the settlement of relations between the Italian state and the Catholic church after the seizure of Rome in 1870, remained the most vexatious and seemingly insoluble problem confronting Italian governments for almost sixty years. Pope Pius IX refused to consider Cavour's proposal in 1860 for "a free church in a free state," which was intended to guarantee the ecclesiastical freedom of the Italian church, uninhibited by government intervention, in return for the renunciation of the pope's temporal claims to Rome. Pius IX noted that Cavour's words contrasted markedly with his record of anticlerical legislation in Piedmont, but, more important, he adamantly stood by the position that papal sovereignty in Rome was essential for carrying out the spiritual mission of the church.

Agitation mounted—especially from Mazzini's republicans looking to discredit the Savoy monarchy—for armed intervention in Rome. When the French garrison was withdrawn in 1870, Italian troops occupied the city. A plebiscite confirmed its annexation, and the next year the Italian capital was transferred to Rome. Still hoping for an equitable accommodation with the papacy, Parliament enacted the Law of Guarantees in 1871, which would establish the Vatican as an independent papal territory within the city of Rome and accord the pope the dignity of a sovereign. Pius IX rejected the offer out of hand, to the disappointment of many Catholics, and proclaimed himself the "prisoner of the Vatican." As far as the Italian government was concerned, the law stood in force awaiting the pope's agreement. For his part, Pius IX refused to recognize the legality of the Italian state, excommunicated King Vittorio Emanuele II, and condemned the occupation of Rome as an aggressive act, appealing to foreign powers to restore the city to the papacy. In retaliation the Italian government sharply restricted the civil rights of the clergy.

The impasse between the pope and the state created a crisis of conscience for Italian Catholics who wanted to

The monument to King Vittorio Emanuele II in central Rome

Crown Prince Umberto I, the son of Vittorio Emanuele II

Umberto I's consort, Queen Margherita of Savoy, the first queen of Italy

The assassination scene of King Umberto's death by an anarchist from the United States on July 29, 1900, at Monza, Italy

King Umberto I, from an official photograph taken in 1900 just before his assassination

reconcile their intense devotion to the church with their natural love for their country, their dilemma made even more difficult by the pope's prohibition of Catholics voting in national elections or participating in national politics as being *non expedit* (inexpedient). Rather than challenge the anticlericalism of the liberals on their own ground—in Parliament—the church chose instead to organize the Catholic masses socially and economically outside the political system through church-sponsored unions and cooperatives. The government was thereby virtually left to the anticlericals; potential Catholic leadership was cut off from the political life of the nation.

The Italian Parliament was composed of the appointed Senate and the Chamber of Deputies, elected by a restricted electorate (about three hundred thousand voters in 1870 or one in every seventy Italians). Early governments were dominated by Piedmontese politicians. The party structure was loose and undisciplined. The right, based on Cavour's liberal coalition, stood for national stability and drawing the parts of the country closer together through a highly centralized state administration. The left, composed of ex-republicans and Mazzini's followers, advocated social reform and a more democratic electorate. With the passing of Cavour's political generation in the 1870s, the quality of leadership in Parliament appeared to diminish. After 1876 the left continually maintained a parliamentary majority, but so many factions within it—usually brought together by a single personality—vied for recognition that clearly defined party government, necessary for rigorous parliamentary life, was impossible.

What the Italians substituted for party government was *trasformismo,* defined as "making it worthwhile for a sufficient number of members [of Parliament] to vote with the government" by using various forms of bribery and political brokering. Seats in the cabinet were allocated to factional or regional leaders, and as a result governments were formed whose members were so divided in outlook that coherent programs could seldom be formulated and, with all good intentions on the part of the government, reform measures were regularly stymied. Only the Italian Socialist party (Partito Socialista Italiano—PSI), organized in 1892, offered a clear-cut program of social and political reform, and by 1900 it controlled 25 percent of the seats in the Chamber of Deputies. The potential strength of the PSI, however, was sapped by ideological divisions within the party. The mounting violence in public life—capped by the assassination of King Umberto I by an anarchist in 1900 and the spectacular growth of socialism—prompted a rapprochement between the ruling Liberals under the reformist prime minister Giovanni Giolitti and the Catholics, who were gradually integrated into political life after the relaxation of the *non expedit* by Pope Pius X in 1904. Giolitti's government introduced universal male suffrage in 1912, raising the number of eligible voters from 3.3 million to 8.6 million.

Italy, an economically underdeveloped country, was late in entering Europe's scramble for overseas possessions, but Prime Minister Francesco Crispi pursued a determined expansionist policy in the 1880s and 1890s to ensure Italy's place among the European colonial powers. Crispi was not contented with the two strips of desert —in Eritrea and Somalia—on the Horn of Africa, acquired in 1889; but an attempt to penetrate Ethiopia in 1896 was ended by the military disaster at Adowa. Imperialism remained an aspect of Italy's foreign policy, and Italy's colonial holdings increased with the occupation of Libya and the Dodecanese during the war with Turkey (1911–12). The Italians also established spheres of interest in the Balkans and Asia Minor through the construction of port facilities and railroads and the exploitation of resources. Throughout the early colonial experience Italy's interests were concerned primarily with economic rather than political expansion.

Italy adhered to the Triple Alliance with Germany and Austria in 1882, but after 1900 Italian foreign policy tended toward closer ties with France and Great Britain. At the outbreak of World War I in 1914 Italy declared its neutrality, explaining that under the Triple Alliance its commitments were solely defensive in nature. Whereas the Giolitti government opposed entry into the war, public opinion, urged on by the popular press, democratic sentiment, and irredentists who saw the war as an opportunity to complete the Risorgimento, prevailed. Under the terms of the secret London Pact, Italy was promised the Italian-speaking areas still held by

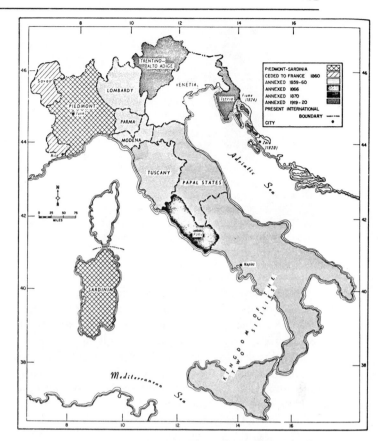

The unification of Italy, 1920

Austria as well as colonial concessions. Accordingly, in May 1915 Italy declared war on Austria. Psychologically Italy was conditioned for war, but the Italian armed forces were woefully unprepared.

By the end of the war Italy had mobilized more than 5 million men, and more than six hundred thousand had been killed. But Italy's case was poorly presented at the Versailles Conference and its bargaining position compromised by unstable conditions at home. Under the terms of the Treaty of Saint Germain in 1919, Austria surrendered Istria, Zara in Dalmatia, Trentino-Alto Adige (South Tyrol), and—of strategic importance— control of the Brenner Pass. However, the extravagant offers made in the London Pact were held to be contrary to the spirit of Woodrow Wilson's Fourteen Points, and the United States refused to support further Italian territorial claims.

MUSSOLINI

For many Italians it seemed that the gains won on the battlefield at such great cost had been thrown away at the peace table, and a sense of frustration and disillusionment—and of betrayal—permeated the country in the years immediately after the war. Italy was saddled with an enormous war debt. Inflation and shortages of basic goods triggered strikes that paralyzed large segments of

Benito Mussolini

Vittorio Emanuele III taking the oath of office as king in 1900. He was the only child of King Umberto I and Queen Margherita.

the economy. Demobilized troops swelled the ranks of the unemployed. Profiteering, often involving public officials, took its toll on public confidence in the government. Socialist gains in local elections inspired fears of expropriation—especially among small landholders—and outbreaks of violence and counterviolence. The government admitted its inability to maintain public order, and amnesties granted to striking workers confirmed the middle class in its belief that the parliamentary government was not only corrupt but weak.

This was the atmosphere that spawned Benito Mussolini's Fascist movement, which for nearly one-quarter of a century demeaned and demoralized Italy's national life. Mussolini had always been a political maverick. Imprisoned and exiled for his political activities, the schoolteacher-turned-journalist from Romagna had begun his activist career as a pacifist and anarchist, later joining the militant wing of the PSI—at one time being the editor of the party's official newspaper. Mussolini broke with the party on the issue of entry into World War I and abandoned Marxism for nationalism.

Mussolini was a manipulative orator; his showmanship was not mere buffoonery but struck a responsive chord in his listeners. He had attracted a personal following as early as 1917. In 1919 he assembled the paramilitary Combat Groups (*Fasci di Combattimento*), called the Blackshirts, from among army veterans and youths, modeled after the *arditi* (commandos), the shock troops of the Italian army. Organized in more than two thousand squads, the Blackshirts were used as strikebreakers (subsidized by industrialists for the purpose); attacked Socialists and Communists, whom they claimed the government was too timid to deal with; terrorized left-wing town governments; and set up local dictatorships while the police and the army looked on—often in sympathy. Mussolini profited from the anxieties of the middle class—their businesses threatened and their savings wiped out by inflation—and from the smallholders' fears of expropriation by the Socialists.

In 1921 Mussolini, seeking a broader following than

among the Fascist squads, formed a parliamentary party, the National Fascist party (Partito Nazionale Fascista), which captured thirty-five seats in the Chamber of Deputies. The party, running on a bloc list with Giolitti's Liberals, was admitted to the coalition government. The party program called in vague terms for social reform, financial stability, assertion of Italy's prestige abroad, and order at home. The Fascists considered themselves a revolutionary party in opposition to nineteenth-century liberalism, middle-class humanistic values, and capitalism, but Mussolini advanced no guiding ideology. Fascism, Mussolini insisted, represented a mood in the country, not ideas, and he wrote, "Fascism . . . was a form of a need for action, and in itself was action."

Despite their relatively minor representation in Parliament, no government could survive without the support of the National Fascist party, and in October 1922 Mussolini was summoned by Vittorio Emanuele III to form a government as prime minister. The much-heralded March on Rome by three hundred thousand armed Fascists, usually credited with bringing Mussolini to power

King Vittorio Emanuele III

King Vittorio Emanuele III's consort, Elena of Montenegro

The royal family was very popular among the populace in Italy. In this World War I photograph of a Red Cross benefit, the king is seen, left; *and* center, *at the table, is Crown Prince Umberto.*

When King Vittorio Emanuele III thought that Mussolini's "Black-shirt" movement was threatening the throne, he asked him to form a new government. They are seen here on their way to a government meeting where Mussolini swore allegiance to the crown. But, this did not keep him from declaring himself dictator of Italy on January 3, 1925.

by a coup, was in fact the result rather than the cause of his appointment to office, a brilliant bluff intended to impress the nation—and Europe—with the strength and determination of his following. Mussolini governed constitutionally, heading a national government comprising the Fascists, some Social Democrats, Liberals, and members of the Italian Popular party (Partito Popolare Italiano, known as Popolari).

The Popolari were a center-left reformist group founded in 1919 by a Sicilian priest, Don Luigi Sturzo. Formation of the party marked the entry of an organized, mass-based Catholic party into parliamentary politics, although without the approval of the Italian hierarchy or the Vatican. In 1919 Sturzo's party won 101 seats in Parliament, second in strength only to the PSI. Mussolini considered the Popolari, parent party to the postwar Christian Democratic party (Partito Democrazia Cristiana—DC), the toughest obstacle in his rise to power. The Popolari withdrew their support from the Mussolini government in 1923.

The Fascists, under a revised electoral law, polled two-thirds of the votes cast in the 1924 elections. Seemingly secure in his parliamentary majority, Mussolini's

confidence was shaken—and his regime endangered—by the public reaction to the murder of a Socialist politician, Giacomo Matteotti, by Fascist toughs. The opposition withdrew from the Chamber of Deputies in protest. Without resistance Mussolini assumed dictatorial powers in January 1925, ruling thereafter by decree, and replacing elected local government officials with Fascist operatives. Although a rump Chamber of Deputies continued to sit, advisory functions passed to a party organ, the Fascist Grand Council, which Mussolini integrated into the state apparatus.

Controlling all the organs of government, Mussolini set about constructing a totalitarian state in Italy that would dominate every aspect of national life. *Il Duce,* as Mussolini was styled, proclaimed the doctrine of "everything within the state, nothing against the state, nothing outside the state," including professional and labor associations, youth groups, and sports organizations. Political parties—other than the Fascists—were suppressed. The press and court system were cowed. Strikes were made illegal and, although the free trade unions were not abolished, they were gradually throttled. Mussolini was less successful in imposing economic control, and the corporate state, which remained part of the myth of the Fascist regime, was never more than its facade. In some respects the Italian character, especially its spirit of individualism, mitigated the worst effects of Mussolini's totalitarianism, which was, as a critic noted, "a tyranny tempered by the complete disobedience of all laws." In addition, totalitarianism in the strictest sense was not possible where an independent church, claiming the spiritual allegiance of a large part of the population, existed. Mussolini's political background was anticlerical, but he understood the importance of the church to Italian life and realized that he could not expect to consolidate political support behind the regime until an accommodation was made with the Vatican—which had not recognized the legality of the Italian state.

The Lateran Pacts of 1929 consisted of a treaty between Italy and the Holy See and concordat regulating relations between the Italian state and the Catholic church. The treaty created the independent state of Vatican City and recognized the sovereignty of the pope there. In the concordat the church was assured of jurisdiction in ecclesiastical matters, and canon law was recognized as superseding the civil code in such areas as marriage. The church was restored to its role in education and allowed unencumbered operation of its press and communication facilities. The clergy were prohibited from membership in political organizations. The solution of the Roman Question, which had vexed Italian politicians since 1860, marked the peak of Mussolini's political leadership and has been considered by some observers the singular positive achievement of an otherwise execrable regime. The provisions of the Lateran Pacts were included in the 1948 constitution.

Imperialism was always a facet of fascism but was not explicit until 1935. The need to provide space for Italian emigration was emphasized by the occupation of Ethiopia in the 1935–36 period. The action might well have been passed over except for Ethiopia's protest in the League of Nations, but to the league's condemnation Italy responded that it had done no more in Africa than other powers had done earlier. France and Great Britain were unwilling to risk war for the sake of Ethiopia, but league members agreed to impose economic sanctions on Italy. The sanctions were halfheartedly enforced and subsequently withdrawn. They provoked bitterness in Italy, especially against Great Britain, and rallied theretofore lukewarm Italians to Mussolini. The sanctions also spurred the drive for economic self-sufficiency, an uneconomic project better suited to propaganda than to feeding the Italian people. Cut off from other sources, Italy relied on Germany as a supplier of raw materials and was drawn within its political orbit.

Mussolini was frankly impressed by German efficiency, overlooking outstanding conflicts of interests in Austria and the Balkans that might otherwise have kept the two dictators at odds. In 1936 Mussolini agreed to the Rome-Berlin Axis, pledging cooperation in central Europe. The next year Italy joined with Germany and Japan in the Anticomintern Pact, directed against the Soviet Union. By the time that Italy had formalized its military ties with Germany in the so-called Pact of Steel in 1939, Mussolini had so identified his country's interests with those of Hitler that Italy had become a virtual German satellite.

Italy aided Franco's forces during the 1936–39 Spanish civil war, contributing supplies, naval and air support, and more than fifty thousand men. Mussolini participated at Munich in the dismemberment of Czechoslovakia in 1938, but his foreign minister, Galeazzo Ciano, had tried to dissuade Germany from attacking Poland. Cut off from advanced notice of its ally's plans, Mussolini's government was acutely embarrassed by the Soviet Pact in 1939 that opened the door for invasion of Poland. Mussolini had pompously bragged about the "8 million bayonets" at his disposal but, as was the case so often during his regime, propaganda had taken the place of actual preparation, and Italy was no more ready for a major war than it had been in 1915. Confident of German strength, Mussolini believed that the war would be short and remarked that it would be humiliating "to sit with our hands folded while others write history," Italy attacked France after the issue of the Battle of France was already decided; nevertheless the French rallied to halt the Italian invasion. Later in 1940 Italy launched an unprovoked invasion of Greece —a fiasco, requiring German intervention to rescue an Italian army fought to a standstill by the Greeks. After a disastrous campaign in Africa, during which entire units surrendered to the Allies en masse, Mussolini squandered another army in the Soviet Union.

The Allies were greeted as liberators when they landed in Sicily in July 1943. In what amounted to a palace coup in Rome, the Fascist Grand Council, including Ciano, forced the resignation of the ailing and beaten Mussolini and returned the power of state to Vittorio Emanuele III. He had the former dictator arrested and called on Marshal Pietro Badoglio to become prime minister. Badoglio formed an interim government that dissolved the National Fascist party and granted amnesty to political prisoners. Although pledging to continue the war, Ba-

King Umberto II, the last of the Italian monarchs

King Vittorio Emanuele III with the crown prince Umberto II in 1939. In 1946 the crown prince became the king of Italy. Umberto II had married the daughter of the king of Belgium, Princess Maria José, in 1930 and she served as his queen.

doglio entered into negotiations with the Allies for an armistice, concluded in September to coincide with Allied landings on the mainland. Hopes for a quick occupation of Rome were disappointed, however, and the king and Badoglio moved the government to Brindisi, out of German reach. The royal government declared war on Germany in October, but the disintegrating Italian army had been left without a commander, and the Germans

were in control of most of the country away from the Allied beachheads. A veteran politician, Ivanoe Bonomi, was called on to form a government of national unity that included both Palmiro Togliatti, head of the Italian Communist party (Partito Communista Italiano—PCI) and the DC leader, Alcide De Gasperi. The new democratic government derived its authority from the all-party Committee of National Liberation, which reorganized local government in liberated areas and directed Italian resistance in occupied regions.

Rescued by German commandos, Mussolini set up a rival government—the Italian Social Republic—under Hitler's patronage in the German-occupied region with headquarters at Salò. Mussolini still commanded some support and, at a National Fascist party congress in Verona in November 1943, called for a return to the revolutionary "fascism of the first hour." The more fanatical Fascist elements were in control at Salò, eager to emulate Nazis in every way. Ciano and others who were held responsible for Mussolini's ouster were executed.

The German army put up stiff resistance to the Allied advance in Italy. Having relatively few troops to spare, the Germans took advantage of the terrain and Allied indecisiveness, stabilizing the battlefront along the Gustav Line during the 1943–44 winter. Rome was liberated in June 1944 after the breakthrough at Cassino in May. A second German defense line to the north, the Gothic Line, held until the last weeks of the war.

Mussolini, protesting at the end his betrayal by the Nazis and berating the Italians as a "race of sheep," made a dash for Switzerland in the last days of the war but was captured by partisans and executed.

ITALIAN REPUBLIC

Although the royal government ended World War II as a cobelligerent with the Allies, Italy was treated as a defeated power when the peace settlements were concluded. Italy was deprived of its colonial possessions; it lost Istria, Zara, and islands in the Adriatic to Yugoslavia and was obliged to recognize Trieste's status as a free territory under Allied supervision.

In June 1946 as the result of a plebiscite, the monarchy form of government was abolished and Italy became a republic.

King Umberto II reigned for one month in 1946.

THE ROYAL SOVEREIGNS OF THE ROMAN EMPIRE AND ITALY

ROMAN EMPIRE

Reign	Title	Ruler	Relationship
753–716 B.C.	Mythical King	Romulus (Quirinus)	
715–673	Mythical King	Numa Pompilius	
672–639	Mythical King	Tullus Hostilius	
639–616	Mythical King	Ancus Marcius	
615–578	Mythical King	Tarquinius Priscus	
578–534	Mythical King	Servius Tullius	
534–510	Mythical King	Tarquinius Superbus	
510–49—The Roman Empire was a republic.			
–44	Ruler	Gaius Julius Caesar	
27 B.C.–A.D. 14	Emperor	Augustus (Octavius)	
A.D. 14–37	Emperor	Tiberius	Stepson of Augustus
37–41	Emperor	Caligula (Gaius Caesar)	Grandnephew of Tiberius
41–54	Emperor	Claudius I	Nephew of Tiberius
54–68	Emperor	Nero	Stepson of Claudius
68–69	Emperor	Galba	
69	Emperor	Otho	
69	Emperor	Vitellius	
69–79	Emperor	Vespasian	
79–81	Emperor	Titus	Son of Vespasian
81–96	Emperor	Domitian	Son of Vespasian
96–98	Emperor	Nerva	
98–117	Emperor	Trajan	
117–138	Emperor	Hadrian	Nephew of Trajan
138–161	Emperor	Antoninus Pius	
161–180	Emperor	Marcus Aurelius	Son-in-law of Antoninus Pius
161–169	Co-regent	Lucius Aurelius Verus	Adopted brother of Marcus Aurelius
180–192	Co-regent	Commodus	Son of Marcus Aurelius
193	Co-regent	Helvidius Pertinax	
193–211	Co-regent	Septimius Severus	
193	Emperor (rival)	Didius Julianus	
193–196	Emperor (rival)	Pescennius Niger	
193–197	Emperor (rival)	Albinus	
211–217	Emperor (rival)	Caracalla	Son of Septimius Severus
211–212	Co-regent	Geta	Son of Septimius Severus
217–218	Emperor	Macrinus	
218–222	Emperor	Heliogabalus (Elagabalus)	
222–235	Emperor	Alexander Severus	Cousin of Heliogabalus
235–238	Emperor	Maximinus Thrax	
238	Emperor (rival)	Gordianus I (Africanus)	
238	Co-regent	Gordianus II	Son of Gordianus I
238	Emperor	Pupienus Maximus	
238	Co-regent	Balbinus	
238–244	Emperor	Gordianus III	Grandson of Gordianus I
244–249	Emperor	Philippus (Philip the Arabian)	
249–251	Emperor	Decius	
251–253	Emperor	Gallus	
253	Emperor	Aemilianus	
253–260	Emperor	Valerian	
260–268	Emperor	Gallienus	Son of Valerian
268–270	Emperor	Claudius II (Gothicus)	
270–275	Emperor	Aurelian	
275–276	Emperor	Tacitus	
276	Emperor	Florian	Brother of Tacitus
276–282	Emperor	Probus	
282–283	Emperor	Carus	
283–285	Emperor	Carinus	Son of Carus
284–305	Emperor	Diocletian	
285–305	Emperor	Maximian	
305–306	Emperor	Constantius I (Chlorus)	
306–311	Emperor	Galerius	Son-in-law of Diocletian
306–307	Emperor	Severus	
307–313	Emperor	Maximinus	Nephew of Galerius
307–337	Emperor	Constantine I (the Great)	Son of Constantius I
306–312	Emperor	Maxentius	Son of Maximian
311–324	Emperor	Licinius	Adopted son of Galerius
337–340	Emperor	Constantine II	Son of Constantine I

Reign	Title	Ruler	Birth	Death	Relationship
337–350	Emperor	Constans I			Son of Constantine I
337–361	Emperor	Constantius II			Son of Constantine I
361–363	Emperor	Julianus (Julian the Apostate)			Cousin of Constantius II
363–364	Emperor	Jovian			
364–375	Emperor West	Valentinian I			
364–378	Emperor East	Valens			Brother of Valentinian I
375–383	Emperor West	Gratian			Son of Valentinian I
383–388	Emperor West	Valentinian II			Son of Valentinian I
379–395	Emperor East	Theodosius I (the Great)			
388–392	Emperor West	Maximus			
392–394	Emperor West	Eugenius			
395–423	Emperor West	Honorius			Son of Theodosius I
395–408	Emperor East	Arcadius			Son of Theodosius I
425–455	Emperor West	Valentinian III			Nephew of Honorius
455	Emperor West	Petronius Maximus			
455–456	Emperor West	Avitus			
457–461	Emperor West	Majorian			
461–465	Emperor West	Livius Severus			
467–472	Emperor West	Anthemius			Son-in-law of Marcian
472	Emperor West	Olybrius			Son-in-law of Valentinian III
473–474	Emperor West	Glycerius			
474–475	Emperor West	Julius Nepos			
474–491	Emperor East	Zeno	426	491	
475–476	Emperor West	Romulus Augustulus			Son of Orestes

476—Western Roman Empire ended when Augustulus was defeated by Odoacer.

ITALY

SCIRIANS

476–493	King	Odoacer	434	493	

OSTROGOTHS

493–526	King	Theodoric (the Great)	454	526	Son of Theodemir
526–534	King	Athalaric	516	534	Grandson of Theodoric
527–565	King	Justinian			
534–536	King	Theodatus		536	
536–540	King	Vitiges			Brother-in-law of Athalaric
540	King	Theodebald (Hildibald)		540	
540–541	King	Eraric			
541–552	King	Tortila (Baduila)		552	Nephew of Theodebald
552–553	King	Teias			

553–565—Italy under Byzantine Empire.

LOMBARDS

568–573	King	Alboin		573	
573–575	King	Cleph			
584–590	King	Autharis		590	Husband of Theodelinda, son of Cleph
590–591	Queen	Theodelinda			Wife of Autharis
591–615	King	Agilulf			Theodelinda's consort
615–625	King	Adaloald			Son of Agilulf
625–636	King	Arioald			Son-in-law of Agilulf
636–652	King	Rotharis		652	Son-in-law of Agilulf
652–661	King	Aribert I			
662–671	King	Grimoald			Son-in-law of Aribert
671–674	King	Garibald			Son of Grimoald
674–688	King	Bertharit			Son of Aribert
688–700	King	Cunibert			Son of Bertharit
701–712	King	Aribert II			
712–744	King	Liutprand (Luitprand)	690	744	
744–749	King	Rachis of Friuli			
749–756	King	Aistulf		756	Brother of Rachis of Friuli
756–774	King	Desiderius		774	

Reign	Title	Ruler	Birth	Death	Relationship
		CAROLINGIAN DYNASTY			
774–814	King	Charlemagne	742	814	Son-in-law of Desiderius
814–818	King	Bernard			Grandson of Charlemagne
818–855	King	Lothair I	796	855	Grandson of Charlemagne
855–875	King	Ludwig II (Louis)	804	876	Son of Louis I
875–877	King	Charles the Bald	823	877	Son of Louis I
877–880	King	Carloman	828	880	Nephew of Lothair I
880–887	King	Charles the Fat	839	888	Brother of Carloman
		VARIOUS KINGS			
888–894	King	Guy of Spoleto		894	
894–898	King	Lambert			Son of Guy of Spoleto
899–905	King	Louis III of Burgundy	880	928	Grandson of Ludwig II
888–923	King (rival)	Berengarius of Friuli		924	Great-grandson of Charlemagne
923–933	King	Rudolf II of Burgundy		937	Son of Rudolf I
933–947	King	Hugh of Arles		947	
947–950	King	Lothair II		950	Son of Hugh of Arles
950–961	King	Berengarius II of Ivrea		966	Grandson of Berengarius of Friuli
961–973	King	Otto (the Great)	912	973	Son of Henry I the Fowler

961–1254—Italy was subject to the Holy Roman Empire.
1861—Italy was divided into many small states until reunification.

Reign	Title	Ruler	Birth	Death	Relationship
		KINGDOM OF ITALY			
1861–1878	King	Vittorio Emanuele II (Victor Emmanuel II)			
1878–1900	King	Umberto I (Humbert I)	1844	1900	Son of Vittorio Emanuele II
1900–1946	King	Vittorio Emanuele III	1869	1947	Son of Umberto I
1946	King	Umberto II (Humbert II)	1904	1983	Son of Vittorio Emanuele III

1946—Italy became a republic.

2
The Kingdom of France

France occupies a geographic position between continent and ocean. France was equally a maritime and a land power with the Pyrenees and Alps guarding the south but totally exposed to the northeast. Its position between north and south made it from earliest times a converging place of peoples. It has also had the task, throughout its history as a kingdom, of defending on the north and east an extended land frontier and on the west and south a long seacoast. The French monarchies have been forever torn between two essential but not always reconcilable policies of land or sea strength.

The founding of Marseilles about 600 B.C. by the Greeks from Phocaea was the first approximate date in French history. At that time the Mediterranean coast and much of the land of what is now France was inhabited by the Ligurians. A second and even more important invasion was that of the Celts (Kelts), a tall, blond race who came from beyond the Rhine and spread themselves throughout Gaul in successive waves of invasion and immigration during the course of two or three centuries until Gaul became a Celto-Ligurian country.

THE OLD CELTS (150 B.C.)

In olden times, before human beings wrote down histories, Europe was overrun by a great people, whom it is convenient to call the Celts—fierce, bold, warrior people, who kept together in large families—or clans—all nearly related, and each clan with a chief. The clans joined together and formed tribes, and the cleverest chief of the clans would be the leader. They spoke a language nearly alike. There were two great varieties of Celts—the Gael and the Kymry (Kewmri). The Gael were the tallest, largest, wildest, and fiercest, but they were not as clever as the little black-eyed Kymry. The Kymry were the people who had the Druid priests. But we know little about the Kymry, as all their knowledge was in verse, which the Druids and bards taught one another by word

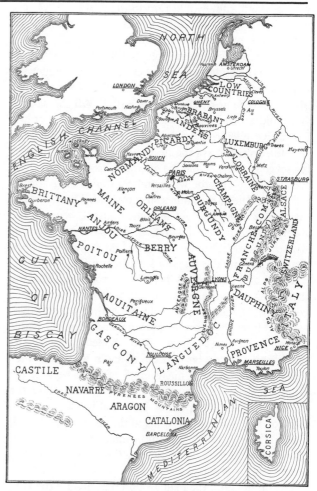

The ancient Provences of France

of mouth, and so was never recorded. What we do know of them was gleaned from their neighbors the Greeks and Romans, who considered them to be very savage, and lived in fear of them.

When the Celts pushed into new territory, it was generally because they were driven from their homes by fiercer, stronger clansmen behind them, coming from the east to the west. When these weaker Celt tribes found that they could not hold their own against the stronger tribes, they put wives and children into wagons made of wood or wickerwork, collected their oxen, sheep, and goats, called their great shaggy hounds, and set forth to find new homes. The men had long streaming hair and beards, and wore loose trousers of wool, woven and dyed in checks by the women—tartan plaids, in fact. The leaders always had gold collars around their necks, and they used round interwoven wicker shields, long spears, and heavy swords. When the country was free to the west, they generally settled down in a woods near a river, closing in their town with a wall of trunks of trees and banks of earth, and setting up their homes of stone or wood within.

If other tribes whom they could not defeat were to the west of them, they would turn to the south into Greece or Italy. One set of Celts, in very olden times, even managed to make a home in the middle of Asia Minor, and it was to their descendants that Saint Paul wrote his Epistle to the Galatians. Another great troop, under the mighty *bran* (chief) who in Latin is called *Grennus,* even broke into the great city of Rome itself. All the women and children of Rome had been sent away, and only a few brave men remained in a strong place called the Capitol, on the top of the steepest hill. There they stayed for seven months, while the *bran* and his Gaels occupied the city, drank up the wine, and consumed long-horned oxen from the surrounding meadowland. The *bran* and his troops never did get into the Capitol, because the Romans paid the chief a great sum in silver not to enter Rome. The tribe that came with him stayed seventeen years in the middle parts of Italy before they were surrounded and defeated. Whenever a group of Celts saw there was no hope of escape, it was their custom to withdraw to within their enclosure and slay their wives and children, set fire to everything, and then kill themselves. Their worst fear was to be made slaves. All the north part of Italy beyond the river Po was filled with Celts, and there were many more of them beyond the Alps. So it came about that from the word Gael the Romans called the north of Italy Gallia Cis-Alpina— Gaul on this side of the Alps, and the country westward, Gallia Trans-Alpina, or Gaul beyond the Alps; and all the people there were known as Gauls, whether they were Gael or Kymry.

Far up in Gaul, the high ground that divides the Rivers Loire, Saone, and Rhine was found by the clever sailors and merchants called Phoenicians. There is a beautiful bay where Gaul touches the Mediterranean, and not only the Phoenicians found it, but the Greeks. The Greeks came to live there, and built the cities of Marseilles, Nice, Antibes, and several more. The Greeks always built lovely cities with marble temples to their gods, pillars standing on steps, and gardens with statues in them and theaters for seeing plays acted in the open

air. Inside these cities and close around them everything was beautiful. The Greeks brought culture and society to southern France and Italy. As a result, the Gauls who lived nearby learned some of the Greek ways and became tamed. They coined money, wrote in Greek letters, and bought and sold with the Greeks. Their wilder brethren beyond did not approve of this, however. Sometimes, indeed, the wilder clans threatened to rob the cities, and the Greeks begged the Romans to protect them. So the Romans sent an officer and an army, who built two new towns, Aix and Narbonne, and went to war with the Gauls.

Then a messenger was sent to the Roman camp. He was an immensely tall man, with a collar and bracelets of gold, and beside him came a bard singing the praises of his clan, the Arverni. There were many other attendants; but his chief guards were a pack of immense hounds, which came pacing after him. He bade the Romans, in the name of his chief, Bituitus, to leave the country and cease harming the Gauls. The Roman general turned his back and would not listen; so the messenger went back in anger and the Arverni prepared for battle.

When Bituitus saw the Roman army he thought it so small that he said, "This handful of men will hardly furnish food for my dogs." He was not beaten in the battle, but by a fluke he and his family were captured just after it, and they were made prisoners and sent to Italy. He was kept a captive all the rest of his life, while his son was brought up in Roman learning and habits, and then sent home to rule his clan and teach them to be friends with Rome. This was about one hundred fifty years before the coming of Christ.

THE ROMAN CONQUEST (67 B.C.–A.D. 79)

The Romans called the country they had taken for themselves in Gaul the Provence, and Provence has continued to be its name. They filled it with numerous colonies— actually cities. When a soldier retired he would receive a grant of land if he promised to defend it. When groups of soldiers combined their land and defense, a city was formed. The first thing they did was to set up an altar and then they built a temple; after that houses, a theater, and public baths, with causeways as straight as an arrow joining the colonies and then cities together. Each city had two magistrates elected every year, and a governor lived at the chief town with a legion of the army to keep the countryside in order.

When the Romans once began in this way, they always ended by gaining the whole country in time. They took nearly a hundred years to gain Gaul. First there came a large-scale invasion of some wilder Kymry, whom the

Romans called Cimbri, from the west, with some Teutons. They broke into Gaul and defeated a great Roman army; and there was ten years of fighting with them before the stout old Roman, Gaius Marius, beat them in a great battle near Aix. All of the Kymry and Teutons were killed on the battlefield, and then the women killed their children and themselves rather than fall into Roman hands. That was 103 B.C.; and Julius Caesar, the same Roman who first invaded Britain, a nephew to Marius, began his conquest of the whole of Gaul. By this time many of the Gaulish tribes had come to be civilized and lived in peace with the Romans and asked for their help. Some wanted help because they feared the less civilized tribes, and others wanted help because the Germans behind them had pushed a big tribe of Kymry out of the Alps, and they wanted to come down and settle in Gaul. Julius Caesar made short work of these Kymry newcomers, and also he defeated the Germans who were trying to get into Gaul. Caesar expected all the Gauls to submit to him—not only those who lived around Provence and had always been friendly to Rome, but all the free ones in the north, too. He was not only a brilliant soldier but also a great civil governor. He conquered all the east side and then he subdued the Belgae, who lived between the Alps and the sea; all the Armoricans along the north; and then the still wilder people on the coast toward the Atlantic Ocean.

But while Caesar was away in the north, the Gaulish chiefs in the south resolved to rise at once, and put themselves under the command of the brave young mountain chief of the Arverni. The Romans called him Vercingetorix. He was not a wild shaggy savage like Bituitus, but a graceful, spirited chief, who had been trained in Roman manners and knew their ways of fighting. The Gauls all rose one night to do battle. It was in the depth of winter, and Caesar at the moment was resting back in Italy. But he immediately started back on first tidings, and led his men through six-foot-deep snow, taking every Gallic town on the way.

Vercingetorix saw that the wisest thing for the Gauls to do would be to burn and lay waste to the land, so that the Romans would have nothing to eat. Caesar followed Vercingetorix to his hills of Auvergne, and fought a battle with him, the only defeat the great Roman captain ever had; indeed, he was obliged to retreat from the face of the brave Arverni. They followed Caesar, and fought another battle, in which he was in great danger. But the Gauls were not as long on strategy as they were on bravery. They fled, and it was all Vercingetorix could do to lead his men to a big camp under the hill of Alesia. He sent horsemen to rouse the rest of Gaul, and shut himself and his troops up in a great enclosure.

Caesar and the Romans came and made another enclosure outside, eleven miles around, so that no help, no food, could reach the Gauls, who had provisions for but thirty days. Their friends outside did try to break through to them, but in vain. Then the brave Vercingetorix offered to give himself up to the Romans, provided the lives of the rest of the Gauls were spared. Caesar gave his word that this should be done. Accordingly, at the appointed hour the gates of the Gallic camp opened. Out came Vercingetorix in his richest armor, mounted on his finest steed. He galloped about, wheeled around once then, drawing up suddenly before Caesar's seat, sprang to the ground, and laid his sword at the victor's feet. Caesar was not touched. He kept a cold, stern face, ordered the gallant chief into captivity, and kept him prisoner with him for six years, while finishing other conquests, and then took him to Rome to walk in chains behind the chariot in which the victorious general entered in triumph. Then with other captives, this noble warrior was put to death in the dark vaults under the hill of the Capitol.

With Vercingetorix ended the freedom of Gaul. The Romans took possession of all the country and made the cities like their own. The Gaulish chiefs thought it an honor to be enrolled as Roman citizens; they wore the Roman tunic and toga, spoke and wrote Latin, and, except among the Kymry of the far northwest, the old Gaulish tongue was soon forgotten. Today, grand temples and amphitheaters still remain in the area of Nismes, Arles, and Autun, and roads, made as only the Romans could make them, crisscross throughout the country. Except in the wilder and more distant parts, living in Gaul was very much like living in Rome.

After Julius Caesar, the Romans had emperors at the head of their state, and some of these were very fond of Gaul. But when the first twelve who had some connection with Julius were all dead, a Gaul named Julius Sabinus rose up and called himself emperor. The real emperor, chosen at Rome, named Vespasian, soon came and overthrew his cause, and hunted him down in his country house. Flames burst out of it, and it was declared that Sabinus had died there. But no; he was safely hidden in a cave in the woods. No one knew of it but his wife Eponina and one trusted slave, and there they lived together for nine years and had two little sons. Eponina twice left him to go to Rome to consult her friends whether they should try to obtain a pardon for her husband. They believed Vespasian was too stern a man. They saw no hope, so she went back disappointed. Once, word got out and she was followed, and Sabinus was found. He was taken and chained and carried to Rome, and she and her two boys followed. She knelt before the emperor and sought his pardon, saying that here were two more to plead for their father. Tears came into Vespasian's eyes, but he would not forgive, and the husband and wife were both sentenced to die. The last thing Eponina said before his judgment seat was that it was better to die together than to be alive under such an emperor. Her two boys were taken care of, and they lived long after in distant places from Rome.

THE CONVERSION OF GAUL (100–400)

Provence was so near Rome that very soon after the Apostles had reached the great city, they went on to Gaul. The people in Provence to this day believe that Lazarus and his two sisters went there. Their first bishop (of Arles) was Trophimus, and he is believed to have been the Ephesian who was with Saint Paul in his third journey, and was at Jerusalem with him when he was made a prisoner.

It was many years before the Gallic Christians suffered any danger for their faith. Then, under Emperor Marcus Aurelius, a governor was sent to the Provence who was resolved to put an end to Christianity. The difficulty was that there were no crimes of which to accuse the Christians. But the Christians were rounded up anyway. The Gallic bishop Pothinus was dragged through the streets, and so ill-treated that after a few days he died in prison. For fifteen days the others were brought out before the non-Christian people in the amphitheater, while every torture that could be thought of was tried on the Christians. The persecution did not last much longer after this, and the bones of the martyrs were collected and buried, and a church built over them, which is now the Cathedral of Lyons.

Almost all the townsmen of Lyons became Christians after that, but the people out in the country were much less easily converted. Indeed, the word *pagan,* which now means a "heathen," was only the old Latin word for a peasant or person who lived in the country. In the year 202, Emperor Septimius Severus put out an edict against the Christians. The fierce Gauls in the adjoining countryside, hearing of it, broke into the city and slaughtered every Christian they could find. There is an old mosaic pavement in a church at Lyons where the inscription declares that nineteen thousand died in this massacre.

The northerly parts of Gaul had not yet been converted, and a bishop named Dionysius was sent to teach a tribe called the Parisii, whose chief city was Lutetia, on the banks of the Seine. He was taken in the year 272, and was beheaded just outside the walls on a hill which is still known as Montmartre, the martyr's mount. His name, cut short into Saint Denys, became one of the most famous in all France.

The three Celtic provinces, Gaul, Spain, and Britain, were together under one governor, and the brave, kindly Constantius I ruled over them and hindered persecution as much as he could. His son Constantine I was also much loved, and it was while marching to Italy with an army that included many Gauls that Constantine saw the vision of a bright cross in the sky, surrounded by the words, "By this conquer." He did conquer and did confess himself a Christian two years later, and under him the church of Gaul flourished. Gallic bishops were at the great council of Nicea, in Asia Minor, when the Nicene Creed was drawn up.

After Constantine's death, his son Constantius II fostered the false doctrine that the Nicene Creed contradicted. He lived at Constantinople, and dressed and lived like an Eastern prince, and the Gauls were growing discontented, especially since the Franks—a ferocious tribe of their Teuton enemies to the east—were trying to break into their lands. A young cousin of Constantius II, named Julianus, was sent to fight with them. He fixed his chief base in a little island in the middle of the River Seine, at Lutetia, among his dear Parisii, as he called his tribe, and from there he came out to drive back the Franks whenever they tried to attack the Gauls. He was a very brave, able man, but he had seen so much selfishness and weakness among the Christians in Rome and Constantinople, that he believed their faults arose from their faith. As soon as Constantius was dead, and he became emperor, he reverted to being heathen again. He only reigned three years, and then, in the year 363, was killed in a war with the Persians. He was the last of his family, and several emperors rose and fell at Rome.

The governor of Gaul, Maximus, called himself an emperor and, raising an army in Britain ruled Celtic provinces for seven years. He was a brave soldier, and not a wholly bad man, for he loved and valued the great bishop Martin of Tours. Martin had been brought up as a soldier, but at eighteen he had become a Christian and was the pupil of the great bishop Hilary of Poitiers. He and the monks used to go out from there to teach the pagans who still remained in the far west. Martin did what no one else had ever done: he taught them to become staunch Christians, though they still spoke their own tongue and followed their own customs.

This was Saint Martin's work while his friend, the false emperor Maximus, was being overthrown by the true emperor Theodosius I. Struggling and fighting continued among the Romans and Gauls, while the dreadful Franks were every now and then bursting into the country from across the Rhine.

Saint Martin had finished the conversion of Gaul just before his death, in his monastery at Marmoutiers, in the year 400. He died in time to escape the terrible times that were coming up all the Gauls, or rather Romans. For all the southern and eastern Gauls called themselves Romans and spoke nothing but Latin.

THE FRANK KINGDOM (450–533)

That race of people which had been driving the Celts westward for six or seven hundred years was finally making its way into Gaul. They had been held back only by Roman skill. This race as a general name was called Teutonic, but it divided into many different nations. The

Julianus declared emperor by his soldiers at Paris

people were large-limbed, blue-eyed, and light-haired. They all spoke a language like rough German, and all had the same religion, believing in the great warlike gods, Odin, Thor, and Frey. They worshipped them at stone altars, and expected to live with them in the hall of heroes after death—that is, all so-called who were brave and who were chosen by the *Valkyr,* or "slaughter-choosing goddesses," to die nobly in battle. Cowards were sent to dwell with Hela, the pale, gloomy goddess of death.

They had lived for at least five hundred years in the center of Europe, now and then attacking their neighbors, when they were being harrassed by another, fiercer race, who was pushing them from the east. The chief tribes were the Goths, who conquered Rome and settled in Spain; the Longbeards, or Lombards, who spread over the north of Italy; the Burgundians (burg or town people), who held all the country round the Alps; the Swabians and Germans, who stayed in the middle of Europe; the Saxons, who dwelt around the south of the Baltic, and finally conquered south Britain; the Northmen, who found a home in Scandinavia; and the Franks, who had been long settled on the Rivers Sale, Meuse, and Rhine. There were two tribes of Franks—the Salian, from the River Sale, and the Ripuarian. They were great horsemen and dreadful pillagers, and the Salians had a family

The meeting between Julianus and the Frank chiefs

King Pharamond, 418–28

King Clodio (Clodion), 428–48

King Clovis (Chlodwig), 482–511

Clovis I's wife, Clothilde, 478–545

King Merovech (Merovee), 447–58

King Childeric I, 459–81

Elevation as king for Clovis

of kings, which, like the kings of all the other tribes, were supposed to have been descended from Odin. The king was always of this family, called Meerwings, after Meerwing—or Merovech—the son of Pharamond, one of the first chiefs.

After the death of the great Theodosius, who had conquered the emperor Maximus, there was no force to keep these Franks back, and they were continually dashing into Gaul and carrying off slaves and plundering. Even worse was the great rush that, in the year 450, was made all across Europe by the Huns, a terrible nation of another race, whose chief was called Etzel (or Attila) and who named himself the Scourge of God. In 451, he invaded Gaul with his army, whose faces had been gashed in infancy by their savage parents, that the warriors might look more dreadful. At Lutetia, the people wanted desperately to flee, but they were persuaded to remain by the holy woman Genoveva. She was a young shepherdess of Nanterre, near Paris, who had devoted herself to the service of God and whose holy life made the people listen to her as a kind of prophet. And she was right. The Huns did not come farther than Orleans, where the good bishop Lupus made the people shut their gates and defend their town until rescued by an army composed of Franks, Goths, Burgundians, and Gauls, under the command of Roman general Aëtius. In 451, he attacked the Huns at Chalons-sur-Marne, beat them, and drove them

back. Chalons was the last victory won under the old Roman rulers, for there now was too much conflict in Italy itself for Rome to help anyone. In came the Franks, and Childeric, the son of Merovech (Meerwig), came to Lutetia, or Paris, as it was now called. He had a great respect for Genoveva, heathen though he was; and when he came home from plundering, with crowds of prisoners driven before him, Genoveva would go and stand in front of him and plead for their pardon. He never could withstand her and always set them free. She died at eighty-nine years of age, and the church named her Saint Geneviève.

Childeric's son was named *Chlodwig,* which means "renowned war," but histories generally called him Clovis. He wanted to marry a Burgundian maiden named Clothilde, and as she was a Christian, he promised that she would be allowed to pray to her God in the churches that still stood throughout Gaul. When her first child was born, she wanted Clovis to let her have it baptized. The child died soon after birth and Clovis feared it was because her God could not save it. However, they had the next child baptized, and when it fell sick she prayed for it, and it recovered. Clovis began to listen more to what she said of her God, and when, soon after, the Germans came with a great army across the

Clovis the champion in hand combat at Mars

A.D. 496 Clovis marched at the head of the Salians.

Baptism of Clovis

Interview of Alaric and Clovis

Rhine and he drew out his Franks to fight with them at Tolbiac, near Cologne, he was in great danger in the battle, and he cried out, "Christ, whom Clothilde calls the true God, I have called on my own gods, and they help me not! Send help, and I will own Thy name." The Germans were routed and Clovis had his victory.

He kept his word, and was baptized at Rheims by Saint Remigius, with his two sisters, three thousand men, and many women and children. And, as he was the first great Teutonic prince who was a Catholic Christian, the king of France, ever since that time, has been called the Most Christian King and eldest son of the church.

Clovis was the first Frank chief who really made a home of Gaul, or who wore a purple robe and a crown like a Roman emperor. He made his principal home at Paris, where he built a church on the little island on the Seine, in honor of the Blessed Virgin, measuring the length of how far he threw an axe; but, though he honored the Gaulish clergy, he was still a fierce and violent savage, who did many cruel things. He generally repented of them afterward and gave gifts to churches to show his sorrow, and the holy men were with him when, in 511, he died at Paris.

The four sons of Clovis divided the kingdom. That is, they were all kings, and each had towns of his own. In the four chief towns—Paris, Orleans, Soissons, and Metz —they all had equal geographical shares. Not that they really governed, but they always were leaders when the Franks went out to plunder in the southern lands of

Provence and Aquitania. There was another part the Franks never conquered, namely, that far northwestern corner called Armorica, which Julius Caesar had conquered, and Saint Martin had converted last of all. The granite moors did not tempt the Franks for the Kymry there were very bold. Moreover, so many of their kindred Kymry from Britain came over for fear of the Saxons that the country came to be called from them Bretagne, or Brittany, and the Kymric tongue is still spoken there to this day.

When Chlodmir, one of the sons of Clovis, died, his three little sons were sent to Paris to be under the care of their grandmother, Clothilde. She was so fond of them that their uncles, Clothaire and Childebert, were afraid she would require that their father's inheritance should be given to them. So they asked her to send the boys to them on a visit, and as soon as they arrived, a messenger was sent to the queen with a sword and a pair of scissors,

Clovis entering Tours

King Childebert, 511–58

Clothaire I, king of Soissons, 558–62

Radegond, wife of Clothaire I

desiring her to choose. This meant that she should choose whether the poor boys should be killed, or have their heads shaven and become monks. Clothilde answered that she would rather see them dead than monks. In the year 533 Clothaire killed the eldest, who was only ten, with his sword. The second clung to Childebert and begged for his life, but Clothaire forced his brother to release him, and killed him too. The third boy, whose name was Chlodoald, was helped by Childebert to escape, and when he grew older he went into a monastery. He was so good a churchman that he became known as St. Cloud.

THE LONG-HAIRED KINGS (533–681)

The Meerwings, or long-haired kings, were the most wicked dynasty to ever call themselves Christian. They murdered, plundered, and married numerous wives, just as if they had been heathens. By the Frank law, a murder might be redeemed by a payment, and it was fully twice as costly to kill a Frank as to kill a Roman, that is to say,

Clothaire discovering the assassins

a Gaul. Except in the cities in Provence and Aquitania, this term *Roman,* once so proud, was now little better than that of a slave.

Out of all the Meerwing names, several have to be remembered above the rest for their crimes. Clothaire I, the murderous son of Clovis, left four sons—Gontram, Charibert, Siegbert, and Chilperic—among whom the kingdom was, as usual, divided. Two of these sons, Chilperic and Siegbert, wished for queenly wives, though Chilperic, at least, had a houseful of wives and among them a slave girl named Fredegond. The two brothers married the two daughters of the king of the Goths in Spain, Galswinth and Brynhild. Siegbert seems to have really loved Brynhild, but Chilperic cared for the beautiful and clever Fredegond more than anyone else, and very soon Galswinth was found in her bed strangled. Fredegond reigned as queen, and Brynhild hated her bitterly and constantly stirred up her husband to avenge her sister's death. Siegbert raised an army and defeated Chilperic, but Fredegond contrived to have him stabbed. She also contrived to have all her husband's other children killed by different means, and, at last, in the year 584, she contrived that he too should be stabbed when returning from a hunting trip. She had lost several infants, and now had only one child left, Clothaire II, a few

King Chilperic I, 566–84

King Charibert, 562–66, a son of Clothaire I

Death of Clothaire I

Fredegond, 561–93, wife of Chilperic I

Brynhild, wife of Siegbert

months old. But in his name she ruled what the Franks called the Ne-oster-rik, or Western Kingdom, namely, France, from the Saone westward; while Brynhild and her son Childebert ruled in the Auster-rik, or Eastern Kingdom, from the Saone to the Sale and Rhine. There was a most bitter hatred between the two sisters-in-law. Fredegond died in 597 at Paris, leaving her son Clothaire II on the throne.

Brynhild quarreled with the Franks chiefs, and when the bishops found fault with her she attacked them, and even caused the saintly bishop of Vienne to be assassinated. In her time there came from Ireland a number of very holy men, Celtic Christians, who had set forth from the monasteries to convert such Gauls and Franks as remained heathen. Brynhild's two grandsons, Theudebert and Theuderick, reigned in Auster-rik. Theuderick listened willingly to the holy men. There was a fierce quarrel finally between her two grandsons. Theuderick was taken prisoner by his brother, and forced to cut his hair and become a monk, but this did not save his life. He was put to death shortly after, and Theudebert soon after died. So Brynhild, after having ruled in the name of her son and grandsons, now governed for her great-grandson, Siegbert, thirty-nine years after her husband's death. But she was old and weak, and her foe, Frede-

Fredegond, wife of Chilperic I

Chilperic dividing his father's treasures

gond's son, Clothaire II, attacked her, defeated her forces, and made her and her great-grandchildren prisoners. The boys were slain, and the poor old Gothic queen, after being placed on a camel and led through the camp to be mocked by all the savage Franks, was tied to the tail of a wild horse, to be dragged to death by it! This was in the year 614 when barbarianism was still a way of life.

Clothaire II thus became king of all the Franks, and so was his son, Dagobert I, who was not much better as a ruler but was not quite so savage. In fact, the Franks were getting gradually civilized by the Romanized Gauls —the conquerors by the conquered.

Twelve more Meerwings reigned after Dagobert. They become less savage and hardly attended at all to the affairs of their kingdoms, only amusing themselves in their palaces at Soissons or Paris, thus obtaining the name of *Rois fainéants,* or "do-nothing kings." The affairs of the kingdom fell into the hands of the *major domo,* as he was called, or "mayor of the palace." The Franks, as they tried to have courts and keep up state, followed Roman patterns so far as they knew them, and gave Roman names from the emperor's court to the men in attendance on them. So the steward, or major domo, master of the royal household, rose to be the chief person in the kingdom next to the king himself. The next most important people were called *comites,* "companions of the king, counts"; and the chief of these was the master of the horse, *comes stabuli,* the "count of the stable" or, as he came to be called in the end, the constable. The leader of the army was called *dux,* a Latin word meaning "to lead," and this word became duke. But the mayor of the palace under these foolish do-nothing Meerwings soon came to be a much greater man than the king himself, and the mayor of the palace of the Oster-rik or Austrasia fought with the palace mayor of the Ne-oster-rik or Neustria, as if they were two sovereigns.

Finally, Ebroin, the last Neustrian mayor, was murdered in 681, the Neustrian army was defeated, and the Austrasians became the more powerful. Their mayors

Death of Siegbert, 575

Clothaire II, 584–628

Brynhild, 534–613, wife of Clothaire II

Clothaire II measuring the prisoners

Death of Brynhild

Chilperic, 566–84, and son Merovire

Death of Merovech

were all of one family, the first of whom was named Pepin I of Landen. He was one of Queen Brynhild's great enemies, but he was a friend of Dagobert I, and he and his family and their armed followers were brave defenders of the Franks from the other German nations.

CARL OF THE HAMMER (714–41)

The son of Pepin I of Landen (the Elder) is commonly called Pepin L'Heristal (Pepin II). He was mayor of the palace through the reigns of four do-nothing Meerwings, and was a brave leader of the Franks, fighting hard with their heathen neighbors on the other side of the Rhine, the Saxons and Thuringians.

He died in 714, and after him came his brave son Carl of the Hammer, after whom all the family are known in history as Carlings. Whether it was meant that he was a hammer himself or that he carried a hammer, is not clear, but it is quite certain that he was the greatest man in Europe at that time. The soft Roman sound softened his name into Carolus and translated his nickname into Martellus, so that he has become known in history as Charles Martel. He was duke of Austrasia and mayor of the palace under Clothaire IV and Theuderick IV.

It was a hundred years since Mohammed had risen up in Arabia, teaching the wild Arabs a strict law, and declaring that God is but one, and that he was His prophet, by which he meant that he was a greater and truer prophet than the Lord Jesus Christ. He taught that it was right to fight for the spread of the religion he

Dagobert I, 628–37

Submission of the Gascons to Dagobert I

The dish of Dagobert

Clovis II, 637–55

King Clothaire III, 655–68

Childeric II, 668–74

Murder of Childeric II and the royal family

taught, and his Arabs fought so well that they overcame the Holy Land and held the city of Jerusalem. Besides this, they had conquered Egypt and spread all along the north of Africa, on the coast of the Mediterranean Sea; and then they crossed over into Spain, and subdued the Christian Goths, all but the few who held fast in the Pyrenees.

And now these Arabs—also called Saracens and Moors—were trying to pass the Pyrenees and make attacks upon Gaul, and it seemed as if all Europe was going to be given up to them and become Mohammedan. Abdul Rhaman, the great Arab governor of Spain, crossed the Pyrenees at the Pass of Roncevalles, burst into Aquitania, and won a great battle near Bordeaux.

Then they marched on toward Tours, but by this time Carl of the Hammer assembled a great army; not only Franks, but Burgundians, Gauls of Provence, and Germans from beyond the Rhine—all who acknowledged owning the sovereignty of Austrasia, and who wanted it saved from the Arabs.

The battle of Tours, between Charles Martel and Abdul Rhaman, was fought in the autumn of 752, and was one of the great battles that decided the fate of the world. For it was this battle that determined whether Europe would be Christian or Mohammedan. It was a hotly

Battle of Testry 682; Pepin II captures Thierry III

King Thierry III, 674–91

Clovis III, 691–95

King Childebert III, 695–711

King Dagobert III, 711–16

fought combat, but the tall powerful Franks and Germans stood like rocks against every charge of the Arab horsemen, till darkness came on. The Hammer had the Franks sleep where they fought, to be ready the next morning to begin the battle again. But all except the dead and wounded Arabs were gone. They had withdrawn in the night, and the battle of Tours had saved Europe. However, the Hammer still had to strike many blows before they were driven back into Spain, and this tended to bring the south of Gaul much more under his power. Charles Martel was looked upon as the great defender of Christendom, and, as at this time the king of the Lombards in northern Italy seemed disposed to make himself master of Rome, the pope sent two nuncios, as pope's messengers are called, to carry him presents, among them the keys of the tomb of Saint Peter, and to beg for his protection. Still, great as he was in reality, he never called himself more than mayor of the palace and duke of Austrasia, and when he died in 741, his sons, Pepin and Carloman, divided the government, still as mayors, for the Meerwing Childeric III. In 747, however, Carloman, weary of the world, had his head shaven by Pope Zacharias, and retired into the great monastery of Monte Cassino. Pepin, commonly called *le bref,* or the Short, ruled alone, and in 751 he asked Pope Zacharias whether it would not be wiser that the family who had all the power should bear the name of king. The pope replied that so it should be. Childeric III was put into a convent, and the great English missionary-bishop, Saint Boniface, whom Pepin and his father had aided in his work among the Germans, anointed Pepin III king of the Franks at Soissons. Two years later, the next pope, Stephen II, came into Gaul again to ask aid against the Lombards, and at the Abbey of St. Denys anointed Pepin again,

Pepin I, 628–39

King Clothaire IV, 717–19

King Chilperic II, 716–21

King Thierry IV, 721–37

Charles Martel, 714–41

Charles Martel receiving the pope's presents

together with his two young sons, Carl and Carloman. And so the Meerwings passed away, and the Carlings began.

Pepin was a great improvement on the do-nothing Meerwings. When the Franks entered Italy and defeated Astolfo, king of the Lombards, Pepin was rewarded by being made a senator of Rome even though he could not read or write. Afterward, the Lombards attacked the pope again. Pepin again came to his help, and after gaining several victories, forced King Astolfo to give up part of his lands near Rome. Pepin made a gift of these to the pope, and this was the beginning of the pope becoming a temporal sovereign, that is, holding lands like a king or prince, instead of only holding a spiritual power over men's consciences as head of the Western church.

Pepin III died at the Abbey of St. Denys in the year 768. In reality he was not the king of France, but king of the Franks, which does not mean the same thing.

CARL THE GREAT— CHARLEMAGNE (768–814)

Carl and Carloman, the two sons of Pepin III, at first divided the Frank domains; but Carloman soon died, and Carl reigned alone. He is one of the mightiest of the princes who ever bore the name of Great. The Franks called him Carl der Grösse, Carolus Magnus in Latin, and this has become in French, Charlemagne.

He was a most warlike king. When the Saxons failed to send him a tribute of three hundred horses, he entered their country, ravaged it, and overthrew an image that they used as an idol—called Irminsul. Thereupon the Saxons burned the church at Fritzlar, which Saint Boniface had built, and so the war went on that way for years. Charlemagne was resolved to force the Saxons to be Christians, and Witikind, the great Saxon leader, was fiercely resolved against yielding, viewing the honor of the god of Odin as the honor of his country. They fought on and on, until, in 785, Charlemagne wintered in Saxony in victory, and at last persuaded Witikind to come

Coronation of Pepin III, the Short

Death of Pepin III

Statue of Charlemagne showing his crown

Charlemagne, 768–814

Baptism of Witikind. Witikind, the chief of the Saxons, defeated by Charlemagne in 785, is forced to be baptized along with all Saxons in the Church of Rome.

Pepin III, 751–68

Pepin III

Charlemagne, from a mosaic in the Church of St. John de Lateran

The coronation of Charlemagne

Although a phenomenal empire builder and administrator, Charlemagne had great difficulty in learning how to write—a skill he attempted only after the age of thirty, when already well on the way to uniting the greater part of Europe under his rule. The most he ever accomplished readily with pen in hand was a monogram of his own name, Karolus, which he inscribed on scores of edicts issued to his Frankish, Saxon, Lombard, and Basque subjects. The example above (greatly magnified) appears on a document of the year 774, at the time of his first visit to Rome. Despite his own difficulties with the alphabet, Charlemagne was instrumental in setting up schools and libraries, in promoting the revival of the Latin language, and in stimulating the Carolingian renaissance.

and meet him at Attigny. There the Saxon chief admitted that Christ had conquered and consented to be baptized. Charlemagne made him duke of Saxony, and he lived in good faith to the new vows he had taken. The Frisians and Bavarians, and all who lived in Germany, were forced to submit to the great king of the Franks.

There was a new king of the Lombards—Desiderio, and a new pope—Adrian I; and as usual they were at war, and again the pope entreated for the aid of the Franks. He came with a great army, drove Desiderio into Pavia, and besieged him there. It was a long siege, and Charlemagne had a chapel set up in his camp to keep the Christmas holiday; but for Easter he went to Rome and was met miles away by all the chief citizens and scholars carrying palm branches in their hands, and as he mounted the steps to St. Peter's Church, the pope met him, saying, "Blessed is he that cometh in the name of the Lord." He prayed at all the chief churches in Rome and then returned to Pavia, which he soon captured. He carried off Desiderio as a prisoner and took the title of king of the Franks and the Lombards. This was in the year 775, while the Saxon war was still going on.

He likewise had a war with the Arabs in Spain, and in 778 he crossed the Pyrenees and overran the country as far as the Ebro, where the Arabs offered him large gifts of gold and jewels if he would stop his campaign before attacking their splendid cities in the south. He consented.

Charlemagne had three sons—Carl, Pepin, and Lodwig (Louis). When the two younger were four and three years old, he took them both with him to Rome, and there Pope Adrian anointed the elder to be king of Lombardy; the younger, king of Aquitania.

Charlemagne had gathered the most learned men he could find at his father's palace at Aachem, and he had a kind of academy where his young nobles and clergy might acquire the learning of the old Roman times. (His son Lodwig was educated there.) In fact, Charlemagne taught there himself. Charlemagne was a Renaissance man. He worked hard to remedy the need for a good education; and such was his ability that he could calcu-

Coronation of Charlemagne

late the courses of the planets in his head. He had an excellent knowledge of Latin; Saint Augustine's *City of God* was his favorite book—a bible of its time; and he composed several hymns, among them the *Veni Creator Spiritus*—that invocation of the Holy Spirit which is sung at ordinations. He also knew Greek, wrote a Frankish grammar book, and collected the old songs of his people.

No one was honored as much and respected in Europe, and after two more journeys to Rome on behalf of Pope Leo III, the greatest honor possible was conferred upon him. In the old Roman times, the Roman people had always elected their emperor. They now elected him. On Christmas day of the year 800, as Carl the Frank knelt down before the altar of St. Peter's, the pope placed a crown on his head, and the Roman people cried out, "To Carolus Augustus, crowned by God, the great and peaceful emperor of the Romans, life and victory!"

So the empire of the West, which had died away for a time or been merged in the empire of the East at Constantinople, was brought to life again in the person of Charlemagne; while his two sons were rulers of kingdoms and all around him were numerous dukes and counts of different subject nations, all comprising his empire. The old cities and Provence—Aquitania, Lombardy, and Gaul—though they had councils that governed themselves, claimed him as their emperor. Moreover, he made the new territories which he had conquered along the German rivers great bishoprics, especially at Triers, Mentz, and Koln, thinking that bishops would more safely and loyally guard the frontier and tame the heathen borderers than fierce warrior counts and dukes.

Aachen was the capital of this empire. There Charlemagne had built a great cathedral, and a palace for himself. His chosen Christian name of David fitted him well, for he was a great benefactor of the church. He gathered together his bishops several times during his reign to consult on the church's good and defense. Indeed, his benefits to her and his loyal service were such that he was placed in the pope's calendar as a saint.

He was a tall figure, with a long neck, and was exceedingly active and dextrous in all exercises—a powerful warrior and very fond of hunting, but preferring swimming to anything else. Nobody could swim or dive as he

Charlemagne in royal costume

Charlemagne crossing the Alps

Charlemagne receiving the emissaries of Haroun-al-Rashid

Charlemagne's wives

Equestrian statue of Charlemagne

*Charlemagne
in later life*

could; and he used to take large parties to bathe with him, so that a hundred men were sometimes in the river at once. His dress was stately on occasion, but he did not approve of mere finery. When he saw some young noble overdressed, he would enjoy taking him on a long muddy ride in the rain.

He had intended his eldest son, Carl, to be emperor, and Pepin and Lodwig to rule Lombardy and Aquitania under him as kings; but Pepin died in 810, and Carl in 811, and only Lodwig was left. This last son he had accepted as emperor by all his chief nobles in the church at Aachen, after which he bade the young man take a crown that lay on the altar and put it on his own head. "Blessed be the Lord, who hath granted me to see my son sitting on my throne," he said.

Louis I, 814–40

Charles the Bald, 843–77

Charlemagne died in the next year, in 814, at the age of seventy-one, and was buried at Aachen, sitting upright, robed and crowned, in his chair, with his sword by his side.

THE CARLINGS (814–87)

Charlemagne's son, Lodwig—Ludovicus Pius, as the Latins called him, or Louis le Debonnaire, as he stands in French books—was a good, gentle, pious man, but his life was one continual fight with his sons. After he—Louis I—had given three kingdoms to his three sons, their mother died; he married again, and had a younger son, Charles; and his desire to give a share to this poor boy led to no less than three great revolts on the part of the elder stepbrothers, until at last their poor father died worn out and brokenhearted, on a little islet in the Rhine, in the year 840.

The eldest son, Lothair, was then emperor, and had for his own, beside the kingdom of Italy and that country where Aachen (the capital) stood, the strip bounded by the Rhine and the Alps to the east, and the Meuse and the Rhone to the west. He was in the middle, between his brothers—Louis, who had Germany and Charles, who had all the remainder of France. They fought over this. When Lothair died, his two sons divided his dominions again—the elder (whose name was the same as his own) got the northern half, between the Meuse and Rhine; and the younger had the old Provence. They both died soon and would not be worth mentioning, but that the name of the two Lothairs remained to the northern kingdom, Lotharick, or Lorraine, and the old kingdom of Arles, or Provence.

Charles survived all his brothers and came to be the head of the family, the second emperor Charles, commonly called the Bald. He was king from his father's death in 840, but emperor only for two years, from 875 to 877; and his life was a time of tumult and warfare, though he was an active, able man, and did his best. He had a good deal more learning than Charlemagne had to begin with, and like him had a school in his palace. He was a great debater and philosopher, and got into trouble occasionally with the pope about some of his definitions.

Charles the Bald had little time to enjoy his palace school, for the Northmen were moving south and were even more dreadful enemies of France than of England. The first fleet of their ships had been seen by Charlemagne, and he had shed tears at the sight; for he perceived that all his efforts to subdue and convert Bavarians, Saxons, and Frisians had not saved his people from a terrible enemy of their own stock, far more earnest in the worship of Odin and likely to come in greater numbers. All through the troubles of Louis I parties of Northmen were landing, plundering any city or abbey that was not strong enough to keep them off; and when

King Alfred the Great had made England too mighty for them, they came all the more to France. Sometimes they were met in battle, sometimes a sum was offered to them to spare a city from their plunder; and if the walls were strong, they would generally accept it. Paris was thus bought off in the time of Charles the Bald from the terrible sea-king, Hasting.

After Charles the Bald there were three very short reigns, only lasting seven years altogether, of his son and his two grandsons, and then the head of the Carlings was Charles II, commonly called *der Dicke* (the Thick or the Fat)—in France known as Charles le Gros. He was the son of Louis II, called the German, the son of Louis I, the Pious, and seems to have been less fit than most of his kindred for the difficulties of his post as emperor of the West, or king of the Franks.

The invasion of Northmen was worse than ever in his time because Harold the Fairhaired had made himself sole king of Norway, driving out all opposition; and those who would not brook his dominion now came southward, intending not only to plunder, but to find homesteads for themselves. One of these was the famous Rolf Gange, or Walker, so called because he went into battle on foot. In the year 885 Rolf and another sea-king named Siguid sailed up the Seine with seven hundred great ships, which stretched for sixteen miles along the stream, and prepared to take Paris.

For thirteen months the city was besieged, until at last the emperor arrived with an army collected from all the nations under him; but, after all of this, he did not fight —he only paid the Northmen to leave Paris and go to winter in Burgundy, which was at enmity with him. In fact, every part of the empire was at odds with poor fat Charles; and the next year (887) a diet, or council, met on the banks of the Rhine and deposed him. Arnulf, a son of the short-lived Carloman, was made emperor; Count Eudes was crowned king of France; Guy (duke of Spoleto) set up a kingdom in Italy; Boso of Arles called himself king of Provence; and Rodolf (another count) was crowned king of Burgundy, so that it appeared as though the whole empire of Charlemagne had been broken up.

THE COUNTS OF PARIS (887–987)

Charles the Fat died of grief the year after he was deposed. He was not the last Carling. Besides the emperor Arnulf, there was a son of Louis the Stammerer (another Carl) who tried to win the old French domains back from the Northman, Eudes. In fact, the westerly Franks, who held Paris and all the country to the Atlantic Ocean, had become very mixed with the old Gauls and had learned to speak Latin, though it was a little altered. In fact, it was the beginning of what we call French. They held with Eudes while the Franks around

Charles II, 884–87

Laon and Soissons were much more German, and chiefly clung to the Carling Charles, though he bore no better surname than the Simple. The farther eastward Franks of Franconia, as it is now called, with all the other German tribes—Swabians, Frisians, Saxons, Bavarians, and so forth—were under Arnulf, and made up the kingdom of Germany. The Franks west of the Rhine never were joined to it again. After the death of Arnulf's only son, Louis III, called the Child, no more Carlings reigned there. The Saxons sustained the leadership.

The counts of Paris were not Gauls but Saxons who had settled in the Frank country and made common cause with the Gauls. They had the same sort of patience with which the first Carlings had waited—until the Meerwings were worn out. Eudes let Charles the Simple govern the lands between the Meuse and Seine, and when Eudes died in 898, his brother Robert the Strong only called himself duke of France, and let Charles the Simple be king of the Franks.

All this time Rolf and his Northmen had gone on conquering in northern Gaul. They did not plunder and

Louis II, 877–79

Charles II, the Fat

Louis III (879–82) and
Carloman (882–84)

Eudes (Odo), count of
Paris, 888–98

Charles the Fat and Count Eudes

Henry I of Germany visiting Charles III, 898–922

ravage like common vikings. Rolf was cleverer, for he spared the towns and made friends with the bishops; and though he and his men fought with the nations beyond, they treated all the country between Brittany and the River Epte as if it were their own. Charles the Simple came to an agreement with Rolf. He said that if Rolf would become a Christian and accept him as his king, he would give him his daughter in marriage and grant him the possession of all these lands, as duke of the Northmen. Rolf consented, and in 911 he was baptized at Rouen, married Gisla (the king's daughter), and then went to swear to be faithful to the king. Now, this ceremony was called swearing fealty. It was repeated whenever there was a change either of the overlord or the underlord. The duke, count, or whatever he was, knelt down before the overlord and, holding his hands, swore to follow him in war and to be true to him always. The overlord, in his turn, swore to aid him and be a true and good lord to him in return, and kissed his brow. In return, the underlord—vassal, as he was called—was to kiss the foot of his superior. This was paying homage. Kings thus paid homage, and swore allegiance to the emperor; dukes or counts, to kings; lesser counts or barons, to dukes; and for the lands they owned they were bound to serve their lord in council and in war, and not to fight against him. Lands so held were called fiefs, and the whole was called the feudal system. Now, Rolf was to hold his lands in fief from the king, and he swore his oath, but he could not bear to stoop to kiss the foot of Charles. So he was allowed to pay this homage by a deputy.

Rolf was a sincere Christian; he made great gifts to the church, divided the land among his Northmen, and kept up such good laws that Normandy, as his domains came to be called, was the most law-abiding part of the country. It was said at that time that a gold bracelet could be left hanging on a tree in the forest for a whole year without anyone stealing it.

Charles the Simple, in the meantime, was overthrown in an odd way. Robert of Paris and Duke Rudolf of Burgundy made war on him, and took him prisoner. Charles's wife was a sister of the English king Ethelstan, and she fled to him with her young son Louis. They stayed there while first Robert was king for a year, and then Rudolf, and poor Charles was dying in prison at Peroune; but when Rudolf died in 936, the young Louis was invited to come back from England and be king. The count of Paris, Hugh the Great, and Rolf's son, William Longsword (duke of Normandy), joined together in making him king. But Louis IV was so afraid of them that he lived at Laon in constant hatred and suspicion. The French people indeed held him as a stranger and called him Louis *d'outremer,* or "from beyond the seas."

William Longsword was murdered by the count of Flanders, when his little son Richard was only seven years old. Louis thought this his opportunity. He went to Rouen, declared himself the little boy's rightful guardian, and carried him off to Laon, and there treated him so harshly that it was plain that he had intentions of getting rid of the child. So Osmond de Centeville, the little duke's squire, galloped off with him to Normandy in the middle of the night. A great war began, and Harold Bluetooth, king of Denmark, came to the help of the Northmen. Louis was made prisoner, and only gained his freedom by giving up his two sons as hostages. Hugh, count of Paris, aided young Richard of Normandy; while the Saxon emperor of Germany, Otto, aided Louis; and there was a fierce struggle, ending in the victory of the count of Paris and the Northmen. One of the young Frank princes died in the hands of the Normans; the other, Lothair, was given back to his father when peace was made.

In the year 954 Louis IV died at Theims, and his widow entreated that the great count Hugh protect Lothair. He did so, and so did his son and successor, Hugh —commonly called Capet, from the hood he wore—who managed everything for the young king.

Peace was made, and the emperor gave Lothair's younger brother, Charles, the province of Lotharick, or Lorraine, as it was coming to be called.

Lothair died soon after, in 986; and though his son Louis V was crowned, he lived only a year. When he died in 987, the great counts and dukes met in consultation with the chief of the clergy and agreed that, as the counts of Paris were the real heads of the state and nobody cared for the Carlings, it would be better to do as the Germans had, and pass over the worn-out Carlings, who spoke old Frank, while the Paris counts spoke the altered Latin, which by now came to be called French. So Charles, duke of Lorraine, was not listened to when he claimed his nephew's crown, but was forced to return to his own dukedom, where his descendants ruled for a full eight hundred years.

And in 987, Hugh Capet, count of Paris, was crowned king of France, and from that time French history begins.

The family that began with Robert the Strong exists still, after more than one thousand years, of which it reigned over France for nine hundred. It is usually called the House of Capet, from Hugh's nickname, though it would be more sensible to call it the House of Paris. In French history there were three great families—Meerwings or Merovingians, the Frank chiefs; Carlings or Carlovingians, the chief of whom was emperor of the West; and House of Paris, or Capetians, the kings of France.

HUGH CAPET (987–96)

The new king was duke of France, count of Paris, and guardian of the Abbey of St. Denys. So in the place called Île-de-France he was really master, and his brother

Rudolf (923–36), son-in-law of Robert, 922–23

Louis IV, 936–54

Louis V, 986–87

Hugh Capet, 987–96

King Capet on the throne

Adelaide, wife of Hugh Capet

Hugh Capet

Election of Hugh Capet

Hugh Capet takes the oath of office as king of France

Henri was duke of Burgundy. But on the Loire was the great county of Anjou, with a very spirited race of counts; and to the eastward were Vermandois and Champagne, also uncompromising counties. In all these places the nobles, like the king himself, were descended from the old Franks. In Normandy the people were Northmen, and in Brittany both the duke and people were still old Kymry, but the Norman dukes always considered that Brittany had been put under them.

In the southern half of the country the people were less Gaul than Roman. These were the dukes of Aquitania or Guyenne, the counts of Toulouse, and the counts of Narbonne. But in the southwest of Aquitania, near the Pyrenees and the sea, were an old race called Basques, who seemed to be older still than the Gauls and did not speak their language, but a strange and very difficult one of their own. The Basques who were mixed with the other inhabitants in the plains were called Gascons in France and Vascons in Spain.

These Romance-speaking counts were considered by the king of France to belong to him, but whether they considered themselves to belong to the king of France or not was quite a different thing. The county of Provence, old Provincia, certainly did not, for it came straight from the Holy Roman Empire. So did the other countries to the east, where a German tongue was spoken, but which had much to do with the history of France—namely, Lorraine, where the old Carlings still ruled, and in Flanders. So the king of France was not really a very mighty person, and had little to call his own.

At this time, in the reign of Hugh Capet, there was very little good to be seen in the world. All over France there were turbulence, cruelty, and savage ways, except, perhaps, in Normandy, where Duke Richard the Fearless and his son Duke Richard the Good kept order and peace and were brave, upright, religious men, making

their subjects learn the better, rather than the worse ways of France. However, there hardly was a worse time in all the history of Europe than during the reign of Hugh Capet, which lasted from 987 to 996.

ROBERT THE PIOUS (996–1031); HENRY I (1031–1060); AND PHILIP I (1060–1108)

Now, as the year 1000 of our Lord was close at hand it was thought that this meant that the Day of Judgment was coming then, and there was great fear and dread at the thought. When the year 1000 began, so many felt it was not worthwhile to sow their corn that a most dreadful famine resulted, and there was great distress everywhere.

But all this time there were good men who taught repentance, and one blessed thing they brought about, while people's hearts were soft with dread, was what was called the Truce of God, namely, an agreement that nobody should fight on Fridays, Saturdays, and Sundays, so that three days in the week were peaceable. The monasteries began to improve, the clergy became more diligent, and the king himself, whose name was Robert II, the Pious, was one of the best and most religious men in his kingdom. He used to come to the Abbey at St. Denys every morning to sing with the monks and wrote and set to music several Latin hymns, which he carried to Rome and laid on the altar at St. Peter's. But he could not manage his kingdom well, and he was exploited. He had married his cousin, Berthe of Burgundy, who was heiress of Arles in Provence. Now, Provence belonged to the empire, and the emperor did not choose that the kings of France should have it; so he made the pope, whom he had appointed, declare that Robert and Berthe were such near relations that they could not be husband and wife, and, with great grief, Robert submitted. Berthe went into a nunnery, and he married Constance of Aquitania. The sons were more like her than like their father, and Robert had a troubled life, finding little peace except in church, until he died in the year 1031.

His eldest son, Henry I, reigned after him, and the second son, Robert, became duke of Burgundy and began a family of dukes that lasted four hundred years. But the spirit of improvement that had begun to stir was going on. Everybody was becoming more religious. The monks in their convents began either to set themselves to rights, or else they found fresh monasteries in new places, with stricter rules. And a very great man, whose name was Hildebrand, was stirring up the church not to go on leaving the choice of the pope to the emperor, but to have him properly appointed by the clergy of the diocese of Rome, who were called cardinals—that is, chiefs.

Henry I had been dead six years, and his son Philip I had reigned forty-eight years, from 1060. William the Great, duke of Normandy, became still greater by winning for himself the kingdom of England. Philip did not want this. He was afraid of William and did not at all wish to see him grow so much more powerful than himself. He spoke contemptuously of the new king of England whenever he could, and at last it was one of his foolish speeches that made William so angry as to begin the war in which the greater conqueror met with the accident that caused his death.

Philip was by no means a good man. After he had lost his first wife, he fell in love with the beautiful countess of Anjou, Bertrade de Montfort, and persuaded her to come and pretend to be his wife. His son Louis, who was so active and spirited that he was called *l'éveillé,* which means "the wide awake," showed his displeasure, and Philip and Bertrade so persecuted him that he was obliged to seek refuge in England.

It was in this reign that a pilgrim called Peter the Hermit came home with a piteous story of the cruelty of the Mohammedans, who had possession of the Holy Land. He obtained leave from the pope, Urban II, to call all the warriors of Christendom to save the Holy Sepul-

cher where Jesus Christ had lain from the hands of the unbelievers. The first great preaching was at Clermont, in Auvergne; and there the whole people were so moved that they cried as if with one voice, "God wills it," and came crowding around to have their left arms marked with a cross, made of two strips of cloth, on an armband. An army came together from many of the lands of the West, and the princes agreed to lay aside their quarrels while the Crusade lasted. The good duke Godfrey led them all through Germany and Hungary and across the narrow straits of the Bosphorus, meeting with many problems and perils as they went. But at last they did get safely to Jerusalem, laid siege to it, and conquered it.

Robert II, 996–1031

Robert II, king of France   *Henry I, 1031–60*

Philip I, 1060–1108   *Philip I*

Louis VI, 1108–37   *Seal of Louis VI*

Louis VI   *Louis VII, the Young, 1137–80*

Then they chose Godfrey to be king of Jerusalem, but he would not be crowned, he said it was not fitting for him to wear a crown of gold where his Lord had worn a crown of thorns. Many nobles and knights stayed with him to help guard the holy places when the others went home. People from England, Spain, Germany, and Italy then joined the Crusade, but there were always more French there than those of other nations.

Louis the Wide Awake was called home by the French barons and ruled for his father for the last eight years of Philip's reign, though the old king did not die till the year 1108.

LOUIS VI, THE FAT (1108–37)

It is disappointing to find that Louis the Wide Awake soon became Louis the Fat (Louis le Gros). But still he was spirited and active, and much more like the old counts of Paris than any of the four kings before him had been; and he was a brave and just man, who therefore was respected.

It should be recalled that when Robert II, duke of Normandy, governed so badly, his Normans asked King Henry I of England, his brother, to help them. Louis did not choose to see the eldest brother despoiled, and he was

glad that the king of England and the duke of Normandy should not be the same person. So he helped Robert, but could not keep him from being beaten at Tenchebray and made prisoner. Afterward Louis befriended poor young William, Robert's son; but he was beaten again at Brenneville. There were nine hundred knights in this battle of Brenneville, and only three were killed, because the armor they wore was so strong. Then Louis helped William to obtain the county of Flanders, which he inherited from his grandmother, Queen Matilda; but the poor young prince had not long been settled in it before he died of an injury to his hand from a lance point.

Men of note lived in the time of Louis VI. One such was Suger. Suger was abbot of the monastery at St. Denys, of which the kings of France, as counts of Paris, were always the protectors; where their most precious banner, the oriflamme, was kept. Also, it was where they were always buried. Suger was a clever and able man, the king's chief adviser, and may perhaps be counted as the first of the men who filled the place of king's adviser or, as we now call it, prime minister. In those times these statesmen were almost always clergy, because few others had any learning.

Louis VI, though not an old man, soon fell into declining health. He thought he had contrived admirably to get more power for the kings by giving his son in marriage to Eleanor, the daughter of the duke of Aquitaine. As she had no brother, her son would have owned that great southern dukedom as entirely as the county of Paris, and this would make a great difference. Young Louis was sent to marry the lady and bring her home; but while he was gone, his father became worse, and died in the year 1137.

Louis VI had begun to govern in his father's name in 1100, just as Henry I of England came to the crown, and he died three years after Henry, while Stephen and Matilda were fighting for power in England.

LOUIS VII, THE YOUNG (1137–80)

The Young is an odd historical name for a king who reigned a good many years. But Louis VII was called so at first because he was only eighteen years old when he came to the throne, and the name clung to him because there was always something young and simple about his character.

The first great event of his reign was that Saint Bernard stirred Europe once more to start a crusade to help the Christians in Palestine, who were hard pressed by the Mohammedans. At Vezelay there was a great assembly of bishops and clergy, knights and nobles; and Saint Bernard preached to them so well that soon all were fastening crosses to their arms and tearing up mantles and robes because enough crosses had not been made beforehand for the numbers who wanted them. The

Louis VII

Louis VII receiving the cross from Saint Bernard

Louis VII on Mount Cadmus

young king and his beautiful queen, Eleanor of Aquitaine, vowed to make the crusade too, and set out with a great army of fighting men and, beside them, pilgrims, monks, women, and children. The queen was very beautiful and very vain; and though she called herself a pilgrim she had no notion of denying herself. So she carried all her fine robes, her ladies, waiting-maids, minstrels, and jesters. The French had no ships to take them directly to the Holy Land, but had to go by land all the way, along the shore of Asia Minor. Great numbers of pilgrims perished along the way, and just as they had passed the city of Laodicea, the Mohammedan army came down on the rear guard in a narrow valley and began to make a great slaughter of them. The whole army would have been cut off had not a poor knight named Gilbert, whom no one had thought much of, come forward, taken the leadership, and helped the remains of the rear guard to struggle out of the valley. Through all the rest of the march, Gilbert really led the army; and yet after this he is never again mentioned in history.

When Palestine was reached at last, there were not ten thousand left out of the four hundred thousand who had set out from home. The prim queen's zeal was quite spent. She despised her pious husband and said he was more like a monk than a king; and as soon as they returned from this unhappy crusade, they tried to find some excuse for breaking their marriage.

The pope allowed the king to rid himself of this faithless lady, and let them both marry again. He married Constance of Castille, and Eleanor took for her husband the young English king, Henry II, and brought him all her great possessions.

The very thing had come to pass that the king of France feared—namely, that the dukes of Normandy should get more powerful than he was. For Henry II was at once king of England, duke of Normandy, and count of Anjou, and his wife was duchess of Aquitaine and Guienne; and, as time went on, Henry betrothed his little son Geoffrey to Constance, the orphan girl who was heiress to Brittany, and undertook to rule her lands for her; so that the lands over which Louis had any real power were a sort of little island within the great sea of the possessions of the English king. Besides that, Henry was a much cleverer man than Louis, and always got the better of him in their treaties. The kings of France and dukes of Normandy always met at Gisors, on their border, under an enormous elm tree, so large that three hundred horsemen could find shelter under the branches; and these meetings never went well for Louis. He was obliged to promise that his two daughters, Margaret and Alice, should marry Henry's two sons, Henry and Richard, and to give them to Henry to be brought up. When Henry had his great dispute with Archbishop Becket over the question of whether or not clergymen were subject to the law of the land, Becket fled to France. Louis loved and respected him very much, gave him shelter in an abbey, and tried hard to make peace between him and Henry, but never could succeed. After six years, Henry pretended to be reconciled, and Becket went home in the year 1170 and was murdered very soon after.

Louis must have been very much surprised when his former wife, Queen Eleanor, came disguised as a man with her three eldest sons to his court, making serious complaints against Henry for keeping the government of their provinces in his own hands and not allowing the children any reign. He must have thought it only what they deserved, but Louis gave them what help he could. Henry was a great deal stronger and craftier than any of them, and soon defeated them. Eleanor was thrown into prison and kept there as long as she lived. She may have deserved it, but her sons and the people of Aquitaine did not think so. Those people of Aquitaine were a curious race—they were very courtly, though not very good; and they thought more of music, poetry, and love-making than of anything else, though they were brave people, too. Every knight was expected to be able to write verses and sing them, and to be able to hold an argument in the courts of love. The best poets among them were called troubadours; and Eleanor herself and her two sons, Richard and Geoffrey, could compose songs and sing them. All were as much beloved in Aquitaine as Henry was hated.

Louis VII was married three times—to Eleanor of Aquitaine, to Constance of Castille, and to Alice of Champagne. These three queens had among them six daughters but no son, and this was catastrophic, since no women had ever reigned in France; for it was held that the old Salian Franks had a law against women reigning. At any rate, this grew to be the rule in France, and it is called the Salic law. However, the problem was not to be settled at this moment in French history, for at last a son was born to Louis in 1165, and in his joy he caused the babe to be christened Philip *Dieu-donné,* or "God-given."

The boy was the cleverest son who had sprung from the House of Paris for ages past, and while still quite young, had concern for all that was important to his father and his kingdom, at an age when other young boys were concerned only for sports and games. When his father met the English king at the elm of Gisors, young Philip was present and saw how Henry overreached and took advantage of Louis, and he was bitterly angered, and swore that some day he would get back all that his father was losing.

One day young Philip was out hunting in a forest with his father when he missed his companions, lost his way, and wandered around all night. When he was found, he

Philip II, 1180–1223

Philip II, Augustus

Philip Augustus

was so spent with hunger and cold that he contracted a bad illness, and was in great danger for some days. When he grew better, King Louis, in great joy, thought this precious life had been granted by the prayers of his old friend Thomas à Becket, and asked Henry's permission to come and give thanks at the archbishop's tomb at Canterbury. He came, and was welcomed as a friend and guest. He gave great gifts to the cathedral in thanks, which became the great treasures of today's Canterbury Cathedral.

He had his beloved son, though only fifteen, crowned, that France might have a king over her while he was in England, and Philip was very soon to be the only king, for good, honest, naive Louis the Young died very soon after his return from Canterbury, in the year 1180, nine years before the death of his great enemy, Henry II.

PHILIP II, AUGUSTUS (1180–1223)

Philip the "God-given" is most commonly known in history as Philip Augustus. Why, is not quite plain; but as he became a very powerful king of France, it is most likely that one of the old names of the Western emperors, Caesar Augustus, got applied to him.

If Philip's father Louis was yet known as the Young in his old age, Philip could have been referred to as Philip the Old in his youth, for he was much older in skill and cunning at fifteen than his father had been most of his lifetime. The whole history of his reign is an endeavor to get the better of the Plantagenet line of England. He so hated the thought of what he had seen under the elm tree of Gisors that his first act was to cut it down. He saw that the best way to conquer his enemies was by pretending to be their friend and helping in their quarrels. The eldest and the third sons, Henry and Geoffrey, were by this time dead, and Richard of the Lion-Heart, the second son, the favorite of the Aquitaine troubadours, was on one of the Crusades.

Then came news from Palestine that the Christians had been conquered by the great Saracen chief Saladin, and that Jerusalem had been taken by him. There was great lamentation, and a fresh crusade was decided on by all the princes of Europe, the king of France, the king of England, and the other royal rulers. The emperor Frederick of the Red Beard set off first, but he was lost by the way while crossing a river in Asia Minor. The two kings waited—arranging their participation. Philip's way of doing this was to get Richard to his court and pretend to befriend him. They became close friends—drank out of the same cup and ate out of the same dish. But Philip was stirring up Richard—who needed it little—against his father, with his brother John joining with him. This was the rebellion that broke the heart of Henry II. He died, and Richard, on his crusade, became king.

It was the first crusade when the armies went by sea

instead of by land. Richard had his own fleet, but Philip was obliged to hire ships of the merchants of Genoa; and when the two fleets reached Sicily, they would not venture to sail on until the winter was over. Now that Richard was king, Philip no longer pretended to be his friend, which resulted in many disputes among the Crusaders. In the spring, they sailed on to help the Christians, who were besieging Acre. Philip arrived first, but no great things were accomplished until Richard arrived. The heat of the climate soon made both kings fall ill, and when the city was taken, Philip's doctors declared that he must go home at once if he wished to recover. Most likely they were right, but he was glad to go, for he hoped to do Richard a great deal of harm while he was away. The pope had forbidden anyone to attack a Crusader's lands while he was away; but Philip could stir up Richard's subjects and his brother against him. And when Richard was made captive in Austria, on his way home, Philip even sent money to the emperor of Germany to keep him a prisoner. At last, when the German princes had forced the emperor to set him free, Philip sent word to John, in a short message: "Take care of yourself, for the devil is let loose."

Oddly, when, two years later, Richard of the Lionheart was killed at Limoges, Philip became John's most bitter enemy, and the friend of the only other Plantagenet left, namely, Geoffrey's son Arthur, duke of Brittany, who appealed to his suzerain, Philip, to make him duke of Normandy and count of Anjou, as son of the elder brother. Philip called on John to give up these lands, but John offered to make peace only by marrying his niece, Blanche, the daughter of his sister and the king of Castille, to Philip's son, Louis VIII, the Lion. Philip was in trouble in France at the time, so he consented to make this peace.

Philip was his own worst enemy. His first wife, Isabelle of Hainaut, was dead, and he had thought to make friends with the king of Denmark by marrying his daughter Ingeborg. But the Danes were then very backward in culture and learning, and poor Ingeborg was a dull, ignorant girl, not at all like a courtly lady. Philip took such a dislike to her that he sent her into a convent, and instead married the beautiful Agnes de Meranie, the daughter of the duke of the Tyrol. At that time one of the mightiest popes who ever lived was ruling—Innocent III. He was determined not to let anyone, however great, go on in sin undisciplined, and he called on King Philip to send Agnes away and take back his only true wife—Ingeborg. And when Philip would not, the pope laid the kingdom under an interdict—that is, he forbade any service to go on in any church except in those of the monks and nuns, and there only with the doors shut against all outsiders. The whole nation was, as it were, cut off from God for their monarch's sin. Philip stood up against this dreadful sentence, but he found the people could not bear it, so he sent Agnes home, and took

Ingeborg back. He was then absolved, and his kingdom went on prospering.

When, in 1203, Arthur of Brittany perished in prison, Philip summoned John, as a vassal of France, to answer for the murder. The great vassals met, the trumpets sounded, and John was called on to appear; but as he did not come, he was sentenced in absentia to forfeiture of his lands of the Normandy and Anjou, and Philip entered them with his army and took the castle, as John could not get men or money to come and stop him. Only the lands of old Eleanor of Aquitaine, who was still alive, remained to the English.

This forfeiture was a great step in the power of the French kings, since not only had the English king lost Normandy and Anjou, but these two great domains were added to the French king's county of Paris. He had no duke or count between him and the barons or cities. Also, Philip's designs against the Plantagenets were favored by John's own misconduct. The quarrel with the pope about the archbishop of Canterbury made Innocent III invite Philip to go and conquer England, and the fear of this brought John to make his peace with the pope.

However, John's nephew, Otho of Brunswick, was emperor, and he too had quarreled with the pope, who wanted to make young Frederick of Sicily emperor.

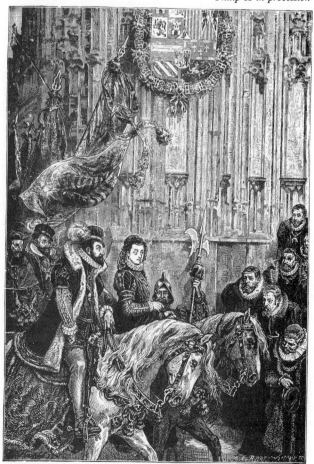

Philip II in procession

Philip took Frederick's part, and Otho marched against him into Flanders. All the French nobles had gathered around their king, and at Bouvines one of the greatest battles and victories in French history took place. Otho had to gallop away from the battle to save his life. This great battle was fought in the year 1214.

Very shortly after, Philip's eldest son, Louis, called the Lion, was invited to England by the barons, because they could no longer bear the horrible cruelties and wickednesses of John; and he would not keep the Magna Charta, which he had signed. Louis went to England, and London was put into his hands; but when King John died, the barons preferred to have his little innocent son, Henry III, as their king, than to be joined on to France. Battles ensued. So, after Louis's troops had been beaten by land and by sea, he came home and gave up the English crown.

But Philip Augustus certainly had the wish of his life fulfilled, for he had seen his foes of the House of Plantagenet humbled and he had recovered the chief of their great possessions in France.

He died in the year 1223, having lived in the reigns of four English kings and done his utmost to injure them all. He was brave and clever and a good friend of the people in the towns. The French people were very proud of him.

THE ALBIGENSES (1190) AND LOUIS VIII, THE LION (1223–26)

Louis the Lion had a very short reign, for most of his activities had been in his father's time. They have been treated lightly, intentionally, so that the reader might have a better understanding of the history of Philip Augustus and his crafty dealings with the House of Plantagenet.

Now, it would be in good perspective to go back and cover Louis before he came to the throne and examine the people he chiefly fought. The south of France, which had first been settled by the Romans and had never been peopled by the Franks, was much more full of "learning" than the northern part. The evil ways of Christians strengthened the notions of these people, who were called Albigenses (from the town of Albi). A great many people followed them. Even some of the great princes of the South began to feel as if the Albigenses were something special belonging to themselves and to the old culture of the Roman Provincia (Provence).

But the great pope, Innocent III, would not permit all this country to fall away from the church. Two men offered to help. One was a Spaniard named Dominic, who wished to found an order of brethren to go forth, preach, teach, and bring back heretics; the other was an Italian, named Francis, who cared above all for holiness and longed to be like the Lord, and wanted to draw

together men within the church to be more spiritual. Both these good men were allowed to institute brotherhoods, orders not like the monks in the old convents, but poorer and not quartered with the nuns. Their brethren were called friars, and went about preaching and hearing confessions, and helping men and women to lead holier lives—friars of Saint Francis went to Christian places, and those of Saint Dominic went wherever there was heresy. Dominic was further allowed to judge and punish with severe penances and captivity those who would not be convinced. The work he and his friars did was called the Inquisition.

But the great dukes and counts in the south of France —in Provence, Toulouse, Foix, Albi, and many others— did not choose to have their people interfered with. The more learned people of this area, the Albigenses, became Provencal princes, being cleverer than their uncultured neighbors. They were less disposed to punish their subjects, but they were also less religious and less honest. Pope Innocent had no doubt but that they should be called to account. So he proclaimed a crusade against them, as if they had been Saracens, and made the leader of it Simon, count de Montfort, a disciplinarian. Pedro II, king of Aragon, joined with the Albigenses, and in the

Louis VIII, 1223–26

Louis VIII

Louis VIII

Blanche of Castille

year 1213 a great battle was fought at Muret, in the county of Toulouse, in which the Albigenses were beaten and the king of Aragon was killed. The count of Toulouse, Raymond, who fought against this crusader, was declared by the pope to be unworthy to rule, and he granted Simon de Montfort all the lands he had conquered in the south of France. In the northern parts Simon was looked on as a saint, and when he went to do homage to the king, people ran to touch his horse and his clothes as if they were something holy. Louis the Lion aided Simon and learned the art of war during these battles, but when the crusaders tried to take the city of Toulouse, the people held out against them. One night, when Simon was attacking the walls, a woman threw down a heavy stone, which struck him on the head and killed him. The year was 1217.

His eldest son, Amaury, took his place in the long struggle but was not as able a warrior, and the Albigenses began to better the Crusaders. But in the year 1223, when Philip died and Louis became king of France, he was called upon by the pope to accelerate the Crusade. He fought well, but Louis was not as capable as he was brave. In the three years of his reign he did

Blanche of Castille

Louis IX freeing the prisoners during his coronation

Louis IX, 1226–70

Marguerite of Provence, wife of Louis IX

little to overcome the Albigenses. While he was passing through Auvergne in 1225, typhoid broke out among his army; he fell ill himself and died in the year 1226.

At his death, his eldest son, Louis IX, was only eleven years old; but the queen, Blanche of Castille, his mother, was a very capable woman and managed the kingdom excellently. She sent fresh troops, who gained such successes that Count Raymond of Toulouse was forced to surrender. And, he had to give his only child into Blanche's care to be brought up as a wife for her third son, Alfonso. The count of Provence had only daughters, four of them, and these girls were "contracted" into marriage in due time to the king of France and his brother Charles, and to the king of England and his brother Richard, and thus all that great country of the Languedoc was brought under the power and influence of the North. The Dominican friars and the Inquisition were put into authority throughout the conquered lands.

SAINT LOUIS IX (1226–70)

The little king, Louis IX, who came to the throne in 1226, when he was only eleven years old, was happy in having a wise mother, Queen Blanche of Castille, who both brought him up carefully and ruled his kingdom for him well. At a young age, he married Margaret of Provence. He was so much stronger and cleverer than the poor, foolish Henry III of England that his barons advised him to take away all of Guienne, which had been left to King John. But he said he would not perform such an injustice. Yet when Henry wanted him to give back Normandy and Anjou, he studied the matter well, and decided that King John had justly forfeited them for murdering Arthur of Brittany.

He was still a young man when he had a very bad illness and nearly died. In the midst of it, he made a vow that if he got well he would go to the Holy Land and fight to free Christ's Sepulcher from the Mohammedans. As soon as he was well he renewed the vow. Though his people didn't want him to leave France, he felt they would be governed well by his mother, so as soon as he assembled an army, one hundred thousand strong, he set out on his crusade with his wife and his brothers.

As the Mohammedans who held the Holy Land came from Egypt, it was thought that the best way of fighting them would be to attack them in their own country. So Louis sailed for Egypt, and besieged and took Damietta; and there he left his queen, Margaret, while he marched on to the Nile, hoping to battle the enemy there. The battle was fought at Monsoureh. The adversaries were not native Egyptians, but soldiers called Mamluks. They had been taken from their homes in early infancy, made Mohammedans, and bred to be soldiers. They were fierce warriors. The French main line charged into battle, but the Mamluks got between them and their main camp, cut them off, and killed them, except for the king, who was

Saint Louis (Louis IX)

Death of Saint Louis

seriously ill with malaria. He recovered, and at last it was settled that he would be set free for a heavy ransom, and he agreed to give up the city of Damietta. Then he embarked with his queen and the remains of his army for the Holy Land, where there was peace just then. After he had fulfilled his vow of pilgrimage, he returned to France. His mother had died in his absence.

Fourteen most happy and good years followed his return. He was a most wise king and thoroughly just. There was a great oak tree near his palace of Vincennes, under which he used to sit, hearing the causes of the poor as well as the rich and administering justice to them all.

The pope had a great quarrel with the emperor Frederick II and tried to make Louis go to war against him, as his father had done against King John of England. But the king knew that the pope's bidding was not right and delayed taking any action.

Louis IX and Henry III and their two brothers, Charles, count of Anjou, and Richard, earl of Cornwall, had married the four daughters of the count of Provence. The earl of Cornwall was chosen to be king of the Romans—that is, next heir to the Western Empire—and when her three sisters were queens, the fourth sister, Beatrice, kept the county of Provence. The pope offered the kingdom of the Sicilies to Beatrice's husband, Charles of Anjou. It rightfully belonged to the grandson of the emperor Frederick so Louis asked his brother to decline the grant. But Charles was an ambitious man. With an army of Provencals he set out and occupied the new kingdom, now called Naples and Sicily. The young Western Empire heir Conradin set off to try to regain his inheritance, but Charles defeated him in battle, made him prisoner, and put him to death on the scaffold. So both the pope and Charles had their way.

Louis had always intended to make another crusade, and Charles promised to join him in it, as had Edward of England. All of North Africa was held by the Moors, who were Mohammedan. Louis had had letters that made him think that there was a chance of converting the dey of Tunis to the Christian faith. So Louis, with his army, landed in the Bay of Tunis and encamped in the

plains of Old Carthage to wait for King Charles and Edward of England. It was very hot and unwholesome, and sickness broke out. The king was soon ill himself. He lay repeating Psalms and dictating a beautiful letter of advice to his daughter, as he grew worse and worse; and at last with the words, "O Jerusalem, Jerusalem!" on his tongue, he died in the year 1270.

Charles of Sicily and Edward of England arrived three days later. As soon as they assembled the armies and satisfied their quest, they sailed for Sicily, taking with them the new young king, Philip III. Louis was buried at St. Denys, and he has ever since borne the well-deserved title of saint.

PHILIP III, THE BOLD (1270–85) AND PHILIP IV, THE FAIR (1285–1314)

Saint Louis left three sons. The second, Robert, count of Clermont, should be remembered, because three hundred years later his descendants, the House of Bourbon, ascended to the throne of France. The eldest son, Philip III, was a man who left little mark in history, though he reigned fifteen years. The most remarkable thing that happened in his time was a great rising against his uncle, Charles of Anjou, in Sicily. The French and Provencal knights that Charles had brought with him were proud and rude in their behavior with the people of the country. At last, on the Easter Monday of 1282, as the people of Palermo were on their way to church to hear vespers, a French soldier openly raped a Sicilian girl, which ended in the people rising up en masse and killing all the Frenchmen on the island. This was called the Sicilian Vespers. The Sicilians then sent a messenger offering their crown to Pedro, king of Aragon, the nearest kinsman left to their old line. The pope was so angry with King Pedro for accepting it that he declared his kingdom of Aragon forfeited, and sent Philip of France to take it from him. But soon after the French army had advanced

Philip III, the Bold, 1270–85

Isabelle of Aragon,
wife of Philip III

Philip IV, 1285–1314

Jeanne of Navarre,
wife of Philip IV

into Aragon sickness broke out among them, the king himself caught it, and died in the year 1285. Pedro of Aragon gained the island of Sicily and kept it, though Charles of Anjou and his sons reigned on in Naples on the mainland.

Philip IV, called le Bel, or the Fair, was only seventeen years old when he came to the crown; but he was as clever and cunning as his granduncle, Charles of Anjou, or his great-great-grandfather, Philip Augustus. His main objective was to increase the territory of the crown by any means possible. He had to deal with Edward I, who was more anxious to make one kingdom of Great Britain than to be powerful in France, and so had little concern for his French duchies. So when Philip seized Guienne, Edward would not draw off his men from Scotland to fight for it, but made a peace which only left him Gascony. He sealed it for himself by marrying Philip's sister Margaret, and betrothed his son Edward to Philip's little daughter Isabel. It was the worst action of King Edward's life—for young Edward was already betrothed to the young daughter of the poor count of Flanders, Guy Dampierre, whom Philip was openly oppressing. When England thus forsook their cause, Philip made the count of Flanders prisoner, and placed him in prison for the rest of his life.

But the most remarkable part of the history of Philip IV concerns the church and the popes. The pope, Boniface VIII, was an old man but full of fiery vehemence. He sent a letter of reprimand, bidding the king release the count of Flanders, make peace, and also, to stop exacting money from the clergy.

Philip, too, was very angry, and the two went on exchanging letters that made matters worse. The pope threatened to depose the king. Philip sent off to Anagni (where the pope lived) a French knight named Nogaret and an Italian called Sciarra Colonna, who had quarreled with the pope and fled to France. They rode into Anagni, crying, "Long live the king of France! Death to Boniface!" at the head of a troop of worthless fellows who had joined them. The people of Anagni were so shocked that they barely moved. The men went on to the

church, where they found the pope, a grand old man of eighty-six, seated calmly by the altar in his robes, with his tiara on his head. They rushed up to him, insulted him, and slapped his face. Colonna would have killed him on the spot but Nogaret interfered. They dragged him out of the church, and kept him prisoner for three days while they physically and mentally tormented him. After the townspeople recovered from their fright, they assembled, rescued the pope, and carried him back to Rome. But the abuse proved too much for him, and a few mornings later he was found dead. This piteous death in the year 1303 was blamed on Philip.

Another pope was chosen, but as soon as Philip found that the new one was determined to control him too, he had him poisoned and then determined to get the future one into his hands. There were a good many French cardinals who would, he knew, vote for anyone he chose. Meeting in secret with the archbishop of Bordeaux, the king told him he would have the cardinals' votes on six conditions. Five of these related to the old quarrel with Boniface; the sixth Philip would not tell then, but the archbishop swore it should be fulfilled. The king then arranged his election as pope, and the archbishop took the name of Clement V.

To everyone's surprise except Philip's, Clement chose to be crowned at Lyons instead of Rome, and then took up residence at Avignon, in Provence, which, though it belonged to the pope's empire, was so much in France that it was in the king's power.

Philip the Fair was a very greedy man, always seeking money and going to any means to obtain it. Soon after Saint Louis's last crusade, the last spot that was held by the Christians—Acre—had been taken from them. The Knights Hospitalers who held it then settled on the nearby island of Rhodes, hoping someday to return to the Holy Land. But the Knights Templars, their leaders, had gone to the royal houses in Europe, where they trained young men in arms. Philip cast his eyes on the Templars' wealth, and told the pope that his sixth condition was that they should be destroyed. Most of them were living in France. They and the others were invited to attend a great meeting in France. When almost all were there, serious charges were made by the church—that they were really heathen, and that no one came into their order without first being made to renounce his baptism and trample on the cross.

The 502 who were assembled were imprisoned and tortured for forty days by the Inquisition. Seventy-two of them confessed.

Then, after being kept in prison one more year, the rest were sentenced, brought out in parties of fifty, and burned to death at the stake. At that time the pope declared the Knights Templars order dissolved, and gave the king all their possessions. The year was 1311.

The Grand Master, James de Molay, was kept in prison three years longer, but then was brought out at Paris and burned at the stake in the king's palace garden. As this very religious man stood in the fire, he called out to Clement, pope of Rome, and Philip, king of France, to appear with him before the judgment seat of God—the pope in forty days, the king in a year—to answer for the torture and murder of his knights.

On the fortieth day, Clement V died; and at the end of one year, Philip the Fair died at age forty-six. The year was 1314.

LOUIS X, THE QUARRELSOME (1314–16); PHILIP V, THE TALL (1316–22); CHARLES IV, THE FAIR (1322–28); PHILIP VI, THE FORTUNATE (1328–50)

Philip the Fair left three sons—Louis, Philip, and Charles—and one daughter, Isabelle, who was married to Edward of England. Louis X was called by the nickname of *Hutin,* which is said to mean the "Peevish" or "Quarrelsome." He was married to the young queen of Navarre, but he only reigned two years and his only son lived but five days. The French barons declared it was against the old law of the Salic Franks that their king-dom should fall to a woman, so Louis's little daughter Joan was only to remain Queen of Navarre, while his brother, Philip V (le Long, or the Tall), became king. Philip was nearly as cruel as his father.

There was a rumor that the drinking water in Paris had been poisoned by the lepers and the Jews, where-upon Philip gave orders that they all should die for it. They were killed on the spot or else burned at the stake throughout France, while the king and his nobles seized their treasures.

The king died young, at only thirty years of age, in the year 1322, leaving only four daughters. His brother, Charles IV, the Fair, succeeded him. It was during the six years that Charles was on the throne that his sister Isabelle came from England with complaints of her husband, Edward II. She succeeded in collecting a number of French knights, who helped her to dethrone Edward. He was brought to a miserable end in prison. The French people were pleased when Charles died in 1328, for their kingdom went to a public favorite, Philip VI, count of Valois, the son of the younger brother of Philip IV.

But Edward III of England called himself the rightful heir, declaring himself a closer blood relative to his uncle, Charles IV, than Philip VI, their first cousin. This was true, for if all the daughters of the three last kings were kept from reigning, it was unreasonable that he should pretend to be a rightful heir through their aunt. At first, though, he put his claim forward and he seemed to have been willing to let it rest for a while. But there was a certain Robert Artois, who had been deprived of what he thought was his lawful inheritance. Philip banished Robert to England. There he induced the king to back his claim, and so, if an oversimplification may be set forth, began the war with France that is called the Hundred Years War. The great cities in Flanders were friendly to the English. But Philip had tried to make them accept a count whom they hated, so they drove him away and invited Edward to Ghent. The French fleet tried to meet and stop him, but their ships were defeated off Sluys in the year 1340 and sunk, with great loss of men.

Louis X (Hutin), 1314–16

Louis X

Philip V, 1316–22

Philip VI, 1328–50

Not long after, there was a dispute about the dukedom of Brittany, which was claimed by the daughter of the elder brother, and by the younger brother, of the late duke. The niece had married Charles de Blois; the uncle was the count de Montfort. The king of France took the part of the niece, the king of England that of Montfort. Before long, Montfort was made prisoner and sent to Paris, but his wife, the brave Joan, defended his cause as well as any knight could have. She shut herself up in Hennebonne and held out the town while de Blois besieged her, even when the townsmen began to lose heart and said they must surrender. She held out until rescued by the English fleet.

The war in Brittany lasted twenty-four years altogether. Montfort made his escape from prison but died very soon after he reached home. His widow sent her little son to be brought up in Edward's court in England, while she took care of his responsibilities at home. The English gradually became very hated and disliked in Brittany, for they had been very cruel in their treatment of the people.

Edward made his greatest attack on France in 1346. Philip had gathered all the very best of his men in the kingdom. The knights and soldiers of France were nearly as strong in troops as those of England, but there was one great difference between the two armies, and that rose from the class consciousness of French counts and barons. Everyone below them was a poor, miserable serf (unless he lived in a town), and had never handled a bow or any other arms before. In England there were farmers and stout peasants who used to practice shooting with the bow once a week. So there were always sturdy English archers available to fight, but the French had nothing of the same kind, and therefore, hired men from Genoa. The battle was fought at Crecy, near Ponthieu; and when it was about to begin, by each troop of archers shooting a flight of arrows at one another, it turned out that a shower of rain which had just fallen had slackened the bowstrings of the Genoese archers. But the Englishmen had their bows safe in leathern cases, and their strings were in good order, so their arrows rained death on the French. A charge was ordered to cut the English archers down. But in the way stood the poor Genoese, fumbling to tighten their strings. The knights were so angry at being hindered that they began cutting them down right and left, thus spending their strength against their own army. So, it was no wonder that they were defeated and put to flight. King Philip himself had to ride as fast as he could from the battlefield.

The English went on to besiege and take the city of Calais, and in Brittany Charles de Blois was defeated and made prisoner. At that point both kings were glad to call a truce and rest their troops for a few years, although Edward still called himself king of France, and the dispute was far from settled. Philip paid his men by bringing to the nation a tax upon salt, while Edward's chief tax was on wool. So while Philip called his rival the wool merchant, Edward said that the Valois did indeed reign by the Sălic law (*sal* being the Latin for "salt").

The counts of the Viennois, in the south of France, used to be called counts dauphin, because there was a dolphin on their coat of arms. The dauphin Humbert, having neither children nor brother, bequeathed his county to the king's eldest grandson, Charles, on condition that it should always be kept separate from the crown lands. After that, the eldest son of the king of France was always called the dauphin.

Philip died in 1350 after a reign that had been little more than one long war.

JOHN II, THE GOOD (1350–64)

If Philip VI had a reign that was all one war, it was much the same with his son John, who considered himself a brave and honorable knight, though he often was cruel and criminal in his actions.

The little kingdom of Navarre, in the Pyrenees, had passed from Louis X to his grandson Charles, called the Bad. In right of his father, the count d'Eveux, Charles was a French noble, and he wanted to hold the highest office a noble could hold—namely, that of constable of France. The constable commanded all the armies, and was the most powerful person next to the king. When John gave the appointment to Lord Charles de la Cerda instead of Charles the Bad, Charles contrived to poison the new constable. The dauphin (Charles) ordered that Charles the Bad be seized and imprisoned. He invited him to dinner, and appeared to be very friendly. But in the midst of the feast the king appeared with a band of soldiers, seized the king of Navarre, and sent him off to prison. Charles the Bad had many friends who were angered by his imprisonment and took his case up with the king of England. Edward, the Prince of Wales, who was in Gascony at this time, took advantage of the opportunity and advanced into the French dominions. John assembled an army to meet him.

Jeanne of Bourgogne, wife of Philip VI

John II, the Good, 1350–64

John the Good

The battle was fought at Poitiers; John was there, with his sons and his brother and all his best knights, and the battle was long and hotly fought. The French did much better than at Crecy but the English were too strong for them. The king fought valiantly with his youngest son Philip close by his side. But at last the father and son found themselves almost alone, with no one but the enemy around them. The king was wounded. So he called to the closest enemy noble he saw—one Denis de Morbeque—and surrendered to him. He was brought before the Prince of Wales, who treated him with the utmost kindness and courtesy, personally dressed his wound, and did his best to lighten the humiliation of captivity.

Things fell into a state of disrepair. Although there was a truce between the two kings, the prince's troops—Free Companions, as they called themselves—roamed about, plundering and robbing all over France, while the king was a prisoner in England. In Paris, a burgher named Stephen Marcel was chosen provost and led the people in terrifying the government officials into doing what he pleased. Believing that the dauphin's friends were giving him bad advice, Marcel stormed into his presence, at the head of a troop of Parisians, and demanded, "Will you put an end to the troubles, and provide for the defense of the kingdom?" "That is not my part," said Charles, "but that of those who receive the money from the taxes." Marcel signaled and his followers murdered the two noblemen who stood beside the dauphin. The prince, in terror, fell on his knees and begged for his life.

But the dauphin eventually escaped from Marcel's custody and took up arms against Marcel. Charles of Navarre had been released from his imprisonment and was fighting in the south of France; and Charles de Blois had been ransomed and was fighting in Brittany. But the peasants, who always had been ill-used by the nobles, began to rise against them. "Bon homme Jacques" was

the nickname given them by the nobles, and hence this rebellion was called the Jacquerie.

The peasants were little more than savages. Whenever they would capture a castle, they murdered everyone in it. They set up a king from among them, and soon one hundred thousand had risen in Picardy and Champagne. But they were armed only with scythes and axes, and the nobles soon cut them down. They were just as brutal themselves in their revenge. The king of the Jacques was crowned with a red-hot tripod and hung, and the poor peasants were hunted down like wild beasts and slaughtered everywhere. No lessons were learned in that rebellion.

The dauphin besieged Paris, and Marcel, finding that he could not hold out, asked the king of Navarre to help him. But another magistrate, who hated Charles the Bad, contrived to attack Marcel as he was changing the guard, killed him and six of his friends, and brought the dauphin back into Paris.

King John was anxious to return, so he promised to give up to Edward of France all of the land that Henry II and Richard of the Lion-heart had held, but the dauphin and the states-general did not choose to confirm his proposal, thinking it better to leave him in prison than to weaken the kingdom so much. So Edward invaded France again and marched up to Paris, intending to fight another battle.

Between the war and the Jacquerie, the whole country was bare of inhabitants, cattle, and crops. The English army was in need of food and the prospect of none in the countryside did hurt their plans. So Edward consented to make peace and set John free on the conditions that two sons should be given up as hostages until payment of a great ransom was received and that a large part of Aquitaine be ceded to England.

King John returned but he found the kingdom in such a dreadful state of misery and poverty that he could not collect the money for the ransom. Nor would his sons agree to be pledges for it. John was very disappointed and ashamed and said the only thing he could do was to return and give himself up as a prisoner since he could not fulfill the conditions of his release. He said, "Where should honor find a refuge if not in the breasts of kings?" and accordingly he went back to London where he was welcomed as a friend by King Edward and there he died in the year 1364. He left four sons—the dauphin Charles; Louis, the duke of Anjou; John, duke of Berry; and Philip, who had married the heiress of Burgundy and was made duke of that province.

CHARLES V, THE WISE (1364–80)

Charles V, in spite of his shortcomings as dauphin, was a much abler man than his father, John. He had learned the best was to handle the English enemy—namely, not to fight with them but to starve them out.

Charles V, 1364–80

The French knights could beat anyone in Europe except the English and at this moment in history there appeared to be peace with Edward III. But with Charles the Bad of Navarre there was still war, until a battle was fought at Cocherel, between the French, under the brave Breton knight Bertrand du Guesclin, and the Navarrese, under the great friend of the Black Prince, the brave Gascon knight Captal de Buch. Du Guesclin gained a great victory and took Captal prisoner, and from that time no French knight was his equal. Charles the Bad had no choice but to make peace.

The young de Montfort, who had been brought up in England, was by this time old enough to try to fight for Brittany; and though the kings were at peace, the Prince of Wales loaned him a troop of English, commanded by the best captain in all Europe, Sir John Chandos. At the battle of Auray, Charles de Blois, who had so long wanted to win the duchy, was killed, and du Guesclin was made prisoner. After this, the king accepted Montfort as duke of Brittany, and the war was over.

When the wars were over, the Free Companions (or Free Lances) had nobody to hire them, so they took "possession' of a number of castles, and lived by plundering the travelers in the nearby countryside. They were a real problem for the king. Therefore, King Charles asked du Guesclin how to get rid of them and Bertrand came up with a plan. Castille, in Spain, had at that time one of the wickedest kings who ever lived, Peter the Cruel, who murdered his wife (a cousin of Charles), and killed, among others, most of his half-brothers. One of the brothers, Henry of Trastamare, managed to escape and came to France to ask for help. Du Guesclin told the king that it would be an excellent way of getting rid of the Free Companions by drawing them off to Spain. Charles consented and du Guesclin invited their leaders to meet him. When the Free Companions found that he would lead them, they all consented. As they rode past Avignon, they frightened the pope into giving them a large contribution, and as soon as they entered Castille,

Peter the Cruel fled and Henry was crowned king. He kept du Guesclin in his service, but sent all the others back to France.

However, Peter the Cruel came to Bordeaux and presented himself to the Black Prince as a distressed king. Edward took up his cause, and undertook to set him upon his throne again. All the Free Companions, who were coming back from Spain, no sooner heard that the prince was going there than they took service with him to restore the very king they had just dethroned. A great battle was fought at Navareta, in which the prince was victorious. Du Guesclin was made prisoner, and Henry of Trastamare fled for his life. Peter was placed on the throne once more; but he kept none of his promises to the English. Sickness broke out among the Black Prince's troops and they went back to Bordeaux, leaving Peter to his fate. France was anxious to have Du Guesclin free again, and even the maidens of Brittany were said to have spun day and night to earn money for his ransom. As soon as the sum was raised and he was at liberty, he returned to Spain with Henry, and then they chased Peter into the castle at Montiel. Peter came out in the middle of one night and attempted to murder his brother but in the struggle was himself killed, to the great relief of all concerned.

The Black Prince was, in the meantime, ill at Bordeaux, and with a problem of how to pay the Free Companions since Peter had not given him a promised payment for helping him. He was obliged to tax his Gascon subjects and this made them very angry. They appealed to Charles V and he summoned the Prince to appear at Paris and answer their complaint.

Edward said he would only come with his "helmet on his head and sixty thousand men" behind him, and so the war began again. But the prince was in poor health, and could not lead in battle as he had in the past.

The war was carried on by sieges of castles that, one by one, fell into French hands because the English prince could no longer rouse himself; and though he couldn't mount his horse, he went in a carriage to besiege the city of Limoges. When it was taken, he sought his revenge in a terrible massacre of all the inhabitants. This expedition was his last. He went back to England a sick man and never recovered. Governors were sent to Bordeaux but they could do little against the continually advancing French, and at last nothing in France was left to Edward but the province of Gascony and the city of Calais. A truce was made. But soon both the great Edwards were dead and Richard II was on the throne, under the regency of uncles who tried to carry on the war but fared no better.

The king had carefully instructed his queen, Jeanne of Bourbon, on how to bring up his two young sons, Charles and Louis, but to his great grief she died first. He was obliged to leave the boys in the care of their uncles. He died on September 16, 1380, after a reign of such

Charles VI, 1380–1422

great success that he is commonly known as Charles the Wise.

CHARLES VI (1380–1422)

Young Charles VI, at twelve years of age, was an orphan king. His uncles—the dukes of Anjou, Berri, and Burgundy (his father's brothers), and the duke of Bourbon (his mother's brother), shared running the government so he was allowed to grow up unrestrained.

The church was in an unsettled state. The popes, while living at Avignon, were at the beck of the French kings and this was not accepted by the other lands of the Western church. At last, in the year 1376, Pope Gregory XI had decided on going back to Rome, though Charles V and all the cardinals of French birth did all they could to prevent him. He died two years later. Then all the cardinals who wanted to stay in Italy chose one pope, and all the cardinals who wished to live at Avignon chose another. So there were now two popes, the real pope and the antipope, and this made for a grievous division which is known in history as the Great Schism. The French and all their friends stood by pope at Avignon, the English and all theirs by the pope at Rome.

One of the proudest nobles was Louis, count of Flanders. He controlled many rich cities in his county where almost all of the best cloth, linen, and lace of the time was made and where the burghers were wealthy. There was always much dislike and distrust between the counts and the cities, and Louis was so tough an administrator that at last the men of Ghent rose up against him and shut their city gates. They chose as their leader Philip van Artevelde, the son of the brewer Jacob van Artevelde, who had been a friend of Edward III. Artevelde led them out to fight with the count, gained a great victory, and drove him into the city of Bruges. In Bruges, he was disliked as much as he was in Ghent. The people rose up against him in the streets and nobody would give him shelter—until at last he found himself in the house of a poor widow who had once received alms from him. He begged her to hide him and she told him to lie under the bed in which her three little children were lying asleep. When his enemies burst through the door, they saw only the bed full of children and went away. In the

morning he managed to get out of the city and escaped to Paris.

He implored the king and his uncles to come to his help. He had but one daughter, who was engaged to marry the son of the duke of Burgundy, so it was in their interests to help—and the young king was very eager to perform in his first campaign. All the burghers involved in the revolt came out to battle with the knights and soldiers but they could not make headway against such an experienced leader as the constable de Clisson. At the battle of Rosbecque twenty-six thousand men were killed, and Philip von Artevelde was trampled to death in his flight from the battlefield.

The young king married Isabelle of Bavaria, a dull, selfish woman, who cared more for food and amusement than for her family.

As there was peace in England, the French knights thought only of crusades. Indeed, the Turks, under their great leader Bajazet, were beginning to make their way into Europe; and the eldest son of the duke of Burgundy, John the Fearless, set out with a party of French knights to help the Hungarians against them. They arrived just as a truce had been sworn to on each side. But the Hungarians broke their word and attacked the Turks. Their breach of faith was met with reprisal, for the whole Hungarian army was defeated and butchered by the Turks, and only John himself, with twenty-seven nobles, survived to be ransomed.

Later, Marshall Boucicault led another army to help the emperor of Constantinople, Manuel Palaeologos, and brought him back to France to visit the king where he asked for further aid for his cause.

BURGUNDIANS AND ARMAGNACS (1415–22)

Nothing could have been worse than the state of France under the mad king Charles VI, the Well-Beloved. As long as his uncle (the duke of Burgundy) lived and the country was under some sort of government, the king was cared for. But when Duke Philip died, and the dukedom passed to his son, John the Fearless, there was a perpetual quarrel between this rough and violent duke and the king's brother Louis, duke of Orleans. The duchess of Orleans—a gentle Italian lady Valentina of Milan—was the only person who could calm the king.

The people of Paris hated Orleans and loved the duke of Burgundy, and were resolved to get the king into his own power on the throne. So one night, as the duke of Orleans was going home from visiting with the queen, Isabelle, he was attacked by murderers and killed in the streets of Paris. The duchess of Orleans came with her sons and knelt at the king's feet, imploring that the murderer be punished, but he would do nothing. Her son, the young duke of Orleans, married the daughter of the count of Armagnac, who took up his cause so vehe-

Henry VII crowned on Bosworth Field in England

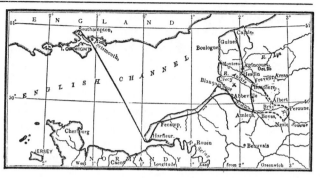

Map illustrating the march of Henry V of England and the Battle of Agincourt, 1415

mently that eventually all the friends of the House of Orleans were called Armagnacs.

The king's oldest son, the dauphin Louis, was sixteen years old and was trying to get into power. He was bright but an "idle" youth, and no one paid much attention to him. When he heard that the new king of England, Henry V, intended to invade France, Louis sent him a present of a basket of tennis balls, saying they were his most fitting weapons, considering his lifestyle "as the madcap prince who loved to play tennis." Henry answered that he could return the balls from the mouths of cannon against Paris, and it was not long before he crossed the channel, and laid siege to Farfleur, in Normandy.

He soon captured it and he proclaimed himself king of France, like Edward III before him. Then he proceeded to conquer the country. The dauphin collected an army and marched to intercept Henry as he was on his way from Harfleur to Calais to obtain fresh supplies. The French army greatly outnumbered the English and thought it would be easy to cut them off in that they were hungry, sick, and worn out from the long march. But the carelessness, dissensions, and insubordination of the French army would have caused it to be beaten by a far less skillful general than was Henry V. Though each French noble and knight was personally an excellent leader, this did little good when they were not united into a single army. There was an immense slaughter at this famed battle of Agincourt, and many noted prisoners were taken by the English, especially the duke of Orleans. Henry kept the nobles in captivity in England until he would win the whole kingdom of France.

The dauphin, Louis, although wounded, escaped from the battle but died soon after. His next brother (the dauphin John) did not survive him much longer. The third brother (the dauphin Charles) was entirely under the power of the Armagnac party.

But the count of Armagnac was so insolent that Queen Isabelle could not bear it any longer and fled to the duke of Burgundy's protection. The people of Paris, hearing of this, rose against the Armagnacs and murdered every one of them they could catch. The count himself was horribly gashed, and his body was dragged up and down the streets. The king was still in a state of mental ill health in the palace, so the dauphin was easily rescued by his friend, Sir Tanneguy du Chastel. For a whole month there was nothing but savage murders throughout Paris of all who were supposed to be Armagnacs. Then the queen and the duke of Burgundy returned, took over, and restored order to the city of Paris.

No one did anything to relieve Rouen, which Henry V was besieging. He captured it in spite of the citizens holding out very bravely. The queen and duke determined to make peace with Henry and met him at a meadow near Pontoise. They held a conference in which Henry asked for the hand of Catherine, the youngest daughter of Charles and Isabelle. And he wanted all of the provinces that had once belonged to the English kings as her dowry—Normandy, Aquitaine, and all of the other smaller territories. If this was refused, he would conquer all of the kingdom for himself.

No absolute promises were made. The duke of Burgundy could not bear to give up such a large portion of his native realm. He considered going over to the dauphin and helping him to defend himself. A meeting was arranged for the duke and dauphin on the bridge of Montereau. But Tanneguy du Chastel and the prince's other friends had no intention of letting the boy join in the power of the great duke, so during the conference they treacherously stabbed John the Fearless in the heart. Thus, he paid for the murder of the duke of Orleans. The consequence was that his son Philip, called the Good, went over to the English. Before long, Henry V was married to Catherine and was to be the regent of

France as long as poor Charles lived, and after his death the dauphin would be disinherited.

All the north of France had been conquered by the English and the dauphin and his friends had retired to the south. They sent to the Scots to ask for help and many brave Scotsmen came, glad for a chance to fight with the English. Henry had gone home to England with his bride and had left his brother, the duke of Clarence, in command. As the English were marching into Anjou, the Scots attacked them at Beauje, defeated them, and killed the duke of Clarence.

Henry came back quickly. He took the town of Meaux, but the siege lasted the whole winter. Henry caught a bad cold there, and was never well again although he attended church services on Sundays at Paris with great pomp and ceremony. Soon after, he set out on another campaign but he became so ill on the journey that he had to be carried back to Vincennes, where he died. King Charles died only three months later, in October 1422, after thirty years of suffering from insanity.

CHARLES VII (1422–61)

Although current history counts the reign of Charles VII as beginning from the death of his father, it was really the infant Henry, son of the king's sister Catherine and Henry V of England, who was proclaimed king of France over the grave in which Charles VI was buried. Henry was acknowledged as king throughout France as far as the Loire, while his uncle, the duke of Bedford, acted as regent.

Charles VII was proclaimed king by the Armagnacs, but most people still called him the dauphin, and many termed him the king of Bourges, for he lived in that little town.

Bedford, in the meantime, was determined to continue the conquest of France and sent the Earl of Salisbury to lay siege to Orleans. But the place was bravely defended and Salisbury was killed by a shot in the throat. Soon after, as some supplies were being sent to the English, a party of French nobles resolved to stop them and attached the wagons. The English came out of their fortifications to defend them and there was a general battle which is known in history as the Battle of the Herrings. It took this name because the provisions chiefly consisted of salt fish intended to be eaten during Lent.

It was a long siege, but miraculous aid came to the French. A young girl named Jeanne d'Arc said that she was summoned by the angel Saint Michael and the virgin saints, Catherine and Margaret, to save her country and lead the king to be crowned at Rheims. At first no one believed her, but she was so persuasive that finally she came to the attention of the king and he sent for her. To test her, he received her by torchlight and stood in the midst of many nobles more richly dressed than he. But she knew him at once from among them. She told him things that he declared no one else could have known about himself, which made him certain she must have some heavenly knowledge. She said her "voices" directed her to get a massive sword from the shrine of Saint Catherine, at Fierbois, and with this in her hand to lead the French troops to drive the English from Orleans. Jeanne d'Arc saved Orleans although she never herself fought or struck a blow. She only led. The French had such trust in her that wherever she led, they willingly followed. The English soldiers, on the other hand, believed her to be a witch, and upon seeing her they fled in horror and dismay, leaving their leaders, who stood in disbelief, to be slain.

She succeeded in entering Orleans and delivering it from the siege. Thereafter she was called the Maid of Orleans, and victory seemed to follow her. She fought in the name of Heaven and did all she could to make her followers holy and good, rebuking them for all bad language and other excesses. Eventually she had the satisfaction of opening the way to Rheims, the city where all French kings had been crowned ever since the beginning of the Meerwings. She saw Charles VII crowned and anointed, and then she asked to return to her home. The king and his council would not permit this because she was such an encouragement to their men and a terror to the English. But her hope, confidence, and blessings were

Charles VII, 1422–61   *Marie of Anjou, wife of Charles VII*

Joan of Arc presented to Charles VII

now gone. The French aristocracy did not like her. At Compiegne, the governor would not open the gates, leaving her outside to be made a prisoner by the Burgundians. She was kept in prison a long time—first in Burgundy, and then at Rouen—and tried before French and Burgundian bishops who decided that her "voices" had been delusions of Satan and her victories his work. Therefore, she was "penanced" to be burned at the stake as a witch. To the disgrace of Charles VII, he never stirred a finger to save her, and she was burned to death in the marketplace at Rouen.

No king ever deserved less to win back a kingdom than Charles. He amused himself with one unworthy favorite after another. But there was a brave spirit among his knights and nobles, and the ablest of them was Arthur, count de Richemont, brother to the duke of Brittany and constable of France. As the French grew stronger, the English grew weaker. The duke of Burgundy made his peace with the king of France; and the duke of Bedford soon after died at Rouen.

Step by step, bit by bit, did the French king regain his dominion. When his cause began to look hopeful, he came in person to receive the release of Paris and to reconquer Normandy. But the war was not finally ended till the year 1453, when Bordeaux itself was taken by the French and thus ended the Hundred Years War that Edward III had begun.

When the war was over and the bands of men-at-arms had nothing to do, Charles VII managed better than his grandfather, Charles V. He put them under strict rules and gave them pay so that they were an asset to him instead of being a torment to the people. This caused the nobles to lose power and they rose in an insurrection, which the dauphin Louis joined, chiefly because he was at odds with his father. But when Louis found the king's soldiers too strong for the rebels, he made his peace with his father and left them to their fate.

Charles became a wealthy monarch and established peace. In the church, too, there was peace; for at the council held by the Lake of Constance, in the year 1415, the rival popes of Rome and Avignon had both been made to resign, and a new one had been elected, who was reigning at Rome.

Through Charles's name in history is the victorious, his son Louis, the dauphin, hated him and in a cunning, bitter way did all he could to vex and anger him. After many quarrels, Louis fled from court and asked for the protection of Duke Philip of Burgundy, who had become the most magnificent and stately of European princes and hoped to make himself or his son king of the Low Countries.

The old king lived in continual fear of this son of his, and believing that Louis would attempt to poison him, he refused to take any food or drink until he lost the power of swallowing, and thus the king died a miserable death in the year 1461.

LOUIS XI (1461–83)

Louis XI wore the most shabby clothes and an old hat topped with little lead images of the saints, which he would take down, one at a time, and invoke to help him. Though his religious attitude was appreciated by the church, he actually was simply superstitious. His court jester once overhead him at his devotions and thought them so absurd and foolish that he could not help telling of them. The truth was that Louis had no love for God or man—he had only fear; and so he tried to bribe the saints with fine promises of gifts to their shrines. And his fear of man made him shut himself up in a grim castle at Plessis-les-Tours, with walls and moats all round, and a guard of archers from Scotland posted in iron cages on the battlements to shoot at any dangerous-looking person. He did not like the company of his nobles and knights but preferred that of his barber, Oliver le Daim, and his chief executor, Tristan l'Hermite. Anyone offending him was imprisoned in the castle of Lockes or put to death.

He had one brother, the duke of Berri, whom he feared and hated, and he persecuted him until the duke of Burgundy took the young man's part. But the king managed

Entry of Henry IV into London

Louis XI, 1461–83

Henry VI released from the Tower

The entrance of Louis XI into Paris

Louis XI and Charles the Victorious at Peronne

to break up their alliance and get his brother back into his own hands. He then poisoned him.

The old duke, Philip the Good, died just after Louis came to the throne; his son, Charles the Bold, was a brave, high-spirited prince, very ambitious and even more bent than his father on making his dukedom into a kingdom. To upset this ambition was Louis's great object. First, he began to stir up the turbulent towns of Flanders to rebel against Charles, and then while this was brewing he went to visit him at his hometown of Peronne, hoping to win him over. But the mischief he had set in motion at Liege broke out suddenly, and the people rose in a tumult, killed the duke's officers, and closed their city gates. Louis had placed himself in his own trap. So Charles though it only fair to leave him there. He left him there until the French army came to rescue him and reduced Liege to nothing.

Now the king and duke hated one another more than ever. Charles, who had married the sister of Edward IV of England, promised to aid the English if they would come to conquer France. Then Edward would have all the western parts, and he all the eastern. Edward came with one of the finest armies that had ever sailed from England, but in the meantime the duke of Burgundy had been drawn into a war with the German emperor, and could not join him. The two kings met one another on the bridge of Pecquiguy, across the Somme, with a great wooden barrier put up between them, for fear they should murder one another. Actually, they kissed one another through the bars, while the two armies looked on—the English ashamed, and the French well pleased.

Charles the Bold would have gone on with the war, but Louis stirred up fresh enemies for him in Switzerland. The town of Basle rose up in arms, murdered Charles's governor, and then joined the young duke of Lorraine, his bitter enemy. Both made war on him. Charles was beaten in two battles, at Morat and Granson, and at last, when he was besieging Nancy (the capital of Lorraine), the wicked Count Campobasso, the commander of his hired Italian troops, betrayed him to

the Swiss by opening the gates of the camp. There was a great slaughter of the Burgundians, and after it was over the body of the brave duke Charles was found, badly mutilated.

He left but one daughter, named Mary. His dukedom of Burgundy could not go to a woman, so it was returned to France. But Mary was sovereign of all Flanders and Holland. Her father had betrothed her to Maximilian of Austria (the son of the German emperor). When Louis was stirring up her towns to rebel against her, she sent her betrothed a ring as a token to beg him to come to her help. He did so at once; they were married and were most happy and prosperous for five years, until Mary was killed by a fall from her horse. Her baby son Philip received her royal inheritance.

Louis had three children—Anne, who married the duke of Bourbon's brother, the lord of Beaujeu; Charles; and Jane, a poor, deformed, sickly girl. She wanted to go into a convent but he forced her to marry her cousin Louis, duke of Orleans. Charles the dauphin was sickly too, and the king himself was in poor health. He was in great dread of death and sent for a spiritualist from Italy (Francis de Paula) to pray over him, vowing to give silver and gold images and candlesticks and shrines to half the saints if they would save him. But death came to him anyway, in 1483, just as Richard III of England had gained the crown.

CHARLES VIII (1483–98)

Charles VIII was but nine years old when he came to the crown. He was a weak lad, with thin legs and a large head, but full of spirit. His older sister, Anne, the lady of Beaujeu, had charge of him and his kingdom. At first, the lady of Beaujeu's time was taken up with quarrels with their brother-in-law, the duke of Orleans, who thought he had a better right to be regent than a woman did. The duke of Brittany had no son, and there was a long line of nobles who wanted to marry his little daughter Anne. Orleans had hopes of getting divorced from his "good wife" Jane and marrying this young girl. A battle was fought between the Bretons and French, in which Orleans was knocked off his horse and made prisoner. He was taken from one castle to another but his good wife Jane always followed him to do her best to comfort him, and never left him except to try to obtain his pardon. But the lady of Beaujeu was smart enough not to try too hard as long as Anne of Brittany was not married. Indeed, the lady thought the best thing would be if young Charles VIII could marry Anne, and join the great dukedom to his dominions.

But, on one hand, Charles was betrothed to Maximilian's daughter Margaret, and Anne to Maximilian himself; and, on the other, there was nothing the Bretons hated so much as the notion of being joined with the French. They wanted the poor girl of fourteen to marry a grim old baron, Alan de Foix, who had eight children already, because they thought he would fight for the duchy. In the middle of all of this, the duke of Brittany died. Anne of Beaujeu, in the meantime, raised an army and entered Brittany, taking one town after another. Anne of Brittany held out in her city of Rennes. Late one evening a young gentleman came to the gates and desired to see the duchess. It was the king. And so sweet and gentle in manner, and so knightly in stature was he, that Duchess Anne forgot her objections and consented to marry him. And so the duchy of Brittany was joined to the crown of France. As soon as Charles and Anne were married, the duke of Orleans was released.

Charles, recalling that he had the right to the kingdom of Naples, which old King René had left to his father, gathered together one of the most splendid armies that was ever seen in France to go and conquer it for himself. No group in Italy was ready to oppose him, for the cities were all quarreling among themselves and the pope who was reigning then, Alexander VI was one of the wickedest and most ineffective men who ever lived. He marched into the territory and was crowned king of Naples. Then he left a division of his army to guard the kingdom. The people had hoped that this young king would set things right—call a council of the church, have the court of

Rome purified. But Charles, a mere youth, who cared more for making a grand knightly display, could not manage his army, and they commited cruel acts on the people of Italy. He rode back the whole length of Italy and on the way claimed the ducy of Milan for his brother-in-law, the duke of Orleans, whose grandmother, Valentina Visconti, had been a daughter of the duke of Milan.

However, the Italian states allied against him, and a great army gathered together to attack him at Fornova. Then he showed all the high spirit and bravery there was in him. He really seemed to grow bigger with courage. He fought like a lion and gained a grand victory.

But there is more to being a king than knighthood. He did not manage well what he had conquered. He had not sent men or provisions to his army in Naples, so they were all driven out by the great Spanish captain, Gonzalo de Cordova. Only a token of them made it back home to France.

Charles began to mature as he grew older. And when he lost both his infant sons, his grief changed him a great deal. He read better books than the romances of chivlary, and he learned piety, justice, and firmness. He resolved to live like Saint Louis, and began, like him, sitting under an old oak tree to hear the causes of the rich and poor, and doing justice for all.

Above all, he realized how vain and foolish he had been in Italy, and what a great opportunity he had thrown away to try to get the terrible things that were going on with the pope and his cardinals ended. By helping the good men left in Italy, together with Maximilian and Henry VII, he hoped to call a council of the church, and set matters straight. He was just beginning to make arrangements for another expedition to Italy when, one day in 1498, while he was riding through a dark passage leading to the tennis court at Blois, he struck his forehead against the top of a doorway, was knocked backward, and after a couple of hours, died. He

Charles VIII, 1483–98

Anne of Brittany, wife of Charles VIII

Anne of Brittany

Meeting of Charles and Anne of Brittany

Louis XII, 1498–1515

was in the twenty-ninth year of his life and the fifteenth of his reign.

LOUIS XII (1498–1515)

Charles VIII had lost both his children, so the crown went to Louis, duke of Orleans, grandson to the second son of Charles V. The first thing he did was to bribe the pope (Alexander VI), to sanction a dissolution of his marriage to Jane, who was sent to a convent. He then married Anne of Brittany in order to keep her duchy united with the crown. She was a very noble and high-spirited queen, and kept her court in excellent order.

Louis was a vain man, and could not rest until he had accomplished as much as Charles VIII. So he allied himself with the pope, marched off into Italy with a big army, and seized Milan. He did not himself go to Naples, but he sent an army who seized a large portion of the kingdom. Then the Spanish king Ferdinand persuaded Louis to make peace, and divide the Kingdom of Naples in half with Spain.

The Italians themselves hated both the French and Spaniards, and only wanted to get Italy free of them; but instead of all joining openly together against them, their little states and princes took different sides, according to which side they hated more. A now famous Florentine, named Machiavelli, wrote a book called *The Prince,* in which he stated that craft and trickery were the right way for small states to overthrow their enemies and prosper. His tongue-in-cheek philosophy is now accepted principle, and is known widely by his name. In any event, the small states prospered by following his advice. Pope Alexander VI was poisoned by drinking by mistake the wine he had intended for another. The new pope, Julius II, made league with Louis and Maximilian against the Venetians. It was called the League of Cambrai, but no sooner had the brave French army gained and given to Julius the towns he had been promised, he turned again to the traditional Italian hatred of the foreigner and deserted their cause. He made another league, which he called the Holy League, with the emperor Maximilian, the Spanish Ferdinand, and Henry VIII of England, for the purpose of driving the French out of Italy.

The French army in Italy was attacked by the Span-

iards and Italians, and though the brave young general Gaston de Foix, duke of Nemours, gained a grand battle at Ravenna, he was killed at the climax of it. The French were driven out of the duchy of Milan, over the Alps, and out of Italy. Louis XII could not send help to them, for Ferdinand was attacking him in the south of France and Henry VIII in the north. The sister of the duke of Nemours was the second wife of Ferdinand and he believed she had a hereditary right to be queen of Navarre. Thus Ferdinand seized the little kingdom and left only the rights that belonged to the French side of the family, so that since that time the king of Navarre has been but a French noble.

Henry VIII had a fine army with him, with which he besieged and took the city of Tournay, and fought a battle at Enguingate in which the French were taken by surprise. A panic seized them and they retreated, leaving their brave knights to be taken prisoners. They galloped off so fast that there were only forty Frenchmen killed. The English called it the Battle of the Spurs. When Terouenne was also taken, Louis thought it was time to make peace.

Louis's wife, Anne of Brittany, had just died. She had had only two daughters, Claude and Renée. As Claude was heiress of Brittany, Louis thought it was a good idea to marry her off to Francis, duke of Angouleme, who was first cousin to her father, and who would be king of France. Francis was a fine, handsome, intelligent young man, but Queen Anne knew Claude would not by happy within Francis's family and tried hard to prevent the match. However, she could not succeed and she died soon after it was concluded. Louis then offered to marry Henry's youngest sister, Mary, the most beautiful princess in all of Europe, and she was obliged to consent. Louis XII was not an old man but he had long been in poor health. The feastings and pageants with which he received his young bride took its toll. He died at the end of six weeks, on New Year's Day of 1515.

Francis I, 1515–47

Equestrian portrait of Francis I

He has been called the Father of His People, although history does not record that he did much for their basic welfare. He taxed them heavily for his wars in Italy. But his appearance was always pleasant, and that meant a great deal to the French.

FRANCIS I (1515–47)

Francis I, the new king of France, was twenty years old when the crown was placed on his head. He had a lot of chivalrous ideas. But he had no sense of morals to keep the truth and honor that are the real part of chivalry.

To conquer Italy was his first notion, and he started to march across the Alps. But the Swiss had turned against him and blocked his way at Marignano. There was a terrible battle beginning at dusk, and when night came everything was in confusion. All night the great cow horns, which were the signal of the Swiss troops, were heard blowing, to gather them together. But the next morning the French rallied and won a great victory. No one had ever defeated the Swiss before. When it was over, Francis knelt down before the famous knight Bayard and asked to be dubbed a knight by him, as the bravest and truest of knights. When this was done, Bayard kissed his sword and declared that it should never be used in battle again. It was retired to the royal palace and may now be seen at the Louvre museum in Paris.

After this, Francis went on to take possession of Milan

and he had a royal audience with the pope at Bologna. There was a new pope, Leo X, a man very fond of art and learning and everything beautiful, though he had little ambition for the duty of his office. However, he made a wise agreement with Francis, which is called the Concordat of Bologna. The king gave the pope certain payments of treasures every year "forever" and gave up the calling of church councils of the French clergy. The pope, in return, gave the king the right for him and his successors of appointing all the bishops, deans, abbots, and abbesses in France forever.

Francis wanted to be emperor of Germany and tried to get Henry VIII to help him. They had a meeting at Ardres (near Calais). That conference was known was the Field of the Cloth of Gold. The two kings were both spirited young men, and they wrestled and played together like two boys. But nothing came of this meeting, for Henry preferred that the emperor be the young king Charles of Spain (who was grandson to the emperor Maximilian and Mary of Burgundy).

When Maximilian died, Francis offered himself to the empire and told the electors they were to think of him and Charles not as enemies, but as rivals for the same lady. This, however, was only a speech, for Francis was very discontented when Charles was chosen emperor, and he started a war at once. But all he got for this was the Italians rising again and driving his army out of Milan. And, another misfortune befell him. His mother, Louise of Savoy, fell in love with another Charles, the duke of Bourbon and constable of France. When the constable rejected her, she resolved to ruin him and made the king take away his lands. The constable was so angry that he went to Spain and offered to serve Charles against his king and country. He was so good a captain that Charles placed him in command of an army.

The constable led a Spanish army to invade France, and ravaged Provence. But the French rallied under Francis and he was driven back. Then Francis crossed the Alps, hoping to recover what he had lost in Italy. There was a great battle fought on February 24, 1525. Francis was too hasty in thinking the victory was his. He charged with all his troops, got entangled in the firmly

Francis I

The dauphin Francis, son of Francis I

positioned Spanish squadrons, and was surrounded, wounded, and forced to give himself up as a prisoner. He was sent as a prisoner to Madrid.

Charles would only release Francis upon the very harshest of terms—namely, that he should yield all his claims to Italy, renounce the sovereignty of the Low Countries, make Henry d'Albret give up his claim to Navarre, and marry Charles's sister Eleanor. Francis was to give his two sons as hostages until this was carried out. Francis declared that he would rather abdicate his throne than cripple his kingdom in such way. However, after ten months' captivity, he agreed to do all that was demanded of him. He was escorted back to the borders, where, on the River Bidassua, he met his two young sons, who were to be exchanged for him. After embracing them and giving them up to the Spaniards, he landed, mounted his horse, made it bound into the air and, waving his sword above his head, cried out, "I am yet a king!"

In France just then, John Calvin, a superintellect and a man of much learning, who had been studying for the priesthood, had, during his course of study, come to think that much of the teaching of the church of Rome was wrong. He wrote books that were eagerly read by great numbers, and his cause was welcomed by the king's sister, Margaret, who had married the dispossessed king of Navarre, and by his sister-in-law, Renée, the duchess of Ferrara. But the Calvinist teaching made Francis angry. Someone broke a statue of the Blessed Virgin in the streets of Paris, and this led to a cry on the part of the people that such things should not be allowed to go on. The persons pointed out as Calvinists were seized, and when they showed how little regard they had for the doctrines of the Roman Catholic church, they were turned over to the clergy of the state. They were burned

alive, according to the laws of France dealing with heretics.

But their brethren were only the firmer in their doctrine and hated the Roman Church all the more. The Calvinists in France were called Huguenots, though no one is quite certain why. One likely explanation is that it is from two Swiss words, meaning "oath-comrades," because they were all sworn brothers. Calvin himself, when he could not safely stay in France, accepted an invitation from the Reformers of Geneva to come and guide them, and from there he sent out rules which guided the French Huguenots.

Margaret, the queen of Navarre, believed like the Huguenots that much was wrong in her church, but she preferred to have the church set these things right. However, her only child, Jane, grew up to be an ardent Huguenot. Jane married Antony, duke of Bourbon, who was called king of Navarre in her right, though the Spaniards had all of the real kingdom of Navarre and she only had the little French counties of Béarn and Foix. But here she fostered the Huguenots with all her assets.

Charles V and Francis kept up a war for most of their lives, but without any more great battles. Francis did everything possible to hurt Charles. Though he was persecuting the Calvinists at home, he helped and made friends with the Protestants in Germany, because they were the emperor's greatest problem. And, because

Sanguine drawing of Francis I in his last years, taken from life

The boundaries of France in the time of Francis I

had no children, and most of Claude's were weak and in ill health—only two survived their father: Henry, who had been the second son, but had become dauphin; and Margaret, the youngest daughter.

HENRY II (1547–59)

The dauphin became king and reigned as Henry II, the son of Francis I. His greatest friend was the constable de Montmorency with whom he had a close friendship all his life, and his one strong romantic feeling was for a beautiful lady named Diana of Poitiers. She was the daughter of the great Florentine family of Medici, Catherine de Medici. She had a large family, and the eldest son, Francis, was betrothed to the infant Mary, queen of Scots, who was sent from her own kingdom to be brought up with her young husband in the court of France.

Henry continued the war with the emperor of Spain. He had one very able general, Francis de Lorraine, duke of Guise (a son of René, duke of Lorraine, who was the grandson to old King René). He sent this general to capture the city of Metz, and there Guise withstood a siege by the emperor himself—until hunger and famine wreaked such havoc on the besieging army that they were forced to retreat.

The emperor was growing old, and suffering badly from gout, so he was longing to retire. He decided on resigning his crowns and spending the remainder of his life in a Spanish monastery. He gave the empire to his brother Ferdinand; and the kingdoms of Spain, the two Sicilies with Lombardy, and the Low Countries to his son, Philip II, who was married to Mary Tudor, queen of England. This made the English join in the war against Henry II, and a small body of men was sent to the Spanish army, which, with Philip himself, was besieging Saint Quentin, a town on the borders of Picardy. One of the bravest men in France, a Huguenot nobleman named Gaspar de Chatillon, admiral de Coligny, was defending the town, and his brother, the sieur d'Andelot tried hard to break through and bring him provisions, but he was beaten back. There was a great battle fought

Charles was at war with the Turks and the Moors, Francis allied himself with them. However, as he deserved, his treachery profited him little, for the emperor gained a fast hold on Italy, and, moreover, invaded Provence. But the count de Montmorency laid waste to every town, village, and farm in his way, so that his army found little to eat. Thus, he was forced to retreat. The poor Provencals suffered just as much from lack of food, but the territory was saved, and Montmorency was made constable of France as a reward.

After this, peace was made for a time, and Charles, who wanted to go in haste from Spain to Flanders, asked permission to pass through France; and Francis received him most courteously, sending the dauphin to meet him, and entertaining him magnificently. But at one of the banquets, Francis pointed to the duchess of Chatelherault, saying, "Here's a lady who says I am a great fool to let you go free." The emperor took the hint and dropped a costly ring into the gold basin that the duchess held to him to wash his hands in. Charles departed in safety but no sooner did Francis hear of him being in trouble in his own domains, than all promises were again broken, and the war began again. This time Henry VIII was also very angry with Francis and joined the emperor to punish him. Charles invaded Champagne, and Henry landed at Calais, and besieged and took Boulogne. However, the Spanish emperor made peace. Then Henry, for a ransom of 2 million crowns, promised, in eight years time, to give back Boulogne. Just after this peace was made Henry died, and Francis only lived two months after him, dying in January 1547, when only fifty-three years old. Queen Claude had long been dead, and Francis had married the emperor's sister, Eleanor. She had

Henry II, 1547–59

The duke of Guise

on August 10, 1557, before the walls, when the constable de Montmorency, who commanded the French, was defeated. He was made prisoner, four thousand men were killed, and Coligny was forced to surrender. France had not suffered such a defeat since the battle of Agincourt. However, it was some comfort to the French that the duke of Guise managed to take by surprise the city of Calais, which the English had held ever since the time of Edward III and which was their last French possession. But other misfortunes forced Henry to make peace; and at Chateau Cambresis, in 1559, a treaty was signed that put an end to the long Italian wars that were begun by Charles VIII nearly seventy years before. After this, there was great rejoicing, but the persecution of the Calvinists was carried on with more rigor, and the king and all his court, including the ladies, used to be present at the burnings at the stake in the marketplace.

One of Francis's acts had been the seizing of the little dukedom of Savoy in the Alps, which he added to his kingdom. The landless duke of Savoy was serving in the Spanish army and was an able general. Indeed, it was his leadership that had won the battle of Saint Quentin. One article in the peace of Chateau Cambresis had been that the French should give him back his dukedom and marry him to Margaret, the only sister of Henry. The wedding festivities were intended to be very magnificent, and Henry began them with a splendid tournament, like those of the olden times of knighthood, when the knights, in full armor, rode against each other with their heavy lances. Henry himself took part in this one, and tried to unhorse the sieur des Lorges, eldest son of the count of Montgomery. There was generally very little danger to men in steel armor, but as these two met, the point of des Lorges' lance pierced a joint in the visor of Henry's helmet, and penetrated his eye and brain. He was carried from the field, and lay speechless for two days. In the meantime, his sister was hastily married in private to the duke of Savoy so that his death might not delay the fulfillment of the treaty. He died on June 29, 1559, leaving four sons (Francis, Charles, Henry, and Hercules) and three daughters (Elizabeth, Claude, and Margaret), all young children.

FRANCIS II (1559–60) AND CHARLES IX (1560–74)

The next two reigns, though they are, of course, called the reigns of Francis II and Charles IX, were really the reign of their mother, Catherine de' Medici. Because Francis was only fifteen when he lost his father, his mother took over the chief management of his affairs. He died of a "swelling in the ear" in his seventeenth year, in 1560. His brother, Charles IX, who was only twelve years old, then began to reign.

At Vassy, where the mother of the duke of Guise lived,

Francis II, 1559–60

there was a barn where the Huguenots used to meet. On one occasion when her son was visiting her, she complained of them. He went to their church and stayed to listen to their singing. His followers were very angry at this and broke into the barn and killed several Huguenots. This was the beginning of the terrible war between the Catholics and the Huguenots. From a historical point of view, it's important to know that a Guise was always at the head of the Catholics and a Bourbon at the head of the Huguenots. The city of Rouen fell into the hands of the Huguenots, and Guise besieged it. But in the course of the siege the duke was shot by a murderer named Poltrot and died in a few hours. His son Henry, who was very young at the time, always believed that the murderer had been sent by the admiral de Coligny and though this is not at all likely, the whole family vowed vengeance against him. During this siege, Antony, duke of Bourbon, was also killed. He was no great loss to the Huguenots, for he had gone over to the other side, and his wife, Queen Jane, was freer to act for them without him.

It the interim, the queen's sons were beginning to grow up. She did not want to put the king on the throne for fear he would learn to govern and take away her power. Her third son, Henry, the duke of Anjou, commanded in the battle of Jarnac. The prince of Condé who was on the other side, had his arm in a sling from a wound received a few days before. And just as he had ridden to the head of his troops his horse reared, fell on him, and broke his leg. But he would not give up, and rode into the battle as he was. He was defeated and taken prisoner. He was lifted off his horse and placed in the shade of a tree, helpless. A friend of the duke of Anjou, riding by, recognized him, stopped, and shot him through the head.

The Queen of Navarre felt that she must come to the head of her party. She had one son, Henry, prince of Béarn. Queen Jane had had him most carefully taught both religion and other studies so that he was a boy of great promise. He was fifteen years old at this time and his cousin Henry, son of the prince of Condé, was about the same age. Queen Jane took them to the head of the Huguenot army and they were trained to be leaders while admiral de Coligny managed their affairs.

Queen Catherine began to realize that she would never

Catherine de' Medici, regent, 1560–63

Charles IX, 1560–74

be able to put the Huguenots down by force. She pretended to make friends with them, and she and her son, Charles IX, made them grants for the sake of getting them into her power. She offered to marry her daughter Margaret to the prince of Béarn, and invited him to her court. Poor Queen Jane could not bear to let her boy go, for she knew what would happen. Catherine kept a contingent of young ladies about her who were called the Queen Mother's Squadron, and who made it their business, with their light songs, idle talk, and pleasant sexual habits, to corrupt all the young men who came in contact with them. By comparison, Jane's little court was grave, strict, and dull, but Henry enjoyed the change. Catherine took care never to have mother and son at her court together. She sent Henry home before she invited his mother to the court.

While at court, Jane fell suddenly ill and died. There was a man about court, a perfumer, whom people called the Queen's Poisoner. History records a fear of the court's that Catherine had had the poisoner kill Jane.

Poor young Charles IX would have been a good king if his mother had allowed him, but she taught him that the way to reign was to deceive, and he had such fear of her that he choked all of his better feelings. She was exceedingly afraid of the Huguenots, and thought they were conspiring against her and the young Henry, duke of Guise, was ready to do anything to be revenged against Coligny, whom he viewed as his father's murderer. So, to get the Huguenots into her power, Catherine invited all their chief nobles to come to the wedding of her daughter, Margaret, with young Henry, who had become king of Navarre. The pope would not give permission for the princess to marry one who stood outside the church, so the queen forged his consent!

Coligny and all his friends had come to the wedding, and the king was so delighted with the brave, honest old soldier that Catherine thought she should lose all her power over him. One day, Coligny was shot in the streets of Paris by a would-be murderer. Though only his hands were shattered, he was so ill that the king came to see him and all his friends gathered round him to protect him. Thereupon, Catherine plotted with her son, the duke of Anjou, and the duke of Guise, that, when the bell of the Church of St. Germain l'Auxerrois, close to the palace of the Tuileries, rang at midnight before Saint Bartholomew's Day, the Catholic people of Paris who were friends of the duke of Guise should rise upon the Huguenots who were asleep in their homes and kill them all. It was hard to get King Charles to consent, for there were many Huguenots whom he had learned to love, but when he found that he could not save Coligny, he said, "Let them all die; let none live to reproach me." However, he called into his own bedroom two whom he most

Charles IX on horseback

Elizabeth of Austria, wife of Charles IX

Charles IX with his second wife, Elizabeth of Austria

wished to save—his doctor and his old nurse. But there were a great many more in the palace who had attended to the young king of Navarre, and every one of these was slaughtered. Everywhere murder was going on. The followers of Guise wore white scarves on one arm, that they might know one another in the dark, and a troop of them rushed in, slew old Coligny in his bedroom, and threw the corpse out the window. All the rabble of Paris joined in the slaying and plundering of their neighbors, and in all the other towns where the Huguenots were the weakest the same horrid slaughter was going on. The Massacre of Saint Bartholomew's Day is the deadliest crime in the history of France. The young king is said to have drawn his sword against the king of Navarre and prince of Condé, and would have struck them if his young wife, Elizabeth of Austria, had not heard of it, and ran in entreating him to spare them. Their lives were spared on condition that they would return to the church, which they did, and they were watched and forced to live like prisoners at court.

When Queen Elizabeth of England heard of his shocking day, she broke off the plans for marrying the duke of Anjou—a scheme which Catherine de' Medici had set up, as it would have made her third son a king without the death of the second. However, a kingdom did come to him, for the old realm of Poland always chose the king by election by all the nobles, and their choice was Henry, duke of Anjou. He did not like going to that wild country, away from all the amusements of Paris, and delayed as long as he could.

Meantime, the poor young king tried to forget the horrors of the night of Saint Bartholomew. The grief of it all was ruining his health. His mother was too busy trying to secure the throne for his brother to attend to him. He died in the year 1574, when only twenty-three years old. His last words were, "If our Lord Jesus will have mercy on me for my crime!"

The war with the Huguenots was still going on when he died, for though Coligny was slain and the king of Navarre was still watched and guarded at court, there were enough nobles left alive to hold out against their enemies. If the troops of the queen and duke of Guise came up on a meeting of the Huguenots, they burned the building and killed everyone who came out of it. And if the Huguenots found a church or convent not defended, they burned it and killed the monks or nuns. Everyone waited anxiously for the arrival of the new king. He was delighted to leave Poland, although he was in no hurry to take all the troubles of his French kingdom upon himself, so on his journey home, he went out of his way to Italy and stayed there a month amusing himself. In the meantime, the duke of Guise was growing stronger and stronger and was becoming a great favorite with the people of Paris. Catherine was hoping to marry off her fourth son, Hercules, the duke of Alençon, to Queen Elizabeth, who pretended to think about it. She even sent for him to see her. But it was all in order to keep peace with France. The duke was an ugly little misformed youth, whom the queen took a fancy to, but it wasn't serious.

HENRY III (1574–89)

On his way home through Savoy, Henry visited with Louise de Vaudemont, a very beautiful girl, a cousin of the duke of Guise, and he desired to marry her. Queen Catherine tried to prevent it, but the king would not let her have a say.

King Henry III was a strange person. He cared for little but fine clothes, his own beauty, and a sort of religion that did him no good. He slept in a mask and gloves for the sake of his complexion, and painted his face; and every day he stood over his wife to see her hair dressed, and chose her clothing and ornaments. He had a set of friends like himself, who were called his "darlings," and were fops like himself. They all wore rosaries, of which the beads were carved like skulls; and they, king and all, used to go in procession, barefoot and covered with sackcloth, to the churches in Paris, with whips in their hands, with which to flog one another in penance for their sins. Yet they were horribly cruel and thought nothing of murder.

Henry III, 1574–89

Louise of Lorraine,
wife of Henry III

Henry III in his favorite
royal garb

Henri, prince of Navarre, in 1557,
later Henry IV

Henry of Navarre stayed in this strange court of his for nearly two years, but at last, in 1576, he fled away to the Huguenot army in the south of France and professed himself a Calvinist again. He soon showed that he was by far the ablest leader that the Huguenots had had, and he obtained another peace.

Even the duke of Alençon, the youngest brother, could not bear the life at Henry's court and fled from it. At one time the Dutch, who had revolted from Philip of Spain, invited the duke to be their "king." But he did them little good and on his way home he died. His death made a great difference because Henry III had no children, and as women could neither reign in France themselves nor leave any rights to their children, the nearest heir to the crown was Henry of Navarre, whose forefather, the first count of Bourbon, had been a son of Saint Louis.

Everybody knew he was the rightful heir, but to have a Calvinist king to reign over them seemed frightful to the more zealous Catholics. They formed themselves into a society, which they called the Holy League for maintaining the church, the great object of which was to keep Henry of Navarre from becoming king of France. The duke of Guise was at the head of this league.

There was a third party—Catholics, but loyal, and with the count de Montmorency at their head—and these were the persons Henry trusted most. He was fond of his bright, kindly brother-in-law, the king of Navarre, and never would do anything to prevent him from succeeding, although he found that it was not safe to remain in Paris and went to his palace at Blois. There he framed a plot for freeing himself from the duke of Guise. He placed guards whom he could trust under the staircase and in his anteroom, and when Guise came to visit the king they murdered him. The duke's brother, the cardinal of Guise, was killed the same day, and Henry went up to his mother, Queen Catherine, who was ill in bed, to tell her that he was free from his enemy, but she saw plainly that he was only bringing more trouble upon himself. "You have a cut," she said; "can you sew? Have you thought of all that you will bring on yourself?" He said he had done so. "Then you must be prompt and firm," she said; but she did not live to help him through his difficulties. She died two weeks later.

Henry was far from able to sew. The Holy League was mad with rage. Guise's sons were little children, so his brother, the duke of Mayenne, took the lead, and though he was not a clever man, the party was so strong that it took no great ability to make it rough for the king. The duke's sister, the duchess of Montpensier, really was like a fury and went about the streets of Paris stirring up the people, who already hated and despised the king and now raged against him. They tried him in effigy, deposed him, carried his figure through the streets heaping insults upon it, and made an anagram of his name, *Henri de Valois—Vilain Herodes.* He was brought to such distress that he was obliged to beg Henry of Navarre to come and help him. The two kings met at Plessis-les-Tours and were most friendly together. They joined their armies and began to besiege Paris. But this made the Leaguers more violent against Henry than ever, and a young monk named Clément, fancying that there was no sin, even virtue, in freeing the church from a man like Henry, crept out of Paris with a packet of important letters, and while the king was reading one, stabbed him with a dagger. Clément was instantly slain by the king's guard, and the king of Navarre was sent for and arrived in time to see his brother-in-law still alive. Henry embraced him, asked his people to make him king of France, and added, "But you will never be able to reign unless you become a Catholic." Then he died (in the year 1589), the last and most contemptible noble in the House of Valois. The Leaguers rejoiced in his death and praised the murdered

Henry IV, 1589–1610

The marriage of Henry IV and Marie de' Medici, 1600

Henry IV in his walking costume

Clément as a saint and martyr, while they set up as king the cardinal of Bourbon, the old uncle of the king of Navarre, declaring that it was impossible that a heretic should ever reign in France.

HENRY IV (1589–1610)

The new king, Henry IV, was so poor, that he was obliged to dress himself in the robes left by his brother-in-law. France was now divided into two parties instead of three, for the Leaguers were against the Huguenots, while the moderate Catholics thought that the birthright of the crown called upon them to be loyal to any sort of king. Both were with Henry.

Henry's uncle, Cardinal Charles, the Leaguers' king, soon died, and then they talked of the throne for Isabelle, a daughter of Philip II of Spain, because her mother had been the eldest sister of the last three kings. But as there was a great hatred of the Spaniards among the French, this plan did harm to their cause and made many more of the Catholics turn to Henry. He was fighting his way to the throne through numerous battles and sieges. At the battle of Ivry, in Normandy, he told his followers that if they wanted a guide in the thick of the fray they had only to follow his white feather, and the saying became a byword after his great victory—"follow the white feather." The Spaniards came to help the league

and the war lasted for years, while Henry still was kept out of Paris. At last he made up his mind that he would return to the Roman Catholic church. He used to say that one of the true things that nobody would believe was that he had changed out of an honest belief that the Calvinists were wrong. But he did gain a kingdom by so doing though the truth was that he had very little religion of any kind at all. But it was true that he did not like the strict ways of the Calvinists. The Catholics were only too glad to have him and accepted him heartily. But the league was not satisfied, and only in the year 1594, when he had been king five years, did he ride into Paris without any opposition from them. Even then the Leaguers went on opposing him, till at last his wisdom and that of his good old friend, the duke of Sully, succeeded in overcoming their objections, and the duke de Mayenne consented to make peace with him.

Only then did Henry IV really begin to reign. He had to put down some of the great nobles who had grown overly powerful and insolent during the long civil war. He tried to bring about peace between the Catholics and

Marguerite of Valois,
wife of Henry IV

Gaston of France,
third son of Henry IV

The entrance of Henry IV into France

A caricature of the older Henry IV

Marie de' Medici

Gabrielle d'Estrées, the duchess of Beaufort, right, mothered three of Henry IV's children. She almost became queen. She is seen in this Louvre Museum painting with her sister-in-law, the duchess of Villars.

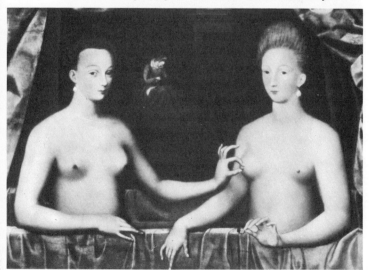

the Calvinists. He had friends on both sides, and was anxious to make them live in unity without fighting with one another or persecuting one another. So he created a law that gave the Calvinists permission to have places of worship, provided it was not where they would annoy Catholics. And they were not hindered from taking offices at court or in the army, or from having schools in certain places. To secure all this to them, they were allowed to hold three towns as pledges—La Rochelle, Montauban, and Montpellier. In this last one, there was a college for educating their pastors. This law was called the Edict of Nantes because Henry had it registered by the parliament of the old duchy of Brittany, since each old province still kept its own laws and parliament. He obtained this Edict of Nantes with great difficulty, for the Catholics thought it wrong to allow any person to remain outside the church. But the people were worn out with the long and bloody civil war and glad for a respite. So the edict was passed and France began on the road to recovery.

Henry had no children and therefore wished to divorce his wife Margaret so that he might marry another who might bear him an heir, instead of having to leave his crown to his young cousin, the prince of Condé. So, as there had never been real consent on the pope's part to the marriage of the cousins and as the bride had been forced into it against her will by her mother and brother, the pope was persuaded to pronounce the wedding null and void, and that the two were free to marry again. It was not easy to find a princess, for all the Spaniards and Austrians and their allies were his greatest enemies. And he could not now marry a Protestant. So he ended up by choosing one of the Medici family, Marie. She gave him two sons and three daughters, and there never was a fonder father. Once, when the Austrian ambassador came to see him, he was found on all fours, with his little son riding on his back. "Are you a father, sir?" he said to the ambassador. "Yes, sire." "Then we will first finish our game," returned the king.

There were many of the remnants of the Leaguers who hated the king for having once been a Huguenot and for the Edict of Nantes. Though the love of the whole country was more and more with him, he still was not willing to gather a great crowd together in Paris for fear of an outbreak. So, as he had been crowned long before he was married, the coronation of Marie de' Medici was put off year after year. Henry was not with her when the coronation finally took place, but looked on from a private box at the pageant.

The next day, just as he had seated himself in his carriage, a man named Francis Ravaillac sprang up on the wheel, held a paper for him to read, and the next moment stabbed him in the heart with a knife. He died instantly, one of the greatest losses his country had ever known. It was on May 14, 1610. He was known to the French as *le Grand Monarque,* "the Great Monarch."

The Coming of Age of Louis XIII, *painting by Rubens*

The later kings of France: Top row, Charles VIII, Louis XVI, Louis XII, second row, Louis XV, John II, Charles V; third row, Francis I, Henry IV, Henry III, Henry II; fourth row, Francis II, Charles VII; bottom row, Charles X, Louis-Philippe, Louis XVIII.

Cardinal Richelieu

Louis XIII, 1610–43

The deathbed of Louis XIII

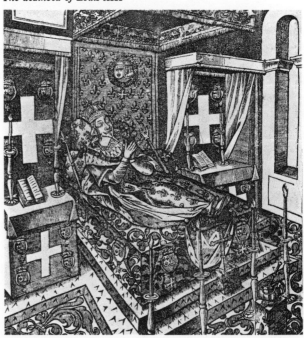

LOUIS XIII (1610–43)

The eldest son of Henry IV, Louis XIII, was but nine years old when his father was killed and his mother, Marie de' Medici, became regent. She was a weak, foolish woman, and let herself be entirely guided by an Italian lady in her court named Galigai, who had married a man named Concini. Marie made her son give him the title of Marshall d'Ancre, and it was they who really ruled France. But all the French nobles hated d'Ancre.

Their rule lasted seven years, but when the young king was sixteen years old, a young nobleman named Luynes told him that, now that he was growing up, he would be secretly killed so that his mother might continue as regent in the name of his little brother. So Louis had his guards arrest Marshal d'Ancre next time he came to the palace, and instructed them to kill him if he resisted. He did resist and was slain, and his wife was tried for bewitching the queen and put to death. Marie was forced to leave the court and go into "retirement" in the country. After some years of wrangling with her son, she went to England, for her youngest daughter, Henrietta Maria, had married King Charles I. Queen Marie later died in extreme poverty.

Louis XIII was a strange person—slow, dull, and cold-hearted, though not ill-disposed. His health was bad, and he hated problems of state more than anything else. There was a very clever man in his court, Armand de Richelieu, bishop of Lucon. Albert de Luynes was the king's first minister after d'Ancre's fall, and when he died of a fever, Richelieu took over the management of everything. He let the king have young men as his companions and young women as his favorites. But if ever one of these showed anything but amusement and fancy —any spirit—or tried to stir the king up to act for himself and overthrow the tyranny he lived under, Richelieu always found it out and put the bold one to death. The king did nothing to save his friends. For in truth he disliked trouble more than anything else, and Richelieu thought and acted for him.

As the pope created him, the cardinal was really one of the greatest statesmen who ever lived and made France a much greater and more mighty power than ever before. He made the king much more powerful too. He was a hard, stern man, and did not bother with justice. He could do but one thing—make the crown of France more powerful. The nobles, who had grown strong and haughty during the long wars, were very sternly, and even cruelly, put down by him. He thought nothing of having them accused of treason, shutting them up in prison, or having them put to death. Thus he managed to get rid of all the great men who had been almost princes, such as the count de Montmorency, grandson of the old constable.

He also made war upon the Huguenots, in spite of the Edict of Nantes, and tried to take La Rochelle from them. There was a long and deadly siege. Charles I of England sent them help but his favorite, the duke of Buckingham, who was to have had the command of the fleet that was coming to help them, died at Portsmouth. When at last the people were starved out, after fourteen months, the cardinal made the king himself come down to personally receive their surrender. La Rochelle was a terrible loss to them. But at least the Roman Catholic Church was in a much better state. There were many very good men among the clergy, especially Francis de Sales, bishop of Geneva, and Vincent de Paul, an outstanding priest, who gathered together the poor desolate children who had no homes and had good families take care of them. He also first established the order of the Sisters of Mercy, who were like nuns, only they were not shut up in convents. Their work was to nurse the sick, take care of orphans, and teach poor children. The great ladies at court used to put on plain dresses and nurse the sick in the hospitals. Even the queen served. She was a Spanish princess, called Anne of Austria—a good, kind, and gracious lady—but not cared for much at court. For many years she had no children, but at last, when all hope had been given up, she had first one boy and then another, and there was immense rejoicing among the people.

Wars had been going on with the Spaniards all through Louis's reign in Italy and the Low Countries, as well as great conflict between the Roman Catholics and Protestants in Germany, which is known as the Thirty Years War. Cardinal de Richelieu managed matters so well that France almost always gained overwhelming advantage in affairs with other countries.

But Richelieu's own iron rule was coming to an end. He had been in very bad health in his later years, yet he never seemed to care about it and was as fierce as ever if a friend of the king appeared to take away any of his power. The baron de Cinq Mars was put to death for conspiring against him when he was almost at the edge of his grave. He declared, when he was receiving his last communion, that he had always meant to work for the honor of God and the good of the state. He died early in his fifty-eighth year on December 4, 1642. On his deathbed he advised the king to put trust in an Italian priest named Mazarin.

Louis seemed to be little bothered by the loss of Richelieu. He only said, "There's a great statesman dead"; and when there was a great storm on the day of the funeral, he said, "The cardinal has a bad day for his journey." But he was in a very weak state of health himself, and only lived five months after Richelieu, dying at the age of forty-two years, on May 14, 1643, and though his reign was a grand one for France, it was no thanks to him, but to the great statesman, Richelieu, who ruled both him and the country.

Louis XIV as a young man   *Louis XIV, 1643–1715*

Cardinal Mazarin

Louis XIV in pomp for the ceremony

LOUIS XIV (1643–1715)

"I am Louis XIV," cried the little five-year-old dauphin, as he stood by his dying father's bedside. "Not yet," the old king was still strong enough to say, though he did not live many more hours. His reign was to be the longest ever of a king (seventy-two years).

At first his mother, Queen Anne, was regent, and she trusted entirely to Cardinal Mazarin. He was not a great man, like Richelieu, but he was clever and cunning and the saying was, "The fox comes after the lion." He was a foreigner and of low birth. The French found it much harder to submit to him than to Richelieu, who was of one of the noblest families in France. Only four days after the accession of the little king, the duke d'Enghien won the great battle of Rocroy in the Low Countries in which the fine old Spanish foot soldiers were annihilated. After two more victories, peace was made between France and Spain. But this did not make things easier for Mazarin, for all the nobles who had been away with the army came home with nothing to do—especially the duke d'Enghien, who soon, on his father's death, became prince of Condé, and who was proud and fiery and hated the young upstart Mazarin.

All this hatred broke out in a great quarrel between the queen and the parliament of Paris. The parliament of Paris was a very different body from the Parliament of England. It did not represent the whole kingdom, for each of the great old provinces had a separate parliament of its own. It was made up only of the lawyers of Paris and the great nobles who belonged to the old duchy of France, along with the bishops and princes of royal blood. It judged peers of France for state offenses, and in matters of property. But it could not make laws or grant taxes. All it could do was to register the laws and the taxes when the king had made them. The king's acts were not valid till this had been done. When Mazarin, in the king's name, laid a heavy tax on all the food that was brought into Paris, the parliament refused to register the act, and there was a great struggle, which was known by the strange name of the Fronde. *Fronde* is the French word for "sling." In the earlier part of the quarrel the speakers used to stand up and throw sharp words at one another, just like little boys slinging stones at one another. But they soon came to much worse weapons.

The Fronde was the effort of the parliament to stand up against the royal power. There were two sieges of Paris in the course of it. The prince of Condé at first would not turn against the king and helped to make a peace. But he insisted on Mazarin being sent into exile, and when he was gone, Condé was found to be such a stern and insolent master that they contrived to get Mazarin back. Then he threw Condé into prison. Condé's wife joined with the other Frondeurs to try to gain his freedom again and he was set free—but only to make another war. Then, he joined the Spaniards, and helped them to wage war against his own country.

Cardinal Mazarin followed up all the plans of Richelieu, and France went on prospering and gaining victories until the Spaniards at last, in the year 1659, made what was called the Peace of the Pyrenees, giving up several towns in the Low Countries. In time the young King Louis was to forgive the prince of Condé and to marry Marie-Therese, the daughter of the king of Spain.

Two years later Cardinal Mazarin died. He had, like Richelieu, cared for the greatness of the kingdom of France and for the power of the crown, but unlike Richelieu, Mazarin shaped the character of the king who held all this power. Louis XIV grew up thinking that the nation was made for his glory. Yet he turned out to be a wonderfully able man. Mazarin said, "There is stuff in him to make four kings, and an honest man into the bargain." When the cardinal died, and the ministers asked to whom they should come, he answered, "To myself," for he was Mazarin's understudy. And for all the half-century after that of his reign, he was always ready for them. His court was exceedingly splendid, and very stiff. Everyone had his place there and never came out of it; who must stand or who might sit, who might be on stools and who must kneel, in the royal presence, was thought a matter of greatest importance. But Richelieu and Mazarin had robbed the nobles of all useful work, so all they cared for was war and ceremony of court and getting money from their poor peasants to support their expense.

Louis XIV had the two best generals then in Europe in the viscount de Turenne and the prince of Condé, and his nobles were very brave and spirited. His victories were all to the credit of his generals. When the king went out to war, he only went to the siege of some city where he rode quite out of reach of danger. And yet his people were all so proud of him that the very sight of him made his soldiers fight all the better, and poets wrote verses comparing him to Jupiter and Mars and every other warlike hero they could think of.

He had married Marie-Therese, daughter of the king of Spain; and when her father died, he pretended that he, rather than her little brother Charles, ought to inherit all the Low Countries. So Louis sent the duchess to persuade King Charles and his minister, with promises of money and concessions, to desert the Dutch; and she succeeded. The brave Dutch were left alone against all the power of France. William, prince of Orange, commanded their armies; and though he was beaten again and again, the little state never gave in. But, finally to keep out the French, it was necessary to open the floodgates that protect Holland from the sea and let in so much water that the enemy could not pass.

Then the emperor of Germany took up the cause of the Dutch, but Louis sent Turenne against his troops and conquered Alsace. Turenne went on into Germany and there his army laid waste to the land. Crops in the fields were burned, houses and villages burned and plundered, the women and girls raped, and the men assaulted and killed. Turenne was killed while standing under a tree near the village of Salzbach, by a cannon shot, which nearly cut his body in two. He was buried among the

kings at St. Denys, and Condé took the command of the army, gaining many hard-fought battles until at last peace was made, leaving Louis in possession of Alsace and of the city of Strasburg.

Besides his great generals, the king had about him many of the ablest men who ever lived in France, both ministers of state and writers, and excellent bishops and clergy. The dauphin was a very dull youth who cared for nothing but playing at cards and hunting, and very little could be taught him. He married a German princess, who was duller still, and they had three sons, the dukes of Burgundy, Anjou, and Berri. To them the king gave as tutor Fénélon, archbishop of Cambrai, one of the best and holiest men then living. The duke of Burgundy was a fiery, selfish, passionate boy; but under Fénélon he learned to rule himself, and his whole thought was how to be a good and religious prince.

Louis lost his wife, Marie-Therese of Spain, and then married a lady named Madame de Maintenon.

In 1688, Louis lost out in his English alliance. Charles II and James II, having spent their youth in France and

Louis XIV and Mademoiselle de la Valliere

The dauphin, son of Louis XIV

Monsieur Philip I, duke of Orleans, brother of Louis XIV

Direct ancestors of Louis XIV

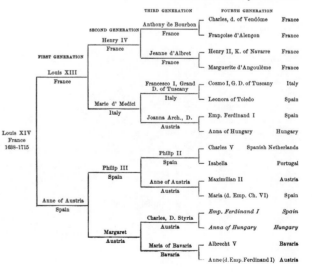

Louis XIV created the greatest of all royal palaces—Versailles and the Trianons.

being Roman Catholics, had always looked up to him and been led by him. But when the Revolution took place and James was driven away to take refuge once more in France, Louis's greatest enemy, William of Orange, became king of England. Louis gave James and his queen a home at his palace at St. Germain's and did all he could for them.

Charles II, king of Spain, died in 1700, leaving no children. His sister and his two aunts had married emperors of Germany and kings of France. But as the Spaniards did not choose to have their kingdom joined on to another, it was always the custom for the princesses to renounce all right to the crown for themselves and their children. However, the whole Spanish line had come to an end and there was really nobody else who had any right to it. Now, Louis XIV had married the sister, so his son was the nearest heir; but, on the other hand, the emperor of Germany was descended from the brother of the great Charles V, who had been emperor and king of Spain both at once. The emperor wanted to make his second son, the archduke Charles, king of Spain; and

Louis put forward his second grandson, Philip, duke of Anjou.

The Spaniards would have preferred Charles, but Louis was ready first. He made the dauphin and the duke of Burgundy give up their rights in favor to Philip, saluted him as king of Spain, and sent him off with an army to Madrid, saying, "There are no more Pyrenees"; by which he meant that France and Spain were now to be like one country. Now this was just what the rest of the world did not wish. France was a great deal too powerful already, so England and all the other states of Europe joined to assist the archduke Charles in winning Spain.

Thus began what was called the War of the Spanish Succession. The archduke Charles went to Spain and the English helped him there. The French army invaded Germany, but they were met there by the English and Austrian armies under the duke of Marlborough and Prince Eugene of Savoy and were badly defeated at Blenheim.

Prince Eugene's father had always lived in France,

The glass gallery of Versailles

The battle gallery of Versailles

and his mother was a niece of Cardinal Mazarin, but he and some other young men had grown tired of the dull court life and had run away to fight in the Austrian army against the Turks. He was very angry and never forgave Prince Eugene, who took service under the emperor of Germany and was then the second-best general in Europe. All the great generals of Louis's youth were dead, and though Marshals Villars and Boufflers were able men, they were not equal to Marlborough and were beaten again and again in the Low Countries. The only victory the French did gain was in Spain, at Almanza, where, strangely enough, the English were commanded by a French Huguenot and the French by Marlborough's nephew, the duke of Berwick, who had left home with James II.

But troubles came fast for Louis XIV. He lost his only son, the dauphin, and all his great men who had made his reign so splendid were dying around him of old age, and nobody was rising up equal to them. His subjects, too, were worn out, all their strongest young men had been carried off to be soldiers, and there were not enough left to till the ground properly. Beside, the money that the king wanted for his wars and buildings was far more than they could pay. It was the tradesmen, farmers, and lawyers who had to pay it all, for in France no priest and no noble ever paid taxes. Moreover, all the family of a

noble was considered as noble forever, instead of, as it is in England, only the head of the house. So all the younger sons and their children paid no taxes and would not enter a profession, but only became clergy or soldiers.

Old as Louis was, his steadiness was admired even by his enemies when he continued dauntlessly to resist, even when there seemed little to hinder Marlborough and Eugene from marching upon Paris. However, this humiliation was spared the proud old king by the change in Queen Anne's councils, which deprived Marlborough of power and led to a peace at last with France, The archduke Charles became emperor after the death of his father and brother; and therefore Philip of Anjou was allowed to remain king of Spain.

The king kept up all his old state, but his strength and spirit were gone; and Madame de Maintenon used to say no one could guess what a dreadful thing it was to have to amuse an unamusable king. The brightest person at court was the young dauphiness, Adelaide of Savoy, wife of the duke of Burgundy, who was now dauphin. She used to play merrily with the king, and coax him into cheerfulness as no one else could. The dauphin was a grave, thoughtful man, very pious and religious, always thinking anxiously of the trouble that the kingdom would be in the state in which his grandfather would

The bedroom of Louis XIV at Versailles

The Grand Trianon on the Versailles grounds was more livable for the royal family.

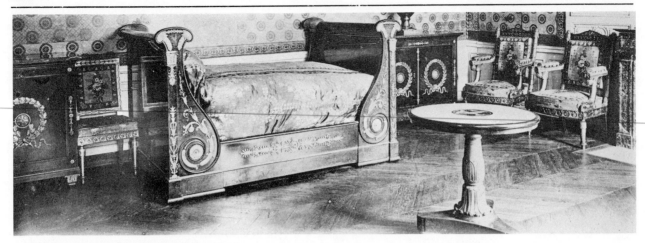

In the Grand Trianon—the bedroom of Napoleon I

leave it. But he never had to bear that load, for a dreadful form of malignant measles spread through the court and the dauphiness caught it and died, then the eldest of her two little sons, and lastly, the good dauphin himself. No one was left of the whole family except the old king and one great-grandson, Louis; the dauphin's second son, a baby; and the king's nephew, Philip, duke of Orleans, the son of his brother.

It was a sad prospect for France when, a year later, Louis XIV died, after a reign of over seventy years, during which he had been one of the greatest monarchs in Europe. But, too, it was a sad reign for the little boy who had become king of France.

Regent Philip II of Orleans

LOUIS XV (1715–74)

The regent was Philip, duke of Orleans, a thoroughly dissipated man, not unlike Charles II of England. He died just as the young king, Louis XV, was growing up. Louis's queen was a Polish princess named Marie Leczinska. She was a gentle, kindly person, though not very intelligent. At first the king was very fond of her. But their moments of bliss soon ended when the king became a glutton and drunkard. He spent most of his spare time in immoral pursuits. The people did not know and had such a love and loyalty for the very name of king that he ended up being called Louis, the Well-Beloved.

There was a great war going on at this time between Marie Theresa, the queen of Hungary and archduchess of Austria, and Frederick II, king of Prussia. The English were allied with the Austrians and the French with the Prussians, and at the battle of Dettingen, George II had been defeated by marshal de Noailles. Again, at Fontenoy, the English were defeated, and Louis XV was with the army.

There was a peace for a little while, but what came to be called the Seven Years' War soon broke out again. This time the English were with the Prussians and the French with the Austrians. There was a great battle at Minden, which the French lost, and soon after there was a more lasting peace in Europe.

The Little Trianon

The bedroom of Marie-Antoinette in the Little Trianon

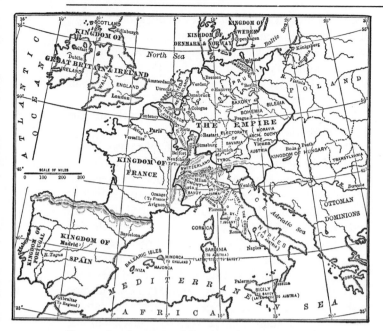

Europe after the treaties of Utrecht and Rastatt

Louis XV as duke of Anjou, 1715–74—the great-grandson of Louis XIV

The older Louis XV

The princesses Adelaide, Victoire, and Sophie, the daughters of Louis XV

Louis XV had only one son, the dauphin, who, although he had grown up in the midst of the king's corrupt court, was himself upright and pious. He lived a peaceful, quiet life with his wife, a Polish princess. The upright dauphin died when only thirty-six years old, leaving five children, the eldest eleven years old, and his wife followed him fifteen months later, begging her four sisters-in-law to watch over her children. The king grew worse than ever and used to amuse himself by going in disguise to the dives of Paris. Yet at the same time he went to church services every morning.

Everyone saw that a great storm was coming for the king and that there must be a terrible downfall of the royal power that Richelieu, Mazarin, and Louis XIV had built up, and which Louis XV used so shamefully. But when the king was told that there was great danger approaching, he only said the kingdom would last his time. His grandson, the young dauphin, had grown up and married the beautiful, bright young daughter of Marie Theresa—Maria-Antoinette. The evening she arrived at Paris, there were grand "illuminations" and fireworks, and in the midst of it a rumor spread that seized the people that there was a fire. A large crowd rushed to the gates of the Champs Elysées, and a number of them were trampled to death. Although the young bride had nothing to do with it the tragedy, this made the people feel that she was a bad omen.

Louis XV died at the age of sixty-four, in the year 1774, after a disgraceful reign of sixty years, in which he performed little or nothing for the people and had constantly fallen deeper into the mire of physical excesses.

LOUIS XVI (1774–92)

The young king, Louis XVI, threw himself on his knees when he heard that his grandfather had died and cried out, "Oh God! help me; I am too young to reign."

It was as if he knew what dreadful times were coming, brought on by the selfishness and wickedness of those who had gone before him. Nobody could have been more anxious to set things right than Louis XVI. But the evils that had been working up for hundreds of years could not be set straight easily, and it was hard to know where or how to begin. And although the king tried, he was not clever enough to solve France's problems.

The great palace that Louis XIV had adorned at Versailles was so grand that nobody could live in it in comfort, not even a king. He had made a smaller one next to it at Trianon, but even this one was too stately for the queen's tastes. So she had another smaller house, with a farm and dairy. The people believed that something very wrong was going on out there. And they hated her because she was an Austrian and her country had been at war with theirs.

It was then that the Americans began their war with George III and England—the American Revolution. A

Louis XVI, 1793–95   *Marie-Therese, daughter of Louis XVI and Marie-Antoinette*

young French nobleman, the marquis de Lafayette, ran away from home to fight in their army. Afterward, Louis XVI sent troops to help them. The sight of the freedom the United States had gained made Lafayette and his friends feel far more bitter about the state of things at home where the poor were ground down to wretchedness by all the old rights of their lords. But until the laws were changed, neither king and nobles, nor clergy, however much they might wish it, could help them. No one felt this more than the king himself. At last, in 1789, he called together his States General—that is, all his peers, and deputies from the towns and provinces—to see what could be done. It was not like the English Parliament, where the peers form one chamber and the commons another; but they were all mixed up together, and there were a great many more deputies than peers, so that they had it all their own way. The people could not bear to wait any longer. It was no wonder, for they were very poor and miserable, and were suffering from starvation. Whenever they saw anyone whom they fancied was against the changes, they used to attack him, crying out, "To the lamp!" and hang him up on the street lamps.

They rushed to the great old prison, the Bastille, where the former kings had kept their state prisoners, and tore it down. But they found few there, for Louis XVI had released all of his grandfather's prisoners. Most of the men at that time were enrolled in what was called the National Guard, and all wore cockades, and scarfs of red, blue, and white. Lafayette was made general of this guard.

The States General called itself the National Assembly, and went on changing the laws. It was at first settled that no law could be passed without the king's consent, but the notion that he could stop any plan added to the people's hatred. At last, when there was a serious scarcity of food in Paris, the mob all rushed out to Versailles. They came and filled the courts of the palace, shouting and yelling for the queen to show herself. She came out on the balcony, with her daughter of twelve and her son of six. "No children!" they cried, and she sent them back

and stood, fully believing that they would shoot her, and hoping that her death might content them. But no hand was raised. In the night they were seized with another fit of anger for lynching, and broke into the queen's room from which she'd escaped while a brave lady and two of her guards were barring the outer door.

The next day the whole family moved back into the Tuileries palace in Paris.

The National Assembly went on to take away all the rights of the nobles and the property of the church, and to decree that the clergy must swear to obey them instead of the church. Those who refused were turned out of their parishes. The National Guard watched the palace and made the life of the royal family so miserable that they tried to escape in disguise. Fearing that they would come back with armies to put down the Revolution, the National Guard seized and stopped them, and they were more closely watched than ever. June 20, 1792, the mob rushed into the palace, threatened all the royal family, and spent three hours rioting and casting personal insults on them. All went well for a few weeks after that, but on the tenth of August another attack was made. The queen longed to let the Swiss guards and the loyal gentlemen fight for her husband, but Louis could not bear to have a drop of blood shed in his defense and hoped to save lives by going to the National Assembly with his wife, children, and sister. But no sooner were they gone than eleven of the gallant men of his guard and household were savagely massacred and their heads were carried about the street of Paris on the tops of poles. It was fear that made the Parisians so ferocious, for the German princes and the French nobles had collected an army to rescue the king, and the mob thought, to destroy them. In bitter hatred the assembly voted that Louis XVI was no longer king of France and the nation was free. So his reign ended on August 10, 1792.

THE GREAT FRENCH REVOLUTION (1792–96)

The government, after the king was deposed, was placed in the hands of the National Assembly—or Convention, as it called itself—of deputies chosen by the people.

The short account of it all is that, for years and years before, the kings, the nobles, and some of the clergy too, had cared for little but themselves, and had done hardly anything to help their people. So now these people were rebelling. The king, queen, his children, and sister (Madame Elizabeth) were shut up in a castle called the Temple, so named because it had once belonged to the Knights Templars, and there they were very roughly treated. Great numbers of the nobles and clergy were shut up in other prisons; and when news came that an army of Germans and emigrant nobles was marching to rescue the king, a set of assassins was sent to murder them all, cutting them down like sheep for the slaughter, men, women, and children. But, the family in the Temple was spared for the time being. The emigrant army was beaten at Jemappes and the brave nobles and peasants who had risen in the district of La Vendee, in hopes of saving them, could not get by the regular French army, all of whom had joined in the Revolution. Three men had the leadership who thought that the only way to make a fresh beginning for France was to kill everyone who had inherited any of the rights that had been so oppressive. Their names were Marat, Danton, and Robespierre, and they had a power over the Convention and the mob that no one dared resist. This period was called the Reign of Terror.

At that time, a doctor named Guillotin had invented a machine for cutting off heads quickly and painlessly. The device to this day has carried his name—the guillotine. This horrible instrument was set up in Paris to do this work of cutting off the old race. The king—whom they called Louis Capet, after Hugh, the first king of his line—was tried before the National Assembly and sentenced to die. He forgave his murderers and charged the Irish clergyman, named Edgeworth, who was allowed to attend him in his last moments, to take care that, if his family were ever restored, there should be no attempt to revenge his death. The last words of the priest to him were, "Son of Saint Louis, ascend to the skies."

The queen and her children remained in the Temple until the poor little prince—a gentle, but spirited boy of eight—was taken from them, and shut up in the lower rooms. His prison guard named Simon was told that the boy was not to be killed or guillotined but to be "got rid of" by any method he should choose. Not long after, Marie-Antoinette was taken to a dismal chamber in the Conciergerie prison until she too was brought to trial, sentenced to die, and guillotined eight months after her husband. Madame Elizabeth was likewise put to death, and only the two children remained, shut up in separate rooms. But the girl was better off than her brother in that she was alone with her little dog, and had not been subjected to torture.

Meanwhile the guillotine was in use every day. Cartloads were carried from the prisons—nobles, priests, ladies, young girls, lawyers, servants, shopkeepers—everybody whom the savage men who were called the Committee of Public Safety chose to condemn to death. There were guillotines in most towns, but at Nantes the victims were drowned and at Lyons they were placed in a square and shot down with grapeshot.

Moreover, all churches were taken away from the faithful. A woman who was called the Goddess of Reason was taken to the great cathedral of Notre Dame, where she was enthroned. Sundays were abolished as a holy day and every tenth day was kept instead. Christianity was called folly and superstition.

Marat was stabbed to the heart by a girl named Char-

lotte Corday, who hoped the assassination would end these horrors. But the other two continued their work of blood, until Robespierre grew jealous of Danton, and had him guillotined. But at last the more humane of the National Convention plucked up courage to rise against him, and he and his associates were carried to prison. He tried to commit suicide with a pistol but only shattered his jaw. In this condition he was guillotined, and then the Reign of Terror which had lasted about two years was brought to an end.

There was much rejoicing at Robespierre's fall. The prisons were opened, and people began to live freely once more. The National Convention governed more mildly and reasonably. But they had a great deal on their hands, for France had gone to war with all the countries around it. The soldiers were so delighted with their new-found freedom that it seemed as if no army could defeat them. The invaders were driven back everywhere. And thus was brought to light the wonderful powers of a young Corsican officer, Napoleon Bonaparte. When there was an attempt of the mob to rise again, Colonel Bonaparte came with his grapeshot and showed that there was a government again that must be obeyed, so that good order was restored.

Some pity had at last been felt for the poor children in the Temple. It came too late to save the life of the boy, Louis XVII, as he was known. For the whole ninth year of his life he had been imprisoned alone in a filthy room, so that he was one mass of infection. He lingered on until June 8, 1795, when he died. In the end of the same year his sister was released and went to Russia to join her uncle, who had fled at the beginning of the Revolution. He was then known by the loyal among the French as Louis XVIII.

In the meantime, the French army had beaten the Germans on the northeast border and had decided to attack the Germans in the north of Italy. Bonaparte made a passage of the Alps, which is considered an

Louis XVII when he was the grand dauphin

Louis XVII in the temple

engineering miracle, and he gained amazing victories. His plan was to get all the strength of his army into one point and, with that, to fall upon the center of the enemy. Since the old German generals did not understand this way of fighting, Napoleon defeated them everywhere and won all of Lombardy, which he set up as a republic, under the protection of the French.

NAPOLEON I (NAPOLEON BONAPARTE) (1799–1814)

When Bonaparte had come back from Italy, he persuaded the governing Directory to send him with an army to Egypt to try to gain the East and drive the English out of India. He landed in Egypt and near Cairo won the Battle of the Pyramids, and tried to promote himself among the people of Egypt by showing great admiration for Mohammed and the Koran. But his ships, which he had left on the coast, were attacked by the English fleet under Sir Horatio Nelson, and every one of them taken or sunk except two, which carried the tidings home. This was called the Battle of the Nile.

The sultan of Turkey, to whom Egypt belonged, fitted out an army against the French, and Bonaparte marched to meet it halfway in the Holy Land. There he took Jaffa, massacred the Turkish garrison, and beat the sultan's army at Tabor. But Acre was so well defended under a brave English sailor, Sir Sidney Smith, that he was obliged to turn back without taking it. He led his troops back, suffering badly from hunger and sickness, to Egypt, but there defeated another Turkish army in the Battle of Aboukir. However, he heard news from home that showed him that he was needed: The pope was a prisoner in France, and the king of Naples had fled to Sicily. The Russians had come to the help of the other nations, and the French had nearly been driven out of Lombardy. Besides, the Directory was not able to keep

Napoleon at an early age when he was in attendance at the military school in Brienne

A schoolmate at Brienne sketched this portrait of Napoleon.

A portrait of Madame Laetitia Buonaparte, Napoleon's mother

Napoleon was arrested on August 10, 1794. Ten days later, "for they [the government] saw nothing to justify any suspicion of his conduct [in the Italy campaign] and, that, taking into consideration the advantage that might accrue to the Republic from the military talents of the said General Bonaparte, it was resolved that he should be set at liberty."

Napoleon as a young lieutenant in the artillery

Napoleon crossing the Alps in the third Italian campaign, 1796

Napoleon's bride, Josephine. The wedding took place on March 9, 1796, and Josephine cut ten years off her age in the certificate.

Napoleon at the Battle of Rivoli

The first meeting between Napoleon and Josephine

Napoleon on the bridge at Arcola, 1796

An engraving of the time showing Napoleon Bonaparte as general in chief of the army of Italy

An allegorical engraving in 1797 showing the humiliation of Austria and the exaltation of Napoleon.

Napoleon before the Sphinx. He defeated the Mamelukes at the plains below the Pyramids and entered Cairo on July 24, 1798.

the unruly people in order; Napoleon felt himself so much wanted, that, finding there were two ships in the port, he embarked in one of them and came home, leaving his Egyptian army to return later.

He was received at home like a conqueror; and the people of France were so proud of him that he soon persuaded them to change the Directory for a government of three consuls, of whom he was foremost. He lived in the Tuileries and began to set up something very much like the old royal court. And his wife, Josephine, was a beautiful, graceful, kind lady, whom everybody loved and who helped very much in gaining people over to his cause. Indeed, he gave the French peace at home and victories abroad and that was what they desired. He

won back all that had been lost in Italy also, and at the Battle of Marengo, on June 14, 1800, when the Austrians were totally routed, he had a great victory. Austria made peace and nobody was at war with France but England. But not all was victory for Napoleon Bonaparte—the last remnant of the French army in Egypt was beaten at Alexandria and obliged to let English ships transport them back home to France. After this there was a peace called the Peace of Amiens, but it did not last long. As soon as Bonaparte had decided on war, he pounced without notice on every English traveler in his dominions, and kept them prisoners till the end of the war.

Napoleon Bonaparte had made up his mind to be emperor of the French, but before declaring this, he

A lithograph of Napoleon in Egypt in 1798

Napoleon Bonaparte, left, and the pasha of Cairo

Napoleon as he appeared to artist Greuze when Napoleon was the first consul of France

On April 25, 1804, the French ruling Tribunate announced that the head of state of France should be entitled emperor. Upon hearing of this, King George III of England took a new look at this upstart Napoleon, which is depicted in this caricature by Gillray.

The day of the coronation for Napoleon and Josephine was set for December 2, 1804. The royal coach is seen here arriving for the coronation at Notre-Dame.

The coronation. After Napoleon placed the crown of the emperor on his head, he then placed the crown of the empress on Josephine's head.

wanted to alarm the old royalists. So he sent a party to seize the duke d'Enghien (heir of the princes of Condé) who was living at Baden, and took him to Vincennes where at midnight, he was tried by a sham court-martial and at six in the morning brought down to the courtyard and shot beside his own grave.

After this, everyone was afraid to utter a word against Bonaparte becoming emperor and on December 2, 1804, he was crowned in Notre Dame in great splendor. The pope was present, but Bonaparte placed the crown on his own head—a golden wreath of laurel leaves and he gave his soldiers eagle standards, in memory of the old Roman Empire. He drew up an excellent code of laws which have been used ever since in France, and are known by his name. His wonderful talents did much to bring the shattered nation into order. Still, England would not acknowledge his takeover. He had an army ready to invade England, but the English fleet never allowed him to cross the Channel. And when he chose to challenge them, his fleet was entirely destroyed by Lord Nelson at the great Battle of Trafalgar on October 21, 1805.

At the same time Napoleon was winning another splendid victory at Ulm over the Austrians, and not long after he beat the Prussians at Jena and had all Germany at his feet. He was exceedingly savage with the Prussians and was insolent in his manners to the gentlewoman, Queen Louisa, when she came with her husband to try to make better terms for their country. The Russians advanced to the aid of Germany, but also, the battles of Eylau and Friedland made them anxious for peace. Indeed, there was never a much abler military man than Napoleon but he had very little honor or honesty. He made his family kings of conquered countries. His brother Louis was king of Holland; Jerome, of Westphalia; and the eldest brother, Joseph, king of Naples. And in 1808 he contrived to cheat the king of Spain of his crown and keep him and his son prisoner in France

while Joseph was sent to reign in Spain. Also at one point, General Murat, the husband of his sister Caroline, was made king of Naples. The Portuguese royal family was obliged to flee to Brazil. But the Spaniards and Portuguese would not submit to the French yoke and called on the English to help them.

Year after year the duke of Wellington was beating Napoleon's generals and wearing away his strength. But Napoleon still went on with his German wars and, in 1809, after two terrible battles at Aspern and Wagram, entered Vienna itself. Again there was a peace.

Napoleon, wanting to have a male child to leave his empire to, had decided on setting aside his loving Josephine and made the emperor Francis of Austria an offer of marriage for the hand of his young daughter, Marie Louise. In 1810, the deed was done.

The marriage was as little liked in France as in Austria, where the people felt that their hero had abandoned them in "giving up on" Josephine. She still had her little court, and was treated and addressed as Empress, however.

The next year, 1811, Napoleon's desire was fulfilled. His new wife presented him with a little son to perpetuate his imperial line, and the baby was promptly crowned king of Rome.

The imperial arms of Napoleon

The French fleet was destroyed at the Battle of Trafalgar on October 21, 1805. Had Napoleon listened to the American, Robert Fulton, seen here trying to sell Napoleon on a steam-powered navy, he might never have had a Trafalgar.

Napoleon in his coronation attire with implements

Empress Josephine as she appeared at the coronation

After the Battle of Austerlitz, the victor, Napoleon, met with the Austrian emperor, Francis II, the loser, and brought about severe conditions to be put into a treaty. A treaty was concluded at Presburg, on the twenty-seventh day of December 1805, by virtue of which Bonaparte was recognized as king of Italy; the Republic of Venice was detached from Austria, and united to his Italian Kingdom; the electors of Wurtemberg and Bavaria, as allies of France and traitors to the national cause, were to be created kings; the duke of Baden, in reward for his having taken in good part the kidnaping and murder of the duke d'Enghien, was to be elevated to be a grand-duke; and these three states were to be enlarged at the expense of Austria. Istria and Dalmatia were ceded. Austria agreed to pay a war indemnity of 140 million francs. Gallant and loyal Tyrol was severed from the crown of Austria, and handed over to Bavaria; and Napoleon was constituted "protector" of a confederation of the Rhine, comprising all the western states of Germany.

There were other secret arrangements, which were speedily carried into effect. Eugene Beauharnais, viceroy of Italy, Josephine's son, was given the hand of Augusta Amelie, daughter of the king of Bavaria; and Stephanie Beauharnais, Eugene's cousin, was united to the son and heir of the grand-duke of Baden. Jerome Bonaparte was to take as wife a daughter of the elector of Wurtemberg. Such were the first royal alliances negotiated, the prelude to others, in which the blood of a Corsican attorney's children was to be mixed with that of the most ancient and princely families in Europe.

Napoleon's brother Louis becomes the king of Holland.

His brother Jerome is given the throne of Westphalia.

The third brother, Lucien. There was no throne for Lucien, but he did marry an Italian princess.

The fourth brother, Joseph, turned down the offer of king of Italy and became the king of Naples. Later Joseph was named the king of Spain by Napoleon.

Jerome Bonaparte married the American beauty, Betsey Patterson, at Baltimore, Maryland, on Christmas Eve, 1803. The Maryland Legislature granted her a divorce in 1815. She lived on as Madame Patterson-Bonaparte until her death in 1879. They had one child, Jerome, who was born in England.

Napoleon meets at Tilsit with Czar Alexander I and Empress Marie-Louise in 1807.

The folly of the successful gambler possessed him. His superstitious belief in his "unconquerable star" increased. He attempted the impossible—and brought about his own destruction. He resolved to crush England, despite her military impenetrable shelter in the seas.

Extending his insatiate hands in an ever wider grasp, Napoleon declared war against Russia, and in 1812 invaded the domain of the czar with an army of half a million men, gathered from all western Europe. Her capital was conquered, but the Russians themselves burned it and left the French to starve and freeze amid the ruins. The terrible Russian winter set in unusually early, and the invaders perished by tens of thousands. They retreated in despair. The French marshal Ney, "the bravest of the brave," held a remnant of the rear guard together; but in that nightmare flight across the Russian steppes, the mighty army was practically annihilated, and the heroic strength of France was broken. Napoleon fled to Paris.

The Prussians rose in eager revolt behind him; the Russians and then the Austrians joined them; but Napoleon wrung yet another army from exhausted France—an army of boys and old men. Despite his transcendent genius, the hitherto invincible conqueror was defeated at Leipzig in the Battle of the Nations, and once more was forced to flee back into France.

Even then he refused the easy terms of peace offered him by the allies, and persisted in struggling against them. So they captured Paris in 1814, and the French Senate, which Napoleon himself had created merely to register his laws, sent notice to him that it had deposed him from his rank as emperor. No other plan seemed possible to save France; and Napoleon, waiting with the

Czar Alexander was asked by Napoleon for the hand of his sister Catherine, but the Russian monarch delayed his answer until Napoleon took a second choice, Princess Marie Louise of Austria.

The French empress Marie Louise in her royal robes. Napoleon told Josephine, "Marie Louise is not beautiful but she is the daughter of the Caesars."

Napoleon breaks the news of the impending divorce to Josephine. She faints upon hearing the news from Napoleon that he wants a wife who can bear him an heir to the throne.

On March 17, 1811, Marie Louise bore Napoleon a son, and he was named Napoleon Francis Charles Joseph, the king of Rome.

The king of Rome at an early age

A medal struck for the imperial family, Francis I, emperor of Austria; his daughter, Marie Louise, the queen of France; and Napoleon, the emperor of France.

The baptism of the king of Rome

Napoleon at Fontainebleau, March 31, 1814, contemplating his future

Napoleon under guard at his place of forced exile. He retains the title of emperor, is to receive 2 million francs a year, and is to have a personal guard of 400 men but is never to leave the island of Elba, and his son cannot remain emperor of France, Napoleon II.

remnants of his troops at Fontainebleau, accepted the decree, surrendered himself to the allies, and was given exile to the little island of Elba, lying in the Mediterranean just off the southern coast of France.

Louis XVIII was summoned by the allies to the throne that, for nineteen years, ever since the death of his little nephew, Louis XVII, he had held in name alone. The various European kings planned to restore France to the position that was hers in Louis XVI's time; but before they could get the ancient system into running order, Napoleon escaped his exile and burst upon them like a sudden thunderbolt. He landed, unexpected, in southern France, and summoned the people to rally once more

around him and drive out their foreign dictators. His magnetic power in speech-making had not deserted him; his former soldiers rushed tumultuously to his standard; and, with an army that grew at every step in obedience to the tune on the flute of the Pied Piper, he advanced upon Paris.

King Louis wrung his hands in bewilderment. He had kept in office some of Napoleon's able generals, and now Ney, the most celebrated of them all, was ordered to lead the king's army against his former emperor. Ney obeyed, saying he would "bring the Corsican back in an iron cage." But when he saw his comrades marshaled around Napoleon, when the great leader himself summoned his lieutenant to rejoin him, old memories were too strong; and Ney, most eager of all, united his deliriously cheering troops with those of Napoleon, who entered Paris and regained his empire without a blow. Louis XVIII fled once more to Germany.

The brief period of Napoleon's restoration to power is called the Hundred Days. It lasted from March to June 1815. The states of Europe declared instant war against him. The armies of Prussia and England took the field at once; and Napoleon determined to crush them before their Austrian and Russian allies could join them. Hence came the celebrated campaign of Waterloo.

The English under Wellington and the Prussians under Blucher lay along the northeastern frontier of France, where Belgium is now located. Napoleon succeeded in driving his army between them and attacked each separately. The English were held in check by Ney at Quatre Bras, while the Prussians were defeated by Napoleon at Ligny. They were not completely destroyed; but, leaving a small force to hold them in check, Napoleon hurled all his strength against the English at Waterloo. If he could drive them back into the sea, the

The famous painting by Meissonier of Napoleon at Waterloo

Polish Countess Marie Walewska. A visitor to Napoleon at St. Helena, where he died, was his favorite of mistresses, Marie Walewska, who mothered a son for him. The offspring of this lifetime affair was Alexander, who was recognized officially by the next monarch, Louis XVIII.

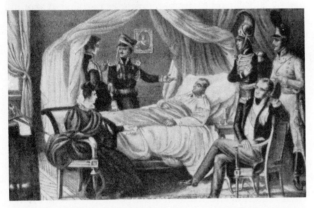

On May 6, 1821, in the midst of the worst storm ever experienced on St. Helena, Napoleon died. He had been sent to St. Helena after a 100-day escape from Elba.

On December 15, 1840, Napoleon's body was interred in Paris. This is an illustration at the time of the funeral cortege.

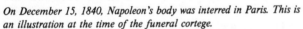

The death mask of Napoleon

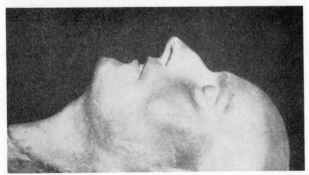

The funeral service inside the Church of the Invalides where Napoleon's body was put to permanent rest

remaining Prussians would be an easy prey.

The struggle was heroic, a death-grapple of giants; seventy thousand Frenchmen against an equal number of English. All day long they fought. Napoleon, by repeated attacks on the English wings, compelled Wellington to send reinforcements there and thus weaken the center of his line. Then the emperor concentrated his best troops for an attack on the depleted center. Just as the charge was ready to begin, Prussian troops appeared on the field, having by a wonderful march evaded the French division sent to hold them in check. The troops aimed against Wellington's center had to be turned against the new arrivals.

The flower of the French cavalry charged the English center; but a ditch lay invisible between them, and into this most of the foremost files of the galloping cavalry fell, until their numbers made a bridge of living bodies over which their surviving comrades rode. The weakened force could not break the solid squares of English infantry. More Prussians reached the field. There was one last, hopeless charge of the French "Old Guard," Napoleon's finest regiments. But the veteran column met devastating English artillery fire. Wellington declared victory and the whole English line advanced with the Prussians. The remnants of the French were swept from the field in disorderly flight amid cries of "Treason!" and "*Sauve qui peut!*" (Save himself who can!)

Both Napoleon and Ney sought death upon this field that saw the final ruin of their hopes. But both were

Napoleon's son, Francis Charles Joseph, reigned as Napoleon II for a few days in 1814 but then became the duke of Reichstadt in Austria. He died of tuberculosis at the age of twenty-one in Vienna, July 22, 1832.

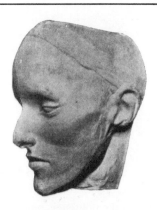

Death mask of the duke of Reichstadt

reserved for sadder fates. Ney had five horses shot from under him, yet escaped without a wound. Napoleon strove to force his way through the crowd of fugitives and advance against the British lines, but his officers surrounded him and forced him away from the field of battle toward Paris. Seeking escape, he went at last to Rochefort and, finding it impossible to get to America, gave himself up to the captain of an English ship, the *Bellerophon.* He was taken to Plymouth harbor and remained on board until his fate was decided by the allied sovereigns. They were determined to send him where he should not again escape to disturb all Europe. He was therefore placed on the little lonely island of St. Helena, out in the Atlantic Ocean, under the custody of an English governor who was to see him every day. He chafed in his confinement and the governor (Sir Hudson Lowe) reacted under warrant, with harsh and insulting treatment. After six miserable years, Napoleon died, in 1821, of cancer of the stomach, and was buried under the willow trees of Longwood, in St. Helena.

His brothers and sisters had all been taken off their thrones. Murat tried to recover Naples, but was "taken out" and shot. But the others submitted quietly. Marie Louise had a little Italian duchy given to her and her son Napoleon (who had been pronounced emperor by his father, but the allies had opposed it) was called the Duke of Reichstadt, and brought up at the court of his grandfather, the emperor of Austria. He died in early youth. The English army had remained for three years in France, to assist Louis XVIII in case of any fresh outbreak. Marshal Ney, the foremost of the generals who had gone over to Napoleon, was tried by court-martial and shot. Almost everyone else was forgiven and Prince Talleyrand, one of the cleverest and most cunning men who ever lived, who had risen under Napoleon, worked on with Louis XVIII.

LOUIS XVIII (1814–24)

The allies had entered Paris—Russians, Austrians, and Prussians—and the duke of Wellington, after winning the Battle of Toulouse at Waterloo, came up from the south to meet them there.

There was a saying in France that in their exile those Bourbons had learned nothing and forgotten nothing. This was not quite true of Louis XVIII, who was clever in an indolent way and resolved to please the people enough to remain where he was until his death, and really gave them a very good charter. His brother Charles, count of Artois, was much more strongly and openly devoted to the old ways that came before the Revolution and, as Louis had no children, his accession was not desired. His eldest son, the duke of Angouleme had no children, and his second son, the duke of Berri, who was married to a Neapolitan princess, was the most amiable and hopeful person in the family. But on February 12, 1820, the duke of Berri was stabbed by one Louvet, as he was leaving the opera, and died in a few hours. His infant son, Henry, duke of Bordeaux, was the only hope of the elder branch of the Bourbons for eventually wearing the crown.

France was worn out and weary of war, so little happened in this reign except that the duke of Angouleme made an expedition to assist the king of Spain in putting down an insurrection. The French nobility had returned to all their titles but many of them had lost their property in the Revolution.

Louis XVIII was in failing health but he kept up much of the old state of the French court and was most careful never to keep anyone waiting, for he used to say, "Punc-

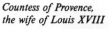

Louis XVIII, 1814–24, at the time he assumed the throne

Countess of Provence, the wife of Louis XVIII

Charles X, 1824–30

The Tuileries, the royal residence in Paris of all of the nineteenth-century monarchs. (It was set afire by the Communists in 1871 and nearly destroyed.)

tuality is the politeness of kings." Even when very ill, he would never give up any of the court duties, and when urged to spare himself, said, "A king of France ought to die standing." But for some years he was unable to walk, being dreadfully tormented by gout, and he was obliged to let his brother manage his affairs. He was shrewd enough to dread the desire of Charles, the count of Artois, to return to the old times of the overgrown royal power. When he found himself dying, he put his hand on the head of his little four-year-old grandnephew, Henry, and said, "Let Charles X take care of the crown for this child." And then he died in September 1824.

CHARLES X (1824–30)

When Charles X had been the young count of Artois, before the Revolution, he had been a playfellow of Marie-Antoinette in those bright, giddy days. After his exile and wanderings, in his old age, he had become very religious; for he was guided entirely by the pope and a few clergy who wanted to bring conditions back to what they were before the Revolution.

The first effort of his rule was made on behalf of the Greeks, who had long been trying to break away from the rule of the Turks. At last the Prussian, English, and French fleets joined and defeated the Turks and Egyptians at the battle of Navarino, after which, Greece was

The coronation of Charles X at Reims

able to become a kingdom, under Christian rule.

On July 26, 1830, the king put out an edict ending the liberty of the press—that is, forbidding anything to appear in any newspapers without being approved by the government. Other distasteful edicts were also made. Everyone begged the king to change his mind and withdraw the edicts, but he thought it was yielding that had ruined his oldest brother, Louis XVI, and nothing would persuade him to give way. There had been fighting throughout Paris, and his troops had been broken and driven out by the National Guard. Then he did consent; but the people would not be satisfied without dethroning him, and he was obliged to leave France again, taking with him his son and daughter-in-law (the last dauphin and dauphiness) and his grandson, the little Henry. They lived first in Scotland, and afterward in Italy and in Germany. The old loyal French still viewed Charles and, after his death, his grandson, Henry V, as the only true kings of France.

Some of the French wanted to have another republic, but most of them wished to try a limited monarchy, like that of England, with a king at the head who had no power to do anything without the consent of the subjects. At that time, they resolved to put at the head of their new constitution the duke of Orleans. He was of the Bourbon royal blood, for he was descended from Louis XIV's brother, the duke of Orleans. He had given up his title of duke of Orleans, and called himself Citizen Philip Egalité (equality), but when, in the Reign of Terror, everyone who had any high birth was put to death, he was guillotined. His eldest son, Louis-Philippe, served in the French army until his father, mother, and younger brothers were thrown into prison, and he was forced to flee to Switzerland, where he was obliged to earn his living as a teacher. Afterward he went to England, where his brothers joined him, but they both fell ill and died, one in England, and the other at Malta. Next he traveled in America.

At the Restoration, he went back to France, with his wife, Marie Amelie, the daughter of the king of Naples, and his sister Adelaide. They brought up their large family at the Palais Royal. When Charles fled, the leaders of the nation all agreed to offer the crown to the new duke of Orleans, but it was not to be as an old hereditary monarch. He was not to be king of France, but king of the French. He was not to be Louis XIX, but Louis-Philippe I, and his eldest son was not to be dauphin, but duke of Orleans. And his power was to be bound by peers and deputies much as the power of the English king is bound by the peers and commons.

This was the revolution of the Three Days of July,

LOUIS-PHILIPPE I (1830–48)

Louis-Philippe of Orleans was called the Citizen King. He used the tricolored flag of the old Revolution instead of the white one of the Bourbons to show that he reigned not as a son of the old royal family but by the choice of the people. There was a chamber of peers and a chamber of deputies, and the constitution was a limited monarchy.

Most of the colonies the French had once made have been lost in the wars since the time of Louis XIV, and Louis-Philippe thought it would be good to form new ones. A settlement was made in Algeria, but it caused a long and fierce war with the Arab chiefs, which lasted nearly throughout the reign. The Arabs were as brave as the French themselves and had a most gallant chief, named Abd-el-Kader. At last, however, after years of fighting, he was forced to surrender and was taken to France.

The French also tried to make settlements in the Pacific Islands, especially New Caledonia and the island of Tahiti. They were not at all welcome in Tahiti, for the native queen, Pomare, had been taught to be a Christian by the English and did not wish for French protection or Roman Catholic teaching. However, the French were the stronger and had taken over the control there.

Louis-Philippe did his utmost to keep the Parisians in good spirits, knowing that he could only reign by their favor, and as the miseries of the old wars were forgotten the French only thought of the victories of the times of Napoleon, praising him as the greatest of heroes. The

In this painting, Louis-Philippe is shown making a public announcement in which he refused the Belgian crown on behalf of his son, the duke of Nemours (on his left). The Belgian National Congress elected the duke as king.

king gratified them by requesting the English to allow him to bring home the corpse of the emperor Napoleon and bury it in the Church of the Invalides, a great asylum for old soldiers at Paris. It was brought to Paris in a huge triumphal car, which was followed through the streets by Louis-Philippe and his sons. A chapel was built, and ornamented with splendid marbles, for the burials of the Bonaparte family. Napoleon's little son was dead, but his brother Louis had left a son, who lived in exile in England and Germany. As it happened, there was a horrible conspiracy by some persons, of whom the chief was named Fieschi, to kill the king as he rode in a ceremony. The king was not hurt but fourteen people were killed. The assassins were traced and Fieschi was put to death.

The republican dislike of having religion taught in schools hindered the growth of the nation. There were the Legitimists, who viewed first Charles X and then his grandson, Henry V, the count of Chambord, as the only true king, and would accept no rule under Louis-Philippe.

The king had five sons, of whom the eldest, the duke of Orleans, was much loved by the people. He married the princess Helen of Mecklenburg Schwerin, and they had two little sons before he was killed by leaping out of his open carriage while the horses were running away.

At last, in February 1848, after the council and the chambers of deputies had decided against measures desired by the people, there was a rebellion of the people throughout Paris. The troops and the National Guard were called out, but when the moment came for action, the National Guard would not fire but made common cause with the people. The army would still have fought, but Louis-Philippe would not allow them to shed blood for him. He sent a message that he abdicated in favor of his little grandson, the count of Paris, with his mother, the duchess of Orleans, as regent. Then he left the Tuileries privately, under the name of William Smith, and safely reached England.

The duchess of Orleans bravely came forward with her two boys but there was no favor, only anger, and her friends saw it was all in vain, and spirited her away as fast as they could. All the family made their way by different means, one by one, to England, where the queen and her people received them kindly. Claremont Palace was lent to them as a home, and there Louis-Philippe and his good queen spent the remainder of their lives. He died in the year 1850, and Marie Amelie a few years later.

THE REPUBLIC (1848–52)

After Louis-Philippe and his family had fled from France, there was a time of confusion. An assembly of deputies met from all parts of France to arrange a new government.

In truth, the Red Republicans, who did not want to see any one in power richer than themselves, were very disappointed that, though noblemen and gentlemen had no more rights than other people, they were still rich men who kept their money and estates.

In the end of June 1848, there were three dreadful days of street riots. It was a fight of the Red Republicans against the Tricolored. Liberty, Fraternity, and Equality were the watchwords of both, but the Red Republicans were tougher than the Tricolored, for they thought that liberty had no order at all. The good archbishop of Paris, Monseigneur Affre, going out on one of these miserable days to try to make peace, was shot through the back from behind a barricade and died a few hours later. However, General Cavaignac, one of the brave men who had been trained to war by the fighting in Algeria, so managed the soldiers and the National Guard that they put down the Red Republicans and restored order.

The Italians rose and tried to shake them off with the help of the king of Sardinia; and at the same time there was a great rising against the pope, Pius IX, at Rome. The popes had held Rome for more than a thousand years, and there ruled the Western church. But there had never been any very righteous princes among their Roman subjects, and things had fallen into a sad state of confusion. When Pius IX first was chosen, he had tried to improve the situation, but his people moved too fast for him and so alarmed him that he fled in the disguise of a servant on a donkey. The Roman Catholics thought the pope could not rule over the church freely unless he had Rome as his own and lived there as a prince. A French army was sent to restore him and Rome was taken, giving the pope his throne again.

After much deliberating in the French assembly, it was settled to have a republic, with a president, like the Americans. Then Charles Louis Napoleon Bonaparte, the son of Napoleon's brother Louis, offered himself as president and was elected, all the "quiet" people and all the Bonapartists joining in the choice. Most of the army were Bonapartists, for the sake of the old victories of Napoleon. Louis Napoleon had great power in his hands. Soon he persuaded the people to change his title from president to that of first consul, as his uncle had once been called.

The next time there was a disturbance at Paris, Louis Napoleon met the mob. He surrounded them with soldiers, had cannon planted so as to command every street, and fired upon the mob before it had time to do any harm; then he captured the ringleaders and had them executed. This certainly was official violence and cruelty, but the Parisians were taught they must obey law and order. This masterstroke is always called the *coup d'etat,* or "stroke of policy," for it settled affairs. And after that, Louis Napoleon did as he chose, for no one dared resist him.

THE SECOND EMPIRE (1852–71)

The entire French nation, in the beginning of the year 1852, was called upon to decide by vote whether or not they would form an empire again, or continue to be a republic. Every man, rich or poor, who was not a convict, had a vote, and the larger number decided for the empire and for Louis Napoleon Bonaparte as the emperor. He considered himself the successor of his uncle, and therefore called himself Napoleon III, counting the little child in whose favor the great Bonaparte had abdicated at Fontainebleau as Napoleon II. He married a Spanish lady of high rank, Eugénie de Montijo, but not of royal blood, whose mother was Scottish. One son was born of this marriage, who was called the prince imperial. The emperor ruled with a strong hand and put things in order again.

The name the emperor wished to be called by was the Napoleon of Peace, as his uncle had been the Napoleon of War. But it was not always possible to keep the peace. In the year 1853, just after he had been crowned, the Russian emperor began to threaten to conquer Turkey and thereupon the French joined with the English to protect the sultan. The French and English armies, together, landed in Turkey and then made an expedition

Louis Napoleon takes the oath of office as president of France.

Napoleon III (Louis Napoleon), 1852–71

President Napoleon after his coup d'etat

Napoleon III in formal wear posing with his royal robe and crown

Empress Eugenie, wife of Napoleon III

Empress Eugenie and her ladies of honor

The royal reception of the Siamese ambassador at Fontainebleau by Napoleon III

Napoleon III at Solferino. In this battle France defeated Austria, 1859.

to the Crimea, where the Russians had built a strong fortified city named Sebastopol, from which to attack the Turks. Marshal Bugeaud was the French general and, with Lord Raglan, commanded in the great battle fought on the banks of the Alma, and then laid siege to Sebastopol, where again they fought a dreadful battle. Peace was made, on condition that all the fortifications of Sebastopol should be destroyed, and no fleet or army would be kept there in the future.

After having been allies in this war, England and France became much greater friends, and Queen Victoria and the emperor made royal visits with one another. The emperor had a love and affection for England, which became a home to him in his later days of exile.

The Italians were more uneasy and miserable than ever under the rule of the Austrians and begged Victor Emmanuel, king of Sardinia, to help them, and become an Italian king over them. Louis Napoleon gave them his help and went in person to Lombardy, where the French and Italians defeated the Austrians at Magenta and Solferino, after which there was again a peace; and Victor Emmanuel was made king of Italy on condition that, in return for the help he had received, he should give to France the little province of Nice, which had always been part of the dukedom of Savoy. But the Romans hoped that they also should have been shaken of the papal government, so a guard of French soldiers was maintained in Rome.

Another undertaking of the French emperor was to bring Mexico in line. Mexico had been settled by Spaniards and belonged to Spain until it revolted. Some of the well-off people in Mexico thought that they might do better if they set up a monarchy, and the French promised to help them. The archduke Maximilian, brother of the emperor of Austria, was chosen, and went out with his young wife, Charlotte, daughter of the king of the Belgians, Leopold I. They were guarded by a French army, but they were soon brought home. And once they had left Mexico, the Mexicans rose up, made their emperor prisoner, and executed him.

The emperor of the French was trying to teach the people to rule themselves to some degree, instead of expecting him to keep order with his power from above. He was anxious to be sure of his son reigning after him and he put it to the vote of all of France whether the empire should be hereditary. The vote was in his favor, and he seemed quite secure. But at this time the Prussians had been gaining great successes against Denmark and Austria, and the French were very jealous of them and expected a fight for some of the provinces along the Rhine. Just then, too, the Spaniards had risen and driven out Queen Isabella. They elected a cousin of the king of Prussia to be their king. He never accepted the Spanish crown, but the motion made the French furious, and there was a great cry from the whole nation that the pride of the Prussians must be put down. The emperor

The Austrian archduke
Maximilian I of Mexico was
the victim of Napoleon III's
plan to establish a monarchy in
Mexico. He was declared
emperor of Mexico in 1863 and
was shot by the Republicans in
1867.

The empress Charlotte,
wife of Maximilian

Napoleon III with the European sovereigns riding to the World's Fair
in Paris, 1867

saw his popularity was failing him and that his only
chance to stay was to please the people by going to war.
The army went off in high spirits to meet the Prussians
on the Rhine—singing, shouting, drinking; and the emperor took his young son with him, trying to seem as
hopeful as they. This was in the summer of the year 1870.

THE SIEGE OF PARIS (1870–71)

It was in the provinces of the Rhine that the big battle
was fought. In that first fight, at Werth, the French were
successful, and a great deal was made of the victory. The
prince imperial fired the first cannon and all the newspapers called it his "baptism of fire." Next, all around the
city of Sedan there was a frightful battle, which lasted
day after day, and in which the French were decisively
beaten, and so surrounded and cut off from retreat by the
German forces, that the emperor was obliged to surrender himself as a prisoner to the king of Prussia. Before
the final battle, he had sent his son to England, as he'd
seen things were going badly. The Empress Eugenie had
been left as regent at Paris, but as soon as the dreadful
news came, all the Prussians rose up and declared that
the emperor be deposed. They wanted to have a republic
again. All that her best friends could do for her was to
help Eugenie steal out of the Tuileries in plain dress, and
she reached England safely.

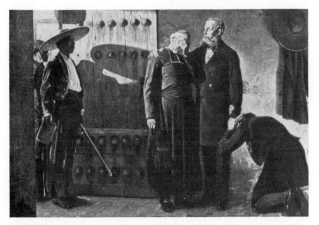

The last moments of Maximilian. Here he is shown trying to console his
friends.

The emperor refused a blindfold before the firing squad.

The Prussians bitterly hated the French ever since the
elder Napoleon had so tyrannically stepped on Prussia
and mistreated Queen Louisa, the mother of the king
William, who was now leading his forces in taking Paris.
King William placed his headquarters in the grand old
palace of Versailles and then besieged Paris, cutting off
all supplies and all communication from outside. No one
could come in or out, except through the German outposts. Letters came and went by carrier pigeons; and tiny
letters on thin paper, and newspapers in print so small
that they could only be read with a magnifying glass,
were prepared for this pigeon post. Starvation set in as
the winter came on; and there was a dire need for fuel
as well as food. Meanwhile, the Germans shelled Paris.

After a half year of siege, the French made terms. The

The Communists destroying the statue of Napoleon I

Napoleon III in "retirement"

*The arrest of Napoleon
at Boulogne*

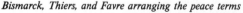
Bismarck, Thiers, and Favre arranging the peace terms

two provinces of Lorraine and Alsace, which used to be German, were given up to Prussia. Prussian troops were to be left for a year in garrison in France and a fine was to be paid. At the same time, quantities of food and fuel were sent in for the famished Parisians, the prisoners were released, and among them the emperor, who went back to England.

THE COMMUNISTS

The terms of the treaty were no sooner known than all the ill will and distrust of the Red Republicans openly broke out. The government withdrew to Versailles to wait for the arrival of all the troops who had been in captivity.

A sort of government was set up, calling itself the Commune—an old word for a town council governing itself—and thus the Red Republicans were known as the Communists. The people's former pride in the first Bonaparte had turned into a ferocious hatred of him. Even the great column in the Place Vendôme, raised in honor of his victories, was destroyed. The Communists were as furious against law, order, property, and religion as even their grandfathers in the Reign of Terror had been. Some of the French leaders had been captured and kept at Versailles. The Communists then seized the archbishop, Monseigneur Darboy, and five more clergy, and threw them into prison, then finally shot them. The good archbishop died with his hand uplifted, as if in the act of blessing his murderers. This was on May 24, 1871.

All France was against the madmen who had possession of their beloved Paris, but the Communists held out desperately. At last, however, the soldiers from Versailles began to force their way in, and then, in their final

The prince imperial Eugene Louis Jean Joseph Napoleon, the only son of Napoleon III and Empress Eugenie. He was the hope of the Bonapartist party to be emperor but his untimely death in a British expedition in Zululand ended their campaign, June 1, 1879.

madness, the Red Republicans set fire to the city. The Hotel de Ville was soon blazing, and so was the Tuileries.

The Versailles government, their troops, were in a frenzy of rage and grief at seeing their beautiful city destroyed before their eyes. And as the soldiers slowly fought their way in, with cannon pointed down the streets, mowing all before them, they made a most fearful slaughter of men and women alike—the innocent with the guilty. There was a last stand made by the Communists in the great cemetery of Père la Chaise, where most of them died and large groups of the captured were marched off toward Versailles—many to be shot at once, others imprisoned, and after trial sent off to prison, and exiled to New Caledonia. Thus the Red Republic was extinguished in fire and blood, and order was restored. For the time Louis Adolph Thiers ruled as a sort of president and set matters as right as possible.

Meanwhile, the emperor, Napoleon III, died in his exile in England and the nation began to consider what should be the government of the future. The old parties still existed—the Legitimists, still loyal to Henry, count of Chambord; the Orleanists, wishing for a son or grandson of Louis-Philippe; the Bonapartists, loving the memory of Napoleon III and hoping to restore his son; and

the Moderate Tricolored Republicans, chiefly seeking rest and order, and revenge upon Germany and the remnants of the Communists.

Henry, count of Chambord, had no children, so the count of Paris, eldest grandson of Louis-Philippe, was his rightful heir. There was a plan that the Legitimist and Orleans parties would join, and a proposal was made to restore the count of Chambord as such a king as Louis-Philippe, and that the count of Paris should reign as he had.

But the count of Chambord's answer was that he would come to his forefather's throne if he were invited, but only to reign as they did, by the right given to his family by God, not as the chosen of the people. He would be the Most Christian King—the king of France, not of the French; with the white flag of the Bourbons, not the tricolor—and the Eldest Son of the Church, obedient to the pope.

Nobody, except the old Legitimists, was in a mood to accept this answer; and so, when the choice of a government was put to the vote of the nation, it was decided to have a republic, with a president, instead of a monarchy. Marshal MacMahon was soon after elected as president and the French were never again ruled by a monarch.

THE ROYAL SOVEREIGNS OF THE KINGDOM OF FRANCE

MEROVINGIAN DYNASTY

Reign	Title	Ruler	Birth	Death	Relationship	Consort
418–428	King	Pharamond		428		
428–447	King	Clodio (Clodion)		447		
447–458	King	Merovech (Meerwig) (Merovee)		458		
458–481	King	Childeric I	435	482	Son of Merovech	
482–511	King	Clovis I (Chlodwig)	467	511	Son of Childeric I	Clothilde
511–558	King	Childebert I	498	558	Son of Clovis	
558–562	King	Clothaire I	500	562	Son of Clovis	Radegond
562–566	King	Charibert	522	566	Son of Clothaire I	
562–575	King	Siegbert	535	575	Son of Clothaire I	Brynhild
566–584	King	Chilperic I	539	584	Son of Clothaire I	Fredegond
584–628	King	Clothaire II	584	628	Son of Chilperic I	
628–637	King	Dagobert I	602	637	Son of Clothaire II	Nanthilde
637–655	King	Clovis II	635	655	Son of Dagobert I	Bathilde
655–668	King	Clothaire III	650	668	Son of Clovis II	
668–674	King	Childeric II	650	674	Son of Clovis II	
674–678	King	Dagobert II				
674–691	King	Thierry III	658	691	Son of Clovis II	
691–695	King	Clovis III	680	695	Son of Thierry III	
695–711	King	Childebert II	684	711	Son of Thierry III	
711–716	King	Dagobert III	700	716	Son of Childebert II	
716–721	King	Chilperic II	670	721	Son of Childeric II	
721–737	King	Thierry IV	715	737	Son of Dagobert III	
737–742—Interregnum						
743–751	King	Childeric III	731	754	Son of Chilperic II	

Reign	Title	Ruler	Birth	Death	Relationship	Consort
		CAROLINGIAN DYNASTY				
628–639	Mayor of the Palace	Pepin I, the Elder		640		
687–714	Mayor of the Palace	Pepin II (Pepin L'Heuristal)		714	Son of Pepin I, the Elder	
714–741	Mayor of the Palace	Charles Martel (Carl of the Hammer)	689	741	Son of Pepin II	
741–747	Mayor of the Palace	Carloman		754	Son of Charles Martel	
747–751	Mayor of the Palace	Pepin III, the Short	714	768	Son of Charles Martel	
751–768	King	Pepin III, the Short				Berthe
768–771	King	Carloman	751	771	Son of Pepin III	Hildegarde
768–814	Joint Ruler	Charlemagne (Carl the Great)	742	814	Son of Pepin III	
814–840	Joint Ruler	Louis I, the Pious (Ludwig)	778	840	Son of Charlemagne	Ermengarde
840–843	Joint Ruler	Lothair, Louis, and Charles the Bald			Sons of Louis I	
843–877	King	Charles I, the Bald	823	877		
877–879	King	Louis II	846	879	Son of Charles I	Adelaide
879–882	King	Louis III	863	882	Son of Louis II	
882–884	Coregent	Carloman		884	Brother of Louis III	
884–887	King	Charles II, the Fat (Charles III)	839	888	Son of Louis II	
888–898	King	Eudes, count of Paris	858	898		Theodorade
898–922	King	Charles III, the Simple	879	929	Son of Louis II	Ogine
922–923	Rival King	Robert	865	923	Brother of Eudes	
923–936	Rival King	Rudolf, duke of Burgundy		937	Son-in-law of Robert	Emme
936–954	Rival King	Louis IV, d'Outremer	918	954	Son of Charles the Simple	Gerberge
954–986	Rival King	Lothair	941	986	Son of Louis IV	Emme
986–987	Rival King	Louis V, the Indolent	967	987	Son of Lothair	Blanche of Aquitaine
		CAPETIAN DYNASTY				
987–996	King	Hugh Capet	946	996		Adelaide of Guienne
996–1031	King	Robert II, the Pious	971	1031	Son of Hugh Capet	Constance de Provence
1031–1060	King	Henry I	1004	1060	Son of Robert II	Anne of Russia
1060–1108	King	Philip I, the Amorons	1052	1108	Son of Henry I	Berthe of Holland
1108–1137	King	Louis VI, the Fat (Louis the Wide Awake)	1081	1137	Son of Philip I	Adelaide of Savoy
1137–1180	King	Louis VII, the Young	1120	1180	Son of Louis VI	Alice of Champagne
1180–1223	King	Philip II Augustus (the God-given)	1165	1223	Son of Louis VII	Isabelle of Hainaut Ingebruge of Denmark
1223–1226	King	Louis VIII, the Lion	1187	1226	Son of Philip II	Blanche of Castille
1226–1270	King	Louis IX (Saint Louis)	1214	1270	Son of Louis VIII	Marguerite of Provence
1270–1285	King	Philip III, the Bold	1245	1285	Son of Louis IX	Isabelle of Aragon
1285–1314	King	Philip IV, the Fair	1268	1314	Son of Philip III	Jeanne of Navarre
1314–1316	King	Louis X, the Quarrelsome (Hutin)	1289	1316	Son of Philip IV	Jean I
1316–1316	King	John I	1316	1316	Posthumous son of Louis X	
1316–1322	King	Philip V, the Tall	1294	1322	Son of Philip IV	Jeanne, duchess of Bourgogne
1322–1328	King	Charles IV, the Fair	1294	1328	Son of Philip IV	Isabelle (reine d' Angleterre)
		VALOIS DYNASTY				
1328–1350	King	Philip VI, the Fortunate	1293	1350	Nephew of Philip IV	Jeanne of Bourgogne Blanche of Evreux
1350–1364	King	John II, the Good	1319	1364	Son of Philip VI	Bonne of Luxemburg
1364–1380	King	Charles V, the Wise	1337	1380	Son of John II	Jeanne of Bourbon
1380–1422	King	Charles VI, the Well-Beloved	1368	1422	Son of Charles V	Isabelle of Bavaria
1422–1461	King	Charles VII, the Victorious	1403	1461	Son of Charles VI	Marie of Anjou
1461–1483	King	Louis XI	1423	1483	Son of Charles VII	Charlotte of Savoy
1483–1498	King	Charles VIII, the Affable	1470	1498	Son of Louis XI	Anne of Brittany

Reign	Title	Ruler	Birth	Death	Relationship	Consort
1498–1515	King	Louis XII, the Father of His People	1462	1515	Brother-in-law of Charles VIII	Jeanne
1515–1547	King	Francis I	1494	1547	Second son of Louis XII	Claude of France
1547–1559	King	Henry II	1519	1559	Son of Francis I	Catherine de' Medici
1559–1560	King	Francis II	1544	1560	Son of Henry II	
1560–1563	Regent	Catherine de' Medici	1519	1589		Henry II
1560–1574	King	Charles IX	1550	1574	Son of Henry II	
1574–1589	King	Henry III	1551	1589	Son of Henry II	Louise of Lorraine

BOURBON DYNASTY

Reign	Title	Ruler	Birth	Death	Relationship	Consort
1589–1610	King	Henry IV, the Great	1553	1610	Distant cousin of Henry II	Marguerite of Valois Marie de' Medici
1610–1617	Regent	Marie de' Medici	1573	1642		Henry IV
1610–1643	King	Louis XIII, the Well-Beloved	1601	1643	Son of Henry IV	Anne of Austria
1643–1651	Regent	Anne of Austria	1601	1666		Louis XIII
1643–1715	King	Louis XIV, the Great	1638	1715	Son of Louis XIII	Marie-Therese of Spain
1715–1723	Regent	Philip of Orleans	1674	1723	Nephew of Louis XIV	Henriette d'Angleterre
1715–1774	King	Louis XV, the Well-Beloved	1710	1774	Great-grandson of Louis XIV	Marie Leczinska
1774–1792	King	Louis XVI, the Beloved	1754	1793	Grandson of Louis XV	Marie-Antoinette of Austria
1793–1795	King	Louis XVII	1785	1795	Son of Louis XVI	

FIRST REPUBLIC

Reign	Title	Ruler	Birth	Death	Relationship	Consort
1799–1804	First Consul	Napoleon Bonaparte	1769	1821		Josephine de Beauharnais Marie Louise of Austria

FIRST EMPIRE

Reign	Title	Ruler	Birth	Death	Relationship	Consort
1804–1814	Emperor	Napoleon I				
1814	Emperor	Napoleon II	1811	1832		

BOURBON DYNASTY

Reign	Title	Ruler	Birth	Death	Relationship	Consort
1814–1824	King	Louis XVIII	1755	1824	Brother of Louis XVI	Louise Marie Josephine of Savoy
1824–1830	King	Charles X	1757	1836	Brother of Louis XVIII	Marie-Therese of Savoy
1830–1848	King	Louis-Philippe I, the Citizen King	1773	1850		Marie Amelie of Naples

SECOND REPUBLIC

Reign	Title	Ruler	Birth	Death	Relationship	Consort
1848–1852	President	Charles Louis Napoleon Bonaparte	1808	1873	Nephew of Napoleon I	

SECOND EMPIRE

Reign	Title	Ruler	Birth	Death	Relationship	Consort
1852–1871	Emperor	Napoleon III (Charles Louis Napoleon)				Eugenie de Montijo

3
England, Great Britain, and the United Kingdom

Little was known of Britain until Phoenician sailors, sailing off the coast of Gaul, saw in the distant horizon the white cliffs of a strange land. The Gauls told them that because of the white color of the cliffs they had given the name of *Albion*—meaning "white"—to the country. The title has lived through all the centuries and was a favorite one with poets and orators. But in the last hundred years, it has become known as the white cliffs of Dover.

The accounts of those remote days are so vague that little dependence can be placed upon them, so we must look at the time of the mighty Caesar for our first knowledge of England.

While Caesar was engaged in conquering Gaul, he discovered that his opponents received great help from their kinsmen, who crossed over from Albion to aid them in repelling the Roman invaders. This fact, added to the strange stories that he heard about the people of the islands, led Caesar, in the year 55 B.C., to sail for Albion—which he, in imitation of the Greeks, called Britain. He took with him two legions, or about twelve thousand men, and that was the first historical invasion of England. The time was late in summer, and the landing place was near the site of the present town of Deal.

The shaggy Britons had watched the approach of the Roman ships, and were in truth more eager for battle than the Romans themselves. The savages had flung off their clothing of skins, so they were literally "stripped for the fight," and many who were on horseback forced their animals far out into the waves, while the riders taunted the invaders, whom they were impatient to reach. Others galloped up and down the beach in their war chariots and filled the air with their defiant cries. The Romans drawing near were awed by what they saw. They had learned from the Gauls of the frenzied devotion of the Britons to the Druidical faith. The Romans knew nothing of that gloomy and fearful religion, and at first were afraid to offend the unknown god whom the savages worshiped.

Old England

Despite their bravery, the Britons were soon scattered in disorder. In his *Commentaries,* Caesar refers to his first campaign in Britain as a reconnoitering expedition, and expressed his intention of returning there later.

Accordingly, the following year he came back with a more powerful force, and penetrated some distance in-

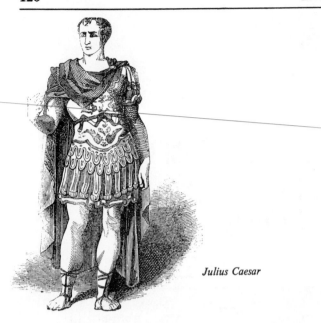

Julius Caesar

the gentleness of Christianity. *Druid* is from a word meaning an oak. The people venerated this tree and also the mistletoe, which still forms a part of our Christmas festivities. They had a regularly organized priesthood and offered up human sacrifices to win the favor of the gods. The priests held all the traditions, administered the laws, and prescribed the customs. Recent research shows this horrible religion was brought from Gaul in the earliest times. The priests kept most of their faith and its ceremonies secret but they believed in a life beyond the grave. They built temples and altars, open to the sky. Some remains of these may still be seen. The most striking is Stonehenge, on Salisbury plain in Wiltshire.

In A.D. 61 Suetonius Paulinus, the Roman governor of Britain, seeing that he could make no real peace with the Druids, set out to extirpate them. The island of Anglesey, off the coast of Wales, was their sacred refuge, and against that he and his men marched. They cut down the Britons, demolished the stone altars, and flung the frantic Druids into their own divine fires.

While Suetonius was in Anglesey, a vicious uprising broke out in the East. The leader was Boadicea, widow of a king of the Icenians. She drew the surrounding tribes to her and led them into battle.

At first it seemed as if the furious and fanatic Britons would sweep the Romans into the sea, but Suetonius returned and stamped out the revolt in one great battle. Eighty thousand Britons were killed, Boadicea poisoned herself in despair, and the Druids disappeared forever.

The real conqueror of Britain was Gnaeus Julius Agricola, who was governor from A.D. 78 to 84. He was an excellent ruler, who built a line of forts from the Firth of Forth to the Firth of Clyde, to keep back the turbulent North Britons. He stopped the merciless tyranny of the Roman tax gatherers, and encouraged the natives to build comfortable dwellings, good roads, and thriving towns.

land. After several months Caesar, finding little pleasure or profit in the wild, bleak island, abandoned it.

Britain was now left to itself for nearly a hundred years. Then in A.D. 43, the emperor Claudius led a third invasion into the country. The islanders made a sturdy resistance, and it was not until nine years had passed that Roman valor and discipline triumphed. Among the captives brought back to Rome was Caractacus, the heroic leader of the Britons. Though in chains, Caractacus held his head unbowed, his spirit unbroken. Brought before Claudius, Caractacus looked him defiantly in the face and refused to kneel or beg for his liberty. The simple majesty and dignity of the prisoner so impressed the emperor that he set him and his family free.

It has been said that the religion of the ancient Britons was Druidical. This faith was hideous in many of its features and of frightful severity, possessing no trace of

Claudius illustrated from a copper coin in the British Museum

Caesar illustrated from a copper coin in the British Museum

Hadrian illustrated from a copper coin in the British Museum

Constantine the Great illustrated from a gold coin in the British Museum

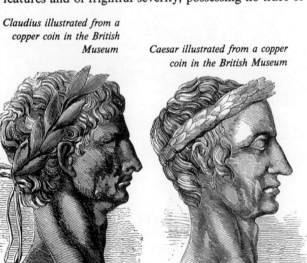

The emperor Hadrian visited Britain in A.D. 120, and not feeling strong enough to hold all the lands gained by Agricola, he constructed an immense wall from the Tyne to the Solway Firth. In 139 the emperor Antoninus Pius built a new dike, which followed the line of that of Agricola. The restless North Britons continued to be troublesome. The emperor Severus made a campaign against them between 207 and 210, and erected a chain of forts along the line of the dike built by Hadrian.

The Romans built some fifty towns, many protected by walls, and of these London soon became the chief, though York was made the civil and military capital of the country. The most notable incident in the history of York was the proclamation of Constantine as emperor in 306. Through him Christianity became the established religion of the empire, though his friendship for the growing faith was that of a statesman rather than of a devout believer.

Rome ruled Britain for three and a half centuries, but by that time the stupendous empire was crumbling to ruin. Her legions were called back to Rome. This left the British people in a state of hopeless collapse. On the north the Picts, on the northwest the Scots, and on the south and east the Teutons were hammering the miserable beings, who meekly bowed their heads to the blows and quarreled among themselves over theological questions, while their enemies swarmed over the border and swept them out of their path like so much chaff.

The foes who came by sea were Teutonic tribes from the mouths of the Elbe and the Weser in North Germany. Most of the country was conquered by these Teutons, of whom the principal tribes were the Angles, Saxons, and Jutes, who finally fused into one people, under the name of Anglo-Saxons, or *Angles* or *English,* while that portion of Britain in which they made their home was called *England.* They were cruel, and the conquered Britons they did not enslave huddled into the western part of the island.

The first of these Teutonic kingdoms was founded in Kent. A despairing British chieftain or king, Vortigern, undertook the dangerous experiment of fighting fire with fire. To save his people from their northern foes, the Scots, he invited the Teutons to come to his aid. Two well-known Jutish vikings, Hengist and Horsa, accepted the invitation with their followers, and in the year 449 landed on the island of Thanet, the southeastern extremity of England.

At first Hengist and Horsa served their host well, driving back the wild northern tribes. Soon, however, larger ambitions took possession of the shrewd sea kings. They recognized their own strength and the Britons' weakness; they sent word to other Jutes to join them and soon accumulated a formidable force.

Legend represents King Vortigern as cowardly, weak, and evil, and tells that he was fascinated by the wiles of Rowena, a daughter of Hengist. At any rate he made

The course of the Viking expeditions

little resistance against the bold robbers and the real defense of the Britons fell to his son Vortimer. There were many fierce combats and in one Horsa was slain. The valiant Vortimer also perished, and gradually the Jutes crushed out all resistance.

Finally, King Vortigern proposed a friendly meeting. Hengist, now sole leader of the Jutes, consented. In the midst of a great love feast held at Stonehenge, the treacherous Hengist cried out suddenly to his men, "Use your swords!"

At the signal every Jute stabbed his British neighbor through the heart. Vortigern alone was spared, for he had wedded Rowena and the murderers thought him more useful alive than dead.

These stories may or may not be the literal facts connected with the first entrance of the great Teutonic race into England. Hengist, Horsa, and Vortigern, however, really existed, and Eric, a son of Hengist, was, in 457, formally crowned king of Kent, that is, of England's southeastern coast. He was the first of her Teutonic kings.

Other Teutonic tribes were naturally drawn to Britain

by the Jutes' success. The Saxons, under a chieftain named Ella, founded a kingdom of Sussex (the South Saxons) in 477. Two Saxon chiefs, coming over in 495, conquered the portion of the country now known as Hampshire, and named it Wessex, or the kingdom of the West Saxons. Then, again, from Jutland came a swarm of Angles, who occupied all that remained of eastern Britain. Increasing in strength and numbers, they became masters of most of the country and gave their own name of Angles, or English, to all the invaders.

According to tradition, the famous King Arthur administered the first real repulse to the Saxons in 520, at Badbury, in Dorsetshire. Arthur has often been looked upon as a mythical hero, but careful research leaves no doubt that he was a valiant patriot who struck many stout blows at the invaders of his country. However, the Saxons pushed inland and their power grew. The kingdom of the Northumbrians was founded in 547, and consisted of the land from the Humber to the Firth of Forth; the kingdom of the Mercians embraced the midland country, while Kent was the kingdom of the Jutes, and Sussex that of the South Saxons. Essex, the kingdom of the East Saxons and that of the East Angles, divided into Norfolk and Suffolk (North-folk and South-folk), were less important. These seven leading kingdoms are often referred to as the Heptarchy.

The religion of the early English was like that of other Teutonic tribes, being a form of heathenism, in which Woden, who was the Odin of the Danes, was worshiped as the leading god, who gave victory. Next to him was Thor, or Thunder, who ruled the sky. There were other less important gods. Our Wednesday is Woden's Day and Thursday is Thor's Day, the names having been preserved to the present time.

Saint Augustine came to Britain in 597 to preach Christianity and was so successful that he established the first cathedral of Canterbury, of which he became archbishop and which is still the mother church of England. The church gained not only great social influence, but was a force in politics.

The kingdom of Wessex now enjoyed a century and a half of prosperity. Egbert, a descendant of Cerdic, the first king, claimed the throne in 787, but was overthrown by a rival, and fled the country. He found refuge in the court of Charlemagne, who was dreaming of reviving the old Roman Empire. Shortly after Charlemagne was crowned emperor of the West, the king of Wessex died, and Egbert was called home to succeed him. He showed the influence of Charlemagne upon his character by resolutely setting out to bring all the neighboring petty tribes into subjection to his sovereignty. His army, "lean, pale, and long-bearded," was a resistless engine, which steadily crushed all opposition, so that in 828 the great task was accomplished and Egbert had fairly won the right to assume the title of king of the English. Caesar had called the land Britain, the Celts had termed it Al-

Egbert, 828–39   Ethelred I, 866–71

LINEAGE OF THE WEST SAXON KINGS FROM EGBERT.

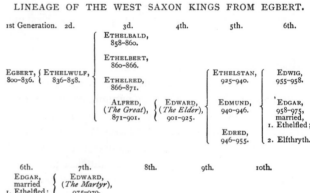

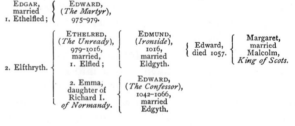

Lineage of the West Saxon kings from Egbert

bion, and it now took the name of Angle-land, or England.

Next England was made to feel the whip of the merciless Northmen, or Danes. These invaders were still heathen and they reveled in the destruction of the Christian churches and monasteries and in the slaying of the priests. Creeping along the coast, hiding in woods and caves, or sailing unexpectedly up the rivers in their galleys and then stealing horses, the Danes galloped through the country on their ferocious forays, sparing nothing they could reach.

The Scots of Ireland had been converted to Christianity in the fifth century mainly through the labors of the great missionary Saint Patrick, and his work was carried on with marvelous completeness by his followers. Learning, therefore, flourished in Ireland, and students flocked thither from England, Germany, and Gaul. The land was luminous with churches and monasteries, but these were blotted out by the Danes, who drove the native Irish back into the swamps and bogs, and then made their own homes along the seacoast.

Such was the miserable condition of England and its immediate neighbors, when one of the greatest characters in English history appeared on the scene, and through his life and achievements accomplished a work for his country whose grandeur and importance have never been surpassed. This heroic figure was Alfred the Great.

ALFRED THE GREAT

Alfred was the fifth son of Ethelwulf, king of Wessex, and of Osburh, his first wife, and was born at Wantage in Berkshire in 849. The father, it is said, had been bishop of Winchester until necessity made him king. He fought the invading Northmen while under-king of Kent, and afterward succeeded his father Egbert on the throne.

Ethelwulf, however, had a side to his character for which the *Witan,* or "wise men," felt little sympathy. He was impressed by the spell that the name of Rome exercised in the Middle Ages, and disregarded many objections of his kingdom in order to make a pilgrimage to the Eternal City. Before leaving, he granted a tenth part of the rents from his private domain for ecclesiastical and charitable purposes. But this grant was afterward mis-

takenly represented as a gift of the tenth of the entire revenue of the kingdom, and was the origin of tithes.

Little is known of the mother of Alfred, who was the daughter of the king's cupbearer, and came of the royal house of the Jutes, settled in the Isle of Wight.

Alfred's visit to Rome with Ethelwulf is supposed to have lasted about two years, and with this visit no doubt should be associated the main part of his formal education. He acquired a fair knowledge of Latin, and thus gained the key to the learning accessible at the time. There, too, he must have imbibed that fondness for literature that led him to translate what he looked upon as the classics in science, literature, and religion. On his way home, he remained for some months with his father at the court of Charles the Bald, king of the Western Franks, and there he tasted the best of medieval monarchy.

When Ethelwulf and his son left the court of Charles the Bald, the father was past sixty years of age, and took with him as his bride Judith, the daughter of Charles, a maiden not more than twelve. His people refused to receive him, for the leaders of Wessex had sworn an oath to bestow the crown upon his son, Ethelbald. The father complacently accepted the situation and withdrew to Kent, where he ruled as under-king for two years. His death was followed by the scandalous marriage of his widow to Ethelbald, but to neither did she bear any children, and her second husband passed away in 860.

Returning to her father, Judith eloped with Baldwin I of Flanders and from the couple descended Matilda, daughter of Baldwin V of Flanders, who became the wife of William the Conqueror. Alfred's daughter married Judith's son.

Ethelwulf set up for the first time in English history the claim to bequeath the crown as he chose. He willed that at his death it should pass to Ethelstan, his eldest son, then to Ethelbald, to Ethelred, and then to Alfred, the children of each being excluded. Ethelbert, standing

Alfred the Great, 871–901

Ethelbald, 858–60

Saint Augustine before Ethelbert (860–66)

affliction that was beyond the skill of the best physicians of the time. Most probably the ailment was epilepsy, so that through the most trying years of his trying life, when engaged upon his grand work, he was liable at any moment to be taken with an epileptic fit. The affliction cannot fail to stir sympathy and deepen admiration of the wonderful man.

In this same year of 868, the Danes withdrew from Northumberland and invaded Mercia, whose people in their panic appealed to Wessex for help. Ethelred and Alfred lost no time in responding. The royal brothers led the brave men of Wessex to the defense of the place, but, though successful at first, were decisively overcome in a great battle. In one of the battles Ethelred was mortally wounded, and with the West Saxon forces withdrawing, the Danes remained masters of the field.

A few weeks after the accession of Alfred, he encountered the Danes again. He surprised them at first, but in the end was repulsed. The enemy, however, had never faced such resistance, nor suffered such severe losses. It did not take long to agree upon terms of peace. Alfred had to pay a heavy price, for he was obliged to debase the coinage, and to put a heavy tax upon landowners. A three-year respite that followed was enjoyed by Wessex only, and London remained in the hands of the Danes until finally reconquered by Alfred.

Alfred believed that his little kingdom could be saved only by action on the sea, and that the relentless invaders of his country must be defeated upon the water or not at all. It came about that, during the three-year breathing spell he created the first English navy. He was able to stop a Danish fleet heading for the Thames.

Stealing along the coast, the enemy found a landing place at Wareham in Dorsetshire. The alert Alfred immediately blockaded them, and the frightened Danes were glad to make a treaty by which they promised "speedily to depart his kingdom." But they found pretexts for breaking their pledge and, seizing Exeter, held it throughout the winter of 876–77. In the following

in order of age between Ethelbald and Ethelred, was to remain after his father's death the under-king of Kent.

While this arrangement suited the persons chiefly concerned, it by no means suited the Witan, who, seeing the need of a united kingdom as a protection against the Danes, set the will aside, and decided to take their kings in order from the ruling family. A condition as unparalleled as it was fortunate was that there was not a bit of jealousy among the brothers. Whoever was king was certain to receive the loyal support of the others. When Ethelbald died in 860, Ethelbert was called from Kent and his rule extended over both that province and Wessex. Six years later, Ethelred, his brother, succeeded. Alfred was at that time seventeen years old, and was the right-hand man of the king, serving as his chief of staff in war, as chief minister in peace, and signing all royal warrants next to the king. During the first three years of Ethelred's reign, the Danes swarmed over Northumbria and East Anglia, and were preparing to overrun Mercia and Wessex.

The first encounter of Alfred with the Danes took place in 868, before he was yet king, and when he was twenty. About that time he was marrying the daughter of Ethelred Mucil, earl of the Gainas.

At Alfred's wedding he was seized with a distressing

Alfred's "jewel"

Alfred's Britain with historical detail

spring, a Danish fleet of more than a hundred vessels sailed around the coast with the intention of reinforcing their countrymen blockaded in Exeter. But at Swanade a severe storm dashed all the ships upon the rocks. This wrested the control of the Channel from the invaders, and the garrison at Exeter was helpless before Alfred. The Danes saw they were defeated and surrendered on the promise of being permitted to leave Wessex. They passed into Mercia and divided some of the choicest lands in Gloucestershire and Warwickshire among themselves.

According to the rules of warfare in those days, it was the practice—to trade the sword for the plowshare. Not doubting the peace, the West Saxon army was disbanded, and the men turned to farming, believing no more fighting would be required. But, without warning, the Danes swarmed back over the Mercian border and surprised Wessex. Wessex passed unresisting into the possession of the Danes and King Alfred followed by his still faithful band, plunged into the swamps and forests of Somersetshire, so hidden in the tangled depths with

which his men were familiar, that his enemies could not trace him to his hiding place.

Between the opening of the year and Easter, 878, Alfred threaded his way to a piece of firm ground in the middle of the marshes formed by the Parret and the Tone. The position was very strong naturally, and he made his headquarters at Athelney, from where he began a guerrilla warfare through which he inflicted considerable damage on the enemy. It is related that, in order to learn the intentions of the Danes, Alfred visited their camp in the guise of a wandering minstrel and stayed a full week, entertaining them and their king, Guthrum, with his music. When he had learned all he wished to know, he quietly departed, without having once drawn suspicion to himself.

Before long Alfred's followers had so increased that he waged war in the open fields. The two forces met at Eddington, near Westbury, and the Danes suffered defeat. After a two-week siege, Guthrum surrendered. The invaders agreed to quit Wessex forever, and Guthrum agreed to turn Christian and be baptized. In the treaty concluded at Wedmore, the boundaries between Danish and English Britain were defined. The rights of Alfred were established over all Wessex, Kent, and London, and a large district extending into Hertfordshire and Bedfordshire.

It was not until 886, however, that the little Saxon chiefs all over England, recognizing Alfred's ability and power, came to him voluntarily, and, placing their hands in his, acknowledged him as their king. In the same year Alfred was able to begin rebuilding London. Being secure now in the possession of the town, the English had no trouble in holding the Thames, and that protected Kent, Wessex, and Mercia.

A tremendous test of Alfred's material work for England came in 893–96, when Hasting, the Northman, landed an army in Britain, but after several defeats at the hands of Alfred, they surrendered. The last days of the illustrious Alfred closed in peace and tranquillity, the

Alfred singing in the Hall of Guthrum

Alfred acknowledged as king by the men of all England

English, ruled for twenty-four years, but there were important events that took place during that time.

Edward passed away in 925, and his eldest son Ethelstan reigned until 940. Three years before his death, he and his brother Edmund gained a crushing victory over a Danish king from Ireland and the Scots, Danes, and Welsh of the north, then there was only one king in all England. His son, Edmund the Magnificent, after reigning brilliantly for six years, was stabbed to death by a banished outlaw. Since the sons of Edmund were still quite young, his brother Edred, who had a sickly body but a strong mind, was chosen king. Upon his death in 955, he was succeeded by his brother Edwy, who reigned for only three years. Dunstan, the archbishop of Canterbury and chief adviser to the king, was virtually sovereign during the reign of the licentious Edgar (959–75), and it was his wise policy that procured for Edgar the title of "the Pacific."

Disorder followed the death of Edgar in 975, and there was a bitter quarrel as to which of the king's sons should succeed him—Edward, about twelve years old, or Ethelred, who was six years younger. The elder was finally selected and Elfrida, the mother of the younger, was incensed, for she had set her heart upon obtaining the crown for Ethelred.

Edward the Elder (901–25) raised on the shield by his followers

entry in the English chronicle being as follows:

"This year [901] died Alfred, son of Ethelwulf, six days before the Mass of All Saints. He was king over the whole English nation, except that part which was under the dominion of the Danes. He held the kingdom one year and a half less than thirty years. And then Edward, his son, succeeded to the kingdom."

Alfred's services to England were those of a patriot and statesman as well as warrior. The code of laws that he compiled in 890 was prefaced by the Ten Commandments, and closed with the Golden Rule, and he remarked, referring to the former: "He who keeps them shall not need any other law book." The real services of Alfred the Great to his people lay less in the framing and codifying of the laws, than in the enforcing of them. He made it clear to his people that the supreme power of the ruler was buttressed by the judicial system, and the executive authority would be used to the utmost to enforce obedience.

THE LATER SAXONS

On the death of Alfred, his followers raised on a shield as their king, his eldest son Edward, surnamed the Elder, an able and ambitious soldier. He became king of all the

Dunstan was still the real king, and it was he who placed the crown upon Edward's head. The stepmother, standing by, vowed a vengeance that was not long delayed. While King Edward was hunting one day, in Dorsetshire, he spurred ahead of his attendants and reached Corfe Castle, where his stepmother lived. The young king blew his hunting horn, and Elfrida hurried out beaming with smiles: "Dear King, you are welcome," she said, "pray dismount and come in!" "I am afraid, my dear madam," he replied, "that my company will miss me and think I have come to some harm. I will be glad to drink a cup of wine here in the saddle to you and my little brother, Ethelred."

Elfrida hurried into the castle to get the wine, and reappeared in a few minutes bearing it in her hand. The king reached down, smilingly took the cup, and lifting it to his lips, said, "Health to you both." At that moment, an armed attendant of the queen, who had stolen around unnoticed to the rear of the king, leaped forward and buried a dagger in his back. The king dropped the cup, and his startled horse dashed off. Weakened from the loss of blood, the dying king soon toppled from the saddle, but his foot caught in the stirrup, and he was dragged over the stones, until his friends came up with the exhausted animal and released the body. Because of the manner of his death, Edward is called the Martyr. His great adviser Dunstan, in great grief, retired to Canterbury and devoted himself solely to religious duties until his death in 988.

Ethelred succeeded his murdered brother on the throne. He was surnamed the Unready, and was a worthless creature who gave himself up to all manner of vices. When the Danes began again their invasions of the country, the cowardly Ethelred and his friends resorted to the disgraceful practice of buying them off. This pleased the robbers, who took the money and then came again, sure of receiving each time a big bribe from the terrified and cringing English. The heavy taxes that it was necessary to impose were called *Danegeld,* or "Dane-gold." When the end of his resources was reached, the worthless Ethelred took refuge with Duke Richard the Good of Normandy, whose sister he had married.

Finally, in 1013, Sweyn the Dane conquered all England. He died the following year, and then Ethelred was recalled, but he, too, soon died, and the war went on between his son Edmund, surnamed Ironsides, and Canute, son of Sweyn. Thus there were two kings in the country. Edmund put up a brave fight, but in the end agreed to accept Wessex, East Anglia, Essex, and London for his share, while the Dane took all the rest. Edmund, however, had reigned only seven months (April 23–November 30, 1016), when he died, and Canute, or Cnut, became the first fully acknowledged Danish king of England, his rule lasting from 1017 to 1035.

Canute began his reign with great harshness, banishing or putting to death the leading Englishmen who had

Ethelstan, 925–40   Edwy (also Eadwig), 955–58

Edgar, 958–75

King Edgar

Edward the Martyr, 975–79

Canute and his queen

Dunstan crowning Edward the Martyr

fought against him; but this severity did not last. He soon sought the goodwill of the people. He rebuked the courtiers who, in flattering his greatness, declared that even the sea would obey him. He had them place his chair on the edge of the waves and commanded the rising tide to come no nearer. When it steadily rose despite his order, he had some harsh words for his flatterers.

Canute's plan was to form a mighty empire that included Denmark, Norway, Sweden, and England. He divided England into four districts or earldoms: Wessex, Mercia, East Anglia, and Northumbria, each ruled by an earl, with absolute authority. The plan began well, but mutual jealousy brought friction, until the safety of the country was imperiled.

Canute visited his different possessions, but lived mostly in England, of which he became very fond. He seems to have been a worthy Christian, for he showed a reverence for all that was good, and one day wrote to his subjects: "I have vowed to God to live a right life in all things, to rule justly and piously over my realm, and to administer just judgment to all."

When Canute died, England was divided between his two sons Harold and Hardicanute. By this time, however, the people had become tired of their Danish rulers.

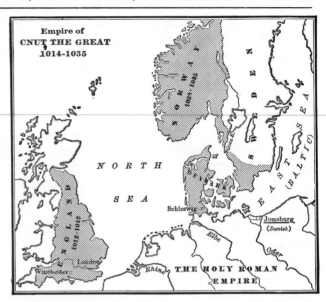

The empire of Canute (Cnut), 1014-35

The Great Council of the Witan sent for Edward, the son of Ethelred, whom they wished to have as their king. He had been taken to the French or Norman court when only nine years old, and had spent nearly thirty years there. He took with him to England a number of French favorites, filled the churches with French priests, and in short ruled like the Frenchman he really was. He even went so far as to give his pledge to Duke William of Normandy, that on his death he would leave the English crown to the Norman duke. The latter never forgot this promise, though Edward chose to disregard it.

Edward married the daughter of Godwin, earl of Wessex, who was the real ruler of the country until his death in 1053, when he was succeeded by his son Harold as earl. The nominal king spent his time in church affairs, and built an abbey at the west end of London, which was called Westminster. His life was so blameless that he was given the name of Edward the Confessor, or the Christian. Hardly had Edward completed and dedicated his abbey, when he died and was buried there. On his death-

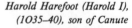

King Canute and the waves

Harold Harefoot (Harold I), (1035–40), son of Canute

Harthacnut (Hardicanute),
1040–42

Edward the Confessor, 1042–66

Great seal of Edward the Confessor

this reward was generally in the form of land, since the king owned most of it. The condition attached to such a gift was the obligation of the receiver to provide a certain number of equipped soldiers to fight for the donor. The nobles and large landholders, imitating the king, gave certain parts of their estates in the same way to tenants, and they in turn, if they chose, could do the same to those below them. This constituted the feudal system, by which every freeman below the rank of a noble was obliged to attach himself to some superior whom he was bound to serve, and who in return became his legal protector.

bed, Edward, despite his solemn promise to the duke of Normandy, and in view of the fact that he had no children, recommended Harold, earl of Wessex, as his successor. His advice was followed. The Witan, or National Council, selected Harold as king, and he was crowned January 16, 1066. Now, the government rested in an elective sovereign, who was aided by the council of the Witan. All freemen had the right to attend this council, but the power really rested with a few of the nobles and clergy. The body could elect the king, but were required to limit their choice to the royal family. If he proved unfit, the Witan had the power to depose him. That body confirmed grants of public lands, and was a supreme court of justice in civil and criminal cases. In conjunction with the king, the Witan enacted laws, levied taxes, and appointed the chief officers and bishops of the realm.

The freemen were compelled to help in the maintenance of roads, bridges, and forts, and were obliged to serve in case of war. Besides the earls, who were nobles by birth, there was a class called *thanes,* or "servants," or companions of the king, who after a time outranked the hereditary nobility. Both classes were rewarded by the king for faithful services, or for valorous deeds, and

The sickness and death of Edward the Confessor (Bayeux Tapestry)

Harold's interview with King Edward on his return from Normandy (Bayeux Tapestry)

Funeral of Edward the Confessor at Westminster Abbey (Bayeux Tapestry)

Edward the Confessor's tomb

Harold

THE NORMAN INVASION

One of the greatest battles in history—Hastings—had its beginnings with the bearing of a king's first message. Duke William of Normandy was about to mount his horse to join his friends on a hunt, when the messenger rode up with the new king's message of the news of the death of King Edward in England, and the accession of Harold II, who sent a demand to Harold that he should respect the promise made by the dead king. Harold's reply was a flat refusal, and the indignant duke resolved to "fight for his rights." He called his Norman barons around him, and promised large grants of land to all who would help him. Since most of the Normans were fond of fighting and adventure, and there was a promise of substantial rewards, they flocked in large numbers to his banner. Not meaning to neglect anything, he sent to the pope asking his favor, and it came back with a consecrated banner that was to be carried by the army. Just as the sun was creeping up in the horizon on September 27, 1066, Duke William's fleet and transports sailed out into the Channel, his own vessel in the lead, with the sacred banner fluttering at the masthead. His archers and cavalry numbered more than fifty thousand.

Now another Harold, who was a Goliath of a warrior and king of the Norwegians, had landed in the north of England. The opposing armies clashed together at Stamford Bridge, on September 25, with the result that the Norwegians were routed, and their leaders slain.

The crown offered to Harold by the people (Bayeux Tapestry)

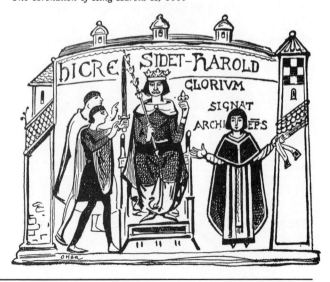

The coronation of King Harold II, 1066

Great seal of William the Conqueror

William the Conqueror, 1066–87

Arms of William the Conqueror (William I)

William the Conqueror landing in England

The English Harold was in high feather over his victory, and held a great feast at York to celebrate it, but in the midst of the merrymaking a messenger galloped up with the news that Duke William had landed at Pevensey. Harold did not waste any more time in celebrating, but, gathering his forces, hurried southward, and camped on the heights of Senlac. Meanwhile, William had landed and built a fort, from which he advanced to Hastings a few miles farther east. No enemy appearing, he began plundering the surrounding country, and was so employed when Harold arrived with his army on the evening of October 13. Full of confidence, the Saxons spent the night in feasting and song, while the Normans engaged in prayer and confession.

The great battle of Hastings opened on the following morning. A huge Norman knight rode forward in advance of his comrades, singing and tossing his great sword high in the air, catching it as it fell. A Saxon rushed forward to meet him and was slain. Then the two armies joined in battle, the Normans attacking, the Saxons defending. Twice the invaders were beaten back. A rumor spread that Duke William was slain, and his men began to flee. Throwing aside his helmet that all might see his face, he galloped among the fugitives and checked them with his voice and lance, threatening death if they did not turn again to battle. Then he bade his archers shoot into the air, so that their descending arrows fell like rain upon the unprotected heads of the Englishmen. King Harold fell, pierced through the brain by an arrow

William I and Tonstain bearing the consecrated banner at the Battle of Hastings (Bayeux Tapestry)

The Battle of Hastings

Edith finding the body of King Harold

and bleeding from countless wounds. Still the sturdy Saxons held their ground, and William resorted to another stratagem. He made his most trusted troops feign flight. The foe broke ranks in a furious pursuit; and the better-trained Normans, turning unexpectedly upon the charging mob, scattered the English in confusion. Still, however, they struggled on, each little detached group fighting for itself, until night enabled the remnant to escape from the field of death. England had been conquered in one of the most desperate and bloody battles of history.

The next day, Harold's old and tottering mother, with tears streaming down her withered cheeks, begged for the body of her son, but the stern duke William would not permit it to have a Christian burial. For a long time it was impossible to find the mangled corpse, and it was only with the help of Edith "of the swan's neck," a

Facsimile of entries in Domesday book, which was a survey of the land and people of William's kingdom. A valuable document for historians, it divided the 2 million people in the land to status as serfs or free people and nobles, and divided real property according to ownership.

former favorite of the king, that it was picked out from the heaps of the slain. On the field of his great victory the Norman conqueror erected the Abbey of Battle, and tradition says he buried the body of his fallen foe under a pile of stones near the sea, whence it was removed by friends, and finally laid at rest at Waltham, near London, in the church (afterward Waltham Abbey) that Harold had built there.

With little delay William marched against London and burned the suburbs. The panic-stricken inhabitants, seeing no hope, threw open the gates without any defense. William repaid them by giving the city a charter that secured for it the same privileges that had been granted by Edward the Confessor. This interesting paper is still preserved among other documents in Guildhall, London. A striking fact connected with it is that William, unable to write his name, signed it with his "mark." He was crowned on Christmas Day, 1066, in Westminster Abbey.

England having been so effectively conquered, William went back to Normandy, where by his appointment his queen, Matilda, was at the head of affairs. Before leaving England, he placed it in charge of his half-brother Eudes, bishop of Bayeux, aided by a trusted

William the Conqueror stricken down by his son Robert

The death of the Conqueror

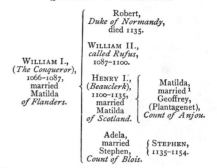

[1] First married to the Emperor Henry V. ; without offspring.

Lineage of the Norman kings from the Conqueror to Stephen

friend William Fitz-Osborn, who had been made earl of Hereford.

These two men were unfitted for the trust, and ruled so harshly that the people revolted and William found it necessary to return to England to quell the insurrection. In 1069, the foreign barbarians swarmed into northern England again and were aided by the English. William swore he would end the continual revolt by laying the country waste, and he kept the fearful oath. Villages, towns, dwellings, crops, cattle, everything beyond York and Durham, was destroyed, and the whole region so desolated that for nine years no one attempted to cultivate a plot of ground. More than a hundred thousand people perished of cold and starvation during the winter that followed. It was an act of dreadful ferocity, and yet there seemed to be a grim necessity for it.

William claimed that he had been the rightful king of England from the time of the death of his cousin, Edward the Confessor, and consequently all who had supported Harold II were traitors whose lands he confiscated, thereby increasing his wealth beyond estimate, and making himself virtually the owner of the whole kingdom. He built numerous strong castles in the different towns—the Tower of London being one of them. These were garrisoned with armed men to hold the surrounding people in subjection. The lands were divided mainly among his followers, so that at the close of his reign England had really only two classes of society —the Norman tenants, known as barons, and the English. They were no longer free, and were known as *villeins,* who were bound to the soil and could be sold with it, but, unlike slaves, could not be sold apart from the land. The word *villain* came from this reference.

Within less than twenty years of his coronation, William ordered a survey and valuation to be made of all the land outside of London, with the exception of a few border counties on the north. These returns, which were complete to the minutest particular, were set down in an immense volume called the Domesday, or Doomsday, Book.

In the summer following the preparation of this book (1086), William summoned all the nobles and chief land-holders, with their vassals, to meet on Salisbury Plain, Wiltshire. There some six hundred thousand men solemnly swore to support him as king against even their own lords—a sweeping and momentous proceeding, which made William supreme. Thus this great man completed his all-important work of blending and fusing together two peoples and civilizations. Still, the English were not conquered by another race, but by a more vigorous branch of their own race. Thus he showed the sea-wolf in his nature, though it was mingled at times with a strange gentleness that proved he was not wholly lacking in better qualities, and well earned for him the title of the Lion of Justice. He did great good to England by infusing the vigor of his Norse nature into the decaying system.

The Great Council, of which mention has been made often, seldom met, but there was need of a court to settle the disputes among the barons. So he organized the King's Court, which was a smaller and more easily handled body. Because of his stern policy many people came from other countries and settled in England. Among them were weavers and farmers from Flanders, who not only grew rich themselves, but added to the wealth of the country.

In 1087, William was so angered by a jest of the French king upon his bulky, awkward figure, that he set out to lay waste the borderland between France and Normandy. While riding through the ruins of Mantes, his horse stumbled and so injured him that he died some six weeks after. His eldest son, Robert, who had rebelled against his father, was not by the bedside of the dying king. So William gave to his second son, Rufus, a letter advising that he would be made king of England to the exclusion of his elder brother. The moment young William received this doubtful heritage, he set out for England to claim it. Henry, the third son, was given a fortune, and he also sped away to make sure of the inheritance.

William II, Rufus, 1087–1100

Great seal of William Rufus

Three sons survived William the Conqueror, besides a daughter Adela, who married Stephen, count of Blois, a prominent French nobleman. Robert, the eldest son, secured Normandy. He had long been in revolt against his father. There is a legend that the father and son fought, unknown to each other, upon the field of battle. Robert unhorsed his father, and would have slain him, but suddenly recognizing his defeated foe, knelt and asked for pardon. A reconciliation followed. It was soon broken again, but Robert in the end was allowed to inherit Normandy.

William, the second son, called Rufus because of the color of his hair, was accepted as king of England on his appearance there. He was elected and crowned king, September 26, 1087, and reigned until 1100. Most of that period was spent in warring with the barons. He reveled in all sorts of vice.

It was during the reign of William that Christendom was filled with wrath by the news that the Saracens in the Holy Land treated with intolerable cruelty the multitudes of devout visitors, who were accustomed to make pilgrimages there. The pope proclaimed a crusade, which set out in 1096 to wrest the Holy Sepulcher from the Mohammedans. Among those caught in the thrill of

the general ardor was Robert of Normandy, who mortgaged his dominions for five years to his brother, in order to raise the expenses of his share in the Crusade. He set out for Palestine, while Normandy dropped like ripe fruit into the hands of William Rufus.

The latter was passionately fond of hunting. On August 2, 1100, he was engaged at his favorite pastime in New Forest, with a number of friends. Some time later, some of his attendants found him dying in agony, from the arrow of a crossbow that had deeply pierced his body. Walter Tyrell, one of the party, was suspected of launching the missile, and saved his own life only by fleeing to France. He always denied having fired the arrow, though suspicion attached to him all his life. A charcoal-burner carried the king's body to Winchester, where it was buried without any religious ceremony, for, even in those days of license and easy-going religion, it was considered a sacrilege to bestow any rites upon such

Matilda, queen of Henry I, from a statue in the west doorway of Rochester Cathedral

Rufus's deathbed, bishops and abbots attending, from a twelfth-century manuscript

Henry I, Beauclerc, 1100–35

Great seal of Henry I

Great seal of Stephen

a viceful person, who had died unrepentant in the midst of his sins. The most that can be said for the reign of William Rufus was that it checked the aggressions of the barons and prevented his kingdom from falling into the anarchy that existed on the Continent.

It was now the turn of Henry, third son of William the Conqueror, to ascend the throne, he being the first of the Norman kings who was born and educated in England. He had enough of his father's administrative genius to carry out and complete the governmental plans that the Conqueror had organized. He created a supreme court, composed of his secretaries and royal ministers, with a chancellor at the head. Another body was formed, representing the royal vassals, the barons of the exchequer. The top of the table around which they assembled was marked like a checkerboard, and it was from this that the title came.

Rufus and Henry I carried out the plan of their father for holding Wales in subjection. This consisted of building castles on the frontiers and placing them in the charge of nobles, to whom were granted all the lands they could conquer from the Welsh. The sons, in addition to this method, planted a colony of Flemish emigrants in the district of Ross in Pembrokeshire, where they gained wealth by weaving cloth and tilling the ground, and defeated every effort of the Welsh princes to expel them.

A pathetic incident is connected with the reign of Henry. His queen, Matilda, died in 1118 leaving a daughter, Matilda, and an only son. The latter was a proud and vicious youth, whose only merit was the manner of his death. In 1120, when nineteen years old, the ship in which he was crossing the Channel was wrecked. He had put off from the sinking vessel, when the shrieks of his half-sister caused him to row back to her rescue. So many leaped into his boat that it went down, and he and all the noble company were drowned. It was said that from the moment the news was carried to King Henry, he never smiled again.

Although he married again, no children were born to the king, and he decided to settle the crown on his widowed daughter Matilda. The barons were displeased at the thought of being ruled by a woman, but had to consent and swore to sustain her in the succession. Then

her father compelled her to marry Geoffrey, count of Anjou, a youth only sixteen years old. This young man was called "the Handsome," and always wore in his helmet a sprig of the broom-plant of Anjou. Because of this fact, their son Henry II is known in history as *Planta-genct,* the Latin name of the plant being *Planta genista.*

Henry died in 1135. Two candidates for the throne immediately came forward. One was his daughter Matilda and the other his nephew Stephen. Despite the pledge of the barons to support Matilda, the feeling against the rule of a woman was so strong that Stephen was allowed to assume the crown. Four years later Matilda landed in England, determined to see that the wish of her father was carried out. The west of England rallied to her support, while the east stood by Stephen, the allegiance of the barons being divided. Stephen himself was one of the barons who had promised to sustain the queen. The king of the Scots, who was Matilda's uncle, came over the border with an army to help her.

It was in 1139 that Queen Matilda landed in England, and at the time a civil war was in all its fury. At the beginning of 1141, Stephen was taken prisoner at Lincoln, was put in chains and shut up in Bristol Castle. Then Matilda entered London in triumph, but was so scornful because of her success that everyone became disgusted, and she was driven out before she could be

*Stephen of Blois, 1135–54,
nephew of Henry I*

Arms of Stephen

crowned. Some months later, Stephen was exchanged for the earl of Gloucester, and the war raged again. The civil war was finally brought to an end by the bishops in 1153, with the agreement that Stephen should keep the kingdom for his life, and then should be succeeded by Henry, the eldest son of Matilda. Stephen died in the autumn of 1154. He was the last of the Norman kings, their combined reigns having covered almost a century.

The Norman conquest did not materially affect the divisions of society, though nearly all the Saxons were compelled to surrender their rank and estates to the Normans. A noble was a member of the National Council, or, in the case of an earl, he represented the king in the government of a county or earldom. He was not exempted from taxation, and his rank could descend to only one of his children. (The aristocracy in France were noble by birth, their rank passed to all their children, and they were generally exempt from taxation.) No changes were made in the organization of the church during the Norman period, but the principal offices in it were also handed over to the Normans. Learning was confined to the clergy, and the meager schools were connected with the monasteries and nunneries. Few books were written, the principal ones being histories. The old Anglo-Saxon chronicle was continued in English, and the chronicles of William of Malmesbury and Henry of Huntington were written in Latin. The best account of the Norman Conquest is the Bayeux Tapestry, worked in colored worsted and done, supposedly, by Queen Matilda. The length of the canvas is two hundred and fourteen feet, the width about twenty inches, and it consists of seventy-two scenes or pictures from which a clear knowledge can be gained of the armor, dress, and weapons of the period.

THE EARLIER PLANTAGENETS

Henry II, who was fond of wearing the sprig of the broom-plant in his helmet, came to the English throne in 1154. He was the first Plantagenet, but twenty-one years old, strong, coarse, and determined to do right.

Before Henry was crowned, he was one of the most powerful of princes. Although a vassal of the king of France, he was the owner of so many fiefs that he was stronger than his king and all the other vassals. From his father he received Anjou, from his mother, Normandy and Maine, and he gained the county of Poitou and the duchy of Aquitaine by marrying their heiress Eleanor directly after her divorce from Louis VII of France.

England contained more than a thousand castles, which, in the language of an early chronicle, were "nests of devils and dens of thieves." All of these Henry leveled to the ground. He told the great landowners they would pay him *scutage,* or shield money, in lieu of military service. His cunning motive was to hire foreign soldiers with this tax, and thus cause his countrymen to lose their

Henry II, 1154–89 (drawn from the tomb at Fontevrault)

Arms of Henry II

Great seal of Henry II

skill with arms, and be less liable to rebel against him.

He was very fond of Thomas à Becket, who was his chancellor, and he secured the election of Becket as archbishop of Canterbury. Becket was the son of a rich citizen of London, and had given his time to secular matters, but upon becoming archbishop he went to the other extreme, resigned the chancellorship, and led the most austere of lives. This displeased Henry, but before long a cause for more serious quarrel rose between them. It was the law that the bishops should hold courts of their own for the trial of ecclesiastics, but Henry insisted that they should be brought under the jurisdiction of the regular courts. Thomas à Becket would not agree to this, maintaining that the special courts for the trial of the clergy should remain as instituted by William the Conqueror. The king had some new laws passed that were called the Constitutions of Clarendon, because they were passed at that place by a council of the prelates and barons, in January 1164. One of the laws was the special enactment demanded by the king, and another was a decree that all appeals in England should be made to the king and not to the pope.

It was necessary for the archbishop to sign these laws. Being summoned to the royal court he entered the hall with his cross held in his hands. Nothing could affect his resolution to oppose the will of the king. To all the appeals and persuasions of the bishops and nobles, who gathered around him, he calmly shook his head in the negative and replied that he must appeal to the pope.

Many grew impatient and angry, and as he passed out of the hall called after him "Traitor! traitor!"

As might be expected, the pope sustained the archbishop, and Becket had to flee to France to escape the persecutions of King Henry. The quarrel went on for six years, and was intensified by the dispute over the coronation of the king's eldest son, whom Henry wished to make his viceroy in England. The pope declared that no one except the archbishop of Canterbury had the right to crown him, but Henry persuaded the archbishop of York to perform the ceremony.

The king, however, dreaded the anger of the pope, and, through the mediation of Louis VII of France, he patched up his quarrel with Becket, who returned to England, where he was joyfully welcomed. But there was no yielding on his part, and he surprisingly announced that he had in his possession the excommunication of the archbishop of York and his assistant bishops. Upon hearing of this, Henry was seized with one of his wild outbursts of rage and, rolling on the floor in a tantrum,

Henry II and his queen, Eleanor (effigies in the abbey church of Fontevrault)

LINEAGE OF THE ANGEVIN, OR EARLY PLANTAGENET, KINGS OF ENGLAND.

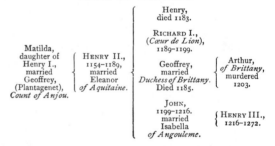

Lineage of the Angevin, or early Plantagenet, kings of England

yelled: "Is there no one who will rid me of this vile priest?"

Four knights who heard the words took it figuratively, riding into the cathedral where the archbishop was celebrating what he knew would be his last church service. The assassins tried to drag him from God's altar; but he resisted them, and they slew him where he stood. Then, they fled in fear.

By his death Becket triumphed. Henry was horrified when told what had been done, and made oath to the pope that he had nothing to do with the crime. He gained general belief in his innocence by kneeling upon the spot reddened by the blood of his former friend, and submitting to a beating like the vilest criminal. The laws that Becket had opposed were not established. The common people of England regarded the archbishop as a martyr, slain for his service to them and the church; and his grave became a shrine to which pilgrimages are made from all over the world.

The close of Henry's life was stormy. His neglected wife and his enemies stirred up his three older sons to rebellion against him. They were Henry, his heir; Richard, who had received the government of Aquitaine; and Geoffrey, who obtained Brittany through his marriage with Constance, the heiress. In 1173, they, in conjunc-

The Angevin Empire of Henry II

tion with a number of nobles of England and Normandy, including the kings of France and Scotland, formed a league against King Henry. He subdued the rebellion and showed leniency toward all except the king of the Scots, who was compelled to submit to a more humiliating vassalage than before, although Henry's successor allowed him to buy back his freedom, with only a shadowy lordship remaining over Scotland.

Henry the younger died in 1183, begging his father's forgiveness; Geoffrey was pardoned, rebelled once more, and died in 1186. Richard was quiet for a time, but it was against his nature, and in 1188 he fled to the king of France for protection, and then seized his father's foreign dominions. In answer to his request for a list of the barons who had joined the league against him, he read among the very first names that of his favorite and youngest son, John. He was so shocked and grieved that he fell into a coma and died in July 1189.

The work done by Henry II was the laying of the foundations of a just government in his country. The Norman method of settling disputes was by trial of battle. This was manifestly so unfair that Henry gave disputants the privilege of deciding their quarrels by reference to the decision of twelve knights of the neighborhood, who were familiar with the facts. This was the real origin of trial by jury, one of the most precious safeguards of modern justice. Another good law was that when the judges passed through a circuit, a grand jury of not less than sixteen was to report to them the criminals of the district. The judges sent the accused to the church to be

Richard Coeur de Lion placing the crown on his own head

Richard I, 1189–99 (from his tomb at Fontevrault)

Great seal of Richard I (Coeur de Lion)

examined by ordeal. If convicted, they were punished, but if acquitted they were ordered to leave the country within eight days. By this method the objectionable characters were effectively removed.

Regarding trial by jury, it must be added that during the reign of John, the son of Henry, in 1215, the church abolished the "ordeal" throughout Christendom. The custom then came into use of choosing a petit jury, familiar with the facts, who decided upon the truth of the accusations laid before the grand jury. In case of disagreement by the petit jury, a decision of the majority was accepted. The objections to this method gradually gave rise to that of summoning witnesses, who testified before the petit jury, with a view of making their decision unanimous. History first records this change in 1350, during the reign of Edward III from which may be dated the modern method of trial by jury, though Henry II was the real founder of the system.

Since the eldest son of Henry had died, he was succeeded in 1189 by his second son, Richard, known in history as *Coeur de Lion,* or the "Lion-Hearted." Richard spent his early years in southern France, the home of music and poetry, and was a dreamer, whose ambition it was to attain military glory. Of magnificent figure, with the physique of a Hercules, and a courage that knew no fear, he was the hero of some of the most marvelous adventures that have ever been related. Although king of England for ten years, he spent less than a year in that country.

Richard went as one of the most valiant of the heroes who sought to rescue the Holy Sepulcher from the Saracens. Hardly had Richard taken the English crown in his strong hands and placed it upon his own head, when he hurried his preparations for a crusade in conjunction with his friend Philip Augustus of France and the emperor of Germany, their Crusade being the third in point of time. Such expeditions demanded enormous sums of money, and Richard resorted to extreme means to obtain what he required. He compelled the Jews to make him loans. He sold earldoms, lands, and public offices. It was at this time that the king of Scotland secured his freedom by the payment of ten thousand marks.

In the summer of 1190, Richard and the French king set out for the Holy Land. They had not gone far before they quarreled, for Richard had a most disagreeable temper, and it was hard for anyone to get along with him. Legend says that in a wrangle with Leopold of Austria the English king delivered a kick that fairly lifted his astounded antagonist off the ground.

Richard failed in his attempt to capture Jerusalem. He forced a landing with his troops at Acre, and performed many heroic feats of individual valor; but the sultan

Saladin was greater than he. When these two were not fighting each other, they met like brothers, and held many talks and discussions over their respective civilizations. Each trusted fully the honor of the other. When King Richard fell desperately ill of a fever, which none of the English physicians could cure, legend says that Saladin asked the privilege of sending his own medical attendant to him. Some of the king's friends suspected treachery and objected, but Richard insisted, and the visitor was led into the English camp at night, and doctored his royal patient so successfully that Richard was soon himself again. Finally, almost broken-hearted over his failure to conquer the Mohammedans, King Richard made a truce with Saladin, and set out to return to his own country.

When the king left England to go on his Crusade, his kingdom was ruled by his justiciars, the first of whom was the chancellor William Longchamp, bishop of Ely. He was honest and faithful to his sovereign, but, being a Frenchman, he hated the English just as intensely as they hated him. He was finally removed from office, and the king's brother John was placed at the head of affairs and he immediately began plotting with the king of France for the throne.

But the weeks and months passed and not a word came from the expected king. The only explanation was that he had met with death on the road. John was delighted, and lost no time in claiming the throne. But, Richard was alive. Various stories have been told of the account of his disappearance. His route compelled him to pass through Germany, and he tried to remain unknown, on account of his quarrel with Leopold, who would have been happy to punish him for the aggravating insult he had received at his hands, or rather his foot. The identity of Richard, however, was discovered.

Richard was seized by Leopold and sold to the German emperor Henry VI, who had him put in irons in a castle in the Tyrol. Blondel, a minstrel who had accom-

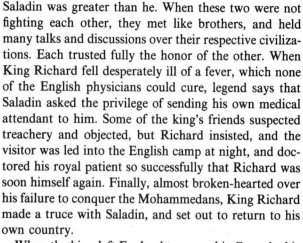

Berengaria, queen of Richard I (from the tomb at Fontevrault)

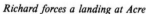

Richard forces a landing at Acre

Blondel hears his master's song

panied Richard to Palestine, set out on a wandering tour through Germany in search of castles rumored to be holding his royal master. At every castle he approached, he sang one of the songs of which the king was fond. At the close of one of those weary days, when he was thus singing at the foot of a tower, he was thrilled by recognizing the voice of his master, who took up the next stanza and sang it through.

All this time, brother John was conspiring with the French king, and urging the emperor to keep Richard in prison, so that John might remain on the throne. But after more than a year's imprisonment, Richard was set free, in February 1194, on condition of paying a ransom so prodigious that it took one-fourth of the personal property of all the noblemen and most of the jewels and silver plate of the churches. It was an outrageous price to pay even for a king.

When Richard came into his own, the only punishment he inflicted on his brother, who had so basely betrayed him, was to take away his lands and castles. In March 1199, Richard quarreled with the viscount of Limoges over a treasure that had been discovered on the estate of the latter and which was claimed by both. While the viscount's castle was being besieged, one of the defenders launched an arrow so well aimed that it pierced the shoulder of the king, who fell, mortally wounded.

Richard, having no children, was succeeded by his brother John, one of the greatest scoundrels that ever cursed England by his rule. When Henry II died he had left John dependent on his brothers, and in jest gave him the nickname of Lackland, which clung to him through life.

Now, the elder brother, Geoffrey, had left a son named Arthur, and the inhabitants of Anjou, which belonged to the English kings from the time of Henry II, wished to have this boy, instead of his uncle John, as their ruler. The French king took the side of Arthur, who had lost his mother a short time before.

"You know your rights," said the king to the young prince, "do you not wish to become king?"

"I do," was the emphatic reply.

"Very well; two hundred knights are ready to march

Richard I (effigy in the abbey church at Fontevrault)

Portrait of King John, 1199–1216 (from his tomb at Worcester)

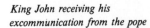

King John receiving his excommunication from the pope

Great seal of King John

King Richard is dying, and the man who shot the fatal arrow has been hauled before him, a terrified prisoner. But for all his faults Richard the Lion-Hearted was as generous as he was brave. He gave orders that the man be set free. But, as soon as their ruler was dead, they put this poor soldier to death.

with you against your own provinces while I advance into Normandy."

Fired by the ambition of asserting his own rights, Arthur placed himself at the head of the little force, which was as eager as he, and advanced against and laid siege to the little town of Mirebeau in Poitou. One of Arthur's noblemen delivered up the town on the night of July 31, 1202, to John, first exacting a promise that no harm should be done to the prince. The besiegers were made prisoners, while Arthur was taken to Rouen and thrown into a dungeon. It is written that on the night of April 3, 1203, the king came to the prison, accompanied by his esquire, Peter de Maulac, and that they took the prince from his dungeon and rowed out in a small boat on the Seine. Arthur, in great fear, begged his uncle to spare his life, promising to do whatever he wished if he would only allow him to live. But the king himself drove a dagger into the body of the poor youth and flung his body overboard. There is little room for doubt that Arthur was slain in this dreadful manner.

Philip, king of France, charged John with the crime and ordered him, as duke of Normandy, to appear at Paris for trial. John was too frightened to obey, whereupon he was proclaimed a traitor, and all his lands on the Continent were declared forfeited. After losing a great deal of territory, he made an effort to regain it, but was crushingly defeated, and Philip seized Normandy and took away from John all his possessions north of the Loire. This seeming misfortune was a great benefit to England, for her kings were now compelled to live among their own subjects and to center their interests and energies in them.

John came back from his defeat soured and revengeful. He insulted and ill treated the clergy to such a degree that Pope Innocent III interfered. With the king still proving stubborn, the pope laid England under an interdict. This meant the entire suppression of all religious services. For two years the church bells were silent. All sacraments were denied to the living and funeral prayers to the dead. The pope next excommunicated John, who laughed with scorn and treated the priests with such brutality that they fled from the country. Then the pope played a trump card by deposing the king and ordering Philip of France to seize the throne.

This brought John to his senses, for he saw himself totally abandoned. He knelt at the foot of the pope's representative, whom he had previously refused to allow to enter England, and promised to make amends with the church and pay a yearly tax of more than £60,000 for permission to keep the English crown upon his head. This satisfied the pope, who removed the interdict and excommunication, and peace was restored. Though the pope had vanquished him, John taxed the people to the point of starvation; he flung those whom he disliked into prison, and refused to bring them to trial.

One day in the summer of 1213, there was a secret meeting in London of the leading men, including Stephen Langton, the newly appointed archbishop of Canterbury. They agreed to form a new code of laws, taken from the ancient charter given by Henry I, and to compel the king to sign it. A few days later, the king was at Mass in the Tower of London, when he was scared almost out of his wits by hearing the angry shouts of the people themselves. In a short time the multitude filed through the streets into the open space in front of the tower. The trembling king went out and timidly asked what it all meant. He was told that the barons had risen against him and the citizens were welcoming them. The terrified John ran out of the back of the tower to the riverside, and escaped by rowing across the river.

As a result of this episode, a monumental historical event took place on the fifteenth of June 1215, at the meadow of Runnymede, on the banks of the Thames. The king's advisers laid before him a parchment that he did not dare refuse to sign. It was the famous Magna Charta, or Great Charter of England. It was the first agreement ever entered into by an English king and his

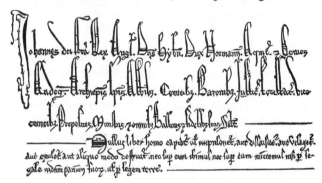

Specimen of Magna Charta, engraved from one of the original copies in the British Museum. The passages are a portion of the Preamble, the Forty-sixth Clause, and the Attestation.

King John (from his monument in Worcester Cathedral)

King John after signing Magna Charta

Henry III, 1216–72 (from his tomb in Westminster Abbey)

Great seal of Henry III

people. It contained sixty-three articles, most of which have become obsolete with time, but three imperishable provisions remain: 1. No free man shall be imprisoned or proceeded against except by his peers or equals, or the law of the land; 2. justice shall not be sold, denied nor delayed; 3. all dues from the people to the king, unless otherwise clearly specified, shall be laid only with the consent of the National Council. The Magna Charta made the English people a united body, and cemented and protected the interests of all classes.

As soon as the assembly had broken up, King John raged like a madman and swore that he would break every one of the laws that he had signed. He begged the aid of the pope who, in response, declared the charter void, promising that if the barons would submit they would suffer excommunication. But they could not be cajoled, and Langton would not pronounce excommunication against them so he was summarily suspended by the pope. John summoned his mercenaries from the Continent, and began ravaging England, invading Scotland to punish the northern barons and their leader, the king of the Scots. It was his custom each morning to burn the house in which he had slept during the night. Finally the barons became so desperate that they offered the crown to Louis, eldest son of the king of France. Louis brought over a French army. In the midst of the fighting, John died, October 28, 1216, and some said from stuffing himself with peaches and ale, while others whispered that he was poisoned by a monk. An epitaph reads that King John died, "a knight without truth, a king without justice, a Christian without faith."

John's eldest son, Henry, was crowned at the age of nine and became King Henry III. During the lad's boyhood, his guardians ruled in his name, and all went fairly well. However, when King Henry came of age, he showed himself to be a degenerate son of a degenerate father. The extravagance of the ruler and his causeless and unsuccessful wars crushed the country under a colossal debt that in these times would be equivalent to $65 billion. To meet the clamors of his numberless creditors, Henry mortgaged the right of extorting money from the Jews to his brother Richard.

When twenty-nine, Henry married Eleanor, daughter of Count Raymond of Provence, a French land bordering on the Mediterranean Sea. Eleanor was brilliant and beautiful.

King John had promised to pay a yearly rental to the pope, who naturally looked upon Henry III as his vassal. The pope sent a legation to England who returned to Rome so laden with treasure that the Great Council of England had to meet to discuss what could be done to avert the financial ruin of the country. The barons were present, and the lesser knights were summoned, but though they conferred earnestly, they were not able to do anything. Finally, one man came to the fore in the person of Simon de Montfort, earl of Leicester. He was a Frenchman, who gained his title from his mother, and had married the sister of the king's wife. Even the king recognized the stern stuff of which his brother-in-law was made. One day, when the royal barge was caught in a thunderstorm on the Thames, the earl, seeing His Majesty's terror, tried to soothe him with assurance that the tempest would soon pass. The king replied, "I fear *you* more than all the thunder and lightning in the world."

When the people came to recognize Simon de Montfort's nobility of character, they gave him the name of Righteous Simon. Simon the Righteous and the Great Council met at Oxford. They resolved that a number of councilors should be appointed whose permission should be necessary before the king could act. To this the king agreed, and the resolutions passed at this meeting were known as the Provisions of Oxford. The government, which promised so much, did not, however, last long, for the members of the council quarreled among themselves, and Henry was soon at war again with the barons. His eldest son, Prince Edward, who had been at times on his father's side, and at other times against him, thought perhaps it would be best to support his parent now, and he joined the royal troops. The two forces met in Sussex, and in the battle of Lewes, in May 1264, Henry and Prince Edward were taken prisoner by the barons. For most of the year following, England was ruled by Simon de Montfort and his councilors.

The most famous act of this patriot was the change he effected in the Great Council of the kingdom. Previously that body had been composed mostly of the barons and bishops, but Simon thought it fair that the lesser tenants, or knights of the shire, should have a voice in making the laws of their country. He therefore arranged that two knights out of each shire should be summoned by writ in the king's name to the national assembly. He provided further that each town and borough should send two citizens, or burgesses, to the Great Council, as the direct representatives of the wishes of the people. This was the beginning of the House of Commons, and the Great Council was, for the first time, called the Parliament, with Simon de Montfort at the head of their affairs.

After a while, the barons fell to quarreling among themselves. Prince Edward effected his escape and began gathering an army. The disaffected barons rallied to him, and the supporters of Simon rapidly fell away, most of them being Welshmen. Simon, the younger, allowed himself to be surprised by Edward and his army at Kenilworth, after which Edward marched against the elder Simon at Evesham, in August 1265. By displaying in front the banners captured at Kenilworth, he deceived Simon and his followers into the belief that friends were approaching. The little company made a valiant fight, but were overpowered, Simon being among the slain. The defeat gave back authority to Henry, who reigned for fifty-six years, his death occurring on November 16, 1272.

EDWARD I AND EDWARD III

Henry's son, Prince Edward, was in the Holy Land on a crusade when his father died, and did not reach home for two years. Though his accession is dated in 1272, he was not actually crowned till 1274. Edward I was surnamed Longshanks, because of his towering stature, which raised him head and shoulders above ordinary men. He was immensely powerful, a fine horseman, his mind was of a superior order, and he ranks as a great statesman and ruler.

He had not been in England long, when he convened a parliament to which the representatives of the people were called. In 1295, toward the close of his reign, the regular Parliament was established with its two branches of Lords and Commons. The term *Lords* included the higher clergy.

The ambition of Edward I was to bring all the island of Britain under his single rule. To the north, Scotland was virtually independent, while Wales on the west was in continual ferment. At the beginning the king set out to annex Wales. He led a strong force there, and, after a number of successes, seemed to have gained his end. To hold his possessions, he built several splendid castles, and garrisoned each with troops, ready to act. Llewellyn, Prince of Wales, after a sturdy resistance was subdued, and peace reigned for several years, though the prince and his people were restless and eager for a chance to free themselves from their yoke. The first one to rise in revolt was David, the brother of the prince. He had fought against Llewellyn, and was under many obligations to Edward. The insurrection became formidable in 1282, but Llewellyn was slain in an encounter with an English knight, and the Welsh chieftains yielded, delivering up David, who was executed in September 1284. Then Wales was united to England, and Edward did all he could to win the goodwill of his new but turbulent subjects.

It is said that the sovereign promised to give the Welsh a ruler who could not speak a word of English, but who

Great seal of Edward I

Queen Eleanor, wife of Edward I (from her tomb in Westminster Abbey)

Edward I, 1272–1307

Edward I on horseback

Coronation chair of Edward I

understood their own language as well as any of his age. The king's son Edward was born in the castle of Caernarvon, in April 1284. Of course he could not utter a syllable of English, and understood the Welsh tongue as well as any other infant of his age, besides which he was unquestionably a native of the country. When, therefore, the king presented the young prince to the Welsh as their future ruler, what could they say? Seventeen years later, the infant was created Prince of Wales, and ever since that time the title has been conferred upon the eldest son of the ruling sovereign of England.

While the king was getting ready to conquer Scotland, a curious opportunity came to him. Two claimants for the Scottish throne presented themselves in the persons of John Baliol and Robert Bruce, the latter a forebearer of the famous king and general of the same name. Both were of Norman descent, and agreed to leave the settlement of their dispute to Edward, who accepted the office of umpire on condition that whoever he selected should first acknowledge the overlordship of England. This was agreed to, and Edward named Baliol; but hardly had the latter been crowned, when he renounced his allegiance and allied himself to France. Edward pushed his campaign so inflexibly against the Scots that they were compelled to yield. Baliol surrendered the crown in 1296, and Edward seized Scotland. He received the homage of the Scottish parliament and placed Englishmen in all the leading offices. At the Abbey of Scone, near Perth, the English seized the piece of rock on which the Scotch kings were always placed at their coronation. According to legend, this stone had been the pillow of Jacob at Bethel, and wherever the talisman was, there the Scots should reign. Edward placed the stone, enclosed in a throne, in Westminster Abbey, where both remain. Every British sovereign since then has been crowned upon them.

Still the struggle continued. Robert Bruce, grandson of the previous claimant to the throne, proposed to Comyn, a powerful Scottish lord, that whichever of the two established his claim to the crown, should bequeath the kingdom by way of indemnity to the other. Comyn made the agreement, but he intended treachery from the first, and took the earliest occasion to send a warning of the conspiracy to Edward. Bruce was in England at the time and would have been arrested but for a warning, which was sent in a curious way to him. One day a messenger called and handed Bruce a pair of spurs. Now, since spurs are used to hasten the speed of a horse, Bruce could not mistake the meaning of the present. He immediately mounted his horse and made off, with no suspicion of the person who had betrayed him. While fleeing, he met a servant of Comyn who was bearing papers to the king. Bruce took the papers from him and thus discovered who the traitor was. Hardly a week later he and Comyn met at Dumfries. The former called his false friend into a neighboring chapel, and told him what he

had learned. The proof was too clear for Comyn to deny the charge, and he blustered. A fierce quarrel followed, and Bruce drove his dagger into the other, who fell on the steps of the altar. Horrified at what he had done, Bruce hurried out and met one of his friends, who, observing his agitated manner, asked what had taken place.

"I think I have killed Comyn," replied Bruce.

"You *think* so," said his friend, "then I will make sure of it."

Hurrying into the chapel he slew Comyn, as well as an uncle who tried to defend him.

Feeling that he was now an outlaw, Bruce raised the standard of independence and, surrounded by a number of priests and lords, was crowned at Scone. Thus on the Day of Annunciation (1306) Scotland had again a king.

The great blot upon the reign of Edward was his expulsion of the Jews. In answer to the demands of the people, who accused them of extortion, he stripped the unfortunates of their possessions, and drove them from the country. So completely did they vanish from English history that not until the time of Cromwell, more than four centuries later, were they heard of again.

It was while marching against Robert Bruce in Scotland that King Edward I died, in the year 1307. He was succeeded by his son Edward II who was a weak, contemptible scamp.

Spurred by the weakness of the king, Robert Bruce resolutely pressed his struggle for the independence of

Edward I and the assassin

Edward II, 1307–27

Great seal of Edward II

Scotland. Edward set out in 1314 with an army to stamp out the rebellion, but in the battle of Bannockburn, June 24, he was utterly routed by Bruce's greatly inferior force.

Again and again during the remainder of Edward's reign Bruce and his forces ravaged the northern counties of England and withdrew unpunished. At last, in 1328, the kingship of Robert Bruce and the full independence of Scotland was formally acknowledged by treaty.

The Scottish king thereon resolved to absolve himself of his many crimes by going on a crusade to the Holy Land. He died before he could follow out his purpose, and his chief lord, James of Douglas, took the dead king's heart from his body to bear it to Jerusalem. James perished in a skirmish with the Saracens, but his followers fulfilled his mission, and the heart of Scotland's greatest leader was entombed in the Holy City. The independence of Scotland was never again disputed, and the two halves of the British island remained separate until they were peaceably united in 1603 under the sway of a common sovereign, James I of England and VI of Scotland.

Isabelle of France, wife of the king, detested Edward II, and openly formed an attachment for Roger Mortimer, one of the chief barons. Under Mortimer's lead a

force was raised that captured and locked up the king in Kenilworth Castle, Warwickshire. Commissioners from Parliament were sent to him with a demand that he should surrender the crown. The coward of a man complied, and then thanked his callers for making his young son his successor. Some time later, his wife incited Mortimer to murder her husband.

Since Edward III was only fourteen years old when his father was deposed, the government rested nominally in a council, but the real rulers were Queen Isabelle and her partner Mortimer. They treated the new king as if he were a prisoner. They were soon to find, however, that he was made of sterner stuff than his father. The dissatisfaction with the queen and Mortimer was so intense that young Edward found friends all around him. With their help he shook off his restraints and, in company with a number of daring companions, entered Nottingham Castle by a secret underground passage, and dashed into the room where the queen and Mortimer were staying. Mortimer was carried off as a prisoner and soon after brought to the gallows (November 1330). The queen was placed in confinement in Castle Rising, Norfolk, and kept there for the rest of her life.

We come now to that period in history known as the Hundred Years' War. For some time, the English and French kings had been bitterly jealous of each other. There were quarrels over the lands owned by England in France, and over the homage that the king of England had to pay because of these lands to the king of France as his "overlord." The enmity was intensified by the action of the French ruler in helping the Scots in their war against England, and by the affrays between the sailors on the French and English ships in the English Channel. Such was the state of affairs when Edward III came to the throne in 1327. He lost no time in allying

Queen Philippa, wife of Edward III (from the tomb of Westminster Abbey)

Effigy of Edward II (Gloucester Cathedral)

The tower in Berkeley Castle where Edward II was murdered. Investigation revealed that he suffered a horrible death, dying of a red-hot poker being forced into his bowels.

Edward III (from a wall painting, formerly in St. Stephen's Chapel, Westminster)

Edward III, 1327–77

Great seal of Edward III

himself with the people of Flanders, against whom the French king had made war.

When the French king died, Edward claimed the throne through his mother, who was the daughter of Philip IV, an earlier king of France. The claim was a poor one, but Edward thought his course would please his Flemish friends, besides giving employment to hundreds of turbulent barons, who were dangerous when they were left idle. Edward gained his first victory with his ships off Sluys, in June 1340.

After several years of desultory fighting Edward, in 1346, was making a raid through the French territories of Normandy, when King Philip of France pursued him with a force far larger than his own. Edward was on the bank of the River Somme, and dared not fight with the stream at his rear. All day he rode along the shore of the Somme looking for a ford. His men were hard pressed and exhausted, the French close behind them. At length

Edward III, and the countess of Salisbury

the ebbing tide gave Edward a chance to cross. Then the returning tide covered the ford, and King Philip and his huge army could pursue no farther till the next day.

Edward, advancing at a leisurely pace, planted his army in a strong place near the village of Crecy. "Here," he said, "we will await the Frenchmen."

The famous Battle of Crecy that followed on the next day, August 26, 1346, was the greatest of King Edward's victories. During the contest Edward, Prince of Wales, only sixteen years old, was placed in such peril that the earl of Warwick, who was near him, became greatly alarmed and sent an urgent request to the king for reinforcements.

"Is the prince wounded?" asked the king.

"Thank God, not yet, sire."

"Is he unhorsed?"

"No, sire, but he is in the greatest possible danger."

"He shall have no aid from me; let him win his spurs."

The son was called the Black Prince, because of the color of his armor, and he won his spurs on that eventful day, for no veteran knight could have acquitted himself more bravely. The French were completely defeated and fled in despair, and Edward the Black Prince became one of the most heroic figures in English history.

Through the efforts of Pope Clement VI, a truce was brought about. But the Scots had taken advantage of Edward's absence to invade England. They were defeated at Nevill's Cross, in October 1346, and David Bruce, their king, was taken prisoner.

The truce ended, and war with France was renewed in 1355. Edward the Black Prince was once more its hero. He started from the English possessions in southern France and made a raid similar to that in which his father had formerly devastated Normandy. The French, under a new king, John the Good, pursued him with a force vastly outnumbering his own. The Frenchmen rode so fast that they got between the prince and his destined goal, shutting him off from escape. He was in a trap.

Before attacking the little band of sturdy Englishmen, King John the Good sent one of his churchmen, Cardinal Perigord, to urge Edward to surrender. The prince, knowing his men were exhausted as well as overmatched, was ready to agree to almost any terms of peace. So all day long Perigord was kept riding between the hostile camps. King John, however, would listen to nothing less than the absolute surrender of Prince Edward with one hundred of his best knights. That would be to accept the battle as lost without fighting it, and the English scornfully refused, besides Edward's troops were now rested.

So on September 19, 1356, the Battle of Poitiers was fought. It was the counterpart of Crecy. The English bowmen and the English knights were invincible. The vast horde of Frenchmen fled. King John was taken prisoner. The Black Prince treated him with the greatest courtesy, complimented him on the courage he had displayed in battle, and entertained him at dinner that evening.

A peace was made at Bretigny in May 1360, which checked the fighting for the time. By the terms of this treaty, Edward yielded his claims to the throne of France, but retained Aquitaine, Calais, and some other districts, while John was given permission to ransom himself for 3 million gold crowns. Being ruler at Bordeaux, as prince of Aquitaine, the Black Prince aided the dethroned king of Castile, Pedro the Cruel, and by a victory at Navarette regained his kingdom for him. Pedro had promised to pay the expenses of Edward, but now refused to do so. The prince was not only deeply involved in debt, but his health was broken and he went back to Bordeaux a changed man. He levied a burdensome tax, and the resentful nobles appealed to the French king, Charles V, who immediately renewed the war. The prince, though weak in body, made a brave fight, and retook Limoges.

After this battle, the Black Prince returned to England and another truce was declared. The king's third son, the duke of Lancaster (also called John of Gaunt) took control of affairs, for the Black Prince was near death, and his next brother was feeble.

And now, with the death of King Edward III, a boy was once more heir to the throne, for Richard, son of the Black Prince, was only eleven years old when he became king in 1377. Parliament decreed that the government during his minority should be vested in a council, but it did not take John of Gaunt long to gain control of affairs. He was unprincipled, extravagant, an enemy of reform, and was detested by the laboring classes.

The country was ready for revolt, and a poll tax was the spark that fired the magazine. A brutal collector went into the house of a workman named Wat Tyler, and so shamefully insulted his daughter that the father took a hammer, ran in, and with a single blow stretched the ruffian dead on the floor. The news of what had been done spread like wildfire, and the excited peasants left their huts and fields, armed themselves with clubs or any rusty weapons upon which they could lay hands, and, with Wat Tyler at their head, hurried to London to demand justice.

They felt that the only way of securing what they wished was by violence, and gave full vent to their anger. Reaching London they held the city for three weeks, burned the law courts and killed the lawyers, looking upon them as their enemies. Then, with their numbers swelled to a hundred thousand, they straggled on to Smithfield, still eager for violence. There the young king rode boldly out to meet them. He assured them that from that time forward they should all be free men and never again be held as serfs. Some were satisfied and went home. But in a few days the storm broke again, and once more the king rode out to meet them. Wat Tyler laid his hand on Richard's bridle, whereon Walworth, mayor of

London, struck the rebel down with a dagger. His death caused consternation in the ranks of his followers, and the insurrection collapsed as quickly as it had risen. Parliament effected a series of merciless executions, and refused to discuss any of the schemes that Richard had promised, and which he was disposed to favor; so the last condition of the peasants was worse than before.

In 1387, the opponents of the king gained the upper hand and banished or executed a number of Richard's friends; but he soon secured control, and took savage

John of Gaunt

Edward III (from his tomb at Westminster Abbey)

Edward III in the seizure of Mortimer

Windsor Castle, erected by Edward III, who was born at Windsor, on the site of an ancient castle presented by Edward the Confessor to the monks of Westminster

St. George's Chapel at Windsor Castle

Edward III crossing the Somme

*Cardinal Perigord and the
Black Prince before Poitiers*

Tomb of Edward the Black Prince in Canterbury Cathedral

*Richard II, 1377–99. When Richard's skeleton was exhumed in 1871
he was found to be nearly six feet tall. It is known that he had thick
yellow hair and he has been credited with inventing the use of the
handkerchief. He has been called "the best and royalest vyander [eater]
of all Christian kings."*

*Anne of Bohemia, 1366–94,
first queen consort of Richard II*

Great seal of Richard II

Richard II in his armor

Penny of Richard II

Banishment of Bolingbroke and Norfolk by Richard II

Funeral of Richard II

vengeance upon those who had opposed him. He governed well for nine years, then his first wife died. This was in 1394, and two years later the king married Isabelle, daughter of Charles VI of France, a girl only eight years old. His purpose in taking this amazing step was to secure an extended truce with France, but the act was very unpopular with his own countrymen, who hated France. Since his uncle, the duke of Gloucester, had led the opposition against him, Richard by a daring act of treachery had him seized in 1397, and carried off to France. He was placed in the charge of the governor of Calais, who soon sent back the desired message that he had died. Since there was no doubt that the duke had been murdered by order of the king, his enemies were terrified into quietude.

Two of the noblemen who had aggrieved him still remained unpunished. They were Mowbray, duke of Norfolk, and Henry of Bolingbroke, duke of Hereford, a son of John of Ghent. Each suspected the other of betraying him, and a duel was arranged. Just as they were about to fight, Richard stopped the contest and banished Hereford for ten years, Norfolk for life. John of Ghent died shortly afterward, and the king seized his estates, which should have passed to Hereford. The latter, now duke of Lancaster, waited until Richard went on an expedition to Ireland. then he came back to England. Accompanied by Archbishop Arundel, another exile, he landed July 4, 1399, with a few armed men, at a seaport on the Humber, where they were immediately joined by the influential northern family of Percy. Followers flocked to them until their number swelled to sixty thousand, while Edmund, duke of York, uncle of the king, who was acting as regent, also turned against his master.

A fortnight passed before Richard heard of what was going on. He was so perplexed that he remained still longer in Ireland, but his troops steadily deserted, and he was persuaded to leave his hiding place by Percy, earl of Northumberland, who turned him over to Henry of Lancaster. The king was brought to London where, under

Derived from the three sons of Edward III.: John of Gaunt, Duke of Lancaster, Lionel, Duke of Clarence, and Edmund, Duke of York ; showing, also, the connection of the Neville family with that of York, and the Beauforts with the Tudors.

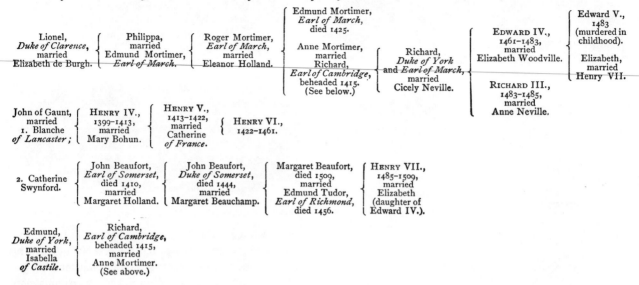

Lineage of the royal houses of Lancaster, York, and Tudor

compulsion, he resigned his crown, and the next day, September 30, was formally deposed by the Lords and Commons on the charge of misgovernment. When this was done, Henry of Lancaster claimed the crown, on the ground of being a descendant of Henry III. Archbishop Arundel conducted him to the throne. Thus Henry of Bolingbroke, duke of Lancaster and son of John of Ghent, became king of England in 1399, as Henry IV. Richard had rebuilt Westminster Hall, and the first Parliament that met there deposed him. He was confined to Pontefract Castle, Yorkshire, where he died after Henry's accession. There is reason to believe that his death was due to violence or starvation, which might have been voluntary or forced upon him.

THE HOUSES OF LANCASTER AND YORK

Next is a study of one of the most absurd and inexcusably criminal episodes in the history of England. The solitary redeeming feature about it is that it affected the upper classes only, and the losses, deaths, and disasters fell upon them. The episode is known as the Wars of the Roses, and, in order to understand it, one must keep a number of historical facts in mind.

Now, you have just learned that Henry IV of Bolingbroke was elected king in 1399. He was not the legal heir, because Edmund Mortimer, earl of March, was de-

The lineage of Lancaster and York—Edward III

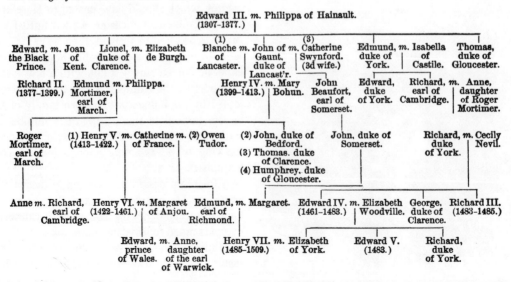

Prince Henry offers his life when his father doubts his loyalty upon return of the crown.

Henry IV, 1399–1413

Great seal of Henry IV

The coronation of Henry IV

Queen Joan of Navarre, second wife of Henry IV (from the tomb at Canterbury)

Signature of Henry IV, consisting of the initials H.R. for Henricus Rex

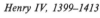

scended from an older branch of the family, and his claim therefore was superior to that of Henry, who was the *elected* king, being chosen by a special act of Parliament. Edmund Mortimer was a young child, and the people had had enough of boy kings, so they willingly assented to a setting aside of the regular succession.

When Henry IV came to the throne, the dethroned king, Richard, was pining in Pontefract Castle. Almost immediately the new monarch learned of a plot to release Richard and restore him to power. The conspiracy was readily crushed, and a month later Richard was found dead in his apartments. There can be little doubt that he was put to death by order of Henry, who had his body brought to London and exposed to public view, in order that the people might not think wrongly in the matter.

A good many believed the body shown was not that of Richard. Among these was Owen Glendower, a prominent Welshman, who had been a devoted friend of Richard, and who proved his sincerity by gathering a large number of men to make a fight for the restoration of Richard's rights. King Henry led his forces in vain against Glendower, who was soon aided by still more powerful friends.

Henry never would have obtained the throne but for the help of the wealthy and influential Percy family. They spent immense sums to aid him, and naturally expected a royal recognition of their services. This being denied, they turned against the king and joined Glendower in the attempt to win the crown for Richard, if still alive, or else for the earl of March. What specially angered Sir Henry Percy was the refusal of Henry to ransom the brother-in-law of Percy, who was a prisoner of Glendower. This relative was Sir Edmund Mortimer, uncle of the boy of the same name, who was the hereditary heir to the English throne. Young Sir Henry was such a fiery fighter against the Scots that they nicknamed him Hotspur. A formidable alliance was made by this impetuous youth, his father, and his uncle, the earl of Worcester, when they joined Glendower and the Scottish earl Douglas in the resolution to dethrone Henry IV.

The two armies met at Shrewsbury, on the border of Wales, July 23, 1403, and fought an obstinate battle. It is said that Henry was told that a number of his enemies had sworn to seek him out and slay him. To baffle the

Tomb of Henry IV and his queen at Canterbury Cathedral

Henry V on horseback

A Parliament of the time of Henry V

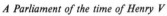

*Henry V being armed
by his esquires*

Queen Catherine, wife of Henry V

Entry of Henry V into London

Henry V of England, 1413–22

Groat of Henry V

Great seal of Henry V

plot several knights donned armor like the king's, and every one paid with his life for the chivalrous act. The revolutionists, however, were routed, Hotspur was killed, and Worcester taken prisoner and executed as a traitor, as were a number of his leading companions. The elder Percy, who was not present, declared that his son had acted contrary to his orders, and he thus escaped punishment, only to lose his life in a subsequent rebellion. Although the power of Glendower was broken, he never made submission, and there were continual insurrections in Wales.

A statute was passed in 1401 against the heretics, which decreed that all who refused to abjure their heresy or, after abjuration, relapsed, should be delivered to the secular authorities to be burned. The first Wycliffte martyr was William Sawtry, a London clergyman, who was burned at Smithfield, in London, February 12, 1401.

Henry's health broke before he was fifty. It is said that he often suffered from the reproaches of his conscience, and had arranged to go on a crusade, but while praying at the tomb of Edward the Confessor, in Westminster Abbey, he was stricken with a fatal illness, and died a few days later, on March 20, 1413.

The son of the dead king reigned from 1413 to 1422, as Henry V. While he was the Prince of Wales he was a wild, roistering fellow, but when he came to the throne, the responsibility of it sobered him, and he gave all of his energies to his new duties.

The opportunity for attacking France was too good to be lost for the country torn by the intriguing and ambitious dukes, who hated one another more than they hated the English. So Henry raised an army and invaded the distracted country. He sailed from Southampton in August 1415. With eight thousand troops he reached a point in France halfway between Crecy and Calais. The French troops were eight times as numerous as the English. But a drenching rain fell during the night, and made the ground so soggy that the land that the French had to cross became a mass of mud in which the horsemen floundered. A great advantage rested with the English bowmen, who, being dismounted, could move readily. The English gained a striking victory, which is known in history as the Battle of Agincourt, because of the name of the castle standing near the battleground.

Great was the rejoicing in England over this wonderful triumph of her yeomen. King Henry was received on his return with acclaim, and there was no longer any question of his right to sit upon the throne.

The young king led a second and larger army to France in 1417, and, profiting by the dissensions of the French, captured one city after another, until all Normandy was in his hands. By the treaty of Troyes in 1420, Paris itself surrendered. Henry married Catherine, the daughter of the French king. The part of France he had already conquered became England's property.

So here was a second crown ready to fall into the hands of this remarkable man, as yet scarcely out of his youth. It was too much good fortune. Henry died in 1422, while still busy crushing out the smoldering sparks of discontent in his new realm of France. Henry's body was brought back to England and buried in Westminster Abbey.

He left a son—also named Henry—only nine months old, whose title was king of England and France, but whose uncle, the duke of Bedford, reigned as regent. This uncle carried on the war in France, where some of the nobles upheld the son of Charles VI to succeed his father who had also died in 1422. This new king, the young Charles VII, was defeated again and again, until the victorious British laid siege to Orleans. The siege of the city was raised through the inspiration of Joan of Arc. In the end, the English were driven out of France, and the Hundred Years War closed in their defeat in 1453. England no longer owned the Norman soil, her only possession being the city of Calais.

By this time Henry VI had been nominally king of England for thirty years, but he was growing feeble. In 1453 a son, Edward, was born to Henry. This promised to perpetuate the rule of the Lancastrian kings who had come into power with Henry IV. Now, there were still living descendants of the older branch of the royal family, who had hoped to be some day recalled to the throne. Chief of these at the time was Richard, duke of York, nephew of the Edmund Mortimer who had been set up as a rival to Henry IV. This Richard ranked as the highest nobleman of the kingdom, and when the feeble King Henry VI became in 1453 temporarily insane, Richard of York was appointed regent.

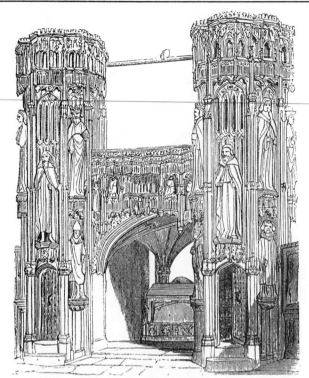

Front of Henry V's chantry, Westminster Abbey

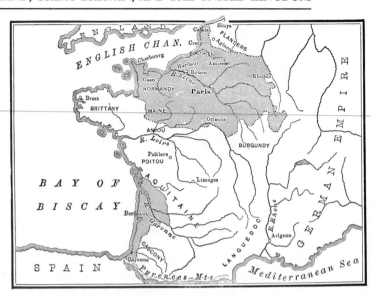

French territory held by the English when Joan of Arc appeared

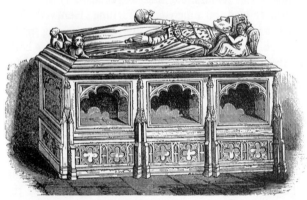

Tomb of Henry V in Westminster Abbey

Henry VI. From a portrait—artist unknown—in Eton College, which he founded. Although the English kings since Edward III had claimed to be kings of both England and France, Henry VI was the only English king ever crowned in France with that title.

Marriage of Henry VI and Margaret of Anjou

Henry VI, 1422–61; 1470–71, in his youth

Queen Margaret

Margaret of Anjou, from an old manuscript

Henry VI

*Tomb of Henry VI,
formerly at Windsor*

Signature of Henry VI

Great seal of Henry VI

He took advantage of his power to crush the leading nobles of the Lancastrian party. The king's friends, alarmed, declared him once more capable of reigning, and would have ousted the duke of York from the regency, but Richard took up arms to defend his position.

The earl of Warwick, the wealthiest and most powerful man in England, joined Richard, and the Wars of the Roses began. They were to devastate England for thirty years. The peculiar name Wars of the Roses was given them because the badge of the party of the king, the Lancastrians, was a red rose, while that of the rebellious Yorkists was a white rose.

This terrible civil struggle, which went on for thirty years, was, in truth, merely a shameless scramble for spoils, there being no real principle involved. In the first conflict at St. Albans, in 1455, the Yorkists gained a victory, as they did at Bloreheath, Staffordshire, and at Northampton, where Henry was taken prisoner, and Queen Margaret fled with the young prince Edward to Scotland. Richard demanded the crown, but Henry made a spirited refusal. Finally a compromise was agreed upon, by which Henry was to remain in possession of his throne till his death, when Richard or his heirs was to succeed him.

But the queen refused to allow her son to be set aside. She hurried down from Scotland to the north of England, and was joined by several powerful lords. The duke of York, with some five thousand men, set out in the winter of 1460 to meet her. He lodged in a castle near Wakefield, and Queen Margaret dared him to come out and fight her. His generals urged him to wait where he was until joined by his brave son, the earl of March. The duke did not heed this advice, and he accepted the challenge. His forces were cut to pieces, and he was made prisoner. His exultant captors set him upon an anthill and mockingly kicked him, while chanting, "Hail, king, who has no kingdom! Hail, prince, without a people; we trust your Grace is well and happy!"

Then they cut off the head of the duke, fixed it to the end of a pole, and handed it to the delighted Margaret. She had some paper doubled up in imitation of a crown, and placed it on the head, which was then fastened on the walls of York. From that time forward neither side gave quarter in their battles.

The next year the Lancastrians suffered a bloody repulse at Towton, where the snow was crimsoned by more than twenty thousand corpses. It is one of the incomprehensible mysteries of human nature that these friends and neighbors should thus murder one another for no other object than to help the ambitious schemes of a wretched set of ambitious nobles.

The earl of Warwick, who commanded the Yorkists at Towton, earned the name of the King-maker. He had made Richard almost king. Now he set the eldest son of the murdered duke firmly upon the throne, as Edward IV. Margaret and Henry took refuge in Scotland and,

Edward IV, 1461–70; 1471–83   *Queen Elizabeth Woodville*

"Angel" of Edward IV

refusing to obey the summons of the new government,
were proclaimed traitors. Henry was captured four years
later and imprisoned in the Tower of London.

All through the reign of Edward IV (1461–83) the
Wars of the Roses raged. The king married Elizabeth
Woodville, who had no rank or money, and he distributed grand titles and estates so lavishly among his lady's
relatives that the earl of Warwick became jealous. To
make good his rights as King-maker he managed to oust
Edward and return Henry to the throne. A few months
later, however, Warwick was killed at the Battle of Bar-
net (1471), and King Henry was sent back to the tower,
where he was secretly murdered on the same day that

Edward IV

Great seal of Edward IV

*Murdered prince called
Edward V, 1483, from
an old manuscript*

Signature of Edward V

Earl Rivers presenting Caxton to Edward IV

The Tower of London at the time of Henry VI

The layout of the Tower of London

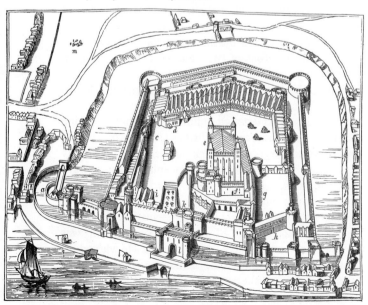

The Bloody Tower

Edward resumed his briefly interrupted reign. Margaret kept up the struggle. In the desperate battle of Tewkesbury (1471) her son was slain and she was made prisoner. After five years of captivity she was ransomed by Louis XI of France, and died in her own country of Anjou.

Edward IV lived a pampered life with no fear of another rebellion, since the Wars of the Roses had killed or financially ruined the barons. He added to his enormous wealth by compelling his subjects to give him large sums of money, which he called benevolences. There was only one person whom he had real cause to distrust, and that was his brother, the duke of Gloucester, who plotted for long years to obtain the throne of England. Miserable and worn out, Edward died in 1483, leaving his widow, five young daughters, and two little sons, Edward, the heir to the throne, and Richard, duke of York. Edward, who is called Edward V, though he never received the crown, was only twelve years old, and was placed under the guardianship of his uncle, the hunchback miscreant Richard, duke of Gloucester, who was appointed lord protector of the realm until the lad became of age.

Meeting the princes on the road to London in charge of their half-brother, Sir Richard Grey, and their uncle, Lord Rivers, the hypocritical duke of Gloucester insisted on taking personal charge of the young king. Then, on the pretense that the prince would be safer in the Tower of London than at Westminster Palace, he sent him to the great prison to pine in solitude.

The incredible villainy of Richard was not long in showing itself. Lord Hastings had voted to make him protector, but he was too honorable to assist him in seizing the crown. Richard accused Lord Hastings of treason, and had him beheaded without a hearing or trial. This left the way clear for the duke to carry out his atrocious purpose toward his two young nephews.

The Bloody Tower—north side

The princes in the Tower

Portrait of Richard III, 1483–85

Anne, queen of Richard III   *Richard III*

The queen mother, sensing the evil intention of her brother-in-law, took her other son and his two sisters, and fled to the sanctuary of Westminster Abbey. After long persuasion, with profuse promises and partial force, Richard induced her to yield her other son to his care. Historians of the period believed that by direct orders of Richard, the princes were smothered to death in the Tower of London, and the finding, a couple of centuries later, of the skeletons of two children corresponding in age to the princes, and buried at the foot of the stairs leading to the room where they were imprisoned, leaves little doubt as to the fate of the lads.

Richard gained enough influential friends to bring about his accession to the throne as Richard III. He strove to win the goodwill of his subjects, but his cruelty created an undercurrent of implacable enmity toward him. Inquiries, too, began to be heard as to what had become of the two princes.

Before Richard became king he persuaded the widow of that Edward (son of Margaret the queen) who was killed at Tewkesbury, to become his wife. He wanted his own son to marry Elizabeth, the eldest sister of the two murdered princes, thereby strengthening the succession of his family to the throne. But the son died and the king

Signature of Richard III

Great seal of Richard III

Richard III forcing his nephew from the protection of Lord Rivers

Bosworth Field—the crown of Richard placed on Henry's head

"disposed" of his own wife, then determined to marry the Princess Elizabeth himself.

But the princess was already engaged to Henry Tudor, earl of Richmond, who had been patiently waiting for years to strike a blow for the crown that he claimed by virtue of his illegitimate descent from the House of Lancaster. Convinced that his opportunity had come at last, he landed with six thousand men at Milford Haven, Wales, in 1485, and pushed on against King Richard.

He met Henry, August 22, 1485, at Bosworth Field, in Leicestershire, where the decisive battle was fought between the rival and pestilent houses of Lancaster and York. Richard strove with a skill and desperation that would have won the day, but for the treachery of many of his followers. At first, his army was twice as numerous as Henry's, but its disaffection more than equalized the strength of the combatants. Richard plunged into the thickest of the fight and, catching sight of Henry among a group of his knights, strove furiously to reach him. He hewed down the Lancastrian standard-bearer, fiercely unhorsed a knight, and struck viciously at Henry himself, but Sir William Stanley parried the blow, and the swarming foes struck Richard from his horse and killed him as he lay on the ground.

Rulers of England during the growth and decline of kingly power

After the battle the crown of Richard was found under a hawthorn bush where it had rolled. Picking it up, stained with blood as it was, Lord Stanley set it on the head of Henry amid cries of "Long live King Henry!" So, it was the only time in English history a king was killed and a king was crowned on the field of battle. On the same night a horse was led up to the church of the Gray Friars at Leicester, with a sack tied across its back. In it was the body of the last of the Plantagenet line, King Richard III, slain in the thirty-second year of his age, after a brief reign of only two years.

THE GROWTH OF ROYAL POWER UNDER THE TUDOR KINGS

The marriage of Henry VII to the princess Elizabeth, sister of the murdered princes and true heiress of the House of York, blended the white and the red roses and ended the civil war. The wedding took place a few months after the king's accession, and today in the east window of stained glass in the burial chapel of Henry VII, in Westminster Abbey, one may see the Roses joined.

With this the beginning of the House of Tudor was ushered in for a long period of almost absolute kingly power. The nobility were so few in number that they were no longer to be feared, and the clergy as well as the people welcomed strong, centralized, conservative government. Henry was cunning and avaricious. By keeping out of foreign wars, he avoided the necessity of calling Parliament together and asking for grants of money. He strove to avoid taxing the poorer classes, since they were the most numerous, for he was anxious to hold his popularity with them. He revived the system of benevolences, and with the aid of his chief minister, Cardinal Morton, wrung large sums from the rich.

Henry VII greatly advanced his own interests through the marriages he arranged. That of his daughter Margaret with James IV of Scotland opened the way for the union of the two kingdoms, while the marriage of his eldest son Arthur to Catherine of Aragon, daughter of the king of Spain, secured the alliance of Spain against France. When Arthur died a few months later, his father obtained a dispensation from the pope that permitted him to marry his younger son Henry to Arthur's widow, and it was this son who became Henry VIII of England. The rapacity of the king enabled him, when he died in 1509, to leave a vast fortune to Henry VIII, who was eighteen years old when he succeeded to the throne.

Within a few years after Henry's accession Martin

Lineage of the Tudor family of English sovereigns, from Henry VII, 1485–1509

HENRY VII., 1485–1509, married Elizabeth, (daughter of Edward IV.).	Margaret, married James IV. of Scotland.	James V., of Scotland, married Mary of Guise.	Mary, Queen of Scots.
	HENRY VIII., 1509–1547 married	1. Katharine of Aragon.	MARY, 1553–1558.
		2. Anne Boleyn.	ELIZABETH, 1558–1603.
		3. Jane Seymour.	EDWARD VI., 1547–1553.

Lineage of the Tudor family of English sovereigns, from Henry VII, 1485–1509

LINEAGE OF HENRY VII. FROM JOHN OF GAUNT, THIRD SON OF EDWARD III.

John of Gaunt, 1340–1399, married (third wife) Catherine Swynford.	John Beaufort, Earl of Somerset.	John Beaufort, 1st Duke of Somerset.	Margaret, married Edmund Tudor, Earl of Richmond.	HENRY VII.

Lineage of Henry VII from John of Gaunt, third son of Edward III

Elizabeth of York, queen consort of Henry VII

Signature of Henry VII

Henry VII. Henry saw two principal duties before him when he came to the throne: (1) to heal the factions in the kingdom; (2) to establish a firm, strong government. It can be said with justice that he did both.

The rose-rial coin of Henry VII

Henry VII on horseback

Luther began his great battle against the doctrines and power of the papacy. It was in 1517 he nailed on the door of the church of Wittenberg his protests that led to the movement against the Church of Rome. Henry VIII was a firm Catholic, and some time later published a reply to one of Luther's works and sent a sumptuously bound copy to the pope, who was so pleased that he conferred on him the title of Defender of the Faith, which, rather strangely, has been retained by every English sovereign since that time.

France and Spain were becoming powerful nations, and Henry was ambitious to take a hand in the continental wars that he might gain some advantage. There was jealousy between the emperor of Germany and the king of France, and each naturally tried to gain the favor of the English king. He coquetted with both. In alliance with the German emperor in 1513, he defeated the French cavalry at Guinegate, who fled in such headlong haste that the conflict was called the Battle of the Spurs. The Scots took advantage of the war and invaded England, but were defeated by the earl of Surrey, September 9, 1513, at Flodden, where their king James IV, with some of the foremost of the nation, was left dead on the field. Peace was made the following year and, in June 1520, a series of friendly meetings took place between the new French king, Francis I, and Henry, which were on

Henry VII delivering to John Islip, the abbot of Westminster, the Book of Indenture (Agreement), which specified the number of masses, collections, and other church obligations "for the repose of the souls of the King's wife, father, and other relatives."

The great seal of Henry VII

Catherine of Aragon. A marriage between Henry's eldest son, Arthur, and Catherine of Aragon, the youngest daughter of Ferdinand V and Isabella of Spain, took place in 1501, the bride being sixteen and the bridegroom fifteen years old. A few months later, the bridegroom died, and negotiations were opened for a marriage of Catherine to the king's younger son, his namesake, Henry, then heir to the throne; but some years passed before that fateful marriage was brought about.

The great brass screen enclosing the altar tomb of Henry VII and his queen in his chapel at Westminster Abbey

such a scale of splendor that the meeting place was called the Field of the Cloth of Gold. The grand display, however, proved of no advantage to the French king, for Henry soon made an alliance with the emperor Charles V, and in 1522 a new war was launched against France, which closed three years later with an agreement of the French sovereign to pay a large annual pension to the English king.

Henry VIII was certain to break before long with the church, of which he was at first so valiant a defender. He had as his adviser one of the ablest and most unscrupulous of men in Thomas Wolsey, a priest who was able to reach the loftiest position. He climbed upward as archbishop of York, chancellor, cardinal, papal legate, and hoped, with seemingly good reason, to become pope himself. The best government of Henry's reign was when Wolsey was at the head of affairs, or from 1515 to 1529. But as the years passed, the pleasant temperament of the king gave way to gloom and dissatisfaction.

When Henry was only twelve years old, he had been betrothed to Catherine of Aragon, the widow of his brother Arthur. He tired of her, and then, under the pretense that he believed the marriage unlawful, he was determined to be divorced in order that he might marry Anne Boleyn, a lady of his court. Cardinal Wolsey favored this divorce because he hated the Spanish royal family and saw in it the means of detaching England from its alliance with that country, while the hope of making a new union with France, through the marriage of the king with a princess of that country, was the scheme that appealed to him. He therefore, in 1527, did his utmost to persuade the pope to consent to the divorce.

Pope Clement VII was in a dilemma. Francis I of France supported England, while, on the other hand, Charles of Spain threatened. The pope temporized, and, to gain time, issued a commission to Cardinal Campeggio and Wolsey to adjudicate the question. Meanwhile, the impatient king discarded Catherine, who was six years older than he, and started living with Anne Boleyn. This turn of affairs knocked Wolsey's schemes awry, and, losing all wish to get the divorce, he favored procrastination as much as did Pope Clement, who revoked the decision, and transferred the question to Rome.

This step virtually ended the papal power in England. The king and Anne Boleyn were exasperated against Wolsey, because they were sure he had tricked them, and they resolved to punish him. (Under a law of Richard II no representative of the pope had any legal authority in England.) Since he had dared to thwart the will of the king, he should now pay the penalty. Feeling his helplessness, Wolsey meekly gave up everything—riches, power, and rank. He was allowed to go into retirement, but a year later was arrested on the charge of treason. While in custody on his way to London, he fell grievously ill, and stopped at the Abbey of Leicester to die.

A new ministry was formed in October 1529, in which, for the first time, the highest places were given to laymen. Sir Thomas More was made chancellor, and the chief adviser of the king was Wolsey's old assistant, Cromwell. About this time, Dr. Thomas Cranmer, of Cambridge, advised the king to lay his divorce question before the universities of Europe. Henry eagerly did so, and with the use of bribes, a favorable response was drawn from the majority. The king was so heartened by this verdict that he charged the whole body of the English church with being guilty of the same offense that Wolsey had committed. Quaking with fear, they bought the pardon of the irate ruler with the payment of a sum amounting to several million dollars. This was clinched by the declaration that the king was the supreme head on earth of the Church in England. Thus, the Reformation entered the kingdom of England.

Henry married Anne Boleyn in 1532, after having lived with her as her husband for some five years. Cromwell succeeded Wolsey as the king's confidential adviser, and Henry and Anne were crowned in Westminster Abbey. The indignant pope ordered the king to leave her, under the threat of excommunication, and to take back Catherine. Henry answered through his obsequious Parliament, which in 1534 passed the Act of Supremacy, which made the king absolutely the head of the church.

Henry VIII. Well-educated, and he had a fairly good mind; but his egotism, his willfulness, and his selfishness had no bounds. Those traits in the king became the cause of infinite suffering to England; but his subjects were so filled with admiration of his stature, his strength, his fine presence, and the bluff freedom of his manner toward them, that they were quite heedless of his character in the first years of his reign.

One of Henry's first acts was to marry Catherine of Aragon, his brother's widow, and he is said to have done so less from policy than from choice. Catherine was twenty-five, while he was nineteen, but her person was attractive to him then, and her manners pleased. For two years he seems to have been contented with the enjoyments of a gay and extravagant court. Then he was seized with the ambition to play a conspicuous part in the eyes of the world. An iniquitous league for the despoiling of Venice had been followed by what was styled a "Holy League" against France, formed by Ferdinand of Spain, the emperor Maximilian, and the pope. Henry was easily drawn into the League, but only to be betrayed. His allies used him to bring pressure on France for secretly securing their own terms of peace.

Meantime, while Henry was making war in France, his Scottish brother-in-law, James IV, acting on the old friendship of Scotland for France, invaded England and suffered the awful defeat of Flodden Field, where he and ten thousand of his countrymen fell. This brought Henry's nephew, James V, the son of his sister Margaret, to the Scottish throne.

The great seal of Henry VIII

Suit of armor presented by the emperor Maximilian I to Henry VIII

Shilling of Henry VIII

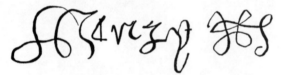

Signature of Henry VIII

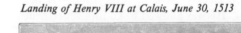
Landing of Henry VIII at Calais, June 30, 1513

This grotesque mask is the only surviving piece of the armor collection given to Henry VIII by Maximilian

Henry VIII at the Field of the Cloth of Gold

Wolsey surrendering the great seal

Henry VIII courting Anne Boleyn

Anne Boleyn. Jane Seymour. Catherine Howard.

Execution of Anne Boleyn. In January 1536, the divorced Queen Catherine died, and by her death she seems to have doomed her rival, Anne. The king had been tiring of the latter for some time, but feared to reopen the old divorce question if he tried to make himself wifeless again. But no sooner was Catherine out of the way than he determined to be rid of Anne Boleyn, and his creature, Thomas Cromwell, lost no time in finding the means. On charges of misconduct and of conspiracy, which few who have investigated the matter give credit to in the least, she was condemned and beheaded (May 1536), while five unfortunate gentlemen, accused of complicity in her crime, shared her fate. Henry married his third wife, Jane Seymour, on the day after Anne's head fell.

The denial of this was to constitute treason. The act of 1534 was the most momentous in the ecclesiastical history of England.

Henry was given the right to declare any judgment and to punish its violation with death. Cromwell was his ready tool in this infamy, it being their rule not to allow any accused person to be heard in his own defense. The venerable Fisher, bishop of Rochester, and the great and good Sir Thomas More could not conscientiously accept the decree that Henry was head of the church, and, for this voice of conscience, both were brought to the scaffold. As More came to the steps leading to the scaffold, he turned to the governor of the Tower of London and said: "If you will see me safely up, I will come down without help."

All Europe was horrified by these atrocious murders, and Henry's only ally, Francis I, remonstrated. The pope declared his excommunication against the tyrant (whom he had once dubbed Defender of the Faith), and Henry retaliated by suppressing the monasteries.

These drastic measures caused a fierce insurrection in the north, where the rebels became so powerful that terms had to be made with them and certain concessions granted, one of which was a general amnesty. The leaders, however, were executed, and the suppression of the rebellion was followed, in 1537, by the dissolution of the larger monasteries. In this same year an order in council placed the English translation of the Bible and six altered articles of religion in every church so that all might read them, and warned all of the penalty of refusing to accept the decisions of the English church. Thus, whoever denied the first article, that of transubstantiation, should be declared a heretic and burned at the stake. Whosoever spoke against the other five articles should, for their first

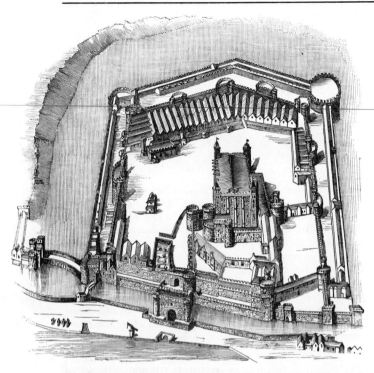

The Tower of London in the sixteenth century, where the executions took place

offense, forfeit their property, and for the second should die at the stake.

This act caught the truculent Cromwell. He had used his influence as a member of the government to thwart the execution of the law by staying proceedings and granting pardons, but Henry had become his enemy and put him to death.

Anne Boleyn, who was the mother of Elizabeth, destined to become one of the greatest queens Europe ever knew, was charged with unfaithfulness, and it is more than likely the charge was true. She was executed, and then Henry married Jane Seymour, who died a year after the birth of a son, who eventually became Edward VI. In 1540, Cromwell arranged a marriage with Anne of Cleves, who was so homely in looks that the king could hardly stand being seen with her and quickly brought about a divorce. It was in that year that Cromwell was beheaded, partly due to the resentment of the king for having cajoled him into the distasteful marriage. His next union was with Catherine Howard, who had been a wanton. She strove to keep the dreadful fact a secret, but Henry found it out, charging her with treason, and she suffered the fate of Anne Boleyn. His sixth and last marriage was with Catherine Parr, who, too, would have gone to the block on the charge of heresy, except that she knew how to flatter the king's conceit and to make him believe she thought him a profound theologian, when in reality he had a lesser than average intellect, compared to those in his court.

War broke out in 1542 with Scotland, where the king,

James V, was a Catholic, and unwilling to form an alliance with his uncle Henry VIII. A Scottish army invaded England, but fled in panic before an insignificant force of English at Solway Moss. James was so mortified that he did not survive long, and left as his successor an infant daughter, Mary Stuart. The politic Henry negotiated a marriage between her and his son Edward, but the Scots repudiated the treaty, and Henry sent an army to enforce it. The troops ravaged the country and sacked Edinburgh. Exasperated with France because of its intrigues in Scotland, Henry made an alliance with Charles V, entered France in 1544, and captured Boulogne, but in the end agreed that it should be returned in eight years, upon the payment of a heavy ransom.

Henry, when but only thirty, was old, diseased, unwieldy, and in continual pain, due to his excesses and debauchery. His condition became worse as he lived on. He succumbed on January 28, 1547, in the fifty-seventh year of his age. He was execrated equally by Catholic and Protestant, for he persecuted both with relentless fierceness. The former were put to death because they would not own him as head of the church, while the Protestants were burned at the stake because they refused to believe the Roman Catholic doctrines. It was Sir Walter Raleigh who said of Henry VIII: "If all the pictures and patterns of a merciless prince were lost to the world, they might all again be painted to the life out of the story of this king." On that dismal winter night when the wretched creature lay dying, he sent for Cranmer, archbishop of Canterbury, to receive his last words, and passed away, "unwept, unhonored, and unsung." The world was well rid of him.

Parliament had given Henry special powers regarding the succession. His son Edward, who was only nine years old, was the rightful heir, but Henry ordered that, if his son died childless, the kingdom should go to Henry's daughters, first to Mary and her heirs, then to Elizabeth and her heirs. After these two, it was to pass to the descendants of his younger sister Mary.

The throne went first to the feeble, sickly son of Jane Seymour, who was crowned as Edward VI in 1547, en-

Edward VI, 1547–53
(from a painting by Holbein)   *Edward VI*

Edward VI entering London in his coronation procession

Great seal of Edward VI

Gold sovereign of Edward VI

Signature of Edward VI

tering London in triumphal procession. The duke of Somerset, uncle of Edward, was appointed to reign during the new king's minority. England then had two great parties—Roman Catholics and Protestants—and the momentous question was which was to become the master of the kingdom. Somerset, the protector, was a Protestant, and he brought that faith to the front. He was ambitious and he was a fine soldier. In the first year of his rule he invaded Scotland with the purpose of compelling the marriage of Mary with the young English king; but Mary eluded him. She was sent to France the next year, became the betrothed of the French dauphin, who was afterward Francis II.

The bitterest enemy of Somerset was his own brother, Thomas, Lord Seymour of Sudeley, high admiral of England, who had married Catherine Parr, the widow of Henry VIII. He aimed to supplant the protector, but was destroyed by a bill of attainder and beheaded March 20, 1549. Somerset was not long in following him, for his rule was detested at home and was a failure abroad, and in 1552 he was beheaded on a charge of conspiring against his rival, John Dudley, duke of Northumberland, and against other lords of the council.

The duke of Northumberland, who now took the management of affairs, resembled Somerset whom he had supplanted, for he had no religion, but professed to be a rigid Protestant. Seeing that Edward could not live long,

Edward VI. A boy-king was once more on the English throne. Authorized by Parliament, his father had left a will that appointed a council of regency to administer government in Edward's name until he should be eighteen years old.

Lady Jane Grey urged to declare herself queen

Edward VI writing his journal

Return of Catholic prelates under Mary I

Lady Jane Grey (from an original picture in the collection of the earl of Stamford and Warrington)

Execution of Lady Jane Grey in the Tower of London, February 12, 1554

Mary I (1553–58). The duke of Northumberland kept King Edward's death a secret until he had proclaimed Jane queen of England. The poor girl knew that a great wrong was being done in her name. She begged that she might not be forced to accept the crown; but she could do nothing to prevent it as her father, her husband, and his father all were bent on making her obey them. So she had to sit as a queen in the royal apartments in the Tower of London.

But as soon as the news reached Mary, she traveled toward London. As everyone knew her to be the right queen, and the people joined her, even Northumberland was obliged to throw up his hat and cry, "God save Queen Mary." Jane and her husband were safely kept, for Mary meant no harm to them had their friends remained quiet. However, the people became discontented when Mary began to have the Latin service used again, and put Archbishop Cranmer in prison for having favored Jane. She wanted to be under the pope again, and she became engaged to marry the king of Spain, her cousin, Philip II. This was very foolish of her, for she was a middle-aged woman, pale, and low spirited; and he was much younger. The English hated it so much that the little children played the queen's wedding in their games and always ended by pretending to hang the king of Spain. Northumberland thought this discontent gave another chance for his plan, and tried to raise the people in favor of Jane, but so few joined him that Mary very soon put them down, and beheaded Northumberland. She thought, too, that the quiet of the country would never be secure while Jane lived, and so she consented to her being put to death. Jane behaved with beautiful firmness and patience. Her husband was lead out first and beheaded, and then she followed. Mary's sister, Elizabeth, was suspected also, and sent to the Tower. She came in a boat on the Thames to the Traitor's Gate; but when she found where she was, she sat down on the stone steps, and said, "This is a place for traitors, and I am none." After a time she was allowed to live in the country but was closely watched.

Philip of Spain came and was married to Mary. She was very fond of him, but he was not very kind to her, and he had too much to do in his other kingdoms to spend much time with her. Her great wish in choosing him was to be helped in bringing the country back to the old obedience to the pope; and she succeeded in having the English Church reconciled again to communion with Rome. But this displeased many of her subjects exceedingly. They thought they should be forbidden to read the Bible and they could not endure the Latin service.

he feared the coming to the throne of Lady Mary, who was sure to bring an end to his arbitrary power. He therefore persuaded Edward to do an illegal thing by altering the succession, and, shutting out his sisters, to settle the crown on his cousin Lady Jane Grey, daughter of the duke of Suffolk and granddaughter of Mary Tudor and Charles Brandon. The hope of the duke of Northum-

berland was to raise his fourth son, Lord Guilford Dudley, who had just married Lady Jane, to the throne of England. Edward died July 6, 1553, and some people in the court believed that the duke of Northumberland used poison to hasten Edward's death.

Lady Jane Grey had married at the age of sixteen, and she and her husband were devotedly attached to each other. They lived in a castle in the beautiful park near Leicester. But one day Lady Jane's father-in-law and several nobles came into her presence and, kneeling at her feet, hailed her as the queen of England. She was terrified, and assured them that she had no wish to reign, and would not do so. They insisted, and when her father and mother urged her for their sakes to accept the honor, she unwillingly consented; but it was with a sinking heart. She was proclaimed on the tenth of July; but Mary was the rightful heir, and at Norwich on the nineteenth of the same month was also proclaimed queen. Mary entered London at the head of a band of friends, without a single hand being raised to defend Lady Jane Grey, whom none were ready to accept as their queen, since she had no moral or legal claim to that honor. The duke of Northumberland was brought to trial and beheaded, and Lady Jane and Guilford Dudley were sent to the tower. Lady Jane and her husband were beheaded February 12, 1554.

Returning to Mary Tudor, whose reign began in July 1553, she was a devout Catholic, the daughter of Henry VIII. She married her cousin Philip II of Spain, who was a languid bigot, and who married her because it suited his father's policy. When he came to England he was received with coldness and distrust. He went back to his own land to become king of Spain and of the Netherlands, after which he returned but once to urge the queen to join him in a war against France. She did so, and the results were disastrous to England. In January 1558 Calais was captured by the French, after the English standard, planted there by Edward III, had waved above its walls for more than two hundred years. It was destined to fall in the course of time, and its loss was no harm to England, though Mary was so oppressed and humiliated that she declared that when she died "Calais" would be found written on her heart.

She was a fanatic, but a resolute one. The dearest ambition of her life was to restore England to the Church of Rome. Like most people of those times, she believed that those who thought differently should be compelled to renounce their opinions and, if they refused to do so, should be punished with death. The fires of persecution that blazed during Mary's reign led to her being called Bloody Mary, for by the close of her reign more than two hundred men and women had perished at the stake. The most notable of the martyrs were John Hooper, bishop of Gloucester; Ridley, bishop of London, and the venerable Latimer. Ridley and Latimer were burned together at Oxford, October 16, 1555. Latimer, exhorting his

Queen Mary (from a painting by Holbein)

King Philip, husband of Queen Mary

Great seal of Queen Mary

Signature of Mary

Gold rial of Queen Mary

the blood of thousands of Protestants, who had died the most cruel of deaths.

Broken in health, neglected by her husband, and hated by her countrymen, Mary died November 17, 1558, after a reign of only five years.

THE GLORIOUS REIGN OF ELIZABETH

The woman who next came to the throne, and whose greatness the whole world now knows, stood for years seemingly much nearer the scaffold than the crown. She was the princess Elizabeth, daughter of Anne Boleyn, the second wife of Henry VIII, whereas Mary, who had just died, was daughter of his first wife, Catherine of Aragon, so that the two queens were half-sisters.

The legitimacy of Elizabeth depended on the validity of her father's divorce from Catherine, and Catholics had always denied that he was legally divorced. So Elizabeth's very existence was an insult to her sister Mary. And Elizabeth was a Protestant! Mary kept her in prison, in constant expectation of death.

Philip II of Spain turned the scale. Mary Stuart of Scotland was the next heir to the throne. She had married the dauphin of France, who was Philip's greatest enemy. Mary Stuart's accession would elevate France, to

Queen Elizabeth, 1558–1603 (from a painting by Zucchero)

friend to die like a man, declared, "We shall this day light such a candle, by God's grace, in England, as I trust shall never be put out." Cranmer, the leader of the church of Henry VIII, recanted, but was also brought to the stake. Yet both Cranmer and Latimer had been zealous in sending others to the stake who had differed with them. But, sad as it was, persecution in England never reached the appalling extent that it did in Spain. The fiendish Philip II reddened the lowlands of Holland with

Queen Elizabeth surrounded by her court (from a print by Vertue)

Great seal of Queen Elizabeth

Signature of Elizabeth

Crown piece of Queen Elizabeth

State carriage of Queen Elizabeth (from Hoefnagel's print of Nonsuch Palace)

the dwarfing of Spain, and, though both Philip and Mary were Catholics, he preferred that England should become Protestant rather than destroy his own political dominance, and give to France the balance of power in Europe.

So Elizabeth became queen of England in 1558, when she was twenty-five years old. She was a most extraordinary woman. Surrounded and advised as she was by some of the ablest of statesmen, she was wiser in some respects than all in her court, and could outwit them at their own games. She was a consummate statesperson, and the forty-five years that she sat on the throne were in many respects the grandest that England has ever known.

Mary Stuart of Scotland had become queen of France, and claimed the English crown through her descent from Henry VII, on the ground that Elizabeth had no such right, because the pope of Rome had never recognized the marriage of her mother Anne Boleyn with Henry VIII. France and Rome maintained this claim, while

Francis Drake knighted by Elizabeth. For more than a dozen years before England and Spain were avowedly at war, Francis Drake and others attacked Spanish-American settlements, fought Spanish warships, plundered Spanish treasure ships, and shared the spoil with English courtiers, and even with the English queen. In 1577, Drake set sail on a memorable voyage, which followed the route of Magellan to the Pacific, gathered booty along the whole Peruvian coast, and then circled homeward by the Cape of Good Hope, having rounded the globe.

Shakespeare before Queen Elizabeth

Queen Mary of Scotland (from a painting by Zucchero)

Sir Walter Raleigh in the Tower awaiting his execution

Mary, Queen of Scots in prison

Elizabeth signing Mary's death warrant. Mary, Queen of Scots' execution cannot be called the cause of war between Spain and England, because war had long existed as a fact, though it was never acknowledged. That singular state of things is not easily understood at the present day.

Mary Stuart led to execution

LINEAGE OF THE STEWART OR STUART SOVEREIGNS OF SCOTLAND, FROM ROBERT BRUCE TO MARY, QUEEN OF SCOTS.

1st Generation.	2d.	3d.	4th.	5th.
ROBERT BRUCE, 1306–1329.	DAVID II., 1329–1370.			
	Margaret, married Walter Allan, High Steward of Scotland (called Walter Stewart).	ROBERT II., 1st of the Stewart or Stuart line, 1370–1390.	ROBERT III., 1390–1406.	JAMES I., 1406–1437.

5th.	6th.	7th.	8th.	9th.	10th.
JAMES I., 1406–1437.	JAMES II., 1437–1460.	JAMES III., 1460–1488.	JAMES IV., 1488–1513, married Margaret, daughter of Henry VII. of England.	JAMES V., 1513–1542, married Mary of Guise.	MARY, Queen of Scots, 1542–1567.

Lineage of the Stewart, or Stuart, sovereigns of Scotland, from Robert Bruce to Mary, Queen of Scots

The surrender of Mary, Queen of Scots at Carberry Hill (from the old picture engraved by Vertue and published by the Royal Society of Antiquaries)

Holyrood House, the ancient royal palace of Edinburgh (from an original drawing made in 1828). Only a portion of the left, or north, wing of the present building existed in the time of Mary.

Philip II supported Elizabeth, whom he hoped to marry and thus add England to his dominions.

Grand as the reign of Elizabeth was, it was harrassed by innumerable plots against her life and against the Protestant religion. Her most formidable enemy was Mary Stuart, queen of Scots, who had married the French dauphin. She claimed the English throne as granddaughter of a sister of Henry VIII, while Elizabeth was excluded from such right on the old ground of illegitimacy. Mary urged Elizabeth to set matters straight by naming her as heir to the throne; but no matter how much inclined Elizabeth might have been to do this, she dared not for fear that the Roman Catholics would then find means of putting her out of the way, to make room for the queen of Scots.

Philip of Spain, her brother-in-law, wanted to marry Elizabeth that he might hold England as a Roman Catholic country. The queen was anxious to keep peace with Spain and France, for she had not the money nor the ships with which to go to war. So she dallied and delayed

her replies to both requests. The pope was also kept waiting and hoping, until he, too, saw through her plans, and issued his edict of excommunication against her. When Mary's husband, the king of France, died, she went back to Scotland, assumed the Scottish crown, and boldly asserted her right to that of England.

Mary was a wonderfully beautiful and fascinating woman and, a few years after returning to Scotland, married Lord Darnley. He became infuriated because of the favoritism she showed her Italian secretary Rizzio, and, with several companions, Lord Darnley seized Rizzio in her presence, dragged him into an antechamber, and stabbed him to death. A year later, Darnley was murdered, and it was generally believed that his wife and the earl of Bothwell, whom she later married, instigated the crime. The people were so outraged that they seized and put her in prison, compelling her to abdicate in favor of her infant son James VI. She escaped and fled to England. Elizabeth feared that if Mary crossed to France, she would stir up that country to war. So she had

Tomb of Mary, Queen of Scots in the south aisle of Henry VII's chapel, Westminster Abbey

Tomb of Queen Elizabeth in the north aisle of Henry VII's chapel, Westminster Abbey

The death of Queen Elizabeth (from the painting in the Louvre)

Interior of Henry VII's chapel

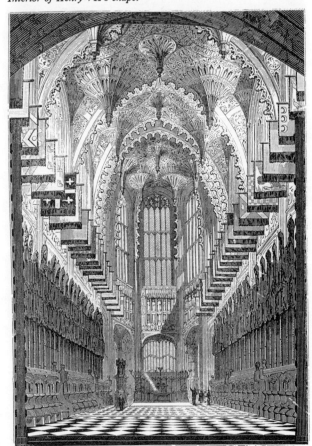

Westminster Abbey and Hall at the time of Elizabeth

her rival thrown into prison, and kept there for some nineteen years.

Finally, Mary became involved in a plot to kill the English queen and seize the government in the interest of the Roman Catholics. William the Silent, who expelled the Catholics from a part of the Netherlands, had been assassinated by one of that faith, and the Puritans in the House of Commons blamed the death on Mary. Impelled by a sense of her own peril, Elizabeth signed the fatal warrant, and Mary was beheaded at Fotheringay Castle, in Northamptonshire.

Mary's devices threatened the destruction of England, for she had been so disgusted with her cowardly son James, who deserted her and accepted a pension from Elizabeth, that she left her claim to the throne of England to Philip II of Spain. He was the most powerful ruler in Europe, determined to conquer England, add it to his own immense possessions, and restore it to the religion of the pope. The fleet that Philip prepared consisted of one hundred and thirty vessels, larger than any other ever in Europe. The land forces were to be lead by the duke of Parma, twenty thousand of them on board the ships of war, while thirty-four thousand more were assembled in the Netherlands ready to be transported to England. Since no doubt was entertained of the success of the fleet, it was called the Invincible Armada.

England was thrown into consternation by news of the coming of the terrible armada, for there seemed no earthly hope of a successful resistance. All that the kingdom had in the way of a navy was thirty ships "of the line," very small in comparison with the huge galleons of the enemy. But, a series of storms and the success of the British in various skirmishes with the armada made it vincible and it returned to Spain defeated.

The great Elizabeth died and her death cast a pall all over England. In her old age she had adopted a young man thirty years her junior, the dashing earl of Essex. For him she seems to have entertained a real affection;

but she expected him to treat her not as a mother, but as a gay young miss. She exacted from him the double devotion of a lover to his lady and of a subject to his queen. She made him captain-general of all her forces, the most conspicuous man in her kingdom. Yet at the same time, his real power was nothing in those moments when he didn't please his sovereign. Once when he attempted to offer some advice, Elizabeth boxed his ears in the presence of the whole court. Essex was with difficulty restrained from returning the assault. "I would not have stood as much from her father," he cried, "and I will not from a petticoat." Later, he led his friends in a minor uprising, endeavoring to drive away by force of arms those of the queen's council whom he deemed his enemies. He was arrested, and after much wavering Elizabeth had him executed for treason. Then she became dejected, and her physical strength gradually passed from her. She died on March 24, 1603, in the seventieth year of her age, after a reign of nearly forty-five years.

THE STUART KINGS

Since Elizabeth was the last of the Tudors, the Stuart line begins with the coronation of James VI of Scotland in 1603. He was the only son of Mary, queen of Scots, and a great-grandson of Margaret, sister of Henry VIII. This made him the nearest heir, and Parliament chose him as James I of England. His accession united England and Scotland under one king, but each had its own parliament, its own church, and its own laws. The strange sight was presented of a sovereign ruling over three kingdoms, each with a different religion, for England was Episcopal, Scotland Independent, and Ireland Catholic.

While on his way from Scotland to receive the crown, an immense petition was presented to him from the Puritan clergy, asking that they might be permitted to preach without wearing a surplice, to perform the marriage ceremony without using the ring, to baptize without making the sign of the cross on the child's forehead, and to

Young James I, 1603–25

James I of England, and VI of Scotland, was the only son of Mary, Queen of Scots, by her second husband, Darnley, who was the grandson of Margaret Tudor, through whom the Scottish line claimed the succession to the English crown. Solomon the Second, as he was called by his obsequious courtiers, or the "wisest fool in Christendom," as he was styled by Henry IV, of France, was a man of shrewdness and considerable learning; but he was mean, vulgar, and undignified, and never really understood his English subjects. His overweening conceit in his own wisdom, and his fixed idea that he ruled by divine right, and was responsible to no earthly power, led to those incessant disputes with the Commons that culminated so tragically in the reign of his son, Charles I.

The first act of James's reign was to put an end to the Spanish war; but the most important question he had to decide was one of religious toleration. A memorable conference was held at Hampton Court in 1604, at which four Puritan ministers, the king, some twenty bishops, and a large number of courtiers were present. Everything was quietly discussed till someone mentioned the word presbytery; *then the king lost his temper and treated the conference to an animated specimen of royal logic, the burden of which was: "No bishop, no king." He needed the bishops to prevent the clergy from gaining ascendancy over the crown. After hearing the royal speech, Bancroft, bishop of London, blessed God on his knees for having sent them such a monarch. The Puritans were flatly told to conform or leave the church. This Hampton Court Conference led the king to order a revised translation of the Bible to be made. This Authorized Version, published in 1611, has, by its power and beautiful diction, contributed more than any other work to the formation and maintenance of the English language in its strength and simplicity, and in widespread use today is still known as the King James version of the Bible.*

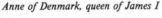

Anne of Denmark, queen of James I

Anne of Denmark, showing the "wheel farthingale" then worn

dispense with bishops. The king held a conference at Hampton Court near London, eager for the chance to display his learning. But he distrusted the Puritans. He was an unshakable believer in the divine right of kings to rule, and looked upon this petition of the Puritans as a dangerous step toward the disputing of that right. To all arguments he replied with a wag of the head, and mumbled his pet maxim, "No bishop, no king," meaning that the two were inseparable. He would not grant any of their petitions and his persecutions of the Puritans became so violent that many of them left the country, and some crossed the Atlantic to settle in New England.

The most notable result of the Hampton Court conference was the order of the king for a new translation of the Bible. This was published in 1611, and constituted the Authorized Version, which is still used by the Protestants everywhere. When the king told the Puritans they must conform to the practice of the Episcopal church, three hundred of their clergymen surrendered their parishes. Parliament was displeased with James's harsh treatment of the Puritans.

The king added to his growing unpopularity by the vehemence with which he insisted upon his "divine rule." He maintained that his authority was derived directly from God and was above and beyond the English constitution, a theory that placed every man's life and liberty completely at his mercy. The claim led James continually to violate the law of the land. He ejected legally elected members of the House of Commons, and thrust in prison those who found fault with his action. This fight lasted throughout the whole twenty-two years of his reign.

Robert Catesby, a prominent Catholic, formed a plot to blow up the Parliament House on the day the king was to open the session, November 5, 1605. With the government out of the way, he expected to persuade the Catholics to rise and proclaim a new sovereign.

A cellar under the House of Lords was rented, and barrels of gunpowder were secretly carried there. Guy Fawkes, a soldier of fortune, of considerable military experience and of dauntless courage, was the most determined of the conspirators. The plan was for him to fire the explosive and then flee to Flanders on a ship that was waiting in the Thames. The Roman Catholic peers, and others whom the conspirators wished to save, were to be prevented from going to the house by some pretended message on the morning of the fateful day. There were so many in on the plot that it is not surprising that it was revealed to the king and those selected for annihilation. On the morning of November 5, a little after midnight, Guy Fawkes was arrested as he was coming out of the cellar under the Parliament House. Three matches were found on him, a dark lantern burning in a corner within, and a hogshead of thirty-six barrels of gunpowder. Under torture Fawkes confessed his guilt, but would not betray his associates, though they were traced out and

James I

Crown piece of James I

Great seal of James I

CROSS OF ST. ANDREW.
SCOTLAND.

A white cross on a
blue field

CROSS OF ST. GEORGE.
ENGLAND.

A red cross on a
white field.

THE "UNION JACK."
GREAT BRITAIN.

The two crosses
combined.

Upon the accession of James I, he issued a proclamation ordering his subjects to use a flag with the two crosses "joined together according to a form made by our heralds." It is said to have received the name Union Jack because the king signed his name in French, Jacques. In 1801, on the legislative union with Ireland, the Cross of Saint Patrick, red upon a white field, was added to the union flag.

Coronation of James I

James ℞

James I (from a letter to his son Charles, while on his Spanish love-making expedition, beginning "My deal bable")

either killed on being captured, or died on the scaffold.

The obstacle to James enforcing his divine right was that he was always in need of money, and Parliament refused grants without the concession of reforms on his part. In order to get money to support his army in Ireland, James created the title of baronet, which anyone could buy for a price. The people did not seem as anxious for the honor as he expected, so he ordered that everyone who had an income of forty pounds or more a year, derived from landed property, must either buy knighthood or pay a big price for the privilege of not buying it.

The name of Sir Walter Raleigh is identified with the settlement of the southern part of the United States. Without the slightest foundation for the charge, he was accused of conspiracy and kept for a number of years in the Tower of London. Then the avaricious king let him out to go on an expedition in quest of treasure in a distant part of the world. Raleigh not only failed to get the treasure, but was foolish enough to become embroiled with the Spaniards on the coast of South America. The Spanish king hated Raleigh because of the part he had taken in the destruction of the Spanish armada, and he demanded of James that the latter should punish his subject for the flurry in South America. The English sovereign was so angry because of Raleigh's failure to secure him the coveted wealth, that he revived the

Guy Fawkes brought before King James

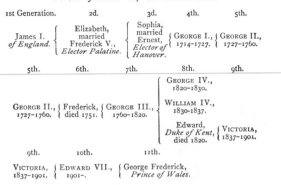

LINEAGE OF THE HANOVERIAN SOVEREIGNS OF ENGLAND, FROM JAMES I., OF ENGLAND.

1st Generation.	2d.	3d.	4th.	5th.
James I. of England.	Elizabeth, married Frederick V., *Elector Palatine.*	Sophia, married Ernest, *Elector of Hanover.*	GEORGE I., 1714-1727.	GEORGE II., 1727-1760.

5th.	6th.	7th.	8th.	9th.
GEORGE II., 1727-1760.	Frederick, died 1751.	GEORGE III., 1760-1820.	GEORGE IV., 1820-1830. / WILLIAM IV., 1830-1837. / Edward, *Duke of Kent,* died 1820.	VICTORIA, 1837-1901.

9th.	10th.	11th.
VICTORIA, 1837-1901.	EDWARD VII., 1901-.	George Frederick, *Prince of Wales.*

Lineage of the Hanoverian sovereigns of England, from James I of England

fifteen-year-old charge of conspiracy, and had the once popular favorite beheaded.

King James I died from drunkenness and gluttony in 1625. The duke of Sully made the pointed remark of him that he was "the wisest fool in Christendom." The marked features of his reign were the planting of the colonies in America, which proved the germ of the present United States; and his prolonged fight with the House of Commons, in which the latter showed themselves the stronger.

The wife of James I was Anne of Denmark, and their children were Henry Frederick, Prince of Wales, who died in 1612; Charles, who was his father's successor; and a daughter, Elizabeth, who married Frederick V, elector palatine of Germany. Because the Bohemians who were in revolt chose Frederick as king, Elizabeth is remembered as the queen of Bohemia. James was the first to take the title of king of Great Britain, and it was he who formed a national flag, which symbolized the patron saints of England and Scotland, Saint George and Saint Andrew, the combination becoming known as the Union Jack.

Charles I was born in November 1600, so that he was twenty-five years old when he succeeded to the throne of Great Britain. He was an extraordinary man, who may be described as having a dual or double nature. In his private life he was conscientious, honorable, and the most courteous of gentlemen. He was what he claimed to be, irreproachable in morals and conduct, scrupulous in all of his personal relations, and a model citizen. As a sovereign, he was exactly the reverse. This may be ascribed to his fanatical belief in the divine right of kings, which he had learned from his father, and which was intensified in the son. He believed himself above all law, and that Parliament, instead of being his master, should be his servant.

He opened his reign with more than one grave mistake. He had imbibed from his father the notion that an Episcopal church was most consistent with the rightful authority of kings, and he adopted severe persecuting measures against the Puritans of England and the Presbyterians of Scotland. He offended his people by marrying Marie Henriette of France, a rigid Catholic, who greatly influenced his religious views, and he made the duke of Buckingham, the unpopular minister of his father, his own prime minister and chief adviser.

The queen, Henriette, had a genius for extravagance, and kept her royal husband busy gathering the immense sums which she insisted she must have. The only way Charles could get the funds was by a grant from Parliament, and there came a time when that body felt strong enough to deny his request, except upon his agreement to sign the "Petition of Right," which would give the people certain reforms and concessions.

Parliament had already drawn up articles of impeachment against the duke of Buckingham for misgovernment, but when the king signed the Petition of Right, they felt that the victory warranted them in dropping proceedings. Soon after the duke was stabbed to death by one of those "nuts" who fancy that such crimes are of help to their country.

It was during this period that the famous Dutch painter, Vandyke, came to England. He painted several appreciative portraits of Charles and the various members of the royal family; and the grateful monarch knighted him as Sir Anthony Vandyke.

All sorts of devices were resorted to for raising money. One of these was to levy "ship money," so called because it was pretended that it was for the purpose of building a fleet. John Hampden, a wealthy country gentleman of Buckinghamshire, who could have paid his tax a score of times over without feeling it, refused as a matter of principle, and his courage heartened others to do the same. On his appeal, the corrupt judges decided against him, but Hampden was raised higher than ever in the estimation of his countrymen.

The story is told that Hampden became so disgusted with the tyranny of the king, that he resolved to join the

Charles I demanding of five members of Parliament

The second Stuart king, Charles I, 1625–49 (painted by Vandyke). Charles was in his twenty-fifth year when he came to the throne. Unlike his father, he was agreeable in person and manner, and could bear himself with the dignity that befits a king. In blamelessness of private life, in many refinements of feeling and taste, he offered an example to be admired. He could be chaste, he could be temperate, he could be courteous; but he could not be upright; he could not be straightforward in what he said and did; he could neither deal honorably with opponents nor be faithful to friends.

This weakness of integrity was balanced in Charles by no intellectual strength. He was narrow in his views, arrogant in his temper, impatient of facts. He had learned from his father to look on royalty as something divine.

"Baby Stuart" (James II), from the painting, 1635, of The Three Children of Charles I *by Anthony Vandyke, in the Royal Gallery at Turin*

Charles I raises the standard of civil war at Nottingham

Puritans who had crossed the Atlantic to America, and that in company with his cousin, Oliver Cromwell, he went on board a vessel in the Thames, but as they were about to sail the king forbade it, and they returned to their homes. The course of the history of England would have been drastically different if King Charles had allowed those two men to leave the country!

The Scots in 1637 rebelled against the attempt to compel them to accept a liturgy like that of England. Two years later Charles marched against them, but his empty treasury and mutinous soldiers forced him to make terms; and, no choice being left to him, he called a Parliament in 1640, of which he was so distrustful that he speedily dissolved it. Then the Scottish war broke out more fiercely than ever, and, when an army actually invaded England, he quickly summoned the law-making body once more. This is known in history as the Long Parliament, because it lasted twenty years—longer than the life of the king.

The Grand Remonstrance, which set forth all the

Trial of Charles I. A. the King; B. Lord President Bradshaw; C. John Lisle; D. William Say, Bradshaw's assistants. E. Andrew Broughton; F. John Phelps, clerks of the court. G. Oliver Cromwell; H. Henry Marten, the arms of the Commonwealth over them. I. Coke; K. Dorislaus; L. Aske, counselors for the Commonwealth. The description of the plate ends with these words: "The pageant of this mock tribunal is thus represented to your view by an eye-and ear-witness of what he heard and saw there."

York half-crown piece of Charles I

The king on his journey to the Scots

At the high Cort of Justice for the tryinge and iudginge of Charles Steuart kinge of England January xxixth Anno Dñi 1648.

Whereas Charles Steuart King of England is and standeth convicted attaynted and condemned of High Treason and other high Crymes And sentence uppon Saturday last was pronounced against him by this Cort to be putt to death by the severinge of his head from his body Of wᶜʰ sentence execucon yet remayneth to be done These are therefore to will and require you to see the said sentence executed In the open Streete before Whitehall uppon the morrowe being the Thirtieth day of this instante moneth of January between the houres of Tenn in the morninge and ffive in the afternoone of the same day wᵗʰ full effect And for soe doing this shall be yoᵘ sufficient warrant And these are to require All Officers and Souldiers and other the good people of this Nation of England to be assistinge vnto you in this Service Given under oᵘ hands and Seales.

The warrant to execute Charles I. The black blots are seals. Notice Cromwell's signature in the left-hand column.

shortcomings of the king's government, was printed and circulated throughout the country, and added much to the distrust already felt for the king. Charles was now at bay. Baffled and furious, the king was determined to make Parliament bend to his will through the use of military force. While England had no standing army, every county had a large body of militia, which was legally under the control of the king, and Parliament now insisted that he should resign that control into its hands. He refused, flung his standard to the breeze at Nottingham, August 22, 1642, and the civil war began.

In this lamentable strife the opponents were Royalists and Parliamentarians, or more the latter name being applied to the Puritans, who, to show their contempt of the prevailing fashion of long hair, wore their own cropped short. They were commanded by an able officer in Robert, earl of Essex, a son of the favorite whom Elizabeth had caused to be executed. He met the Royalists at Edgehill, in Warwickshire, on the twenty-third of October, and fought an indecisive battle. The commander of the Cavaliers was Prince Rupert, son of the queen of Bohemia, and nephew of the king, a brave, dashing officer, whose practice of looting caused many to look upon his acts with disfavor. The king was well provided with gentleman cavalry, whose horses were much superior to those of the raw levies of the Parliamentarians; but he had insufficient artillery and ammunition. The queen, who had withdrawn to Holland, sold her own and the crown jewels, and bought considerable ammunition, which she sent to him. She herself returned to England in February 1643, with four ships, and landed at Bridlington. A few months later the gallant patriot, Hampden, was killed in a skirmish with Prince Rupert.

Parliament now formed an alliance with the Scots,

who, in 1644, sent an army, while Charles made a treaty of peace with the Catholics in Ireland, so as to allow him to bring troops home from that country. He then summoned those of the Peers and Commons who were loyal to him to meet in Parliament at Oxford, and they thence directed his cause. It failed because of the transcendent ability of one man—Cromwell.

Oliver Cromwell was born at Huntingdon in 1599, his father being a country gentleman of some means. Little is known of his boyhood, but he left college in 1616 to take over the management of the estate of his father, who had died. In 1620, he married the daughter of Sir James Bourchier. He associated himself with the Puritan party, who respected his earnestness and sagacity. He made his first appearance in Parliament in 1628, but had hardly taken his seat when he and his fellow commoners were sent home again by the king. Cromwell devoted the next eleven years to farming, but was sent to Parliament in 1640 as a member for the town of Cambridge.

Oliver Cromwell

Mr. Oliver Cromwell visits Mr. John Milton

Oliver Cromwell on horseback (his signature appears below)

In July 1642 Cromwell moved in Parliament for permission to raise two companies of volunteers, having first supplied the necessary arms at his own cost. A month later he seized the magazine at Cambridgeshire. Now that the opportunity came, Cromwell exhibited astonishing military genius. The troop of cavalry that he formed, his "Ironsides," resisted the efforts of Rupert, who hurled his gallant cavaliers in vain against them. As a lieutenant colonel on the bloody field of Marston (July 2, 1644), and in the second battle of Newbury, three months later, Cromwell displayed admirable bravery and skill, but the backwardness of his superiors prevented them from reaping the full fruits of victory. Cromwell complained in Parliament, and declared that unless greater vigor was shown a dishonorable peace would be forced upon them. He had already so demonstrated his ability that he was excepted from the provision of the "Self-denying Ordinance." In the new model army which was formed, Lord Fairfax, one of the new noblemen on the Puritan side, was appointed general, with Cromwell as lieutenant general of the horse. At Naseby (June 1645) Cromwell commanded the right wing of the parliamentary forces, and the royal army was utterly routed and ruined. After the disorderly flight, the papers of the king were picked up on the battlefield, and proved him more perfidious than even his enemies had suspected. These papers revealed that he meant to betray those who were negotiating with him for peace, and was arranging to bring foreign troops to England.

Naseby practically ended the first civil war. The Royalists in the west were soon brought under submission. Bristol was carried by storm, and everywhere the cause of the king rapidly crumbled. In May 1646 he escaped from Oxford in disguise, and finally, in his extremity, surrendered to the Scottish army, which delivered him to the English Parliament. After remaining a state prisoner for more than four months, he was carried off by Fairfax's guard to the army, chiefly Independents. The soldiers became so threatening that, believing his life in danger, he escaped from Hampton Court and, in his bewilderment, flung himself into the custody of Colonel Hammond, governor of the Isle of Wight, who confined him in a castle, from which he tried in vain to escape.

At this time the country was in a critical condition. The Welsh were in revolt; a hostile Scottish army, made up of Presbyterians and Royalists, was bearing down from the north, and Rupert, to whom seventeen English ships had deserted, was preparing for a descent from

Charles I and armor-bearer (by Vandyke)

Holland, while Ireland was rampant in its royalism. The promptest and most energetic measures were necessary to save the country, and Cromwell was the man to take them. The Welsh were forced to surrender, and Cromwell routed the Scots at Preston Moor.

The Presbyterian element dominated in Parliament, and the Independent in the army. They were jealous of each other's power, but Cromwell, with his usual sagacity, had the king removed from the commissioners' hands into those of the army, in June 1647. Then some of the leading Presbyterians were turned out of Parliament by the army, and the Independents with Cromwell gradually gained the ascendency.

Charles I

Charles I's queen, Henriette Marie

Signature of Charles I

Vandyke painting the portrait of King Charles's family

Great seal of Charles

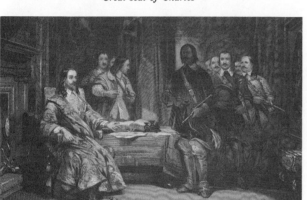

Seizure of the king of Holdenby

Execution of Charles I

"A shadow moved across his forehead!" Cromwell viewing the body of Charles I

Queen Henriette interceding for Charles I

Two years were spent in fruitless negotiations, when Charles, who was still a prisoner on the Isle of Wight, made a treaty with the Scots, in which he promised to establish the Presbyterian church in England if they would send an army to re-place him on the throne. The advance of the Scots into England and the flocking of the Royalists to their aid caused the civil war to break out again. On the return of the victorious parliamentary army to London the Presbyterians were still temporizing with the king. In December 1648, Colonel Pride drove more than one hundred of the Presbyterian members out of Parliament, the process being known in history as Pride's Purge. Cromwell did not order this summary proceeding, but approved of it. Some sixty Independents were left, and the body was derisively called the Rump Parliament.

The Rump Parliament voted that the king should be brought to trial on the charge of treason against the government. The Lords refused to agree, whereupon the Commons declared that the supreme authority rested in them, and closed the House of Lords. A High Court of Justice was organized for the trial of the king, Cromwell, of course, being a member of it. On January 20, 1649, the king was brought before this court. He bore himself with a dignity that compelled the respect of his enemies. He was found guilty, and the sentence of death was pronounced upon him as a "tyrant, traitor, murderer, and public enemy to the good people of the nation." He calmly accepted his fate, bade farewell to his children, and was beheaded on the scaffold before Whitehall, on January 30, 1649.

CROMWELL AND THE COMMONWEALTH

Before the multitude which stared with mingled awe, exultation, and pity upon the beheading of Charles I had separated, the House of Commons declared that no person should be proclaimed king of England, or Ireland, or the dominions thereof. So in 1649, England ceased to be a kingdom and took the name of a Commonwealth. Within two months the House of Lords was abolished, not only as an encumbrance but as a dangerous menace to the nation. England, then, claimed to be a republic, governed by a Council of State, with John Bradshaw as president and the famous poet, John Milton, the foreign secretary. Fairfax and Cromwell commanded the army, but the heart of the Commonwealth was the grim, relentless, iron-willed Cromwell.

The young republic, like our own, was pestered by anarchists, who contended that all offices should be done away with and rank and property placed on an equality. These people called themselves Levelers, and broke out in a vicious mutiny, which Cromwell crushed.

Fairfax soon resigned, and Cromwell became the sole head of the military forces of his country. The Royalists were numerous and daring, and the Presbyterians detested the army and the Rump Parliament, from which they had been excluded. The dead king had left six children—Charles, Prince of Wales, born in 1630; James, duke of York, born three years later; Henry, who died young; and three daughters—Mary, Elizabeth, and Henrietta. Mary married Prince William of Nassau, stad-

Cromwell taking the oath as lord protector

The children of Charles I. Charles, afterward Charles II, 1630–85; Elizabeth, who died unmarried at Carisbrooke, 1635–50; and Mary, afterward princess of Orange and mother of William III, 1650–1702. Charles had two other children, James, duke of York, afterward James II, 1630–1701; and Anne, who died in infancy.

Cromwell's daughter begs him to refuse the crown

Oliver—protector, a signature changed (from a patent dated July 5, 1655)

Cromwell's great seal for Scotland

holder of Holland. It is remarkable that both of the older sons afterward became kings of England, as also did the son of Mary. The daughter Elizabeth died in 1650, a prisoner held by the Parliamentarians, in Carisbrook Castle. The daughter Henrietta Maria, born in 1644, married the French prince, Philip, duke of Orleans.

The Royalists in Ireland proclaimed Prince Charles, king, and Cromwell went there to quell the uprising. He made a cyclone campaign, his fanatical soldiers showing no mercy, and in the space of nine months he had so nearly crushed the revolt that he left his son-in-law, Ireton to finish the work, while he passed over Scotland to stamp out the rebellion there. Young Charles had reached that country and been received as king, but Cromwell attacked the Scots at Dunbar, September 3, 1650, and routed them "horse, foot, and dragoons." While the great general was still engaged in subduing Scotland, Charles led his army across the border and pressed on as far as Worcester, where Cromwell overtook and defeated him on the anniversary of the victory at Dunbar. Charles made his escape, but three of his leading supporters were executed, Parliament having declared all his adherents rebels and traitors.

Cromwell yearned to get hold of Charles, and offered a reward of a thousand pounds for his capture. Charles and his friend, Lord Wilmot, sailed in a collier from the small fishing town of Brighton. After passing more dangers the prince landed in Normandy, where even the powerful arm of Cromwell was not long enough to reach him. Meanwhile the war in Scotland was brought to a successful conclusion by General George Monk, one of Cromwell's officers.

War broke out with Holland in 1652, and was noted for the resolute strife between the great Dutch sailors,

Martin Tromp and Michael de Ruyter, on one hand and Admiral Robert Blake on the other. Tromp, having defeated Blake, sailed through the Channel with a broom at his masthead, as an intimation of the manner in which he had swept the seas of the British. But Blake had his revenge. Tromp was slain in a naval battle in 1653, and peace was made with the dejected Holland the following year.

Cromwell had urged the need of calling a Parliament which should represent the country and provide the necessary reforms. The leading member of the house was young Sir Harry Vane, who had made an excellent governor of the colony of Massachusetts. Feeling that there was imminent danger of the country falling into the power of Cromwell as military dictator, Vane urged with all the earnestness in his power, that the bill should be passed without delay. Cromwell never hesitated in such crises. With a squad of soldiers he strode to the building and, leaving them at the door, entered the house and sat down to watch what was being done. He could not restrain himself long, and springing to his feet, charged the Commons with misgovernment and the abuse of their power. As he talked, his anger rose, until exclaiming, "You are no Parliament!" he called in his soldiers, had them pull the presiding officer from his seat and throw him outside. The other members scrambled after. When

Cromwell dissolving the Long Parliament (from a painting by Benjamin West)

Silver crown piece of Cromwell

Cromwell and his family listening to Milton playing the organ at Hampton Court

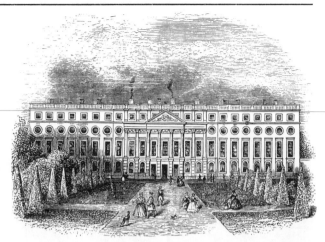

Hampton Court Palace (from a print of the time)

all were gone, Cromwell locked the door, thrust the key into his pocket, and went home.

The old Parliament out of the way, Cromwell called a new one to his own liking. It had one hundred thirty-nine members, and was nicknamed the Barebones Parliament, because one of its members bore the curious name of Praise-God Barebones. It was ridiculed from the first; but it cannot be denied that it did good work, and that some of the laws originated by it proved very helpful to the country.

A constitution was presented by a council which, on December 16, 1653, made Cromwell lord protector of England, Ireland, and Scotland. A few years later a second constitution offered him the crown. Tradition represents him as desiring to take it, but being withheld by the entreaties of his favorite daughter, Elizabeth Claypole. So, Cromwell refused the crown of England. He tried, however, to restore the House of Lords, failing only because the members would not attend. Most of the old forms of the constitution were revived, though they were veiled under other names. Since Ireland and Scotland were at this period added to the English Commonwealth, the representatives of those two countries took seats in the English Parliament, but an army of ten thousand men under General Monk was required to hold the Scots in subjection.

Tyranny of the Stuart kings had sent hundreds of Puritans to Massachusetts and other New England colonies. There was now a reversal of these conditions, and many of the Royalists fled to Virginia, where they founded one of the greatest states of the American Union. It seems singular that these roystering Cavaliers, with their horse-racing, cock-fighting, gambling, and convivial dispositions, should have laid the foundation of a state which until long after the revolution was the leading member of the Union. Virginia remained true to the king all through the troublous times of the Commonwealth. When Charles I was beheaded, the Virginians recognized his exiled son as the rightful sovereign, and were the last subjects to submit to the Commonwealth. Cromwell showed both generosity and sagacity in dealing with these rebels across the ocean. In 1652 he sent a strong fleet to Virginia, but at the same time offered such liberal concessions for a simple declaration of allegiance, that the colony reluctantly accepted him as its overlord. When Charles II came to the throne, he expressed his gratitude for the loyalty of the colony by ordering the arms of the province to be quartered with those of England, Scotland, Ireland, as an independent member of the kingdom. That is why Virginia is called the Old Dominion.

It is wonderful that a man who didn't turn his attention to war until he was forty years old should have developed so astounding a genius in that direction. The success of Cromwell's foreign policy was amazing, and to him is due the chief glory of England's advance to one of the foremost powers of Europe. He built a great navy and, under the mighty Blake, her fleets smote the Dutch, until they took down the brooms from their mastheads and promised forever after to salute the English flag wherever met on the high seas. It was Blake who compelled the duke of Tuscany to pay for injuries to England's commerce, and who scourged the pirates of Barbary till they cowered before him. The West Indian possessions of Spain were hammered into submission in 1655. Two years later, in the face of a terrific fire from the shore batteries, Blake destroyed the Spanish treasureships in the harbor of Santa Cruz, in Teneriffe. Having won one of the most illustrious names in naval annals, the grim old veteran lay down and died off Plymouth in the summer of 1657. The following year the allied English and French forces captured Dunkirk from the Spaniards, and the French king, by way of thanks, presented the city to the English, who thus received a consolation for the century-old loss of Calais.

Cromwell, who had been so absolutely fearless in bat-

Richard Cromwell

Great seal of Richard Cromwell, obverse; Great seal of Richard Cromwell, reverse

tle, grew so afraid of secret assassination that he wore armor concealed under his clothing. Then came the finishing blow to his strength in the death of his beloved daughter, Elizabeth. Cromwell passed away on September 3, 1658.

How seldom a great genius is succeeded by one worthy of wearing his laurels! Cromwell left two sons, Henry and Richard, the elder of whom was proclaimed protector. But, the dissatisfaction with him was so deep that the old Rump Parliament was called together at the end of eight months, and demanded his resignation. As gently as a lamb he stepped down and withdrew to private life, where he was followed by his brother, Henry, who had shown considerable capacity in governing Ireland during the Protectorate. Richard was nicknamed "Tumbledown Dick," and caricatures of him were displayed in many public places. He was given a pension, and lived in strict privacy until his death, in 1712, in his eighty-seventh year.

Under Richard Cromwell the Commonwealth had existed only in name. The country was placed under the control of the Rump Parliament, which represented only itself. The quarrel between it and the army was immediately renewed, and before long the body was expelled by the military leader, General John Lambert, who hoped to travel in the footsteps of the great Cromwell. General Monk, commander of the English army in Scotland, however, refused to recognize the government thus set up, and advanced with his forces toward England and made his headquarters at Coldstream-on-the-Tweed. It is in memory of this fact that one of the regiments composing his vanguard is still known as the Coldstream Guards.

The people on hearing the news rose against the government, and the fleet, sailing up the Thames, at the same time declared for the Parliament. General Lambert, who had expected to play the role of the great Cromwell, moved to the north to check Monk, but his soldiers fell away from him, and the triumphant Monk entered London in February 1660. He was a grim, silent man, who kept his own counsels, and for several days he

gave no sign of his intentions. Then he declared in favor of a free Parliament. The announcement was received with the blazing of bonfires, the ringing of bells, and the joyful shouts of the people. The Presbyterian members hurried back to their seats again, and, after issuing writs for a general election, dissolved March 16. Thus passed away the notable Long Parliament, which had been in existence for twenty years.

The new assembly was termed a Convention Parliament, because it was called without royal authority. It met about a month later, including ten members of the House of Lords. Meanwhile Monk had been in communication with the exiled Charles, who issued a declaration of pardon to all for past offenses, "excepting only such persons as shall hereafter be excepted by Parliament." One week after this declaration was received, May 8, Charles II was proclaimed king, and the fleet which had been sent to convey him from Holland to Dover arrived at London, May 29. Bells clanged, flags waved, and bonfires flashed all the way to London.

THE RESTORATION AND SECOND EXPULSION OF THE STUARTS

By a pleasant fiction the beginning of his reign was dated back twelve years before, that is, from the day of his father's execution. The Commonwealth troops were disbanded, but the King retained a select guard of five thousand men, from which in time a large standing army grew.

No reign could have begun under more promising prospects than that of Charles II. He was heartily welcomed by the great majority of his people. He had talents, a pleasing temper, and a courteous manner, but he was utterly lacking in moral principle. He secretly favored the Catholic religion, but it was as a matter of policy, for he would accept no faith that put the least restraint on his shameless life. In short, the times that were ushered in by his reign were a complete and abso-

Charles II as a boy

Charles II, 1660–85

lute reaction from the rigid morality of the Puritan rule. Immorality reigned everywhere in the Commonwealth.

The new Parliament passed an Act of Indemnity, granting a general pardon, but excepting from its benefits the judges who had condemned Charles I to death. Some of these were imprisoned for life, and thirteen were executed; but most of the others had already fled from the country. One of the silliest revenges conceivable was the digging up of the bodies of Cromwell, Ireton, Bradshaw, and Pride on the anniversary of the late king's death and hanging them in chains at Tyburn, after which they were buried at the foot of the gallows among the remains of highway robbers and the lowest of criminals. The Episcopal form of service was restored. It was in 1662 that the Act of Uniformity was passed. This ordered every clergyman who did not assent and consent to everything in the prayer book, and who did not use it in his Sunday services, to surrender his church. It meant that he must leave his home and go out in the world, to seek in the best way he could a living for himself, his wife, and children. On August 24 of that year two thousand clergymen abandoned their homes. During the reign of Charles II eight thousand religious Dissenters died in the jails. The Scottish Parliament was as merciless as the English in persecuting the Dissenters, for Scotland had again become a separate kingdom.

Catherine of Braganza, wife of Charles II

Charles II and the English ambassadors at The Hague, arranging the terms of his restoration

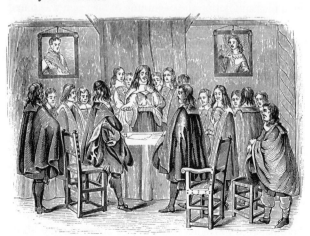

Charles II welcomed back to London

King Charles II landing at Dover

Charles II at Lady Castlemaine's house

Top: *view of Worcester. The battle was fought on the foreground meadows.* Center: *the fight of Charles before the parliamentary soldiers, designed from various contemporary portraits of Charles II, Harrison, Lilburne, Bradshaw, and others.* Bottom: *the old wooden house in the corn market, Worcester, in which Charles lodged.*

One of the shameful acts of Charles II was the seizure of New Amsterdam—the present city of New York—in 1664. The infamy of the proceeding lay in the fact that England and Holland were at peace, and the former in a treaty had recognized the justice of Holland's claim to the territory through the discovery of Henry Hudson.

The marriage of the king in 1662 to the Infanta of Portugal, Catherine of Braganza, brought him the fortress of Tangier in Africa and the island of Bombay in India. The latter was soon turned over to the East India Company, and Tangier was abandoned as worthless. In the year mentioned Charles, in order to procure funds with which to keep up his debauchery , sold Dunkirk to the king of France, much to the displeasure of the English.

Charles had shown himself as ambitious as his father to rule without a Parliament, but he needed money. How to get it without the help of Parliament was the great problem of his reign. Louis XIV of France, the greatest monarch in Europe, was anxious to conquer Holland, that he might add it to his own kingdom and extend the power of Romanism. He made the secret treaty of Dover with Charles (May 22, 1670), by which the latter, for the price of three hundred thousand pounds, was to aid him in carrying out this scheme for destroying the liberty and Protestant faith of Holland. Charles started a war with the Dutch, but quickly found he must have more funds with which to carry it through. There was then lying in the government treasury a sum equal to 10 million dollars in these days, which was pledged to repay the leading merchants and bankers who had made loans to the government. The king deliberately stole this enormous sum and used most of it in pandering to his vices. A financial panic resulted, which ruined some of the oldest firms in London.

Charles's declaration of war against Holland in 1672 earned him the bribe promised by the king of France, and he was eager for more, but was too cautious to come out openly as a Catholic. The nearest he dared go was to issue a proclamation of indulgence to all religions, and under this he may have intended to bestow special favors on the Catholics. Parliament replied, however, by requiring every government officer to declare himself a Protestant. This compelled the duke of York, the next heir to the throne, to resign as Lord High Admiral, for he was a Catholic and not such a coward as to be ashamed of his religious belief.

Charles was frightened by the vigor of Parliament, and tried to wheedle it into granting him more money by marrying his niece, the princess Mary, to William of Orange, head of the Dutch Republic and the foremost Protestant on the Continent. Thus peace was once more made with Holland only two years after the declaration of war.

The Magna Charta had declared that no freeman should suffer arbitrary imprisonment, but many ways

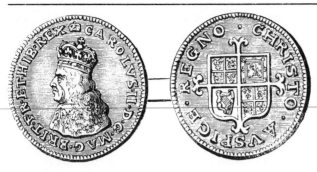

Shilling piece of Charles II

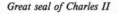

Signature of Charles II (from the original in Harleian Library)

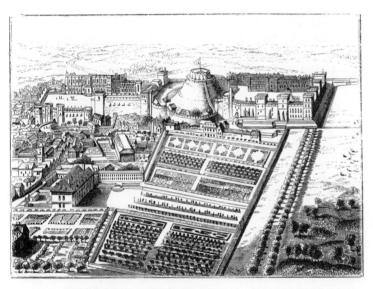

Windsor Palace at Charles II's time

Great seal of Charles II

were found of breaking the law. So, in 1679, Parliament passed the famous Habeas Corpus Act, which declared that no man should be detained long in prison on a criminal charge without being brought before a judge, who should inquire into the legality of the imprisonment and arrange for a speedy trial. This merciful and just provision is one of the most precious rights guaranteed in any country.

It was at this time that the two political parties came to be known by the respective names of Whig and Tory, which still prevail, though, of course, the meaning of the terms has undergone many shadings and changes. The first Whigs were the Scottish Puritans or Covenanters who rejected the episcopacy that Charles I had tried to force upon them. The word was a term of reproach, as was that of Tory, when applied to the Roman Catholic outlaws of Ireland. The name Tory was now given to those who supported the claim of the duke of York as the successor of the king. This duke was James, the brother of Charles, and he was of the Roman Catholic faith. The Whigs were those radical Protestants who endeavored to shut him out from the accession. The excitement ran so high that the country was on the verge of civil war.

What undoubtedly prevented an outbreak was the discovery of the Rye House Plot. This was formed by a number of desperate Whigs, and its object was the assassination of the king and his brother at a place called the Rye House, not far from London. The purpose was to place the highly popular duke of Monmouth on the throne. He was the illegitimate son of the king, who had no legitimate descendants. The plot was betrayed. The leading advocates of the bill for excluding James from the succession had been Algernon Sidney, Lord Russell, and the earl of Essex. Probably none of them had any real connection with the Rye House Plot; but the opportunity seemed too good to lose, and they with others were arrested for the conspiracy. Sidney and Russell, who were clearly innocent, were tried, condemmed, and executed. The earl of Essex, to avoid the fate of his comrades, committed suicide while imprisoned in the Tower of London. The duke of Monmouth was banished to Holland.

While considering his future policy, Charles was seized with a fit, and after lingering several days, died February 6, 1685. He refused at the urging of the bishops to take the last rites, but, his brother quietly brought a monk into the chamber and insisted on the sacrament being administered. So, the king died a Catholic.

The duke of York now came to the throne as James II. While his accession was dreaded because of his religious faith, general confidence was felt in him because of his courage and honesty, and when he declared he would respect the laws and defend the Church of England, few doubted him. Still, one of the dearest wishes was to restore the Roman Catholic religion in England. The Protestants were indignant when, on the Easter Sunday

James II, 1685–88

Maria Beatrix of Modena,
queen of James II

Halfpenny, James II

Mary, daughter of James II

James II

Great seal of James II

James II at an indoor tennis court

Signature of James II

preceding his coronation, he went to Mass in royal state.

Four months after the accession of James, the duke of Monmouth was led to believe by a number of refugees that if he would return to England and claim the throne as a Protestant he would be welcomed with open arms. Landing at Lyme on the coast of Dorsetshire, he issued a proclamation denouncing James as a usurper, tyrant, and murderer, because, like Nero, he had applied the torch to London, cut the throat of Essex, and poisoned his brother, Charles II! It was so preposterous a charge that it caused ridicule even among the friends of the duke.

On July 8, 1685, at Sedgemoor, "King Monmouth" was captured. He prayed his captors to take him to the king. They did so, and he flung himself on the ground at his royal uncle's feet, weeping and begging for life, no matter how hard the terms. When his pleadings were received with contempt, he regained a spark of manhood, and walked with some dignity to the Tower, from which he was taken to the scaffold and hanged.

Henry IV of France had issued the Edict of Nantes, granting liberty of worship to Protestants in his kingdom, but in 1685 the edict was revoked by Louis XIV, who thereby drove thousands of Huguenots to England and America. This encouraged James II to take steps in the same direction. While he did not dare go so far, he began violating the English law by placing Catholics in the most important offices of church and state. At the same time he stationed an army of thirteen thousand men near London, that they might be ready to quell any rebellion. Then he superseded the Protestant duke of Ormond, as governor of Ireland, with Richard Talbot, earl of Tyrconnel, a notorious Catholic, with orders to

James II receiving news of the coming of William of Orange

James Francis, the Old Pretender

Landing of William III at Torbay

recruit an Irish Roman Catholic army to sustain the king. In following this policy, it should be stated that the king went contrary to the wishes of Pope Innocent XI, who desired and even entreated him to rule according to law.

At this time an event took place whose consequences were of momentous importance to the kingdom: This was the birth, on June 10, of James Francis Edward, son of the king and of his second wife, Mary of Modena. By his first wife the king had already two daughters—Mary,

William and Mary requested by Parliament to become king and queen

The flight of James's queen

who had married William, prince of Orange, and lived in Holland, and a younger daughter, Anne, married to George, prince of Denmark, and then living in London. Both daughters were ardent Protestants, and it was because of the prospect that one of them would ascend the throne upon the death of James that the English people had submitted to his many violations of law.

The birth of a prince, however, dashed all these hopes, for he would of course be reared by his father as a strict Catholic. The angry people declared that no prince had been born, and that the infant was the child of obscure parents whom the royal couple were trying to palm off upon them as the legal successor to the throne. The disappointment was so bitter that a number of leading citizens sent a secret and urgent invitation to William, prince of Orange, to come to England with an army to defend the claim of his wife, Mary, to the English throne. William took time to consider the important matter and then decided to accept the invitation. He was greatly influenced in taking this step by the warm support of the leading Catholic princes of Europe—excepting the king of France—and by the friendship of the pope himself, who made no secret of his disgust with the idiotic rashness of the English king.

On November 5, 1688, William landed with fourteen thousand troops at Torbay. He issued a declaration that he came to protect the liberties of England and to secure the calling of a free Parliament, which should redress grievances and inquire into the facts concerning the birth of the Prince of Wales. The scared James tried to rally a force to resist the invader, but was terrified when his son-in-law, Prince George, and Lord John Churchill, afterward duke of Marlborough, went over to William's side. James's troops kept slipping from him, and finally his younger daughter, Anne, passed over to the enemy. "God help me," exclaimed the despairing king, "when my own children desert me!"

Unwilling to make terms with his enemies, he hastily arranged the escape of himself and his family. In the darkness of a stormy night the queen stole out of Whitehall with her infant child and was safely carried to France. This babe, whose birth caused all the trouble, never received any more royal title than that of "The Pretender," which he passed to his son, Prince Charles Edward Stuart, the Young Pretender.

Shortly after midnight, on December 11, the king followed his wife in flight. Crossing the Thames, he dropped the great Seal of State into the river, foolishly imagining that without it his adversary could not legally decide the questions left unsettled at his departure. When the king reached the coast, he was captured by some fishermen and brought back; but William did not want him, and allowed him to escape a second time. James reached France, where he was welcomed and supported by Louis XIV.

The extraordinary feature of the revolution of 1688

William III, 1689–1702

was that it was accomplished without bloodshed. With James II out of the kingdom, the situation was simplified. A Convention, or Parliament, met and declared that James had broken the original contract between king and people, and that the throne as a consequence was vacant. On the invitation of an assembly of peers and commoners, the prince of Orange assumed charge of the government, and called a Convention of the Estates of the Realm, which assembled January 22, 1689.

WILLIAM OF ORANGE AND ANNE

William of Orange was a silent, reserved man, devoid of all personal magnetism, but with stern qualities and virtues that commanded respect. The Declaration of Rights having been read to him and his wife, Mary, they assented to it, and were formally invited to accept the joint sovereignty of the realm, with the understanding that the duties were to be administered by William alone.

It was not in the nature of things that the accession of William and Mary should be acceptable to all. The extreme Tories still clung to James II. These adherents became known as Jacobites, from the Latin *Jacobus* for James. There were many of them in the south of Ireland and the Highlands of Scotland. They kept up communication with James, and were forever plotting for his restoration.

Parliament having drawn up the "Bill of Rights," it was signed by the king, and became the law of the realm.

Queen Mary II

Costume of William III

Costume of Queen Mary

Arms of William III

Great seal of William and Mary

Great seal of William III

Crown piece of William and Mary

The divine right of kings to rule; which had cost more than one of them his life, vanished into the mists of the Dark Ages. It was distinctly declared that only with the consent of Parliament could a standing army be maintained in time of peace; that the people could not be taxed in any form whatever without permission of the same body; that every man, no matter how humble his station, had the right to petition the crown for redress of any wrong; that no interference would be permitted with the election of members of Parliament; that the laws should be faithfully executed regardless of the king's wishes or views; and finally that no Roman Catholic, or one marrying a Roman Catholic, should ever be eligible to the throne of England.

In those days, as at the present time, an overwhelming majority of the Irish were Roman Catholics, but they had been gradually ousted from their hold on the land, most of which was owned by a comparatively few Protestant settlers. His loyal supporter, Tyrconnel, now rallied the Catholics, and invited James to come over from France and claim his own, assuring him that he was certain to secure it. It was because the Protestants in the north of Ireland stood by the prince of Orange that they have ever since been known as Orangemen.

Louis XIV of France was profoundly interested in this movement, and furnished money, arms, and troops to James, who landed in Ireland in March 1689. He made his headquarters at Dublin, where he issued his famous Act of Attainder, which ordered all who were in rebellion against his authority to appear for trial on a certain day, under penalty of being declared traitors, hanged, drawn and quartered, and their property confiscated. It was a tremendous document, and that there might be no mistake about it, more than two thousand people were warned by name that if they failed to do as commanded, they would be put to death without trial.

Having launched this thunderbolt, James and his troops next laid siege to the Protestant town of Londonderry, which held out for more than three months. When all hope seemed gone, an English force sailed up the river, dashed through the obstructions, and rescued the brave city.

In the following summer William himself went over to Ireland and commanded at the battle of the Boyne, fought in the east, on the banks of the river of the same name. He had a more numerous force than his opponent, and it was better disciplined and well armed. Because of a wounded right arm William was compelled to handle his sword with his left. Yet he was foremost in the battle, and fought with splendid valor. James took care to keep beyond reach of the lusty blows and viewed the fight from the top of a neighboring hill. His own Irish soldiers were so disgusted with his cowardice that they cried out after their defeat, "Change kings with us and we'll fight you over again!" James waited only long enough to see that the day was lost, when he galloped off, denouncing his Irish army, and, reaching the coast, sailed for France, where he was safe from harm. The conquest of Ireland was ended, and peace came with the treaty of Limerick, in 1691, when a large body of Irish soldiers who had fought under James were allowed to leave the country for France.

The terms of the treaty were shamefully violated by the Protestants, who hunted down the Catholics like so many rabid dogs, and seemed never sated with the vengeance they were able to inflict for James's foolish and unfortunate Act of Attainder and to this day the fight between them continues.

When William went to Ireland, the French in concert with the Jacobites struck a blow at England and won a naval engagement off Beachy Head. In 1692, while William was absent on the Continent, another French invasion took place, but England demonstrated her claim of being mistress of the seas when, with the Dutch fleets, she decisively defeated the French fleet in the Channel and, chasing the ships to the Bay of La Hogue, burned them there. The land struggle against the French king was carried on chiefly in the Netherlands, where William led his troops in person. Louis was finally exhausted by the seemingly endless wars, and consented, in 1697, to the Treaty of Ryswick, which acknowledged the prince of Orange as king of Great Britain.

Queen Mary died at the close of 1694 from smallpox, a fearful disease of the times, against which the physicians were powerless until the discovery of vaccination a century later. In February 1702, while the king was riding at Hampton Court, his horse stumbled over a molehill and he was thrown with such violence that his collarbone was broken. He was not able to survive the shock, which resulted in his death on the eighth of March, when in his fifty-second year.

Since Queen Mary left no children, the crown went to Anne, her younger sister, who had married George of Denmark, and who was as Protestant as Mary. She was a meek soul, without any force of character, who meant well, but had not enough intelligence and experience to know the best thing to do. Though a fervent upholder of the Church of England, she was as resolute as her be-

Queen Anne, 1702–4. Younger daughter of James II and Anne Hyde. She succeeded to the throne in 1702 on the death of her sister's husband, William III, and was the last reigning sovereign of the Stuart Dynasty. In 1683, she married Prince George of Denmark; none of their offspring survived childhood.

Prince George of Denmark

headed grandfather in the belief of the divine right of kings to rule. The London *Gasette* of March 12, 1712, had an official notice that on certain days the queen would "touch" for the cure of "king's evil," or, *scrofula,* which was devine healing. Thousands were foolish enough to try the "sovereign remedy," and no doubt some fancied they received benefit from it.

The peace of Ryswick had brought humiliation to King William, for the Commons compelled him to send away his favorite Dutch troops and disband most of the army. He had given nearly all of the forfeited lands in Ireland to his friends, but he was now forced to assent to an act which annulled these Irish grants and applied the forfeiture monies to public service in the government.

William took alarm in 1700 when, on the death of Charles, king of Spain, it was found that he had be-

Great seal of Anne (before the union with Scotland)

Arms of Anne

Great seal of Queen Anne (after the union of England and Scotland)

Signature of Queen Anne

Halfpenny piece of Queen Anne

queathed all his dominions to Philip of Anjou, a grandson of Louis XIV. There were grounds for fear in this tremendous increase of the power of his great rival. In the following year James II died, and, disregarding the Treaty of Ryswick, Louis recognized the Pretender, son of James as king of England, Scotland, and Ireland. The angry Parliament requested William to make no peace with Louis until this insult was repaired. It was at this time that William met his death as a result of the stumbling of his horse, and the quarrel descended to Anne, who had hardly come to the throne when hostilities broke out with France, the war which became known as the Spanish Succession.

It was the recognition of the Pretender by Louis XIV that roused the English to the fighting point, for, should he gain the throne, it meant the restoration of the realm to the Catholic church. But there was much more involved, for it was necessary to defend Protestant Holland, now a valuable ally of England, and to protect the English colonies on the other side of the Atlantic from France, who was actively extending her settlements in America. It was, in fact, the opening of that gigantic struggle for supremacy in the New World which reached its culmination more than half a century later.

In the war that now broke out England had the services of two of the greatest military leaders of the age. These were John Churchill, duke of Marlborough, who commanded the English and Dutch forces, and Prince Eugene of Savoy, who led the German armies. Those allies supported the claims of the archduke Charles of Austria to the Spanish crown. Marlborough was conscienceless and treacherous, but no one could deny his masterly ability. James II had leaned on him, but he deserted to William, and then opened a secret correspondence with James. But Marlborough was a soldier of consummate genius, and earned the compliment of Voltaire, who remarked that the duke never besieged a fortress which he did not take, nor fought a battle which he did not win.

Eugene of Savoy was another kind of man. He was born in Paris, and was intended for the church, but his liking for a military life led him into the army. Being refused a regiment by Louis XIV, he volunteered under the emperor against the Turks, where his bravery and skill quickly won him the command of a regiment of dragoons. Afterward he was placed at the head of the army of Hungary. By this time Louis had discovered his genius, and offered him a marshal's staff, a pension, and the government of Champagne, but the prince could not forget the earlier slight, and indignantly refused the offer.

In 1704, by superb strategy, Marlborough shifted the scene of war from the Netherlands to Bavaria, and there, at the village of Blenheim, he and Prince Eugene won a crushing victory over the French. Marlborough, dismounting, led his troops to the attack, in person. The battle saved Germany from falling into the hands of Louis. England was so grateful to the duke that she presented him with the ancient park of Woodstock and built for him the Palace of Blenheim, near Oxford, where his descendants still live.

The war against France was prosecuted in Spain as well as in Germany. The rock and fortress of Gibraltar were taken by Admiral Sir George Rooke, yet on the whole, the allied arms were not successful in the Spanish Peninsula.

But, there was no checking the momentum. In 1706, the duke of Marlborough riding gloriously at the head of his charging troops, won the battle of Ramillies, in the Netherlands, thereby recovering the whole of that country from the French. Two years later the French armies came back to the Netherlands determined to regain the territory they had lost. Marlborough defeated them at Oudenarde, and the next year pushed the war into northern France, where he fought his last battle and won the victory of Malplaquet. He effectually broke the power of poor old King Louis, who had kept all Europe in a tremor for so many years.

Marlborough, for all his many vices, was the most devoted of husbands, and adored his wife, Sarah Jennings, duchess of Marlborough, to whom he wrote: "I would rather face twenty thousand men than meet a frown on your brow." She and Queen Anne were for years the most intimate of friends, corresponding almost daily under the names of Mrs. Morley, for the queen, and Mrs. Freeman, for the duchess. The latter was mentally the superior of the queen, and for a long time dominated her. But the time came when even the meek, stupid Anne rebelled at the domineering manner and methods of her mistress of the robes. They quarreled, and she was superseded by a Mrs. Masham, who speedily gained as complete control of the queen as had been held by the duchess. She brought about the abandonment of the Whig policy, made her cousin a prime minister, and secured the recall of Marlborough in disgrace.

The Tories, or peace party, having triumphed, negotiations were opened for bringing the tiresome war to a close. This was finally accomplished in 1713, at the city of Utrecht in Holland, where the treaty signed by all the nations interested bound Louis XIV to acknowledge the Protestant succession in England, to expel the Pretender from France, to renounce the union of the crowns of France and Spain, and to surrender to England all claims to Newfoundland, Nova Scotia, and the immense territory long known as the Hudson Bay Company's Possessions. On the part of Spain she agreed to yield her Netherlands to Austria and to allow the Dutch a line of forts to defend their frontier against France, while England was to have a monopoly of the slave trade for thirty-three years with the Spanish-American colonies.

From the time of James I, England and Scotland had been governed by one sovereign, but each country had its own parliament and religion. In 1707 the countries were united under the name of Great Britain, and the national flag, which had been ordered by James I but which had fallen into disuse, was "appointed" for the English, Scotish, and Welsh. In 1801, when Ireland was joined to Great Britain, the red cross of Saint Patrick was added to the flag, which united the cross of Saint George, the patron saint of England, and Saint Andrew, the patron saint of Scotland. The name "Jack," as applied to the flag, comes from *Jacques,* French for James.

A violent quarrel between the bitter rivals, Oxford and Bolingbroke in the presence of Queen Anne, hastened her death, which took place from apoplexy a week later, August 1, 1714. Seventeen children had been born to her, but all had died young. As prescribed by the Act of Settlement, the crown went to George, elector of Hanover, a Protestant descendant of James I of England. Thus in the death of Anne the Stuart line came to an end and that of the Brunswick line began.

THE HOUSE OF HANOVER

George I (1714–27) was a little, stupid Dutchman, fifty-four years old, fond of his long clay pipe and beer. He did not know and did not wish to know much about England, honestly preferring to live a country gentleman's life amid his homely German court. But he was persuaded that he would have to make a move; so, after waiting for six weeks, he took an extra swig from his

George I, 1714–27

Sophia Dorothea of Zell, wife of George I

mug, grunted, rose to his feet, and leaving his wife shut up in a castle, started with his eldest son for Greenwich. The loyal English people received him for the great argument he represented: Protestantism, with religious and civic liberty. But it was impossibly for anyone to feel enthusiasm over the coarse, awkward fellow, who had to be taught a few Latin sentences to repeat by rote at his coronation.

Although unable to speak a word of English, and having no English friends, this king did institute much of the form of government that is used there today. Instead of selecting a cabinet from his supporters, as did his predecessors, he chose one man for prime minister, who picked the cabinet from his own party. Thus, since Anne, no sovereign has been present at a cabinet council or refused assent to any Act of Parliament.

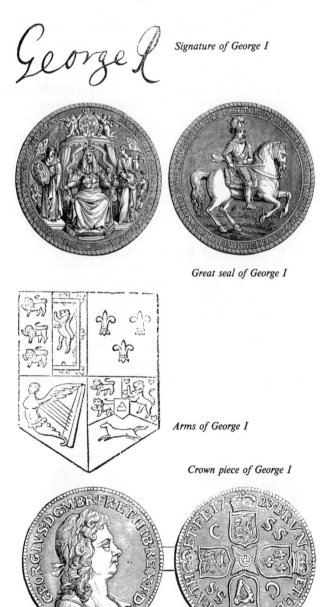

Signature of George I

Great seal of George I

Arms of George I

Crown piece of George I

The king understood that the Whigs were his friends, so he gave them the control of affairs, with the able Sir Robert Walpole at their head. Walpole was the first official prime minister of England. This marked a friendship for the Whigs, offended the Tories, but did not disturb the king, since his pet indulgences continued unmolested.

The Jacobites in Scotland, having a secret understanding with a considerable number of influential malcontents in England, rose in 1715 with the object of placing James Edward Stuart, son of James II, known as the Chevalier, or Pretender, on the throne. John, earl of Mar, shrewd in court intrigues, but without military talent, led the revolt, and an indecisive battle was fought at Sheriffmuir, in Perthshire, Scotland. Mar counted on a Jacobite uprising in the west of England, but prompt measures on the part of the government crushed it, and a number of the leaders were arrested. On the same day of the fight at Sheriffmuir, a party of Scots surrendered at Preston, Lancashire, without offering resistance. The earl of Mar fled and escaped to the Continent, but almost all of his more important followers were surprised, captured, and were sentenced to death for treason. A few escaped, but some thirty persons taken with arms in their hands were executed, while many of the common soldiery were sold as slaves to English colonists. Soon after the defeat of his friends, the Pretender visited Scotland, but he did not stay long.

This, however, was not the last to be seen of him. The king of Sweden, in revenge for George's purchase of the duchies of Bremen and Verden from Denmark and their annexation to Hanover, planned an invasion of Scotland, where he was invited by a number of Jacobites. But the conspiracy was discovered in 1717 and crushed.

George I left England for his beloved Hanover in the summer of 1727, but was stricken with apoplexy while in his carriage on the road to Osnabruck, and died on the night of the tenth of June. He left only one son, George Augustus, Prince of Wales, with whom the crusty old Dutchman was on bad terms. Before his death the Septennial Act was passed, which lengthened to seven years the term for which a Parliament might last, thus preventing the danger of dissensions and riots from frequent elections.

George II (1727–60) was forty-four years of age when he became king, and he had one advantage over his father: he knew how to speak English. Like his father, he was on poor terms with his son, Frederick, Prince of Wales, who possessed very little ability, but was popular because of his father's unpopularity. The king was miserly, stubborn, of ugly temper, and fond of war. He was restrained, however, from plunging the country into disaster. A wise and able woman shared his throne, and without appearance of mastery discreetly guided her husband. The queen trusted Sir Robert Walpole, and retained him as prime minister, though the king disliked

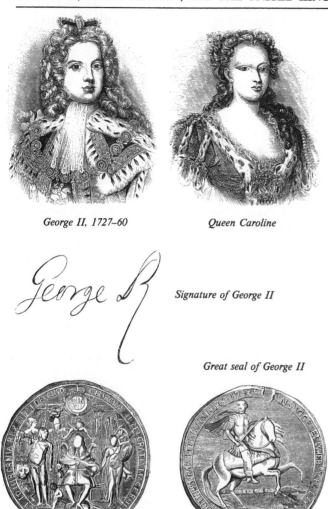

George II, 1727–60

Queen Caroline

Signature of George II

Great seal of George II

severe losses in their expedition against Carthagena. The capture of Porto Bello was about the only substantial English success of the war.

Walpole's opposition to this war, in which it is charged he was influenced not so much by his wish of peace for his country as peace for his administration, made him so unpopular that he was forced to resign in 1742, when he was created earl of Orford, with a pension of $20,000 a year. Charges of corruption were made against him but were dropped in the end, and he died three years later at the age of sixty-eight.

It is said in the history of Germany and of Austria, that when Charles VI, who was of the House of Austria and emperor of Germany, died in 1740, his daughter, Maria Theresa, succeeded to the Austrian dominions. This was one of those occasions when one hears so much about the "balance of power" being endangered, as France, Prussia, and other nations united to upset the balance to secure some of the Austrian possessions for themselves. It was to the interest of England and Holland to hold Austria as a check against the aggressions of their old rival and enemy, France, and they, in company with Austria, declared war in 1741. The sweetest perfume to the nostrils of George II was the smell of gunpowder. Hurrying to Germany, he joined his army and, leaping out of his saddle, fought on foot—the last time an English sovereign appeared in battle. He proved himself the fine soldier he was, too, doing more than any one else to win the battle of Dettingen, in 1743.

In 1745, however, the French, under Marshal Saxe, defeated the allies at Fontenoy, in the Netherlands. Crossing the ravine which protected Fontenoy, the English advanced as though on parade. Each major, having a small cane in his hand, rested it lightly on the muskets of the soldiers to regulate their fire. The fusillade was fatal to the French guard. Saxe begged Louis XV to retreat. "I stay where I am," said Louis. Fortunately for the proud Frenchman, he had in his service the Irish brigade, composed of Jacobite exiles. These charged furiously on the English, overwhelmed them, and won the day for France. In 1748 a peace was arranged at Aix-la-Chapelle.

And now the time had arrived for the Stuarts' last effort to regain loyalty. The War of the Austrian Succession led the French to encourage Charles Edward, grandson of James II, known as the Young Pretender, to make an attempt for the English crown. An expedition to invade England put to sea in 1744, but was shattered by a storm. The following year Charles landed on the northern coast of Scotland with seven comrades.

Being joined by a considerable number of followers, the Young Pretender defeated the British at Prestonpans, near Edinburgh, his Highlanders sweeping away their opponents in one tremendous and successful charge. Greatly enspirited by his success, he advanced into Derbyshire, on his way to London, his army

him. Thus, guided by the minister's wisdom, the government continued to prosper. Nevertheless, at the end of twelve years a war did break out with Spain, and it was all on account of a man's ear!

A Captain Jenkins, an English navigator, was cruising in the West Indies—and most likely smuggling—when he fell into the hands of the Spaniards. Angered because they believed him to be violating the law, they clipped off one of his ears, which he wrapped in paper and thrust into his pocket. When he reached London, boiling with fury, he strode into the House of Commons, unwrapped the ear, and holding it up so all might see, demanded that something be done to revenge the outrage.

England had long been vexed with Spain because she interfered in her contraband trade with the South American colonies. Captain Jenkins's shriveled ear brought matters to an issue. Walpole could not stem the tide, and was forced to declare war (1739), the step being received with ringing of bells and shouts of rejoicing. "Ah," said Walpole, "ring the cords of all your bells today, but how long before you will wring your hands!"

The prime minister was right, for the English suffered

Charles Edward Stuart, the Young Pretender

Crown piece of George II

amounting to about four thousand men. The capital was thrown into consternation and Charles was grievously disappointed by the failure of the people to rise in his favor, as he had been sure they would do. The English "Jacobites" were discontented with the government, but had not reached open rebellion. Charles held an earnest conference with his officers, who insisted that it was folly to go on, and only one course remained to them: that was to leave England without delay. Charles sorrowfully obeyed, and withdrew into Scotland, where he gained a victory at Falkirk, but was routed at Culloden, April 16, 1746, by William, duke of Cumberland, son of the king. The slaughter of the wounded men and the atrocities perpetrated in the neighborhood made a foul blot upon English arms and earned for the duke the name of the Butcher.

Charles never could have escaped after Culloden but for the devoted loyalty of the Highlanders. Hundreds of them knew where he was hiding, and though the people

were in the depth of poverty and could have earned more than a hundred thousand dollars by betraying him, not a man dropped a hint of where he was hidden under cover, with the English beating the bushes and wood, hunting for him as if he were royal game, as in truth it may be said he was. However, he escaped, and finally reached France, never returning to Scotland. He died in 1788 at Rome, a miserable drunkard, and thus the house of Stuart vanished form the troublous stage of action, though the younger brother of the Pretender, Henry Benedict, Cardinal York, did not pass away until 1807.

Terrible punishment was administered to the leaders of this revolt, of whom some eighty were put to death. Among them were the earl of Kilmarnock, Lords Balmerino and Lovat, and Charles Radcliffe, a brother of the late earl of Derwentwater. The uprising itself, on account of the year in which it took place, is called by the Scots the Forty-Five.

George II died of heart disease at Kensington on October 25, 1760. His eldest son having passed away nine years before, he was succeeded by his grandson, George William Frederick, Prince of Wales, who was born in 1738 and was of English birth.

GEORGE III AND THE STRUGGLE WITH NAPOLEON

George III was king for sixty years (1760–1820), and his long reign saw greater events and more important changes for England than perhaps any other period of equal length. He came to the throne several years after the breaking out of the French and Indian War in America. This was the supreme struggle between England and France for the mastery of the North American continent.

The first few years of the French and Indian War went against the British, because the French were better organized and were wise enough to win the support of most of the fierce Indian tribes. Then, under the splendid guidance of William Pitt, who became prime minister of England, a great change was wrought. The best officers

George III, 1760–1820

William Henry (afterwards Duke of Clarence).   GEORGE III.   QUEEN CHARLOTTE.   Princess Mary.
George, Prince of Wales.   Frederick (afterwards Duke of York).   Princess Augusta.   Princess Elizabeth.
Ernest Augustus.   Augustus Frederick.   Adolphus Frederick.

George III and his family, 1775

Attempted assassination of George III on his way to the House of Lords

were sent across the ocean, and they were given enough troops to organize and carry out decisive campaigns. The crowning victory was won by General Montcalm Wolfe at Quebec in 1759. Spain then ceded Florida to Great Britain, and, when peace was made in 1763, the Union Jack waved over the eastern half of the continent, and France was left with scarcely a foothold between the Atlantic and the Mississippi.

The next important war in which Great Britain became engaged was with her thirteen American colonies, the war of which we speak as the "Revolution." Opening in 1775, it was pressed with the greatest valor under General George Washington, and through cold,

heat, sufferings, and starvation, was brought to a successful conclusion in October 1781, by the surrender of Lord Cornwallis at Yorktown, Virginia. The final treaty by which England recognized the independence of the United States was signed September 3, 1783, and the last of the English forces in the United States left New York on November 25.

In 1782 Ireland secured the independence of her Parliament, though she remained subject to the kingdom of Great Britain. Rebellions were put down with crushing severity, and through the most flagrant bribery of members of the Irish Parliament, Ireland was, on January 1, 1800, united to Great Britain under the title of the United Kingdom of Great Britain and Ireland.

England had to fight a long time in India to maintain her supremacy. The first governor general, Warren Hastings (1774), through his great ability, extended England's power there while it was losing in other quarters. But he was as unscrupulous in many respects as the duke of Marlborough, and, in 1786, was impeached by the Commons for injustice, oppression, and extortion. The English dominion was extended later, and in 1815 Ceylon was annexed to Great Britain. The exposure of the corruption of the East Indian Company caused it to be broken up, and, in 1784, a Board of Control was created for the administration of Indian affairs. A formidable rebellion broke out under Tippoo Saib, an Indian prince whose capital was at Seringapatam. He led his army in several open battles against the English, but finally his capital was stormed and he himself slain (1799). India was absorbed into the regular system of English government.

George III was a man of excellent character, conscientious but stubborn to the last degree. When he had made up his mind to follow a certain cause, argument was wasted upon him: he was ready at any time to walk straight to the scaffold for conscience's sake. But for this immovable obstinacy there would have been no American Revolution, for the best men in his kingdom opposed coercing the colonies into submission to the tyrannous acts of the king.

In September 1761 he married the princess Charlotte Sophia, daughter of Charles, duke of Mecklenburg-Strelitz, and the two were the parents of fifteen children. He suffered strokes several times—in 1764, in 1788, in 1801, and in 1804. In 1810, his final total incapacitation occurred. He was so provoked by the marriages of two of his brothers that he secured the passage of the Royal Marriage Act in 1772, by which the descendants of George II, excepting the issues of princesses married into foreign families, were not allowed to marry under the age of twenty-five without the consent of the sovereign. After that age marriages were contracted upon due notice, unless both houses of Parliament express their opposition. The enormous debts and the scandalous dissipation of his eldest son, who became George IV, the young man's private marriage with Mrs. Fitzherbert, the Roman Catholic widow of two husbands, and the scandals of his public marriage with his cousin, Caroline of Brunswick, proved that even a marriage bill cannot cure all the domestic miseries of a sovereign.

During this period England's long and glorious struggle against Napoleon occurred. The war began as early as 1793, the new and amazingly vigorous French Republic having included England in the number of her foes in that defiant declaration of war against all Europe. The early land operations brought England no honor, but she at once established her superiority at sea. The French ships were defeated and driven out of the English Channel. British fleets controlled the Mediterranean and the Atlantic. Spain and Holland, the great sea powers, allied themselves with France. England crushed them both in two famous naval battles in 1797.

The Spaniards were defeated off Cape St. Vincent in the Atlantic. It was this battle that first centered attention on England's greatest naval hero, Nelson. He had already risen to the rank of commodore, and, although not nominally in command, he bore the brunt of the fighting at St. Vincent. He led his men on board a huge Spanish ship with the cry, "Victory or Westminster Abbey!" meaning that if he failed he would, by a glorious death, earn a burial place in the great abbey where England enshrines her heroic dead.

Tippo Saib

Tippo Saib leading his troops to the defense of Seringapatam

The Dutch were soon afterward defeated off Camperdown by Admiral Duncan. They made a sturdy and gallant fight, but almost their entire fleet was either sunk or captured. It was in the same year of 1797, in fact, in the interval between the two great seafights.

In 1798, Napoleon, having risen to the head of French affairs, undertook his expedition to Egypt. Nelson, now admiral, was in command of the British fleet in the Mediterranean, and gained worldwide fame by attacking Napoleon's ships at Aboukir, in the mouth of the River Nile, defeating and almost wholly destroying them. By the "Battle of the Nile" the French conqueror and his entire army became practically prisoners in Egypt. Napoleon got back to France by a daring flight through the British blockade, but his army could not follow him, until a treaty of peace with England allowed them to be carried home by the very ships that had held them in exile.

The powers of the North—Russia, Sweden, and Denmark—next formed a naval league against England. Denmark's strong fleet was defeated by Nelson off Copenhagen in 1801. So determinedly did the Danish fleet and shore batteries return the English fire that the nominal commander (over Nelson) had enough of the cannonade and hoisted a signal for the Britons to retreat. Nelson, white with the rage of the battle, raised his telescope to one eye, the sight of which had been destroyed in a previous battle. "I really cannot see any such signal," he said to his men. "We will have to go on fighting." And they did—and won.

The short-lived peace between England and France was followed in 1803 by deeper and more deadly war, a war that ceased only with Napoleon's downfall. Its sudden announcement found over ten thousand Englishmen in France. Napoleon promptly arrested them, and they remained prisoners for eleven years.

During all these years, Napoleon conquered all of central Europe, but England conquered all the waters of the earth. Her fleet was victorious over Frenchman, Spaniard, Hollander, and Dane. Now, in the greatest triumph of all, Nelson defeated the French and Spanish navies combined, and perished in the hour of his most glorious victory.

This celebrated battle of Trafalgar was fought because of Napoleon's attempt to invade England. All his forces were gathered at Boulogne to cross the Channel, but first he must be rid of the enemy's fleet. So his admirals were ordered to deceive Nelson by pretended flight, and as he pursued them, they were to evade him on the ocean and return to Boulogne. "If I can be master of the Channel for only twelve hours," said the great conqueror, "England is ended."

Nelson pursued the fleeing ships with scorn. Some of them escaped him, and were returning; but off Cape Finisterre, on the Spanish coast, he had a small English squadron under Admiral Calder meet them. Calder checked them, and drove them to seek shelter in the harbor of Cadiz.

This battle of Finisterre may have saved England. At any rate, Napoleon abandoned his camp at Boulogne, and found another use for his armies. Meanwhile, all the French and Spanish men-of-war gathered at Cadiz, and there Nelson, still following in pursuit, found them. They outranked his ships in both size and number, and sailed out of the harbor to attack him off Cape Trafalgar.

Nelson hoisted from his flagship the stern and simple signal, "England expects every man to do his duty!" and the battle began. It raged for four hours, and resulted in the complete defeat of the Spaniards and the French. The great admiral was shot in the height of the contest and, though mortally wounded, remained listening with joy to the cheers of his men as one of the enemy's ships surrendered after the other. He died just at the close of the battle.

England, unmolested at sea, sought to meet her mighty foe on land, supporting each nation that revolted under Napoleon's oppression. Most important of these struggles was that known as the Peninsular War, which broke out in Spain in 1808.

Sir Arthur Wellesley, afterward the duke of Wellington, who had already gained fame in India, was sent by England to the aid of the Spanish patriots. He won an important battle at Vimiero and then was given the chief command. He drove the French from Portugal without a battle, and defeated them in Spain at Talavera, for which he was made Lord Wellington. It was not, however, until 1812 that Wellington felt himself sufficiently strong to make an aggressive campaign. He defeated the French in a great battle at Salamanca, and again at Vitoria, in 1813.

By this time Napoleon was in the toils of his Russian disaster, and the weakened forces that he left in Spain were easily swept back into their own land. The last battle of the Peninsular War was fought in 1814, at Toulouse, on the soil of France itself. At that moment the Prussian and allied forces were already masters of Paris.

England with historical detail, 1800–1900

When Napoleon, escaping from Elba, made one more bid for power, he knew well that England and Prussia were his chief opponents. They were once more first in the field against him, and it was they who under Wellington's command defeated him at Waterloo. All day long in that last great battle the squares of English infantry resisted the assaults of France's bravest veterans. At length, when it seemed as if human flesh and blood could endure no longer, the Prussian reinforcements arrived. Wellington, who had been anxiously studying the field with his spyglass, closed it. "Let the whole line advance!" he said; and the Britons rolled in one huge wave over the despairing foe.

Napoleon fled to a British frigate. This big war was over, the French emperor an exile, and Wellington the hero of all the world. Alas! that Nelson had not lived to share the glory!

Let us look back, to speak of what was to England but a side issue in this tremendous struggle. Her arrogance and oppression upon the ocean proved unendurable to the United States; and the War of 1812 resulted. America had no fleet to match England's, but neither could England spare her entire fleet. And ship for ship U.S. sailors taught her that there were seafighters as good, perhaps better, than hers. The English statesmen were loud in the complaints of the child they had reared to strike at them; and the peace treaty of 1815 left a still smoldering fire of ill will between the kindred nations, which it took over a half a century to obliterate.

Turn now to the puppet king, who, during all these great events sat immovable upon England's throne. In 1810, Princess Amelia, the youngest and most loved child of King George, died. His heart was broken by the blow, and his insanity returned. The remaining ten years of his life were brightened only by flashes of lucidity. Because of his condition, his eldest son was appointed regent, and acted as such from 1811 until his father's death, in 1820.

Sovereigns of England, 1689–1910

Victoria

Anne	Edward VII	William IV
George I	Mary II	George IV
George II	George III	William III

GEORGE IV

George IV was fifty-seven years old when he came to the throne. While Prince of Wales, his income had been more than half a million dollars; but he was always swamped by debt. By 1795 his debts had become so mountainous that Parliament undertook to wipe them out by an appropriation of 3 million dollars. But soon he was as deeply involved as before, and had not help been given him again by the taxpayers, he would have been hopelessly bankrupt.

When he became king, matters grew worse than before. The nation paid more than a million dollars for his coronation. The jewels in which he appeared were borrowed, and he stole them, for his neglect to return them amounted to nothing less than that, and Parliament, as meek as ever, paid for them. Added to his incredible extravagance, he did all he could to oppose reforms.

The marriage of the Prince of Wales with his cousin, Caroline, was entered into by him on the demand of his father, because it offered a prospect of his debts being paid. She was a coarse woman, from whom the prince soon separated. Shortly after he became king, a bill was brought into Parliament to divorce her for criminal misconduct. The examination of witnesses before the House of Lords disclosed such baseness in the king that the bill was dropped. His wife had the sympathy of the people, but the king was resolute that she should not be crowned as his consort. She appeared on the morning of the coronation before the doors of Westminster Abbey only to be turned away. She died shortly after.

Three important reforms were made law during the reign of George IV. The first was the repeal of the Corporation Act, which had excluded Dissenters from all town or corporate offices; the second was the repeal of the Test Act, passed under Charles II to keep Catholics and Dissenters out of government offices, whether civil or military. The third and most important reform was the passage in 1829 of the Catholic Emancipation Act. This was bitterly opposed by the duke of Wellington, who was Prime Minister, and by the king; but it went through in spite of them. It gave the Catholics the right to sit in Parliament, a privilege which had been denied them for more than a century. Daniel O'Connell, an honorable Irish gentleman, possessing great ability, became the leader of the Catholics. He succeeded after much difficulty in securing his seat in the House of Commons.

The most popular thing done by George IV during his reign occurred at Windsor Castle, June 26, 1830, when he stopped living. Since the dead king had left no direct heir, his brother, William Henry, duke of Clarence, succeeded to the throne. He had certainly reached the age of discretion, for he was in his sixty-sixth year. He had spent his early life in the navy, was a bluff, hearty fellow, with a contempt for pomp and ceremony, and was well liked by the people, who called him the Sailor King. He

King George IV, 1820–30

George IV. "A Voluptuary under the horrors of digestion," colored etching by J. Gillray (National Portrait Gallery)

King William IV, 1830–37

Adelaide, queen consort of William IV

was the first William of Hanover, the second William of Ireland, the third William of Scotland, and the fourth William of England.

Simon de Montfort, in the reign of Henry III, labored to give the people a share in the making of the laws, and he sent two men from every town and borough in England to speak and act for the people who lived in them. That was the way the House of Commons came into existence six hundred years before the time of William IV. Many of the old towns had decayed and vanished since the time of Montfort, and new ones, like Manchester, Leeds, Birmingham, and Glasgow and grown into big cities. But there had been no change in the system of representation. Thus many large cities were totally unrepresented. After William IV came to the throne Lord John Russell, on March 1, 1831, brought in a Reform Bill, which was so sweeping that it roused violent opposition. The Ministry was defeated, and persuaded the king to dissolve Parliament. Then a new House of Commons was elected under the battle cry of "The Bill, the whole Bill, and nothing but the Bill." The measure was sent to the House of Lords, who rejected it. It was not until a third Reform Bill had been brought in by the Ministry and passed by the Commons that the Peers yielded, and it became a law, June 7, 1832. Even this would not have been accomplished had not the king, in obedience to the pressure put upon him, notified the House of Lords that if they refused their assent he would create a sufficient number of Whig lords to carry the measure.

This Reform Bill, one of the most important measures ever passed by Parliament, abolished the "rotten boroughs," gave a vote to every householder who paid a rent of fifty dollars.

Many of the Tories were sure that this reform meant the ruin of England. Even the brave old duke of Wellington wrote: "I don't generally take a gloomy view of things, but I confess that, knowing all that I do, I cannot see what is to save the Church, or property, or colonies, or union with Ireland, or eventually monarchy, if the Reform Bill passes."

With the coming of the new Parliament the Whigs began to take the name of Liberals and the Tories of Conservatives.

Although the slave trade had been extinguished wherever the English power reached, slavery still existed in the colonies. In 1833, in the face of the king's opposition, a bill was passed by Parliament, which set free all black slaves in British colonies. There were also thousands of white slaves in England at that time—women and children who toiled in the factories and in the mines.

William IV passed away at Windsor Castle, June 20, 1837. His two daughters by his wife, Princess Adelaide of Saxe-Meiningen, died in infancy. This left as the heir to the throne Princess Alexandrina Victoria, the only child of his brother, Edward, duke of Kent. Victoria was living with her widowed mother at the time, and was only eighteen years old. She was a religious girl, conscientious to the last degree, and destined to become one of the noblest queens who ever lived. Early that bright summer morning in 1837 she was suddenly awakened and told, much to her amazement, that she was queen of Great Britain.

On the night that King William IV died in 1837, Victoria was aroused from her sleep to be told she was the queen of England. Her retort was: "My Lord Archbishop, pray for me."

THE VICTORIAN PERIOD (1837–1901)

No sovereign could have received a more enthusiastic welcome than Queen Victoria, and this loyalty and affection increased until her death, after the longest reign of any sovereign over Great Britain.

On February 10, 1840, the queen married her cousin, Prince Albert of Saxe-Coburg and Gotha. The marriage was what is almost unknown among royal couples—a genuine love match, and the two lived ideally happy lives until the death of the prince consort, in December 1861.

The king or queen of England has much less power than the president of the United States. If a measure after passing both houses of Congress is submitted to the President, and he dislikes it, he sends it back with a statement of the reasons why he disapproves, and it then requires a two-thirds vote to pass it over his veto. It is in his power to defeat a measure that is preferred by a majority of Congress, and he frequently does so. Again, the president chooses his own members of the cabinet. True, he sends the names to the Senate for confirmation, but the political situation must be very remarkable when the Senate is discourteous enough to refuse its approval. Moreover, the president has unlimited power in removing any member of his cabinet. When Victoria became queen, she accepted the principle that she could not remove the minister or his cabinet without the consent of the House of Commons, nor would she venture to keep a Ministry which that body refused to support.

Another custom has acquired the force of law: the sovereign has no veto power whatever. The king or queen, as it may be, must approve every bill passed by Parliament. As has been said, if the two houses should agree upon the king's own death warrant and send it to him, he must sign it or abdicate.

The Opium War in which England engaged in 1839, was disgraceful to that country. In the year named the Chinese emperor forbade the importation of the poisonous drug into China. England was largely engaged in cultivating opium in India for the Chinese market, and forbade the emperor to interfere. War followed, with the result that the Chinese were compelled to allow the drug which destroyed the bodies and souls of countless of Chinese people, to be brought into their country as before, while the opium planters of India and the British traders reaped a golden harvest in thus violating the

Queen Victoria, 1837–1901, at the time of her coronation (from a portrait—painter unknown—in Westminster Abbey)

The marriage of Queen Victoria, in the Chapel Royal, St. James's Palace

His Royal Highness Prince Albert

sacred rights of a heathen people. Great Britain compelled the opening of Hong Kong and several important ports to British trade, with subsequent wars adding others.

It seems to be the decree of perverse fate that Turkey was the bone of contention among the leading powers. Any disturbance of her government or boundaries must threaten the "balance of power," as it is termed, and the mutual jealousy of those powers will not permit that. Turkey, therefore, was the intolerable nuisance among nations. She was corrupt, treacherous, and cruel to the last degree, her most cherished amusement being that of massacring Christians. Gladstone well named the sultan the Great Assassin. Nicholas, czar of Russia, who had long cast covetous eyes upon Constantinople (Istanbul), thought the time had come, in 1852, for him to take a step toward acquiring that city. His pretext was the restrictions laid by the sultan upon Christians in Palestine. He demanded that he should be made the protector of Christianity throughout Turkey, and the scheme he proposed would have made St. Petersburg (Leningrad) the real capital of the Ottoman Empire.

Turkey declared war against Russia in 1853, and soon after England and France joined as allies of Turkey. The British campaign was marked by the worst blunders conceivable. While ships laden with provisions and clothing, enough for ten times as many troops, lay within sight of Sebastopol, thousands of the soldiers starved and froze to death in their rags. Hardly one out of ten of those who were sent to the hospitals lived to come out again. To Florence Nightingale and her assistants is due the credit of redeeming the unpardonable failure of the nation.

The allied armies triumphed in the end. Russia was forced to give up her demands, and suffered the humiliation of being shut out from the waters of her own Black Sea.

The Sepoy Mutiny of 1857–58 was one of the most terrible uprisings in British history. It was due to several factors, the principal being the belief of the fanatical population that the British were trying to undermine their religion. The native Indian troops were ordered to use cartridges lubricated with hog's grease, and they had at times to hold the cartridges in their teeth. Now everything connected with hog-eating is an unspeakable abomination to the Mussulman and the Hindu, who are ready at all times to face death for the sake of their faith. The revolt broke out at Meerut in June 1857, and ran like a prairie fire. The native troops, or sepoys, were good soldiers, but they turned against their British officers and cut them down without mercy. The mind can conceive of no more horrifying ferocities than were committed by these fiends upon the helpless women and children, nor can England be blamed for inflicting upon some of them the only punishment they dreaded—that of being blown to pieces at the cannon's mouth, since that made it impossible to give the remains proper religious burial.

After the crushing of the revolt all political power was withdrawn from the East India Company, and the country was brought under the direct rule of the British crown. The governor-general became viceroy, with a council, and the supreme power of India was subject to the secretary of state in England. In 1876, Queen Victoria was proclaimed empress of India.

Let us finish our glance at that part of the world by saying that after many revolts and much strife, England succeeded in placing a friendly ruler at the head of affairs in Afghanistan, and kept him there until his recent death, by the payment of a yearly allowance of six hundred thousand dollars. In January 1886, the king of Burma, who had misused British traders, was ousted and Upper Burma was annexed to India. In 1887, Russia, which was very jealous of England's growing power in that region, agreed upon a new boundary between Russian territory and Afghanistan, with a view of preserving peace, which had been threatened more than once.

Theodore, king of Abyssinia, barbarously abused two representatives of England and refused to give satisfaction for just claims against him. War was declared, and, in the autumn of 1867, an army of ten thousand men, under the command of Sir Robert Napier, landed at Massouah. Magdala was conquered the following April, and the death of King Theodore followed. The repairing of the wrong done her two representatives cost England $44,895,000.

The death of King Theodore of Abyssinia

In the spring of 1861 the American War for the Union, the most tremendous struggle of modern times, broke out and lasted four years. Napoleon, emperor of France, was one of the most malignant enemies of the Union, and Queen Victoria was one of its warmest friends.

Honorable Abram Hewitt, formerly mayor of New York, has publicly stated that in 1862, while on a confidential mission for our government to England and France, Minister Dayton asked him to leave for London at once to notify Minister Adams that Napoleon III had proposed to the British government to recognize the Southern Confederacy. There was imminent danger that England would join in such recognition, and Hewitt made all haste to London. Lord John Russell was so evasive that Minister Adams demanded the privilege of seeing the queen, for it was evident to him that something of the most momentous importance was afoot. It was an unusual privilege that was asked, but Minister Adams went to Windsor, where he saw the queen personally. He laid the case before her and appealed against so monstrous a wrong, declaring that it would produce universal war, for the United States would fight the whole world rather than give up the Union. In the presence of Prince Albert the queen said:

"Mr. Adams, give yourself no concern; my government will not recognize the Confederacy."

"The queen was the friend of peace," said Mr. Hewitt; "she was the friend of the United States; and it is a debt of gratitude, which can never be discharged by any amount of homage which we Americans can bring and offer upon the tomb of this great sovereign and this good woman."

Down to 1858 the Jews were shut out from Parliament by the provision that they should make oath "on the faith of a Christian." This law was so changed that Baron Rothschild, the famous Jewish banker, was able to take his seat among the legislators of the country. Disraeli, leader of the Conservative party, carried through a Reform Bill in 1867 that gave the right to vote to every householder who paid a tax for the support of the poor, and to all lodgers paying a rental of fifty dollars yearly. In 1886, under the Liberal ministry of Gladstone, a third Reform Bill gave all the residents of counties in the United Kingdom the right to vote.

The Second Irish Land Act was carried through by Mr. Gladstone in 1881, and was popularly known as the Three F's—Fair rent, Fixity of tenure, and Free sale. It gave the tenant the right to appeal to a board of land commissioners, appointed to fix the rate of his rent, when the demands of the landlord were unreasonable. Provided he paid the rate fixed, he was allowed to hold the land for fifteen years, during which the rent could not be increased, nor could the tenant be evicted, except for violation of the agreement or continued neglect of the land. Finally, he was at liberty to sell his tenancy whenever he chose.

After the Second Land Act had become law, Lord Frederick Cavendish, chief secretary of Ireland, and Mr. Burke, a leading government official, were assassinated in Phoenix Park, Dublin, after which the members of different secret societies made use of the fearful explosive, dynamite, in perpetrating outrages in London and elsewhere. These crimes were denounced by the chiefs of the Irish National party, who demanded home rule, under the lead of Charles S. Parnell, "the uncrowned king of Ireland," a member of Parliament. In 1886, Gladstone brought in a bill for the establishment of an Irish Parliament, but it was defeated. On his return to power, in 1893, he introduced a similar measure, which was carried through the Commons, but all his masterful eloquence could not save it from defeat in the House of Lords.

When Queen Victoria was born in the apartments of her father, the duke of Kent, in Kensington Palace, her godfathers were the emperor Alexander of Russia and her uncle, the prince regent, who was afterward George IV. Her father seemed to believe from the first that she would come to the throne of England, and wished her to be named Elizabeth, probably because he hoped her reign would rival in splendor that of the great queen. The prince regent wanted her to be called Georgianna, and when the archbishop of Canterbury asked him at the font what the child's name was to be he replied, "Alexandrina"—the feminine form of the czar's name. The duke of Kent begged that some other name might be added, whereupon his eldest brother said: "Then give her the name of her mother also, but it may not precede that of the emperor." Thus it was that she received the name of Alexandrina Victoria.

Her father died from pneumonia before she was a year old, and she was raised by her mother, the duchess of Kent, who lived to see her become queen and the mother of a large family. She was educated with the utmost care, and grew to be one of the most admired of women. From the very beginning of her reign the court life of England underwent a radical change. Referring to the purer and higher tone that prevailed in royal circles under Victoria, the London *Times* said:

"It is hard to overstate, for example, the effect of such a purification of the court as her reign has witnessed: one may perhaps measure it by imagining what would have happened to England had the reign of Carlton House (George IV) lasted for sixty years."

There was an early assassination attempt. The young queen and her husband were riding in an open carriage up Constitution Hill, accompanied by their usual attendants, when a young man suddenly aimed a pistol at her and pulled the trigger, but missed. Before he could be stopped, he drew a second weapon, fired, and again missed. At this juncture he was seized, disarmed, and handed over to the police. He made no resistance, and at the police station identified himself as Edward Oxford, a barman. He was sentenced to imprisonment "during the queen's reign," but it appearing afterward that he was insane, he was released and went to Australia.

The first child born to the queen, November 13, 1840, was the princess royal, Victoria Adelaide, who became the wife of the emperor Frederick of Germany. Four days less than a year later Albert Edward, who was to become Edward VII, was born. The remaining children were Alice Maud Mary, grand duchess of Hesse (1843); Alfred, duke of Saxe-Coburg-Gotha, duke of Edinburgh (1844); Helena, princess Christian (1846); Louise, duchess of Argyll (1848), Arthur, duke of Connaught (1850); Leopold, duke of Albany (1853); Beatrice Mary Victoria Feodore (1857).

There was great rejoicing over the birth of the prince of Wales. The queen directed that the convicts who were on good behavior should have their sentences commuted, and she issued a "patent" creating the month-old baby prince of Wales and earl of Chester. He was already duke of Saxony, duke of Cornwall and Rothesay, earl of Carrick, baron of Renfrew, lord of the Isles, and great steward of Scotland. The principal guest at the young prince's christening was the king of Prussia, who stood as sponsor. The prince married Princess Alexandra of Denmark, on March 10, 1863.

In 1842, there was rioting in the mining districts and fear of an uprising. The queen opened Parliament in person and read the speech from the throne. To relieve the distress in London, she gave a great fancy ball, hoping thereby to stimulate trade. It was famous as the Plantagenet ball, the queen appearing as Philippa, consort of Edward III, and the prince consort as Edward III.

About this time two further attempts were made on the queen's life. As she was driving down Constitution Hill a man named John Francis fired a pistol at her, but the weapon was grabbed by a policeman who saw it drawn. Her Majesty and her husband, as in the former instance, remained cool, and appeared at the opera that night. Francis was tried for high treason and sentenced

The royal family: the queen; the Prince of Wales (Edward VII); Empress Frederick (Victoria Adelaide), and her son, William II; and other children and grandchildren of the queen

Queen Victoria and her signature

to death. The queen made the mistake, committed by more than one sovereign, of reprieving the assassin. She was rewarded the following Sunday by a similar attempt by William Been, a druggist's assistant, but his pistol misfired. It seems to take sovereigns a lot longer to learn that leniency in such cases encourages anarchists and seekers of notoriety. A bill introduced by Sir Robert Peel, which became law, made all attempts on the queen's life high misdemeanors, punishable only by seven years of imprisonment, and "the culprit to be whipped publicly or privately not more than three times."

The queen made her first visit to Scotland in 1842 and was greeted everywhere with great enthusiasm. Later she and the prince consort went to France and were received with much ceremony by King Louis-Philippe. It was the first time that an English monarch had gone there since the Field of the Cloth of Gold, when Henry VIII met the French sovereign.

In 1848, Louis-Philippe, who had received the queen with so much pomp and splendor, presented himself in England under the name of plain "John Smith," being a fugitive from the uprising in his own country, and Victoria was most hospitable to the exiled king and queen.

In May 1848, William Hamilton fired a pistol at the queen, but missed. He narrowly escaped lynching. He was tried and sentenced to seven years. The same year saw the queen's first visit to Ireland. She and her husband were greeted with wild enthusiasm by the people of Dublin.

In 1850, soon after the birth of Prince Arthur, a Lieutenant Pate struck at the queen with his cane as she was leaving Cambridge House. Her face was bruised, but her big bonnet saved her from serious injury. As usual, the plea of insanity was set up and all the punishment he received was the regulation seven years.

The principal domestic event of 1851 was the opening of the Great Exhibition in Hyde Park, which proved the beginning of the world's fairs that have been held so many times in different countries.

Queen's Jubilee, Queen Victoria leaving palace

The court reception during Victoria's Diamond Jubilee

Prince Albert, who had been in poor health for some time, died December 14, 1861. Everyone sympathized with the sovereign, left a widow at the age of forty-two.

In 1887, there occupied the jubilee of the queen's accession to the throne. London swarmed with visitors, and many princes took part in the procession to Westminster Abbey. Ten years later, the celebration of her Diamond Jubilee was still more imposing. On June 21, a Sunday—the queen went to St. Paul's church in great state to return thanks on the completion of the sixtieth year of her reign. Later she held a state reception at Buckingham Palace surrounded by all the great dignitaries of the realm. Before she left the palace she telegraphed the message to all parts of the empire: "From my heart I thank my beloved people. May God bless you."

The dearest wish of Victoria was that her closing years should not be disturbed by war, but her prayer was not to be granted. The conflict in South Africa came. She was strongly opposed to it, but could not stay the sentiment in its favor. It depressed and made her melancholy, and her sadness continued till her death, which took place January 22, 1901. Her reign was the longest in English history.

THE TWENTIETH CENTURY

After Queen Victoria's death there was a succession of kings and queens in her stead but the monarch was never again a strong ruler, more a figurehead. There followed her son, Edward VII (1901–10); and his son, George V (1910–36); and his son, Edward VIII, who reigned for only a matter of days in 1936—a period limited by his country's displeasure with his love for a commoner, a divorced American woman; and his brother, George VI (1936–52) next in line. Upon his death in 1952, George VI's older child, Queen Elizabeth II, succeeded him.

Queen Elizabeth was born on April 21, 1926; married Prince Philip, the duke of Edinburgh, on November 20, 1947; acceded to the throne on February 6, 1952; and was crowned on June 2, 1953. She celebrated her Silver Jubilee (the twenty-fifth anniversary of her accession to the throne) during 1977. Her title in Britain is: Elizabeth the Second, by the Grace of God of the United Kingdom of Great Britain and Northern Ireland and of Her Other Realms and Territories Queen, Head of the Commonwealth, Defender of the Faith. The queen's eldest son— Charles, Prince of Wales— is the heir to the throne. Next in line of succession are, in order: Prince Andrew, Prince Edward, Princess Anne, and her son, Peter.

As the head of state, the queen is informed and consulted on every aspect of national life. On the advice of her ministers she performs certain important acts of government. She is the center of much of the nation's ceremonial. Royal duties include visiting many parts of Britain each year to inaugurate scientific, industrial, artistic, and charitable works of national importance; paying state visits to foreign countries; and undertaking tours of other countries in the Commonwealth, of which the Queen is recognized as the head.

The wedding of Edward VII to the princess Alexandra

King Edward VII, 1901–10. Albert, in his sixtieth year, became king at his mother's death and was proclaimed as such with the ancient formal ceremonies in London and throughout the United Kingdom, on November 24, 1901. The more solemn ceremony of coronation was subsequently appointed to take place on June 26, 1902; but a serious illness of the king, developed a few days before that date, and requiring an immediate surgical operation, caused it to be postponed until the ninth of August following, when the health of the sovereign had been nearly restored.

The new occupant of the throne chose to be known in his regal office as Edward VII, rather than Albert I, saying that he wished the name of his father, who had been called Albert the Good, to stand alone. His firstborn son, Albert Victor, who was duke of Clarence, died in 1892. The only son living, George-Frederick, duke of York, born in 1865, was made Prince of Wales, heir to the crown.

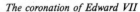

The coronation of Edward VII

Coronation of King Edward VII—procession passing arch

Alexandra, 1844–1925, queen consort of Edward VII. Daughter of Christian IX, king of Denmark. Born at Copenhagen. Married the Prince of Wales, at Windsor, 1863. Her matchless grace of form and manner reflected a lasting youthfulness of heart and soul that won her the love of the English people.

Windsor Castle at the turn of the century

Funeral of King Edward, who died May 5, 1910

King Edward VII and Queen Alexandra opening Parliament, 1901

King George V, 1910–36

There were nine kings at Windsor Castle for the funeral of Edward VII
on May 10, 1910. Standing, left to right: *Haakon VII of Norway,
Ferdinand of Bulgaria, Manuel II of Portugal, William II of Germany,
George I of Greece, Albert of Belgium.* Seated, left to right: *Alfonso
XIII of Spain, George V, Frederik VII of Denmark.*

Their Gracious Majesties King George V and Queen Mary in their coronation robes

The waiting crowds outside the Sandringham Palace saw a solitary figure walk across the courtyard, remove one notice, and replace it with another. A man read it and removed his hat. One of the best-loved monarchs in the world was dead.

SANDRINGHAM, NORFOLK.

DEATH CAME PEACEFULLY TO THE KING AT 11.55 p.m. TONIGHT, IN THE PRESENCE OF HER MAJESTY THE QUEEN, THE PRINCE OF WALES, THE DUKE OF YORK, THE PRINCESS ROYAL, AND THE DUKE AND DUCHESS OF KENT.

(Signed) Frederic Willans,
Stanley Hewett,
Dawson of Penn.

20th January, 1936.

The family of Prince George (later King George V) and Princess Mary at Abergeldie in 1906. The baby, Prince John, died in 1919. The other children, left to right, *are Princess Mary, Prince Henry, Prince George, Prince Edward, and Prince Albert.*

Great crowds of silent people watched the brief procession, shorn of almost every semblance of state in its simple majesty, which accompanied the king's body to Westminster. The imperial crown, the wreaths, and the royal standard on the coffin were the only touches of color; mounted police and Guardsmen the sole escort.

Her Majesty Queen Mary

His Royal Highness the Prince of Wales in the robes he wore at his investiture at Carnavon

The Prince of Wales and General John H. Pershing, USA, review troops at the French front.

The young prince's vacations were spent on the Continent in travel. Here he is pictured skiing in Norway.

The duchess of Windsor, ironically, was never allowed in Windsor Castle. Her hair styles and clothing led the fashion world. She was first married to U.S. Naval Lieutenant E. Winfield Spencer, and then, after a divorce, to Ernest Simpson, an English broker. The Simpsons moved to London from New York City in 1928, and it was then that she met the duke of Windsor on many occasions in the circle of society's parties that included the prince.

The photograph used for the proposed coinage of King Edward VIII

Proposed coinage

In his first radio speech, on March 10, 1936, King Edward VIII addressed his listeners as "my fellow men" and not as "my subjects," as the previous kings of England had spoken to the people.

The baby princess Elizabeth, born 1926, with Queen Mary

The duke and duchess of Windsor on their wedding day, June 3, 1937, at the Château de Condé, France (photograph by Sir Cecil Beaton)

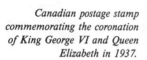

Canadian postage stamp commemorating the coronation of King George VI and Queen Elizabeth in 1937.

King George VI, 1936–52. The king and queen with Princess Elizabeth and Princess Margaret

His Majesty King George VI

"Conversation piece at the royal lodge, Windsor" (National Portrait Gallery)

The royal family at Sandringham in 1951. Standing, left to right: the Duke of Kent, Princess Margaret, Princess Alexandra, Princess Marina, the duke of Gloucester, Princess Elizabeth, Prince Philip, the duchess of Gloucester. Seated, left to right: Queen Mary, King George, Princess Anne, Prince Charles, Queen Elizabeth. Seated on the floor, left to right: Prince Richard of Gloucester, Prince Michael of Kent, Prince William of Gloucester.

Queen Elizabeth II, whose reign began in 1952

An early formal pose of Queen Elizabeth II and Prince Philip in Buckingham Palace.

Funeral of King George VI (photograph by the author)

Princess Margaret, left and her husband Lord Snowdon, third from the left, visit with Prince Ranier and Princess Grace in Monaco in May, 1966.

Queen Elizabeth II in the royal carriage on the return from her coronation.

This first day cover commemorates the royal wedding of Princess Anne and Captain Mark Phillips. The ceremony took place on November 14, 1973.

The queen and Prince Philip on a royal visit to the Bahamas, February 27 and 28, 1966. First day cover, February 4, 1966

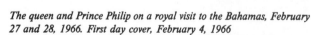

Coming ashore from the royal barge

Prince Charles in Washington, D.C., with the President, Ronald W. Reagan, and the First Lady, Nancy. The photograph was taken on May 2, 1981, when the Prince of Wales was entertained for dinner at the White House in the U.S. capital.

Buckingham Palace, the royal residence of over 600 rooms, is a self-contained community of its own. The Victoria Memorial is in the foreground.

Queen Elizabeth II stamps commemorate the twenty-fifth anniversary of her coronation.

A number of Canadian postage stamps were issued to commemorate events in Queen Elizabeth's reign including her visits there with Prince Philip from 1951 to 1973.

The first day cover for the wedding

"The Royal Wedding (The Prince of Wales and Lady Diana Spencer)"

The Prince of Wales and his bride-to-be, Lady Diana Spencer, on the grounds of Buckingham Palace at the time of the announcement of their engagement. The couple were married in St. Paul's Cathedral in London on July 29, 1981, at which time Lady Diana became Princess Diana. The royal couple make their home in Highgrove House in Gloucestershire.

Prince William playing with his toy bear on March 15, 1983.

The christening of Prince William took place on August 4, 1982, at Buckingham Palace with the archbishop of Canterbury, Dr. Robert Runcie performing the baptism. He used water flown in from the river Jordan and a nineteenth-century silver-gilt lily font that was brought over from the Tower of London where it is kept along with the crown jewels. This is the official christening photograph. From left to right: Queen Elizabeth II, Prince Charles, Princess Diana and Prince William, Prince Philip and the queen mother.

The Isle of Man postage stamp commemorating Princess Diana's twenty-first birthday and a welcome to her child, Prince William of Wales, born on June 21, 1982.

THE ROYAL SOVEREIGNS OF ENGLAND, GREAT BRITAIN, AND THE UNITED KINGDOM

ANGLO-SAXON LINE

Reign	Ruler
828–839	King Egbert
839–858	King Ethelwulf
858–860	King Ethelbald
860–866	King Ethelbert
866–871	King Ethelred I
871–901	King Alfred the Great
901–925	King Edward the Elder
925–940	King Ethelstan
940–946	King Edmund I, tne Magnificent
946–955	King Edred
955–958	King Edwy
959–975	King Edgar the Pacific
975–979	King Edward the Martyr
979–1016	King Ethelred II, the Unready
1016–1016	King Edmund II, Ironsides

DANISH LINE

Reign	Ruler
1013–1014	King Sweyn I, the Splitbeard
1014–1035	King Canute (Cnut)
1035–1040	King Harold I Harefoot
1040–1042	King Harthacnut

SAXON LINE RESTORED

Reign	Ruler
1042–1066	King Edward the Confessor (or Christian)
1066–1066	King Harold II

Reign	Title	Ruler	Birth	Death	Relationship	Consort
					NORMANDY LINE	
1066–1087	King	William I, the Conqueror	1027	1087	Son of Robert, duke of Normandy	Matilda, daughter of Baldwin, count of Flanders
1087–1100	King	William II Rufus	1056	1100		
1100–1135	King	Henry I Beauclerc	1070	1135	Brother of William II	Matilda, daughter of Malcolm III of Scotland Adelicia, daughter of the duke of Louvain
1135–1154	King	Stephen	1101	1154	Son of Stephen, count of Blois	Mathilde, daughter of the count of Boulogne
					HOUSE OF ANJOU (later called PLANTAGENET LINE)	
1154–1189	King	Henry II	1133	1189	Son of Matilda, the daughter of Henry I, and Geoffrey Plantagenet, count of Anjou	Eleanor of Poitou
1189–1199	King	Richard I, Coeur de Lion	1157	1199	Eldest surviving son of Henry II	Berangaria, daughter of Sancho IV of Navarre
1199–1216	King	John Lackland	1166	1216	Brother of Richard I	Hadwisa, heiress of the earl Gloucester Isabelle, daughter of the count d'Angouleme
1216–1272	King	Henry III	1207	1272	Eldest son of John	Eleanor of Provence
1272–1307	King	Edward I Longshanks	1239	1307	Eldest son of Henry III	Eleanor, daughter of Ferdinand III of Castille Marguerite, daughter of Philip III of France
1307–1327	King	Edward II	1284	1327	Son of Edward I	Isabelle, daughter of Philip IV of France
1327–1377	King	Edward III, the Black Prince	1312	1377	Son of Edward II	Philippa of Hainaut
1377–1399	King	Richard II	1367	1400	Son of Edward III, the Black Prince	Anne, daughter of Charles IV of Bohemia Isabelle, daughter of Charles VI of France

Reign	Title	Ruler	Birth	Death	Relationship	Consort
LANCASTER LINE						
1399–1413	King	Henry IV of Bolingbroke	1367	1413	Son of John of Gaunt and grandson of Edward III	Mary, daughter of the earl Hereford
						Jeanne, daughter of Charles II of Navarre
1413–1422	King	Henry V	1387	1422	Son of Henry IV	Catherine, daughter of Charles VI of France
1422–1461	King	Henry VI	1421	1471	Son of Henry V	Margaret of Anjou
YORK LINE						
1461–1483	King	Edward IV	1442	1483	Eldest surviving son of Richard, duke of York	Elizabeth Woodville
1483–1483	King	Edward V	1470	1483	Son of Edward IV	
1483–1485	King	Richard III	1452	1485	Brother of Edward IV	Anne, daughter of the earl of Warwick
HOUSE OF TUDOR						
1485–1509	King	Henry VII	1457	1509	Son of Edmund Tudor and Margaret, daughter of the duke of Somerset	Elizabeth, daughter of Edward IV
1509–1547	King	Henry VIII	1491	1547	Son of Henry VII	Catherine of Aragon Anne Boleyn Jane Seymour Anne of Cleves Catherine Howard Catherine Parr
1547–1553	King	Edward VI	1537	1553	Son of Henry VIII and Jane Seymour	
1553–1558	Queen	Mary I (Tudor)	1516	1558	Daughter of Henry VIII and Catherine of Aragon	Philip, who became King Philip II of Spain
1558–1603	Queen	Elizabeth I	1533	1603	Daughter of Henry VIII and Anne Boleyn	
HOUSE OF STUART						
1603–1625	King	James I	1566	1625	Son of Mary, Queen of Scots	Anne, daughter of Fredrick II of Denmark
1625–1649	King	Charles I	1600	1649	Son of James I	Henriette Marie, daughter of Henry IV of France

1649–1660—The Commonwealth
  Charles II was proclaimed king in Scotland, 1649, later in Ireland. The Commons voted the House of Lords and the office of the king abolished. Cromwell was declared lord protector, 1653. Lord Cromwell died 1658.

Reign	Title	Ruler	Birth	Death	Relationship	Consort
1660–1685	King	Charles II	1630	1685	Son of Charles I	Catherine of Braganza, daughter of John IV of Portugal
1685–1688	King	James II	1630	1701	Brother of Charles II	Anne Hyde, daughter of the earl of Clarendon
						Mary d'Este, sister of the duke of Modena
HOUSE OF ORANGE AND STUART						
1689–1702	King	William III	1650	1702	Son of William of Orange	
	Queen	Mary II		1694	Daughter of James II	
HOUSE OF STUART						
1702–1714	Queen	Anne	1665	1714	Daughter of James II	Prince George of Denmark
HANOVER LINE (also called HOUSE OF BRUNSWICK)						
1714–1727	King	George I	1660	1727	Son of electress Sophia, the daughter of James I	Sophia Dorothea of Zell
1727–1760	King	George II	1683	1760	Son of George I	Caroline of Anspach
1760–1820	King	George III	1738	1820	Son of Frederick, prince of Wales, and grandson of George II	Charlotte Sophia of Mecklenburg-Strelitz

Reign	Title	Ruler	Birth	Death	Relationship	Consort
1820–1830	King	George IV	1762	1830	Son of George III	Caroline of Brunswick
1830–1837	King	William IV	1765	1837	Brother of George IV	Adelaide of Saxe-Meiningen
1837–1901	Queen	Victoria (empress of India, 1877)	1819	1901	Only daughter of duke of Kent, fourth son of George III	Albert, prince of Saxe-Coburg

HOUSE OF SAXE-COBURG-GOTHA

1901–1910	King	Edward VII	1841	1910	Son of Queen Victoria	Alexandra of Denmark

HOUSE OF WINDSOR

1910–1936	King	George V	1865	1936	Son of Edward VII	Mary of Teck
1936–1936	King	Edward VIII	1894		Son of George V	Mrs. Wallis Warfield
1936–1952	King	George VI	1895	1952	Brother of Edward VIII	Lady Elizabeth Bowes-Lyon
1952–	Queen	Elizabeth II	1926		Daughter of George VI	Philip Mountbatten, duke of Edinburgh

Queen Elizabeth II visits President Reagan Ranch on an overseas trip during the summer of 1983. Queen Elizabeth II and Prince Philip visited the ranch home (*Rancho de Cielo*—ranch in the sky) of President and Mrs. Ronald Reagan located near Santa Barbara, California.

Upper right: *It rained a lot.* Left to right, *in informal attire: President Reagan, Queen Elizabeth II, the First Lady Nancy Reagan, and Prince Philip.* (White House photographer, Mary Anne Fackelman)

Middle right: *A formal walk in the garden.* Left to right: *Queen Elizabeth II, President Reagan, Nancy Reagan, and Prince Philip.* (White House photographer, Karl Schumacher)

Lower right: *The President and the queen on the bridal path.* (White House photographer, Michael Evans)

Below: *The arrival—Queen Elizabeth II and President Reagan.* (White House photographer, Bill Fitz-Patrick)

4

Imperial Germany, the Holy Roman Empire, and Prussia

The German lands lay in the paths of early invaders from the east and came to occupy a mediating position between classical Western civilization and semibarbarous cultures of the east and north. After a period during the Middle Ages when German kings were the most powerful monarchs in Europe, political fragmentation weakened Germany, leaving it vulnerable to papal intervention and French incursions.

Religious struggles affected several centuries of German life. In the eleventh and twelfth centuries the controversy over state versus church authority brought more chaos and further weakened secular authority. The issue was partially settled in 1122 by a compromise that granted the church the right to bestow spiritual authority on the clergy and permitted nobles to invest political authority on clerics.

Martin Luther rekindled the religious debate in the early 1500s by criticizing church conditions and practices and papal authority. Dissension followed for more than one hundred years and left Germany not only divided into a predominantly Protestant north and Roman Catholic south but weakened politically and economically.

As Prussian influence grew in the seventeenth century under Hohenzollern rule, its absolutist regime spread throughout Germany. By the time of Frederick the Great, in the mid-eighteenth century, Prussia was strong enough to challenge Austria for hegemony among the more than two hundred German sovereignties, but it was still unable to develop a unified nation-state. Only in the second half of the nineteenth century, under Otto von Bismarck's vigorous leadership, was the country united in the North German Confederation and was able to match its western neighbors politically and economically through national unification and industrial development.

THE ANCIENT PERIOD
TO A.D. 800

During the second century B.C., as Roman authority was extended throughout the Mediterranean area and into western Europe, Germanic tribes began to move westward and southward from central Europe and collided with Roman forces, inaugurating several centuries of hostilities between the so-called barbarians and the Romans. Eventually, the Rhine and Danube rivers constituted the frontier beyond which Roman power did not extend. Rome fortified the frontier and, after a severe defeat of three Roman legions east of the Rhine in A.D. 9, was content to defend the frontier rather than try to extend it into German territory. Until the final collapse of the Western Roman Empire in the latter part of the fifth century A.D., Roman forces generally fought off the incessant incursions of Germanic raiders. At the same time, however, many thousands of German settlers crossed the frontier and lived peacefully under Roman rule. During the fifth century, Roman power was so weakened that German marauders and other invaders crossed the frontiers at will, and before the end of the century the Roman Empire in the west had disintegrated.

Gradually, as the power of the Romans declined, a group of closely related Germanic tribes known as Franks became the dominant power in the Rhine River area and, under King Clovis I, expanded their territory through military conquests and became the successor to the Roman Empire in much of western Europe. Under Clovis, who converted to Christianity in 496, the expansion of Frankish temporal power was accompanied by the spread of the Roman religion and the establishment of new monasteries and churches. At the time of his death in 511, Clovis's Merovingian Dynasty was firmly entrenched in the former Roman province of Gaul, but

Thusnelda, the wife of Hermann, was the daughter of Segestus and therein lies the tale of the angry father-in-law. Arminius carried off Thusnelda and married her over her father's objections. She soon became Arminius's chief counselor in his role of the leader of the rebellion of A.D. 9. This was humiliating to Segestus, for he was the Roman-appointed governor of his native Germany.

Arminius (Hermann) who lived from 18 B.C. to A.D. 21 was considered by historians of old to be the first German chieftain. He was the liberator of the Germans over the dominion of the Romans.

An allegory of the "interview" between Attila the Hun and Pope Leo I

Attila the Hun, also surnamed the Scourge of God and the Sword of Mars, is probably the best heralded in history of the early European rulers. He was king of the Huns from A.D. 434 to 453. In 451 he invaded Gaul and beseiged Orleans but was defeated at Chalôns-sur-Marne by the Roman army under Aetius and the Visigoths under Theodoric. In the next year (452) he invaded northern Italy where he and his savages murdered every man and ravished the women caught in their route. He laid seige to Rome and Pope Leo I met with him in a truce and spiritual "interview" during which the savage Hun chieftain gained religion, granted the Romans a "Truce of Hostilities" and Attila retired to Pannonia, where he died in 453. He was buried in the middle of the night and the prisoners who dug his grave were executed in order to keep the burial place from ever becoming a shrine or memorial to this Hitler type of character.

Clovis I, 481–511, is recorded in history as the first king of Germany. He became the king of the Salian Franks, succeeding his father Childeric in 481. Known as the Constantine of France, he held his court in Paris and was married to the beautiful Christian princess Clotilda (Saint). He defeated the Romans and Gauls at Soissons in 486 and personally killed Alaric, king of the Visigoths, at Poitiers in 507. Clovis I was the founder of the Merovingian line of Frankish kings, leaving four sons to carry on the throne.

he had little success in subjugating the Germanic peoples east of the Rhine.

After Clovis a series of weak Merovingian kings dissipated Frankish power, but the dynasty survived for two centuries until Charles Martel, a councilor to the king, led a Frankish army to an important victory by halting invading Muslims at Poitiers in 732. Martel subsequently became the most powerful leader in the kingdom, although he did not take the throne. His son, Pepin the Short, finally deposed the last Merovingian king and became the first ruler in the new Carolingian Dynasty. Once again the Franks were united under a powerful ruler and began to expand when Pepin's son Carl (Charlemagne) succeeded to the throne in 768.

THE HOLY ROMAN EMPIRE

Charlemagne succeeded through relentless military and missionary campaigns in bringing the areas of present-day Germany, France, Switzerland, Austria, northern Italy, and the Low Countries within a precariously unified administration. His coronation as emperor by Pope Leo III in Rome on Christmas Day, A.D. 800, marked the emergence of a successor in western and central Europe to the defunct Western Roman Empire, which could protect the papacy and assume equality with the Byzantine successor of the empire in the east. Charlemagne's empire remained, however, essentially a Frankish kingdom having its center in Aachen. The centrifugal forces of such Germanic tribes as the Saxons and Bavarians were too strong to permit more than a tenuous and uneasy unity. The death of Charlemagne in 814 was followed by the rapid dissolution of the empire. One or two generations of Frankish administration had been insufficient to fashion a cohesive political tradition centering on royal authority in the comparatively newly conquered regions of Germany as it had in France. The lack of a clear rule of succession led to the division of the empire among rival heirs of Charlemagne's son, Louis the Pious. In 843 the three chief claimants signed the Treaty of Verdun, which divided the empire into three strips running north to south: the westernmost constituting roughly medieval France, the easternmost roughly the German lands east of the Rhine, and a central strip of territory stretching from the North Sea to the city of Rome.

In 855 the ruler of the Middle Kingdom died, and within a few years that territory had been divided between the remaining two, making boundaries similar to those of modern France and modern Germany. The two regions quickly developed different solutions to the problem of rule. In the German area, where both rulership and individual free status had retained greater vitality, feudalism came later than it did in France. Power devolved upon those Carolingian administrators who stood

Clovis I standing beside his throne with crown, scepter, and battleaxe

An allegory of Clovis's triumph over the Romans. Clovis died young, in 511, and was replaced by Theodoric I, 511–34. It should be pointed out that Clovis left his domain to his four sons, but it is a difficult and sordid story to tell. Clovis's sons and grandsons fought each other, and father and son fought on occasion for control of the throne. Maybe they weren't far enough removed from their heritage. Clovis's grandfather, Merovaeus, often told him the legend that the Merovingian line was derived from another Merovaeus, a reptilelike man with webbed hands and feet who lived in the Rhine river banks many, many centuries back.

King Clothaire I (Clotar), who reigned from 558 to 562. He was the fourth son of Clovis I. He usurped the "right" to the throne in 558.

King Charles Martel leading his men at the Battle of Poitiers and Tours in 732.

Depicted in this early woodcut is the ceremony in which Radegond, the wife of Clothaire, receives the robes of a saint from Saint Medard.

Saint Boniface declaring Pepin the Short king of Germany in 751

Queen Brynhild (575–613), the wife of former King Siegbert, reigned by terror, which included arranging the death of her husband. She is shown in this sketch "meeting her maker" at the bidding of Clothaire II. She was tied to the hooves of a wild horse and met her death in this fashion in 613. Clothaire's remark at the time is believed to be the origin of the saying: "You live by the dagger (sword) and you die by the sword."

Pepin le Bref (the Short) was king of Germany from 751 to 768. He was the son of Charles Martel and he founded the Carolingian Kingdom. The pope (Stephen II) visited with him in Germany in an atmosphere of complete reverence on the part of Pepin, so it was no wonder that the fugitive pope conferred on him the title of Patricius Romanorum.

Charlemagne, who ruled Germany as king from 771 to 800, and then as emperor from 800 to 814, was considered by future historians as the greatest European ruler of all time. Even Napoleon and Kaiser Wilhelm admitted that they "dreamed of being another Charlemagne." He had not been formally schooled but he was a great educator of his people. In fact, he taught classes, as seen in this painting. He also changed the names of the days of the week and the wind directions to establish more order in the realm of things. In early life he disciplined himself to learn to read Latin and Greek, but he never thought it important to learn to write. Because he was crowned emperor in 800 by Pope Leo III, he is considered by many scholars as the father of the Holy Roman Empire.

In 773, Charlemagne led his Frankish soldiers across the Alps into Lombard and captured it for the German people in his plan for the expansion of territory for Germany.

An allegorical painting of Pope Leo III crowning Charlemagne at Rome as the emperor of German territory in 800

Charlemagne imposing baptism on the Saxons

A manuscript prepared by Charlemagne that contains his signature, which is in the lower part and consists of a cross with the letters K,L,R,S at the ends of the bars.

Charlemagne was buried in the Aachen Cathedral in 814, but with his death his domain, which was the old Western Roman Empire territories, went back into the "dark ages."

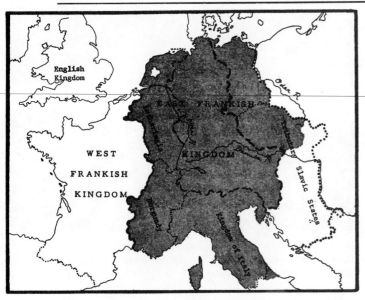

········ **Farthest eastward extention of the Carolingian Empire (843)**

≡≡≡ **Boundary lines fixed by Treaty of Verdun (843)**

▓▓ **The Holy Roman Empire of the German Nation**

The Carolingian Empire (843) and the Holy Roman Empire (1097)

Conrad was elected king of Germany in 911 in hopes that he could bring the German lands back together again. But alas, his counts, Arnulf, Berthold, and Erchanger rebelled, desiring to rule as independent princes. And Hungary twice attacked his security, so on his deathbed he asked his weakling brother, Eberhard, to bear the crown and scepter to Henry of Saxon, whom he thought to be the strongest prince in Europe.

out as effective military leaders. Five great German duchies—Franconia, Bavaria, Swabia, Saxony, and Thuringia—evolved and gradually assumed the trappings of petty kingdoms. The ties of legitimacy were broken when the Carolingian line died out, and the imperial crown faced the continuing problem of asserting its power successfully against the territorial dukes.

Two great dynasties, the Saxon and the Salian, which dominated during the tenth and eleventh centuries reversed the particularist trend. The Saxon homeland was the Schleswig-Holstein area of present-day Germany, and the Salian center was the Rhineland. The territorial dukes were circumvented by a monarchy that succeeded, during the tenth century, in governing with major assistance from a German church subservient not to the dukes but to the crown, and during the eleventh century through a developing Salian imperial administration. Strong central authority went far toward eliminating regional peculiarities and loyalties, and rising trade and cultural advances introduced a new sense of kinship among the German provinces. At the same time, however, absorption in the conflict with the dukes caused the monarchy to ignore the classes of freemen and aristocracy—neither of them bound as yet by feudal hierarchical ties—which were developing a political consciousness that would later cause trouble for the empire.

The Saxon kings, who ruled from 919 to 1024, revived the idea of an "empire." Inheriting a tradition of kingship and monarchical rights from the Carolingians, the Saxon Empire was, nevertheless, far different from the Frankish Kingdom. Lacking the ecumenical motive of

Charlemagne and superseding old tribal loyalties, it became under the forceful leadership of the Saxon kings a truly German empire. The Saxon kings established the hereditary principle of succession, increased the crown lands, important as a basis of power, and extended their influence in several directions.

One great enterprise during this period was the conquest of eastern territories, accompanied by limited settlement. The church moved along in the wake of conquest, ostensibly to convert the pagans, but it was motivated at least as much by a chance to increase holdings and gain an economic advantage. The severe treatment accorded the conquered Slavs aroused their hostility and stimulated the political cohesion of Poles and Bohemians. As they gained strength they successfully prevented further German expansion at the end of the tenth century.

The formal revival of the Holy Roman Empire dates from 962, when Otto I (the Great) received the title *Imperator et Augustus* in Rome. The Saxon kings turned their attention southward toward Burgundy and, even more, toward Italy, which was a wealthy but weak neighbor. Their aims in Italy were limited, whereas the legacy of the imperial tradition greatly strengthened the crown in its northern home. The German hold on Italy waned in the eleventh century.

The Salian rulers, inheriting the accomplishments of the Saxon Dynasty, were the most powerful kings in Europe during the eleventh century. At this time Germany was well ahead of both France and England in the modernity of its political and governmental conceptions.

Otto I, who was the king of Saxony from 936 to 962, became the first Holy Roman emperor in 962 and ruled until his death in 973. Under Otto I, the Great, Germany became the greatest nation in Europe in the tenth century. But Otto the Great was not without his challenges to the throne. His older half-brother, Thankmar, waged war for the crown but lost. Wounded in battle, he sought refuge in a church but died of his wounds on the steps of the altar. Otto is seen here viewing the remains.

Otto the Great pardons his brother Henry for starting a rebellion with Eberhard to take the throne. This scene took place in the Frankfort Cathedral after Eberhard was killed and Henry captured.

Otto II, who succeeded his father Otto the Great in 973, is seen in this ivory plaque of the time in Christ's hands along with his wife, Theophano, who was the daughter of Romanus II. Otto II had a reign of continuous warfare. Among his victories was a defeat of King Harold Blaatand of Denmark.

Otto III, called the Wonder of the World, was as religious as his father Otto II, but he had a bent for the mystic. He ruled from 983 to 1002. In this miniature, which is from a personal collection of his in the Munich Museum of Art, he is seen with his priests and knights advising him on the throne.

Under Conrad II, Henry III, and Henry IV, from 1024 to 1106, the constructive features of monarchy reached fruition.

The most obvious of the Salian accomplishments was the development of a permanent administrative system based not on personal or dynastic relations but on a class of *ministeriales,* officials of the crown. The Salian administrative machinery proved effective, though not as directly influential on the people as in feudal France. The monarchy was challenged unsuccessfully in 1075 by an uprising of the peasantry, which sided with the nobility in opposing the administrative burdens imposed by the monarchy.

A more compelling challenge, the Investiture Contest, which endangered the throne itself, came to a climax in 1077. The controversy was a clash between church and state, between Pope Gregory VII and Henry IV, that pitched Germany into disorder for a generation. Essentially it was a struggle for the German church, which recognized the emperor as its head and was, hence, largely outside papal authority. Gregory insisted that Henry IV give up his rights over the church, eventually extending his argument to an outright attack on divine right of kings and hereditary monarchy. The pope was joined by large elements of the German aristocracy whose motives were not reform of the church but release from imperial control. Henry IV was eventually forced to submit to the personal humiliation of his famous journey to Canossa to conciliate the pope and outwit the German opposition. But he did not renounce his impe-

Otto III was carried back to Germany for burial by Henry II after dying in Rome at the tender age of twenty-three. He had served as king for twenty years, coming to the throne when he was but three years of age.

Henry II was called Henry the Saint because he greatly supported the clergy during his reign (1003–24). Although he was known as the Saxony Saint, he was not Saxon, for his father was the outcast Henry, brother of Otto the Great. As there was no other heir to the throne, the Germans finally accepted him.

Henry II was crowned in the great Cathedral of Aix in 1003.

Henry II's consort, Empress Cunegund, was given the "ordeal by fire" to test her innocence of a "crime." She walked barefoot, miraculously, on red-hot plowshares, and survived the ordeal. The Church in Rome made both of them saints.

Henry III, the Black, who ruled from 1039 to 1056 as king of Germany, was the emperor of the Holy Roman Empire from 1046 to 1056. He started the fight to subordinate the papacy.

The emperor Henry III had two popes die out from under him, but in the case of the third, he selected his cousin Bruno to be pope. Bruno was celebrated as Leo IX. Henry III set out to reform the Church in the empire. The priests at that time owned about 50 percent of the land. While Henry the emperor was busy with his reform, the king of France, Henry I, invaded Burgundy and Lorraine. In this sketch the emperor Henry can be seen during a meeting in 1056 at Ivois with King Henry, throwing down his glove in a challenge to the French monarch to a personal duel. King Henry declined and hastily left Ivois and German territory to return nevermore.

rial role as head of the German church, and the struggle was prolonged beyond the deaths of both opponents.

The contest was accompanied by rampant civil war, devastation of religious establishments, and general loss of central control. The disorder lasted, to some degree at least, until the middle of the twelfth century and the rise of the Hohenstaufen Dynasty. The crown had become dependent upon the aristocratic factions. Its control over Italy was lost; its control over Germany was so impaired that the governing edifice built up over two centuries by Saxon and Salian kings was scarcely viable when Frederick I, also known as Friedrich Barbarossa, began to restore the empire in 1152.

Exploiting their opportunity fully, the aristocracy took over administration and organized it around increasing numbers of castles, which came to form the visible expression of territorial fragmentation and a particularism that was to influence eight centuries of German history. Feudalism advanced rapidly, making vast inroads on the class of freemen. A full-fledged German feudal order eventuated, lacking only the capstone of the hierarchy; the monarchy had lost, at least for the time being, its preeminence in the German lands.

During the century of Hohenstaufen rule over the empire, the reigns of Frederick I (1152–90) and Henry

VI (1190–97) constituted a period of brilliance and were followed by a period of decline. Frederick I's accession in 1152 was welcomed as a remedy for the disorder that had characterized the empire for more than a generation. The loyalty that he engendered, even among dukes and clergy, was proof against further interference by the papacy in imperial affairs. By combining favorable conditions and a firm but circumspect policy he was able to refurbish and extend the empire. Through his efforts the crown was restored to its position of preeminence in the feudal organization; concessions to the feudal aristocrats as well as gains to the crown were implied in the policy.

His son, Henry VI, continued the vigorous Hohenstaufen policies, though more recklessly than Frederick. His addition of Sicily to the empire as a result of marriage, although constituting a further check on antiimperial papal ambitions, was to prove fateful for Germany, for later Hohenstaufens would ignore Germany in favor of Italy, where they felt more at home.

What the first two Hohenstaufen emperors gained, however, their successors either lost or neglected. The decay of the empire as a genuine political force—it remained a compelling idea for centuries—left Germany thoroughly disunited and subject to the desires of territorial interests. The decline, however, coincided with a

Henry IV (1056–1106) vowing to drag the pope, Gregory VII, from his throne in Rome

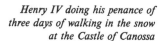

After the Pope outmaneuvered and overpowered Henry IV, the emperor sought the help of the abbot Hugh of Cluny and the countess of Tuscany —Matilda, to intercede for him with the pope.

Henry IV doing his penance of three days of walking in the snow at the Castle of Canossa

period of cultural enlightenment; the towns gained in economic strength; German literature was introduced; architecture developed rapidly; and German influence moved steadily eastward with the colonizers. For most of the thirteenth century, as a contrast, Germany was relatively powerless in European politics, while both France and England had developed viable central monarchies and political institutions.

The early thirteenth century was a transitional period in German history. The empire, neglected in favor of Italy, was allowed by the Hohenstaufens to decay at the center. With the passing of the Hohenstaufens the empire entered a period of decline. The houses of Luxembourg, Wittelsbach, and Habsburg succeeded each other, and the Habsburgs retained the imperial throne from the mid-fifteenth century until the end of the empire at the hands of Napoleon Bonaparte in 1806.

Beginning in the fourteenth century, the ruling houses based their strength upon dynastic holdings rather than upon imperial claims or prerogatives; consequently, their policies were dynastic rather than imperialistic in character, and specifically German interests were usually ignored by the crown. The Luxembourgs had established Bohemia as their dynastic center, and it was under their

tutelage that Prague became a cultural and educational center. Charles IV founded the first German university in Prague in 1348 on the pattern of Oxford, Paris, and Bologna, setting in motion an educational movement of profound importance for the future of Germany. The universities of Vienna, Heidelberg, Cologne, and Erfurt were founded within the century. In 1356 Charles promulgated the Golden Bull, which accepted the reduction of imperial power by establishing the elective principle of monarchy, granting the territorial princes virtually regal powers in such matters as coinage and foreign policy and setting up the seven electors as the keys to imperial stability. The Golden Bull, by tacit exclusion of the papacy from any role in the election, also brought to an end the extended and, for Germany, destructive history of papal intervention in imperial affairs. This compromise in favor of the status quo left effective power securely in the hands of the princes, and German political history developed, henceforth, in the principalities.

The territorial state, which thus succeeded the personal bonds of the feudal order as the chief agency of government in the territories, became the carrier of political developments leading to the emergence of the nation-state. But that process, which was proceeding so

Henry V (emperor, 1106–25), almost as if in defense of his father's humiliation before an earlier pope, challenges Pope Pascal II's proclamation that the clergy give up their worldly riches in return for the "right of investiture." Both the churchmen and the knights objected to this philosophy and in 1111 the emperor Henry V had his knights seize the pope and all of his cardinals, and kept them in prison until the pope gave in to all of Henry's demands.

A coin of Frederick I, or Barbarossa (1152–90). He was crowned in Aix-la-Chapelle on March 9, 1152, and by the pope in Rome as the emperor of the Holy Roman Empire on June 18, 1155. The emperor was the son of Frederick the One-eyed, the duke of Swabia, and Judith, daughter of Henry the Black, duke of Bavaria, thus in him was united the blood of two longtime rival families.

It was the custom in Berlin to pay homage to the ruler on religious holy days. Frederick I and his family accept these tributes in this sketch.

Lothair was the emperor of Saxon (Saxony) from 1125 to 1137. He was the first of eight emperors to hold that title. This costume is typical wear of the emperor of the time.

·RVDOLFVS·I·

Rudolf I of Habsburg (1273–91) was the first of a number of emperors from various houses who ruled from 1273 until 1438, when the House of Habsburg started a continuous reign until the Holy Roman Empire ended in 1806.

Albert I of Austria (1298–1308), the son of Rudolf I, was "voiced" against the pope, Boniface VIII, but when the pope recognized him as king of Germany in order to gain an ally against King Philip of France, Albert I recanted his stance against the pope. But the aspirations of greater control escaped Albert when King Philip took Boniface VIII captive and the pope died a prisoner in 1303. Just five years later Albert I was murdered under very bizarre circumstances.

·ALBERTVS·I·

The official seal of Albert I

Charles IV of Luxemburg was emperor from 1347 to 1378. He became the king of Germany in 1347 and the emperor, crowned at Rome in 1355. This print is an exact likeness of the emperor made in a print in 1356 at the Golden Bull, which was a document, one of the most important in history, in which regulations were made for the election of a king, the duties of the elected princes, and for the public order of peace. The Golden Bull remained in effect for 450 years. The preamble to it reads: "Every kingdom which is at odds with itself will fall. For its princes are the companion of robbers; and, therefore, God hath removed the light from their minds. They have become the blind leading the blind; and with blinded thoughts they commit misdeeds."

vigorously in France and England during the fourteenth and fifteenth centuries, was late in developing in Germany for several reasons. All but the most vigorous territorial sovereignties in Germany were limited by their fragmentary nature and their lack of land, wealth, and military power; they were also challenged by the counterclaims of cities and emerging commercial classes for political power. The result, in the west at least, was that the German states became pawns in great power rivalries, suffering particularly form French incursions along the western frontier, which were a constant feature of French policy form the time of Philip the Bold at the end of the thirteenth century through Cardinal Richelieu and Louis XIV to Napoleon. In the long run, however, the course of events in the east was to be more decisive.

Colonization had been moving eastward ever since the organization of marches for defensive purposes by Charlemagne. It had been especially intense in the region later comprising Austria, but by the Hohenstaufen period the emphasis was in the northeast. As the German center of power shifted to the east, the princes were increasingly freed from imperial control by basing their power on holdings beyond the imperial frontiers. In general, colonization was carried out with little bloodshed or racial animosity. The Slavs often welcomed and profited from the methods introduced by German settlers and worked with them in developing the areas east of the Elbe River.

Not only did this movement lay the foundations for later development of Prussian and Austrian domains; it also provided impetus for the spreading of German influence along the Baltic area. An example was the colonization of East Prussia and Livonia by the Teutonic Knights in the thirteenth and fourteenth centuries. The Teutonic Order's rule—despite its demise after its defeat at Tannenberg in 1410 by the rising Polish state—resulted in the effective germanization of East Prussia and the establishment of German cities along the Baltic, such as Danzig, Riga, Dorpat, and Reval.

For most of the individual German colonizers the eastward move meant an opportunity to obtain their own land and to enjoy comparative freedom. Many of the later Prussian landowners, the Junkers, were descended from the colonizers who had amassed large holdings. Another major element in the extension of German influence eastward was the commercial league known as the Hanse, a group of cities generally dominated by Lübeck, of paramount importance to Baltic trade from about 1350 to 1500. Like the colonization of the east, the Hanse developed on private initiative without reference to, or significant assistance from, the empire. Comprising at its peak some seventy north German cities, plus Novgorod and other non-German trade centers, the Hanse not only carried on its lucrative trade operations, it even maintained its own foreign policy and fought a war with Denmark over trade privileges. Only toward the end of

Sigismund of Hungary was the last of the separate emperors, having ruled from 1410 to 1437. After that reign, the House of Habsburg began a long period of rule beginning with Albert II in 1438.

Albert II, the king of Germany, is credited by most historians as the first ruler of the House of Habsburg.

·ALBERTVS·II·

·FRIDERICVS·

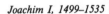

Frederick III, crowned in a coronation in Rome in 1452, was also known as Frederick IV, king of Germany. He served in one of the longest reigns as emperor of the Holy Roman Empire—from 1440 to 1493.

Joachim I, 1499–1535

Frederick I, 1417–40

Frederick II, 1440–71

Albert Achilles, 1471–86

John Cicero, 1486–99

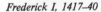

the fifteenth century did Hanse dominance over northern trade decline because of national competition from Holland and England. The fall of the Teutonic Order contributed to the loss of Hanse power, as did the lack of agreement among the cities, the closing of Novgorod by the Russians in 1494, and the absorption of many of the cities in the expanding territorial German states.

The German cities, although not as advanced as those of northern Italy or Flanders, had long been in the center of a developing commercial bourgeois culture. With the protection granted by the crown and despite opposition from territorial princes and clerical authorities, the cities flourished as commercial centers and developed a distinctive order characterized by the commercial law that was to form the basis for city law, by guilds of artisans, and by bourgeois freedom contrasting markedly to the dependent condition of the peasantry. In the thirteenth and fourteenth centuries some of the trading cities formed leagues for the protection of their special privileges against the territorial princes. But these centers fell prey to the rising power of the princes at a time when the empire was powerless to protect them. By the mid-seventeenth century, however, only Lübeck, Bremen, and Hamburg remained as members of the Hanse diet.

At the end of the medieval period no single political force represented anything that could be called a German interest. The Habsburg Dynasty, which kept the empire alive, was concerned with its Austrian base and with its status in Spain; Germany figured in dynastic policy only as a possible tool in its rivalry with France. The princes pursued particularist interests without refer-

MAXIMILIANVS

Emperor Maximilian I, who lived from 1459 to 1519, was called the Penniless but in reality was a very wealthy ruler. He is best known for joining Henry VII of England in the invasion of France. He fought against Charles VIII and Louis XII of France. His only goal in later life was to see to it that his grandson Charles V succeeded him. He succeeded him (from a woodcut of the time).

Emperor Maximilian I, son of Frederick III, served as ruler from 1493 to 1519. This portrait is by Albrecht Dürer.

The emperor Maximilian I and his family

Maximilian I posing for a painting by Albrecht Dürer

ence to the whole of Germany, and the middle class, having risen during the commercial revolution, had no channel through which to become a unified or unifying force.

THE REFORMATION

The Reformation was an attempt at readjustment between religious and secular forces. It also involved a reconciliation between the hierarchical social organization of feudalism and a new emphasis upon the individual arising out of Renaissance humanistic thought.

Martin Luther (1483–1546), an Augustinian monk and professor of theology at the University of Wittenberg, was one of the purifiers who tried from within church polity and discipline to reform ecclesiastical practices. In objecting to such abuses as the sale of indulgences, Luther was a loyal cleric striving for reform. From the outset Luther's ideas contained a fundamental challenge to the Roman Catholic hierarchy—the belief in justification by faith that lay at the center of his teaching. In this respect, Luther was a heretic.

The ground had been prepared for Luther's deviation by the influence of the Renaissance; by the teachings of humanists such as Erasmus; by a popular, mystical religious revivalism growing out of frustration with the religious examples offered the people by the church; and by social and economic grievances. Not least among the factors accounting for the success of the Reformation was the spread of printing, which enabled the reformer's message to reach the masses.

Luther's strong personality and leadership catalyzed conditions that were ripe for revolution. His famous ninety-five theses, nailed to a church door in Wittenberg in 1517, included criticism of conditions within the church, several teachings that contradicted official dogma, and an attack on the assumption of papal authority to grant indulgences. Within a short time the theses were known throughout Germany, and Luther was called before the papal legate, where he refused to renounce his position. In 1520 Luther published his three great reformist pamphlets. They called for the destruc-

Charles V reigned from 1519 to 1566. He was the duke of Brabant; count of Flanders and Holland; king of Spain, Sicily, and Naples; and the Holy Roman emperor. It was during his reign that Martin Luther's time had come.

Martin Luther as he appeared in 1520

Martin Luther defends himself before Charles V at Worms.

Joachim II, the Hector   *John George, 1571–98*

Charles V meets with Francis I in the Church of the Royal Families in St. Denis, France, to discuss their differences in January 1540.

Joachim Frederick, 1598–1608   *John Sigismund, 1608–19*

Ferdinand II, in an illustration from an engraving of the time. He is pictured in his royal dress (state robes) wearing the crown of Charlemagne

Emperor Ferdinand II (1619–37)

tion of papal power by the German princes and the rejection of the orthodox system of the seven sacraments and stated the conviction that every man is his own priest, requiring gospel and faith but not priestly intercession.

In 1521 Luther again refused to recant before the emperor Charles V at the Diet of Worms. The emperor was opposed Luther's teachings, but Luther had the support of most of the princes and the people. Charles outlawed Luther and his teachings, but the reformer was given sanctuary by one of the imperial electors, Frederick the Wise of Saxony.

Despite Luther's strong language in condemning princely misrule, he stated that a Christian must obey the ruler even if his commands are unjust. The peasants, however, had read into his religious teachings a message of social reform and were stimulated to revolt. The Peasant War of 1524–1525 testified to their depressed condition but was crushed by the princes and nobility, with the support of Luther, who relied essentially on upper-class support to effectuate his religious revolution.

Nevertheless, the Reformation was important for Germany because it involved all elements of the population. Princely support was based on resistance to papal authority over churches in their domains; popular support, on grievances against clerical abuses of power in both temporal and spiritual realms; and intellectual support, on the congruence of Lutheran teaching along with the contemporary trend toward individualistic emphasis in science and thought.

The political working out of the implications of the Reformation occupied the remainder of the sixteenth century and culminated early in the next century in the Thirty Years War (1618–48). External pressure from the Turks, defeated near Vienna in 1529, and the repeated wars of Charles V against France preoccupied the emperor and permitted the ideas of the Reformation to spread without arousing overt violence. A legal solution

Ferdinand II refusing to sign the writ of the Protestant insurgents, June 11, 1619.

to the growing religious disunity was the Augsburg Religious Peace in 1555, which enunciated the doctrine *cuius regio, eius religio,* meaning that the religion of subjects was determined by that of the prince.

But this formula did not quiet religious dissension, which was further stimulated by the Counter-Reformation under Jesuit leadership and by disagreement among Protestants of Lutheran, Calvinist, and sectarian persuasion. The Counter-Reformation had great success in the south and west of Germany, as well as in Poland and France; and by the early 1600s Germany was sharply divided, the Catholic League led by Bavaria in opposition to the Protestant Union led by the Palatinate. The Protestant churches had by this time become territorial institutions and served ultimately to reinforce the princely regimes. But the religious passions engendered by the Reformation remained much in evidence as contributing factors to the devastating series of battles and depredations known as the Thirty Years War.

The several sets of opposing forces active during the years from 1618 to 1648 included Roman Catholic imperial Austria-Spain under the Habsburgs against the Protestant countries; the empire against the estates (classes) represented in the Reichstag; and the Habsburgs against France. Furthermore, Sweden found itself having an opportunity to extend its power in the German areas of northern Europe in the absence of a unified national power that could prevent its incursions on the Continent.

Most of the wars that resulted were fought on German soil. The devastation was enormous; thousands of towns, villages, and castles were destroyed. The economy received a setback that was not reversed until the nineteenth century. The population was reduced by perhaps one-third, and the general level of culture fell markedly as life became a simple struggle for survival. Except for Johann Sebastian Bach and Gottfried Wilhelm von Leibniz, the renewal of a flourishing German culture had to wait for the age of Johann Wolfgang von Goethe and Johann Christoph Friedrich von Schiller.

Despite the brilliant exploits of the emperor's military leaders, Albrecht von Wallenstein and Johann Tserclaes Tilly, the Counter-Reformation as embodied in the Habsburg forces registered no gains in the series of wars. The mixture of religious discord and national rivalry dictated the outcome as incorporated in the Peace of Westphalia ending the war in 1648. It did not end religious strife, but it established a workable formula for the German territories, essentially a reaffirmation of the Augsburg principle of *cuius regio, eius religio* and; therefore, a confirmation of German fragmentation.

Political atomization was also enhanced by ensuring the sovereign status of each principality. This meant the final nullification of the empire as a political force and the establishment of numerous incipient German nation-states too weak to compete with the modern European powers. France and Sweden were left in a position to interfere at will in German affairs. Among the German states only Brandenburg emerged from the wars with a foundation for growth. But in European perspective it, too, remained a second-rate power for another century. More than ever, Germany was a mere geographical expression. The consciousness of national purpose and identity, awakened at times in the past by external threats to the empire, was stultified in the atmosphere of petty absolutism that followed the Thirty Years War. The German people, except for the few bureaucrats and professional men employed by the system, ceased to count as a political factor, becoming merely an object of exploitation. Popular endorsement was neither granted to nor sought by the princes.

ABSOLUTISM AND THE RISE OF PRUSSIA

After papal interference had been largely eliminated, the urban middle class ruined, and imperial power shunted to the sidelines, the principal force the princes had to appease after 1648 was that of the aristocratic landowners. This they did by extensive grants of privilege and authority.

Modeling their courts and conduct of state affairs on the resplendent example of Versailles, the principalities required efficient bureaucracies and some semblance of military strength, but most of all they needed abundant financial resources to support what was more often extravagant display than constructive state activity. To secure the resources, the courts imposed crushing taxation upon the peasantry.

Owing to the decay of the commercial bourgeoisie and the deterioration of the status of the peasantry, the older commercial centers declined; new cities grew around local courts, and in the rural areas landholdings were markedly consolidated in the hands of wealthy landowners. It was the period when the Junkers, the landed aristocracy, developed as an independent, conservative political power in the east, while the middle class was being increasingly subordinated to the state. Large-scale appeasement of the Junkers in the form of privileges of rule over their domains often secured their acquiescence in the destruction of the remaining organs of parliamentary expression. Moreover, the ruling class had such a monopoly of power that it could, in its petty concern for self-protection, bring about a rigidity of social stratification hitherto unknown. The era of absolutism was, for the most part, only a system of preserving privilege, unrelieved by major cultural advance or renewal.

In the late seventeenth century Prussia appeared as a new political power, although it was not until a century after the Peace of Westphalia that it emerged as a great European power under the strong rule of the Hohenzollerns. The erection of a powerful Prussian state did not

Charles VI (1711–40) was another warrior emperor. He was in battle with Spain and claimed its throne, and was also the king of Bohemia and Hungary. Also, Charles played a big role in helping fight the Turks, giving assistance to Venice and Russia.

George William, 1619–40

Frederick William, the Great Elector, 1640–88

alter the repressive, socially and politically rigid pattern of absolutism; on the contrary, the reactionary order was strengthened by the expansion of Prussian influence throughout Germany. And the very success of Prussia as a European power made its illiberal social organization seem justified as a prop of effective state policy.

In 1618 the Hohenzollern rulers of Brandenburg inherited the Polish fief of Prussia, as they had, in equally passive fashion, acquired possessions on the Rhine a decade earlier. But Frederick Wilhelm, who became elector in 1640, began to pursue a more active policy of expansion. Known as the Great Elector because of his vigorous fostering of Brandenburg's interests, he pressed the Hohenzollern claim to Pomerania during the settlement after the Thirty Years War and acquired the eastern portion of it despite Sweden's conflicting claims. The victory over Sweden at Fehrbellin in 1675 confirmed the state as a power in the Baltic area. In 1701 Frederick William's successor took the title of king of Prussia and was crowned at Königsberg. The new title indicated clearly the eastern outlook of the leading German Protestant state.

The Hohenzollerns were distinguished from other German ruling houses by their concept of duty to the state. The regime of austerity established in Brandenburg by Frederick William was designed to stabilize the finances of the state while permitting it to undertake mainly military projects that would make it a power to be reckoned with. And because the ruling house followed the same spartan regimen, it was able to awaken a sense of loyalty among its subjects that had no particular relation to their economic well-being. The Hohenzollern rulers, sparing neither themselves nor their subjects in a century of building, were able to establish Prussia's power and its tacit claims to German leadership.

The extent of Brandenburg-Prussian territory, coupled with its lack of internal cohesion and shared tradition, required an efficient administrative apparatus for its management. Its internal problems had to be solved before it could presume to genuine great power status. Along with centralizing the administration, Frederick William had to impose his terms on the still viable estates, especially the landholders and their parochial and selfish interests. Although conceding to the Junkers their right to keep the peasants in virtual serfdom, Frederick William succeeded in forcing the Junkers to accept the

burden of maintaining a standing army, which he had concluded was required to meet the political needs of the state. The well-trained permanent professional Prussian army may be dated from 1655.

Frederick William I (who bore the same name as the Great Elector of Brandenburg) ruled Prussia from 1713 to 1740 and devoted himself largely to the army and to inculcating the population with the idea of unconditional obedience. At the end of his reign he had an army of eighty thousand, half recruited at home from a population of roughly 2 million. His financial austerity enabled him to leave a surplus in the treasury, which was increased by his successor, while maintaining the army out of Prussian resources without the foreign subsidies that rendered many other German states so vulnerable. The army, like the administration, was rigidly hierarchical; the officers stemmed exclusively from the nobility and enjoyed enormous social prestige. The army was probably the best drilled army in Europe, but it constituted an

Frederick William I became the king of Prussia in 1713. During the twenty-seven years he reigned, Frederick William built a well-trained large army and kept them intact by not allowing the country to go to war.

King Frederick William I was an enthusiastic amateur painter. This is a self-portrait.

The coat of arms of Frederick I

The royal palace in Berlin, 1733

Frederick II, the Great, became the king of Prussia at the young age of twenty-eight when in May 1740, Frederick William I passed away. The new king said that in his reign the king "would make all of the decisions of state and that the prime minister had nothing to do but to issue these to the cabinet, without ever being consulted upon the subjects." The makings of a great king.

Frederick the Great leading his soldiers to victory in the Battle of Kolin in 1757

Frederick the Great (1740–86) surprises the enemy Austrian officers at the Castle of Lissa the evening after the Battle of Leuthen, December 5, 1757. Having ridden ahead faster than his frontline soldiers could move, he came across the Austrians when he was looking for a night's lodging. The calm, collected king of Prussia simply said, "Can a tired, victorious general find a room here for the night?"

Emperor Joseph II (1765–90) was erudite, speaking fluently and intelligently in French and Italian as well as his native tongue. He is considered as the best of the Habsburg-Lorraine administrators as far as political power is concerned, even better than Maria Theresa.

Leopold II was the emperor of the Holy Roman Empire from 1790 to 1792. He was the third son of Maria Theresa and was forty-three years old when he replaced Joseph II on the throne. Leopold was a wise and able administrator as the archduke of Tuscany, from 1765 to 1790.

enormous burden on the taxpayers because it consumed two-thirds of the state budget. As the landholders were largely tax exempt, the peasants and the middle class assumed most of the tax burden.

Under the stern rule of Frederick the Great (1740–86), Prussia emerged clearly as a European power and as the counterweight to Austria among the more than two hundred parochial sovereignties that had formed the crazy-quilt German map since the Peace of Westphalia. Internally Frederick continued to build on the foundation of the earlier Hohenzollerns. Keeping administrative authority completely in his own hands, he devoted himself wholly to efficiency, frugality, and absolutism. He was not despotic toward his subjects in the sense of needless repression, but the peasants were kept above the threshhold of starvation mainly so that the Prussian state might continue to enjoy tax revenues and the supply of soldiers.

Frederick's devotion to the Enlightenment, symbolized by his friendship with Voltaire, was a matter of private indulgence more than a policy of state, for nothing mitigated the stern Prussian doctrine of service to the state. Frederick called himself the first servant of the state.

Externally, during Frederick's reign Prussia acquired territory that made it an extended but continuous area spreading across northeastern Europe from the original Brandenburg province to East Prussia; Silesia stretched southeastward along the Oder River; and there were scattered possessions in the western areas. Frederick's major acquisitions were Silesia, separated from Austria in 1742 in a major test of strength, and West Prussia, Prussia's portion resulting from the first partition of Poland in 1772.

The growth of Prussian territory was of secondary importance compared to the profound implications of Frederick's reign in terms of power. Prussia became a power to be reckoned with in European perspectives, and before the end of Frederick's reign it had become the leading German power, supplanting a weakened Austria, which was increasingly absorbed in its multinational empire in Italy and the Balkans. Foreign influence was not diminished; on the contrary, the inability of either Prussia or Austra to gain clear hegemony enabled other powers—chiefly France and the Russia of Catherine the Great—to assume the function of arbiter in Germany. But Prussian power ended Germany's role as a mere pawn in great power manipulations.

After twenty years of pursuing an aggressive foreign policy, which kept Prussia almost constantly at war, Frederick spent the last half of his reign maintaining a balance of power in Europe. Prussia needed time to recover from the devastating effects of the Seven Years War (1756–63) and time to solidify its economic base. To this end Frederick was instrumental in founding the League of German Princes, including the rulers of Prussia, Saxony, Hanover, and other smaller states, to oppose Austrian attempts to upset the power balance. Because neither side expressed a genuinely German policy, the league cannot be regarded as foreshadowing a unified German state. It was not until Napoleon and the ideas of the French Revolution were introduced that the pioneers of German nationalism and patriotism were awakened.

Under strong leadership the Prussian system had proved itself a capable defender of its own interests within the absolutist state pattern of the eighteenth century. Frederick's successors, however, were not strong leaders. And, more important, at the turn of the century Prussia and all of Germany were confronted with a new set of ideas introduced in the wake of Napoleon's national army. Prussia withdrew from the Rhine as early as 1793 to avoid a conflict with the volunteer army of the French Revolution and devoted itself exclusively to interests in the east. When Austria also, after resisting somewhat more resolutely, gave way before the French, Napoleon had a free hand to reconstitute the entire pattern of German politics in the west.

THE DEVELOPMENT OF NATIONAL SENTIMENT

In the absence of any spirit of nationalism in Germany until the early nineteenth century, the country's cultural and intellectual life was dominated by a cosmopolitan spirit that rose above the petty concerns of the principali-

The House of Hohenzollern—the kings of modern Prussia and Germany: Left, top to bottom: Frederick William II (1786–97), Frederick William IV (1840–61), and Frederick II, the Great (1740–86). Center, top to bottom: the Great Elector (Frederick William of Brandenburg, 1640–88); Frederick I (1701–13); William II (1888–1918) and William I (1861–88); and Frederick William III (1797–1840), Frederick III (1888), and Frederick William I (1713–40).

ties. This spirit set an example for all of Europe in its breadth of vision and universal appeal.

The intellectual ferment of the early nineteenth century was confined to a small segment of the population. But as these ideas filtered into popular thought throughout the century, the cosmopolitanism and humanism of the Enlightenment were buried under the statist and nationalistic attitudes stimulated, at least in part, by the imposition of Napoleonic rule over large areas of Germany. The War of Liberation that followed represented a genuine awakening of national consciousness within the limited sphere of effective public opinion. At the same time, there is little evidence that the reaction against foreign domination reached very far down into the masses of the people. Particularly in the western portions of Germany, French examples proved highly durable; even the educated statesmen and intellectual leaders often preferred French to Prussian models. Throughout Germany the peasantry remained essentially indifferent to the struggle against Napoleon.

Napoleon dominated the early nineteenth century in Germany. The welcome accorded him displayed a lack of national feeling. The French Revolution had aroused intellectual enthusiasm in Germany, and Napoleon was described by Goethe as the "expression of all that was reasonable, legitimate, and European in the revolutionary movement." Beethoven originally dedicated his *Eroica* Symphony to him, although growing evidence of despotism caused the composer to withdraw that homage. More important than the intellectuals, however, were the German princes who flocked to Napoleon's camp in preference to Prussian or Austrian hegemony.

Napoleon's policy in Germany was to isolate the two principal powers, Prussia and Austria, and to erect a third force, the Confederation of the Rhine, which would

King Frederick William III ruled from 1797 to 1840 and was married twice, to Louisa of Mecklenburg-Strelitz and Augusta von Harrach.

The beautiful Queen Louisa of Prussia

The world-famous meeting of Queen Louisa, consort of Frederick William III, with Napoleon at Tilsit before the peace terms were signed that directed severe losses to Germany. Napoleon wanted to meet privately with the beautiful queen, but it never quite came off the way he expected it to, and in the end neither made any concessions.

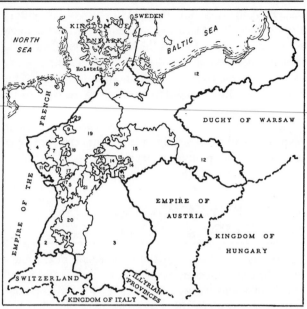

1	Anhalt, Principality of	11	Nassau, Duchy of
2	Baden, Grand Duchy of	12	Prussia, Kingdom of
3	Bavaria, Kingdom of	13	Reuss, Principalities of
4	Berg, Grand Duchy of	14	Saxon Duchies
5	Frankfurt, Grand Duchy of	15	Saxony, Kingdom of
6	French Territory	16	Schwarzburg, Principality of
7	Hesse, Grand Duchy of	17	Senberg, Principality of
8	Hohenzollern, Principality of	18	Waldeck, Principality of
9	Lippe, Principality of	19	Westphalia, Kingdom of
10	Mecklenburg, Duchy of	20	Württemberg, Kingdom of
	21　Würzburg, Grand Duchy of		

Germany in the Napoleonic period (1812)

be dependent on him. Prussia's failure to act against this move meant the technical end of the Holy Roman Empire. Prussian neutrality after 1795 gave Napoleon a free hand to defeat Austria in the field and strengthen his alliance on the Rhine by rewarding the princes of Bavaria, Baden, Württemberg, and Hesse-Darmstadt generously for their support. With Prussia's influence sharply delimited within its own borders, Frederick William III roused himself and his armies to fight the French less than a year after Napoleon's victory over the Austro-Russian forces at Austerlitz (1805). The Prussian army was routed at Jena in October 1806, and presently the French troops were "sharpening their swords on the statue of Frederick the Great" in Berlin. Prussian humiliation was emphasized by the maintenance of French garrisons in Prussia until 1813.

The Holy Roman Empire was formally dissolved in 1806. The Confederation of the Rhine, including all German states but Austria and Prussia, took its place under French protection. Napoleon's principal allies gained lands, and the electors of Bavaria, Saxony, and Württemberg were elevated to kingly status. The number of sovereign entities was reduced from about eighteen hundred to fewer than forty.

Some of the direct reforms that Napoleon brought to Germany, as to his other domains, survived the restoration that followed the Congress of Vienna. He abolished the lingering feudalism that had prevented the growth of a class of peasant proprietors, as well as the anachronistic ecclesiastical states. The Napoleonic Code was intro-

duced in western Germany and, thereafter, remained the basis of law in that area. Napoleon removed the legal disabilities affecting the Jews and inaugurated freedom of worship. His influence was also visible in the spread of a decimal system of coinage and the adoption of the metric system of weights and measures.

Although Napoleon desired a unified Europe contiguous with the area of his conquests, his measures elicited national responses making him at least the godfather of the discrete nation-state pattern of Europe. He also released forces of secularism, middle-class political awareness, and commercial striving. The first evidence of a German counteraction to Napoleon's system was the reform movement in Prussia. Reform of the military system was undertaken by Frederick William III's military leaders Gerhard von Scharnhorst, Karl von Clausewitz, and August von Gneisenau. Their program was to build an army of patriots on the French model, eliminating the earlier dependence of mercenaries and the exclusion of all but nobles from the officer ranks.

Like the military regeneration, administrative reforms were stimulated by French example and carried through by men such as Heinrich vóm und zum Stein and Prince Karl von Hardenberg, who had entered Prussian service from other states.

The remnants of feudal obligation were eliminated and the status of serfdom abolished, although the landowners were generally confirmed in their manorial privileges, local manorial police power surviving until 1872.

In 1812 Napoleon's forces were in retreat from Moscow. Napoleon's Confederation of the Rhine dissolved as he fled westward, and the states joined a resurgent Prussia in the alliance with England and Russia against their former patron in return for the preservation of their territory and sovereignty. The Congress of Vienna had begun its deliberations when Napoleon returned in 1815, calling forth another coalition against him. His second defeat at the hands of the English and Prussian forces resulted in the second Paris peace treaty, which gave Prussia additional territories along the Rhine but left France in the position of a great power.

The Congress of Vienna, designed to reestablish the shattered European order, awarded Prussia, as one of the vistors, the remainder of Pomerania, the northern half of Saxony, part of Westphalia, and the Rhenish province. Prussia thus became a westward-looking country and, at England's behest, a bulwark against French ambition along the Rhine. Conservatism predominated at Vienna and was further mirrored in the Holy Alliance advocated by the Russian czar; Russia, Austria, and Prussia were the exponents of a return to the prerevolutionary order and combined their forces in protection of absolute monarchy. This backward-looking policy was initiated by the representative of Habsburg Austria, Clemens von Metternich, whose leadership Prussia accepted. It also characterized the constitutional arrangement devised for Germany.

Reform agitation grew for a constitutional order and German unification. A desire for German nationalism was growing but lacked large-scale support. It was a time of frustration for liberals and reformers. By 1820 five states had constitutions that granted the people representation in parliamentary government, but sovereign authority remained in the hands of the monarch.

In 1848 discontent was stimulated by revolutionary events in France. The ideas and social forces contributing to the unrest were mixed. In the southwest of Germany the uprising was particularly influenced by liberal ideals and republican goals of opening politics to popular participation. In the Rhineland Karl Marx and Friedrich Engels were involved. Proletarian agitation occurred in Berlin and Leipzig. Extensive pamphleteering among the workers injected social and economic demands into the struggle for political change. The unrest included strains that were primarily nationalistic rather than liberal and even some peasant discontent that was essentially reactionary and often anti-Semitic. The central issues of the movement consisted of middle-class demands for a political role.

Uprisings in Vienna and Berlin in 1848 elicited from the Prussian monarch a promise of aid in achieving German unification. On the basis of general elections a German national assembly convened in May 1848 in Frankfurt, although the assembly was powerless against state authorities. It substituted a central authority for the Confederation diet and adopted the Declaration of Fundamental Rights, modeled on the French Declaration of Rights of Man and the United States Declaration of Independence. The Revolution of 1848 failed, but the document on fundamental rights assumed importance as an indigenous liberal tradition after both world wars when new political forms were being sought.

Queen Louisa with two of her nine children. These two became kings of Prussia as Frederick William IV and William I.

King Frederick William IV (1840–61) of Prussia was an advocate of unlimited power for the crown. In 1849 he was offered the imperial crown of Germany but refused, attempting to assert Prussian hegemony.

Ludwig II was the most famous of the Bavarian kings. He reigned over Bavaria from 1864 to 1886 when he was found drowned along with an "alien" friend, Dr. Bernhard von Gudden, the doctor who had gathered the evidence against which Ludwig was officially declared insane. The king, who was known to be bisexual, led a gay life during his time on the throne.

The Dream King built the Linderhof Palace in the image of the French Versailles.

King Ludwig II's most beautiful Castle Neuschwanstein in Bavaria is now known as the "dream castle of the mad King Ludwig" (German Information Service, New York City).

A close-up of the Castle Neuschwanstein

Prince Otto Eduard Leopold von Bismarck-Schoenhausen, the great Prussian statesman, who was known as the Iron Chancellor.

The constitutional problem revealed division within the assemble over the question of including Austria in a unified Germany. Opponents of inclusion, who also wished to enthrone the Prussian monarch, won. Effectuation of the constitution, however, depended on the willingness of the Prussian King to accept the proffered crown, but Frederick William IV refused the crown unless offered by his peers, the sovereign princes of the states, thus reasserting monarchical authority.

The actual failure of the Revolution of 1848 often obscures its importance in German history. The partial realization and partial frustration of the ideas and aims expressed by the Frankfurt assembly form the substance of German history up to World War I. That liberalism largely gave way before nationalism is only partly attributable to the failure of the revolution, although the subsequent repression drove some of liberalism's best spokesmen into exile.

William I (1861–88) became the first German emperor in 1871, after his successes in the Franco-Prussian war. He was made the king of Prussia in 1861 after having been the regent on behalf of his brother, Frederick William IV, since 1858.

BISMARCK AND UNIFICATION

The prerevolutionary lack of a broad middle-class economic base and parliamentary governments was resolved in the 1850s. Not only was there a burst of economic energy, but commercial interests were encouraged by the state. Although parliaments were restricted, they existed in Germany before unification. Another significant change before unification was the transformation of political thought; much of the liberal tradition in Germnay had been diluted.

In this setting Otto von Bismarck was named chief minister of Prussia. He was a conservative Prussian Junker who believed that Germany would profit from anything that was good for Prussia. His objective on assuming office was to strengthen the power of the crown over military matters and to defeat the attempts of the Prussian diet to infringe upon the authoritarian nature of the Prussian state. Public opposition to him mounted as he ignored the diet in some matters, restricted the press, and limited the actions of some local governments that criticized his policies.

The coronation of William I in 1861

Proclamation making William I the German emperor was made by the Bavarian king, Ludwig II, in the Hall of Mirrors in the Palace of Versailles on January 18, 1871.

Bismarck resorted to war, and this action silenced some liberal opposition. The wars of 1864 to 1866 proved decisive not only for Bismarck's policy but also for Prussia's position within Germany. Bismarck collaborated with Austria, the enemy of German unity, to wrest Schleswig from the Danes and to resolve the question of the rule of Schleswig-Holstein. The German campaign was successful, and the two powers agreed that Austria would manage Holstein and that Prussia would administer Schleswig.

Difficulties over the joint governance of the northern provinces gave Bismarck a pretext to initiate war with Austria in 1866. The Prussian forces defeated Austria in less than one month, and the Treaty of Prague confirmed the end of the German Confederation and Austria's role in German affairs.

The North German Confederation was established in 1867 under the presidency of the Prussian king, and Bismarck served as chancellor and the only responsible minister. Bismarck supplied a constitution that stipulated equal, direct, and secret elections to the Reichstag (Lower House), which was empowered to participate in legislation and budget approval.

Bismarck remained occupied primarily with foreign affairs. He was convinced that war with France was inevitable, and the question of possible Hohenzollern succession to the Spanish throne served as provocation. The outbreak of war in 1870 received popular approval in both Germany and France, but by January 1871 the German victory had stemmed French enthusiasm.

The Germans immediately proclaimed the new German Empire—the Second Reich—and William I was crowned emperor. Bismarck had united Germany and had obtained the nearly unanimous support of the people while maintaining the predominance of the Prussian state. Elections took place for a Reichstag genuinely representative of all Germany. The Reichstag adopted the Constitution of 1867.

Bismarck found it difficult to preserve the balance he desired, and beginning in 1871 he had to shuffle alliances to stave off war. Conflict over political strategy developed between Bismarck and the last German emperor, William II. Bismarck's forced resignation in 1890 left European nations with no one to restrain the power that had developed during the previous twenty years. The degeneration of Bismarck's system eventually led Europe, which was in an age of national self-assertion, into World War I, which nobody wanted but nobody knew how to avoid.

Bismarck was equally skilled in the maneuvers of domestic politics, the consequences of which were as far reaching for Germany as World War I and directly at-

King William I with his lead generals on the way to meet with Napoleon III at Sedan

William I reentering Berlin in a blaze of glory after becoming the emperor of Germany

tributable to Bismarckian fallacies. He was bent on preserving the authority of the crown and thwarting the people from actively participating in the governing processes. This was at a time when the people were strong enough to contribute to national solidarity and to modify the narrow official orientation to consideration of state power alone, which prevented Germany from undergoing a further state of modernization in responsible political operation. Bismarck's frustration of republican and democratic tendencies was probably the most damaging part of his legacy to Germany.

Bismarck was faced with a basic division in German society and economy. Western Germany was modern and industrialized, and eastern Germany was agrarian, semifeudal, and autocratic. Makeshift measures and superficial constitutionalism could not abolish this split. In fact, the reactionary policy of Prussia intensified the splintering of Germany into incompatible segments by treating all opposition as a force hostile to the state. Political parties thus came to represent not competing

interests or programs but incompatible ideologies, each of which wished to eliminate the others. Parliament, without effective power either to direct or restrain the government, became a debating society in which the opposed ideologies were aired to no particular purpose. Bismarck used it largely as a tribunal for berating and bullying the members and for conveying his messages to the public.

Opposition to Bismarck was futile, as the emperor remained the actual power in Germany, having a veto over all legislation through his power to appoint or dismiss the chancellor. The parties and the parliament had to wait until the Weimar Republic to obtain real authority.

The conflict with the Roman Catholic church, the so-called *Kulturkampf* of 1872 to 1878, originated in Bismarck's belief that the Roman Catholic church and the Center party were potential threats to German unity under the crown. The Center party was antagonistic toward a secular Prussian monarchy, protective of its own religious schools, and it advocated federalism and social harmony. In order to restrain the party, laws were passed to reduce the authority of the bishops, ease apostasy, and interfere with the educational prerogatives of the church. Yet the Center party continued to increase its parliamentary strength in each election, and the church adopted an effective passive resistance to restrictive measures. Conservative Lutherans, who feared Bismarck might include them in his anticlerical moves, supported the Center party. By 1878 Bismarck wanted to seek a way out of the impasse, and some of the anticlerical measures were repealed. Bismarck's defeat on the religious issues made a popular party of the Center party.

Germany became economically prominent among the industrial nations of Europe under the Second Reich. By 1870 its iron, steel, and textile industries were highly developed; rail and canal transportation facilities were being expanded rapidly; and banks and joint-stock companies were flourishing in support of the capitalist boom. After unification the government gradually became responsive to the needs of the national economy, and by 1897 agricultural opposition to high tariffs diminished enough to allow tariff protection for new industries. By World War I Germany had become Europe's foremost iron and steel producer. Governmental policy was closely related to economic interest by this time, and the state was deeply involved in the economy through ownership of many public utilities and transportation facilities.

Bismarck began to look for means of suppressing socialism. By exploiting an attempt on the emperor's life as a socialist plot, Bismarck secured passage of the Socialist Law, giving the government power to suppress labor organizations and publications. The party was forced underground and became more radical. It contin-

Four generations are shown in this picture: Emperor William I with his son, grandson, and great-grandson.

The crown prince Frederick William (III) was married to Princess Victoria in Windsor Castle in January 1858.

Emperor William I in a portrait done in the year of his death, 1888

Crown Prince Frederick (III) and King William (I) on a trip to the Balmoral Castle in Scotland in 1864. The father and son were close friends all their lives. Both eventually became emperors of Germany.

Princess Victoria, the namesake of her mother, the queen of England (1857)

Emperor Frederick III was the emperor of Germany but a short period of time in 1888. He died in that year shortly after becoming the emperor at the age of fifty-seven.

Frederick III on his deathbed, June 16, 1888. A heavy tobacco smoker, he became the first famous person in history who died of cancer of the throat attributed to his smoking habits.

Empress Frederick (Victoria Adelaide) with her mother, Queen Victoria of England, consoling each other over the death of Frederick III, who served but ninety-nine days in his reign in 1888

Prince William as he looked in 1886, sketched on a hunting trip

Dowager Empress Victoria, consort of Frederick III, as she appeared in 1888. Their son, the reckless and audacious William II, became the emperor of Germany at the age of twenty-nine.

Kaiser William II announces that he is demanding the resignation of Bismarck. The great chancellor resigned on March 18, 1890.

Prince Leopold of Hohenzollern

"Dropping the pilot" was the caption given to this political cartoon by Sir John Tenniel in the Punch magazine published in London, March 20, 1890. It refers to William II firing Bismarck. Among other things, they disagreed on Prince Leopold of Hohenzollern's being named the king of Spain. Bismarck had failed to notify the king of his decision and nomination of the prince for the position. As it turned out, the prince declined the offer.

Prince William (II) at the age of four in a sailor suit

The Princess Augusta Victoria in a portrait painted in 1880, a year before her marriage to William II

William II. On February 27, 1881, Prince Frederick William of Prussia married Princess Augusta Victoria of Schleswig-Holstein-Sonderburg. They began their reign as emperor and empress in 1888.

As the result of a visit made in 1898 by William II and Augusta to Palestine, while the guests of the sultan of Turkey, a decoration honoring them was painted on the ceiling of the German Protestant Church of the Redeemer in Jerusalem.

A 1918 photograph of William II and his empress. Emperor William was the last royal ruler of Germany.

ued to register electoral gains until Bismarck's dismissal and its reconstitution as a legal party in 1890. The more radical party program of 1890 bore the imprint of the new leader Karl Kautsky and followed the main tenets of Marxist ideology.

In one major respect the reign of William II (1888–1918) departed from the Germany of Bismarck. The emperor cloaked his uncertainty in brash and intemperate displays of power. The resulting tendency toward national assertiveness and imperialism supported a new trend in foreign policy. The desire for a commanding role in world affairs was rooted in the conviction held by many German leaders at the time that Germany had been denied its place in history because of the predominance of France and England. The historian Ludwig Dehio observed that Germany entered upon an imperial course having no motive other than national self-assertion, a mission that could not secure allies in its undertaking. Germany, striving for colonies and for a commanding naval position, brought its policy into conflict with every major power except Austria.

With the possible exception of England, all of the top nations were intoxicated with national power during the late 1800s and early 1900s and were determined to advance their political goals at all costs. Rivalries were exacerbated by the rising nationalism of eastern Europe. The diplomatic record shows an even distribution of responsibility for the outbreak of war in 1914. Germany's responsibility, however, is determined by the reckless spirit of its policy and its determination to overthrow rules of diplomacy, if necessary, to achieve its objectives. Because these objectives were conditioned by an exaggerated estimate of German military strength, the country was led into war against superior powers.

Germany entered the war in a jubilant mood. Its generals were confident of the superiority of the German military forces, and its people were convinced of the rightness of their cause.

The army failed in the opening phase of the war to achieve the lightning victory in the west that German strategists intended. The war soon settled into a slogging campaign in the trenches, and only the news of brilliant victories in the east under the leadership of Paul von Hindenburg and Erich Ludendorff compensated the civil population for its patriotic sacrifices. By 1916 this team of generals had taken over the civil government as well as the conduct of the war. Ludendorff, the more dynamic individual, became, in effect, a military dictator.

The breakdown of the final German offensive in March 1918 and the defection of Germany's allies persuaded Ludendorff that the military cause was hopeless. With unrest at home bordering on revolution and with mutiny in the navy, there remained only the Ludendorff

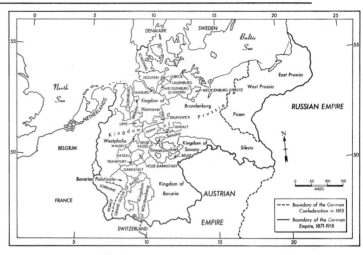

Germany in the nineteenth century

decision to turn command over to a broadly constituted government under the liberal prince Max of Baden. This government, including Majority Socialists, Centrists, and Progressives, presided during October and November 1918 over the liquidation of the empire, the abdication of the emperor, and the initiation of peace negotiations. This marked the end of the royal reign for Germany.

THE ROYAL SOVEREIGNS OF IMPERIAL GERMANY, THE HOLY ROMAN EMPIRE, AND PRUSSIA

Reign	Title	Ruler	Birth	Death	Relationship
		IMPERIAL GERMANY			
		MEROVINGIAN KINGS			
481–511	King	Clovis I (Chlodwig)	467	511	
511–534	King	Theodoric I (Thierry)		534	
558–562	King	Clothaire I (Clotar)	500	562	
562–575	King	Siegbert (Sigibert) (Sigbert)	535	575	
575–613	Queen	Brynhild (Wife of Siegbert) (Brunehaut)		613	
613–628	King	Clothaire II (Clotar)	584	628	
628–637	King	Dagobert	602	637	
		MAYORS OF THE PALACE			
628–639	Mayor of the Palace	Pepin of Landen (Pepin) (was the royal steward of Clothaire II)		640	
656–681	Mayor of the Palace	Grimoald		681	
687–714	Mayor of the Palace	Pepin (Pepin d'Heuristal) (Pipin)		714	

Reign	Title	Ruler	Birth	Death	Relationship
714–741	Mayor of the Palace	Charles Martel	689	741	
741–751	Mayor of the Palace	Pepin the Short	714	768	

CAROLINGIAN KINGS

Reign	Title	Ruler	Birth	Death	Relationship
751–768	King	Pepin III, the Short			
		Carloman (Son of Charles Martel)		754	
768–771	King	Charles			
771–800	King	Charlemagne	742	814	
768–771	King	Carloman (Son of Pepin)	751	771	

CAROLINGIAN EMPERORS

Reign	Title	Ruler	Birth	Death	Relationship
800–814	Emperor	Charlemagne	742	814	
814–840	Emperor	Louis the Pious (Ludwig)	778	840	
840–855	Emperor	Lothair I		855	

CAROLINGIAN KINGS

Reign	Title	Ruler	Birth	Death	Relationship
843–876	King	Ludwig II, the German (Louis)	804	876	
876–881	King	Charles the Fat	839	888	
881–899	King	Arnulf	850	899	
899–911	King	Ludwig III, the Child	893	911	

FRANCONIAN KING

Reign	Title	Ruler	Birth	Death	Relationship
911–918	King	Conrad		918	

SAXON KINGS

Reign	Title	Ruler	Birth	Death	Relationship
919–936	King	Henry I, the City-Builder (Fowler)	876	936	
936–962	King	Otto I	912	973	Son of Henry I

962—Holy Roman Empire commences

HOLY ROMAN EMPIRE

SAXON EMPERORS

Reign	Title	Ruler	Birth	Death	Relationship
962–973	King/Emperor	Otto I, the Great			
973–983	King/Emperor	Otto II	954	983	Son of Otto I
983–1002	King/Emperor	Otto III	980	1002	Son of Otto II
1003–1024	King/Emperor	Henry II, the Saint	973	1024	Great-grandson of Otto I, the Great

HOUSE OF FRANCONIAN (SALIAN)

Reign	Title	Ruler	Birth	Death	Relationship
1024–1039	King/Emperor	Conrad II	990	1039	Descendant of Otto the Great
1039–1056	King/Emperor	Henry III, the Black	1017	1056	Son of Conrad II
1056–1106	King/Emperor	Henry IV	1050	1106	Son of Henry III
1106–1125	King/Emperor	Henry V	1081	1125	Son of Henry IV

EMPEROR OF SAXONY

Reign	Title	Ruler	Birth	Death	Relationship
1125–1137	King/Emperor	Lothair II	1070	1137	

Reign	Title	Ruler	Birth	Death	Relationship

HOUSE OF HOHENSTAUFEN

Reign	Title	Ruler	Birth	Death	Relationship
1138–1152	Emperor	Conrad III	1093	1152	Grandson of Henry IV
1152–1190	Emperor	Frederick I (Barbarossa)	1122	1190	Nephew of Conrad III
1190–1197	Emperor	Henry VI	1165	1197	Son of Frederick I
1197–1208	Emperor	Philip of Swabia	1177	1208	Brother of Henry VI
1208–1215	Emperor	Otto IV of Saxony	1182	1218	Son of Henry the Lion
1215–1250	Emperor	Frederick II	1194	1250	Son of Henry VI
1250–1254	Emperor	Conrad IV	1228	1254	Son of Frederick II
1248–1256	Emperor	William of Holland		1256	
1256–1271	King of the Romans	Richard, earl of Cornwall	1209	1272	Son of King John
1254–1273—The Great Interregnum (nominal emperors)					
1257–1273	Emperor	Rudolf of Habsburg	1218	1291	Son of Albert IV of Habsburg
1257–1273	Emperor	Alfonso of Castile			

SEPARATE EMPERORS

Reign	Title	Ruler	Birth	Death	Relationship
1273–1291	Emperor	Rudolf I of Habsburg			
1292–1298	Emperor	Adolf of Nassau	1255	1298	Son of Walfram II
1298–1308	Emperor	Albert I of Austria	1250	1308	Son of Rudolf I
1308–1313	Emperor	Henry VII of Luxemburg	1269	1313	
1314–1325	Rival King	Frederick III of Austria	1286	1330	Son of Albert I
1314–1347	Emperor	Ludwig IV of Bavaria	1287	1347	

HOUSE OF LUXEMBURG

Reign	Title	Ruler	Birth	Death	Relationship
1347–1378	Emperor	Charles IV of Luxemburg	1316	1378	Son of John of Luxemburg
1378–1400	Emperor	Wenceslaus (Wenzel) of Bohemia	1361	1419	Son of Charles IV
1400–1410	Emperor	Rupert of the Palatinate	1352	1410	
1410–1410	Emperor	Jossus of Moravia			Nephew of Charles IV
1410–1437	Emperor	Sigismund of Hungary	1368	1437	Brother of Wenceslaus

HOUSE OF HABSBURG

Reign	Title	Ruler	Birth	Death	Relationship
1438–1439	Emperor	Albert II of Habsburg	1397	1439	
1440–1493	Emperor	Frederick III	1415	1493	Great-great-grandson of Albert I
1493–1519	Emperor	Maximilian I	1459	1519	Son of Frederick III
1519–1556	Emperor	Charles V	1500	1558	Grandson of Maximilian I
1556–1564	Emperor	Ferdinand I	1503	1564	Brother of Charles V, abdicated 1555
1564–1576	Emperor	Maximilian II	1527	1576	Son of Ferdinand I
1576–1612	Emperor	Rudolf II	1552	1612	Son of Maximilian II
1612–1619	Emperor	Matthias	1557	1619	Son of Maximilian II
1619–1637	Emperor	Ferdinand II	1578	1637	Nephew of Maximilian II
1637–1658	Emperor	Ferdinand III	1608	1658	Son of Ferdinand II
1658–1705	Emperor	Leopold I	1640	1705	Son of Ferdinand III
1705–1711	Emperor	Joseph I	1678	1711	Son of Leopold I
1711–1740	Emperor	Charles VI	1685	1740	Son of Leopold I

BAVARIAN EMPEROR

Reign	Title	Ruler	Birth	Death	Relationship
1742–1745	Emperor	Charles VII	1697	1745	Son of Maximilian Emanuel, elector of Bavaria

HOUSE OF HABSBURG-LORRAINE

Reign	Title	Ruler	Birth	Death	Relationship
1745–1765	Emperor	Francis I	1708	1765	Son of Leopold, duke of Lorraine and consort of Maria Theresa
1765–1790	Emperor	Joseph II	1741	1790	Son of Francis I and Maria Theresa
1790–1792	Emperor	Leopold II	1747	1792	Brother of Joseph II
1792–1806	Emperor	Francis II (abdicated 1806) (Emperor of Austria as Francis I from 1804–1835)	1768	1835	Son of Leopold II

The Holy Roman Empire was formally abolished under France's Napoleon.

1806—Francis II declares Holy Roman Empires end.

Reign	Title	Ruler	Birth	Death	Relationship

GERMAN AND PRUSSIAN RULERS—HOUSE OF HOHENZOLLERN

KINGS OF PRUSSIA

Reign	Title	Ruler	Birth	Death	Relationship
1701–1713	King	Frederick I	1657	1713	Son of Frederick William the Great Elector of Brandenburg
1713–1740	King	Frederick William I	1688	1740	Son of Frederick I and Sophia Charlotte
1740–1786	King	Frederick II, the Great	1712	1786	Son of Frederick William I
1786–1797	King	Frederick William II	1744	1797	Grandson of Frederick William I
1797–1840	King	Frederick William III	1770	1840	Son of Frederick William II and Frederica Louisa
1840–1861	King	Frederick William IV	1795	1861	Son of Frederick William III and Louisa
1861–1888	King/ Emperor	William I	1797	1888	Son of Frederick William III and Louisa
1888–1888	King/ Emperor	Frederick III	1831	1888	Son of William I
1888–1918	King/ Emperor	William II	1859	1941	Son of Frederick III

GERMAN BAVARIA (BAYERN)

Reign	Title	Ruler	Birth	Death	Relationship
1806–1825	King	Maximilian I Joseph			
1825–1848	King	Ludwig I	1786	1868	Son of elector Maximilian
1848–1864	King	Maximilian II Joseph	1811	1864	Son of Ludwig I
1864–1886	King	Lugwig II	1845	1886	Son of Maximilian II
1886–1912	King	Otto	1848	1916	Brother of Ludwig II
1886–1912	Regent (Prince)	Luitpold	1821	1912	Brother of Maximilian II
1912–1913	Regent (Prince)	Ludwig III	1845	1921	Son of Prince Luitpold
1913–1918	King	Ludwig III			

GERMAN SAXONY (SAXON)

Reign	Title	Ruler	Birth	Death	Relationship
1806–1827	King	Frederick Augustus I, the Just	1750	1827	
1827–1836	King	Anthony	1755	1836	Brother of Frederick Augustus I
1836–1854	King	Frederick-August II	1797	1854	Nephew of Anthony
1854–1873	King	John	1801	1873	Brother of Frederick Augustus II
1873–1902	King	Albert	1828	1902	Son of John
1902–1904	King	George	1832	1904	Son of John
1904–1918	King	Frederick Augustus III	1865	1932	Son of George

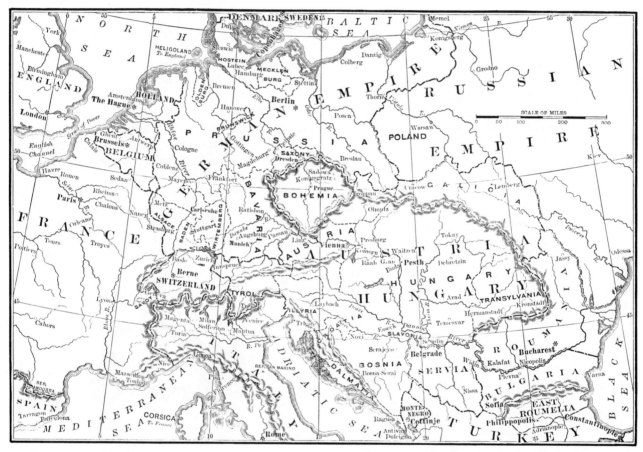

The old empires of Austria and Germany

The land encompassed by the borders of modern Austria experienced great tribal migrations from the earliest appearance of man in Europe, many thousands of years before the time of Christ. The Venus of Willendorf, a small sandstone statuette of an apparently pregnant woman, was carved, according to archaeologists, by a Stone Age sculptor who inhabited the Danube River valley some 15,000 or more years B.C. In a later epoch a thriving culture existed in the Salzkammergut region near the present-day village of Hallstatt, which gave its name to the early Iron Age culture that existed in much of western and central Europe for several centuries of the first millennium B.C.

The Celts, who had displaced or absorbed earlier Illyrian inhabitants, established a kingdom known as Noricum about the middle of the first millennium B.C., which included much of the area of the present-day provinces of Upper Austria, Lower Austria, Styria, Ca-

Austria today

never fully regained as the barbarians to the north and east remained a constant threat until the final collapse of the Western Empire in the fifth century A.D.

In the approximately three centuries between the death of Marcus Aurelius and the final demise of the empire, Christianity was introduced into the lands that later bacame Austria, and the centuries-old movement of peoples continued as various Teutonic, Slavic, and Asian tribes tested Roman power. By the year A.D. 400 the Romans had lost control of the Vienna basin. Visigoths, Marcomanni, Quadi, Huns, and Avars all pressed into the area at various times, disrupting the life of the inhabitants and eventually eliminating Roman hegemony.

In the sixth century A.D. a branch of the Marcomanni known as Bayuvarians entered the area from the north and west at the same time that the Avars—nomadic Asian horsemen—entered from the east. The Avars were eventually destroyed by the Frankish emperor Charlemagne, but the Bayuvarians—sedentary tillers of the soil—settled in the area and provided the main ethnic roots of the modern Austrians and Bavarians. Invasions and migrations did not cease with the arrival and settlement of the Bayuvarians; Slavic tribes had entered Carinthia, Styria, and Lower Austria; and Magyar tribes had occupied Pannonia, from which they launched constant forays into the western countries until their disastrous defeat at the hands of the Saxon king Otto I (the Great) at Lechfeld in A.D. 955.

After defeating the Magyars, Otto I attempted to restore the Carolingian Empire and, toward that goal, designated the area east of the Enns River as a *mark* (frontier zone) to provide security against further attacks from the east. Later, in 976, Leopold of Babenberg (in

rinthia, and Salzburg, plus a part of Bavaria. The small area east of ancient Noricum that would fall within the borders of present-day Austria—the Vienna basin and Burgenland—was peopled by Illyrians. In the western part of the area—present-day Tirol and Vorarlberg—a confederation of tribes known as Raetian-Illyrians had managed to maintain their ethnic identity. By 15 B.C., however, the Romans had conquered the entire region and eventually created the Roman provinces of Raetia, Noricum, and Pannonia.

For the first one hundred-fifty years of the Christian era, Roman power maintained relative peace in the area and kept the Teutonic tribes at bay beyond the Danube River. The Romans developed the country by constructing roads and camps and by exploiting the natural resources, particularly iron. The Roman camps eventually grew into settlements and towns and the Celtic and Illyrian inhabitants were romanized.

In the late second century A.D. the Marcomanni and the Quadi—Teutonic tribes—perhaps pressured by other peoples to the north, invaded the Roman Empire, initiating several years of warfare. The Roman emperor Marcus Aurelius finally succeeded in driving back the barbarian invaders, but his apparent desire to expand his realm beyond the Danube had been thwarted, and he died at Vindobona (Vienna) a short time later. The security that had been known under the Roman Empire was

Attila the Hun

During the fifth and sixth centuries, after Attila and his Tatars vacated the Danube River area that is now Austria, there sprang up from among the northland people who came into the area two leaders of their tribes known as the Sclavs. These two were the Prophetess Libussa and the first king Premysl. Here Libussa is shown telling her chief councilor and followers to allow her unmounted horse to wander until Fate stops him at the feet of their future king.

The horse stops at Premysl and paws the ground. Premysl is brought back to Libussa and crowned King Premysl. The shoes he wore when he was found plowing in a field were used in the coronation ceremony of the kings of Bohemia for the next 500 to 600 years. Today there is a statue of Premysl on the site where the horse found him. But there is no evidence to verify the legend.

King Ottokar Premysl, king of Bohemia and the former "king" of Austria from 1253 to 1276, spent the rest of his life (two more years) fighting Rudolf, trying to regain his throne in Austria.

Rudolf I. There was a period of exactly 300 years from 976 to 1276 during which various margraves and dukes ruled the Austrian area, starting with Margrave Leopold I (976–94) and ending with Duke (King) Ottokar II of Bohemia (1253–76). Then the Habsburg reigns began with Duke Rudolf I in 1276.

the German duchy of Franconia) was named margrave, that is, commander in chief of the mark, thus beginning the political history of Austria. The Babenberg Dynasty lasted for two-hundred and seventy years, expanding the territory and forging a powerful political entity by means of military conquests or threats as well as by judicious marriages. In 1156, the *Mark* was designated a duchy, and the Babenberg margrave (Henry II) became a duke with all the attendant trappings of the new rank.

All during the Babenberg period the missionary activity of the Church of Rome continued, spreading Christianity throughout the area, establishing bishoprics in the important centers of culture and commerce, and building monasteries in the hinterlands at an amazing rate. Beginning late in the tenth century, the area was referred to as Ostarichi, which eventually bacame Österreich. Because it was a crossroads country, it benefited economically during the Crusades and established trade links that remained important. The court life of Vienna reflected a cultured and prosperous society: the Babenberg dukes became patrons of the arts and furthered the early cultural development of the area. Two of the greatest epic poems in the German language, *Nibelungenlied* and *Gudrun,* attest to the artistic achievements of the court at Vienna, and Walther von der Vogelweide, one of the greatest lyric poets of the Middle Ages, gave credit

Emperor Rudolf I crosses into Austria and takes possession.

to the Babenberg court as his mentor and inspiration. The Babenberg Dynasty, which had reached the apex of its power and prestige in the early years of the thirteenth century, ended in 1246 with the death of Duke Frederick II (Frederick the Fighter), who was killed in battle against the Magyars and left no heirs.

HABSBURG AUSTRIA (1276–1918)

Fighting among the Babenbergs, Magyars, and Bohemians had been frequent. After Duke Frederick was killed by Magyars, the ensuing struggle for succession was settled when the Austrian nobility elected Przemysl Ottokar, the future King of Bohemia, as duke in 1251. He extended Austria by adding Styria, which had been previously lost in battle; Carinthia; and part of Carniola (in present-day Yugoslavia).

The land, however, changed hands again in the 1270s. Count Rudolf of Habsburg, the strongest ruler in southwest Germany, in 1276 fought and defeated Ottokar, who had refused to recognize his authority. Thus began the Habsburg rule over the duchies of Austria, Styria, and Carinthia that would last six-hundred and forty years. Rudolf established the lands as hereditary possessions.

The coronation of Rudolf as the king of Austria in 1276

From the thirteenth-century victory of Rudolf until 1918, the history of Austria is to a large degree only part of the history of the Habsburg family. The territories that compose most of present-day Austria were but a small part of the Habsburg domains, which expanded until, under Charles V in the sixteenth century, they included large parts of North and South America, the Low Countries, Germany, Italy, and all of Spain. In 1556 Charles V divided his realms with his son, Philip II of Spain, and his younger brother, Ferdinand, who succeeded him as Holy Roman emperor in 1558.

Until the dissolution in 1806 of the Holy Roman Empire of the German Nation, as the loose German confederation came to be called, the Austrian Habsburgs were concerned with internal German affairs and with the problems raised by the Reformation, the rising power of France, the almost constant Turkish threat, and the necessity for reorganizing and developing an administrative system for their territories. Austria itself was merely a headquarters for their activities. Usually a Habsburg was chosen Holy Roman emperor by the electors of the empire.

The Habsburgs opposed the Reformation and made every attempt to destroy it; in the territory of Austria they were almost completely successful in preventing the new movement from gaining a foothold. In the political struggle with France the Habsburgs were less successful, and the conclusion of the Thirty Years War in 1648, in which France had intervened against them, produced a considerable weakening of the imperial power. As a result the Habsburgs tended to concentrate more attention on the expansion and consolidation of the immediate territories. The chief expansion was at the expense of the Turks. For about a century after the end of the Thirty Years War, Austria's major thrust in international affairs was against the Turks. After the two-month Turkish seige of Vienna in 1683 was broken, the Turks were pushed out of Hungary, Transylvania, and Croatia. The process of expanding at the expense of the Ottoman Empire ended only with the annexation of Bosnia-Herzegovina in 1908.

Internally, as the Habsburgs consolidated their rule and reestablished the supremacy of the Roman Catholic church, the country experienced one of its greatest periods of artistic and architectural achievement. This era in the seventeenth and eighteenth centuries, known as Austrian baroque, saw the building of some of Europe's most magnificent churches and palaces as well as high levels of achievement in painting, sculpture, and music. The court in Vienna took on a truly international flavor as Austrian noblemen were joined by Italians, Frenchmen, Germans, and even by Scots and Irishmen, all of whom pledged loyalty to the Habsburg monarch.

The administrative system necessary to govern the German, Czech, Hungarian, Polish, and other territories acquired through marriage and conquest was developed

Rudolf I receives the news that he has been elected emperor of Germany (1273). His rise from obscurity was so rapid that the bishop of Salzburg said: "Lord God, sit fast upon Thy throne or Rudolf will have that, too."

The Austrian emperors of Germany. Left, top to bottom: *Matthias (1612–19), Francis II (Francis I, 1792–1835), and Maximilian II (1564–76).* Center, top to bottom: *Maria Theresa (1717–80), Charles V (1519–56), and Maximilian I (1493–1519).* Right, top to bottom: *Ferdinand II (1619–37), Joseph II (1765–90), and Ferdinand I (1556–64).*

in the eighteenth century by Maria Theresa and her son Joseph II and given a form that still survives to a large extent in the modern bureaucracy. Laws were codified during this period, and educational programs were established that required communities to provide elementary schooling. Programs for secondary schools were also set up, but education was not mandatory at this level. To oversee the educational establishment a forerunner of a modern ministry for education was established.

In international affairs Maria Theresa participated with Frederick the Great of Prussia and Catherine the Great of Russia in the first partition of Poland, in which Austria received Galicia and other Polish territories containing about 2.7 million people. The peaceful development of Habsburg rule was interrupted at the end of the eighteenth century by the outbreak of the French Revolution in 1789 and by the subsequent wars which, under Napoleon Bonaparte, destroyed much of the structure of old Europe.

Duke Rudolph IV, the Silent, had all of the markings of being a great leader, but he died in 1365 at an early age—twenty-six. He was also called the Founder because he created the University of Vienna.

The crown of the Holy Roman Empire made in Germany for the coronation of Otto I in 962. It has an enameled front plate on which King David and King Solomon are shown on the right and left hand of God. It is kept in the Treasury of the Hofburg at Vienna.

Emperor of Austria (1493–1519), Maximilian I, as he appeared at the Diet of Augsburg in 1519, the year of his death. The painting is by Albrecht Dürer.

Announcement of the marriage-to-be of Maximilian and Mary of Burgundy

Emperor Charles V painted by Titian at the Diet of Augsburg in 1548. He reigned from 1519 to 1522 as the emperor of Austria.

Emperor Maximilian I and his family: Maximilian, Archduke Ferdinand, Archduke Charles, Philip the Handsome, Mary of Burgundy, and Prince Lajos of Hungary.

The youthful archduke Ferdinand, who became Emperor Ferdinand I and had a long reign—from 1519 to 1564

Emperor Maximilian II (1564–76), the son of Ferdinand I, and his family, painted in 1553 by Giuseppe Arcimboldo. The queen is his consort, Maria, daughter of Charles V. Left to right: *the children, Anna, who became the wife of King Philip of Spain; Rudolf, who succeeded his father as Emperor Rudolf II; and Archduke Ernst.*

The church solemnizes the engagement contract of the grandchildren of Emperor Maximilian I in the Cathedral of St. Stephen in Vienna, July 22, 1515. "Bella gerant fortes: tu felix Austria nube; Nam que Mars aliis, dat tibi regna Venus" is the old saying that applies to Maximilian more than any other Habsburg ruler: interroyal marriage adds to the crown. In this arrangement the marriage between his grandchildren, Ferdinand and Mary, was set with Louis and Anne, children of Ladislas, king of Bohemia and Hungary.

Rudolf II, the Holy Roman emperor, was quite mad but, upon his death in 1612, his court scientist, John Kepler, dedicated his (Kepler's) astronomical tables to the emperor calling them the Rudolphine Tables. A mad emperor receives a memorial that will outlast matter itself and of the "important" emperors of the Holy Roman Empire we have little to bear tribute destined to carry into the twenty-first century.

Emperor Ferdinand II, the nephew of Maximilian II, served as ruler of Austria from 1619 to 1637.

Leopold I (1658–1705) was called the little man in the Red Stockings. The great writer Savous said of Leopold: "In him were united and intensified all of the faults of his ancestors and none of their greatness." Leopold fled Vienna when the infidel, Kara Mustapha, laid siege to the city. Pope Innocent XI implored the great Polish king John Sobieski to fight against the Turks by leading the armies of the allies of Austria. On September 12, 1683, the Polish king attacked the Turkish forces on the heights of Kahlenberg and defeated them, inflicting over 20,000 fatalities among their masses. But the returning Leopold was more jealous than grateful. He ordered the city commandant to fire upon the Poles if they came into the city looking for provisions for themselves and their horses. King John described the condition in his letter to his wife, Maria Kazimira: "We should be less miserable if they constructed a bridge across the Danube and allowed us to go and live among our enemies."

Matthias I replaced his brother Rudolf II on the throne when the electors feared that Rudolf was insane. Matthias ruled from 1612 to 1619.

Emperor Ferdinand III succeeded his father, Ferdinand II, and ruled Austria from 1637 to 1658.

Emperor Charles VI, Emperor of Austria from 1711 to 1740, invariably dressed for formal occasions in the attire of the royal Spanish style in memory of the lost Spanish throne.

The Polish king John Sobieski after having raised the siege of Vienna by the Turks met with the commandant of the city and asked for provisions for his men and their horses. There were great stores of grain in the city but they were not made available to the Polish forces. The emperor Leopold I had the concurrence of the city fathers to save the stores in the event the Turks ever returned.

Archduchess Maria Theresa (right) was in fact the empress of Austria from 1740 to 1780 when she placed her son Joseph II on the throne. She was an outstanding horsewoman, as seen in this painting, reviewing the troops with ease and professionalism.

Archduchess of Austria and queen of Hungary and Bohemia, Maria Theresa, born May 13, 1717, is seen in this painting as she appeared in her premarriage days. In 1723, she was declared the sole heir of the House of Habsburg by the Pragmatic Sanction of 1713.

In 1741, France, Spain, Bavaria, and Saxony invaded Austria. Maria Theresa fled Vienna with Joseph, her son, and galloped like the wind to Presburg, where the Hungarian nobles were meeting. They crowned her with the crown of Saint Stephen, and after she addressed them in Latin with a stirring speech, they shouted; "Moriamur pro rege nostro," which translates, "Let us die for our sovereign." Austria then also rallied behind her and the two armies planted themselves between Vienna and the invaders, who soon turned their conquest toward Bohemia, whose capital they entered, proclaiming Charles Albert as king.

In a drawing by Archduchess Marie Christine, a scene in the private lives of Maria Theresa and Francis is captured. The occasion is Christmas Day morning when three of their younger children have examined what Saint Nicholas has left them in their shoes. The little girl Marie-Antoinette (later queen of France) is seen with a doll, and the boy on the floor munching on sweetmeats (candy cakes) is Maximilian (who became the archbishop of Cologne and the benefactor of Beethoven). The boy on the left, crying, is the future archduke Ferdinand who apparently was a bad boy, for he received a shoe full of switches.

The brother emperors, Leopold, left, and Joseph. Emperor Joseph II reigned first from 1765 to 1790. The majority of the people were not ready for the ideas of liberalism and religious tolerance fostered by this sovereign, and he must have realized their sentiments, for he wrote the following for the epitaph on his tomb: "Here lies a prince whose intentions were pure, but who was unfortunate in all of his undertakings." He died in 1790 and his younger brother became Leopold II and served but two years before he died. In his two years he did more for the people and the nobles than his brother had done in twenty-five years. Historians in the field of economics credit him with being the first in the modern world to open a nation's borders to free import of foreign goods.

The Palace of Schonbrunn in the eighteenth century.

It was built on the outskirts of Vienna by Maria Theresa and her son Joseph, beginning in 1744. Situated on 500 acres of gardened grounds, it contained 1,441 rooms and 139 kitchens in its 100-by-660-foot building of four stories.

Francis I (1804–35). Francis II, who had been the Holy Roman emperor since 1792, became the emperor of Austria in 1804 and reigned until his death in 1835. When he took over the reign of Austria, he did so as Francis I. Austria renounced her connection with Germany on August 6, 1806, and Emperor Francis II abdicated the throne of Germany but remained the emperor of Austria as Francis I. The official consummation of the severance took place with the Peace of Schonbrunn on October 14, 1809.

Francis I of Austria seated on his throne as Emperor Francis II of the Holy Roman Empire

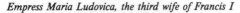

Emperor Francis and his family

Empress Maria Ludovica, the third wife of Francis I

AUSTRIAN EMPIRE (1804–67)

The Holy Roman emperor Francis II, assumed the title Francis I, emperor of Austria in 1804, two years before the dissolution of the Holy Roman Empire. The Habsburgs tried to rule their domains as a unit. From 1815 (the Congress of Vienna) until 1866 (the Austro-Prussian War) they tried to control the German Confederation, which had replaced the old Holy Roman Empire. For a time they were successful in both enterprises, and during the period industrialization began to have an effect on the economy. Railroads and communications were developed as Austria began to enter the industrial age.

In 1847 an economic decline engendered more dissatisfaction with the government, and in the next year a February revolt in Paris sparked the March 1848 revolt in Vienna, a revolt that had been smoldering for years. Students, the bourgeoisie, and workers rose against the government, but the revolution foundered because of lack of organization. There were, however, some short-term effects, such as freedom of the press and Austria's first elected parliament. Furthermore, Prince Klemens von Metternich, Austria's chancellor and the leading

Emperor Francis I took his fourth wife, the empress Caroline Augusta, for a carriage ride around the Schonbrunn Palace every morning, weather permitting. He was the first emperor of Austria and served from 1804 to 1835.

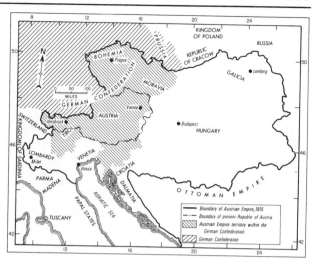

The Austrian Empire in 1815

European statesman of the first half of the nineteenth century, was forced out of office and into exile. By October of 1848 the revolution had ended. Ferdinand I, who had ruled since 1835, abdicated in December, and the eighteen-year-old archduke Francis took the throne and the name Francis Joseph I. The new emperor ruled over Austria, Hungary, and Bohemia, as well as parts of Italy, Poland, and the Balkans.

The empire of Austria might have succumbed to the revolutionary forces of the mid-nineteenth century if it had not been for Russian military assistance against Magyar revolutionaries. Until 1867 the empire was held together only by force. In the German Confederation, Austria was faced with growing Prussian strength and the pan-German ambitions of the famed "Iron Chancellor," Otto von Bismarck. Finally, Austria was defeated by the Prussians in a brief war in 1866.

AUSTRO-HUNGARIAN EMPIRE (1867–1918)

In order to preserve his empire, Emperor Francis Joseph made a deal in 1867 with the Hungarians, who were the strongest of the empire's non-German ethnic groups. The Compromise of 1867 (Ausgleich) established a mode of relationship between the Habsburgs and their Hungarian subjects, after which the empire of Austria was reorganized as the Dual Monarchy of Austria-Hungary, that is, the empire of Austria and the kingdom of Hungary. The compromise set forth the details of control over matters of common concern, such as defense, finance, and foreign affairs. Failure to act in concert on these common matters during the turbulent year of 1848

Francis Joseph I in the first official painting prepared after his enthronement in 1848

Archduchess Sophie of Bavaria was the wife of Emperor Ferdinand I's brother, Francis Charles Joseph. This first of four boys turned out to be the emperor Francis Joseph I (1848–1916). Their second son became the emperor of Mexico—Ferdinand Maximilian Joseph.

Empress Elizabeth's portrait by F. X. Winterhalter

Emperor Francis Joseph and Empress Elizabeth early in their reign

At the Battle of Solferino, June 23, 1859, Francis Joseph was outfoxed by Napoleon III and badly defeated. The Austrian emperor is seen here urging his soldiers on to battle.

Francis Joseph was the emperor of Austria from 1848 until his death in 1916. This sketch shows him in early life.

The royal family in 1860. Left to right: Francis Joseph, Archduke Maximilian, Empress Elizabeth with Rudolf and Gisela, Archduchess Charlotte, Archduchess Sophia, Archduke Louis-Victor, Archduke Francis-Charles, and Archduke Charles-Louis.

Maximilian, who was the emperor of Mexico

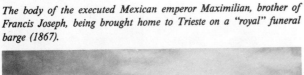

The body of the executed Mexican emperor Maximilian, brother of Francis Joseph, being brought home to Trieste on a "royal" funeral barge (1867).

Empress Charlotte,
wife of Maximilian

Emperor Charles I, the last of
the Austrian emperors, was first
crowned the king of Hungary
in December, then later as the
emperor of Austria.

Crown Prince Rudolf, the only
son of Francis Joseph, committed
suicide in 1889.

Empress Zita, wife of Charles I

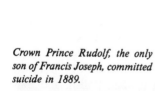

After a long life of personal
tragedy but a reign of great his-
torical significance, Emperor-
King Francis Joseph died on
November 21, 1916, at the age of
eighty-six. This is one of the last
photographs taken of the em-
peror.

Emperor Charles I, the last of
the Habsburg monarchs. He
reigned from 1916 to 1918 as
the king of Hungary.

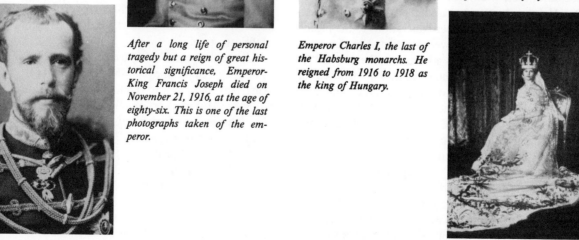

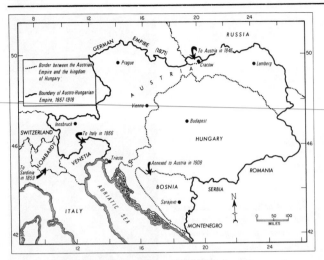

Austrian-Hungarian Empire, 1867–1918

A comparison map to show how the empire was broken up into Austria and successor states

had aroused suspicions in the Habsburg court that the Hungarians were seeking complete independence. The compromise estabished the legal link between the two countries that was necessary for concerted action.

The common monarch and the obligation to render support on matters of general concern were accepted by both parties to the 1867 agreement. Parliamentary bodies were to function in both states, and any suggestion of a general legislature was abandoned as an affront to Hungarian autonomy. The ministers who were concerned with matters of defense, finance, and foreign affairs were responsible to equal delegations from the two parliaments sitting alternately in Vienna and Pest (after 1872, Budapest). The delegations decided what part of the budgets were allocated for matters of joint concern, and a special committe periodically determined the relative financial contributions of the two countries. Arrangements concerning commerce and the customs were made subject to periodic review every ten years.

Seeing the Hungarians achieve a measure of independence, several other ethnic groups that had been chafing under Habsburg rule increased their demands for national recognition, but further concessions to the principle of national autonomy were disdained by Emperor Francis Joseph. Particularly adamant in the demand for national recognition were the Czechs, who agitated for a Bohemian kingdom that would have a status similar to that of Hungary with Francis Joseph as the common monarch. Prime Minister Eduard von Taaffe placated the Czechs and other ethnic groups by granting minor concessions but refusing actual autonomy. Von Taaffe's goal, in his own words, was "to keep all the nationalities in a balanced state of mild dissatisfaction" and thus avoid major upheaval. For several years during the 1880s and early 1890s von Taaffe was successful in keeping a lid on the more extreme expressions of nationalism, but

after his resignation in 1893 the voices of dissent became more shrill.

By the time of the outbreak of World War I in August 1914, it had become obvious that the Austro-Hungarian Empire could not survive military defeat. From the Austrian point of view the declaration of war on Serbia following the assassination of the archduke Francis Ferdinand, heir to the throne, had been necessary in order to stamp out the dangerous nationalistic movement supported from outside the Dual Monarchy. Ironically, Francis Ferdinand (who had a Czech wife) had been sympathetic to the idea of a Habsburg state organized with full recognition of national differences. As the war progressed, Czech, Romanian, Polish, and South Slav demands for the division of the Dual Monarchy into new national states became increasingly strong.

Some attempts were made by Charles I, the last Habsburg ruler, to make concessions to nationalism that might have held his realms together, but they were too late. The collapse of the Central Powers in 1918 meant the loss of Czech, Slovak, Romanian, Polish, and Balkan territories. The tie with Hungary was broken. An "Austria" was left as a sort of German residue of the Habsburg rule.

Although present-day Austria is only a part of the old Habsburg realm, the Habsburg rule is not forgotten. Austrians look back to the long reign of Francis Joseph I (1848–1916) as a sort of golden age. They like to recall the eighteenth-century reigns of Maria Theresa and her son the reforming emperor Joseph II, who is even now referred to affectionately as the People's Kaiser. Heroes of the Habsburg rule such as Prince Eugene of Savoy, the great eighteenth-century general, are still heroes in Austria. All these memories, however, belong to a past that was terminated by complete collapse in 1918 of Habsburg Austria-Hungary.

THE ROYAL SOVEREIGNS OF THE EMPIRES OF AUSTRIA

Reign	Title	Ruler	Birth	Death	Relationship
976–994	Margrave	Leopold I			
994–1018	Margrave	Henry I			Son of Leopold I
1018–1055	Margrave	Adalbert			Son of Leopold I
1055–1075	Margrave	Ernst			Son of Adalbert
1075–1096	Margrave	Leopold II			Son of Ernst
1096–1136	Margrave	Leopold III, the Pious			Son of Leopold II
1136–1141	Margrave	Leopold IV			Son of Leopold III
1141–1156	Margrave	Henry II	1114	1177	Brother of Leopold IV
1156–1177	Duke	Henry II			Grandfather of Leopold VI
1177–1194	Duke	Leopold V			Son of Henry II
1194–1198	Duke	Frederick I			Son of Leopold V
1198–1230	Duke	Leopold VI, the Glorious	1176	1230	Brother of Frederick I
1230–1246	Duke	Frederick II, the Fighter			Brother of Leopold VI
1246–1248	—To the empire				
1248–1250	Duke	Herman von Baden			Nephew-in-law of Frederick II
1250–1253	—Anarchy: several claimants				
1253–1276	King	Ottokar II of Bohemia	1230	1278	

HABSBURG DYNASTY

Reign	Title	Ruler	Birth	Death	Relationship
1276–1282	Duke	Rudolf I	1218	1291	Son of Albert IV of Habsburg
1282–1308	Duke	Albert I	1250	1308	Son of Rudolf I
1308–1330	Duke	Frederick	1286	1330	Son of Albert I
1308–1326	Coregent	Leopold I	1290	1326	Son of Albert I
1330–1358	Duke	Albert II			Son of Albert I
1330–1339	Coregent	Otto			Son of Albert I
1358–1365	Duke	Rudolf			Son of Albert II
1358–1397	Duke	Albert III			Son of Albert II
1365–1379	Coregent	Leopold III	1351	1386	Son of Albert II

HOUSE OF ALBERT

Reign	Title	Ruler	Birth	Death	Relationship
1379–1395	Duke	Albert III			
1397–1404	Duke	Albert IV			Son of Albert III
1404–1439	Duke	Albert V	1397	1439	Son of Albert IV; Holy Roman emperor Albert II, 1438
1440–1457	Duke	Ladislaus			Son of Albert V

HOUSE OF LEOPOLD

Reign	Title	Ruler	Birth	Death	Relationship
1379–1386	Duke	Leopold III			
1386–1406	Duke	William			Son of Leopold III
1386–1411	Duke	Leopold IV			Son of Leopold III
1406–1424	Duke	Ernst			Son of Leopold III
1457–1463	Duke	Albert VI			Brother of Frederick
1457–1493	Archduke	Frederick V	1415	1493	Cousin of Ladislaus; Holy Roman emperor Frederick III, 1440
1493–1519	Archduke	Maximilian	1459	1519	Son of Frederick V
1519–1522	Archduke	Charles	1500	1558	Grandson of Maximilian I, Holy Roman emperor, 1519
1519–1564	Archduke	Ferdinand	1503	1564	Brother of Charles V; Holy Roman emperor, 1556

(See Holy Roman Empire for the periods 1564–1740; 1780–1804.)

Reign	Title	Ruler	Birth	Death	Relationship
1740–1780	Archduchess	Maria Theresa	1717	1780	Daughter of Charles VI
1804–1835	Emperor	Francis I	1768	1835	Son of Leopold II of Habsburg-Lorraine; Holy Roman emperor, 1792
1835–1848	Emperor	Ferdinand I	1793	1875	Son of Francis I; abdicated 1848
1848–1916	Emperor	Francis Joseph I	1830	1916	Nephew of Ferdinand I
1916–1918	Emperor	Charles I	1887	1922	Grandnephew of Francis Joseph

1918—Austria became a republic.

6

The Kingdom of Hungary

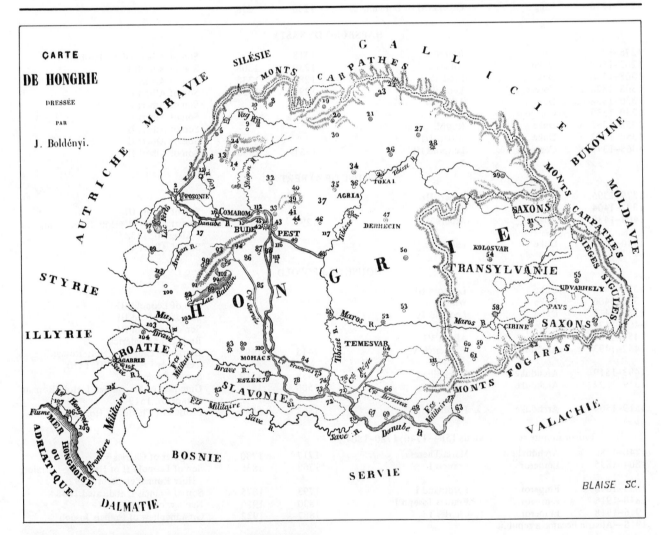

An early map of Hungary (then spelled Hongrie). It includes Transylvania and other parts of Hungary that have since become parts of other countries. The Treaty of Trianon attempted to limit Hungary to the part of its territory occupied by the Hungarian, or Magyar, people. Thus, a great part of the traditional kingdom of Hungary was divided among neighboring countries and its population was reduced by nearly 40 percent.

For long periods in their history the Hungarians have been an oppressed people trying to escape imperial power and foreign control. On the other hand, their efforts to control the Carpathian Basin have expressed a determination to impose a type of Hungarian imperial control. The Hungarians have been ethnically and linguistically isolated in a region coveted by more powerful peoples, often in conflict with one another.

Ever since the Hungarians came from the east to the Carpathian Basin roughly eleven hundred years ago, some tension has existed between the orginal Eastern cultural heritage and the new Western cultural accretions.

The problem of national groups or minorities has been a recurrent factor, especially since the latter part of the nineteenth century. During much of the past, other peoples had been assimilated into Magyar culture, but in recent decades the ambition of the Magyars to continue this process in the face of competing nationalisms had been labeled "chauvinism" or "irredentism."

Long periods of the nation's history have been marked by religious conflict. The politics of the very early period revolved around the conflict of the original paganism and the acquired Christianity. Paganism was defeated, but its remnants were preserved in local culture. Later, after the emergence of Protestantism during the Reformation, a conflict between the Roman Catholic church and the new, more national Christianity also developed. The struggle quickly took on political implications.

EARLY HISTORY

The Hungarians, or Magyars, arrived in the Carpathian Basin, that is, the general area of modern Hungary, at the end on the ninth century A.D. The date usually ascribed by historians to this migration is 896, but it is likely that Magyar raiding parties were already familiar with the region from previous incursions. Before moving into the area that eventually became their new homeland, the Magyars had lived in the Khazar state, north of the Black Sea, to which they had earlier migrated, probably from the region between the great bend of the Volga River and the Ural Mountains. Little is known about the Magyars before they began the migration that took them south to the Black Sea and eventually west to the middle Danube River. Their language, which became modern Hungarian, is of the Finno-Ugric language group and has strong influences from the Turkic languages with which it came in contact during the Magyars' indeterminate stay in the Black Sea area. These early Magyars were a seminomadic pastoral people, who associated in a loose tribal confederation for offense as well as defense.

The Finno-Ugric family of languages had over 19 million speakers in 1970, the majority of whom—over 13

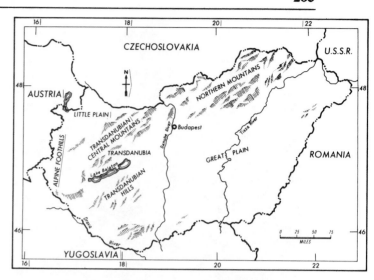

Hungary as it appears today

million—were Hungarian. Although Finnish is a very distant relative of Hungarian, the two languages are not mutually understandable; neither are the nearest Ugric relatives, such as Vogul (Mansi) and Ostyak (Khanty), which are spoken by a few thousand herdsmen and fishermen living in Siberia. During the migrations of the early Magyars, their language was influenced by contacts with Turkic peoples and later incorporated loanwords from the Slavic, Germanic, and Romance languages.

The Magyars were merely one among many of the warlike, nomadic hordes that swept into Europe from the East, bent on conquest and plunder. Their warriors were as competent at fighting from horseback as were the Huns who preceded them or the Mongols who came later; but the Magyars were not as numerous as these other hordes, nor, it would seem, did their leaders entertain the grandiose schemes of conquest that motivated such men as Attila the Hun or Genghis Khan. The seven

Hungarians of today are descended from fierce, cruel warriors who were constantly raiding their neighbors and confiscating or destroying nearly everything in their path. These Magyars, as they were called, adopted religion (Christianity) in Saint Stephen's time, about A.D. 1000, and proved to be the most mature people in the Austrian Empire.

Arpad was the first chieftain of Hungary (875–907).

King Stephen I on his throne with orb and scepter. He ruled from 997 to 1038. The Catholic Church canonized him in 1087, and he is to this day the patron saint of Hungary. Pope Sylvester III gave him the title of Apostolic King of Hungary and all following kings of Hungary used the title.

Tradition holds that Pope Sylvester II gave the crown of Saint Stephen to Hungary's first Christian king in the year 1000. It came to symbolize the essence of the Hungarian people and as such played a central role in the course of Hungarian history. At the end of World War II, the custodial guard gave over the treasure without condition to elements of the U.S. Army. This is a detailed sketch of the crown.

The crown of Hungary, the one first used by Saint Stephen, has had a stormy career since it rested on the head of the saint. The first recorded time that it was "removed" from Hungary was when Countess Helen Kottanner stole it so that Albert II's son, born after his death in 1439, could be crowned king of Hungary on the day of his birth. Albert's queen performed the rite but the Hungarians refused to be governed by a baby, so they elected Ladislaus, the king of Poland, as their king. (In 1444, he lost his head to the top of a lance after losing a battle with the Turks.) Hunyaadi, the great Hungarian general who survived that very battle, had been named "governor" of Hungary by the people and officials of Hungary, but in Austria the boy, "Ladislaus of Austria," was elected king of Hungary, invested by the stolen crown.

Two 1938 postage stamps of Hungary honor Saint Stephen (wearing the crown) and the crown itself

tribes that easily and rapidly defeated the Slavs and other peoples living around the middle course of the Danube River in A.D. 896 were led by Arpad, an elected chieftain. Although Arpad was a tribal chieftain rather than a king, his successors later became kings of Hungary, and the Arpad Dynasty lasted until the male line died out at the beginning of the fourteenth century.

For the first few decades after settling along the Danube, the Hungarian tribes seemed to consider the area more as a base of operations than a new homeland. The majority of the people maintained the seminomadic existence they had known in the East—moving with their herds from mountain pastures in summer to milder lowlands in winter. In the meantime, marauding armies of the tribes swept from Constantinople to the North Sea and from southern Italy to the Pyrenees, returning with booty and slaves but instilling fear and incurring wrath in the countries they invaded. Finally, the Hungarians

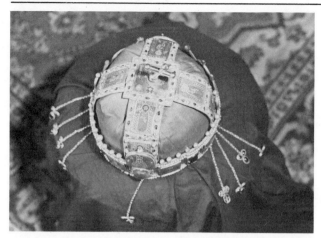

The crown as it appeared in 1945 when it was turned over to the U.S. Seventh Army for safe-keeping. The crown was returned to Hungary in 1977.

Another important crown is the ancient one from earlier rulers of Hungary, the Monomachos crown, which is kept in the Hungarian National Museum.

A contemporary portrait of King Stephen on the back of the coronation cloak currently stored in the Hungarian National Museum

suffered a catastrophic defeat by a coalition of forces of the Holy Roman Empire. The defeat at Augsburg proved to be a turning point in Hungarian history as the tribes ceased their depredations and became more sedentary along the waterways of the Carpathian Basin. After giving up their incursions into the territories of other peoples, the Hungarians themselves endured centuries of invasions and incursions as their adopted land proved to be a crossroads for Eastern hordes moving into Europe as well as for Germanic forces raiding the Balkans.

In A.D. 972 Prince Geza, great-grandson of Arpad, became the leader of the entire Hungarian confederation and succeeded in curbing the power of the individual tribal chieftains. Geza, recognizing that a pagan nation surrounded by the Eastern and Western forms of Christianity would be in constant danger and fearing domination from the East, admitted missionaries from the West and permitted his son, Stephen Istvan, to be baptized a

Roman Catholic. Stephen's later marriage to a Bavarian princess, the conversion to Roman Catholicism of the Hungarian people, and the development of a Latin alphabet for the Magyar language solidified the Western orientation of the country.

When Geza died, Stephen became ruling chieftain and worked strenuously to erase paganism among his people, to convert them to Roman Catholicism, and to resist any encroachment by the Eastern Orthodox church. As a reward Stephen received a crown from the pope (a story doubted by some modern historians but indelibly inscribed in Hungarian tradition) and, about the year A.D. 1000, became the first king of Hungary. Stephen was later canonized by the Roman Catholic church and, as Saint Stephen, became the most famous king in Hungarian history. Stephen's crown was revered as the symbol of Hungarian nationhood until World War II.

King Stephen asserted the unity of the state, the supremacy of the royal authority, and the need for the unquestioning obedience of the people. Under Stephen much of the country became crown land, personal domains of the monarch from which he could derive revenue as well as manpower for military service. The crown lands remained a foundation of power for many of Stephen's successors. It was also during Stephen's reign that the vast territory of Transylvania was brought under Hungarian hegemony.

In addition to the vast domains he already possessed, Stephen occupied large tracts of uninhabited territories lying between existing settlements and added land to the royal domain. In these areas, he fortified strategic points

Saint Stephen was succeeded by his son-in-law, Peter Orseolo in 1038. King Peter served until 1041.

Margaret of France and her husband, King Bela III (1173–96) see the Crusaders off to the Holy Land.

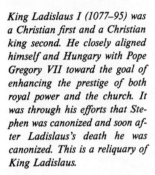

King Ladislaus I (1077–95) was a Christian first and a Christian king second. He closely aligned himself and Hungary with Pope Gregory VII toward the goal of enhancing the prestige of both royal power and the church. It was through his efforts that Stephen was canonized and soon after Ladislaus's death he was canonized. This is a reliquary of King Ladislaus.

A fifteenth-century woodcut depicting King Ladislaus rescuing a fair maiden from a Kumanian knight who was trying to abduct her. The woodcut is based on an old legend about the king.

The seal of King Andrew II (1205–35). This golden seal was issued in 1222 as an official decree of the Golden Bull, which was a proclamation of importance in Hungarian history. It provided that reduced taxes would be levied against certain citizens and that there would be restrained ecclesiastic exploitation.

and, in time, towns grew up around the fortresses. The king appointed administrators to guide the affairs of the fortified areas and towns, which were embryos of future counties, thus facilitating the development of the medieval state.

In the three centuries from the coronation of Stephen until the death of the last Arpad King in 1301, the kingdom acquired vast new territories and assumed a multinational, multilingual character. In addition to the indigenous peoples who were brought under Hungarian control, foreign colonists were invited in great numbers to occupy the uninhabited lands of the kingdom. Many of the peoples, particularly those from the East, were absorbed and became completely magyarized. Others, such as the Germans (called Saxons) who colonized Transylvania for the Arpads in the early thirteenth cen-

In 1242, the Tatars crossed the Danube in hope of capturing or killing the king of Hungary, Bela IV. They knew they couldn't occupy the country because they didn't have the organization to do it, as they were in the throes of the disintegration of the Mongol (Tatar) Empire and too far from home bases. This old museum miniature shows the Tatars pursuing the king. They never caught him, even though there were some anxious moments. The result was that Bela IV reviewed the country's defenses and was able to take remedial actions that safeguarded the borders for centuries.

In this sketch, Mary of Hungary is seen being rescued by Venetians. She and her mother, the widow of Louis of Anjou, were captured by dissidents who wanted someone else on the throne. Her mother was tortured and strangled before her eyes. When Louis the Great (of Anjou) died in 1382 he left no male heir to the throne of Hungary; except for Mary there was no other available ruler. She found so many would-be kings that she could not cope with the situation. At that time, Hungary extended to the Adriatic Sea, hence the Venetians held their former queen in dear favor. During her captivity, when her husband Sigismund was elected King of Hungary, the Venetians, having put down the Hungarian nobles who were laying claim to the throne, came in and rescued their queen.

Mary, queen of Hungary from 1382 to 1387, was also known as King Mary. The daughter of Louis the Great, who was the king of Poland and Hungary, Queen Mary was the first queen to rule a major country in Europe. The future female monarchs based their claim on their thrones against the precedence of King Mary's reign.

King Louis I, son of Charles I, was the king of Hungary from 1342 to 1382. He was also the king of Poland.

tury, retained their own cultures and languages and never were assimilated.

One of the most important developments in Hungarian constitutional history occurred in 1222 when the people compelled the king to sign the Golden Bull. The Golden Bull has often been compared to the English Magna Charta in that both documents placed limitations upon the crown. The Golden Bull, unlike the Magna Charta, however, was realized through the pressures of small landholders, the so-called freemen, rather than barons. The Golden Bull set limits on the king, but it also had the unfortunate effect of further isolating the landless peasants, as they had no voice in its establishment.

Despite the Golden Bull, the thirteenth century was a century of trouble for the country. In 1241 the Mongols invaded Hungary, eventually gaining control of territory

Louis I's royal palace, the Château de O-Zolyom

to the east and north of the Danube. This was Hungary's first experience as a buffer state between East and West, but it was a costly experience in that the Western monarchs allowed the Hungarians to bear the brunt of the Mongol onslaught, which actually endangered all of Europe. Hungary stood alone, and her forces were not equal to the task presented by the overpowering Golden Horde of the Mongols. Although the Mongol invasion lasted only until 1242, the country was devasted and depopulated. The Mongols withdrew to the Russian steppes, from which they still presented a threat. Twice during the next twenty years the Mongols offered to join the Hungarians as allies, but both offers were refused as Hungary chose to retain its strongly developed Western orientation.

The death of Andrew III, the last Arpad in the direct male line, initiated a period of crisis that lasted for over two hundred years. The crises were created by growing Turkish pressure upon Europe, in which Hungary again became a buffer between East and West; the Habsburg ambition to absorb Hungary into its empire; the political and social power of the great nobles who placed their personal welfare before that of the kingdom; and the periodic lack of effective rulers. Hungarian feudalism reached its fullest development during this period, and the serfs suffered as the nobles gained power.

During the more than two centuries from the end of the Arpad Dynasty until the Turkish conquest, Hungary suffered from a seemingly endless power struggle, during which various royal houses of Europe vied for the crown of Saint Stephen. A Bohemian King rapidly gave way to a Bavarian who, in turn, was succeeded by Charles Rob-

ert of the House of Anjou. Charles Robert gradually brought some stability to the court while maintaining peace and a measure of prosperity in the country. Under his son, Louis the Great, Hungary extended its influence into the Balkans and into Poland (the throne of which Louis also held).

A tight rein was maintained on the nobility. A new military system was organized in which royal forces were supported by the militia of the magnates (leading nobles) and the county forces fo the lesser nobility. Financial reforms, through which the state treasury became independent of the large estates, were accomplished. The maintenance of the royal fortified areas was based on the crown lands and the original counties, which became autonomous under officials appointed by the king. New sources of revenue were tapped in the form of customs duties, direct taxes, and a monopoly on precious metals.

Commercial transactions with other countries were improved, and by the end of the fourteenth century the country had achieved an enviable measure of prosperity. As a result of a growing number of villages and towns, a viable economy, and a flourishing of the arts and sciences, Louis enjoyed a successful reign; moreover, his reissuing of the Golden Bull in 1351 helped to stabilize the social order.

Sigismund of Luxemburg followed the Anjous on the

Hungarian peasants bearing gifts of food to the king Sigismund, as was the custom at Easter

Sigismund was already king of Hungary (1387–1437) when he was elected German king and Holy Roman emperor in 1410.

The Ville de Presburg, royal castle of Ladislaus V, King of Hungary. He was king from 1444 to 1457 and built the ville in 1453.

A 1971 stamp commemorating the 450th anniversary of the death of Prince Neagoe Basarab of Walachia

King Hunyadi, historically known as Matthias Corvinus (1458–90). He is shown here in an allegory depicting the life of his court.

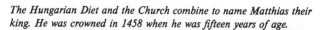

The Hungarian Diet and the Church combine to name Matthias their king. He was crowned in 1458 when he was fifteen years of age.

Hungarian throne but, because he also became the Holy Roman emperor, his interests were diffused to the detriment of Hungary. At the same time, the Ottoman Turks were becoming more menacing around the fringes of the vast Hungarian domains. Janos Hunyadi, one of Hungary's greatest heroes, came to power as a regent and initiated a long overdue policy of defense against the Turks. He defeated them decisively at Belgrade in 1456, delaying their advance into Europe for seventy years. After Hunyadi's death, his son Matthias was elected king and brought to the country significant talents for administration, social justice, cultural development, and military operations at a time of great need.

Matthias Corvinus (Matyas Hunyadi), ruling from 1458 until 1490, gave Hungary a period of prosperity and national glory. He fought the country's enemies and established a standing army of mercenaries, which he used as quickly against dissenting magnates as against foreign enemies. Matthias restored the public finance and improved the system of taxation so that the nobility's traditional exemption was eliminated, and he reduced the power of masters over serfs. In foreign affairs he succeeded in becoming ruler of Bohemia, Silesia, Moravia, Lower Austria, and other principalities. He maintained defenses against the Turks but also recognized the fundamental nature of the struggle with the growing power of the Habsburgs. Matthias also found time to become a great patron of the arts and of learning in general.

After the sudden death of Matthias, the inevitable power struggle eventually culminated in the election of a weak king, whom the magnates could manipulate. Many of the foreign territories that Matthias had incorporated broke away immediately and, internally, most of the curbs that he had effected against the nobles were cast aside. New law codes widened the cleavage between the nobility and the peasantry and weakened the power of the monarchy. Internal conditions deteriorated to the point that, in 1514, a serious serf uprising occurred. The uprising was suppressed with great loss of life and bloodshed, but the reprisals that followed were even more debilitating to the country as a whole. Tens of thousands

Coins commemorating King Matthias Corvinus

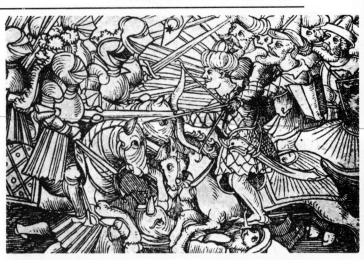

The Mohács Disaster (1526). *Both the internal and the external position of Hungary worsened during the reign of Louis II. The double marriage contract of 1515, by which Archduke Ferdinand Habsburg married Ladislaus's daughter and Louis married Ferdinand's sister Maria, finalized the country's association with the Habsburgs. This contract was made on the eve of the fight between the Habsburgs and the Turks for the hegemony of the Mediterranean basin and central Europe. In 1519 Charles Habsburg became the German emperor, but his preoccupations in the west and the internal anarchy of the German Empire prevented him from using his immense power to help Hungary against the Turks. Nándorfehérvár (today Belgrade) fell in 1521.*

King Louis II (1516–26) was the last of the kings of Hungary, the end of the native kings. In 1526, Hungary was divided between Turkey and Austria. After 1526, the only native sovereigns were the princes of Transylvania, and they came under outside control in 1711, when Hungary came under Austria, and remained so until their independence in 1919.

of serfs were executed because of their participation in the rebellion, and the conditions against which the serfs had rebelled became more burdensome than ever before. Twelve years later, the Turkish and Hungarian armies met in the Battle of Mohács, which proved to be utterly disastrous for the Hungarians and which initiated 150 years of Turkish rule. Hungary never regained unqualified control of the Carpathian Basin homeland that the original Magyars had secured over six centuries earlier.

After the defeat at Mohács and a period of internecine strife, Hungary was partitioned; the western and northern section was drawn into the Habsburg domains, the central area was under direct Turkish control, and Transylvania was governed by Hungarian princes under Turkish suzerainty. The three-way partition lasted for almost 150 years and finally ended in Habsburg domination rather than in independence. Hungarian nationalists were active at all times during the long occupation; various leaders arose to champion the cause of self-determination and, although they fought valiantly against Turks and Austrians alike, the Hungarians could not match the power of the Ottomans and the Habsburgs. When the Turks were finally forced to withdraw from Hungary, the Habsburgs were in control and forced the Hungarians to accept Austrian succession to the Hungarian crown.

The area of western and northern Hungary, ruled by the Habsburgs during most of the Turkish period, witnessed the orginal outbreak of the conflict between the

King Louis II was killed on August 29, 1526, at the Battle of Mohács when a small, badly organized Hungarian army was heavily defeated by superior numbers of Turks.

John Zapolya, the first voivode (prince) of Transylvania

The voivode's wife, Princess Isabelle Zapolya

The prince of Transylvania, Stephen Bathory, was also the king of Poland.

Stephen Bocskai, prince of Transylvania (1605–06), with his Haiduks. The Haiduks were the bands of homeless Hungarian warriors who had fled from the Turkish destruction and the despotism of the landlords. Prince Stephen solved the problem of the roaming bands of Haiduks by alloting land to 10,000 of them and making them nobles in reward for their military service.

Commemorative stamps, 1975. Top to bottom: Michael in the Battle of Calugareni, Michael the Bold, and Ottoman messengers bringing gifts to Michael.

Habsburg loyalists and the Hungarian nationalists, although the Nationalists later became associated with Transylvania. As a result of the Habsburg success, the kingdom of Hungary began to experience a type of absolutism that came to stand for foreign interference or intervention.

The feudal bases of the nobility's position were becoming weaker, and their ability to resist was weakened as well. The Hungarian administrative apparatus declined, and the chief organs of government were almost totally staffed by non-Hungarians. Public finance, foreign affairs, and defense of the kingdom were made subordinate to those of Austria. Foreign troops were stationed in the country, and their commanders were always foreigners. The diet was ineffectual and was largely reduced to registering protests.

The chief aim of Turkish officials had been to take as much as possible from the country in the shortest possible time. The Hungarian population was sharply re-

Protestantism had taken deep root in Hungary by the end of the sixteenth century. With the Emperor Rudolf II being very anti-Protestant in policy, his brother Matthias, a strong Protestant, gathered an army and was able to force his views on the emperor. Here the emperor Rudolf II is conferring the crown of Hungary on Matthias in 1605. Matthias took over the control of affairs in Hungary.

Prince Gabriel Bethlen (1613–29) was one of the finest horse generals of all Europe at the time. He proved his prowess as a cavalryman by invading Hungary proper, but in the end he made peace with Ferdinand II of Germany.

George Rakoczy II was the prince of Transylvania from 1648 to 1660. He operated on an anti-Habsburg policy and his master plan was to conquer Poland, which he attempted with the help of Sweden. However, because he had poorly prepared for the campaign, he was soundly defeated in 1657. The Turks, standing by for decades hoping to destroy the independence of Transylvania, invaded Transylvania and in that war the prince was killed (1660). The country was laid waste and the Voivodes were never again a serious threat to the Habsburgs. This coin is reported to have a near likeness to the prince.

Michael Apafi, although listed as a prince of Transylvania, was in reality the Turkish governor and he reigned longer than any other ruler of Transylvania (1661–90). He was succeeded by his son Michael Apafi II (1690–99). Michael II abdicated in 1699 when the rule was taken over by Habsburg Hungary.

duced, and the people who survived were in a condition of servitude. For defense purposes many left their individual farms and joined large cooperative farms, which incorporated the lands of outlying farms and villages and formed the basis of new kinds of towns. Many of the former towns almost disappeared. The people in outlying regions often paid taxes not only to Turkish authorities but also to Hungarian nobles.

Transylvania was able to maintain a semi-independent status, usually balancing the power of the Turkish sultan against that of the Habsburg emperor. The maintenance of Hungarian culture and national independence was promoted by a line of able princes and statesmen, such as Gabriel Bethlen and George Martinuzzi. Their internal policies brought about a measure of religious tolerance that was unique in Europe at that time. The Transylvanian princes also broadened the base of the privileged classes, but they did not go as far as to eliminate serfdom. Probably the Turks did not take over the principality because the gold coming from it—the richest source of the precious metal in Europe—was important to them, and they no doubt believed that its uninterrupted production and receipt by the sultan's government were more certain under conditions of semi-independence than under absolute control. Transylvania remained as a symbol of the survival of the Hungarian potential for independence, of both the Turks and Habsburgs, as well as the ideal of east-central European cooperation.

THE HABSBURG ERA

The final expulsion of the Turks and the confirmation of Habsburg rule initiated a long struggle between the absolutist empire and a reviving country. In 1711 conditions were desperate. In the central areas, depopulated under Turkish rule, the Austrian government introduced

Prince Francis Rakoczy (1704–11) was an instigator of the Insurrection of 1703, which was a peasant revolt. The Habsburgs offered Francis Rakoczy the crown rather than take a chance on the revolt spreading into Austria.

alien and more docile groups to weaken the unruly Magyar element. Much of the land was parceled out to foreign beneficiaries of the monarch's favor, who were recipients of political and social power, and some parts of the country were exempted from the jurisdiction of the diet, especially the military frontier district of the south. The state apparatus on the whole was Hungarian, although for long periods the sovereign ruled by executive fiat rather than through traditional constitutional procedures. A discriminatory tariff policy was used to keep the country economically repressed in order to maintain it as a source of cheap raw materials and food supplies. Peasants lived miserably, and the agricultural enterprise of the countryside was hampered by outmoded systems of land tenure.

Nevertheless, the Hungarian will to independence survived, and forces of national revival emerged. Their origin was essentially the persistence and determination at this time of the lesser nobility and small farmers in defending the traditional rights of Hungary and Hungarians. Their activities were effective mainly on the level of county government, where many officials continued to be locally elected and within whose assemblies national interest could be maintained. At this level the effectiveness of the lesser nobility and a measure of democracy could be maintained.

Toward the end of the eighteenth century a national renaissance, notably in general literature and political theory, began in Hungary. Much influenced by the French, the movement opposed intolerance and fostered the nobility's opposition to the Austrian monarchy. A significant aspect of the literature was its nativistic emphasis upon the contribution of the pagan Magyars to the mainstream of Hungarian culture. More importantly, a large group of academicians, lawyers, writers, and other professionals strove for the abolition of feudal privileges and emphasized the peasantry as the founda-

The princess Rakoczy was often pictured carrying a musket rifle because she said in the barbarian state of Hungary a woman always had to be prepared for the worst. The former princess of Hesse-Rheinsfeld is recorded in history as possessing "heroic courage" in the revolt.

tion of the nation. The group's activities culminated in a conspiracy in 1795; the conspiracy was discovered, and many of those involved were executed or imprisoned. The development, however, became evidence of the need for reform. Also at this time the issue of the right of the Hungarian people to employ their own language, especially in contact with officialdom, was expanding in importance.

During the reigns of Charles III and Maria Theresa the Habsburgs had such a diversity of interests that it was important for them to preserve peace in the east. Under Charles III a permanent army was stationed in Hungary, administered by a war council and supported by a general war tax. Although Hungarian troops served in the army, no Hungarian could reach the higher ranks. The Royal Court Chancery and the Hungarian Deputy Council were entirely dependent on the king. The Austrians often retained control over the subordinate nationalities, and under this administration Transylvania and Croatia were administered separately.

After a long period of political quiescence, Hungarians again opposed Austrian absolutism, and a great reform movement began about 1830. Count Istvan Szechenyi, a wealthy aristocrat, became a leader of the second Hungarian renaissance and led the forces of the lesser nobility supporting evolutionary reform. More importantly, he became, in effect, a national educator defining the situation and necessities of Hungary. Szechenyi, filled with religious devotion and sensitive to the forces moving about him, called especially for the nation to turn its attentions to its own weaknesses. He analyzed the faults of the nobility, attacked their special privileges, and strove to incite them to enthusiasm for national reform. Some of his followers were conservative and evolutionary in their thinking and willing to work under the authority of the Habsburgs, but he also inspired those who believed that reform could be accomplished only by a disestablishment of the existing political regime, an idea to which he was opposed. Szechenyi called for cultural, economic, and social reforms under the rule of the Habsburgs rather than a revolution to overthrow the alien rule.

Whereas Szechenyi counseled economic and social improvement, Lajos Kossuth, a landless noble, advocated political revolution and independence. Szechenyi called for a revolution from the top, but Kossuth wanted an uprising of the common people. The one desired the mass educated; the other, the mass unleashed. The one counseled looking inward for the assessment of the nation's problems; the other prescribed looking abroad for the national enemy and found him in Vienna. The one's sternest lesson was hard, critical realism; the other's message was nationalist idealism. Szechenyi's evolutionary approach was enhanced by his great respect for Great Britain and its culture and civilization. Kossuth's revolutionary position was the product of a more active

French influence. In effect, these two leaders became opposite poles of the Hungarian response to the revolutionary influences of the nineteenth century.

Repression followed every demand for reform, and each repression made each future demand more violent. Szechenyi's reform plans, which would have preserved the legal framework of evolutionary change, were not enough. Kossuth assumed leadership; his prestige was only enhanced by imprisonment between 1837 and 1840 for the political offense, among others, of publishing the proceedings of the county assemblies. Greatly influenced by French literary and political figures and French and American revolutionary events, Kossuth transformed a journalistic career into a career of national political leadership and gained renown through his slogans calling for a free people and a free fatherland.

The diet, which opened in November 1847, was presented a program of conservative reform proposing the establishment of responsible government in Hungary (as opposed to Vienna) and an elected legislature, a system of uniform and general taxation, freedom of the press, and reinclusion of Transylvania in Hungary. Kossuth, however, soon demonstrated his control over the diet, which went through a period of unproductive controversy until news of the revolution in Paris was received. Realizing the opportunity to initiate events and force change, Kossuth demanded the abolition of serfdom, popular representation, and the replacement of control from Vienna by control in a Hungarian government. These demands were presented to King Ferdinand, who responded favorably by appointing Count Lajos Batthyany as president of a Hungarian council.

Following the model of the Belgian constitution, the king was to exercise his power and prerogative through responsible ministers, whose countersignatures were required to give validity to his acts. The diet, established as a bicameral legislature (the Chamber of Deputies and the Chamber of Magnates), was to be elected for three years. Representation was related to the payment of taxes, educational qualifications, and knowledge of the Hungarian language. Several aspects of the new constitutional laws revealed the implicit radical Hungarian assumption, found also among the conservatives, that the ethnic minorities could be included within the Hungarian state without regard to their own national aspirations.

Certain aspects of relations with Austria remained vague, and control over such matters of common concern as public finance, defense, and foreign affairs was left in doubt. Austrian reactionaries and Hungarian counterrevolutionaries tried to undo what had been accomplished; in 1848 they contrived to set the national minorities against the Hungarians, at first covertly and then openly. King Ferdinand, who had granted the concessions in March 1848, was forced to abdicate in favor of Francis Joseph, who stated that he was not bound by the concessions made by his predecessor. The Austrians then moved with direct military force against the Hungarians; in 1849, when their efforts fell short, the Austrians asked the Russians for military assistance. The national minorities aroused to anti-Hungarian activity were Croats, Serbs, Romanians, Ruthenians, and Slovaks. The sporadic outbreaks of violence in Transylvania between Romanians and Hungarians in 1848 and 1849 were especially bloody.

Despite the bravery and skill of the Hungarians, the imperial Austrian and Russian forces defeated them. This defeat was hastened by internecine strife, and the head of the revolutionary government, Kossuth, was not above reproach in his role in such internal controversy. The Declaration of Independence of April 14, 1849, which had been insisted upon by Kossuth, proved to be a tactical blunder. It confirmed the worst suspicions of the Vienna reactionaries—that Kossuth was intellectually unprepared to remain in a moderate position. It created difficulties for the national forces in that it required a violation of the oath of loyalty to the king. The declaration made even more determined the efforts of the imperial and Russian armies to put down the Hungarian revevolution, just as it doubtless increased the fears of the British and the French. Although they generally supported the development of constitutional monarchy, the British and the French could not but be alarmed at the prospect of the dissolution of the Habsburgs, whom they considered necessary to the European balance of power.

The decision of the government in Vienna was to make use of Hungary's defeat to destroy it as a state and to incorporate it into the empire as a province; some of its historic lands, such as Croatia and Transylvania, were separated from it in order to reduce its unity and strength. The new emperor, Francis Joseph I, had assumed the direction of the monarchy upon the abdication of Ferdinand. The first seventeen years of his rule were characterized by the last attempt at absolute rule under the monarchy. The national minorities, which had been used against the Hungarians during the revolution, fared equally badly during the period of reaction and came to detest Austria as much as did the Hungarians.

Although the regime was soon changed from a military into a civil administration, no amelioration of the situation took place. A gigantic and corrupt state bureaucracy and system of political police imposed persecution and repression at great expense. For years it was controlled by Alexander von Bach, minister of internal affairs and revolutionary agitator turned tool of absolutism. Austrian, Galician, and Czech officials dominated the Hungarian administration, through which the emperor ruled by decree—entirely without reference to a constitution. Kossuth was forced into exile.

The general reaction was the development of a more intense national patriotism accompanied, at least among moderate and radical groups, by a hatred of everything German or Austrian. Many significant groups—their educational function for the time neglected—retired into political inactivity. Formal education itself declined in quality; much of it remained adequate only to train those who could fit into the bureaucracy.

The remaining political groups were all united in the view that historic Hungary had not lost its continuity and rejected the Austrian view that by reason of rebellion the Hungarians had forfeited the right to independence. They nevertheless were divided with respect to the type of reform they supported. The old conservatives called for a return to the constitutional arrangement of 1847, which presupposed Hungarian autonomy under a general monarchy. They also desired the reestablishment of county autonomy. In addition to desiring the maintenance of traditional relations with Austria, this group strove for some modernization. They were more politically passive than some other groups, but they became more active in general cultural affairs.

Another general group followed the leadership of Ferenc Deak, a conservative reformer, in demanding a return to the laws of April 1848, which the group declared

1943–1945 Hungarian stamps honoring her heritage. **Top, left to right:** *Arpad, King Ladislaus I, and Miklos Toldi;* **second row, left to right:** *Janos Hunyadi, Paul Kinizsi, and Count Miklos Zrinyi;* **third row, left to right:** *Franz Rakoczy II, Count Andrew Hadik, and Arthur Georgei;* **bottom row:** *Virgin Mary, Patroness of Hungary, and the crown of Saint Stephen.*

to have an organic relationship with the traditional constitution. A third group, made up primarily of émigrés who had fled the country, insisted upon the principles of the April 1849 Declaration of Independence. The leader of the group was Kossuth, who over decades of exile never wavered from the position. On two occasions during the period they were able to continue the fight against the Habsburgs: the Italo-French War against Austria in 1859, as a result of which Austria lost Lombardy; and the war with Prussia in 1866, which removed Austria from any pretense of control in Germany.

The group led by Deak proved to have a compromise solution between the unitary concept of the Habsburgs and the complete independence of the radicals. Defeat in war and diplomatic isolation, especially from Russia, whose ambitions in the Balkans were causing a breach with that power, stimulated the emperor to choose the compromise position. His decision was supported by the official British desire to see the monarchy maintained as a bulwark against the Russian drive toward the Balkans and the Dardanelles.

Before the compromise advocated by Deak and his followers was passed by the diet and accepted by Francis Joseph, Count Gyula Andrassy had been appointed as the responsible head of a Hungarian ministry, and Transylvania was brought again into union with Hungary. Thus, although the Revolution of 1848 had proved abortive, it in effect produced the compromise establishing the Dual Monarchy, finally adopted in 1867, which provided a workable arrangement between Austria and Hungary for fifty years.

THE DUAL MONARCHY

The Compromise of 1867 established a mode of relationship with Austria and the Habsburgs. It set forth the details of control over matters of common concern to the two countries—defense, finance, and foreign affairs. Failure to deal with them in 1848 had aroused the suspicions of court circles that the Hungarians were seeking complete independence. The arrangement of 1867 established a legal link between the two states.

A common monarch and the obligation to render mutual support on matters of general concern were accepted. Parliamentary bodies were to function in both states, and any suggestion of a general legislature was abandoned as an affront to Hungarian autonomy. The ministers involved with the matters of common concern were responsible to equal delegations from the two parliaments sitting alternately in the two capitals. The delegations fixed the budget for the matters of common concern, and a special committee periodically determined the relative financial contributions of the two countries. The army was made subject to the king with respect to its leadership and internal organization and to the Hungarian parliament on matters of the draft, recruitment, and the general system of defense. Agreements concerning commerce and the customs were made subject to periodic review every ten years.

The politics of the period from the compromise to World War I were almost entirely dominated by the issue of relations with Austria. Every Hungarian government was caught between unpopularity at home and an obstructive Austrian officialdom that remained adamant about the idea of a centralized monarchy, although Emperor Francis Joseph was consistently loyal to the 1867 arrangement. The dominating role of the question of public law tended to prevent concentration by the government upon the solution of social and economic problems.

The problem of minorities loomed ever larger. The one involving the Croats was the most critical and, perhaps, the most revealing. The Croats received considerable autonomy, especially in local administration, education, and justice. It was provided that their language would be employed in matters connected with civil administration and justice and in education below the higher levels. They were made responsible to the Hungarian government through the governor and were empowered to send forty deputies to the Hungarian parliament. Despite such concessions, the Croats and other ethnic groups were no more satisfied with their status than were the Hungarians with dualism.

At the outbreak of World War I, after the assassination of Archduke Francis Ferdinand, the Hungarian government faced a dilemma. If the Hungarians failed to support the imperial government, minorities in the empire and the governments of peoples of similiar ethnic background would exert pressure for the independence of those minorities on the assumption that the Dual Monarchy could not survive. On the other hand, a victory for the Central Powers might result in the inclusion of a larger number of Slavs in the Dual Monarchy. The situation forced the Hungarian leaders to accept the decision already taken. The Hungarian decision was made easier by the fact that the killing of the wife of the archduke had turned political assassination into an even more heinous type of murder. The war policy could be supported, or rationalized as necessary, in order to withstand Russian imperial aggression. On this basis most parties in the country, including the Social Democratic party, were able to bring some enthusiasm to the prosecution of the war.

Before Emperor Francis Joseph died in the fall of 1916, he recognized the need for peace if the Dual Monarchy was to be preserved. The Serbs were the only minority that had actively attempted to obstruct entry into the war, but it became increasingly difficult to use troop units made up of minorities at critical points on the war front; more and more the strain on Hungarian contingents became disproportionate to their number. Economic conditions deteriorated; hunger and privation became widespread. Despite the relatively large production of foodstuffs in the country, the drain imposed by the requirements of the Central Powers found production unequal to demand.

The successive failures of Russian military campaigns and the subsequent appearance of revolution in Russia encouraged Germany and Austria-Hungary to believe that they could win the war. The decision of the German high command to carry through offensives on the western front made it difficult to entertain the idea of a negotiated peace. Moreover, Germany's unrestricted submarine warfare raised an issue that ruled out any result except the unquestionable victory of one side or the other. Finally, the entry of the United States into the war made the Hungarians believe that their Hungarian national state could be preserved only if they persisted in the fight long enough to make unreasonably high the price the Allies would have to pay to destroy it. At the same time the minorities became more confident of an independent future, and the chance that conciliation could make them accept a status within the Hungarian state became more remote.

In October 1918 Count Mihaly Karolyi, a leader of the left wing of the Party of Independence, was appointed premier and formed a cabinet made up of Social Democrats, radicals, and members of his own group. In November this government declared Hungary a republic. Karolyi believed that a new policy of toleration toward the minorities and an orientation toward the Triple Entente could preserve a larger Hungary. The Allies, however, accepted Italian, South Slav, Romanian, and Czech demands. Serbian, Romanian, and Czech army units then established areas of occupation on Hungarian territory.

Gradually, the Karolyi government was infiltrated at all levels and at key points by Communists, who had in many cases returned from Russian prisoner-of-war camps where they had been influenced by the followers of Lenin. The Hungarian military forces on their return from the front had been disarmed before the security of the state had been established, and the Social Democrats proved incapable of withstanding pressure from the left. In March 1919 the leftist group formed a bloc with the Communists. After Karolyi's resignation the Communist leader, Bela Kun, formed a cabinet and, although technically not the head of government, reserved to himself full powers, including those over foreign affairs. A reign of terror was conducted by Bela Kun; its memory was a powerful factor in Hungarian resistance to communism and Russian influence. Bela Kun defended the country against the Czechs but, defeated by the Romanians, was forced to resign after five months in power.

The leader of the new counterrevolutionary regime was Admiral Miklos Horthy, commander in chief of the armed forces that entered Budapest in November 1919.

In the absence of any possibility of a return of the Habsburgs, Admiral Horthy was elected regent of Hungary by the parliament in 1920. The government he headed was one of reaction and initially one of terror, and it carried out stringent reprisals against many who could be identified with the Bela Kun and Karolyi regimes, especially Jews.

The National Assembly on March 1, 1920, confirmed the selection of Horthy as regent. It also abolished the legislation of 1867 that had established the Dual Monarchy arrangement, but it did not settle finally whether the Habsburgs retained the right of succession. Even after two attempts by Charles I to resume the throne in 1921 caused pressure to be applied on the legislature to declare the Habsburg succession revoked, there remained a division in Hungarian political thought on this subject. Horthy was most instrumental in bringing about the

Regent Miklos Horthy of Nagybanya was the principal royal person who served as the head of state in the kingless monarchy that existed in Hungary between World War I and World War II.

expulsion of Charles from Hungary. Charles I's removal eliminated the last remnant of a royal family who could possibly rule Hungary in the form of a monarchy.

THE ROYAL SOVEREIGNS OF THE KINGDOM OF HUNGARY

Reign	Title	Ruler	Birth	Death	Relationship
875–907	(Chieftain)	Arpad		907	
972–997	Duke	Geza			Great-grandson of Arpad
997–1038	King	Stephen I (Saint Stephen) (Istvan)	975	1038	Son of Geza
1038–1041	King	Peter Orseolo	1011	1050	Son-in-law of Stephen I
1041–1044	King	Aba Samuel			Brother-in-law of Stephen I
1044–1046	King	Peter Orseolo			
1046–1060	King	Andrew I		1060	Cousin of Peter Orseolo
1060–1063	King	Bela I			Brother of Andrew I
1063–1074	King	Salomon			Son of Andrew I
1074–1077	King	Geza I			Son of Bela I
1077–1095	King	Ladislaus I (Saint Laszlo)	1040	1095	Son of Bela I
1095–1116	King	Salomon (Coleman Beauclerc)	1070	1116	Nephew of Ladislaus I
1116–1131	King	Stephen II (abdicated 1131)	1100	1131	
1131–1141	King	Bela II			Grandson of Bela I
1141–1161	King	Geza II			Son of Bela II
1161–1162	King	Stephen III, the Lightning		1164	Son of Geza II
1162–1163	King	Ladislaus II	1134	1163	Son of Bela II
1163–1165	King	Stephen IV		1166	Son of Bela II
1161–1173	King	Stephen III			
1173–1196	King	Bela III		1196	Grandson of Bela II
1196–1204	King	Emeric			Son of Bela III
1204–1205	King	Ladislaus III	1179	1205	Son of Emeric
1205–1235	King	Andrew II	1175	1235	Son of Bela III
1235–1270	King	Bela IV	1206	1270	Son of Andrew II
1270–1272	King	Stephen V	1239	1272	Son of Bela IV
1272–1290	King	Ladislaus IV	1262	1290	
1290–1301	King	Andrew III		1301	Grandson of Andrew II
1301–1305	King	Wenceslaus Wenzel of Bohemia	1289	1306	
1305–1307	King	Otto of Bavaria		1312	
1308–1342	King	Charles I	1298	1342	Grand-nephew of Ladislaus IV
1342–1382	King	Louis the Great	1326	1382	Son of Charles I
1382–1387	Queen	Mary	1370	1395	Daughter of Louis the Great
1387–1437	King	Sigismund	1368	1437	Husband of Mary
1437–1439	King	Albert	1397	1439	Son-in-law of Sigismund
1439–1440	Queen	Elizabeth		1443	Wife of Albert
1440–1444	King	Ladislaus I of Poland	1424	1444	Grandson of Mary
1444–1457	King	Ladislaus V	1440	1457	Son of Albert
1458–1490	King	Matthias Corvinus	1440	1490	
1490–1516	King	Ladislas of Bohemia	1456	1516	Nephew of Ladislaus V
1516–1526	King	Louis II	1506	1526	Son of Ladislas V of Bohemia

1526—Hungary was divided after 1526 between Turkey and Austria.

Reign	Title	Ruler	Birth	Death	Relationship

TRANSYLVANIA (1344–1711)

1344–1376—Six members of the Lackfy family ruled (beginning of formal rule).

Reign	Title	Ruler	Birth	Death	Relationship
1415–1438	Prince	Vice-voivode Lorand Lepes			
1441–1456	Prince	Iancu of Hunedoara		1456	

Sixteenth century—Under control of the Turkish government

Reign	Title	Ruler	Birth	Death	Relationship
1526–1540	Prince	John Zaoolya	1487	1540	
1540–1571	Prince	John Sigismund	1520	1571	
1571–1572	Prince	Gaspar Bekesy		1572	
1571–1576	King	Stephen Bathory (king of Poland)	1533	1586	
1576–1581	Prince	Christopher Bathory	1530	1581	
1581–1598	Prince	Sigismund	1572	1613	
1599–1600	Prince	Andrew	1562	1600	
1600–1601	Prince	Michael the Brave			
1602–1603	Prince	Moyses Szekely			
1602–1605	Emperor	Rudolph II			
1605–1606	Prince	Stephen Bocskai	1557	1606	
1607–1608	Prince	Sigismund Rakoczi	1544	1608	
1608–1613	Prince	Gabriel Bathory	1589	1613	
1613–1629	Prince	Gabriel Bethlen	1580	1629	
1630–1630	Prince	Stephen Bethlen			
1630–1648	Prince	George Rakoczy I	1591	1648	
1648–1660	Prince	George Rakoczy II	1621	1660	
1658–1660	Prince	Achatius Bocskai			
1661–1662	Prince	Johann Kemeny			
1682–1699	Prince	Emerich Tokoli			
1661–1690	Prince	Michael Apafi	1632	1690	
1690–1699	Prince	Michael II Apafi	1680	1713	

1699–1821—Habsburg authority in Transylvania

Reign	Title	Ruler	Birth	Death	Relationship
1704–1711	Prince	Francis Rakoczy	1676	1735	

1711–1918—Hungary under Austria

1919—Kingless monarchy established

Reign	Title	Ruler	Birth	Death	Relationship
1919	Regent	Joseph of Austria	1872		
1920–1944	Regent	Miklos Horthy of Nagybanya	1868	1957	
1944–1945	Regent	Ferenc Szalasi	1897	1946	
1944–1945	Regent	Bela Miklos	1890	1948	

1946—Hungary became a republic.

7

The Yugoslav Kingdoms

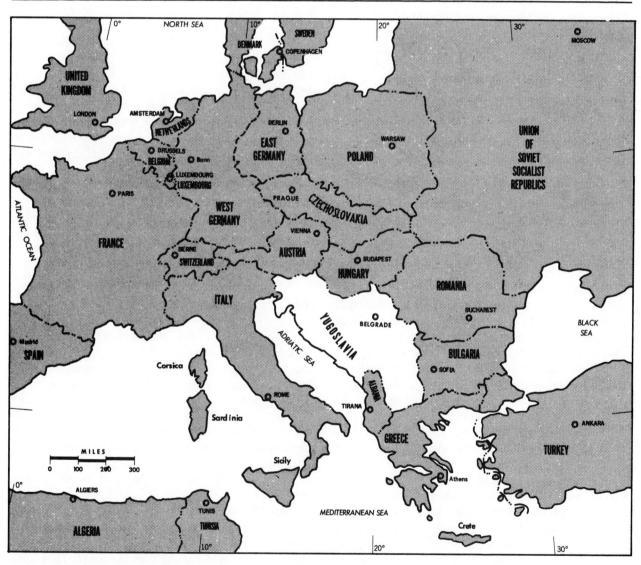

Geographic position of Yugoslavia in Europe today

The South Slav groups in present-day Yugoslavia became linguistically and culturally differentiated after they entered the Balkan Peninsula in the sixth and seventh centuries A.D. Their subjection to various non-Slav powers occupying the Balkan area during the next twelve centuries fostered even greater variations among them in religion, language, culture, and political development. For some six hundred years before 1914, Croats and Slovenes were subordinated to the Germanic and Roman Catholic Habsburg Empire. The Eastern Orthodox Serbs, Macedonians, and Islamized Slavs were under the rule of the Ottoman (Turkish) Empire for much of the period between the fourteenth and nineteenth centuries.

Centuries of foreign rule, however, did not prevent the development of a strong sense of ethnic identity within each of the South Slav groups. Slovenes, Serbs, Croats, Montenegrins, and Macedonians sought to maintain separate character and identities. Serbia's successful struggle to regain independence in the early nineteenth century stimulated the other groups to strive for independence.

During the nineteenth century, some Slovene, Croat, and Serb intellectuals began to advocate the creation of a united and independent Yugoslav state. By 1914 the sentiment for a union of the South Slavs was widespread and, at the end of World War I, the Western Allies agreed to the concept of a Yugoslav kingdom to be formed by uniting the South Slav territories of the defeated Austro-Hungarian Dual Monarchy (the former Habsburg Empire) with Serbia, Montenegro, and northern Macedonia. (Until 1929 the new state was known as the Kingdom of the Serbs, Croats, and Slovenes.)

In 1915 exiled Slav leaders from Austro-Hungarian regions had formed a Yugoslav Committee, based in London. It gained broad support among the Slovenes, Croats, and Serbs. In July 1917 Ante Trumbic, president of the committee, signed an agreement with Serb premier Nikola Pasic at Corfu, providing for the creation of a South Slav kingdom under Alexander Karadjordjevic (1921–34). The new state was to be "a constitutional, democratic, and parliamentary monarchy" based on the equality of the Serbs, Croats, and Slovenes. The Latin and Cyrillic alphabets, the Slovene and Serbo-Croat languages, and the Catholic, Eastern Orthodox, and Islamic religions were to be given equal recognition. Parliamentary representatives and local government officials were to be elected through universal manhood suffrage.

After formation of the kingdom, the sense of separateness that was the legacy of the past continued to exert a significant influence on each group. Forces of unity and cohesion were counterbalanced by the influences of ethnic extremism. Threats to the internal order of the state by ethnically based political extremist groups led to the establishment of a dictatorship in 1929, a situation that continued until the outbreak of World War II and the occupation of Yugoslavia by the Axis powers.

THE PRE-SLAV PERIOD

The earliest recorded inhabitants of the area now included in Yugoslavia consisted of two obscure groups of tribes known collectively as the Illyrians and the Thracians. The Illyrians occupied much of the region west of the Vardar River and north of what is now Greece, including the area of present-day Albania. Thracian tribes occupied the regions to the east of the Illyrians, an area that included much of the territory that later was a part of the Serbian Kingdom.

At the beginning of the Christian Era, the western portion on the Balkan Peninsula came under the control of the Roman Empire. Much of this territory was incorporated into the Roman province of Illyricum, with an administrative center at Salona, the present-day city of Split, on the Dalmatian coast. When the Roman Empire was divided into the Eastern and Western empires in A.D. 395, the region east of the Drina River bacame part of the Eastern Empire. The border between the two empires cut through Bosnia and Hercegovina.

During the fifth century the area was subjected to waves of raiding tribes of Visigoths, Huns, and Ostrogoths. In the sixth century the Slavs began their incursions into the Balkan Peninsula and gradually assimilated the remnants of the Illyrians and Thracians, except for small Illyrian groups that retreated into the mountainous regions along the Adriatic coast—the ancestors of the present-day Albanians.

THE COMING OF THE SLAVS

The Slavic peoples who entered during the course of approximately one hundred years eventually developed into five main groups, differentiated in language and customs: Serbs, Croats, Slovenes, Montenegrins, and Macedonians. The area came to be divided not only between the two Roman empires, but also between rival branches of the Christian church. The religious estrangement between Rome and Constantinople began in the fifth century, and the schism dividing the Roman Catholic and Eastern Orthodox faiths came in the eleventh century.

Generally, the boundary separating the Eastern and Western churches coincided with that which divided the empires. For several centuries both empires and churches contested control over the Slavs. Thus were introduced the diverse political and cultural influences that were to continue for more than a thousand years and which were to cause divisions among the South Slavs even after political unification in 1918.

SOUTH SLAV HISTORY TO WORLD WAR I

THE SLOVENES

Slovene tribes began to settle in the northwest corner of the Balkan Peninsula in the sixth century. By the eighth century they had submitted to the domination of the Franks. Under Charlemagne, German Catholic missionaries had converted them to Christianity and introduced German culture. With the increase of German influence, the Slovene peasants became serfs under the German feudal nobility. During the tenth and eleventh centuries the Slovene lands were divided into the marches (borderlands) of Carniola, Carantania (the name given in the eighth century to the region known more recently as Carinthia), and Styria.

Throughout the next two centuries the Slovenes were ruled by a variety of petty princes until the region came under the control of the Habsburgs in the the late thirteenth century. From then until 1918 the Slovene lands were an integral part of the Habsburg domains.

During the fifteenth to the seventeenth centuries the Slovenes, like the Slav groups to the south, were repeatedly subjected to Turkish raids. In the sixteenth century the Protestant Reformation had considerable influence among the Slovenes, but the severity of the Counter-Reformation, combined with the efforts of the Austrian nobility to retain power, served to reinforce both the feudal system and the discipline of the church over the peasant population. The centralization policy of the Habsburg rulers during the seventeenth century resulted in an even greater degree of germanization. German was made the official language for all government affairs as well as for education, but Slovene national consciousness remained strong, and the masses continued to speak the Slovene language.

French troops came into the Slovene regions during Napoleon's campaign against Austria and, in 1809, the Treaty of Vienna brought most of the Slovene lands and Croatia under the control of France. These areas, along with Dalmatia, the coastal region along the Adriatic Sea, were formed into the Illyrian provinces under a French proconsul. During the brief period of French control, there was substantial improvement in the material conditions of the Slovenes. Additional schools were established, and the Slovene language was given renewed status.

With the defeat of Napoleon's forces in the Russian campaign, the 1815 agreements of the Congress of Vienna restored the Slovene lands, as well as Dalmatia and part of Croatia, to the Austrian Empire. Although Slovenes were again subjected to German control, Slovene national consciousness continued to grow, and sentiments developed favoring not only Slovene unity and independence but the union of all the South Slavs as well.

THE CROATS

During the sixth and early seventh centuries Croat tribes migrated from the Dnieper River region (Ukraine) into the area between the Sava and Drava rivers (Slavonia), the land directly south of the Slovene area (Croatia), and into the northern Adriatic coastal region (Dalmatia). In the seventh century these tribes were converted to Christianity.

Largely in response to military pressure from both the Eastern and Western Roman empires, organization on a family and tribal basis evolved into broader units during the eighth century. Two principal Croat units developed, Dalmatian Croatia along the Adriatic, and Pannonian Croatia to the north, centering in the valley of the Sava. During the first quarter of the ninth century, the northern Croatians were brought under the hegemony of the Franks, and Dalmatian Croatia came under the nominal control of the Eastern Empire. Because of their relative isolation from the two power centers, the Croatian groups were eventually able to shake off foreign domination and by the early tenth century had begun to develop a sense of common identity.

About 924 a powerful *zupan* (tribal leader), Tomislav, from Nin, a city on the Adriatic, united the Pannonian and Dalmatian Croats and was recognized by the pope as king. He extended the borders of his territory inland to include part of Bosnia and established a kingdom that continued for nearly two hundred years.

During this time the original tribal structure of Croat society was gradually replaced by feudalism. A class system developed, based on landholdings. The leaders of the more powerful clans assumed the status of a hereditary nobility; the royal family and the church accumulated extensive properties formerly held as a common tribal land, and the peasants were reduced to serfdom.

In the late eleventh century the increasing strength of the nobility limited the authority of the king, and his power bagan to wane. When the throne became vacant in 1089, a long struggle ensued between rival Croat claimants. In 1102, with no leader strong enough to unite

King Tomislav, about the year 924, emerged as a powerful tribal leader (zupan) having united the Pannonian and Dalmatian Croats. The pope recognized him by crowning him king. This Yugoslavian postage stamp shows him on the throne.

the Croat lands, the Croat nobles offered the crown—with the blessing of Pope Paschal II—to the king of Hungary. Although at times the Croatians enjoyed a special status, during most of the ensuing eight hundred years (until 1918) Croatia remained tied to Hungary.

In the late fourteenth century the Turks began their incursions into the more northern regions of the Balkan Peninsula; and, after Bosnia fell to Turkish forces in 1463, the sultan's armies pushed into Croat lands. For sixty years both the Croats and Hungarians sought to resist the periodic raiding of the Turks, but in 1526 the Hungarian army was defeated in a disastrous encounter, their king was killed, and Hungarian resistance ended. The next year Croatian nobles opted to submit to the Habsburg emperor Ferdinand, who that same year had become ruler of most of Hungary. The Turks continued to press northward and by the end of the sixteenth century had absorbed much of Croatia and almost all of Slavonia.

In 1578 the Habsburg emperor established a "military frontier province" in the depopulated southern borderland of what remained of Croatia and Slavonia. Expropriated from Croat nobles, these lands were subject directly to the emperor, who granted them to soldier-peasants, free from feudal obligations, in return for military service.

In 1699, when the Habsburgs recovered all of Croatia and Slavonia from the Turks, the military frontier province was extended to include the southern half of Croatia, Slavonia, and the Vojvodina—the southern part of the Hungarian Danubian plain, directly east of Slavonia. The land was settled not only by Croat peasants but by Germans and a large number of Serbs who had migrated into the area to escape Ottoman oppression. The descendants of these Serb immigrants later became a controversial factor in the nineteenth-century issue of Croatian nationalism.

The Croat feudal nobility opposed the efforts of the emperor to retain the frontier lands under his direct control, but the system was continued until the late nineteenth century. The frontier soldier-peasants became the most loyal of the emperor's subjects; as late as World War I, these frontier elements resisted Croat nationalist sentiment in favor of the emperor.

The Dalmatian coastal area of the medieval Croat state was the object of three hundred years of conflict between Hungary and the growing power of Venice. Some of the Dalmatian cities changed hands repeatedly. From the fifteenth century to the end of the eighteenth, most of the coastal area was subordinate to Venice and shared in its art, commerce, and wealth. The Republic of Ragusa, present-day Dubrovnik, however, remained independent of foreign control throughout most of the period and developed its own high level of economic prosperity and culture. By the eighteenth century, the commercial power of Venice and Ragusa had passed to other European states, and the Dalmatian cities were in a state of decay.

Like the Slovene lands, part of Croatia was incorporated into the Illyrian provinces by Napoleon in the early years of the nineteenth century. During the four years of French control, schools were established; the first Croat-language newspaper appeared; commerce was stimulated; and Croat nationalist sentiment was fomented.

After Napoleon's defeat, Slovenia, Dalmatia, and the Croatian military-frontier province were restored to Austria; the rest of Croatia went to Hungary within the Habsburg Empire. Feudalism was formally ended by the Habsburg emperor, and the Slovene and Croat peasants were permitted to buy their land from their former feudal lords.

THE SERBS

Serb tribes settled in the interior of the Balkan Peninsula south and east of the Croat lands during the seventh century. Throughout these early years clans engaged each other in a continual struggle for dominance. During most of the period from the eighth through the eleventh centuries the Serbs were under the control of either Bulgar or Byzantine rulers. In the latter half of the ninth century, Byzantine monks—the most important of whom were Methodius and Cyril—converted the Serbs to Christianity and introduced Byzantine culture into the area.

Byzantine control was weak, however, and by the twelfth century strong tribal leaders were able to unite the Serbs into two independent Serb states: Zeta, in the mountainous region of present-day Montenegro and Hercegovina; and Raska, in Serbia proper. Shortly before 1170, Stephen Nemanja became the grand *zupan* of Raska. He shook off Byzantine hegemony, united the two states into a Serb kingdom, and founded a dynasty that in the next two hundred years made Serbia the strongest state in the Balkans.

The Serb rulers enlisted the Eastern Orthodox church in their efforts to unite the dissident tribes. In 1196 Nemanja abdicated the throne and with his son helped found the great Serb Orthodox Monastery of Hilander on Mount Athos in present-day Greece. The younger Nemanja later gained recognition from the Byzantine patriarch for an independent Serbian archbishopric, and in 1219 (under the name of Sava) he became the first Serb archbishop. The Serb rulers developed a fierce loyalty to the church among their people.

The Serbian Empire reached its zenith under its last emperor, Czar Stephen Dusan (1331–35). Guided by Dusan's genius, Serbian economy and arts were greatly developed. In 1349 he promulgated an important legal code, known as the Dusanov Zakonik, which fused Byzantine law and Serbian custom into a formal legal and political system. Dusan expanded the empire to include all of modern Albania, Macedonia, Epirus, and Thessaly. With Dusan's death, however, rebellion by subordinate nobles brought about the disintegration of the empire.

Encouraged by the disunity of the Serb state, the Ottoman Turks, who had expanded into the southern Balkans in the middle of the fourteenth century, advanced against the Serbs. In 1389 the Turks met and defeated the Serbian armies at Kosovo in what was to become the most legendary battle of Serbian history.

Turkish power in the Balkans steadily increased, and after the second great defeat of the Serbs at Smederevo in 1459 the Serb lands were placed under Turkish military occupation and so remained for more than three hundred and fifty years. Bosnia fell to the Turks in 1463, Hercegovina in 1483. Only the most inaccessible mountainous Serb area north of Lake Scutari—present-day Montenegro—was able to resist Turkish domination.

When the Ottoman Turks overran Serbia, Macedonia, and Bosnia, the Slav nobles of Serbia and Macedonia were killed or forced to flee to the mountains or into Hungary. The Turkish sultan granted large landholdings to *spahis* (Muslim cavalry officers), who subjected the Christian *raja* (serfs) to a new, oppressive feudal system. The Serbs continued to be tied to their land and forced to pay heavy taxes in kind to the *spahis* and other Turkish administrators. In addition, every four years they had to submit to the seizure of a portion of the healthiest and most gifted boys in each village, whom the *spahis* sent to Constantinople to be educated as Muslims and trained as part of the sultan's elite military corps, the Janissary. Many came to occupy high positions in the Ottoman government.

During the first two hundred years of Turkish occupation, when the Ottoman Empire was expanding and the newly conquered lands ere able to support the increasing numbers of Muslim aristocrats, their rule was not intolerably oppressive. As long as the Christian serfs paid their taxes, they were permitted to live according to Serb customs and to govern their own local affairs without direct interference from the Turkish administration. They could not be removed from their land, which continued to be treated as private family property. The Turks were tolerant of the Christian religion, although they impoverished the Serbian Orthodox church by seizing most of its lands and its richest buildings.

The Serbs reverted to the egalitarian rural society that had characterized their social structure before the rise of feudalism. They avoided town living, and towns were inhabited solely by the Turkish nobility and administrators, along with the non-Slav craftsmen and traders who supplied them. The Serb villagers retained a high degree of autonomy under the administration of village councils elected by the head of each Serb family. In the absence of a native nobility, the members of the church hierarchy were recognized by the Serbs as their leaders, and the Serbian Orthodox church became the major perpetuator of the Serb tradition and national consciousness.

During the late seventeenth century and the first half of the eighteenth, the Serb peasants supported several vain attempts by the Habsburg armies to force the Turks out of Serbia. Brutal reprisals by the Ottoman administrators triggered a mass migration of thirty thousand to forty thousand Serb families, who moved northward in 1691 and settled in Habsburg-controlled Vojvodina. During the second half of the eighteenth century, Constantinople lost most of its control over its officials in Serbia, who then entered a period of unrestrained oppression and plundering of the defenseless Serb peasants. As the power of the Ottoman Empire declined, Habsburg Austria and Czarist Russia attempted to extend their hegemony over the Balkans. During the late eighteenth century the two powers joined together to oust the Turks, but their efforts were indecisive until the expansion of Napoleon's empire began to threaten Turkish territories.

With the sultan's forces under pressure from Napoleon in the Mediterranean area, Russia moved to occupy Turkish provinces in the eastern region of the Balkans. In 1804, sensing that the time was ripe for revolt, a Serbian peasant, Djordje Petrovic—known to his followers as Karadjordje (Black George), led the Serbs in an uprising against their Turkish rulers. The revolution was successful for a time, and Karadjordje established a short-lived government in Belgrade. When Napoleon's forces attacked Russia in 1812, Russian troops were withdrawn from the Balkan area, and Turkey took advantage of the situation to move against the Serbs. By October 1813 the Serbs were defeated and Karadjordje fled to Austria.

In 1817 a second revolt, led by the peasant Milos Obrenovic, forced the Turks to grant the Serbs a considerable degree of autonomy. The mysterious murder of Karadjordje that same year began a blood feud between his descendants and those of Obrenovic that affected Serbian politics until the early twentieth century.

Although Serbia remained nominally a province of Turkey after 1817, the Serbs were virtually independent. By 1830, with the support of Russia, they were able to force Constantinople to establish Serbia as an autonomous principality. Russia took the new state under its protection, but it was not until 1878 that complete freedom from Turkish domination was achieved with the signing of the Treaty of Berlin. In 1882 the Serbian ruler took the title of king.

Unlike the development in Croatia, where nationalist sentiment was fostered by an intellectual minority, Serbian independence was created by the peasant masses. Milos Obrenovic gained additional support among the peasants by dividing the confiscated Turk properties among them. Under the Turkish landlords the peasant class had been given no opportunities for education, and almost none, including the leaders, were literate. Much

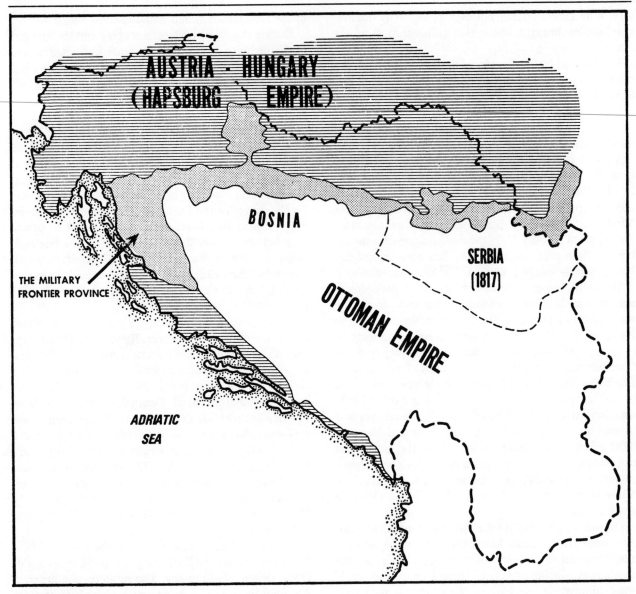

Yugoslavian lands divided between the Habsburg and Ottoman empires in the early nineteenth century.

of the leadership in the government established in 1817 was provided by educated Serb immigrants from Vojvodina. These introduced into Serbia a romantic nationalist passion for the native language and folkways that strengthened the people's self-consciousness as a nation.

In 1839, after much dissension over the autocratic nature of Milos Obrenovic's rule, he was forced to abdicate in favor of his son Milan. Milan died of illness after reigning only twenty-five days and was succeeded by his seventeen-year-old brother, Michael. The sultan named a group of advisers and, in 1842, the advisers, some of whom belonged to a group called the Defenders of the Constitution (Ustavobranitelji), forced out the Obrenovic prince and installed Alexander Karadjordjevic, son of the first Karadjordje, on the throne. Internal conflicts were aided by Russian and Austrian influences

who used the Serbian rivalries as a means of keeping Serbia weak. Serbia remained neutral in the Crimean War and accepted the terms of the Treaty of Paris in 1856, which ended Russia's position as exclusive protector of the Serbs and placed Serbia under the protection of Austria, Great Britain, France, and Turkey. Amidst complex internal dissensions, the Serb Parliament (Skupstina) deposed Alexander in 1858 in favor of the return of the Obrenovic Dynasty.

Milos Obrenovic again became prince of Serbia for a brief, autocratic period. Upon his death in 1860, he was succeeded by his son Michael, also ruling for a second time. In 1868 Michael was assassinated, and for the next twenty years Serbia was ruled by his cousin Milan Obrenovic, whose scandalous private life and inattention to state affairs led to widespread unrest. In 1889 Milan,

Milos Obrenovic, the prince of Serbia, was driven from reign by the Revolution of 1839 but was recalled. After his death his son Michael was appointed to replace him.

The postage stamp showing Prince Milan (Obrenovic IV)

who had been recognized by that time as the king of Serbia, attempted to regain popular support by promulgating a new liberal constitution, but in 1893 his successor Alexander set the constitution aside and instituted an oppressive oligarchic rule. Disorders and plots multiplied toward the end of the century.

Serbian political parites developed during the reign of Milan. By the 1880s, two larger parties, the Liberals and the Radicals, had emerged, as well as an embryonic Socialist party. The Liberal party advocated the centralization of government authority, whereas the Radicals were distinguished by their passionate nationalsim and advocacy of local government.

The latter part of the nineteenth century was a period

of international unrest throughout the Balkans. Serbia declared war on Turkey in support of the Bosnian peasant uprisings in 1876 and was rewarded by the Congress of Berlin, which recognized its complete independence from the Ottoman Empire. Serbia's internal weakness, however, enabled Austria to gain considerable influence over Serbian foreign affairs and trade. In 1882 Serbia was declared a kingdom, but neither its international prestige nor its internal affairs improved. Austrian influence increased to the point where, by 1905, 90 percent of Serbian exports and 60 percent of its imports were controlled by the Austro-Hungarian Dual Monarchy.

In 1903 opposition to Obrenovic rule culminated in the brutal assassination of Alexander and his wife. The Parliament elected Peter Karadjordjevic to the throne. An intelligent ruler, he revived and further liberalized the Constitution of 1889. He reorganized the country's finances and reasserted Serbian independence of action from Austria. In 1905 the Serbs began trade negotiations with Bulgaria and planned to shift Serbian munitions orders from Austria to France. The Austrians tried to bring the Serbs to heel by placing a prohibitive tariff on all Serbian livestock. The so-called pig war of 1906 threatened disaster, for pigs were Serbia's main export. The Serbs succeeded in finding other markets, but the pig war reinforced hostility toward the Habsburg Empire among Serbian peasants.

This hostility had its counterpart in Austrian fear and mistrust of Serbia's expansionist policies. The foreign policy of the Radical party governments, which ruled Serbia under the constitutional Karadjordjevic monarchy after 1903, was based on the slogan "Serbia must expand or die." Expansionist efforts were directed toward the south into Macedonia and west toward the Adriatic through Bosnia and Hercegovina. These aims brought Serbia into direct conflict with the Austro-Hungarian Empire and Bulgaria. The Austrians were particularly anxious because of the rapprochement that took place just after the turn of the century between Serbia and Habsburg-controlled Croatia.

A serious crisis was created in October 1908 when the Austrian government annexed Bosnia and Hercegovina, ostensibly to frustrate Serbian plans to move into the two provinces. This unilateral move produced intense resentment in both Serbia and Montenegro. Serbia received encouragement—but no military support—from Russia. The British government also supported Serbia's diplomatic protests. Germany staunchly defended Austria's right to the territory. Thus were drawn the major outlines of the competing alliances that were to evolve into World War I.

Deprived of Bosnia and access to the Adriatic, Serbian hopes for expansion came to center on Macedonia, then part of the Ottoman Empire. In the 1890s a number of anti-Turk secret societies developed in Macedonia, chief of which was the Internal Macedonian Revolutionary

Organization (Vatreshna Makedonska Revolutsionna Organizatsa), whose slogan was "Macedonia for the Macedonians." Violent pressure groups representing Greek, Serbian, and Bulgarian interests also proliferated and kept the region in constant turmoil. From 1911 to 1912 various alliances were formed between Bulgaria, Greece, Serbia, and Montenegro, marking a temporary triumph over centuries of disunion and distrust. In 1912 the quick victory of the Balkan allies over Turkey, in the first Balkan War, led to a dispute between Serbia and Bulgaria over the sharing of Macedonia, which the war had freed from Ottoman rule. During June and July of 1913, supported by Greece, Montenegro, and Romania, Serbia defeated the Bulgarians. By the subsequent Treaty of Bucharest, the Serbs acquired a much larger share of Macedonia—extending almost to the southern boundary granted the new state of Yugoslavia after World War I. The simultaneous creation of the independent state of Albania, however, frustrated Serbia's plans to reach the Adriatic.

Serbian successes in the Balkan wars acted as an impetus for the other Slavic peoples within the Austro-Hungarian Dual Monarchy, and the Austrian government decided to eliminate the Serbian threat. Therefore, when Archduke Francis Ferdinand, heir to the Habsburg throne, was assassinated in Sarajevo (Bosnia) in June 1914 by a member of a secret pro-Serb terrorist group, the Austrian government presented Serbia with an ultimatum whose terms were so harsh as to preclude acceptance by the Serbs. The Serbian government suggested international arbitration of the question, but Austria declared war on July 28, 1914. Within a week Germany had aligned with Austria, while Great Britain, France, and Russia came to Serbia's defense. The war was destined to end Habsburg hegemony over the Balkans and to forge a Yugoslav state.

BOSNIA AND HERCEGOVINA

Serb groups settled the region of Bosnia and Hercegovina during the seventh century, but the area was separated from Serbia in the tenth century and experienced a different history. Bosnia or Bosna (from the Bosna River) appears to have originated as a small principality in the mountainous region of the upper reaches of the Bosna and Vreba rivers. The name Hercegovina orginated in the fifteenth century when a powerful Bosnian noble, Stephen Vuksic, gained control of lands in the southern part of Bosnia and took the title of Herzog, the German equivalent of duke, from which came the name of the region.

Situated on the dividing line between the areas of Roman Catholic and Eastern Orthodox religious influence, Bosnia and Hercegovina suffered from constant internal turmoil from the tenth through the fifteenth centuries. This situation was complicated by the introduction from Bulgaria of an ascetic heretical Christian cult—Bogomil-

Francis Ferdinand, nephew of Francis Joseph, Austria, the heir apparent after the suicide of Crown Prince Rudolf, did not fare much better, for he was assassinated along with his wife in Sarajevo on June 28, 1914, in what history records as the "opening shot of the Great World War." His wife was Sophie, the countess of Chotek and the duchess of Hohenberg.

Archduke Francis Ferdinand in his royal naval uniform

The archduke in an official royal photograph with the duchess Sophie and their children

ism—during the twelfth century. It gained widespread popular adherence as a protest against the proselytism of both existing major religions. Many Bosnian nobles and a large portion of the peasantry persisted in the heresy despite repeated attempts by both the Catholic and Eastern Orthodox churches to extirpate the cult. The chaos caused by this religious struggle laid the country open to the Ottoman Turks after their defeat of the Serbs in 1459. By 1463 the Turks controlled Bosnia and, twenty years later, gained control of Hercegovina; many Bogomil nobles and peasants accepted the Islamic religion of their conquerors.

The Islamized nobles were allowed to retain their lands and their feudal privileges, and the peasants who

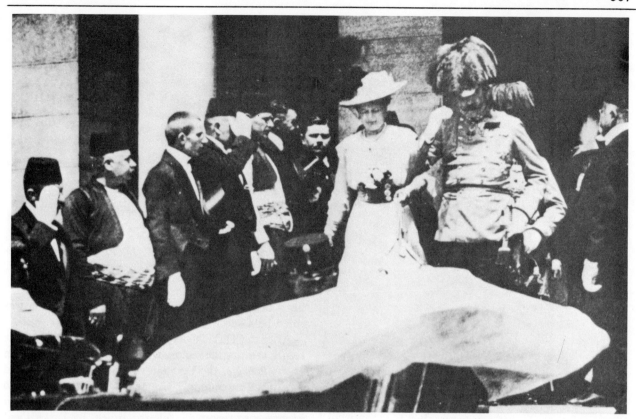

Archduke Francis Ferdinand and his wife about to enter their official car moments before their assassination

accepted Islam were granted land free from feudal obligations. The Christian nobles were killed and Christian peasants subjected to the same oppressive rule—but by the converted nobility—as their Serbian counterparts. The Bosnians became the most conservative Muslims in the Ottoman Empire, opposing every attempt by the sultan to modernize the empire through secularization of the administration and to moderate the oppressive subordination of non-Muslim subjects.

Early in the nineteenth century, the Christian peasants revolted against the Islamic nobility in a series of uprisings, which were bloodily suppressed. In 1850 the Turkish government itself put down the Bosnian aristocracy and established a centrally controlled Turkish administration. The Christian serfs continued to rebel against the new administration, and by 1875 both Bosnia and Hercegovina were in a state of general revolt. The following year Serbia and Montenegro declared war on Turkey in support of the insurrection. In 1877 Russia entered the war against Turkey in order to increase its influence among the Balkan Slavs. The Russian army defeated the Turks in January 1878, and the Treaty of San Stefano, which the Russians dictated in March 1878, provided for the recognition of an autonomous government in Bosnia and Hercegovina.

The Habsburg and British governments, fearing the growing influence of Russia in the Balkans, called the Congress of Berlin in July 1878, which revised the basic terms of the Treaty of San Stefano. The congress placed Bosnia and Hercegovina temporarily under the administration of Austria-Hungary, and in 1908 the Austro-Hungarian Dual Monarchy unilaterally annexed the two provinces.

Under Austro-Hungarian control, the Bosnians were not permitted any degree of self-rule. Individuals from other parts of the Dual Monarchy were brought in to administer the area. Material conditions in Bosnia and Hercegovina improved considerably, but the peasants were still subject to the basic features of the old feudal system. Nationalist tendencies developed among the population as a result of influences from neighboring Serbia and Croatia. In 1914 the population was divided: the Catholics, many of whom wished to retain their ties with the monarchy; the Eastern Orthodox Serbs who wanted to unite with Serbia; and the Muslims who were divided on the issue, some fearing both proposals. Revolutionary sentiments were widespread, particularly among the youth, and it was a young Bosnian, Gavrilo Princip, who on June 28, 1914, assassinated Archduke Francis Ferdinand and his consort the duchess of Hohenberg, during their visit to Sarajevo.

THE MONTENEGRINS

In medieval times the area north of Lake Scutari was known as Duklja, or Zeta. In the twelfth century it came under the rule of Stephen Nemanja of Serbia, but after

The first prince-bishop of
Montenegro was Danilo
Petrovic (1697–1737).

King Alexander I of Serbia (1889–1903) and Queen Draga. Both were
assassinated in 1903.

The wedding picture of King Alexander and Queen Draga

King Nicholas I of Montenegro (1910–18) first served as the prince of
Montenegro for fifty years, from 1860 to 1910.

his death Serbian power dwindled, and the region was
ruled by a succession of local rulers.

After the Turkish victory over Serbia in the late fourteenth century the region, which had come to be known
as *Montenegro,* the Venetian variant of the Italian word
for "black mountain," became a refuge for Serbs who
refused to live under the Islamic Ottomans. Although
Montenegro repeatedly suffered attacks by Turkish and
other external forces over a period of some four centuries, it was never fully subdued. The constant struggles
of the Montenegrins, particularly those with raiding
Turks and Albanians, resulted in the development of the
Montenegrin reputation for bellicosity.

In the early sixteenth century Montenegro became a
type of theocracy with *vladike* (Eastern Orthodox bishops) exercising both temporal and spiritual control. The
vladike were elected by local assemblies until 1697 when
succession was restricted to the family of Danilo Petrovic Njegus. Since the *vladike* were celibates, the line
passed from uncle to nephew. The Njegus family ruled
Montenegro as bishop-princes for more than one hundred and fifty years. Under the successive *vladike* the
territory was doubled in size.

In 1851 the offices of bishop and prince were sepa-
rated, but the Njegus family continued to rule. Nicholas
I become the prince in 1860 and remained the ruler of
Montenegro until the outbreak of World War I.

The Treaty of Berlin (1878) greatly increased the size
of Montenegro and granted formal recognition of the
country as a princedom. Nicholas I established a parliamentary constitution in 1905 and took the title of king
in 1910. At the outbreak of World War I, in 1914, he
went into exile. An opposition political movement,
known as the Montenegrin Committee, was formed in
Geneva and began to press for the incorporation of Montenegro into a union of all South Slavs. In 1918 Nicholas's rule was ended, and Montenegro became part of the
Yugoslav Kingdom.

A political cartoon of Peter I with
his sword holding the heads of his
assassinated predecessors, King
Alexander and Queen Draga.

Peter I of Serbia (1903–21). King
Peter I united the three kingdoms
of Serbia, Croatia, and Slovenia.

King Peter I Karadjordjevic. This postage stamp shows him as he appeared later in life.

THE MACEDONIANS

Long an area of contention and competition between the powers that figured prominently in the history of the Balkans, the territory covered by the historical-geographic term *Macedonia* has been divided among the states of Yugoslavia, Bulgaria, and Greece. Strategically located and ethnographically complex, Macedonia typifies the Balkan problem of conflicting interests and rival peoples.

Slav tribes settled in the region, an area considerably larger than Yugoslavia's Macedonian Republic, in the seventh century, at which time the territory was under the control of the Eastern Empire. During the ninth century much of Macedonia was incorporated by the Bulgars (also South Slavs) into the first Bulgarian Empire. In the latter half of the tenth century the region again came under Byzantine domination, which was troubled by repeated uprisings of the Macedonian Slavs.

During the fourteenth century most of Macedonia was conquered by the Serbian ruler Stephen Dusan, who set up his capital at Skopje. After the death of Dusan the Serbian Empire disintegrated and, following the historic battle of Kosovo in 1389, the major part of Macedonia again came under Turkish control and remained so until the twentieth century.

As Bulgarian nationalism developed in the nineteenth century, the Bulgarians, after much controversy, were successful in gaining Turkish approval for a separate Bulgarian Orthodox church (the Exarchate). Since the authority of the Exarchate covered most of Macedonia and part of Serbia as well as Bulgaria, the church became a means of extending Bulgar influence, a fact particularly resented by the Serbs.

Rivalry between Serbs, Bulgars, Greeks, and Turks was increased in the late nineteenth century. Russian troops invaded Turkey in 1877 and dictated terms of the Treaty of San Stefano (1878), providing for a greatly enlarged, autonomous Bulgaria that was to include most of Macedonia. Opposed by the Austro-Hungarian and British governments, the Treaty of San Stefano was quickly nullified by the Treaty of Berlin (1878), which was to prove a great disappointment to almost all elements of the Balkan population. The Treaty of Berlin returned Macedonia to Turkey, established an independent but greatly reduced Bulgaria, and allowed Austrian forces to occupy Bosnia and Hercegovina. Along with renewed Turkish control of Macedonia, the Austrian presence in Bosnia and Hercegovina came as a bitter blow to Serbian aspirations. The end result was to increase Serbian and Bulgarian rivalry in Macedonia, and Bulgaria continued to use the Treaty of San Stefano as a basis for its claims to the area.

Bulgarian, Serbian, and Greek organizations launched intensive propaganda campaigns in Macedonia to strengthen their particular claims. Even Romania entered the contest, basing its claim on the Vlach population scattered throughout the Macedonian area. In 1896 an underground independence movement, the Internal Macedonian Revolutionary Organization, was organized within Macedonia. Torn between the competing forces, the Macedonian peasants responded to the organization's slogan "Macedonia for the Macedonians."

Competition over Macedonia eventually led to the Balkan Wars of 1912–13. Montenegro, Serbia, Greece, and Bulgaria joined together in a successful campaign to drive the Turks from Macedonia. Once this goal was achieved, however, the victors were unable to reach agreement on the division of the territory, and Bulgaria attacked the Greek and Serbian forces in Macedonia. Montenegro, Romania, and Turkey joined with Greece and Serbia to defeat Bulgaria. A peace treaty, signed in Bucharest in 1913, ceded north and central Macedonia to Serbia, granted the southern region to Greece, and provided for a small extension of the Montenegrin frontiers. Bulgaria retained a small portion of eastern Macedonia. The areas of old Macedonia that came under Serbian control in 1913 were included within the Serb territory under the Yugoslav Kingdom, then were given the status of a republic in post-World War II Yugoslavia.

ROOTS OF THE YUGOSLAV MOVEMENT

The movement for the unification of all South Slavs into an independent Yugoslav state originated during the brief period of French control of Slovenia and Dalmatia early in the nineteenth century. The ideal of South Slav unity first gained momentum among linguists and poets and, until the early years of the twentieth century, the unity movement was restricted to the literary intelligentsia. The small part of the population that took an interest in politics tended to be primarily focused on local partriotism, and the most powerful political parties

Yugoslavia, Slovene lands before 1918

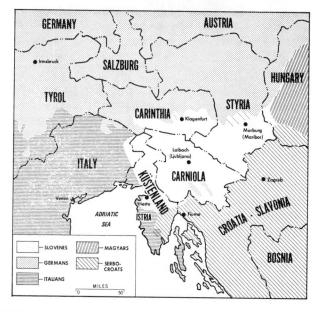

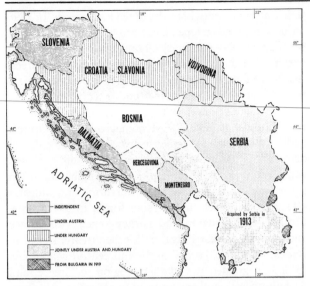

South Slav territories are formed into the Yugoslav state (1918).

World War I found Slavs fighting on both sides. The Serbian army strongly resisted repeated Austrian invasions, but Bulgaria's entry into the war on the side of the Austrians tipped the balance. By the end of 1915 a joint German-Austrian-Bulgarian attack forced the Serbian government and army to retreat across Albania whence, with Allied help, it reached the island of Corfu, and Serbia became divided administratively between Bulgaria and Austria-Hungary. The Serbian army regrouped on Corfu and was transported to the Salonika front. By 1918 it was able, with French, British, and Italian forces, to march up the Vardar River valley from Salonika back into Serbia. By the beginning of November 1918 the Serbs had cleared most of their homeland of enemy occupation.

In the independent kingdom of Montenegro, the people rebelled, in October 1918, against the wartime Austrian occupation and set up a national assembly that deposed the anti-Serbian king and declared for union with Serbia. In November 1918 the Croatian nationalists voted in the Zagreb council for immediate union with Serbia and Montenegro, without waiting to establish any agreement on the terms of the union, and invited the Serbian prince, Alexander, to assume regency over the new nation. Only Croat Peasant party leader Stephen Radic dissented, demanding guarantees of the integrity of Croatia in the new union. On December 4, 1918, the various Slavic groups declared Alexander head of the kingdom of the Serbs, Croats, and Slovenes.

in both Serbia and Croatia developed in support of these particularist sentiments. The repression by Croatia of a Serb minority—comprising about 25 percent of the total population of Croatia after 1881—and rival Serb-Croat interests in Bosnia and Hercegovina dimmed the prospects for unity among the Yugoslavs during the last years of the nineteenth century.

After the turn of the twentieth century, however, a new generation of political leaders emerged, inspired with the ideal of South Slav unity. In 1903 the leader of the nationalistic Croat Peasant party hailed the newly crowned Serbian king, Peter, with "Long live the King of Yugoslavia." In 1905 forty deputies from Dalmatia to the Imperial Diet in Vienna demanded a union between Dalmatia and Croatia and the granting, by the Hungarian government, of political freedoms to Croatia. Serbian political leaders seconded this demand and proposed joint political action between Croats and Serbs. In 1908 the Austrian government put a number of Serbs on trial, using fabricated treason charges in an attempt to discredit Serbia by allegedly proving its complicity in a plot to absorb Croatia. The trial served, rather, to draw the two Slav peoples closer together. Serbian successes in the Balkan Wars of 1912–13 aroused enthusiastic demonstrations among the Croats, Slovenes, and the inhabitants of Bosnia and Hercegovina. When World War I began, even Montenegro, which was independent and in some ways a rival to Serb expansionist aims, was officially considering unity with Serbia.

By 1914 every Slav province within the Austro-Hungarian Dual Monarchy had at least one major political party that supported Yugoslav unity. The Serb Radical party, which had been a proponent of a Greater Serbia, split shortly after the war started, and its younger faction shifted its support to a democratic Yugoslav state.

THE YUGOSLAV KINGDOM

The kingdom of the Serbs, Croats, and Slovenes was constituted of seven disparate elements: the independent kingdom of Serbia, including part of Macedonia; the independent kingdom of Montenegro; Croatia-Slavonia, formerly somewhat of a home rule area under Hungary; Vojvodina, plus two small districts between Slovenia and Hungary, formerly integral parts of Hungary; the Slovene lands, long Austrian provinces; Dalmatia, an Austrian province of Serbo-Croatian inhabitants; and Bosnia and Hercegovina, formerly administered jointly by Austria and Hungary.

The kingdom comprised several ethnic groups speaking a variety of languages and adhering to three major religions. About 74 percent of the 12 million inhabitants spoke Serbo-Croatian, 8.5 percent spoke Slovene, and several other languages were represented. About 46 percent of the population was Eastern Orthodox, 39 percent Roman Catholic, and over 11 percent Muslim. Most Croats and Slovenes were Roman Catholic, and almost all the Serbs were Eastern Orthodox. Economically, the state was largely rural: 80 percent of the population was supported directly by agriculture, and only three towns had populations of over one hundred thousand. Much of the area had been depopulated by war. A long history of foreign rule by non-Slavs uninterested in the economic or cultural development of the area was reflected in poverty and a high illiteracy rate.

The overwhelmingly rural character of the population as well as its ethnic and cultural heterogeneity had a marked effect on developments during the interwar period. The peasant had a deep-seated mistrust of city dwellers, large absentee landowners, and representatives of foreign governments. After independence the peasants remained aloof and suspicious of the complex political and economic ideas originating in the cities. Thus, only a small minority of the population, particularly special-interest groups, were represented in the government. Autocratic government and ethnic nationalist groups characterized the country's political life.

THE DEMOCRATIC EXPERIMENT (1919–29)

Border disputes delayed efforts to settle the internal order of the new state until November 1920. The disputes involved borders with Austria, Hungary, Bulgaria, Italy, and Albania. The dispute with Italy continued until 1924, but boundaries with Yugoslavia's other neighbors were settled more amicably, for the most part on the basis of ethnographic distribution of population.

Before elections to the Constituent Assembly were held in November 1920, the kingdom was administered by the king, assisted by the Serbian Parliament. The Parliament, however, had last been elected in 1911 and after the war represented neither Yugoslav nor even Serbian public opinion. The self-appointed provisional governments of Croatia, Slovenia, and Bosnia, established during the last days of the war, had difficulty functioning.

Political party activity, however, was not lacking. The conservative Serbian Radical party, led by Nikola Pasic, was the strongest single party, representing the new ruling group of the remnants of the former large landholders and some of the emerging urban professional and business class. The more liberal Democratic party, formed by a union of the dissident Radicals, the former Serb-Croat coalition of Zagreb, and the Slovene Liberals, also appealed to the urban middle class. Stephen Radic had formed a Peasant party in Croatia before the war and continued after the creation of the Yugoslav state to lead the only major party that claimed to represent the peasants. His program, however, made few concessions to the peasants but stressed rather his political aims for a federated, republican state.

Social Democratic parties had gained support among peasants and workers during the 1890s in Serbia, Croatia, and Slovenia. In 1919 the Serbian Social Democrats took the lead in fusing the three parties into a new Socialist Worker's party (Communist) of Yugoslavia, which affiliated with the Communist International (Comintern). This revolutionary party basically followed a Greater Serbia policy in regard to the nationalities problem.

No party gained an absolute majority in the elections to the Constituent Assembly, and a coalition of the Radicals and Democrats, which had dominated the Parliament since the war, held the power to formulate the new constitution. King Alexander swore allegiance to the constitution on Saint Vitus Day, a Serbian national holiday, in June 1921, and it was thenceforth known as the Vidovdan (Saint Vitus Day) Constitution.

After the assassination of the newly appointed minister of the interior, Milorad Draskovic, by a Bosnian Communist terrorist, the Parliament, as one of its first acts, outlawed the Communist party. Communist deputies were forced to vacate the 58 seats that they had won in the 419-seat Parliament, largely as a result of a protest vote against the Radical policies. From then until 1941 the Communist party operated underground.

Pasic, who had become premier, followed an essentially Serbian program that alienated the Slovenes and Croats. In 1924 Pasic dissolved the Croat Peasant party and imprisoned its leader, Radic, for denouncing his regime and demanding semiautonomy for Croatia. Radic gained his freedom by abandoning his demands, reforming his program, and entering into an alliance with Pasic. It was short-lived, however, for Pasic died in 1926, and Radic reversed himself, moving back into the opposition. In June 1928 Radic was assassinated on the floor of the Parliament by a fanatical Montenegrin and was succeeded as leader of the Croat Peasant party by Vlatko Macek, who continued Radic's intransigent support for Croat autonomy.

During this entire period neither the Radical party nor the Croat Peasant party was strong enough to govern by itself, and neither was able to form a durable coalition with the other parties. Twenty-four governments succeeded each other in rapid succession between 1919 and 1929. Serbian hegemony remained predominant, and Croatian resentment increased markedly. By January

King Alexander I of Yugoslavia (1921–34)

1929 the parliamentary system had broken down, and King Alexander decided to step in. He dissolved the Parliament, abolished the Vidovdan Constitution, and assumed all governing authority.

Despite the unstable political situation, economic progress had not been seriously impaired during the first ten years of Yugolavia's existence. Agriculture was encouraged, and a series of good harvests permitted the export of an agricultural surplus. Railroad communication and a sizable Yugoslav merchant marine were developed.

In 1921 Yugoslavia entered into bilateral treaties with Czechoslovakia and Romania to guarantee mutual defense against any possible aggression by Hungary and Bulgaria. This Little Entente was supported and financed after 1924 by France.

THE PERIOD OF THE DICTATORSHIP (1929–34)

King Alexander declared his assumption of power to be temporary, to last only until the abuses of the previous party regimes could be overcome. Initially, the king's move was well received by most segments of the population, and many looked to Alexander's personal rule for relief from the country's political tensions.

During the first two years, however, King Alexander issued a series of decrees that greatly restricted individual rights and strengthened the monarchy. The death penalty or a long prison sentence was imposed for all acts of terrorism, sedition, or dissemination of Communist propaganda. Political parties based on a regional or religious character were declared illegal, and freedom of the press was eliminated. All municipal and departmental councils were abolished. The crown assumed the power to remove judges, and the Council of Ministers was made responsible solely to the king.

Queen Marie-Mignon with the newborn son, Crown Prince Peter

King Alexander and his son, Crown Prince Peter

Kings Tomislav and Alexander in a 1929 stamp

Many of these measures were directed toward unification of the divided country. In October 1929 Alexander changed the name of the state to the Kingdom of Yugoslavia and replaced the former provinces with nine regions *(banovine)*, in many cases disregarding ethnic and historical boundaries. Despite the fact that Croatia proper was left almost intact, the Croats interpreted these measures as simply a means of preserving Serbian hegemony. A number of Croat leaders fled the country. Some sought assistance from Bulgaria, Italy, and Hungary; others began a press campaign in western Europe, propounding the justice of Croatian claims for autonomy. Within and without the country extremist Croat nationalists formed a political movement—the Ustasi—which developed into a Fascist organization. The exiled Ustasi leader, Ante Pavelic, was given refuge in Italy and had the support of the Mussolini government.

Faced by growing discontent in Croatia, as well as among the Serbs, and feeling the need to gain the confidence of foreign governments, particularly of France, Alexander decided to revive the parliamentary system. In September 1931 he promulgated a new constitution, but all the legal restrictions declared in the preceding two years remained in effect. An upper house was created, its members partly elected and partly appointed by the king, to share power with the previously established Parliament (Skupstina). The new constitution gave legal sanction to Alexander's strict personal control.

Alexander I of Yugoslavia was the second son of Peter I of Serbia. He changed the name of his kingdom to Yugoslavia in 1929. He is seen here in 1922 at the wedding ceremony with Princess Maria of Romania, his future queen of Yugoslavia.

Queen Marie-Mignon

King Alexander with the French foreign minister, Louis Barthou, in Marseilles, France, moments before they are assassinated on October 9, 1934

The assassination scene. The murderer, Vlada Georguiev, has struck and the king is dead. His military escort, Lieutenant Colonel Piollet, can be seen beating the murderer's head with his sword.

The economic depression that had swept the United States and western Europe also had a major effect on Yugoslavia. The collapse of agricultural prices and a run on the banks in 1931 were followed by the loss of foreign credits and a serious shortage of foreign exchange. A severe winter added to the difficulties by sharply reducing the exportable agricultural products.

The combination of King Alexander's strong personal rule and a catastrophic deterioration in Yugoslavia's economic position lent additional impetus to the growth of extremist groups. The Ustasi movement gained rapidly. The University of Belgrade became a center of political intrigue and student disorders. Secret terrorist organizations began to be active throughout the country, but the underground Communist party lacked strong leadership and remained largely ineffective. Demands by opposition political leaders for a return to constitutional monarchy and for the protection of the rights of the various national groups led to large-scale arrests, including that of Vlatko Macek.

To seek outside support for his weakening government King Alexander sought a rapprochement with Bulgaria in 1933. The next year he was instrumental in the creation of a Balkan entente between Yugoslavia, Romania, Turkey, and Greece. During the same year he sailed to France to strengthen the ties between France and the states of the Little Entente (Yugoslavia, Romania, and Czechoslovakia), and in October he was assassinated in Marseilles by Ustasi terrorists, reportedly aided and financed by Italy and Hungary, both under Fascist control. Although the majority of Yugoslavs had disapproved of Alexander's dictatorial policies, he had been personally liked and had been a symbol of Yugoslav unity and independence. His assassination brought an outburst of grief and rage from all but the most radical among the Croat extremists.

THE REGENCY PERIOD (1934–41)

Alexander's son, Peter Karadjordjevic, was eleven years old at the time of his father's death. In his will, Alexander had named his cousin, Prince Paul, to act as regent until Peter reached his maturity. After assuming the regency, Prince Paul did not take advantage of the mood of conciliation and hope that greeted the new king, but continued Alexander's controversial policies. Although Macek was released from prison, opposition parties still were forbidden to operate. In May the first general elections to the Parliament in eight years were held. Opposition candidates were not allowed to campaign on party programs, but they won more than 1 million out of 2.8 million votes. Nevertheless, the complex electoral system allowed the government party to attain 301 seats, with 67 going to the opposition.

The opposition deputies boycotted the Parliament and met in a counter-Parliament in Zagreb. As leader of the major Croat poltical movement, Macek was able to come to an agreement with the Serbian Democratic and Agrarian party leaders conderning their goals. This marked the beginning of a Serb-Croat rapprochement in opposition to the authoritarian government.

Alexander's son became Peter II after the death of his father. He was but eleven years old at the time, so Alexander's will was followed and his (Alexander's) cousin Paul was named regent until Peter reached his majority.

Peter II (1940)

Princes Tomislav and Andrei, brothers of King Peter II (1936)

Prince Paul ruled as regent from 1934 until he was ousted by the revolution of March 27, 1941. His downfall came after he met with Hitler at Berchtesgaden, Germany, in March 1941 and agreed to have Yugoslavia join Bulgaria and Turkey in the Tripartite Pact with Germany, Italy, and Japan. Peter II then took over but by April 15, 1941 had to flee to London in exile.

In June 1935 Prince Paul appointed a young Radical party businessman, Milan Stojadinovic, as premier. Although the premier promised a democratic government and a wide measure of autonomy for Croatia, no progress was made in either direction, and opposition to Stojadinovic quickly developed among Croats, as well as among Serbs within the Radical party. In December 1936 Prince Paul reopened negotiations with Macek toward the granting of semiautonomy to Croatia within a federalist state. Negotiations became stalemated, however, over the disposition of Bosnia—whether it should be included in the Croatian autonomous region, be tied to Serbia, or become autonomous.

Paul's foreign policy added to the internal political tensions. As France's power to guarantee Yugoslavia's security system based on the Little Entente weakened, Paul felt constrained to seek security in closer relations with the rising German and Italian states. Yugoslavia became economically dependent on Germany. In 1936 and 1937 Paul concluded agreements with Bulgaria and Italy that strained Yugoslav relations with France and the Little Entente.

Hitler, the dictator who controlled Germany during World War II, talked Prince Paul into having Yugoslavia join in an alliance with Germany.

In the midst of the growing international tensions in the period immediately preceding World War II, Prince Paul apparently recognized the urgency of reaching a settlement in the Serb-Croat problem before the Ustasi and other extremist national groups hopelessly divided the country. After several months of negotiations between Dragisa Cvetkovic, who was then premier, and Prince Paul on the one hand, and Macek, leader of the Croat Peasant party, on the other, a *sporazum* (agreement) was reached that allowed the Croatian people to establish a local assembly (diet) of their own and have a measure of autonomy. At the same time Macek became vice premier of the Yugoslav government. The *sporazum* satisfied most of the Croats but was denounced by the Slovenes and the Serbs whose regions were still under the direct control of Belgrade.

On March 27, 1941, the British government recognized King Peter II as the head of the Yugoslavian government (in exile). This was the first postage stamp the exiled government issued from London.

EVENTS LEADING TO WORLD WAR II

Faced by the growing threat of German and Italian aggression, Yugoslavia tried to maintain its neutrality. When the Yugoslav leaders became aware of the ultimate Nazi and Fascist intentions, the country had neither internal strength nor foreign support to oppose them effectively. Although Yugoslav public opinion was incensed against Berlin and Rome, the government re-

Peter II takes the Oath of Accession on March 28, 1941, with Patriarch Gavrilo officiating at the Dedinye Palace, and becomes king of Yugoslavia.

mained diplomatically neutral when Italy attacked Greece and Germany invaded Romania in mid-1940.

Early in 1941 Premier Cvetkovic was summoned to Berchtesgaden, where Hitler suggested that Yugoslavia, Bulgaria, and Turkey join the Tripartite Pact between Germany, Italy, and Japan. By the beginning of March Bulgaria had agreed, and Prince Paul flew secretly to Berchtesgaden to negotiate with Hitler. By March 20 he was resigned to the necessity of signing the pact but still hoped that Yugoslavia would be guaranteed its territorial integrity and spared the demand for troops. Under orders from Prince Paul, Cvetkovic went to Vienna and on March 25 agreed to German terms.

On his return two days later Cvetkovic found Belgrade in an uproar. The news of his secret mission had reached the public. That night a group of Serbian army and air force officers led a coup d'etat against Prince Paul, who was forced to resign as regent and seek exile. King Peter assumed the throne before reaching his majority, Cvetkovic and other members of his government were arrested, and a new government headed by General of the Army Dusan Simovic was formed with Macek as a vice premier.

Although Simovic assured the Germans that the Vienna agreement would be honored, the new govern-ment was greeted with wild enthusiasm throughout the country as a defiance of Hitler. The Russians, British, and Americans congratulated the government, and Churchill said that in the coup d'etat "Yugoslavia found her soul."

On April 6, without a declaration of war, the German air force began the bombing of Belgrade—which Simovic had declared an open city—and the German army crossed the border into Yugoslavia. The bulk of the invading forces came from Bulgaria; other armies entered from Hungary, Romania, and Albania with the support of Hungarian and Italian troops.

Germany and the Soviet Union were still bound by the Molotov-Ribbentrop nonaggression pact, and the Yugoslav Communists saw in the defeat of Yugoslavia their opportunity to come to power. The animosity of the Croats toward the Serb-dominated Yugoslav government and their desire for a fully independent Croatia led many to welcome the German invasion. These factors, along with poor equipment, inadequate communications, and problems with troop disposition, made early defeat inevitable. By April 15, 1941, King Peter and the government had fled—first to Palestine and ultimately to London, England, thus ending the monarchy form of government for Yugoslavia.

King Peter visits with the president of the United States, Franklin D. Roosevelt, at the White House in Washington, D.C. in 1942.

Joseph Broz Tito became president of Yugoslavia in 1953. He is seen here, center, on a state visit to Greece in 1954. King Paul and Queen Frederica were his host and hostess.

Peter II's wedding. Standing, left to right: duke of Gloucester; duchess of Kent; King George VI; King Peter II; King Haakon VII (Norway); the bride and queen, Princess Alexandra of Greece; Princess Aspasia of Greece; King George II of Greece; and Prince Bernhard of the Netherlands. Seated, left to right: Queen Elizabeth; Prince Thomas, brother of Peter II; and Queen Wilhelmina of the Netherlands. The wedding took place in London, England, on March 20, 1944.

King Peter II as he appeared in England during World War II. When the British government backed Tito as the leader of postwar Yugoslavia, King Peter moved to Paris. He moved to Monte Carlo in the 1950s and, after several visits to the United States, made his permanent residence in New York and California. He died in Denver, Colorado, on November 4, 1970, and was buried at the Serbian Monastery in Libertyville, Illinois.

THE ROYAL SOVEREIGNS OF THE YUGOSLAV KINGDOMS

SERBIA

Reign	Title	Ruler	Birth	Death	Relationship
600—Serbia established by emigrants from the Carpathian Mountains					
1459–1829—Serbia ruled by Turkey					
1804–1813	National leader	Karadjordje (George Petrovic)	1766	1817	
1817–1839	Prince	Milos Obrenovic	1780	1860	
1839	Prince	Milan	1819	1839	Son of Milos Obrenovic
1839–1842	Prince	Michael	1823	1868	Son of Milos Obrenovic
1842–1858	Prince	Alexander Karadjordjevic	1806	1885	Son of Karadjordje
1858–1860	Prince	Milos Obrenovic			
1860–1868	Prince	Michael			Son of Milos Obrenovic
1868–1882	Prince	Milan	1854	1901	Grand-nephew of Milos Obrenovic
1882–1889	King	Milan I			
1889–1903	King	Alexander I	1876	1903	Son of Milan I
1903–1921	King	Peter I Karadjordjevic	1844	1921	Son of Alexander
1915–1918—Occupied by Austria					
1918—Serbia part of Yugoslavia					

CROATIA

1091—Under Hungary
1526—Under Turkey
1809–1813—Part of France; under Austria-Hungary when it became part of Yugoslavia
1813–1918—Croatia declared independent 1941
1944—Kingdom created by Italians

1941–1943	King	Aimone of Spoleto			

1943–1945—Croatia under Germans
1945—Reunited with Yugoslavia after World War II

MONTENEGRO

Reign	Title	Ruler	Birth	Death	Relationship
1697–1737	Prince-Bishop	Danilo Petrovic	1677	1737	
1737–1756	Prince-Bishop	Sava		1782	
1756–1766	Prince-Bishop	Vasili		1766	
1766–1774	Prince-Bishop	Stephen the Little		1774	
1774–1782	Prince-Bishop	Sava			
1782–1830	Prince-Bishop	Peter I	1760	1830	Nephew of Sava
1830–1851	Prince-Bishop	Peter II	1812	1851	Nephew of Peter I
1851–1860	Lord	Danilo II	1826	1860	
1860–1910	Prince	Nicholas I	1841	1921	Nephew of Danilo
1910–1918	King	Nicholas I			

YUGOSLAVIA

Reign	Title	Ruler	Birth	Death	Relationship
1918—Kingdom proclaimed					
1919–1921	King	Peter I (of Serbia)	1844	1921	
1918–1921	Regent	Alexander	1888	1934	Son of Peter I
1921–1934	King	Alexander I			
1934–1941	Regent	Paul	1893	——	Cousin of Alexander I
1934–1945	King	Peter II	1923	1970	Son of Alexander I
1945—Yugoslavia becomes a Communist republican regime.					

The ancient kingdoms of Spain

8
The Kingdoms of Spain

An important and productive region in the Roman Empire, Spain's national history can be dated from the fifth century A.D., when a Germanic successor state was established in the former Roman diocese of Hispania. Although it lacked internal political unity throughout the Middle Ages, Spain is nevertheless one of the oldest nation-states in Europe. It acquired its present-day borders and was united under a personal union of crowns by Ferdinand II of Aragon and Isabella of Castile in the late fifteenth century. For a period in the sixteenth and seventeenth centuries Portugal was also part of that Iberian federation.

Spain was deeply involved in European affairs from the sixteenth into the eighteenth century and in the sixteenth century was the foremost European power. Spain's kings ruled provinces scattered across Europe. The Spanish Empire was global, and the impress of Spanish culture was so pervasive, especially in the Americas, that in 1975 Spanish was the native tongue of 200 million people outside Spain.

Modern Spanish history has been marked by recurrent political instability, military intervention into politics, frequent breakdown of civil order, and periods of repressive government. Spain possessed the constitutional framework in the nineteenth century for parliamentary government not unlike that of Great Britain and France but was unable to develop institutions capable of surviving the social, economic, and ideological stresses of Spanish society. The hopes placed in the Second Republic after 1931 by advocates of liberal parliamentary democracy in Spain and throughout Europe were never realized.

The Spanish civil war (1936–39), which claimed more than half a million lives, was a recapitulation on a larger scale and in an infinitely more brutal context of conflicts that had erupted periodically for generations. Not only did it divide Spain, but it polarized European opinion as well, tested the idealism of the Western democracies, and served as a proving ground for the weapons and tactics of World War II.

After the civil war Spain became identified worldwide with Generalissimo Francisco Franco y Bahamonde, the leader of the Nationalists. Although indebted to the Axis powers for their support during the civil war, Franco kept Spain nonbelligerent during World War II.

IBERIA

The people who were later named Iberians, or dwellers along the Ebro, by the Greeks, migrated to Spain in the third millennium B.C. The origin of the Iberians is a subject for debate, but archaeological evidence of their metallurgical and agricultural skills supports the theory that they came from the eastern Mediterranean. Other peoples of Mediterranean origin settled on the coast during the same period and together with the Iberians fused with the diverse autochthonous inhabitants.

The Iberians lived in small, tightly knit, sedentary tribal groups, isolated from one another by geography. Each developed distinct regional and political identities. Intertribal warfare was endemic.

Celts crossed the Pyrenees into Spain in two major waves of migration in the ninth and seventh centuries B.C. Celtic settlement was concentrated north of the River Duero and the River Ebro where the Celts fused with the Iberians to form distinct groups, called Celtiberians. They were farmers and herders, who also excelled in the metalworking crafts, which the Celts had brought with them from their Danubian homeland by way of Italy and southern France. Celtic cultural influence was dominant, and the Celtiberians appear to have had no social or political organization larger than their matriarchal, collective, and tenaciously independent clans.

Another distinct ethnic group in the western Pyrenees, the Euskera or Basques, predated the arrival of the Iberians. Their pre-Indo-European language has no links with any other language, and attempts to identify it with pre-Latin Iberian have not been convincing. The name Vascones, from which Basque is derived, was given them by the Romans.

The Iberians shared in the Bronze Age revival (ca. 1900–1600 B.C.) common to the Mediterranean basin. In the east and south urban settlements were established, possibly through the amalgamation of tribal units that developed into a system of city-states. Their governments followed the older tribal pattern and were despotic, governed by warrior and priestly castes. A sophisticated urban society emerged with an economy based on the export of gold and silver and the trade in tin and copper, plentiful in Spain, for bronze. The most important of the Iberian city-states was Tartessos, the biblical Tarshish, which, after a period of domination by the Phoenicians, flourished in the sixth and fifth centuries B.C. The Greek historian Herodotus mentioned Tartessos, and a later Greek commentator, Phylarchus, related with some exaggeration that the Tartessians drank water "though they are the wealthiest of mankind (for they possess very great quantities of silver and gold) and . . . they never eat but once a day from thrift and wear the most magnificent clothes."

The Iberian towns were the beneficiaries of cultural currents that moved with commerce across the Mediterranean from Greece and the Near East. The Iberians adopted alphabets for their non-Indo-European language from Greek and Punic sources, and a wide variety of inscriptions indicate that literacy was not confined to a cultural elite.

Phoenicians, Greeks, and Carthaginians competed with the Iberians for control of Spain's coastline and the sources of the interior. Merchants from Tyre may have

The Iberians were driven as slaves in the days of Roman conquest. In this allegorical illustration the Roman emperors Julius Caesar and Augustus are seen holding court over their subjects in Spain.

established their outpost at Cadiz, "the walled enclosure" (Punic, Gadir; Greek, Gades), as early as 1100 B.C. as the westernmost link in what became a chain of Punic cities and outposts lining the southern coast. If the accepted date of its founding is accurate, Cadiz is the oldest city in western Europe and older than Carthage, the greatest of the Punic colonies. From Cadiz, Phoenician seamen explored the west coast of Africa as far as Senegal and reputedly ventured far out on the Atlantic.

Greek pioneers from Rhodes landed in Spain in the eighth century B.C., and later Colaeus, a merchant from the Greek island of Samos, returned home with a cargo of silver after having sailed through the Straits of Gibraltar. The Greek colony at Massilia (later Marseilles) maintained commercial ties with the Celtiberians in what is now Catalonia. In the sixth century B.C. Massilians founded a polis at Ampurias, the first of several established on the Mediterranean coast of the peninsula.

HISPANIA

After its defeat by the Romans in the First Punic War (264–241 B.C.), Carthage compensated for the loss of Sicily by rebuilding a commercial empire in Spain. From Cartagena (Carthago Novo), three generations of the Barcid Dynasty directed Carthaginian expansion, establishing new towns and subduing the Iberians in the interior. Spain became the staging ground for Hannibal's epic invasion of Italy during the Second Punic War (218–201 B.C.).

Roman armies also invaded Spain, using it as a training ground for officers and a proving ground for tactics during the campaigns against the Carthaginians and Iberians. Resistance from the Iberians was fierce and prolonged, and it was not until 19 B.C. that the Roman emperor, Augustus, was able to complete the conquest of Spain.

Romanization of the Iberians proceeded quickly upon conquest. Called Hispania by the Romans, Spain was not a political entity but was originally divided into three provinces (nine by the fourth century A.D.), each governed separately. More important, Spain was for more than four hundred years part of a cosmopolitan world empire bound together by law, language, and the Roman road. From every part of the empire men of many races, united in a common Roman identity, came to Spain as government officials, as merchants and, in the greatest numbers, as soldiers who settled on Spanish land, often with native wives, after their long terms of service. In addition Iberian soldiers, employed as mercenaries for several centuries by the Carthaginians, enlisted in large numbers in the Roman army. Emperor Hadrian, who ruled from A.D. 117 to 138, used tough Iberian legionnaires to man his wall across Britain.

Tribal leaders and urban oligarchs were admitted into the aristocratic class and played a part in governing Spain and the empire. The latifundia, extensive estates controlled by powerful magnates, were superimposed without difficulty on the landholding system already operative among the Iberians.

The Romans laid out the new cities of Zaragoza, Mérida, and Valencia and improved existing ones. They provided amenities found throughout the empire—theaters, arenas, baths fed by aqueducts, and the forum, focal point of every Roman city. The local administrative division was the *civitas*, which often corresponded to an Iberian tribal area but always centered on a city or town. The economy expanded under Roman tutelage as part of the imperial system. With North Africa, Spain served as a granary for the Roman market, and its harbors exported gold, wool, olive oil, and wine. Agricultural production was extended by the introduction of irrigation projects, some of which remain in use. The Hispano-Romans—the romanized Iberians and the Iberian-born descendants of Roman soldiers and colonists—had all achieved the status of full Roman citizenship by the end of the first century A.D. The emperors Trajan (reigned 98–117), Hadrian (117–38), and Marcus Aurelius (161–80) were born in Spain.

The Vulgar Latin developed into a distinct provincial usage, which in turn evolved into Spanish regional dialects. Spain remained in the mainstream of Hellenistic culture throughout the Roman period and produced its share of Silver Age writers, among them the Stoic philosopher Seneca (5 B.C.–A.D. 65), who was born in Cordova. Some authorities read Seneca's Spanish background (his mother is thought to have been an Iberian) into his Stoicism.

Christianity was introduced into Spain in the first century and had become popular in the cities by the second century. Little headway was made in the countryside, however, until the late fourth century, by which time Christianity was the officially recognized religion of the Roman Empire. The major heresies of the early church were in evidence, but the Spanish church remained orthodox. Orosius, a Spanish bishop, was the author of the creed formulated at the Council of Nicaea (325) to refute Arianism. Bishops, who had official civil as well as ecclesiastical status in the late empire, continued to exercise their authority to maintain order when civil government had broken down in Spain in the fifth century, and the Council of Bishops, which met at Toledo, became an important instrument of stability during the Visigothic ascendancy.

In 405 the Vandals and Suevi crossed the Rhine, ravaging Gaul until driven by another Germanic tribe, the Visigoths, into Spain. The Suevi established a kingdom in the remote northwestern corner of the peninsula. The hardier Vandals, never more numerous than eighty thousand, occupied the region that bears their name—Andalusia.

Because large parts of Spain were outside his control, the Western emperor, Honorius (395–423), commissioned the willing Visigoths under their king, Ataulphus, and his Roman consort, the emperor's sister, Galla Placida, to restore order, giving them the right as *foederati* to settle in and govern Spain in return for defending it. The Visigoths were among the most highly romanized of the Germanic peoples. The Visigoths subdued the Suevi and compelled the Vandals to sail for North Africa. In 484 they established Toledo as the capital of their Spanish monarchy. The Visigothic occupation was in no sense a barbarian invasion. Successive Visigothic kings ruled Spain as patricians holding imperial commissions to govern in the name of the Roman emperor. Though the authority of the emperor in Constantinople was nominal there, Spain remained in theory a part of the Roman Empire.

The Germanic peoples in Spain numbered no more than three hundred thousand in a population of 4 million, and their overall influence on Spanish history is generally seen as minimal. They were a privileged warrior elite, though many of them lived as herders and farmers in the valley of the River Tajó and on the central plateau. Hispano-Romans continued to run the civil administration, and Latin remained the language of government and commerce. The two peoples retained separate and distinct legal codes, though the distinctions over the years tended to be blurred.

Religion was the most persistent source of friction between the Catholic Hispano-Romans and their Arian Visigoth overlords. At times it invited open rebellion and was exploited by restive factions within the Visigothic aristocracy to weaken the monarchy. In 589 Recared renounced his Arianism before the Council of Bishops at Toledo, accepting Catholicism and assuring an alliance between the Visigothic monarchy and the Hispano-Romans, who proved themselves more reliable than his own rebellious chieftains.

The Visigothic monarchy was elective. A new king was nominated from the royal family, according to Germanic tradition, on the basis of the candidate's "throne-worthiness." In Spain after Recared's conversion the Council of Bishops functioned as a legislative assembly to ratify royal elections and to confer on the king the charismatic character of a theocratic monarch. This was symbolized in the rite of coronation, which Spain's Visigothic monarchs were the first among the Germanic rulers of the successor states to use and which was modeled on the forms used by the Christian Roman emperors. The kings also were entitled to intervene in the administrative affairs of the church, inaugurating a royal prerogative that persists in Spain.

Court ceremonials from Constantinople that proclaimed the imperial sovereignty and unity of the Visigothic state were introduced at Toledo. In fact warlords and great landholders had assumed wide discretionary powers. Bloody family feuds went unchecked. Civil war, royal assassinations, and usurpation were commonplace. The Visigoths had acquired and cultivated the apparatus of the Roman state but not the ability to make it operate to their advantage. Without a well-defined hereditary succession to the throne, rival factions encouraged foreign intervention by the Greeks, Franks, and finally the Muslims in domestic disputes and royal elections.

AL-ANDALUS

Early in the eighth century armies from North Africa began probing the Visigothic defenses of Spain, initiating the centuries-long Moorish epoch. The people who became known to western Europeans as Moors were the Arabs who had swept across North Africa from their Middle Eastern homeland and the Berbers, inhabitants of Morocco whom the Arabs had conquered and converted to Islam.

In 711 Tarik ibn Zizad, a Berber and the governor of Tangier, crossed into Spain with an army of twelve thousand (landing at a promontory that later bore his name, Gib al-Tarik or Gibraltar). They came at the invitation of a Visigothic clan to assist it in rising against King Roderic, who died in battle, leaving Spain leaderless. Having decided the outcome of an internal Spanish feud, Tarik returned to Morocco, but the next year Musa ibn Nusair, the Muslim governor in North Africa, led the best of his Arab troops to Spain, intent on staying. In

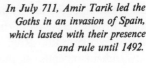

In July 711, Amir Tarik led the Goths in an invasion of Spain, which lasted with their presence and rule until 1492.

The first Moorish amir, Tarik

A native princess brought before Amir Abderraman (730–32) for his approval. The Moorish amirs had an eye for Spanish women.

three years he subdued all but the mountainous region in the extreme north and initiated forays into France, which were stemmed at Poitiers in 732.

Al-Andalus, as Islamic Spain was called, was organized under the civil and religious leadership of the caliph of Damascus. Governors in Spain were generally Syrians whose political frame of reference was deeply influenced by Byzantine practices. The largest contingent of Moors in Spain, however, were the North African Berbers, recent converts to Islam, hostile to the sophisticated Arab governors and bureaucrats, and given to a religious enthusiasm and fundamentalism that were to set the standard for the Islamic community. Berber settlers fanned out through the country and made up as much as 20 percent of the population of the occupied territory. The Arabs constituted an aristocracy in the revived cities of Spain and on the latifundia, which they had inherited from the Romans and Visigoths.

Most of the Gothic nobility converted to Islam and retained their privileged position in the new society. The countryside, only nominally Christian, was also successfully Islamized. An Hispano-Roman Christian community survived in the cities. Jews, who constituted more than 5 percent of the population, continued to fill an important place in commerce, scholarship, and the professions.

The term *Mozarabs* (Arablike), used to identify the Christians in al-Andalus, indicates the impact of the new cultural influences on the country. Social customs and mores, dress, food, and artistic styles were significantly influenced. The native Romance dialect was regularly written in Arabic characters, and in some cities use of Arabic had become so widespread among Mozarabs that it was used in the Christian liturgy.

The Arab-dominated Umayyad Dynasty at Damascus was overthrown in 756 by the Abbasides, who moved the caliphate to Baghdad. One Umayyad prince fled to Spain and, as Abder-Rahman I (756–88), founded a politically independent emirate with its capital at Cordova in what was then the farthest extremity of the Islamic world. His line flourished for two hundred and fifty years. Nothing in Europe compared with the wealth, power, and sheer brilliance of al-Andalus during the Cordovan period.

In 929 Abder-Rahman III, who was half European as were many of the ruling caste, elevated the emirate to the status of a caliphate, cutting Spain's last ties with Baghdad and establishing that thereafter al-Andalus's rulers would enjoy complete religious as well as political sovereignty. A similar process attended the breakdown of Arab hegemony throughout the Islamic world in the tenth and eleventh centuries.

Hisham II, grandson of Abder-Rahman III, inherited the throne in 976 at age twelve. The royal vizier, Ibn Abi Amir (al-Mansur), became regent and established himself as virtual dictator. For the next twenty-six years the legitimate caliph was no more than a figurehead, and al-Mansur was the actual ruler. Al-Mansur wanted the caliphate to symbolize the ideal of religious and political unity as insurance against any renewal of civil strife. He reinforced this by insisting on strict conformity with religious orthodoxy and by creating a professional army personally loyal to the vizier to replace the unreliable regional forces under local lords. Notwithstanding the fact that al-Mansur employed Christian mercenaries, he preached *jihad*, or "holy war," against the Christian states on the frontier, undertaking annual summer campaigns against them, which served not only to unite Spanish Muslims in a common cause but also to extend Muslim control in the north temporarily.

The Cordovan caliphate did not long survive al-Mansur's dictatorship. With his firm and often cruel grip off the reins of government, the caliphate was torn apart by rival claimants to the throne, local aristocrats, and army commanders who staked out *taifas*, independent regional city-states. Some of them, such as Seville, Granada, Valencia, and Zaragoza, became strong emirates, but all were subject to frequent political upheavals, warring among themselves and making long-term accommodations with the emerging Christian states.

In the ninth century Cordovan Mozarabs, led by their bishop, invited martyrdom by denouncing Mohammed in public, but physical violence remained the exception until the eleventh century, when the Christian states became a serious threat to the security of al-Andalus and Mozarabs there were harassed. Many Mozarabs fled to the Christian north, where their artistic talent and technical skill, the product of two cultures, had a fructifying effect.

CASTILE AND ARAGON

Active resistance to the Muslim invasion in the eighth century had been limited to small groups of Visigoth warriors. They took refuge in the mountains of Asturias in the old Suevian Kingdom, the least romanized and

Pelayo, the first Christian king of Asturias (and León), the son of Favila, the duke of Cantabria, is seen presiding over his council in this sketch.

King Ordono III of León (950–55) was the first Spanish king to be buried at León.

King of Aragon, James I, the Conqueror (1213–76), saying goodbye to his wife before departing for the Balearic Islands

least Christianized region in Spain. According to tradition Pelayo (d. 737), a king of Oviedo, first rallied the natives to defend themselves, then urged them to take the offensive beginning the seven-hundred-year-long Reconquest (Reconquista), which became the dominant theme in medieval Spanish history. What began as a matter of survival in Asturias became a crusade to rid Spain of the Muslims and an imperial mission to reconstruct a united monarchy in Spain. The two ideals were inextricably bound together.

The kings of León, as Pelayo's successors were styled as they extended Christian control southward from Asturias, tore away bits of territory, which were depopulated and fortified against the Muslims and then resettled as the frontier was pushed forward. The kingdom's center of political gravity always moved in the direction of the military frontier.

In the tenth century, strongholds were built as a buffer for León along the upper Ebro in the area that became known as Castile, the "land of castles."

In 981 Castile became an independent county and in 1004 was raised to the dignity of a kingdom by the Sanchez Dynasty. Castile and León were reunited periodically through royal marriages, but their kings had no better plan than to divide their lands again among their heirs. The two kingdoms were permanently joined as a single state in 1230 by Saint Ferdinand III of Castile (d. 1252).

Under Frankish tutelage a barrier of pocket states was constructed along the range of the Pyrenees and on the Catalonian coast to hold the frontier of France against Islamic Spain. Out of this Spanish march emerged the kingdom of Aragon and the counties of Catalonia, which expanded, as did León-Castile, at the expense of the Muslims. (Andorra is the last independent survivor of the march states.)

The counts of Barcelona were descended from Wilfrid the Hairy, who at the end of the ninth century declared his fief free of the French crown and monopolized lay and ecclesiastical offices on both sides of the Pyrenees, dividing them, according to Frankish custom, among members of the family. By 1100 Barcelona had dominion over all of Catalonia and the Balearic Islands. Aragon and the Catalan counties were federated through a personal union after the marriage of Ramon Berenguer IV, count of Barcelona, and Petronilla, heiress to the Aragonese throne, in 1137. He assumed the title king of Aragon but continued to rule as count in Catalonia. Berenguer and his successors thus ruled over several realms, each with its own government, legal code, currency, and political orientation.

Valencia, seized from its Muslim emir, became federated with Aragon and Catalonia in the thirteenth century. With the union of the three crowns, Aragon (the term most commonly used to describe the federation) rivaled Venice and Genoa for control of Mediterranean trade. Aragonese commercial interests extended to the Black Sea, and the ports of Barcelona and Valencia prospered from the traffic in textiles, drugs, spices, and slaves.

Weakened by their disunity, the eleventh-century *taifas* fell piecemeal to the Castilians, who had reason to anticipate the completion of the Reconquest. When Toledo was lost in 1085, the alarmed emirs appealed for aid to the Almoravids, a militant Berber party of strict Muslims, who in a few years had won control of the Maghreb (northwest Africa). The Almoravids turned back the Christian advance and incorporated all of al-Andalus, except Zaragoza, into their North African Empire. They attempted to stimulate a religious revival based on their own evangelical brand of Islam, but in Spain the movement soon conformed with the religious attitudes of the *taifas*. The Almoravid state fell apart by the mid-twelfth century under pressure from another religious group, the Almohads, who extended their control from Morocco to Spain and made Seville their capital. The Almohads shared the crusading instincts of the Almoravids and posed an even greater military threat to the Christian states, but their expansion was stopped decisively in the epic battle of Las Navas de Tolosa (1212), a watershed in the history of the Reconquest. Muslim strength ebbed thereafter. Ferdinand III took Seville in 1248, reducing al-Andalus to the emirate of Granada, which had bought its safety by betraying the Almohads' Spanish capital. Granada remained a Muslim state but as a dependency of Castile.

Aragon's territorial aims were fulfilled in the thirteenth century when it annexed Valencia. The Catalans, however, looked for further expansion abroad, and their economic views prevailed over those of the parochial Aragonese nobility, who were not enthusiastic about foreign entanglements. Pedro III, king of Aragon from 1276 until 1285, had been elected to the throne of Sicily when the French Angevins (House of Anjou) were expelled from the island kingdom during the uprising in 1282. Sicily and later Naples became part of the federation of crowns, and Aragon was brought into the center of Italian politics, where Spanish interests remained embroiled into the eighteenth century.

Catalan expansionism was not limited to the actions of the legitimate authorities. The Grand Catalan Company, a corporation of *almogávers* (light infantry troops), freebooting mercenaries sometimes in the service of the Byzantine emperor, carved out an independent duchy of Athens in Greece and governed it throughout most of the fourteenth century. The Catalan economy was controlled by the independent, highly individualistic, and often ruthlessly competitive entrepreneurs of the urban oligarchy. The Catalan nobility competed with the merchants and bankers of Barcelona for a share in the commercial market.

Feudalism, which bound nobles to the king-counts

Queen Berengaria, wife of Richard I of England, became the regent in 1217.

King Ferdinand III, the Saint

King Pedro III, the Great (1276–85), monarch of Aragon and Catalonia, watches from a mountaintop as the French flee Spain.

Pedro I, the Cruel, was the king of León and Castile from 1350 to 1369. For which of his crimes he received his nickname is not certain, but ranking high would be the imprisonment and murder of his wife, Queen Blanche of Bourbon.

Henry II of Castile (1369–79) was known in history as the count of Trastamara. He was, in character, nearly as cruel as Pedro the Cruel; as loose in morals and only slightly inferior as a tyrant. His was the reign with the rivalry of Pope Urban VI and the antipope Clement, so he withheld the customary contribution to the Holy See. Henry also recovered the vast amounts of gold and other fortunes of Pedro's and this very money today represents the wealth of the royal family.

Henry IV in a portrait from life by Camarauz

King Henry IV of Castile (1454–74) was called Henry the Impotent because after he married Blanche of Navarre in 1440, he failed to produce an heir. Blanche, after thirteen years of marriage, "complained that the 'debitum conjugale' was not paid," and as damages received an annulment in 1453.

economically and socially as tenants to landlords, had been introduced into Aragon and Catalonia from France. It produced a more clearly stratified social structure than Castile's and consequently greater tension among classes. Castilian society was less competitive, more cohesive, and more egalitarian. The labor-free production of wool left far fewer occasions for class struggle than did the labor-intensive commerce and industry of Barcelona and racially diverse Valencia. Castile attempted to compensate through political means, however, for the binding feudal arrangements between crown and nobility that it lacked. The guiding theory behind the Castilian monarchy was one of political centralism to be won at the expense of local *fueros*, but the kings of Castile never succeeded in creating a unitary state. Aragon-Catalonia accepted and developed, not without conflict, the federal principle, and no concerted attempt was made to establish a political union of the Spanish and Italian principalities outside of their personal union under the Aragonese crown. Beyond conflicting local loyalties, therefore, the principal regions of Spain were divided in their political, economic, and social orientations. Catalonia particularly stood apart from the rest of the country.

Both Castile and Aragon suffered from political instability in the fourteenth and fifteenth centuries. In Castile the Trastamaras, who took the throne in 1369, created a new aristocracy to whom significant authority was granted. Castilian kings were often dominated by their *validos* (court favorites) and, because the kings were weak, nobles competed for control of the government.

Aragon, where another branch of the Trastamaras succeeded to the throne in 1416, was affected by the social disruption and decay of institutions common to much of Europe in the late Middle Ages. For long periods the overextended Aragonese kings resided in Naples, leaving their Spanish realms with weak, vulnerable governments. The economic dislocation caused by plague and the commercial decline of Catalonia was the occasion for repeated revolts by regional nobility, town corporations, peasants and, in Barcelona, the urban proletariat.

THE GOLDEN AGE

Stability was brought to both kingdoms in 1469 through the marriage of royal cousins, Ferdinand of Aragon (1452–1516) and Isabella of Castile (1451–1504). Ferdinand had grown up in the midst of civil war, and Isabella's succession had been bloodily disputed by her niece Juana in a conflict in which rival claimants had been given assistance by outside powers—Isabella by Aragon and Juana by the king of Portugal, who was her suitor. The direction in which Iberian unification would proceed, linking Castile with Aragon, was determined by the outcome of that struggle, concluded in 1478. Ferdinand succeeded his father in Aragon the next year. Both Isabella and Ferdinand understood the importance of unity: she, in terms of ideological uniformity, and he, as part of a politcal process. Together they effected institutional reform in Castile and left Spain one of the best administered countries in Europe.

John II on a medallion of the time

King Don Juan II (John) of León and Castile (1406–54). John II was the weakest and most despicable of the princes that ever ruled in Spain.

In 1469, Ferdinand of Aragon, son of King John II, married Isabella of Castile, which united the two countries into one Spain.

Blanche the Tattler, as she was known, became the "Heiress of Navarre" upon the death of her brother Charles in 1461. But her male competition for the throne of Navarre led to her imprisonment in the Castle Orthez in Béarn, where she was under continual sexual assault and torture for two years, until her captors poisoned her in 1464. Her death paved the way for that ancient kingdom to be partitioned between France and Spain.

The leading sovereigns of Spain from 1474 to 1886. Left, top to bottom: Isabella II (1833–68), Isabella I (1474–1504), and Philip I (1504–6). Center, top to bottom: Charles I (V, 1519–56), Alfonso XII (1874–86), and Philip V (1701–24). And right, top to bottom: Maria Cristina (1886), Ferdinand V (1506–16), and Philip II (1556–98).

By marrying Ferdinand, Isabella had united Spain, but she had also inevitably involved Castile in Aragon's wars in Italy against France, hitherto Castile's ally. The motivation in each of their children's marriages had been to circle France with Spanish allies—Habsburg, Burgundian, and English. The succession of the Habsburg Dynasty with its broader Continental interests and commitments drew Spain onto the center stage of European dynastic wars for two hundred years.

Even with the personal union of the Castilian and Aragonese crowns, Castile, Aragon, Catalonia, and Valencia remained constitutionally distinct political entities and retained their separate councils of state and parliaments. Ferdinand, who had received his political education in federalist Aragon, brought a new emphasis on constitutionalism, consultation with the estates, and respect for local *fueros* to Castile, where he was king consort (1479–1504) and remained as regent after Isabella's death in 1504. Greatly admired by Machiavelli, Ferdinand was one of the most skillful diplomats in an age of great diplomats and assigned to Castile its predominant role in the Dual Monarchy.

Ferdinand and Isabella resumed the Reconquest, dormant for more than two hundred years, and in 1492 captured Granada and earned for themselves the title Catholic kings. After the long history of Islamic Spain was brought to an end, attention turned to the internal threat posed by a Muslim population increased by sev-

Queen Isabella as a child

The marriage of Isabella and Ferdinand in 1469

An authentic sketch of Queen Isabella's crown

The queen in her youth, from an original print of the time

Isabella and Ferdinand receive the keys to Granada from Abou Abdilehi (Boabdil), Moorish king of Granada (1482–92) on January 2, 1492. The place still bears a plaque with the inscription "El ultimo suspiro del moro," which translates as "The last sigh of the Moor."

The queen's armor as it has been preserved

During his coreign, Ferdinand was known as Ferdinand the Catholic.

A portrait of Isabella I, the Catholic

A famous painting of The Education of Boabdil, *the last King of Granada*

Isabella and Ferdinand welcoming Columbus on his return from the Americas

Christopher Columbus explaining his forthcoming trip to the Americas to Isabella and Ferdinand in a famous painting by Vacslav Brozik

Tomb of Prince Juan, son of Isabella and Ferdinand, located in the Church of St. Thomas in Avila

eral hundred thousand by the incorporation of Granada. "Spanish society drove itself," J. H. Elliott writes, "on a ruthless ultimately self-defeating quest for an unattainable purity."

Everywhere in sixteenth-century Europe it was assumed that religious unity was a necessary ingredient of political unity. Insistence on religious conformity was therefore not unique to Spain, but there was a greater sense of urgency in enforcing it. Spain's population was more heterogeneous than that of any other European nation and contained significantly large non-Christian communities. In Granada especially they constituted a conquered majority of doubtful loyalty. *Moriscos* (Granadan Muslims) were given the choice of voluntary exile or conversion to Christianity. There was a precedent for Jewish conversion, and *Conversos* (Jewish converts to Christianity) had filled important government and ecclesiastical posts in Castile and Aragon for more

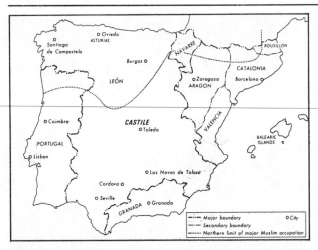

Spain in the fifteenth century

Queen Juana and Philip I reigned from 1504 to 1506, when Philip died and the queen grieved herself into insanity. Here she is shown in a vigil at Philip's gravesite.

than one hundred years. Many had married or purchased their way into the nobility. Muslims in reconquered territory, Mudejars, also had lived quietly for generations as peasant farmers and skilled craftsmen. Valencia retained a Mudejar majority in 1500.

After 1525 all residents of Spain were *officially* Christian, but forced conversion and nominal orthodoxy were not sufficient for complete integration into Spanish society. Purity of blood *(pureza de sangre)* regulations were imposed on candidates for positions in the government and the church, not only to prevent Moriscos from becoming a force again in Spain but to eliminate participation by Conversos as well, though their families might have been Christian for generations. There was a scramble to reconstruct family trees in many of Spain's oldest and finest families.

The task of enforcing uniformity of religious practice was put in the hands of the Inquisition, a state-controlled Castilian tribunal authorized by papal bull in 1478 and soon extended throughout Spain. It was originally intended to investigate the sincerity of Conversos, especially those in the clergy, who had been accused of being crypto-Jews.

For years laws were laxly enforced, particularly in Aragon, and nominally Christian Jews and Moriscos continued to observe their religions in private. In 1568 a serious rebellion broke out among the Moriscos of Andalusia, who sealed their fate by appealing to the Turks for aid. The incident led to mass expulsions throughout Spain and the eventual exodus of hundreds of thousands of Conversos and Moriscos, some apparently devout Christians. The last of them was expelled in 1609. "Wherever we are, we weep for Spain," laments a Morisco in *Don Quixote*, "for after all, there we were born, and it is our natural fatherland."

In the fifteenth century Portuguese mariners were opening a route around Africa to the East and, together with the Castilians, they had planted colonies in the Azores and the Canaries, the latter islands assigned to

The church in an attempt to exorcise Queen Juana

The tomb in Granada of King Philip and Queen Juana, the parents of Charles I

The birth of Charles I in 1500. He was king of Spain from 1519 to 1556. He also reigned as Charles V, emperor of the Holy Roman Empire.

Charles V at the Battle of Mühlberg

The triumphant entry of Charles V and Pope Clement VII into Bologna for Charles's coronation in 1530

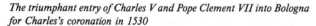

Queen Isabella of Portugal, the consort of Charles V

Spain by papal decree. The conquest of Granada allowed the Catholic kings to divert their attention to exploration but, though blessed by Isabella, Christopher Columbus's first voyage in 1492 was financed by foreign bankers. In 1493 Pope Alexander VI (Rodrigo Borgia, a Catalan) sanctioned the division of the unexplored world between Spain and Portugal. The Treaty of Tordesillas signed by Spain and Portugal one year later moved the line of division westward and allowed Portugal to claim Brazil.

In the exploration and exploitation of the New World, Spain found an outlet for the crusading energies stimulated by the war against the Muslims. New discoveries and conquests came in quick succession. Vasco Núñez de Balboa reached the Pacific in 1513, and the survivors of Ferdinand Magellan's expedition completed the circumnavigation of the globe in 1522. In 1519 the conquistador Hernando Cortés subdued the Aztecs in Mexico with a handful of followers, and between 1531 and 1533 Francisco Pizarro overthrew the Inca Empire and established Spanish dominion over Peru.

In 1493, when Columbus brought fifteen hundred colonists with him on his second voyage, a royal administrator had already been appointed for the Indies. The Council of the Indies (established in 1524) acted as an advisory board to the crown on colonial affairs, and trade with the colonies was regulated by the House of Trade (Casa de Contratación). The newly established colonies were not Spanish but Castilian. They were administered as appendages of Castile, and the Aragonese were prohibited from trading or settling there.

Ferdinand and Isabella were the last of the Trastamaras, and Spain was not again ruled by a native dynasty. When their sole male heir, John, who was to have inherited all his parents' crowns, died in 1497, the succession passed to his sister Juana (a younger sister was Catherine of Aragon, first wife of Henry VIII). Juana had become the wife of Philip the Handsome, heir through his father, Emperor Maximilian I, to the Habsburg patrimony and through his mother to the Burgundian domains, which included the Netherlands and Franche-Comté. Their son, Charles of Gaunt (Ghent), was recognized as lord in the Netherlands provinces on Philip's death in 1506. On Ferdinand's death in 1516, Charles inherited Spain and its colonies and Naples (Juana, called the Mad, lived until 1555 but was judged incompetent to rule) and, when Maximilian I died in 1519, the Habsburg domains in Germany. Shortly after-

Charles I loved the sport of bullfighting from horseback.

Philip II, king of Spain, was born in 1527, the only son of Emperor Charles V (of the Holy Roman Empire). He was known as the Demon of the South. He had no equal among Spanish monarchs, for he was invested with the duchy of Milan, 1540; married Maria of Portugal, 1543; succeeded to the kingdoms of Naples and Sicily, 1554; married Mary Tudor of England, 1554; succeeded to the lordship of the Netherlands, 1555; became king of Spain on abdication of his father, 1556; married Elizabeth, daughter of Henry II, of France, 1557; proclaimed himself king of America, 1565: married Anne of Austria, the former betrothed of his son Don Carlos, 1572; and acquired the throne of Portugal in 1580.

ward he was selected Holy Roman emperor to succeed his grandfather. In such a way the most diverse empire since Rome's, stretching around the globe, was brought together in a matter of a few years under Charles V—Charles I of Spain.

Charles's closest attachments were to his birthplace, Flanders, and he surrounded himself with Flemish advisers who were not appreciated in Spain. The town corporations *(comunidades)* of Castile and León rose in revolt against their absentee king in 1520 and 1521. His duties as Holy Roman emperor and king of Spain never allowed him to rest too long in one place. As the years of this long reign passed, Charles drew closer to Spain, which because of its manpower and the wealth of its colonies was increasingly called upon to maintain the Habsburg Empire.

When he abdicated in 1556 to retire to a Spanish monastery, Charles divided his empire. His son, Philip II (reigned 1556–98), inherited Spain, the Italian possessions, and the Netherlands (the industrial heartland of Europe in the mid-sixteenth century). For a brief period (1554–58) Philip was king of England as Mary Tudor's husband. In 1580 Philip was acknowledged king of Portugal through succession from his mother, and the Iberian Peninsula had a single monarch for the next sixty years.

Philip II was a Castilian by education and temperament. He was seldom out of Spain and knew no other language but Spanish. He governed his scattered dominions through a system of councils, such as the Council of the Indies, staffed by professional civil servants, whose activities were coordinated by a council of state responsible to Philip. Its function was advisory only. Every decision was Philip's, every question required his answer, every document his signature. His father had been a peripatetic emperor, but Philip, a royal bureaucrat, administered every detail of his empire from the Escorial,

Philip II, as a young man (photograph, duke of Wellington estate)

Anne of Austria, the young bride promised to Don Carlos, ended up the fourth wife of Philip II. (By Velasquez)

the forbidding palace-monastery-mausoleum begun in 1563 on the barren plain outside Madrid.

Well into the seventeenth century music, art, literature, theater, dress, and manners from the Golden Age were admired and imitated, setting a standard by which the rest of Europe measured its culture. Spain was also Europe's preeminent military power and had occasion to exercise its strength on many fronts—on land in Italy, Germany, North Africa, and the Netherlands and at sea against the Dutch, French, Turks, and English. Spain was the military, diplomatic, and spiritual standard-

In 1651, a daughter was born to Philip II and Anne and named Margaret Maria. In the christening scene by Velasquez, the ''Infanta'' is seen, center, *with her godmother, Infanta Maria Theresa,* left.

Philip II with the royal architect and engineer at the site planning the building of the Escurial Royal Palace, which Philip wanted to be the biggest in the world.

Elizabeth of Valois, queen of Spain, the third wife of Philip II

Philip II suffered from gout. He is seen here receiving a delegation from Holland with his foot propped up on a chair. Philip said that he would prefer living with his inflamed big toe to giving up drinking.

Anne of Austria (in later life), the fourth wife of Philip II.

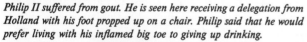

The Escurial (Escorial) built by Philip II in memory of his father, Charles I, is the former residence (near Madrid) of many kings of Spain. It is a massive palace, monastery, and church that contains royal tombs and a priceless collection of rare paintings.

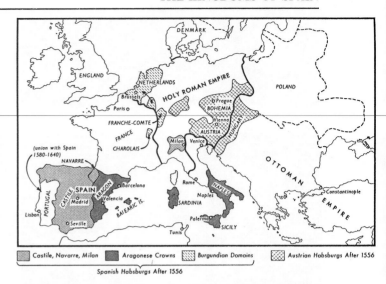

Spain in its European setting in the sixteenth century

Philip II in later years

Philip III (1598–1621). He is recorded in history for his helplessness, imbecility, dissipation, and idleness.

A painting of Philip IV (1621–65) by the famous artist Velasquez

The last of the Moorish people being expelled from Spain by Philip III

bearer of the Counter-Reformation. Spanish fleets defeated the Turks at Malta (1565) and at Lepanto (1572) —events celebrated even in hostile England—preventing the Mediterranean from becoming an Ottoman lake. The defeat of the Grand Armada in 1588 averted the planned invasion of England but was not a permanent setback for the Spanish fleet. It recovered and remained an effective naval force in European waters.

Sixteenth-century Spain was ultimately the victim of its own wealth. Military expenditure did not stimulate domestic production. Bullion from American mines passed through Spain as through a sieve to pay for troops in the Netherlands and Italy, to maintain the emperor's forces in Germany, for ships at sea, and to satisfy conspicuous consumption at home. Dutch commercial interests, for instance, so prospered from supplying the Spanish army that they resisted concluding the war in the Netherlands.

The seventeenth century was a period of unremitting political, military, economic, and social decline. Neither Philip III(1598–1621) nor Philip IV (1621–65) was competent to give the kind of clear direction of which Philip II in his prime had been capable. Responsibility passed to aristocratic advisers, as it had to the *validos* of Castile in the fifteenth century. Gaspar de Guzman, count-duke of Olivares, attempted and failed to establish the centralized administration that his famous contemporary Cardinal Richelieu introduced in France. In reaction to his bureaucratic absolutism, Catalonia revolted and was virtually annexed by France. Portugal, with English aid, reasserted its independence in 1640, and an attempt was made to separate Andalusia from Spain. In 1648 at the Peace of Westphalia, Spain assented to the emperor's accommodation with the German Protestants and in 1654 recognized the independence of the northern Netherlands.

During the long regency for Charles II (1665–1701), the last of the Spanish Habsburgs, Spain's treasury was milked by *validos,* and its government operated principally as a dispenser of patronage. The country was wasted by plague, famine, floods, drought, and renewed war with France. The Peace of the Pyrenees (1659) ended fifty years of warfare with France, but Louis XIV, the young king of that expansionist country, found the temptation to exploit Spain during its enfeeblement too great. As part of the peace settlement the Spanish infanta Marie-Therese had become the wife of Louis XIV. On the pretext (technically a valid one) that Spain had not paid her dowry, Louis instigated a war of devolution to recover the debt, in territory, in the Spanish Netherlands. Most of the European powers were ultimately involved in Louis's wars in the Low Countries.

BOURBON SPAIN

Charles II was the unfortunate product of generations of inbreeding. He was unable to rule and remained childless. The line of Spanish Habsburgs came to an end at his death. Habsburg partisans argued for allocating succession within the dynasty to its Austrian branch, but in one of his last official acts Charles II left Spain to his nephew, Philip of Anjou, a Bourbon and the grandson of Louis XIV. This solution appealed to Castilian legitimists, as it complied with the principle of succession to the next in the bloodline. Spanish officials had been concerned with providing for the succession in such a way as to guarantee an integral, independent Spanish state that, along with its possessions in the Netherlands and Italy, would not become part of either a pan-Bourbon or a pan-Habsburg Empire. "The Pyrenees are no more, " Louis XIV rejoiced at his grandson's accession, but it was the prospect of the Spanish Netherlands falling into French hands that alarmed England and the Dutch estates-general.

The acceptance of the Spanish crown by Philip V (1701–46) in the face of counterclaims by Archduke Charles of Austria, who was supported by England and the Netherlands, was the proximate cause of the War of the Spanish Succession (1702–14), the first world war fought by European powers. In 1705 an Anglo-Austrian force landed in Spain. Its advance on Madrid was halted by a Franco-Castilian army, but the invaders occupied Catalonia.

The Bourbon Dynasty had been received enthusiastically in Castile but was opposed by the Catalans not so much out of loyalty to the Habsburgs as in defense of their *fueros* against the feared imposition of French-style centralization by a Castilian regime. The war, fought on a global scale, was also a Spanish civil war. England agreed to a separate peace with France, and the allies withdrew from Catalonia, but the Catalans continued their resistance under the banner "Privilegis o Mort" (Liberty or Death). Catalonia was devastated, and Barcelona fell to Philip V after a prolonged siege (1713–14).

The main European theaters of operation were in Germany and the Low Countries, where the allied coalition, led by Randolph Churchill, duke of Marlborough, had won a military advantage over the French. The Treaty of Utrecht (1713), which brought the war to a close, recognized the Bourbon succession in Spain on the condition that Spain and France *never be united under the same crown*. The Spanish Netherlands (Belgium) and Spain's Italian possessions, however, reverted to the Austrian Habsburgs. England retained Gibraltar and Minorca, seized during the war, and was granted trade concessions in Spanish America.

Philip V reigned from 1701 to 1724.

Charles II, king of Spain (1665–1701). In the thirty-six years of his reign he was credited with little but debited with much. He was utterly destitute of discernment, energy, and skill. Sickly and hypochondriacal, it is surprising that he lived to be thirty-nine years of age.

Philip V built the Orientè Palace for himself in Madrid but did not live to see its completion.

Charles III (1759–88), Spain's enlightened despot par excellence, served his royal apprenticeship as king of Naples. He was one of Europe's most active patrons of the Enlightenment, which had as its goal the reform of society through the application of reason to political, social, and economic problems. Charles promised a generation of happiness and more efficient collection of taxes. Despite the attempt to restructure the economy on a rational basis, the impact of the Enlightenment was essentially negative. Anticlericalism was an integral part of Enlightenment ideology but, because of government sponsorship, it was carried to greater lengths in Spain than elsewhere in Europe. Considered antisocial because they were thought to discourage initiative, public charities financed by the church were abolished. Monasteries were suppressed and their property confiscated by the state. The Jesuits, outspoken opponents of regalism, were expelled, virtually crippling higher education in Spain. The teachings of medieval philosophers and of the sixteenth-century Jesuit political theorists who had argued for the "divine right of the people" over their kings were banned. Even the plays of Pedro Calderón de la Barca were prohibited from performance, reputedly because of their "jesuitical" bias. The Inquisition was employed by the government to discipline antiregalist clerics.

Spain emerged from the war with its internal unity and colonial empire intact but its political position in Europe weakened. The Bourbon succession, which ended the interminable wars that had pitted Spain against France since the fifteenth century, called for a basic reorientation of foreign policy. The two Bourbon monarchies were linked diplomatically by a series of family pacts, which were as much an expression of common national interests as of dynastic solidarity. Spain conducted an aggressive campaign to recover the lost Italian possessions and regained a measure of prestige under the protection of the French alliance.

Philip V also undertook to ratonalize Spanish government through his French and Italian advisers. Centralized government was institutionalized, local *fueros* were abrogated, regional parliaments abolished, and the independent influence of the aristocracy on the councils of state destroyed.

The Bourbon regime had its ideological foundation in regalism, a concept of statism that went beyond administrative centralization to attack all autonomous bodies that in the past had placed limitations on the authority of the monarchy and were therefore viewed by its advocates as obstacles to progress. The church and its religious orders were the most important of these bodies. In effect regalism combined an absolute monarchy with bureaucratic dictatorship.

Economic recovery was noticeable, and government efficiency greatly improved at the higher levels during Charles III's reign. The Bourbon reforms, however, made no basic changes in the pattern of property holding. Neither land reform nor an increase of land in use was accomplished. Creation of a middle-class movement was hindered by the rudimentary nature of bourgeois class consciousness in Spain. Despite the development of a national bureaucracy in Madrid, government programs foundered because of the lethargy and passive resistance of administrators at lower levels as well as by a rural population that remained wedded to aristocratic ideals. The reform movement could not be sustained without the patronage of Charles III and did not survive him. Reform in general was cast in a suspicious light after the outbreak of the French Revolution and was seen as for-

Charles III was the king of Spain from 1759 to 1788.

Manuel de Godoy, the lover of Queen Maria Louisa and a close "friend" of King Charles IV (1788–1808). He was appointed Spanish premier in 1792. The queen had hoped to have Godoy made king on the death of Charles III, who objected, but she could not overcome the royal line of succession.

eign innovation hostile to Spanish traditions. The chaos of the next generation seemed to traditionalists to prove the point.

Spain joined France in aiding the fledgling United States and declared war on Great Britain in 1779. A two-year siege of Gibraltar failed, and the natural fortress remained in British hands. In the Treaty of Paris (1783), however, Spain recovered Florida, lost in 1763, and Minorca.

Charles IV (1788–1808) retained the trappings of his father's enlightened despotism but was dominated by his wife's favorite, a guards officer, Manuel de Godoy, who at the age of twenty-five was chief minister and virtual dictator of Spain. When in 1792 the French National Assembly demanded Spain's compliance with the family pacts, Godoy rode the popular wave of reaction building in Spain against the French Revolution and joined the coalition against France. Spanish arms suffered repeated setbacks, and in 1796 Godoy shifted allies and joined the French against Great Britain. Promised half of Portugal as his personal reward, Godoy became Napoleon Bonaparte's willing puppet. Louisiana, Spanish since 1763, was restored to France. A regular subsidy was paid to France from the Spanish treasury, and fifteen thousand Spanish troops were assigned to garrisons in northern Europe. Spain lost Trinidad to the British, saw its fleet destroyed at Trafalgar (1805), and failed in another attempt to seize Gibraltar.

With Godoy discredited, Napoleon in 1807 demanded Charles IV's abdication and forced his son and heir, Ferdinand, to renounce his claim to the throne. Joseph Bonaparte, Napoleon's brother, was named king of Spain, and a large French army was moved in to support the new government and to invade Great Britain's ally, Portugal, from Spanish soil. The Bonapartist regime was welcomed by the *afrancesados,* a small but influential group of Spaniards who favored reconstructuring their country on the French model.

In a move to ingratiate himself with the *afrancesados,* Joseph Bonaparte proclaimed the dissolution of religious houses. Defense of the Roman Catholic church, long attacked by successive Spanish governments, now became the test of Spanish patriotism and the cause around which resistance to the French rallied. The War of Independence (1808–14), as the Iberian phase of the Napoleonic wars is known in Spanish historiography, attained the status of a popular crusade that united all classes, parties, and regions in a common struggle. It was a war fought without rules or regular battlelines. The brutality practiced on both sides was made vivid by the Spanish painter Goya.

A British expeditionary force, originally intended to occupy part of Spanish America, was dispatched to the peninsula in 1808, followed the next year by a larger contingent under Arthur Wellesley, later duke of Wellington. Elements of the Spanish army held Cadiz, the

Charles IV reigned from 1788 to 1808. He preferred hunting to ruling.

Queen Maria Louisa, wife of Charles IV, was described by Napoleon: "Maria Louisa has her past and her character written on her face and it surpasses anything you dare imagine." The queen had pronounced masculine features.

Charles IV presiding over his court in 1804

The older brother of Napoleon, Joseph Bonaparte, was made king of Spain under the name of King Jose I and reigned from 1808 to 1814.

Joseph Bonaparte's triumphant entry into Madrid in 1808

only major city not taken by the French, but the countryside belonged to the guerrillas, who held down 250,000 of Napoleon's best troops under Marshal Nicolas Soult while Wellington waited to launch the offensive that was to cause the defeat of the French at Vitoria (1813).

THE LIBERAL ASCENDANCY

A central junta sat in Cadiz. It had little actual authority, except as surrogate for the absent royal government, but it did succeed in calling together representatives from local juntas in 1810, with the vague notion of creating the Cortes of All the Spains, so called because it would be the single legislative body for the empire and its colonies. Many of the overseas provinces had by that time already declared their independence. Some saw the Cortes at Cadiz as an interim government until the Desired One, as Ferdinand VII was called by his supporters, could return to the throne. Many regalists could not admit that a parliamentary body could legislate in the absence of a king. The two parties most in evidence at Cadiz, the Medievalists and the Liberals, favored the continuance of parliamentary government as provided for by a written constitution and the restoration of the monarchy—but for very different reasons. The Medievalists, who

formed the majority in 1810, favored the Cortes, with its medieval origins, as a vehicle for returning Spain to the traditions it had cast away in the previous century. They proposed, in effect, wiping out the eighteenth century and restoring in a constitution the liberties of regional, economic, and social associations that would prevent any one of them or the monarchy from becoming too strong. The restoration of the liberties of the church and the return of its property were other important aspects of the Medievalist program.

The Constitution of 1812 provided for a limited monarchy, a centralized administration, and a parliament to which the government would be responsible. Suffrage was limited by property qualifications favoring constituencies where liberal sentiment was strongest. Individual liberties, the right to the free use of property among them, were guaranteed. By Spanish standards it was a revolutionary document.

Ferdinand VII (reigned 1808, 1814–33) dismissed the Cadiz Cortes when he reassumed the throne, refusing to recognize the constitution drawn up by it. He was determined instead, to rule as an absolute monarch.

Spain's American colonies took advantage of the postwar chaos to proclaim their independence, and most had established republican governments. By 1825 only Cuba and Puerto Rico remained under the Spanish flag in the New World. When Ferdinand was restored to Madrid, he expended wealth and manpower in a vain effort to reassert control over the colonies.

In 1820 Major Rafael del Riego led a revolt among troops quartered in Cadiz while awaiting embarkation to America. Garrison mutinies were not unusual, but Riego issued a *pronunciamento* (declaration of principles) to the troops, which was directed against the government and called for the army to support adoption of the Constitution of 1812. Support for Riego spread from garrison to garrison, toppling the regalist government and forcing Ferdinand to accept the liberal constitution. The pronunciamento, distributed by barracks politicians among underpaid members of an overstaffed officer corps, became a regular feature of Spanish politics.

Ferdinand VII, who reigned in 1808 and then after Joseph Napoleon, from 1814 to 1833, made a most unusual proclamation on March 29, 1830, to the effect that the Salic Law of 1713 instituted by Philip V be abolished. This action reestablished that women had the right to inherit the throne of Spain.

Army support was required for any government to survive and, if a pronunciamento received sufficient backing, the government was well advised to defer to it. This "referendum in blood" was considered within the army to be the purest form of election because the soldiers supporting a pronunciamento were expressing their willingness to shed blood to make their point—at least in theory. In fact it was judged to have succeeded only if the government gave in to it without a fight. If it did not represent a consensus within the army and resistance to it was offered, the pronunciamento was considered a failure, and the officers who had proposed it dutifully went into exile.

The three years of liberal government under the Constitution of 1812, called the Constitutional Triennium (1820–23), were brought to an abrupt close by French invervention ordered by Louis XVIII on an appeal from Ferdinand and with the assent of his conservative officers. The arrival of the French was welcomed in many sectors. Ferdinand was restored as absolute monarch and chose his ministers from the ranks of the old *afrancesados.*

Ferdinand VII, a widower, was childless, and Don Carlos, his popular, traditionalist brother, was heir presumptive. In 1829, however, Ferdinand married his Neapolitan cousin Maria Cristina, who gave birth to a daughter, an event followed closely by the revocation of provisions prohibiting female succession. Ferdinand died in 1833, leaving Maria Cristina as regent for their daughter, Isabella II (1833–68).

Don Carlos contested his niece's succession and won the fanatical support of the traditionalists of Aragon and of Basque Navarre. The Carlists held that legitimate succession was possible only through the male line. Agrarians, regionalists, and Catholics, they also opposed the middle-class, centralist, anticlerical Liberals who flocked to support the regency. The Carlists fielded an army that held off government attempts to suppress them for six years (1833–39), during which time Maria Cristina received aid in arms and volunteers from Great Britain. A Carlist offensive against Madrid in 1837 failed, but in the mountains the Basques continued to resist until a compromise peace in 1839 recognized their ancient *fueros.* Sentiment remained strong in Navarre for Don Carlos and his successors, and the Carlists continued as a political force to be reckoned with. Carlist uprisings occurred in 1847 and from 1872 to 1876.

The regency had come to depend on liberal support within the army during the first Carlist war, but after the end of the war against the traditionalists both the Liberals and the army tired of Maria Cristina. She was forced to resign in 1840, and responsibility for the regency was taken over by a series of Liberal ministries.

The Liberals were a narrowly based elite. Their abstract idealism and concern for individual liberties contrasted sharply with the paternalistic attitudes of Spain's

Queen Isabella II as she appeared on assuming the throne of Spain. She was ruler from 1833 to 1868. She followed the path of her father, Ferdinand, one of pursuing an administrative policy of military despotism and ranged to clerical absolutism. The queen was of loose morals and her children's legitimacy was in doubt. She even had a serious attempt made on her life in 1852 by a priest named Merino. Her life was saved in the stabbing attempt by the whalebones in her corsets. She had the priest "garroted and his body burned."

The marriage procession at the wedding of Isabella II. She married her cousin Francis de Asis.

Queen Maria Christina, the wife of Ferdinand VII, after the king's death turned to England and France, and the Quadruple Alliance of April 22, 1834, to conclude with these states and Portugal that her daughter Isabella II would be the ruler of Spain.

Queen Isabella with her son, Don Alfonso, from a portrait by Winterhalter in the royal palace

rural society. There was no monolithic Liberal movement in Spain, but all factions were unified by their anticlericalism, the touchstone of liberalism. Like the regalists of the previous century, nineteenth-century Liberals held that no one within the state could exercise authority independent of it, and hence no aspect of national life could be excluded from political concern. The state, they assumed, was the sum of the individuals living within it and could recognize and protect only the rights of individuals, not of corporate institutions, such as the church or universities, nor of the regions as separate entities with distinct customs and interests. Because individuals were subject to the law, only individuals could hold title to land. As nothing should impede the development of the individual, so nothing should impede the state in guaranteeing the rights of the individual.

Liberals also agreed on the necessity for a written constitution, a parliamentary government, and a centralized administration, as well as the need for laissez-faire economics. All factions found a voice in the army and drew leadership from its ranks. All had confidence that progress would follow naturally from the application of Liberal principles. They differed, however, on the methods to be used in applying them.

The Moderates saw economic development within a free market as the cure for political revolution. They argued for a strong constitution that would spell out guaranteed liberties. The Progressives, like the Moderates, were members of the upper and middle classes, but they drew support from the urban masses and favored creation of a more broadly based electorate. They argued that greater participation in the political process would ensure economic development and an equitable distribution of its fruits. Both factions were constitutional monarchists. The more radical Democrats, however, countered that political freedom and economic liberalism could only be achieved in a republic.

The Moderates, who dominated the new regency in coalition with supporters of Isabella's succession, were backed by the army and assured parliamentary majorities by caciques, local political leaders who regularly

The queen Isabella in later life. She was expelled to France in 1868 and died in 1904.

Amadeo, the duke of Aosta, second son of Italy's Vittorio Emanuele II, was offered the throne of Spain and after accepting was given a tumultuous welcome when he arrived in Madrid.

Marshal Juan Prim rallied the patriots against the reactionary party and the queen. This effort by the Spanish Liberals resulted in the dethronement and flight of Isabella and her family in 1868. Prim led a successful revolution but fell victim to assassins in 1874.

delivered the vote for government candidates in return for patronage. The Progressives courted the Democrats enough to be assured of regular inclusion in the government. Relations with the church remained the most sensitive issue confronting the government and the most divisive issue throughout the country. Despite their anticlericalism, the Moderates concluded a rapprochement with the church, which agreed to surrender its claim to confiscated property in return for official recognition by the state and a role in education. They looked in vain, however, to reconciliation with the church as a means of winning conservative rural support.

In 1868 Don Juan Prim, an army hero and popular Progressive leader, was brought to power by an army revolt led by exiled officers determined to force Isabella from the throne. Her abdication inaugurated a period of experimentation with a liberal monarchy, a federal republic, and finally a military dictatorship.

As prime minister, Prim canvassed Europe for a ruler to replace Isabella. A tentative offer made to a Hohenzollern prince was sufficient spark to set off the Franco-Prussian war (1870–71). Prim found a likely royal candidate in Amadeo of Savoy, son of Victor Emmanuel II, king of Italy. Prim was assassinated shortly after Amadeo's arrival in Spain, leaving the new king without

Amadeo (Amadeus) I, king of Spain, 1871 to 1873, followed Isabella II to the throne. (There was a provisional government from 1868 to 1871.) A serious attempt on his life was made in 1872, and he abdicated in 1873. He lived until 1890.

King Alfonso XII was proclaimed king of Spain on December 29, 1874, by General Martinez Campos, the top military leader, who was an adherent of the overturned Bourbon Dynasty. At the time, Alfonso was living in Paris with his mother, the ex-queen Isabella II. Alfonso XII arrived in Madrid on January 14, 1875, at the head of the government troops, and although not yet eighteen years of age, he took over the reins of government.

a mentor and at the mercy of hostile politicians. The constitution bequeathed to the new monarchy did not leave Amadeo sufficient powers to supervise the formation of a stable government and, mistrustful of Prim's foreign prince, factional leaders refused to cooperate with or advise him. Deserted finally by the army, Amadeo abdicated, leaving a rump parliament to proclaim Spain a federal republic.

The constitution of the First Republic (1873–74) provided for internally self-governing provinces bound to the federal government by voluntary agreement. Jurisdiction over foreign and colonial affairs and defense was reserved for Madrid. The federal Republic had four presidents in its eight-month lifespan, none of whom could find a prime minister to form a stable cabinet. The government could not decentralize quickly enough to satisfy local radicals. Cities and provinces made unilateral declarations of autonomy in imitation of the Paris Commune. Madrid lost control of the country, and once again the army stepped in to rescue the "national honor." A national government taking the form of a unitary republic briefly served as the transparent disguise for an interim military dictatorship.

THE CONSTITUTIONAL MONARCHY

It required no more than a brigadier's pronunciamento to restore the Bourbon monarchy, calling Isabella's son, the able, British-educated Alfonso XII to the throne (1874–86). Alfonso identified himself as "Spaniard, Catholic, and Liberal," and his succession was greeted with a degree of relief even by supporters of the Republic. He cultivated good relations with the army (Alfonso was a cadet at Sandhurst when summoned to Spain), which removed itself from politics, content that a stable, popular civilian government was being provided. Alfonso insisted that the church be confirmed constitutionally in its official status, thus assuring the restored monarchy of conservative support.

Alfonso XII brought the unrest of Spain to an end by 1876. He married twice. His first wife was his cousin, Marie de las Mercedes, daughter of the Duke de Montpensier; and his second wife, Maria Christina, archduchess of Austria, was the mother of Alfonso XIII.

Alfonso XII in the robes of the Order of the Golden Fleece

Queen Regent Maria Christina (1886–1902) and Alfonso XIII

King Alfonso XIII and his queen visit the royal family in Belgium. Standing, left to right: Prince Leopold and King Albert of Belgium, and King Alfonso. Seated, left to right: the queens of Spain and Belgium.

Queen Maria Christina

The royal palace in Madrid where the queen lived with the young king Alfonso XIII

The birth of Alfonso XIII is announced to the awaiting statesmen. His father having died in 1885, Alfonso XIII became king at birth.

King Alfonso XIII in his first royal military uniform

The young king Alfonso XIII horseback riding—his favorite sport

In its political provisions the new constitution was consciously modeled on British practices. The new government used electoral manipulation to construct and maintain a two-party system in parliament, but the result was more a parody than an imitation. Conservatives and Liberals exchanged control of government at regular intervals after general elections. Once again the elections were controlled at the constituency level by caciques who delivered the vote to one party or the other as directed in return for the assurance of patronage from whichever was scheduled to win. Considering Spain's turbulent political history through the first three-quarters of the century, it was a remarkable example of compromise and restraint.

Alfonso XIII (1886–1931) was the posthumous son of Alfonso XII. His mother, another Maria Cristina, acted as regent until her son came officially of age in 1902. (Alfonso XIII abdicated in 1931.)

Emigration to Cuba from Spain was heavy in the nineteenth century, and the Cuban middle class, among whom ties to the mother country were strong, favored keeping Cuba Spanish. Cuba had experienced periodic uprisings by independence movements since 1868. Successive governments in Madrid were committed to maintaining whatever armed forces were necessary to combat insurgency. Hostilities were renewed in 1895, supported clandestinely from the United States, and required Spain's sending substantial reinforcements under General Valerio Weyler. Public opinion in the United States was stirred by reports of his suppression of the independence movement, and the mysterious explosion of the battleship U.S.S. *Maine* in Havana harbor led to a declaration of war by the United States in April 1898. Antiquated Spanish naval units were destroyed at Santiago de Cuba and in Manila Bay. Despite a pledge by Madrid to defend Cuba "to the last peseta," the Spanish army surrendered after a few weeks of hostilities against an American expeditionary force. At Paris in September Spain gave up Cuba, Puerto Rico, and the Philippines.

The suddenness and the totality of Spain's defeat and the realization of its lack of support during the war with the United States (only Germany had offered diplomatic backing) threw the country into despair.

The traumatic events of 1898 and the inability of the government to deal with them prompted political reevaluation. Solutions were sought by a plethora of new personalist parties, most of them short-lived, and by regional groupings on both the left and the right that broke the hegemony of the two-party system and ultimately left the parliamentary structure in disarray. By 1915 it was virtually impossible to form a coalition government that could command the support of a parliamentary majority.

Spain was neutral in World War I, but the Spanish army was constantly engaged from 1909 to 1926 against Abd al-Krim's Riff Berbers in Morocco, where Spain

The coronation of King Alfonso XIII

Alfonso XIII with his queen riding in a carriage in spite of the many threats of assassination plots to kill him during this exposure to all elements of the public. Note the miniature royal crown on the queen's head.

King Alfonso XIII as he appeared later in life

Queen Victoria Eugenia, the consort of King Alfonso XIII, was the grandmother of King Juan Carlos I.

An early picture of Don Juan, the third son of King Alfonso XIII. In 1969, when Franco designated Juan Carlos as his successor, the senior pretender, Don Juan, had not yet given up his claim to the throne.

had joined France in proclaiming a protectorate. Successive civilian governments in Spain allowed the war to continue but refused to supply the army with the means to win it. Spanish losses were heavy to an enemy that was fierce, skillful, and equipped with superior weapons. Riots against conscription for the African war spread disorder throughout the country, and opposition to the war was often expressed in church burning. Officers, who often had served in Morocco, formed juntas to register complaints that were just short of pronunciamentos against wartime inflation, low-fixed salaries for the military, alleged civilian corruption, and inadequate and scarce equipment.

Conditions in Morocco, increased anarchist and Communist terrorism, industrial unrest, and the effects of the postwar economic slump prompted the pronunciamento that brought a general officer, Miguel Primo de Rivera, to power in 1923. His authoritarian regime originally enjoyed wide support in much of the country, and he had the confidence of the king and the loyalty of the army, but the regime was without an ideological foundation. Its mandate was based on the general disillusionment with the parliamentary government and the divisiveness caused by partisan party politics.

Primo de Rivera's government sponsored public works to curb unemployment. Protectionism and state control of the economy led to a temporary economic recovery. A better led and better supplied army brought the African war to a successful conclusion in 1926.

The precipitous economic decline in 1930 undercut support for the government from special-interest groups. For seven years Primo de Rivera had remained a man on horseback. He had established no new system of government to replace parliamentary government. Criticism from academics mounted. Bankers expressed disappointment at the state loans that his government had tried to float. An attempt to reform the promotion system cost him the support of the army—which, in turn, lost him the support of the king. Primo de Rivera resigned and died shortly after in exile.

REPUBLICAN SPAIN

Antimonarchist parties won a substantial vote in the 1931 municipal elections. Alfonso XIII interpreted the elections and the riots that had acclaimed their results as an indication of imminent civil war, and he left the country with his family, appealing to the army for support in upholding the monarchy. When General José Sanjurjo, army chief of staff, replied that the armed forces would not support the king against the will of the people, Alfonso abdicated.

A multiparty coalition in which regional parties held the balance met at a constitutional convention at San Sebastian, the summer capital, to proclaim the Second Republic. The convention set as the goals of the new Republic to reform the army, to grant regional autonomy, to carry through social reform and economic redistribution, to separate church and state, and to deprive the church of a role in education. Niceto Alcalá Zamora, a nonparty conservative, was named president and called elections for June.

The first general election of the Second Republic gave a majority to a coalition of Left Republicans, middle-class Radicals led by Manuel Azaña, who became prime minister, and labor leader Francisco Largo Caballero's Socialists, backed by the UGT. Azaña's government was pledged to the gradual introduction of socialism through the democratic process. His gradualism alienated the political left; his socialism, the right.

Azaña's greatest difficulties derived from doctrinal differences within the government between his non-Marxist, bourgeois Republicans and the Socialists, who after an initial period of cooperation obstructed Azaña at every step. Attempts at labor legislation were blocked by opposition from the UGT. The Socialists complained that Azaña's reforms were inadequate to produce meaningful social changes, though there was no parliamentary majority that would have approved Largo Caballero's proposals. If Azaña's legislative program did not satisfy his ally, it did rally moderate and conservative opinion against the coalition on the eve of the second general election in November 1932.

Azaña's principal parliamentary opposition came from the two largest parties that could claim a national constituency, Lerroux's moderate, middle-class Radical Republicans and the right-wing Catholic organization, the Spanish Confederation of the Autonomous Right (Confederación Española de Derechas Autonómas— CEDA). Lerroux, who had grown more conservative and tolerant than in his days as an antimonarchist firebrand, capitalized on the left's failure to reach a compromise with the church or to deal with industrial unrest and the extragovernmental power of the UGT and CNT. President Zamora was hostile to CEDA and urged Lerroux to head a minority government, which he did for more than a year before entering into a parliamentary alliance with CEDA. The center-right coalition was not welcomed by Lerroux, but it was the only means by which a parliamentary majority that included his party could be obtained. Gil Robles was appointed minister for war, with a role in maintaining public order, in the new government.

The unions used the strike as a political weapon much as the army used the pronunciamento. Industrial disorder climaxed in the miners' strike in Asturias, which Azaña openly and actively supported. The miners were crushed by the police and army commanded by Francisco Franco. The strike confirmed to the right that the left could not be trusted to abide by constitutional processes, and the suppression of the strike proved to the left that the right was "Fascist." Azaña accused Gil Robles of using Republican institutions to destroy the Republic.

The Lerroux-Gil Robles government had as its first priority the restoration of order, although its existence was the chief excuse for the disorder. Action on labor's legitimate grievances was postponed until order was restored. The most controversial of Gil Robles' programs, however, was finding the means to effect a reconciliation with the church. Within the context of the coalition with Lerroux, he also attempted to expand his political base by courting the support of anti-Republican elements. The government resigned in November 1935 over a minor issue. Zamora refused to sanction the formation of a new government by CEDA, without whose cooperation no moderate government could be put together. On the advice of the left, Zamora called a new general election for February.

In polarizing public opinion the Asturian miners' strike had consolidated the parties on the left from Azaña's Republicans to the Communist Party of Spain (Partido Comunista de España). The Socialists had been increasingly "bolshevized," and it was difficult for a Social Democrat such as Largo Caballero to control his party in its leftward drift. In 1935 Stalin had sanctioned Communist participation in popular front governments with bourgeois and Democratic Socialist parties. The success of Léon Blum, the French Socialist leader, in bringing the Popular Front to power in France had conferred respectability on the project. The Left Republicans, the Socialists, the Catalan Left (Esquerra Catalana), the Communists, a number of smaller regional and left-wing parties, and the Anarchists, who had boycotted previous elections as a matter of principle, joined to present a single leftist slate to the electorate.

In contrast to Blum's experiment in France, however, the Spanish Popular Front was to be an electoral coalition only. Its goal was not to form a government but to defeat the right. Largo Caballero made it clear that the Socialists would not cooperate in any government that did not adopt their program for nationalization, a policy as much guaranteed to break Spain in two and provoke

a civil war as the appointment of the CEDA-dominated government that Zamora had worked to prevent.

The general election produced a number of irregularities that led the left, right, and center to claim voting fraud on a massive scale. Two subsequent runoff votes, recounts, and an electoral commission controlled by the left provided the Popular Front with an impressive number of parliamentary seats. Azaña formed his minority government, but the front's victory was taken as the signal for the start of the left's long-awaited revolution, already anticipated by street riots, church burnings, and strikes. Parallel governments were set up by workers' councils, which undertook to circumvent the slow-grinding wheels of the constitutional process. Zamora was removed from office on the grounds that he had gone beyond his constitutional authority in calling the general election. Azaña was named to replace him, depriving the Left Republicans of his strong leadership.

THE SPANISH CIVIL WAR

Gil Robles' influence waned as a spokesman for the right in the new parliament. CEDA's role was assumed by the National Block, a smaller coalition of monarchists and Fascists led by José Calvo Sotelo, who had sought the army's cooperation in restoring Alfonso XIII. Calvo Sotelo, who had been eloquent in opposition in the opening sessions of the new parliament, was murdered in July 1936, supposedly in retaliation for the killing of a police officer by Fascists. Calvo Sotelo's death was a signal to the army to act, on the pretext that the civilian government had allowed the country to fall into disorder, which on the face of it was true. A pronunciamento was issued. A coup was expected, however, and revolts by army garrisons in Madrid and Barcelona were beaten down by the urban police and workers' militia loyal to the government. Navy crews spontaneously purged their ships of officers. The eleventh-hour efforts of Indalecio Prieto, who had succeeded Azaña as prime minister, to arrive at a compromise were rejected both by the army and by the left.

The army was most successful in the north. Old Castile, Leon, and the Carlist strongholds in Navarre and Aragon rallied to the army. In Morocco elite units seized control under Franco, Spain's youngest general and a hero of the Riff campaigns, where he had commanded the Foreign Legion. Franco's African army, including Moorish auxiliaries, were ferried to Andalusia on transport supplied by Germany and Italy. Franco occupied the major cities in the south before turning toward Madrid to link up with Mola, who was advancing from Burgos. The relief of the army garrison besieged in the Alcazar at Toledo, however, delayed the attack on Madrid and allowed time for a preparation of the defense of the capital. Army units penetrated the city limits but

The dictator, Francisco Franco

were driven back on the grounds of the University of Madrid.

A junta of generals, Franco included, formed a government at Burgos that was immediately recognized by Germany and Italy. Sanjurjo, who had been expected to lead the army movement, was killed in a plane crash during the first days of the uprising. In October 1936 Franco was named head of state, with the rank of generalissimo and the title *el caudillo* (the leader).

Franco, who did not have a reputation as a political soldier, had opposed Sanjurjo in 1932, but Azaña had considered him unreliable and made him captain general of the Canaries, virtual exile for an ambitious officer. Though by nature a conservative, Franco was not wedded to any political creed. He set about reconciling all right-wing, anti-Republican groups in one Nationalist organization. The catalyst was provided by the Falange, a Fascist party founded by José Antonio Primo de Rivera, the dictator's son. The Carlists, revived after 1931, merged with the Falange in 1937, but the association was never harmonious. José Antonio's execution by the Republicans provided the Falange with a martyr. The more radical of the early Falange programs were pushed aside, and the syndicalism adopted by the Nationalists was only a shadow of what José Antonio had intended, but the Nationalist organization kept its Fascist facade. Franco's strength, however, lay in the army.

Nationalist strategy called for separating Madrid from Catalonia, which was firmly Republican, and from Valencia and Murcia, which the Republic also controlled. The Republicans stabilized the front around Madrid, defending it against the Nationalists for three years. Isolated Asturias and Vizcaya, where the newly organized Basque Republic fought to defend its autonomy without assistance from Madrid, fell to Franco in October 1937. Otherwise the battlelines were static until July 1938, when Nationalist forces broke through to the Mediterranean Sea south of Barcelona. Throughout the civil war the industrial areas, Asturias and the Basque provinces excepted, remained in Republican hands while the chief food-producing areas were under Nationalist control.

The Republic lacked a regular trained army, though a number of armed forces cadres had remained loyal, especially in the air force and navy. Many officers who were loyal were either purged or not trusted to hold command positions. The brunt of the fighting in the early months of the civil war was borne by the workers' militia and independently organized armed political units like those of the Trotskyite Workers' Party of Marxist Unification (Partido Obrero de Unificación Marxista— POUM), described by George Orwell in *Homage to Catalonia.* The army garrison in Barcelona, for instance, had been crushed by the anarchist UGT militia and the Assault Guards, the urban police corps established by the Republic to counterbalance the Civil Guard (Guardia Civil), the paramilitary rural police, generally considered reactionary. Advisers, logistics experts, and some field-grade officers were provided by Moscow. Foreign volunteers, including more than two thousand from the United States, formed the International Brigade. The Communists pressed for and won approval for the creation of a national, conscript Republican army.

Nationalist strength was based on the regular army, which included large contingents of Moroccan troops and the battalions of the Foreign Legion, which Franco had commanded in Africa. The Carlists, who had always maintained a clandestine military organization *(requetés)* and some of whom had received training in Italy, were among Franco's most effective troops and were employed with the Moroccans as a shock corps. More than fifty thousand Italian "volunteers," most of them army conscripts, were dispatched to Spain by Mussolini, along with air and naval units. The German Condor Legion, made infamous by the bombing of Guernica, provided air support for the Nationalists and tested the tactics and equipment used a few years later by the Luftwaffe.

A nonintervention commission, including representatives from France, Great Britain, Germany, and Italy, was established at the Lyon Conference in 1936 to stem the flow of supplies to both sides. France and Great Britain were concerned that escalating foreign intervention not turn Spain's civil war into a European war.

Largo Caballero, who became prime minister in September 1936, had the support of the Socialists and of the Communists, who were becoming the most important political factor in the Republican government. The Communists, after successfully arguing for a national conscript army that could be directed by the government, pressed for elimination of the militia units. They also argued for postponing the revolution until the Fascists had been defeated and encouraged greater participation by the bourgeois parties in the Popular Front. The UGT, increasingly under Communist influence, was brought into the government, and the more militant elements within it were purged. POUM, which had resisted disbanding its independent military units and merging with the Communist-controlled national army, was ruthlessly suppressed as the Communists undertook to eliminate competing leftist organizations. Anarchists were dealt with in similar fashion, and in Catalonia a civil war was fought within a civil war.

Fearing the growth of Soviet influence in Spain, Largo Caballero attempted to negotiate a compromise that would end the civil war. He was removed from office and replaced by Juan Negrin López, a pro-Communist Socialist with little previous political experience.

The Republican army, its attention diverted by internal political battles, brave but often poorly led, was never able to mount a sustained counteroffensive or to exploit a breakthrough such as that on the Ebro in 1938. Negrin López realized that the war could not be won by Spaniards in Spain, but he hoped to prolong the fighting until the outbreak of a European war, which he thought imminent.

Barcelona fell to the Nationalists in January 1939, and Valencia, the temporary capital, in March. When factional fighting broke out in Madrid among its defenders, the Republican army commander seized control of what remained of the government and surrendered to the Nationalists on the last day of March, thus ending the civil

FRANCO'S SPAIN

Although Franco made no secret of his Axis sympathies in the early years of World War II and was a signatory of the Anti-Comintern Pact, he kept Spain neutral. Hitler attempted to encourage more active cooperation from Franco at their one meeting at Hendaye on the French border in 1941, but Franco was determined to make no commitments.

Juan Carlos was always a very popular person with the Spanish people. He is seen here arriving in Madrid in 1955 for a royalist demonstration.

Franco prepared for the likelihood of postwar criticism of his regime by reinstituting the Cortes in 1943, though not as an elected legislature, and by providing a constitution in 1945.

Stalin proposed an attack against Spain, the last Fascist stronghold, after Germany's defeat, but his suggestions were rejected by Winston Churchill and Franklin D. Roosevelt. At the conclusion of World War II the United Nations bound its members to observe diplomatic and economic sanctions against Spain, and for several years Spain was ostracized by the world community.

The United States resumed the exchange of ambassadors with Madrid in 1951, and an agreement calling for the establishment of American air and naval bases in Spain was concluded in 1953. Efforts to include Spain in the North Atlantic Treaty Organization (NATO) were vetoed by the Western European members, whose official attitudes toward Spain remain cool.

THE MONARCHY RETURNS

Spain was proclaimed a monarchy without a king in 1957. Don Juan de Borbón y Battenberg, the heir of

Juan Carlos Víctor María de Borbón y Borbón was born at 1:05 P.M. on January 5, 1938, at the Anglo-American Hospital in Rome. He was the first son of Don Juan de Borbón y Battenberg and Doña María de las Mercedes de Borbón y Orleans, and consequently the grandson of King Alfonso XIII and Queen Victoria Eugenie—the granddaughter of Queen Victoria of England—on his father's side, and of the Infante Don Carlos de Borbón and the Infanta Dona Luisa de Orleans on his mother's side.

The two dynastic branches that had been separate since the death of Ferdinand VII have come together once more in his person, "through the design of Providence," as Juan Carlos himself was to proclaim on July 23, 1969, at the ceremony of his oath-taking as successor to the office of head of state as king.

A few hours after his birth, he was baptized in the church of the Master's Palace of the Sovereign Military Order of Malta, by the then secretary of state of the Vatican, Cardinal Eugenio Pacelli, who a year later was to become pope under the name of Pius XII.

Finally, by virtue of the Law of Succession dated July 26, 1947, Prince Juan Carlos de Borbón y Borbón was designated successor as king on July 22, 1969, with a view to his ascending the throne in due course. This actually took place on November 22, 1975.

Alfonso XIII, was considered too liberal and was removed from the line of succession, but in 1969 his son, Don Juan Carlos de Borbón y Borbón, groomed by Franco to assume the monarchy, was named to succeed to the throne. Prince Juan Carlos, upon being named heir to the throne, swore to uphold the principles of the National movement, Franco's umbrella political organization. Franco had taken an active interest in the prince's education, making certain that Juan Carlos attended the three military academies—army, navy, and air force—as well as the University of Madrid. After formal schooling the prince was assigned at various times to positions in the different ministries in order to learn government operation firsthand.

Admiral Luis Carrero Blanco, a longtime confidant of Franco's, replaced the aging dictator as head of government in 1973 and was considered to be Franco's handpicked political successor. Carrero Blanco was assassinated in 1974 by Basque terrorists. In the cabinet reshuffle that followed the appointment of his successor, former security chief Carlos Arias Navarro, Opus Dei ministers were dropped. During Franco's illness in the summer of 1974 and the fall of 1975, Prince Juan Carlos assumed temporarily the duties of the head of state. Franco died November 20, 1975, and Prince Juan Carlos became the king of Spain, returning the monarchy to control of the country.

In May 1962 Prince Juan Carlos married Princess Sophia of Greece. In this photograph of the ceremony King Paul of Greece (1947–64), the father of the bride, appears to the left, and behind Sophia is her brother Constantine, who became the king of Greece (1964–73).

King Juan Carlos I is commemorated on many stamps in his country and its possessions.

On September 13, 1961, Juan Carlos's engagement to Princess Sophia, the daughter of King Paul I and Queen Fredericka of Greece was announced. She was born on November 2, 1938, in Athens, and in her family tree there are two German emperors, eight kings of Denmark, five kings of Sweden, seven czars of Russia, one king and one queen of Norway, one queen of England, and five kings of Greece.

The wedding took place in Athens on May 14, 1962. The marriage, for which the Latin Catholic rite was used, took place at the Catholic church of Saint Dionysius, and was followed by an Orthodox ceremony at the Metropolitan Church for civil purposes. More than a half-million people cheered the bride and groom through the streets of the Greek capital. The marriage ceremony was attended by 137 kings and princesses from different countries.

Up to the present time, the king and queen of Spain have had three children:

The Infanta Doña Elena. She was born on December 20, 1963, at the Nuestra Señora de Loreto Hospital in Madrid. The christening took place at the Zarzuela Palace on December 27. The godparents were the countess of Barcelona and the Infante Don Alfonso of Orleans.

The Infanta Doña Cristina. She was born at the same hospital as her sister, on June 13, 1965, and was also christened at the Zarzuela Palace, on June 21. Her godparents were the Infanta Maria Cristina, countess of Marone; and Don Alfonso de Borbón Dampierre.

The Infante Don Felipe. He was born on January 30, 1968, at the same hospital as his sisters. The king and queen's first son, Felipe Juan Pablo Alfonso de Todos los Santos Borbón Schleswig-Holstein Bourbon Sonderburg-Glücksburg, is the rightful heir to all his father's titles of nobility and will eventually succeed him as head of state and king. At his christening, which took place on February 8, his godparents were Don Juan de Borbón, count of Barcelona; and Queen Victoria Eugenia, who, after thirty-one years' absence, had set foot on Spanish soil once more for this purpose.

A stamp honoring the crown prince Felipe (Philip) and future king of Spain

In 1976, the king and queen visited the United Nations headquarters in New York City. Left to right: Mrs. Kurt Waldheim, King Juan Carlos, Secretary-General Waldheim, and Queen Sophia.

Spain in its geographic setting today

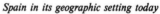

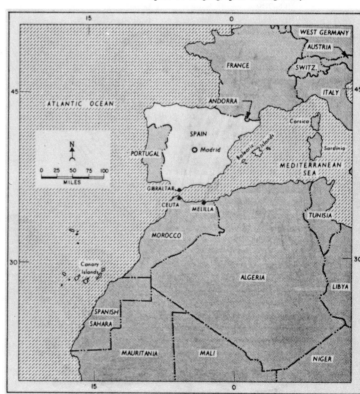

Recent rulers of Spain commemorated in a special series of stamps. Left, top to bottom: *Philip V (1701–24), Charles IV (1788–1808), and Alfonso XII (1874–86).* Center, top to bottom: *Luis I (1724), Ferdinand VI (1746–59), Ferdinand VII (1808), and Alfonso XIII (1886–1931). And* right, top to bottom: *Charles III (1759–88), Isabella II (1833–68), and Juan Carlos I (1975–   ).*

THE ROYAL SOVEREIGNS OF THE KINGDOMS OF SPAIN

Reign	Title	Ruler	Birth	Death	Relationship

206 B.C.–A.D. 411—Under control of Romans
411—Spain conquered by Visigoths

VISIGOTHIC RULE

Reign	Title	Ruler	Birth	Death	Relationship
412–415	King	Ataulphus (Atauf) (Ataulfo)		415	
415–417	King	Wallia		417	
417–451	King	Theodoric		451	
451–456	King	Theodoric II		456	
466–484	King	Euric (Eurico)		484	
484–507	King	Alaric (Alarico)		507	
508–531	King	Amalaric (Amalarico)		531	
531–554	King	Theudes		554	
554–567	King	Athanagild (Athanagildo)		567	
567–571	King	Theodomir		571	
571–572	King	Leuva		572	
572–586	King	Leuvigild (Leovigildo)		586	
586–601	King	Recared (Recaredo) (Reccaredo)		601	
601–612	King	Sisebut (Sisebert)		612	
612–621	King	Recared II (Recaredo) (Reccaredo)		621	
621–631	King	Swintilla (Suintila)		631	
631–640	King	Sisenando		640	
640–642	King	Tulga		642	
642–653	King	Chindaswind (Cindasuinto)		653	
653–672	King	Recceswinth (Recesuinto)		672	
672–680	King	Wamba		680	
680–687	King	Euric (Ervigius)		687	
687–702	King	Ergica		702	
702–709	King	Witiza		709	
709–711	King	Roderic (Rodrigo)		711	

MOORISH AMIRATE

Reign	Title	Ruler	Birth	Death	Relationship
711–714	Amir	Tarik and Musa			
714–717	Amir	Abdelaziz		717	
718–719	Amir	Alhor		719	
730–732	Amir	Abderraman of Gafeki		732	

AMIRS OF CORDOVA

Reign	Title	Ruler	Birth	Death	Relationship
756–788	Amir	Abder Rahman I	731	788	
788–799	Amir	Hisham I	742	799	Son of Abder Rahman I
799–822	Amir	Hakam I	760	822	Son of Hisham I
822–852	Amir	Abder Rahman II	788	852	Son of Hakam I
852–886	Amir	Mohammed I	816	886	Son of Abder Rahman II
886–888	Amir	Mondhir	844	888	Son of Mohammed I
888–912	Amir	Abdallah	868	912	Son of Mondhir

CALIPHS OF CORDOVA

Reign	Title	Ruler	Birth	Death	Relationship
912–961	Caliph	Abder Rahman III (Abderraman)	891	961	Grandson of Abdallah
961–976	Caliph	Hakam II (Alhaken)	913	976	Son of Abder Rahman III
976–1008	Caliph	Hisham II (Hixen)	975	1016	Son of Hakam II
1008–1008	Caliph	Mohammed II	976	1008	
1009–1009	Caliph	Suleyman	980	1017	
1010–1012	Caliph	Hisham II (rethroned)		1016	
1012–1017	Caliph	Suleyman (rethroned)	980	1017	
1017–1021	Caliph	Ali bin Hamoud		1021	
1021–1022	Caliph	Abder Rahman IV		1022	
1022–1022	Caliph	Alcasim		1022	
1022–1023	Caliph	Abder Rahman V		1023	
1023–1024	Caliph	Mohammed III		1024	
1024–1027	Caliph	Yahya bin Ali		1027	
1027–1031	Caliph	Hisham III		1031	

Reign	Title	Ruler	Birth	Death	Relationship

SULTANS OF ALMORAVIDE

Reign	Title	Ruler	Birth	Death	Relationship
1067–1107	Sultan	Yousouf bin Teshonfin		1107	
1107–1144	Sultan	Ali bin Yousouf		1144	
1144–1147	Sultan	Teshoufin bin Ali		1147	

SULTANS OF ALMOHADE

Reign	Title	Ruler	Birth	Death	Relationship
1147–1163	Sultan	Abd el-Moulmin		1163	
1163–1178	Sultan	Yousouf abou Yacoub		1178	
1178–1199	Sultan	Yacoub bin Yousouf		1199	
1199–1213	Sultan	Mohammed bin Yacoub		1213	
1213–1223	Sultan	Abou Yacoub		1223	
1223–1225	Sultan	Abou Malik		1225	
1225–1238	Sultan	Mamoun		1238	

KINGS OF GRANADA

Reign	Title	Ruler	Birth	Death	Relationship
1238–1273	King	Mahommed I			
1273–1303	King	Mahommed II			
1303–1309	King	Mahommed III			
1309–1312	King	Nazar			
1312–1325	King	Ismail I			
1325–1333	King	Mahommed IV			
1333–1354	King	Youcef I			
1354–1359	King	Mahommed V			
1359–1361	King	Ismail II			
1361–1361	King	Abou-Said			
1361–1391	King	Mahommed V (rethroned)			
1391–1396	King	Youcef II			
1396–1408	King	Mahommed VI			
1408–1425	King	Youcef III			
1425–1427	King	Mahommed VII			
1427–1427	King	Mahommed VIII			
1427–1431	King	Mahommed VII (rethroned)			
1431–1431	King	Ebn Alhamar			
1432–1445	King	Mahommed VII (rethroned)			
1445–1454	King	Ebn Ostman			
1454–1456	King	Ebn Ismail			
1456–1482	King	Moulay Hacen			
1482–1492	King	Abou Abdilehi (Boabdil)			

CHRISTIAN KINGS

KINGS OF ASTURIAS

Reign	Title	Ruler	Birth	Death	Relationship
718–737	King	Pelayo			
737–739	King	Favila			
739–757	King	Alfonso I, the Catholic			
757–768	King	Fruela I			
768–774	King	Aurelio (Aurelius)			
774–783	King	Silo			
783–788	King	Mauregato the Usurper			
788–791	King	Bermudo I, the Deacon (Veremund)			
791–842	King	Alfonso II, the Chaste		842	
842–850	King	Ramiro I		850	Son of Bermudo I
850–866	King	Ordono I		866	Son of Ramiro I
866–910	King	Alfonso III, the Great	848	912	

KINGS OF LEÓN

Reign	Title	Ruler	Birth	Death	Relationship
910–914	King	Garcia		914	
914–924	King	Ordono II		924	Son of Alfonso III
924–925	King	Fruela II		925	

Reign	Title	Ruler	Birth	Death	Relationship
925–930	King	Alfonso IV, the Monk		930	
930–950	King	Ramiro II		950	
950–956	King	Ordono III		956	Son of Ramiro II
956–967	King	Sancho I, the Fat		967	Brother of Ordono III
967–982	King	Ramiro III		982	Son of Sancho I
982–999	King	Bermudo II		999	Son of Ordono III
999–1027	King	Alfonso V, the Noble		1027	
1027–1037	King	Bermundo III		1037	

KINGS OF LEÓN AND CASTILE

Reign	Title	Ruler	Birth	Death	Relationship
1037–1065	King	Ferdinand I, the Great		1065	Son of Sancho III of Castile
1065–1072	King	Sancho II		1072	Son of Ferdinand I
1072–1109	King	Alfonso VI	1030	1109	Son of Sancho II
1109–1126	Queen	Urraca	1081	1126	Daughter of Alfonso VI
1126–1157	King	Alfonso VII, the Emperor	1106	1157	Son of Urraca

KINGS OF LEÓN

Reign	Title	Ruler	Birth	Death	Relationship
1157–1188	King	Ferdinand II		1188	Son of Alfonso VII
1188–1230	King	Alfonso IX		1230	Son of Ferdinand II

KINGS OF CASTILE

Reign	Title	Ruler	Birth	Death	Relationship
1157–1158	King	Sancho III		1158	Son of Alfonso VII
1158–1214	King	Alfonso VIII	1155	1214	Son of Sancho III
1214–1217	King	Henry I	1202	1217	Son of Alfonso VIII
1217–1217	Queen	Berangaria			Mother of Ferdinand III
1217–1252	King	Ferdinand III, the Saint	1199	1252	Son of Alfonso IX of León
1252–1284	King	Alfonso X, the Wise	1225	1284	Son of Ferdinand III
1284–1295	King	Sancho IV	1258	1295	Son of Alfonso X
1295–1312	King	Ferdinand IV	1285	1312	Son of Sancho IV
1312–1350	King	Alfonso XI	1310	1350	Son of Ferdinand IV
1350–1369	King	Pedro I, the Cruel	1334	1369	Son of Alfonso XI
1369–1379	King	Henry II	1333	1379	Brother of Pedro I
1379–1390	King	John I	1358	1390	Son of Henry II
1390–1406	King	Henry III	1379	1406	Son of John I
1406–1454	King	John II	1405	1454	Son of Henry III
1454–1474	King	Henry IV	1425	1474	Son of John II

KINGS OF NAVARRE

Reign	Title	Ruler	Birth	Death	Relationship
840–851	King	Inigo Arista			
905–925	King	Sancho Garces			
925–970	King	Garcia Sanchez I			
970–994	King	Sancho Abarca			
994–1000	King	Garcia Sanchez II			
1000–1035	King	Sancho the Great			
1035–1054	King	Garcia Sanchez III		1054	
1076–1094	King	Sancho III Ramirez (Sancho I of Aragon)		1094	
1134–1150	King	Garcia Ramirez IV		1150	
1150–1194	King	Sancho V, the Wise		1194	
1194–1234	King	Sancho VI, the Strong		1234	
1234–1253	King	Teobaldo I		1253	
1253–1270	King	Teobaldo II		1270	
1270–1274	King	Henry I		1274	
1274–1305	Queen	Juana I		1305	
1305–1316	King	Luis Hutfn		1316	
1316–1322	King	Philip		1322	
1322–1328	King	Charles I		1328	
1328–1349	Queen	Juana II		1349	
1349–1387	King	Charles II, the Bad		1387	
1387–1425	King	Charles III, the Noble		1425	
1425–1479	Queen King	Blanca and Don John			
1479–1479	Queen	Leonor		1479	
1479–1481	King	Francisco Febo		1481	
1481–1512	Queen	Catalina (and Don John of Aragon)			

1512—Joined with Castile and Aragon

Reign	Title	Ruler	Birth	Death	Relationship

KINGS OF ARAGON

Reign	Title	Ruler	Birth	Death	Relationship
1035–1065	King	Ramiro I		1065	
1065–1094	King	Sancho Ramirez		1094	
1094–1104	King	Pedro I		1104	
1104–1134	King	Alfonso I, the Fighter		1034	
1134–1137	King	Ramiro II, the Monk		1137	Brother of Alfonso I
1137–1162	Queen	Petronilla		1162	
1162–1196	King	Alfonso II		1196	Son of Ramon Berenguer IV
1196–1213	King	Pedro II		1213	Son of Alfonso II
1213–1276	King	James I, the Conqueror		1236	Son of Pedro II
1276–1285	King	Pedro III, the Great		1285	Son of James I
1285–1291	King	Alfonso III		1291	Son of Pedro III
1291–1327	King	James II		1327	Brother of Alfonso III
1327–1336	King	Alfonso IV		1336	
1336–1387	King	Pedro IV, the Ceremonious		1387	Son of Alfonso IV
1387–1395	King	John I		1395	Son of Pedro IV
1395–1410	King	Martin I, the Humane		1410	Brother of John I
1412–1416	King	Ferdinand I		1416	Brother of John II of Castile
1416–1458	King	Alfonso V, the Magnanimous		1458	Son of Ferdinand I
1458–1479	King	John II		1479	
1479–1516	King	Ferdinand II	1452	1516	

KINGS OF SPAIN

Reign	Title	Ruler	Birth	Death	Relationship
1474–1504	Queen	Isabella and Ferdinand V			
1504–1506	King	Philip I and Queen Juana (Joanne)			
1506–1516	Regent	Ferdinand V			
1516–1517	Regent	Cardinal Cisneros			

HOUSE OF AUSTRIA

Reign	Title	Ruler	Birth	Death	Relationship
1519–1556	King	Charles I (Emperor Charles V)	1500	1558	
1556–1598	King	Philip II	1527	1598	Son of Charles I
1598–1621	King	Philip III	1578	1621	Son of Philip II
1621–1665	King	Philip IV	1605	1665	Son of Philip III
1665–1701	King	Charles II	1661	1701	Son of Philip IV

HOUSE OF BOURBON

Reign	Title	Ruler	Birth	Death	Relationship
1701–1724	King	Philip V	1683	1746	Great-grandson of Philip IV
1724–1724	King	Luis I	1701	1724	Son of Philip V
1724–1746	King	Philip V (rethroned)	1683	1746	Great-grandson of Philip IV
1746–1759	King	Ferdinand VI	1713	1759	Son of Philip V
1759–1788	King	Charles III	1716	1788	Son of Philip V
1788–1808	King	Charles IV	1748	1819	Son of Charles III
1808–1808	King	Ferdinand VII	1784	1833	Son of Charles IV
1808–1814	King	Joseph Bonaparte	1768	1844	
1814–1833	King	Ferdinand VII (again)	1784	1833	Son of Charles IV
1833–1868	Queen	Isabella II	1830	1904	Daughter of Ferdinand VII
1868–1871—Provisional Government					
1871–1873	King	Amadeo I of Savoy	1845	1890	
1873–1874—First Republic					
1874–1886	King	Alfonso XII	1857	1886	Son of Isabella II
1886–1886	Regent	Maria Cristina (Christina)	1858	1929	Widow of Alfonso XII
1886–1931	King	Alfonso XIII	1886	1941	Posthumous son of Alfonso XII
1931—Second Republic					
1975–	King	Juan Carlos I	1938		Grandson of Alfonso XIII

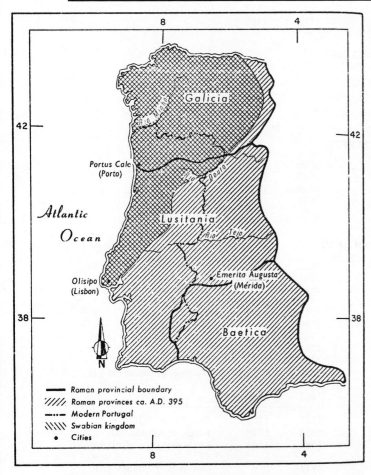

9

The Portuguese Monarchy

The ancient Portugal—Roman Lusitania and the Swabian Kingdom

Portugal derives its name from the medieval Latin term *Portucalense,* which designated the country surrounding the Roman town Portus Cale (modern Porto), roughly the northwestern region between the River Douro and the River Minho. First mentioned in the ninth century A.D., the Portucalense was an administrative area on the frontier of the Christian Kingdom of León, without tra-

ditional borders or a previous history as a separate political unit. The Douro-Minho core had been part of larger regions—the tribal lands of the Lusitanians and the Swabian kingdom that had left it with a legacy of isolation and separateness—but until the twelfth century its history was indistinguishable from that of Spain. It was from this core area, however, that the Portuguese state emerged and before the end of the thirteenth century had extended southward to the borders it retains in the twentieth century.

Many historians, Portuguese and Spanish alike, have considered it an accident that Portugal, exposed and peripheral, developed as an independent entity. The country has no distinctive natural borders. Apart from the western littoral its several regions are geographical extensions of larger ones in Spain. In its origins Portugal lacked ethnic cohesion. Its language had a common root with that of the dialects spoken by the people of Galicia, which has never ceased to be a part of Spain. Historians have seen the maintenance of Portuguese independence as resulting from the early development of a colonial empire, an extraordinary political and economic relationship with England, and Spain's untimely preoccupation with matters more urgent than Iberian unification.

Clearly a Portuguese government existed before a Portuguese nation. Nationality developed around allegiance to the king during the twelfth and thirteenth centuries, and from that grew political and cultural unity and a common Portuguese existence for all the king's subjects. The selection of Lisbon as the national capital tied Portugal's future to the Atlantic, making the Portuguese, in the words of the Spanish writer Salvador de Madariaga, "a Spaniard with his back to Castile." Portugal was the first European nation to establish a sea-borne overseas empire. Its dominion and civilization were extended to parts of Africa, Asia, and America. Small, poor, and marginal in a European context, Portugal ensured its continued existence in large measure by its ability to exploit far-flung colonies, and developments in the colonies often had a decisive effect on domestic Portuguese affairs. Throughout its history as a separate state Portugal has had an ambiguous relationship with Spain. It was an imperative of Portuguese policy to resist absorption and the loss of national identity, but nonetheless the history of inter-Iberian relations was marked by repeated efforts by Portugal and Castile to achieve dynastic union. Ironically, in order to maintain the integrity of its empire and its independence from Spain, Portugal became an economic dependency of England.

In the absence of an easily defined national character it is impossible to determine which of the distinct regional characters is authentically Portuguese. Family oriented, generally apolitical, basically conservative and individualistic, the Portuguese are intensely patriotic but not public spirited. Forgetting whatever in it has been unpleasant, they are given to nostalgia for an idealized past. They tend to be phlegmatic but not practical in their political attitudes. Foreign influences are often rejected because they come from a mentality too different from their own to be assimilated.

Contemporary Portuguese historians have been reluctant to study the unstable and weak governments of the early twentieth century. Although proud and boastful of their country's past achievements, they have been embarrassed by the failure of liberal democratic government to take root in Portugal and by the easy resort to authoritarian alternatives.

LUSITANIA

The west flank of the Iberian Peninsula has known human habitation for many thousands of years; however, the prehistory of the area is even more obscure than that of most parts of Europe, and the origin of those earliest inhabitants as well as the origins of subsequent waves of migrants who each in turn absorbed their predecessors is a matter of scholarly debate. Archaeological finds in southern Portugal are similar to those excavated in sites stretching across North Africa to the Middle East and are evidence of participation in a common southern Mediterranean Paleolithic culture that had its roots in the African continent. Although later Mesolithic settlers and megalith builders, active before 3000 B.C., probably came into the region from the north, all prehistoric cultures there appear to bear the impress of African cultural influence. Compared with adjacent areas, however, the territory lying within the geographic confines of modern Portugal was an isolated backwater in prehistoric times.

IBERIANS

During the course of the third millennium B.C. the Iberians spread over the peninsula that came to bear their name. They provided the genetic base for the populations of both Portugal and Spain. Archaeological evidence has been variously interpreted as indicating an African or an eastern Mediterranean origin, the weight of opinion leaning to the latter, but it is likely that the Iberians who emerged into recorded history after 2000 B.C. were an amalgam of several groups of migrants and still earlier inhabitants who after generations of mingling came to share a number of cultural traits and adopt similar modes of social organization. They differed greatly among themselves, however. In some areas a sophisticated urban society emerged based on trade with the Aegean in tin and copper—the components of bronze—and supported by a prosperous agriculture. By contrast the Iberians who settled in the region bounded by the River Tejo and the River Minho were primitive. Called Lusitanians, they were described by the classical geographers Polybius and Strabo as a loose, quarrelsome federation of tribes, living behind the walls of fortified villages in the hills, engaging in banditry as their primary occupation, and carrying on incessant tribal warfare.

The Lusitanians were marked by their contact with the Celtic herders and metalworkers who moved across the Pyrenees in several waves after 900 B.C. to settle in the northern half of the peninsula. The heaviest concentration of Celts was north of the River Douro in Galicia, where they easily adapted to the damp, relatively cool climate similar to that of their Danubian homeland. The Celtic settlers soon were fused racially and culturally with the native Iberians among whom they lived. The degree to which there was a Celtic genetic intrusion south of the Douro is a matter of discussion, but the Lusitanians would seem to have been Iberians who assimilated Celtic culture rather than a racial admixture of Celts and Iberians. Similar though they were in many ways, even in their language, there was nonetheless a clear dividing line at the Douro between the patriarchal bandits of Lusitania and the matriarchal pastoralists of Galicia.

From about 1200 B.C. the Phoenicians, later their Carthaginian colonists, and by 800 B.C. the Greeks moved up the western Iberian coast to Galicia and beyond in search of trade, but the Lusitanian coast held no interest for them. Although they established colonies elsewhere in Iberia, there were no substantial settlements in what later became Portuguese territory, apart from several Phoenician and Carthaginian trading stations exploiting the salt basins and fig groves of the Algarve, at the southern extreme of modern Portugal. The Carthaginians, however, did hire the bellicose Lusitanians as mercenaries, some probably serving under Hannibal during his Italian campaign in the late third century B.C.

ROMANS

Roman armies invaded Iberia in 212 B.C. to cut Hannibal off from his source of supplies and reinforcement. Resistance by the Iberians was fierce and prolonged, and it was not until 19 B.C. that the Roman emperor Augustus was able to complete the conquest of the peninsula, which the Romans renamed Hispania. The people south of the River Tejo, Mediterranean in outlook, were docile in the face of the Roman advance, but it took seventy years to subdue the Lusitanians. Their banditry had a barbarizing effect on areas far beyond their own tribal territory and compelled the Romans to launch repeated expeditions against them. Native chieftains such as Viriato, leading light cavalry skilled in hit-and-run tactics, harried army after army and occasionally decimated them. Viriato, the first of the Hispanic world's caudillos, or popular military leaders, remains one of Portugal's folk heroes.

Once subdued, however, the Lusitanians were quickly and thoroughly romanized. Their fortifications were dismantled, and the tribes moved down from the hills to the more fertile lowlands, where they were introduced to agriculture. So complete was the process of pacification that no troops were permanently garrisoned in Lusitania. Eventually the territory included in modern Portugal was divided into three Roman provinces, but none was coterminous with subsequent Portuguese borders. The capital of Roman Lusitania was at Emerita Augusta, the site of present-day Mérida in Spain. Roman towns of some size were laid out at Baracara Augusta (Braga), Portus Cale (Porto), Pax Julia (Beja), and Olisipo (Lisbon), which according to legend had been founded by Ulysses. Settlers from Italy were few in the north, but large estates or latifundia were staked out in the Alentejo and the Algarve, where the names of Roman villas survive in Portuguese villages.

Unlike other parts of Hispania, Lusitania played no significant part in the history of the Roman Empire. It was neither populous nor prosperous, produced no luminaries of Roman political life or Latin culture, and was without strategic significance. It was for five hundred years, however, part of a cosmopolitan world empire, bound together by the Roman road, sharing a common language and legal system, and its people, at peace, united in a common Roman identity and citizenship.

Christianity was introduced in the second century A.D., later than in the rest of Hispania, but an ecclesiastical hierarchy active in church councils had been established by the next century. Despite severe persecution Christianity was popular in provincial towns and cities but made little progress in the Lusitanian countryside until the late fourth century, by which time it had become the officially recognized religion of the Roman Empire. Bishops, who had civil as well as ecclesiastical status, maintained order after government had broken down in that part of the empire in the fifth century.

SWABIANS

In A.D. 409 the Vandals and the Swabians (Suevi), driven by other Germanic tribes, crossed the Pyrenees into Hispania. The Swabians, never more numerous than sixty thousand settled eventually in Galicia and Lusitania. Before the migration they had been peaceful farmers in Saxony and Thuringia, where they had benefited from several centuries of contact with romanized Celts in Helvetia (Switzerland), and they attempted to recreate their former patterns of life in the kingdom that they established in Hispania. In contrast to the nucleated villages and large estates that survived in the south, the Swabian farms, tilled with heavy quadrangular plows brought from the upper Rhine, were dispersed, single small holdings to be divided among heirs in smaller portions from one generation to the next. They bequeathed few place-names to the land, but they set a pattern for landholding and agricultural technology that persisted in the Douro-Minho area over the centuries.

With large parts of Hispania outside his control, the emperor Honorius in 415 commissioned the Visigoths, the most highly romanized of the Germanic peoples, to restore order there. They compelled the Vandals to sail for North Africa and asserted hegemony over the Swabians, who retained autonomy under their own kings, managing a well-organized government with its seat at Braga, an old Roman provincial capital. The Swabian kings and their Visigothic overlords held commissions to govern in the name of the Roman emperor and, although the emperor's authority was nominal, their kingdoms remained in theory a part of the Roman Empire. The Swabians tilled the land and left the towns to the Luso-Romans. Some towns, such as Coimbra, remained entirely outside Swabian control. Elsewhere Luso-Romans continued to operate the civil administration for the Swabian farmer-warrior elite, and Latin remained the language of government and commerce. By the middle of the fifth century the royal house and most of the Swabians had accepted Christianity.

The Swabians lost their autonomous status within the greater Visigothic state at the end of the sixth century, but by that time they had come to identify their interests entirely with those of the Visigoths. The Swabian Kingdom retained its territorial integrity, however, as a viceroyalty traditionally reserved for the heir to the Visigothic throne, but geography served to isolate it from the turmoil of Visigothic politics, of which civil war, usurpation, and assassination were commonplace instruments.

MOORS

In A.D. 711 an army of Moors (Arabs and the Moroccan Berbers whom they had conquered and converted to Islam) crossed to Spain as allies of Visigothic nobles who had rebelled against Roderic, their king. Having killed the king in battle and decided the issue against the monarchy, the Moors returned home; but the next year Musa ibn Nusair, Muslim governor of North Africa, led the best of his troops back to a Spain bereft of leadership, intent on annexing it to the expanding domains of the caliph of Damascus. By 715 all but the mountainous region of Asturias in the extreme north of the peninsula had been subdued and was in the process of being reorganized as al-Andalus, the name by which Islamic Spain, including its western provinces, was known.

In Lusitania land was apportioned among the Moorish troops. Bad crops, rebellion against their Arab overlords, and dislike for an inhospitable climate put an end to the short-lived Berber colonization along the River Douro. The Moors preferred the familiar dry country below the River Tejo, especially in the Algarve (from the Arabic *al-Gharb,* "the west"), an area where the Moorish stamp remained the strongest. An Arab aristocracy assumed ownership of the latifundia or gravitated toward the towns, where they revived lagging urban life. The Berber majority fanned out across the countryside as small farmers. For native rustics the transition from Visigothic to Moorish domination posed no problems. Only superficially Christianized, they readily became Muslims although remaining a caste distinct from Arabs and Berbers. Some Visigothic nobles who held to their Christian faith were reconfirmed by the Moors as local governors, but many others converted to Islam and achieved status in the new society. Jews, who were always an important element in the urban population, continued to exercise a significant role in commerce and scholarship and as artisans. The Christian Luso-Roman urban and landholding classes retained freedom to practice their religion and remained largely self-governing under separate laws and institutions. Called Mozarabs (Arablike people), they were, however, profoundly affected by Islamic culture and adopted Arab social customs, dress, language, and artistic styles. In almost every respect except that of religion they were integrated into Moorish society.

For two hundred fifty years a united al-Andalus flourished under the emirs (later caliphs) who had their capital at Cordova. Nothing in Europe approached Cordova's wealth, power, culture, or the brilliance of its court. But, as the strength of the local nobles increased at the expense of a divided royal house, it became more difficult to hold the state together. The caliphate was torn apart in the eleventh century as rival claimants to the throne, military commanders, and opportunistic aristocrats staked out *taifas* (independent regional city-states), among them the emirates of Badajoz, Mérida, Lisbon, Evora, and a number of lesser states that warred among themselves and made accommodations with the emerging Christian state to the north.

The divided and leaderless Visigothic state had crumbled before the initial Moorish onslaught. Active resistance was limited to small groups of Visigothic warriors who took refuge in the mountain fastness of Asturias in the old Swabian Kingdom. There they halted the Moorish advance and, according to tradition, were rallied by the Visigothic chieftain Pelayo (d. 737) to take the offensive, beginning the seven hundred-year-long Reconquest

that became the dominant theme in Portuguese as well as Spanish history.

Within fifty years of the Moorish conquest the Christian kings of Asturias-León, who claimed succession from the Visigothic monarchs, had retaken Braga, Porto, Viseu, and Guimarães in the Douro-Minho area, and peasants and craftsmen had gathered for protection around their strongholds. For two hundred years the region was a buffer zone across which the frontier shifted back and forth with the ebb and flow of Moorish attacks and Christian counterattacks.

THE EMERGENCE OF PORTUGAL

As the Christians extended the Reconquest, life for Mozarabs in the Muslim-controlled south became precarious. In the late ninth century A.D. a large number of them fled to the north, arriving at a time when the so-called desert zone between Galicia and the Moorish territory was being reorganized, under counts *(comes)* appointed by the kings of León, as the Provincia Portucalense (Province of Portugal), a term first recorded in 883 to designate the Douro-Minho region. Separated from León by the rugged Trás-os-Montes province and called on to deal with the Muslims and Viking raiders by their own devices, the counts, who had their stronghold at Porto, developed local connections and governed with a substantial degree of autonomy. By the mid-eleventh century they had carried the frontier southward to Coimbra.

ALFONSO HENRIQUES

In 1096 King Alfonso VI of Castile-León gave hereditary title to the counties of Portugal and Coimbra as a dowry to the crusader Henry of Burgundy on his marriage to the king's illegitimate but favorite daughter, Theresa. Henry was to be sovereign there, but it was recognized by all parties that he held the counties as a

Count Henry of Burgundy became the first king of Portugal. He founded the royal reigning House of Burgundy (1094–1383), and King Henry was the first sovereign of it, ruling until 1112.

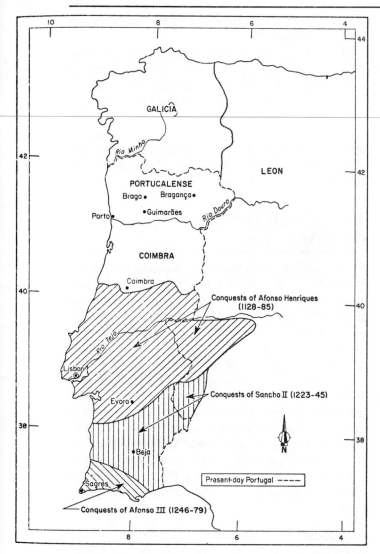

Portugal as it was reconquested by Alfonso Henriques (1128–85) and Sancho II (1223–45)

title of king of Portugal by virtue of his independent conquest of Muslim territory and his direct descent from Alfonso VI. When his cousin Alfonso VII of Castile demanded his homage as a vassal, he refused. Alfonso Henriques' assertion of royal dignity and his defiance of Alfonso VII coincided with a renewed Moorish offensive that absorbed Castile's energy and limited the king's ability to chastise a recalcitrant vassal. Although later Alfonso Henriques reluctantly performed his act of homage, his royal title and Portugal's separate national identity were well established. He assured recognition of Portuguese political independence by swearing fealty to the pope, he and his successors holding Portugal thereafter as a fief of the papacy rather than of Castile.

Portugal benefited from one hundred fifty years of wise and strong leadership by the line of unusual kings descended from Alfonso Henriques, who in his long reign of fifty-seven years laid a firm foundation for subsequent state building. He left a compact kingdom, which grew from a core area—the Douro-Minho—that had a tradition of independence and separateness dating from the Lusitanians and Swabians and a corps of lay and ecclesiastical lords who were tied by allegiance directly to the crown. Using their entrenched royal power his successors founded towns, compiled the law, and carried forward the distinctly Portuguese Reconquest that Alfonso Henriques had begun on the field of Ourique.

THE RECONQUEST

To the Moors the Portuguese were the "bravest of the Christians," but the Portuguese Reconquest regularly relied on the aid of Crusaders and adventurers from abroad. A papal bull in 1100 called on European chivalry to assist the Hispanic kingdoms in a great western crusade. In 1147, when he succeeded in taking Lisbon, and during an earlier, unsuccessful siege of the city, Alfonso Henriques counted as many as fifteen thousand English, French, Flemish, Rhenish, and Danish Crusaders at his side. Many returned home enriched by the booty they had taken during the Crusade, and others went on to Palestine after the fall of Lisbon, but some of the Crusaders remained as settlers on the land they had helped to conquer. Large tracts in the new territory were given to the knights of military orders to gain their support for future efforts in the Reconquest.

The Alentejo was occupied after 1225 by Sancho II (1223–1245), the weak and divided *taifas* there preferring the Christian Portuguese to the Muslim Berbers who had asserted hegemony over what remained of al-Andalus. The Algarve fell in 1249 to Alfonso III (1245–1279), completing the Portuguese phase of the Reconquest. Although the Portuguese were continually called upon to defend the country against the Castilians, they also fought beside them against the Moors. Portuguese knights had served with distinction at Las Navas

vassal of the Castilian king. When Henry died in 1112, Theresa was left as regent for their son, Alfonso Henriques. Theresa alienated the Portuguese barons and townsmen by appearing too willing to sacrifice their hard-won liberties and immunities to the designs of her kinsmen in Castile. They turned to Alfonso Henriques, whom they encouraged to oust his mother and claim his hereditary right to Portugal.

Alfonso Henriques (reigned 1128–85) made war on the Moorish *taifas* to the south, decisively defeating them at Ourique (ca. 1139), a battle acclaimed in legend but its site lost and even its date obscure. Ourique remains an event of great significance in Portuguese national mythology, in which Alfonso Henriques, like Constantine, experienced a vision of the labarum, a sign of the cross in the heavens, and so gained assurance of victory on the field of battle.

Backed by his nobles, Alfonso Henriques assumed the

de Tolosa (1212), a turning point in the Reconquest, where a Castilian chronicler reported that they had "rushed into battle as if at a feast."

Lisbon became Portugal's capital in 1298, finally bringing to rest a peripatetic royal government that had made its seat at Braga, Guimarães, Coimbra, and other points along the road south during the Reconquest. A predominantly Christian city, even under Moorish rule, with an excellent sheltered harbor in the River Tejo, Lisbon was already the economic, social, and cultural center of Portugal before it was chosen as its political center. It enjoyed a good climate and a scenic location, and one Crusader had described its buildings as *"artissime coriglobata"* (crowded together with great skill). The prominence of Lisbon ensured Portugal's future orientation toward the Atlantic, but the city, surrounded by the country's most productive area—favored by both Romans and Moors—grew at the expense of the countryside. It was not part of the Portuguese heartland and remained remote from it.

THE MEDIEVAL MONARCHY

King Diniz (1279–1325) introduced Portuguese as the official language of the realm in place of Latin and imposed its use on the south. Called *O Lavrador* (the Farmer), he encouraged his nobles to bring their wastelands into cultivation and to take an active interest in agricultural development. It was not an easy step for a warrior aristocracy to settle down as estate managers, and Diniz found it necessary to reassure them that "no baron shall lose caste by dedicating himself to the soil." The new lands in the south, whose development he supervised, provided an abundance of fruits, olives, wine, almonds, and grain that was turned for the first time toward stimulating Portugal's export trade but, despite increased production, Portugal remained a poor country even by medieval standards.

Portugal's kings were fruitful in their children, legitimate and illegitimate. Favors granted by doting royal fathers to their numerous bastard offspring, those of Diniz more plentiful than most, frequently provoked rebellions by legitimate heirs. The daughters of prolific Portuguese monarchs were married well, however, extending Portugal's political contacts to England, Flanders, Burgundy, France, and Denmark, as well as cementing dynastic connections with other Hispanic states.

The Portuguese monarchy had fewer constitutional limitations placed on its authority than those imposed by custom and law on other medieval kingdoms. The king's government was administered by a centralized bureaucracy. The *forais* (charter rights) defined the relationship of individual subjects and communities to the king both directly and through intermediate lords or town corporations. In return for immunities and privileges on their own lands nobles were obliged to provide for the defense of a sector of the country. Rural collectives were encouraged by grants of tax relief and local self-government to farm the poor soil of Trás-os-Montes. The Portuguese Cortes (parliament), composed of representatives of three estates—the church, the nobility, and the towns—had a continuous history beginning in 1254.

Early medieval monarchs were expected to be self-sufficient and to operate the government out of their own resources but, as government became more complex and expensive, they were forced to call on the resources of their subjects as well. In return for a vote of subsidies to the royal government, the estates, through their representatives in the Cortes, compelled the king to listen to their grievances, seek advice, and get their consent for the projects for which the revenues that they granted were intended. The stronger the king, the more willing was the Cortes to provide the funds that he requested; the weaker the king, the more demands were made on him by the estates.

Though feudal terminology was used in charters and deeds in Portugal for lack of a more specific vocabulary, feudalism (that is, hereditary title to the use of land and to legal jurisdiction on that land in return for personal allegiance and service to the donor) did not exist de jure in any developed form in medieval Portugal; in practice, however, situations very much like it did occur. According to Portuguese custom landholders were limited to economic control of the property they held. Legal jurisdiction on that property might be granted, but it was separate from title to the use of the land. All governmental and judicial power was vested ultimately in the crown, but in time it was delegated to landlords acting as the king's agents on their property. As the origin of grants of jurisdiction was obscured by the years, lords assumed that they exercised it as a right, and the crown had to review grants and titles to land continually in order to reclaim and reallocate its own property and authority.

Portugal's borders with Castile were stabilized after 1295. But the threat of war with the stronger Spanish Kingdom was a constant concern to a succession of kings in the fourteenth century. To keep the tenuous peace, Alfonso IV (1325–57) had ordered the murder of Inês de Castro, heroine of a romance with his heir, Dom Pedro, on suspicion that she was involving Portugal in Castilian politics. When Dom Pedro became king as Pedro I (1357–67), *O Justiceiro* (the Judge)—as he was called because he punished the wicked indiscriminately regardless of rank—proclaimed Inês his queen and forced his court to do homage to her corpse, clothed for the occasion in the robes of state. When he died, Pedro was buried with Inês at the abbey of Alcobaça, where his tomb was embellished with the scene in stone of her murderers in hell. Their son, John, became grand master of the military Order of Aviz.

SOCIAL, ECONOMIC, AND CULTURAL DEVELOPMENT

The social and economic structure of medieval Portugal differed radically from region to region. A frontier society developed in the north that persisted after the region ceased to be a frontier. Liberties had been granted to soldier yeomen who were willing to take responsibility for defending their holdings. A petty nobility or gentry had risen among those who had succeeded in consolidating their holdings and those of their dependents, as had a caste of commoner knights *(cavaleiros vilãos)* who were granted land to defray their military expenses. But the dominant pattern in much of the north remained that of the small-holding yeoman farmer who, according to the Germanic landholding system inherited from the Swabians, divided his land among all his heirs in plots that shrank in size with each generation. For the man who possessed it, his land was as much an heirloom as it was a piece of potentially productive property.

Peasants in the Douro-Minho as well as in Trás-os-Montes formed collective associations *(pactos de bemfeitoria)* to pay rent on fields and pastures that went toward the support of the military aristocracy, which also agreed in the bargain to defend them. Originally they retained full freedom to negotiate contracts with their protector and if unsatisfied to choose a new lord. As the frontier was pushed forward, however, peasants were usually tied to one lord. The crown, particularly after Diniz, encouraged family and collective farming by alienating aristocratic and ecclesiastical land to peasant proprietors.

Above them all was a small number of interrelated great families, relatively poor in liquid income. From the crown they regularly received subsidies that allowed them to meet their obligations and that also tied them tightly to the crown.

In the central regions and on the lands in the south added in the thirteenth century, the military and monastic orders, the hierarchy, and military aristocrats had been vested with vast latifundia to support their services to the crown and church. The land was tilled by sharecroppers, by peasants contracted to the land (though dependent serfdom appears to have been rare) and, most numerously, by wretched masses of itinerant rural laborers who worked without the protection of a lord or a manorial contract that would have regulated their status and assured them of minimal rights.

The Sesmarias Decree (1375) brought about government regulation of agriculture and served to stimulate a stagnating economy. It ordered that all arable land be put under the plow and allowed seizure by the crown of underproductive estates.

The hierarchy and many religious houses grew enormously wealthy by Portuguese standards from the lands granted them during the Reconquest, and their wealth often implied great political power as well, which engaged the crown in a running dispute with the church over title to land.

THE HOUSE OF AVIZ

Ferdinand (1367–83), last of the House of Burgundy, left no male heir, but his daughter was the wife of John I of Castile, and it was intended that their offspring should inherit Portugal. Until issue was forthcoming, however, Portugal was to be governed under the regency of Ferdinand's unpopular widow, Leonor Teles. John, grand master of Aviz, expelled the regent and was proclaimed king as John I (reigned 1385–1433), by a Cortes called at Coimbra in 1385. In response a Castilian army invaded Portugal to uphold the rights of an as yet unborn Castilian heir to the Portuguese throne. What had taken place was a dynastic revolution that had provoked foreign intervention, but the struggle that followed was also a Portuguese civil war. The traditionalist north supported John of Castile and the cause of legitimacy; the towns and the south where the Order of Aviz was one of the great landholders, backed their John. The future of the House of Aviz and, from the perspective of John's followers, the independence of Portugal were decided at the epic battle of Aljubarrota near Lisbon. Fewer than seven thousand Portuguese on foot, under Nuno Alvares Pereira, the Constable, and a contingent of English longbowmen faced an opposing army of ten thousand infantry and twenty thousand cavalry, the cream of Castilian chivalry. As the Constable's men held their positions, the longbowmen shattered the enemy's heavily armored cavalry and won the day for John of Aviz.

English aid to the Aviz Dynasty set the stage for the

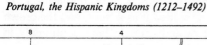

Portugal, the Hispanic Kingdoms (1212–1492)

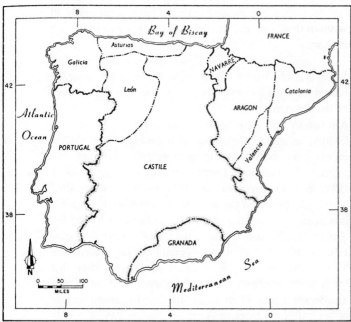

King John I (1385–1433) had a long reign—forty-eight years—during which he achieved much in the way of creating administrative and organizational order for the cities of Portugal and was called the Great because he invested the money in sea exploration, and was responsible for the settling of the island of Madeira in 1418. His was the first reign of the House of Aviz (1385–1580).

*A stamp honoring
King John I
issued in 1948*

The first Independence Issue of postage stamps in 1926 honored Alfonso I, the Conqueror, son of Count/King Henry. Most Portuguese historians claim Alfonso as their first official king.

cooperation with England that would be the cornerstone of Portuguese foreign policy for more than five hundred years. In 1386 the Treaty of Windsor confirmed the alliance born at Aljubarrota with a pact of perpetual friendship between the two countries. The next year John of Gaunt, duke of Lancaster, son of Edward III and father of Henry IV, landed in Galicia with an expeditionary force to press his claim to the Castilian throne with Portuguese aid. He failed to win the support of the Castilian nobility and returned to England with a cash compensation from the rival claimant, but the war with Castile continued for Portugal until 1411.

John of Gaunt left behind his intelligent and cultured daughter, Philippa of Lancaster, as the wife of John I to seal the Anglo-Portuguese alliance. She introduced an English element at court—an "icy influx," according to the Portuguese, that reformed the morals of their court

and imposed uncomfortably rigid standards of behavior on them. More important, Philippa provided royal patronage for English commercial interests that sought to meet the Portuguese desire for cod and cloth in return for wine, cork, salt, and oil through the English-run warehouses at Porto. Philippa also became the mother of an extraordinary line of royal princes who led Portugal into its Golden Age. For the poet Luís de Camões they were the "marvelous generation," the brothers Durate the king, Pedro the regent, António the Crusader, John, and Dom Henrique—Prince Henry the Navigator.

John I distrusted the old aristocracy that had opposed his rise to power. He promoted the growth of a lower nobility attached to the crown and rewarded the urban commercial oligarchy with position and influence in the realm in return for its support of Aviz. He surrounded himself with skilled bureaucrats who professionalized royal administration and extended royal jurisdiction at the expense of the old aristocracy. A strong and confident monarch, John nonetheless summoned the Cortes biennially to approve his legislation and lend legitimacy to the title that he had seized by force. The future of the Aviz Dynasty seemed assured by the presence of John's five legitimate sons, but the king also provided for his illegitimate children as he had been provided for by his father. John conferred on his bastard son Alfonso the hereditary title of duke of Braganza and endowed him with lands and jurisdiction that amounted to creation of a state within a state supported by a huge reserve of armed retainers. The House of Braganza accumulated wealth to rival that of the crown and assumed leadership of the old aristocracy in opposition to Aviz.

THE EXPANSION OF PORTUGAL

In 1415 the Portuguese seized Ceuta in Morocco, the western depot for the spice trade, and began a campaign that by the end of the century had put them in control of most of Morocco's western coastline. From strongholds on the coast the Portuguese manipulated satellite Muslim states in the interior and provided cover for settlers who had carved out estates in North Africa but derived most of their income from raiding along the frontier between Portuguese and Muslim-held territory. Portuguese efforts throughout most of the fifteenth century were focused on Morocco rather than on exploration by sea and colonization of unknown territory.

HENRY THE NAVIGATOR

Prince Henry the Navigator (1394–1460), to whom much credit for early Portuguese exploration has gone, was not himself a scientist, nor was he well traveled, but he possessed intellectual curiosity and surrounded himself with skillful and imaginative minds at his retreat, the Vila do Infante, on the promontory of Sagres. As master of the Order of Christ, one of the crusading orders, he commanded a permanent military force and had access to substantial resources. His order paid for fitting out expeditions of which the risks outweighed the expectations of profit, and it bore the cost of their failures. Henry prodded his mariners to explore beyond Cape Bojador on the west coast of Africa, a psychological as well as physical barrier that was thought to be the outer boundary of the knowable world. In 1420 Portuguese seamen reached Madeira and by 1427 the Azores. In 1434 Gil Eanes rounded Cape Bojador and reported back to Henry that it was not the end of the world.

Although Henry's motives were obviously many, he saw exploration primarily in terms of outflanking the Moors and contributing to the success of the conquest of Morocco. His attitudes matured over forty years, however, as his knowledge increased and he began to recognize the separate advantages of overseas expansion. The expeditions he sponsored were better planned and organized, and they began to turn a profit in gold and slaves. By midcentury Portuguese mariners had mapped twenty degrees of latitude south from Cape Bojador and had perceived the curve of the African continent.

ROYAL PATRONAGE

A conflict over priorities continued to brew between the factions: the old aristocracy, led by the duke of Braganza and demanding expansion in Morocco, and commercial interests in the towns and among the lower nobility, favoring expanded trade overseas and looking to Prince Henry's older brother Dom Pedro for leadership. Pedro was made regent for his young nephew, Alfonso V (1438–81). A scholar and collector of maps, the regent saw the Moroccan wars as a wasted effort and emphasized commercial expansion. In the practical matter of securing profit from exploration Pedro was more effective than his brother Henry. But Pedro's attempts to pull back from Morocco led to armed conflict within Portugal in which the regent died in 1449. An aristocratic reaction took place during the reign of Alfonso V, and for a decade after Pedro's fall no further expeditions set sail, but interests revived as even the duke of Braganza saw profit in the importation of slaves from Africa. In fact the renewed wars in Morocco, championed by him, had the desired effect of rechanneling the Sudan gold trade away from North Africa to the Guinea coast, where the gold was picked up by Portuguese ships and conveyed to Europe.

Official patronage of exploration and trade was renewed under John II (1481–95), and to him belongs credit for the first comprehensive plan for overseas expansion and the idea of rounding Africa to open a new trade route to India. The crown would thereafter take its "royal fifth," or share of the profit, on all chartered commercial ventures, assume direct management of trade, and reap most of the benefits.

THE PASSAGE TO INDIA

The Portuguese conducted their expeditions in greatest secrecy. Foreign investment, except by the Genoese merchants living in Portugal, was discouraged. The advantages that Portugal derived from advanced ship design and navigational devices and maps, charts, and reports from earlier voyages were carefully guarded. In 1484 Christopher Columbus's recommendation for a westward approach to the Indies was rejected; the Portuguese had an accurate measure of the earth's circumference that had confirmed them in their commitment to finding an eastward route.

To head off conflict between Portugal and Spain after Columbus's initial discoveries in America, the Pope's Line of 1493 was devised by Alexander VI, a Spaniard, to divide the world between the two countries, Spain having title west of a line passing near the Cape Verde Islands and Portugal to the east of it. The next year the line was redrawn in the Treaty of Tordesillas and moved more than one thousand miles westward.

RENAISSANCE PORTUGAL

John II, called the Perfect Prince, was a ruthlessly efficient royal bureaucrat of the kind described by Niccolò Machiavelli. Commercial expansion overseas had altered the political balance of power within Portugal and allowed John and his successor, Emanuel I (1495–1521), enriched by trade, to live on their own without need to seek subsidies or to require advice and consent from the Cortes in order to operate the government. They humbled the long-troublesome old aristocracy, which would survive only as a court-bound nobility, dependent on the

Dom Antonio in 1580 declared himself king. He was the illegitimate Pretender to the throne in that King Henry (1578–80) did not have a male heir. Antonio raised an army from his followers but was defeated by the infamous duke of Alva.

crown and incapable of challenging its authority. In addition to being an astute politician Emanuel was a man of taste and refinement who used Portugal's new wealth to embellish his court—art and literature, theater and architecture flourishing under his patronage within its narrow circle.

Sebastian (1557–78) was the sole surviving heir of John III (1521–57), whom he succeeded at the age of three. Unintelligent and fanatical in his maturity, he launched a campaign in Morocco, where Moorish counterattacks had reduced Portuguese holdings. His fourteen thousand ill-equipped troops were overwhelmed at Alcázarquivir and destroyed. Sebastian was presumed killed in battle with large numbers of the nobility. More were captured and held for ransom, draining noble households of their substance and of potential investment capital. The natural leadership was depleted, the treasury emptied, and the government at a standstill during the brief interim reign of Sebastian's uncle, the aged Cardinal Henry (1578–80).

HABSBURG PORTUGAL

The royal House of Aviz died with Henry. Philip II of Spain (reigned 1580–96 in Portugal as Philip I) had a better claim to Portugal than any of the several other possible candidates. His first wife and his mother were daughters of kings of Portugal. The master of the greatest military machine and naval power in Europe, he was also the strongest candidate in terms of enforcing his claim. Resistance was slight, and Philip's title was duly recognized by the Portuguese Cortes.

The succession of a Spanish Habsburg king had been anticipated for some years since it became obvious that Sebastian lacked the inclination to perpetuate his dynasty. The union of the Hispanic crowns—Portugal, Castile, and Aragon—had been promoted for generations by dynastic marriages. For a few years at the end of the fifteenth century Portugal and Spain had shared an heir apparent. A carefully negotiated scheme to link Castile with Portugal by the marriage of Isabella of Castile to Alfonso V (1438–81) had been wrecked when she chose instead his rival, Ferdinand of Aragon, and set the course of modern Spanish history.

Philip II inherited several crowns in Spain, Italy, and the Netherlands from his father, the Holy Roman emperor Charles V, and the addition of Portugal fit comfortably into the federal structure of the Spanish Habsburg Empire, in which several kingdoms, each retaining its own separate institutions, recognized one king. Contrary to the opinion put forth in some nationalist histories, Portugal was not annexed to Spain and did not lose its independence, nor was it an occupied country during sixty years (1580–1640) under three Habsburg kings. In Portugal Philip II and his successors ruled as kings of Portugal. The government and the Cortes, courts, laws, local customs, and currency remained Portuguese. Taxes were collected by Portuguese for use in Portugal. Portuguese troops manned the garrisons. The colonies were under Portuguese administration, the church under Portuguese bishops. Indeed Portuguese held positions throughout the Habsburg Empire out of proportion to their numbers. The Council of Portugal sat in regular attendance on the Habsburg kings wherever they made their capital to advise on Portuguese affairs. For two years (1581–83) Philip II made Lisbon his capital, and in later years it was not Spanish oppression that his Portuguese subjects complained of but rather neglect by a distant king.

There was a current of resistance among the masses in the countryside that took form in a messianic cult of the "hidden prince," Sebastian, who they believed did not die in battle but would return again and somehow right all wrongs. Practically Sebastianism has been explained as symptomatic of deep-seated social unrest among tenants exploited by landholders who approved of the Habsburgs and as a demonstration of hostility directed at all forms of authority. Several so-called false Sebastians surfaced in Portugal to claim the throne with the backing of this popular sentiment. Some scholars have seen the origin of the cult in New Christian fears of persecution by the Inquisition. Others have pointed out that nostalgic longing for the unattainable is at the basis of much of Portuguese art and literature or have seen it as a continuing feature of Portuguese political life.

More concrete political and economic causes for the dissolution of the dynastic union can be found in the demands made on Portugal as part of the larger Habsburg Empire deeply engaged in European religious and dynastic wars. Portugal was inevitably involved in these wars, for which the Portuguese had little sympathy, and its colonies were exposed to attack by Spain's enemies. The Dutch pounced on Portuguese holdings throughout the East: Ceylon, Malacca, and numerous East Indian islands fell to them, as did the depots in Angola and a

John IV (1640–56) was the first king of Portugal to reign under the House of Braganza (1640–1910).

large part of Brazil. The Habsburg kings of Portugal were helpless to defend the Portuguese Empire.

With Spain at war across Europe and the burden borne almost entirely by Castile, the count-duke of Olivares, chief minister to Philip IV (reigned 1621–40 in Portugal as Philip III), contrived in the 1630s to give greater direction to the Hispanic states, pooling their resources, integrating their administration, and exploiting untapped manpower. Catalonia rebelled in protest in 1640, and Portugal followed suit when required to assist Philip IV against the Catalans.

John IV (1640–56), duke of Braganza and nominal commander of the Portuguese forces ordered to Catalonia, reluctantly placed himself at the disposal of his country when called upon by some of the nobility to be king. The move was popular in the countryside, in Brazil, and in the urban merchant community. John IV also had the powerful backing of the Jesuits, who offset the influence of the pro-Habsburg hierarchy. The break with Spain was, however, as much a civil war as it was a revolution.

It was argued that throwing off the Spanish connection would mean peace with Spain's enemies and save the Portuguese Empire from destruction at their hands. In fact the Dutch returned nothing they had taken but took more territory after 1640 and demanded concessions in return for support against Spain. Spain did not have the resources to press its cause against the Portuguese, who rated low among Spain's priorities, but neither could the Braganzas force recognition of their claim on the Habsburgs. Only in 1668 was peace made between them.

Portugal for its part had chosen to protect its overseas empire rather than participate in a common Hispanic nationhood. Some historians have argued that the choice condemned Portugal to be a small, underdeveloped country dependent on England for survival.

THE HOUSE OF BRAGANZA (SEVENTEENTH AND EIGHTEENTH CENTURIES)

The House of Braganza was an illegitimate line of the royal family of Aviz and dated from the early fifteenth century. Its dukes had been leaders of the Portuguese aristocracy, and their wealth and holdings in land equaled those of the crown. John IV, who was essentially a businessman in outlook, had profitable interests in the Azores and Brazil and at one point had considered selling Portugal back to the king of Spain. His son Alfonso VI (1656–67) was a degenerate whose brother, Pedro II (1683–1706), seized control of the government and imprisoned Alfonso in 1667 with the aid of the king's wife. He ruled as regent until Alfonso's death and then in his own right. Pedro introduced absolutist rule into Portu-

gal after the pattern set by Louis XIV in France, and the Cortes ceased to meet after 1697.

ANGLO-PORTUGUESE RELATIONS

John IV had renewed the Anglo-Portuguese alliance during the long stalemate with Spain, and Oliver Cromwell had exacted trade concessions as the price for England's support. The marriage of a Portuguese princess, Catherine of Braganza, to the English king Charles II in 1661 added prestige to the fledgling royal house, and English troops served in Portugal against the Spanish, participating at the decisive battle of Vila Viçosa in 1665. England sheltered the rich but vulnerable Portuguese Empire but took in return a mortgage on its economy.

Portugal's domestic economy had been static since the fifteenth century. Crop production never kept pace with the increase in population and, though an agricultural country, Portugal was an importer of grain. No serious attempt was made to organize domestic industries until 1670, when one of the periodic depressions in colonial trade deprived Portugal of the means to pay for manufactured imports. The first effort at industrial development lapsed when colonial trade perked up after 1690.

It was Brazil's apparently bottomless wealth in gold and later in diamonds that assured Portugal of the means to pay for imports and destroyed for several generations the initiative for development at home. Brazilian gold also encouraged England to update its commercial relations with Portugal.

POMBAL

Eighteenth-century Portuguese government was a highly centralized bureaucracy managed by ministers responsible to the king and exercising as much power as he saw fit to allow them. John V (1706–50) had been an energetic king until the last years of his reign when he sank into melancholy and turned over his government to ecclesiastical advisers who were not up to the task. His successor, Joseph Emanuel (1750–77), was indolent, eager to reign but not to bear the burden of ruling his country and empire. He put direction of his government in the hands of a diplomat, Sebastião José de Carvalho e Melo (1699–1782), later marquis of Pombal, a man of genius and energy at once remarkable for his accomplishments and controversial for the methods he used to achieve them. Pombal became the veritable dictator of Portugal, using the absolute authority of the crown without check and operating the most authoritarian regime known in eighteenth-century Europe.

On November 1, 1755, the feast of All Saints, Lisbon was destroyed by an earthquake, followed by fire and a tidal wave, that killed sixty thousand and shook the confidence of "Enlightened" Europe. The direction that Pombal gave in the aftermath of the disaster—"Bury the dead and relieve the living"—brought him to prominence.

King John VI, after acting as regent for his mother, Queen Maria I, succeeded to the throne in 1816. As a result of the Rebellion of 1820, he agreed to a constitution limiting the power of the crown.

Pombal took charge of rebuilding the city. He also undertook the restructuring of state administration to deal with Portugal's recurrent economic problems, stimulating industry—in the face of British opposition—to overcome another trade slump and regulating the export of gold and the production of wine to keep up price levels. Portugal paid a price for the rational government that Pombal sought to give through enlightened despotism. Opponents of his regime were arrested, tortured, and some executed. It was a token of his confidence in his own power that Pombal turned to challenge the position of the church, which had retained a degree of independence from state control and which Pombal despised for its opposition to his reforms. He initiated official anticlericalism in Portugal, intervening in ecclesiastical affairs, confiscating church property, and expelling the Jesuits.

With King Joseph's death Pombal's dictatorship was dismantled as quickly as it had been built. The restrictive monopolies that he had sponsored were suspended, allowing the growth of a class of independent merchants who brought relative prosperity to the country at the end of the century and permitted the old regime in Portugal to pass through the revolutionary 1790s unscathed.

THE PENINSULAR WAR

Portugal resisted participating in the continental blockade imposed in 1804 by Napoleon Bonaparte against importation of British goods. For a short time in 1807 Portugal was occupied by French troops, Napoleon claiming that he had sent an army to liberate the Portuguese people from British economic domination. The royal family—Maria I (1777–1816) and her son John VI (1816–26), who acted as regent during her long mental illness that began in 1799—took refuge in Brazil, where a government-in-exile was established under British protection. A British expeditionary force under Arthur Wellesley, duke of Wellington, compelled a French withdrawal from Portugal and repelled two subsequent invasions. Wellington used Portugal as a base of operations for the offensive that drove the French from Spain in

1813. The Portuguese army was reorganized during the war under British tutelage and put under the command of William Carr Beresford, one of Wellington's officers, who remained in Portugal as regent in the absence of the royal family.

THE CONSTITUTIONAL MONARCHY (1822–1910)

The war passed from Portugal, but the royal family stayed in Brazil, which in 1815 was the political center of the so-called United Kingdom of Portugal, Brazil, and the Algarve. In 1816 John VI succeeded to the Portuguese throne—in Rio de Janeiro.

In Portugal itself discontent at Beresford's regency, the absence of the king, and the country's diminished status in the empire was expressed by the small middle-class intelligentsia and commercial oligarchy, who were identified as liberals and called for constitutional government. The officer corps, which had gained self-esteem during the war, also demanded a larger role in national life. Both groups had confidence that a constitution and a responsible parliamentary government were the remedies needed for curing the country's economic and social ills. Although they wanted to emulate Great Britain's political example, they chafed at the influence exerted by the British in Brazil. It was the army, however, that took the lead in 1820 by demanding the reestablishment of the Cortes and the writing of a constitution. What followed were years of experimentation with constitutions, a succession of attempts to provide stable government, and repeated foreign intervention in Portuguese affairs.

The 1822 Constitution, written by a Cortes composed mainly of civil servants, academics, and army officers, called for strong central government, a limited monarchy, and ministerial responsibility to a unicameral legis-

Queen Maria II reigned from 1826 to 1828, and from 1834 to 1853.

King (Regent) Miguel became the regent of Portugal for his niece Maria in 1828. But in 1834 Queen Maria recovered the throne from the self-proclaimed king and he had to flee to Italy.

lature elected by literate males. John VI, accepting his status as a constitutional monarch in Portugal, returned from Brazil, leaving his heir Dom Pedro behind as co-king. The Cortes was willing to accept representatives from Brazil but would not concede autonomous status within an imperial framework. Having won the fight for a parliament vested with executive authority, the Portuguese liberals did not believe that they could relinquish any sovereignty without compromising the sum of it. More representative of commercial interests than its predecessor, the first Cortes elected under the new constitution attempted to reassert Lisbon's economic control over Brazil. With British support Pedro declared Brazil an independent state and took the title of emperor, but he remained heir to the Portuguese throne.

Opinion was polarized in Portugal in reaction to the loss of Brazil. Politically aware moderates were caught between those who gravitated toward the militantly anti-clerical radicals, who demanded a continuing political revolution, and the traditionalists, who were allied with the church and hostile to the drift in affairs under the rule of an urban, middle-class Cortes. Traditionalist juntas, supported by smallholders and peasants, were formed in the north to protect the communal liberties threatened by the liberal central government. Calling for a return to absolutism, the traditionalists found a champion in Dom Miguel, younger son of John VI, who was seen to exult in martial, rural, and Catholic virtues.

If the new emperor of Brazil chose to remain in America, his brother Miguel would succeed their father in Portugal, and there was no doubt that Pedro preferred Brazil. When John VI died in 1826, Pedro reluctantly returned to Portugal, pressured by the British to leave his prosperous Brazilian Empire for an impoverished country with an unstable constitutional regime. Backed by the army, which was easily disenchanted by civilian rule, Pedro demanded an accommodation from the liberal Cortes in the form of the compromise Charter of 1826, which replaced the 1822 Constitution and remained substantially in force until 1910. The charter returned executive authority to the king, who governed through a ministry responsible to him. It provided for a bicameral Cortes, consisting of the Chamber of Deputies, elected indirectly by a reduced electorate, and an upper house appointed by the crown.

After the charter was adopted, Pedro returned to Brazil, leaving title to the Portuguese throne to his young daughter Maria da Gloria, later Maria II (1834–53). Miguel was to act as regent on condition that he accept the new constitution. Miguel duly swore to abide by the settlement, was given command of the army, and promptly seized power, abolished the charter, and appointed an absolutist government that offered him the Portuguese crown.

There had been little resistance to Miguel, but Pedro abdicated his Brazilian throne and recrossed the Atlantic

determined to restore the charter and remain in Portugal as constitutional monarch. Leading an expeditionary force from the Azores, where he had established a provisional government, Pedro landed near Porto in 1832 and defeated Miguel with substantial British assistance in a two-year-long civil war that pitted liberals against traditionalists.

The church had overwhelmingly supported Miguel. The government under Mosinho da Silveira, which carried on the regency for Maria II after her father died, purged the hierarchy and abolished the religious orders, about one-third of Portugal's thirty thousand clergy. In 1834 the government ordered the expropriation of church property. Intended to raise funds to pay the debt of the civil war, the lands and buildings of five hundred religious houses were sold at auction at prices below their market value to approximately six hundred new owners who used government credits to make their purchases. The sale of church property resulted in a shift in the ownership of more than one-fourth of all land and created a new class—wealthy landholders who were drawn from the ranks of the liberal politcal oligarchy and were indebted to the policies of the constitutional monarchy for their position. This group had the dominant influence in the political life of the country throughout the rest of the nineteenth century.

THE LIBERAL OLIGARCHY

Anticlericalism, economic freedom achieved through unregulated trade, and an overweening confidence that national honor could be restored through constitutional government were the chief tenets of Portuguese liberalism in the nineteenth century. In reality the governments that it supported came to office through manipulated elections. Revolts by an activist army divided in its polit-

King Pedro V (1853–1861) left his mark as one of the poorest administrators to sit on the throne. He is blamed for the neglect of sanitary conditions in the cities, which brought on devastating epidemics of yellow fever and cholera in Portugal. The king and his brothers, John and Ferdinand, died of cholera.

ical sympathies were regular occurrences. British and French intervention was required to forestall civil war and protect investments. Despite anticlerical legislation the country remained officially Roman Catholic, and royal patronage in nominating bishops was confirmed in a succession of concordats with Rome. The Cortes was representative of a social and economic elite, middle class in its origins, that was determined to retain its position by restricting suffrage. One percent of the population was enfranchised. Property qualifications for candidates limited to forty-five hundred the number eligible to sit in the Chamber of Deputies. From the Senate, or upper house of the Cortes, a new bourgeois aristocracy emerged, the product of an inflation of titles to encompass the wealthiest of the elite.

Parliamentary politics consisted of working out personal rivalries within the liberal oligarchy. Large working majorities set the stage for arbitrary government by successive liberal ministries that interpreted constitutional guarantees very flexibly. Opposition to the oligarchy was centered in Porto, where the demand for a broader electorate and decentralization was strongest from the industrial—as distinct from commercial and landholding—sector of middle-class opinion. By 1836 a national movement known as the Septembrists had developed around the issue and had entered into loose and unruly coalitions with both radicals and traditionalists, as the disparate extremes of the political spectrum challenged—ineffectively—the entrenched and static center.

An artificial two-party system developed in the Cortes by midcentury. The parties—the Regenerators somewhat the more conservative, the Progressives somewhat the more liberal—agreed on policies and political tactics. Shared patronage was the most cohesive force in keeping the party system functioning. After 1856 the practice of

alternating parties in power at regular intervals, called rotativism in Portugal, was all but institutionalized. Because political power was concentrated in so small a group of like-minded men, compromises were easily struck, and reformist factions were quickly absorbed by the established parties. Rotativism produced relatively stable governments that nonetheless failed to come to grips with Portugal's underlying social and economic problems. On the whole, successive governments introduced constructive programs that failed in execution.

JOÃO FRANCO

The year 1890 was a watershed in Portuguese political history. It marked the beginning of a growth in political awareness that contributed to the downfall of the monarchy twenty years later. The government's retreat in the face of the British ultimatum was denounced roundly by the Republicans, who were organized as a political party in 1878. The Republicans' strongest appeal was to nationalism. Portugal, they argued, would never be honored in the world as once it had been until an outworn constitutional monarchy was replaced by a modern democratic republic. Republican propaganda played on fears of Portugal's becoming a British colony or a province of Spain.

The government reacted to the drive for broader suffrage by revising the electoral law in 1896 in order to eliminate minor parties from the Cortes. The king's hand was also strengthened to permit him greater latitude in appointing ministers and dissolving the parliament, but King Carlos (1889–1908), an artist and a distinguished scientist, refused to rule by decree as his advisers insisted.

In 1900 João Franco, a conservative reformist in the Cortes, led a minority of Regenerator delegates with him out of the parliamentary party. Working to reinvigorate parliamentary institutions, Franco appealed for electoral reform directly to the people—a new and unsettling phenomenon in a depoliticized society. In 1906, although Franco had only a small following in the Cortes, Carlos summoned him to form a coalition government with the Progressives. The unwillingness of one wing of the Progressives to cooperate in the coalition splintered that party just as Franco's defection had broken the Regenerators.

The Republicans were the immediate beneficiaries of Franco's program as prime minister to encourage greater participation in political debate. They turned on the well-meaning king, blaming him for the corruption of the political parties that rotativism had made inevitable. Demands were made for a parliamentary investigation of royal finances, as the monarchy was made the symbol of all that was perceived to be wrong in the country.

The established parties had become so badly splintered that no alternative could be found to Franco's

King Carlos I (1889–1908) was the last important king of Portugal to reign. His son, Manuel II, reigned for two years upon the death of Carlos but had to abdicate in 1910 when Portugal became a republic.

Manuel II as he appeared on postage stamps in 1910

minority government, nor could the prime minister win approval of his legislative program. The parliamentary process had ceased to function when in 1907 Carlos dissolved the Cortes and granted Franco authority to rule by decree. An attempted military coup backed by the Republicans in January 1908 led to the cancellation of elections for a new Cortes and a crackdown against opposition. In February Carlos and his heir were assassinated in Lisbon, leaving the eighteen-year-old Manuel II (1908–10) as king. Manuel could rely only on Franco, against whom all parties were ranged. In an effort to save the young king, Franco called for an election and stepped down as prime minister.

THE PARLIAMENTARY REPUBLIC

The Republicans became the party of urban, middle-class radicalism, nationalistic, libertarian, and intensely anticlerical in temper. Their active ranks included a high proportion of journalists, and the publicity received by the party in the press was out of proportion to its actual size. Republican candidates in the 1908 and 1910 parliamentary elections got a small vote—and that localized in Lisbon—but factionalism prevented the established monarchist parties from forming a stable government capable of resisting them. (Six governments fell during the period between the two elections.)

In October 1910 troops in Lisbon refused to put down a mutiny aboard two warships, and some went over to the dissidents. With no one in a position of authority willing to take charge of the situation and his appeals for advice left unanswered, Manuel II fled with the royal family to exile in England.

Portugal in its European setting today

THE ROYAL SOVEREIGNS OF THE PORTUGUESE MONARCHY

Reign	Title	Ruler	Birth	Death	Relationship
–1094—Portugal under control of Romans and Moors					
1094—Portugal becomes an independent state					
HOUSE OF BURGUNDY					
1094–1112	Count/King	Henry of Burgundy	1057	1112	Grandson of Robert I of Burgundy; consort, Theresa of Castile
1128–1185	King	Alfonso I	1112	1185	Son of Henry of Burgundy
1112–1140	Regent	Theresa			
1140—Portugal became an independent monarchy.					
1185–1211	King	Sancho I	1154	1211	Son of Alfonso I
1211–1223	King	Alfonso II, the Fat	1186	1223	Son of Sancho I
1223–1245	King	Sancho II	1209	1248	Son of Alfonso II
1245–1279	King	Alfonso III	1210	1279	Son of Alfonso II
1279–1325	King	Diniz	1261	1325	Son of Alfonso III
1325–1357	King	Alfonso IV	1291	1357	Son of Diniz
1357–1367	King	Pedro I	1320	1367	Son of Alfonso IV
1367–1383	King	Ferdinand I	1345	1383	Son of Pedro I
HOUSE OF AVIZ					
1385–1433	King	John I	1358	1433	Son of Pedro I
1433–1438	King	Edward I	1391	1438	Son of John I
1438–1481	King	Alfonso V (Africano)	1432	1481	Son of Edward I

Reign	Title	Ruler	Birth	Death	Relationship
1481–1495	King	John II	1455	1495	Son of Alfonso V
1495–1521	King	Manuel I	1469	1521	Grandson of Alfonso V
1521–1557	King	John III	1502	1557	Son of Emanuel I
1557–1578	King	Sebastian	1554	1578	Grandson of John III
1578–1580	King	Henry	1512	1580	Brother of John III
1580–1580	King	Antonio	1531	1595	Nephew of Henry

1580–1640—Controlled by King Philip II of Spain (Philip I of Portugal).

HOUSE OF BRAGANZA

Reign	Title	Ruler	Birth	Death	Relationship
1640–1656	King	John IV	1604	1656	Descendant of John I
1656–1667	King	Alfonso VI	1643	1683	Son of John IV
1667–1683	Regent	Pedro II	1648	1706	Son of John IV
1683–1706	King	Pedro II			
1706–1750	King	John V	1689	1750	Son of Pedro II
1750–1777	King	Joseph Emanuel	1714	1777	Son of John V
1777–1816	Queen	Maria I	1734	1816	Daughter of Joseph Emanuel
1777–1786	Joint Ruler	Pedro III	1717	1786	Son of John V, husband of Maria I
1799–1816	Regent	John	1767	1826	Son of Maria I
1816–1826	King	John VI			
1826–1826	King	Pedro IV	1798	1834	Son of John VI
1826–1828	Queen	Maria II	1819	1853	Daughter of Pedro IV
1828–1834	King	Miguel	1802	1866	Uncle of Maria II
1834–1853	Queen	Maria II			(Rethroned)
1853–1861	King	Pedro V	1837	1861	Son of Maria II
1861–1889	King	Louis I	1838	1889	Son of Maria II
1889–1908	King	Carlos I	1863	1908	Son of Louis I; (assassinated)
1908–1910	King	Manuel II	1888	1932	Son of Carlos I; abdicated 1910

1910—Portugal became a Republic.

10

The Kingdom of Belgium

Map of Belgium today

Historically, the country now known as Belgium was, at one time or another, the property of many other European powers, including the Romans, the French, the Spanish, the Austrians, and the Dutch. It achieved its independence from the Netherlands in 1830 after many centuries of foreign domination.

When the country was liberated in 1830, the people yearned for total independence, although necessity dictated a certain degree of dependence on other European states. Moreover, neutrality was forced upon Belgium by the other European powers. This neutrality was maintained for over one hundred years, but just before World War II Belgium proclaimed a policy of "armed neutrality," indicating that it no longer wanted to be dependent militarily on others. After World War I and particularly after World War II, Belgium developed strong economic and military ties with its European neighbors and North America.

Internally, the country's history has been marked by

ethnic problems, principally between the Flemings—who live in the northern areas and speak Flemish—and the Walloons—who live in the southern section and speak French. The linquistic and cultural differences between these two groups can be traced back to their earliest association.

Strained relations between the Flemings and Walloons, which the government of Belgium has tried to solve in a variety of ways, profoundly affect the education of Belgian children, politics, economic affairs, and religion. Until after World War II, the major political parties—apart from the Belgian Socialist party (BSP—PSB for Dutch and French designations)—were the Belgian Catholic party, which was supported for the most part by the Flemings, and the Belgian Liberal party, which was generally supported by the Walloons.

In this country that contains such great differences of opinion and culture, the two ostensible unifying forces are the church and the institution of the monarchy. The Roman Catholic church encompasses the vast majority of Belgians. There are great differences, however, between the generally devout Flemings and the frequently anticlerical Walloons. The monarchy—despite the fact that Belgium has one of the world's more democratic constitutions—is another force for unity in that the king brings antagonistic elements together under his rule. As one authority on the country has written: "Monarchy in Belgium is indispensable to national unity in that the King stands above conflict so that through him alone can Fleming and Walloon, Catholic and anticlerical identify himself as Belgian."

EARLY HISTORY

In his *Commentaries on the Gallic Wars,* Julius Caesar referred to the Belgae as "the most courageous" of the peoples his legions had encountered in their conquest of Gaul. The Belgae were a Celtic people who had migrated earlier from middle Europe and had settled in the area

A Belgian stamp commemorating Caesar crossing the Rubicon

Ambiorix, chief of the Eburones and the last warrior to fight Julius Caesar's occupation of Gaul, depicted in a statue near the location in Belgium where the action took place.

that later became known as the Low Countries—modern Netherlands, Belgium, and Luxemburg. After being conquered by Caesar's forces in the first century B.C., the Belgae adopted the language of the conquerors and began to assimilate Roman culture. By the second century A.D. the Belgic tribes began accepting the Christian religion, which was spreading through the Roman Empire of which they were a part, but paganism remained strong among them. During the early Roman period the Belgae retained contact with, and were influenced by, the Greek Mediterranean settlements, particularly the one at Massilia (Marseilles).

In the third century A.D., Germanic tribes—the Franks—moved into northern Gaul, pushing the Belgae toward the general area of modern Belgium. The Flemish-Walloon ethnic troubles that still persist in the 1980s had their origins in the differences between the Franks and the Belgae in the third century. The modern Flemings of northern Belgium are descended from the Germanic Franks, and the Walloons of the south are the descendants of the Celtic Belgae.

Over the next few centuries as the power of Rome declined, Frankish kings challenged Roman hegemony in northern Gaul and eventually incorporated the land into their empires. Under Clovis in the late fifth and early sixth centuries A.D., the Belgians were re-Christianized, having lapsed back into paganism after their earlier conversion. Although the veneer of Christianity remained thin, this time the new religion took root, and Christianity eventually flourished among the people of the Low Countries. Both Clovis and Charlemagne established powerful empires, but both were followed by weak rulers who could not avert long periods of strife and turmoil. Clovis's Merovingian Empire plunged into two centuries of troubles after his death in the early sixth century, and it was not until the Carolingian Dynasty was established that some semblance of stability was restored. After Charlemagne, the greatest Carolingian

leader and head of the Holy Roman Empire until his death in A.D. 814, the empire was divided into three kingdoms and subjected to civil war as well as to disastrous raids by the Norsemen. The weakness of the later Carolingian emperors brought on a proliferation of powerful nobles, who fortified their castles and walled their cities as protection against the Norse raiders; in the process these nobles assumed prerogatives that had been exercised by the emperors, thus giving rise to a fractionated society.

Before the Norsemen were finally defeated at the end of the ninth century A.D., the Middle Kingdom had already disappeared; the territory of the Low Countries had been divided between the kingdom of France and the Holy Roman Empire; and feudalism had been established throughout the area. The feudal system, which was essentially rural, lasted for about three centuries; during that period the Belgian area developed as a center of industry and trade. Belgian textile and metalworking industries became famous throughout Europe, and Belgium's location on the North Sea made it a crossroads of maritime trade and travel. The easy access to the interior by way of navigable waterways and the old Roman roads also made the Low Countries the terminus of much overland commerce.

The growth of industry and trade conflicted with the agrarian feudal system as merchants and manufacturers established themselves as a class of freemen between the feudal overlords and the serfs. The new industrial and commercial centers attracted serfs from the rural areas. The serfs became freemen, but a rigid class distinction evolved between them and the merchant class. As towns grew, powerful merchant guilds secured charters from

Baldwin and Queen Judith. Important to the recording of the royal history of Belgium is the mention of the counts and countesses of Flanders, for Flanders, the main province of Belgium, was ruled by them from the time of Charlemagne's demise to 1384 when the country came under Burgundy. History records the first count of Flanders as Baldwin, the Flemish chieftain, who started the reign in 862. In 864, Judith, the daughter of Charles the Bald, king of France, and the widow of Ethelwulf, king of England, "attached herself" to Baldwin. The king, after many attempts to break up the union, finally, upon the advice of the pope, who feared a lack of recognition by France would turn Baldwin to the Normans, conferred the title of count of Flanders on Baldwin I.

Baldwin II, the second count of Flanders (878–918)

Arnuff I, the third count of Flanders (918–50; 961–64)

Arnuff II, the sixth count of Flanders (964–89)

Baldwin IV, the seventh count of Flanders (989–1035)

Arnuff III, the tenth count of Flanders (1070–71)

Robert I, the eleventh count of Flanders (1071–93)

Baldwin III, the fourth count of Flanders (950–61)

Arnuff I, the Elder, the fifth count of Flanders (961–64).

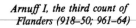

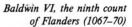

Baldwin V, the eighth count of Flanders (1035–67)

Baldwin VI, the ninth count of Flanders (1067–70)

Robert I and his son Robert II, who became the twelfth count of Flanders (1093–1111)

Baldwin VII, the thirteenth count of Flanders (1111–19)

feudal overlords for the establishment of law and municipal institutions. The charters usually granted rights to merchants that were denied to workers, and the class system that emerged severely inhibited upward mobility. In the thirteenth century, dissatisfaction on the part of the workers led to a series of uprisings that, toward the end of the century, became virtual revolution. The upper classes, terrified by the worker uprisings, called on the French king for help in putting down the unrest. England, fearing undue French influence in the area, also intervened.

The history of the Low Countries for the next several centuries was one of foreign intervention and domination, dynastic struggles, worker unrest, and rising and falling economic fortunes.

In the late fourteenth century the Low Countries came under the political hegemony of the dukes of Burgundy, who initiated a reign during which the economy flourished and the area experienced a golden age of scholarship, culture, and commerce.

By the middle of the sixteenth century the Burgundian period had ended, and the Spanish had gained control over the Low Countries. Philip II of Spain tried to reduce the autonomy of the prosperous cities and towns and, in so doing, unleashed almost a century of warfare that finally resulted in the independence of the Netherlands but left the Belgian provinces under Spanish rule. From that point on, Belgium was a pawn in the power struggles and the religious conflicts of the great European nations, passing from the Spanish Habsburgs to the Austrian Habsburgs to the French to the Dutch and often serving as a battleground for the contesting armies of the major European powers. As a result of the religious strife of the sixteenth and seventeenth centuries, great numbers of Protestants from the Belgian provinces migrated to England, America, and Scandinavia, taking with them their skills in commerce and industry.

During the seventeenth and early eighteenth centuries, the linguistic differences of the Flemings and the Walloons became more intense. Under the later Burgundian dukes, all oaths of office in the northern provinces had been taken in the Flemish language. Under Philip II, however, French became the administrative language of the entire area. During the years of the Spanish Inquisition when Protestants fled northward, the language frontier—between the Flemish speakers in the north and the French speakers in the south—was again reinforced. When the area was ceded to Austria in 1713, the language of administration for the entire area was again French.

During the seventeenth and eighteenth centuries, Belgians had little or no control over the international events that shaped their destiny. They had no voice in the councils that decided on war or peace in Europe, even though Belgium was often the battleground, nor were they consulted on the peace treaties that ended the

Charles the Good, the fourteenth count of Flanders (1119–1127)

William Clito of Normandy, the fifteenth count of Flanders (1127–28)

Dirk of Alsace, the sixteenth count of Flanders (1128–57)

Philip of Alsace, the seventeenth count of Flanders (1157–91)

Baldwin VIII, the eighteenth count of Flanders united the countships of Flanders and Hainaut (1191–95)

Countess Margareta of Constantinople, the eighteenth count(ess) of Flanders (1191–94)

Margareta in later life, just before her death in 1194

Baldwin IX (1195–1206), the nineteenth count of Flanders (1195–1206)

Joanna of Constantinople, the twentieth count(ess) of Flanders, was the daughter of Baldwin IX.

Ferdinand of Portugal, the twentieth count of Flanders, was the husband of Joanna (coregent with her from 1212 to 1233).

Thomas of Savoy was the second husband of Joanna and served as coregent with her from 1237 to 1244. He was considered the twenty-first count of Flanders.

many wars and often changed their territorial borders. The Peace of Westphalia in 1648, which ended the Thirty Years War, recognized Holland as an independent country and, with a subsequent treaty in 1661, confirmed the closing of the Schelde estuary and thus strangled the port of Antwerp. From 1609 to 1715 the Belgian provinces were known as the Spanish Netherlands and suffered heavily from wars fought by Spain, France, England, and Holland. In the early part of the eighteenth century, once again by treaties engineered by the major powers, the Belgian provinces became the Austrian Netherlands.

Under Austrian rule during most of the eighteenth century, the Belgian provinces made great progress in both agriculture and industry. A great deal of effort was put into the building of roads and canals. Despite Austrian efforts during their period of rule, the port of Antwerp continued to languish as Belgian ships were denied use of the Schelde estuary. In another area of conflict with the Dutch, however, the Austrians were successful. This involved the barrier fortresses—a series of military garrisons in Belgian towns—that the Dutch maintained and forced the Belgians to pay for. The Austrian emperor, Joseph II, finally forced the Dutch to abandon the forts and leave Belgium. The Austrian efforts to weaken Dutch influence in the area were appreciated by the Belgians, but efforts to impose autocratic rule by the Austrians met stiff resistance. The French Revolution of 1789 spurred the Belgians to action, and they declared independence; but powerful Austrian armies quickly ended the life of the United States of Belgium.

In the early 1790s the French revolutionary armies invaded Belgium and, eventually, drove out the Austrians. By 1795 the Belgian provinces had been annexed by France. French rule, however, was short-lived. Napoleon's disaster in Russia and his final defeat at Waterloo (a few miles south of Brussels) ended the twenty-year period of French hegemony in the area. The major European powers, meeting in the Congress of Vienna, decided that the Low Countries should be united and

Countess Margaret (1244–80), daughter of Joanna, is honored on a Belgian commemorative stamp.

Guy de Dampierre, the twenty-second count of Flanders (1280–1305)

Robert III of Bethune, the twenty-third count of Flanders (1305–22)

Louis I of Newers, the twenty-fourth count of Flanders (1322–37)

Louis II de Male, the twenty-fifth count of Flanders (1345–84), was secretly murdered by his son-in-law's brother, the duke of Berri. The son-in-law, Philip the Bold, duke of Burgundy, then had his wife Margaret, the daughter of Louis II, placed in reign (1384–1405).

created the United Kingdom of the Netherlands, which combined Holland, Belgium and Luxemburg under William of Orange, the Dutch king. The new kingdom prospered and, because Antwerp was reopened, Belgian trade again became important.

For a time it seemed as though the United Kingdom of the Netherlands might succeed in spite of ethnic and religious differences, but old problems and old enmities were never far beneath the surface. Before long the Belgians believed that they were being treated as second-class citizens in the new arrangement. The Belgians were bothered by edicts that directed them to assume half the national debt even though Holland had entered the union with an indebtedness many times larger than Belgium's. In addition, seats in the legislature were divided equally despite the fact that Belgium's population outnumbered the Dutch by more than 1 million. Finally, both the Flemings and Walloons of Belgium were intensely Roman Catholic and were concerned about being ruled by a Dutch Calvinist. Tensions mounted until the summer of 1830, when the Belgians successfully revolted and declared their independence.

THE NEW KINGDOM

William of Orange sent armies to the Belgian provinces to prevent their secession, but the Belgians were deter-

mined to win their freedom. The great powers—Austria, France, Great Britain, Prussia, and Russia—intervened to impose a cease-fire and, eventually, to approve of an independent Belgium. The bulk of the fighting in the revolution had fallen on the urban workers and the peasants but, ironically, the bourgeoisie, many of whom had not favored independence, acquired political power in the new state. A provisional government was established and soon declared independence and arranged for elections to the Belgian National Congress. The great powers had advocated that the Belgians accept a son of the Dutch king as the new king of Belgium, but the congress voted to exclude the House of Orange from the throne of Belgium. Once the constitution was drafted in February 1831, a search was undertaken to select an appropriate king. The throne was first offered to the duke of Nemours, who was the son of Louis-Philippe of France; the British were opposed to this choice, and it was abandoned. It was then offered to Leopold of the House of Saxe-Coburg.

The constitution, which was liberal in most respects, guaranteed not only freedom of the press but also freedom of association, education, and worship. It assured citizens of the inviolability of the home, the right of petition, and equality under the law. The constitution allowed for little future change, however. In fact it has been amended only three times since 1831.

One of the essential features of the constitution was the concept of the monarchy. The monarchy was to be hereditary, and women were excluded from succession to the throne. The king was to have the power to dissolve the National Congress, appoint ministers and judges, issue currency, and make war and peace; he was also to be commander of the armed forces.

Leopold had been in the Russian army that fought Napoleon and had been married to the heiress to the English throne. Since his first wife had died, he was free to marry the daughter of the French ruler Louis-Philippe. In fact, one of the primary motives for choosing Leopold was that he had relationships with Belgium's allies. He was Protestant but relatively objective in religious matters; in addition, according to Belgian law, his children would be raised in the Roman Catholic church.

Leopold accepted the throne on the condition that the great powers ratify Belgium's proposed Treaty of Eighteen Articles, which would allow Belgium to retain Limburg and Luxemburg. After Leopold had taken the throne in July 1831, the Dutch began another march against Belgium, and Leopold asked for and received the aid of French troops. At this point, the London Conference drew up an amended version of the original treaty, which was called the Treaty of Twenty-four Articles. Although the treaty guaranteed international protection to Belgium and recognized its independence, parts of both Limburg and Luxemburg were lost.

The first king of the Belgians, Leopold I. The crown was offered to Prince Leopold of Saxe-Coburg, and on June 4, 1832, he was proclaimed king of the Belgians.

Princess Charlotte and Maximilian in their official engagement photograph

Princess Charlotte. Leopold I had three children, Leopold II, Prince Philip, the Count of Flanders (Father of King Albert I) and a daughter, Princess Charlotte. The princess married Maximilian of Austria, who became for a short period of time the emperor of Mexico. His firstborn, the crown prince Leopold, succeeded him to the throne in 1865.

This satirical print was published in 1833 when constitutional conflict was disturbing several countries whose sovereigns were of tender age. Isabella of Spain, right, was only three when her proclamation as queen led to the first Carlist war. In Portugal, Dom Miguel claimed the crown of Maria II, aged fourteen. Otto, left, shown as a boy of twelve, was king of a newly independent Greece; and the imperial crown of Brazil overweights the head of Pedro II, five years old.

The liberation of Belgium tended to intensify the Flemish-Walloon dispute. The revolution not only dissolved the political union with the Dutch but also weakened any sense of community with them. The political leaders of the revolution in Belgium, both Fleming and Walloon, had long admired the French—not only for their politics but also for their language and culture. As one authority has written, the Liberal party regarded the Flemings as set apart from the entire revolution: "In their [the Liberals'] eyes the Flemish masses had been dangerously cut off, through their ignorance of the French language, from the ideals of the French Revolution which had so deeply influenced Belgium's constitution." Once the independence of the country had been achieved, French became the official language of the country, but the Flemish masses continued to speak their own tongue. In fact, the full impact of Flemish-Walloon differences was severely felt at precisely the moment when the two ethnic groups were forged into one country.

Religion and politics, inextricably intertwined in Belgium, continued to be sources of dispute. The Constitu-

tion of 1831 had—in an attempt to satisfy both the Catholic and Liberal parties—guaranteed complete freedom of worship. The Roman Catholic clergy, however, were subsidized by the state.

Belgium was one of the few European countries that did not undergo the turmoils of the 1848 revolutions. Leopold's chief goals were to fend off the Dutch, in the early years, and to keep the French and the Prussians from absorbing the country. At the time of independence Prussia had been opposed to a free and independent Belgium. Later, however, the Prussians tried to entice the Belgians into a customs union (Zollverein). Although Belgium signed treaties with Prussia in 1844 and 1852, it refused to enter the proposed union.

The French had not been eager to see a totally independent Belgium, principally because they hoped to annex the country again. Between 1838 and 1843 the French, like the Prussians, made various proposals for an economic union, which Belgium again refused. A simple commercial treaty was, however, signed with France in 1845. Relations with France deteriorated when, in the latter part of the century, it was learned that the French had submitted a secret draft treaty to Prussia in which France proposed that both Belgium and Luxemburg be annexed to France. This plan was never carried out, largely because of Great Britain's pledge of protection to Belgium.

THE BELGIAN CONGO

In the late 1860s King Leopold II, who succeeded Leopold I in 1865, became interested in expanding his territory overseas, although the Belgian population was indifferent to his aims. In 1876 Leopold II convened a conference of European explorers in Brussels and set up a committee called the International African Association (Association Internationale Africaine—AIA); Leopold was its first president. By 1879, with the assistance of the famous explorer, Henry M. Stanley, Leopold laid plans for a free state in the Congo. While Stanley was founding Leopoldville—named after the Belgian king— the French were also ceded certain territories in the Congo. By 1882, however, Leopold created the International Association of the Congo (Association Internationale du Congo—AIC) and persuaded the United States and Germany to accept the association's territorial status.

By 1884 the Berlin Conference, which had been convened to mediate the claims of European powers to African territory, recognized the new state of the Congo. One year later, in May 1885, a royal decree proclaimed the establishment of the Congo Free State with Leopold II as its ruler. Five years after the proclamation, Leopold persuaded the leading European powers to allow the Congo to impose customs duties. Shortly thereafter the boundaries of the free state—which itself was wealthy in rubber and ivory—were expanded to include the province of Katanga, which was extremely rich in copper.

Because the native population of the country was exploited, while Leopold II was draining its wealth, other countries—most notably Great Britain—began to pro-

King Leopold II (1865–1909). His greatest claim to fame was the founding in West Africa of the Congo state (Belgian Congo), with the help of the famous explorer, Sir Henry Stanley. King Leopold died in December 1909.

Prince Albert enters Brussels in 1909 after the death of King Leopold II

test. Even within Belgium itself, the Catholic party joined with the Socialists in opposition to Leopold's activities in the Congo. By 1890 Leopold had decided, despite the reactions of his Belgian citizens, to leave the Congo to Belgium in his will. After long struggles and opposition, a bill of annexation was passed by the government in 1908, one year before Leopold died.

WORLD WAR I

In the years before the outbreak of World War I, Belgium's industry, banking, and railroads boomed; the country was one of Europe's leading exporters. Poverty, however, existed on a large scale. Conditions for workers were dismal—urban conditions were poor, and wages were low. Education did not become compulsory until 1914; approximately one-fourth of all workers were illiterate. Therefore, the domestic situation was difficult when the war began.

Because Belgium was a passageway to France, it was crucial to German strategy in the war. On August 2, 1914, the Germans crossed the frontier of Luxemburg, which like Belgium was a neutral state. Two days later the Germans marched on Belgium. In two weeks the city of Liège fell to Germany; the Germans entered Brussels on August 20. The Belgians under the leadership of King Albert, who had assumed the throne in 1909, attempted to resist German incursions at Antwerp. When the Belgians were driven from the city in October 1914, they located themselves in a narrow strip of the country west of the IJssel River, where they remained for four years.

The German strategy was based on a dual plan: to encourage the Flemish movement, thereby dividing the country internally, and to make a separate peace with Albert. Although both plans met with what appeared to be success, neither plan succeeded completely. The Flemings were still frustrated by the government at the beginning of the war; an extremist group of Flemings, known as the Activists, wanted complete separation from the Belgian state. In 1916 the German governor general agreed to split the Ministry of Arts and Science into separate Flemish and Walloon sections; at the same time he reopened the University of Gent as a totally Flemish institution. In 1917, two hundred Activists met in Brussels and formed the Council of Flanders. They demanded that the country be completely divided into two administrative units, with Brussels as the capital of Flanders and Namur as the capital of Wallonia.

The other aspect of the German plan was also partially successful. Albert, much like the Activists, was interested not in aiding and abetting the German cause but in restoring a free and independent country. The Germans first approached Albert on the basis of a separate peace in October 1915; he was definitely opposed to their plan at that time. By 1916, however, he appeared to be more responsive. Although Albert sought peace for the

Albert I (1875–1934), king of Belgium (1909–34). Second son of Prince Philip Baldwin, count of Flanders, and Princess Marie of Hohenzollern, he married (1900) Elizabeth, duchess of Bavaria. Their children were Prince Leopold (who succeeded his father as Leopold III), Prince Charles, and Princess Marie-José, who married (1930) Prince Umberto of Italy.

Queen Elisabeth, wife of King Albert, 1876–1965, honored on a Belgian birth centenary stamp. She was born on July 25, 1876, at Possenhoven, in Bavaria, the daughter of Carl Theodore, duke of Bavaria, and Marie-José of Braganza, princess of Portugal.

On October 2, 1900, she married Prince Albert in Munich, nephew of the then-reigning monarch of Belgium, Leopold II.

King Leopold II died without an heir and Prince Albert became king of the Belgians on December 22, 1909. From the time of her arrival in Belgium, Her Majesty showed interest in the cultural life of her new country. She encouraged young artists by visiting exhibitions of painters and attending concerts, and was a gracious hostess of artists in all fields.

Three children were born of her marriage to King Albert of the Belgians: Prince Leopold, who reigned in Belgium after his father's death in 1934, under the name of King Leopold III; Prince Charles, who was regent of the kingdom immediately after World War II until 1952; Princess Marie-José, who married King Umberto of Italy.

The heroic defense of the Belgians in 1914, during World War I, gave Britain and France time to complete mobilization and prepare for the battle of the Marne. Albert remained in the field at the head of his troops throughout the war. He died years later in a mountain-climbing mishap.

sake of his country, there was no real opportunity to negotiate with the Germans because of the basic hostility of Albert's cabinet, the overall attitude of the Belgian people, and the opposition of the Allies.

When the war ended and the armistice was signed in November 1918, Albert returned to Brussels with Belgian and Allied troops. He found his country in a better political situation than before the war, but it had been devastated by human and material damage. From the

On October 25, 1918, King Albert I, Queen Elisabeth, and the crown prince Leopold make their state return to Bruges, Belgium, after the Germans were defeated.

war there emerged—despite the collaboration of the Activists—a new spirit of national unity that continued to prevail in peacetime.

THE INTERWAR YEARS

During the period between 1918 and the beginning of World War II, Belgium was in a state of constant flux. Out of the turmoil of war, a sense of national identity emerged for the first time since independence in 1830. Although Belgium was excluded from the inner circle of the Versailles conference and treaty, it attempted to demand the revision of the Treaty of Twenty-four Articles, written in 1831, which would return Limburg and Luxemburg to Belgium. This demand was rejected by the Versailles conference.

In other postwar negotiations, however, Belgium gained a certain amount of ground. It was given 2,500 million gold francs and promised a thirty-year indemnity from Germany through the Treaty of Versailles. The same treaty ensured that Belgium's historic neutrality clause—dating back to the 1830s—would be abandoned. Through this renunciation of neutrality, Belgium was able to safeguard its territory by means of military alliances as was true of any other sovereign state. Belgium also made a slight territorial gain in the previously German-held territory near Liége.

Domestic politics also went through a period of change and upheaval. Albert continued as ruler until his death in 1934, at which point he was succeeded by his son Leopold III. The political parties passed through a number of changes.

By 1935, a year after the death of Albert, a three-party coalition took power under the leadership of a Catholic party member, Paul van Zeeland. Eventually, despite a series of economic reforms designed to reduce unemployment and taxes, his government fell, and leadership passed to Paul-Henri Spaak.

A photograph of King Albert taken to make an engraving for a postage stamp

Crown Prince Leopold

Crown Prince Leopold, left; the Prince of Wales, center; and King Albert during a state visit by the prince to Belgium

The Prince of Wales, left, with the crown prince Leopold

A royal group photograph taken during the visit of the Prince of Wales. Sitting, left to right: Princess Marie-José, Queen Elisabeth, the Prince of Wales, and King Albert. Standing, left, Crown Prince Leopold and Prince Charles, the count of Flanders.

The various crises that the country had undergone in this period of turmoil assisted the development of the Rexist movement. The Rexists—who took their name from Christus Rex (Christ the King)—were a quasi-Fascist organization, led by Léon Degrelle, a former student at the University of Louvain. Most of his supporters were from the capital of the country and the south. The organization had its roots in the nazism of Hitler and the fascism of Mussolini. In the elections of 1936 the Rexists achieved great success at the polls, gaining twenty-two seats. Because of Hitler's actions in Europe, by 1937 the country began to turn against the Rexists; by 1939 the Rexist party had only four deputies left in Parliament. The Rexists were at one point closely related to extremists of the Flemish population, such as the Flemish National party (Vlaamsch National Verbond—VNV), which was formed in 1925 and campaigned for Flemish autonomy from the state of Belgium in 1935.

The frustrations of the Flemish population during this period—which were exacerbated by the Belgian alliance with France after the war—came to a head in the 1930s. By 1935 the VNV began to make demands on the government on purely Flemish grounds. By 1939 seventeen VNV deputies were sent to Parliament; they were determined to do away with the Belgian state. The cry of the Flemish extremists at that time was *"Weg met Belgie"* (Away with Belgium).

In 1936 a new expansionist Germany was again appearing on the European scene. King Leopold III withdrew Belgium from the Locarno Treaty and advocated a policy of armed neutrality. By 1937 Belgium's independence from the pact was recognized by Great Britain and France, although they continued to offer assistance if it should be needed. Leopold's armed neutrality policy reflected a desire on the part of Belgium to stand aside from the disputes of Europe and to defend its own territories. This desire had been provoked and aggravated by Belgium's awareness of the significance of Hitler's invasion of Austira; the Czechoslovakian crisis; and the Munich agreement between Germany, Italy, France, and Great Britain. On September 3, 1939, Belgium formally

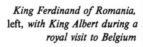

King Ferdinand of Romania, left, with King Albert during a royal visit to Belgium

King Albert birth centenary stamps (1875–1934)

King Leopold III and Queen Astrid in a wedding pose

On August 29, 1935, the beautiful queen Astrid, consort of the young king Leopold III, was killed in a motoring accident in Switzerland. Queen Astrid, who was thirty years old and a niece of the king of Sweden, is seen here with her children, left to right, *Princess Josephine-Charlotte, Prince Albert, and the crown prince Baudouin.*

Deep sympathy was felt for King Leopold, who less than two years previously had lost his father as the result of a mountaineering accident. King Leopold, who was driving the car when it crashed into a stone parapet near Kusnacht, a resort on Lake Lucerne, was himself injured and appeared at the funeral with his arm in a sling.

The king's palace in Brussels

declared its neutrality to the world, but Europe was engulfed in another war.

WORLD WAR II

In September 1939 Germany invaded Poland; two days after the invasion, France and Great Britain declared war on Germany. At the same time that Belgium renounced its neutrality, it began to mobilize. In accord with Belgium's new policy of independence, it refused to allow British and French troops to be stationed on Belgian soil during the first months of the war.

On May 10, 1940, Germany attacked Belgium. With an abrupt about-face, Belgium called on the British and French for military aid. The Germans began to bomb the country and issued a statement declaring that Germany was forced to occupy Belgium in order to forestall invasions by the British and the French. Germany successfully cut off the Allied armies in the area and encircled the country. Belgian refugees fled in panic, and the British and French were forced to retreat. By June 1940 the Germans had occupied Belgium. Leopold III decided to remain in Belgium against the wishes of his cabinet, which moved the government to England. Disapproval of his decision was based on the belief that the king's presence in the country could be used to the advantage of the Germans. In fact Leopold eventually became a German prisoner and was severely condemned for his conduct during the war.

Criticism of the king grew even as the war was winding to a close. During the last year of the war, Leopold III had been transferred first to Germany and later to Austria. On May 7, 1945, he was freed by American troops. Belgium was liberated on September 3, 1944, by General Bernard Montgomery's forces. Although the war was officially over for Belgium, German bombs continued to fall through the winter, damaging both Liége and Antwerp. Eventually, in the spring of 1945, all fighting ceased in Belgium, and peace was restored to Europe.

THE POSTWAR YEARS

The years between World War II and the early 1970s were characterized by five major themes. The first theme was Belgium's desire for a role in international politics. The second major issue was the resolution of the Congo crisis. The third issue was the conflict between clerical and secular forces in education. This was exacerbated by the fourth problem, the increasing tensions between the Flemings and the Walloons. The most severe initial problem, however, in the postwar years was the so-called royal issue regarding Leopold's right to the throne.

In 1945 the Catholic party became the Christian Social party (CVP-PSC). In the elections of 1946 this party obtained a large number of seats in Parliament, gaining mostly from the loss of VNV and Rexist representatives. Eventually, a coalition was formed of Socialists, Liberals, and Communists, all of whom were overtly hostile to the continuation of Leopold III as king of the Belgians.

At approximately the same time, the Flemish-Walloon situation was aggravated by a language census taken in 1947. The results were shattering to the Walloons. The census showed that 51.3 percent of the country spoke Dutch; 32.9 percent spoke French; 1 percent spoke German; and the remaining 15.7 percent, who were located in Brussels, spoke both French and Dutch. The Walloons not only were shocked by these statistics but also felt that the government favored the Flemings.

The issue of Leopold's retention of the throne was the focal point for political, religious, and ethnic grievances. Because of Leopold's alleged collaboration with the Germans during the war, he had been for the most part repudiated by his fellow countrymen. Generally, however, the Roman Catholic Flemings hoped to see Leopold return to the throne, but the more anticlerical Walloons did not. Achille van Acker, the first cabinet leader in the postwar years, felt that the king would unite the two antagonistic groups by sheer force of the monarchy.

Meanwhile, the Socialists and the Communists demanded Leopold's abdication in favor of his older son, Prince Baudouin. The CVP-PSC, which was initially in favor of Leopold's retention of the throne, now also objected. At this point, the more liberal coalition asked for a popular vote on the issue. In the elections of 1947 the CVP-PSC gained another thirteen seats, and a new coalition was formed between the CVP-PSC and the Liberals.

A vote was taken in 1950 regarding the king. Of the total vote, 57 percent favored Leopold's retention of the throne. There were, however, regional and ethnic differences: 72 percent of the Flemish provinces voted in favor of Leopold, whereas only 42 percent of Wallonia and 48 percent of the residents of Brussels voted similarly.

In the same elections of 1950, the CVP-PSC won an absolute majority. When Leopold III was returned to the throne, approximately 1.5 million Communists and Socialists went on strike in Wallonia, crying "Hang Leopold." The continuing strikes and destruction of property forced the government to recognize that the only way to prevent a civil war was for Leopold to abdicate. Even members of the CVP-PSC, who had previously favored Leopold, were opposed to his leadership when they realized the destruction that his return had caused. By August 1950 the government had announced that Leopold would be replaced by Prince Baudouin, who took the title of prince royal. In July 1951 Leopold III turned over all power to Baudouin, who assumed the title of king. The struggle, however, went far deeper than

politics. The basic cleavage between the Flemings and the Walloons had been intensified through the royal issue.

The domestic situation in Belgium during the 1950s was still volatile, and foreign relations became increasingly troubled by the situation in the Congo. When Baudouin assumed the throne in 1951, social agitation was momentarily quieted. The CVP-PSC still retained power, although its popularity dropped to some extent, primarily because of controversial school legislation in the 1950s. By 1954 the CVP-PSC vote had dropped significantly. A sentiment of anticlericalism, which had pervaded certain elements of politics since 1830, led to the formation of a coalition of Socialists and Liberals.

By the 1960s, although most of Belgium's foreign problems had been resolved, the domestic situation was fraught with difficulties. The essential problems revolved around Flemish-Walloon relations, which in turn impinged to a great extent on the country's educational system. Other major issues were the economic and political situation, the question of constitutional reform, and the proposal of federalism as the form of government best suited to the needs of the country.

King Baudouin paid a visit to the United Nations headquarters in New York City in 1959. He is seen here, left, with UN Secretary-General Dag Hammarskjold at the podium in the General Assembly Hall.

Their Majesties King Baudouin and Queen Fabiola. They were married in Brussels on December 15, 1960.

A close-up of Queen Fabiola

King Baudouin, king of the Belgians, is a constitutional monarch, the country's fifth sovereign since Belgium acquired its independence in 1830. Together with the Chamber of Representatives and the Senate, he exercises the legislative power. In addition, he possesses, with the assistance and under the responsibility of his cabinet ministers, the sole executive power. The king reigns, he does not govern, but it is an unwritten rule of the Belgian political system that as an arbiter standing above the parties, the king does, through persuasion and the prestige of his office, guide the decisions of his government. He is, thus, far from being just a figurehead, and may even be in times of stress the cornerstone of the political edifice.

The king's youth was marred by tragedy: the death in a mountaineering accident of his grandfather, King Albert (1934), and the death of his mother, Queen Astrid (who was a Swedish princess), victim of an automobile accident in Switzerland (1935). Later, the invasion of Belgium in May 1940 forced him to seek refuge and safety first in France and finally at San Sebastian, Spain. He returned to Laeken in September 1940 and spent two years at the Castle of Ciergnon. In June 1944, the royal family was deported to Germany after the landing of the Allies in Normandy, and the king became one of Hitler's youngest political prisoners. The royal family was first interned in a decrepit medieval castle, Hirschtein near Heimar, where comfort was at a minimum. After the final Allied breakthrough in March 1945, the royal family was transferred by the Germans to Strobl in Austria. On the way, the party was caught in a severe air attack on Munich and forced to take refuge under a railroad bridge while comparatively safe shelters were available at a short distance.

Queen Fabiola in a formal appearance at a theatrical performance

The king and queen in an informal pose on the grounds in front of the royal palace in Laeken

The royal family was freed by a detachment of the Seventh American Army on May 7, 1945; Prince Baudouin knew freedom again after five years. He resumed his studies in Geneva, where King Leopold and the royal family lived temporarily pending the settlement of what became known as the question royale. He then returned to Brussels with King Leopold in the summer of 1950.

After his return to Belgium in July 1950, Prince Baudouin first acted as ruler of the kingdom under the title of prince royal; he acceded to the throne in July 1951 as king of the Belgians, following his father's abdication.

King Baudouin was born in Brussels, September 7, 1930, the son of King Leopold III, born November 3, 1901 (son of King Albert and Queen Elizabeth) and of Queen Astrid (daughter of Prince Karl and Princess Ingeborg of Sweden). Besides King Leopold, his wife Princess Liliane, the royal family consists of: Princess Josephine-Charlotte, born October 11, 1927, married to the grand-duke Jean of Luxemburg; Prince Albert, born June 6, 1934, president of the Red Cross of Belgium, who visited the USA in 1955; Prince Alexander, born July 18, 1942; Princess Marie-Christine, born February 6, 1951; Princess Marie-Esmeralda, born September 30, 1956 (as of 1982).

Prince Alexander and the Princesses Marie-Christine and Marie-Esmeralda are the children of King Leopold's marriage to Princess Liliane, born in London, November 28, 1916, and married to King Leopold in 1941. Prince Charles, who was regent of the kingdom from 1945 to 1950, is the king's uncle (as of 1982).

THE POLITICAL PARTIES

In 1961 a coalition government—formed of Christian Socialists and Socialists—came to power. By the late 1960s there were three major political parties and two relatively ineffectual ones. The major party of the 1960s was the Christian Social party (CVP-PSC), formerly known as the Belgian Catholic party. Its support came primarily from the Roman Catholic church, the Roman Catholic-allied trade unions, the business community, and the Flemish workers and farmers. The second strongest political party at that time was the Belgian Socialist party (BSP-PSB). It was supported principally by Wallonian industrial workers but also gained some support from businessmen and some of the population in Flemish industrialized areas. The third major political party was the Party of Liberty and Progress (PVV-PLP), formerly known as the Belgian Liberal party. It was the most conservative of the three and had roughly equal strength in the Flemish and Walloon areas. The Belgian Communist party and the Flemish People's Union—an extreme Flemish group—were the minority parties.

ETHNIC RELATIONS

In 1965 the Commission for Institutional Reform met to discuss the Flemish-Walloon problem. It favored the establishment of cultural councils, one for the French-speaking and one for the Flemish-speaking population. There was also to be a cultural council for the small German-speaking segment of the population. Each council would promote and supervise the spreading of its particular culture within its own area. Ministers of the government would submit legislation to the cultural councils on such matters as the use of a particular language; education in general; literature, libraries, and museums; mass education; youth activities; radio and television; and cultural relations with foreign countries.

Meanwhile, the Flemings remained dissatisfied with the educational situation. The country's bishops were opposed to the idea of a completely autonomous Flemish section that the Flemings proposed at the University of Louvain—a traditionally Roman Catholic and originally French-speaking university—and refused to tolerate the idea. In 1965 and 1966 there were widespread riots by Flemish students. Rioting in Antwerp by the Flemings also occurred during the same period.

In 1967 the bishops declared in a rather ambiguous way that the Flemish department of the University of Louvain would be autonomous, although the university was still to be united. By 1968 the French faculties of the university were so overcrowded that it was proposed that the university expand to an area between Leuven and Brussels. This proposal was deeply disliked by the Flemings, who felt that all French-speaking faculties should be transferred to Wallonia rather than to another Flemish area.

In 1968 street riots broke out throughout Flanders. When eight members of the PSC, who were members of the cabinet under Paul Vanden Boeynants, resigned en masse over the issue, the government fell, and Vanden Boeynants was succeeded by Paul-Henri Spaak. After the government fell from power, the new coalition government acceded to the demands of the Flemings and agreed to move the French-speaking faculties to Wallonia. Since that time the crown has been relegated to a very respected position of trust by the populace.

The principal members of the Belgian royal family. Left to right: *Princess Paola, Prince Albert, Queen Fabiola, and King Baudouin*

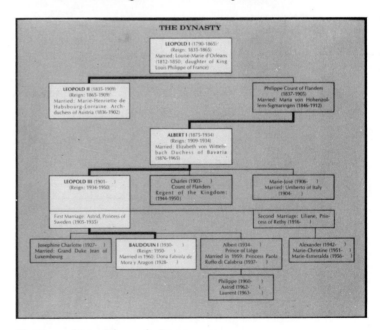

The House of Saxe-Coburg—the Dynasty

THE ROYAL SOVEREIGNS OF THE KINGDOM OF BELGIUM

Reign	Title	Ruler	Birth	Death	Relationship
862–878	Count of Flanders	Baldwin I, the Iron Hand		879	
878–918	Count of Flanders	Baldwin II		918	Son of Baldwin I
918–950	Count of Flanders	Arnuff I (Arnold) (Arnulf)		964	Son of Baldwin II
950–961	Count of Flanders	Baldwin III		961	Son of Arnuff I
961–964	Count of Flanders	Arnuff I, the Elder		964	Son of Baldwin II
964–989	Count of Flanders	Arnuff II, the Younger		989	
989–1035	Count of Flanders	Baldwin IV, of the Handsome Beard		1035	
1035–1067	Count of Flanders	Baldwin V, the Debonnaire		1067	Son of Baldwin IV
1067–1070	Count of Flanders	Baldwin VI of Mons		1073	Son of Baldwin V
1070–1071	Count of Flanders	Arnuff III		1071	Brother of Baldwin VI
1071–1093	Count of Flanders	Robert I	1013	1093	Brother of Baldwin VI
1093–1111	Count of Flanders	Robert II	1039	1111	Son of Robert I
1111–1119	Count of Flanders	Baldwin VII	1058	1119	Son of Robert II
1119–1127	Count of Flanders	Charles the Good	1084	1127	Cousin of Baldwin VII
1127–1128	Count of Flanders	William Clito of Normandy		1128	Grandson of William I of England
1128–1157	Count of Flanders	Dirk (Didrik) of Alsace		1177	Grandson of Robert I
1157–1191	Count of Flanders	Philip I		1191	Son of Dirk
1191–1195	Count of Flanders	Baldwin VIII of Hainaut	1150	1195	
1191–1194	Countess of Flanders	Margareta			Wife of Baldwin VIII and sister of Philip I
1195–1206	Count of Flanders	Baldwin IX (emperor of Constantinople, 1204)	1171	1206	
1206–1244	Countess of Flanders	Joanna		1244	Daughter of Baldwin IX
1212–1233	Count of Flanders	Ferdinand of Portugal		1233	Husband of Joanna
1237–1244	Count of Flanders	Thomas of Savoy			Husband of Joanna
1244–1280	Countess of Flanders	Margaret	1201	1280	Daughter of Joanna
1280–1305	Count of Flanders	Guy de Dampierre		1305	Son of Margareta
1305–1322	Count of Flanders	Robert III of Bethune	1240	1322	Son of Guy de Dampierre
1322–1337	Count of Flanders	Louis I of Nevers (Crecy)	1304	1346	Grandson of Robert III
1337–1345	Governor of Flanders	Jacob van Artevelde	1290	1345	
1345–1384	Count of Flanders	Louis II de Male	1330	1384	Son of Louis I
1384–1405	Countess of Flanders	Margaret	1350	1405	Wife of Philip of Burgundy; daughter of Louis II
1384–1405	Count of Flanders	Philip the Bold of Burgundy			Husband of Margaret; son of King John II of France

1384–1477—Under the control of Burgundy
1477–1795—Under the control of the Habsburgs
1795–1814—Under the control of France
1814–1830—United with Holland (the Netherlands)
1830—Independence as a monarchy

HOUSE OF SAXE-COBURG

Reign	Title	Ruler	Birth	Death	Relationship
1831–1865	King	Leopold I	1790	1865	Son of Francis Frederick, duke of Saxe-Coburg-Saalfeld
1865–1909	King	Leopold II	1835	1909	Son of Leopold I
1909–1934	King	Albert I	1875	1934	Son of Leopold II
1934–1951	King	Leopold III	1901	1983	Son of Albert I
1944–1951	Regent	Charles, count of Flanders	1903		Son of Albert I
1951–	King	Baudouin I	1930		Son of Leopold III

The Kingdom of the Netherlands

The medieval provinces of the Netherlands

Caesar gives us our earliest glimpse at these Netherlanders. He found the district occupied by tribes partly Gallic, partly German, the fiercest fighters he had anywhere encountered. The southern more Gallic region having been longer snatched from the sea, was covered with a vast, dense forest, amid whose twilight deeps he fought ferocious tribes. Among them were the Nervii, who saw resistance hopeless yet refused all submission and were well nigh exterminated; and the Belgae, whose name became a general term for the entire region, hence our modern Belgium.

Farther north Caesar found the Batavians or people of the *bet-auw* (good meadow land) the group of islands formed by the diverging mouths of the Rhine. From them *Holland* (hole-land, hollow-land) was long called the Batavian Republic. These Batavians in their impenetrable swamps were never really mastered by the Romans. They became allies of the great conquerors, famous as the dashing "Batavian cavalry." From them was drawn the trusted body guard of Augustus.

Beyond the Rhine, the strange half-land, half-water region was occupied by the Frisians, a wild Germanic race who, like the Batavians, became the dependent allies but never the defeated slaves of Rome. Indeed, the Romans relied much upon these friendly tribes in the attempt to conquer Germany. Batavia was the gathering place of the Roman troops and ships against the German national hero, Arminius.

The name of the Roman general Drusus, or Germanicus, as his countrymen entitled him, is the first that can be distinctly associated with the development of the Netherlands. Drusus built embankments or dikes to protect his armies from the sudden tides, and he dug canals that his ships might pass from river to river without venturing on the dangerous North Sea, for whose terrors Tacitus cannot find words, declaring it inhabited by strange monsters and frightful water birds.

Drusus also began the apportioning of the land west of the Rhine into regular provinces. The Netherlands and the region just south of them were thereafter known as Germania Inferior or Lower Germany. Cities sprang up, Cologne and Nymwegen. Civilization progressed rapidly even among the slow Batavians, who were ridiculed by the poet Martial for being as stupid as they were sturdy, as foolish as fierce.

The knowledge of these people and of their day closes abruptly with the last fragment of Tacitus. He tells with full detail of the revolt of Germania Inferior during the confusion caused by the fall of Nero (A.D. 68). Claudius Civilis, a Batavian leader, whose services had made him a general under Rome, urged his people to rebel. In a famous speech he cried out that the Romans no longer treated the Batavians as allies, but ground them down as slaves. A prophetess called Veleda, deeply revered by the Germanic race, lent Civilis her aid. The Belgae and other Gauls joined him, and the Roman legions were defeated and wholly driven out of the region (A.D. 69). A year later, they returned. The Gauls were subdued; Batavia was ravaged, but the Batavians and some Germans from beyond the Rhine continued the struggle, roused to frenzy by the impassioned prophecies of Veleda. Civilis made a determined and skillful resistance, and after several battles, a conference between him and the Roman general was arranged to take place upon a bridge over the River Yssel. The center of the bridge was purposely broken away; Civilis advanced upon the ruin from one shore, the Roman from the other—and there our only manuscript of Tacitus breaks off and leaves them standing. What became of Civilis and the prophetess, we do not know.

Vaguely from other sources, we gather a general impression that the Batavians thereafter were treated with greater wisdom and justice. They remained loyal to the empire even in the days of its decline, and their race was almost exterminated in the constant strife with the hordes of Franks, Burgundians, and other Germans who in the fourth and fifth centuries surged over the feeble barrier of the Rhine and swept into Gaul. In the confused maelstrom of seething, wandering tribes that followed the downfall of Rome, the people of the Low Countries must have become widely scattered over Gaul. The Frisians, indeed, remained upon their barren coasts, which no one coveted. But the Batavians disappeared as a separate race, and their "good meadow land" became the chief home of the Salian Franks.

These Salians gradually extended their power southward, over the ancient land of the Belgae, and finally Clovis, the leader of the Salian Franks, rose to be the first king of France. Most of the Franks moved southward in the wake of Clovis, and by degrees portions of the Frisians occupied the land thus left almost vacant. Hence, the Hollanders of today are the descendants of the Frisians with some small admixture of Batavians and Franks. The race, therefore, is almost wholly Teutonic, though with traces of the Roman and the Gaul. The Belgians are Franks and ancient Belgae with a fuller Roman tint, half Teuton and half Gaul.

THE FEUDAL AGE

Batavia, the "good meadow" in the delta of the Rhine, remained for centuries a doubtful border district between Frisians and Franks. The Frisians were heathen and wholly barbarian; the Franks adopted Christianity and assimilated something of the culture of the Roman world they had overrun. One Frankish king, Dagobert I, a descendant of Clovis, made a determined effort to convince the Frisians of the force and reasonableness of Christianity. He marched an army into their unprotected land and in 622 erected a church at Utrecht. But the sand dunes and the mists and marshes soon grew wearisome to Dagobert, so he marched home again. The Frisians came to examine his church, and it disappeared. After that the Frankish kings grew feeble, and the defense of the Batavian border was left to the local chiefs. We find the Pepins, who were to supersede the family of Clovis on the Frankish throne, first rising into prominence in this valiant strife. Both of the royal races which supplied the early sovereigns to France and Germany had thus their origin in the Netherlands, which today belong to neither country.

Pepin of Landen, the earliest distinguishable ancestor of the mighty Charlemagne, was lord of Brabant, the frontier land along the Maas River, which he held against the Frisians. His grandson, Pepin d'Heurista, defeated Radbod, king of the Frisians, and compelled him to diminish his title to that of duke, as a subject of the Franks. This Pepin was the real chief of the Franks, "mayor of the palace" to a sluggard king. Yet despite Pepin's power his son, Charles Martel, had to fight Radbod again, and later was obliged to defeat Radbod's son before the resolute Frisians would yield him even a nominal sovereignty.

Charles Martel refounded Dagobert's vanished church at Utrecht and made the Irish Saxon Willibrod, the first bishop of the northern Netherlands. Willibrod's labors extended from 692 to 739 and under him such small portion of the Frisians as accepted the Frankish yoke began the practice of a sort of hybrid faith, mingling their ancient superstitions and barbarous rites with fragments of the Christian ritual, little understood. Willibrod was followed in his episcopate by Winfred or Boniface, an English Saxon, the celebrated converter of the Germans. Boniface, dissatisfied with the debased and debasing worship of his Utrecht flock, insisted upon fuller conformity with the teachings of the church, and met a martyr's death, welcoming his slayers with open arms (775).

The first real conqueror of the Frisians was Charlemagne himself. He was probably born in one of his family's ancestral homes in Belgium near Liège and gained his earliest warlike training in strife with these wild pagans of the marshland. During his first Saxon wars, the Frisians aided their Saxon kinsmen; but by degrees the mingled kindness and sternness of Charlemagne won them to his side. Half of them, however, were slain before his result was achieved, or they were transported by the resolute monarch to other portions of his domains.

By wisdom rather than by force Charlemagne attached the remainder to his empire. They were confirmed in the proud title by which they called themselves, the Free Frisians. Thus reassured, they were induced to look with some favor upon Christianity, hitherto sternly rejected as being a mark of submission to the Franks. Charlemagne gave them a written constitution guaranteeing their ancient laws. "The Frisians," so runs the wording, probably far older than the date when it was written down, "shall be free so long as the wind blows out of the clouds and the world stands."

The bright promise of Charlemagne's reign faded, as we know, in every portion of his broad empire. His son and grandsons exhausted in civil war the lives and resources of their people. The Northmen plundered the coasts almost with impunity.

Then ensued a period of direst tragedy. The North Sea coast was of all lands the most exposed to the Norse raids, and it was harried without mercy. Utrecht, the bishop's city, was plundered as early as 834. Soon all Friesland lay wholly in the invaders' power. They came there year after year and established permanent camps to avoid the necessity of returning home between expeditions. Ghent was seized by them in 851. They learned to use horses instead of ships, and rode unopposed over all the Netherlands.

What portion of the original inhabitants remained in the conquered lands, it would be difficult to say. Those who survived were ruled by Norse dukes, Heriold, Roruk, and Godfrey. The last named is even called king of Friesland. He extended his ravages beyond Cologne, and his men stabled their horses in its cathedral built by Charlemagne. The feeble Carolingian emperor made Godfrey duke of the regions he had plundered (882); the inhabitants were little better than his slaves. During his reign every "free Frisian" was compelled to go about with a halter looped around his neck.

But the relief of the peasantry was near. Duke Godfrey enlarged his demands. His territories, he said, produced no wine, therefore he must have lands higher up the Rhine. He interfered in the civil wars of the Carolingians, and was slain (885). A few years later, the German emperor Arnulf completely broke the power of the Netherland Norsemen in the great battle of Louvain (891).

After Louvain, the Netherlanders were left to themselves. The emperors were too desperately beset elsewhere to give much attention to this impoverished portion of their domains; the influx of the Norse sea robbers had exhausted itself. Dukes, counts and bishops, acknowledging some vague allegiance to emperor or pope or to the king of France, bore such rule as to themselves seemed good, over such regions as they could master. Most prominent of the lordships that thus developed, were those of the counts of Holland and of Flanders, the dukes of Lorraine and of Brabant, and the bishops of Utrecht and of Liège.

Flanders was the district west of the Scheldt, that is the most Gallic portion of the Netherlands, adjoining France and partly belonging to it, though the inhabitants, the Flemings, were mainly Germanic and regarded themselves as a race wholly separate from the French. The first remembered count of Flanders was Baldwin of the Iron Hand, who ruled from 862–878. He had been a chief forester in the service of the emperor Charles the Bald, and managed after the reckless fashion of the time to wed his master's daughter, Judith. The lady had already been queen of England, was widow, indeed, of two successive English kings, Ethelwulf and Ethelbald, when Baldwin carried her off from her villa at Senlis and made her his bride. The Northmen were not the only robbers of the age. The emperor after much show of empty wrath, finding that Judith herself seemed not overly angry, made peace with Baldwin and confirmed the marriage, was glad to make such peace perhaps, for along all that coast the iron-armed Fleming stood alone as a bulwark against the Norsemen.

The sons and grandsons of Baldwin and his queen inherited the fame and the rank of their sire, and upheld them well. They acted as independent monarchs, not hesitating to war against the king of France or even the emperor when occasion came. Indeed Baldwin IV, of the Handsome Beard, defeated both emperor and king and extorted additions to his territory from both Germany and France. His son, Baldwin V, was count of Flanders when William the Conqueror won England and William wedded the Fleming's daughter after having been twice repulsed by the haughty lady. Baldwin VII was known as Baldwin of the Axe. Armed with his favorite weapon, an iron axe, he established peace and insisted on its preservation throughout the land. Many a robber baron fell beneath the axe or was seized and executed at the complaint of the peasantry. Another Baldwin, the ninth, headed a crusade and made himself emperor of Constantinople (1204) rather neglecting his government at home for the sake of his glory abroad, and leaving Flanders to much internal disaster and civil war.

Farther north the counts of Holland emerge from obscurity when a certain Count Dirk of Kennemerland, having shown himself a gallant warrior against the Northmen, was by Charles the Simple entrusted with the defense of the entire region around him and given the title of Dirk I of Holland. He was followed by a long line known among their people as Dirk (Dietrich, Theodoric) or Floris (Florence) several of whom rose to prominence and extended their sway over Friesland and Zealand, as well as over their own smaller province among the Rhine morasses to which the name Holland was at first confined.

These counts were at constant war with their rivals, the bishops of Utrecht. The German emperors, dreading the ever-increasing influence of the Holland counts over the wild Frisians, sought to weaken the rebellious noble-

The first ruler of the Netherlands was Count Dirk, appointed by Charles IV (the Simple) of France.

men by conferring their fiefs upon the more loyal bishops. But not even to the emperor would the sturdy Dirks yield an inch of territory. So between Utrecht and Holland there was constant strife. One war specially memorable began in 1058, when Holland was invaded by the warlike bishop William I, at the head of his own troops, a large number of neighboring allies and also a great force sent in the name of the Franconian child emperor, Henry IV. Count Floris I of Holland met the overwhelming masses of his enemies at Dordrecht, entrapped their cavalry in pits, and then scattered their infantry. The chronicles of the time with their usual prodigality of numbers, assert that sixty thousand of the allied troops were slain.

Undiscouraged by the disaster, Bishop William, the mightiest prelate of his age, raised a second army of invasion. This Floris also repelled; but exhausted by his personal efforts in the battle, he, rather imprudently it would seem, lay down beneath a tree to sleep. There he was found by some of the enemy who, having killed him, attacked and slew the larger portion of his men (1060).

The defeat seemed to portend the total extinction of the county of Holland; for Dirk, the little son of Floris, was but a child. Bishop William took possession of the helpless land; whereupon the desperate widow of Floris sought aid from the Flemings and married Robert, a son of their great count Baldwin V. Robert fought so valiantly for Holland that the emperor, Bishop William's protector, sent to the scene and imperial army under Godfrey the Hunchback, duke of Lorraine (1071). Robert was driven back upon the coast lands, forced to take refuge among the marshes and the dunes. "Count of the waters" he is dubbed by the jesting chroniclers.

For a time Godfrey and Bishop William held all Holland and Friesland in their hands. This, however, was the period of the first great strife between emperor and pope. The young emperor Henry IV had not yet bowed to Pope Gregory at Canossa; instead he was upheld and encouraged in his defiance of the papal power by both Duke Godfrey and Bishop William, the two most powerful of his subjects. So long as they lived the emperor was triumphant. It was William who led the council of Worms in passing the resolution to depose the "perfidious monk on the papal throne"; and from his great cathedral at Utrecht, William preached to the imperial court a most fiery sermon against the pope. On the very day of his preaching, according to the story, lightning blasted his cathedral. That same year he died (1076); Godfrey of Lorraine perished also, assassinated in the city of Delft, which he himself had built to be the capital of his new posessions in Holland. The sudden death of these, the two strongest supporters of the emperor, was very generally regarded as an evidence of the wickedness of upholding him against the pope.

In the civil war that broke out everywhere against Henry, little Dirk of Holland recovered his possessions, the more readily since his stepfather Robert had now become count of Flanders, and the new duke of Lorraine was that Godfrey of Bouillon who headed the first Crusade.

The strife of emperors and popes continued. In 1248, the pope having declared the emperor Frederick II deposed, Count William II of Holland was chosen as the emperor's successor and solemnly inaugurated. Soon however, he was compelled to hurry home to suppress a formidable revolt among the Frisians. It was winter, and the marshmen lured him onward over the frozen shallows until he and his heavily armored horse broke through the ice. He could neither fight nor flee, and the peasants slew him in triumph (1256).

Holland was thus plunged again into turmoil; and indeed all Germany suffered for twenty years from the Great Interregnum, during which there was no emperor, and every locality, every little town, had to depend upon itself for defense against the swarms of robber bands, which reveled in the universal anarchy. In the tumult and disaster Friesland almost disappears from our view, but we know that in 1282, a great storm of the water swept away the protecting sand dunes, and the ocean flooded much of the ancient land. The broad Zuyder Zee, or "sea" was formed where before had been only a lake. Towns and villages were destroyed, and fifteen thousand people drowned despite boats and dykes and every other aid. The whole face of the land was changed. Friesland was cut in two. What little was left of the province south of the Zuyder Zee was easily annexed by Holland. The isolated northern portion became practically independent, a republic of the poor, a dangerous, far-off wilderness which no army would dare to penetrate, where no noble would care to live.

RISE OF THE GREAT CITIES

But by the year 1300, the Low Country cities had grown greater than their lords. In this land and in this alone of all Europe, do the citizens stand out during the last two centuries of the Middle Ages, as holding a more prominent place than either the nobility or kings.

It is worth noting that there had never been any real monarchs of the Low Countries. The Romans accepted the Batavians as allies. Even Charlemagne left the Free Frisians their own laws. The shadowy Norse king endured but for a moment. France never claimed supremacy except over part of Flanders; and the German emperors were constrained to exercise their feeble authority over the Netherlands by deputy through its own local rulers, bishops of Utrecht or Liège, or dukes of Lorraine. The counts of Flanders or of Holland might indeed be regarded as independent kings of their domains, especially after the Great Interregnum, during which young Dirk of Flanders completely humbled Utrecht. Both of these semiregal houses, however, waned in power, while the cities of the land grew strong and, recognizing their strength at last, asserted their supremacy.

How was it that these cities had so advanced in wealth, in population and intelligence? The story is not clear, though much study has been expended on it and argument has waxed hot. Dimly we know that the great Flemish municipalities, Ghent and Bruges, came down from Roman times and were never wholly destroyed. Utrecht and Liège grew up as bishop's courts, then turned upon their feeble masters. The other more northern cities were of later growth. Wealth came to all of them through industry and trade. The Flemings were the cloth weavers of Europe; the towns of Holland held control of the fisheries at a time when all Catholic Europe dined on fish during the long periods of abstinence commanded by the church. The Netherlanders, like the Frisians of old, were bold travelers by both land and sea, shrewd traffickers, and sturdy holders of their own. They became the merchants of Europe. As to their liberties, these had been granted inch after inch by generations of Dutch and Flemish counts who, cautious bargainers themselves, had seen that there was much more to be gained by a steady income of taxation from prosperous merchants than could be secured by a single complete plundering, which would leave the victims without means to continue their profitable toil. So the Dirks and Baldwins, the Godfreys of Lorraine and the Johns of Brabant had encouraged trade.

Various Netherland cities seem to have had charters or some sort of grant which made them partly self-governing, as early as 1060. Belgium celebrates its civic independence as originating in a document conferred on the municipalities of Flanders by Baldwin VI. Then comes a more definite event. In 1127, when Charles the Good was count of Flanders, there was a famine in Bruges. A few of the leading merchants and lesser nobles gathered all the grain into their barns and held it for famine prices. Despite their protests, Charles ordered the granaries thrown open to the people. A conspiracy was formed against him by the disappointed speculators, and

he was slain. Then the people rose in their fury against the murderers, besieged them in their castles and mansions and killed them all, those who were captured being tortured to death.

Following on this grim tragedy and grim reprisal, the men of Bruges and other places took oath to one another (1128) that they would acknowledge no prince who did not rule the country honestly and well. From this period we may fairly date the beginning of the supremacy of the cities or, as they and their people are sometimes called, the communes. These did not yet assert independence, but they began to recognize their own strength, to trust in themselves. Their era of wealth and splendor also commenced. A writer of the times asserts that in 1184, Ghent sent twenty thousand armed men to aid the king of France, and Bruges sent many thousands more. We need not accept the numbers as exact, but it is certain that at this time Flanders held over forty cities, Brabant had twelve, Hainaut seven, Liège six. By the year 1240, the preponderance of the cities was so established that Count Guy of Flanders was aided in his government by an advisory council, consisting of the head magistrates of the five principal communes.

In the north the cities were slower to develop. In all of what we now call Holland, there were at the close of the twelfth century not more than seven or eight chartered cities, and it was not until 1296, that the northern towns imitated their neighbors of the south by combining in opposition to the nobles. The occasion was similar to that which had roused the Flemings against the murderers of Charles the Good. Floris V of Holland had been shifting his alliance between England and France. Moreover, his nobles were jealous of his great popularity among the common people; they distrusted his designs. So a dark conspiracy was formed, which certainly involved the king of England, and perhaps other foreign rulers as well, though all the secret windings of the treachery may never be unveiled. Floris was decoyed to Utrecht and there separated from his personal attendants during a hawking party. Deep in the woodlands, he was seized by some of his own nobles, who until the last moment had remained fawning on him with false pledges. Bound hand and foot, he was hurried to the seashore to be sent to England. But news of the seizure had become noised abroad. All along the coasts, the people rose in arms for his rescue; so that the conspirators, unable to escape with their victim by sea, strove to carry him off inland. Again they found themselves encircled by the infuriated people; and in desperation they slew their dangerous prisoner. His sad story has become one of the chief themes of the poetic literature of Holland.

The murder did not save the conspiring nobles. So devotedly had Floris been loved that the people everywhere swore to avenge his death. The false lords who were proved to have been in the plot were executed;

others fled in terror from Holland; and the enfeebled remainder lost much of their authority. The burghers and even the country peasants assumed some voice in governing the land. The line of Floris died out with his weak son John, and there was much war both at home and with the Flemings. Finally whatever dignity still remained attached to the vacant throne of Holland, passed through the female line to the counts of Hainaut.

Meanwhile, the power and splendor of the Flemish cities were reaching to their fullest assertion. Ever since the early days of the partition of Lothair's kingdom (843), the Flemish counts had vaguely acknowledged the king of France as their overlord. But his supremacy remained an idle name until the great battle of Bouvines in 1204. In this decisive contest, the German emperor Otto, backed by all the forces of the Netherlands, was defeated by the French. Thereafter the Flemings were left without German help and could scarcely maintain their independent stand alone. The French king asserted more and more authority over them, until the Flemish counts retained but a shadow of their ancient greatness.

In 1297, Count Guy rebelled against King Philip IV, the Fair, the shrewdest, craftiest, strongest monarch of his time. After four years of wrangling, Philip deposed and imprisoned the count, declared Flanders confiscated, and ruled it through his own officials. With his haughty queen, Jeanne of Navarre, he paid a visit to the great cities there, Lille and Ghent and Bruges. The royal pair were astounded. "I thought I was the only queen here," said Jeanne, "but I find a thousand who can dress as richly as I."

From that time, both Philip and she seemed to set their evil hearts on ruining Flanders, on bringing its proud citizens to the same hideous yoke of slavery that ground French peasants in the dust. The charters and privileges of the cities were ignored; magistrates who protested were cast into prison; taxes were heaped upon taxes; French troops insulted the citizens; French officials laughed at them.

In 1302, rebellion flared up everywhere. The lower classes of Bruges took the first step, as they had in the days of Charles the Good. Issuing suddenly from their city, they attacked and slew the French in the forts around. Then, returning secretly to Bruges by night, they fell upon the Frenchmen there, in the early dawning. The foreigners were caught wholly unprepared, while the townfolk had made thorough plans for the assault. Some portion of each French soldier's equipment had been stolen by his hosts; chains were stretched across the streets to prevent a charge. Even the women took part in the fray, tossing the hated Frenchmen out of the windows, or helping to drag them to the shambles where they were slaughtered like cattle. The *Bruges matins* as it is called, was a massacre rather than a fight.

The old Flemish standard was at once unfurled everywhere in the province. Only Lille and Ghent, whose strong garrisons were now upon their guard, remained in possession of the French. King Philip hastened to raise a powerful army. All the nobles of his kingdom marched against Bruges. Most of the nobility of Flanders, of Brabant, and Hainaut joined them. Only a few Flemish lords cast in their lot with the commons.

The opposing forces met at Courtrai in the noted Battle of the Spurs (1302). The Flemings are said to have numbered sixty thousand, the French still more. So confident were the latter of success that we are told they brought with them casks of ropes to hang every rebel who had slain a Frenchman. Queen Jeanne with the chivalry of the time, had sent her soldiers a message that when they were killing the Flemish pigs they must not overlook the Flemish sows.

But the French knights quarreled amongst themselves; they sneered at their Netherland allies; and, the spirit of rivalry being thus aroused in many breasts, each faction charged forward blindly to outdo the other. Thus in tumultuous rush they came upon the Brugeois—or rather they came upon a ditch, a small canal that lay as an unseen trap in front of the burgher army. Into this ditch plunged the chivalry of France, so that the burghers had little more to do than beat their enemies' brains out as the victims lay helpless before them. The French were utterly defeated. Twenty thousand were slain. Of gilded spurs, emblems of highest rank, seven hundred, or according to some accounts, four thousand were gathered from the battlefield. The nobility of France was almost exterminated in that fatal charge.

King Philip hastened to raise fresh forces. The Flemings, drunk with pride and self-confidence, began a war of invasion against Holland, in which they were defeated and their fleet destroyed. The cities quarreled among themselves. Fresh battles, less decisive than Courtrai, were fought against the French. Amid all these difficulties the resolution of the sturdy merchants seemed only to increase. Their cities were practically emptied of men, the whole nation took the field. King Philip in despair cried out that it seemed to rain Flemings; and he made peace with them, granting almost all they asked.

From this time forward, the Flemish counts became practically exiles from their own land, mere servants of the French king, warring against the Flemish cities with his aid. United, the cities might have defied all foes, but they were generally quarreling among themselves. Their merchants were rivals for the trade of Europe, and the disasters of one metropolis meant the aggrandizement of others. Only some common danger, imminent and obvious, could ever unite them for a moment.

Ghent was aristocratic in its government and hence was usually to be found in alliance with its count; Bruges was democratic and relied for support upon the smaller towns and countryfolk. Lille soon became separated from the rest of Flanders, fell into the power of the French king, and was united permanently to France. In

1328, twelve thousand Brugeois were defeated at Cassel by their count Louis and his Frenchmen, the Flemings standing up heroically against their foes and fighting till the last man fell. After that, Bruges sued for peace, and Ghent became the chief city of the Netherlands.

In 1335, began the long war, the Hundred Years War between France and England. This had a vast influence upon the fortunes of the Netherlands. In the first place, England was at that time the chief sheep-raising country; and Flanders and the other Belgic provinces, the cloth makers of Europe, imported English wool in vast quantities. This mutually profitable commerce drew England and Flanders into close economic relations. The Flemish count, Louis, after crushing the army of Bruges, grew more and more domineering. He insulted the burghers, and they endured it; he interfered with the English trade, and they rebelled.

At the head of this new rebellion stood the weavers of Ghent, and at the head of the Ghent weavers, chief of their guild, stood Jacob van Artevelde, sometimes called the great Fleming, a far-seeing social reformer and revolutionist, destined to become one of the main economic forces of his age. The Arteveldes had long been among the leading families of Ghent, and Jacob, brilliant and eloquent, shrewd and energetic, came naturally to be the chief burgher of the city. As "captain" of Ghent he was the recognized leader of the people's party throughout Flanders and commanded their forces in a battle in which he overthrew the aristocratic adherents of Count Louis.

So strong became the position of Artevelde, that when the war broke out between France and England, the rival monarchs dealt with him as with an independent prince. Each sought his alliance. Philip of France reminded him of his feudal allegiance. Edward came in person to the Netherlands, visited the Ghent captain as an equal, and offered him vast commercial advantages for Flanders. Artevelde saw only too plainly that, whichever side he joined, the Netherlands would become the theater of the war and be exposed to all its miseries. Hence he sought to maintain a middle position between the two contestants. So skillfully did he manage that it was actually agreed by treaty that Flanders, despite her feudal dependence upon France, was to remain neutral throughout the war.

This neutrality did not long continue. Count Louis naturally intrigued to reestablish his shrunken authority. His efforts caused an angry outbreak against him in Bruges. The people sought to make him prisoner; and, barely escaping with his life, he fled to France. When he returned with French troops, Artevelde allied himself openly with England.

The main difficulty in persuading the Flemings to this step was their oath of allegiance to France. Therefore upon the Ghent captain's advice, Edward reasserted an ancient hereditary claim to the French throne. The burghers were thus relieved of their conscientious scruples, and readily joined this newmade "king of France" in his attacks upon his rival. English and Flemings combined drove the French out of the Netherlands. Flemish marines aided Edward in his great naval victory off Sluys, in which the French navy was destroyed. Into such distress was King Philip driven that he negotiated a separate peace with Flanders, remitting all taxes and making the province practically an independent state under Jacob van Artevelde (1340).

The Ghent captain, or Ruward of Flanders, as he was now called, proceeded to a reorganization of his country, giving the common people power above the aristocracy. The main opposition encountered was in his own city, where the aristocrats had still the upper hand. Artevelde joined the popular brewers' guild, whence he has been called the brewer of Ghent, though he probably knew nothing of the actual trade. There were street battles, a massacre of aristocrats at Bruges, five hundred armed men slain in a strife between the guilds in the public square at Ghent. Finally the commons triumphed everywhere. Artevelde reached the summit of his career.

His influence extended far beyond Flanders. The poor folk throughout Europe heard of this land where the commons ruled. Uprisings were attempted in other countries. The Italian poet Petrarch sang of Artevelde and encouraged the rebellion of Rienzi at Rome. The hideous revolt of the Jacquerie in France is attributed to the Flemish example.

In the end, the Great Fleming fell a victim to the rash forces he had evoked. Edward of England became too friendly with him, visiting him repeatedly in Ghent, calling him "dear comrade." They stood as godfathers to each other's children. All this aroused the suspicion and perhaps the jealousy of Artevelde's fellow citizens, a suspicion which Count Louis of Flanders knew well how to fan into flame. The intrigues of Louis became so dangerous that Artevelde formed the bold project of stripping him of his rank, and creating a new count of Flanders, the young English Edward, Prince of Wales, afterward famous in history as the Black Prince.

This was further than the Flemings would go. They might quarrel with Count Louis, hold him prisoner, slay him even; but they were still loyal to his house, their rulers for uncounted centuries. They accused Artevelde of having sold himself wholly to England. There was a sudden tumult; and the great chieftain was slain in the streets, struck down, torn to pieces almost, by a mob of those commons who had been his most devoted adherents (1345).

Though he could not save himself, Artevelde did not die unavenged. The people recovered from their sudden frenzy and repented of their deed. They accused Count Louis of having fomented the disturbance, and when he came hurrying to reassert his power, they drove him once more out of Flanders. The next year he perished in the English victory at Crecy and was succeeded by his son Louis de Male, the last of the ancient race.

Meanwhile Flanders, released from Artevelde's restraining hand, fell into anarchy. City fought against city; guild against guild. Louis de Male was able to reassert his dominion, but France was too exhausted by the English war to give him aid. Finally another revolt broke out in Ghent in 1380, and Louis laid siege to the city.

Finding themselves in utmost danger, the men of Ghent went to the house of Artevelde's son Philip, the godson of the English queen. Philip had lived quietly among his neighbors until he was past the age of forty years. Now, despite his protests, he was forced for his father's sake to become the leader of the city; and once aroused, Philip proved not unworthy of his people's faith. At first he counseled submission. Ghent was starving; and Philip, going himself to Louis's camp, pleaded for mercy. The count fiercely demanded that all the citizens should come out to him unarmed and barefoot, with ropes about their necks, to be dealt with as he chose. Philip refused to submit to these grim terms; and the burghers, finding courage in despair, became soldiers again, as their fathers had been under Philip's father.

A famous contest followed. Louis was forced to raise the siege of Ghent; but the merchants of Bruges aided him against their rivals. The lands of Ghent were ravaged. Artevelde with his fleets gathered provisions from distant lands. He captured city after city from the count. Suddenly the troops of Ghent marched upon Bruges and stormed it. Louis and his knights were defeated, and the haughty count had to hide for his life in the house—under the bed, says one narrator—of a poor widow till he found a chance to flee. Bruges was sacked. So were the other cities that upheld the aristocratic cause. Once more an Artevelde of Ghent became undisputed master of Flanders.

For two years Philip defended his land against all the forces of France and Burgundy combined. But at last his troops were defeated by overwhelming numbers and he himself perished, sword in hand, at the battle of Roosebeke (1382). The town of Roosebeke is close to Courtrai, and the French felt that this victory balanced the defeat "of the spurs." In fact Froissart pauses to point out the importance of Roosebeke as checking the vast movement of peasant revolt which was everywhere in progress. The downfall of the Flemish burghers was a calamity to the common folk through all of Europe.

For two years afterward the men of Ghent still heroically defended their city. But the rest of Flanders yielded to Count Louis. He died in 1384, and as he left no direct heirs, the countship passed through his daughter to her husband, Philip the Bold, duke of Burgundy. Philip made peace with Ghent. His supremacy was acknowledged, and as he ruled mildly, yet with all the power of Burgundy behind him, his authority was not opposed.

THE BURGUNDIAN PERIOD

Gradually the house of Burgundy obtained possession of the entire Netherlands. Philip the Bold was a son of the French king John, and was given the duchy of Burgundy by his father in recognition of his knightly conduct at Poitiers (1356), where almost alone, he had defended his father and striven to protect him from capture by the English.

How Flanders fell to Philip in 1384, we have seen. His grandson Philip the Good secured Holland, Hainaut, and Brabant. In Holland the ancient line of the Dirks and Florises became extinct (1345), and the sovereignty passed through the female line to what was called the House of Bavaria. There was a long civil war between mother and son, during which the Dutch cities, courted by both sides and taking small part with either, rose to a commercial prosperity rivaling that of the Flemish towns. The north made such giant strides in advance upon the south, that during the early years of the fifteenth century, William VI of Holland shared equally with the Burgundian dukes in the rule over not only the territory but also the wealth of the Netherlands.

William VI of Holland left no sons, only a daughter Jacqueline whose tragic, romantic, pitiable career is celebrated in history. Even the dry chronicles of the time cannot tell Jacqueline's story without lamentation, without bursts of poetry. They describe her as being good as she was beautiful, gentle yet strong, and pure and heroic, a worthy rival of her contemporary, Joan of Arc, who was freeing France from England, while Jacqueline fought for Holland against Burgundy.

Her father laid careful plans that she should succeed him in his rule. To this end he wedded her when but a child of five (1406) to the equally youthful John, second son of the king of France. The marriage was of course only nominal at first, but in 1415 the youthful pair were released from their schoolbooks and formally united. In 1417, John became heir to the French throne, and his father being insane, he set out with his fair young bride to rule over France as regent. The two journeyed southward together in the springtime, but hardly had they entered France when John suddenly died. He had been a weakling all his life, but both the manner and the moment of his death caused a widespread rumor that he had been poisoned.

The youthful widow was hurried home. Her father, who had accompanied her happy entry into France, now hastened her return. He knew how loath the Hollanders were to be governed by an unprotected woman, and he must make new arrangements for her. Before these could be established, he died. In less than two months poor Jacqueline, barely seventeen years old, lost husband and father, both powerful potentates and her natural protectors. The next male heir to Holland was her uncle, the bishop of Liège, called John the Pitiless.

For a moment, misfortune seemed to hesitate at further pursuing the child widow. She made a brave, brilliant progress through her domains and was everywhere received with noisy loyalty. When Bishop John sought to assert his claim to Holland, she rode on horseback at the head of her army and defeated him. John appealed to the German emperor, who, glad of the opportunity to assert himself, declared that the countship of Holland had lapsed to the empire by the failure of male heirs, and that he now conferred the rank upon his faithful and submissive servant, John. The matter being thus put to a plain issue, a general assembly of the Dutch knights and burghers was summoned, and this representative body flatly contradicted the emperor, declaring that Holland was not a fief of the empire, and that Jacqueline was their lawful ruler.

Nevertheless, in order that she might have a man to assert her rights and to settle the dispute decisively, Jacqueline's advisers urged her to wed again and at once. Yielding to their aged wisdom, the poor countess within less than a year of her first husband's death married another John, the third of that name to become prominent in her life. The suitor thus chosen out of the many who sought the honor of wedding the great heiress, was her cousin, the duke of Brabant. He was selected by Jacqueline's advisers as a matter of policy, not only because he was ruler of a neighboring state, but because being a member of the House of Burgundy, he would have the support of its powerful duke.

As the man for the place, John of Brabant proved a failure. He was even younger than his wife, and a feeble, enervated youth, one of those sapless, worthless branches so common to the French royal stock. Jacqueline's first husband had been the same, only his early death leaves his figure less clearly outlined on the historic page. John of Liège, on the other hand, was at least a man. The pope took up his cause and relieved him of his priestly vows that he might found a new family of counts of Holland. Hence he was Bishop John no longer, but only John the Pitiless.

When he and young John of Brabant met in battle or diplomacy the result was a foregone conclusion. John the Pitiless won contest after contest. City after city of Holland declared in his favor, until Jacqueline's feeble husband, abandoning the strife, retreated into Brabant, making a treaty with his rival which left the latter in practical possession of Holland. Naturally Jacqueline protested; but her husband found that bullying her was a far easier and more congenial task than matching himself against John the Pitiless. He ignored her complaints and made her life a misery.

She fled suddenly from his court, from what was really a prison, and escaped to England (1419). There she was received with high honor. Humphrey, duke of Gloucester, the king's brother and afterward regent of the kingdom for the child Henry VI, became a suitor for her

hand. Her marriage to her cousin John of Brabant had been performed in opposition to an express command from the pope. Advantage was now taken of this to declare the unahppy union void, and Jacqueline and Humphrey were wed. In 1424 the couple led an English army to Holland to reestablish the bride in her inheritance.

They were partly successful. Humphrey defeated the forces of Brabant; the royal pair were welcomed in Hainaut; and John the Pitiless died, poisoned by one of their adherents. But even in death he avenged himself by willing Holland to John of Brabant. Now this childless and feeble Brabant duke had for heir the mighty Duke Philip the Good of Burgundy, who, seizing the opportunity, espoused his nephew's cause with all the strength of his powerful domains. England had long been allied with Burgundy against France; and Duke Humphrey of Gloucester was thus placed in a peculiar position, maintaining his wife's cause against his country's ally. He and Philip had hot words and finally agreed to settle their differences in ancient knightly style by personal combat. Before the contest could take place however, Humphrey, doubtless moved by many mingled emotions, abandoned Holland and withdrew to England.

Poor Jacqueline, thus left once more to her own resources, defended herself desperately against the Burgundians, and sent passionate appealing letters to Humphrey. Her moving words were of no avail. Her English husband solaced himself with another lady; her subjects in Holland hesitated between her and her discarded John, and at last, seeking peace most of all, surrendered her to Burgundy. She was imprisoned in the castle of Ghent.

Still, however, the resolute woman refused to yield. Some of her adherents both in England and Holland yet clung to her. Disguised in boy's clothes, she escaped from her confinement and for three years led a wild life of adventure, fighting at the head of such troops as she could raise. She held her castle of Gouda against all comers, and in the field achieved more than one brilliant victory over the Burgundian forces. Duke Humphrey roused himself sufficiently to send a fleet from England to her aid, but it was wholly defeated. John of Brabant died in 1427.

His death brought the great duke of Burgundy, Philip the Good, more directly into the struggle against Jacqueline. Philip now claimed Holland as his own, and summoned England as his ally to counsel the countess to peace. On the other hand, Jacqueline, freed from the last traces of her marital chain to John, entreated Duke Humphrey to reestablish their abandoned union. The English duke most ungallantly obeyed Philip, urged his deserted wife to yield, and wedded the English mistress who had been her rival.

In face of these blows, Jacqueline surrendered (1428). It was agreed that she was still to be called countess of

Philip the Good, the duke of Burgundy, was sovereign over the Netherlands from 1419 to 1467. He should be credited with being the first to concentrate the administration of all of the Low Countries under one ruler.

Philip of Burgundy riding through the streets of Utrecht with his wife, the countess of Burgundy. He was generally accompanied by his entourage, including the court jesters.

Holland and to receive some part of the revenues of the state; but she made a progress through all her cities in company with Philip, formally releasing them from allegiance and bidding them be obedient to the Burgundians. She also promised not to wed again without Philip's consent. Her claims might still have been dangerous in some strong king's hands.

Here Jacqueline passes out of political history, the tale of jangling states. But romance was still to be hers, happiness perhaps, after all her sorrows. Philip's governor over Holland was Lord Francis Borselen. The governor's duties threw him much into the company of Jacqueline. Love sprang up between the two. In 1432, they were secretly married. Philip, learning of this, threw Borselen into prison and threatened his death. To save him Jacqueline abandoned everything that remained to her, renounced her empty title, and with her liberated husband retired to a secluded estate, where the two dwelt in peace and apparent devotion until her death in 1436. Lord Francis was then restored to a post of trust, and had what must have been the keen satisfaction of defeating Duke Humphrey of England when the latter, his alliance with Burgundy having failed at last, attacked the Netherlands once again.

Jacqueline's long struggle is important historically. It must be compared to that of the Arteveldes in Flanders; for little as the Dutch cities realized it, their liberty was dependent upon her victory. She ruled in the policy of her ancestors who had encouraged them in self-reliance and assertion. Her fall placed her people with Flanders under the House of Burgundy, a race of rulers who guarded the material prosperity of their subjects, but vigorously trampled every liberty underfoot.

With the establishment of the supremacy of Philip the Good, the history of the Netherlands becomes merged for a time in that of Burgundy. Philip, though in name only a duke, was in reality more powerful than any sovereign of his time, imposing his will upon the enfeebled rulers of both France and Germany. At this period only Italy could rival the Low Countries in wealth; and Italy was divided into many petty states; the Netherlands had now been all absorbed into one. Moreover, its military strength while vigorous in Philip's hands, was useless for defense against him, since each city was antagonistic to the others, easily to be brought to Philip's side by some promise of commercial advantage over its rivals.

Hence, playing one metropolis against another, Philip became the despotic master of all. One by one, he took away their ancient privileges. He heaped taxes on them till his was the richest court in Europe. Bruges rebelled (1436), and seized upon the persons of the duke's wife and little son, afterward Charles the Bold. Philip liberated the captives, half by force, half fraud, and blockaded the city until its people starved and surrendered, so trampled down as never to regain their former splendor. Ghent also resented the duke's exactions and was vigorously suppressed.

In return for the liberty he took away, Philip gave the Netherlanders security. The nobles who had preyed upon the country from their strong castles and, arms in hand, exacted toll from what merchandise they could, now become dependents of Philip, mere silk-clothed courtiers idling in his train. Hence the Netherland tradesfolk, valuing prosperity and quiet far more than any abstract ideal of self-government, gradually acquiesced in the new order of life. They were in fact the first to give their new ruler the name of the Good, which sounds oddly enough when contrasted with some of his treacheries and unsurpations.

Admirers of the beautiful are also wont to speak in highest terms of the period of Burgundian supremacy in the Netherlands. The splendor-loving Philip and his successors encouraged art and literature. The van Eycks, earliest of the great Flemish painters, flourished under Philip. Literature of the most elaborate sort became the amusement of the wealthy citizens. They established "chambers of rhetoric," which held poetic contests called Land jewels. These grew to be national institutions and were accompanied by gorgeous pageants. Lawrence Coster of Haarlem is said to have invented the art of printing in 1440; and though the claim of the German, Gutenburg, is more generally accepted, the new art found immediate and wide support in Holland and the other Low Countries as well. Wealth, splendor, and the gradual stirring of the intellect to deeper thoughts—these are the keynotes of the Burgundian period.

In 1467, Philip, grown very old and feeble, died and was succeeded by his even more widely known son, Charles, whose nickname we have translated into English as the Bold. Really it is *le téméraire,* "the rash; the overbold," a qualification of far different significance. The story of the long struggle of Charles the Overbold against the crafty Louis XI belongs with the tales of France and Burgundy. The Netherlands were to Charles only the storehouse whence he drew supplies of men and money. When the cities rebelled, he chastised them, especially Liège, which he ruined completely, battering down its walls and executing all of its chief citizens. In his brief regin of ten years, he outraged every feeling of his subjects, trampled on their every privilege, and squandered all the enormous wealth his father had accumulated. Then he perished in the Battle of Nancy, falling as much a victim to the disgust and hatred of his own subjects, as to the valor of the Swiss.

This sudden death of Charles the Overbold left his rich domains to his daughter Mary of Burgundy, an heiress whose unhappy career has been made the theme of many comparisons with that of Jacqueline, the countess of Holland, whom Philip, Mary's grandfather, had found in similar plight and so mercilessly despoiled. Much of Mary's inheritance was seized by Louis XI. The Netherlands remained to her, only because they were strong enough to choose a ruler for themselves; and with shrewd merchant craft, the people saw they could make a better bargain with Mary than with Louis or any other.

The States General of Flanders, a body organized under the Burgundians and consisting of the chief nobles and burghers, met to decide the succession to the realm. Its members were joined by deputies from the other

At the Battle of Nancy in 1477, Charles the Bold, duke of Burgundy, lost the battle and his life, leaving his position to his eighteen-year-old daughter, Mary of Burgundy. Congress met at Ghent on February 11 and gave a formal grant to Mary called the Great Privilege. She is seen here accepting it. But on August 18 of the same year she married Maximilian and, unfortunately, died shortly thereafter.

provinces. They exacted from Mary the Great Privilege (1477), the celebrated document which still stands at the base of all Netherland law and freedom. It was a charter confirming to the people every right they had ever possessed.

For a brief period the cities resumed over the court that control which the Burgundian dukes had wrested from them. So helpless was Mary in the hands of her tyrannical subjects, that they executed two of her chief officials before her very eyes. These men had been detected in treacherous correspondence with Louis XI against Flanders; and though Mary rushed before their judges with disheveled hair and robe and appeared afterward at the place of execution in the same desperate plight to plead for her friends upon her knees, the two courtiers were beheaded in the marketplace of Ghent.

Then came the problem of Mary's marriage, that like Jacqueline she might have "a man to defend her heritage." Her arrogant father had once refused her hand to Maximilian, the son of the impoverished German emperor. Now the rejected suitor was selected by Mary and her Flemish advisers as the most available of the long list of candidates who approached her. Maximilian, afterward emperor and head of the great Austrian house of Habsburg, thus became the bridge by which the Low Countries passed under the dominion of Austria and afterward of Spain, both of which states came under Habsburg rule.

Yet Maximilian was never himself the titular sovereign of the Netherlands; he was only guardian of the provinces for Mary, and when she died five years later, he became guardian for their baby son, Philip. The hatred bred in the Netherlands against Charles the Bold passed down as an inheritance against Maximilian. During Mary's lifetime it did not break into open violence, especially as the Flemings dreaded Louis of France and his dangerous schemes. Maximilian put an end to these by defeating the French in the battle of Guinegate (1479) and Flemish independence of France was again secure. The power of Maximilian seemed to the burghers to become more dangerous with each of his successes; and on his wife's death, instead of admitting his authority, the States General of Flanders made virtual prisoner of his son Philip and claimed the regency for itself in Philip's name.

Civil war followed between Maximilian and the cities. Step by step the Habsburg lord reestablished his authority. In 1485, he defeated the troops of Ghent and rescued his little son from the hands of the burghers. In 1488, it was their turn. Maximilian was made prisoner in Bruges and confined there for seven months, until he yielded all that his jailors demanded. The French king, not Louis XI but his successor, was made guardian of little Philip; and Maximilian agreed to abandon the Netherlands and return to Germany.

No sooner was he released from confinement, then he repudiated the oaths he had taken under compulsion, and reinvaded the Netherlands at the head of a German army raised for him by his father, the emperor. He was not especially successful, and for four years more the war dragged on. It was no longer conducted by Maximilian, who as heir to the dominions of his aged father had other tasks, but by his German generals. These in 1492 were able to report to him that the Netherlands was once more beaten into subjection. The Great Privilege was abrogated, though not forgotten by the people. And thus in the very year of the discovery of America, the persistent struggle of the Dutch and Flemish people for liberty again met temporary defeat. They sank back into an enforced submission, no longer as a Burgundian but as a Habsburg province.

Maximilian's son, young Philip the Fair, ruled in his own name from 1494. He wedded the half-insane Juana, daughter of the Spanish soveriegns Ferdinand and Isabella; and when, through the death of nearer heirs, Juana became ruler of most of Spain, Philip took control of her possessions in her name. He died, and all the domains of his family, Spain, Austria, Italy, the Netherlands, gradually gathered to his young son Charles, afterward the celebrated emperor Charles V.

Charles was born in Ghent while his father reigned there (1500) and was practically a Fleming. During his childhood, his grandfather Maximilian was once more regent of the Netherlands; though, being emperor now, Maximilian wisely delegated the protection of Charles's domains to his daughter, Charles's aunt Margaret. She was a capable and vigorous ruler, and despite many difficulties preserved for her young nephew an undiminished power and sovereignty in the Netherlands. In 1515 Charles entered Antwerp in royal procession, and there began his varied and tumultuous experience as a ruler of many nations.

Whatever opinion we may form of the mighty emperor in his dealings with the rest of Europe, it cannot be denied that to the Low Countries he was a wise and upon the whole a popular sovereign. For one thing, he reduced them to a unit. We hear no more of the separate prov-

Charles V entering Antwerp in 1515. He served as ruler from 1506 to 1555.

The signature Charles V used in Holland on documents

inces of Flanders, Brabant, Holland, Zealand, Friesland, and so on, each acknowledging a different ruler and rushing into war against the others. He attached the entire region firmly to the German Empire, to which before it had sometimes acknowledged, sometimes refused allegiance, but which had never given it military protection or received from it effective military aid.

Moreover, under Charles the burghers were prosperous. A Fleming himself, he knew how to win the merchants' hearts, and he did everything to aid them in their trade. For this he secured bountiful return. In the period of his greatest splendor when his income from all his other vast possessions combined, Germany, Italy, Spain and the golden Indies of America, amounted to 3 million ducats, the little Low Countries by themselves supplied him with 2 million. Ghent was probably at this time the wealthiest and perhaps the largest city in the world. When Charles one year laid a tax of 1,200,000 ducats upon Flanders, he expected Ghent to supply one-third the whole, an exaction which in our day would scarcely be equaled by 20 millions of dollars. At this the burghers of Ghent planned another rebellion, insisting upon laying their own tax in accordance with the Great Privilege.

The outbreak was not even under way when Charles learned of it; and hastening from Spain, he gathered his imperial armies and advanced into the city. For a month, he gave the burghers no warning of what he intended. Then he suddenly declared that the unhappy metropolis had forfeited all its rights and privileges whatsoever. The leaders of the recent movement were seized and executed; all the communal property of the city and of the guilds was confiscated; and the tribute demanded of the citizens was heavily increased. The great bell Roland used through all the heroic struggles of Ghent to summon the people hastily together, the palladium of their liberties, was removed from its tower. The people were to assemble for conference no more. Having gone thus far and ruined Ghent, Charles forgave its contemplated rebellion because, as he explained, he had been born there.

It is not, however, to Charles alone that we must attribute the decay of Ghent and the other Flemish cities. Natural causes were at work. The discovery of America was shifting the commercial routes of the world. England had learned to turn her wool into cloth in manufactories of her own. Above all, the Low Countries were, as we have said, still unfinished by the hand of Nature. Gradually the rivers of Flanders were extending their mudbanks into the sea, choking up their own courses with shallow bars. Ships, moreover, were increasing in size. Bruges ceased to be available as a seaport. Ghent also lost much of its trade. By degrees, instead of Ghent and Bruges, we hear talk of Brussels and Antwerp. Thither the merchants removed with their ships and storehouses; and thither the nobles followed, and the artists, and the kings.

The new cities, upheld by imperial favor, inclined to be far more submissive to Charles than were their more ancient rivals. Yet it was from these new cities and their merchants that sprang up the final, great and celebrated "rebellion of the Netherlands," the heroic story which we now approach.

THE GREAT REBELLION

The era of Charles V was the era of the Reformation, and it was this religious upheaval that led to the great Netherland revolt. Yet the Netherlanders were not as a rule enthusiastic in the support of Luther. The attitude of Erasmus, the Dutch scholar of Rotterdam, the most learned writer of his time, may be taken as typical of that of his countrymen. They desired reform within the church, not a violent breaking away from it. Most of the Dutch and Flemish churchmen were agreed that changes should be made. Even Charles V himself was convinced of this. Lutheranism was robbing him of his power in Germany; he would take no risk of its gaining permanent root in the Netherlands. Hence he introduced there a form of Inquisition conducted by churchmen instead of civilians. This had already crushed out heresy in his Spanish domains; and, as the easygoing Dutch and Flemish prelates seemed to him too mild, he brought Spanish Inquisitors to introduce their sterner judgments and crueler tortures. The Netherlanders were alarmed; they protested; a rigid, uncompromising Spanish priest might easily call every one of them a heretic. Yet they

disapproved actual rebellion against the church; they liked Charles; and so they submitted, though unwillingly. The Inquisitors began work; and though for some years they confined themselves to slaughtering the more extreme reformers, yet the stream of blood expanded into awful volume. Estimates disagree widely as to the number of these executions during the reign of Charles. They have been set as low as a single thousand, and as high as a hundred thousand.

Despite the persecution, the emperor himself, the hearty, good-natured comrade, "one of themselves" as the Flemish burghers called him, retained his popularity in the Netherlands and looked upon the country with a friendly eye. When, worn out with his life of toil, he resolved to abandon all his many thrones, Brussels, which he had made the capital of the Low Countries, was the city he selected for the ceremony of abdication.

As he closed his farewell speech to his "well-beloved subjects," the listening multitude were moved to honest tears, regretted their rebellions, and pledged themselves readily to be loyal to the son of this kindly monarch. That son, a youth of twenty-eight, afterward the celebrated Philip II of Spain, then arose to address the Estates, and, speaking through an interpreter, promised to be even more devoted than his father to the interests of the Netherlands.

Probably no one of all those present suspected the terrible war that was to come. Philip himself, secret and subtle, knowing his own heart, may have seen nearest to the truth; but what Philip did not know was the sturdy spirit of these Netherlanders, whom he counted on crushing into submission to his will. Therein lay Philip's blunder. Unlike his father he had been neither born nor bred in Flanders. He was a Spaniard through and through. His haughtiness took constant offense at the free manners of the Flemings, and he hated as much as he despised them. Charles had ruled them through their own officials; he had even placed some of his trusted Netherland nobles in high position in Spain. Philip, despite his father's warning, reversed this and brought his Spanish associates to govern the unruly lowlands.

For a time all seemed well. The young sovereign promised many reforms. There was a war with France, and a great victory at St. Quentin (1557), due largely to Flemish troops and to the brilliancy of their general, Count Egmont. A year later Egmont and his Flemish cavalry crushed another French army at Gravelines. The enemy was forced to a humiliating peace; and one of the secret articles of the treaty between Philip and the French king was that all the military forces of the latter were to be loaned to Spain, if needed to crush revolt in the Netherlands. Thus did their new sovereign measure and reward the loyalty of his people.

Here enters William, prince of Orange, called William the Silent, the great antagonist of Philip. He ranked at the time with Egmont among the chief nobles of the

Netherlands, and so high was his repute for ability that though only twenty-two at the time of Charles V's abdication, he had already become that monarch's most trusted counselor. Indeed Charles, disappointed in his own son, who constantly opposed and defied him, had made the young Dutch noble a protégé, introduced him to the most secret interviews of state, and trained him in the methods of diplomacy. It was on the shoulders of this youthful counselor already nicknamed the Silent, that Charles leaned as he made his abdication speech; and the loyalty which William had given the father he seemed ready to transfer to the son. Philip, as we know, trusted no one; but the French king, not realizing this and seeing William apparently high in his sovereign's confidence, talked freely to the young man of the secret treaty against the Netherlands. The silent William, true to his name, listened without comment, and so learned of the destruction intended for his country.

In 1558 Philip, leaving the Netherlands for Spain, appointed as regent Margaret of Parma, his half-sister, an illegitimate daughter of his father. The departing sovereign had planned a trap for the States General; he hoped that body, lulled by his professions of goodwill, would resign all its powers to Margaret until his return. Thus through his regent he would be able to rule as an absolute monarch, unrestrained by a protesting assembly. Instead the States General, at Williams's suggestion, urged Philip to withdraw all the Spanish troops which upon one pretext and another he had quartered upon the country to overawe it.

Philip unprepared as yet to face open revolt, yielded with such grace as he could; but for one moment, as he stepped on shipboard, his wrath flamed out in his celebrated last interview with William. "It is you who have done this," he said, gripping the young prince of Orange by the arm. "Nay, it is the States General," responded William. "No," flashed out Philip, using an untranslatable form of address, insolent and contemptuous, "it is you, you, you!" Keen of insight as always, he knew that if strife came, it was not with a confused and many-headed States General he would have to deal, but with this one composed and self-reliant youth.

From the safe distance of Spain, Philip sent word to the Netherland Inquisitors to increase their severity. He also commanded Margaret, his regent, to ignore the advice of the States General and the charters of the people. A general protest arose and grew more and more determined. Margaret, dreading the consequence, entreated her brother to be more lenient; and at his suggestion Count Egmont, the popular military leader, was sent to Spain to lay the matter more fully before him. The wily sovereign, seeking only delay, listened to Egmont's complaints with seriousness and apparent respect, promised to give heed to his mild advice, and then gave him to bear back to Brussels sealed letters which contained orders for yet greater cruelty (1565).

William I, the Silent, was the stadholder from 1579 to 1584, when he was assassinated. He is looked upon by many Hollanders as the father of the country. He was also called William of Orange.

Anne of Buren was the first of four wives of William the Silent. They married in 1551.

Anna of Saxony was the wife of William the Silent from 1566 to 1575.

The third wife of William the Silent was Charlotte of Bourbon. They were married in 1575.

Princess Louise of Coligny was the fourth wife of William the Silent. They were married but one year before his death.

King Philip II of Spain threatens William the Silent and puts a price on his head (1580).

Open revolt now flared out at last. The magistrates in many places refused to obey the commands of the Inquisitors. A petition protesting against the king's orders was signed by thousands of prominent nobles, citizens, and even priests, and was presented to Margaret by the leaders of a vast procession representing every class of society. Trembling and distraught, the regent promised to do what she could.

"Are you afraid of these beggars?" demanded one of her courtiers, scornfully, referring not only to the rabble but to the lesser nobles among them, impoverished now that their ruler bestowed on them no favors. The sneer was repeated at a banquet held by many of the younger nobles who favored the revolt. Some cried out that they would accept the name thus given them in scorn. Their leader, de Brederode, promptly secured a beggar's bowl and wallet, and passing these around the tumultuous assembly swore to give up everything to the cause. The others joined him in the oath. William of Orange, Count Egmont, and Count Horn, another member of the more conservative nobility who were striving to keep peace between the court and the people, happened in upon the banquet and drank the toast that was going round, "Long live the Beggars." From this event (1566) is usually dated the great Revolt of the Netherlands.

There were a few minor contests between small forces of Beggars and Royalists; then William and Egmont succeeded in restoring a temporary peace, Margaret yielding to the demands of the insurgents for religious toleration. The Protestants, thus released from immediate danger, appeared everywhere in great numbers; they seemed suddenly a majority among the people. The "image-breaking" furor swept over the country. Bands of frenzied peasants burst into churches and cathedrals, desecrating and destroying every object of worship and of art. The nobility and the Catholic members of the Beggars sought to punish these excesses; and so dislike and distrust were sown among the various forces of rebellion. King Philip by many treacherous devices increased the mutual suspicion that spread among the Netherlanders; and at the same time he dispatched to the country a Spanish army under his lead general, the duke of Alva.

A united resistance might have held back the invaders; but few of the patriot leaders felt themselves compromised beyond hope of pardon. Count Egmont, having received from Philip letters of personal friendship and approval of his course, declared that he would again trust wholly to the sovereign who had deceived him; he would be loyal to the end, and oppose all rebellion. Count Horn took a similar attitude; and so high was the veneration in which these two were held that their course induced thousands of others to do the same. In vain William of Orange pleaded with Egmont. "You will be the bridge," he told the somewhat pompous general, "over which the Spanish will enter our country." And he added with characteristic keenness, "Having entered, they will destroy the bridge."

Finding Egmont inflexible, and deeming resistance impossible without him, the prince of Orange and his immediate associates withdrew into Germany. The two leaders parted amid tears, each lamenting what he considered the suicidal decision of the other.

"Farewell, landless prince," said Egmont.

"Farewell, headless count," responded William.

To the common people was also presented the same momentous problem, and while many took Egmont's course, many took William's. A hasty exodus began. Thousands fled to England; other thousands wended their way in long caravans across the German border. The regent Margaret entreated them to stay, she entreated Philip to recall his army. He would find himself ruling, she wrote, over naught but a desert. Finally on Alva's arrival, learning that his authority exceeded hers, she left the Netherlands in despair and retired to a religious life of quietude.

Alva and his army came (1567). The general received Egmont's welcoming speech with ominous scorn. His first public act was to summon the nobles to a general council, at which he arrested not only Egmont, but Horn and every other patriot who had ventured within his grasp, who had trusted Philip's promises. The Inquisition was revived in its most awful form. In addition to this a civil council was created to try the Netherlanders for treason. Its members were tools of Alva, and under his leadership the body soon became known by the frightful name the Council of Blood. It condemned thousands of patriots to the gibbet. It confiscated the estates of those who had fled. As soon as its authority was fully established, it sent Egmont and Horn the way of its other victims. They were beheaded in 1568.

Meanwhile the silent William, seeing his forewarning

No history of the Netherlands would be complete without a mention of the duke of Alva and his infamous Council of Blood. The duke was a very successful Spanish general who was made the governor of the Netherlands. He arrived on May 5, 1567, and left to return to Spain on November 17, 1573. He was a total tyrant who excelled in hangings, beheadings, quartering, and burning at the stake, which were everyday spectacles, for he made the townspeople watch. History records no parallel of horrors.

fulfilled, had resolved upon new effort. All Europe was in protest against the horrors being enacted in the Netherlands. The emperor Maximilian II wrote to Philip, his nephew, warning him that such severity must produce a revolution of despair. William raised an army. In addition to his exiled friends, he found thousands of volunteers, German, French and English, to assist him.

Even before the execution of Egmont, William invaded Brabant, while his brother Louis led a detachment into Friesland. Louis, after one victory, was defeated by Alva; but with William, Alva avoided a contest. There was clever maneuvering on both sides; then William, unable longer to support his army without funds, was obliged to disband it and withdraw. Alva returned unopposed to his executions and his extortions, to his Council of Blood.

Suddenly, not in Brussels but in distant Holland, the turning of the tide had come; the "revolution of despair" began, and even Alva saw that he must halt (1572).

The first success with which the Netherlanders now reopened their desperate war was gained by the "sea beggars." These were a few scattered members of the "beggars'" conspiracy who, driven into exile, had become sea robbers, roving vikings like the Norsemen of old. Many a ruined merchant joined them with a ship saved from the destruction of his fortunes; and, urged on by hunger, the wanderers plundered the coasts of the unhappy Netherlands, or seized the treasure ships of Spain, fleeing for shelter to the ports of England or Germany. At length, yielding to King Philip's repeated protests, both the emperor and Elizabeth of England excluded the sea beggars from their ports. This, which seemed to portend the ruin of the sturdy patriot pirates, proved their salvation. They appeared suddenly before the town of Briel in Holland, captured it almost without resistance, and held it in the name of William of Orange. Before his exile William had been governor or stadholder of Holland and Zealand; he was known to be still trying to raise funds for another army to rescue his people. Now the daring exploit of the sea beggars was like a spark set to the waiting train. All the northern provinces flashed into revolt. City after city expelled its Spanish garrison and declared for Orange. They did not, be it noted, claim independence; those were days when "independence" was still an unknown word in the mouths of common folk. The cities still acknowledged Philip as their overlord; they merely rejected Alva, and declared that, under Philip, William was their rightful governor.

Alva, driven by necessity, made truce with the semirebellious merchants in Brussels and hurried northward to check this vaster outbreak. For seven months Haarlem resisted a Spanish siege. William, enabled to raise another army at last, sought to relieve the city, but in vain. Haarlem surrendered to starvation in the summer of 1573. The city was plundered, and every man of its garrison was slaughtered. The next spring Louis of Nassau, William's brother and chief aid, was slain and the troops under his command totally defeated by Alva. Leyden, besieged in its turn by the advancing Spaniards, held out with desperate heroism through thirteen weary months.

Then came relief. The defense of the northern sections lay in the hands of the assembly of Holland, the largest province. The only successes of the patriots had been on the ocean, where the sea beggars had repeatedly defeated the Spanish ships; and now William urged upon the assembly that the dykes must be opened in order that the ships of the sea beggars might sail over the submerged farms and rescue Leyden. After some dispute and considerable deliberation this course was adopted. The ocean was unchained; its destructive power was made welcome; and, aided by a favoring storm, the ships swept up to the very walls of the despairing city. The Spaniards fled and Leyden was saved (1575).

This was the turning point of the heroic war. The assembly of Holland asked the citizens of Leyden to name their own reward for the service their long resistance had done the common cause; and the burghers, to their glory be it recorded, chose to have a university founded in their town. So rose the University of Leyden, the great center of religious freedom in northern Europe.

Alva had failed. His influence over King Philip was lost and he was recalled. His successor tried to rule by mildness, but it was too late. The sea beggars held the ocean. Trade, driven by taxation from the southern provinces, poured into the north. The men of Holland were triumphant in their success, determined in their resistance. They insisted on retaining William as their leader, and would listen to no terms of agreement which did not include self-taxation and complete religious toleration, terms wholly impossible to Philip's views.

The Spanish soldiers, unpaid for years, broke into open mutiny against their leaders. Instead of marching against Holland, they plundered the submissive southern provinces. The "Spanish fury" swept over many cities, most notably Antwerp, which was seized by the mutineers and ravaged for three days with most hideous accompaniments of outrage and slaughter (1576). Driven by such miseries, the south joined the north in its resistance. The ancient privileges of Flanders and Brabant were once more insisted on, and a treaty of alliance, "the Pacification of Ghent," was arranged among all the "seventeen provinces" of the Netherlands.

In the face of this united opposition even Philip yielded, or at least he postponed the subjugation of the Low Countries to a more convenient period. He was completely bankrupt. He could neither pay his troops nor compel their obedience. No alternative was left him but submission. Another new governor was therefore sent to the Netherlands, Don John, the hero of Lepanto, most famous of the illegitimate children of Charles V. Don John agreed to the "Pacification of Ghent," agreed to everything. The Spanish soldiers were paid by the southern provinces and marched for home.

Don John endeavored to undermine the prince of Orange. So also did the Flemish nobles, who were jealous of his power. But the common people everywhere learned to cling to him more and more, to see in him the one earnest patriot not to be duped by Spanish trickery, not to be bought by Spanish gold, nor even by promises of an almost imperial dignity. That these were offered him we now know from Spanish sources; but he remained true to his cause and his people. By these he was elected governor of Brabant as well as of the northern provinces; and finally he became the acknowledged leader of the entire Netherlands.

In 1581, the Assembly of Holland finally took the decisive step of declaring Philip deposed for all his misgovernment. Then asserting its own right to select another king, the Assembly offered the nominal rank to the duke of Anjou, while reserving the real authority to William.

So a Frenchman came to be king of the northern Netherlands, while the Spaniards still fought in the south. Soon the French ruler and his courtier followers found they had little real power, and no opening for

The assassination of William the Silent

wealth. They planned a conspiracy of their own, and suddenly attacked the Antwerpers in the street, trying to gain possession of the city. The Frenchmen were soon defeated, and with their feeble chief took refuge in France, where Anjou died.

The Spaniards meanwhile had begun a more subtle warfare. By fair promises they lured many of the prominent patriot leaders to their side. William was declared an outlaw, and a huge price was set upon his head. The church promised to forgive all the sins of any man who could reach and slay him. Five separate times assassins, lured by the promise of earthly gain or spiritual reward, attempted William's life. His friends guarded him jealously, but at last a religious fanatic eluded their every precaution, reached William under pretense of being a messenger from France, and shot him down (1584).

GLORY AND DECAY OF HOLLAND

The way in which William's sudden assassination was met must have gone far to convince all Europe that these Dutch merchants were resolute as any knightly warrior and watchful as any courtly statesman. On the very day of the disaster, the Holland Council of State sent to each of its generals and absent members a grave and noble letter urging all to stand firm, since now the need of the land was greater than before.

The Netherlanders had not yet realized either their own strength or Spain's increasing weakness. They despaired of being able to continue the strife alone, and despite their disastrous experience with the duke of Anjou, they sent ambassadors to both France and England, entreating that the royal houses would supply them with a king. Henry III of France and Elizabeth of England both seemed to look with favor on these appeals; and trusting upon kingly promises, the Netherlanders were slow in preparing for self-defense.

King Philip had at last secured a leader of real genius, Alexander, prince of Parma, son of Margaret, the former regent. Parma took advantage of the momentary lassitude of his foes. He acted while others stood at gaze. By threats and bribery and clever chicane, he detached one southern city after another from what seemed a falling cause. Soon, in all Flanders and Brabant, Antwerp was the only important center which held out against him. This he besieged with rare military skill. The city was headless, a turmoil of confused, excited, and incapable advisers. "It is easily seen," cried he, as he noted the lack of unity and wisdom in the defense, "that the prince of Orange is dead."

Antwerp lies on the bank of the Scheldt, which in its breadth and turbulence is rather an arm of the sea than it is a river. Parma constructed a marvel of engineering skill, a bridge that blockaded the Scheldt and resisted all the storms and tides of winter. The men of Antwerp sought to destroy the bridge, to blow it up with powder ships. Failing in the effort, they were starved into surrender. The Protestant merchants were compelled to return to Catholicism, or else were given two years to wind up their affairs and leave the country. Most of them departed into exile even before the time appointed. In the southern Netherlands, the region which is Belgium today, the revolt was over. The land became definitely separated from the better defended provinces of the north, and sank back into the grasp of Spain.

King Philip, grown wiser through disaster, encouraged the burghers' feeling of nationality by making their land a semi-independent state. He conferred the sovereignty upon his daughter, Isabella, and her husband, the duke of Austria. The entrance of Isabella into each city of her domain was made a celebration of peace, and hundreds of unhappy political prisoners were given their release. The years that followed are known as the Austrian or Austro-Spanish period of Belgium's history.

Isabella and her husband made the Netherlands their permanent home, and so also did their successors. They encouraged trade, they became patrons of art. Rubens and other famous painters flourished under them. Belgium's prosperity gradually revived. For two hundred years the Spanish Netherlands remained a sort of family estate, conferred by the Habsburg sovereigns of Austria and Spain upon the younger sons and daughters of the house. Its story during this period was uneventful; and upon the whole, for a people who had apparently lost all desire for self-government, the centuries were neither unhappy nor unprosperous.

Meanwhile, in the north, the war continued. Of the "Seven United Provinces" which still defied the might of Spain, Holland was by far the largest; and gradually its name came to be used for the entire land. Henry III of France refused the sovereignty which the rebels offered him; but Queen Elizabeth sent them English troops and an English leader, her favorite, the earl of Leicester. The alliance of England with the Dutch had also much to do with King Philip's despatching the Spanish Armada against England, and Dutch ships took no small part in the succession of naval victories by which the armada was destroyed. Its defeat meant fully as much to Holland as to England.

The prince of Parma, unaided by Spain with either men or money, continued toiling at his impossible task of making armies out of nothing, until he died of despair. Leicester offended the Dutch burghers by his arrogance, and withdrew to England, as dissatisfied with them as they with him. Philip II also died; and his successor, Philip III, inherited the feeble struggle, inherited a bankrupt Spain exhausted of every military resource.

Two men rose to be leaders of Holland. One was John of Olden-Barneveldt, who stands among the purest patriots of any age, a statesman and financial genius. The other was Maurice of Nassau, younger son of the martyred William. Maurice became the chief military figure of the war. He originated a new system of siege and defense, by which he gradually forced back the Spaniards upon the frontier, capturing their fortresses one by one. As a general he was greater than his father, but as patriot and statesman he sank far lower. William had repeatedly been offered the kingship of the land, and had refused it. Maurice sought the high rank all his life, he schemed and planned for it, and was refused. His chief opponent was the patriot Barneveldt and at length Maurice so roused the people against their aged protector that Barneveldt was condemned and executed as a traitor (1619).

A reaction followed the excitement, and Maurice found himself farther than ever from his goal. He had long been governor or stadholder of the United Provinces; that was the highest he could rise. Fortune deserted him. The cause of freedom, stripped of the statesmanship and financial wisdom of Barneveldt, sank in the scale. Even those who had supported Maurice began to point at him in horror. He died in 1625 a gloomy, disappointed man.

Still the war continued. From 1609 to 1620 there had been a truce in Europe, but in Asia the fighting was continued. Then the worldwide Thirty Years War of Germany drew both Holland and Spain once more into the vortex of religious strife. Maurice was succeeded as stadholder by his young half-brother Frederick Henry, who upheld the high reputation of his race. In 1628 the Dutch admiral, Piet Heijn, captured the Spanish silver fleet and brought treasure worth millions of dollars into Holland. In 1639, Admiral Tromp attacked and completely destroyed a Spanish fleet of fifty ships in the Battle of the Downs off England's coast. This completed the destruction of the vast navy of Spain, and raised the naval repute of Holland to the highest point.

Prince Maurice of Orange succeeded his father William the Silent and reigned from 1584 until 1625. He was the son of Anna of Saxony.

Frederick Henry, prince of Orange (1625–47). When he died on March 14, 1647, he left behind him a character of unblemished integrity, prudence, tolerance, and valor.

The haughty House of Habsburg, rulers of Spain and of the German Empire, saw their sea power crushed by Holland and their armies exhausted by the Swedes in the German war. So at last the emperor and the king of Spain, another Philip by this time, the fourth of the name, consented to the general peace of 1648, by which the entire independence of Holland was formally acknowledged. She took her place among the great powers of Europe, not as a monarchy but as a republic. The House of Orange retained a very high authority as stadholders, but the burghers had become fully accustomed to self-government. The States General was the acknowledged authority of the land; and its members, dreaming of empire in the East, assumed all the airs of royalty. They officially styled themselves the High and Mighty Lords.

To any far-seeing eye, a business war between the two rivals, both keenly grasping, both superbly self-confident, must have appeared inevitable. The quarrel grew rapidly. At length Admiral Blake in command of an English fleet fired a shot at a Dutch vessel; Admiral Tromp responded with a broadside; the memorable naval war began (1652). There were two years of desperate, deadly, glorious naval fights. On the whole the advantage was with the English, who had the heavier ships. But both Admiral Tromp and Admiral de Ruyter defended the Dutch coast with vigor and success, and won for themselves and their countrymen undying renown.

The man who had led Holland to this height of influence and renown, was John de Witt, chief of the celebrated family of that name. Unfortunately it was he also who brought his country to the very verge of destruction. His attitude and that of the Dutch people in general was construed as an insult by the new "rising sun" in France, the youthful monarch Louis XIV. Or rather, to put it more broadly, the very existence of Holland, a republic, was felt as an insult by every sovereign of Europe. Here were these "mere tradesfolk" assuming airs of equality and even of superiority toward the most eminent royal houses. When in 1672, Louis suddenly proclaimed himself offended and without warning hurled his armies upon Holland, not a voice was raised in its favor. The English mindful of recent injuries rather than more recent treaties, sent their fleet to join France in the attack.

Once more as in their memorable war with Spain, the Dutch stood alone, friendless and apparently overwhelmingly outnumbered. But now their cause seemed even more hopeless than before, because they were wholly unprepared for an attack by land. De Witt had persisted in courting alliance with France, in trusting upon Louis's friendship. No precautions had been taken against attack; the invading Frenchmen found their work at first a mere pleasure trip, a plundering expedition amid a helpless people. The infuriated Dutchmen cried out that de Witt was a traitor, that he had expected, nay invited this disaster. He and his brother Cornelis were slain by a mob in the streets of The Hague, savagely beaten, and trampled almost out of recognition as human forms.

The martyrdom of these two pure and high-souled patriots left the way open for the return to power of the princes of Orange. The young heir of the house, now grown to manhood, was at once made stadholder as William III. In fact it was his partisans who had slain the de Witts, nor was the prince himself ever wholly cleared of complicity in the crime.

His sudden appearance at the head of affairs roused the people from the despair into which they had been thrown by Louis's sudden attack. Half the country was already in French hands; but Amsterdam set example to the remainder by cutting her dykes, flooding her own surrounding fields, and so opposing a barrier of water to the enemy's advance. Yet so desperate seemed the situation that William and the States General, finding every overture for peace rejected, discussed in solemn council the necessity of destroying all the dykes, taking the entire nation on board their ships and sailing away to their empire in the East—leaving a drowned land to an insatiable foe.

Fortunately this extreme of heroism was not demanded of them. The partial flooding of the land by Amsterdam and other cities, sufficed to check Louis's progress. Moreover, on the checkerboard of European politics, the Habsburg rulers of Germany and Spain seeing their rival the French king apparently on the point of subduing Holland, lent their aid to the very land that had broken down their ancient supremacy. William also secured the friendship of England by marrying Mary, the

Prince William II, who succeeded his father Frederick Henry, reigned but three years—from 1647 to 1650.

Prince William III of Orange was the stadholder from 1650 to 1702. This proud, slight man was also the king of England, but he served the two countries differently, in that he was the restorer of liberty from foreign conquest and its staunchest defender in England; however, he served Holland as a vassal state.

king's niece (1677). Against this array, France fell back, baffled. Holland was once more saved by a prince of the House of Orange.

From that time William III devoted his life to his celebrated strife against King Louis. Again and again he managed to draw Europe into an alliance against France. In 1689 he became king of England; and that high office also he employed to defeat Louis. In the end he was successful. At the time of William's death (1702), England, the United Provinces, and the German Empire were attacking Louis in the War of the Spanish Succession; the towering might of France was already crumbling.

William left no nearer heir than a youthful cousin, so the provinces elected no new stadholder to succeed him. Once more the States General took entire charge of the government. Its members resolutely continued William's plans for war with France; and their troops took a prominent part in those great victories of Blenheim, Ramillies and Malplaquet, for which England is so apt to claim entire credit.

Yet the provinces were becoming exhausted both in men and money. These perpetual wars were at last sapping their vitality beyond its power to recuperate. England was crowding them from the ocean; their trade was languishing. When in 1712 the English queen suddenly decided to make peace with France, the provinces had no choice but to acquiesce in the arrangement.

LATER HISTORY OF THE NETHERLANDS

The southern portion, the Spanish or as they had come to be called, the Austrian Netherlands, had been the main battleground between Louis XIV and the European coalition. The land lay wasted and desolate. Holland, impoverished and exhausted, was in little better condition. Peace slowly restored both regions to a material prosperity, but not to that high national pride and vigor which had once made them famous.

Holland joined in the war of 1744 against France and lost what little prestige remained to her. The people, in an outbreak of resentment against their feeble government, not only restored the stadholdership to the House of Orange (1747), but declared it a permanent office and hereditary in the family forever. William IV, the stadholder thus appointed, was a nephew of William III; and his patriotism and ability seemed to promise him worthy of the renowned race from which he sprang. But his sudden death in 1751 left his rank to an infant son, William V, so that the difficult duties of the position fell into the hands of regents.

The first of these was the child's mother, Anne, a daughter of King George II of England; and after her death came the duke of Brunswick, who was also inti-

William IV was the stadholder of the Netherlands from 1747 to 1751.

Stadholder William IV Friso (1747–51) was the son of John Friso, a distant relative of William III.

mately allied with the English royal house. The people of Holland felt that their interests were deliberately sacrificed to those of their formidable commercial rival. Dutch ships were openly seized by the British. Dutch colonies were appropriated, and finally in 1780 England, declaring war upon the helpless and wholly unready provinces, seized what was left of their trade and their colonial empire. Only a few small districts in the farthest east remained to remind Holland of the vast regions she had once possessed.

By this time the young stadholder, William V, had grown to manhood; but matters failed to improve under his guidance. The people grew more discontented and rebellious; Prussian troops were loaned to William to strengthen his position; and the chiefs of the opposition or Republican party were compelled to flee from the country. William became practically as absolute a sovereign as any of the little German princes along his borders (1787).

Then came the French Revolution. Already its spirit had invaded Holland. It had inspired the party in rebellion against William V. It roused the Belgians, and in 1789 they engaged in a short but fierce revolt against Austria. This was suppressed the following year, but it is no wonder that neither in Belgium nor Holland was there much desire to resist the advance of the French when the aroused revolutionists burst upon them proclaiming freedom with the sword, reasserting those doctrines of "Liberty, Equality, and Fraternity" which the Netherland burghers themselves had been the first to champion in the face of monarchical Europe.

The Austrians were driven out of Belgium by the French victory at Jemappes (1792), and the land was annexed to France. Holland resisted longer; yet many Dutchmen fought on the side of the invaders; and, aided by the severity of the winter—the French winter it was called by the Hollanders—General Pichegru took possession of the land in 1795.

William V fled to England. The Republican party among the Dutch formed an alliance with the Frenchmen, welcomed them as liberators, and formed a new government under a new constitution. Holland became the Batavian Republic. The name was an empty form which did not long survive. In reality the land was a mere dependency of France, savagely tyrannized over by the French deputies sent to "advise" its government. In 1806, Napoleon converted it into a kingdom of Holland for his brother Louis; and in 1810 it was formally incorporated, as the southern Netherlands had previously been, in the rapidly expanding empire of France.

The downfall of Napoleon in his Russian campaign found the Dutch common people as eager as the Germans to throw off a yoke which had become intolerable. They bore a valiant part in the struggles of 1813–14, and in the final campaign of Waterloo. The stadholder William V had died in exile; but his son, another William, returned from England to lead his people in their struggle. He was received with a warm affection that forgot former causes of dispute and remembered only his race, the great race of Orange, and its long devotion to the

Prince William V ruled the Netherlands from 1751 until 1795, when he had to flee to England to escape the French. He was the last of the stadholders.

The first king of the Netherlands was Louis Bonaparte, who reigned at the behest of his brother, Napoleon Bonaparte, from 1806 to 1810.

King William I (Willem), who served as the sovereign over both Belgium and Holland after the fall of Napoleon. He ruled until 1840, when he abdicated.

cause of Holland. The nation had been surfeited with republican forms of government; the stadholdership was abolished; William was eagerly invited to become a king and in March 1814 was solemnly inaugurated as King William I.

In the general rearrangement of European affairs undertaken by the Congress of Vienna in 1814–15, it was universally agreed that this new "kingdom of Holland" should not only be accepted but enlarged, so that it might become a real restraint upon France's northern border. Austria, receiving compensation elsewhere, surrendered its outworn claim upon Belgium; and once more after the lapse of centuries all the low countries were reunited into a single state, the "Kingdom of the Netherlands," under the sovereignty of William I, no longer prince of Orange, but king of the Netherlands.

This ill-advised union of Belgium and Holland lasted only fifteen years. It had indeed been hopeless from the beginning, a purely geographical alliance which took no account of the differences of religion and race, nor of the even keener antagonisms roused by centuries of alienation and war. Nobody really desired the union except a few purblind diplomats and the ambitious King William. The Dutch accepted it with hesitation. The Belgians were not consulted at all. They felt themselves treated as a conquered and dependent people; and when the French Revolution of 1830 gave them the impulse and opportunity, they rushed immediately to arms and proclaimed their independence.

The Dutch however, had become proud of their superior position in the union; they would not lightly relinquish it. King William, grown old and narrow, was haughty and uncompromising. A Dutch army attacked Brussels and was vigorously resisted by the citizens. There were four days of fighting in the streets. Barricade after barricade was stormed by the Dutch troops, but always there were others beyond, and at length the invaders were compelled to retreat. Belgian independence had been sealed in blood.

Everywhere throughout the country the people rose in arms. The Dutch garrisons were driven out. The most notable struggle was in Antwerp, where the Dutch troops, driven from the streets, took possession of the citadel and bombarded the city they were supposed to be protecting. Both France and England intervened. If Belgium was so determined on independence, the great powers would no longer stand as sponsors for the union they had created. So the Netherlands were again declared divided. Belgium was allowed to select a king of its own from the royal families of Europe, and after negotiation with two or three candidates conferred the dignity upon a German prince, Leopold of Saxe-Coburg. Lines of demarcation between Belgium and Holland were then agreed to by the powers, though naturally the boundaries assigned satisfied neither of the belligerent little disputants. Scarcely indeed had King Leopold entered his new kingdom when an army of nearly eighty thousand Dutch troops poured into it. William of Holland had decided to defy Europe and reassert his sovereignty (1831).

The astonished Belgians were defeated in two slight battles. Leopold appealed to France and England for aid; and a French army entered Belgium, while a British fleet descended upon the coast of Holland. Confronted by such overwhelming odds, King William yielded as ungraciously as possible, disputing every step of the negotiations, which were only finally completed in 1839.

Belgium thus stands as a sort of godchild to the neighboring great powers, fostered by their care. King Leopold proved a model constitutional sovereign, undertaking seriously and successfully the duties of his position. His death in 1865 was deeply mourned by his people, and his son, Leopold II, was enabled to begin his reign under the most favorable auspices. Unfortunately he has devoted himself less to the guidance of his country than to a career of pleasure and the accumulation of enormous wealth.

In Holland meanwhile there has been far greater national sentiment, greater unity of feeling; and her course has been one of peace and progress. King William I abdicated in 1840, soon after he had been finally compelled to consent to the formal release of Belgium. His son William II ruled until 1849, when he was succeeded by his son, William III. The revolutions which shook Europe in 1848–49 had their echo among the Dutch, but a truly great statesman appeared to guide the country through the crisis. To Jan Rudolf Thorbecke, Holland owes not only the peaceful solution of the many problems of this difficult era, but also the development of many of her industries and the establishment of her present broad-minded and liberal constitution. Thorbecke died in 1872.

King William III, grown old and feebleminded, died in 1890 without male heirs, so that the throne passed to his ten-year-old daughter, Wilhelmina. For several years the child's mother ruled as regent, but in 1898 Wilhelmina assumed full sovereignty amid the congratulations of all nations. She soon selected a husband suited to her taste, a dashing young Prussian officer, Duke Henry of Mecklenburg. The choice was approved by her devoted people; Duke Henry was created a general, and also prince of the Netherlands, and in 1901 the happy pair were wedded with splendid ceremonials at The Hague. Rumor has since represented them as proving less congenial to each other than their subjects hoped. A daughter was born to the queen in 1909, and became the heiress of her mother's crown.

Wilhelmina made an excellent ruler; she was devoted to her people, and they to her. During the Boer War in South Africa, Holland showed that she had not forgotten her former sovereignty over those distant climes and people. The queen's offer to mediate between the Boers and England was refused, but the expatriated Boers were

King William II (1840–49) was the son of William I and the leader of the Dutch army against Belgium in its efforts to gain independence. He had conducted himself with valor at Waterloo but didn't make much of an impression on the Belgians. History also records that he had serious deficiencies as a statesman and diplomat.

King William III had a long (1849–90) reign, but it was not noteworthy.

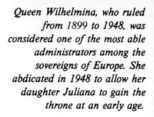

Queen Wilhelmina, who ruled from 1899 to 1948, was considered one of the most able administrators among the sovereigns of Europe. She abdicated in 1948 to allow her daughter Juliana to gain the throne at an early age.

The wedding of Queen Wilhelmina to Henry of Mecklenburg-Schwerin in 1901

warmly received in Amsterdam and elsewhere. Wilhelmina had also brought her country into note as the seat of the International Peace Conference, which held its first meeting at The Hague in 1899. A second great peace conference was held there in 1907, on which occasion a splendid Palace of Peace, gift of Andrew Carnegie, was erected as a home for the tribunal.

In 1940 German troops invaded the Netherlands and Queen Wilhelmina left the country for England. The period of her exile showed clearly that the link between the Netherlands and the House of Orange is not based merely on the constitutional position of the monarch in the Dutch state. By giving strong personal and spiritual leadership the queen inspired the Dutch people and gave them courage in their resistance to the occupying forces. The Netherlands, like the royal house, is fully aware of the moral value that the monarchy represents in the country.

The queen in exile took a step of historic significance when in 1942 she held out the prospect of a conference between the Netherlands on the one hand and the Dutch East Indies, Surinam, and the Netherlands Antilles on the other to revise the constitutional links between the several countries.

In 1948 Queen Wilhelmina abdicated, to be succeeded by her daughter Juliana. Queen Juliana too was deeply aware of the heavy responsibility of her office, as is evident from the words with which she defined the importance of the monarchy: "I have been called to a task so difficult that no one who has given it a moment's thought would wish to do it, but also so splendid that I can only say—who am I, to be permitted to perform it?"

For security reasons Queen Juliana and her children spent the war years in Canada. She had four children by her marriage in 1937 with Prince Bernhard: Princess Beatrix (married to Prince Claus), Princess Irene (married to Prince Charles Hugo of Bourbon-Parma), Princess Margriet (married to Mr. P. van Vollenhoven), and Princess Christina. In 1949 the queen signed the treaty transferring sovereignty over the former colony of the Dutch East Indies to the government of the Republic of Indonesia. In 1954 the queen gave the royal assent to the Charter of the Kingdom of the Netherlands proclaiming the equality of Surinam, the Netherlands Antilles and the Netherlands.

The main themes of her speeches at home and abroad were respect for life, international solidarity, and close cooperation in Europe. She also championed the cause of development cooperation and was anxious to keep in touch with the younger generation in the Netherlands and other countries.

As head of state she studied government affairs very carefully indeed and was closely involved in the formation of new governments. She regularly received members of Parliament for exchanges of views which enabled her to keep abreast of the latest developments in society. Every year she opened the session of the States General by reading the speech from the throne. In recognition of her services to society the State University of Groningen conferred upon her an honorary Doctorate in Social Sciences.

Prince Bernhard spent most of his time during the war in England with Queen Wilhelmina. As commander of the Dutch armed forces he was actively involved in the liberation of the Netherlands. Although the prince of the Netherlands has no constitutional function, his activities were manifold. In 1970 his military duties were combined in one function: inspector general of the armed forces. As curator of the Netherlands Economic Institute and the Netherlands School of Economics in Rotterdam the prince was closely involved in the development of the economic sciences.

Immediately after World War II the prince began to take an active part in the work of promoting the economic recovery of the Netherlands. To foster trade relations he traveled widely in South and Central America, the United States, Canada, Africa, and Asia. His interest in cultural matters was reflected in his chairmanship of the international board of the European Cultural Foundation, which promotes cultural cooperation in Europe. He is also the founder and trustee of the Praemium Erasmianum Foundation, a Dutch body that awards money prizes annually to persons or institutions which have made an important contribution to European art, science, or culture in general. In the last few years the prince has done a great deal for nature conservation as president of the World Wild Life Fund.

Since 1954 he has been chairman of the Bilderberg group. A meeting of seventy-five to eighty leading politicians, businessmen, academics, and journalists from Western Europe, the United States, and Canada was held under his chairmanship every year to discuss cur-

Queen Wilhelmina addresses a joint session of the United States Congress on August 22, 1942, to announce that the Netherlands was ceasing its neutrality position.

Prince Bernhard and Princess Juliana meet with the first lady of the White House, Eleanor, the wife of President Franklin D. Roosevelt, in 1942.

The royal family in 1955

It is September 1948 and Queen Wilhelmina has just abdicated and is greeting her daughter and the people with a cheer, "Long live the Queen!" from the balcony of the royal palace. Prince Bernhard looks on with anticipation as the queen Juliana appears to be stunned by the emotion of the moment.

Netherlands arms. The coat of arms of the Netherlands state is also that of Her Majesty the queen. It bears the motto of the princes of Orange: "Je maintiendral." The arms are surmounted by the royal crown as a symbol of the dignity of the Dutch Commonwealth since 1815, when the monarchy was founded.

After World War II, Queen Juliana comes to the United States on a state visit and speaks before the joint houses of Congress.

Soestdijk, the palace residence of the royal family

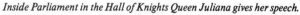

The golden coach awaits in the Binnenhof as Queen Juliana delivers the opening address before the Parliament.

Inside Parliament in the Hall of Knights Queen Juliana gives her speech.

Queen Juliana with Queen Elizabeth II of England

Queen Juliana and Prince Bernhard visited the United Nations New York headquarters in 1952. Seated (left to right) are Prince Bernhard, the queen, and UN Secretary-General Trygve Lie.

Her Royal Highness Princess Beatrix made an official visit to the United Nations headquarters in 1963. The princess is seen here during the visit conversing with the secretary-general. Left to right: *Ambassador Muhammad Zafrulla Khan, permanent representative of Pakistan to the UN, the princess, Secretary-General U Thant, and Ambassador C.W.A. Schurmann, permanent representative of the Netherlands to the UN.*

Her Majesty Queen Juliana and His Royal Highness prince of the Netherlands Bernhard.

rent foreign politics and economic and social problems.

Since her mother became queen, Princess Beatrix (born 1938) had been the heiress presumptive to the throne. She had been a member of the Council of State since she was eighteen. She has always shown a great interest in social and cultural matters, both within the kingdom and elsewhere.

Prince Claus has chosen to work in the field of physical planning, concentrating on the environment. In 1967 he was appointed a member of the Advisory Council for Physical Planning. He is also interested in aid to developing countries. His knowledge and experience in this domain led to his appointment as a member of the Netherlands Advisory Council on Development. He is also very much interested in trade and industry.

On April 30, 1980, Queen Juliana abdicated in favor of Princess Beatrix. In six hours of festivities, the abdication and inauguration ceremonies took place at the royal palace and at the Nieuwe Kerk (New Church) in Amsterdam's downtown Dam Square. It was Queen Juliana's seventy-first birthday. The queen, upon abdicating, said, "For the sake of the Kingdom of the Netherlands, for the sake of all of us who are Dutch, it is better that my place should be taken by someone new and vigor-

Crown Princess Beatrix (later queen) with Prince Claus and their three sons, left to right: *Prince William Alexander, Prince John Friso, and Prince Constantijn.*

ous." Orange confetti honoring the House of Orange-Nassau showered down from the buildings in the square as the mother and daughter appeared on the balcony of the palace. They were joined by Queen Beatrix's husband, Prince Claus, and their three sons, including thirteen-year-old Willem Alexander, the first male heir to the throne in ninety-six years. At the inauguration Queen Beatrix wore a twenty-three-foot-long velvet robe lined with ermine which was made in 1840. The crown, however, remained on a table beside the throne, for the Dutch do not crown the sovereigns, reflecting the two centuries of Republican rule that preceded the monarchy.

Under the 1815 constitution, amended slightly on this point in 1922, the monarchy in the Netherlands is hereditary in both the male and female lines. The throne passes to the eldest son or, if there are no sons, to the eldest daughter of the monarch and his or her descendants. If the monarch has no children, the eldest brother or—if there are no brothers—the eldest sister succeeds to the throne. The succession then passes to his or her descendants. Succession like this in the collateral line goes as far as the third line removed. If there is no legitimate successor on the death of a monarch, the two chambers of the States General meet in joint session to appoint a king or queen.

Members of the royal house who marry without the permission of the States General forfeit their right of succession. No such approval was requested when Princess Irene, Queen Juliana's second daughter, married; so she is excluded from the succession under the relevant clause in the constitution.

Those who are legally entitled to succeed to the throne are not allowed to abjure that right. The succession to the throne is of great Dutch concern and an established duty of the ruling royal house. The country's interests would be prejudiced if possible successors were to alter the succession to the throne by giving up their right to succeed to it. When the monarch dies the heir to the throne succeeds immediately: the rule in the Netherlands is "Le Roi est mort, vive le Roi."

The duties of the monarch are both legislative and executive. No statutory provision can come into force unless one or more ministers are answerable to Parliament for it. They give evidence of their responsibility by countersigning acts and royal decrees. Neither the monarch, nor ministers, nor Parliament can on their own change any act of government.

Queen Juliana appeared on many of her country's postage stamps.

The April 30, 1980, stamp commemorating the coronation of Queen Beatrix.

A 1964 postage stamp honoring the BE-NE-LUX countries and their sovereigns. Left to right: *King Baudouin of Belgium, Queen Juliana, and Grand-duchess Charlotte of Luxemburg.*

Before the formal dinner. Left to right: President Ronald Reagan, the First Lady, Nancy Reagan, Queen Beatrix and her husband Prince Claus. (White House photographer, Bill Fitz-Patrick)

Queen Beatrix's arrival at the White House on April 20, 1982, to commemorate the 200th anniversary of diplomatic relations with the United States. The queen, Beatrix Wilhelmina Armgard, queen of the Netherlands, Princess of Orange-Nassau and Princess of Lippe-Biesterfeld, is seen here with President Ronald Reagan during the playing of the national anthems of the two countries. (White House photographer, Cynthia Johnson)

THE ROYAL SOVEREIGNS OF THE KINGDOM OF THE NETHERLANDS

Reign	Title	Ruler	Birth	Death	Relationship	Consort	Birth	Death
					THE COUNTS OF HOLLAND (843–1299)			
–923	Count	Dirk I		923	Appointed by Charles the Simple			
923–988	Count	Dirk II		988	Son of Dirk I			
988–993	Count	Arnold		993	Son of Dirk II			
993–1039	Count	Dirk III		1039	Son of Arnold			
1039–1049	Count	Dirk IV		1049	Son of Dirk III			
1049–1061	Count	Floris I		1061	Brother of Dirk IV			
1061–1091	Count	Dirk V		1091	Son of Floris I			
1091–1121	Count	Floris II, the Fat		1121	Son of Dirk V			
1121–1157	Count	Dirk VI		1157	Son of Floris II			
1157–1187	Count	Floris III		1187	Son of Dirk VI			
1191–1203	Count	Dirk VII		1203	Son of Floris III			
1203–1204	Countess	Ada		1224	Daughter of Dirk VII			
1204–1224	Count	William I		1224	Brother of Dirk VII			
1224–1235	Count	Floris IV		1235	Son of William I			
1235–1256	Count	William II		1256	Son of Floris IV			
1248—William II becomes the king of Germany								
1256–1296	Count	Floris V		1296	Son of William II			
1296–1299	Count	John I		1299	Son of Floris V			
1299—Count of Hainaut assumes control as John II								
1300–1356—Under the control of the House of Hainaut								
1356–1435—Under control of independent sovereignties								
1436–1493—Under the control of the Habsburgs and the House of Burgundy								
1494–1506	Count	Philip the Handsome	1478	1506	Son of Maximilian I	"Mad" Juana		1482
1506–1555	Count	Charles V	1500	1558	Son of Philip the Handsome			
1555–1581	Count	Philip II	1527	1598	Son of Charles V			
1579—Dutch Republic								
1579–1584	Stadholder	William I, the Silent, prince of Orange	1533	1584	Son of William the Rich	Anne of Buren Anna of Saxony Charlotte of Bourbon Louise of Coligny	1533 1544 1555	1558 1577 1582 1620
1584–1625	Stadholder	Maurice of Orange	1567	1625	Son of William I			
1625–1647	Stadholder	Frederick Henry	1584	1647	Half-brother of Maurice	Amalia of Solms	1602	1675
1647–1650	Stadholder	William II	1626	1650	Son of Frederick Henry	Maria Stuart	1631	1661
1650–1702	Stadholder	William III of Orange	1650	1702	Son of William II	Mary Stuart	1662	1694
1702–1747—Republic without a stadholder								
1747–1751	Stadholder	William IV Friso	1711	1751	Nephew of William III; son of John Friso	Anne of Hanover	1709	1759
1751–1795	Stadholder	William V	1748	1806	Son of William IV	Wilhelmina of Prussia	1751	1820
1795–1806—France established the Dutch Republic as the Batavian Republic								
1806–1810	King	Louis Bonaparte	1778	1846	Brother of Napoleon Bonaparte			
1810–1813—The Netherlands incorporated into France								
1813–1840	King	William I	1772	1843	Son of William V	Wilhelmina Frederika of Prussia	1774	1837
1840–1849	King	William II	1792	1849	Son of William I	Anna Paulowna of Russia	1795	1865
1849–1890	King	William III	1817	1890	Son of William II	Emma of Waldeck-Pyrmont	1858	1934
1890–1948	Queen	Wilhelmina	1880	1962	Daughter of William III	Henry of Mecklenburg-Schwerin	1876	1934
1948–1980	Queen	Juliana	1909		Daughter of Wilhelmina	Bernhard of Lippe-Biesterfeld	1911	
1980–	Queen	Beatrix	1938		Daughter of Juliana	Claus of Germany		

12
The Kingdom of Denmark

SWEDEN, NORWAY,
AND DENMARK
after the
Treaty of Westphalia 1648.

This map shows the most significant period in Denmark's history with its relationship to Sweden and Norway, immediately after the Peace of Westphalia in 1648.

of the Scandinavian peninsula, in the east. For a long time it was Danish policy to control the foreign bases, markets, and shore stations of the trade routes leading to the west and to the Slav and Arab worlds. This drew Denmark into the struggle for the three seas: the North Sea with the coasts of Britain and western Europe; the Skagerrak with the Norwegian and Swedish coasts; and the Baltic with the states of Germany, Sweden, Poland, and Russia. Denmark became at once a Baltic and an Atlantic power, with all the political, economic, and cultural consequences that that has entailed. She came to occupy a key position at the outlet of the Baltic. In successive combinations she clashed with the English, German princes, and Norwegian and Swedish kings. The period of expansion lasted until about 1600 and was followed by the struggle to preserve the national territory against expanding rivals: Swedish power in Scania; Germany in the border regions of southern Jutland. In the long run Danish foreign policy was dictated by her relations with the western maritime powers on the one hand and the great continental powers on the other.

Migrations and invasions from the Continent flowed across the open borderland of Jutland. By the same route came cultural currents from western Europe and Germany which Denmark received and adapted to her own. But, even in the Iron Age, with its vigorous economic and social development, Danish tribes also trekked across Europe toward Germany and Italy and sailed their vessels to Britain. This first great expansion was followed from about A.D. 500–600 by another, which, along with Norwegian Viking raids to the west and Swedish raids to the east, continued for several centuries and culminated around A.D. 900–1000.

While the Norwegians settled on the Atlantic islands and in parts of Scotland and Ireland, and the Swedes

Denmark was created at the great junction of the northern seas, in the region of transit between north and south, east and west. The twin pillars of this maritime realm dependent on sea connections for its cohesion, its outward lines of expansion also governed by shipping, were the continental peninsula of Jutland in the west and the island of Zealand together with Scania, the southern part

Odin died in 55 B.C. and was buried at sea in a flaming Viking ship, which was the traditional burial for their leaders.

Odin's first invasion to the south and into Danish territory

made their way along the great Russian rivers to the Black Sea, Danish Vikings overran the Frisian coast and about A.D. 800 swung across the North Sea to England. From the middle of the century one great campaign followed another in an almost unbroken assault, and in 886 the king of Wessex was forced to cede the land north of a line running from London to Chester, where the Danes had settled permanently. It was not until around 900 that Alfred the Great succeeded in checking the expansion.

THE FIRST KINGDOM

At Jellinge in 910 King Gorm built a memorial stone. It bore the inscription in letters called runes: King Gorm set up this monument for his queen, Thyri, Denmark's guardian. The queen was given the title because she had brought together workers from all over Denmark to build a wall—the *Danevirke* (Danes' work) as a bulwark to deter their enemies. This tribute of King Gorm to his queen is the first recording of Danish history from the Danes themselves. King Gorm is considered to be the first king of all Denmark—the man with whom Danish history becomes separate from the history of Norway and of Sweden. It was hundreds of years before the three young nations learned to live on peaceful terms with one another. Danish history, like the history of the other two countries, is distressingly full of wars against the rest of

Gorm the Old (883–941) is historically considered to be the first king of Denmark who had an organized government. It was, also, the first government free of political or geographical connection with Sweden and Norway.

Queen Thyri, consort of King Gorm, directing the building of Danevirke. Legend has it that King Godfred built Danevirke but recent discoveries evidenced it to be the work of Queen Thyri. Therefore she has been called the Danebod, *"the mender of Denmark."*

In the east Jutland township of Jelling are Denmark's oldest royal monumental tombs: the burial mounds—the largest in the country —of Gorm the Old and Queen Thyri with two runic stones. The small one was erected by Gorm to Thyri, and the large one was raised in about A.D. 980 to Gorm and Thyri by their son Harold the Bluetooth.

An early (1591) sketch of Jelling as it appeared in 900. A is the church; B, center, is King Harold's stone with the figure of Christ on it (in that history records as the first-known depiction of Christ in Scandinavia). C and D are a burial mound with a funerary chamber. E is a burial mound without a funerary chamber, and F is a memorial stone.

Scandinavia—and other nations. Harold Blaatand, the Bluetooth, King Gorm's son, who ruled Denmark from 941 to 991, won a place for himself and Denmark by fighting Norway and making their leader, Earl Haakon, his "citizen." King Harold was also the first king of Denmark to be baptized a Christian and he tried to spread the new religion among his subjects and organize the early Danish church. Harold's son, Sweyn I, the Splitbeard (991–1014), was also a great warrior and leader. It was he who, in league with the Swedish king and some of the Norwegian earls, defeated the heroic King Olaf Tryggvason of Norway in the great sea fight (A.D. 1000) that ended with King Olaf leaping with his armor into the sea in an apparent suicide. Then Sweyn took his Viking warriors to Britian to avenge the killing of Danish settlers there and by 1013 was master of all England.

THE MEDIEVAL STATE

By the middle of the tenth century, there were churches in Jutland towns and the monarchy had undertaken to assist the church in winning over the Danes. The church brought to Denmark the culture of medieval Europe. But in organization and doctrine it was foreign to the old community. Its leaders and its loyalty were outside the old organization of the clans. Such were the forces on which the monarchy was building its power, assisted by the Viking wars and the church. It is true that the kings

Denmark's Viking kings played chess, often with fatal results for one of the players. In 1026, Canute the Great and his brother-in-law Ulf Jarl had a match, and Ulf Jarl angrily overturned the board when the king altered a move. The following day Ulf Jarl was murdered.

Roskilde was the first center of church-building in stone. After the murder of Ulf Jarl in Harold the Bluetooth's wooden church, the jarl's widow pulled it down and built a stone church, ca. 1026. A cathedral was erected on the site later, but it was Bishop Absalon who built the present cathedral in the 1170s; one of the first brick structures, it is still the finest, although a conglomerate of various periods, surrounded, for example, by built-on chapels, where Danish kings have been buried for 600 years.

The Danish coat of arms, three blue lions among red hearts on a gold escutcheon, is one of the kingdom's oldest treasures. The picture shows the earliest preserved example of the coat of arms as used in the seal of Canute (Knud) IV dating from about 1080.

The small coat of arms, showing only the three lions and nine hearts, is the oldest Danish arms, having been borne around 1190 by King Canute VI.

The large coat of arms in its composition illustrates the history of Denmark from the Middle Ages, the Viking raids, and their English possession, the Danelaw (Danelagen).

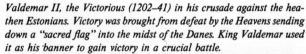

Valdemar II, the Victorious (1202–41) in his crusade against the heathen Estonians. Victory was brought from defeat by the Heavens sending down a "sacred flag" into the midst of the Danes. King Valdemar used it as his banner to gain victory in a crucial battle.

belonged to the old clans and were originally only *primi inter pares* who acquired special authority in war, but the constantly recurring mobilizations of the Viking period, with its discipline, its fleets, and a large system of fortified camps, strengthened the monarchs.

In a serious struggle with the time-honored authority of the clan community the monarchy gained ascendancy. During the twelfth century it obtained further support from the small towns that had arisen as special areas outside the jurisdiction of the old "moots."

When King Sweyn died in 1014, his second son, Canute, became king of England, and four years later succeeded to the throne of Denmark. This was Canute II, the Great (1018–35), who in every way was a greater king than Sweyn. Canute was a mighty warrior. He conquered England all over again when it slipped away after his father's death. Also, before he died he added Norway to his kingdom. What is most remarkable is his idea of how a king should rule—not by force. He did not rule England as a conquered land, but with the same equal rights for the people as in Denmark. He built churches and monasteries, and had welfare programs for the poor. "In his realm," reports a historian, "was so good a peace that no one dared break it." The English people were better off under Denmark than under their own rule.

History records that great kings rarely have great sons to carry on their rule. It happened with Canute as it happened with Alexander the Great and with Charlemagne—his heirs were weak and quarrelsome, and his empire fell apart into confusion and war.

King Sweyn II Estrithson (1047–74), a nephew of Canute the Great, tried to reconquer England, but did not succeed. Another descendant of Canute's, Canute the Holy (1080–86), is worthy of note, for he was made the patron saint of Denmark because he had served the Danish church so well. From 1147 to 1157 the quarrels of the kings and would-be kings kept Denmark continually torn with civil war. And then, out of the confusion, rose another great king—Valdemar the Great (1157–82).

At Valdemar's right hand stood one of Denmark's greatest statesman, Absalon, who was warrior and archbishop besides. It was he who built the stronghold which later became Denmark's capital—*Copenhagen*, which means "merchants haven." And it was Absalon who counseled Valdemar to carry Christianity to the land of the Wends on the southern shore of the Baltic, overturning their worship of the four-headed idol. In 1169 the Wends were baptized into the Christian faith.

The struggle against German influence was already in full swing. Under the Valdemars (1157–1241) a counteroffensive was gradually launched. They forced the provinces into greater unity and reorganized the military system; at the beginning of the thirteenth century, crown and church succeeded in repelling the great north German commercial town of Lübeck and in conquering Estonia (1219–1346).

An undoubted reminder of the Danish period in Estonia is the Tallin (Reval) coat of arms as it remained down to the Second World War: three blue lions on a yellow escutcheon. Only the red hearts are absent. In a naval engagement against the Hanseatic League, in the Sound in 1427, the Danes won a great victory, but the men of Lübeck succeeded in capturing a Danish ship, from which the Danneborg flag, the oldest to survive into modern times, probably originated. It was found, about the year 1880, by a Danish museum official in the Maria Church at Lübeck, but is thought to have been destroyed in the Second World War. The flag was four and a half meters (14¾ feet) long and shows a white cross on a red ground; in the four quarters are the devices of Denmark, Sweden, Norway, and Pomerania. The field nearest the staff shows the Virgin and Child and Saint James.

One evening later in life, while hunting, King Valdemar II was kidnaped by the German lord Count Henry and imprisoned in an impenetrable castle for three years during which he suffered the severest of tortures. In this scene, Danish nobles and church figures bargain with Count Henry for his release. The discussions were successful but the price was that the king would have to give up his throne.

The murder of King Eric IV the Plowpenny in 1250 as seen on a fresco in the Ringsted Church

Another Valdemar, called the Victorious, became king in 1202. He, like Canute, was a great conqueror. He made the Baltic nothing more than a Danish lake. Indeed, this "age of the Valdemars" was the highest point of Denmark's power in Europe. There is an interesting legend in the lore of the crown which tells of how the king thought his power came from Heaven. In a battle against the heathen Estonians, as the story goes, the Danes had lost their banner and were near defeat. Then a red banner with a white cross floated down on the battlefield from Heaven above. As the Danes fought under this God-sent flag, the tide turned in their favor. So the white-cross banner—the Dannebrog, has ever since been the national flag of Denmark.

But even before Valdemar the Victorious was dead and buried the proud Danish Empire crumbled away. The unfortunate king was betrayed and taken prisoner in Germany, but he won his freedom by trading his Baltic provinces as part of his ransom. And when he died in 1241, the Danish historians wrote, "the crown fell off the head of the Danes."

In the next century of Danish history kings murdered their ambitious brothers or were murdered by them, bishops and kings struggled for power, and most often the kings lost and were put out of the church. Civil wars raged. The country was broken up, with parts of it coming under the power of the dukes of Schleswig-Holstein.

Denmark became seriously involved in the struggle to maintain her power in the Baltic region; a struggle for over a century, until the north German princes and commercial towns pressed the kings so hard that for a period around 1320 they were forced to abandon the entire country to conquest or mortgage. Meanwhile the aristocratic families had long been endeavoring to suppress the monarchy from within; and in 1282 they forced the king to sign a Great Charter (Handfaestning), establishing an annual parliament to control the king's activities. The only bright spot in an otherwise sad period of time is that charter signed by King Eric V Klipping. It was a constitution that can be compared to the Magna Charta of England. Under the charter, the king agreed to rule with

King Valdemar IV Atterdag (1340–75) and his consort, Queen Helvig, on a fresco in St. Peter's Church in Naestved

a council of nobles, the Council of the Danish Realm (Danmarks Riges Rad), which endured until 1660 when absolute monarchy prevailed over the nobility and Denmark.

The prime task now was to restore the kingdom, an aim which was largely completed by about 1370 under King Valdemar IV, the Restorer (Atterdag) (1340–75).

Queen Margrethe I, the sovereign of Denmark, Norway, and Sweden from 1387 to 1412

THE RISE OF
AN ABSOLUTE MONARCHY

By 1340, when King Valdemar IV came to the throne, Denmark's state of affairs had sunk into a dismal low. This new king, by his personal bravery and leadership, subdued his enemies at home and abroad, and made Denmark once more a great power in the Baltic. At home he showed himself to be a great organizer. Under his rule the national assembly began to meet every year. Also, he acted as supreme judge in the courts.

The struggle for Denmark and the Baltic thus entered a new phase. Through royal marriage and a general policy of war against the powerful German commercial towns, now combined in the Hanseatic League and dominating the merchant trade of Scandinavia, a new Danish Empire grew up: Norway fell to the royal family by inheritance, and Sweden chose personal union (the Union of Kalmar) under the Danish monarchy in the common struggle against German interests. With Norway came the Atlantic islands, the Faroe Islands, Iceland, and Greenland; with Sweden, large parts of Finland. This union, in character at once Atlantic and Baltic, was to last in the case of Norway until 1814.

The Danes strove persistently to dominate the union, and Sweden's membership was of short duration. During internal conflicts the union disintegrated in the course of the fifteenth century and in 1525 it broke down altogether in the face of an increasingly powerful Sweden.

The beaver used to be widespread in Denmark, as witness this tapestry, which shows Eric of Pomerania standing beside a beaver dam. This is one of a series of tapestries, executed about 1580 by the Netherlands artist Hans Knieper to the command of Frederik I for the banqueting hall of Kronborg Castle. Against a historically interesting background of small everyday scenes they show Frederik and his 111 predecessors on the Danish throne.

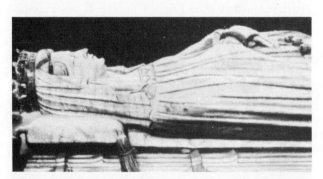

In his resolute policy of restoring the country and strengthening the throne Valdemar Atterdag was generally supported by church and aristocracy. His daughter, Queen Margrethe, however, prohibited private building of castles, and had many old ones demolished. Queen Margrethe united Denmark, Norway, and Sweden in the Union of Kalmar, 1397. She died in the plague of 1412, but well into the nineteenth century two schoolboys sang every morning at her tomb in Roskilde Cathedral. The tomb bears the likeness of her in alabaster.

Copenhagen Castle, or Copenhagen House, was the royal residence from the time of Eric of Pomerania, ca. 1400. Christian IV added the elegant openwork spire to the Blue Tower, little suspecting that his favorite daughter, Leonora Christine, would spend nearly twenty-two years in its prison. Christian VI demolished the castle and in 1733–45 built the first Christiansborg, a magnificent structure that was destroyed by fire in 1794. The second Christiansborg, erected 1820–28, was burned down in 1884, the existing, third Christiansborg being built in 1907–28.

MARGRETHE

Queen Margrethe became the ruler in 1387 and was an even stronger ruler than her father, Valdemar. When she was only ten years old she had been married to King Haakon VI of Norway. As a result, her little son Olaf became heir to both Haakon's throne and Valdemar's. Also, Margrethe claimed that Olaf was the rightful heir to the throne of Sweden, but a German prince was wearing the Swedish crown. In quick succession King Valdemar died in 1375, King Haakon in 1380, and the young King Olaf in 1387. Thus according to the law at that time Olaf should have been succeeded by a male. Instead, the regent Margrethe, who had been ruling for Olaf in a proper balance of cunning, tact, and political genius, was elected queen in her own right, not only of Norway and of Denmark but of Sweden too. She then wore the triple crown of the largest empire in all of Europe. Margrethe groomed her grandnephew, Eric VII of Pomerania, to be king. But in reality she continued to do all of the ruling herself until her death in 1412. She had united the three countries in a formal union called the Kalmar Union in 1397. Without force, she persuaded the nobles to give back some of the wealth and power they had taken from the crown. She ruled wisely and well.

PEASANTS VERSUS KING VERSUS NOBLES

When Margrethe died in 1412 the state of affairs of Denmark began to sour. The fact that Margrethe did not give any control to Eric resulted in his becoming a weak and foolish ruler. He was finally driven by the nobles into exile and removed from the throne for a number of stupid decisions. Legend has it that he beacme a highwayman and pirate preying on the nobles. The Kalmar Union came to an end in 1448 when Sweden elected a separate king. But Norway remained united with Denmark for nearly four centuries more, even though the Danes took advantage of the union.

The House of Oldenburg came to the throne in 1448 and stayed in power until 1863. This period is a story of the struggle for power between the nobles and the king at the sacrifice of the peasants. The king eventually became an absolute monarch but later lost his power again to the nobles and, then, the nobles had to share it with the people. The truth of the story is that the poor peasants had a rather hard time of it no matter who had the power. But history reveals that the nobles were crueler masters than the kings. The Danish peasants, until 1863, never managed to acquire as many of the democratic freedoms as the peasants of Sweden and Norway.

THE OLDENBURG PERIOD

Christian I (1448–81), the first Oldenburg king, managed to win back Sweden, and he ruled there for seven years (1457–64). But Christian II (1513–23) lost Sweden forever. He succeeded in crushing a rebellion of the brave Sten Sture and Sten's gallant widow Christina. After he was crowned at Stockholm he caused to be murdered in cold blood a hundred or so of Sweden's foremost nobles and citizens, in what is called the Stockholm Massacre. On his way back to Denmark he set up a gallows in every town through which he passed, and in each he hanged all of the leaders of the rebellion his soldiers could find. But, the Swedish peasantry rallied behind their great leader Gustavus Vasa, who had somehow escaped the hangman's noose. The successful rebellion dropped Sweden from the union forever.

But in other ways Christian II was an admirable king. He did great things for the peasants of Denmark, forbidding that they be sold along with the land when nobles sold their property. But his reforms were too sweeping for the proud nobles. They rose against him and the king was soon driven from his throne and spent the last twenty-seven years of his life languishing in prison. The

King Hans (1481–1513) and his three sons in prayer—in a reredos rubbing from an old tomb in St. Knud's Church in Odense. Left to right: *Prince Frants, Prince Hans, the king, and Prince Christian, who became Christian II.*

Christian II had great gifts as a ruler, but his morbidly suspicious nature and hot temper prevented him from applying his talents to lasting advantage. Lacking balanced judgment, he pushed through his reform program with such impetuosity that the nobility rose against him.

For mercantile and other reasons, Christian II married the thirteen-year-old Elizabeth (Isabella) of the Netherlands. Although neglected, she held her husband in warm affection and admiration. She died in 1526 when only twenty-five years old. This excellent portrait of the gentle young queen with the protruding lower lip of the Habsburgs was carved by Claus Berg on the altarpiece of St. Knud's Church in Odense.

The signatures of Christian II and Queen Elizabeth

two centuries. At the same time the Danish kings, especially Hans (1481–1513) and Christian II, endeavored to consolidate the monarchy by means of a more despotic policy toward the aristocratic landowners, assisted by the townspeople, especially in Copenhagen, the capital. These attempts led to a bitter civil war, markedly political and social in character. The revolt at first was a failure. Three-fourths of the land was owned by the lords temporal and spiritual, and in the political struggles and economic troubles of the preceding centuries they had secured control over nearly four-fifths of the peasants. The nobles had further strengthened their position through the development of a closed aristocratic group of about two hundred and fifty families, who monopolized the land as well as national offices and authority.

The nobility, on the whole, emerged victorious from the struggle. The real loser, besides burghers and peasants, was the church. The Lutheran movement had pene-

Frederik II and Prince Christian (King Christian IV) in a tapestry woven for Kronberg (Kronburg) Castle. The castle appears in the tapestry on the left and on the right is Frederiksborg (Frederiksburg) Castle, both royal residences in their time.

Kings from the "later" period of Denmark's history. Left, top to bottom: *Christian III (1533–59), Frederik IV (1699–1730), and Christian VII (1766–1808).* Center, top to bottom: *Frederik III (1648–70), Christian II (1513–23), Christian IX (1863–1906), and Frederik V (1746–66).* Right, top to bottom: *Christian IV (1588–1648), Christian V (1670–99), and Frederik II (1559–88).*

Christian IV (1588–1648) was one of the most colorful kings of Denmark. He is seen here on horseback. He was a great warrior as well as an able ruler.

minstrels wrote many ballads about him and the peasants sang them and passed them on to their children. In one he was "the eagle lost in the wilderness who would one day return to protect the peasants from the hawks." But Christian II never returned, and the nobles dominated the peasants and, then, the noble's children ruled the peasant's children.

The struggle for the Baltic between the two leading Scandinavian powers dominated high policy for the next

He was also a fashion plate: left, ca. 1625; above, ca. 1640.

King Christian IV knew many ups and downs of fortune, but the thing that made his name famous in Danish story was a deed of heroism when he was already sixty-seven years old. Denmark was once more at war with Sweden, and things had gone so badly that the Swedes held the whole peninsula of Jutland. Then, in February 1644, the king with his fleet of thirty ships met the forty-six Swedish ships in battle. In the midst of the fight a bursting cannonball struck Christian, wounding him in thirteen places. Blinded in one eye, he fell to the deck of his ship, the Trinity. But instantly he was up again, shouting that he still lived and still could fight. In this painting he thanks God for his life and urges the Danes to fight on.

trated to Denmark from Germany through southern Jutland and it soon gained the monarchy's support. When the civil war was over, and the monarchy and temporal nobility restored, the Reformation was carried through. The state took over church lands and the king became supreme head of the new church, with the bishops as his officials.

During the next reign, that of Frederik I (1523–33), Denmark, like the rest of Europe, had to decide the question of the Reformation—whether they should turn Protestant or stay in the Catholic church. When Frederik died the question was answered with a civil war. Not until 1536 was Christian III, the Protestant candi-

date, secure on his throne without internal strife. Then he began reorganizing and strengthening the war-torn country. He made the government more economical and efficient than ever before. He built a large fleet and did all he could to encourage commercial trade.

But the next king, Frederik II (1559–88), fell back into the pattern and tried again to conquer Sweden. However, the Seven Years War which followed brought nothing but debts and devastation to both sides, with Denmark suffering most. But to show that Denmark was still mistress of the northern seas, she required every ship that passed a Danish man-of-war to dip its topsail in a salute. And the Danes had a very strong castle at Elsinore where a toll was taken from all of the ships that passed through The Sound.

From the middle of the sixteenth century Denmark experienced a period of economic prosperity. The landed nobility with their large cattle exports and the monarchy with its Sound dues levied on the rich trade passing through The Sound, recovered their former strength. The Renaissance came in with its handsome Netherlands style. In this flourishing period Christian IV (born 1577; 1588–1648) strove hard for a more modern system of

After a costly and unsuccessful intervention in the Thirty Years War, King Christian IV of Denmark to the best of his ability endeavored to pursue a policy of retrenchment. In 1631 he discontinued the expensive but popular ceremony of the bed at aristocratic weddings. Yet he himself ordered the most extravagant wedding in Denmark. This was the wedding of the crown prince to Magdalena Sibylla, daughter of Johan Georg I, elector of Saxony, and a member of one of the foremost royal families in Europe. The grandeur of the celebrations was therefore related to their political importance. The day preceding the ceremony of the bed began with the appointment of twelve Danish noblemen as Knights of the Elephant. The event, which took place in the royal antechamber at Copenhagen Castle, is illustrated by the court engraver, Simon de Pas, of Cologne. The first of the knights, in the foreground, is kneeling before the king, who with a sword of gold touches his left shoulder three times, as he says: "I appoint thee knight in the name of the Father, the Son, and the Holy Ghost. Arise, knight!" The appointment was then proclaimed through the open window by the herald, "whereupon drummer and trumpeter in the square commenced to beat and play." The drapery behind the king bears his motto, Regna Firmat Pietas (piety fortifies the realm), which also appears on the Order of the Elephant. The procedure is witnessed by the bride-to-be from a balcony, and by the diplomatic corps on the floor.

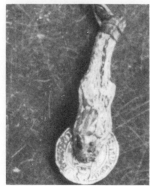

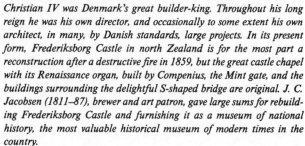

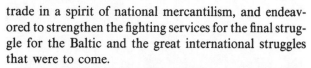

Christian IV was Denmark's great builder-king. Throughout his long reign he was his own director, and occasionally to some extent his own architect, in many, by Danish standards, large projects. In its present form, Frederiksborg Castle in north Zealand is for the most part a reconstruction after a destructive fire in 1859, but the great castle chapel with its Renaissance organ, built by Compenius, the Mint gate, and the buildings surrounding the delightful S-shaped bridge are original. J. C. Jacobsen (1811–87), brewer and art patron, gave large sums for rebuilding Frederiksborg Castle and furnishing it as a museum of national history, the most valuable historical museum of modern times in the country.

Outside the ramparts of medieval Copenhagen in 1610–25 Christian IV built a summer house, afterward called Rosenborg, and now a museum of the highest international standard, containing the crown jewels and thousands of other royal treasures. The picture shows the ear pendants that Christian IV's mistress, Vibeke Kruse, had made from the metal fragments that had robbed the king of an eye at the naval battle of Kolberger Heide. She also kept the bloodstained pillowcase from his bunk, unwashed. The scabbard of his admiral's sword held a knife for eating with, a nail file, and a number of gilt instruments, among other uses for measuring guns. Christian IV's charm: one day the king dropped a gold coin, which was seized by a snake, whereupon he cut off its head with his sword.

trade in a spirit of national mercantilism, and endeavored to strengthen the fighting services for the final struggle for the Baltic and the great international struggles that were to come.

Christian IV was one of Denmark's great kings. He founded towns, built ships from his own designs, fostered trade, and won fame in battle. Two of the castles he designed and built are still standing in Copenhagen. Christian IV did not have the backing of the quarrelsome nobles, and this was the reason his ventures into the Thirty Years War in Germany were disastrous. As a result Denmark lost two Norwegian provinces and two islands in the Baltic in 1645. It was this king's heroism in a hard-fought sea battle that is celebrated in Denmark's national anthem.

In spite of every effort it was too late. There were great internal differences between king and nobles and many mistakes were committed on both sides; in particular Denmark, for all her former leadership in Scandinavia, had gradually exhausted herself in the ceaseless struggle and had been fundamentally incapable of renewing her political or military organizaitons since the Middle Ages. The leading class, the nobility, in whom the privileges and obligations of the nation were vested, were now for

many reasons less qualified to perform their special duties. Dissension between the classes was once more rapidly increasing. Furthermore, Sweden, in her national revolt against the union with the Danes, had produced a strong and ruthless monarchy which modernized the national organization and relied on fresh resources that, in marketable terms, had greater economic value in the seventeenth century than Danish agricultural goods. The balance of power in Scandinavia was silently and steadily shifting, long before the decisive clash took place within the compass of the Thirty Years War.

The final clash came with the Thirty Years War (1618–48) and the subsequent Danish-Swedish War with European participation (1657–60). Step by step Denmark was pushed back as the Swedes, in a succession of brilliant campaigns, advanced across the Baltic countries and occupied Jutland and later the Danish islands. In 1660, Denmark was obliged to sign a peace treaty limiting her sway to the territory west of The Sound. The richest provinces, those of Scania, Halland, and Bleking, were lost, The Sound now being divided between the two leading Scandinavian powers.

An even worse result was prevented by European interests, as Denmark's ally, the Netherlands, with her

Behind a magnificent iron grating is the chapel of Christian IV, with Thorvaldsen's bronze statue of the king and Marstrand's well-known painting of the Battle of Kolberger Heide, where he lost an eye

Celebration in front of the castle of Copenhagen on the introduction of hereditary absolute monarchy, October 18, 1660. Painted 1666 by Wolfgang Heimbach. The citizens and the military are lined up on each side of the red runner that goes from the castle gate to the throne. The castle roof, the decks and masts of the vessels and all the windows are full of spectators. In the background Holmens Church and the Exchange, two of the most distinguished buildings of Christian IV.

Portrait of Frederik III in the Royal Act, which he signed in 1665, but which was at first kept secret. It set him above the law, but did not grant him the title to the national territory.

Frederik III, silent and retiring, was strangely unknown. The coup that made him the first absolutist king, however, reveals determination and single-minded tactical abilities. He also busied himself with contemporary learning, including alchemy, and laid the foundations of Danish museums. Despite national poverty, he redeemed his father, Christian IV's, sumptuous crown, mortgaged in Hamburg, and even lavished enormous sums on new regalia.

vital trading interests in the Baltic, had succeeded in relieving the heroic defenders of Copenhagen and preventing all of The Sound from becoming Swedish.

When the next king, Frederik III (1648–70) was crowned, he had to sign away most of his power to the nobles who controlled the wealth. But the nobles did not back him when the king declared war against Sweden at the moment when the Swedes were very busy fighting in Poland. The city of Copenhagen withstood a heroic siege by the Swedes but the nobles deserved small thanks for that either. It was the people who rallied to the king. But the terms of peace lost Denmark more territory.

ABSOLUTE MONARCHY

The Danish state was now bankrupt and the country laid waste. A political and social settlement in the wake of the war and defeat was inevitable. Relying on enlisted troops and on the townspeople and peasants, Frederik III assumed absolute power for himself and his heirs. Instead of personal despotism, the result was a more highly centralized bureaucracy.

Frederik felt that he had the people behind him and was determined to overpower the nobles. The Estates, or national parliament, met in 1660 and forced the nobles to join them in offering the king absolute power. The king was "instructed" that the peace terms were that he was to draft a new constitution. But he never got around to it. Instead, he and his counselor, the great statesman Peder Schumacher, later Count Griffenfeld, drew up the Lex Regia, or Royal Law. The Lex Regia gave the people of Denmark an absolute monarchy. So the common people in this new type of government were taking two steps forward and one step back.

Count Griffenfeld continued to be chancellor under Frederik's successor, Christian V (1670–99) and he con-

The "Estates" give back the coronation charter to Frederik III. Left to right: the king, Peder Reetz, Hans Svane, and Hans Nansen.

The royal crown of absolutism is still used in stylized reproduction by Danish institutions and purveyors to the court.

Christian VI "had no mistresses and waged no wars." Deeply religious, he laid the country under puritan pressure, yet was led by his, and especially Queen Sofie Magdalene's, view of the dignity of the absolutist monarch into very costly building works and to surrounding himself with a magnificent court. But the many splendid apartments were not employed in their time for greater amusement or festivities than were required by representative arrangements, and the already stiff tone ended in sterile abnegation. His son's reign, Ludvig Holberg said, was a "reign of bliss, when everything seemed to gain new life and energies," and despite excesses Frederik V was almost idolized by the public.

tinued to make the government very efficient and tried to keep the country at peace. But the impatient king longed for the heritage of fame in war and overthrew his wise chancellor. He quickly entered into another war with Sweden (1675–79) and lost. Also, there were two more of these disastrous wars with Sweden in the next reign, that of Frederik IV (1699–1730). Besides this the country at this time was inundated by the plague, and crop-damaging floods in Schleswig-Holstein. But Frederik not only won the hearts of the common people by building schools, starting a postal system, and reducing the national debt but by being a very charming person. The people forgave him all of his faults.

The whole machinery of government was modernized. The early period of autocracy (1660–1750) imposed greater national unification in place of the medieval provincial system. Unified systems of legislation, finance, local administration, main roads, and weights and measures were established, and greater equality for all the king's subjects was aimed at as an essential condition for greater national unity.

Royal rule proved of vital importance to modern Denmark in several significant respects. The kingdom became more integrated. The church was already subject to the state and now a standing army was established; new economic enterprise was displayed by the state, and later the first attempts to create a uniform school system were made. The old aristocracy paid the political price of this bloodless revolution. Economically and socially, they had already suffered because of the war. But the peasants also suffered because of the war. They suffered through heavier labor services to the lords of the manors and through military service to the states.

In external affairs, the early absolutist rule refused to accept the peace terms of 1660 as definitive. Several costly wars followed, until, in a new peace treaty of 1720, the settlement had to be reaffirmed. The Scandinavian balance had been maintained.

The people hated the next king—Christian VI (1730–46) because he was as negative in the pious sort of way his father, Frederik IV, was positive as a cheerful person. He let the clergy censor all literature and art, and fined people if they did not go to church. In spite of his strong religious beliefs, which angered the people, Denmark was prosperous and at peace during his reign.

Christian VI's son, Frederik V (1746–66) was a very different sort of king. He was gay and pleasure-loving. He did away with his father's law for compelling people to go to church. But he paid scant attention to the affairs of state. He really didn't need to for he had two wise counselors, Counts Bernstorff and Moltke, who ruled for him and did it well.

From the mid-eighteenth century fresh currents began to assert themselves in the Danish autocracy. Baroque gave place to Rococo, and European enlightened despotism slowly began to manifest itself in freer and more humane outlooks. They appeared first in agriculture, realizing the need for a radical transformation of the medieval village community through land consolidation. Starting under favorable conditions for agricultural exports in the Europe of the Prussian Seven Years War and subsequent revolutionary wars, it involved another revolution: the emancipation of the Danish peasant from 1788 onward and a gradual transition from copyhold to freehold tenure. Thus in time a free class of peasant proprietors was formed that was to prove of crucial importance to modern Denmark.

Other social reforms followed: the abolition of the slave trade in the few Danish overseas colonies from 1792; the granting of civil rights to Jews from 1814; and the great educational reforms of the same year, with the introduction of general compulsory education. In the economic field, the land reforms were followed by an extremely liberal tariff reform of 1797. With this early liberalization, the autocracy itself sponsored an agrarian revolution while the French Revolution was in progress.

For a long time Denmark derived economic advantage from the European wars which she strove to avoid, but when Napoleon's troops had overrun Europe, the net closed around her.

In 1801 in a fierce naval battle off Copenhagen, the British forced Denmark out of the armed alliance of neutral states; and when the French and Russian emperors had agreed on the continental blockade, the war returned in an even more menacing form. In 1807, the Danish government rejected a British ultimatum to surrender its large navy before Napoleon's troops, marching northward, could seize it. This was the signal for a British attack, and after a devastating bombardment of Copenhagen the Danes were forced to deliver up the fleet, and they later concluded an alliance with Napoleon.

The French Revolution had one good effect on Denmark's people as it had on people elsewhere in Europe and throughout the rest of the world, later. The rights of the common people became apparent. In Denmark the tide turned again to the people—the peasants. The nobles and kings had their times of power. Now the common people as a whole began to desire to have a voice in government.

There was a continuing need for great statesmen during the next reign, that of Christian VII (1766–1808), for this king was mentally weak and vicious as a tyrant. In the end he became insane. For a while a clever German adventurer named Struensee, the king's physician, had control of the government. He advocated democratic ideas of the king that led to the French Revolution, and in line with these beliefs, he instituted all sorts of reforms in favor of the common people. He was watched closely by the nobles and the lords of property and when he took one step too fast in 1772 his enemies had him put to death.

King Christian VII (1766–1808) rides among the peasants with his son, Crown Prince Frederik VI (1808–39).

Queen Caroline Matilda

For a short period of time the king's physician, John Struensee, had gained control of the throne of Christian VII. But the nobles and lords tried him and arranged to have him put to death. Before he was beheaded on April 28, 1772, Struensee confessed that the king's consort, Queen Caroline Matilda, was his accomplice and "more."

Queen Matilda faints when required to sign a statement of guilt of conspiracy, which included an automatic divorce from the king and banishment. She was kept at Celle, where her life came to an end on May 10, 1775.

The Celle castle

Prince Christian (VIII) married Caroline Amalie of Augustenborg in 1815. The couple, shown at about the time of their wedding, were rightly referred to afterward as the handsomest pair to have occupied the throne of Denmark. As king of Norway for three and one half months in 1814 he was celebrated for having introduced "the most liberal constitution in the world." As king of Denmark, however, this cultured aesthete, perhaps against his will, became increasingly conservative, faced with the insoluble problem of meeting contemporary demands for a liberal constitution and national self-determination while keeping Danish and German-speaking provinces united.

Frederik VI was the son of Christian VII and succeeded him to the throne.

As prince regent in 1784–1808, Frederik VI was responsible for radical reforms, but in the course of his reign, 1808–39, he became the embodiment of reaction, maintaining the principle "We alone know." The small, undemonstrative king, in stature and dress more like a lean, bony officer of the squirearchy, was none the less popular as paternal monarch and paterfamilias. Victim of misfortunes in his calling and in private life (he lost several of his children), he became the picture of the elderly man whom time had left standing. His death released long-pent-up forces in society that were soon to bring about its economic, political, and social transformation.

The crown prince, later Frederik VI (1808–39), firmly took the reins of the crown but was wise enough to call back Count Bernstorff, whom Struensee had dismissed. Frederik VI put through many reforms to replace Struensee's acts of prerevolution. The most important of these was in 1788 when he ended serfdom for the peasants.

But the train of events outside the nation proved disastrous. Denmark was cut off from Norway, where separatist trends were already perceptible. Sweden formed a wartime alliance with Britain and Russia against Denmark. In 1813 the state went bankrupt, and the following year Frederik VI was forced to make peace and cede Norway to Sweden, Denmark retaining Iceland, Greenland, and the Faroe Islands. This was the second division of the Danish realm.

NATIONAL STRUGGLE AND LIBERAL CONSTITUTION

The cession of Norway was a radical solution of a serious national problem that had faced the old dual monarchy. Norway had in fact been governed as a Danish province. As late as in the eighteenth century outstanding Norwegians had served the monarchy without national antipathies, but toward the end of the century a new nationalist trend had developed among townspeople and free peasants. Various local demands were rejected by the royal government, which feared a split in the kingdom. The war and the peace treaty cut short this growing discord.

The loss of Norway had twofold significance. First, this second great defeat gave many in impoverished Denmark a sense of being left behind in a small, weak kingdom without any prospects; and, second, the Norwegian situation was an ominous reminder that even in the areas still subject to the Danish king new and serious national problems were developing on the southern border fronting the German states. Here were two border duchies, where a nationalistic trend might soon ignite a political powder magazine. The northern duchy, Schleswig, was an ancient Danish borderland; the southern, Holstein, had always been German but had gradually become subject to the Danish kings. The links between the duchies were old and close, and they had grown steadily stronger during the centuries in which kings and their sons had reigned without much discrimination and increasingly under one administration. German culture had penetrated strongly into Schleswig.

As early as 1460, Christian I had been obliged to promise the Holstein nobles that Schleswig and Holstein would remain forever united *(ewich tosamende ungedeelt)*. Dynastic and aristocratic ties had caused an even greater integration before the nationalistic winds of the nineteenth century finally ignited the powder.

This flare-up began in earnest about 1830, when the movement for the unification of the German states based on national liberalism began. The political demand was for liberal constitutions, with democratically elected parliaments which would limit the powers of the ruling princes. From that moment the absolute monarchy was confronted with a dangerous dual problem: that of national and liberal opposition in a nationally heterogeneous region within the monarchy's limits. Under growing pressure from increasingly stronger German states such as Prussia, the young liberals in the monarchy were split into pro-German and pro-Danish liberals. King and government were aware that if they yielded to either, the consequence would be the final disruption of the monarchy and the collapse of the autocracy.

In 1834, Frederik VI had tried to grant some of the purely liberal demands by establishing consultative provincial assemblies *(radgivende staenderforsamlinger)*, but the only result was to intensify both the liberal and the national demands. The Holstein movement demanded a free and united Schleswig-Holstein as part of the German Confederation. In order to save Schleswig, their liberal Danish opponents demanded a free and united Denmark including Schleswig, but granting Holstein a liberal constitution as a member of the German Confederation was precisely the outcome the king and government had feared. Neither of the two national movements would admit that the Schleswig population was nationally mixed; an attitude which only aggravated the whole problem. A further complication was the threatening international situation, with Prussia and

Russia approaching the great struggle for the control of the Baltic, which the Scandinavian countries had lost. Not only was it to be feared that the Danish monarchy would split, but also that it would, sooner or later, be absorbed by a powerful Germany.

Through the 1840s the internal and external pressures rose swiftly, until the explosion occurred in March 1848, in the trail of the February revolution in France. Knowing in advance that the Danish liberals would prevail over the government in Copenhagen, the Holsteiners revolted against their policy and Denmark was plunged into civil war. This quickly developed into an international struggle when Prussia came to the assistance of the pro-Germans and invaded Jutland. Thanks to international support, principally from Russia, the Prussian troops were forced to withdraw. But the Danish government had to promise the great powers not to make any change in the status of Denmark, Schleswig, and Holstein, or link any of them more closely. To insulate the future from the past in this way, however, was impossible, and the first war of 1848–49 was only the portent of the next and greater one.

The Danish liberals eventually obtained the internal revolution they had striven for.

Frederik VI's successor, Christian VIII (1839–48),

Frederik VII (1848–63) and his queen. Frederik VI was the king of soldiers and father of the constitution, loved and acclaimed uncritically, later criticized, and unjustly denigrated. Difficulties and frequent crises arose between the king and his ministers because the new liberal constitution had to be worked out, but in fact he coped gallantly with the teething troubles, at times with lively humor. His relations with Countess Danner (1815–74), a former ballet dancer and milliner, also led to political complications, while consolidating his popularity among commoners who saw her as a guarantee of democracy. The king insisted on signing the constitution on her son's birthday, and he used to say that without her he would long ago have lain "nose up." King of Denmark from 1848, his tyrannous rule in Schleswig-Holstein was bitterly resented, and by his death, in 1863, the main line of the royal house became extinct.

On the death of the Danish king in 1863, the duke of Augustenburg raised claims to the duchies of Schleswig-Holstein, but by the War of 1864 these went to Prussia and Austria.

was a king with a liberal mind and heart. The Danish people expected him to let them have their way in this new world government of the common people. But it was his son, Frederik VII (1848–63), last of the Oldenburg line, who turned the trick. In 1849 Frederik cheerfully signed away the absolute monarchy by accepting a very liberal constitution developed by the national assembly. He took for his motto, "The love of my people is my strength." And the free common people of Denmark loved him, until his dying breath.

Since the end of the Oldenburg line, five kings and one queen have reigned—Frederik VII (1848–63), Christian IX (1863–1906), Frederik VIII (1906–12), Christian X (1912–47), Frederik IX (1947–72) and the sovereign queen Margrethe II who replaced her father, Frederik IX. He died January 15, 1972, at the age of seventy-two after a reign of twenty-five years.

Margrethe II was the oldest of three daughters by Princess Ingrid of Sweden. The constitution was amended in 1953 to allow for female succession to the throne in the absence of a male heir. Five centuries earlier when Margrethe I ruled, it was without being

The coronation parade of Christian IX, 1863. He succeeded to the throne of Denmark on the death of Frederic VII. His eldest daughter, Alexandra, married King Edward VII of Great Britain.

King Christian IX of Denmark (1863–1906) was called Europe's Father-in-law because marriage had formed ties to the thrones of Britain, Greece, and Russia. Frequently the royal family met at Fredensborg Palace, north Zealand, where the painter Lauritz Tuxen (1853–1927) made this group picture, which now hangs in the Royal Reception Room at Christiansborg Palace, Copenhagen, the seat of the Danish government.

Christian IX and Queen Louise are sitting on the sofa. Seated on the left is the Prince of Wales (later Edward VII), and behind him are his wife Alexandra and their son the duke of Clarence, Albert Victor. In the center, Czar Alexander III with his wife Empress Dagmar. Crown Princess Louise is on the sofa to the right of the czar. Behind her, King George of the Hellenes and Crown Prince Frederik. Standing, Queen Olga. Behind the king and queen of Denmark are Thyra, duchess of Cumberland, and Prince Valdemar. The two boys near the door are Prince Christian (X) and the later czar Nicholas II. Nearer the gilt fireguard is Prince Carl, later Haakon of Norway.

Christian IX. A sketch of the King in his eighty-fourth year at work at his desk.

crowned queen. Margrethe II's sisters are Benedikte, born in 1944, and Anne Marie, who is now the former queen of Greece, born in 1946.

Since 1849, Denmark has been a constitutional monarchy. Legislative power is held jointly by the sovereign and the parliament. The unicameral parliament, called the Folketing, which was authorized by the Constitution of 1953, consists of one hundred seventy-nine members who are elected in general voting every four years. The cabinet is presided over by the sovereign.

Royal family gatherings were the vogue in Europe just prior to World War I. This is a gathering of the Danish clan in the early 1900s. The center of the photograph has the principals. Seated, left to right, are Frederik VIII; Dagmar, Dowager Empress of Russia; Christian IX, and Queen Alexandra. Behind her, standing, is George I of Greece.

Crown Prince Frederik in 1929

Public ovations to King Frederik IX and Queen Ingrid, standing on the balcony of Christianborg Castle on the occasion of their accession to the throne on April 21, 1947. (On May 24, 1935, the crown prince had married Princess Ingrid of Sweden.)

Christian X (1912–47)

King Christian X in a formal pose with his consort, the Queen Alexandrine

Frederik IX (1947–72)

Greatly cheered by the people, King Christian X takes his daily ride through the streets of Copenhagen during the German occupation in World War II.

Some Danish coins honoring King Frederik IX

Postage stamps of the king were also issued during his lifetime and in commemoration.

The official portrait of King Frederik IX and Queen Ingrid

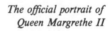

The royal Danish family photographed in 1964. Left to right: Princess Benedikte; the then Princess Anne Marie (Queen Anne Marie of Greece); King Frederik; Queen Ingrid; and Princess Margrethe, now Queen Margrethe of Denmark.

Youngest queen in oldest monarchy. Queen Margrethe II (born April 16, 1940) succeeded her father, King Frederik IX, when he died January 15, 1972. She is married to French-born Prince Henrik (born June 11, 1934) and they have two boys, Crown Prince Frederik (born May 26, 1968) and Prince Joachim (born June 7, 1969).

Having been queen a year she told a press conference, held at one of the royal castles, that the monarch's duties were to her both an obligation and a gift: "I have been privileged to live a very rich life now. Gaining an insight into so many things and people in a manner never experienced before. It has been an immense unexpected thrill."

The official portrait of Queen Margrethe II

A recent stamp honoring Queen Margrethe II

By a revision of the constitution in 1953, female hereditary succession was introduced in Denmark. Accordingly, the king and queen's eldest daughter, Princess Margrethe, born 1940, became successor to the throne. Having come of age in April 1958, the princess, together with the king, for the first time presided over a cabinet meeting. She is pictured with her father driving in an open coach from the Folketing to the palace (photo: Aue, Copenhagen).

Queen Margrethe II and Prince Henrik in formal dress

In 1976, Queen Margrethe II spoke at a dinner in her honor at the United Nations headquarters in New York City. She is seen here, second from right, *during the visit, with Prince Henrik, Mrs. Kurt Waldheim, and UN Secretary-General Kurt Waldheim.*

The Royal Christiansborg Palace. Christiansborg Palace occupies a large part of the islet of Slotsholmen. Of the first great palace only the two pavilions near the Marble Bridge have survived, but this is a considerable baroque monument even by international standards. The only minor alteration is in the southern wing, where Christian VII incorporated a theater, now the Theater Museum. The extensive stables have marble pillars and cribs, and the original royal box has survived in the riding hall. The present palace, the third Christiansborg, is the seat of Parliament (the Folketing), the Supreme Court, and the Foreign Ministry, and here, too, royal audiences and banquets are held.

Prince Joachim and Crown Prince Frederik photographed in the park of the Palace Caix in France, August 1976

The throne room at Christiansborg Palace

In the spring and autumn the queen moves their residence to Fredensborg Palace in north Zealand. The oldest parts were built in the 1720s by J. C. Krieger, architect and landscape gardener, as a remarkably high-domed central section with an octagonal forecourt bounded by rather low wings.

THE ROYAL SOVEREIGNS OF THE KINGDOM OF DENMARK

Reign	Title	Ruler	Birth	Death	Relationship
70–55 B.C.	King	Odin of the North		55	
55–40	King	Skiold		40	
40–23	King	Fridlief I		23	
A.D. 23–35	King	Frode I		35	
35–47	King	Fridlief II		47	
47–59	King	Havar		59	
59–87	King	Frode II		87	
87–140	King	Vermund the Sage		140	
140–190	King	Olaf (Olav) the Mild		190	
190–270	King	Dan Mykillati		270	
270–310	King	Frode III, the Pacific		310	
310–324	King	Halfdan I		324	
324–348	King	Fridlief III		348	
348–407	King	Frode IV		407	
407–436	King	Ingild		436	
436–447	King	Halfdan II		447	
447–460	King	Frode V		460	
460–494	King	Helge and Roe		494	
494–510	King	Frode VI		510	
510–522	King	Rolf Krake		522	
522–548	King	Frode VII		548	
548–580	King	Halfdan III		580	
580–588	King	Rorik Slyngebaud		588	
588–647	King	Ivar Vidfadme		647	
647–735	King	Harold Hildetand		735	
735–750	King	Sigurd Ring		750	
750–794	King	Ragnar Lodbrok		794	
794–803	King	Sigurd (Sigfred) Snogoie		803	
803–810	King	Godfred		810	
803–850	King	Harde-Knud (Hardicanute) Canute I		850	
850–854	King	Eric I (Haarik)		854	
854–883	King	Eric II (Haarik)		883	
883–941	King	Gorm the Old		941	
941–991	King	Harold Blaatand, the Bluetooth		991	Son of Gorm the Old
991–1014	King	Sweyn I, the Splitbeard		1014	Son of Harold the Bluetooth
1014–1018	King	Harold		1018	Son of Sweyn I
1018–1035	King	Canute II, the Great	1001	1035	Son of Sweyn I
1035–1042	King	Harthacnut (Canute III)	1018	1044	Son of Canute II
1042–1047	King	Magnus the Good	1015	1047	Son of King Olaf (Norway)
1047–1074	King	Sweyn II Estrithson	1020	1074	Nephew of Canute II
1074–1080	King	Harold Hen	1046	1080	Son of Sweyn II
1080–1086	King	Canute IV, the Holy	1040	1086	Son of Sweyn II
1086–1095	King	Oluf I (Olaf), the Hungry	1042	1095	Son of Sweyn II
1095–1103	King	Eric I, the Evergood	1049	1103	Son of Sweyn II
1103–1134	King	Niels the Elder	1054	1134	Son of Sweyn II
1134–1137	King	Eric II Emune	1071	1137	Son of Eric I
1137–1146	King	Eric III Lam	1112	1146	
1146–1157	King	Sweyn III Grade	1114	1157	Son of Eric II
1157–1157	King	Knud III Magnussen	1135	1157	Son of Magnus Nielsen
1157–1182	King	Valdemar I	1131	1182	Son of Knud Lavard
1182–1202	King	Canute VI	1163	1202	Son of Valdemar I
1202–1241	King	Valdemar II Sejr, the Victorious	1170	1241	Son of Valdemar I
1241–1250	King	Eric IV, the Plowpenny	1216	1250	Son of Valdemar II
1250–1252	King	Abel	1218	1252	Son of Valdemar II
1252–1259	King	Christopher I	1219	1259	Son of Valdemar II
1259–1286	King	Eric V Klipping	1249	1286	Son of Christopher I
1286–1319	King	Eric VI Maendved	1274	1319	Son of Eric V
1319–1332	King	Christopher II	1276	1332	Son of Eric VI
1340–1375	King	Valdemar IV Atterdag	1320	1375	Son of Christopher II
1375–1387	King	Olaf II	1370	1387	Grandson of Valdemar IV; son of Haakon VI of Norway
1387–1412	Queen	Margrethe I	1353	1412	Daughter of Valdemar IV; consort of Haakon VI
1412–1439	King	Eric VII of Pomerania	1382	1459	Grandnephew of Margrethe I
1440–1448	King	Christopher III of Bavaria	1418	1448	Nephew of Eric VII
1448–1481	King	Christian I	1426	1481	Son of Count Dederik of Oldenburg and Deimenhorst
1481–1513	King	Hans	1455	1513	Son of Christian I
1513–1523	King	Christian II	1481	1559	Son of Hans

Reign	Title	Ruler	Birth	Death	Relationship
1523–1533	King	Frederik I	1471	1533	Son of Christian I
1533–1559	King	Christian III	1503	1559	Son of Frederik I
1559–1588	King	Frederik II	1534	1588	Son of Christian III
1588–1648	King	Christian IV	1577	1648	Son of Frederik II
1648–1670	King	Frederik III	1609	1670	Son of Christian IV
1670–1699	King	Christian V	1646	1699	Son of Frederik III
1699–1730	King	Frederik IV	1671	1730	Son of Christian V
1730–1746	King	Christian VI	1699	1746	Son of Frederik IV
1746–1766	King	Frederik V	1723	1766	Son of Christian VI
1766–1808	King	Christian VII	1749	1808	Son of Frederik V
1808–1839	King	Frederik VI	1768	1839	Son of Christian VII
1839–1848	King	Christian VIII	1786	1848	Cousin of Frederik VI
1848–1863	King	Frederik VII	1808	1863	Son of Christian VIII
1863–1906	King	Christian IX	1818	1906	Son of William, duke of Schleswig-Holstein-Sonderberg-Glucksborg
1906–1912	King	Frederik VIII	1843	1912	Son of Christian IX
1912–1947	King	Christian X	1870	1947	Son of Frederik VIII
1947–1972	King	Frederik IX	1899	1972	Son of Christian X
1972–	Queen	Margrethe II	1940		Daughter of Frederik IX

13
The Kingdom of Norway

A map of the Nordic countries

The history of man in Norway dates back some eight to ten thousand years, possibly more. The most ancient finds have been made along the coast of Finnmark and Møre. From the earliest times people kept to the coastal regions, making their living by hunting and fishing. During the third millennium B.C. (the early Neolithic age) however, agriculture slowly began to make itself evident, and gradually the interior of the country became colonized. From the Bronze Age (about 1500–500 B.C.) comes the first testimony of a social organization in Norway; huge sepulchral mounds tell the story of mighty men commanding the labor of others.

A KINGDOM DEVELOPS

The oldest form of a state government in the country probably dates from about the commencement of our chronological order. During the early centuries A.D. tribal races such as the Heids, Raums, and Ranrikings formed in the east of Norway small kingdoms, founded on common councils and sanctuaries. Somewhat later, the districts surrounding the Trondheimsfjord also apparently united into a single kingdom. During the period of the migration of nations (from about A.D. 400) the Hords and Rygers, coming by sea from the south to the west of Norway, forced the earlier inhabitants into submission. The small kingdoms in the east of the country subsequently met in common council and established commercial intercourse with the kingdoms along the coast.

The name *Norge,* or *Norvegr* (the northern way), signifying the coastal regions from Haalogaland to Vestfold, is encountered in a source more ancient than the political consolidation under Harald Fairhair (Haarfagre), the first recognized king of Norway.

Legend tells us that King Harald, son of Halfdan Svart (the Black), had sent ambassadors with a proposal of marriage to the Princess Gyda. But the fair maiden—so goes the story—turned him down. "Tell your master," she said, "I, Gyda will not wed a king who has only a few poor territories to rule over. If he wants to win me, let him first rule all of Norway!"

The ambassadors recommended that he should take her by force. But the king, having listened to them quietly, said, "I like this maiden's spirit. Furthermore, I wonder why I had not thought of this myself." And he vowed not to cut his hair nor comb it until he became king of all Norway.

So he set out to conquer all the other earls and political rulers in Norway. It took several years and many battles, but finally, in 872, his task was complete. By this time his uncombed hair was such a wild sight that men called him, Harald the Tousle-headed. He cut and combed it in a token of his victory, and it turned out so beautiful that ever after he was known as Harald Fairhair. And as the legend goes, he married the fair maiden, Princess Gyda.

Harald Fairhair reigned almost until his death in 934. He was a strong king, but the turbulent earls and vassal lords did not take very kindly to the heavy tariffs and taxes he made them pay. Many of them gathered their wealth and vassals and sailed for Iceland or Normandy and other lands where the Vikings were reported to be discovering, ravaging, and settling. In the same period, Harald took his warriors beyond his borders and conquered the Orkney and Shetland islands and the Hebrides. There he established Norwegian earls in control. Rich from the new conquests, the king had a splendid court, with many fine *skalds,* or bards, to sing of his glory.

Long before his death Harald's many sons were fighting among themselves as to who would succeed him. Harald's favorite son had been a fierce young Viking named Eric Bloodaxe, and he won out for he was designated king in Harald's will. The brothers, the landowning earls, and the people hated Eric and equally hated his "wicked" queen, Gunhild, In 934, when Eric's younger brother Haakon finally managed to overthrow the throne, the governing body, the *thing,* or assembly of the citizens, officially crowned him the king.

Eric fled to England and died a few years later. But his queen raised her sons to one day return to Norway and fight for their rightful place on the throne.

For a short time, Norway experienced a time of peace under Haakon the Good (934–61). He was a devout Christian and strove to wipe out heathen ways of his country. But hard as he tried, the people would not give up their ancient gods. Haakon soon gave up. He fell in battle, fighting against tremendous odds when the sons of Gunhild invaded Norway to regain their father's throne.

King Olaf Tryggvason (995–1000) is officially credited with converting Norway to Christianity. When he was a small child, Queen Gunhild had fled with him. Dressed like a beggar she'd traveled with young Olaf from farm to farm and then headed east over the border. But, once in Russia, they were sold into slavery. Many stories, fact and fiction, are told of Olaf's adventures there. He had next sailed long-oared Viking ships on expeditions to England and while there he had become a Christian. Finally he came back to Norway and won his throne from the earl Haakon. Because he was a legend returned, the people looked very kindly on him for he was from the house of Haakon the Good.

The fiery but clever Olaf was made of different stuff than Haakon the Good. He believed in Christianity with the same fierce zeal that later caused men to go on Crusades to fight the Turks in Palestine. The earls and the landowners obejcted to changing their country's faith

because they thought that Christianity would give the people too much freedom. He told them then to choose between being baptized or sacrificed to their god Odin. When confronted by them, he knocked over their principal statue of Odin with a heavy sword and then challenged them to accept Christ or fight him. None accepted his challenge and all of Norway was "converted" to Christianity. But the earls never forgave Olaf.

The revolting earls joined the Swedes and the Danes against Olaf. And as a result he died after fighting valiantly at the prow of his mighty dragon ship *Long Serpent.* When the battle was lost the king made a choice. Rather than be taken alive, he raised his heavy shield above his head and leaped into the water and, together with his armor, the weight soon sunk him out of sight.

Then for a time Norway was divided between Denmark and Sweden. But, in 1015, King Olaf Haraldson seized the throne.

No sooner was Olaf Tryggvason in his watery grave when Olaf Haraldson (his successor) had to attempt to convert Norway back to Christianity all over again, for the people had largely gone back to their old gods. This Olaf used much the same methods as the earlier Olaf had used, and used them very well indeed. He knew that if the earls and all of the people had the same religion it would make it easier to hold the nation together. Many revolted against him, as they had against the other Olaf. Then, to help them, the mighty King Canute of Denmark, who was also king of England, defeated Olaf and drove him out of Norway. Two years later Olaf came back at the head of a small army. He proved how sincere he was in his battle for "Christ" by sending away hundreds of badly needed soliders because they were not

King Olaf II Haraldson (1016–30)

This tapestry of King Olaf and the three heathen gods depicts the king bringing Christianity to Norway. He was later canonized and is commonly referred to in history as Saint Olaf.

The wrongness of the law of the times that the sons of the king were to rule in parallel rests in the demise of King Eystein (1142–57), who was assassinated by a brother. This wooden statue of him is located in the Munkeliv monastery in Norway.

At left: *The Norwegian kings have always been fond of boating. This allegorical fresco shows Saint Olaf in a race with Harold Hardrade (1047–56).*

Christians. So when he fell (1030) in a hopeless battle, his brave death probably did much more to make people think well of him than all his strong-arm missionary work had done. The church made him Saint Olaf.

Misrule by Denmark quickly made the earls change their minds about not wanting Olaf. They invited his son Magnus to come and take his father's throne. Magnus was only ten at this time. He soon matured into a very able ruler and won from his grateful people the title of Magnus the Good (1035–1047). He was so just and

peace-loving that when his uncle Harald Sigurdson demanded half of the kingdom, Magnus let him be joint king to avoid another family brawl. His successor, Harald Hardrade (1047–66), was much more fierce and warlike than Magnus. Men called him Harald Hard-Ruler—but he left Norway stronger than he found it. He fell in battle in England, trying to conquer Harold, last of the Saxon kings.

The national unification under King Harald and his successors was a phase in the enormous expansion that characterized the Viking period (about 800–1050). A marked increase in population provided the cause presumptive for the Norwegian raids on territories bordering the North Sea and, with them, partly the settlement of Norwegians in west European countries already inhabited (the British Isles and Normandy), and partly the acquisition of uncolonized areas (North Atlantic islands, Iceland, and Greenland). Simultaneously, however, both during and after the Viking period, an extensive settlement took place within Norway's own borders, especially in the inland districts of the east.

The political fusion of the country was by no means concluded under Harald Fairhair. In fact, it might be said that the period of consolidation did not cease until the fall of Olaf Haraldson at Stiklestad in 1030, and his canonization in the following year. Proceeding apace with the political consolidation effected by the previous generation was the Christianization of the people, or, more precisely, of the chieftains. With the death of Olaf,

Christianity emerged officially, and in the course of the eleventh century the church became permanently established throughout the country, gradually coming into possession by gift and purchase of considerable land property. At the same time the royal power was strengthened by alliance with the landowners, and class distinction became steadily more apparent. A minority of aristocrats displaced the freeholders, the majority of whom became leaseholders of the church, crown, or nobility. This vital change in social conditions did not proceed without violent clashes.

For a while there was tranquillity in Norway. During the reign of Olaf the Peaceful (1066–93) Norway had a long period of peace and prosperity.

King Eystein I (1103–22), the grandson of Olaf the Peaceful, was another beloved king. His brother, Sigurd the Crusader (1103–30), ruled with him and after him. Sigurd had been on a Crusade for he was an impetuous and haughty man. The peaceful Eystein was pressed to

King Magnus VI, the Lagabaeter (Lawmender), reigned from 1263 to 1280. He structured the laws of the land into a written code. While this took power from the thing *(Storting) and the nobles there, it also created a new status, peasant nobility, by giving more power to wealthy farmers.*

When King Haakon IV (1217–63) was a baby, the loyal party of Birchlegs feared that the child would be caught up in the civil war that was raging at the time in Norway (1204), so they spirited him away for safekeeping. He outlived the danger and came back to be one of the finest kings of Norway.

Two stamps commemorating King Magnus VI and the written code of laws

keep on good terms with him. But times were good during his reign and when he died the people mourned him.

It was to be a century and a decade more after his death before Norway was to know peace again. All that time, with only the briefest interruptions, civil wars raged among the royal blood who wanted the throne. The Norse law read that all the sons of a king had equal right to the throne. And it is not difficult to see that only men with much tact could rule jointly as had Olaf the Peaceful and Eystein I.

There arose one great and heroic figure, who in another time might have done much for Norway. This was King Sverre Sigurdson (1184–1202). Sverre's story is one of the most stirring of all the stories told in the old legends. As a youth he came out of the Faroe Islands, friendless and unknown, and put himself at the head of a band of ragamuffin rebels called the Birchlegs. Their name came from the fact that they could not afford anything but birchbark for shoes. For years they lived perilously in the mountains, an outlaw band like Robin Hood's. By amazing feats of heroism and skill, Sverre won every battle against all of his opponents and became king of Norway. He never had a chance to accomplish much with his throne, for bands of rebels kept forming and were forever trying to dethrone him. His enemies lied about him to the Pope until he was excommunicated. Once put out of the church, even the peasants (now Christians) who had been his friends, were pitted against him. The irony of it. The common people, who had raised him to power, were the ones he favored over the chieftains. Norway had become much more democratic under his rule.

Haakon the Old (1217–63), Sverre's grandson, managed at long last to end the century-long civil war. After trying desperately to keep the peace with him, Haakon had to fight one last pretender. He defeated him (1240) and was formally crowned with the blessing of the church. He was especially interested in architecture and put up many fine buildings. He brought the power of Norway among the nations to the highest point it had ever reached before or since. The emperor Frederick II was his devoted friend, and Haakon gave his daughter in marriage to a Spanish prince, Philip of Castile.

During the second half of the twelfth century the temporal aristocracy became a feudal nobility, and in the course of the thirteenth century this form of government was firmly established. The most prominent chieftains (the Royal Council) sided with the king; relations with the church were regulated by means of a concordat (1277); the right of succession to the throne was agreed upon, and a common legal code for the whole country was adopted (about 1270). It was during this period that Iceland and Greenland submitted to Norwegian rule, whereas the Suderoys were lost (1266).

Haakon's son Magnus (1263–80) won the name of Lawmender by reforming the Norse laws. In a way this was a good deed, but it took away from the *thing*'s power to pass on laws and made Norway much less free and democratic—more like the feudal lands to the south. At the same time certain wealthy farmers began to win more and more power till they became a sort of peasant nobility. During this reign Norway lost some of the Scottish islands, and her power among the nations began to wane. During the next two reigns it waned even further, especially because of commercial quarrels with the powerful Hanseatic League of German cities. When Haakon V Longlegs (1299–1319) died, the male line of Harald Fairhair came to an end.

This, as it turned out, meant the end of Norway as a separate independent kingdom for nearly six hundred years.

Already in the eleventh century the church had promoted the development of several towns; others owed their origin and rise to commerce. Among the latter, Bergen was in a class by itself. In the twelfth century the town had become the trading center for the fisheries of north Norway and a haven for merchant ships from many countries. A determining factor in the relations with foreign countries arose in the middle of the thirteenth century, when Norway found herself dependent upon imports for her supplies of grain. Such imports, however, could only take place from states adjoining the Baltic and the sole means of communication with them lay in the hands of the Hanseatic merchants upon whom, as was evident in a war about 1285, Norway had become entirely dependent.

Before 1300 the Hanseatic merchants had secured their most important privileges in the country. A national reaction against this German commercial hegemony during the ensuing decades proved of no avail, with the result that, before the royal line became extinct in 1319 with the death of King Haakon V, and the country merged into Scandinavian unions, the economic foundation necessary for Norway's independence had been weakened. In her need for grain, and in her dependence upon the Hanseatic towns of the Baltic, may be seen the most important premise for the decline of Norway in the latter part of the Middle Ages. The decline was thus due to a particular problem in national life. Grave consequences also ensued when, in the middle of the fourteenth century, the people were afflicted with the black death. The loss of lives was enormous.

THE UNION OF SCANDINAVIA

The most natural person to elect as a successor to the Norwegian throne was the son of Haakon's daughter, King Magnus Eriksson II of Sweden. Then Norway and Sweden, until 1380, had one king between them. In that year Denmark, also, came into the union. Norway had drifted into a union with Denmark which was to bring them nothing but misfortune. From the first, the formal treaty in 1397 which set up the Kalmar Union had Denmark as the head of it. This was because Queen Margrethe, who created the union, lived in Denmark. After her death, the Danish kings gave little attention to the welfare of Norway. And in 1537 Christian III made Norway into a mere province of Denmark.

So history records the story of the kings and wars and great events of these centuries as the story of Denmark, not that of Norway. And Denmark had a way of paying for her own defeats in war by giving away parts of Norway. In this fashion the last of Norway's foreign possessions slipped away, and parts of Norway proper were passed over to Sweden.

Trade languished and Norway became poorer and poorer. The peasants, used to expressing their ideas fearlessly in the *things,* found foreign officials over them who tried to grind them down as the serfs of the land. And when they appealed to the king, he was too busy with Danish affairs to bother with them. An uprising in 1436 brought a promise of reform, but the promises were not kept. A treaty in 1450 promised a separate Norse legislature, but this promise, too, was not to be kept. When the Protestant revolt against the Catholic church came, Norway was converted to Lutheranism by force, though the new Protestant clergy were at first so few and so ignorant that many of the Catholic priests had to be retained for a while. In the latter half of the 1500s the plague—which had carried off a third of the population two hundred years before—again swept through Norway.

Following the economic decline, political consequences made themselves seriously felt when, toward the end of the fourteenth century, the three northern kingdoms had become united under Queen Margrethe's centralized rule. To an increasing extent alien nobles now became chatelains in Norway, bishoprics were similarly held by foreigners, and state revenues flowed from the country. In 1449 Sweden broke away from the union, but Norway continued with Denmark from 1450, by virtue of a special treaty of union, drafted in Danish and serving Danish interests. In 1496 the Orkneys and Shetlands were lost to Norway, and when under the leadership of Archbishop Olaf Engelbrektson, the country rose against Danish dominance, the State Council of Denmark resolved that Norway, in the future, should cease to exist as a separate kingdom (1536). It was by a foreign dictate that the Reformation was introduced into Norway, and with the fall of the Catholic episcopacy the last national entrenchment fell, Norway being henceforth a mere vassal of Denmark.

THE RISE OF MODERN NORWAY

The sixteenth century, however, preluded a new era of prosperity for Norway. The forests, which during the Middle Ages had been of minor significance, now became the most important source of national wealth, owing to the increasing demand in west Europe for timber products. Exports increased voluminously during the fifteenth and sixteenth centuries and until the second half of the seventeenth century, the Dutch were the most important shippers. In the seventeenth and particularly during the eighteenth century, however, Norway's own shipping grew to displace the foreigners in the transport of goods to and from Norwegian shores. Progress continued, and before the year 1800 Norwegian vessels were even trading between foreign ports.

Gradually, with the razing of forests in the coastal regions of east Norway, the timber had to be floated down from inland areas, with the consequence that exports became confined to fewer places and left in fewer hands. From Ryfylke (Rogaland) to the Swedish frontier this gave rise to the foundation of a number of towns at river mouths, while increasing the importance of the older market towns. A new class of prosperous townspeople, mainly immigrants, acquired the principal profits of the timber trade; they acquired the sawmills and, in addition, frequently engaged in navigation and ship owning, some also amassing wealth as iron founders, an industry which in this period played an important role in the economic life of the country.

In Bergen, which was the main entry of grain for the north of Norway, the Hanseatic merchants maintained their established power longer than elsewhere in northern and western Europe, but here also they were gradually displaced by Norwegian citizens, partly by the naturalization of Germans permanently domiciled and married into Norwegian families.

As in all European countries, the new commercial activity about 1500 had the effect in Denmark-Norway of promoting the power of the state. The increasing customs' revenues benefited the crown, which consequently became less dependent upon the feudal lords. A modern

King Christian II (1513–23) lived to be seventy-eight years of age. This is a contemporary painting of him. He succeeded to the thrones of Norway and Denmark in 1513, and by force of arms also recovered the crown of Sweden.

King Christian V (1670–99) is remembered in history as the Norwegian king who tried to put a stop to superstition and the burning of witches at the stake, but he did much to advance society by putting into motion a new set of modern laws.

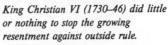

King Frederik IV (1699–1730), the Danish king who more than any other caused the people's rebellion against rule by Denmark because he showed his gratitude for the Norwegian warriors (who had defeated the invading Swedes) by selling off their trading rights.

King Christian VI (1730–46) did little or nothing to stop the growing resentment against outside rule.

King Frederick V (1746–66). During his reign the Norwegian peasants rebelled successfully against excess taxes.

bureaucracy took the place of the old feudal system, a development concluded in 1660 by the institution of the Royal Autocracy. A joint central administration for both kingdoms was now created, Denmark and Norway being governed as one state. Nevertheless, contributing to their geographical separation was Denmark's loss of the Skånean provinces about 1660 and Norway's loss of Bohuslän, Jemtland, and Herjedalen, all of which became parts of Sweden. Moreover, the new Norwegian merchant patriciate were, in their activities, little concerned with Denmark, which promoted the interests of Copenhagen at the expense of Norwegian towns.

With the reign of Christian IV (1588–1648) conditions slowly began to improve. This king actually took the trouble to visit Norway and see what was going on there. Mines were opened and new towns were built. Chritian's successor, Frederik III (1648–70), gained more power over his nobles, and this worked to the advantage of the common people. The next king, Christian V (1670–99), put in force a new set of laws, some of which still stand.

But it was during this period that part of Norway had been given to Sweden (in 1645 and 1658). And when, in 1715, the Norwegians rose in heroic resistance to the invasion of the impetuous warrior Charles XII, king of Sweden, and defeated him, Frederik IV (1699–1730) gave them little thanks for it. He sold the rights to Norwegian trade and church offices to private parties, and in this way gave the nobles power to oppress the people. During the reign of Frederik V (1746–66) the peasants

Signature of Christian VI as it appeared on official documents

rebelled successfully against excess taxes. In 1789 the French Revolution broke out, and the ideas of freedom for which Norway had always stood began to be voiced everywhere in the country.

TWO KINGDOMS

The conflicting interests of the two kingdoms became strikingly apparent during the Napoleonic wars. The Danish hostilities with England affected Norway very adversely and brought to a conclusion the period of remarkable prosperity which the country had experienced from 1793 to 1807. The demand for a separate Norwegian foreign policy was not accordingly raised and was, in fact, met during the years 1809 to 1812, when communication between the two kingdoms was severed by the English-Swedish blockade. The Danish alliance with France led to the dissolution of the Danish-Norwegian union. By the peace treaty of Kiel, January 14, 1814, Norway was ceded to Sweden, whereas the ancient Norwegian tributary countries, Iceland, Greenland, and the Faroe Islands, were retained by Denmark.

During the war, in 1813, Charles Frederick, the heir to the Dane-Norwegian throne, arrived in Norway as viceroy. When the peace treaty of Kiel became known in Norway, he contemplated his proclamation as absolute monarch but, acting on the advice of leading Norwegians, he recognized the sovereignty of the people and promised to summon a constituent assembly. The assembly met at Eidsvoll on April 10, 1814, and had concluded its labors by May 17, when the Constitutional Law was signed and Charles Frederick was elected king. The new constitution was based upon a division of power between the royal authority, on the one hand, and the representatives of the people (the Storting), on the other. The work of establishing the constitution had been carried through without disturbance from abroad, but upon the conclusion of the campaign against Napoleon the Swedes demanded the observance of the Kiel treaty. The great powers sided with Sweden, but Norway refused to yield. War accordingly broke out on July 27 but was over by August 14. An armistice was concluded and the Convention of Moss was signed. The convention stipulated the summoning of an extraordinary Storting, in order to pass legislation sanctioning the union of Norway with Sweden; the Constitutional Law of Eidsvoll was to remain in force; but Charles XIII Frederick was to abdicate and leave the country. The union was approved by the Storting on November 4, and in 1815 the relevant conditions were the subject of a separate agreement (Act of Union).

MODERN BUREAUCRACY

Primarily it was due to the bureaucratic class that the work at Eidsvoll was concluded; the resistance made by the civil servants to the union with Sweden was due to the powerful position they held in Norway, and in order to protect its own status, the bureaucratic majority in the Storting, during the years immediately following 1814, rejected all attempts on the part of the king, Charles XIV John (1818–44), to strengthen the royal power and to extend the common interests of the union. A merging of the civil services of the two countries could only have been carried out at the expense of the Norwegian officials.

The depression which began in 1807 made itself strongly felt after 1814. The development of the new state institutions entailed heavy expenditure, and taxa-

tion accordingly became a great burden. The political movement which the French July Revolution occasioned also in Norway led to strong agitation among the farmers against a bureaucratic government, and demands were raised for a reduction in state expenditure, restrictions on departmental management, and for the institution of municipal self-government. The last mentioned was introduced in 1837. In 1833, for the first time, the farmers had a majority in the Storting, but it was not maintained for many years, and with the advent of better times toward the end of the 1830s, their demands for reductions became less acute.

Christian VII's official signature as king

King Frederick VI (1808–14) served as the joint ruler from 1808 and after Norway declared away from Denmark, the king continued to serve as the king of Denmark from 1814 until his death in 1839.

The men of Eidsvoll in a country mansion of that name just north of Oslo, on May 17, 1814, completed the Norwegian constitution. It is one of the most remarkable of modern times. Its first paragraph reads "The Kingdom of Norway is a free, independent, indivisible and inalienable kingdom. Its form of government is a limited and hereditary monarchy."

In Norway, as elsewhere, a movement now set in toward a liberalistic industrial legislation, the foremost spokesman of which was A. M. Schweigaard, and, at the same time, internal communications were being developed under the direction of Father Stang. The economic expansion enhanced class distinction, and the French February Revolution of 1848 produced a Norwegian political labor movement with M. Thrane as its leader. This movement found special support among the rural laborers, but its demand for universal suffrage was rejected by the Storting.

During the second half of the nineteenth century a profound internal political transformation took place and in the Storting two distinctly separate groups came to be formed—one, a conservative party supporting the bureaucratic government in power; the other, an apposition in definite antagonism. The leader of the latter, and larger party was John Sverdrup. A resolution of 1869 for an annual Storting (as against the previous triennial)

contributed to the strengthening of the Storting at the expense of the king and government, and it was attempted to promote this tendency still further by the Storting's Resolution of 1872, regarding the access of ministers of state to the debates of the Storting. The government, believing that this would mean the complete adoption of parliamentarism and the abandonment of the principle of the division of power as laid donw in the constitution, procured a refusal of sanction. This was the prelude to a bitter struggle between the two governing bodies, the issue being whether the Storting had the right, constitutionally and of its own accord without the cooperation of the crown, to amend the constitution (the so-called Veto issue). The political conflict culminated in the ruling given by the High Court of the Realm in 1884, whereby the members of the cabinet were deprived of their offices. After a short transitional period the king was obliged, in 1884, to appoint a cabinet with Sverdrup as its head. A change of system had thus taken place: the

Oscar

Oscar I's signature

Oscar II (1872–1905) had closer ties with Sweden, so he discouraged movements toward independence. But in 1905, the Storting announced that the union with Sweden would be dissolved.

King Haakon and Queen Maud as the prince and princess of Denmark

The document from the Norwegian Storting is read by King Christian IX, November 20, 1905. It states a desire for independence but offers the throne to the Danish Prince Charles, who would become King Haakon VII of Norway.

King Haakon VII with the crown prince arrives in Norway.

personal power of the king had come to an end and the Storting had become the decisive governing body.

With the greatest anxiety this development had been followed in Sweden where, with all good reason, a weakening of the union was feared. As early as the 1850s the Storting had claimed equality for Norway, and from then onward to 1905 the attitude to be adopted toward Sweden received steadily increasing prominence in Norwegian politics. Not least of the reasons for the fall of the Sverdrup ministry, in 1888, was its obscure attitude on this question. The Left party (founded in 1884) split in 1887, as a result of its cultural and ecclesiastical polity (the Radical Left and Moderate Left wings).

During the reign of Oscar I (1844–59) Norway won the right to use her own national flag and started to work for separate consuls in foreign countries. In 1905 the Norwegian ministry resigned against the protest of the king, Oscar II (1872–1905), and announced that the union ought to be dissolved altogether.

The official coronation photograph of King Haakon and Queen Maud

The coronation of King Haakon at Trondheim Cathedral. The crown is placed on his head.

It was put to a vote among the Norwegian people; for since 1898 all the grown men among them had had the right to vote. The referendum was counted 368,208 for independence and only 184 against it! The Danish prince Charles was chosen as king, and crowned as Haakon VII. Since then Norway is listed among the independent nations.

Sverdrup's successor was Smil Stang, the organizer of the Conservative party (founded in 1884) as a parliamentary and democratic people's party. The conservative government fell in 1891, on its proposals for a solution of the union conflict, and the Radical Left took office with J. Steen as prime minister. In 1893, upon the refusal of the king to sanction the Storting's resolution in favor of a separate Norwegian consular service, Stand again formed a government. The prominence of a claim for a separate consular service was due to the demands made by the growing Norwegian shipping. A coalition cabinet was formed in 1895 under F. Hagerup, and the Storting resolved to commence negotiations with Sweden with a view to the reorganization of the entire diplomatic and consular service. The negotiations, however, fell through and the Liberals again assumed office under Steen. In 1902 fresh negotiations were commenced for a separate consular service under a joint Foreign Office, and with this as his program, Hagerup in 1903 again formed a coalition government. The proposals put forward by Sweden, however, proved altogether unacceptable and Hagerup had to make way for a coalition government under Christian Michelsen (March 1905).

An act establishing a separate Norwegian consular service was unanimously passed by the Storting but did not meet with royal sanction (May 27). As King Oscar II refused to accept the resignation of the government, the cabinet, on June 7, put their portfolios in the hands of the Storting. The Storting, however, requested the cabinet to retain office and thereupon declared the union with Sweden dissolved.

THE UNION CONFLICT

Concurrent with the union conflict, a mighty economic expansion in the domains of shipping, commerce, industry, agriculture, and breeding fish was taking place. The development of industry considerably attracted the rural population, and agriculture thus became commercialized. Class distinction in the country districts decreased and the number of freeholds increased. In the towns, on the contrary, class distinction became enhanced as a result of the growth of industrial capitalism.

In 1887 industrial workers founded their own party, but they had at an earlier date started to organize in trade unions. The first demand put forward by the Norwegian Labor party was for universal suffrage which, with the assistance of the Liberal party, was granted for men in 1898, but not until 1913 for women.

A commemorative stamp for Queen Maud, who died in 1938. She was the daughter of King Edward VII of England.

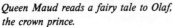

Queen Maud reads a fairy tale to Olaf, the crown prince.

The party collaboration seen in 1905 did not continue. With the consolidation of the Liberal party (1906–7) its moderate wing broke away and, in 1909, formed the Independent Liberal party, which until 1927 was conservatively inclined. The Labor party, which in 1905 played no part of importance and was not represented in the Storting until 1903, thereupon grew considerably and became, in 1938, the largest party in the kingdom. Influenced by the events in Russia, the revolutionary wing triumphed in 1918 and it was not before 1921 that the Social Democrats broke away. In 1923 the Labor party severed relations with the Third International and this led the same year to the formation of a separate Communist party. The latter, however, rapidly lost its influence. In 1927 the Social Democrats rejoined the Labor party. In 1920 the Agrarian party was formed, the fourth of the large political fusions in Norway.

For a great part of the time subsequent to 1905, the Liberal party held office or, at all events, determined the political course of the country. The first important issue the party dealt with was foreign capital in respect of the exploration of the natural resources of the country.

THE WORLD WARS

In Norway, the period from 1905 until World War I was characterized by prosperity, increasing industrialism, and rising prices, a tendency which was accelerated during the war. The economic situation during the war led to an enormous rise in shipping revenue. Industry attracted all available labor and the difficult conditions governing imports stimulated agriculture and encouraged the breaking of fresh soil. Under the leadership of Gunnar Knudsen, the Liberal party, supported by a compact majority in the Storting, carried through a comprehensive regulation of prices and rationing of foodstuffs. To avoid labor conflicts, a law for compulsory mediation was passed in 1916 and, at the same time, social legislation became more comprehensive.

The policy adopted in connection with maintaining neutrality during this critical period entailed a heavy increase in the national debt.

In 1921, with the end of this boom period, there set in, as everywhere else, a marked and prolonged period of depression involving curtailment in industry, permanent unemployment, and numerous labor conflicts.

The international depression after 1929, however, hit Norway less severely than many other countries, due to the relatively marked variation in Norwegian production. Nonetheless, the fall in prices, in conjunction with the monetary fluctuations, had unfortunate consequences in agricultural circles. The situation thus brought about induced, in the spring of 1935, the political alliance between the Agrarians and the Labor party which resulted in the forming of a Labor government.

The most important political task of the government was to combat unemployment, and this resulted in a marked increase in national expenditure. The increased sums that were voted for national defense, which were a result of the international tension prevailing in the late 1930s, had a similar effect. As it turned out, these grants were made too late. Because of a policy of neutrality, which had the support of all parties, the years following World War I in Norway were marked by a far-reaching program of disarmament that was to have tragic conse-

The marriage photograph of Crown Prince Olaf and Princess Martha of Sweden, March 21, 1929. The best man was the duke of York, later to become the king of England.

The Germans invaded Denmark and Norway in April 1940. This is King Haakon and Crown Prince Olaf just prior to leaving for England with the cabinet and their families, a few days before the Germans entered Oslo.

Vidkun Quisling, the World War II prime minister placed in control by the German government during the occupation. On a 1942 stamp.

King Haakon and Crown Prince Olaf in their home near London where they resided during World War II while they led the Norwegian government-in-exile.

King Haakon and the royal family return to Oslo on June 7, 1945.

quences in April 1940. It would thus be wrong to place all the blame for Norway's lack of preparedness on the Labor government, especially when reminded that Norway was entirely dependent on the import of finished munitions of war to be able to carry out her armament program.

On April 9, 1940, Germany invaded Norway. There was fighting in southern Norway until May 5, and in northern Norway until June 7. The king (Haakon VII), the crown prince, and the government left the country with the Storting and continued the fight from England.

After a short period of coalition government in 1945,

the first postwar elections gave the Labor party a majority in the Storting, and during a number of succeeding elections the party continued to poll more than half of the votes cast. In 1961, however, the Labor party obtained only 74 of the 150 mandates to the Storting. After a heated debate in the summer of 1963, chiefly concentrated on questions of industrial policy of the Labor government, this administration was defeated in the Storting, and a coalition government of the four non-Socialist opposition parties, headed by Mr. John Lyng (Conservative), was formed. But barely four weeks later a new Labor government took power.

GOVERNMENT

In the general elections of 1965, the non-Socialist parties won a majority of seats and formed a coalition government, headed by Per Borten (Center party).

The issue of Norwegian membership in the European Economic Community (EEC) contributed to a government crisis that led to the resignation of the cabinet of Prime Minister Per Borten on March 2, 1971, followed by the return of the Labor party to government power. For the same issue the Labor party lost control in September 1972, but in the elections of 1973 and 1977, it became the minority party in charge of government.

The government is dependent upon the majority of the Storting, and it is compelled to carry out its functions by means of the help of the permanent employees of the bureaucracy. The government, however, will still be able to exert considerable influence on the general course of events through its day-to-day operations.

The head of the government is the prime minister, and the next after him in rank is considered to be the foreign minister. The prime minister's primary role is that of coordinating the functions of the cabinet ministers, drawing up the basic policy lines and ensuring that these are followed. In connection with the present-day intense international involvement, he also represents the country to a considerable extent, in addition to the foreign minister. Among other things, the premiers of the Nordic countries meet from time to time to consider questions of common interest. The prime minister is also a central figure in connection with the government's contact with officialdom, in that he, inter alia, gives press conferences where he issues statements and where the representatives of the press are able to question him.

The cabinet normally meets in the king's presence every Friday. In addition, there are informal meetings between the government members, preferably a couple of times a week. Matters are discussed at these meetings which, among other things, require interdepartmental cooperation in order to carry them out. Such matters have increased in number during recent years by virtue of the state having assumed heavier tasks and responsibilities, and the various spheres of social life having become more dependent upon each other.

THE KING AND
THE ROYAL FAMILY

King Olaf V, born in 1903, has reigned since 1957, when he succeeded his father Haakon VII, who had sat on the throne since 1905. The king symbolizes the unity of the country. He presides over the cabinet, but has otherwise no political function. When necessary he may intervene if the apportionment of elected representatives from the various parties makes it uncertain which of the parties should be called upon to form an administration that would be able to cooperate with the Storting.

King Olaf is the commander in chief of the country's armed forces. Today this is of mere symbolic significance, although the right was actually invoked during World War II. The king can use his right of veto to suspend legislation. He is the head of the Church of Norway, to which he himself and at least half of his cabinet must belong. In law, the king can do no wrong. He cannot be censored or indicted. The throne is hereditary, succession being in direct male descending line.

King Olaf was married to Martha, princess of Sweden, who died in 1954. The marriage resulted in three children, the princesses Ragnhild and Astrid, who are married to Norwegian commoners, and Crown Prince Harold, born 1937 and married in 1968 to a Norwegian commoner, Miss Sonja Haraldsen. Crown Prince Harold and Crown Princess Sonja have two children, Princess Martha Louise, born 1971, and Prince Haakon Magnus, born 1973. Their residence is at Skaugum, some kilometers west of Oslo, while King Olaf remains at the Oslo palace in the center of the capital.

A commemorative stamp for King Haakon VII, 1905–57.

The blessing of the new king in the Nidaros Cathedral in Trondheim. In 1957, Prince Olaf succeeded his father, King Haakon VII, to the Norwegian throne.

The official portrait of King Olaf V. The functions of the king are mainly ceremonial, although he has influence as the symbol of national unity. Though the present constitution grants important executive powers to the king, these are almost always exercised by the Council of Ministers in the name of the king (King in Council). The Council of Ministers consists of the prime minister, chosen by the political parties that enjoy the confidence of Parliament, and other ministers.

King Olav V leaving the Security Council Chamber with Secretary-General U Thant, right, after a speech made to the General Assembly during a visit to the UN headquarters in 1968.

Crown Prince Olav of Norway visits the United Nations building in New York City in 1950 and meets with Secretary-General Trygve Lie, right.

King Olav V visits the United Nations building again, in 1975, and addresses the General Assembly on an important issue. Secretary-General Kurt Waldheim is on his left.

Norwegian stamps honoring King Olaf V

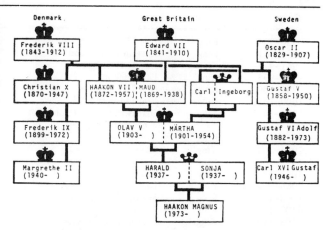

This genealogy chart shows the interrelationships among the Norwegian and other European royal families.

Norway today

Norway's royal family lives at Skaugum, west of Oslo. Here we see Crown Prince Harald, left, with Princess Martha Louise on his knee, and, right, Crown Princess Sonja with Prince Haakon Magnus.

The crown prince Harald and the coat of arms

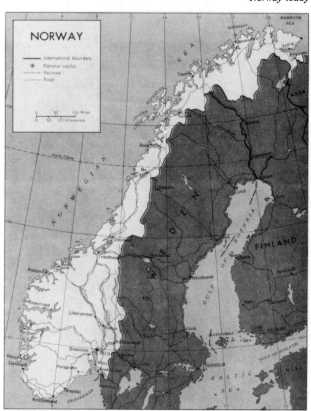

THE ROYAL SOVEREIGNS OF THE KINGDOM OF NORWAY

Reign	Title	Ruler	Birth	Death	Relationship
	King	Olaf Traetelia		640	
	King	Halfdan Huitben		700	
	King	Eystein		730	
	King	Halfdan Millde		784	
	King	Gudrod Mikillati		824	
	King	Olaf Geirstada		840	
	King	Halfdan Svart		863	
872–930	King	Harald Fairhair (Harold I)	849	934	Grandson of Harold Goldenbeard, ruler of Sogne

Reign	Title	Ruler	Birth	Death	Relationship
930–934	King	Eric I Bloodaxe (Erik)		940	Son of Harold I
934–961	King	Haakon I, the Good	913	961	Son of Harold I
961–977	King	Harold II Graypelt	929	977	Son of Eric I
977–995	King	Earl Haakon	937	995	Son of Haakon I
995–1000	King	Olaf I Tryggvason	969	1000	
1000–1016	Kings	Eric and Sveyn			Sons of Earl Haakon
1016–1030	King	Olaf II Haraldson (Saint Olaf—cannonized in 1164)	995	1030	
1030–1035	King	Canute the Great	1001	1035	Son of Sweyn I, the Splitbeard
1035–1047	King	Magnus I, the Good	1015	1047	Son of Saint Olaf
1047–1066	King	Harold III Hardrade	1015	1066	Descendant of Harold I
1055–1066	King	Magnus II	1035	1066	Son of Harold III
1066–1093	King	Olaf III, the Peaceful		1093	Son of Harold III
1093–1103	King	Magnus II Barefoot	1073	1103	Son of Olaf III
1103–1122	King	Eystein I	1089	1122	Son of Magnus II
1103–1130	King	Sigurd I, the Crusader	1090	1130	Son of Magnus II
1130–1135	King	Magnus III, the Blind	1115	1139	Son of Sigurd I
1130–1136	King	Harold IV Gilchrist	1104	1136	
1136–1161	King	Inge I		1161	Son of Harold IV
1136–1161	King	Sigurd II Mund	1134	1155	Son of Harold IV
1142–1157	King	Eystein II		1157	Son of Harold IV
1161–1162	King	Haakon II	1147	1162	Son of Sigurd II
1163–1184	King	Magnus IV	1156	1184	Son of Erling Skakke
1184–1202	King	Sverre	1152	1202	Son of Sigurd II
1204–1204	King	Haakon III Sverreson		1204	
1204–1217	King	Inge Baardson			
1217–1263	King	Haakon IV	1204	1263	Son of Haakon III
1263–1280	King	Magnus VI, the Lawmender	1238	1280	Son of Haakon IV
1280–1299	King	Eric II (Erik)	1268	1299	Son of Magnus VI
1299–1319	King	Haakon V Longlegs	1270	1319	Son of Magnus VI
1319–1355	King	Magnus VII	1316	1374	Grandson of Haakon V
1355–1380	King	Haakon VI	1339	1380	Son of Magnus VII

KINGS OF NORWAY AND DENMARK 1380–1814

Reign	Title	Ruler	Birth	Death	Relationship
1380–1387	King	Olaf IV	1370	1387	Son of Haakon VI
1387–1412	Queen	Margrethe	1353	1412	Mother of Olaf IV; consort of Haakon VI
1389–1442	King	Eric III of Pomerania	1382	1459	Grandnephew of Margrethe
1442–1448	King	Christopher III of Bavaria	1418	1448	Nephew of Eric III
1448–1481	King	Christian I	1426	1481	Son of Dederik, count of Oldenburg
1481–1513	King	Hans I	1455	1513	Son of Christian I
1513–1523	King	Christian II	1481	1559	Son of Hans
1523–1533	King	Frederik I	1471	1533	Son of Christian I
1533–1559	King	Christian III	1503	1559	Son of Frederik I
1559–1588	King	Frederik II	1534	1588	Son of Christian III
1588–1648	King	Christian IV	1577	1648	Son of Frederik II
1648–1670	King	Frederik III	1609	1670	Son of Christian IV
1670–1699	King	Christian V	1646	1699	Son of Frederik III
1699–1730	King	Frederik IV	1671	1730	Son of Christian V
1730–1746	King	Christian VI	1699	1746	Son of Frederik IV
1746–1766	King	Frederik V	1723	1766	Son of Christian VI
1766–1808	King	Christian VII	1749	1808	Son of Frederik V
1808–1814	King	Frederik VI	1768	1839	Son of Christian VII

KINGS OF NORWAY AND SWEDEN 1814–1905

Reign	Title	Ruler	Birth	Death	Relationship
1814–1818	King	Charles XIII (Carl)	1748	1818	Son of Adolphus Frederick
1818–1844	King	Charles XIV John (Bernadotte)	1763	1844	
1844–1859	King	Oscar I	1799	1859	Son of Carl XIV
1859–1872	King	Charles XV	1826	1872	Son of Oscar I
1872–1905	King	Oscar II	1829	1907	Son of Oscar I

1905—Norway became an independent kingdom.

KINGS OF NORWAY

Reign	Title	Ruler	Birth	Death	Relationship
1905–1957	King	Haakon VII	1872	1957	Son of Frederik VIII of Denmark
1957–	King	Olaf V (Olav)	1903		Son of Haakon VII

14
The Kingdom of Sweden

Map of early Sweden and her neighbors

"Ship-settings" are an impressive feature of certain burial grounds from the Migration Period. The largest ship-setting in Sweden, the Ale Stones (not unlike Stonehenge), is located at Kaseberga on the south coast of the province of Skåne.

We now know that the southernmost parts of Sweden began to emerge from the Ice Age about 12,000 B.C. This is the oldest date in Swedish history and perhaps the oldest dependable one in the history of the world.

The primitive tribes who followed the ice as it withdrew northward carried on the first and decisive struggle for a settlement on Swedish soil. They were helped by inventions and discoveries which make those of later times fade in importance: fire employed to serve human beings; the art of making tools from flint and bowls from clay; taming of the first domestic animals; cultivation of crops. About 3000 B.C. agriculture was begun. Imposing tombs made with huge blocks of stone enable us to trace the spread of this early peasant culture.

Copper and bronze became known about 1500 B.C.

The Bronze Age can be studied through the richly decorated weapons of the chieftains as well as in ornaments preserved in the earth, and in the stone carvings that depict fertility rites. Common and extensive use of a metal in this early civilization was not possible until relations with countries to the south had acquainted the northerners with iron, which they learned to extract from bog ore found on the bottom of lakes and marshes; on the other hand, it was impossible for them to work deposits of rock ore. During the first centuries A.D. the provinces around Lake Mälaren and the Suiones, or Svear, residing there began to assume their leading position. The first recorded mention of the Suiones, who were to give the whole country its name, is found in the *Germania* written by the Roman historian Tacitus in A.D. 98. Cultivation of the land was accelerated with the help of iron and because the farmers joined together in village teams that shared the work. These villages are still in existence, and the names they received during those early years are still in use.

Silvermynt coin of King Olaf Skottkonung

King Birger II Magnusson

*King John I (Johan) Sverkersson
(1216–22)*

Noble King Birger II, 1317

Silvermynt coin of King Anund Jacob, 1022–50

THE VIKING AGE AND EARLY CHRISTIANITY

The comparative isolation of Scandinavia was not broken until the Viking age (A.D. 700–1000), when intrepid travelers brought back foreign goods and knowledge, new methods and new thoughts, in short, the contributions of more southerly civilizations. The coastal regions around and north of present-day Stockholm were the base of Viking power and the starting point for great forays and trading expeditions—sometimes involving hundreds of ships—to the east. Whether as plunderers or merchants—and no clear distinction appears to have been made—the Vikings kept up the contact between Sweden and the east (Russia, Constantinople) and Sweden and western Europe, including the British Isles and Ireland. The latter countries were the favorite goals of the men from southern Sweden who joined with Danish and Norwegian Vikings, then their countrymen, in pillage, trade, or conquest.

Calmer centuries followed the Viking expeditions and their tremendous display of energy. Eastern contacts ceased, and Sweden turned instead to the west and the south. Christianity gradually made headway with the aid of missions sent from England and northern Germany. Churches were built, first of wood, then of stone. Several hundreds of the latter from the twelfth and thirteenth centuries still stand. Sweden was incorporated in the huge organization of the Roman Catholic church.

At the same time, the realm became more firmly established; it included Finland and all of modern Sweden, except the provinces of Bohuslän, Blekinge, Halland, and Skåne. Rival dynasties did not succeed in breaking the fundamental unity, definite procedures for electing the rulers were established, and a council, drawn from the foremost families of the country, took its place by the king's side. Villages were expanded and new ones founded; in each century the frontier was pushed a little farther into the wilderness. During the thirteenth century the provincial statutes were compiled in law books which remain unique in their age and clarity. By these

A recently uncovered wall painting of King Magnus Ladulas

the life of the whole province was regulated in detail from the most elevated aspects to the commonest everyday concerns: "Christ is foremost in our law, next to Him our Christian dogma and all Christians: the King, peasants and all legal residents, bishops, all men of book-learning," but also "if horse rolls or swine roots in grainfield, [owner] pays fine therefore with such grain as was sown in the field, one skep for every third rolling or every third rooting." Differentiation into social groups took place in this period; in addition to the clergy a class of nobles emerged, the latter composed of estate owners and those high in the service of kings or lords. The nobles were exempt from taxes in exchange for military service in heavy armor.

Eventually this society of farmers and foresters came into contact with the commercial cities of Germany, organized into the famous Hanseatic League. One of the league's foremost trading centers was on Swedish soil, the city of Visby on the island of Gotland. Sweden thereby gained full entry to European trading and obtained an international market for her products, such as copper, iron, butter, and pelts. Even in regard to culture the fourteenth century was a flourishing time: a Swedish chivalric poetry modeled after European prototypes was created, and the first internationally famous Swede appeared in the person of Saint Birgitta, author of remarkable revelations and founder of a new monastic order that included both monks and nuns (Vadstena Monastery). Soon after 1350 a national code was compiled. Based in part on the provincial laws, it aimed above all to safeguard peace and personal security. Acts of violence in church, at the *ting* (tribal courts), personal attacks in another man's house or against a defenseless woman, made a man an outlaw without rights and property. The "law of the land" included a brief constitution in which the powers of the king, the council, and the citizens were delimited. Even in the modern world order the duties of the king could hardly be defined more succinctly than in the old text: "The King shall all justice and truth strengthen, love and preserve, all wrongs and falsehoods destroy, both by law and by his royal power."

King Magnus II Eriksson

King Magnus II Eriksson, 1319

THE KALMAR UNION

The period from 1397 to 1520 was a time of great political experiment in the north. Queen Margrethe of Denmark and Norway succeeded also in becoming ruler of Sweden. This was during a strong, intra-Nordic reaction against the expansionistic efforts of the Germans. An

For many centuries the famous Kalmar Castle on the Baltic served as part-time residence for the royal families. Parts of the castle date back to the twelfth century. It was at the nearby seaport town of Kalmar that Sweden along with Denmark and Norway signed the treaty that set up the Kalmar Union.

King Albert of Mecklenberg and his queen in effigy on their tomb

Seal of Regent Engelbrekt, 1436

·CHRISTIERNVS·Z·DANORVM·
·REX·SVETIE·NOR·
VEGIE·ZC·
·1·4·17·

King Christian II

Seal of Regent Karl Knutsson, 1440

Detail from Queen Margrethe's sepulcher in Roskilde Cathedral, Denmark. Whether the noble features of this alabaster sculpture resemble the queen's actual appearance is difficult for posterity to determine.

King Christian II's armor

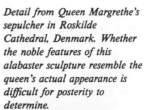

Sten Sture the Younger wounded in battle at Lake Asunden dies as he is being transported back to Stockholm in his sledge.

enormous kingdom emerged. The Kalmar Union was the name of this alliance (important negotiations regarding it had been held in the Swedish city of Kalmar), and it gave undeniable evidence of a statesmanlike ability to think in broad terms, but after several decades of strife it failed nevertheless. Margrethe's successor in 1412 and nominal king since 1396, Eric of Pomerania, sought to extend the royal power throughout the triple realm and fought the German princes as well as the Hanseatic League while seeking political alliances in England and elsewhere. But Sweden was dependent on the Hanseatic League, especially in respect to a market for her metals; furthermore, the country was little inclined to tolerate increased tyrannical power on the part of the king.

In the mining districts of Bergslagen the people rose in revolt under the leadership of a simple mine owner by the name of Engelbrekt. The nobles, viewing with alarm the king's bid for greater power, made common cause with him. After bitter struggles between Denmark and Sweden the union was dissolved. During these turbulent decades in the fifteenth century a notable innovation was made in the Swedish political system: the *Riksdag,* or Parliament, was instituted, which on behalf of the people made important political decisions. Even the peasants were represented in this new body.

Christian II, King of Denmark since 1513, soon became a new threat to Sweden's independence. Hope of a successful defense against the repeated attacks faded when the Swedish regent, Sten Sture the Younger, fell in one of the losing battles against the Danes in 1520. By the Stockholm Massacre, a mass execution in the conquered capital, Christian attempted to eliminate the leaders of the independence party and with them all opposition. Once more it appeared that a great northern kingdom was in formation, this time by violence. But the king had underestimated the Swedish tradition of freedom.

THE AGE OF GUSTAVUS VASA

A revolt against the Danish king, led by a young, rather unknown relative of the Stures, Gustavus Eriksson Vasa, began in Dalarna in 1520–21. Vasa definitely put an end to the union and made Sweden into a national state of the type which had arisen on the Continent during the late Middle Ages.

Gustavus Vasa placed the stamp of his personality on Sweden's history from 1523, when at the age of twenty-seven he was elected to the throne, until his death in 1560. His first royal concern was the stabilization of the state finances; by resolute measures at the Västerås Parliament in 1527 he created the conditions necessary for the confiscation by the state of all property in the hands of the Roman Catholic church. Since the end of the Middle Ages the church held 21 percent of the Swedish soil, as compared with only 5.6 percent owned by the

When we think of Regent Gustavus Vasa, we like to imagine him looking just like this, with a black beret and white plume, a prominent nose and straight-cropped hair and beard. This painting from 1542 shows Gustavus Vasa at the age of forty-six.

Princess Margarta, sister of Gustavus Vasa

King Gustavus I's helmet

Regent Gustavus Vasa

Queen Margaret Leijonhufvud, second wife of King Gustavus I

King Eric XIV, 1560–68

King Eric XIV, who sought the hand of Queen Elizabeth of England, sent her this portrait showing himself standing in a well-chosen setting, magnificently attired, and with a self-consciously royal bearing (National Museum of Fine Arts, Stockholm. Photo, P. Jalkman).

Gustavus Vasa (Gustavus Eriksson) was not content to be king in name alone. He sought to stop the consumption of alcohol by the populace. Here he is seen bursting a barrel of grog with his sword in one of his frequent visits of "temperance" to the taverns.

Signature of King Gustavus I

Eric XIV, the eldest son of Gustavus Vasa, succeeded his father to the throne but was a weakling and eventually went insane. He imprisoned the famous Sture family in 1567 and, as seen here, in a rage one day while talking to Nils Sture, stabbed him to death.

"Riksdaler" coin of King Gustavus I

Before his insanity, Eric XIV was deposed and imprisoned. Here he is seen at the time of his notification that he was deposed as king. His queen, Karin Mansdatter, stood by his side until his death.

King Sigismund, 1592–99

King John III, 1568–92

King Charles IX, 1604–11

crown; this represented an immense addition to the strength of the state. Gustavus Vasa found a certain amount of justification for this measure in the Lutheran teachings that had begun to spread in the country, with the full approval of the king. Gradually the Swedish church was separated from Rome, became Lutheran in character, and was organized into a state church which survives to this day. The decree of the Västerås Parliament established the new religious phase with the goodly statement that "the plain and true word of God shall be preached in the realm." Simultaneously with the great confiscation of church property, the king and his men reorganized the government administration and developed unprecedented efficiency. Various provinces, such as Dalarna and Småland, objected strenuously to having their local interests set aside for the common good. When they rebelled against the king, they were severely castigated. Foundations for modern literature were also laid during the reign of Gustavus Vasa with a complete translation of the Bible, and in the hymns and theological writings of Olaus Petri, Swedish reformer.

For half a century after the death of Gustavus Vasa his sons, Eric XIV, John III, and Charles IX ruled Sweden in the order named. All three were interesting, talented, but contradictory men, engrossed in the confusing international relations of the day. From the south, Denmark plotted against Sweden, while the Swedes repeatedly waged war against Lübeck, Poland, and Russia. One of their more consistent efforts was to gain control over Russia's foreign trade in the Baltic Sea, to which she had no direct access. When Estonia became Swedish (1561, 1595), this objective was partly attained, for Sweden thereby obtained considerable strength in the Baltic area and control over some of the important trade routes to Russia.

A new attempt at a north European union was made by Sigismund, son of John III, who through his mother first became king of Poland, then in 1592 succeeded his father on the throne of Sweden. His Catholicism and prolonged absences in Poland caused great opposition in Sweden and paved the way for his uncle, Charles, to depose him in 1599. The only consequence of Sigismund's abortive enterprise was that acute enmity replaced the former alliance between the two countries. Charles remained protector of the realm and did not assume the title of King Charles IX until 1604. During the last years before his death in 1611 Sweden was waging a losing struggle against Denmark, Poland, and Russia.

GUSTAVUS ADOLPHUS

Sweden's greatest expansion grew out of the ensuing struggle for existence. If Gustavus Vasa was the dominating figure in Sweden during the sixteenth century, the most important role in the first part of the seventeenth century was played by his brilliant grandson, Gustavus II Adolphus, son of Charles IX. His enormous task was to liberate Sweden from the paralyzing grip in which she was held by her neighbors and into which she had, to some extent, voluntarily entered in her long-range plans for expansion. He succeeded in this task, and he expanded the empire in the east by conquests at the Russian border and by annexing the previously Polish Livonia to the Swedish possession, Estonia. But this did not suffice: he gradually added to his program a battle against the political expansion of the Catholic Counter-

King Gustavus II Adolphus

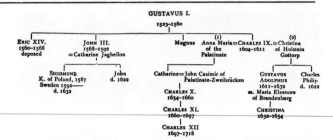

The House of Vasa in the sixteenth and seventeenth centuries

*King Gustavus II Adolphus
about 1629 wearing armor*

*King Gustavus II entering Elbing, Germany, in 1626, on his conquests
to the south*

*King Gustavus II Adolphus on horseback (engraving by Crispin van der
Passe)*

Seal of Gustavus II Adolphus

Medal of Gustavus II Adolphus coronation, 1617

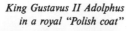

*King Gustavus II Adolphus
in a royal "Polish coat"*

*Painting of King Gustavus
II Adolfus, 1641 (Vandyke)*

*Queen Maria Eleonora, wife
of King Gustavus II*

*Gustavus Adolphus the Great,
original drawing by L. Strauch,
dating from 1632 and recently
discovered in the schoolhouse in
Madenhausen, Bavaria*

A minnespinning *(medal) depicting the death of Gustavus Adolphus*

Reformation. Even Charles IX's campaigns against Sigismund and Poland had acquired that character, but the new conflict spread to include all of Europe in the Thirty Years War. The House of Habsburg was in the process of crushing the Protestant princes in Germany and advanced toward the Baltic with the intent of becoming a great power also in northern Europe. Gustavus Adolphus decided to participate in the historic struggle. He first launched an attack against Poland, and seized the most important towns in eastern Prussia, which were vital to Poland's commerce. Then he led his army into Germany against Habsburg and the Catholic League, received support from France, and in 1631 routed the famous General Tilly in the Battle of Breitenfeld (near Leipzig) in Saxony. The next winter he held court in Mainz and Frankfurt on the Main, marched through Bavaria in the summer of 1632, and on November 6 that year encountered Wallenstein, the emperor's chief commander, at Lützen, not far from Breitenfeld. Wallenstein was forced to retreat, but Gustavus Adolphus fell in battle.

An almost inevitable question presents itself as these extensive campaigns are reviewed: how could a small country like Sweden, modest in its resources, generate and maintain such military power?

Throughout the war the king had the people's approval. Parliament, including nobles, clergy, burghers, and peasants, had been in full accord with him on the necessity of entering the war in Germany. In presenting and justifying his plans and actions before the representatives of the people the king was indefatigable. His armies were largely composed of Swedish farmers, their sons and farmhands. A source of financial support was the copper mine at Falun, whose exports were then in great demand throughout Europe. The political genius of Gustavus II Adolphus, his talent for military organization, and his advanced ideas on strategy and tactics were important contributory factors in the success of his campaigns. In addition, the king possessed outstanding administrative ability.

When Gustavus Adolphus fell, his heir and only child, Christina, was six years old. The regency was placed in the hands of a group from the upper nobility, headed by Chancellor Axel Oxenstierna, Sweden's greatest statesman. For sixteen more years the war in Germany continued. The Peace of Westphalia (1648) gave to Sweden a number of important possessions on the southern shore of the Baltic and on the North Sea, but the Polish ports had to be relinquished; in addition, the Catholic German states were to pay reparations.

Sweden's strategic position was entirely changed. Queen Christina abdicated in 1654 and was succeeded by her cousin, Charles X Gustavus, who was waging war in Poland when Denmark joined Sweden's enemies. He then departed from Poland with his army in 1658, marched through Schleswig-Holstein, and forced the

The tomb of Gustavus in the Riddarholm Church

Queen Christina (1632–54) in her youth

By most narrators and artists, King Charles Gustavus is represented as fat and bloated, but as a young man he made a different impression. This portrait from the early 1640s gives an idea of how he looked to Christina, his enamored playmate and cousin, up till 1645, when her personal liking for him suddenly ceased.

King Gustavus Adolphus and the child Christina in a painting showing Christina as a small girl together with her father. There is probably no question of likeness, yet the picture gives some idea of Christina's boyish appearance when young.

Portrait of Queen Christina, painted 1650, the year of her coronation

Queen Christina loved horseback riding.

Map of the Swedish Empire after the death of Gustavus in 1660

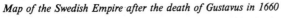

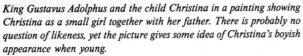

Stockholm Castle in the middle of the seventeenth century

Queen Christina in a portrait painted during her reign

On June 6, 1654, Queen Christina officially renounced the Swedish crown at a solemn ceremony in Uppsala Castle.

Queen Christina in 1670

Danes to transfer to Sweden the provinces of Blekinge, Skåne, Halland, and Bohuslän. In a surprise move the king had led his army over the newly frozen Belts—one of history's most daring exploits—and Denmark had to relinquish her control over The Sound, main inlet to the Baltic Sea.

SOCIAL CRISIS—CHARLES XI'S FINANCIAL REORGANIZATION

Since that time the southern provinces have remained Swedish and represent the lasting gain from the period of power politics. However, this policy also had a very negative aspect. A large portion of the monies and much of the support needed for the wars had been secured through the transfer or sale of crown lands or tax concessions to the nobility. In a country still having an economy largely operating in kind, it was necessary to resort to such means. European power politics could not, after all, be financed with taxes paid in butter and grain. The result was that the nobles ended up with the possession of about 72 percent of Sweden's soil, while the crown and the independent farmers had to be satisfied with the remaining 28 percent. Those farmers who had become subject to nobles and paid their taxes to them obviously had difficulty in maintaining any measure of independence, especially since the lords in question had acquired on the Continent a purely feudal attitude toward subordinates.

Sweden's Vasa kings had not always seen eye to eye with the nobles. Gustavus Vasa's three sons had severe clashes and sanguinary reckonings with them. Gustavus II Adolphus had maintained good cooperation with the great men of the realm, but for his daughter, Christina, the situation was more difficult. To curb the nobles, restore order in the state finances after the wars, and assist the peasants in the struggle for their ancient freedoms combined into an immense task, even for as talented a woman ruler as Christina. Furthermore, her personal position was changed when she secretly became a convert to Catholicism. She found herself in a complex quandary of conscience and decided to abdicate, but not until she had secured the throne for her cousin Charles Gustavus, and forestalled his being faced with increased power on the part of the nobility. The almost constant wars and his early death (1660) at the age of thirty-eight prevented Charles X Gustavus, too, from solving the great internal problems. During the long regency for his minor son, Charles XI, the influence of the nobles grew even more. Early in Charles XI's own reign, which began in 1672, he had to lead a bitter struggle against Denmark for the retention of the southern provinces. When peace was concluded in 1679, the king began a gigantic task of reorganization reminiscent of Gustavus Vasa's a century and a half earlier. This is customarily referred to as

King Charles X Gustavus

King Charles XI

Charles XI's reduction; that is, by vote of Parliament the nobles were "reduced" as the crown repossessed a large part of the estates they had obtained for themselves. At the end of this reorganization the property distribution was once more radically changed; the crown now held 35.6 percent of the soil, the nobles only 32.9 percent, and the independent farmers 31.5 percent. In accordance with a detailed plan, the king used the income from state properties to cover all expenses of the crown, such as military and civil service payrolls. An important by-product of the reorganization was that the status of the freeholders was restored and secured. The nobles retained their extensive privileges, but their rule was replaced by that of an absolute monarch.

A few years of peace quickened the economic life of the nation. Copper had declined in importance, but iron exports had increased, and wood tar also became a major item in the shipments abroad at the time. This peaceful period gave Charles XI an opportunity to carry out his sometimes harsh but generally beneficial reforms. They affected every phase of Swedish life: commerce, finances, defenses, legal procedures, the church, and education.

A note signed by King Charles XI on August 20, 1664

This painting of King Charles XII, 1697–1718, below, *provides the generally accepted image of the young warrior-king in his classical Carolinian uniform. The portrait reflects the ascetic simplicity that was typical of the king throughout his life, depicting him as remote and dignified, an autocratic monarch by the grace of God.*

King Charles XII

CHARLES XII

Nearly two decades of peace under Charles XI were followed by the last major war period in Sweden's history. Under Charles XI an absolute monarchy had developed, and the importance of the king's council and of the Parliament had begun to diminish. The autocracy was taken over by the young Charles XII, who has become a classic figure in the character gallery of world history as a man of his word and a spartan warrior-king.

The first task of Charles XII was to defend Sweden against a new encirclement from three directions.

A portrait of King Charles XII

Charles XII as he appeared in 1707

Charles XII hunting bear

Charles XII handing the quill to a hesitant recruit for his army

Queen Ulrica Eleonora

First meeting of King Charles XII of Sweden and Stanislaus I of Poland

Drottningholm Castle at Stockholm was built in the period 1662 to 1686 for Queen Hedvig Eleonora. In Swedish drottning *means "queen."*

Queen Eleonora's bedroom

Charles XII was killed in battle in Norway, struck in the head by a cannonball. He is shown here being borne back to Sweden by his personal officers.

The queen in later life

Russia, Poland-Saxony, and Denmark, after careful preparations, began an attack in the year 1700, and Sweden's situation seemed as difficult as it had been a hundred years earlier. In brilliant victories—the most famous in 1700 at Narva against Russian forces five times as great—Charles crossed the plans of the hostile coalition, eliminated Denmark, gave the czar a setback at Narva, pursued the Polish king Augustus through Poland, and forced the Peace of Altranstädt in 1706.

A bold expedition against Russia's heart in 1709 anticipated the trail of both Napoleon and Hitler; in each case the outcome was about the same. It led to Charles's defeat at Poltava, the capitulation of his army, and his

own flight to Turkey. There he was virtually interned for
years, during which he was partly successful in persuading the Turks to attack Russia. The home country held
out against the extended coalition which now included
Russia, Poland-Saxony, Denmark, Hanover-England,
and Prussia. In 1715 the king managed to return to
Sweden.

Charles pinned his hopes on the Anglo-Russian rivalry, but in the midst of complicated diplomatic maneuvers he was killed as he besieged the Norwegian fortress
of Fredriksten (near Fredrikshald) in 1718. Sweden then
had to conclude a series of peace treaties which left her
with few of her far-flung possessions, except most of
Finland and a couple of small holdings on the south
shore of the Baltic. Again Sweden's situation was completely changed.

ERA OF LIBERTY—
INTRODUCTION OF
PARLIAMENTARISM

A total but almost bloodless revolution to establish a new
constitution was the first internal move after the collapse. This document gave by far the greatest authority
to Parliament, whose wishes were carried out by the king
and his council. In the council the king had only two
votes.

The Era of Liberty, as the next fifty-three years are
called, has been severely criticized for its partisan
animosity and political befuddlement. But it has become
increasingly clear that this era was of great significance
in shaping the Swedish heritage of freedom. A real parliamentary system was gradually developed, which to be
sure labored under very heavy and cumbersome juridi-
cally formulated procedures. Nevertheless, it is of great
interest in many respects and a notable parallel to the
English system.

Two parties, the Hats and the Caps, came into being
and contended for political power. In their theories of
national economy the Hats were strictly mercantilistic.
Their foreign policy aimed at an alliance with France
whereby they hoped to regain the foreign possessions
recently lost; this led to badly prepared wars and correspondingly unfortunate outcomes.

The Caps were more restrained in respect to state
subsidies in the national economy, and their foreign policy strove for rapprochement with England and Russia.
Toward the end of the era the Caps also gathered into
their ranks the commoners in opposition to the prerogatives of the nobles.

Alternately in power—the Hats being at the helm
somewhat longer—the two parties developed far-reaching assumptions regarding the authority of Parliament.
"The idea that the Estates (of Parliament) may err is
contrary to the fundamental law of the realm" is a sam-

*Frederick of Hesse
(later to become Frederick I)*

Frederick I

*King Adolphus Frederick's
signature*

*Queen Louisa Ulrika,
wife of Adolphus Frederick*

ple of their claims; if the king refused to sign the council
decisions, it was not unheard of that a facsimile stamp
of the royal signature was used. During these years of
acrid party feuds, however, a truly significant political
development took place which proved of great importance to the subsequent evolution of the Swedish constitution. Considerable economic and cultural progress also
characterized the era. Land reforms came under discussion, there was an interest in the advancement of the
frontiers of science, and the Swedish press was born. Carl
von Linné (Linnaeus) created his botanical classification
system and Emanuel Swedenborg his unique philosophy
of religion.

Violent struggles over the prerogatives of the nobility flared up during the last years of the Era of Liberty. The foreign policy of the Hats had cost Sweden part of Finland. A certain weariness with the constant tug-of-war between the two parties was in evidence. All in all, a number of circumstances paved the way for a new coup d'état.

THE GUSTAVIAN PERIOD

Gustavus III, a nephew of Prussia's Frederick the Great, ascended the throne in 1771. The following year he placed himself at the head of the forces opposed to the status quo, and the ensuing revolution took place without bloodshed. A new constitution accorded the king greater power, but parliamentary opposition, especially on the part of the politically powerful nobility, was not to be downed. Consequently, in the midst of a provoked and ill-conducted war with Russia, Gustavus III put over a second coup which increased the royal prerogatives to such an extent that the next twenty years (1789–1809) are referred to as the Gustavian Absolutism. Gustavus III himself was assassinated three years later (1792) by a fanatic group of young noblemen in the opposition. A patron of literature and the arts, endowed with brilliant personal qualities, Gustavus III remains one of the most captivating and colorful figures in the whole succession of Swedish rulers. During his reign, literature and art flourished. Gustavus III founded the Swedish Academy after the French pattern and he wrote a large number of dramatic works himself.

This period brought certain important reforms, among them an equalization of civil rights and a fundamental land act, but the extenral events became predominant. Sweden was drawn into the struggle against Napoleon and soon found herself in an extremely precarious situation. In 1805 Gustavus IV Adolphus, son and heir of Gustavus III, had chosen to side with Britain in the contest for supremacy among the great powers. The king took this step with an eye to Britain's great importance for Sweden's foreign trade and stood firm in spite of Napoleon's overwhelming success. The outcome was something resembling a catastrophe.

In the Treaty of Tilsit (1807), Napoleon gave his new ally, Alexander I of Russia, a free hand to proceed against Sweden, hoping to force her into the camp of Britain's enemies. The aim was to make the Continental Blockade against Britain wholly effective. As Gustavus IV Adolphus remained loyal to his ally, Russia fell upon Finland, which was lost in her entirety (1809). Gustavus

King Gustavus III

Portrait of King Gustavus III painted to commemorate the coup d'etat of 1772

Gustavus III's Haga Pavilion, built for the king in 1787–90 by Olaf Tempelman and originally intended as a temporary residence during the construction of Desprez' much larger Haga Palace, which was never completed. (Photo: P. Jalkman)

Charles XIII, 1809–18

King Gustavus IV Adolphus

King Gustavus III receiving surgical aid after the attempt on his life in 1792. After two weeks the king died of his wounds.

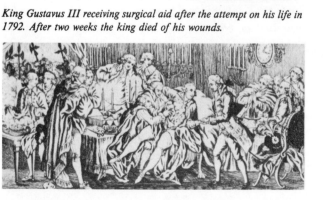

IV Adolphus's ability was by no means great enough to meet the crisis, and his temperament further emphasized the absolute nature of his office. In the eyes of the public officials, the military, and all liberty-professing citizens he became the scapegoat for the unhappy outcome and was removed in a new revolution (also in 1809), again without bloodshed. A new constitution was adopted, which in its fundamental features is still in effect, and the deposed king's uncle became ruler as Charles XIII.

CONSTITUTIONAL DEVELOPMENT

Since 1521 Sweden had undergone six major dynastic or constitutional readjustments, the last four without bloodshed. Within the same three hundred years she went through three sweeping changes of a social nature, for the most part peacefully. Gustavus Vasa's confiscation of church property and Charles XI's repossession of crown lands have already been traced; the third social change spanned the years 1719–1809 and may be described as a gradual and more equitable redistribution of rights and privileges.

What the French Revolution achieved by means of numerous violent upheavals came about undramatically but quite effectively in Sweden. For example, the farmers obtained the right to purchase clear title to crown lands. Commoners could own exempt land and were admitted even to high government posts previously held only by nobles. Several of these innovations were made by Gustavus III despite the fact that he, in principle, befriended the nobles. Some archaic elements remained in the constitution and the social structure, however, and the political struggles of the nineteenth century pivoted to a large extent around them.

In the Constitution of 1809 the attempt was made to profit from previous experience in achieving a balance among the various authorities: king, cabinet, Parliament, and government officials. The success of this attempt depended in part on the leaders involved.

Charles XIII was childless, and a successor had to be found outside the dynasty.

CHARLES XIV JOHN (1818–44)

In July of 1810 the French marshal Jean Baptiste Bernadotte was chosen in the midst of great enthusiasm by Parliament (Riksdag) to be crown prince of Sweden. Behind him Bernadotte had a brilliant career as a soldier and official in the France of Napoleon. In 1780, when Bernadotte was seventeen years of age, he enlisted as a soldier. Twelve years later he became an officer, and in 1794 general of a division. In 1804 he became marshal of France and alone commanded the forces in northern Germany. He became known for his humane treatment of occupied peoples. On returning to their native country, captured Swedish officers praised his civility.

Eventually Bernadotte came into serious conflict with

Coronation of Charles XIV John

Marshal Bernadotte. This engraving by P. M. Alix was shown to the Parliament in 1810 and contributed greatly to the choice of Bernadotte as successor to the throne.

the despotic emperor. He was in a very difficult situation at the time he was chosen as Swedish crown prince.

It was a difficult time for Sweden too. The country had just suffered a major defeat at the hands of Russia. In the peace, Finland had been torn from the realm and become a Russian grand duchy. The Swedes believed that Bernadotte enjoyed high favor with Napoleon and that, with French assistance, he would help them to revenge themselves upon Russia and regain Finland. Bernadotte chose a completely different path. He entered into an alliance with Russia and the other major European powers. He participated in the struggle against Napoleon and exploited the alliance to win compensation for Finland by conquering Norway from Denmark.

In 1818 the French marshal ascended the ancient throne of Sweden. As king he assumed the name of Charles XIV John. For a long time he experienced difficulty in adjusting to "the winterland." The marshal, who had spent most of his life in the open air, stayed indoors as king. He never learned to understand the Swedish language and was long suspicious of the people whom he ruled. He had reason for suspicion. How badly the Swedes had treated their rulers before he came to the country! Gustavus III had been shot, and his son Gustavus IV Adolphus had been driven into exile. The same year that he came to Sweden, the leading nobleman of the country, Count Axel von Fersen, had been beaten to death by a mob in the Old Town, while the troops stood at ease. Charles John was fearful of a new revolution.

Charles John had a need to be popular, but his fear of revolution and proclivity toward secret agents and intrigue repelled many. It is easy to understand his suspiciousness. He had grown up during the bloody French Revolution when the monarchy was overthrown. He had seen Napoleon's military dictatorship replaced by the Holy Alliance of the reaction and now heard the hammerstrokes of new popular movements. As quickly as the world was changing, he considered it better to be over-cautious than overtaken. He was without illusion about people.

Charles John could feel somewhat more secure after his first grandson was born in 1826 and the future of the dynasty was assured. The founder of the new dynasty showed his increasing self-assurance a year later when he gave the name Gustavus—a traditional name for Swedish kings—to the second son of the crown prince.

Charles John attempted to understand the Swedes by studying Swedish history diligently. The Caroline fulfillment of duty, the simplicity, and the moderation during the final phase of Sweden's era as a great power appealed to him. Finally he discovered a Swedish characteristic that he understood. He approved of such popular movements as the temperance movement, which he supported in every way, and he often aided poor, struggling young students.

Thus it was all the more tragic that despite all his splendid talents and his worldliness, he did not understand the new liberal movements in his time. During the final ten years of his life, he was to clash violently with both the Riksdag and the press. He saw sedition all about him. Opposition became, for him, synonymous with conspiracy. Yet he still had the ability to convince people by means of his charm and chivalry.

Though the relationship between Charles John and the Swedish people was not free from suspicions, it has been easier for later generations to understand the greatness in the kingly deeds of the first Bernadotte. By means of the union with Norway he reestablished the self-confidence of the country after the catastrophes in Finland. During his continued consistent peace policy he laid the foundation for a splendid development in the business and cultural life of the country. For the first time in centuries, Sweden's relations with Russia were stabilized by means of a friendship policy on the basis of equality.

THE POLITICAL DEVELOPMENT

At the conclusion of the Napoleonic wars Sweden, in common with other Nordic lands, was hard hit by the economic slump which lasted up to 1830 and which was characterized by stagnation and great economic difficulties, manifested by abortive attempts by the state to redress the value of the currency. After devaluation in 1834 the value of the currency was stabilized.

Charles XIV John pursued a strictly conservative policy. The king's power, invested in him by the constitution, was exploited to the limit, and the ministers were recruited from his courtiers and others dependent on royal favor without regard to the wishes of Parliament. In accordance with an amendment to the law on the freedom of the press implemented in 1812, the government had the right to censor newspapers without having first to institute legal proceedings. The amendment which was originally instituted to enable the government to guide public opinion when the country's foreign policy was altered, was still being exploited after 1815 by Charles John to control the growing opposition against his conservative policy. In the 1820s the liberal opposition raised steadily increasing demands for reforms, and 1830 was for Sweden, as for the rest of Europe, the year in which the liberal currents made a breakthrough. In Sweden this was indicated by, amongst other things, the establishment of a newspaper *Aftonbladet,* which with L. J. Hierta as editor became the leading organ of the liberal opposition. Simultaneously, the king's one-man rule, which was exercised through his powerful favorite Magnus Brahe, became even more pronounced. The struggle against the growing liberal opposition which reached its climax at the end of the 1830s was conducted on the one side by actions involving restrictions on freedom of the press and arrests for high treason, and on the other side by sharp criticism, demonstrations, and street riots.

The pressure of the opposition, however, at last forced the king to yield and the Parliament of 1840 in which the liberal opposition had the majority, forced through the so-called Departmental Reform, which meant in fact that the ministers actually became the heads of their own ministries, each responsible for his own definite part of the administration and not, as formerly, merely the king's advisers. The stronger position which the ministers had won was the first step toward a more parliamentary form of government. Another reform of great significance for the future was the introduction of compulsory school education in 1842.

OSCAR I (1844–59)

After the death of Charles John in 1844, his only son, Oscar I, ascended the throne. He had received a very careful Swedish upbringing. He was talented and possessed good comprehension of the affairs of the day.

King Charles XIV John, 1818–44

King Charles XIV John and his queen, Desiree

King Oscar I, 1844–59

King Oscar I of Norway and Sweden. The son of Charles XIV, he succeeded to the dual throne of Norway and Sweden.

King Oscar's queen, Josephine de Beauharnais, 1848

Aside from extensive artistic and literary talents, he had thorough insight into social problems. His general viewpoint was that of an occidental liberal, and he was highly interested in reforms. In a booklet entitled "On Punishment and Penal Laws," which he published anonymously in the 1830s, he urged the adoption of more just laws and more humane treatment of the prisoners.

The relationship between the liberal Oscar and his strictly conservative father had been strained. Charles John considered his son so liberal-minded that he would not permit him to attain any greater influence. Oscar's ascent to the throne was greeted with enthusiasm by the opposition. Oscar immediately selected a moderately liberal-minded government and accomplished a series of moderate reforms within the economic life, legislation, and education. The king himself played a major role in domestic politics. He made a thorough study of every question.

Despite his devotion to duty and conscientiousness,

Oscar never became as popular as Charles John. He lacked his father's charm. He was colorless and stood so firmly upon his royal dignity that he was unjustly considered stiff and lacking in temperament. The long period as heir apparent under a dominating father had repressed his own personality and robbed him of the ability to show spontaneity and enthusiasm.

Oscar wanted to be his own minister for foreign affairs. During the German-Danish War of 1848–49, he conducted a wise and cautious policy. His position was more criticized during the Crimean War, during which he was exposed to severe pressures from the western side to participate in the war against Russia. Like the liberals of the opposition, Oscar was anti-Russian, and dreamed of playing a leading role in the north by snatching Finland away from Russia. The peace in Paris came as a hard surprise for him, and the relations between Sweden and Russia were long cool.

The disappointments during the Crimean War contributed to the deterioration of the king's constitution. During the summer of 1857 he was forced to surrender the governmental power to his oldest son, Charles. For two long years he lay paralyzed. He was forgotten by his people, and died in the summer of 1859 shortly after reaching the age of sixty.

During his illness, Oscar was cared for by his self-sacrificing queen, Josephine, the daughter of Napoleon's stepson Eugène de Beauharnais. Josephine was both beautiful and wise, one of the most intellectual of the Swedish queens. Under very trying conditions, she maintained her Catholic faith in arch-Protestant Sweden. As time passed, she became generally appreciated for her great fortitude and her extensive charity work. In his marriage to Josephine, Oscar I had five children. Two of the sons—Charles and Oscar—were to ascend the throne.

When Charles XIV John died, he was succeeded by Oscar I, the liberal reform period which was characteristic of Sweden in the middle of the nineteenth century was already underway.

Amongst the most important of the reforms was the introduction in 1846 of free enterprise, which meant abolition of the guilds which had formerly held the monopoly of trade and industry. They were now replaced by free industrial and trade associations. Simultaneously, the monopoly of trade which the towns had held since the Middle Ages was also abolished. Finally a statute passed in 1864 established complete freedom of enterprise in trade and industry. The lifting of almost all bans on exports and imports in 1847 together with a reduction in customs duties were the first steps toward free trade, though it was the tariff charges of 1857 and the trade agreement with France in 1864 which caused the real breakthrough in free trade. A number of other liberal reforms were introduced: equal right of inheritance for men and women (1845); single women's rights (1858); a more humane penal code through a number of reforms (1855–64); religious freedom (1860); and local self-government (1862). Another step of importance for the future was the decision in 1854 that the state should be responsible for the building of mainline railways and that they should be run by the state.

Oscar I, who himself took the initiative in many of these reforms, became more conservative after the disturbances in Stockholm in the revolutionary year of 1848. By the time he was succeeded by his son Charles XV (1859–72) the substance of the power had gradually passed into the hands of the Privy Council who, under the leadership of the minister of finance, J. A. Gripenstedt, and the minister of justice, Louis de Geer, completed the process of reform.

From the beginning of the nineteenth century the most important of the liberal demands had been for a reform of the old form of representation. It was not until 1865–66, during Charles XV's reign, that agreement was reached on a proposal by Louis de Geer to replace the old Parliament with its four estates—nobility, clergy, burghers, and peasantry—with a Parliament consisting of two chambers with equal rights, the members of the first chosen by indirect vote and with such a high eligibility qualification that it bore the stamp of an upper chamber representing great landowners and magnates of commerce and industry, while the members of the second were chosen by direct vote, which was limited, however, by a property qualification and which therefore put the farmers in a strong position.

The reform of the representative system can be said to round off the liberal reform period (1840–66). During the following twenty years Swedish politics were dominated by two issues: the demand for an abolition of the land tax which had been levied from ancient times, and the defense question where the demand was for an abolition of the military system termed *indelningsverket,* that is, an army organization where the soldiers were given small holdings to live on. The defense system was to be modernized by, among other things, an increase in conscription. However, the First Chamber's demand for a rearmament of the armed forces was impossible to combine with the Second Chamber's demand for an abolition of the land tax. These issues had been linked together by the so-called Compromise of 1873 and it was not until 1892 that they were resolved, at which time it was decided to abolish the land tax and to replace the old army organization with a larger and better-trained National Service army. The latter reform was completed through the Defense Reform (1901), which introduced a purely conscriptive army with a call-up period of two hundred and forty days.

With the appearance of the Social Democrats in 1889, Liberals in 1900, and Conservatives in 1904 there came into being around the turn of the century the parties which today still dominate Swedish politics.

FROM ALLIANCE TO NEUTRALITY

Up to the end of the nineteenth century foreign policy was still regarded as the monarch's personal province. Already as crown prince, Charles John had concluded an alliance with Russia against an almost unanimous opposition, and by so doing, initiated the pro-Russian policy which was characteristic of the whole of his reign. Oscar I's succession to the throne in 1844 indicated no immediate alteration. The only deviation lay in his somewhat cautiously demonstrated sympathy for the growing Scandinavianism. When the German nationals rebelled against the Danish king in 1848, Oscar I aligned himself with Frederik VII and contributed, together with the czar, to a cease-fire and armistice.

During the negotiations on Scheswig-Holstein, Oscar I, still on the side of Czar Nicholas, ranged more or less against radical nationalism in Germany; but in reality he endeavored to extricate Sweden from the conservative pro-Russian line which Charles John had initiated in 1812. The opportunity came during the Crimean War when the conflict on Turkey and control of the Bosporus led to war between the western powers and Russia in 1853. From the beginning Oscar I adopted a friendly attitude to the western powers and, among other things, opened Swedish harbors to British and French warships. By articles in British and French newspapers Oscar I prepared the way for Sweden's entry in the war and with the promise of help from Swedish troops tried to induce the western powers to attack St. Petersburg. With this intention he signed a pact with the western powers in 1855, the so-called November Pact. However, the peace treaty which was concluded in Paris shortly afterward put an end to the hopes cherished in Sweden of winning Finalnd, or at least Åland back again. All that was gained was the Åland Convention which forbade Russia to build fortifications or have other installations of a military nature on Åland.

CHARLES XV (1859–72)

Scarcely any Swedish king has been so popular as was Oscar's son Charles XV. He was the first Bernadotte born in Sweden and had Swedish as his native language. With his stately appearance and natural manner, he won devotion wherever he went.

Charles XV was a practical individual. He was a man of action. He liked to drill soldiers and wanted to share their hardships during maneuvers. But the faults in Charles's character were serious and conspicuous to those close to him. He was impulsive and was easily swayed by the spirit of the moment. He lacked endurance and the inclination toward the dutiful, intellectual, everyday work.

King Charles XV, 1859–72

King Oscar II, 1872–1907

As far as domestic affairs were concerned, the reign of Charles XV was a period of major liberal reforms. Sweden acquired greater religious freedom, total freedom of trade, and a completely new form of popular representation with a bicameral Riksdag and municipal self-government. To the common man, the king appeared to be the driving force behind these reforms, and this further increased his popularity. Actually, most of the reforms were accomplished against his will. He himself had a generally conservative viewpoint.

As far as foreign policy was concerned, the king was still able to assert his personal authority, and here he attempted to have his revenge for failures on the domestic front. Nevertheless, he experienced his greatest defeat in this area. As a firm adherent of Scandinavianism he wanted to assist Denmark in its struggle over Schleswig on the German border. He hoped for a dynastic union, with himself as king of all three countries. On several occasions he promised liberal military aid to the Danes in case of a German attack upon Schleswig. His government advised caution, and when the Danish-German war broke out in 1864, they forced him to retreat. The treaty of alliance was disregarded for the time being, and only volunteers came from Sweden and Norway to the aid of Denmark.

Scandinavianism disintegrated; and the king, who lacked the strength of will to put up a fight, was highly compromised. At the same time he was at variance with his younger, pro-Danish brother, Oscar. After this failure, Charles withdrew more and more from the business of government. Due to his great love of France, he experienced the Franco-German War of 1870–71 as a great disappointment. He died in the fall of 1872.

OSCAR II (1872–1907)

When Oscar II in 1872 succeeded his brother Charles XV as the king of Sweden and Norway, he was little known and scarcely popular. He was considered to be haughty and to stand upon his dignity. No one who knew him, however, could deny his strong ambition and con-

siderable ability to accomplish the tasks entrusted to him.

Oscar was widely read and interested in many subjects. When he ascended the throne he was considered, with some justification, to be the most scholarly and enlightened monarch in Europe. He was the first of the Bernadottes to receive training with the Fleet. He wrote several books which illustrated his command of naval matters and also wrote poems about the fleet and the sea that were highly appreciated in his time.

His contemporaries often had difficulty in understanding the king's conscious effort to smooth out and reconcile opposites, to be in favor with everyone. The memoirs he started to write immediately after his ascent to the throne are, however, an excellent source of understanding of the king's political viewpoint and actions. They have, until now, been lying sealed in tin boxes in the Bernadotte family archive in the palace in Stockholm. The remarkable thing about these reminiscences is that they were written in stages, shortly after the events described.

When fifty years had passed after Oscar's death, Gustav VI Adolf in 1957 gave his permission that the memoirs could be published.

Oscar had great aspirations. He wished to reestablish the power of the monarchy as it had been exercised by his grandfather and father. He wished to be a modern king and had great ambitions of influencing the formation of public opinion and leading the people. He also had good qualifications: he was talented and receptive and possessed great charm and ability to adjust. Oscar wanted to arouse confidence and win approval, but he had difficulty in being appreciated by the common man. Queen Josephine is reported as having once said of her sons, "Oscar does everything to be popular, without success; whereas Charles does everything to injure his popularity, without success." Nevertheless he honestly meant well and possessed a strong sense of responsibility for the realm. In his memoirs he describes a conservative, monarchical program. He was a completely constitutional king but did not approve of parliamentarism, which he considered to be demoralizing to the executive power.

The king also had an eye for Norrland's growing economic and military importance. He took action personally and carried through the bill on the establishment of a fortress in Boden as a base of support for the country in the north. In 1897 Oscar could celebrate his 25-year jubilee as king of the union. During the same year a large exhibition was arranged in Stockholm, which testified to the growth of Swedish industry. Despite the fact that the king had by no means accomplished all that he himself had hoped for during the first years of his reign, he could, at any rate, look back upon his achievements with a certain quiet satisfaction.

Oscar II also took advantage of those opportunities offered him to act in matters of foreign policy. Only in the middle of the 1880s was the power of the monarchy forced to give way to that of the prime minister in that area as well. He was an active driving power in that change in foreign policy which, in the middle of the 1870s, resulted in a rapprochement with Germany. There were several reasons for this step. The German Empire was making strong progress economically and industrially, and it was therefore a sound economic policy for the young industrial country of Sweden to seek contacts to the south. In addition, there was concern for the defense situation. According to the opinion of the king and his advisers, Russia constituted a constant threat against the existence of Sweden and Norway, and in the German Empire they saw support against Russian aggression. Toward the end of his life, the king also exhibited a strong interest in England. He hoped for English support against Russia, and also had a feeling of monarchic solidarity with the king of England.

Despite his close cooperation with Germany, the king wished to maintain neutrality. The king was clearly conscious of the fact that the power of the monarchy was the unifying factor in the Swedish-Norwegian union. Preserving the union was also the central idea of his policy. Oscar was well educated for his task as king of the union. He spoke both Swedish and Norwegian and had a thorough knowledge of Norwegian economic and cultural conditions. He liked being in Norway.

The growing nationalism was the most dangerous enemy of the union: in Sweden it became conservative, in Norway radical. Oscar considered it his most important task to act as mediator between the conflicting parties. During his efforts to smooth out the differences, the king assumed a position—to use a rather pointed expression—to the left of the Swedish right and to the right of the Norwegian left, and thus lost support for his policy in both camps.

After the breach of the union in 1905, Oscar II was a broken man. He died two years later, both tragically misunderstood and himself unable to comprehend the course of events. He had a faithful adviser in his firm and wise queen Sophia of Nassau. She was affected by the strivings of the day toward peace. It was her cautions and propitiatory adivce that prevailed when the question of the union was finally solved.

Oscar II had four sons. The oldest of them, Gustavus, succeeded him on the throne. Oscar, who married a Swedish noblewoman, renounced his right to succession and other royal prerogatives. He adopted the title of Prince Bernadotte and devoted himself to extensive religious and welfare activity. Charles chose a military career. His greatest contribution was his forty-year chairmanship of the Swedish Red Cross. The youngest son, Eugene, devoted his life to painting and, as an interpreter of the Stockholm countryside, he became one of the most noted artists of his day. His extensive artistic patronage was centered in his home at Valdemarsudde, Djurgården.

THE SWEDISH-NORWEGIAN UNION

The union with Norway was a factor which played a central role in Swedish politics during the whole of the nineteenth century. Relations between Sweden and Norway during the period 1814–1905 were colored by re-

A sketch of Oscar II in later life in a sea setting that he loved so much

Gustavus V as he appeared when crown prince of Sweden and Norway

peated and progressively sharper conflicts. From the very advent of the union there was dissension due, as later, to conflicting interpretations of Sweden's and Norway's joint position in the union: on the one hand Sweden attempted to assert her hegemony, strengthen the bands of the union and in the end accomplish a coalescence of the two peoples, while Norway, on the other hand, demanded equality of status with Sweden and a completely independent position in the union.

From the Swedish viewpoint the union with Norway was a disappointment. Instead of a coalescence of the two countries as hoped for, the incompatibilities grew and the union remained a personal union, on the whole confined to a joint monarchy and foreign policy. One of the few positive results of the union was the statute of 1825 which abolished or greatly reduced customs duties between the countries. The union question furthermore had an important influence on Sweden's domestic affairs; Norway served as a model for the Swedish radicals who demanded parliamentarism and increased democracy. Thus the government exploited the conflict on the governor-general question to strengthen its position against the king and the demand for control by Parliament over the government was further strengthened when parliamentarism won its decisive victory in Norway in 1884.

As the union king usually resided in Sweden, he was represented in Norway by a governor-general. When Charles XV as crown prince was viceroy in Norway, he had promised the Norwegians that on his succession to the throne he would abolish the governor-generalship, which in Norway was regarded as a sign of the country's subordinate position in the union. This was a relatively unimportant issue, as the governor generalship had not been occupied by a Swede since 1829 and had in fact been vacant since 1855. However, when Charles XV succeeded to the throne and in accordance with his pledge tried to sanction in his Norwegian government the Norwegian Parliament's resolution to abolish the post, the Swedish Parliament together with the government headed by the powerful minister of finance, J. A. Gripenstedt, opposed the resolution. Their argument was that the issue concerned a union provision and could not, therefore, be decided by the Norwegian government alone but required a decision in a joint council of ministers. When the Norwegians declined to accept this view, the Swedish government threatened to resign and won strong support in Parliament. The king was forced to give way and withdraw his support for the abolition of the post. From a Swedish point of view this implied that the government, with support from Parliament, had strengthened its position against the king. The governor-general question, one might say, was the beginning of the tug-of-war for power between the king and Parliament which was characteristic of Sweden's internal political history during the latter part of the nineteenth century.

One of the problems raised by the king's interference in the governor-general question (which was not resolved until 1873 at which time Sweden had yielded to the most essential of Norway's demands) was that in Norway the king was regarded as purely Swedish and his right to nominate the government in Norway was considered a danger to the country's autonomy. The conflict revolved around the question of the Parliament's confidence in the government. Matters came to a head during the reign of Oscar II when a conservative government in Norway refused to pass a bill which Parliament had three times accepted. After a trial before the Court of Impeachment (riksretten) the government was forced to resign in 1844. Parliament and not the king had herewith acquired the decisive influence on the government, and Norway became the first country in Scandinavia to be governed by parliamentary means.

Although Norway had won full self-government on the domestic front, the union was represented externally by the Swedish-Norwegian king and the country's foreign policy was conducted by the Swedish foreign minister. From the 1880s, therefore, there was an increasing demand for an independent Norwegian foreign minister. In 1891 the left won an impressive majority at the polls with the foreign minister question, amongst other things, on its program. In spite of this, the left government headed by Johannes Steen, which the king had had to appoint in Norway after the election, did not take the question up but put forward instead the rather more limited demand for a Norwegian consular service. Even this, however, was flatly refused in 1892 by the Swedes. When Parliament subsequently attempted to carry out this reform independently, they were forced under threat of military action to negotiate with Sweden on a revision of the whole question of the union. Although Sweden soon indicated her desire to be most compliant, the incompatibilities had become so marked that there was no real chance of a compromise. On the collapse of the negotiations in 1898 when Norway at the same time demonstrated her independence by, inter alia, abolishing the so-called union emblem on her merchant flag—and this in spite of the king's veto—new negotiations were opened in an attempt to solve the more limited problem of an independent consular service. When even these negotiations did not lead to any result, Norway took the matter into her own hands, and a decision was taken in Parliament to pass a bill establishing Norway's own consular service. When the king refused to sanction the bill, the Norwegian government resigned, and the Norwegian Parliament declared on June 7, 1905, "the Union with Sweden dissolved as a result of the King ceasing to function as Norwegian King."

The Swedish Parliament refused, in the meantime, to accept this unilateral Norwegian decision. Under threat of military action and the partial mobilization of both countries, Norway was forced to give way and enter into negotiations with Sweden on conditions for the dissolution of the union. In Karlstad in September 1905, a settlement was reached which embodied concessions from both sides. The Swedish-Norwegian union was herewith legally dissolved.

GUSTAVUS V (1907–50)

During the final years of King Oscar's life, Gustavus was his best assistant and adviser in political questions. At the time of the dissolution of the union in the summer of 1905, the crown prince proposed a radical line of action. When all roads were closed for continued union, he considered that Sweden should take the initiative for an amicable separation.

He lacked the Bernadotte vivacity. He was shy, reserved and reflective. A trip to England, which he made in 1879, meant a great deal for the spiritual development of the twenty-year-old. At the same time that the English appreciated his innate sense of tact and his simple and natural manner, he drank in strong impressions of the country. He freed himself from the influence of his mother, and became self-assured and independent. He devoted himself to the ideal of the English gentleman, which he himself later was to embody during his many travels abroad as the tennis-playing "Mr. G.," and sharpened his awareness of international relationships.

In 1907 Gustavus V ascended the Swedish throne. His first decade as king was stormy. The forces of parliamentarism were advancing, and Gustavus, who adhered to the old balance of power between king and Riksdag, came into conflict with them. The struggle developed especially over the requirements of the armed forces. Whereas the king wished to build up defenses, the forces of the left, with Liberal leader Karl Staaf at the helm, demanded general suffrage and social reforms.

The conflict increased due to the fact that the king listened all too much to his queen, the strong-willed Victoria of Baden. As a child of the Germany of William, she believed in the power of the monarchy and detested parliamentarism. She considered every concession to its forces to be treachery. In the political activity of the queen were certain elements of fanaticism and hysteria, and during World War I it appeared that she felt more like a German princess than the Swedish queen. She lacked adaptability and an understanding of psychology, but it cannot be denied that she fought for her outdated, traditionalistic principles with great consistency and loyalty.

The domestic tension within the country became an open breach in February 1914—a few months before the outbreak of World War I. It occurred when a farmers' demonstration to the king, consisting of thirty thousand participants, marched to the courtyard of the palace in Stockholm. In his acknowledgment the king said that he intended to support immediate accomplishment of the military armament program which his Liberal government only wished to carry out in stages. The speech brought about a political crisis. The Staaff government resigned, whereupon Province Governor Hjalmar Hammarskjöld, father of Dag Hammarskjöld, was called upon to form a new government. The outbreak of the war could be seen as a confirmation of the fact that a defense reform was necessary.

During the final years of the war the king worked intensely for common Nordic neutrality, which was evident in the meetings of the three Scandinavian monarchs. In his speech at the meeting of the monarchs in Kristiana in November of 1917, he did away with the remaining distrust between Sweden and Norway. After the end of the war, he continued this policy of Nordic unity, which had its main expression in the declaration of neutrality issued jointly by the heads of state of the four Nordic countries at their meeting in Stockholm in October of 1939 after the outbreak of World War II.

Great changes in Swedish domestic policy came about in 1918. The fall of the German and Austrian dynasties also caused repercussions in Sweden, where the risk of a revolution appeared imminent. A government of Liber-

Gustavus V became king of Sweden in 1907

King Gustavus V in World War II

als and Social Democrats presented a proposal on universal suffrage. The proposal, however, was met by strong Conservative opposition in the Upper Chamber. Then the king and the crown prince intervened to support the government and succeeded in breaking down the opposition, after which a solution could be reached on good terms. In the future, as well, the king complied with public opinion, and cooperated very well with radical politicians. The relationship between him and the Social Democratic prime ministers Hjalmar Branting and Per Albin Hansson was congenial.

The king followed questions of foreign policy and defense with special interest. With his long experience and unerring sense of tact, he could act as a wise and knowledgeable "adviser to his advisers" on these matters. During World War II he undertook several personal actions to clarify Sweden's position and resources.

During the long reign of Gustavus V—without doubt the longest in the history of Sweden—the opposition between "power of the monarchy" and "power of the people" was wiped out. The king became the first citizen of a parliament-governed land. At the time of his death in 1950, he had long been an institution in political life.

Queen Victoria died in 1930. After World War I, when all she had hoped for crumbled to dust, she devoted herself mainly to social aid work. King Gustavus and Queen Victoria had three sons: Gustavus Adolf, who succeeded his father on the throne; William, who devoted himself to an extensive authorship; and Erik, who died young.

THE ROAD TO PARLIAMENTARISM AND DEMOCRACY

In the nineteenth century Sweden was a poor country in which about eighty percent of the population still earned their living from agriculture, and which together with Ireland and Norway had proportionally the largest number of emigrants among the European countries. Swedish industry did not expand to any great extent until late in the 1890s and around the turn of the century. A prerequisite for the quick industrialization which followed was the great influx of capital. Up to World War I Swedish railways and Swedish industry were largely built with the support of foreign capital.

The turning point in Swedish economy came during and immediately after World War I. Sweden suddenly became a rich country. There was a worldwide demand for Swedish commodities such as steel and pulp, matches and ball bearings, Aga light-houses and separators, telephones and vacuum cleaners. The economic progress which started in the first decades of this century laid the foundations for internal developments in Sweden during the twentieth century. Industrialization led to a rapid growth in the numbers of factory workers and the towns grew correspondingly. The composition of the population underwent a decisive change; Sweden was transformed from an agricultural country into an industrial society of the most modern kind where more than 50 percent of the inhabitants lived in urban areas.

The political consequences of the economic development were that around the turn of the century there was greatly increased pressure for a universal and equal franchise. No sooner had the union question been settled in 1905, than the dominating question in Swedish politics became the demand for universal and equal suffrage. The issue was solved by a compromise submitted by a Conservative government under the leadership of Arvid Lindman. The motion embraced universal and equal franchise to the Second Chamber, a certain democratization of the First Chamber, and proportional representation to both chambers of Parliament. The reform was implemented by a parliamentary motion in 1909. The election to the Second Chamber in 1911, on which occasion the new provisions where adapted for the first time, was a landslide for the Liberal party and as Lindman, in view of this, resigned, Gustavus V (1907–50) was forced to request Karl Staaff to form a Liberal government. Although the king hereby acted in accordance with the rules of parliamentarism, he had by no means accepted parliamentarism, and still regarded the members of the government as the representatives of the king and not of Parliament.

On the outbreak of war, Sweden issued a declaration of neutrality. The neutral policy which the country carried out under the leadership of Hammarskjöld was, however, doctrinaire which meant, inter alia, that Sweden attempted to assert her right to trade freely with the belligerent countries. As the blockade was used by Britain as an important weapon in the war, Sweden's insistence on free trade favored Germany exclusively. The result was that the Allies intensified their control and stopped a major part of Sweden's trade. This, however, not only hit Sweden's exports to Germany but from 1916 caused a severe shortage of supplies and strict rationing. The situation, which was further exacerbated by unrestricted submarine warfare and America's entry into the war in 1917, gave rise to intense dissatisfaction in the country and Hammarskjöld and his government were forced to resign in 1917. A new foreign policy was thereafter introduced and in May 1918 an agreement was reached with Britain and the United States which allowed Sweden again to import products from the west on condition that she limited her exports to Germany and placed a major share of her merchant fleet at the disposal of the Allies.

In the general elections of 1917 the left-wing parties, that is, the Social Democrats and Liberals, gained a victory which further increased their majority in the Second Chamber of Parliament. As a consequence of the defeat the Conservative government resigned; up to this time they had held office with the support of the king and the Conservative majority in the First Chamber. Now the king was obliged to designate a government based upon a majority of the Second Camber. With the Liberal–Social Democratic government of Nils Edén, parliamentarism had obtained definite recognition in Sweden.

One of the first measures of the new government was to propose a constitutional amendment. The main issues were female suffrage and the abolition of the forty-degree scale in local elections, meaning the introduction of a universal and equal franchise which would also cover election to the First Chamber. As expected, the Conservative majority in the First Chamber rejected the bill. However, when the government in November 1918—under the pressure caused by the news of Germany's defeat and the consequent clamorous demands from the workers for democracy and with the republic—reintroducing the bill which now embodied measures designed to democratize the Second Chamber still further, then the First Chamber was forced to acquiesce. The Constitutional Reform which was carried through between 1918 and 1920 signified the introduction of democracy in Sweden.

FROM MINORITY PARLIAMENTARISM TO MAJORITY RULE

It was the demand for parliamentarism and for the introduction of democracy that had above all constituted the basis for cooperation between the Liberal and the Social Democratic parties. When these demands had been realized, the two parties went their separate ways. Led by a young and radical phalanx within the party, the Social Democrats now demanded nationalization of the natural resources of the country and socialization of the means of production, or that they should at least be placed under the control of society. Confronted by these demands, the Liberal party defended private property and free enterprise. Up to 1918 the great dividing line in Swedish politics was drawn between the right and the left, between those who wanted to retain a class society and those who demanded democracy and equal rights for all citizens. From 1920 onward the main line was drawn between the Socialist parties on one side and the Liberals and Conservatives on the other. This grouping has remained in being since 1920.

The regrouping of the parties in Swedish politics did not produce new, fixed combinations. The break between the Social Democrats and the Liberals meant that the basis of Edén's left-wing government was gone. But the regrouping did not bring about a union of the right-wing parties, that is of the Conservatives, the Liberals, and a growing group representing agricultural interests who

had formed their own party, *Bondeförbundet,* "the Farmers' party." It was only in their opposition to the move toward socialization that these three right-wing parties were really united. On most other questions they disagreed in one way or other. Consequently there was no basis for any long-term cooperation between the parties. As a result it was impossible to form a majority government and thus, paradoxically enough, one of the consequences of the recognition of parliamentarism and the breakthrough of democracy in Sweden was that it became almost impossible to create in Parliament any firm basis for a government. In the years from 1920 to 1932 the parties held power alternately, but no government—whether Social Democratic, Liberal, or Conservative—had any chance of gaining firm support for its policy in Parliament. It became impossible for any one party to carry through its individual policy. From a political point of view the 1920s were a period of stagnation.

From an economic point of view, however, the picture was quite different. Once the depression that followed the war had been overcome, the 1920s were marked by steadily improving trade conditions, and in this period Sweden was one of the countries that prospered exceedingly from the boom. Swedish timber products and pulp, steel, and manufactured goods were exported and sold all over the world.

Like the rest of the western European countries, Sweden suffered severely during the depression in the early 1930s. Unemployment rose, and simultaneously reductions in wages caused a series of harsh labor conflicts. This was the state of affairs when the Swedish people went to the polls in the autumn of 1932. The result was a considerable advance for the Social Democratic party and to some extent for the Farmers' party as well. Even so, the Social Democrats did not obtain a majority in Parliament. The election did lead, however, to the resignation of the Liberal government, which was replaced by a Social Democratic administration under the leadership of Per Albin Hansson.

The steps taken by the Social Democrats to fight the crisis in Sweden were built on the theory of an active market policy, an idea which was later theoretically worked out by J. M. Keynes. The most important point on the Swedish program was the starting of great public works, where the wages were to be the same as in the rest of the labor market and which, for the most part, were to be financed by state loans. Alone, the Social Democrats had little chance of carrying through this program, which was received with scathing criticism by the right-wing parties. It was under these circumstances, and after the program had been amended with various moves in support of agriculture, that an agreement was reached with the Farmers' party in 1933, enabling the program to be realized.

The economic crisis of the 1930s was overcome in

Sweden more rapidly than in most other countries. As early as 1936 wages had reached the same level as before the crisis and by the end of the decade unemployment had become insignificant. Business was characterized by steadily improving trade conditions. Swedish industry once again enjoyed a period of rapid expansion.

From a political point of view the 1930s were in fact a time of preparation. A series of bills for radical reforms were worked out in that decade covering many fields: fiscal policy, old-age pensions, social services, medical care, education, and so on. All these reform bills aimed at a leveling of class divisions, at a higher degree of social security for all citizens; and at equal opportunities for everyone. The whole program could be summarized in the term *folkhemmet,* society viewed as a home for the people, taking care of their needs in unemployment, sickness, and old age. From an ideological point of view this program meant that the idea of nationalization had been weakened and even abandoned. The main interest was shifting toward a policy of social welfare which, while it would certainly give the state a considerable increase in influence, did not necessarily mean that the state had to nationalize the means of production to achieve it.

But during the 1930s themselves, only a few rather moderate reforms were realized. When the war came in 1939, it placed a great economic strain even on a neutral country like Sweden and consequently the reforms had to be postponed. The first consideration was to secure the country's defenses and, when trade with the western world was cut off after April 9, 1940, to deal with economic questions connected with the provision of food and other essential raw materials. From the domestic point of view the most important change during the war was the increase of power given to the state: it was found necessary to demand not only rationing but also detailed planning of the use of the resources of the country. Strict regulations were therefore introduced immediately after the outbreak of war. By this means the government obtained practically complete control over business and industry. The planned economy which had been the desideratum of the Social Democrats during the 1930s was carried through during the war as a matter of necessity and with the support of all parties.

NEUTRALITY AND SOLIDARITY

The two factors which above all others dominated Sweden's foreign policy during both the interwar years and the Second World War were, the Soviet Union's attempt to gain a stronger position in the Baltic area, and the threat from Germany in the south.

When the First World War ended, both Russia and Germany belonged to the conquered nations and for a period remained greatly weakened. Sweden's security during the 1920s, therefore, was unusually sound and in 1925 a new defense agreement was reached which em-

bodied a drastic reduction in the country's defenses. External affairs during the 1920s were confined partly to Sweden's application for membership to the newly formed League of Nations, which was granted in 1920, and partly the country's relationship with Finland.

The news of Finland's Declaration of Independence on December 6, 1917, was received with pleasure in Sweden. During the civil war which broke out shortly afterward in Finland an active right-wing group in Sweden desired Swedish intervention on the White government's side, while the majority within the right-wing parties would have been satisfied with support in the form of armaments and so forth. Within the left wing the Social Democrats viewed the civil war as a class struggle in which their sympathies lay with the Reds and where Sweden ought to follow a strict policy of nonintervention. Although the Liberals had greater sympathy with the White government, they were forced by the Social Democrats to conduct a neutral policy.

When the civil war ended the question of Åland became acute. The inhabitants of the Åland islands were purely Swedish speaking, had from ancient times an affinity with Sweden, and had on many occasions expressed a desire for affiliation with Sweden. In November 1918 application was made to the victorious powers to consider these wishes at the approaching peace negotiations. When the question was not dealt with at Versailles it was referred to the League of Nations. In spite of a plebiscite that revealed an almost unanimous desire from the population of Åland for affiliation with Sweden, the League of Nations decided in 1921 to award Finland the sovereignty of the islands, certain conditions being attached, however, pertaining to internal self-government and limiting the right to fortify or otherwise utilize the islands for military purposes. The decision aroused bitterness in Sweden and for a short period was the cause of friction between the two countries.

When Hitler came to power and Germany commenced rearmament Sweden's security deteriorated. This led to a reexamination of defense policy, and in 1936 a new defense ordinance was implemented which resulted in a strengthening of the country's defense. Concerning foreign policy, Sweden followed a strictly neutral course in close collaboration with the other Scandinavian countries plus Holland, Belgium, and Switzerland. Consequently Hitler's proposal of a nonaggression pact in the spring of 1939 was rejected. The feelers put out by Sweden at this time for a Nordic defense union or, when that could not be realized, Swedish-Finnish collaboration on defense came to nothing, due mainly to the objections raised by the Soviet Union.

THE SECOND WORLD WAR

During the Second World War Sweden was placed in a difficult and delicate position. Already in the years immediately preceding the outbreak of war the friction between Germany and the Soviet Union in the Baltic area had proved an insuperable obstacle to the Swedish plans for a Nordic-oriented security policy.

When the war came in September 1939, Sweden in concurrence with the other northern countries issued a declaration of neutrality which was put to the test almost immediately during the Finno-Russian war in the winter of 1939–40. A strong political popular movement in favor of Finland's cause then made itself felt but did not result in any official participation in the conflict. On the other hand, a number of volunteers joined the Finnish forces, and Sweden placed extensive material aid at Finland's disposal. When later the Allies, primarily Britain, wished to send troops through Sweden to aid Finland (March 1940), the request was refused. This was motivated by the government's desire to avoid having the country drawn into the conflict between the Great Powers. Toward the end of the "winter war" Sweden undertook the role of mediator between the two belligerents.

Close on the heels of the Finno-Russian armistice came the German occupation of Denmark and the attack on Norway (April 9, 1940). German plans to attack Sweden as well were known to exist; Sweden's rearmament was not completed and her strategic situation was extremely difficult. It became a serious problem to resist the German demands for permission to send military transports over Swedish territory against the defenders of Norway. Such demands were repeatedly turned down in April and May 1940, and only Red Cross transports to northern Norway were permitted. But in June, "when the hostilities in Norway had ceased," the government felt constrained to permit transit of military equipment and personnel on leave between Norway and Germany via Sweden. Both the government and the High Command were convinced at the time that a hopeless war with Germany would be unavoidable if the demands were refused. In many quarters the reaction of public opinion was very strong. A popular movement on behalf of Norway's cause gathered numerous supporters in the months that followed.

The government was forced to make one more major concession. In connection with the German attack on Russia in June 1941, the transfer of a German division from Norway to Finland over Swedish territory was permitted. Further requests of that nature were refused.

The Swedish people had to realize that they were living on an almost entirely isolated and threatened, but still independent isle in the north European sphere of German conquest. It was a year of poor harvests and only with great difficulty was it possible to tide the nation over the shortages, as extensive rationing was put into effect and a speedy conversion of the industries undertaken. Ships given safe conduct by both belligerent sides maintained some contact with the outside world, and a certain amount of trade was carried on with Germany.

On April 9, 1940, about one-half of the Swedish merchant marine was in foreign waters outside the German blockade; this tonnage was chartered to Britain and the United States.

An intensive debate on foreign policy was conducted during this period by both the Swedish press and the general public. Frequently the question was whether the concessions made to the peremptory requests of the Germans had been necessary and whether still more refusals could have been risked, for many of their demands had been firmly declined time and again. These discussions repeatedly led to a stream of coarse invective heaped upon Sweden by the Nazi press.

During the final stages of the war Sweden became increasingly active in humanitarian work. Much had, of course, been done since the outbreak of hostilities; thus in 1939–40 during the "winter war" many Finnish children were received and cared for in Swedish homes. When the Germans attacked Norway, a stream of refugees began to flow into Sweden and finally totaled about fifty thousand.

When the Nazi persecution of Danish Jews began, approximately seventy-five hundred found asylum in Sweden. Large numbers of refugees from the Baltic countries to the east were also admitted during the war years. King Gustavus V addressed a profound personal plea to the Nazi "government" in Budapest, asking for and obtaining humane treatment of the Hungarian Jews. After long and intricate negotiations with the Germans it became possible to extend further aid in an unexpected manner. Count Folke Bernadotte, a nephew of the king, organized in the spring of 1945 the removal of the Danes and Norwegians—and later prisoners of other nationalities—from the German concentration camps and their transportation to Sweden.

THE WELFARE STATE

Toward the end of the war expectations ran high within the Social Democratic party; their hopes seemed about to be realized as the chances of a Socialist success were undeniably good. Since the election in 1940 the Social Democratic party had had an absolute majority in both chambers of Parliament. The increase of governmental power and the planned economy that had been introduced during the war had made it possible to control business and industry to a far greater extent than ever before. Finally, after long discussions, the great reform bills worked out by the planners during the 1930s were now ready to be carried out.

The coalition government with representatives of the four democratic parties which was formed in 1939 was replaced shortly after the end of the war in 1945 by a purely Social Democratic government under the leadership of Per Albin Hansson. After his death in 1946 Tage Erlander became prime minister, a post which he held continuously until his resignation in 1969 from the chairmanship of the Social Democratic party and therewith also as prime minister. He was succeeded by Olof Palme who took over the leadership of the government without any other changes being made in its composition.

The period 1946–50 may justly be called the Great Period of Reform during which new comprehensive laws were adopted: on old-age pensions, child allowances, health insurance, rent allowances, educational reforms, and the expansion of universities and other institutions of higher education and research. The welfare society planned in the 1930s has thus largely been realized. Those parts of the Social Democrats' postwar program that aimed at the nationalization of certain branches of industry were not, however, carried through. In this respect the Social Democratic government contented itself with preserving a good deal of the control over manufacturing and service industries which had been obtained during the war. By redistributing taxation they tried at the same time to achieve an economic leveling. Political discussion centered more and more on these two items. Thus the Conservative opposition demanded the abolition of economic regulations and attacked such items as rent and housing control. The income tax policy was, however, the subject of the most vehement debate. The great social reforms, especially the sharp rise in old-age pensions and the introduction of child allowances, were very costly. In order that the rise in taxes necessary for the reforms should not fall upon low incomes, a new steeply graduated scale of taxation was introduced in 1947. The result was tax relief for low incomes and an increase in taxation on middle and high incomes.

What characterizes the early fifties is the absence of proposals for important reforms. There was good reason for this pause. It was not only the rise in old-age pensions and child allowances that were expensive for the state. There was the introduction of a general heatlh insurance, which required an increase in medical resources; educational reform similarly required a radical enlargement of

King Gustavus VI Adolph with his queen Louise walking among the villagers of Sweden as was their habit (1953)

The late king of Sweden, Gustavus VI Adolf, had a profound knowledge of archaeology. To relax from his royal duties he traveled to Italy every autumn to spend his vacation doing research. In this photo from 1957, we see His late Majesty busily unearthing Etruscan relics at San Giovendale, north of Rome.

the educational system, including universities and colleges. Certainly all these reforms had been decided on in the forties but they were not effected until the early fifties. This automatically meant greatly increased public expenditure as the economic consequences of the reforms made themselves felt. All available resources were exploited to create the material basis of the reforms, housing for old-age pensioners, doctors and hospitals, teachers and schools. In these circumstances any new initiatives were severely limited. In addition to this, the favorable trade conditions changed for the worse in the early 1950s.

GUSTAVUS VI ADOLF (1950–73)

Gustavus VI Adolf became king in 1950 when he was 67, an age when ordinary Swedes begin to collect their pension benefits. Even so he was firmly resolved to perform the important tasks required of a Swedish monarch. The motto he chose for his reign was "Duty above all." He was also exceptionally well qualified: he knew his country and his people through countless journeys, his inquiring mind was legendary, and he had a memory that seldom failed.

Gustavus VI Adolf was to stand out as an ideal king for a modern nation. He came very close to his people. A combination of amiability and natural dignity made him highly popular among broad sections of the community. He made brilliant contributions to the humanities as an archaeologist, a collector of Chinese pottery and

King Gustavus VI Adolf

porcelain, and connoisseur of fine art. For many summers he would go abroad to excavate on his own, mainly in Greece and Italy. With the donations collected by the Swedish people for his seventieth and eightieth birthdays, a fund for Swedish culture was formed called the Royal Foundation which acquired great importance for Swedish cultural activities.

Gustavus VI Adolf died in 1973 in Helsingborg. When the coffin was taken to Stockholm about three hundred and seventy five miles away, hundreds of thousands of people stood along the roadside to pay tribute to their beloved monarch.

Since the death of Crown Prince Gustavus Adolf in an air accident in 1947, and due to a series of marriages of the princes to commoners, the Bernadotte Dynasty dwindled. The succession now rested upon the grandson of Gustavus VI Adolf, King Carl XVI Gustaf.

PROBLEMS BEGIN IN FIFTIES

Contrary to what had been expected, the years after World War II had been marked by stable trading conditions. Among other things this meant scarcity of labor. During the Korean War in 1950–51 the boom reached its climax, with steeply rising prices and a violent inflationary tendency. In reaction to this a recession came at the end of 1951. In Sweden this meant that the movement upward of prices and incomes was interrupted, and for the first time since the war there was a rise in unemployment. Even though the crisis of 1951–52 cannot be said to have been a serious or long one, it drew attention to the problem of economic stability. The policy of the Social Democrats came now to concentrate primarily on the task of securing the advances already achieved. To reach this goal they strated a new collaboration with the Farmers' party. In the autumn of 1951 the purely Social Democratic government was replaced by a coalition government consisting of Social Democrats and Farmers. It was not until 1957—when the Social Democrats effected an important new reform in the matter of workers' pensions—that the collaboration with the Farmers' party collapsed.

The background to the demand for the reform which was then proposed was that at that time there was still a striking discrepancy between the economic situation of manual workers and that of public servants and officials. The discrepancy lay in the provision of retirement pensions. Whereas the worker at pensionable age had only the ordinary old-age pension, the public servant or person in a similar situation had, in addition, his pension as a public servant, which normally amounted to two-thirds of his previous income. The general old-age pension which despite all rises did not amount to more than SKr 1,500–2,000 a year at this date, only sufficed for the most elementary living expenses. The pension was, as it has been said, too small to retire on and too big to expire on.

The quick rise in workers' wages in Sweden after the war made the difference very considerable between a worker's normal income—in industry about SKr 12,-000–15,000 a year—and the old-age pension of only a little more than a tenth of this amount. The demand for an obligatory pension for all employees was vigorously made by the Social Democratic party.

In the later part of the 1950s the question of this pension became predominant in Swedish politics. The main reason the opposition so energetically opposed an obligatory pension for all citizens was the enormous pension fund that would be necessary. In Conservative and Liberal quarters it was thought that in the power over economic life which control over this fund would give, there was a latent risk of socialization. The government had to fight hard before it succeeded in carrying the bill through.

First a referendum was taken. The Social Democrats' bill introducing an obligatory pension received, however, only 46 percent of the votes, while the other parties were divided and received 15 percent and 35 percent respectively. When subsequently the government proposed the bill in Parliament, it was rejected by the majority which the 1956 election had given the other parties in the Second Chamber. Under the circumstances the government dissolved the Second Chamber, but in the following election they won only enough seats to produce a balance of 115 on the Labor side against 115 on the right-wing side. At a dramatic second ballot in the new chamber the government's bill was passed by a majority of one vote as a result of the abstention of one of the Liberal members. In this way the great obligatory pension reform was decided and carried through.

After the decision had been taken the reform was soon accepted by all parties, and the fact that it could be successfully carried out in practice further contributed to strengthen the Social Democratic party's position in Swedish politics.

By 1960 the fluctuating trade conditions of the 1950s had again been replaced by more stable conditions. The increase in the economic resources of society has, however, been used primarily for making good, and in certain cases improving, the actual value of old-age pensions, child allowances, health insurance, and other social benefits whose purchasing power was reduced by the rise in prices since the fifties. But at the same time problems other than the social ones have begun to attract attention.

PRESENT-DAY SWEDEN

The Swedish Constitution of 1809 together with the statute of 1866 was by the middle of the 1950s completely obsolete, and a regular practice had developed alongside the provisions of the constitution which in many instances reduced the latter to a mere formality. To comply with the demand for a modernization of the constitution, a Committee of Enquiry was appointed in 1955. The most important result of its work to date has been the replacement in 1970 of the old two-chamber Parliament by a one-chamber Parliament comprising three hundred and fifty members elected by proportional representation, mathematical justice being achieved by means of supplementary seats—forty in all—while the number of parties is restricted by the rule whereby any one party must obtain 4 percent of the votes cast in order to be represented at all. In the election of 1970, which was the first to be held under the new system, the Social Democrats lost the absolute majority which they had held since 1968 but control, together with the Communists, the majority in the new Parliament.

Sweden's foreign policy since 1945 has been strictly neutral. When the international situation became acute in 1948 after the coup in Czechoslovakia and during the Berlin blockade, the Swedish government took the initiative in negotiations on a defensive alliance between Sweden, Norway, and Denmark. However, when Sweden insisted that the alliance should be not merely nominal, but factual and independent of the Great Powers, while Norway desired cooperation with the Western Powers, the negotiations fell through. When Denmark and Norway at this time accepted the invitation to join NATO while Sweden declined to join, Sweden stood alone as the only alliance-free state in the North.

Neutrality and freedom from alliance have been the guidelines for Sweden's foreign policy during the whole of the postwar period. The hallmark of her trading policy has been her attempt to liberalize trade, and this has been pursued in close connection with Great Britain with whom she participated in the establishment of the European Free Trade Association (EFTA) in 1959. Although the Nordic defensive alliance was not realized, Nordic collaboration has been intensified by—among other things—the Nordic Council (1952). Important results of the council's work are that passports are not required between Nordic countries, a free Nordic labor market has been created, and a far-reaching coordination of economic and social legislation has taken place. On the other hand, the plans for a Nordic customs union which had been discussed during the 1960s and which aimed at a more extensive cooperation than that which already existed within the framework of EFTA led to no result. The so-called Nordek plan submitted in 1969, which, moreover, also aimed at far-reaching economic cooperation between the Nordic lands, met with opposition, primarily from Finland, and was abandoned in 1970. Concerning the negotiations for entry into EEC which Denmark and Norway took part in in 1971, Sweden has declared that she does not intend to seek membership as this would be incompatible with the country's policy of neutrality. Sweden has instead in 1972 concluded an agreement with EEC on a gradual winding up of customs.

Sweden today is characterized by a high average standard of living and by a well-developed system of social security, but at the same time by sharply rising prices and a decline in certain sections of trade and industry which has resulted in locally rising unemployment. In foreign relations Sweden's goal is to remain independent of alliances and the country has adopted a neutral attitude in the conflicts between the Great Powers. Support to underdeveloped countries plus an active contribution to the environment question both in Sweden itself and in an international context are among the salient issues in Swedish politics today.

CARL XVI GUSTAF (1973–   )

With the death of King Gustavus VI Adolf, on Saturday, September 15, 1973, his grandson, the former crown prince Carl Gustaf, twenty-seven, succeeded to the throne of Sweden.

At a special cabinet meeting the new king announced his accession to the throne, and announced his royal name, title, and motto. He indicated his official name and title as Carl XVI Gustaf, king of Sweden. His motto, he said, reflected the responsibility of a constitutional monarch to adjust to a changing society and to value and benefit from experiences of the past. He chose; *"För Sverige i tiden"* (For Sweden—with the times).

The new king was born on April 30, 1946, in the Haga palace, as heir apparent, and was created duke of Jömtland. He is the only son of the late king's eldest son, Prince Gustavus Adolf, who was killed in an airplane accident in 1947, and the late princess Sibylla, nee princess of Saxe-Coburg-Gotha.

The king was confirmed in the summer of 1962 in Borgholm's Church on the island of Öland, where the late Princess Sibylla and her family used to spend their summer holidays.

Immediately after graduation from Sigtuna the prince began his two-year military service in different branches of the armed services. The main emphasis was laid on naval training and the prince participated, among other things, in a long voyage with the minelayer *Älvsnabben* during the winter of 1966–1967. After further practical and theoretical training, he was commissioned as a naval officer in the autumn of 1968. The king had then also devoted four months to studies and intensive exercises at the Military Cadet Schools of the army and the air force and served in a coast artillery unit for some weeks. The king is also second lieutenant of the Royal Svea Life-Guards, the Commando Regiment of Jömtland, and the air force.

King Carl XVI Gustaf studied Swedish labor market organization—the Swedish Employers' Confederation, the Swedish Central Organization of Salaried Employees, and the Swedish Confederation of Trade Unions. He spent one month in New York in order to familiarize himself with the United Nations and its work and a few weeks at the Swedish embassy in London. He then visited Gothenburg for press studies at the newspaper *Göteborgs-Posten* and to be briefed on the activities of the Swedish Ball-Bearing Company and the Gothenburg port facilities. Later he studied the activities of the Swedish Church, the Swedish Central News Agency, and the banking system.

During the early 1970s the king devoted a great deal of time to visiting and studying the Swedish ministries, the Royal Chancery, and the Riksdag (Parliament). King Carl XVI Gustaf was married to Miss Silvia Sommerlath on June 19, 1976, and on July 14, 1977, their daughter Victoria was born.

King Carl and Queen Silvia in 1977 (Swedish Institute, photo: Lennart Nilsson)

The new Swedish monarch, King Carl XVI Gustaf, giving a speech in memory of his grandfather, the late King Gustavus VI Adolf, and expressing his own attitudes to his position in modern society. Bodyguards in the Throne Room wear uniforms dating from the days of Charles XI, seventeenth century.

The king and queen in 1978 (Swedish Institute, photo: Claes Lewenhaupt)

King Carl XVI Gustaf, left, visited the United Nations headquarters in New York City in 1976. The king is seen here with UN Secretary-General Kurt Waldheim.

1980—The king and queen in a family birthday party with their children

King Carl XVI Gustaf and Queen Silvia, 1976

THE ROYAL SOVEREIGNS OF THE KINGDOM OF SWEDEN

Reign	Title	Ruler	Death
		THE YNGLINGS	
		Odin arrived in the North	(70 B.C.)
		Njörd	20 B.C.
		Frey-Yngve	A.D. 10
		Fiolner	14
		Svegdir	34
		Vanland or Valland	48
		Visbur	98
		Domald	130
		Domar	162
		Dyggve	190
		Dag-Spaka, the Wise	220
		Agne	260
		Alrek and Eric	280
		Yngve and Alf	300
		Hugleik	302
		Jorunder and Erik	312
		Aun hinn Gamle (the Old)	448
		Egill Tunnadolgi	456
		Ottar Vendilkraka	460
		Adils	505
		Eystein	531
		Yngvar	545
		Braut-Onund	565
		Ingiald Illrada	623
		Olaf Traetelia (exiled about 630)	
		ACCESSION OF THE SKIOLDUNGS	
		Ivar Vidfadme	A.D. 647
		Harold Hildetand	735
		Sigurd Ring	750
		Ragnar Lodbrok	794
		Björn Ironside	804
		Eric Bjornson	808
		Eric Raefillson	820
		Emund and Björn	859
		Eric Emundson	873
		Björn Erickson	923
		Eric the Victorious	993
		Eric Arsaell	1001
		Olaf the Lap-King	1026
		Arund Kolbrenner	1051
		Edmund Slemme	1056
		Stenkil (raised to the throne 1056)	
		HOUSE OF STENKIL	
1056–1066	King	Stenkil	
1066–1080	King	Inge the Elder, Stenkilsson with	
1066–1070	King	Halsten Stenkilsson, joint rulers	
1080–1130	King	Inge the Younger, Halstensson with	
1080–1110	King	Filip Halstensson, joint rulers	
		HOUSE OF SVERKER AND ERIK	
1130–1156	King	Sverker, the Elder	
1150–1160	King	Erik IX, Jedvarsson (Saint Erik)	
1160–1161	King	Magnus Henriksson	
1161–1167	King	Charles VII (Karl Sverkersson)	
1167–1196	King	Knut Eriksson (Knut VI)	
1196–1208	King	Sverker the Younger, Karlsson	
1208–1216	King	Erik Knutsson (Erik X)	
1216–1222	King	Johan Sverkersson (John I)	
1222–1229	King	Erik Eriksson (Erik XI)	
1229–1234	King	Knut Holmgersson (Lange)	
1234–1249	King	Erik Eriksson	

Reign	Title	Ruler	Death

HOUSE OF FOLKUNG

Reign	Title	Ruler	Death
1250–1275	King	Valdemar I Birgersson (His father, Birger Jarl, was regent until 1266)	
1275–1290	King	Magnus I Birgersson (Ladulas)	
1290–1318	King	Birger II Magnusson	
1319—Union of Kalmar unites Sweden and Norway			
1319–1364	King	Magnus II Eriksson	
1356–1359	King	Eric XII	
1365–1389	King	Albert of Mecklenburg	
1389–1521—Various families ruled.			
1389–1412	Queen	Margrethe	
1396–1439	King	Eric XIII of Pomerania (Eric VII of Denmark)	
1397—Union of Kalmar unites Sweden, Norway, and Denmark			
1435–1436	Regent	Engelbrekt Engelbrektsson	
1438–1440	Regent	Karl Knutsson	
1440–1448	King	Christopher of Bavaria	
1448–1457	King	Charles VIII (Karl Knutsson)	
1457–1464	King	Christian I of Denmark	
1464–1465	King	Charles VIII (Karl Knutsson)	
1465–1466	Regent	Jons Bengtsson Oxenstierna	
1466–1467	Regent	Erik Axelsson Tott	
1467–1470	King	Charles VIII (Karl Knutsson)	
1470–1497	Regent	Sten Sture the Elder	
1497–1501	King	Hans (John) II of Denmark	
1501–1503	Regent	Sten Sture	
1503–1512	Regent	Svante Nilsson Sture	
1512–1520	Regent	Sten Sture the Younger	
1520–1521	King	Christian II	

HOUSE OF VASA

Reign	Title	Ruler	Death
1521–1523	Regent	Gustavus Eriksson Vasa	
1523–1560	King	Gustavus I	
1560–1568	King	Eric XIV	
1568–1592	King	John III	
1592–1599	King	Sigismund	
1599–1604	Regent	Charles IX	
1604–1611	King	Charles IX	
1611–1632	King	Gustavus II Adolphus	
1632–1654	Queen	Christina	

HOUSE OF PALATINATE

Reign	Title	Ruler	Death
1654–1660	King	Charles X Gustavus	
1660–1697	King	Charles XI	
1697–1718	King	Charles XII	
1718–1720	Queen	Ulrica Eleonora	
1720–1751	King	Frederick I of Hesse	

HOUSE OF HOLSTEIN-GOTTORP

Reign	Title	Ruler	Death
1751–1771	King	Adolphus Frederick	
1771–1792	King	Gustavus III	
1792–1809	King	Gustavus IV Adolphus	
1792–1796	Regent	Charles	
1809–1818	King	Charles XIII	
1814–1905—Sweden unites with Norway			

HOUSE OF BERNADOTTE

Reign	Title	Ruler	Death
1818–1844	King	Charles XIV John	
1844–1859	King	Oscar I	
1859–1872	King	Charles XV	
1872–1907	King	Oscar II	
1907–1950	King	Gustavus V	
1950–1973	King	Gustavus VI Adolf	
1973–	King	Carl XVI Gustaf	

15

Imperial Russia

Map of early Russia

Slavic tribes, the earliest ancestors of the Russians, inhabited various river valleys in what is now the European part of the Soviet Union from a very early time. Just how early and where they came from are subjects of great controversy among historians, but Slavs were present in the area for many centuries before the appearance of the first Russian state. The historical heritage of the Soviet Union is the sum of the lasting influences exerted on the people and on their institutions during the centuries of development from primitive times to the present.

The early Slavic clans and tribes, which were relatively peaceful, agriculturally oriented, and spread out over large areas, were easy prey for mounted nomads from Asia or for the warlike Germanic tribes from the north. The vast open steppes and the north-south river routes provided natural avenues for invasion by seemingly endless waves of peoples who swept back and forth across the country for centuries. These invasions were not merely fleeting moments in history; more often they were mass migrations, spearheaded by powerful warrior groups, which left indelible imprints on the people and the land. The Scythians held sway for five hundred years; the Sarmatians, for four hundred; and the Goths, Huns, Khazars, and Avars, among others, all ruled for varying periods of time.

Meanwhile, the Slavs paid taxes and tribute to their conquerors, fought when possible, retreated when necessary, assimilated many of the invaders, multiplied in numbers, and continued their cultivation of the land, their hunting, fishing, and beekeeping. Pushed by invaders or simply seeking more peaceful lands, the Slavs themselves moved in all directions, and their migrations during the early Christian Era resulted in three general groupings. The West Slavs include the Poles, Czechs, Slovaks, and Lusatians; the South Slaves became the Serbs, Croats, Macedonians, Slovenes, Montenegrins, and Bulgars. The East Slavs are the Russians, Ukrainians, and Belɔrussians.

By the middle of the eighth century A.D., the land of the East Slavs consisted of several city-states, each of which dominated its surrounding territory. Extensive trade in foodstuffs and furs had been carried on for centuries, usually through foreign overlords, but now a class of Slavic merchants had developed and had built prosperous trading centers. The most pressing problem of the merchants was the vulnerability of their profitable commerce. They needed protection against Viking marauders and Asian nomads, as well as against their own subject peoples, who often rebelled against exploitation by the wealthy merchants. In the ninth century A.D. the protection of trade was provided by a group of Vikings known as Varangians, and a new epoch in Russian history began.

Whether the Varangians were invited by the Slav merchants to "come rule and reign over us," as related in the ancient chronicles, or whether they forcefully appropriated a profitable commercial structure is still a subject of controversy but, in either case, by about the year A.D. 862 the Varangians had assumed control. Their semilegendary leader was a Dane called Rurik, a trader-pirate-adventurer who founded a dynasty that would rule for more than seven hundred years. With the advent of Rurik it is proper to use the term *Rus*. Once again historians differ as to whether the Varangians brought the term or adopted it from an indigenous Slavic tribe but, from the time of Rurik on, the most numerous and most powerful branch of the East Slavs would be known as Rus or Russian. Although the new rulers were Scandinavian in origin, they did not lead a great migration. They took over a Slavic civilization and culture and called themselves Rus, and within two or three generations they had been absorbed, completely Slavicized.

Rurik himself settled in the northern trading town of Novgorod, but Oleg, his successor, moved south and established himself as prince of Kiev. The subsequent flowering of Kievan commerce and culture marks the beginning of the first truly Russian state. At the height of its power, Kievan Russia encompassed a vast territory that included several large, prosperous trading centers. From the beginning, Kievan Russia was expansionist in nature, a trait passed on to future Russian states. The lifeblood of Kiev was trade, and the princes fought continually to expand that trade and encompass more potential routes and territories.

The flourishing commercial enterprises of the Kievan Russians, however, were paralleled by other aspects of their society. Most important in the rich Kievan legacy was the Orthodox religion, which the princes had adopted from the Byzantine Empire and had urged on their subjects in place of primitive pagan beliefs. Orthodox Christianity became a dominant theme in Russian life, and the considerable influence of the church affected development of the character of the people, whether of the nobility or of the peasantry. Religion as a dominant theme in Russian life remained until the Bolshevik revolution proclaimed official atheism but, even after more than fifty years of militant antireligion, Orthodoxy continued to be a force in the lives of many Russians.

In addition to the large ecclesiastical establishment and the commercial structure, Russia also inherited from Kiev a system of agriculture, a money economy, a mili-

The Early Rulers of Russia: top, *Vladimir, Rurik, Demetrius Donski;* center, *Michael Romanoff, Alexis, Ivan the Great;* below, *Ivan the Terrible, Fedor III, Yaroslav the Just*

The Funeral of Rurik

Saint Olga, ruler of Russia, 945–55

Saint Andrew preaching Christianity to the Russians

Grand Duke Sviatopolk ruled
Russia from 1015 to 1019.

Grand Duke Yaroslav I
(also Iaroslav), 1019–54

Grand Duke Sviatoslav,   *Saint Vladimir I rules*
ruler of Russia, 955–72.   *Russia from 980 to 1015.*

Grand Duke Dmitri (Demetrius)
Donski (Donskoi) was the ruler of
Russia from 1359 to 1389.

tary tradition, and a stratification of society. The beginnings of Russian art, architecture, and literature are also traced to the Kievan period.

Weakened by internal strife and constant warfare, Kievan Russia was in an advanced stage of decline when the last great mass movement of Asians swept over the land, eventually occupying much of Eurasia. The Golden Horde, led by the successors of Ghengis Khan, held Russia in bondage for over two hundred years, and Mongol influences are integral to subsequent development. The Horde destroyed the city of Kiev in 1240; Genghis Khan replaced the prince as ruler of practically all of what had been Kievan Rus. Thus, the first East Slavic state disappeared and Russia was again subject to an Asian invader.

The Mongols were ruthless in their treatment of Russia and the Russians. They destroyed cities, slaughtered or enslaved citizens, and forced princes to swear allegiance to the khan and to collect taxes for his treasury. They did not, however, systematically eradicate Russian culture and customs. The Mongol aim was to maintain control and exploit the wealth of the country even though at first their terrible campaigns laid waste most of the cities. After the initial waves of destruction,

the Mongols adopted the role of absentee landlord, humiliating the Russian princes and intimidating the country with their military might, which had so far proved to be nearly invincible.

Victory over the Horde in the battle of Kulikovo in 1380 was an event to be commemorated ever after. Led by a prince of Moscow, a Russian army defeated a Mongol force in a battle fought over nonpayment of tribute. The battle was actually inconclusive, and tribute payments continued, but the victory was very important to the developing state of Muscovy. A century later Ivan the Great of Moscow refused to pay tribute, and the khan did not force the issue. The stranglehold of the Mongols was broken.

Two and a half centuries of a harsh, brutal occupation designed for utmost exploitation inhibited the development of all aspects of Russian life. Russia was effectively cut off from contact with the west during the Mongol period. Its cities with their crafts, industries, and trade declined, and the country became predominantly agricultural. The Orthodox church, although suffering great losses of churches and monasteries, emerged stronger than before because religion had gained a wider base among the people. Arts and literature suffered as the

Demetrius Donski refusing the Tatar tribute

Ivan III tearing up the letter of demands of the Tatar khan

civilizing influences that had taken root in Kiev withered under the occupation. Most important during this period was the emergence of Muscovy as a new Russian state, establishing itself as the true successor to Kiev, the foundation of modern Russia.

MUSCOVY

The town of Moscow was first mentioned by the ancient chroniclers in 1147, at which time its only claim to fame was its location on a river route. Moscow was ranked low among Russian principalities, but after the decline of Kiev ambitious princes took steps to raise Moscow to first rank. All of the Russian princes had served at the sufferance of the khan during the period of domination. The prince of Kiev had been known as grand prince, but later that title was given to more important cities such as Novgorod and Tver.

In 1328 Ivan I of Moscow convinced the khan that he should be named grand prince, with the result that the prestige of Moscow soared. Ivan I was known to his people as Moneybags, apparently with good reason. As grand prince, his duty was to collect taxes from all lesser princes to be given as tribute to the Mongol overlords.

Enough of this wealth stayed in Moscow to enable Ivan to purchase various poorer princedoms as well as towns and villages surrounding Muscovy. Ivan also convinced the metropolitan of the Russian Orthodox church to transfer the metropolitanate to Moscow, a move that did much to enhance the prestige of Moscow and its prince. Ivan I succeeded so well in the enlargement and aggrandizement of Muscovy that his immediate successor assumed the new title of Grand Prince of All the Russias.

As the power of the Muscovite princes increased, that of the lesser princes proportionately decreased, and a trend toward centralization was definitely in evidence. The importance of towns and cities was reduced under the Mongols, whereas agricultural landlords tended to increase their control over the land and, with it, over the peasantry. In embryonic form, the institution of serfdom was slowly taking hold. When Ivan III (the Great) came to power in 1462, Muscovy was almost as large as Kiev had been in its heyday. It was difficult to administer such a large territory and there were enemies on the borders, but during his forty-three-year reign Ivan III solidified central control, created a bureaucracy, ended the Mongol domination, and regained large territories in the west which had been absorbed by the Polish-Lithuanian Empire. Ivan also broke the power of such Russian strongholds as Novgorod, Tver, and Ryazan, incorporating them into Muscovy.

Ivan III referred to himself as Sovereign of All Russia and in international relations, called himself czar. Early chronicles tell of a prince of Kiev who had led his cavalry into battle, roasted his own food over an open fire, and slept on the ground with his saddle for a pillow. The dynasty of Rurik had come a long way from that early warrior-prince. The court of Ivan III had become regal and ritualistic, with Ivan declaring, "we hold our appointment from God." Thus, divine right was introduced, and autocracy was firmly established with the Russian Orthodox church as its handmaiden.

Sixteenth-century Russian history is dominated by Ivan IV (the Terrible), whose reign lasted from 1530 to 1584. Since Ivan was a child of three when he succeeded to the throne, Russia was ruled by a regency council for several years. At age seventeen, however, Ivan was crowned czar in a glittering ceremony designed to im-

Ivan IV, the Terrible

press every Russian with the fact that the grand prince of Moscow was indeed czar of All the Russias with all the power inferred by that lofty title. Ivan, despite his youthfulness, ruled with an iron fist. For the next thirty-seven years he was the complete autocrat, running the country as if it were a private estate, changing its size and shape as well as its internal complexion.

The high priest Philip rebuking Ivan the Terrible

During the years before his coronation, Ivan the Terrible learned to hate the nobles, known as boyars, who wielded extensive power at the Muscovy court. Scheming and conniving for influence, various noble families offended the young czar and, in so doing, sealed their fate by leading Ivan to the conviction that he would have to destroy the influence of the hereditary boyars and eliminate all differences between boyars and the service gentry created by his grandfather, Ivan the Great. Under Ivan IV, it became impossible to be a landlord without paying homage and rendering service to the czar.

In the years immediately following his coronation, Ivan was advised by a small council, chosen by himself from among the middle classes rather than from the nobility whom he despised. Various enlightened reforms were initiated during this period which contrast sharply with the mad excesses of the latter part of Ivan's reign. A new legal code was enacted, new church regulations were enforced, and a new system of local government was adopted which gave some citizens a voice in selecting local officials. Ivan also called the first *Zemsky Sobor* (Assembly of the Land), which contained representatives of the merchant class in addition to hereditary nobles and service gentry. Ivan called the assembly to advise him, but the inclusion of merchants and service gentry was simply another step to lessen the prestige of the boyars who had traditionally formed the czar's advisory council.

On the international scene, Ivan established close commercial relations with England but was unsuccessful in his attempt to form a military alliance with that country against his Baltic enemies. For the most part, Ivan's other international relations consisted of warfare with Russia's neighboring states. The remnants of the Golden Horde still maintained independent khanates in Siberia, Kazan, Astrakhan, and Crimea. During Ivan's reign the first three of these Tatar khanates were conquered and incorporated into Muscovy, extending the eastern and southeastern boundaries far beyond Ivan's inheritance. The Crimean tatars, eventually under Turkish suzerainty, held out for another two centuries. On his western borders, Ivan was less successful and lost the Baltic outlet at Narva, which had been secured by his predecessors. Western Europe was becoming alarmed by the burgeoning Muscovite giant; consequently the Scandinavian countries allied themselves with the German Baltic knights to reinforce Poland-Lithuania against incursions by the forces of Ivan the Terrible.

In the midst of his foreign wars, Ivan instituted a reign

Cathedral of St. Basil in Moscow. It was built by Ivan IV, who considered it so beautiful that he had the architect's eyes put out so that he might not build another.

of terror designed to eliminate all opposition and resistance to his policies. A six-thousand-man political police, Russia's first and answering only to the czar, ravaged the country, terrorizing boyar and peasant alike. Tracking down traitors became the chief task of Ivan's police, and the designation "traitor" was applied loosely and arbitrarily as the regime used any measure to establish czarist absolutism. As with later purges, the terrorism of Ivan ultimately turned inward as his purgers destroyed one another. Russian cities, such as Novgorod, which the czar suspected of mass disloyalty, were completely devastated. When the terror finally subsided, the state, although weakened and almost ruined, was completely under the control of its central authority.

Shortly before his death, Ivan the Terrible struck and killed his son and heir, an event that had far-reaching effects on the development of Russia. Ivan's remaining son, the simple-minded Fedor I, died without an heir,

The death of Ivan the Terrible

ending the Rurik line and setting the stage for a dynastic struggle.

The Time of Troubles brought such great strife and upheaval throughout the land that it is remarkable that Muscovy managed to survive as a political entity. The struggle for the crown between 1605 and 1613 became a confusing succession of pretenders, charlatans, and foreign princes, all trying to ascend Muscovy's throne. Poland and Sweden, seeing opportunity for territorial gain and settlement of long-standing disputes, intervened in force. Cossack freebooters arose in the steppes, swept north, enlisting thousands of peasants into their armies, and sometimes threatened Moscow itself. At one time, a cossack band installed its own czar in a town near Moscow and, in effect, Muscovy had two czars with rival courts, rival armies, and rival tax collectors.

In 1610, with Polish armies occupying Moscow, both czars were deposed and a council of boyars took control. At this point, feelings of nationalism stirred in the Russian people and, rallied by the patriarch of Moscow, they came to the defense of Holy Russia. Freebooters and foreign armies were finally driven out, and in 1613 the interregnum ended with the election by a Zemsky Sobor of Czar Michael Romanov, the first of a new dynasty that would rule Russia for three hundred and four years.

The first three Romanov czars, whose reigns covered most of the seventeenth century, were all weak rulers. Although the Time of Troubles, historically speaking, ended in 1613, the foreign wars, peasant uprisings, and boyar intrigues continued to plague Russian czars. With the help of strong personal advisers, the Zemsky Sobor, and various boyar councils, the first three Romanovs did manage to bring about a measure of internal order. The cossacks were won over by treaty, resulting in the annexation of the Ukraine. The Poles and Swedes were bought off in the west, postponing what seemed to be an inevitable military confrontation. A new law code was promulgated which bound every Russian to service to the crown, legalizing the hated institution of serfdom. In religious affairs, a blunt, undiplomatic patriarch forced corrections in liturgy and ritual, which alienated great

Michael Feodorovich Romanov. Michael I was the founder of the House of Romanov. On February 12, 1613, after rejecting all members of foreign royal families as prospective candidates to the Russian throne, the National Assembly (Sobor) considered suitable Russian candidates and finally selected an elected nobleman, Michael Feodorovich Romanov.

During his reign, he gradually built the czar's powers above those of the elected assembly.

On July 12, 1645, while attending church services, he suffered a stroke but before dying he named his son, Aleksei, by his second wife Evdokia Loukiahovna (his first wife, who died early, was Maria Vladimirovna Dolgorourky), to succeed him to the throne. Michael I had reigned for thirty-two years.

The coronation of Michael I took place on his seventeenth birthday, July 11, 1613, at the Assumption Cathedral in Moscow.

Aleksei Mikhailovich Romanov. Czar Aleksei, (1645–76), son of Michael I, was crowned on September 28, 1645, and he died twenty-one years later without leaving any historical milestones for Russia.

At the time of Michael I's coronation, his father, Filaret Nikitich, was a captive of King Sigismund III in a Polish prison.

Martha, the mother of Michael I, after the coronation entered the royal mansion, blessed her son, and then returned as mother-nun to the convent of the Ascension.

The royal jewel-laden throne

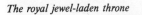

The crown, scepter, and orb of the early czars

Fedor Alekseevich Romanov. Czar Fedor III, son of Aleksei, ascended to the throne on January 29, 1676. Like his father, Czar Fedor was recorded in history as a ruler who left no mark for himself or his country. He died in 1683.

Regent Czarevna Sophia Alekseevna, reign 1682–89

A modern-day photograph of the Assumption Cathedral, the church of coronation for the czars

numbers of Russians and caused a schism in Russian Orthodoxy that has never been healed. The religious dissension made it easy for the next ruler, a strong czar, to usurp church prerogatives and downgrade clerical authority among the people.

IMPERIAL RUSSIA (1721–1917)

Near the end of the seventeenth century, a powerful Romanov came to the throne—Peter I (the Great). During his reign he transformed Russia from a backward principality into a powerful empire. Peter's furious energy drove him to interest himself in almost every aspect of Russian life. Impatient with the old, lethargic, inward-looking ways of his homeland, Peter determined to modernize it, using western Europe as his model. He changed the administrative structure of the government to make it more efficient as well as more responsive to the czar. He modernized the army and built a navy—necessary reforms for a monarch who was at war for forty of the forty-two years of his reign. He changed the structure of society, establishing a table of ranks for military and civil service in which ability rather than heredity determined position. He abolished the office of patriarch in the Orthodox church, putting a layman in Russia's top religious office and making the church an extension of the autocracy.

Peter considered beards to be a symbol of backwardness and personally sheared some of his boyars; others quickly decided that a clean-shaven face was best in court circles. Nothing was too small or insignificant to escape the czar's personal attention if it contributed to ending Russia's backwardness. Among other achievements, he changed the ancient Russian calendar, introduced Arabic numerals, revised the Cyrillic alphabet, published the first newspaper, established compulsory schools for children of the gentry, and founded an Academy of Sciences.

Peter, however, was not a systematic reformer nor a great theoretician. He was a man of action who brooked no opposition and little procrastination. Although his reforms were sometimes ill conceived and poorly executed, some of his achievements had lasting effects on the development of the empire over the next two hundred years. Peter did nothing for the Russian serf except to make him more of a slave than he had ever been before; later, peasant uprisings became epidemic throughout the countryside.

Russia was at war with Sweden from 1700 until 1721, fought Turkey during many of the same years, and also was forced to use regular troops to put down serf insurrections. Peter suffered some humiliating defeats at the hands of the Swedes, but setbacks engendered greater efforts and, after studying the tactics of the enemy and adapting them to his own forces, the czar personally led an army that destroyed Swedish land power, and his

Ivan V and Peter I (reign of 1682–89). Czar Aleksei had five sons by his first wife, Maria Miloslavskaya, and one by his second wife, Natalie Narishkina. Natalie bore Aleksei, one of the greatest rulers of Russia— Peter I, the Great.

Peter was preceded to the throne by a son of Maria—Fedor III—who, along with his brother Ivan, survived the children's diseases of the day. Fedor III left no heir so the succession to the throne went to brothers, Peter I and Ivan V. They reigned under their older sister Sophia's regentship. In 1689 Ivan V was deposed in favor of Peter I.

When Peter the Great died on January 28, 1725, like other great general rulers he left his country with enlarged border lines, an immense treasury, and a large military force. If he is to be remembered for any one achievement, it must be the defeat of King Charles XII of Sweden at Poltava in June of 1709. Until that month in history Charles XII, the king of Sweden, was considered the greatest military commander of modern times.

The coronation of the two children, Ivan and Peter the Great

The regent Sophia seized and carried to a convent

Peter had his sister Sophia removed to the convent on the grounds of this monastery, Novodevitchy.

Russia at the time of Peter the Great

Peter the Great

At the time of Peter the Great, the Kremlin in Moscow was used as his palace. Succeeding czars also used it as their residence grounds while in Moscow. A period sketch of the times.

Eudoxia Lopukhin, first wife of Peter the Great. They were married February 6, 1689, and formally divorced in 1698, when he sent her to a convent for the rest of her life.

navy was equally victorious at sea. Sweden was eliminated as the preeminent power in northern Europe, and Peter obtained his long-sought outlet to the sea and his "window on Europe," as he termed the new capital of St. Petersburg. Upon his return from the Swedish war, Peter accepted the title of emperor from the Senate (one of his administrative creations), and Russia emerged as a full-blown power on the European scene.

With all of his reforms, Peter carefully avoided any innovation that might limit the authority of the czar. In his view, Russia could only progress under the direction of an absolute monarch. Therefore, importation of European political thought did not accompany importation

Eudoxia preparing for her wedding to Peter

of goods, services, and techniques. Peter the Great also used terror in eliminating opposition, and his reign was marred by excesses reminiscent of the time of Ivan the Terrible. Like Ivan, Peter participated in tortures and executions, including the torture of his own son, who subsequently died from his injuries.

A series of weak rulers followed Peter, resulting in rule by court favorites and cliques from the time of Peter's death to the rise of Catherine the Great in 1762. This was not, however, a retrogressive period for Russia. Peter had established his country as a European power, and certain processes went forward despite the quality of rule. In external affairs, Russian armies warred successfully against the Turks and, at the same time, brought Frederick the Great of Prussia to the brink of disaster. Internally, the position of the peasantry became worse than ever, leaving little to distinguish serfdom from slavery. At the coronation of Peter's daughter, Elizabeth, serfs were omitted from the classes swearing allegiance to the new monarch, and in a revised law code they were listed simply under the heading of property. As the official status of the serfs degenerated into slavery, the gentry class accumulated greater wealth, prestige, and privileges. During the short reign of Peter III in 1762, the gentry managed to push through repeal of the law that bound them to state service. Thus, the gentry

became a free class with few restraints on their power and control over the serfs.

Peter the Great had created elite Guards regiments for the protection of the czar and of the capital. These regiments became the czar's personal army, often performing secret police functions under Peter's supervision. In the power vacuum brought about by the death of the strong czar, the St. Petersburg regiments became politically potent, twice determining the succession to the throne.

Catherine, princess of the small German state of Anhalt-Zerbst, married the grandson of Peter the Great, was converted to Orthodoxy, and took up residence in the court of St. Petersburg in 1744. Catherine was intelligent, determined, and supremely self-confident. Her position as a German princess in a Russian court that often despised and distrusted all Germans, was tenuous, but the force of her personality, her willpower, and her dexterity in court intrigue served her well in the long years of waiting for her husband to become czar. In 1762 Catherine (later to be called the Great), backed by the Guards, deposed her husband, bypassed her son, and had herself proclaimed empress of Russia. As empress, she quickly established herself as the absolute autocrat and became the most powerful monarch since Peter the Great.

Peter the Great learning ship building in Zaandam (near Amsterdam), Holland

Peter and Catherine visiting Poland

Peter was an artist. This sketch of his depicts himself as a "God over Russia."

Peter embracing Louis XV of France

The Later Russian Czars: top, Nicholas I, Peter the Great, Alexander I; center, Alexander III, Catherine the Great, Nicholas II; below, Catherine I, Alexander II, Peter II.

Peter designed the flag of Russia, which shows himself on horseback ready for combat.

Peter the Great founding St. Petersburg

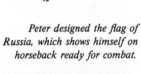

Peter's royal sledge

Empress Catherine I, 1725–27. The first Russian empress, Catherine, reigned but two years and three months after the death of her husband, Peter I; she died on May 7, 1727. She continued to carry out Peter's programs in every field.

Empress Anna was in constant disagreement with her male advisers and is seen here tearing up an edict prepared by them that would have deprived her "common" subjects of their rights.

Anna Leopoldovna, 1740–41

Peter II, 1727–30. Peter II was but twelve years of age when he was called upon to wear the heavy crown of the Romanovs. His mother, who died when her son was only three years old, was a niece ·of Peter the Great. During his short reign (1727–30) a trade treaty was signed with China and Bering discovered the famous strait between Siberia and Alaska.

Empress Anna Ianovna, 1730–40. On the day after the death of the short-reigned emperor, a successor was selected. Special deputies were sent to Mitau to offer the crown to Anna Ivanovna, duchess of Courland and daughter of Czar Ivan Alekseevich. Anna Ivanovna not only agreed to accept the crown but she set out immediately for Moscow for the coronation. On February 10, 1730, she arrived at the village of Vsesvyatskoye, five miles from Moscow, and stopped over while her triumphant entry was arranged. Five days later Anna entered the capital, and on April 28 the coronation took place.

Elizabeth Petrovna. After the death of Anna Ivanovna (1740), Biron and then Anna Leopoldovna, the mother of the young czar Ivan VI, were appointed regents. The Orthodox church did not welcome either. The reign of Ivan Antonovich was short lived. Elizaveta (Elizabeth), on November 25, 1741, finally yielded to the pressure of her following and proclaimed herself the empress of Russia. She had a most celebrated coronation, for a direct descendant of the crown was once again on the throne. The clergy, the army, the nobility, and the people rejoiced. Representatives of all of the tribes to the east joined in the festivities. The empress from her coronation at the age of thirty-two years ruled in a reign of peace and prosperity for Russia and is credited with abolishing the death penalty. She served the people well and on her death, Christmas Day, 1761, she was acclaimed by all of Russia as a true descendant of Peter the Great.

Emperor Ivan VI at an early age.
He was murdered in 1764.

The old residence of the Romanov czars in Moscow

Catherine II at age eleven. Catherine Alekseevna, Empress Catherine II,
proclaimed herself the sovereign of Russia. She was crowned on June 28,
1762, and the following day had Peter III, the rightful heir, imprisoned.
Catherine II performed this extraordinary take-over of the throne with-
out any blood being shed. Her proclamation was that Russia was in dire
danger from foreign domination of her government, the church and the
culture of the country were at stake, and the "safety" of the nation's
welfare was in jeopardy.

Catherine II did alter the course of Peter III. She broke off with King
Frederick II of Prussia and succeeded in having a friend, Stanislaus
Poniatowski, elected king of Poland. She won two wars with Turkey,
extending Russia's border to the Black Sea. Catherine II died of natural
causes on November 5, 1796.

Catherine the Great taking communion during her coronation at the
Dormition Cathedral (September 22, 1762). Her coronation (at the
Kremlin) was the most spectacular ever recorded.

Peter Karl Ulrich. Emperor Peter III was the son of Anna Petrovna,
daughter of Peter the Great. Elizabeth Petrovna, during her reign,
brought Duke Peter Ulrich from Holstein to become the emperor. On
December 25, 1761, he ascended to the throne but it was to be short lived
—six months. Czar Peter III was closely aligned with Frederick II of
Prussia and this relationship was looked upon with suspicion by the
Russian court. So it was no surprise when the nobles and the church
backed his wife Catherine Alekseevna to replace him on the throne.

The empress Catherine II at the height of her reign

Paul Petrovich. Czar Paul I wanted his coronation to be the greatest, so he chose April 5, 1797—the first day of Easter week. He redesigned the crown of Empress Catherine II to fit it with larger pearls, the scepter was fitted with the 200-carat Orlov diamond, and the new orb was made of solid gold. (These then served all of the successive sovereigns at their coronations.)

He strove to better the lot of the serfs by limiting the landowners to working them only three days a week and exempting them from work on Sundays or church feast days. Militarily he defeated the French in northern Italy. But the palace guard plotted with the nobles who were his closest advisers and "friends" to assassinate him. On March 11, 1801, they murdered him in his sleep.

After consolidating her power, Catherine fostered administrative reforms but, despite her celebrated correspondence with Voltaire and other philosophers of the Enlightenment, she believed that Russia could only succeed under an absolute monarch, and she intended to be that monarch. Much of Catherine's liberal philosophy fell victim to Russian reality, and the shock of the

French Revolution finally converted her to conservatism. Revolution was anathema to Catherine. She vowed never to recognize the new United States of America, for example, and at her death in 1796 recognition had not been granted. (Official diplomatic relations between the United States and Russia were inaugurated in 1809.) With all her fear of revolutions and uprisings, Catherine would not confront serfdom, the root cause of Russia's internal problems. On the contrary, she compounded the problem by placing hundreds of thousands of peasants in bondage during her reign. Following the examples of earlier rulers, Catherine made lavish gifts of state lands to her favorites. Each gift included the peasants living on the land, thus swelling ranks of bonded serfs year after year.

Part of the reality of Russia during Catherine's time was the growing gap between gentry and peasantry. Peter the Great had wrenched his country out of its backwardness and had transformed it into a more or less modern European power, but had left the semifeudal structure of serfdom that could only impede progress. During Catherine's reign, the growing animosity between the relatively few landowners and the millions of serfs exploded into Russia's most famous serf rebellion. Led by Yemelyan Pugachev, a Don cossack, the insurrection spread rapidly, encompassing a huge territory and recruiting thousands of adherents to the cause. The Pugachev revolt (1773–75) was similar to many that had preceded it and many more that followed, but for sheer size and audacity it was a landmark in Russian history. Doomed to failure by poor organization and poor leadership, the revolt nevertheless frightened the privileged gentry class for decades to come. Instead of reform, Pugachev's escapade fostered further repression. Catherine attempted reforms but, because she sought always to maintain central authority, the reforms merely served to solidify the semislave status of the serfs and the feudal lord status of the landowner.

In foreign affairs Catherine followed the centuries-old expansionist policies of her predecessors. Vast new lands were acquired, and Russia's position as a participant in European power politics was reinforced. At the expense of Turkey, Russia finally reached the Black Sea coast and occupied the Crimean Peninsula. The empress also participated with the Prussian and Austrian rulers in three partitions of Poland that gave Russia most of the Ukraine and Belorussia along with several million new citizens. At the end of Catherine's reign, the Russians, though overwhelmingly poor and illiterate, possessed one of the most glittering courts in Europe, a huge standing army, and a smothering bureaucracy. Russia was acknowledged as one of Europe's foremost powers. Catherine was succeeded by her son Paul I, who for thirty-four years had waited for the throne that he had always considered to be rightfully his. Five years of Paul's madness brought about a palace revolt, Paul's

The Kremlin in 1800

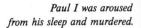

*Paul I was aroused
from his sleep and murdered.*

Alexander I reviewing the troops

murder, and the placing of his son, Alexander I, on the Romanov throne.

REFORM AND REPRESSION

Alexander I became czar in 1801 in the midst of a revolutionary age. The new Russian ruler appeared at first to be a liberal reformer, and the early years of his reign seemed to forecast a relaxation of the all-pervasive power of the autocracy. He reorganized the central administrative organs to reduce bureaucratic confusion. He instituted educational reforms, financed the building of universities and schools, and decreed that education would be open to all classes rather than just to upper-class children. He made obvious his own distaste for serfdom, but did not take official steps to abolish it. The high promise of Alexander's early years was eventually worn down by the size of Russia's problems and, in the

middle of his reign, the czar despaired of finding solutions to those problems. He complained that he needed thousands of officials to administer the huge country, but could not find fifty who were trustworthy.

Externally, Alexander's reign was essentially a continuation of the expansionist policies of his ancestors. Worried about Napoleon's designs on the Continent, Alexander abrogated an inherited alliance with France, then sent his troops to engage French forces in Prussia. The Russian army suffered two severe military defeats, but distance saved the homeland and Napoleon was generous in his treatment of the czar at their famed meeting in Tilsit. Russia was once again aligned with France. The new Franco-Russian alliance was barren, however, because of the incompatibility of national interests, and in 1812 Napoleon led the Grand Army in its ill-fated invasion of Russia. Two years later Alexander rode triumphantly into Paris. With the czar playing a leading role

The meeting between Napoleon and Alexander on the Nieman River

Alexander Petrovich. Czar Alexander I, upon the death of his father, Paul Petrovich, ascended to the throne (March 12, 1801). But his coronation didn't take place until September 15, 1801. The czar became known to the people as the blessed. The religious ceremony of the coronation "moved" the twenty-three-year-old czar, and as a result he forgave public debts and penalties, deferred the draft, allowed the Vatican to enter into religious ceremony along with the Orthodox church, etcetera. He wanted to abolish serfdom but had to settle for a ukaze reform under which landowners could free villages, and stopped the granting of inhabited land to nobles, and penalized landlords for abusing serfs.

But Alexander I's biggest test of his rule came on June 12, 1812, when the militarily invincible Napoleon invaded Russia with 600,000 troops. When Alexander I's offer of terms was rejected by Napoleon, the czar vowed to fight until the last Frenchman was driven from Russian soil. He told his 200,000 soldiers, the noblemen, the clergy, and the people to "unite, and fight with a crucifix in your heart and a weapon in your arms and no human power will be able to prevail against you."

By November 1812 the last of the French soldiers had retreated from Russia and in 1813 Czar Alexander I entered Paris at the head of his victorious armies. The Blessed died on November 19, 1825, going to his grave with the firm conviction that the other foreign sovereigns would embrace Christianity and that it was only a question of time that Russia would also follow suit.

Napoleon's flight from his "Waterloo"

The Imperial Russian flag at the time

Alexander declined to enter into the peace treaties after the Battle of Austerlitz and joined Prussia in another war against France. He visited with the Prussian king Frederick William and his queen Louise and while in their country visited the tomb of Frederick the Great, where all three pledged to fight to the death against Napoleon.

Alexander meeting the Prussian and Austrian sovereigns in Leipzig

as peacemaker at the Congress of Vienna in 1815, Russia gained in prestige and Alexander emerged as one of Europe's leading monarchs.

Internally, Russia remained an absolute monarchy even though Alexander granted constitutions to the kingdom of Poland, of which he was king, and to the grand duchy of Finland, of which he was grand duke. He had one of his closest advisers draw up a constitutional plan for Russia, but nothing was ever done with it. Alexander discontinued the practice of crown grants in land and peasants, and the serfs of the Baltic provinces were emancipated, but the vast majority of Russian serfs were unaffected by the wave of liberalism that rolled over Europe in the wake of the French Revolution and the Napoleonic wars.

Official opposition prevented the infiltration of revolutionary ideas, but many of the officers who had followed Alexander across Europe returned with liberal ideas and imprecise notions of doing something to relieve the oppression of the masses in their homeland. Alexander's sudden death in 1825 while on a trip in the south brought confusion concerning the succession and a seemingly opportune time for a revolutionary movement. An abortive revolution known as the Decembrist Uprising followed. The Decembrist leaders, with no agreed goals or plans of action, tried to incite various army garrisons to revolt and to demand a constitution, but no revolutionary preparation had been accomplished among the soldiery or among the people, with the result that the revolt was quickly suppressed and the leaders were either hanged or exiled to Siberia.

Although the Decembrist movement ended in disaster and was little more than a caricature of a revolution, it became a symbol for revolutionaries, radicals, liberals,

The coronation of Nicholas I

and patriots for the remainder of the turbulent nineteenth century. It was also a symbol for Nicholas I, brother and successor to Alexander, who devoted his thirty-year reign to the suppression of liberal ideas. Nicholas I became the defender of the status quo, and his reign was notable for autocratic oppression even to the point of sending Russian troops abroad to quell revolution in neighboring states. The days of Russian influence in European affairs were numbered, however, as the government of Nicholas I blundered into the Crimean War against a coalition of powers. The bravery of the individual Russian soldier and sailor could not hold back the modern weapons and tactics of the French and British forces, and in a humiliating defeat Russia was exposed as a giant without power. Nicholas I died in 1855 and was succeeded by his son Alexander II before the Crimean debacle was finally concluded.

The new czar, as conservative as his father but more practical, realized that the harsh measures of the past had to be tempered and, more important, that serfdom was an anachronism which Russia could no longer afford. From an economic viewpoint, serf labor was expensive and inefficient. Writers decried the system for what it did to human values and human dignity. Alexander II, more and more concerned over the fifteen hundred peasant uprisings of the first sixty years of the century, freed the serfs by imperial proclamation in March 1861.

The evils of a system that had virtually enslaved millions of Russians for centuries lived on after the abolishment of the system. Former serfs found themselves in a new type of bondage as they borrowed money to buy land which they had to have for simple existence. Landowners felt that they should be paid for the loss of serf labor. The emperor proclaimed emancipation, but could not proclaim peace and prosperity for the emancipated.

Alexander II initiated a series of reforms but, attempting to retain complete autocracy, he often tried to emasculate the measures that his government introduced. Reforms once initiated, however, proved difficult to re-

Nicholas Pavlovich I. From the time of Czar Nicholas I's coronation on August 22, 1826, until his death (February 18, 1855) he upheld a balance of church, monarchy, and democracy. Like his father, he sheltered Christianity but was a shrewd diplomat and gave his people solid sovereign rule through his efforts, both, at the negotiation table (the Treaty of Turkmanchaisk) with Persia, and on the battlefield with Poland and Turkey. Prior to his death he gave his people eighteen years of uninterrupted peace. This painting shows him as he looked early in his reign.

Czar Nicholas I as he appeared later in his life

Alexander II guarded in the streets of St. Petersburg

Alexander Nicolaevich. This czar, Alexander II, ascended the imperial throne at the height of the Crimean War and his first request of the people was to turn to God. Once the Crimean War ended in the east, Alexander II announced his intention to abolish serfdom in Russia and he signed the great manifesto ending it on February 19, 1861.

Known as the Liberator, he accomplished more for the people of Russia than any other czar. In his twenty-six-year reign he brought the telegraph system to the country, by the Treaty of Peking in 1860 extended the Russian Empire into China, created a school system, saw to it that women were also sent to school and brought about many other national and public achievements.

But the nobility wasn't pleased with his humanitarian ways and five unsuccessful attempts were made on his life. His response each time was, "Upon God, I place my trust. His will be done." It was on March 1, 1881, when the next assassination attempt was successful. An exploding bomb inflicted mortal injury on the czar during Lent in a period of prayer with his family.

The coronation procession of Alexander II

strain, and Alexander II is often referred to in histories as Czar-Liberator and Great Reformer. The reforms carried through in local government, the judicial system, the military forces, in education, and in the fiscal system placed Russia on the threshold of a new era while the rigidity of the autocracy kept the door open to the past.

On the international scene, Alexander could do little to regain prestige and influence in Europe so soon after the Crimean defeat. On the Asian mainland, however, the czar could and did continue the tradition of expansion that had been going on since Muscovy first added to its original six hundred square miles. Alexander's armies conquered the remaining khanates and secured the trans-Caspian region. At the expense of troubled China, Russia acquired vast territories around the Amur and Ussuri rivers, leading to years of claims, counterclaims, and continual boundary disputes. The Caucasus mountain region also came under effective control after years of conflict with the various nationalistic Caucasian tribes.

Despite the aggrandizement of empire through new conquests, the freeing of millions of subjects, and the host of reforms, Russia remained a troubled country. A spirit of revolution, growing out of abject poverty and fed by the writings of the radical intelligentsia, was prevalent throughout the cities and towns. Overthrow of the czarist system was the aim of the most radical groups, whereas moderates thought that constitutionalism could cure Russia's ills. Anarchistic and nihilistic underground groups sprang up.

A secret society called Land and Freedom had as its goal a mass peasant uprising, but thought it necessary to educate the peasantry toward this goal before success could be possible. In this movement hundreds of revolutionaries were arrested by the czar's police, and many others were beaten or turned over to the police by the suspicious peasants. With the countryside proving to be unreceptive to, and suspicious of, city-bred revolutionaries, the latter turned their propagandizing efforts toward the more fertile areas of the universities and factories.

Extremists turned to acts of terrorism, making several attempts on the life of Alexander II, who was finally killed by a terrorist's bomb in 1881.

The reactionary attitude introduced by Alexander III after the murder of his father became the hallmark of the remaining years of Russian czardom. The few political and individual rights that were gained so slowly over the centuries slipped away as many reforms were annulled or ignored. People were subjected to arbitrary arrest, trial, and sentencing with little or no recourse to legal proceedings as the regimes of Alexander III and Nicholas II sought to perpetuate absolute monarchy. Russia, in effect, was a police state.

In areas other than political, the Russian Empire under its last two czars was not stagnating. Industrialization, arriving late in Russia as compared with western Europe, once started, grew at an amazing rate. In the

The assassination of Czar Alexander II

Alexander Alexandrovich. Alexander III reigned from 1881 until his death on October 20, 1894, and was determined to preserve the peace both at home and abroad. He was called the czar-peacemaker. When Germany, Italy, and Austria banded together to threaten the peace of Europe, Alexander III entered into a pact with France, thus maintaining the balance of power and peace. He promoted industrialization of the nation as a means toward economic independence. As a result, the vast resources of Russia for the first time were developed and exported. He created the Farmer's Bank throughout Russia in 1882 so the emancipated serfs could purchase land at low interest rates.

wake of Russia's industrial revolution came all the adverse effects that had earlier beset other industrialized nations. Poor peasants flocked to new industrial centers, depressing the labor market and creating instant slums. Women and children were exploited in factories and mines alongside their husbands and fathers. The unsafe, unhealthy working and living conditions were as bad or worse than those in the industrialized west.

Russia also had the problem of a shortage of indigenous capital and was flooded by foreign investment with the concurrent lack of concern for local conditions. Because of the poverty of local consumers, Russian producers were forced to seek export markets, but their products could not compete with those of the more industrially developed countries. New markets were found in the east, while the government, prodded by its enlightened and able finance minister, Serge Witte, aided industrialization by establishing banks and building railroads. The famous Trans-Siberian Railway, completed in 1904, provided a necessary link between European Russia and the Pacific coast.

In the face of industrialization and the complexities of modernization, Alexander III and his son Nicholas II both persevered in their attempts to run the empire in the style of Peter the Great or Ivan the Terrible—as a personal estate. Alexander was strong willed and reactionary in the mold of Nicholas I and so many other predecessors who had reacted to liberal trends with severe repression. Nicholas II had inherited his father's reactionary attitudes but not his strong will. Nicholas's weakness of character and his tendency toward vacillation eventually contributed to the downfall of imperial Russia.

REVOLUTION

At the turn of the century the economy, still overwhelmingly agricultural, was staggered by a depression that further impoverished the populace, increased dissatisfaction with the government, and gave impetus to the growing forces of revolution. Nicholas, surrounded by incompetent advisers (he had a propensity for dismissing good ones), allowed Russia to stumble into what proved to be a disastrous war with Japan. A series of defeats revealed the ineptitude of the czar as a leader and demonstrated the gross inefficiency of the bureaucracy in administering the affairs of the nation.

The spark needed to ignite revolution came when an order to fire on a workers' demonstration was given to the St. Petersburg militia. The demonstration had been peaceful. The workers of the capital with their wives and children had marched to the Winter Palace to petition the czar to intervene on their behalf against the intolerable conditions brought about by depression and war. The demonstrators, carrying religious icons and pictures of the czar, sang hymns as they marched to the palace. The militia opened fire at close range, and the resulting massacre, known in Russian history as Bloody Sunday, was the first act of violence of the Revolution of 1905.

For the remainder of the year Russia was torn by strikes and civil strife, and at times the czardom itself seemed to be in danger of collapse. By granting concessions of certain civil liberties and, more important, a legislature (Duma), Nicholas managed to survive. The importance of the Revolution of 1905 lay in the fact that the masses of Russian people had risen against extreme oppression. This was not a revolt instigated by the Marxist Bolsheviks or Mensheviks, the Socialist Revolutionaries, or any other radical group. This was the voice of the long-suffering Russian people making themselves heard by means of a popular revolution—a fact seemingly missed or ignored by Nicholas, who returned to his autocratic ways.

By the end of 1905 revolutionary fervor was waning, and opposition to the monarchy was divided between the Bolshevik-led groups that wanted complete overthrow and those less radical factions that were willing to settle for the minimal constitutionalism promised by the czar. Elections were held in December, and the first Duma convened in St. Petersburg in May 1906. Nicholas, expecting a subservient Duma because of the restrictive election laws, was horrified by the liberal demands of the new legislative body and forthwith dissolved the first Duma by imperial decree. New elections were held, but a second Duma was heavily Socialist in membership and, after meeting for only three months, met the same fate as its predecessor.

After considerable manipulation of the electoral laws, a third Duma met with the czar's grudging approval and served its full five-year term. The fourth and final Duma sat through the war years until it was abolished by the Bolsheviks, ending Russia's brief experiment with parliamentarism. Despite the extreme limitations placed on the Duma, it was a rudimentary legislature. Nicholas thought of his powers as God-given and viewed any constitutional limitation as sinful and heretical. He was guided by the idea that the throne of the Romanovs should be passed on to his son as he had received it from his father: absolute and autocratic.

In the face of inevitable change presaged by the Revolution of 1905, the intransigent czar gave ground slowly and only when there was no alternative. During the Duma period of limited constitutionalism, a strong man emerged as prime minister. Peter Stolypin, a monarchist who dedicated himself to preservation of the autocracy, was also a practical man who realized that certain reforms were necessary for the survival of the regime. Stolypin's first move was a program of pacification by which he planned to eliminate the nuclei of revolution. The new prime minister established military courts to deal with revolutionaries, and soon references to the "Stolypin necktie" became common as more and more

Czar Nicholas II at the time of his coronation

Empress Alexandra Feodorovna

The coronation of Czar Nicholas II in the Cathedral of the Ascension in Moscow

The coronation of Nicholas II—illumination of the Kremlin

The taking of the Communion during the coronation

The handing of the scepter during the coronation

The procession after the coronation of Their Imperial Majesties.

The Imperial Bodyguard swearing allegiance to Nicholas II

enemies of the regime were summarily tried and hanged.

As pacification progressed, Stolypin introduced land reforms, which began the transformation of the Russian countryside from the centuries-old communal system to a capitalistic farming structure. During the reform period hundreds of thousands of peasants were allowed to break their ties with the village communes and acquire land in their own names. The reformers hoped to create a new class of independent farmers who, as landowners, would be conservative in their politics and loyal to the czar. The reforms were rather slow moving, however, and Stolypin, a hard-driving person impatient with inefficiency and corruption, was making enemies on all sides. In 1911 he was assassinated by a revolutionary. A class of small landholders had been established, but the reforms had not progressed to the desired extent and, without the forcefulness of Stolypin, the reform movement languished. Meantime, along with Europe's other nations, Russia blundered along the path toward World War I.

When Russia entered the war in August 1914, the czar was able to mobilize millions of men, but despite the progress of the previous decade, the industrial base was not equal to the task of supplying and moving a modern war machine. Russian troops fought valiantly, inflicting serious defeats on Austrian and Turkish armies and forcing the Germans to engage in a two-front war at a time when France and England were in dire need of help; however, Russian losses in killed, wounded, and prisoners were huge and, with the breakdown of supply and transport, there were times when as many as 25 percent of the frontline troops were without weapons. Soldiers were instructed to retrieve rifles of fallen comrades on the battlefield.

As the fierce fighting and massive losses failed to halt the German advance, morale at the front deteriorated dangerously, and at home similar discontent grew as every village watched rapidly mounting casualty lists. Political unrest, fostered by active revolutionary propaganda, became endemic and was increased when Nicholas assumed personal command of the forces. Petrograd, which had formerly been known as St. Petersburg, was left in the hands of Empress Alexandra, the German-born wife of the czar, whose autocratic views had never endeared her to the Russian people and who was now widely accused of being a German agent. Alexandra's chief adviser and confidant was the ignorant peasant-monk Rasputin, whose escapades offended the Orthodox sensibilities of most Russians, whether nobles or peasants. Rasputin's hold over Alexandra, and through her over Nicholas, gave him such enormous power that he actually held the reins of government, dismissing and appointing officials at a dizzying rate.

Once again in the midst of a disastrous war, the Russian monarchy was shaken and, despite the murder of Rasputin in December 1916, the whole structure of czar-

The czar Nicholas II visits with the president of France, Felix Faure, during French naval maneuvers in an attempt to pacify age-old feeling of conflict.

The czar, walking behind the priest, attending church services

Gregori Rasputin as he appeared shortly before his murder in 1916

dom crashed in the revolution of March 1917. As in 1905, it was the people of Russia, almost leaderless, revolting against conditions that had become intolerable. Spurred on by revolutionary propaganda but reacting to conditions rather than to exhortations, the masses stirred as the housewives of Petrograd took to the streets demanding bread. The women were soon joined by workers. Troops ordered to suppress the disturbances joined the demonstrators. Four days later Nicholas II was forced to abdicate, ending the three-century rule of the Romanovs. The Russian monarchy, which traced its beginnings to Rurik in the year 862, passed into history.

Nicholas II imprisoned at Tsarskoe Selo, 1917

Grand Duke Michael of Russia. As the revolution in Russia caught hold Nicholas acted under this new influence as readily as he had succumbed to the influence of his former reactionary advisers and signed a document that left his throne vacant.

"But I cannot consent to part from my son," he said, "so I abdicate in favor of my brother Michael."

The grand duke Michael wisely refused to accept the honor thus bestowed on him unless at the request of a Constituent Assembly, thus leaving the throne vacant. By that time the manifestation of public opinion in favor of abolishing entirely the monarchical form of government asserted itself so strongly that no further effort was made to find a candidate for the throne, and the provisional government remained the supreme authority of the state.

The ex-czar Nicholas for several days remained at liberty, traveling aimlessly back and forth in his sumptuous drawing-room car, until finally he was arrested and imprisoned at Tsarskoe Selo, together with the rest of his family.

The royal portrait of His Imperial Majesty, the sovereign emperor, Nicholas II, and his august family. Taken at the royal grounds at Tsarskoe Selo, June 3, 1913. In the back row, left to right: grand-duchesses Marie, Titiana, and Olga, with Anastasis seated on the far right. Empress Alexandra Feodorovna and the emperor seated in the center with Czarevitch Aleksei at their feet. All seven members were imprisoned first at Tsarskoe Selo in 1817 and later murdered at Ekaterinburg by their captors on July 17, 1918.

THE ROYAL SOVEREIGNS OF IMPERIAL RUSSIA

Reign	Title	Ruler
GRAND DUKES OF KIEV		
862–879	Grand Duke	Rurik of Novgorod
879–912	Grand Duke	Oleg (Helgi)
912–945	Grand Duke	Igor
945–955	Regent	Saint Olga
955–972	Grand Duke	Sviatoslav
973–980	Grand Duke	Yaropolk
980–1015	Grand Duke	Saint Vladimir the Sunny
1015–1019	Grand Duke	Sviatopolk
1019–1054	Grand Duke	Yaroslav the Just
1054–1073	Grand Duke	Izhaslav (Isiaslav)
1073–1076	Grand Duke	Sviatoslav
1078–1093	Grand Duke	Vsevolod
1093–1113	Grand Duke	Sviatopolk
1113–1125	Grand Duke	Valdimir Monomachus
1125–1132	Grand Duke	Mstislav
1132–1139	Grand Duke	Yaropolk
1139–1146	Grand Duke	Vsevolod
1146–1154	Grand Duke	Izhaslav II

Reign	Title	Ruler
GRAND DUKES OF VALDIMIR		
1154–1157	Grand Duke	Yuri (George) Dolgoruki
1157–1175	Grand Duke	Andrey Bogolyubski
1176–1212	Grand Duke	Vsevolod
1212–1218	Grand Duke	Konstantin
1218–1238	Grand Duke	Yuri II
1238–1246	Grand Duke	Yaroslav II
1246–1253	Grand Duke	Andrey
1253–1263	Grand Duke	Aleksandr Nevsky
1263–1272	Grand Duke	Yaroslav of Tver
1272–1276	Grand Duke	Basil
1276–1293	Grand Duke	Demetrius
1293–1304	Grand Duke	Andrey
1304–1318	Grand Duke	Michael of Tver
1318–1326	Grand Duke	Yuri Danilovich of Moscow
1326–1328	Grand Duke	Alexander of Tver

CZARS OF RUSSIA

(Ivan I called himself czar, but it wasn't an official title until the reign of Ivan IV.)

Reign	Title	Ruler
GRAND DUKES OF MOSCOW		
1328–1341	Grand Duke	Ivan I (Kalita)
1341–1353	Grand Duke	Simeon
1353–1359	Grand Duke	Ivan II
1359–1389	Grand Duke	Demetrius Donski
1389–1425	Grand Duke	Basil I
1425–1462	Grand Duke	Basil II
1462–1505	Grand Duke	Ivan III, the Great
1505–1530	Grand Duke	Basil III
1530–1584	Czar of all Russia	Ivan IV, the Terrible
1584–1598	Czar	Fedor I
1598–1605	Czar	Boris Godunov
1605–1605	Czar	Fedor II
1605–1606	Czar	Dimitri the Imposter (Demetrius I)
1606–1610	Ruler	Basil IV Chouiski
1607–1610	Czar	Dimitri (Demetrius II)
1610–1612	Ruler	Ladislaus IV of Poland

Reign	Title	Ruler
CZARS (EMPERORS) HOUSE OF ROMANOV		
1613–1645	Emperor	Michael I
1645–1676	Emperor	Aleksei (Alexis)
1676–1683	Emperor	Fedor III
1682–1689	Emperor	Ivan V
1682–1689	Regent	Sophia
1682–1725	Emperor	Peter I, the Great
1725–1727	Empress	Catherine I
1727–1730	Emperor	Peter II
1730–1740	Empress	Anna (Duchess of Courland)
1740–1741	Emperor	Ivan VI
1741–1762	Empress	Elizabeth Petrovna
1762–1762	Emperor	Peter III
1762–1796	Empress	Catherine II, the Great
1796–1801	Emperor	Paul I
1801–1825	Emperor	Alexander I
1825–1855	Emperor	Nicholas I
1855–1881	Emperor	Alexander II
1881–1894	Emperor	Alexander III
1894–1917	Emperor	Nicholas II

16

The Polish Kingdoms

Throughout its one thousand-year history Poland has maintained a sense of unity and nationhood despite losses of independence and drastic frontier shifts brought about by foreign conquests, invasions, partitions, and occupations.

During its first eight centuries as an independent state, Poland grew to be one of the largest countries in Europe, particularly after the union with Lithuania. As Poland expanded, it collided with its expansionist neighbors, Prussia and Russia; in addition, it also had to defend its territory from Czechs, Turks, Swedes, and other enemies. Weakened by foreign wars, but more so by internal dissension and political instability, Poland was finally reduced to impotency and was dismembered by Prussia, Russia, and Austria. Polish territory was divided among the three powers in 1772, 1793, and 1775—the last date marking the disappearance of Poland as a great nation in Europe.

EARLY ORIGIN

Although the exact origin of the Slavs is obscure, archaeological evidence supports the theory that Slavic tribes inhabited areas in the Wisla (Vistula) River basin as early as the second millennium B.C. These tribes migrated in many directions from the Wisla area and eventually formed differentiated groupings generally referred to as East, West, and South Slavs. Early in the Christian Era those groups that migrated to the west had reached the fertile valley of the Elbe River and had penetrated as far northward as the Baltic Sea. Among the largest and the best organized of these tribes was the Polanie, a group located along the Warta River that forcibly united several tribes. The Polanie are generally considered to have taken their name, which was eventually passed on to the state, from the word *pole,* meaning "field" or "plain." Thus the Polanie were field dwellers or plains people. Modern Poles are descended from the Polanian union of West Slavs.

Since the plains area offered few impassable barriers into surrounding areas, the Polanie lived in a loose grouping of shifting communities. Among these communities a limited network of more permanent settlements had been established in which primitive buildings were erected, which generally included the dwelling of the tribal chieftain, or prince, and which served as the nucleus of a small town. The Polanie tribe, although primarily dependent upon an argicultural economy, also pursued certain handicrafts, engaged in a limited form of trade, and developed a somewhat sophisticated culture.

THE PIAST KINGDOM

The impetus for the creation of a unified state among the Polanie and the neighboring tribes came with the need to resist the increasing invasions of the area by the Germanic tribes from the west. To meet this danger, the tribes united in the middle of the ninth century A.D. under the Polanie princes of the Piast Dynasty, who developed the region into a viable political entity. One of the earliest Piast kings, Mieszko I, in 966 established the first recorded capital of the state at Gniezno, to the northeast of the present-day city of Poznan. He also secured the new state from German intrusions by placing the kingdom under the protection of the Holy Roman Empire and by accepting Christianity for himself and the Polish people.

The kingdom was drawn further into the orbit of Rome and western civilization under Mieszko's son, Boleslaus I, who expanded the state and extended its authority and influence as far east as the Dnepr River in Russia. This eastward push did much to sustain the prosperity of the nation through the Middle Ages by opening commercial routes to the Black Sea area, but at the same time it led to an overextension, which ultimately resulted in the loss of much of the state's territory in the west.

The power and independence of the Polish state were maintained by succeeding Piast kings until the reign of

The Polish prince Mieszko I (960–92) was the first official king of Poland. Faced on his borders by the triumphant armies of Otto I of Saxony, founder of the Holy Roman Empire, conqueror of France, Denmark, Burgundy, and Bohemia, King Mieszko promptly and smartly recognized the sovereignty of the German Empire, forsook the faith of his fathers, and embraced Christianity.

Boleslaus the Brave (992–1025), the eldest son of Mieszko, having disposed of his brothers, with whom he was joint heir to the domains of his father, became the single ruler of Poland and determined to push her boundaries far and wide. After having successfully checkmated the Bohemian and Ruthenian invasions, Boleslaus defeated the Pomeranians and conquered the Baltic seacoast. In the year 999 the old commercial town of Cracow was annexed, and after beating back a Hungarian invasion, Boleslaus added Trans-Carpathian Slavonia to Poland.

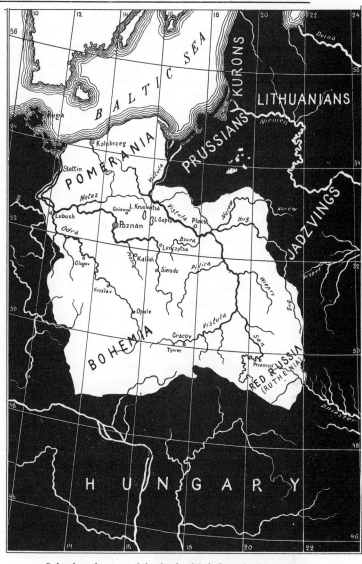

Poland at the time of the death of Boleslaus the Brave, 1025

Three coins of Boleslaus the Brave from his period

To curb the Bohemian ambition the Germans lent their aid to Casimir the Restorer (1034–58), who restored unity and peace and began to devote himself to internal reorganization along German lines. He established a bureaucracy and an ecclesiastical hierarchy, rebuilt cities and churches, and imposed very heavy taxes and duties on the people in an effort to reduce them into complete subjugation to the warriors and clergy. In compensation for the aid of Germany, Casimir recognized the sovereignty of the German emperor and renounced the title of king.

Boleslaus III who, before his death in 1138, decreed that the appanage system of inheritance would be instituted whereby the kingdom would be divided into principalities and each of his four sons would reign as a prince. The oldest son became prince of the strong and rich southern principality of Silesia and was supposedly senior in authority, but the division of loyalties among the princes brought on a long period of dynastic struggle, intrigue, and national weakness. As generation followed generation, the original principalities were continually subdivided among male heirs, creating further dissension and inviting invasion from Poland's powerful neighbors. During the almost two hundred years during which the appanage system held sway, the northern region of Pomerania and the port of Gdansk (Danzig) were lost to the Teutonic knights, depriving Poland of access to the sea. Silesia, which had been subdivided into sixteen minuscule principalities, was taken over by the expanding kingdom of Bohemia.

In the early part of the fourteenth century the Polish state was reunited under Casimir the Great, the last of the Piast kings and one of Poland's greatest rulers. During his nearly forty-year reign Poland became a full member of the European community, capitalized on a constructive foreign policy that enlarged its territory to the east, and underwent a series of enlightened reforms that accelerated the country's constitutional and cultural development. Under Casimir, Polish law was codified, the currency was reformed, and western administrative methods were introduced in both towns and rural areas. In addition, he introduced a system of efficient administration throughout the country; founded the first Polish university at Krakow; fostered the growth of towns, art, and commerce; and encouraged the development of the church as a unifying force in the restoration of stability and order. During Casimir's reign Jews were welcomed as immigrants and came in great numbers because of persecution in many other countries. Jews quickly moved into mercantile pursuits that were looked upon with disdain by the Polish gentry.

King Ladislaus I Herman (1079–1102)

The seal of Ladislaus I Herman

During the reign of Boleslaus II, the Bold (1058–79), there occurred that famous struggle for supremacy between Pope Gregory VII, Hildebrand, and the emperor Henry IV. In recognition of the assistance shown him in this conflict, the pope crowned Boleslaus as independent king in 1076. Seeking revenge, the emperor recognized the Bohemian ruler as king and offered him the Polish provinces of Cracow and Silesia. A war followed that led to internal dissensions in Poland. In carrying out rigorously the reforms of Hildebrand, the king made many enemies among the clergy. His despotic character was also resented by the nobility. Under the leadership of the king's brother, Wladyslav Herman, a revolution broke out. The bishop of Cracow interdicted the king and joined the Bohemians. For this he paid the penalty of death. The story goes that the infuriated king personally murdered the bishop in the church at Mass. Recent studies, however, show that the bishop was tried for treason by the King's Court, was found guilty, and was executed.

The civil war resulted in the king's defeat and he fled the country. Cracow and southern Poland went to Bohemia, and Poland once more became a feudatory of the German Empire, and the new ruler, Ladislaus I Herman (1079–1102), lost his title of king.

By a skillful playing off of Poland and Bohemia against each other, and by the active encouragement of internal hereditary strifes, the German emperors kept both of these Western Slavic nations from developing into powerful states.

The years following the death of Ladislaus I Herman witnessed one of those terrific internal strifes that, in this instance, was aggravated by a German invasion, finally repelled by Boleslaus the Wrymouthed (1102–1138), who succeeded also in conquering Pomerania and extending the Polish possessions on the Baltic seaboard, far across the Oder up to and including the island of Rugia (Rugen). He died, however, a feudatory of the German emperor.

The ruler of Cracow obtained the title of *dux Poloniae*, the duke of Poland, but the security of his office depended upon his relations with the aristocracy and clergy. Casimir the Just (1177–94) had been obliged to summon a council of nobles and clergy and to surrender certain of his rights and privileges. He was also compelled to promise to call such councils when important matters of state were to be decided upon. At the Council or Synod of Lenczyca, held in 1180, the church, under the threat of an interdict, enjoined the duke from the exercise of his right to the personal property of deceased bishops (Ius Spolii) and to certain levies for his officials and representatives. In return for these concessions or immunities the council abolished the seniorate and vested in the line of Casimir the Just the perpetual right to the principality of Cracow. Thus the right of seniority in the House of Piast the Wheelwright gave way to the law of primogeniture in the line of Casimir the Just. This right was frequently contested by armed interference. The authority of the duke of Cracow was not adequately defined by law and was nil in actual practice. The heads of the smaller principalities were, in fact, independent rulers.

One of the princes of Great Poland, Ladislaus I Lokietek (1306–33), an able and enterprising man, who, by the unification lost his title to sovereignty, fled abroad, enlisted the help of the powerful Pope Boniface VIII, and, choosing an appropriate moment when Bohemia became involved in a war with Hungary, appeared in Poland. He met with a cordial reception in all the parts of the country. Lokietek was but an incarnation of the national spirit that had produced Boleslaus the Brave and Boleslaus the Wrymouth and that revealed itself most powerfully in the days of Jagiello and on many subsequent occasions in the course of Polish history. The union brought about by the leadership of Lokietek was, however, personal at first. The sovereign was the only bond that kept the various provinces together. In their internal organization the component parts of the unified state were completely autonomous and governed in exactly the same way as they had been before the consolidation took place. To give to the political unity an adequate outward expression Lokietek strove for royal dignity. With the consent of the pope he was crowned in 1320 in Cracow as an independent king of Poland.

The historians record Casimir III, the Great (1333–70), as the first official king of Poland. He served well in unifying the independent factions in a common effort.

The period preceding the unification of the country abounded in warfare and bloodshed. Prince Przemvsi of Great Poland, with the consent of the pope, crowned himself king of Poland in Gniezno (Gnesen) in 1295, but a few months later was murdered by the agents of Brandenburg. After his death the struggle between the various princes who strove for the high dignity again became acute. As a compromise Wenceslaus, king of Bohemia, was crowned king of Poland in 1300. All Poland, except Mazovia, came under his scepter. The unification, however, entailed the loss of national independence and subjected Poland to a rigid administrative rule of Bohemia and to a strong German influence, which at that time had already become predominant in Bohemia.

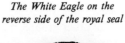

The seal of Casimir the Great   The White Eagle on the reverse side of the royal seal

THE JAGIELLON DYNASTY

Because there was no direct heir when Casimir died in 1370, a series of rapid dynastic changes occurred that continued until 1386. In that year Queen Hedwig, one of Casimir's descendants, who had gained the throne through concessions to the Polish nobility, married Ladislaus Jagiello, grand duke of Lithuania. The union established between the two countries later was formalized at the state level and lasted for nearly two centuries. Although less well developed than Poland at the time of the union, Lithuania was a vast state consisting of its homeland near the Baltic Sea and also encompassing large parts of modern Belorussia and the Ukraine to the south and east. Within the union Jagiello, who had accepted Christianity for himself and Lithuania, ruled both countries as king of Poland, although each maintained its own separate government.

Under the Jagiellonians, Poland became one of the greatest powers in eastern Europe. After the Poles defeated the Teutonic knights early in the fifteenth century, Polish Pomerania and Gdansk were regained, and the country entered into an extended period of cultural and economic development. The influence of the Renaissance of the sixteenth century was expressed in architecture and science; the Polish language was developed as a medium for an expressive national literature; and new universities were established as centers of secular learning. Although Roman Catholicism and its culture remained predominant and were a rallying point for Polish nationalism, Protestantism, introduced with the Reformation, enjoyed widespread toleration and also made its contributions to the Western orientation of the general cultural achievements of the country.

After the two countries became affiliated, the Polish and Lithuanian nobility quickly became assimilated and gradually increased their prestige and influence. Members of the lesser nobility (landed gentry), in particular, acquired privileges and rights that greatly reduced the authority and strength of the crown. Polish kings became increasingly dependent on the goodwill of the nobles, particularly for the funds and manpower needed to support political and military undertakings. The rise in power of the landed gentry was generally accompanied by the deterioration of the political and social status of other groups, mainly the burghers and peasants. Deprived of freedom of movement and the ability to buy land and heavily taxed, increasing numbers were forced into the service of the nobility and were gradually reduced to serfdom.

By the middle of the sixteenth century a national parliament had emerged consisting of a senate, representing the greater nobles, and a lower house, called the Sejm, which was composed of delegates from the more numerous landed gentry. This parliament, or diet, became the supreme legislative organ of the state, and the king could

In 1370, Louis, then king of Hungary, ascended the throne of Poland. Ambitious but narrow-minded, he soon came into conflict with the Polish nobles, whom he desired to subdue as he had subdued the barons of his native land. Feeling against him rose high when he tore Red Russia from Poland and gave it to one of his friends with a feudatory title. Great Poland openly rebelled. Soon, however, he entered into a compromise with the nobles, particularly those of Little Poland, over the matter of succession to the Polish throne.

Lithuanian Prince Jagiello married Queen Hedwig and the two countries were joined. Prince Jagiello took the name of Ladislaus II and began the reign as king of Poland in 1386. He ruled until his death in 1434, when he was replaced on the throne by his son, Ladislaus III.

King Ladislaus III of Varna (1434–44)

The royal castle at Podhorce at the time

King Casimir IV Jagiello (1447–92). When Ladislaus III died in 1444, his brother, Casimir Jagiello, who had been discharging the office of grand duke of Lithuania, was very slow in ascending the Polish throne to which he was elected by the nobility, assembled in April 1445, at Sieradz. The chief reasons for his procrastination were his ambition to restore to Lithuania the provinces of Volhynia and Podolia, which were administered by Polish governors, and his disinclination to subscribe to the liberties and privileges of the clergy and nobility. When, after many fruitless presentations, the king remained recalcitrant and insisted that the two provinces be put under Lithuanian control, and that he not be compelled to sign the pacta conventa, the magnates conditionally elected Boleslav of Mazovia. Thus threatened, Casimir accepted the crown on June 18, 1447.

His first act after the coronation was to curb the power of the clergy by subordinating the church to the state. His war with the church and the pope made it possible for him to press his claims to the thrones of Bohemia and Hungary, after the childless death of Wladyslav Habsburg, son of Emperor Albert, whose beautiful sister he had married. The Hungarians proclaimed Matthias Corvinus, the son of John Hunyadi, as their king, and the Bohemians chose George of Poděbrad, a Hussite. The dissatisfied Catholic element in Bohemia turned to Poland. Casimir intervened, and as a consequence his son ascended the throne of Bohemia. Soon afterward Hungary, at the death of Matthias Corvinus, who left no legal sons, united with Bohemia under the same scepter. Polish influence was, in this way, established over a wide area and in foreign lands.

King John Albert. Immediately after the death of Casimir IV, John Albert was elected king of Poland (1492–1501). The Lithuanians elected his younger brother, Alexander, as grand duke of Lithuania in violation of the existing agreements. The new king was educated in accordance with the principles of Humanism, and, like his father, was determined to resist the power of the secular and temporal lords, and in these efforts sided with the nobility, whose idol he had become.

King Alexander (1501–6), before taking the throne, agreed with the Council of Magnates that he would abide by their direction. This made him little more than the "president of the Senate."

King Sigismund I (1506–48) started his rule with the "Nihil novi" statute, which did more harm to Poland than any other document to date. It provided that no new business could be conducted without the unanimous consent of the three estates—the king; the Senate; and the representatives of the landowners, the nobles. Because the nobles feared to give the king a big standing army, the country had a period of military unpreparedness.

He had four children: Isabella, whose husband was John, king of Hungary; Sigismund, who became king of Poland; Anne, who married the king of Poland, Stephen Bathory; and Catherine, whose husband was John III Vasa, king of Sweden.

The duke of Prussia swearing allegiance to Sigismund I at Cracow in 1525

Sigismund I, the Old, in his Renaissance sarcophagus in the Sigismund Chapel in Wawel Cathedral, the burial place of the Polish kings

pass no new laws without its consent. Eventually an extraordinary legislative practice called the *liberum veto* evolved, which in later years was widely abused and weakened the state by severely curtailing central authority and by perpetuating internal political weaknesses, confusion, and corruption. Under the *liberum veto* an individual legislator could block consideration of a proposal and, by interposing an outright veto, any delegate could dissolve the body and require resubmission of all current measures to a new assembly.

King Sigismund II (1548–72). Before the death of his father, Sigismund the Old, the Diet agreed to his accession but only on the condition that after Sigismund II's reign the kings would be elected. He had a serious encounter with the Senate for marrying Barbara Radziwill without their permission. The Senate for two years tried to make the king divorce her, but he held out and finally the Senate allowed her to be crowned queen.

THE ELECTIVE MONARCHY

In 1572 King Sigismund II, the last of the Jagiello line, died without an heir, and succession to the Polish crown became elective. Domestic affairs were in disorder, there being no recognized authority to curb political excesses and intrigues. Members of the Polish nobility had never developed the concept of service to the throne, and their continued struggle for position and wealth continually deprived the state of the cohesion it needed to maintain its independence. Succession to the throne became a competition among the royal houses of Europe and degenerated largely into a contractual arrangement in which the new monarch, before election, was required to sign a pact that severely limited his prerogatives and guaranteed the full rights and privileges of the nobility.

In the late sixteenth century and during most of the seventeenth, wars were fought with Russia, Turkey, and Sweden, primarily over outside vested interests held by the foreigners who occupied the Polish throne. Some Polish victories were won, particularly under the leadership of King John Sobieski between 1674 and 1696. Toward the close of the seventeenth century internal political decay and impotence had grown to such proportions that Polish efforts to resist external pressures were ineffective. After King John Sobieski's death in 1696, no fewer than eighteen foreign candidates competed for the vacant throne, which went to Augustus II of Saxony. His inept, thirty-six-year rule did little to retard further divisiveness and internal disintegration.

When Augustus II died in 1733, parliament elected a Polish nobleman king, but a Russian army sent into Warsaw prevented his accession and forced parliament to choose the son of Augustus II as the new ruler. The low state of effectiveness to which the Polish governmental institutions had sunk persisted throughout the undistinguished reign of Augustus III. Toward the end

Queen Barbara Radziwill

The Polish Republic in the year 1569

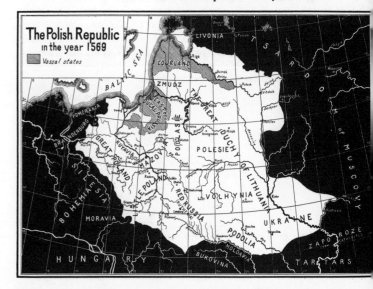

The Polish Republic in the year 1569

Vassal states

In April 1573, with 40,000 eligible voters present, a new king of Poland was elected. The candidates were Henry of Valois, the brother of the French king Charles IX; Archduke Ernest Habsburg, who was the younger son of the emperor Maximilian II; King John of Sweden; Czar Ivan the Terrible; Prince Stephen Bathory of Transylvania; and some lesser Polish candidates. The French candidate carried the vote because of the strong tie to the church. However, Henry was in Poland as the new king for only five months when his brother died. Henry fled to France, where he became King Henry III. The Polish people, particularly the noble families—who were very well educated and by far the most cultural people in the world at that period in history—were shocked that Henry chose to leave Poland. The honored historian Morfil explains this difference in a history book of Poland, "The Poles had a facility to speak Latin, French, German and Italian while in the entire Court of France (over a hundred members) only two spoke Latin."

Stephen Bathory (1574–86). After the flight of Henry of Valois from Poland, there proceeded an election for a new king. The Senate voted for the Austrian emperor, Maximilian II, and the nobles chose Stephen Bathory who was married to Anne Jagiello, sister of Sigismund II Augustus. Bathory was the first to arrive in Cracow and entered the city when the nobles were in control. He was crowned the king in 1576. All of Poland and Lithuania recognized him but Danzig and West Prussia rebelled. He soon put down the opposition. A rare king, schooled in both diplomacy and warfare, he won over his opposition and did in his enemies. He executed Samuel Zborowski, who with the help of foreign monarchs, came to Poland to upset the king and he dealt summarily with George Dscik, the leading Lithuanian magnate who was plotting with the czar of Muscovy. This king carried out judiciary reforms with the same justice for all including the nobles. His reign is noted for his success in curbing anarchy and also for convincing the Diet to finance him to a big army. He stopped the raids of the Turks and the Tatars, and drove Ivan the Terrible out of his invasion of Livdnia (1577). Ivan sued for peace but King Bathory wanted to move on and take control of Moscow. Ivan went to a foolish pope, who sent the famous Jesuit Antonnio Possevino to negotiate with the Polish king, after Ivan promised to turn himself and his country over to the Catholic church. Stephen Bathory accepted the terms of Ivan and the pope, and stopped his victory march with possession of Livdnia and the duchy of Polotsk. He died young on December 12, 1596, at the age of fifty-three, after serving as one of Poland's greatest Catholic kings.

The royal castle at Krasiczyn

The royal castle at Warsaw

King Bathory at Pskov settling his terms with Ivan the Terrible and Jesuit Antonnio

The Interregnum of 1586–87 ended in a war. The chief candidates were the Swedish archduke Sigismund Vasa, the son of King John and Catherine Jagiello, who was the second sister of Sigismund II Augustus; and Maximilian, the brother of the emperor Rudolf II. The archduke won and became King Sigismund III Vasa (1587–1632). Thought to be a tabula rasa, he soon proved to be the opposite—a king of strong character. He married an Austrian princess without the Senate's permission, an action that led to a secret agreement on his part to cede Estonia from Poland to the possession of Ernest Habsburg's Austria. This charge brought about an Inquisitorial in 1592 but the king survived it and ruled on until his death in 1632. He was noted in Polish history as one of the staunchest supporters of the church.

King Ladislaus IV Vasa (1632–48). Under this Polish king's reign, the nobles became "kinglets" and took possession of the people and the cities. The Radziwills came into ownership of 16 cities and 583 villages with a standing army of 6,000 to maintain control of their deedship, and the Potockis "royal" family ended up with 3 million acres and 130,000 serfs to work them.

Ladislaus IV died on May 20, 1648, on a journey to the Ukraine, where the brilliant and wise ruler had hoped to put down a rebellion by the peasants and cossacks against the "magnates, Jews, and Jesuits."

of the eighteenth century Poland maintained neither a standing army nor a diplomatic service and no longer attempted to follow any semblance of an independent foreign policy.

The political stagnation and decline of the country were accompanied by increasing social, cultural, and economic disintegration. The life of the peasant became harsher as the landed estates were more heavily exploited, and the towns and cities diminished in importance as a result of heavy taxation and a decline in commerce and trade. The lack of economic progress coupled with poor Polish attitudes toward commercial pursuits were significant factors in the retarded development of a prosperous middle class, the absence of which served to emphasize the great cleavage that existed between the nobility and the extremely large peasant class. The Roman Catholic church was the only important element of cohesion and unity that remained as a base of identity for the bulk of the population. This sense of identity was nurtured by the fact that most foreign invaders and rulers had been of different religions, including Protestant Swedes and Prussians, Orthodox Russians, and Muslim Turks. As a consequence, strong nationalistic Catholic feeling developed to the point where the dissident religious minorities were denied political recognition and were restricted in many of their religious activities.

John II Casimir Vasa (1648–68) served in a period when the constituency wanted a separation of church and state as well as banishment of the Jesuits who by now were well in control of the politics of Poland.

The Polish Republic at the time of her greatest expansion, 1634–60

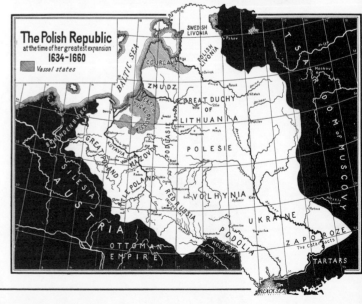

The Polish Republic at the time of her greatest expansion 1634–1660
Vassal states

The Polish winged Hussar, the elite personal soldier and officer in the king's army. These light cavalry troops were begun by King Bathory and were used by every king thereafter, with King John III Sobieski using them for battle and ceremonial royal guard.

King John III Sobieski (1674–96). This Polish king is considered the greatest of all of Poland's warrior-kings. In his early youth he showed great promise in the military by distinguishing himself against the invasions by the cossacks, Tatars, and Russians. He defeated the Turks under Mahomet IV and took their fortress of Kotzim in 1671, and was elected king of Poland in 1674. He went to the relief of Vienna when it was beseiged by the Turks in 1683, was successful and expelled the Turks from the country. In this action he became the first Supreme Commander of combined military forces, all of the Austrian, Bavarian, and Saxon armies.

The family portrait of King John III Sobieski, at right

Wilanow Palace (near Warsaw), at left and below. *The palace residence of King John III Sobieski whose wife, Queen Marie Casimire, designed the building and the grounds. At the end of World War II, it was looted and destroyed by the retreating Germans. Most of the treasures were recovered and the building was completely restored and rebuilt to its original splendor from 1956 to 1965 and is now a national museum and open to the public.*

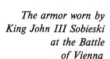

The gateway entrance to King Sobieski's palace at Wilanov

The armor worn by King John III Sobieski at the Battle of Vienna

King Stanislaus Leszczynski

A souvenir medal of the election of Stanislaus Leszczynski in 1733

The Supreme Allied Commander King John III Sobieski at the head of his troops before the Battle of Vienna

Augustus II, the Strong, reigned from 1697 to 1706 and lost the throne from 1704 (1706) to 1709 but regained it in 1709 and reigned again until 1733. The elector of Saxony, he became a Catholic in order to mount the throne as king of Poland. Poland served as his springboard for expansionist plans to conquer the Swedish Baltic possessions. The Polish Diet denied him support in his plans, so he used his Saxony troops to invade Lithuania and the great Northern War of 1700–21 began. Augustus II was defeated by King Charles XII of Sweden and abdicated his Polish throne, whereupon Stanislaus Leszczynski, his choice as successor, was elected to be king. Stanislaus remained as king of Poland until Charles XII was defeated by Russians in the Ukraine in 1709. Augustus II then withdrew his abdication, declaring it illegal, and reigned until 1733. Upon Augustus's death in 1733, Stanislaus was reelected and served in a very shaky political period from 1733 to 1736.

THE PARTITION PERIOD

Shortly after becoming empress of Russia in 1762, Catherine II (the Great) exerted pressure on the Polish state to restore full rights and privileges to the Orthodox and Protestant religious minorities. This campaign sparked a violent outbreak of armed conflict within the country, which lasted for nearly four years and was eventually put down by Russian military forces. Concerned over the large possible territorial gains that could accrue to Russia after this victory, Austria and Prussia concluded an agreement with Russia in 1772 whereby none of the three interested powers would acquire Polish territory to the exclusion of the others. This led to the first partition of Poland and the loss to the three competing powers of contiguous areas comprising almost one-third of its territory and one-half of its population.

The effects of this partition shocked the Polish nobility and stimulated them to undertake reforms that would strengthen the country. Their efforts resulted, in 1791, in a new constitution that abolished the *liberum veto,* established a hereditary monarchy, strengthened the executive power of the king, and gave political recognition to the urban middle class. This new constitution was opposed by a group of disgruntled nobles who appealed to Catherine II for full restoration of their privileges. As a result Russia, in collusion with Prussia, launched a second invasion of Poland in 1792 and within three months forced the country to accept a second treaty of partition. This second loss reduced Poland to less than one-third of its original prepartition area and left the country with a population of only about four million people.

The second partition also led to an insurrection in 1794, under the leadership of Tadeusz Kosciuszko, a Polish patriot who had distinguished himself earlier in

Augustus II as he appeared at the beginning of his second reign, 1709–33

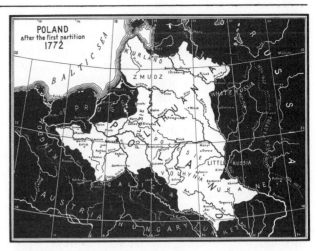

Poland after the first partition by Russia in 1772

King Augustus III (1734–63). In 1733, the people of Poland elected Stanislaus Leszczynski as king of Poland but on January 17, 1734, under protection of Russian and Saxon armies, Augustus III, the son of Augustus II, was crowned king of Poland in Cracow. The Diet of 1736 recognized Augustus III as king. Under his reign the beginning of the end of Polish royalty went through its stages with the formation of political parties that were in their very nature opposed to a monarchy in any form, including an elective one.

In the final election in Poland of a king, it ironically fell to the leader of the Russian conquerors, Empress Catherine, to make the choice. She "expressed" the view that her Polish lover, Stanislaus Augustus Poniatowski, be elected the king of Poland and the elective machinery obliged her. His coronation took place in Warsaw on November 25, 1764, the name day of Russian Empress Catherine. He served Poland and Russia until Poland was partitioned away by Russia, Austria, and Prussia.

Although Austria joined with Prussia and Russia in 1772 to divide up the kingdom of Poland, only ninety years before, Austria had been saved by the Poles from destruction. The Austrian Empire had been overrun by a Turkish army, which was on the point of capturing Vienna, when John Sobieski, the king of Poland, appeared on the scene with an army, relieved the capital, and drove the Turks out of the Austrian dominions. Here are the Polish troops with their prisoners after they had beaten the Turks.

A sketch of Ujazdow Castle in Warsaw as it appeared early in the reign of King Stanislaus Augustus. The dukes of Mazovia erected Ujazdow Castle in the sixteenth century and early in the next century King Sigismund III erected on the grounds a new castle. Partially destroyed during the Swedish wars, Ujazdow Castle was sold in 1674 to Lubomirski, the marshal of the crown. King Augustus II of the Saxon Dynasty in 1720 took a lease on the reconstructed "Ujazdow" from Lubomirski's heirs. In 1764 Ujazdow was bought by Stanislaus Poniatowski, who later in that year was elected king of Poland and assumed the name of Stanislaus Augustus and thus the castle reverted back to the monarch. But the castle proved to be too small for the king, and in 1775 he ceased to live there. At the same time, the king chose the Lazienka—one of the pavilions on the vast Ujazdow grounds—as his summer residence.

Lazienka was built shortly before 1690 on an island on a small rectangular lake. Described as "un 'edifice dans le goût grotesque," its centerpiece was a spacious circular and domed hall with a large water basin and fountain in a grotto setting. Lazienda Palace was known to the Poles as the Palace on the Waters. The grounds are now the Lazienki Park in the center of Warsaw.

This complex of Lazienki Park includes the White House (erected 1774–75), Myslewicki Palace.

the American Revolution. Although scoring some initial successes, Kosciuszko's forces were crushed by combined Russian and Prussian troops. The defense of Warsaw was a heroic but futile struggle that was concluded by the virtual massacre of its defenders by the Russians. After their victory, Russia and Prussia shared with Austria the remaining Polish territory in a final partition in 1795. This action totally eliminated Poland as a political entity for more than one hundred years.

After 1795 many Polish intellectuals, political leaders, officers, and patriots emigrated to France and organized military units within the French forces with the hope of returning to Poland with the revolutionary French army. In 1807 Napoleon defeated Prussia and fashioned from its Polish provinces the grand duchy of Warsaw, a puppet state, which enjoyed a liberal form of local government under a firm but tolerant French administration. Although the life of this revived Polish state ended with the defeat of Napoleon in 1815, the ideals of liberal democracy that were visible under French administration during this period had a lasting influence on the development of Polish nationalism and its survival during the nineteenth century.

The grand duchy of Warsaw was replaced at the Congress of Vienna by a much smaller kingdom of Poland, which was made semiautonomous within the Russian Empire with the czar as hereditary monarch. This small, so-called Congress Kingdom showed considerable political progress under the moderate rule of Czar Alexander I. Industry, mining, and education were fostered, and a separate Polish administration and a small army were permitted to function. The kingdom was caught up, however, in a series of anti-Russian uprisings beginning in 1830, which finally resulted in the full incorporation of the Congress Kingdom into the Russian Empire and the ultimate imposition of a harsh russification program in all the Polish areas under Russian rule.

During the nineteenth century and up to the period of

Belvedere Palace. A drawing room corner on the upper floor—a room frequently used by King Stanislaus Augustus

Belvedere Palace (north view). The king had more elaborate plans for the site and the adjoining Belvedere Palace, but he abdicated and left Poland in 1795. However, until his death (1798) he directed from St. Petersburg (Leningrad) the work for the completion of Lazienki Park. In 1798 his heirs sold the estate to Emperor Alexander I of Russia who used it as a summer palace. After World War I, when Poland regained her independence, the Polish authorities removed all traces of the Russian modifications. During World War II the Germans in retreat in January 1945 destroyed all of the buildings and removed all of the furnishings and collections of Lazienka. The Poles completed a reconstruction of Lazienka in 1965 and recovered most of the artifacts. Lazienka rivals the French Palace of Versailles and Trianon.

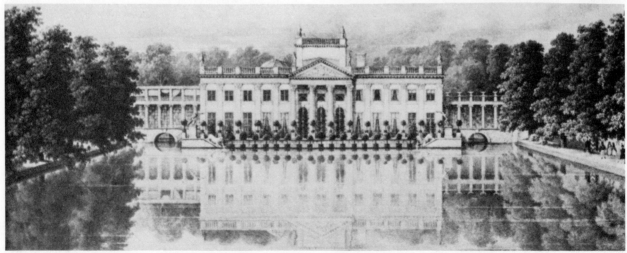

World War I each of the three partitioned areas of Poland received a distinctive imprint from its occupying power. Important social, cultural, and economic changes were experienced, but at varying times. Indicative of this was the final emancipation of the peasant from serfdom. Prussia abolished the practice in its occupied areas in 1823; Austria, in 1849; and Russia, in 1864—three years after eliminating the custom in the native Russian lands. In all three areas the landed gentry gradually decreased in number and wealth, and sons of the lesser nobility turned to the towns for careers in business and the professions. This was was the last stage of the disintegration of the Polish monarchy.

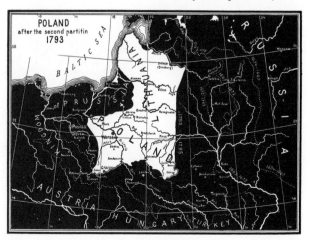

LEGENDA

1. Zamek Ujazdowski
2. Pałac Na Wyspie
3. Ermitaż
4. Biały Dom
5. Pałac Myślewicki
6. Dom Turecki
7. Stara Pomarańczarnia
8. Rezerwuar
9. Wielka Oficyna
10. Kordegarda Wschodnia
11. Kordegarda Zachodnia
12. Amfiteatr
13. Budynek stajni
14. Domek Letni
15. Pałac Belwederski
16. Nowa Pomarańczarnia
17. Obserwatorium
18. Świątynia Opatrzności
19. Pomnik Chopina

Sketch of the Lazienki Park grounds

A painting of King Augustus

Voting on the Constitution of May 3, 1791, in the debating chamber of the Warsaw Castle

Myslewicki Palace

Poland after the partition of 1793

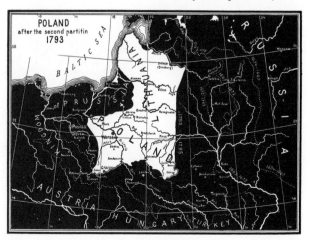

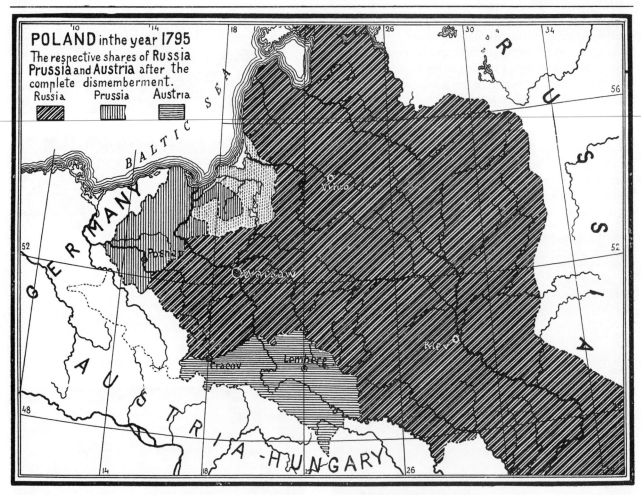

POLAND in the year 1795
The respective shares of Russia
Prussia and Austria after the
complete dismemberment.

Russia   Prussia   Austria

Poland in the year 1795

*Wewel Cathedral—
coronation and burial site
of Polish kings*

*Wilanov Palace as it appears today. It was the former residence of King
John III Sobieski.*

*Tourists get this view today across the lake, of the Royal Castle of Wewel
in Cracow.*

The Ambassadors' Hall in the royal castle of Wewel. It is a room used by the later kings of Poland in which they received foreign royalty and dignitaries.

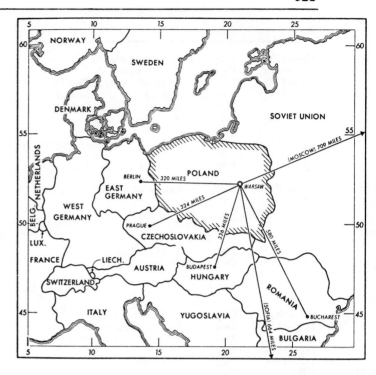

Poland today

THE ROYAL SOVEREIGNS OF THE POLISH KINGDOMS

Reign	Title	Ruler	Birth	Death	Relationship

PIAST DYNASTY

EARLY FEUDAL MONARCHY

Reign	Title	Ruler	Birth	Death	Relationship
960–992	King	Mieszko I	922	992	
992–1025	King	Boleslaus I, the Brave (crowned in 1025)	967	1025	Son of Mieszko I
1025–1034	King	Mieszko II Lambert	990	1034	Son of Boleslaus I
1034–1058	King	Casimir I, the Restorer	1016	1058	Son of Mieszko II
1058–1079	King	Boleslaus II, the Bold (king from 1076)	1039	1081	Son of Casimir I
1079–1102	King	Ladislaus I Herman	1043	1102	Son of Casimir I
1102–1107	King	Boleslaus II, the Wrymouth	1039	1107	Son of Casimir I
1107–1138	King	Boleslaus III, the Wrymouth	1085	1138	Son of Ladislaus I

FEUDAL DISINTEGRATION PERIOD (DUKES RULING IN CRACOW)

Reign	Title	Ruler	Birth	Death	Relationship
1138–1146	King	Ladislaus II, the Exile	1105	1159	Son of Boleslaus III
1146–1173	King	Boleslaus IV, the Curly	1120	1173	Son of Boleslaus III
1173–1177	King	Mieszko III, the Old	1126	1202	Son of Boleslaus III
1177–1194	King	Casimir II, the Just	1138	1197	Son of Boleslaus III
1194–1202	King	Mieszko III, the Old	1126	1202	Son of Boleslaus III
1202–1202	King	Ladislaus Spindleshanks	1138	1202	Son of Boleslaus III
1202–1210	King	Leszek, the White	1186	1227	Son of Casimir II
1210–1211	King	Mieszko, the Stumbling	1190	1211	Son of Mieszko III
1211–1227	King	Leszek, the White	1186	1227	Son of Casimir II
1227–1229	King	Ladislaus Spindleshanks	1169	1229	Son of Ladislaus Spindleshanks
1229–1232	King	Conrad of Mazovia	1197	1232	
1232–1238	King	Henry I, the Bearded	1163	1238	Son of Boleslaus of Silesia
1238–1241	King	Henry II, the Pious	1191	1241	Son of Henry I
1241–1243	King	Conrad of Mazovia	1181	1247	Son of Casimir II
1243–1279	King	Boleslaus, the Chaste	1226	1279	

Reign	Title	Ruler	Birth	Death	Relationship
1279–1288	King	Keszek, the Black	1240	1288	Son of Casimir I of Cuyavia
1288–1290	King	Henry Probus	1257	1290	Son of Henry III of Silesia
1290–1291	King	Przemysi II (king 1295–1296)	1257	1296	Son of Przemysi
1291–1305	King	Wenceslaus II of Bohemia, Premyslid Dynasty (king of Poland from 1300)	1271	1305	Son of Ottokar of Bohemia
1305–1306	King	Wenceslaus III of Bohemia, Premyslid Dynasty	1273	1306	Son of Ottokar of Bohemia

UNITED POLISH KINGDOM

Reign	Title	Ruler	Birth	Death	Relationship
1306–1333	King	Ladislaus I, the Short, Lokietek (king from 1320)	1261	1333	Son of Casimir I
1333–1370	King	Casimir III, the Great (first king of Poland)	1310	1370	Son of Ladislaus I

ANGEVIN DYNASTY

Reign	Title	Ruler	Birth	Death	Relationship
1370–1382	King	Louis of Hungary	1326	1382	Nephew of Casimir III
1383–1399	Queen	Hedwig (Jadwiga)	1374	1399	Daughter of Louis of Hungary

JAGIELLON DYNASTY

Reign	Title	Ruler	Birth	Death	Relationship
1386–1434	King	Ladislaus II Jagiello	1348	1434	
1434–1444	King	Ladislaus III of Varna	1424	1444	Son of Ladislaus II
1447–1492	King	Casimir IV, the Jagiellonian	1427	1492	Son of Ladislaus II
1492–1501	King	John Albert	1458	1501	Son of Casimir IV
1501–1506	King	Alexander	1460	1506	Son of Casimir IV
1506–1548	King	Sigismund I, the Old	1467	1548	Son of Casimir IV
1548–1572	King	Sigismund II Augustus	1520	1572	Son of Sigismund I

ELECTORAL KINGS

Reign	Title	Ruler	Birth	Death	Relationship
1573–1574	King	Henry of Valois	1551	1589	
1576–1586	King	Stephen Bathory	1533	1586	Son-in-law of Sigismund I
1587–1632	King	Sigismund III Vasa	1565	1632	Grandson of Sigismund I
1632–1648	King	Ladislaus IV Vasa	1594	1648	Son of Sigismund III
1648–1668	King	John II Casimir Vasa	1609	1672	Son of Sigismund III
1669–1673	King	Michael Korybut Wisniowiecki	1640	1673	
1674–1696	King	John III Sobieski	1629	1696	
1697–1706	King	Augustus II, the Strong (Wettin)	1670	1733	Son of John George of Saxony
1704–1709	King	Stanislaus Leszczynski	1677	1766	
1709–1733	King	Augustus II, the Strong	1670	1733	
1733–1736	King	Stanislaus Leszczynski	1677	1766	
1734–1763	King	Augustus III (Wettin)	1696	1763	Son of Augustus II
1764–1795	King	Stanislaus Augustus Poniatowski	1732	1798	

Poland was partitioned by Russia, Austria, and Prussia in 1772, 1793, and 1795; central Poland was created as grand duchy of Warsaw by Napoleon with Frederick Augustus I of Saxony as ruler, 1807–1814, and Poland regained independence in 1918.

Romania and her historic provinces

17

The Kingdoms of Romania

Romania's history as an independent state dates from about the middle of the nineteenth century; as a Communist state, from about the end of World War II. The history of the Romanian people, however, is long, complex, and important when considered in the context of the overall history of the Balkan region. The origin and development of the Romanians remain controversial subjects among Romanian and Hungarian historians, whose arguments serve to support or deny claims to rightful ownership of large areas within Romania's borders.

Until the end of World War II Romania's history as a state was one of gains and losses of territory and shifting borders. As the Ottoman Empire in Europe receded, the Romanians found themselves pressured by the Russian and Austro-Hungarian empires. Borders arranged by the victorious powers after World War I increased Romania's territory but also increased its minority population, particularly the Hungarian. Between the two world wars the country experienced a period of Fascist dictatorship and aligned itself with Nazi Germany early in World War II, but it eventually overthrew the Fascists and finished the war on the side of the Allies.

In the postwar chaos of the late 1940s, with Soviet troops occupying the country, Romania deposed its king and emerged as a Communist state under the close scrutiny and supervision of its powerful northern neighbor, the Soviet Union.

EARLY ORIGIN

The earliest recorded inhabitants of the area included in present-day Romania were Thracian tribes, known as Dacians, who settled in the area well before the Christian Era and established a major center in Transylvania. These people practiced a primitive form of agriculture and engaged in limited trade with Greek settlements along the western coast of the Black Sea. By the middle of the first century A.D. the Dacians had grouped themselves into a loosely formed state ruled by a series of kings who attempted to expand their power to the north and west and, most aggressively, to the south into the area below the lower Danube River.

In their advance southward the Dacians came into conflict with the Romans who, during the same period, were attempting to extend their control over the Balkan region and to push the northern border of their empire up to the natural barrier formed by the Danube River. In a series of campaigns between A.D. 101 and 106, the Roman emperor Trajan succeeded in conquering the areas known as Banat, Oltenia, and Walachia and in finally reducing the Dacian stronghold in Transylvania. After consolidating and unifying his control over the people, Trajan fortified the area, stationed Roman legions in garrisons at strategic points, and organized the region to serve as a province of the Roman Empire.

As a border province, Dacia developed rapidly and became one of the most prosperous in the empire. Colonists were brought in from other parts of the empire, cities were built, agriculture and mineral resources were

The story of the Romanian people begins with the original inhabitants of Romania who were Dacians. The Romans under Trajan first conquered and occupied Dacia. This is a Roman coin found in Romania that is of Trajan's time, and bears his image.

FORMATION OF THE PRINCIPALITIES

WALACHIA AND MOLDAVIA

As the threats of invasion diminished, the Vlachs gradually moved farther into the foothills and plains of the Danube basin and fused with a population that, while retaining a small Vlach element, had by then acquired a heavy mixture of Slavs and Tatars. Two distinct groups eventually emerged, one settling in the area now known as Walachia and the other settling farther to the east and north in Moldavia. The earliest events surrounding the development of these areas are not known, but after a period of colonization the two regions emerged, in the thirteenth and fourteenth centuries, respectively, as the semi-independent principalities of Walachia and Moldavia.

When the Ottoman Empire overran southeastern Europe in the fifteenth century, these Danubian principalities were forced to accept Turkish suzerainty and remained Turkish dependencies until the middle of the nineteenth century. Unlike other areas under Turkish

developed, and profitable commercial relations were established with other regions under Roman control. The province proved vulnerable to periodic barbarian incursions, however, and toward the end of the third century the Roman emperor Aurelian was forced to abandon Dacia and withdraw the Roman troops to defend similarly threatened areas farther to the south.

Aside from the romanization of the native population, little evidence of the occupation survived the Roman evacuation of Dacia. Among the traces of the Roman presence remaining were the vestiges of Christianity introduced in the second century and the legacy of the name of the future state of Romania as well as the Latin basis for its language.

Lacking natural geographical barriers to invasion from the east and south, the greater part of the Dacian territory was overrun by successive waves of barbarian invaders for ten centuries after the withdrawal of the Romans. Little is known of the fate of the Daco-Roman population during this long, turbulent period until new settlements inhabited by a Latin-speaking people known as Vlachs emerged on the Romanian plains in the eleventh century. Although historic records are lacking, these Vlachs were believed to be descendants of the earlier Daco-Roman colonists, many of whom either sought refuge in the Carpathian Mountains of Transylvania or migrated south of the Danube River to escape the invaders. Having survived, they returned to reestablish themselves in their historic homeland.

The succession of barbaric invasions exploited and devastated the country. The Germanic Goths were followed by Slavs and Avars, and not until the Bulgars overran the area in the seventh century was a semblance of civic order established. The region developed a rudimentary form of cultural life, and Christianity in the Eastern Orthodox form was introduced after the conversion of the Bulgar Czar Boris in 864. The Bulgars were eventually displaced by Hungarians, who, in turn, gave way to Asiatic Tatars, all of whom left limited, but lasting, influences on the land and its inhabitants.

Basarab I (1317–52) shown on his white horse, foreground, *commanding a battle being fought against Charles Robert's soldiers in the mountain passes of Romania*

Mircea the Old, a Walachian prince, who reigned 1386 to 1418, exemplifies the royal princes of the early days of Romania and their place on the field of battle at the head of their armies. Prince Mircea in 1388, 1394, and 1397 turned back the Turkish expeditions of Vizier Ali Pasha, and in 1404 he again stopped the Turks.

Iancu of Hunedoara (1441–56) was another fierce fighter against the Turks and defeated them regularly when they invaded his territory of Transylvania. A powerful politician, he also was able to place the princes on the thrones of Moldavia and Walachia to help in the battles against the Ottoman invaders.

The royal Hunyad Castle survives the ravages of time.

Stephen the Great, the Prince of Moldavia (1457–1504), defeated the Turks at Rakova in a decisive battle but the Turks with heavy reinforcements drove him from his dominions. But as events altered the balance of forces, he regained his throne and once more came to the aid of his country by defeating a massive invasion of the Polish army.

Vlad the Impaler (1456–62), the ruling prince of Walachia, became the leading Romanian military leader to fight off the Turks after the death of Iancu. In 1461–62, Vlad attacked and destroyed the Ottoman garrisons on both banks of the Danube from Zimnicea to the mouth of the river. Mohammed II himself pursued Vlad and his men. Vlad at this time and point in history received his name Impaler. He impaled the enemy soldiers he had captured, nude, on ten-foot poles, every 100 feet on both sides of the road being used by the Turks. After seeing this sight of their impaled comrades in an erect position on the top of these tall poles along their route for mile after mile, they soon lost the stomach for continuing the pursuit of Vlad, for they considered him the worst of barbarians. On the night of June 16, 1462, he attacked the sultan's main camp and in a continuing hit-and-run tactic drove the Ottoman's best army out of Romania by the end of the month. But his brother, Radu the Handsome, sold him out to the boyars and he was also betrayed by Matthias Corvinus, the king of Hungary, who captured him and imprisoned him at Buda. But our story doesn't end here. Matthias Corvinus, to discredit Vlad, blackened his name during his imprisonment by spreading stories about him that resulted in the hero Vlad becoming infamously known from that time as the bloodthirsty villain—Dracula.

rule, the Romanian principalities were controlled by native princes, who maintained their position through concessions to the nobles, from among whom they had gained preeminence, and through the concurrence of the Turks, to whom a substantial annual tribute was paid. This system of political control led to intrigues and a long succession of rulers who, assisted by the nobles, systematically exploited the peasantry, from whom the heavy annual tribute was collected.

Continued misrule and long-term economic exploitation of the regions seriously affected the social structure within the principalities. The lesser nobility, including the landed gentry, was reduced to the level of free peasants; the peasantry itself was placed in virtually complete serfdom; and cultural activity became almost nonexistent. Even the appearance of outstanding political and military leaders, such as Michael the Brave of Walachia (1593–1601) and Stephen the Great, prince of Moldavia (1457–1504), could not reverse the general trend of deterioration, although the harshness of the feudal system was somewhat lessened during their tenure in office.

At the beginning of the eighteenth century the Otto-

*A 1957 postage stamp
honoring Stephen the Great*

man Empire began to decline, and the Turks instituted a system of direct control over Walachia and Moldavia, in order to ensure the continued receipt of maximum revenue from the countries. Greek merchants known as Phanariots, named for the Phanar district of Constantinople, which was their center, were invested as rulers in the principalities upon direct payment of large sums of money. Since their period in office was indefinite and generally lasted only until outbid by a successor, an even more intensive system of exploitation within the countries was introduced to extract greater tribute in shorter periods of time. This period of oppressive rule lasted until 1821 and proved to be the most disastrous experienced by the inhabitants. Conditions under this corrupt system became almost intolerable and led to massive resistance and eventually to the heavy migration of the peasantry into neighboring areas, particularly Transylvania.

TRANSYLVANIA

The historic development of Transylvania was substantially different and more complex than that experienced by the principalities of Walachia and Moldavia. Overrun by Asiatic Magyars as early as the ninth century, the region was organized originally as a province in the eleventh century. In order to strengthen this eastern outpost, the Hungarians encouraged two groups of people—Sze-

After Neagoe Basarab's death in 1521, the Turkish governor in the area was forced to appoint Radu of Afumati (1521–29) as the prince of Walachia because of pressure from Transylvania. The political move by Transylvania saved Walachia from having a Turkish prince. This gravestone of Radu is still in good condition at his burial site. The Romanian people today still have a great respect for their ruling princes of old and their historic places are well kept.

Prince John the Terrible of Moldavia (1572–74) appealed to the countrymen to bear arms against the Turkish rule when they doubled the taxes in 1573. He led the army, fought well, but in the end was captured and although promised no personal harm in return for a surrender, he was quartered alive by his captors—the Turks and the Tatars. They tied him to four camels and drove them in different directions. The Tatars then went on to lay waste to the country. This is reported to be a good likeness of him on a coin of the time.

Neagoe Basarab of Walachia and his family as they appeared at the time of his reign, 1512–21. During his time on the throne Walachia enjoyed the best period of internal stability and important cultural growth ever achieved in the country.

Michael the Brave (1593–1601) came to Walachia's throne at a time when the Ottoman taxes were at their peak. Michael was considered the greatest of all of the Romanian princes. During the eight years of his reign, he liberated Walachia from the Turks and had achieved the unity of the three Romanian countries. Unfortunately, he was assassinated on August 19, 1601, by a group of professional soldiers who were purportedly aiding him in putting down a rebellion in Transylvania.

Prince Matei Basarab of Walachia (1632–64) and

Prince Vasie Lupu of Moldavia (1634–53) were noted in history for their periods of reign at a time when the prince's authority was considerably enhanced.

Constantine Brancoveeanu and his four sons. He was the prince of Walachia from 1688 to 1714. For the first time in the history of Walachia, the prince received the wholehearted support of the boyars. This was probably because as a wealthy landowner he was not far from the same background as the nobles. He brought about an understanding with Czar Peter of Russia for support in getting out from under the Ottoman yoke. His four sons spent their entire lives helping their father in his goal toward this end.

klers, or Szekelys, an ethnic group of people akin to the Hungarians, and Germans—to emigrate from the west into the area. Although these colonists eventually reached substantial numbers, the native Romanian speakers remained in the majority.

With the expansion of Turkish power, Transylvania became the battleground for opposing Turkish and Hungarian forces. Under Turkish pressure Hungarian control declined in the fifteenth and sixteenth centuries, and by 1526 the region had become a semiautonomous principality ruled by Hungarian princes but still subject to Turkish authority. At the end of the sixteenth century Michael the Brave, the ruler of Walachia and Moldavia, succeeded in revolting against Turkish rule and united Transylvania with the other Romanian territories. This union, however, was short-lived, and all three principalities subsequently reverted to Turkish control. Toward the end of the seventeenth century Austria conquered Hungary, and Transylvania as part of Hungary then was included in the Austro-Hungarian Empire.

From the earliest times the position of the Romanians in Transylvania was inferior to that of the other nationalities, and accounts of the long-term measures practiced against them have been perpetuated among their descendants. The Romanians were mostly serfs, and their social and economic status was the lowest in the province. Their Orthodox Christianity was not recognized, in contrast to the Lutheran, Calvinist, Unitarian, and Roman Catholic faiths practiced by the various other nationalities. To gain religious equality and to win a larger measure of economic and social recognition, many of the Romanians gradually abandoned their Eastern Orthodox creed and became Uniates by accepting papal authority in 1698.

Although the Romanians were slow to benefit from the relatively high cultural and political level reached in Transylvania under the Austro-Hungarians, an appreciable number of concessions had been made to them by the middle of the nineteenth century. They began to share in the political life after political parties were established, schools were opened for Romanian children, and education became more widespread among the general population. Progress in these and associated fields stimulated the Romanian desire for full equality and the hope for eventual unification of all Romanians in their own national state.

WESTERN INFLUENCES

Although Romania was late in achieving national recognition, many of the factors that were to influence its western orientation after independence began to evolve as early as the seventeenth century. In Transylvania the Uniate church became an important medium by which Romanian national identity was fostered in the struggle

The Brancoveeanu's Palace at Mogosoaia

Constantine Mavrocordat for nearly four decades (1730–69) ruled alternately Walachia and Moldavia. He was reported to have had a remarkable personality, as well as a great ability at fiscal, administrative, social, and judicial matters. He is known best today in Romania for having abolished serfdom in a charter he issued August 5, 1746.

Alexander Ypsilanti, prince of Walachia from 1774 to 1782, became the first ruler to separate the judiciary from administration, creating courts of law. This opened up the process whereby common law was to be replaced by written law.

against foreign assimilation. The Habsburg rulers favored the expansion of the church and permitted the opening of seminaries for the training of young Romanian clergy. Many of these young clerics were sent to Rome to complete their studies and, while there, became aware of their Roman ancestry. They saw the famous column of Trajan, which recorded, in stone, the early conquest of their Dacian ancestors by the Romans, and they also discovered that Romanian was an essentially Latin language.

The contacts established with Rome encouraged the scholarly development of a "Latinist" movement in the homeland in the late eighteenth century, which produced many adherents among the Transylvanian Romanians. It was the efforts of this group that led to the replacement of the Cyrillic alphabet, then in common use, with the Latin, the writing of the first latinized Romanian grammar and, later, the introduction of the first dictionary that traced the full historical development of the Romanian language. These reforms helped to create a uniform literary language as an essential basis for the broad development of Romanian culture.

During their long experience under the Habsburgs and Hungarians, the Transylvanian Romanians also became intimately associated with the events of central and western Europe. Opportunities for travel and cultural contacts that later developed were also predominantly within western areas and intensified the political consciousness of the Romanians along western lines.

Meanwhile, in Walachia and Moldavia interest in western ideas and affairs was provided by French influences introduced initially by the Greek Phanariot princes, who were in power during most of the eighteenth century. These rulers established French as the court language, and many of the Greek merchants, clergymen, and teachers who followed them into the areas helped spread the use of French among the urban population in Bucharest and Iasi, the respective capital cities. Gradually, French was introduced into Romanian schools, and eventually Romanian students from the principalities were sent abroad in considerable numbers to study at French universities.

In addition to Romanian students, many of the young sons of Romanian nobles traveled in France. These two groups gradually formed the nucleus of an intellectual class, which favored French philosophy and thought and which became receptive to the liberal ideas of the French Revolution and later periods.

NATIONAL INDEPENDENCE

A phase of major significance and a turning point in Romanian history began in 1821 with a revolt led by Tudor Vladimirescu, a Romanian and former officer in the Russian army. This uprising against the harsh Phanariot rule was the first with a national character,

After Walachia and Moldavia were united in 1859, the postrevolutionary (1848) army general was elected to be the royal head of Romania—Alexander Ioan Cuza (1859–66). In his short reign he solidified the two countries into one government and established the capital at Bucharest. He was forced to abdicate in 1866.

and it attempted to give expression to the revolutionary ideas of emancipation and independence. Although the outbreak was suppressed by the Turks, it did achieve the objective of bringing about the early abolition of the Phanariot regime and the restoration of Romanian princes as rulers in the Danubian principalities.

After the Russo-Turkish war from 1826 to 1828 Russian forces occupied both Walachia and Moldavia to ensure the payment of a large war indemnity by the Turks. Under the ensuing six-year enlightened and competent rule of the Russian governor Count Pavel Kiselev, the foundations were laid for a new Romanian state. The first constitutional assemblies were organized along identical lines in each province; a rudimentary governmental administration was established and modeled on that of the French; an educational system was begun; commerce and a modest industry were encouraged; and provisions were made for the creation of a national militia. The intentional similarity in the fundamental laws that were also enacted in each area further encouraged the two principalities to develop side by side.

During the two decades after the departure of Russian occupying forces, the national movement within the two principalities continued to grow under the rule of native princes who had been restored to power. Considerable stimulation was provided by the 1848 revolutionary events in France, the basic ideas of which were imported by the French-educated Romanians. Dissension arose, and street demonstrations took place during which demands were made for freedom of speech, assembly, and the press, as well as for the unification of all Romanians in one independent state. Similar emancipation efforts were also organized in Transylvania, but they too, were forcibly repressed, as were those in Walachia and Moldavia.

Despite the setbacks suffered by the intellectuals and other leaders of the revolutionary movement, the modern ideas of liberal government took firm root and con-

tinued to flourish. The dispute between Russia and Turkey that culminated in the Crimean War, however, provided the actual opportunity for the first step toward ultimate independence. French and Russian collaboration at the Congress of Paris, which concluded the war in 1858, succeeded in producing agreements that finally led to the establishment of the autonomous United Principalities of Walachia and Moldavia in 1859.

Although still subject to Ottoman authority, the United Principalities moved rapidly under their newly elected leader, Alexander John I Cuza, to further unify and modernize themselves. Cuza fused the administration of the two principalities into a single government, established a single capital at Bucharest, and changed the name from United Principalities to Romania. Domestic reforms were also undertaken, among which were the emancipation of the serfs in 1864, the institution of a broad land distribution program, the introduction of free and compulsory education, and the adoption of the French civil and penal codes as the basis for a revised legal system. Political parties on the western pattern began to take form as well, the conservatives representing the large landowners and the liberals representing the new urban class.

The reforms instituted by Cuza were bold and progressive, but his methods proved to be harsh and unpopular. Forced to abdicate in 1866, he was succeeded by a German prince, Charles of Hohenzollern-Sigmaringen. Charles, who reigned from 1866 to 1914, extended the reforms initiated by Cuza. He gave the country its first formal constitution modeled after that of the Belgians, built the country's first railroad, and modernized and enlarged the small army. In 1878 the country's full independence was recognized by the Treaty of Berlin, which ended the two-year Russo-Turkish war in which Romania participated as an ally of Russia. The kingdom

Princess Elizabeth of Wied became the bride of the future King Carol I and as his queen led a marvelous double life. She was known to the rest of the world as the poet queen Carmen Sylva.

King Carol I (1881–1914), who served as the reigning prince of Romania from 1866 to 1881 when the country became a kingdom

of Romania was proclaimed formally in 1881 with the crowning of Prince Charles in Bucharest as Carol I.

The period from 1878 to 1918 brought significant advances in Romania, largely in the economic and political fields. Under the initiative of King Carol I and with considerable backing from German capital, new industries were started, and others were expanded; railroad and port construction was emphasized; and the considerable petroleum resources of the country were developed and exploited. The goals of political parties and leaders became more clearly defined, and modern government institutions, including a bicameral parliament, were organized.

Economic and formal political progress, however, was not matched by similar advancement of democratic processes in the social field. The liberal provisions of the 1866 constitution were circumvented under the authoritarian governmental system, leaving much actual power in the hands of the landed aristocracy. The slowly rising middle class and small number of industrial entrepreneurs were granted some rights, but the increasing number of industrial workers and the great peasant majority shared very little in the political life of the country.

A major peasant revolt in 1907 attempted unsuccessfully to rectify the serious social imbalance. The uprising was forcefully suppressed with extensive loss of life, and although some corrective measures were later instituted that improved working conditions and resulted in the division of more large landholdings, the general political strength and living standards of the peasants and workers were not materially improved. Related also to this social unrest was another problem that grew more intense during the latter half of the nineteenth century— that of the increasing size and economic importance of a large Jewish minority.

Forbidden to own land and subject to many other restrictions, the Jews had settled in urban areas, engaged successfully in commercial activities, and, as a class, gained economic influence and position generally out of proportion to their overall numerical strength in the population. To an unusual degree, they formed the prosperous urban middle class, overshadowing the far smaller number of native Romanians in that category. In rural centers, as moneylenders, they also became the middlemen between landlords and peasants; as such, the Jew became a symbol of oppression, which over the years was transferred into intense anti-Semitism. Consequently, the Jews were included as a target in the 1907 uprising, and the animosity shown then remained a feature of later Romanian society.

WORLD WAR I

At the outbreak of Word War I in 1914 Romania's leaders were indecisive and proclaimed an armed neutrality, which lasted for nearly two years. Much of the pro-

On June 14, 1914, the Russian royal family visited the Romanian Royal family at Constantsa. Standing, left to right: King Carol I, Grand Duchess Anastasie, Princess Marie Mignon of Romania, Prince Carol of Romania, Princess Ileana of Romania, the crown prince of Romania Prince Ferdinand, Queen Elizabeth, and the czar of Russia. Seated, left to right: Grand Duchess Marie, Empress Alexandra Feodorovna, Grand Duchess Tatiana, Crown Princess Marie of Romania, Grand Duchess Olga holding Prince Mircea of Romania. Foreground: the Czarevitch Alexei and Prince Nicholas of Romania. Elizabeth married the king of Greece—George II; Marie Mignon; the king of Yugoslavia, Alexander, and their first son became Peter II, king of Yugoslavia; and Ileana married Anton, the archduke of Austria.

King Ferdinand I (1914–27) succeeded King Carol I on October 11, 1914.

Queen Marie in an official portrait in 1920

Princess Marie of Edinburgh turned down marriage to the future king George V of England to marry Prince Ferdinand of Romania. The prince became the king of Romania and the princess developed into the most vivacious queen of modern times.

Russian and pro-French political orientation of the 1840s and 1850s still existed in the country, but this was offset in large measure by the strong ties of King Carol I with Bismarck's Germany and by the rapprochement with Germany that had resulted from the large investment of German capital in the country. In addition, territorial inducements, which were attractive to Romania, were made by each side to influence its entry into the conflict. The Central Powers offered Bessarabia to be taken from Russia, and the Allies promised the cession of Transylvania from Austro-Hungary.

After the death of King Carol I and the accession of his nephew, King Ferdinand, to the throne, Romania entered the war on the Allied side in 1916. By December 1917, however, Romania was forced to conclude an armistice when the Russian forces disintegrated on the Balkan front after the Bolshevik revolution of that year. Before the armistice was ratified, however, and as the defeat of the Central Powers was becoming apparent, the Romanian army, which had not been demobilized, reentered the war, liberated Bucharest from the Germans, and occupied much of Bessarabia and Transylvania. After the war, in response to the expressed will of the popular assemblies in Transylvania, Bessarabia, and Bukovina, those provinces were united with the kingdom of Romania—often called the Old Kingdom. Formal treaties in 1919 and 1920 confirmed these decisions, and virtually all Romanians were finally reunited within the historic homeland.

INTERWAR YEARS, 1918–40

With the annexation of Transylvania, Bessarabia, and Bukovina, postwar Romania, sometimes referred to as Greater Romania, doubled in size, as well as in population. Included among the newly acquired population were large ethnic minorities—principally Hungarians, Germans, and Jews—whose diverse backgrounds and development presented complex social, political, economic, and administrative problems for the Romanian government. The various traditions of the people within the acquired lands could not easily be transformed into new patterns, largely because of the government's reluctance to share power with any political leaders except those representing the Transylvanian Romanians. As a result, minority elements were largely excluded from national affairs, and discriminatory policies developed that bred resentment and increased political instability.

The immediate postwar years were dominated by the Liberal party of the Old Kingdom. The party instituted a series of land reforms, fostered increased industrialization, and sponsored a broadly democratic constitution in 1923, which made the new state a centralized constitutional monarchy. The Transylvanian Romanians, long accustomed to considerable autonomy and self-govern-

King Ferdinand I in an official photograph later in life. He served until his death in 1927.

Queen Elizabeth (Carmen Silva) in later life

Crown Prince Carol II with Princess Helen on their engagement. She was his second wife. His first wife was Zizi Lambrino by whom he had a child, Mircea. His third wife was Elena Lupescu.

Queen Marie at age sixty

Princess Helen with her son, the future king Michael. He was born in 1921.

A tableau of the king of Greece's daughters, Princess Helen, left, and Princess Irene. Princess Helen married Carol II, who became king of Romania in 1930.

King Michael, at age six, on his way, in a royal carriage, to his accession to the throne in 1927

King Michael in an official portrait during his first reign

King Carol II (1930–40)

ment under Hungarian rule, resented the imposition of central control, especially under the administration of officials from Bucharest. In protest, a new party, the National Peasant party, was formed in 1926 by a fusion of the Transylvanian National party with the Peasant party in the Old Kingdom.

Other parties were active during this early period, but all were overshadowed by the Liberal party and the National Peasant party. The Social Democratic party had been organized at the beginning of the twentieth century but, lacking any sizable number of industrial workers, the Socialist movement remained weak. After the Russian revolution, however, the radical left-wing elements of the Social Democratic party seceded and formed the Romanian Communist party in 1921. The Communists went underground after being banned in 1924 and were largely ineffective until after World War II.

The death of King Ferdinand in 1927 and the elections of the following year brought significant changes in the Romanian government. Ferdinand's son, Carol II, was

excluded from the succession because of his earlier renunciation of all claims to the throne to accept exile with his mistress, Magda Lupescu. A regency was therefore appointed to rule in the name of Carol's young son, Michael, and a new government led by Iuliu Maniu and the National Peasant party was elected, thus ending the six-year tenure of the Liberals.

Although Maniu's government instituted a series of reforms intended to improve general economic and social conditions, its efforts were largely offset by the adverse effects of the worldwide depression of the early 1930s. Also, early dissatisfaction with the regency resulted in the return of Carol II from exile and his assumption of the crown in late 1930. His agreement to sever relations with Magda Lupescu was not kept, however, and in protest Maniu resigned the premiership. In the unstable conditions that followed, King Carol II emerged as the chief political figure in the country, and his rule evolved into a royal dictatorship.

King Carol's assumption of power was aided initially by the rise of a fanatical Fascist and anti-Semitic group known as the Iron Guard. This group was strongly pro-German and employed tactics similar to those of the Nazi party, which was then emerging as the dominant political force in Germany. The Fascist movement, with financial and indirect support from Germany, increased the influence of the Iron Guard, which was reflected in the 1937 elections. The coalition government that resulted supported King Carol but was later overthrown, bringing to power a new coalition of right-wing extremists.

In order to halt the increasing threat to his power, Carol proclaimed a personal dictatorship in 1938 and promulgated a new constitution that abolished all political parties and instituted censorship and other control measures. This action was followed by the suppression of the Iron Guard, whose leader, Corneliu Codreanu, was shot. Absolute authority was maintained by the king, who was supported by the army and by the National Renaissance Front, a monopoly party that he founded later in the same year.

Internal instability and uncertainty were aggravated by rapidly developing international events that threatened the security of the state. The swift rise of Germany under Adolf Hitler resulted in the annexation of Austria in 1938 and the subsequent dismemberment and absorption of Czechoslovakia. These actions, unopposed by the western powers, were early warnings of weakness in the western-oriented collective security system on which Romania had depended since World War I. The lessening of confidence in the west led Romania in 1939 to conclude a treaty of economic collaboration with Germany. This agreement greatly increased German influence in the country and placed the extensive Romanian oil and other resources at Germany's disposal for later wartime use.

Although Romania's territorial integrity had been guaranteed by both Great Britain and France after the fall of Czechoslovakia, these assurances were nullified by the early German military successes achieved following the outbreak of World War II. After the conclusion of a nonaggression pact with the Soviet Union in August 1939, Germany invaded and occupied Poland and, by mid-1940, had defeated France and forced the evacuation of the European mainland by British forces. Faced with the loss of its two strongest partners in the alliance system and with the aggressive ambitions of the two strongest totalitarian powers on the European continent —Germany and the Soviet Union—Romania had little chance of continued independent survival.

WORLD WAR II

The first claims against Romania were made by the Soviet Union, which in June 1940 demanded the immediate cession of Bessarabia and northern Bukovina. Under German pressure Romania acceded to these demands, as well as to the later loss of northern Transylvania, which Germany and Italy transferred to Hungary at a joint conference held in Vienna on August 30, 1940. A third loss of territory, also under German pressure, followed one week later with the return of southern Dobruja to Bulgaria, which had already entered the war on the side of Germany.

The crisis caused by these territorial losses had a serious impact within the country. King Carol was forced to appoint a pro-German cabinet, and the government was heavily infiltrated with members of the Iron Guard, most of whom were released from custody under German pressure. A national protest against the king in early September culminated in his abdication in favor of his son, Michael. A new government under General Ion Antonescu was formed, composed almost entirely of members of the Iron Guard, whose leader was made vice premier. German troops entered the country under the pretext of protecting the oil fields, and on November 23, 1940, Romania joined Germany, Italy, and Japan in the Anti-Comintern Pact.

In January 1941 members of the Iron Guard, attempting to seize full control of the government, initiated a terroristic campaign that was suppressed with much bloodshed by the Romanian army, which had remained loyal to the government. With the continued support of the Germans, Antonescu dissolved the Iron Guard and formed an almost exclusively military dictatorship. After stabilization of the government, Romania entered the war against the Soviet Union and incurred heavy losses in the prolonged fighting on the eastern front.

After the defeat of the German and Romanian forces at Stalingrad in early 1943, the Soviets mounted a counteroffensive, which by mid-1944 had liberated the southwestern portions of the Soviet Union and had advanced

A 1947 postage stamp picturing King Michael

deep into Romania and threatened Bucharest. On August 23, 1944, King Michael, with the support of the major political and military leaders, overthrew the regime of Antonescu, halted all fighting, and installed a new, moderate coalition government. Under the terms of the armistice that followed, Romania reentered the war on the side of the Allies, agreed to reparation payments, and accepted the military occupation of the country until the conclusion of a final peace settlement.

Romanian forces that continued the war were committed in support of the Soviet army in Transylvania, Hungary, and Czechoslovakia. Those engaged on the Moldavian front were disarmed, and control over the greater part of the country was maintained by the Soviets. Among the occupation troops stationed in Romania was the Communist-indoctrinated "Tudor Vladimirescu" division, a force composed of captured Romanian prisoners that had been organized after the German-Romanian defeat at Stalingrad. In addition, the Soviets were given the chairmanship of the Allied Control Commission, the joint body that was established to administer the occupied country.

COMMUNIST SEIZURE OF POWER

The several conferences held by the Allied powers concerning postwar arrangements and the understandings that resulted from bilateral discussion among individual leaders indicated that the Soviet Union was to become the dominant military and political power in the Balkans. As a result, the Soviets, from the outset of their period of occupation, acted determinedly to consolidate their position within Romania and to influence the development of a permanent postwar governmental system designed along communist lines.

Although Romania had surrendered in August 1944, it took several months to create a government stable enough to carry out essential programs. The first postwar coalition regimes included relatively few Communists who ostensibly cooperated with the revived traditional political parties. Despite their small numbers, however, they vigorously engaged in disruptive antigovernment tactics to prevent the stabilization of political authority along democratic lines. This course of action was dictated by the general weakness of the Communists who had surfaced after the war and was handicapped by the absence of partisan or resistance organizations, which could have been used as a basis for expanding political control.

In February 1945, during a staged demonstration, the Communists provoked an incident in which several participants were killed. Using this incident as a pretext, Soviet Deputy Commissar for Foreign Affairs Andrei Vyshinsky, who arrived from Moscow within two days of the event, forced King Michael to accept a National Democratic Front government to be headed by Petru Groza, the leader of the Plowman's Front and longtime Communist sympathizer.

The government installed by Groza on March 6, 1945, was dominated by Communists and fellow travelers and represented an effective seizure of power by relatively peaceful means. Although a few dissident former members of the Liberal and National Peasant parties were given posts to maintain the facade of representative government, no leaders or representative members of the historic political parties were included.

After recognition by the Soviet Union in August 1945 and by the United States and Great Britain in February 1946, the Groza government held rigged elections for the Grand National Assembly and emerged with 379 of the 414 seats. Having thus achieved legislative as well as executive control, the Communists proceeded methodically during the following year to eliminate all political opposition.

By the end of 1947 the only remaining link with the prewar system was the monarchy. King Michael, in addition to being a popular ruler, represented a national symbol around whom anti-Communist opposition could rally and, as such, was an unacceptable threat to the embryonic Communist dictatorship. Accordingly, in a meeting in December requested by Groza and Gheor-

ghiu-Dej, King Michael was forced to abdicate under the threat of civil war. On the same day the government announced the creation of the Romanian People's Republic. The action represented the last step in the seizure of power and placed Romania under complete Communist control and for the foreseeable future this meant a monarch would not rule the people.

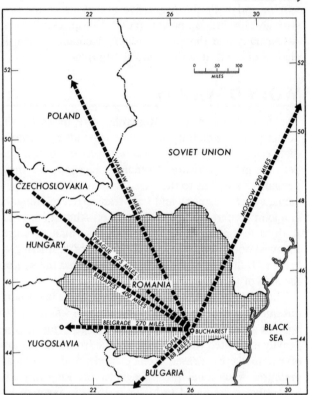

Romania today

THE ROYAL SOVEREIGNS OF THE KINGDOMS OF ROMANIA

Reign	Title	Rulers (principal ones)	Reign	Title	Rulers (principal ones)

Thirteenth century—The Romanian states of Walachia, Moldavia, and Transylvania were founded.

WALACHIA

Reign	Title	Rulers (principal ones)	Reign	Title	Rulers (principal ones)
1317–1352	Grand Voivoide and Prince	Basarab I	1556	Prince	Patrascu the Kind
			1583–1585	Prince	Petru Cercel
			1593–1601	Prince	Michael the Brave
1352–1364	Prince	Nicholas Alexander	1601–1611	Prince	Radu Serban
1364–1377	Prince	Vladislav Vlaicu	1611—Ottoman Empire control		
1386–1418	Prince	Mircea the Old	1611–1616	Prince	Radu Mihnea
–1456	Prince	Petru Aaron	1623–1626	Prince	Radu Mihnea
1456–1462	Prince	Vlad the Impaler	1629–1632	Prince	Leon Tomsa
1462–1475	Prince	Radu I	1632–1654	Prince	Matei Basarab
1494–1508	Prince	Radu the Great	1654–1658	Prince	Constantine Serban
1512–1521	Prince	Neagoe Basarab	1660–1664	Prince	Grigore Ghica
1521–1529	Prince	Radu of Afumati	1678–1688	Prince	Serban Cantacuzino

Reign	Title	Rulers (principal ones)	Reign	Title	Rulers (principal ones)
1688–1714	Prince	Constantine Brancoveeanu	1556	Prince	Alexandru Lapusneaunu
1716—Phanariot Regime installed			1561–1563	Prince	Iacob Eraclid, the Despot
1716–1717	Prince	Nicholas Mavrocordat	1572–1574	Prince	John the Terrible
1719–1730	Prince	Nicholas Mavrocordat	1574– ?	Prince	Peter the Lame (at this point in history the Turks frequently changed the princes.)
1735–1741	Prince	Constantine Mavrocordat			
1741–1744	Prince	Michael Racovita			
1744–1748	Prince	Constantine Mavrocordat	1595	Prince	Stefan Razvan (failed to regain his throne)
1774—Ottoman domination					
1774–1782	Prince	Alexander Ypsilanti	? –1606	Prince	Ieremia Movila
1802–1806	Prince	Constantine Ypsilanti	1606–1607	Prince	Simeon Movila
1806–1812—Russian occupied			1611—Ottoman Empire restored		
1812–1818	Prince	John Caragea	1626–1629	Prince	Miron Barnovschi Movila
1818–1821	Prince	Alexander Sutu	1633–1633	Prince	Miron Barnovschi Movila
1834—Russian occupation ended			1634–1653	Prince	Vasie Lupu
1834–1842	Prince	Alexander Ghica	1685–1693	Prince	Constantine Cantemir
1842–1848	Prince	Georghe Bibescu	1711—Phanariot Regime installed		
1848–1859—Walachia and Moldavia unified			1711–1714	Prince	Nicholas Mavrocordat
			1714–1716	Prince	Stephen Cantacuzino
			1717– ?	Prince	Michael Racovita
			1726–1733	Prince	Gregory Ghica
			1741–1743	Prince	Constantine Mavrocordat
			1730–1769	Prince	Constantine Mavrocordat (ruled alternatively between Moldavia and Walachia)

MOLDAVIA

Reign	Title	Rulers (principal ones)	Reign	Title	Rulers (principal ones)
–1365	Prince	Bogdan (the founder)			
1365–1374	Prince	Latcu	1774—Ottoman Empire domination		
1374–1391	Prince	Petru Musat	1774–1777	Prince	Gregory Ghica
1391–1394	Prince	Roman I	–1806	Prince	Alexander Moruzi
1394–1399	Prince	Stephen I	1806–1812—Russian occupation		
1400–1432	Prince	Alexander the Good	1812–1819	Prince	Scarlat Calimah
1457–1504	Prince	Stephen the Great	1834—Russia leaves the country		
1517–1527	Prince	Stefanita	1834–1849	Prince	Mihai Sturdza
1527–1538	Prince	Petru Rares	1849–1859—Moldavia and Walachia united		
1538—Turks defeat Moldavia and end their independence					

Reign	Title	Ruler	Birth	Death

TRANSYLVANIA

Reign	Title	Ruler	Birth	Death
1344–1376—Six members of the Lackfy family ruled (beginning of formal rule).				
1415–1438	Prince	Vice-voivode Lorand Lepes		
1441–1456	Prince	Iancu of Hunedoara		1456
Sixteenth century—Under control of the Turkish government				
1526–1540	Prince	John Zapolya	1487	1540
1540–1571	Prince	John Sigismund	1520	1571
1571–1572	Prince	Gasnar Bekesy		1572
1571–1576	King	Stephen Bathory (king of Poland)	1533	1586
1576–1581	Prince	Christopher Bathory	1530	1581
1581–1598	Prince	Sigismund	1572	1613
1599–1600	Prince	Andrew	1562	1600
1600–1601	Prince	Michael the Brave		
1602–1603	Prince	Moyses Szekely		
1602–1605	Emperor	Rudolph II		
1605–1606	Prince	Stephen Bocskai	1557	1606
1607–1608	Prince	Sigismund Rakoczi	1544	1608
1608–1613	Prince	Gabriel Bathory	1589	1613
1613–1629	Prince	Gabriel Bethlen	1580	1629
1630–1630	Prince	Stephen Bethlen		
1630–1648	Prince	George Rakoczy I	1591	1648
1648–1660	Prince	George Rakoczy II	1621	1660
1658–1660	Prince	Achatius Bocskai		
1661–1662	Prince	Johann Kemeny		
1682–1699	Prince	Emerich Tokoli		
1661–1690	Prince	Michael Apafi	1632	1690
1690–1699	Prince	Michael II Apafi	1680	1713
1699–1821—Habsburg authority in Transylvania				
1704–1711	Prince	Francis Rakoczy II	1676	1735
1821–1848—Revolutionary period				
1919–1920—The Old Kingdom of Transylvania, Bessarabia, and Burkovina annexed to Romania.				

Reign	Title	Ruler	Birth	Death	Relationship

KINGS OF ROMANIA (OFFICIALLY ESTABLISHED 1881)

1859—Moldavia and Walachia united

Reign	Title	Ruler	Birth	Death	Relationship
1859–1866	Prince	Alexander John I Cuza of Moldavia	1820	1873	
1866–1881	Prince	Charles Eitel Frederick of Hohenzollern-Sigmaringen	1839	1914	
1881–1914	King	Carol I (Charles Eitel Frederick			
1914–1927	King	Ferdinand I	1865	1927	Nephew of Carol I
1927–1930	King	Michael	1921		Grandson of Ferdinand I
1930–1940	King	Carol II	1893	1953	Son of Ferdinand I
1940–1947	King	Michael (regained the throne)			Son of Carol II

1947—Creation of Romanian People's Republic

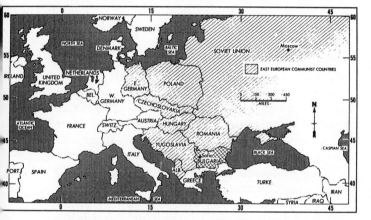

Bulgaria's geographic relationship to the rest of Europe

18

The Kingdom of Bulgaria

The history of Bulgaria is marked by four interrelated motifs or themes. The first motif is that of regional rivalry coupled with irredentism. The second is Bulgaria's strategic significance for the leading powers of Europe and the varying relationships with those powers. The third theme is Bulgaria's constant conflict between loyalty to, and alliances with, the east—particularly Russia and the Soviet Union—on the one hand and to the west —particularly Italy and Germany—on the other. The fourth major theme in Bulgarian history is the influence exerted by Russia (and the Soviet Union) on the internal and external affairs of Bulgaria. This influence was intermittent from the late nineteenth century until World War II but was constant after that war.

From its earliest history Bulgaria was in continual conflict with its Balkan neighbors. The area that eventually became Bulgaria was the object of regional disputes as early as the fourth century B.C. Later, when that area was taken over by the Slavs in the sixth century A.D. and the Bulgars in the seventh, a state evolved that proceeded to encroach on the territory of the mighty Byzantine Empire itself. Despite successful raids and conquests during the periods of the First Bulgarian Kingdom and

the Second Bulgarian Kingdom, Bulgaria was eventually reduced to subject status by the Byzantines and later by the Ottoman Turks. During Turkish rule the country was not only under constant attack by neighbors but was also utilized by the Turks as a base for Turkish expansion. When Bulgaria was finally liberated from the Turks by the Russians, irredentism and regional rivalry became the prime focus of its foreign policy. Macedonia, a much-valued land throughout Bulgarian history, became the major object of Bulgaria's irredentist campaigns, although eventually most of the land reverted to Serbia and was later incorporated into Yugoslavia. Macedonia, in addition to Thrace, which was valued because it provided access to the sea, was the primary motive for Bulgaria's role not only in the two Balkan wars of 1912 and 1913 but also in the two world wars.

Bulgaria was not only struggling for power throughout its history, it was also a pawn in the power struggles of the so-called great powers. Before the Christian Era the area was conquered first by Greece and later by Rome and was influenced strongly by both of these early cultures. Later, when the Slavs and Bulgars succeeded in forming a united state, the country was still besieged by both Byzantium and Rome. Although the Romans eventually lost their hold over Bulgaria, the Byzantine Empire took both political and religious control of the country for two centuries. When Bulgaria managed to reassert its autonomy in the time of the Second Bulgarian Kingdom, independence was short-lived, and the country again fell under alien control, this time to the Ottoman Turks. The Turks dominated Bulgaria for five centuries, until liberation by the Russians temporarily gave the country full sovereignty. Before each of the two world wars of the twentieth century, Bulgaria was actively courted by both sides as a potentially strategic ally. Realizing Bulgaria's territorial aspirations, Germany played upon Bulgarian irredentism in order to gain its collaboration in the wars, and both times Bulgaria emerged on the losing side. When World War II ended for Bulgaria in 1944, it fell under Soviet influence, where it has remained ever since.

EARLY HISTORY

The history of the country that became modern Bulgaria can be traced back many hundreds of years before the time of Christ, predating by fifteen or more centuries the arrival of the people known as Bulgars, from whom the country ultimately took its name. The earliest people to have a viable political organization in the area were the Thracians, whose loosely organized tribes occupied and controlled much of the Balkan Peninsula. Later, when their society began to disintergrate, the Thracians fell under Greek influence and joined forces with Athens to overrun neighboring Macedonia. In the fourth century B.C., however, Philip of Macedon, competing with the Greeks in a power struggle over Thrace, conquered Thrace and made the Thracians a subject people.

This invasion was followed in the second century B.C. by a Roman invasion of Macedonia and a subsequent conquest of Thrace. By the first century A.D. the Romans totally dominated the area. Despite their strict and unpopular military control over the population, under their tutelage cities grew, roads were constructed, and mining and farming were developed.

In the third century A.D. a series of mass migrations into the Balkans began; these migrations lasted for several centuries. The Goths came in four separate waves during the third century. In the fourth century the Huns swept across the country, razing cities and villages. They were followed in the fourth and fifth centuries by the Visigoths and Ostrogoths who, like the Huns, continued to ravage the country. These invasions culminated in the eventual conquest and settlement by the relatively civilized Slavs in the sixth century.

In A.D. 330 the Emperor Constantine established what was to be considered a second Rome and named it Constantinople. In this period the Roman Empire in the Balkans was split into two parts: in the East, Thrace was once again under Greek domination, and the West was dominated by the Romans. Constantinople was growing in power, and Greek influence was eroding the political and cultural influence of the Romans. By the mid-fourth century Rome and Constantinople were actively struggling for domination over the Balkans.

In the sixth century A.D. the Slavs crossed the Danube River and occupied much of the Balkan Peninsula. Although the Byzantines built fortresses to protect themselves, they were unable to hold the Slavs at bay. Once the Slavs had taken over most of the Balkan Peninsula, they succeeded in destroying the existing social system, rapidly replacing it with their own. Soon the entire Thracian population became slavicized.

In the seventh century A.D. the Bulgars in turn began to migrate into the Balkans. They had come originally from central Asia and were said to be related to the Huns. They were of the same stock as the Turks and spoke a language similar to Turkish. Before migrating to the Balkans, they had lived north of the Black Sea. Their social order was vastly different from that of the Slavs, although eventually the Slavic system became dominant. The Bulgars, unlike the Slavs who repudiated the concept of kingship, were governed autocratically by khans. The Bulgars were warriors who fought on horseback, and their customs and dress were Asiatic.

When the Bulgars overran what is now northeastern Bulgaria, they found Slavic tribes already established and quickly made peace with them in order to strengthen themselves against the Byzantines. As the Slavs were far more numerous than the Bulgars, the latter were assimilated, and within two centuries the Bulgars had been completely slavicized. The Slavic language and culture were adopted, although the Bulgarian name and political structure were retained. A Slav-Bulgarian state was formed with the capital at Pliska.

The First Bulgarian Kingdom lasted from A.D. 679 to 1018, when it fell to Byzantium. During this period the social system resembled the feudal system of western Europe. The king, or czar, was the leading nobleman. As the political situation of the period varied, he was alternately supported or opposed by the boyars (large landowners). The great majority of the people were serfs.

During the seventh and eighth centuries A.D. the Bulgarians consolidated and further reinforced their power. By the ninth century they were so powerful that they challenged the Byzantine Empire itself. Twice in this period the Bulgarians controlled areas of Greece, Turkey, Yugoslavia, Romania, and even Russia. In a battle in 811 the Bulgars completely devastated the Byzantine army that had invaded their country, killed the Byzantine emperor, Nicephorus; and went on to lay seige to Constantinople itself. The seige failed, but Bulgaria had established itself as a power with which to be reckoned.

During the ninth century A.D. Bulgaria once again became the focus of Greek and Roman cultural and political rivalry. The dispute was finally terminated when Bulgaria, under Czar Boris I, accepted Christianity from Constantinople rather than from Rome. As early as 836 the Byzantine Empire had sent two brothers, Cyril and Methodius, to convert the Slavs. When the brothers were in Venice, they argued in favor of church services and literature in the Slavic language, opposing the Roman bishops who believed that only Hebrew, Greek, and Latin were suitable languages for worship. This dialogue further exacerbated the tensions between Byzantium and Rome. By 870 Boris made Orthodox Christianity the official religion of the state. At this juncture Bulgaria fell under the Byzantine sphere of influence, completing—for the moment—its break with the Roman religion and culture.

The influence of Cyril and Methodius upon the Bul-

Czar Simeon I (893–927). Simeon's reign was known as the golden age for Bulgaria. Bulgaria had extended its borders from the Black Sea in the east and to the southern Carpathian Mountains to the north. It was in this period that Bulgaria made its greatest territorial expansion, penetrating deep into the Byzantine Empire.

Prince Samuel, who ruled Bulgaria from 976 to 1014, was the sovereign and general who lost the battle to invading Byzantine emperor Basil II in 1014 and surrendered his soldiers and himself to a fate worse than death.

Basil II (Lucius Basilius) was the Byzantine emperor (976–1025) who is recorded in history by the name "the Slayer of the Bulgarians" for having led his army into Bulgaria in 1014, capturing 14,000 Bulgarian soldiers and putting out their eyes out with hot coals and other equally cruel methods. He performed this hideous "deed" in retaliation for the defeat and death of Nicephorus, the Byzantine emperor, on the field of battle in 811.

In 1186, Bulgaria came out from under the Byzantine rule. The three Asen brothers served in succession as kings—Peter and John Asen, and Kaloyan, starting the Second Bulgarian Kingdom. In 1186, they gained independence from the Byzantine Empire.

garian language and culture is incalculable. They not only carried a new liturgical form to Bulgaria but also devised a new alphabet known as Cyrillic. This new alphabet soon replaced Latin and Greek as the only form of writing, and on its base a new Slavic literature and culture grew up.

When Bulgaria adopted Christianity from Byzantium, it also adopted Byzantium's territorial ambitions. Under Czar Simeon (A.D. 893–937), a period known as the Golden Age, Bulgaria extended its territories from the Black Sea in the east to the southern Carpathian Mountains in the north, to the Sava River in the west, and to Macedonia in the southwest. It was in this period that Bulgaria reached the peak of its territorial expansion, penetrating deep into the Byzantine Empire. Macedonia and Albania became Bulgaria's new frontiers; in 924 Serbia fell under Bulgarian rule. With these victories Simeon claimed the title czar of all the Bulgarians and the Greeks.

With the territorial expansion came a domestic flourishing in the arts and an increase in trade. The arts and architecture of the period were significant for their beauty and vitality. Preslav, then the capital city, became the center of culture. Crafts, such as goldsmithing, pottery, stonemasonry, and blacksmithing grew, and shops sprang up everywhere. At the same time literature flourished, and education and scholarship took on a new importance. Knowledge of Slavic literature became widespread, and writers treated such varied topics as religion, grammar, logic, and patriotism.

By the end of the tenth century A.D., however, the First Bulgarian Kingdom was beginning to decline. Internally, the local population was weary from continual warring and from the oppression of feudalism. The boyars continued to struggle against the king and his council for their own autonomy. Because of the internal weakness of the country, Bulgaria's neighbors began to encroach on her borders. The Magyars (Hungarians) attacked from the northwest, seizing territory north of the Danube River. The Byzantines in 967 formed an alliance with the prince of Kiev in Russia and, because of this alliance, succeeded in invading Bulgaria repeatedly.

In the late tenth century there was a brief revival of Bulgarian power under Samuel, when the Bulgarians succeeded in liberating the northeastern sector of the country from Byzantine control and captured southern Macedonia. But the revival was short-lived. The Byzantine emperor, Basil II, was determined to regain his lost land and once again recaptured the northeastern sector. In 1014 Basil again invaded Bulgaria; defeated Samuel's army; and, in an act of matchless cruelty, blinded fourteen thousand Bulgarian soldiers. From 1018 until 1185 all of Bulgaria was under Byzantine rule.

The eleventh and twelfth centuries witnessed a period of extreme hardship for the country. Byzantine domination was harsh and punitive. Monetary taxes, which added to the already heavy burdens of the peasantry, were levied in 1040. Bulgarian feudalism was replaced by Byzantine feudalism. The Byzantine church itself was a vehicle of oppression as it was later to become under Turkish rule; the church owned entire estates and villages and the people who inhabited them. There were a series of revolts during the eleventh century, but none was successful in overthrowing Byzantine tyranny. During this period the first and second Crusades made their way through the Balkan Peninsula, wreaking havoc among the local populations.

The Second Bulgarian Kingdom was established in 1186 and lasted until 1396, when—like the First Bulgarian Kingdom—it was conquered by a powerful enemy and neighbor. Ironically, history came full circle to spell defeat for the Bulgarians. In the twelfth century, when the Byzantine Empire was declining because of internal weakness, the Bulgarians were able to free themselves from domination. In the fourteenth century, when Bulgaria itself was weakened by domestic strife, it was conquered by an enemy whose oppression was greater than that of the Byzantine Empire: the Ottoman Turks.

At the close of the twelfth century the internal situation in Bulgaria was deteriorating. Taxes had been increased, and the burden borne by the peasants became still heavier. The feudal lords openly began to proclaim their independence from Byzantium, whose empire was by now steadily declining. Bulgaria was surrounded by its enemies: the Ottoman Turks, the Magyars, and the Normans. In 1183 the Magyars invaded, penetrating as far as Sofia. Realizing the vulnerability of the Byzantine Empire, the Bulgarians rebelled under the leadership of two brothers, John Asen and Peter Asen. The brothers first liberated northeastern Bulgaria and then proceeded into Thrace, where they were opposed by Isaac Angelus, then emperor of Byzantium. In 1187 a peace treaty was concluded in which Byzantium conceded autonomy to Bulgaria.

Despite the peace treaty, however, the Bulgarians continued to wage war against the empire, hoping to regain northern Bulgaria and Macedonia—a contested territory and bitterly disputed issue throughout Bulgarian history. In 1201 the empire again concluded a peace treaty with the Bulgarians, ceding all of northern Bulgaria and a large part of Macedonia. Eventually, in 1207, Constantinople recognized the complete independence of Bulgaria, and Bulgarian freedom was firmly established.

This new-found independence, however, did not extend to the Bulgarian church, which was still under the aegis of the empire. For that reason Kaloyan, the Bulgarian ruler, negotiated with the Roman pope, Innocent III, in order to ally the Bulgarian church with the Church of Rome. The motives of Rome and those of Kaloyan were similar: to isolate the influence of Byzantium from Bulgaria. In 1204 Kaloyan was crowned king

John Asen I and Kaloyan

by the papal nuncio in Turnovo. Although this union lasted only briefly, it served the purpose for which it was designed, and Bulgaria was effectively cut off from Byzantium.

During the thirteenth century the Holy Roman Empire replaced the Byzantine Empire on the borders of Bulgaria, and Byzantine aggression was replaced by that of the Holy Roman Empire. When Rome declared war on Bulgaria, the Bulgarians invaded Thrace, defeating the Crusaders at Adrianople in 1205. The reestablishment of the Bulgarian patriarchate in 1235 represented the end of the short-lived alliance between the Bulgarian church and Rome.

Under the reign of John Asen II in the mid-thirteenth century peace was again restored, and the country once more extended its territories. The Bulgarians succeeded in capturing eastern Thrace, the Aegean coast, Albania, and Macedonia. Bulgarian territory at this time was as great as under the reign of Czar Simeon; with these conquests Bulgaria became the largest state in the Balkans. The country was now surrounded by three seas— the Black Sea, the Aegean Sea, and the Adriatic Sea— opening the country's doors to foreign trade and culture.

Again, as in the time of Simeon, the arts and cultural life of the country flourished. Monasteries, churches, and

King George I Terter founded a new dynasty in 1280 and served until 1292.

fortresses were constructed. Religious literature and art achieved a high level of excellence, and secular works became popular. The first chronicle of Bulgarian history was written, and an interest in history grew among the people. The first Bulgarian coins were minted at this time. Trade, particularly with Italy, increased greatly because of Bulgaria's free access to the sea. Merchants and ambassadors came to Bulgaria from abroad, lending their influence to Bulgaria's economic and cultural life.

By the second half of the thirteenth century, however, internal conditions in the country had deteriorated. The feudal system, which had been further consolidated during the thirteenth century, had exacerbated the tensions of the peasants, and hostilities among the boyars increased. The throne was contested between 1257 and 1277 and was eventually taken forcibly by Ivalio, known as the swineherd czar because of his leadership of a peasant uprising in 1277.

Meanwhile, Bulgaria's neighbors again sensed an opportune time to attack because of the internal divisions in the country. The Byzantines conquered several parts of Macedonia and Thrace, and the Hungarians and Tatars invaded on another front. At one point the Hungarian king declared himself king of Bulgaria. In 1242 there was a large-scale Mongol invasion. Tatar raids went on continually between 1241 and 1300. The country was totally fragmented; each separate area attempted to ally itself with its former enemies, whether Russian, Hungarian, or Tatar, in order to prevent widespread damage.

By the fourteenth century the Turks began to envision the conquest of Bulgaria. Internally the boyars continued to fight among themselves, and externally the country was threatened alternately by Byzantium and by Serbia. By the mid-fourteenth century all of Macedonia was under Serbian control, and the Serbian czar—much like the Hungarian king before him—called himself the czar of the Bulgars. The area of the country retained by the Bulgars by this time was divided into three parts: the last Bulgarian czar maintained his capital at Turnovo in the central highlands; the so-called Vidin Kingdom, ruled by the czar's brother, existed in the far northwest; and a principality of Dobrudzha was established in the northeast.

At the same time the Ottoman Turks were beginning to advance. Having seized areas of Asia Minor, they proceeded to raid the Balkans from 1326 to 1352. Under their leader, Murad I (1319–1389), they began to attack Thrace, Macedonia, and parts of Bulgaria. By 1371 they were attacking territories in northeastern Thrace. At this point they marched against Sofia and, despite active resistance, succeeded in capturing it. Despite an alliance with the Serbs, the Bulgarians were too weak to resist further; in 1388 the Turks easily won a battle against the Serbs. The fall of Turnovo was followed by the fall of Vidin and Dobrudzha. By 1396 all of Bulgaria was under Turkish domination.

TURKISH RULE

The Second Bulgarian Kingdom, like the first, had ended in total defeat, and the darkest period in Bulgarian history began with the Turkish conquest. Only the priests of the Bulgarian Orthodox church—despite its takeover by the Greeks—were able to preserve Bulgarian national literature and culture to some degree. The Bulgarians once again were subjected to foreign domination, only this time foreign rule lasted for five centuries. Historians agree that Turkish rule was a deathblow to the creative forces that had been responsible for the development of the country to that time. With Turkish domination the normal economic, political, and social life of Bulgaria ground to a halt.

The Ottoman Turks were at a far lower stage of social development than either the Byzantine Empire, which preceded them in their occupation of the Balkans, or the Balkan states themselves. The Turks lived an almost nomadic life in primitive communal systems that were headed by tribal chiefs. When the Turks occupied Bulgaria, they replaced the established feudal system with their own more rudimentary and conservative feudalism. Many boyars were executed or rendered powerless if they failed to convert to Islam. The peasants were more completely under the feudal yoke than they had ever been under Byzantine rule. The Turks imposed heavy taxes and hard labor on the people of the conquered country, whom they considered cattle. Young boys were taken from their homes, proclaimed Muslims, and conscripted into the army.

The Turks ruled Bulgaria by means of a sharply delineated administrative system. Bulgaria as an entity did not exist for the Turks; the entire Balkan Peninsula was known as Rumili (Rumelia) and was ruled for the sultan by a *beylerbey* (governor-general) whose headquarters was located in Sofia. Rumili was divided into *vilayetlar,* which were further subdivided into *sanjaklar,* each in turn ruled by lesser officials. Bulgaria itself was divided into five *sanjaklar:* Kyustendil, Nikopol, Silistra, Sofia, and Vidin. Although all land was considered to be the property of the sultan, on the local level the land was distributed to feudal lords and was tilled by non-Muslim serfs.

A second vehicle for both administration and oppression that the Turks employed—in addition to the land administrators—was the Greek Orthodox church. By 1394, before the final conquest, the See of Turnovo had been subordinated to the patriarchate of Constantinople, where it remained until 1870. Greek bishops replaced Bulgarians, as Greek liturgy replaced the Slavic. The patriarchate, in turn, was totally subordinate to the sultan. The Greek clergy destroyed Bulgarian books and banned Slavic liturgy. The Bulgarian language and all Slavic literature were forbidden. Greek became the language in all schools.

The hellenization of the Bulgarian church was used by the Turks as a means to negate the nationalism of the people and thus dominate them. The Turks attempted to some extent to convert the Bulgarians to Islam in order to assimilate them more fully. Although many Bulgarians fled to the mountains with the coming of the Turks, others stayed on and accepted the Muslim faith, often for purely opportunistic purposes. Those who did were generally placed in strategically significant positions; frequently, as a reward for their conversion, they paid no taxes to the state. The Bulgarian converts to Islam were called Pomaks.

The plight of the peasants grew worse. Agricultural production dropped as their exploitation continued. Although landowners were not persecuted to the same degree as the peasantry, they were frequently displaced from the land. Turkish cattle breeders entered the country to settle on their lands. Lands were also taken to reward army commanders, provincial governors, and knights in the service of the sultan. Still other lands were given to immigrant Turkish peasants. The only food that was not subject to requisition by the conquerors was pork, which was not allowed in the Muslim diet.

As the life of the Bulgarian countryside declined, so too did urban life. Bulgarians were expelled from most urban centers and replaced by Greeks, Armenians, Jews, and Turks. By the end of the sixteenth century two-thirds of Sofia's population was Turkish. Trade was virtually halted for a time, and, when resumed, it also was dominated by Greeks, Armenians, and Jews rather than Bulgarians. The towns themselves were in a state of deterioration. The crafts had declined, economic life was stagnant, and the Black Sea was closed to all foreign ships.

As life within Bulgaria declined, the Turks began to perceive the country as a springboard for further aggression against other territories. Although Bulgarian hopes rose briefly when it appeared that the Turks might be destroyed by their enemies, such hopes eventually were dashed when the Turks emerged victorious throughout a period of two centuries of conquest and aggression.

In the early years of Turkish domination, the Turks waged continuous war with Albania, Bosnia, Serbia, Walachia, Moldavia, and what remained of the Byzantine Empire. Bulgarian hopes of liberation were fueled by the Turkish defeat at the Battle of Ankara in 1402, when the Turkish army was defeated by the Tatars. Resistance was eventually crushed, however, and the Turks began to renew their conquests after capturing Salonika in 1430. In the Battle of Varna the Turks succeeded in capturing Constantinople itself.

After the defeat of Constantinople the Turks overran Serbia, Walachia, Bosnia, and Albania. Their conquests expanded to include Mesopotamia, Syria, Arabia, and North Africa. In the sixteenth century Turkish conquests continued under Suleyman the Magnificent, who succeeded in capturing Serbia and Hungary in 1526. This triumphant expansion of the Turkish state caused Bulgarian dreams to be destroyed, although sporadic struggling within the country continued intermittently.

THE RISE OF NATIONALISM

During the sixteenth and seventeenth centuries the first seeds of real resistance to Turkish rule were planted in Bulgaria. On the foreign front the Turks were constantly beseiged by the Austrians and the Russians. By 1683 the Austrian army succeeded in liberating Hungary and Transylvania; they also were able to penetrate areas of Bulgaria and Macedonia. These victories over the Turks again sparked Bulgarian hopes.

During the same period the internal situation in Bulgaria continued to signal the eventual decline of Turkish power and the rise of a Bulgarian national spirit. Because of the increase in corruption and oppression by the Turks, the Bulgarians began to rebel openly. In the 1590s, the 1680s, and the 1730s significant local uprisings took place. Although these rebellions were not successful, they gave rise to the *haiduk* (forest outlaw) movement, which continued to carry out acts of rebellion against the Turkish overlords. The people praised their acts of daring and wrote folk songs detailing their adventures and exploits. In addition to the revolutionaries the *chorbadzhi* (squires), who were on the whole a progressive force, were able to gain some concessions from the Turks.

In the eighteenth and nineteenth centuries this latent nationalism grew swiftly under the influence of outside forces penetrating the country. The French Revolution —with its democratic ideals—had a widespread and vital impact on Bulgarian national sentiment.

By the early 1870s the seeds of revolution were sown as Bulgarians won some political victories over their conquerors. In 1870, primarily because of the activity of the Bulgarian priests, the Bulgarian Orthodox church was reestablished. Although the Bulgarian clergy was in large part responsible for this action, it was probably tolerated by the Turks because of their anger with the Greeks, who were then embroiled in a revolt in Crete. In 1872 the Bulgarian Revolutionary Central Committee was formed in Bucharest; by 1875 this group became active in the uprisings in Bosnia and Herzegovina, uprisings that were not easily quelled by the Turks.

As Bulgarian revolutionary sentiments grew, the Bulgarians turned to Russia to help win freedom from the Turks. Although the motives of the Russians and the Bulgarians were not identical, both wanted to rid the Balkans of Turkish oppression. The Russians perceived the Ottoman Empire as a very dangerous rival that they hoped to annihilate, thus gaining control of western European trade. The Bulgarians, although their motives were also pragmatic, felt a deep sense of kinship with the

THE KINGDOM OF BULGARIA

Russian people. The Russians, like the Bulgarians, were Slavs. Their religion was identical. Even their language was similar. Thus, they sensed a commonality not only of interest but also of cultures.

The precursor to the liberation in 1878 was an unsuccessful uprising in 1876. The Bulgarians, at this point, were ill prepared for war, politically and strategically. Thousands of Bulgarians were killed in April of that year. Soon thereafter Turkish reprisals followed. Fifteen thousand Bulgarians were massacred in Plovdiv alone. The savagery of these reprisals was so brutal that western public leaders spoke out in protest. The governments of the west, however, fearing an increased Russian penetration in the area, refused to act against the Turks.

Although the revolution of 1876 had met with failure, it had succeeded in loosening the Turkish grip on the country and in increasing the feeling of the Russians that the time to attack was imminent. Finally, after the Russo-Turkish War of 1877, the Russians invaded Bulgaria, liquidating the Turkish army by March 1878. In these battles for Bulgarian liberation, the Russians lost over two hundred thousand lives, a sacrifice the Bulgarians never failed to recognize.

The results of 1878 were mixed, and the outcome of the original peace treaty was reversed within five months of its signing. Bulgaria became an autonomous tributary of the Turkish sultan; complete independence was not established until 1908. The original peace treaty, the Treaty of San Stefano, signed on March 3, 1878, granted Bulgaria additional territories, including Thrace and the much-valued Macedonia. This treaty was reversed, primarily because of Western fear of Russian encroachment, by the Congress of Berlin; the Treaty of Berlin, signed on July 13, 1878, unlike the Treaty of San Stefano, delimited Bulgarian territories. The Bulgarians were forced to give Thrace and Macedonia back to the Turks. Bulgaria itself was carved into two separate entities: the principality of Bulgaria, including northern Bulgaria and Sofia, and eastern Rumelia, or southern Bulgaria.

LIBERATION AND ITS AFTERMATH

Although the 1877–1878 war freed Bulgaria from Turkish rule, the outcome of the Congress of Berlin once again denied to Bulgaria the land that it perceived to be rightfully Bulgarian, thus setting the tone for an irredentist foreign policy that lasted through World War II. Because the west, particularly Great Britain, played a significant role in carving up the Balkans, and Bulgaria in particular, in hopes of curbing Russian power, many historians speculate that Bulgaria's alliances with Germany in both World War I and World War II were products of irredentist sentiment that grew out of the Treaty of Berlin.

Bulgaria moved to recapture its lost territory only seven years after the Treaty of Berlin. In 1885 it annexed eastern Rumelia—or southern Bulgaria—by means of a military coup. The British were in favor of the annexation as it represented an obstacle to Russian ambitions in the Balkans; the Russians quite naturally were disturbed by the act. This was the first in a series of Bulgarian moves designed to reestablish earlier boundaries.

The establishment of a Bulgarian government in 1878 was relatively easily accomplished, and that government achieved a certain degree of stability in the aftermath of Turkish rule. The Turnovo Constitution (1879)—originally drafted by the Russians but rewritten by Bulgarians—established an essentially advanced and democratic system. It set up a unicameral parliament, which was to be elected on the basis of universal suffrage; the parliament was to control the executive. The monarchy, which lasted from the 1880s until World War II, was established at this time under a German dynasty that was acceptable to the European powers. Although the first prince was forced to abdicate by the Russians, his successor established firm and advanced economic and administrative institutions in the country. Eventually, because of a crisis in Bosnia and Herzegovina, the country was able to declare itself an independent kingdom in 1908.

Alexander as he appeared in later life as prince of Bulgaria

With guns aimed at his head, Prince Alexander is forced to abdicate in 1886

*King Ferdinand I as he looked
during his reign of 1908–18.*

One historian has described the postliberation period as the "only prolonged period of peaceful development" for Bulgaria. After the liberation, land rose in value. Peasants were able to purchase land from the Turks, and agricultural production rose markedly. Modern industry grew up at a relatively rapid pace, although the country remained primarily agrarian. The state began to take steps in education and culture. All levels of education were expanded; students of higher education studied both in Bulgaria and abroad; and illiteracy, which was overwhelming at the period of liberation, was reduced to 76 percent by 1900 and to 54 percent by 1920. Science and the arts were actively encouraged, and literature flourished once again.

Financial burdens, however, escalated rapidly between 1886 and 1911. In 1911 the national debt was actually more than three times the size of the national budget. At the same time, as industry increased, two antagonistic goups developed: the urban middle class—composed of merchants and white-collar workers, and the poor, who were generally laborers or peasants. Working conditions in factories were nearly intolerable, causing factory workers to interest themselves in the cause of socialism, while on the farms the peasants began to organize a movement known as the Bulgarian Agrarian Union (also called the Agrarian party), which was designed to offset the growing power of the urban groups. In 1891 the Social Democratic party was established; this party later formed the base of the Communist party in Bulgaria.

THE MACEDONIAN ISSUE

By the early twentieth century the country was once again embroiled in war; the Balkan wars of 1912 and 1913 impeded economic and social development in the country. Once again, as in the case of eastern Rumelia, irredentism was the Bulgarian motive for war. Both eastern Thrace and Macedonia, the lands ceded to Bulgaria by the Treaty of San Stefano, were still under Turkish rule. The lands had not only large Bulgarian populations but also strategic and economic significance. Macedonia, more than Thrace, was of extreme importance to Bul-

garia; Bulgarians believed the population of Macedonia to be composed almost exclusively of Bulgarians. The issue of Macedonia was, in fact, a focal point around which Bulgarian political life revolved after 1878, because that issue was seen by the Bulgarians as involving the territorial integrity of their nation.

Between the tenth and fourteenth centuries Macedonia was alternately occupied by the Bulgarians, the Serbs, and the Turks. At the time of liberation Macedonia was ceded to the Bulgarians by the Treaty of San Stefano, only to be returned to the Turks by the Treaty of Berlin. In 1893 the Internal Macedonian Revolutionary Organization (IMRO) was founded. This terrorist organization, with the battle slogan "Liberty or Death for Macedonia," fought a continual underground war of terrorism against the Turks. In 1903 there was a major Macedonian uprising in which two factions participated. Although the predominant faction favored Bulgarian annexation of Macedonia, another group favored complete autonomy for Macedonia. In 1908, when King Ferdinand proclaimed Bulgaria completely independent, memories of the medieval Bulgarian Empire, which included Macedonia, were rekindled.

The existence of a Macedonian minority has been disputed over many decades by Yugoslavia and Bulgaria. Bulgaria has consistently claimed that Macedonians are ethnically Bulgarians, that their language is a dialect of Bulgarian, and that their land is a part of Bulgaria. Yugoslavia, on the other hand, has given legal recognition to a Macedonian nationality be establishing the People's Republic of Macedonia and by designating the Macedonian language one of the official languages of the federal Republic.

The vast majority of Bulgarians have been born into the Bulgarian Orthodox church ever since the ninth century, when Boris I adopted Christianity for his people. Until World War II a person had no legal existence without a baptismal certificate from the church. In keeping with Eastern Orthodox tradition, the Bulgarian Orthodox church is an independent national church. It is inseparably linked with Bulgarian nationhood in the minds of most Bulgarians because of the role it played in preserving a national consciousness during the centuries of Turkish rule and in spearheading a national revival in the nineteenth century.

A tradition of religious freedom and tolerance allowed religious minorities to exist without friction. Even during World War II the Jews in Bulgaria suffered little persecution in comparison with those in other parts of eastern Europe. No census of religious affiliation has been taken since the Communists took power; however, according to various estimates in 1965 there were about 750,000 Muslims; 26,000 Protestants; 32,000 Roman Catholics; and between 3,000 and 7,000 Jews. The Muslim population included most Turks and some 50,000 Pomaks (Bulgarians who converted to Islam during Turkish rule) living in the rugged Rodopi mountain range.

Religious freedom is guaranteed by the constitution, but churches are subject to strict governmental control. Formal religious education is restricted to the training of priests. Children, however, continue to be instructed in the rudiments of faith and ritual by their families. Despite government efforts to secularize the milestones in the life cycle, a large percentage of Bulgarians continue to regard the priest as an essential officiant at baptisms, weddings, and funerals. Churchgoing and the strict fasts prescribed by the Eastern Orthodox church have not been carefully observed by most Bulgarians since the 1930s; nevertheless, the people often exhibit strong religious feelings tempered by traditional beliefs in the powers of nature, the evil eye, and other forces.

THE BALKAN WARS

The tumultuous history of Macedonia set the stage for the two Balkan wars. In 1912, at the onset of the First Balkan War, Serbia, Bulgaria, Montenegro, and Greece formed an alliance to drive the Turks from Europe. Turkey, who was at war with Italy at the time, was weak and disunited. Macedonia and Thrace were hotbeds of internal disorder. In October 1912 Turkey declared war on Serbia and Bulgaria, a move that was countered by a Greek declaration of war on Turkey. In 1913 the Bulgarians succeeded in capturing Adrianople, and the Greeks captured Salonika, Crete, and Samos. Eventually, the Turks were badly defeated. But the question of Macedonia remained. Serbia, Greece, and Bulgaria all laid claim to the land at the end of the First Balkan War. Eventually a compromise was reached: the northern section went to Serbia and the eastern section, to Bulgaria.

Despite this compromise, the Serbs and Greeks remained wary of the Bulgarians. In 1913 the Second Balkan War began, the Greeks, Montenegrins, Serbs, and Romanians joining forces with their previous enemy, the

Prince Boris ascended to the throne October 5, 1918, upon the abdication of his father, King Ferdinand. King Boris III served from 1918 to 1943.

Turks, against their former ally, the Bulgarians. This rivalry had been fostered by both Austria and Russia. Eventually, the Bulgarians turned to the Russians for arbitration and finally signed a mutual defense treaty with Russia. When the Romanians crossed into Bulgaria, the Bulgarians—who were simultaneously fighting in Macedonia and were therefore weakened by fighting on two fronts—were forced to surrender. As a result of this loss, when the peace treaty of Bucharest was signed in August 1913 and Macedonia was partitioned between Greece and Serbia, Bulgaria managed to retain only a tiny fragment in the eastern sector.

Macedonia, however, remained an issue for Bulgaria. In World War I Bulgaria succeeded in invading Macedonia. During the interwar period Macedonia was divided between Greece, Bulgaria, and Yugoslavia, Yugoslavia retaining the largest portion of the land. In the 1923–34 period Macedonian terrorism plagued the country and wreaked havoc on Bulgarian political and social life. During World War II the Bulgarians invaded both Greek Macedonia and Yugoslav Macedonia once again. Although the Macedonians themselves were divided in their sentiments between loyalties to Greeks, Yugoslavs, and Bulgarians, the land eventually reverted to Yugoslavia during World War II. As an issue, however, it still burns in the minds of the Bulgarians. The Macedonian question has been aptly referred to as "that eternal Balkan sore spot of rival nationalism."

WORLD WAR I

As was the case in the Balkan wars, Bulgaria's primary motivation for engagement in World War I was irredentism. Again the country was determined to regain the two lands that had escaped her grasp in the past: Macedonia and Thrace. Although Macedonia was prized for political and social reasons, Thrace represented a strategically more significant objective. In order to develop foreign trade, Bulgaria required an outlet to the sea; Thrace represented that outlet.

The domestic situation in the country before World War I was mixed. Although Bulgaria's army had been demobilized at the end of the Second Balkan War (1913) and economic conditions were rapidly improving, the mood of the monarchy and the middle class was one of vindictiveness and retaliation against those countries that had stripped Bulgaria of its territories. The country became divided between those who wanted closer relations with Russia and the Triple Entente and those who preferred an alliance with the Central Powers. As the war neared, the struggle between these camps intensified.

Bulgaria, of all the Balkan states, was the only one to join the Central Powers, led by Germany and Austria, in World War I. It was deeply ironic that Bulgaria chose to side with her former enemy and oppressor, Turkey, and against her former friend and protector, Russia.

Again, the issue for Bulgaria was the Macedonian question. Serbia and Greece, which had triumphed over Bulgaria in the Second Balkan War, were allied with the entente powers. Bulgaria chose to fight against these enemies in order to regain Macedonia. Although the entente powers hoped to woo Bulgaria to their side, they refused—because of Serb and Greek pressures—to cede Macedonia to Bulgaria. The Central Powers, on the other hand, who were already at war with Serbia, were willing to promise Macedonia to the Bulgarians in exchange for their collaboration.

In the early stages of the war Germany won victories in France and on the eastern front. Although the government then ruling Bulgaria was already inclined to join the Central Powers, these early successes made German promises even more appealing. In August 1915 a secret treaty of alliance was signed by Bulgaria and Germany, containing a clause that promised Serbian, Greek, and Romanian territories to the Bulgarians. Thus the quadripartite alliance was born, composed of Germany, Austria-Hungary, Turkey, and Bulgaria.

By September 1915 Bulgarian troops were mobilized and began to deploy along the borders of Greece and Serbia. On October 1, 1915, Bulgaria declared war on Serbia and, with the assistance of Austrian and German troops, succeeded in defeating the Serbian army. At the same time the Bulgarian army began to advance on Macedonia. There the local population, a proportion of which was openly sympathetic to Bulgarian aspirations, joined in the fighting on the side of the Bulgarians. Although the Bulgarian army attempted to drive the entente forces from southern Macedonia, it met with failure. This defeat was followed by a period of prolonged trench warfare on the Balkan front. By 1916 Bulgaria was also at war with Romania and, with the help of German and Austrian units, managed a victory over the Romanians.

By 1918 Bulgaria and the Central Powers were defeated, leaving Bulgaria in a worse position than before the war. Hopes of regaining Thrace and Macedonia were dashed, and the country was immeasurably weakened by external fighting and internal division. The people were frustrated and bitter. Although the war had stimulated Bulgaria's industry—there were 345 industrial enterprises in 1911 and 1,404 in 1924—it had been costly in other respects. Bulgaria was forced to pay both reparations and payments for the Allied occupation that followed. Taxes rose, and the value of the currency declined. As a result, King Ferdinand was forced to abdicate in 1918, shortly before the armistice was signed.

The Treaty of Neuilly-sur-Seine was signed on November 27, 1919, ending Bulgaria's role in the war and establishing her boundaries. Once more Bulgaria had entered a war on the losing side, and once more its irredentist ambitions had resulted in no territorial gains. At the end of the war Bulgaria lost Thrace to Greece—

thus failing in her attempts to gain access to the sea—and a small area in the Rodopi (or Rhodope Mountains) and a portion of its western frontier to Yugoslavia. As a result of these losses, Bulgaria was left with a still greater sense of frustration and hostility toward its Balkan neighbors.

THE INTERWAR YEARS

The period between the first and second world wars was one of political unrest and Macedonian terrorism. The country was in an almost untenable economic situation at the close of the war: prices skyrocketed, people died of starvation, and strikes were almost continuous. Out of this situation two extreme political groups grew up. On the extreme right was a faction of the IMRO, which at that time demanded the annexation of Greek and Yugoslav Macedonia. On the left was the Bulgarian Agrarian Union, the only party at the time more popular than the Communists.

When Ferdinand was forced to abdicate, he was succeeded by his son, Boris III. Real political power was, however, in the hands of Alexander Stambolisky, the leader of the Bulgarian Agrarian Union. He led the country as its prime minister from 1919 to 1923. When Stambolisky took power, the peasants formed 80 percent of the population. Stambolisky and the Bulgarian Agrarian Union were dedicated to improving the lot of these people; in his words "to raising the standards both economic and educational, of the desperately poor and depressed peasant class."

Stambolisky, on behalf of the peasant populism movement, made several sweeping reforms. He instituted various social reforms, spread education, and built roads. His strong dislike of the commercial and professional classes in the cities led him toward the objective of a peasant republic. When in power he instituted tax and land reforms and radically altered the legal system. His domestic policies were not popular with all strata of society; his foreign policies were even less popular. He favored reconciliation with Yugoslavia over the Macedonian issue. In 1923 he was overthrown by a group composed of IMRO, military, and other factions and was beheaded.

The murder of Stambolisky was followed by a Communist attempt to foment revolution in the country. The leaders were Georgi Dimitrov and Vasil Kalarov, later leading figures in the Bulgarian Communist state. The country was in a state of civil war, which was subsequently crushed by the right-wing political factions of the country. Thousands of Bulgarians were killed, and Dimitrov and Kalarov were exiled. In 1925 the Bulgarian Communist party (BKP) was officially outlawed. Although Boris continued as monarch, the country was ruled by coalition governments and military dictatorships for a decade following Stambolisky's death.

From 1923 until the putsch of 1934 IMRO terrorism dominated the country. Bulgaria's position toward Macedonia was clear and unequivocal: it sought to annex Macedonia completely as it considered the land to be Bulgarian and the people to be Bulgarians. In the Bulgarian sector of Macedonia the Macedonians were given a high degree of latitude, some Macedonians even holding high offices in Bulgaria. In the Yugoslavian sectors of Macedonia, however, most Macedonians felt oppressed and restricted. As a result of this mixed status and treatment, there was a certain ambivalence in Macedonian sentiment, the IMRO terrorists favoring complete independence and self-rule. Among Macedonian patriots, two predominant factions grew up. The Federalists favored an autonomous Macedonia—which could, if necessary, be allied with Yugoslavia and Bulgaria—and the Supremists sought to incorporate Macedonia within Bulgaria, with aspirations of dominating the entire Balkan area. The results of these divergent opinions were expressed in acts of violence and terrorism that wreaked havoc in Bulgaria and eventually culminated in Federalist collaboration with the Ustashi—a group of Croat separatists—and the murder of King Alexander of Yugoslavia.

Macedonian terrorism was virtually ended by the putsch of 1934. The government, the People's Bloc, which was a coalition of four parties including the Bulgarian Agrarian Union was overthrown by the so-called Zveno—or link—group. The Zveno group was headed by Kimon Georgiev and was aided by the League of Reserve Officers. As soon as it seized power, Zveno suspended the constitution and dissolved parliament. The king was left with only nominal powers. Although the group did succeed for the most part in ridding the country of Macedonian terrorism, its rule was overtly authoritarian. By 1935 the king, with the aid of the military, had regained his power and replaced the Zveno group with a more moderate government.

With the reestablishment of the monarchy, a royal dictatorship took power and ruled over Bulgaria until 1943, when Boris died. There were at this time no forces left to oppose the king, political parties were negligible, and only a shadow parliament existed. Ironically, the military, which had aided the Zveno in the overthrow of the king, now was an instrument of his control.

Foreign relations under Boris III before World War II were leading the country again inevitably into a war that would bring it to total defeat. In 1934, despite the suppression of IMRO by the newly formed government, Romania, Yugoslavia, Greece, and Turkey, as in the Second Balkan War, were once again wary of Bulgaria's irredentist ambitions. In that year the four powers signed the Balkan Pact, from which Bulgaria naturally was excluded, in order to prevent Bulgarian encroachment in the area. Although Bulgaria and Yugoslavia later established a rapprochement in 1937, the potential of a Bulgarian annexation of Macedonia was still considered a threat by its neighbors.

During the 1930s, while Bulgaria was viewed with suspicion by its neighbors, it began to form new friendships with Germany and Italy. Boris had married the daughter of King Vittorio Emanuele of Italy, a country that had already become Fascist, thus strengthening ties with that country. At the same time, Bulgaria began to solidify its ties with Germany, principally by means of trade. A new-found prosperity was based almost exclusively on German trade, an arrangement that eventually weakened the country. Within a short period German agents were pouring into the country. Thus, Bulgaria was on one side alienated from its neighbors and on the other being drawn into the Nazi-Fascist camp.

WORLD WAR II

Bulgaria's motives for entering World War II were once again based on irredentism, coupled with almost total economic dependence on Germany. Once more it hoped to regain the lands of Thrace and Macedonia, which were lost after the Treaty of San Stefano was reversed by the Congress of Berlin. The lesson of the two subsequent Balkan wars and World War I had fallen on deaf ears. Bulgaria was still estranged from its Balkan neighbors and once more was being courted by the former ally of World War I, Germany. Germany, again realizing Bulgaria's territorial aspirations, hoped to bribe the Bulgarian leadership with southern Dobrudzha, which was eventually ceded to Bulgaria in 1940.

In December 1941 Bulgaria placed herself squarely on the German side by declaring war on Great Britain and the United States and joining the Rome-Berlin Axis. This alignment, which derived primarily from Bulgaria's irredentist policy, was given further force by dislike of the British, who were held to blame by the Bulgarians for the loss of Macedonia to Yugoslavia and Greece.

Despite the declaration of war against Great Britain and the United States, Bulgaria refused throughout World War II to declare war on the Soviet Union. The Russians, unlike the British and Americans, were popular with the Bulgarian people. They were still remembered for their assistance to the Bulgarians in the past and were viewed by the people as their liberators from Turkish rule. Not only did Bulgaria refuse to declare war on its former liberator, but it also refused to make its army available to Adolf Hitler for his eastern campaign. When Germany declared war on Russia, Bulgaria continued to retain neutrality toward, and to maintain diplomatic relations with, the Soviet Union.

In the early stages of the war, before Bulgaria had declared war on the Allies, it had already begun to regain some of the land lost during the Balkan wars and World War I. Southern Dobrudzha, which had been ceded to

Romania in 1913, reverted to Bulgaria by August 1940. In the spring of 1941, supporting Germany against Yugoslavia and Greece, Bulgaria regained Macedonia and part of Greek Thrace. When Bulgaria was rewarded with these lands by the Nazis, Bulgarians perceived their gains as a "historical national unification." By 1941 Yugoslavia was overrun, and some of its territories were taken by Italy, Hungary, and Bulgaria. Italy received Montenegro, Hungary took part of northern Yugoslavia, and Bulgaria gained, in addition to the much-prized Macedonia, the frontiers of southeastern Serbia. The Bulgarians at this point were once again approaching the frontiers that had been established by the Treaty of San Stefano.

Internally, the country was in relatively good condition during the early stages of the war. The economy, based primarily on active trade with the Germans, was booming. The Bulgarian people perceived the fighting as essentially a "paper war" and were generally apathetic regarding their role in the war. There was little suffering within Bulgarian boundaries and little expression of hatred toward Bulgaria's ostensible enemies. Despite Bulgaria's alliance with the Nazis and Fascists, within the country Jews were for the most part protected rather than persecuted.

By 1943, however, the war began to change for the Bulgarians. Slowly the Allies began to turn back German power. At this time Bulgaria was hit frequently by British and United States air raids. Because of Bulgaria's strategic significance and its declaration of war, albeit symbolic, against Great Britain and the United States, Sofia and other major Bulgarian cities became targets for American and British bombers. Sofia was reduced to little more than rubble at one point, and over thirty thousand casualties were suffered by the Bulgarians.

In 1943 Boris died and was succeeded by his six-year-old son, Simeon. In fact, however, a three-man regency retained power, with Ivan Bagrianov as premier. The regency was less actively pro-Axis in orientation than was the late king; with its coming to power, thousands of political prisoners were released from jail, and all persecution of Jews was terminated.

By 1944, when Germany and its allies were clearly losing the war, the Bulgarian leaders sought to reverse the earlier decision of the king and to seek peace with the Allies as well as with the Greek and Yugoslav governments-in-exile. Despite sub rosa attempts to release itself from agreements with the Axis, Bulgaria was unable to extricate itself from the alliance. On August 22, 1944, the Bulgarian government publicly announced that it was ready for a peace agreement with the Allies.

The war was ended for Bulgaria when, on September 4, 1944, the Soviets, after taking over Romania, entered Bulgaria. The exact sequence of events has been interpreted differently by various historians. There are, however, two major interpretations. One suggests that, once

the Soviets had occupied Romania and declared war on Bulgaria, Bulgaria—under a hastily formed anti-Axis coalition government—immediately quit the pact with the Axis and declared war on its former ally, Germany. The other interpretation posits the theory that, on August 26, the Bulgarian government had declared itself neutral, thus withdrawing from the war. At this time it ordered German troops on its soil to disarm. When Soviet troops arrived in Bulgaria, they found this so-called neutrality unacceptable and insisted on a Bulgarian declaration of war against Germany. This declaration was promptly carried out on the eve of the day that it was requested.

When the Soviets occupied the country in September 1944, the government of the so-called Fatherland Front (Otechestven Front) seized power from the existing government within five days of the occupation. On September 9, 1944, the Fatherland Front—under the leadership of Georgiev—officially took control of the country on what was then termed an interim basis. On October 28, 1944, an armistice was signed between Bulgaria and the Soviet Union, which stated that all territories gained by Bulgaria since 1941 would be surrendered. Only southern Dobrudzha, taken from Romania in 1940, was to be retained. The agreement also established the Allied Control Commission in Sofia under direct Soviet control.

The results of the war for Bulgaria were mixed. In terms of financial burdens Bulgaria's position was relatively favorable compared with that of other countries on the losing side. In terms of territorial losses, which resulted in a legacy of bitterness and continued irredentism, its position was poor. As Bulgaria had suffered over thirty thousand casualties in the war, the Allies imposed relatively light peace terms. The Soviet Union extracted no reparations from Bulgaria, despite the fact that reparations were demanded from Germany, Hungary, and Romania. Yugoslavia also canceled Bulgaria's debts. Overall war damages to the country itself were generally moderate.

In terms of losses, however, Bulgaria not only lost most of the territories it had regained at the beginning of the war but also ultimately lost its constitutional monarchy and became a Soviet satellite. Although it was allowed to retain southern Dobrudzha, all the territories that were of significance to Bulgaria's sense of nation-

Tsar Simeon II on a June 12, 1944, stamp.

hood were gone. Macedonia reverted to Yugoslavia, and Thrace to Greece. The Treaty of Paris, signed in February 1947, confirmed Bulgaria's pre-1941 boundaries. Not only had Bulgaria lost these prized territories, but her sovereignty as a nation was severely curtailed by the Soviet military occupation. Both the armistice agreement of September 1944 and the British-Soviet agreement of October of that year recognized Soviet dominance in the country. Although this power over the country was not expected by the Western powers to endure indefinitely, this illusion was dispelled as Bulgaria soon succumbed completely to Soviet influence.

THE COMMUNIST STATE

GROWTH OF THE COMMUNIST PARTY

In 1891 the Social Democratic party was founded; the Communist party was eventually an offshoot of this movement. By 1903 the Social Democrats had begun to split into what were known as the "broad" and "narrow" factions. The broad faction retained the ideology of social democracy, but the narrow faction became the Bulgarian counterpart of the Russian Bolsheviks; its leader was Dimiter Blagoev, the so-called father of Bulgarian communism. In 1919 the narrow faction split off from the Second Socialist International and assumed the name Bulgarian Communist party (BKP). Although the party had great prestige abroad, it failed to enjoy domestic popularity. The most popular party at the time—and that favored by the peasant class, which was predominant in this still-agrarian society—was the Bulgarian Agrarian Union. The BKP, on the other hand, was composed almost exclusively of intellectuals and students and held little appeal for the working and peasant classes.

In 1923 there was an unsuccessful attempt by the Communists to bring the country to revolution. When this uprising was quelled, the Communists turned to terrorism in order to gain their goals, and in 1925 a plot to assassinate King Boris was formulated. Once again the Communists met with failure, as the king not only lived but grew more powerful. In the last half of the 1920s the party faded from the scene, but by the early 1930s it was again revived and grew in popularity.

During the late 1930s the party went underground as the king increased his power. In 1939 the Communists reappeared and merged with the left-wing Workers party; in the 1939 elections the party doubled its representation and took on an air of greater respectability. In 1941, while the war was under way, the Communists realized that Bulgaria was falling into the German camp. Although they were powerless to stop this alliance, their activity in evoking pro-Soviet sentiment was successful to the extent that—coupled with the basically favorable sentiments of the Bulgarian people toward the Russians

—it prevented the monarchy from declaring war against the Soviet Union.

Once the Germans began to invade the Soviet Union itself, the Bulgarian Communists committed themselves to a policy of armed resistance, known as the partisan movement. Historians dispute the extent of partisan activity; some state that it did not become active until the Soviet victory at Stalingrad in 1943, and others claim that the movement was active from the onset of the German invasion of the Soviet Union.

In 1942, on the initiative of Dimitrov, the Fatherland Front was established. The organization was essentially a coalition, composed of members of the Workers party, the Bulgarian Agrarian Union, the Social Democratic party, and the BKP. Its purpose was to overthrow Boris and rid the country of the Germans, simultaneously forming a new government that could more adequately meet the needs of the workers and the peasants.

In 1943 the National Committee of the Fatherland Front was formed, and this committee became the vehicle for the Communist takeover in 1944. In the same year the so-called National Liberation Army, composed of partisans and certain units of the Bulgarian army who had joined forces with them, was established. In the fall of 1944 there were approximately eighteen thousand people in the National Liberation Army, augmented by some two hundred thousand people who sheltered and assisted them.

Before 1944, however, the Communists were still not widely popular. The apathy of a large portion of the population was due primarily to the fact that the country had remained relatively untouched by the war; but, as the country was not actually at war with the Soviet Union, little rationale was provided to the Soviet-backed Communists in their attempts to enlist the support of the partisans. The Bulgarian army and police were active in hunting down the known Communists. All of these factors precluded the possibility of the country becoming totally committed to either the Communist cause or armed resistance. By 1944, however, when Soviet troops entered Romania, activity became widespread within Bulgaria. In August 1944 Romania completely capitulated. By early September the Soviet Union declared war on the Bulgarian government, an act more symbolic than real, as Soviet armies met no Bulgarian resistance. On September 9, 1944, the Fatherland Front was installed, and the Communists were firmly entrenched in the country.

DEVELOPMENT SINCE WORLD WAR II

At the time of the Fatherland Front takeover in Bulgaria the Soviets, with the assistance of the partisans and units of the National Liberation Army, occupied many Bulgarian towns and cities. It is said that they were received by the people with gifts of bread and salt, a traditional Bulgarian gift of welcome. At the same time, on the political front, the Soviets and their Bulgarian collaborators took over the key ministries in the capital city and arrested members of the government.

The Fatherland Front—a coalition composed at that time of Communists, members of the left wing of the Bulgarian Agrarian Union, members of the left wing of the Social Democratic party, and the Zveno group—was led by Georgiev as the new premier. Dimitrov and Kalarov returned from Moscow, where they had been in exile since 1925, to assist the new government in its takeover. The Communists proceeded to rid the coalition of certain opposing elements within its ranks. Nikolai Petkov of the Peasant Union and Kosta Lulchev of the Social Democratic party were temporarily retired from the coalition. Large-scale purges were initiated against German collaborators and sympathizers; many thousands were either executed or imprisoned by the Communists.

When plans for elections were made in 1945, both Great Britain and the United States made a strong bid for the holding of popular elections. Their hopes were temporarily defeated when, on November 18, 1945, Communist-controlled elections were held. The Fatherland Front won a decided victory, eventually resulting in Georgiev's formal installation as premier. His tenure in office was brief, and he was quickly succeeded by Dimitrov. At this point Great Britain and the United States protested, insisting that the Communists broaden their governmental base. Thus, although the two leading figures of the BKP, Dimitrov and Kalarov, were installed eventually as premier and president, respectively, Petkov and Lulchev were allowed to take over control of the Ministry of the Interior and the Ministry of Justice, two vital organs of the government.

By 1946, however, the Communists had whittled down all opposition. In July 1946 control over the army had been transferred from non-Communist members of the ostensible coalition government to exclusively Communist control. At this time two thousand so-called reactionary army officers were dismissed. A plebiscite held in September abolished the monarchy, declared Bulgaria a republic, and gave all power to Dimitrov as premier. He officially took the title on November 4, 1946, and held it until his death in 1949. When Dimitrov took power, any opposition that remained was quickly eliminated. Once the United States had ratified the Bulgarian Peace Treaty —a moment for which the Communists waited anxiously in order to rid themselves of all Western control over Bulgarian affairs of state—Petkov was summarily arrested and executed. His party, the Peasant Union, had been dissolved one month before his death.

On December 4, 1947, a new constitution was adopted, modeled on the Soviet Constitution of 1936. King Simeon, at this point, seeing that there was little room in Communist Bulgaria for a monarch, took up residence in Paris and Philadelphia.

THE ROYAL SOVEREIGNS OF THE KINGDOM OF BULGARIA

Reign	Title	Ruler	Birth	Death	Relationship
679–1018—First Bulgarian Kingdom					
852–893	Czar	Boris I (Michael Simeon)	827	907	
893–927	Czar	Simeon I	862	927	Son of Boris I
927–969	Czar	Peter I		969	Son of Simeon I
969–972	Czar	Boris II			
976–1014	Prince	Samuel			
1014–1015	Prince	Gabriel Radomir			
1015–1018	Prince	John Vladislav			
1018–1185—Under the control of the Byzantine Empire					

ASEN DYNASTY

Reign	Title	Ruler	Birth	Death	Relationship
1186–1197	Czar (Coregent)	Peter Asen II		1197	Brother of John Asen
1186–1196	King	John Asen I		1196	Brother of Peter
1197–1207	King	Kaloyan		1207	Brother of Peter and John
1218–1241	King	John Asen II		1241	Son of John Asen I
1241–1246	King	Kaliman I		1246	
1246–1257	King	Michael Asen		1257	
1258–1277	King	Constantine Asen		1277	
1278–1279	King	Ivalio (Ivailo)			
1279–1280	King	Ivan III Asen			

Reign	Title	Ruler	Birth	Death	Relationship
		TERTER DYNASTY			
1280–1292	King	George I Terter			
1292–1300	King	Smilitz			
1300–1300	King	Caka			
1300–1322	King	Theodore Svetoslav			
1322–1323	King	George II Terter			
1322–1330	King	Michael		1330	
1330–1331	King	Ivan II Stephen			
1330–1371	King	Ivan I Alexander		1371	
1365–1393	King	Ivan III Sishman		1393	
1396–1878—Under the control of the Turkish government					
1879–1886	Prince	Alexander Joseph of Battenberg	1857	1893	Nephew of Alexander II of Russia
		COBURG DYNASTY			
1887–1908	Prince	Ferdinand of Saxe-Coburg-Gotha	1861	1948	
1908—Bulgaria becomes an independent kingdom					
1908–1918	King	Ferdinand I	1861	1948	
1918–1943	King	Boris III	1894	1943	Son of Ferdinand I
1943–1944	Regent	Cyril	1895	1945	Brother of Boris II
1943–1946	King	Simeon II	1937		Son of Boris III
1946–1947—Bulgaria became a Communist republic.					

19

The Ancient and Modern Kingdoms of Greece

Greece with its ancient regional territories

By one historical yardstick Greece is a relatively young country. Its history as an independent European nation-state begins only in the 1820s. The greater part of the territory occupied by contemporary Greece was acquired in the past one hundred years. By another important yardstick—the one by which Greeks and most Westerners measure the country's past—Greece is the seat of Europe's oldest civilization, the one that has been the archetype for the cultural, intellectual, and spiritual development of succeeding civilizations.

Some aspects of the patriotism, cultural consciousness, and ethnic cohesion felt by modern Greeks are reflected in each of the historical periods that preceded Greek independence and the establishment of a Greek

state in the nineteenth century. The heritage of ancient Greece is the common property of the Western world, and modern Greeks take great pride in this fact. In spite of the political differences and habits of individualism that separated the numerous city-states of which the Greek world was comprised, the Greeks of antiquity were bound together by common cultural values and moral ideals, which were expressed as Hellenism—the character and spirit of the Hellenes, or Greeks. Acceptance of these values and ideas was synonymous with being a Greek.

Using Greece as his base, Alexander the Great created a world empire. Greece was later a vital constituent of the Roman Empire, which was in turn made over by medieval Greeks as the Byzantine Empire, Greek in language and culture but politically the continuation in the Middle Ages of the old Roman Empire. The Orthodox church of Greece is the legacy of the Byzantine epoch. Political attitudes and social institutions crucial to the development of modern Greece are also attributed to that one-thousand-year period of Greek history. For nearly four centuries after the fall of Constantinople in 1453 the Greeks were the conquered subjects of the Ottoman Empire. The Greek nation survived through its identification with Orthodox Christianity and its retention of self-governing communal institutions. Many historians have found the roots of modern Greek national consciousness in the struggle for survival during this period of subjugation.

Modern Greece is a homogeneous nation. Its people have a definite national identity and, although modern Greeks have a complex family tree, ethnic minorities are of insignificant size. But modern Greeks have required a national myth to demonstrate their historical continuity as a nation. The independence movement has been regarded as signaling the rebirth of Hellenism in a new age, and Hellenism has provided the means by which Greeks could trace their descent. There is, however, more than one version of the national myth. *Hellenism* is a value-laden term that can be interpreted to suit its translator. Hence modern Greeks have at different times and for different reasons sought their national wellspring in different places. This ambiguity has contributed to schisms within the political fabric of Greece and has usually meant that political opponents were, by the very fact of their being in opposition, considered anti-Greek.

Greeks do not lack for patriotism, but their closest ties have traditionally been to church, community and family, and patron. Modern Greece has experienced difficulty in creating stable national institutions outside the framework of these traditional ones. Both church and community have been weakened in contemporary Greece, the former by secularism and the latter by mobility. Patronage is increasingly absorbed by political ideology. But another institution—the military—has remained a constant force in Greek political life. The military coup is a specter that has haunted generations of civilian politicians.

It has been observed that ancient Hellas and the Byzantine Empire were far larger than they needed to be. Expansionism—expressed in terms of *enosis* (union) of all Greeks within a Greek state—has been a constant feature of modern Greek history as well. The energy of the Greeks, however, has often exceeded the resources of their country. Greece has been both poor and weak, conditions dangerous in a country so strategically located that it is important in the struggles of the great powers to maintain a balance or to win domination in the eastern Mediterranean. For the great powers of Europe, Greece was in a sense too important to be left to the Greeks to manage alone, and governments were sometimes imposed or deposed in accordance with the strategic requirements of other countries. Greece achieved independence only after foreign intervention in its revolution. As an independent state it has been dependent for its defense and for political and economic survival on the periodic intervention of protecting powers—France, Russia, Great Britain and, more recently, the United States. A corollary of that dependence has been the Greek's outraged sense of betrayal of his country's interests by foreign powers and his frustration at its inability to break free of such influence.

Indeed the very term *Greek* is foreign to Greeks. It is derived from the Latin *Graeci,* used to identify one Hellenic tribe and later applied to all Hellenes. For centuries even Greeks referred to themselves as Romaioi (Romans) rather than as Hellenes, an ancient name that was revived among the Greeks only in the eighteenth century.

The expectations of Western philhellenes for a Greece restored to independence were often disappointed by Greek realities. No less than foreigners, Greeks have idealized their past. Greek historiography has a tendency to stress the continuity of Greek history—ancient, medieval, and modern—as well as its otherness. Its ethnocentricity has often obscured the fact that Greek history in many ways transcends the boundaries of territory and nationality.

ANCIENT GREECE

Archaeological evidence suggests that continental Greece and the Aegean Islands supported a sparse Neolithic population as early as the sixth millennium B.C. It was displaced by bronze-working Helladic (pre-Greek) tribes who entered the peninsula overland from Asia and had spread to the islands sometime before 3000 B.C. On Crete they developed an advanced, culturally and technically sophisticated civilization that benefited from its proximity to Egypt and the cultures of the Near East. The Minoans—named for Minos, their legendary king, whose successors ruled from the massive palace complex at Knossos—dominated the Aegean world, relying on sea power to protect their commerce and to defend their unwalled cities.

Helladic development on the mainland was markedly slower. At about the beginning of the second millennium B.C. the Achaeans (proto-Greeks) invaded the peninsula from the north, settling there and on the islands among the indigenous inhabitants. Much of classical Greek mythology was an attempt to explain the process by which the two cultures—that of the patriarchal Achaeans, accompanied by their sky-gods, and that of the Helladic earth-goddess worshipers—were fused.

By 1600 B.C. the Minoans had extended their political, economic, and cultural hegemony over the Achaeans, whose tribal kings employed Minoan craftsmen to build palaces in emulation of their overlords on Crete. The interaction of the Minoan and Achaen cultures gave rise to a new civilization that had its center at Mycenae in the Peloponnesus. The Minoan civilization declined after 1400 B.C., succumbing finally to a combination of natural disasters and conquest by the Mycenaeans. The period from 1400 to 1100 B.C. was the Mycenaean heroic age that inspired the Homeric epic, the *Iliad,* describing the assault of the Achaeans on Troy. After 1100 B.C. the steady migrations of the Dorians, primitive Hellenic tribesmen from the north, overwhelmed the Mycenaeans and ushered in the three-hundred-year-long Greek Dark Ages.

The beginnings of the *polis,* or city-state, are found during this chaotic time when, for security, the people of the countryside moved within the shadow of an *acropolis* (literally, high town), the fortification of a local lord or tribal chieftain constructed on defensible high ground that dominated the countryside. Athens, for instance, had its origins in villages clustered around one such acropolis in Attica. The polis became the distinctive form of political and social organization in classical Greece. (It forms the root of the word *politics,* meaning the "business of the city." But the idea of the polis meant more to the Greeks than just a city and its surrounding countryside.)

The governments of some city-states evolved gradually, as in Athens, from monarchy to oligarchy to democracy, the transitions from one form to another eased by the rule of tyrants; but democracy was by no means the common end of them all. There could have been no greater contrast than that between the two most prominent city-states, Athens and Sparta. Athens, which in the popular imagination epitomizes Hellenic civilization, was a direct democracy and a cosmopolitan state—in the words of Pericles, "thrown open to the world." Sparta—authoritarian and isolated in the mountains of the Peloponnesus—was a completely militarized state existing to support an exclusive caste of warriors. Often a city-state's form of government was reflected in its urban plan. The adoption of a democratic constitution, for instance, usually coincided with the construction of walls around the city to enclose its agora, or marketplace, and marked the triumph of commercial over landed interests. Even in democratic Athens, however, citizenship was restricted to a small part of the city's population. Slavery was a common institution, rationalized on the grounds that it released citizens to participate in public affairs and was necessary to sustain civilization on a high level in a poor country.

A shortage of arable land in Greece encouraged individual city-states to establish colonies for their excess

King Aristodemus, the reputed first king of Sparta, circa ninth century B.C.

The tyrant (ruler) Gelon (or Gelo) was the first sovereign of Syracuse.

The first tyrant (ruler) of Athens, Pisistratus, returning from a victory to the celebration dance of the city. Research shows that he and his subjects were but five feet tall.

The wedding ceremony of Alexander III to his second wife, Statira

*Medallion of the time
of Philip II*

*A sketch of the bust of
Alexander III in the Capitoline
Museum in Rome. He
authorized only one artist to
make a bust in bronze,
Lusippus. But he had many
wax figures made of himself,
including an entire collection of
his life from birth to death.*

Alexander III was a pupil of Aristotle.

population. Although they retained cultural ties with their mother cities, the colonies were politically independent of them. Hundreds of Greek city-states were spread from Spain to the Black Sea. Political fragmentation, implicit in the city-state system, led inevitably to the sometimes suicidal internecine warfare that plagued the classical Greek world. But even when geography separated them and politics set them against each other, the Greeks were united by their collective cultural consciousness, expressed in Panhellenic festivals at such religious centers as Delphi, Olympia, and Eleusis. They displayed an attitude of superiority to other peoples. Not to be a Hellene was to be a barbarian.

Greece is a geographic and cultural bridge between Europe and Asia. Early in the fifth century B.C., however, it served as a barrier against the westward expansion of the Persians. The conflict between the Greeks, led by Athens, and the Persians has been explained as an early example of East-West confrontation. Whatever the merits of that argument may be, the century after the Persian defeat was the golden age of the Greek polis and saw full flowering of Hellenic civilization. Athens emerged from

the Greek victories at Marathon (490 B.C.), Salamis (480 B.C.), and Plataea (479 B.C.) at the peak of its prosperity and creativity. It was also recognized as the leader of an alliance of Greek city-states known as the Delian League. There was a popular demand within the Athenian democracy to use the resources of the league to spread democratic institutions in areas liberated or conquered during the Persian wars. A conflict of interest with Sparta and other nondemocratic Greek states as well as resentment by some Delian allies at high-handed Athenian domination of the league precipitated the Peloponnesian Wars, which were fought intermittently over many years (440–404 B.C.) and left both Sparta and Athens exhausted. Plato and Aristotle produced their philosophical works in the more introspective mood of the next century.

The weakness of the Greek city-states invited the military intervention of Philip, king of Macedonia—a primitive and peripheral region that had not wasted itself in the wars. Having subjugated the city-states by force, Philip presided over a Panhellenic congress at which the city-states were joined in a confederation under

A vintage statue of Alexander III, one of the few that have survived that holds a good likeness of him

The only case in history when a great general and king sired a great general and king is that of Philip II and Alexander III, the Great. Philip is seen here reviewing his troops. In his generalship and demeanor he has been likened to General George Patton of United States World War II fame. King of Macedonia, he served from 359 to 336 B.C. It was during the siege of Methone that Philip lost one of his eyes. It is told in legend that he was approached by an archer soldier who told him that he wanted to be one of Philip's royal archers and that he could shoot a small bird in flight. Philip scoffed at this, saying, "Well, well, I shall make use of you when I go to war with the starlings." Astor joined the Methones and during the siege, it seems that an arrow was shot into Philip's right eye. It had a message tied to it: "Astor to Philip's right eye." Astor was assassinated in 336 B.C. at the wedding celebration between his daughter Cleopatra and the king of Epirus, by Pausanias, a soldier in his own bodyguard.

"Astor to Philip's Right Eye"

Macedonian protection. Philip's son, Alexander, mobilized the Greeks behind a Macedonian attack on the vast Persian Empire that carried Greek influence in a few short years to the banks of the Indus. The syncretic cultural style generated as a result of Alexander the Great's conquests is called Hellenistic, or Greeklike, sometimes described as Hellenic culture orientalized to accommodate non-Greeks; among its characteristics was

Before Alexander could embark on his father's dream of the conquest of Asia, he first had to be certain that affairs would be settled at home. In his deliberate destruction of Thebes, he made his point and all who opposed him were brought to severe judgment.

Roman Emperor Hadrian conquered Greece and stayed long enough to attempt to beautify Athens. He built the Pantheon, which stands today (in ruins) as a memorial to this great Roman general and engineer.

The dying Alexander. It is believed that he passed away in the final stages of syphilis, the dread social disease of the time. He returned to die at Babylon, the city from which he set out to conquer Asia. He returned to the same place where he had his farewell dinner—the palace of the king Nebuchadnezzar.

an emphasis on a universalism, crucial in the development of Western thought and Christian theology.

When Alexander died in 323 B.C., his empire was divided among his generals. Greece fell under the control of Macedonia, but its kings had difficulty restraining the independence of the city-states. A Macedonian alliance with Carthage during the Punic Wars and appeals by restive Greek city-states for aid against their overlords caused Rome to intervene as the "protector of Greek freedom." Macedonia became a Roman province in 148 B.C., followed in short order by the rest of Greece. A favored part of the empire, Greece was prosperous and —for the first time—peaceful under the mantle of the Pax Romana. Although the city-states had forfeited their political liberty, Greek culture continued to flourish. It was readily absorbed by its Roman patrons, giving rise to the epigram, "Captive Greece Took Her Captors Captive."

THE BYZANTINE EMPIRE

In A.D. 285 Diocletian undertook the reorganization of the Roman Empire, dividing jurisdiction between its Latin-speaking and Greek-speaking halves. Diocletian's successor, Constantine, established his capital at the site of the Greek city of Byzantium as a "New Rome," strategically situated on the European shore of the Bosporus. The city was renamed Constantinople for its founder. For nearly twelve centuries, until its capture by the Ottoman Turks in 1453, Constantinople remained the capital of the Roman Empire—better known in its continuous development in the East during the Middle Ages as the Byzantine Empire.

Though Greek in language and culture, the Byzantine Empire was thoroughly Roman in its law and administration. Justinian's codification of Roman law was compiled—in Latin—in Constantinople in the sixth century. The Byzantine Empire was seen as being ecumenical— intended to encompass all Christian peoples—not as a specifically Greek state, and it was described as God's earthly kingdom working to fulfill the divine will. Its Greek-speaking citizens called themselves Romans, not Hellenes. Absolute and theocratic in principle, the emperor in practice delegated considerable authority in the provinces to a military aristocracy.

Christianity was recognized throughout the Roman Empire as the official religion of the state before the end of the fourth century, and a patriarchate was established in Constantinople with ecclesiastical jurisdiction over the Greek East. In contrast to the Latin church, whose patriarch in Rome asserted the church's independence of secular control, the Greek church was not only identified with but was subordinated to the interests of the state. It was not surprising, therefore, that political dissidence within the empire was often expressed in terms of theological heterodoxy. The decisive break between the Latin

Alaric, the great Gothic leader who destroyed Rome, invaded Greece in 396, and once he entered Athens he was greeted with gold instead of iron. The people of Greece had lost the manliness that was always evident in this period of their civilization.

and Greek churches in the eleventh century was due in no small part to the prerogatives in ecclesiastical affairs claimed by the Byzantine emperors. The Greek church, for its part, maintained that it alone had remained faithful to the Christian orthodoxy taught by the Apostles and the early church councils from which the Latin church had departed. Christian Byzantine culture was hostile to Hellenism and repudiated it for its paganism. The classical heritage as a moral force was thereby dismissed among medieval Greeks, to whom the Hellenes were simply the people who once occupied Roman provinces that had since become a poor and primitive backwater far removed from the centers of Greek culture and economic development in Constantinople and Asia Minor.

Gradually, as stronger demands were made on imperial resources to defend the empire's eastern and southern flanks against Persians, Arabs and, later, Seljuk Turks, the European provinces were left open to invasion first by Goths and, from the sixth century, by repeated waves of Slavs, who eventually overran the interior of the peninsula and settled there in such large numbers that Byzantine sources frequently referred to continental Greece as Sclavinia (Slav-land). The church was the means through which the Slavs were gradually assimilated into the Greek population. The Slavs contributed significantly to the genetic pool of the Greek people, and pockets of them retained their separate identity into the modern era.

Western European merchants and adventurers were attracted to the Byzantine Empire both by its wealth and, after the dynastic strife of the late twelfth century, by its relative weakness. In 1204 Constantinople, the Aegean Islands, and most of the European provinces fell to the largely French contingents of the Fourth Crusade and their Venetian allies. Count Baldwin of Flanders was

installed in Constantinople by the Crusaders as emperor of the so-called Latin Empire, and territory conquered from the Greeks was dismembered into a number of tributary feudal states, creating "New France" in Greece where Western political, social, ecclesiastical, and economic institutions were transplanted intact. Large tracts, especially on the islands, were annexed by Venice and other Italian states or were seized by Catalan and Navarese mercenaries. The Greeks referred to the Western conquerors collectively as Franks. Independent Greek kingdoms were established in Epirus and at Nicaea and Trebizond from remnant provinces of the Byzantine Empire. Constant warfare pitted Frank against Frank or against Greek, Slav, or Turk, and territory changed hands frequently. In 1205, for instance, the acropolis of Athens became the residence of a Burgundian duke and the Parthenon his church; in 1311 Athens was taken by the Catalans, and in 1388 it passed to the Florentines, in whose hands it remained until conquered in turn by the Turks in 1456.

The Latin Empire lasted for fifty-seven years before Constantinople was retaken by the Greek Palaeologi Dynasty of Nicaea under which the Byzantine Empire was restored. Some of the feudal states survived for two hundred years, however, and Italian domination of many Greek islands and mainland enclaves persisted for an even longer time. Venice held Crete until 1669 and still retained the Ionian Islands at the time of the Venetian Republic's collapse in 1797.

THE OTTOMAN OCCUPATION

Greece was partitioned by the Turks into administrative districts organized along military lines. The principal task of their governors was to oversee the collection of taxes from the sultan's non-Muslim subjects. Greeks kept the use of their land, but they paid a fixed part of the revenue from it for the upkeep of Turkish soldier-landlords. Another form of taxation levied by the Turks was a capitation fee paid by Christian families through the conscription of their children for the corps of Janissaries. Every four years—until 1676—one out of every five young Christian males in the European provinces was sent to Constantinople to be reared as a Muslim and serve in the sultan's bodyguard.

Western historians have tended to underrate the severity of the Ottoman occupation. For all but an elite among the Greek population, it was anything but benevolent. Institutions were left intact, however, and were encouraged by the Turks. These institutions were crucial to the survival of the Greek nation through nearly four hundred years of foreign rule. The most important of them were the Orthodox church of Greece and the organs of local self-government. Greeks also had freedom of trade under Turkish rule, and education in the Greek language was allowed to continue under the auspices of the church and the patronage of the merchant community.

The concepts of nationality and religion were inalienable qualities to both Greeks and Turks, and nationality was determined according to religion. To be an Orthodox Christian was to be a Greek—just as a Greek who apostacized to Islam thereby became a Turk. The sultan's Orthodox Christian, or Greek, subjects were regarded as a separate nation, or millet, having a degree of autonomy within the Ottoman Empire. The patriarch of Constantinople was recognized not only as the head of the Orthodox church but also as the temporal leader of the Christian millet. He bore the title *ethnarch* and was responsible for the civil administration of the people through a separate system of courts with distinct laws and customs based on the Roman Law of the Byzantine Empire. Local government operated under the clergy and landowners, who were the leaders of the Greek communities. Ironically, the Turks referred to the Greek Christian millet as the Roman Nation.

For Greeks, whose communities were dispersed over a large and alien empire, the Orthodox church was their "common fatherland." The Orthodox hierarchy was allowed more latitude by the Turkish sultan than it had been by the Byzantine emperor. As late as the eighteenth century the patriarch spoke of the Ottoman Empire as sent by God to preserve the Orthodox faith after Greek emperors had compromised it in an effort to win Western support for their tottering throne. The Turkish turban, it was commonly observed, was preferable to the Roman miter.

The Turks were a nation of warriors with little head for business or bureaucratic administration, and they were eager to assimilate the experience of those whom they had conquered. Greeks rose to high office in the Ottoman civil service, conducted the sultan's diplomacy, governed provinces, controlled many of the empire's financial institutions, and in time dominated its trade and commerce. Of particular importance in government and finance were the Phanariots, residents of the Phanar district in Constantinople, where the patriarch had established his headquarters. A privileged class, their position in the Turkish administration was all but institutionalized in the eighteenth century.

INDEPENDENT GREECE, 1821–1912

The Greek War of Independence was complex in its origins, conduct, and final resolution. Greeks fought not only Turks but also each other in a civil war for control of the revolution. The standard of rebellion was first raised at a monastery in the Peloponnesus in 1821 by Bishop Germanos. Leaders came from among the lower clergy, *klephts* (mountain bandits), pirates and merchant

captains, and the chieftains of the independent Mani region, whose irregular, autonomous, locally recruited guerrilla bands quickly won control of the countryside and cut off Turkish units dispersed in small garrisons across southern Greece. The massacre of Muslims at Tripolis and of Greeks at Chios set a standard of violence for the war on both sides, turning it into a religious war and ruling out compromise or the offer of quarter.

Despite the initial success of the rebellion, the Greeks had difficulty establishing government on a firm basis. Regional differences and political factionalism were already apparent at the assembly that met in Epidaurus in 1822 to frame a constitution. Strongly influenced by the ideals of the French Revolution, the Constitution of Epidaurus put a check on executive authority by diffusing it through an annual national legislature and three autonomous regional assemblies. The klephts resented any government that restricted their mode of operation, and they refused to submit to civilian control. Elected officials represented the communal governments developed under Ottoman rule; power thereby remained in the hands of landowners, many of whom had reluctantly supported the rebellion only after intimidation by the klephts and peasants. The new government relied on the administrative talents of Phanariots, merchants from the towns and islands, and intellectuals from the diaspora to give shape and direction to the Hellenic Republic.

In 1825, his forces beaten on land and prevented by Greek corsairs from reinforcing the Peloponnesus, the sultan called on the pasha of Egypt, an Ottoman tributary state, for aid. A condition for the intervention of Egyptian troops and naval forces was that Ibrahim, the pasha's son, would become governor of the Peloponnesus. Ibrahim brought to Greece a disciplined, European-trained army of eleven thousand men and conducted a lightning campaign through the Peloponnesus. The uncoordinated Greek guerrilla bands, so successful in small-scale actions, were scattered in disarray. The Turko-Egyptian forces mounted a pincer movement converging on Missolonghi, the key fortress guarding the Gulf of Corinth, which fell in 1826 after a year's siege. With the capture of Athens the next year, the rebellion appeared to be at an end.

Public opinion in Europe had favored Greek independence, but the European powers had hoped for a Greek defeat in order to preserve Turkey's integrity and maintain the balance of power. It was the prospect that the Peloponnesus might become an Egyptian province—and British suspicions that Russia was prepared to act unilaterally to aid the Greeks—that prompted Great Britain, France, and Russia to intervene diplomatically to end the conflict, recommending an autonomous status for Greece within the Ottoman Empire. When the Turks, flushed with their recent military success, refused mediation, the three powers dispatched a joint naval force, which destroyed the Turko-Egyptian fleet anchored in the Bay of Navarino and forced an Egyptian evacuation. Czar Nicholas I, acting in his self-appointed role as protector of Orthodox Christians, declared war on Turkey, and a Russian army pushed to the outer defenses of Constantinople. By the Treaty of Adrianople (1829) Russia compelled Turkey to recognize the independence of Greece, but Crete and Thessaly—claimed by the Greeks—were left in Turkish hands.

In reaction to Russia's stance as sole protector of Greece, Great Britain forced a renegotiation of the border settlement, which was spelled out in the first London Protocol (1829). Of greater significance, the European powers also gave Greece their formal recognition in the protocol. Greek leaders protested that eighty percent of the nearly four million Greeks in the Ottoman Empire had been left under Turkish rule, and Greece's pro-Russian president, John Kapodistrias, rejected the settlement. When Kapodistrias, who had made domestic enemies by his attempts to disarm the klephts and to centralize the Republic's government, was assassinated in 1831, the country lapsed into anarchy.

The European powers convened once again and in the second London Protocol (1831) declared Greece a monarchy under joint British, French, and Russian protection. It was further decided that a foreign monarch was required to avoid identification of the executive with one of the native factions. In both areas the protecting powers were eventually disappointed, but many responsible Greeks, recalling the violent end of Kapodistrias's presidency, concurred in the judgment embodied in the second protocol.

The protecting powers offered the Greek crown to Otto, the seventeen-year-old younger son of the king of

Bavaria. He had the advantage of coming from a country that was not aligned with any one of the three powers, and it was hoped that this would ensure that Otto (or Otho, as he was known in Greece) would be neutral in his relations with them. He was accompanied to Greece by a council of Bavarian regents, who took over direction of the Greek government.

The regency imposed a complicated judicial code, modeled on that of Bavaria. It replaced the familiar decentralized forms of local government, inherited from the occupation, with a modern centralized bureaucracy that the Greeks considered distant and unsympathetic. Impersonal crown officials, appointed to posts in local administration by the central government, attempted to assume the role played for centuries by clergy and landowners. Tax collecting under the Bavarian regency was no less efficient than it had been under the Turks. Unfortunate standards of patronage, bribery, and violence were set early in Otto's reign.

Accomplishing what Kapodistrias had failed to do, the regency disarmed the Greek irregulars who had fought in the War of Independence and replaced them with a corps of Bavarian mercenaries. As a result many Greek soldiers returned to their old habits of brigandage in the mountains, increasing a problem that would plague Greece for decades. Brigandage remained an accepted method of political intimidation, and the countryside showed greater loyalty to the klephts than to the representatives of the national government. Klephts were subsequently employed by the king to terrorize his opposition and to create border incidents intended to demonstrate to the protecting powers the extent of irredentist sentiment in Greece.

In 1843 Greek officers commanding the Athens garrison executed a coup that forced Otto to dismiss his Bavarian advisers and consent to constitutional monarchy and parliamentary government. Even the Greeks, however, were frightened by the prospect of renewed factionalism in a parliamentary context, and the new constitution left the king with considerable prerogatives, especially in defense and foreign affairs. During the Crimean war (1854–56) Otto's efforts to annex Thessaly and Epirus—tilting Greek neutrality in Russia's favor—won him popular support but provoked a humiliating Anglo-French occupation of the port of Piraeus. The political figures who grew to maturity after the Crimean War came into sharp conflict with the king. In 1862 they took advantage of demonstrations in Athens to depose Otto and call on the protecting powers to nominate a successor to the Greek throne.

The protecting powers bypassed the candidacies of the czar's nephew and of Queen Victoria's second son, Alfred—which, though seriously proposed, violated the principle laid down in the London protocols that members of reigning families of protecting powers were ineligible for the Greek throne. A compromise candidate,

The seventeen-year-old boy-king of Greece, Otto I, enters Nauplia on January 25, 1833, to take over the reins of the country. In 1828, the Greeks defeated the Turks and regained their freedom. The Greek leaders accepted Otto, the son of the king of Bavaria, as their king in 1832. But, Otto I had little capacity for administering a government the size and enterprise of Greece and he was expelled in 1862 and forced to leave.

William George, son of Christian IX of Denmark and brother-in-law of the heirs to both the British and Russian thrones, was selected and approved by a plebiscite in 1863. The Danish prince thereby became George I, king of the Hellenes. Great Britain rewarded the Greeks for returning a favorable vote by ceding the Ionian Islands. The new constitution under which George agreed to govern provided for a unicameral legislature, extended male suffrage, and placed strict limitations on royal prerogatives. George maintained the constitutional system that he was pledged to uphold, but his reign was marred by political violence and military revolts that frustrated the growth of secure parliamentary institutions. Political factions vied for the support of army units, and parliamentary elections took on some of the aspects of civil war.

George eventually found a capable prime minister in Charles Tricoupis, whose evenhanded policies in the 1880s and 1890s permitted the beginnings of a two-party system to emerge. Tricoupis's Liberal party represented urban, commercial, middle-class interests; the National party found support in the traditional landowning class in rural constituencies. During his tenures in office Tricoupis curbed runaway government spending, especially for the armed forces, and followed a cautious policy in his relations with Turkey. Apparent political stability, the prospect of peace, and Tricoupis's fiscal policy gave Greece better access to foreign loans and encouraged investment for economic development. But the edifice of his work came to ruin with his death in 1896 and the outbreak of war with Turkey the next year.

Since independence the passions of the Greek irredentists had been focused on Crete, Epirus, and Thessaly. Crete was the scene of continuous revolts by the Greek majority against the Muslim landlords. In 1877, when

There were a number of attempts to assassinate George I

George in his youth as a naval cadet

war broke out in the Balkans between Russia and Turkey, there were uprisings by Greeks in other Turkish territories, but the Treaty of San Stefano (1878), which ended the Russo-Turkish war and provided generously for the aspirations of Serbia and Bulgaria, made no concessions to Greek territorial claims. Proposals offered by German chancellor Otto von Bismarck at the Congress of Berlin the following year—that the disputed provinces be ceded to Greece—were rejected by the British, who also used the threat of naval blockade against Greece to discourage irredentist sentiment. The issue of these Turkish-held provinces troubled Anglo-Greek relations until 1881, when the British—confident that Russia could gain no advantage from it—obtained the sultan's reluctant agreement to turn over Thessaly and southern Epirus to Greece.

Reports of a massacre of Greeks on Crete led to war with Turkey early in 1897. The well-equipped Turkish army, recently reorganized by German advisers, routed the ill-prepared, poorly led Greek forces in a thirty-day campaign in Thessaly. The protecting powers intervened to prevent the Turks from pursuing their victory against the demoralized Greeks. Minor territorial adjustments were made in favor of Turkey, and Greece was assigned to pay an indemnity. An international commission was created by the powers to manage bankrupt Greek state finances. But, despite Greece's defeat, the Cretans gained the substance of their original demands for greater self-government. The second son of George I, Prince George, was named high commissioner of Crete and given a mandate by Great Britain to organize an autonomous regime there under the Turkish flag.

For many Greeks, however, any arrangement short of enosis was unacceptable. In 1906 Prince George resigned after a disagreement with his Cretan adviser, Eleutherios Venizelos, on the question of enosis, which the high commissioner—and the royal government in Athens—

George I, a son of the king of Denmark, was chosen in 1863 to replace the despotic ruler Otto I. After fifty years on the throne George I, on March 18, 1913, was assassinated by an insane man at Salonica. His reign was marked with seven notable accomplishments. They were: the acquisition of the Ionian Islands, the union with Crete, the establishment of radical parliamentary procedure, creation of a beautiful city in Athens from its former dirty village status, participation in the Balkan Alliance, the quieting of internal revolutions, and the possession of unanimous approval from the people. It is an irony of fate that he was assassinated at the very moment in history when Greece was to become a great world power, and the moment died with him.

opposed. Two years later, when the Cretans took advantage of political turmoil in Turkey to proclaim enosis, the Athens government rejected the offer. Threatened with another Turkish war and economic sanctions imposed by the international commission, the royal government admitted that Greece was not in a position to deal with the consequences of annexing the island. The king's unwillingness to risk a new war provoked a revolt by an antiroyalist officers' group, the Military League, that made the most of public disgust with the old-line political elite who had backed away from fighting the Turks. For the next two years the Military League virtually dictated government policy. Its calls for sweeping reforms had unsettling effects on the economy and relations abroad and opened a lasting breach between royalists and antiroyalists in the armed forces and the civil service.

The Military League found an ally in Venizelos, who had no previous party connections. His first act was to call a convention to revise the constitution and make parliamentary government effective. Elections the next year—which were a referendum on the revised constitution—gave Venizelos's newly formed Liberal party 300 of the 364 seats in Parliament. Firmly in control of the government, Venizelos introduced agrarian reforms and social legislation, encouraged the growth of trade unions, improved the technical efficiency of the armed forces, and restructured the bureaucracy.

The sheer activity of Venizelos's government gave Greece an immense psychological uplift. It also left the impression that massive changes in the established order had occurred. But Venizelos was no radical; he was a nationalist committed to shoring up old structures, such as the monarchy and Parliament, by making them work more effectively in the interests of the country. He understood that patronage was the key to power in Greece and tied the reformed permanent civil service to the fortunes of the Liberal party. Vocal opponents of his government were retired from the officer corps. Control of these two institutions—the military and the bureaucracy—and his activist foreign policy, an area that had been the crown's preserve, strained relations between Venizelos and George I. When the king appeared as the leader of the opposition, Venizelos took steps to remove the monarchy from politics.

EXPANSION AND DEFEAT, 1912–23

In 1912 Greece joined Serbia and Bulgaria in a war against Turkey, after Venizelos had rejected a Turkish appeal for Greek neutrality. The Treaty of London (May 1913), which ended the war, forced Turkey to surrender all its European territory, except eastern Thrace and Albania, to the Balkan allies. Each member of the alli-

ance had laid claim to a share of Turkey's remaining European provinces—Greece to northern Epirus and Macedonia and to the city of Salonika, which had been occupied by the Bulgarians. Each of the Balkan allies put forward claims in ethnically mixed Macedonia. In June

King Constantine, the former duke of Sparta, oldest son of George I, replaced him on the throne. Constantine was fresh from a wave of personal feats of military glory. He had led a triumphant army from Athens to Salonica, and captured the second biggest city of Turkey. And he captured Janina, which was believed by the Turks to be impregnable. The terms of peace were that Turkey was to give up most all of her European territories. The biggest blow of all to Turkey was the loss of Adrianople to Bulgaria. This ancient Thracian town of unknown antiquity had been built before the Roman emperor Hadrian swept in from the West and gave it his name. It was a city much to be desired, for it was a crossroad of trade from East to West. The Goths held it in the fourth century and the Huns in the fifth. Then it went to the Byzantines. In 1361 Sultan Murad I captured it for Turkey and made it their capital and residence of the sovereign. They kept it as their capital until 1453 when Constantinople was captured and made the capital. There was strong Turkish national sentiment for Adrianople. Constantine was deposed in 1917 but was restored in 1920; however, in 1922 he was forced to abdicate.

Members of the Greek royal family leave Athens (Piraeus) for exile in Switzerland in 1917 aboard a British warship. The Allies—Great Britain, France, and Russia—called for the removal of the king (Constantine) and the crown prince George but allowed the crown to name his younger son Alexander as his future successor. On board the warship, right to left: Prince Alexander, the ex-king, and behind the queen is the ex-crown prince George.

1913 Greece and Serbia combined with Romania and their enemy of a few weeks before, Turkey, to overwhelm Bulgaria. The peace agreement at Bucharest, monitored by the great powers, awarded southern Macedonia, including Salonika, to Greece, and Turkey acquiesced in enosis for Crete.

In foreign affairs Venizelos pulled Greece closer to France and Great Britain, a move that further complicated his relations with the crown at the start of World War I. Constantine I, who had become king after the assassination of his father, George I, in 1913, was pro-German and committed to keeping Greece neutral in the European war. Venizelos, however, pushed for intervention on the side of the Allies to advance Greece's frontier. The Gallipoli campaign in 1915 gave new life to the so-called Great Idea *(Megali Idéa)*, the dream of adding Constantinople and Ionia, on the Aegean coast of Asia Minor, to a Greater Greece to create the "New Byzantium" envisioned by Venizelos. A constitutional struggle ensued over the question of foreign policy, and the Great Idea, which had been an issue above politics and had united Greek opinion for decades, became a divisive issue. Despite his parliamentary majority, Venizelos resigned as prime minister when Constantine repudiated his offer of aid to the Allies. When general elections confirmed the Liberal majority, Venizelos argued that the people had voted for war, but the king countered that foreign policy could not be allowed to become a matter of partisan politics.

Constantine's subsequent refusal to allow the Serbian army to retreat across Greek territory and his surrender of a strategic fortress in Macedonia to the Central Powers provided the pretext for the Allied occupation of Salonika, to be used as a staging area for operations in the Balkans. Military action was coupled with a demand for the demobilization of the Greek army. In October 1916 Venizelos established a provisional government at Salonika with Allied backing. Greece had two governments and two armies, frequently in conflict, one loyal to Constantine and the other to Venizelos.

The Allies imposed a blockade on royalist-controlled Greece and gave Constantine the choice of abdication or the bombardment of Athens. The king chose exile and named his son, Alexander, to succeed him. Venizelos returned to Athens as prime minister and in July 1917 brought Greece into the war against the Central Powers. Ten Greek divisions fought on the Macedonian front, and Greek troops were among the Allied contingents that entered Constantinople in 1918.

Venizelos trusted the Allies to back Greek demands for territory. He argued his case well at the Versailles Conference and obtained permission for the Greek occupation of Smyrna (Izmir), thereby gaining a toehold for Greece in Asia Minor. The Treaty of Sèvres (1920), formally concluding the war with Turkey, allotted eastern Thrace (excluding Constantinople) and Smyrna and its hinterland to Greece for five years, the final disposition of the territory to be determined by a plebiscite. Venizelos ordered troops to occupy Smyrna, effecting a landing under cover of an Allied flotilla that included United States warships, and prepared for a campaign to fulfill Greek demands in the interior of Anatolia.

In contrast to his diplomatic triumphs, Venizelos's political strength at home deteriorated during his attendance at the peace conferences. In November 1920 Alexander died, and Constantine was recalled to the throne. The Liberals were defeated by proroyalist parties in general elections, and Venizelos went into exile.

The Greek army took the offensive in 1921. Mustafa Kemal (Ataturk) lured the overextended Greeks to within sixty miles of Ankara before launching a counterattack that sent them reeling in a disorderly retreat back to the coast. Smyrna was captured and sacked, and a large number of the Greeks who lived there were massacred by the Turks. As shiploads of refugees poured into Greece, a military committee took control of the government, ousted the king, and executed six royalist ministers, whose death for their alleged role in the debacle absolved the army from blame. Constantine was succeeded by his son, George II.

The Treaty of Lausanne (1923) canceled Greece's gains at Sèvres and provided for the exchange of Greek and Turkish minorities. More than 1.3 million Greeks were expelled from Asia Minor and four hundred thousand Muslims repatriated from Greece to Turkey. Greece was faced with the problem of absorbing a 20 percent increase in population.

INTERWAR PERIOD, 1923–40

Modern Greece passed through its period of greatest political instability during the 1920s and early 1930s. As the Orthodox church had united the Greeks under Ottoman rule, so the Great Idea had transcended regional or factional loyalties. For many politicians and army officers the defeat of the Great Idea had deprived Greece of its future. The perceived enemy was no longer the Turks but other Greeks—royalist or republican. In 1924 army officers deposed George II and established a republic, which was confirmed in a plebiscite the following year. After four years of ineffective government, punctuated by a military dictatorship, the party leaders summoned Venizelos to unify Greece under a national government.

The thrust of Venizelos's postwar foreign policy was to end Greek dependence on any single European power. He established friendly relations with countries that had obvious interest in the Mediterranean area. Venizelos assured the Turks that Greece had given up territorial ambitions at their expense, and for the first time in modern Greek diplomatic history Greece and Turkey had cordial relations. In Athens, however, Venizelos had difficulty holding the Liberal party together. A series of

King George II was the only modern-day sovereign to be restored to the throne twice. He served from 1922 to 1924, from 1935 to 1941, and from 1946 to 1947.

abortive military coups and assassination attempts accompanied his personal decline. Venizelos, for all his expansive vision, was a narrowly partisan politician who was not above using political allies in the armed forces to keep his opposition from power. Beaten at the polls in 1931, Venizelos was later implicated in an abortive naval coup aimed at forcing out the conservative Populist government. Venizelos fled again into exile and was condemned to death in absentia.

Voters in a 1935 plebiscite called overwhelmingly (97 percent) for the return of George II. Parliamentary elections the next year, however, produced a deadlock between royalist and republican parties in Parliament, fifteen Communist seats holding the balance. In desperation George II called on General John Metaxas, former army chief of staff and Greece's outstanding soldier, to form a government as prime minister. Metaxas had no support in Parliament, but he was popular among royalist army officers. He temporarily adjourned Parliament (thereby defusing its influential Communist bloc) and governed the country by decree during a proclaimed state of emergency, but in 1936 Metaxas dropped all pretense of constitutional government. He dissolved Parliament with royal assent and initiated a dictatorship, claiming that the action was necessary to forestall a Communist-inspired coup within the armed forces.

THE TERRIBLE DECADE, 1940–49

Metaxas reorganized and reequipped the army in preparation for the European war that he believed was inevitable. At best he hoped to keep Greece neutral, but there was no question that if Greece were drawn into war it would be on the side of Great Britain. On October 28, 1940, the Italian ambassador in Athens demanded that Italian troops be allowed to occupy "certain strategic points" on Greek territory. Metaxas rejected the ultimatum in a one-word reply—*"Ochi"* (No). He recalled republican officers who had been dismissed in 1936, and he united the armed forces and the nation in a common

front. This was in marked contrast to the situation that had prevailed during World War I.

The Italian forces that invaded Greece expected an easy victory. Within a month, however, an inspired Greek army had counterattacked and driven the Italians deep into Albanian territory. But Metaxas's death in January 1941 deprived the Greek war effort of his determined leadership. Metaxas's strategy had been to defeat Italy before Germany was drawn into the Balkan theater, a position that was tenable as long as Greece's ally, Yugoslavia, stayed neutral. In April Germany invaded both Yugoslavia and Greece. The British provided naval support and sent fifty thousand troops to aid the Greeks, but within three weeks the Allied defense lines were overrun by a combination of air and armored attacks. The Greek commander in Epirus surrendered his army in the field. Prime Minister Alexander Koryzis, depressed by the discovery of treason within his cabinet, committed suicide. Crete was captured in June by German airborne units. The king and his government were evacuated to Egypt, where Greek naval units and the remnants of the army were reorganized to continue the war under British command.

The Axis powers occupied Greece for almost three years. The Germans were interested in holding only the principal communications routes and positions of vital strategic importance. Bulgaria annexed Thrace, but most of the country was nominally under Italian control. A collaborationist government provided day-to-day administration and internal security in occupied areas, but the greater part of the country—two-thirds of its more mountainous territory containing one-half of the population—was left virtually a no-man's-land.

The royal family resided in South Africa during the war years, and a government-in-exile, headed by noncommunist, pre-Metaxas politicians, operated from Egypt under British sponsorship. Greek naval and ground forces served in North Africa and the Near East under British command. The Allied Middle East Command supplied the Greek resistance and was responsible for its overall direction through the British Mission working inside Greece.

The German army withdrew from Greece in October 1944. Through the Soviet military mission in Athens the KKE (Kommunistikon Komma Ellados—the Greek Communist party) was ordered to "avoid opposition" and to participate in George Papandreou's government. Although the EAM-ELAS (Ethnikon Apeleftherotikon Metepon—the Greek National Liberation Front, and Ethnikos Laikos Apeleftherotikos Stratos—the National People's Liberation Army) had effective control of all of Greece outside the capital, the Communists bowed to Moscow's directive. The government installed in Athens by the British had six ministers from the EAM in the cabinet—all with portfolios that were useless as instruments of power. What the Greek Communists had not been aware of was the bargain struck between Winston Churchill and Joseph Stalin guaranteeing that Greece would fall into Great Britain's postwar sphere of influence.

Three immediate problems confronted the new government in Athens: reconstruction, the return of the monarch, and the disarming of guerrilla forces. More than five hundred thousand Greeks had perished from military action, in concentration camps, or from cold and hunger. Only two thousand of a prewar Jewish community of seventy thousand survived the occupation. Some fifteen hundred villages had been destroyed, leaving seven hundred thousand Greeks homeless. Communications and transportation networks were in ruins. Two-thirds of the merchant fleet had been sunk. Fruit and tobacco crops, strong prewar export items, were gone. Food production was half of what it had been in 1940.

Opinion was divided on whether George II should be allowed to return to Greece. The EAM conducted a campaign against restoration of the monarchy, accusing the king of responsibility for the Metaxas dictatorship and denouncing him for having fled the country in 1940. Demobilization of the guerrilla army was, of course, the most dangerous problem in the short term. For ELAS to disarm would take from the Communists the means to hold the country by force—a situation both sides understood. The British command proposed retaining two brigades—one royalist, one drawn from ELAS—until a national army could be formed. ELAS disregarded British general Sir Ronald MacKenzie Scobie's order to lay down its arms, reminding him that his authority extended only to operations against the Germans. The EAM ministers resigned from the government and held a demonstration in Athens on December 3, 1944, to protest the British demand. The police fired into the crowd to disperse it, and that action set off a chain reaction of violence between government troops and ELAS.

The Battle of Athens—the second round in the civil war—lasted one month. The British, who intervened against ELAS, were compelled to withdraw two divisions from the Italian front to reinforce their hard-pressed forces in the Greek capital. The renewed fighting also had the unpleasant aspect of pitting Greek government forces, which now included some who a short time before had been active collaborationists, against men who had taken leading parts in the resistance. The United States Mission in Athens had been instructed to remain neutral, but British colleagues generally considered the Americans to be pro-EAM.

On Christmas Eve 1944 Churchill and Anthony Eden, British foreign secretary, flew to Athens in an attempt to find a political solution that would end the violence. Their personal intervention failed to resolve the conflict, but Churchill temporarily defused the controversial

question of the monarchy by persuading George II to appoint as regent the archbishop of Athens, Damaskinos, a heroic figure during the occupation who was respected by both sides. Papandreou resigned as prime minister, and the regent appointed a republican to succeed him. The change in government paved the way for a cease-fire.

Thirty-three days of street fighting cost eleven thousand lives and left sections of Athens in ruins. Under the provisions of the armistice ELAS laid down its arms, the KKE and the EAM agreed to reorganize as legal political parties, and parliamentary elections and a plebiscite on the king's future were scheduled to be held within the year.

In November 1945 a caretaker government, composed of a broad coalition that excluded the Communists, announced parliamentary elections for the following March. When a Communist request for postponement of the election until after the plebiscite was denied, the KKE pulled out its candidates and asked supporters to abstain from voting. An Allied commission monitored the elections, which were marked by a swing to the right and gave the conservative Populists a clear majority, but only 60 percent of the electorate went to the polls. The plebiscite, held in September, returned a 69 percent majority in favor of George II's returning to Greece as king. He died the next spring and was succeeded by his brother, Paul.

During 1946 a series of isolated uprisings by leftists in various parts of the country escalated into a third round in the civil war. The KKE organized the so-called Democratic Army of Greece as ELAS's successor, and it conducted a classic guerrilla war against a static defense by conventional forces. The main guerrilla activity was in the Peloponnesus and in Macedonia and Epirus close to the sanctuary of the Yugoslav, Bulgarian, and Albanian borders, across which the Communist forces could retreat to rest and regroup before returning to combat. Across these borders also ran the lines of supply for the Greek Communists.

The government imposed martial law, permitting arrests without warrants. In 1947 it outlawed the KKE, but during three years of civil war constitutional processes were retained remarkably intact. Though in a seemingly invulnerable military position and apparently able to continue the fighting for an indefinite period, the

King Paul I began his reign in 1947 and on his death in 1964 was succeeded by his son Constantine II.

*The young queen Frederika
in a formal pose*

Communists lost much of their popular support in the countryside. The wanton cruelty of the guerrillas and the atrocities committed against whole communities that had given less than enthusiastic support disillusioned many Greeks who had previously backed the EAM. Peasants in Communist-controlled areas were conscripted for forced labor and military service.

By 1947 the British had reluctantly admitted their inability to continue substantial aid to the Greek government. In March of that year, by covering Greece in the Truman Doctrine—which sets limits on American tolerance to Communist expansion in the area—the United States replaced Great Britain as Greece's protecting power.

Perhaps the decisive element in the failure of the Communist military effort was the break in relations between the KKE and its most generous patron, Marshal Josip Broz Tito of Yugoslavia. The KKE was sharply divided by the Tito-Stalin rift, but the leaders remained faithful to Moscow. Early in 1949 Tito, who was anxious to cement good relations with the West as a check against Soviet pressure after his break with Stalin, closed the Yugoslav border with Greece, choking off supplies and ending the tactical flexibility that the guerrillas had previously enjoyed.

STABILITY AND CRISIS, 1949–67

The Liberal and Populist parties had lost strength in the immediate postwar years, and after 1949 neither could command a substantial enough following to lead a viable coalition government. In 1951 Field Marshal Alexander Papagos left the army to form a new right-wing party, the Greek Rally (Ellinikos Synagermos—ES), that would be free from association with established conservative politicians. He was inspired by France's Charles de Gaulle, and the ES was closely modeled on the Gaullist Reassemblement. Papagos was a popular figure who had led Greek forces in Albania early in World War II and had been chief of staff during the successful final phase of the civil war. General elections in 1952 brought the ES 49 percent of the vote and, through a system of plurality representation introduced that year, gave it 247 of 300 seats in Parliament. The new electoral system, which had been suggested by American advisers, replaced a method of proportional representation that had discouraged single-party majorities.

Papagos's administration, on the basis of its secure parliamentary majority, put an end to petty struggles within conservative ranks, fought corruption and nepotism in government, and cut the size of the bureaucracy.

Papagos died in 1955. King Paul appointed as prime minister a relatively unknown conservative politician, Constantine Karamanlis, who like Papagos enjoyed American backing. Karamanlis formed a new party, the National Radical Union (Ethniki Rizopastiti Enosis— ERE), which continued the basic policies of the ES. In the 1956 elections the ERE won 45 percent of the vote and 80 percent of the seats in Parliament.

After the mid-1950s Greek foreign policy was marred by the prolonged dispute over Cyprus that led to a steady deterioration of relations with Turkey. The Greeks had long hoped for the cession of the island, with its 80 percent Greek majority, by Great Britain.

By 1954 the movement for enosis had come under the direction of Archbishop Makarios, ethnarch of the Greek community on Cyprus, and a Cypriot-born Greek army officer, Colonel George Grivas. Grivas, at the head of the right-wing National Organization of Cypriot Combatants (Ethniki Organosis Kyprion Agoniston— EOKA), waged a campaign of violence and terror first against Greeks who did not back the movement and later against Turkish Cypriots and British authorities.

Karamanlis resigned in 1958 after criticism of his handling of the Cyprus question, but he returned to power when elections the following year confirmed the ERE's majority. In the meantime Great Britain, Greece, and Turkey had compromised on the issue of enosis by agreeing to the establishment of an independent Republic of Cyprus. Greece and Turkey were recognized as the protectors of their respective populations on the island.

In 1960 George Papandreou returned to politics, forming a new party, the Center Union, that was based on support for the old Liberal party. The United Democratic Left (Eniea Dimokratika Aristeras—EDA) also campaigned for parliamentary seats, allegedly as a front for the outlawed KKE and former EAM activists. Despite the introduction of new and united opposition parties, Karamanlis's ERE increased its majority still further in the 1961 elections. Papandreou and his liberal allies picked up only a third of the vote in the Center Union's first electoral contest, far less than they had anticipated. Claiming election fraud, the one hundred Center Union delegates boycotted the opening of Parliament. When they finally took their seats, Papandreou denounced the Karamanlis government as unconstitutional.

Karamanlis's position was complicated by the deterioration of his personal relations with King Paul and his influential consort, the German-born Queen Frederika. The royal family had become the focus of parliamentary debate when the liberal and left-wing opposition attacked Karamanlis for supporting a dowry for Princess Sophia on her marriage to Don Juan Carlos of Spain. Papandreou had also challenged the king for his comments linking the interests of the army with those of the crown. Conservative governments had profited from the king's confidence and from the loyalty of royalists in the officer corps, but Karamanlis was careful to keep the image of the monarchy as an institution above partisan politics.

In the summer of 1963 Paul and Frederika accepted an invitation to make a state visit to Great Britain. When radical groups threatened to demonstrate against the monarchs, Karamanlis advised the king to cancel the trip in order to avoid embarrassment to the government. Paul rejected his prime minister's recommendation—reportedly at Frederika's urging—and Karamanlis resigned on the grounds that he no longer had the king's confidence. The overall effectiveness of the ERE was damaged by his departure from office.

The "old" royal palace in Athens is now used as the parliament building.

Stamps of Greece honoring King Constantine II and his family

Elections in November showed a sharp but not decisive swing to the Center Union. Papandreou's party won 140 seats in the new Parliament, just short of a majority, as against 123 for the ERE, and 30 for the Communist-linked EDA. Papandreou was called on to form a government but resigned in a matter of weeks rather than rely on left-wing support to stay in power. Karamanlis, in the meantime, had retired from politics and left Greece, consigning the ERE leadership to Panayiotis Kanellopoulos. New general elections in February 1964 gave the Center Union an absolute parliamentary majority and enabled Papandreou to establish a one-party government. Papandreou had emerged as the first genuinely popular political figure since Venizelos. Like Venizelos, however, Papandreou had a domineering and highly personal style of politics, and it alienated the more independent-minded members of his own parliamentary party and led to a gradually widening breach in the Center Union.

King Paul died in 1964 and was succeeded by his son, Constantine II, a young, athletic prince, married to an attractive Danish princess and presumably possessing the qualities needed to make him a popular monarch. According to some observers, however, he compensated for his political inexperience by reliance of dubious constitutionality on royalist officers and the advice of his mother. The question of royal prerogative in military affairs soon brought the twenty-three-year-old king into conflict with Papandreou, an elder statesman with an impressive mandate in Parliament and broad support in the country.

The immediate cause of the confrontation between the king and his prime minister was Cyprus. Kanellopoulos accused Papandreou of condoning Cypriot president Makarios's negotiations with the Soviet Union for arms purchases, and the conservative leader called for the prime minister's resignation. Center Union deputies retaliated by publishing the Pericles Plan, an alleged army plot to rig the 1961 elections in favor of the ERE. The army responded to Center Union allegations by leaking news of the Aspida conspiracy, a suspected plot laid to radical officers—members of a secret group, Aspida—who planned to overthrow the monarchy and set up a left-wing government. The prime minster's son, Andreas Papandreou, was implicated in the plot. The younger Papandreou was a member of his father's cabinet as minister for the prime minister's office. In that capacity he had attempted to assert supervisory control of the military intelligence section, used by the army for surveillance of subversive activities. His radical reputation had made him feared by conservatives and by the army—and by members of the Center Union who resented his obvious grooming for party leadership in succession to his father.

The king ordered Petros Garoufalias, minister of national defense, to investigate the Aspida group and charges of conspiracy involving army officers and government officials. The prime minister, questioning Garoufalias's impartiality, moved to dismiss him and take over the defense portfolio himself. Many even within the Center Union interpreted this as an attempt by Papandreou to protect his son, and Garoufalias refused to resign without a writ from the king. When Constantine declined to issue the writ, although such action should have followed the prime minister's request, Papandreou resigned.

Demonstrations were staged in support of Papandreou, who commanded the loyalty of the largest single bloc in Parliament if not the confidence of the king. A series of caretaker governments had difficulty scraping together even slim majorities to support them in Parliament, but Constantine delayed ordering the prescribed elections, which observers recognized would also be a referendum on the royal prerogative. Papandreou pledged to bring the armed forces under civilian political control and to remove the monarchy from politics. Politically vocal elements in the army cautioned about the consequences of a Papandreou victory for national security, but Constantine was finally compelled to set a May 1967 date for elections.

THE COLONEL'S REGIME, 1967–74

On April 21, 1967—less than a month before the scheduled elections—a military junta composed of middle-rank army officers ousted the government of the caretaker prime minister, Kanellopoulos, dismissed Parliament, suspended key articles of the constitution, and banned all political activity in the country. Many officers were disgruntled by the government's decision not to prosecute Andreas Papandreou for complicity in the Aspida conspiracy, and the colonels justified the coup on the grounds that it had been necessary to save the nation from an imminent Communist takeover. The purpose of

In 1967, King Constantine XIII and Queen Anne-Marie visited the United Nations headquarters in New York City. They are seen here with Secretary-General U Thant, center.

the action taken by the so-called Twenty-first of April movement was to prevent the May elections and George Papandreou's return to power. A civilian, Constantine Kollias, was installed as prime minister at the king's insistence. In December Constantine fled into exile with his family after a hapless attempt at a royal countercoup. Kollias, who had backed the king, was dismissed by the junta; and an artillery officer, Colonel George Papadopoulos, took over the prime minister's office at the head of a military government.

In November 1968, the military regime firmly entrenched in power, Papadopoulos submitted a new constitution to a referendum. The document, which called for reinstatement of the monarchy but reserved definitive authority for the prime minister, was approved by 92 percent of the voters. Although due process was theoretically reintroduced with the lifting of martial law, guarantees embodied in the constitution were held in abeyance to be applied at the regime's discretion, and no timetable was set for the return of civilian rule or the restoration of political liberties. Papadopoulos vaguely promised to implement the constitution when he was assured that the Greek people had acquired "sufficient maturity" to prevent their lapsing back into the chaos from which the junta had supposedly rescued Greece.

By 1970 some junta members had become uneasy at the extension of Papadopoulos's personal power. An attempt to force him from power not only failed but even appeared to consolidate his position. Papadopoulos monopolized cabinet portfolios and neutralized potential rivals by sending them out of Athens as provincial governors. Civilian technocrats were brought in to replace military men in high government offices.

Greece had remained a monarchy under the military regime, but Constantine had steadfastly refused to lend legitimacy to the Papadopoulos government. In May 1973 naval units staged an abortive coup against the regime. Although mutineers denied contact with the king—and in fact resented the suggestion of it—Constantine was charged with having conspired in the plot from Rome. In June Papadopoulos issued a decree abolishing the monarchy and calling for the establishment of a republic. Observers abroad saw the Papadopoulos Republic as being the result of a deadlock within his government. The regime clearly lacked both a legal basis and popular support, and Greece had been ostracized by the international community. Economic difficulties had led to growing unrest at home. Papadopoulos put forward a new constitution, modeled on that of the French Fifth Republic, providing for a presidential Republic and a Parliament. Papadopoulos was the sole candidate for a seven-year term as president. Despite compulsory voting regulations, 25 percent of the electorate abstained from the referendum that followed, but Papadopoulos and the constitution were approved by 77 percent of those who went to the polls.

The Supreme Court subsequently ruled that Papadopoulos's decree abolishing the monarchy had been legal because it was "an act of revolution" aimed at "restoring normal conditions in the country." The new president claimed that the people had shown "great political maturity and a high sense of responsibility" in approving the constitution. Given a supposedly legitimate mandate to rule through 1981, Papadopoulos set about demilitarizing the regime and preparing for parliamentary elections scheduled for 1974. Papadopoulos's Republic was, however, little more than a military dictatorship in civilian clothes.

It was also destined to be short lived. Tension continued to build in the country. In November crowds attending a memorial service marking the anniversary of George Papandreou's death were fired on by the police, setting off a chain reaction of violence. When police killed nine university students—protesting the rescinding of draft deferments—workers joined the students in a general strike. Determining that Papadopoulos had lost control of the situation, Brigadier Dimitrios Ioannides, commander of the military police and an original junta member, arrested the erstwhile president, pledging to return the country to the "ideals of the 1967 revolution" and "to save the nation" from an "electoral travesty." Ioannides set free politicians imprisoned by Papadopoulos and reopened island prison camps to receive supporters of the former president. The constitution was modified and Lieutenant General Phaedon Ghizikis named president. Ghizikis spoke of promoting so-called guided democracy, and a civilian technocrat was appointed prime minister; but Ioannides and the army remained the real power behind the new government. It was a military regime with the spurs on.

The Cyprus question—an issue that had refused to go away and had defied solution by successive Greek governments—proved the undoing of the Ioannides regime. Greek regular army officers who had been assigned to the Cypriot National Guard carried forward a plot in July 1974 to seize the government of Cyprus and kill President Makarios as steps toward proclaiming enosis for the island. The military regime in Athens had become impatient with the independent-minded Makarios, and some Greeks who were not sympathetic to the colonels nonetheless agreed that the ethnarch was a traitor to enosis. Makarios and many observers abroad believed that Ioannides had masterminded the conspiracy to bring about a confrontation with Turkey that would divert popular attention from domestic problems. The military regime had engaged in a similar saber-rattling exercise with the Turks earlier in the year over oil exploration in the Aegean Sea. On July 20 Greek troops made a desperate six hundred-mile airborne dash from bases in Greece to reinforce the Cypriot National Guard against counteraction from Turkish bases only forty miles from the island. The Turkish reaction was quicker and more determined

than the Greeks had bargained for. Turkish troops—eventually numbering thirty thousand—landed on Cyprus the same day, supported by vastly superior air and naval forces. Athens called a general mobilization, and troops were moved into offensive positions in Thrace, where units of the two NATO allies exchanged artillery fire across the Evros River.

The Greek general staff protested the mobilization order and requested that President Ghizikis call in civilian political leaders for consultations, signifying that the armed forces had lost confidence in the military regime. At this point the military regime came unstuck. On July 22 the military leaders ordered a cease-fire and submitted themselves to civilian authority "to save the nation." Karamanlis, who had been living in Paris sincd 1963, accepted an invitation by Ghizikis to form a new government.

Backed by an ERE-Center Union coalition, Karamanlis reinstated the precoup constitution and entered into negotiations with Turkey in Geneva to work out a permanent cease-fire. Papadopoulos, Ioannides, and other junta leaders were arrested; the military police was disarmed and stripped of its power; and the democratizing of the armed forces under civilian control was begun. Constantine remained in Rome but welcomed the change in government and expressed his desire to return to Greece eventually. The plebiscite in December 1974 rejected proposals for a return to constitutional monarchy, and in June 1975 a new republican constitution provided for a parliamentary democracy.

Expansion of Greece from 1832 to 1947

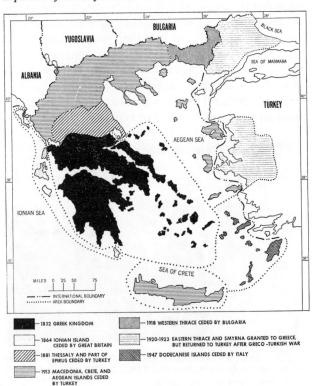

THE ROYAL SOVEREIGNS OF THE ANCIENT AND MODERN KINGDOMS OF GREECE

Reign	Title	Ruler	Birth	Death	Relationship

SPARTA (SOUTHERN GREECE)

1100 B.C.—Conquered by the Dorians
1100–192—Dual hereditary kings
146—Conquered by the Romans

ATHENS

1000–683—Various forms of monarchies
638–288—Mixture of forms of governments including monarchies
146—Conquered by the Romans
88—Merged with the Mithridates
86—Conquered by Sulla

SYRACUSE (SOUTHEAST SICILY)

733—Founded by the Corinthian settlers
733–215—Rulled by numerous sovereigns called tyrants
215—Conquered by the Romans

MACEDON (MACEDONIA) (NORTHERN GREECE)

Reign	Title	Ruler	Birth	Death	Relationship
500–498 B.C.	King	Amyntas I		498	
498–454	King	Alexander I		454	
454–413	King	Perdiccas II		413	Son of Alexander I
413–399	King	Archelaus		399	Son of Perdiccas II
399–370	King	Amyntas II		370	Nephew of Perdiccas II
370–368	King	Alexander II		368	
368–360	King	Perdiccas III		360	Brother of Philip II
360–359	King	Amyntas III		359	Grandson of Amyntas II
359–336	King	Philip II		336	Brother of Perdiccas III
336–323	King	Alexander III, the Great	356	323	Son of Philip II
323–323	King	Philip III Aridaeus		317	Son of Philip II
323–310	King	Alexander IV		310	Son of Alexander III
316–297	King	Cassander		297	Son of Antipater
297–297	King	Philip IV		297	Son of Cassander
297–294	King	Alexander V		294	Son of Cassander
306–283	King	Demetrius I Poliorcetes		283	Son of General Antigonus Cyclops
283–273	King	Antigonus II Gonatas		273	Grandson of Antigonus
273–272	King	Pyrrhus of Epirus		272	
272–239	King	Antigonus II Gonatus		239	
239–232	King	Demetrius II		232	Son of Antigonus II
232–229	King	Philip		229	
229–221	King	Antigonus III Doson		221	Nephew of Antigonus II
220–179	King	Philip V		179	Son of Demetrius II
179–168	King	Perseus		160	Son of Philip V
150–148	King	Philip VI		148	

146—Conquered by the Romans

GREECE FROM THE TIME OF CHRIST

Reign	Title	Ruler	Birth	Death	Relationship
146 B.C.–A.D. 395—Ruled by Rome					
1460—Conquered by Turkey					
1827—Independence from Turkey					
1832—Monarchy established					
1832–1862	King	Otto I (Otho)	1815	1867	Son of King Ludwig I of Bavaria
1863–1913	King	George I	1845	1913	Son of King Christian IX of Denmark
1913–1917	King	Constantine I	1868	1923	Son of George I
1917–1920	King	Alexander	1893	1920	Son of Constantine I
1920–1922	King	Constantine I (rethroned)			
1922–1924	King	George II	1890	1947	Son of Constantine I
1924–1935—Greece is a republic					
1935–1935	Regent	Georgios Kondylis	1879	1936	
1935–1941	King	George II (rethroned)			
1941–1944—Occupied by Germany					
1946–1947	King	George II (again rethroned)			
1947–1964	King	Paul I	1901	1964	Son of Constantine I
1964–1973	King	Constantine II (exiled in 1967)	1941		Son of Paul I

20

The Byzantine and Ottoman Empires, and the Sultanates of Turkey

The Turkish nation of 1973 is at once new and old. The Republic of Turkey, created in the Anatolian heartland from the disintegration of the Ottoman Empire after World War I, was founded in 1923. In the background, however, was a long and diversified historical tradition including Turkish, Ottoman, Islamic, and European elements and influences. The Western influence was most recently added; the basic Turkish current appeared in the eleventh century A.D. with the arrival from central Asia of Islamized Turkoman tribes that gradually established their predominance over the heterogeneous population then present in Anatolia.

The vast Ottoman Empire, lasting from the fourteenth to the twentieth century, was established and expanded in the *gazi* (warrior) spirit of a militant Islamic society advancing its frontiers against the infidel. Eventually, however, Islam within the empire became static, the Ottoman sultanic dynasty, with its hierarchical bureaucracy, declined into corruption and stagnation, and the decaying Ottoman realm became subject to the competing interests and expanding power of European states.

Buffeted both by external pressures and by internal conservative opposition, a reform program attempted during the nineteenth century finally expired. The Young Turks nationalist reform of 1908 failed to produce a successful administration, and the empire, drawn into World War I on the side of Germany against the western Allies and Russia—the latter a traditional Turkish enemy—went down to final defeat.

Harsh terms were imposed by the victors. The external empire was divided among the victors, the sultanate was limited to northern Anatolia, and Greek forces invaded the western region of the country. Mustafa Kemal, commander of the successful Turkish defense of Gallipoli in 1915, had, however, become leader of the nationalists in the central plateau region of Anatolia. Turkish forces, rallied and reorganized under his leadership, drove the Greeks from Turkey by the end of 1922, and a new treaty restoring the Turkish homeland includ-

ing Thrace was secured from the western Allies in 1923. The Ottoman sultanate was abolished, and the Republic of Turkey was proclaimed at Ankara, the new capital, on October 29, 1923, with Mustafa Kemal as president. Later designated *Atatürk*, or "Father of the Turks," he continued in the presidency until his death on November 10, 1938.

ANCIENT HISTORY

The great land bridge of Asia Minor that constitutes most of the modern state of Turkey was known to ancient geographers by the Greek word *Anatolia* (the rising of the sun). The term survives in such regional references as Anatolian Plateau and in Turkish as Anadolu, meaning Asiatic Turkey. Archaeologists have found evidence of prehistoric peoples in the seventh and sixth millennia B.C. These people, different from the later Hittites and much later Turks, are known as the Hatti and their language as Hattic. By the third millennium B.C., central and eastern Anatolia, after earlier progress, apparently reverted for a time to a more primitive culture.

Along the Aegean coast in the west, the land projection between the Dardanelles and the Gulf of Edremit—corresponding roughly to the present-day province of Çanakkale—was known in antiquity as Troias, or land of Troy. There, at the Hisarlik mound about sixteen miles southwest of the modern city of Çanakkale, the nine successive settlements, or levels of ancient Troy were identified in the late nineteenth century. Troy, the center of a periodically prosperous small kingdom, was first established some time in the period between 3000 and 2500 B.C. The seventh layer of settlement, from about 1250 to 1200 B.C., is accepted by most scholars as the Troy of Homer's *Iliad* and *Odyssey*. Between 1100 and 700 B.C. the site seems to have been abandoned, but it was then reoccupied by Greek settlers and continued under the name Ilion, or Ilium, until declining into obscurity in the fourth century A.D.

Elsewhere in Anatolia, a revival of cultural development occurred somewhat after the early settlements at Troy. During a copper age that occurred from about 2500 to 2000 B.C., tribes from the north and east, coming mostly by way of the Caucasus, began appearing in Anatolia and to the south in Syria and Mesopotamia. These people, superimposing their Indo-European speech on the indigenous Hattic, are known as the Hittites. Their empire covered Anatolia and most of northern Syria and Mesopotamia during the period from 2000 to 1200 B.C.

The Hittites introduced Mediterranean cuneiform writing in Anatolia and were noted for the early working of iron. At the site of their capital of Hattusas (present-day Bogazkoy), thousands of clay tablets illustrating eight languages have been found. The Hittite Empire reached its zenith in the period from 1450 to 1200 B.C., when it held power and prestige comparable with the Egyptian Empire of the time.

In about 1200 B.C., corresponding closely in time with the fall of Homer's troy, the Hittite civilization came to an abrupt end. The capital city of Hattusas was captured by raiders sweeping eastward from ancient Thrace and across the Aegean Sea into western and central Anatolia, thus ushering in what are sometimes called the Dark Ages of 1200 to 700 B.C. In southwestern Anatolia a neo-Hittite state showing strong Assyrian influence endured from about 900 to about 600 B.C. Soon after the collapse of that state, the Armenians first became identifiable in history in the eastern reaches of Anatolia near Mount Ararat (Agri Dagi) and the area between the Black and Caspian seas lying south of the Caucasus Mountains. These Armenians had come earlier from the east and had merged with and absorbed the Hittites of the region. They spoke and preserved a distinct Indo-European language and were to endure in the area as a separate ethnic group.

The invaders from the west who overthrew the main Hittite Empire are known as Phrygians. A strong Phrygian state was maintained in west-central Anatolia between 750 and 300 B.C.; its capital was at Gordium, about forty-five miles southwest of modern Ankara. At Gordium the fabled King Midas reigned, from 725 to 675 B.C.; and there, more than three centuries later, Alexander the Great is supposed to have cut the Gordian knot. Meanwhile in western and southwestern Anatolia, the city-states of Lydia, Lysia, and Caria rose and flourished briefly as part of the Ionian-Greek civilization of Asia Minor. In 546 B.C. the Lydians were defeated by the Persian king, Cyrus the Great, and Anatolia was then brought under the Persian Empire of the Achaemenid Dynasty for the next two centuries.

Alexander the Great, having established his authority in Greece, began his advance into Asia Minor in 334 B.C. and during the next four years incorporated the region into his far-flung empire. After Alexander's death in 323 B.C., political control in Anatolia became divided among a number of small splinter kingdoms. During the third century B.C. an incursion from Europe by Gallic peoples resulted in settlements in central Anatolia; during Roman times this region became known as Galatia.

ROME AND THE RISE OF BYZANTIUM

Rome had begun its conquest of Asia Minor as early as 190 B.C. In 133 B.C. the Province of Asia was formally designated and organized, and the Roman period in Anatolia is often considered to commence at this date. Other sources prefer to assign the start of the period to the imperial unification of Roman power in 30 B.C. under Augustus, the first emperor.

The cultural progress and economic prosperity of the Hellenistic age continued under Roman rule, especially in western Anatolia, and the first two centuries A.D. have been described as a golden age. By this time the ethnic map of the area showed the extreme complexity that had been developing in the cultural, political, and economic crossroads of Asia Minor since the earliest recorded times. Writing in the first century A.D., the Greek geographer Strabo attempted to describe the peoples of Anatolia but noted what he called "the confusion which has existed among the nations in this district, with their many different fables of origin."

Christianity was introduced to Anatolia in the first century A.D., particularly by the four missionary journeys of Paul of Tarsus, or Saint Paul—the Apostle to the Gentiles—and by the Pauline Epistles to the churches in

Constantine the Great. Roman emperor Constantine the Great began his reign in the West in 306. He decided to transfer the capital of the empire to Constantinople. But it wasn't until 330 that he was able to "dedicate" Constantinople as the new capital and it wasn't until 364 that his plan took shape with a division of the empire into an East and West separation. Although Constantine died in 337, his plans were more or less carried out. His son Constantine was to take the West, Constans the center, and Constantius the East. Constantius was too busy fighting the wars of the empire in the East and administering in the West to establish a throne in Constantinople, and his early death by execution in 354 slowed the master's plan. When Valentinian became emperor in 364 he put the partition into effect and named his son Valens to be the first emperor of the East.

Emperor Valens, the first emperor of the East. He reigned from 364 to 378.

The empress Theodora in legend had a long-term affair with Belisarius, who was the greatest general of all Byzantine time (having conquered the Italians and the Huns). He lived from 505 to 565. The empress in later years served as the coruler.

Theodosius I was the emperor of the East from 379 to 395 and was the founder of the Theodosian Dynasty, which lasted until 450.

The emperor Marcianus, founder of the Thracian Dynasty (450–518), reigned from 450 to 457.

Empress Theodora, the beautiful actress Justinian married. She is seen here with her attendants.

The emperor of the East, Justinian (527–65), and his court. This sketch is from a mosaic at St. Vitale in Ravenna.

Emperor Phocas, who killed Maurice in 602 so that he could replace him on the throne, died likewise eight years later when he was strangled by Heraclius.

Heraclius reigned from 610 to 641 and was the founder of the Heraclius Dynasty, which ran from 610 to 717. On this coin Heraclius is on the left with his eldest son, Constantine III, right. Constantine succeeded his father and was emperor for a short time in 641. Both he and his father died in 641. Their reigns were troubled, with Islam becoming more in conflict with Christianity.

Asia Minor, written probably between A.D. 50 and 60, which survive in the New Testament. The first seven Christian churches in Asia were all in Anatolia, notably at Ephesus, Antioch (present-day Antakya), and Nicaea (present-day Iznik), where the Nicene Creed was formulated in A.D. 325.

The Christian religion spread widely in Anatolia, survived Roman persecutions, such as that of the emperor Diocletian (reigned 284–305) and was ultimately to endure strongly in the forms of Greek and Armenian Orthodoxy. Roman imperial political control, however, and its attendant prosperity came to an end in the eastern border warfare with Persia when the emperor Valerian was defeated by the Sasanian Persian king Sapor I in the year 260, subsequent to which there was a brief period of ostensible Persian dominion in the east.

In 313 the Roman emperor Constantine, having accepted Christianity, sponsored the Edict of Milan, by which Christianity became the established religion of the empire. In 330 he shifted his capital to the old town of Byzantium on the Bosporus Strait. The new capital was called Constantinople, but in local use it became known as Istanbul. In the de facto partition of the old Roman Empire into western and eastern segments in 395, Constantinople became capital of the vast eastern and North African domains. Thus the period of the Byzantine Empire began, and all or part of Anatolia, in decreasing proportions, remained under it for nearly eleven hundred years until the empire's demise in 1453.

The early Byzantine centuries were, in the main, prosperous for Anatolia, and in the sixth century a period of grandeur like that of the old Roman Empire was temporarily reached under Emperor Justinian (527–65). The level of energy and prosperity attained under Justinian was not maintained by his successors, however, and a combination of internal difficulties and external pressures gradually weakened and crumbled the Byzantine imperial structure.

ISLAM AND THE ARABS

By the time of his death in 632, the Prophet Mohammed and his followers had brought most of the tribes of the Arabian Peninsula under the banner of the new monotheistic religion of *Islam* (submission), uniting the individual, state, and society under the all-powerful will of God. True Islamic rulers therefore exercised both temporal and religious authority; consequently, to them the much later Western idea of separation of church and state would have appeared not only heretical but fundamentally illogical. Adherents of Islam, called Muslims, collectively formed the *Dar al-Islam* (abode of Islam); all others lay outside in the *Dar al-Harb* (abode of war).

By the early eighth century A.D. the mobile armies of

the Prophet's successors had carried the conquests of Islam north, west, and east from the Arabian Peninsula in a sudden political-religious tidal wave. Historians have pointed out, however, that this great surge was at least as much sociological and economic as religious. The new unity of Islam was the vehicle enabling the

Emperor Heraclius has been a well-thought-of ruler for the Christians in the United States, for it was his victory over Chosroes that restored the true wood of the Holy Cross to the Holy Sepulcher in Jerusalem and brought a fragment of it to Constantinople, which in time found its way to America. The fragment enshrined in this gold triptych is now located in the Metropolitan Museum of Art in New York City.

The Prophet Mohammed

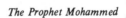

Murder and mayhem were no less in evidence in the East than in the West empires. Justinian II (685–95), a tempestuous psychopath, had to be deposed and banished to the Crimea in 695, but he recovered his throne in 705 and for six years he killed everyone who opposed his sordid way of life until he himself was murdered.

Emperor Leo III, the Isaurian, founded the Isaurian Dynasty (717–867) and was its first sovereign (717–41). He saved Constantinople from the Saracens in 717 and defeated them again in 727 and 740.

Empress Irene, who served as regent for her son Constantine VI and in her own right from 797 to 802 after his death. She was strongly anti-iconoclast and in 787, while the regent, met with the Council of Constantinople; they issued a policy of return to idol and image worship. The Council of Nicaea later overrode her wishes and reversed the decision.

expansion to new lands required by the growing problem of population pressures in the peninsula.

Initially, the major antagonist encountered in the spread of Islam was the Byzantine Empire. By 642, however, Egypt and the Fertile Crescent of Palestine, Syria, and Mesopotamia were conquered by the Arab Muslim forces. In the west the next three decades saw the conquest carried along North Africa to the Atlantic Ocean. In the east the forces of the Persian king succumbed to the Arabs in 651. To the north, in the Byzantine heartland of Anatolia, Islamic Arab military and political conquest did not succeed. Islam as a religion, however, was later to become the most significant single influence in the national life of Turkey.

Naval forces under Muawiyah, the Arab governor of Syria, won important victories over Byzantine naval forces in the Aegean Sea in 655 but were unable to capitalize upon these successes. The Byzantine emperor Constans II, who ruled from 641 to 668, resisted Arab attacks so strongly as to force a tributary truce upon Muawiyah.

Sporadic border warfare continued between Byzantines and Arabs for the next two centuries. During this time, as during the earlier wars of Muawiyah, the declining Byzantine Empire was battered not only by Arabs from the south but by attacks from the west by Slavic peoples out of the Balkans. But of even greater importance, by the tenth century, were the growing incursions of Islamized, warlike tribes from the east—the Turks.

TURKISH ORIGINS AND THE SELJUKS

The Turks are first recorded in history as living in the present-day border areas of the Soviet Union and the Mongolian People's Republic (Outer Mongolia), bounded by the Altai Mountains, Lake Baikal, and, to the south, the edge of the Gobi Desert. Chinese records of the second millennium B.C. identify certain tribal peoples in Outer Mongolia north of the Gobi Desert as Hiong-Nu, who are believed to have been Turkish.

The earliest specific references to Turks, as such, appear in Chinese sources of the sixth century A.D. referring to the Tu-Kiu tribal kingdom on the Orkhon River south of Lake Baikal. The earliest known writings in

Turkish, dated about A.D. 730, have been located in this area. Other Turks from the Altai base area set up a Turkish tribal kingdom south of the Aral Sea, in what later became known as Turkestan and its people as Turkomans or Turkmen. In modern times this is the general area of the Uzbek and Turkmen Soviet Socialist Republics of the Soviet Union. Neither of the early nomadic tribal kingdoms long endured, but by the eighth century Turkish peoples had spread throughout the area between the Aral Sea and Lake Baikal.

Both Christianity, in several of its doctrinal schismatic forms, and Buddhism appeared among the Turks. Apparently neither took hold, however, and the Turks remained mainly influenced by their own ancient shamanist beliefs. With the Arab-Islamic conquest across Iran in the seventh century, Sunni Islam began spreading rapidly and effectively among the Turks—first among those to the west and then to the still-nomadic Turks of central Asia, where conversion became generalized in the tenth century.

Islam not only provided a framework of religious worship and faith; it also constituted a systematic, organized way of life governing all human and divine relationships. With it, the Turks acquired the Arabic alphabet and system of writing, which superseded earlier forms.

Among the Turks, two trends in the practice of Islam were to have long-lasting effects on the history of the Turkish nation: on the one hand, the more austere and more demanding orthodoxy of Sunni Islam and, on the other, what may be called folk Islam, involving extensive mysticism and magical accretions. Folk Islam was susceptible to influence from the Shiite Persians and congenial to the rise of fraternal religious brotherhoods, such as the dervish orders. The early Turkish *gazi* were often identified with folk Islam. On the other hand, in the early conversions a strong Turkish tribal chief named Seljuk and his people accepted and maintained Sunni orthodoxy.

The first Arab dynasty of the Ummayads had given way to the Abbassides, who ruled from Baghdad. Early in the ninth century the Abbasside ruler, or caliph, began utilizing Turks in increasing numbers in his armed forces, a process that contributed to the rise of Turkish power. In 1055 a Seljuk leader named Tughrul Beg, a descendant of the first Seljuk chief, occupied Baghdad with a Turkoman army, and while retaining the Abbasside caliphs as figureheads, effectively imposed a Turkish government under Seljuk sultans over much of the eastern caliphate. From the tenth century onward, Turkish tribes had moved across Iran into Iraq and eastern Anatolia; and by the mid-eleventh century the *gazi* raiders, noted for endurance, mobility, and military prowess, had penetrated at least halfway across Asia Minor to present-day Konya (Iconium). These movements brought about the second great encounter in Turkish history—the first being with Islam, the second with the Byzantine Empire.

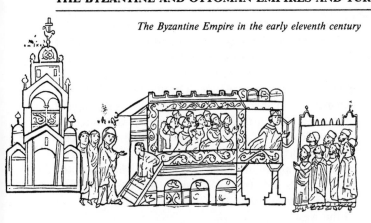

The Byzantine Empire in the early eleventh century

Empress Zoe, the daughter of Constantine II, married successive husbands who became the rulers by mercy of the marriage—Romanus Argyrus (1028–34) and Michael IV (1034–41). She outlived them both but her real troubles began when she adopted one Michael Calaphates, who had her thrown in prison. The people rebelled to have her released. She is seen in this old manuscript illustration thanking the people upon her release.

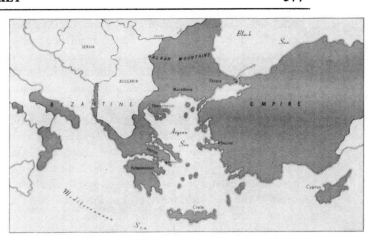

Emperor Nicephorus the Usurper, so called because he usurped the throne of the Eastern Empire from Michael Ducas in 1078. But in the end he found out that he "bit off more than he could stomach," for the Turks were, in the latter part of the eleventh century, starting their move to conquer Europe and Nicephorus and his generals could not drive them out of the foothold they had in Asia Minor. This manuscript page from the time shows Nicephorus and his wife, Empress Maria, being crowned by Christ.

This illumination from an old manuscript shows Alexius I Comnenus, left, and his son John II being crowned from above by Jesus Christ. They reigned respectively from 1081 to 1118 and 1118 to 1143. They started the House of Comnenus, which was the ruling dynasty from 1081 to 1185. All five of the dynasty's rulers were very capable and performed ably.

The Seljuk Sultan Alp Arslan apparently had intended to pursue further conquests southward into Syria and perhaps to Egypt. The Turkish advances in Anatolia, the need to control the tribes there, a preference for the more northerly climate, and the approach of a Byzantine army caused a redirection northward, however. In 1071, at the decisive battle of Manzikert, near Lake Van, Alp Arslan defeated the Byzantine forces, and the way was opened for a rush of Turkish expansion westward. The result, as the historian Roderic H. Davison has noted, was the shattering of Byzantine administration by Turkish control of the countryside and lines of communication.

The Turkish incursions and the harassment of the Christian pilgrimage routes through southern Anatolia let the Byzantine emperor to call for assistance from Europe. Thus the First Crusade began, and in 1097 the Byzantines regained about one-third of Anatolia. The Turks were not driven out, however, but were compacted in central and eastern Anatolia, where they continued to be reinforced by further immigration from the east. In the central region, with its capital at Konya, the powerful Sultanate of Rum (Rome) was established and became one of the three principal centers of medieval Seljuk Turkish rule—the other two being the Seljuk rulers in Iran (until 1117) and the Seljuk regent-sultans in Baghdad (until 1194).

The sultanate of Rum reached its peak about 1230 and expired in 1307. During its period of greatness the Sufi mystic Jalal al-Din al Rumi founded the Mevlevi dervish order known in the West as the "whirling dervishes." A distinct Seljuk Turkish culture developed in central Anatolia, where the sultanate ruled in balance between Byzantium to the west and Armenia to the east. In Seljuk times the joint process of Islamization and Turkification (the adoption of the Turkish language and customs) of Anatolia spread rapidly and permanently. The historian Philip K. Hitti has observed that "it was the Seljuks who held back the Byzantines, dealt the first blows to the Crusaders, and paved the way for their Ottoman kinsmen."

The Crusades continued at intervals from 1095 to

about 1450. The sultanate of Rum did not fall in these assaults, but in 1243 it was defeated from the east by distant relatives of the Turks, the Mongol forces of Genghis Khan's descendants. Mongol control was tributary and nominal rather than administrative; and after the destruction of Baghdad in 1258 by Hulagu, or Kublai Khan, the Mongols gradually retired to Mesopotamia and, in particular, to Iran. Rum, although not completely destroyed, had been fatally weakened, and other scattered centers of Turkish power developed. During these times, extensive new Turkish emigrations also occurred in the westward movement of Turkish tribes fleeing from the Mongol pressure in central Asia. These developments set the stage for the next major era in Turkish history—the six centuries of the Ottoman Empire.

THE OTTOMAN EMPIRE

ESTABLISHMENT AND SURVIVAL OF THE OTTOMAN SULTANATE

In the fragmentation of the sultanate of Rum, one of the emergent principalities became the nucleus of the Ottoman Empire. Centered on Sogut, near modern Eskisehir, it was by no means the largest of the princedoms. It is believed to have been formed by the Kayi tribe, originally from the Oghuz Turkish tribes of central Asia, and was initially held by its first ruler, Ertugrul, in fief from the Seljuk sultan of Rum. Ertugrul was succeeded, about 1299, by his son Osman, who ruled until 1326. From him, the Turkish Osmanli Dynasty and state derived—becoming known to Europeans as Ottoman and to Arabs as Uthman. The thirty-six Ottoman sultans who followed Osman, ending with Mehmed VI (also known as

Timur the Lame (Tamerlane) was the Turkic-Mongol successor to the earlier conquerors from the East. He defeated Sultan Bayezid I in 1396 at the Battle of Nicopolis in Greece and took the sultan prisoner. Timur attempted to set a new order. He replaced the Turkish and Mongolian tradition with Islamic tradition. For the old sovereign law (yassak) and the customary law (edeb), he substituted a new sovereign law (teuzuk) and a religious law (sheriat). As a result of his changes the highest class of people would be the descendants of the Prophet replacing the "king's household" (tarkhans), which were first in the Turkish and Mongolian society. They (the tarkhans) rebelled.

Vahidedin) in 1922, were all descended from him.

Osman's small princedom, located on the crumbling Byzantine frontier near Constantinople, attracted men of the Islamic *gazi* spirit from the Anatolian interior and, in effect, became a *gazi* state. The impulses of Ottoman expansion, moving slowly at first and then with rapidly increasing momentum, swung alternately west and east. In practical terms, what became in time a dominant westward orientation may be accounted for by geography, the opportunities that presented themselves, the internal wars and disunity in Europe, and the *gazi* nature of the Ottoman state—the frontier of Dar al-Islam was to the west.

During the fourteenth century the new Ottoman sultanate consolidated its hold over the western two-thirds of Anatolia, isolated Constantinople, extended its control over the Balkans, and began probing into Hungary. Responding finally to the Ottoman advance, in 1396 a western European coalition army challenged Sultan Bayezid I at the Battle of Nicopolis in northwestern Greece and was crushingly defeated. In the east, however, a Turkic-Mongol successor to the earlier conquerors had appeared—Timur Lenk, known to the West as Tamerlane, or Timur the Lame. At a battle near Ankara in 1402, Timur not only defeated the Ottoman forces but also captured Bayezid I, who died in captivity the following year.

Timur, after briefly overrunning Anatolia, was satisfied with the reduction of the Ottoman threat. He restored some of the neo-Seljuk minor princes in eastern Anatolia and withdrew. After Bayezid I's death, his four sons fought for a decade to settle the succession in what was left of the realm. During this time neither disunited Europe nor beleaguered Byzantium took advantage of the situation. In the east, Timur died in 1405, and the internal struggle for the Ottoman succession proceeded without external intervention. Eventually one of Bayezid's sons was victorious, and in 1413 he took the throne as Sultan Mehmed I. The Ottoman state thus survived and, after a time of consolidation, entered into the period of its maximum growth and splendor.

The time of the first four sultans (about 1299–1413) was one of founding, expansion, crisis, contraction, and bare survival. Nevertheless, some of the governmental and administrative institutions characteristic of the later Ottoman Empire took form in these early years. During the reign of Orhan the executive office of chief minister (*veziriazam*, or grand *vezir*) first appeared, a development consonant with practice in earlier Eastern empires. This office evolved centuries later into the office of prime minister under the Constitution of 1876. The use of the title pasha (*pasa*; plural, *pasalar*) to designate civil or military officials of high rank and place probably also began during Orhan's reign.

The early Ottoman Empire, like the later one, was a patchwork of diverse ethnic and religious minorities and

Sultan Mehmed II (Mohammed II) in 1451 succeeded to the throne of the Ottoman Empire and immediately began a bloody career that oddly was mixed with savagery and scholarship. He solemnly promised to maintain peace with the emperor of Constantinople but at the same time was plotting for his overthrow. This painting of the sultan is by Gentile Bellini.

Mehmed II entering into Constantinople where he killed Constantine XI, ending the Byzantine Empire rule. This was May 29, 1453, after Mehmed II had the capital under siege for two years. After this famous date in history, the sultan became known as Mehmed the Conquerer. The triumph of the Crescent over the Cross had much greater meaning in history than as a military victory. The far-reaching effect of this event in history is that it drove the scholars and intellectuals into Italy from the East, which greatly helped the revival of learning and led directly to the Reformation.

After his victory and new status, Mehmed II built himself a big, beautiful new palace on the Bosphorus.

was not completely Muslim even in Anatolia. Troops were raised from the minorities as well as from the Turkomans. By the late fourteenth century, under Murad I, troop requirements caused the establishment of a corps of professional infantry—the Janissaries (*yeniçeri*, or new troops)—who were later to exercise an important but troublesome political role. Almost constant warfare produced many captives. What came to be known as the slave administration began to develop in the Ottoman use of prisoners and minority members to form a loyal, well-rewarded, but captive bureaucracy. Among other things, this prevented the rise of a hereditary nobility with its hands on the organs of government.

IMPERIAL EXPANSION AND POWER

Under Mehmed I and Murad II consolidation and development of administration continued, along with continual warfare in both Anatolia and Rumelia, as the Balkan area was called. A Hungarian attack in the Balkans was defeated at Varna in 1444; the maritime-commercial warfare with the Venetian city-state began its long course, and naval organization was undertaken.

Historians believe that the practice of *devsirme* (collection) was instituted during the reign of Murad II to fill and expand the Janissary corps. This practice involved the impressment of young Christian boys into the imperial service, where they were raised, Islamized, and trained for professional duties in the Ottoman administrative bureaucracy and the Janissaries—particularly in the latter.

The city of Constantinople, although isolated since 1365, continued as the last remnant of Byzantium despite several tentative Turkish assaults. Mehmed II, upon succeeding to the throne in 1451, immediately undertook a systematic, well-organized campaign against the ancient city. Having acquired gunpowder, technical advisers, and cannon from the West, the Ottomans bombarded and periodically assaulted the walls for fifty days. On May 29, 1453, the city fell, and the last Byzantine emperor, Constantine XI, was killed in this final assault. Thereafter Mehmed II became known as Fatih Mehmed, or Mehmed the Conqueror.

The effect upon Europe of the Ottoman seizure of Constantinople was important but, modern historians point out, not critical. The rise of the European national states, the Renaissance, the age of exploration, and the search for new routes to east Asia were already under way. To the Ottomans, however, the capture of Constantinople (which the Turks called Istanbul, although the name was not officially changed until 1930) had symbolic, religious, and political importance. The *gazi* Ottoman frontier sultanate had come of age and become an empire. A revived Islam was again triumphant. Fatih Mehmed, reportedly a man of culture and education as well as warlike prowess, moved his capital at once to Istanbul and began to rebuild the city.

Sultan Mehmed (Mohammed) the Conqueror built the Mosque of Mohammed the Conqueror in Constantinople in an attempt to make it better than the temple of St. Sophia.

The expansion westward under Bayezid II, successor to Fatih Mehmed, was chiefly maritime; the sultan's new navy and his use of subsidized corsairs largely displaced the declining power of Venice in the eastern and central Mediterranean. At about the same time Bayezid conducted a successful defense of eastern Anatolia against the forces and influence of the Persian shah Ismail, who had established Shia Islam as the official religion of Persia. The work of quelling dervish uprisings and Shiite heresy in the east was continued by Bayezid's son, Selim I—known to history as Selim the Grim.

Selim I extended the Ottoman conquests southward beyond the Taurus Mountains, which had formed a

The many mosques of Constantinople (Istanbul) are all copies of the St. Sophia. The term mosque means "to adore." The principal place in the mosque is the niche, or mihrab, which is sunk in the wall at right angles to a line drawn from Mecca, the sacred city of Islam, and birthplace of Mohammed.

Sultan Selim I (1465–1520), the conqueror of Persia, Syria, and Egypt, was the first Ottoman caliph. This portrait sketch was accomplished by a highly regarded artist, Haidar Bey in the sixteenth century.

Suleyman I (1520–66) was known in the West as Suleyman the Magnificent. He tried to conquer far and wide, from India to the east and Malta to the west. His name is also spelled Suleiman and Solyman. As he appeared as a young man.

Suleyman I—a sketch of him later in life

Sultan Suleyman I built the Mosque of Suleyman in 1557.

rough division between Ottomans and Arabs and, earlier, between Byzantium and the Arabs. The conquests of much of the Arabian Peninsula, Syria, Palestine, and Egypt, where the last Mamluk sultan was defeated in 1517, constitute the major developments of his reign. The three sacred cities of Islam—Mecca, Medina, and Jerusalem—and the famous cities of Damascus and Cairo were thus brought into the empire.

Selim I's son, Suleyman I, is known to the Turks as the Lawgiver (Kanuni) because of the codification during his reign of the religious law of Islam, the *seriat (sharia)*, and its application in the Ottoman society. In the West he is known as Suleyman the Magnificent. During his long reign (1520–66) the empire reached its peak of power and drive, and arts and trade flourished. The period from approximately 1550 to 1650 is sometimes called the Ottoman golden age.

Wars of conquest continued. The island of Rhodes was taken in 1522; between 1520 and 1551 the Mediterranean corsairs extended the sultan's fiat along the North African coast as far as Morocco; suzerainty over Hungary was established at the Battle of Mohacs in 1526. King Francis I of France, as part of his conflict with the Austrian Habsburg Dynasty, conciliated the sultan and urged him into continued warfare against Charles V, the Habsburg emperor. In retaliation Charles V cultivated the Persians and urged them into hostilities against the Turks. In several eastern wars Suleyman's forces were successful in taking much of the Kurdistan area of northwest Iran and added lower Mesopotamia (Iraq) to the empire in 1534—bringing another famous Arab capital, Baghdad, under the Ottoman domain. Two inauspicious omens appeared, however. In the westward drive the sultan's forces, at the end of long lines of communication, were unable to take Vienna in 1529; this was to mark the greatest advance in central Europe. Secondly, after reaching the Persian Gulf, the Turks failed in their attempt to drive European seafarers out of the Indian Ocean.

When Suleyman I, still on the campaign trail, died in Hungary in 1566, the Ottoman Empire was one of the major world powers. Of the four Islamic monarchies of the time—the others being Morocco, Iran, and Mughal India—the Ottomans were preeminent in their impact on Europe and were rivaled only by the Mughals in splendor, power, and wealth. The Ottoman system of administration exemplified the patriarchal-absolutist, military-dynastic nature of the realm and the concept of commingling of the religious and the temporal in a Muslim society. Although modified in later centuries, much of the early structure of administration was still identifiable at the end of the empire.

The sultan, at the apex, was theoretically responsible only to God and to God's law—the Islamic *seriat*, of which he was the chief executor in all its judicial and executive ramifications. All offices were filled by his authority. He legislated by decree, or *firman*; he was supreme military commander; and he had basic title to all land.

The office of the sultan, regardless of whether it was held by a strong or a weak ruler, was of utmost importance because all authority, law, and administrative procedures were geared to it. The question of succession was therefore particularly serious. Strong sultans were virtually absolute. In practice, however, all sultans were limited by pragmatic political requirements for support from the military forces and from the collegial body of senior Islamic theologians, the *ulema*. Both of these centers of influence and support were from time to time the source of factionalism and intrigue.

Assisting the sultan was the *divan* (imperial council), a relatively small body of the most senior officials who met regularly at the sultan's palace in Istanbul to direct and coordinate government business and to formulate policy recommendations. Some sultans presided personally over the divan; others did not. In the sultan's absence the chief minister presided. The entrance to the palace for official purposes of access to the chief minister, representing the sultan and the government, was called the Sublime Porte. Diplomatic correspondence and histories of the Ottoman period frequently refer to the government simply as the Porte.

The Ottoman state had been built in the *gazi* spirit of military organization and conquest by an absolutist, monarchical regime directing an Islamic society dominated by a Turkish elite. This *gazi* spirit, becoming mythologized, long persisted among the ruling class. Military concepts and patterns permeated the whole system of government; no clear-cut distinction between military and civilian functions was made in Ottoman thinking and administration.

Members of the ruling elite at all levels were those associated with the Ottoman regime in some position of hierarchal authority or influence. Entry to this class was based neither on a hereditary nobility nor on family wealth and prestige but could be gained by ability, training in the imperial palace schools, and, of course, absolute loyalty.

Collectively, the Ottoman elite, both civil and military, became known as the *askeri* (military) class—again reflecting the pervasive *gazi* mythology. The members necessarily had some education, almost always Islamic; spoke Ottoman Turkish, with its heavy infusion of Arabic and Persian words; and thought in Ottoman imperial terms. Those holding the topmost ranks, again both civil and military, were called pashas. The designation *bey* was used for positions somewhat lower than those held by a pasha; and the term *effendi*, for members of the ulema and for officers of the lower middle and lower grades of the bureaucracy.

In the early Ottoman years regional administration was divided between two governors general, one for

Anatolia and the other for the European holdings, or Rumelia. Others were designated in later years. The governor general might individually have the title of pasha, but the name of this office was *beylerbey* (governor of governors). His region was divided into provinces, each called a *sanjak* and each under a bey (governor). Provinces, in turn, were divided into fief-holdings. They were not necessarily hereditary but were subject to confirmation by the sultan upon the death or removal of the fief-holder. In each holding (*timar*) the fief-holder was called the *sipahi* (literally, cavalryman). He was the senior official of local administration and was responsible for carrying out the directives of the sultan, maintaining order, collecting taxes, and providing on call a designated number of mounted troops. He answered to the *sanjak-bey*.

Each fief was surveyed, and its people, cattle, and other property were recorded in a register *(defter)* of the imperial revenue service, whose director, in Constantinople, was often a member of the divan. As historians have often pointed out, the old Ottoman Empire was essentially a warmaking and revenue-collecting organization.

As military forces became larger and more regularized and as the costs of warfare materially increased, the system of fief-holder levies and fief-holdings became less effective. A system of tax farming was then employed in some areas. In this system, numbers of fiefs were combined under major landholders, whose responsibility was agrarian management and collection of taxes, from which they took their percentages. This led to the rise of a class of landed provincial notables *(ayan)*, who were to become politically influential in the nineteenth century.

In addition to the semimilitary structure of executive administration and the military forces themselves, the system of justice—the Islamic law of the *seriat* and its application—was an essential component of the Ottoman system. The Kuran (Quran) and the *seriat* do not provide for an organized hierarchical clergy, and Islamic states generally did not produce this form. The Ottoman regime was an exception. A *kadi-asker* (chief judge) was appointed for Anatolia and one for Rumelia. In each province a *kadi* (judge), with assistants, was appointed by the sultan and (at least in theory) was independent of the *sanjak-bey*. Thus, the *kadi* was both an Ottoman official and a member of the ulema.

The ulema, one of the most influential elements in Ottoman internal politics, were headed by the chief mufti *(müfti)* of Constantinople, who soon after the establishment of the capital became known as the *şeyhülislam* (Arabic: shaykh al-Islam). By the end of the sixteenth century, this office had increased in power to become second in ministerial prestige only to the chief minister. The *şeyhülislam* was a distinctively Ottoman development, becoming something like a combination of minister of justice and archbishop—although not exactly like either. The *şeyhülislam* influenced the appointment of each *kadi-asker*, and a term in the latter office became virtually a precondition for the former. The *fetva* (theological judgment) of the *şeyhülislam* was an instrument of importance and was used in the deposition of sultans from time to time.

Several notable exceptions to the system of provincial administration pertained throughout the Ottoman period. The empire was from the start a heterogeneous mixture of races, languages, and creeds. Turkish Muslims predominated only in Anatolia proper. Conquered territories were sometimes held as vassal states in which existing rulers were allowed to remain, subject to tribute and allegiance to the sultan. This device was more frequently employed in the early days of the empire than later, although it continued to prevail, in theory at least, in Egypt until World War I. The other notable exception was the *millet* system for governing non-Islamic creedal minorities as semiautonomous ethnic groups through their own religious channels. In particular, this system was applied to the millions of Christians and Jews in the empire.

Within Anatolia itself the three largest minorities in Ottoman times were found in the Greek Orthodox communities of western Turkey and in the Armenian and Kurdish concentrations of the east. The Greek Orthodox community had been closely identified with the Byzantine Empire, although its origins were earlier. All three major groups figured prominently in the later days of the Ottoman Empire and in the history of modern Turkey.

ONSET AND FACTORS OF DECLINE

The first ten Ottoman sultans, ending with Suleyman I (the Magnificent), were on the whole strong and able rulers and reigned an average of about twenty-six years each. Thereafter, with some partial exceptions, the sultanate was not characterized by a comparable pattern of leadership and went into decline. For example, Suleyman's son, Selim II, became a famous libertine with the nickname of Selim the Sot. His son, Murad III, followed a like course of dissipation and, in the process, sired more than one hundred children.

Some minor imperial gains and consolidations of territory were made, however, after the time of Suleyman I, and the empire reached its maximum physical extent in the mid-seventeenth century. Nevertheless, the reign of Suleyman I is usually described as the summit era of effective Ottoman power. This is a convenient historical generalization and is broadly true, but modern historians have pointed out that signs of decline had actually appeared before the death of Suleyman I.

For nearly two hundred fifty years after Suleyman I, in contrast with the phenomenal political, scientific, commercial, and industrial advances in Europe for which no Ottoman counterpart occurred, the internal

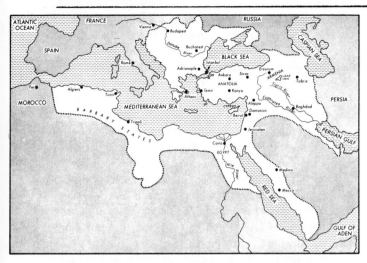

Turkey, the Ottoman Empire, at mid-seventeenth century

The most infamous of the sultans must surely be Ibrahim I (1640–48), for in a rage he drowned all the women in his harem.

Suleyman II ruled from 1687 to 1691 as the sultan of Turkey. This is a woodcut of him as he appeared early in his reign.

Sultan Mehmed IV (Mohammed) was the ruler of Turkey from 1648 to 1687. He conquered Greece without too much military effort but his invasions to the north and northwest into the Hungary and Austria territories were stopped by the Polish general and king, John III Sobieski.

The wife of Suleyman II

Kara Mustafa, the grand wazir for Mehmud IV, had a "brilliant" scheme for the conquest of the West but was defeated by the Polish king Sobieski at Vienna in 1683, which was the second defeat of Mehmud IV by King Sobieski. Therefore, Kara Mustafa was beheaded in Belgrade shortly thereafter.

Sultan Suleyman II later in life wearing the official crown of the sultans

King John III Sobieski who was known as the terror of the Turks

Abdul Hamid I ruled from 1774 to 1789. In the fashion of the customs of the ruling classes, Abdul Hamid was kept in total isolation from society for the first forty-nine years of his life to prepare him for the throne. As a result, when he became the sultan he was at the least unprepared, and at the worst, insane. But he ruled for fifteen years until he died.

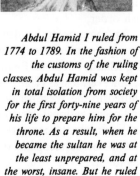

stagnation and corruption in the Ottoman regime brought about the gradual crumbling away of its power. Although often at war between 1560 and 1800, the Ottoman Empire was not confronted with sustained massive attacks, such as the earlier Crusades from the west or the Mongol invasions from the east, and the empire continued to be a factor of significant importance in European power politics.

During the reign of Selim II, in the longstanding maritime war with Venice, a combined Venetian, Spanish, and Austrian fleet destroyed the Ottoman fleet at the Battle of Lepanto in 1571. The European coalition broke up, however, and Venice ceded Cyprus to the Turks. Under Mehmed IV the empire by 1670 had acquired Crete and part of the Ukraine. In the Balkans, on the other hand, three defeats were suffered between 1664 and 1700. Vienna was vainly besieged for the second and last time in 1683. After a ruinous war against the combined forces of Austrians, Venetians, Poles, and Russians, Sultan Mustafa II was forced to accept the Treaty of Karlowitz in 1699. Under this treaty, the first to be signed by Ottoman Turkey as a defeated power, most of Hungary was relinquished, along with cessions to Poland and the cession of Azov to Russia.

Several wars with Austria in the early eighteenth century further weakened the Ottomans, and war with Russia between 1768 and 1774 let to further defeat and the important Treaty of Küçük Kainarça in 1774. Under this treaty indemnities were exacted, further territories were lost to Russia, and free access to Turkish waters by Russian ships was granted. Russia also gained certain vaguely worded rights of protection over Eastern Orthodox Christians in the Ottoman Empire, and these clauses were thereafter utilized to justify Russian intervention in Ottoman affairs. By 1787 Russia and Austria evinced designs, not then accomplished, of dismembering Ottoman Rumelia. In the Treaty of Jassy in 1792, the Ottomans lost all their holdings in the Crimea and southern Russia. These reverses and the stress of frequent wars occasioned extensive civil unrest in Anatolia. The long-pampered Janissary corps, having lost its old discipline and military effectiveness, became instead a focus of political intrigue and factionalism and was heavily influenced by the Bektaşi dervish order.

The Ottoman Empire had for some centuries dealt with the states of Europe from a position of strength in the *gazi* spirit of the conquering Islamic offensive. By the end of the eighteenth century, however, it was clear that the military advantage had shifted to the West because of economic, technological, and organizational developments. Nevertheless, Ottomans, secure in the conviction of their own supremacy, had been slow to recognize the shift in power and the reasons for it.

Of the early Ottoman contacts with Europe, those with France were of particular importance. In 1525 the Ottomans had fought the Austrians as allies of France, and the long period of preeminent French interest in Turkey was initiated by a treaty of friendship between Suleyman I and Francis I of France in 1535. What began then as voluntary concessions from an empire at the height of its prowess evolved into the system known as the capitulations, which in later years was to become a major irritant in Ottoman-European relations.

The capitulations granted to certain European powers commercial and financial privileges that over a period of time were greatly extended. In addition, those residents of the empire who were under European protection were subject to European rather than Ottoman law. Although originally confined to foreign residents, rights under the capitulations were eventually extended to some non-Muslim citizens of the empire.

Capitulatory rights were extended to Great Britain in 1579, to Austria in 1615, to Holland in 1680, and to Sweden in 1737. The United States obtained similar rights in 1830 by treaty with the Ottoman government in which the latter undertook to accord the United States a status equal to that of the "most favored nation."

The events of the eighteenth century showed that the expansion of the Russian Empire had become the most serious external threat to the Ottomans. The dominant Russian interest was to secure yearlong access to the sea, that is, warm water ports. Control of the Bosporus Strait, and therefore access to the Mediterranean, remained in Ottoman hands. Russian actions against the Turks were not always successful but increasingly became so as the Russian pressure was maintained. Other European nations in the seventeenth and early eighteenth centuries actively or inactively supported Russian expansion at the expense of the Ottoman Empire. By the nineteenth century, however, some interests had shifted to limiting the growth of Russian power by preserving the faltering Ottoman regime. Great Britain emerged increasingly as the advocate and protector of what remained of Ottoman territorial integrity.

One of the causes of the decline of the empire was the shift of military and technical superiority to the West; the gap was increased by the absence of any comparable developmental experience in the East. The only ideological-philosophical system the Ottomans accepted was Islam and, under the Ottomans, Islam became ossified and ultraconservative. The old administrative system, once fairly efficient, had decayed at all levels into stagnation and corruption. As in most Islamic states, the absence of fixed rules of succession to the throne within a dynastic family led to intense intrigue and factionalism. In the Ottoman realm the practice of fratricide had been legalized by ordinance as early as Mehmed II. Upon accession, some sultans extended this practice to include nephews, cousins, and other male relatives.

At the same time, it was desirable to ensure the Ottoman succession. Hence the system developed about 1603 of confining, or "caging," a chosen successor—the oldest son or other male relative—in complete luxury but under strict political surveillance, cut off from the world and any effective training for office. In this effete environment, harem politics and the influence of favorite concubines became a significant element of internal factionalism. By the chances of history, not all sultans were to grow up in this atmosphere of debilitating fantasy, but many did. Abdül Hamid I, for example, was isolated in this fashion for forty-three years and was mentally unbalanced when he at last came to the throne. The system was not conducive to strong sultanic leadership.

THE NINETEENTH CENTURY AND REFORM EFFORTS

During the nineteenth century the implications of the decline of Ottoman power, the vulnerability and attractiveness of its vast holdings, the stirrings of nationalism among the minorities of the empire, and the periodic crises resulting from these and other factors became collectively known to European diplomatists as "the Eastern question." In 1833 Czar Nicholas I of Russia described the Ottoman Empire as "the sick man of Europe." Austria and Russia were rivals for control in the Balkans, at Ottoman expense. France sought to gain a position of predominant influence. Great Britain's objective was to prevent either Russian or French ascendancy in the Ottoman region, particularly any threat to British communications with India and the Eastern markets. The Eastern question was a major and vexing issue throughout the century and into the next because the empire had become a troublesome anachronism.

The "sick man," however, was not without a certain residual toughness that endured almost to the empire's demise. From about 1800 to 1839, and particularly during the reform period of 1839 to 1878, known as the *tanzimat* (reorganization), specific efforts at political, social, and economic modernization were made. A small class of political leaders and intellectuals emerged, known as the Young Ottomans, who were competent in European languages and schooled in European thought. These sought to redirect and reinvigorate imperial affairs. Several reforming or, at least, moderate sultans stimulated the effort. Although this effort left enduring influences, it finally foundered.

During the Napoleonic era, from 1796 to 1815, the Ottomans were pitted against their main European contact, the French. Napoleon seized and held Egypt from 1798 to 1801. In the latter year, combined British and Turkish military operations forced withdrawal of the last French forces, and the country was ostensibly returned to Ottoman sovereignty. A period of internal chaos ensued, until effective control was reestablished in 1805 by an Ottoman officer named Mohammed Ali. The sultan then designated Mohammed Ali as pasha of Egypt, and he began the dynastic line of semi-independent rulers of Egypt that lasted, first under Ottoman and then under British domination, until 1952.

The first primarily Ottoman crisis to bring about European intervention in the nineteenth century was the Greek War of Independence of 1821–29. Russia, France, and Great Britain supported the Greeks; a British and French fleet destroyed the Turkish-Egyptian fleet at the Battle of Navarino Bay in 1827, and Russian armies advanced into the Balkans to Adrianople. Greek independence was established by the Treaty of Adrianople in 1829 and the London Convention of 1832.

Mohammed Ali of Egypt had supported the sultan by quelling an uprising in Arabia in 1818 and later by substantial aid in the Greek war. Not having been rewarded for this assistance, in 1831 he invaded Syria with French backing and pursued the Ottoman forces deep into Anatolia. The sultan, in desperation, appealed to the Russians, who sent forces. Great Britain and France then intervened to mediate, and Mohammed Ali was constrained to withdraw to Syria; but the price the sultan paid for this support was the Treaty of Hunkar Iskelesi in 1833.

Under this controversial treaty, the Dardanelles Straits was to be closed by the sultan, on Russian demand, to naval vessels and troops of other powers. War with the Egyptian pasha was resumed in 1839, the Ottoman forces were again defeated, and Egypt seemed on the verge of seizing Anatolia. Great Britain once more intervened; France, having favored Mohammed Ali, abstained. Russia, to break the British-French entente, waived its rights under the Treaty of Hunkar Iskelesi and aligned itself with the British. By the London Convention of 1840, Mohammed Ali was forced out of Syria and compelled to abandon certain other claims, but he was made hereditary ruler of Egypt under nominal Ottoman sovereignty. In a further protocol of 1841 the sultan undertook to close the straits to warships of all powers. The sultan, in fact, had very little to say about any of this complex power play.

The empire was involved in two more major conflicts with Russia before the end of the nineteenth century. A French and Russian dispute concerning their respective rights in the traditional holy places of Palestine led to the Crimean War of 1854–56, a bloody and costly conflict in which Great Britain, France, Turkey, and Sardinia fought Russia. The prospect of Austrian entrance on the allied side caused Russia to concede, and the Crimean War was terminated by the Treaty of Paris of March 30, 1856. Under this treaty Russia abandoned its claim to protection of Christians in the Ottoman realm, renounced rights of intervention in the Balkans, and agreed to unrestricted navigation on the Danube under an international commission. The Bosporus and the Black Sea were opened to all commercial shipping but closed to naval ships except for minor Turkish and Russian coast guard vessels.

The Ottoman and Russian empires were again major combatants in the war of 1877–78. The Russian declaration was prompted by Turkish repression of nationalist agitation in the Balkans, principally in Bulgaria. After initial defeats the Russians, with extensive Romanian assistance, succeeded in forcing upon the sultan the Treaty of San Stefano in 1878. The European powers, particularly Great Britain, did not concur with the harsh terms imposed by this treaty, and it was revised at the 1878 Congress of Berlin, at which the powers attempted to formulate a final settlement of the Eastern question.

The treaty at the end of the Congress of Berlin gave Bulgaria independence but returned Thrace to Ottoman control. Serbia, Romania, and Montenegro were also made independent; Bosnia-Hercegovinia was placed under Austrian administration. Cyprus passed to British control, and Russia made some territorial gains in Bessarabia and at the eastern end of the Black Sea.

During this long period of intrigue, power politics, and war from 1800 to 1881, the European powers had not been so concerned with Russian designs, the Balkans, and the straits as to fail to notice the Ottoman weakness and vulnerability in its vast North African territories. Algeria had been invaded by France in 1830 and made a French possession. In 1881 France similarly invaded and seized Tunisia, forestalling Italian designs in that area. Egypt from 1882 onward was controlled by a British resident agent and consul general, although, as in Cyprus, Egypt was still nominally under Ottoman sovereignty through a peculiar legal fiction agreed to between Great Britain and the Sublime Porte.

Throughout this long period of external pressure and successive imperial disasters, mitigated only by survival as a buffer in European politics, the Ottoman government had simultaneously been engaged in a sequence of efforts aimed at internal reform and reorganization. These attempts began piecemeal about the start of the nineteenth century, initially in the interest of military improvement.

Selim III (1789–1807) is recognized as the first sultan to undertake serious efforts at modernization and reform. He endeavored to reorganize the military forces, to reimpose discipline on the Janissary corps, and to initiate reforms in the bureaucracy and provincial government. He was opposed at every turn by the Janissaries, by the Bektaşi dervish order, and by corrupt officials. The Janissary leadership forced Selim III to abdicate and later murdered him. He was succeeded by his nephew, Mustafa IV, who canceled every progressive measure directed by Selim III but was himself dethroned by forces favoring reform. Mustafa's brother, Mahmud II (1808–39), was then installed on the throne.

Mahmud II has been called the greatest of the reform-minded sultans. The emphasis he gave to education and the study of European languages, always with the primary objective of military improvements, allowed the

Sultan Selim III tried to overthrow the powerful Janissaries, but the attempt failed and he was deposed and assassinated in 1808. He was in reign from 1789 to 1807.

Mahmud II became the next full-time sultan after the death of Selim III. He served from 1808 to 1839. There was an interim when Mahmud II's brother, Mustafa IV, served as sultan of Turkey for a few months before being assassinated.

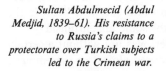

Sultan Abdulmecid (Abdul Medjid, 1839–61). His resistance to Russia's claims to a protectorate over Turkish subjects led to the Crimean war.

Sultan Abdul Aziz acceded to the throne in 1861 and during his reign (until 1876) the conditions of the country grew worse. Turkey had to declare national bankruptcy. On May 30, 1876, the sultan was discovered dead in his royal apartments and it was declared officially that he was a "suicide," but in later years documents were unearthed that show he was assassinated.

The last visit of Abdulaziz to the mosque at Baddsch in 1876

When Abdulaziz was deposed on May 29, 1876, his place was taken by Murad V, who reigned for only three months before he was declared insane and deposed in August.

The sultan Abdul Hamid II (1876–1909). The sultan was the brother of Murad V and he succeeded to the throne in 1876. In the following year he gave Turkey its first Parliament, which was soon after withdrawn. But because it was so sound a change with the times, it was restored in 1908.

Sultan Abdul Hamid II opening Turkey's first Parliament in 1877

growth of a small, but increasing number of administrators, scholars, and diplomats educated in, and acquainted with, Europe. Most notably, however, Mahmud destroyed and disestablished the Janissary corps when it revolted again in 1826, and he outlawed the Bektaşi dervishes.

Mahmud's successor, Abdulmecid I (1839–61), inaugurated the *tanzimat* period of 1839 to 1878 with the Hatt-i Serif of Gulhane (Royal Edict of the Rose Chamber). This document, which reflected the influence of Mustafa Resid Pasa, one of the ablest and most enlightened of the reform ministers, promised further reforms, an end to corruption and the equality of non-Muslim and Muslim subjects. Some legal and organizational changes were implemented, but the momentum of change died out in confrontation with conservative inertia.

Abdulmecid's inept and weak successor, Abdul-Aziz, who was the first sultan to travel abroad, brought the Ottoman Empire to the verge of bankruptcy. During his reign, however, a group of liberals known as the Young Ottomans emerged among the intellectuals of the empire. Abdul-Aziz was deposed in 1876. Murad V, next in line, was deposed three months later because of insanity. His successor, during a thirty-three-year reign of absolutist paranoia, was to acquire the unenviable nicknames of the Red Sultan and Abdül Hamid the Damned.

Abdul Hamid II (1876–1909) came to the throne with the approval of the liberal reformers of the empire, including the influential Midhat Pasa, the father of the first constitution. On December 23, 1876, Abdul Hamid accepted and promulgated a constitution modeled on French and Belgian lines as drafted by a number of senior political, military, and religious officials. This constitution, in addition to establishing a representative parliament, guaranteed religious liberty and freedom of thought within the law. Islam was recognized, however, as the state religion, the sultan for the first time was officially designated as caliph, and all citizens of the empire were to be known as Ottomans.

Abdul Hamid soon showed that his acceptance of constitutionalism was a temporary tactical expedient, as he began the assertion and centralization of his own authority. On February 5, 1877, Midhat Pasa was dismissed; he was exiled and later murdered. The sultan called the empire's first Parliament in 1877 but, encouraged by an Ottoman victory over the Russians at Plevna in December 1877, he dissolved the parliament in February 1878. The *tanzimat* was ended.

Abdul Hamid acquired a reputation for despotism throughout Europe. The European powers particularly disliked his methods of dealing with nationalist currents among the empire's Christian minorities. The brutal suppression of this kind of movement among the Armenians in 1894 and 1895, although overshadowed by the far more extensive massacres of twenty years later, took about one hundred thousand lives and aroused horror

The sultan's palace on the Bosphorus as it appeared at the turn of the twentieth century

throughout Europe. Abdul Hamid tended to be suspicious of those around him; he lived in seclusion under heavy security in the royal palace, where he mixed his own medical potions and pulled his own teeth.

During the reign of Abdul Hamid II, German influence greatly increased. Germany had emerged unified and victorious from the Franco-Prussian War of 1870, and the sultan saw imperial Germany as a more congenial alternative to the previous British and French influence. The Germans were interested in railroad construction, especially a Berlin-to-Baghdad line, and won a ninety-nine-year concession from the sultan in 1902. This project exacerbated Anglo-German relations. The visit of Kaiser Wilhelm II in 1898 dramatized German interest in the Ottoman realm, especially the kaiser's declaration that Germany would be its protector.

Abdül Hamid sought to revive the ideology of pan-Islam throughout the empire and the Muslim world. Jamal al-Din al-Afghani, the advocate of a revived Islam in which Western technology would be absorbed without accepting Western philosophy and "moral corruption," was welcomed from time to time at the capital. This pan-Islam policy further alarmed and alienated the minorities of the empire and developed no real strength.

THE YOUNG TURKS AND WORLD WAR I

The repressive policies of Abdul Hamid fostered disaffection, especially among those educated in Europe or in the westernized schools. Small groups of conspirators developed as successors to the Young Ottomans of several decades earlier. The first was the Committee of Union and Progress, founded in 1889 by students at the Turkish Military Academy. A number of its members eventually fled to France, where they joined other Turks in conspiracies against Abdul Hamid.

Similar groups of officers and students sprang up, largely outside Constantinople, where the sultan's spy network was most efficient. Mustafa Kemal organized a secret *vatan* (fatherland) society among officers in Damascus and thereafter a second in Salonika. The *vatan* society merged with another Salonika group, the Ottoman Society of Liberty. A further merger took place in September 1907 when the enlarged Salonika group joined with a Paris organization to form the secret Ottoman Committee of Union and Progress. This group, which became known as the Young Turks, sought the restoration of the 1876 Constitution, other liberalizing steps, and unification of the diverse elements of the empire into a homogeneous nation.

In July 1908 parts of the army revolted and demanded the restoration of the constitution. Abdul Hamid, outwardly appearing to yield, announced the restoration on July 24 and ordered the abolition of press censorship, the termination of the intense internal security surveillance, and the release of political prisoners. A wave of enthusiasm swept the empire, accompanied by demonstrations of solidarity between Turks and minority groups, and the Ottoman Committee of Union and Progress then engaged openly in its activities. Reactionary forces in the capital, encouraged by the sultan, then staged a counterrevolution on April 13, 1909. Abdul Hamid immediately pardoned the leaders of the counterrevolution and formed a new cabinet. The Young Turk leadership reacted by dispatching forces from Salonika, which retook the capital and liberated parliament. The legitimizing *fetva* was secured from the *şeyhülislam,* and the Young Turks deposed Abdul Hamid. His aged and compliant brother was enthroned as Mehmed V (1909–18). Abdul Hamid himself was thereafter kept under close confinement and died at the Beylerbey palace on the Bosporus in 1918.

The Young Turk government was subject to a number of serious external and internal threats, finally culminating in World War I. Austria had annexed Bosnia-Hercegovinia immediately after the 1908 revolution, and Bulgaria had secured complete independence. Both actions were accepted by Turkey on the basis of reparations paid or credited by Austria and Russia. Soon afterward the Italian government of the time, having already penetrated Libya commercially, evinced designs of colonial annexation. On the pretext that Turkish operations and influence in the Balkans were hostile to Italy, the Italian government declared war on September 29, 1911, and, after a naval bombardment, landed troops on the Libyan coast at Tripoli on October 3. The Italo-Turkish War was ended by a treaty on October 18, 1912, in which Italy gained paramount interest in Libya, the annexation being later confirmed in the post-World War I settlements.

Mehmed V was the last sultan of any consequence, and he ruled from 1909 to 1918, but under the tight control of the Young Turk revolutionists.

Pressure from the Balkans and not defeat in Libya had forced the Turkish concession. The Christian states of the Balkans, aided and abetted by both Russia and Italy, wished to prevent the Young Turk revolution from succeeding to the point where a rejuvenated Ottoman Empire might regain its old position west of the Bosporus. In March 1912 Greece, Serbia, and Bulgaria formed a secret alliance and on October 17, 1912, the alliance declared war and attacked. Turkish forces were defeated, and in the settlements of December 3, 1912, and May 30, 1913, the empire lost all of its European holdings, including Thrace. Albania had successfully proclaimed its independence on November 12. These disasters led to internal political change. A faction called the Liberal Union had formed a government in July 1912. This regime was overthrown in January 1913 in a coup engineered by Enver Bey, thereafter Enver Pasa, and the most authoritarian elements of the Young Turk movement gained full control

The Balkan allies fell to fighting among themselves in the Second Balkan War, commencing on June 29, 1913. Taking advantage of this situation, Turkish forces scored a number of tactical victories, and in a new series of settlements between August 10, 1913, and March 14, 1914, regained Thrace and reestablished the western boundary at the Maritsa River, where it was ultimately to remain.

The assassination of Archduke Francis Ferdinand of Austria on June 28, 1914, proved to be the spark, relatively unimportant in itself, that set off World War I. Between August 1 and August 4 war was declared, and operations commenced between the Allied powers of France, Russia, and Great Britain on the one side and the Central Powers of Germany and Austria-Hungary on the other. Ottoman Turkey remained officially neutral for about three months. On August 3, however, general mobilization of the armed forces was ordered; on the previous day Enver had concluded a secret treaty of alliance with Germany.

Despite the debilitated state of the Ottoman Empire, its contribution to the cause of the Central Powers during the next four years of war was enormous. Turkish troops fought well, the government did not collapse, and the Ottoman effort outlasted that of imperial Russia by

a year. The Turkish forces were expanded to fifty-two divisions, or about eight hundred thousand men and, fighting on far-distant fronts, tied up at least 1 million Allied troops for most of the war.

During the 1914–1915 winter, against the advice of German general Otto Liman von Sanders, Enver undertook an unsuccessful campaign against Russia in the Caucasus. During this campaign some assistance was given to the Russians by Armenians of eastern Anatolia.

A combined British and French naval assault, commencing on March 18, 1915, to force the Dardanelles was inconclusive, and British troops were landed on April 26 on the Gallipoli Peninsula. In the campaign that ensued, Turkish forces were initially under Liman von Sanders. Toward the end, command passed to Colonel Mustafa Kemal, who directed five divisions in containing and driving the invasion forces back to the beaches, from which they were then withdrawn commencing on December 19, 1915. Constantinople was thus secured for the rest of the war. This great success heartened the Turkish spirit, and Mustafa Kemal, the successful Turkish commander, became known as pasha.

To the south the Ottoman army in Iraq defeated and took the surrender on April 26, 1916, of a British-Indian invasion force. The British mounted a new invasion, however, and in March 1917 took Baghdad and drove the Ottoman forces out of Mesopotamia. In eastern Anatolia, Russian armies won a series of battles that carried their control west to Erzincan by July 1916. Mustafa Kemal was then given command of the eastern front and took up a successful counteroffensive that checked the Russian advance and began rolling it back. By the end of 1917 Turkish forces had retaken most of eastern Anatolia. The revolution of November 7, 1917, in Russia took that country out of the war. Its new government concluded the Treaty of Brest-Litovsk on March 3, 1918, under which Turkey regained its eastern provinces.

Sharif Husayn bin Ali, the sultan's appointed prince of Mecca and the Hejaz region of western Arabia, had launched the Arab revolt on June 5, 1916, supported by British supplies and naval forces as well as British advisers with the Arab forces. Of these advisers, T. E. Lawrence was to become best known. Aqaba was taken, and in October 1917 the British launched an offensive across Sinai into Palestine. Jerusalem was taken on December 9, 1917. Arab and British forces, after hard fighting against the Turkish Fourth Army, entered Damascus on October 1, 1918. Late in the campaign, Mustafa Kemal had succeeded Liman von Sanders in command of Turkish forces in Syria and withdrew them successfully northward through the Taurus Mountains and back into Turkey.

Turkish resistance was now exhausted. Early in October 1918 the central figures of the Young Turk leadership—Enver, Talat, and Cemal—fled to Germany. Sultan Mehmed V died in July 1918 and was succeeded by Mehmed VI. The new sultan and the remaining government apparatus were compelled to sue for peace, and Ottoman representatives signed the Allied-directed armistice at Mudros on October 30, 1918.

STRUGGLE FOR THE NEW TURKISH STATE

The future of Turkey was dark when the Turks signed the armistice at Mudros. None of the victorious powers was interested in the Ottoman Empire except to dismember it. Bolshevik Russia was, in its own interest, opposed to the western European plans for postwar settlement with the remnant Ottoman state but was unable to prevent them. British, French, and Italian troops occupied Istanbul, as Constantinople was now known to all Turks. The compliant sultan dismissed nationalist-minded ministers and formed a government with ministers willing to implement Allied demands without question.

A number of secret inter-Allied agreements concluded during World War I so divided the Ottoman Empire that Turkey would have been reduced to northern Anatolia. Other arrangements, such as the Sykes-Picot agreement of May 16, 1916, between Great Britain and France, concerned the disposition of the Arab provinces of the empire, in which were included the present-day states of Iraq, Syria, Lebanon, Jordan, and Israel. The British had promised Izmir (Smyrna) to the Greeks in the negotiations that preceded the Greek entry into the war in July 1917.

On March 29, 1919, Italian troops had landed in their intended area of occupation, and Greece soon gained the authorization of the Supreme Allied War Council to land troops at Izmir. These landings, commencing on May 15, 1919, were followed by further advances to the northeast with the apparent intent of annexing large areas. The Greek landing was an important factor in stimulating Turkish national resistance. Turkish public opinion, after the sufferings of war, did not react intensely against the loss of the external provinces, but the invasion of the homeland itself aroused fierce resentment.

The Allied victory terms were worked out by the interested parties at San Remo in April 1920. These terms were embodied in the Treaty of Sèvres, which, as presented to the Ottoman government in June 1920, was an extremely severe document. Turkey was reduced to northern Anatolia and Constantinople, the sultan was placed under European protective custody, the straits were placed under a European commission (without a Turkish member), the remainder of European Turkey was given to Greece, an autonomous Kurdish state and an independent Armenia were created, and the empire was demilitarized. Italy and France had zones in southern Turkey. The Arab Kingdom of Hejaz became inde-

pendent, but control of the other Arab provinces was divided among Great Britain, France, and Italy; all Turkish external claims were annulled. The sultan's representatives signed the treaty on August 10, 1920, thereby further discrediting the Ottoman government. Although the external dispositions finally took place generally as stated in this treaty, the Treaty of Sèvres, as such, was never enforced, for events in Anatolia rendered it unworkable.

While the diplomats bargained, a Turkish nationalist movement was organized, and the war for independence was launched, with Mustafa Kemal as leader. Kemal had been sent by the Ottoman government to central Anatolia as inspector general—ostensibly to supervise the demobilization of Turkish forces and the disposition of supplies but, more particularly, to get him out of the capital. Upon his arrival at Samsun on May 19, 1919, he proceeded to rally men to the nationalist cause. Support grew in all sectors of the population as a result of the foreign invasion. Resistance gradually moved from guerrilla warfare to the full-fledged military campaigns of 1920, 1921, and 1922.

Negotiations continued between the nationalists and the Ottoman government but without avail. Kemal resigned from the army when relieved of his duties; communication between the capital and Anatolia was later cut. The naming of a chief minister sympathetic to the nationalist cause, Ali Reza Pasa, had brought a brief improvement, and a parliament, which met in January 1920, approved the National Pact. Such developments brought about reinforced Allied occupation of the capital and the seizure of public buildings on March 16. Numerous national leaders were sent to Malta for detention. Reza fell from power, and Parliament was dismissed on April 11. That same day the *şeyhülislam* issued a *fetva* that proclaimed that the killing of nationalist rebels was a religious duty; on May 11 Kemal and other nationalist leaders were sentenced to death in absentia.

The actions of the Ottoman government brought quick response from the nationalists. Parliament was summoned to Ankara, and that city became the nationalist headquarters. On April 24, 1920, the nationalists established the Turkish Grand National Assembly; Mustafa Kemal was elected president of this body. Numerous religious leaders in Anatolia asserted that the *fetva* of the *şeyhülislam* was invalid because it had been issued under duress. The Law of Fundamental Organization (also known as the Organic Law) was passed on January 20, 1921, proclaiming that sovereignty belonged to the nation and was exercised for it by the Grand National Assembly.

The nationalist military campaign of 1920 against the Greek invaders had been at best a draw, but the nationalist cause was then strengthened by a series of military victories in 1921. İsmet Pasa (who was later to take his name from the battles) defeated the Greeks twice at Inonu, about twenty miles west of Eskişehir, once in January and later in April. The Turkish army, under the personal leadership of Kemal with İsmet as second in command, decisively defeated the Greeks at the twenty-day battle of the Sakarya River starting on August 24, 1921. Kemal was thereafter awarded the title of *gazi* by the Grand National Assembly.

An improvement of Turkey's diplomatic situation accompanied these decisive military victories. Treaties granting Turkish claims in the east and setting the boundary essentially as it remained in 1973 were signed on March 16 and October 13, 1921, with the Soviet Union, the first European power to recognize the nationalists. Turkish forces in eastern Anatolia by midsummer had disestablished the nascent Armenian republic. Impressed by the viability of the nationalist government, both France and Italy withdrew from southern Turkey by the end of October 1921.

The final drive against the Greeks began in August 1922; the last battle, referred to in Turkish sources as the Battle of the Commander in Chief, was launched on August 30. The Greek forces were again defeated and forced to evacuate, and on September 9 the Turks moved into Izmir. The Turkish army then turned its attention to Thrace, where the British barred the way. After careful negotiation, the Armistice of Mundanya on October 11, 1922, averted a clash with the British and returned to the Turks control of Thrace as far as the historic line of the Maritsa River.

At the end of October 1922 the Allies invited both the Ankara and the Istanbul governments to a conference at Lausanne, but Kemal was determined that the nationalist government should be the only spokesman for Turkey. The action of the Allies prompted a resolution by the Grand National Assembly on November 1, 1922, that separated the offices of sultan and caliph and abolished the former. The assembly further stated on November 4, 1922, that the Istanbul government had ceased to be the government of Turkey when the Allies seized

the capital on March 16, 1920. The essence of the latter statement was the abolition of the Ottoman Empire. Sultan Mehmed VI, evacuated by a British naval vessel on November 17, 1922, fled to exile on Malta. His cousin, Abdülmecid, was named caliph.

Turkey was the only power defeated in World War I to negotiate with the Allies as an equal and to influence the provisions of the peace treaty. İsmet was the chief Turkish negotiator at the Lausanne Conference that opened on November 21, 1922. The National Pact of 1919 was the basis of the Turkish negotiating position; its provisions were, in fact, recognized in the treaty concluded by Turkey on July 24, 1923, with Great Britain, France, Italy, Japan, Greece, Romania, and Yugoslavia. The United States participated in the conference but, because it had never been at war with Turkey, did not sign the treaty.

The Treaty of Lausanne recognized the present-day territory of Turkey with two exceptions: the Mosul area and the Hatay district, sometimes referred to as the *sanjak* of Alexandretta, which included the port of İskenderun, or Alexandretta. The Mosul boundary with Iraq was settled by a League of Nations initiative in 1926, and İskenderun was added to Turkey on July 23, 1939, by disposition of France in its capacity as League of Nations mandatory power for Syria. Detailed provisions regulated the Bosporus and the Dardanelles straits, which were to be open to merchant vessels at all times. In peacetime, or if Turkey should be neutral in war, warships could pass the straits within certain limitations. If Turkey were at war, it could close the straits to all but neutral warships. General supervisory powers were given to the Straits Commission under the League of Nations. Represented on the commission were Turkey as president and the other signatories of the treaty plus the Soviet Union and Bulgaria. The straits area was to be demilitarized.

The capitulations and the Council of Administration of the Ottoman Public Debt, which infringed upon the sovereignty of Turkey, were abolished. Turkey, however, assumed 40 percent of the Ottoman debt, the remainder being apportioned among other former Ottoman territories. The Treaty of Lausanne reaffirmed the equality of Muslim and non-Muslim Turkish nationals. In a separate treaty, concluded on January 30, 1923, Turkey and Greece agreed to a mandatory exchange of their respective Greek and Turkish minorities with the exception of some Greeks in Constantinople and Turks in western Thrace. Massive population exchanges were then carried out.

On October 13, 1923, the Grand National Assembly declared Ankara to be the capital of the country and on October 29 proclaimed the Republic of Turkey, with Mustafa Kemal as president. The Ottomans and the empire were gone, and the modern state of Turkey was born.

The president, Kemal Ataturk, who was the first leader to serve in place of the sultanate in 1923, served until 1938.

A 1957 stamp commemorating the 400th anniversary of the opening of the Mosque of Suleyman I in Istanbul (Constantinople)

THE ROYAL SOVEREIGNS OF THE BYZANTINE

AND OTTOMAN EMPIRES, AND THE SULTANATES OF TURKEY

Reign	Title	Ruler	Birth	Death	Relationship
		BYZANTINE EMPIRE			
		THEODOSIAN DYNASTY			
379–395	Emperor (East) (West, 394)	Theodosius I (the Great)	346?	395	Father of Arcadius
395–408	Emperor	Arcadius	378	408	Son of Theodosius I
408–450	Emperor	Theodosius II	401	450	Son of Arcadius
		THRACIAN DYNASTY			
450–457	Emperor	Marcianus	392	457	Brother-in-law of Theodosius II
457–474	Emperor	Leo I the Great	401	474	
474–474	Emperor	Leo II		474	Grandson of Leo I
474–491	Emperor	Zeno	426	491	Father of Leo II
491–518	Emperor	Anastasius I	430	518	Son-in-law of Leo II
		JUSTINIAN DYNASTY			
518–527	Emperor	Justin I	450	527	
527–565	Emperor	Justinian I	483	565	Nephew of Justin I
565–578	Emperor	Justin II		578	Nephew of Justinian I
578–582	Emperor	Tiberius II Constantinus		582	
582–602	Emperor	Maurice	540	602	Son-in-law of Tiberius II
602–610	Emperor	Phocas		610	
		HERACLIAN DYNASTY			
610–641	Emperor	Heraclius	575	641	
641–641	Emperor	Constantine III	612	641	Son of Heraclius
641– ?	Coregent	Heracleonas	614		Son of Heraclius
641–668	Emperor	Constans II	630	668	Son of Constantine III
668–685	Emperor	Constantine IV	648	685	Son of Constans II
685–695	Emperor	Justinian II	669	711	Son of Constantine IV
695–698	Emperor	Leontius		705	
698–705	Emperor	Tiberius III Apsimar		705	
705–711	Emperor	Justinian II (rethroned)			
711–713	Emperor	Philippicus			
713–716	Emperor	Anastasius II		721	
716–717	Emperor	Theodosius III		718	
		ISAURIAN DYNASTY			
717–741	Emperor	Leo III, the Isaurian	680	741	
741–775	Emperor	Constantine V	718	775	Son of Leo III
775–780	Emperor	Leo IV	750	780	Son of Constantine V
780–790	Empress (Regent)	Irene, wife of Leo IV	752	803	
780–797	Emperor	Constantine VI	770	797	Son of Irene
797–802	Empress	Irene	752	803	
802–811	Emperor	Nicephorus I		811	
811–811	Emperor	Stauracius		811	
811–813	Emperor	Michael I		845	Son-in-law of Nicephorus I
813–820	Emperor	Leo V, the Armenian		820	
		AMORIAN DYNASTY			
820–829	Emperor	Michael II		829	
829–842	Emperor	Theophilus		842	Son of Michael II
842–857	Empress (Regent)	Theodora		867	Mother of Michael III
842–867	Emperor	Michael III		867	Son of Theophilus
		MACEDONIAN DYNASTY			
867–886	Emperor	Basil I the Macedonian	813	886	
886–912	Emperor	Leo VI	866	912	Son of Michael III
913–919	Emperor	Constantine VII	905	959	Son of Leo VI
919–944	Emperor (Regent)	Romanus I		948	Stepfather of Constantine VII
944–959	Emperor	Constantine VII			
959–963	Emperor	Romanus II	939	963	Son of Constantine VII
963–969	Emperor	Nicephorus II	912	969	
969–976	Emperor	John I Zimisces	929	976	
976–1025	Emperor	Basil II	958	1025	Son of Romanus II

Reign	Title	Ruler	Birth	Death	Relationship
1025–1028	Emperor	Constantine VIII	960	1028	Son of Romanus II
1041–1042	Emperor	Michael V			Nephew of Michael IV
1042–1055	Emperor	Constantine IX	1000	1055	Son-in-law of Constantine VIII
1055–1056	Empress	Theodora	980	1056	Daughter of Constantine VIII
1056–1057	Emperor	Michael VI			
1057–1059	Emperor	Isaac I Comnenus		1061	

DUCAS DYNASTY

Reign	Title	Ruler	Birth	Death	Relationship
1059–1067	Emperor	Constantine X Ducas	1007	1067	
1067–1071	Emperor	Romanus IV		1071	
1071–1078	Emperor	Michael VII			Son of Constantine X
1078–1081	Emperor	Nicephorus III Botaniates		1081	

COMNENUS DYNASTY

Reign	Title	Ruler	Birth	Death	Relationship
1081–1118	Emperor	Alexius I Comnenus	1048	1118	Nephew of Isaac I
1118–1143	Emperor	John II Comnenus	1088	1143	Son of Alexius I Comnenus
1143–1180	Emperor	Manuel I Comnenus	1120	1180	Son of John II Comnenus
1180–1183	Emperor	Alexius II	1168	1183	Son of Manuel I Comnenus
1183–1185	Emperor	Andronicus I	1110	1185	Grandson of Alexius I Comnenus

ANGELUS DYNASTY

Reign	Title	Ruler	Birth	Death	Relationship
1185–1195	Emperor	Isaac II Angelus		1204	
1195–1203	Emperor	Alexius III		1210	Brother of Isaac II Angelus
1203–1204	Emperor	Alexius IV		1204	Son of Isaac II Angelus
1204–1204	Emperor	Alexius V		1204	

LATIN EMPERORS

Reign	Title	Ruler	Birth	Death	Relationship
1204–1205	Emperor	Baldwin I	1171	1205	Son of Baldwin V, count of Hainaut
1205–1216	Emperor	Henry	1174	1216	Brother of Baldwin I
1216–1217	Emperor	Peter		1217	Brother-in-law of Baldwin I
1217–1219	Empress (Regent)	Yolande		1220	Wife of Peter
1219–1228	Emperor	Robert		1228	Son of Peter
1228–1261	Emperor	Baldwin II	1217	1273	Brother of Robert

LASCARIS DYNASTY

Reign	Title	Ruler	Birth	Death	Relationship
1206–1222	Emperor	Theodore I Lascaris		1222	Son-in-law of Alexius III
1222–1254	Emperor	John III Ducas	1193	1254	Son-in-law of Theodore I Lascaris
1254–1258	Emperor	Theodore II Lascaris	1221	1258	Son of John III Ducas
1258–1261	Emperor	John IV Lascaris	1250	1269	Son of Theodore II Lascaris
1259–1261	Regent	Michael Palaeologus	1234	1282	

PALAEOLOGUS DYNASTY

Reign	Title	Ruler	Birth	Death	Relationship
1261–1282	Emperor	Michael VIII Palaeologus			
1282–1328	Emperor	Andronicus II	1260	1332	Son of Michael VIII Palaeologus
1328–1341	Emperor	Andronicus III	1296	1341	Grandson of Andronicus II
1341–1347	Emperor	John V Palaeologus	1332	1391	Son of Andronicus III
1347–1355	Emperor	John VI Cantacuzene	1292	1383	
1376–1379	Emperor (Rival)	Andronicus IV		1385	Son of John V Palaeologus
1379–1391	Emperor	John V			
1391–1425	Emperor	Manuel II Palaeologus	1350	1425	Son of John V Palaeologus
1391–1412	Emperor (Coregent)	John VII	1360	1412	Son of Andronicus IV
1425–1448	Emperor	John VIII	1390	1448	Son of Manuel II Palaeologus
1448–1453	Emperor	Constantine XI	1403	1453	Son of Manuel II Palaeologus

1453—The Eastern Roman Empire ends with the capture of Constantinople by the Turks

OTTOMAN EMPIRE

Reign	Title	Ruler	Birth	Death	Relationship
1288–1324	Emir	Osman I (Ottoman)	1259	1324	
1324–1360	Sultan	Orhan (Orkhan)	1279	1360	
1360–1389	Sultan	Murat I (Murad) (Amurath)	1319	1389	

Reign	Title	Ruler	Birth	Death
1389–1402	Sultan	Bayezit I (Lightning) (Bajazet)	1347	1402
1402–1413	Interregnum	Bayezit's sons Suleman and Musa fought for the sultanate.		
1413–1421	Sultan	Mehmet I (Mohammed I)	1387	1421
1421–1444	Sultan	Murat II (Murad II)	1404	1451
1444–1446	Sultan	Mehmet II (Mohammed)	1430	1481
1446–1451	Sultan	Murat II (Murad II)	1404	1451
1451–1481	Sultan	Mehmet II (Mohammed)	1430	1481
1481–1512	Sultan	Bayezit II (Bajazet)	1447	1513
1512–1520	Sultan	Selim I (The Grim)	1467	1520
1520–1566	Sultan	Süleyman I (Suleiman)	1497	1566
1566–1574	Sultan	Selim II	1524	1574
1574–1595	Sultan	Murat III (Murad)	1546	1595
1595–1603	Sultan	Mehmet III (Mohammed)	1566	1603
1603–1617	Sultan	Ahmet I (Ahmed) (Achmet)	1589	1617
1617–1618	Sultan	Mustafa I (Mustapha)	1591	1630
1618–1622	Sultan	Osman II (Young Osman)	1604	1622
1622–1623	Sultan	Mustafa I	1591	1630
1623–1640	Sultan	Murat IV (Murad)	1609	1640
1640–1648	Sultan	Ibrahim I	1615	1648
1648–1687	Sultan	Mehmet IV (Mohammed)	1636	1687
1687–1691	Sultan	Süleyman II (Suleiman)	1641	1691
1691–1695	Sultan	Ahmet II (Ahmed)	1642	1695
1695–1703	Sultan	Mustafa II	1664	1704
1703–1730	Sultan	Ahmet III (Ahmed)	1673	1736
1730–1754	Sultan	Mahmut I (Mahmud)	1696	1754
1754–1757	Sultan	Osman III	1697	1757
1757–1774	Sultan	Mustafa III	1717	1774
1774–1789	Sultan	Abdülhamit I (Abdul-Hamid I)	1725	1780
1789–1807	Sultan	Selim III	1761	1808
1807–1808	Sultan	Mustafa IV	1779	1808
1808–1839	Sultan	Mahmut II (Malmud)	1785	1839
1839–1861	Sultan	Abdülmecit I (Abdul-Medjid)	1823	1861
1861–1876	Sultan	Abdülaziz (Abdul-Aziz)	1830	1876
1876–1876	Sultan	Murat V	1840	1904
1876–1909	Sultan	Abdülhamit II (Abdul-Hamid)	1842	1918
1909–1918	Sultan	Mehmet V (Mohammed)	1844	1918
1918–1922	Sultan	Mehmet VI (Mohammed)	1861	1936

1922 Ottoman Sultanate abolished
1923 Republic of Turkey established

SELJUK EMPIRE

(The Seljuk Empire included what is now Turkey, Iran, Iraq, and Syria)

1037–1063	Grand Sultan	Tughrul Beg
1063–1073	Grand Sultan	Alp Arslan
1073–1092	Grand Sultan	Malik Shah
1092–1104	Grand Sultan	Barkiarok
1104–1116	Grand Sultan	Mohammed
1116–1157	Grand Sultan	Sandjar

1157–1092—Divided into four separate states

SULTANS OF RUM (ROME)

1092–1106	Sultan	Kilidy Arslan I
1107–1117	Sultan	Malik Shah
1117–1156	Sultan	Masoud I
1156–1193	Sultan	Kilidy Arslan II
1193–1211	Sultan	Khaikhosru II
1211–1222	Sultan	Azeddin Kaikus I
1222–1237	Sultan	Alaeddin Kaikobad
1247–1261	Sultan	Azeddin Kaikus II
1261–1267	Sultan	Kilidy Arslan III
1267–1276	Sultan	Kaikhosru III
1276–1283	Sultan	Masoud II
1283–1307	Sultan	Alladdin

Appendix

A

The Kingdom of Albania

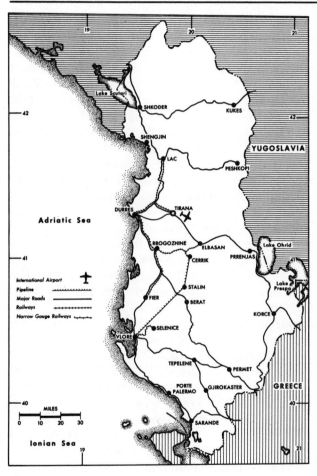

Albania

The modern Albanians call their country Shqiperia and themselves Shqipetare. In antiquity the Albanians were known as Illyrians, and in the Middle Ages they came to be called Arbereshe or Arbeneshe, and their country Arberia or Arbenia. The present European forms, Albania and Albanians, are derived from the names Arbanoi and Albanoi or Arbaniti, which appeared in the eleventh century.

In antiquity the Albanians formed part of the Thraco-Illyrian and Epirot tribes that inhabited the whole of the peninsula between the Danube River and the Aegean Sea. Until 168 B.C. the northern and central part of present-day Albania comprised parts of the kingdom of Illyria, whose capital was Shkoder. The Illyrian Kingdom was conquered by the Romans in 168–167 B.C., and thereafter it was a Roman colony until A.D. 395, when the Roman Empire was split into East and West, Albania becoming part of the Byzantine Empire.

Under the Roman Empire, Albania served as a key recruiting area for the Roman legions and a main outlet to the East. The present port of Durres (the ancient Durrachium) became the western terminum of Via Egnatia, an actual extension of Via Appia, by which the Roman legions marched to the East. It was during the Roman rule that Christianity was introduced into Albania.

From the fifth century to the advent of the Ottoman Turks in the Balkans in the fourteenth century, invasions from the north and east, especially by the Huns, the Bulgarians, and the Slavs, thinned the indigenous Illyrian population and drove it along the mountainous Adriatic coastal regions. During the Crusades in the twelfth and thirteenth centuries, Albania became a thoroughfare for the crusading armies, which used the port of Durres as a bridgehead. By this time the Venetian Republic had obtained commercial privileges in Albanian towns and, after the Fourth Crusade (1204), it received nominal control over Albania and Epirus and took actual possession of Durres and the surrounding areas. In the middle of the thirteenth century Albania fell under the domination of the kings of Naples, and in 1272 armies of Charles I of Anjou crossed the Adriatic and occupied Durres. Thereupon, Charles I issued a decree calling himself Rex Albaniae and creating Regnum Albaniae (the kingdom of Albania), which lasted for nearly a century.

In the period after the defeat of the Serbs by the Ottoman Turks in 1389 in the battle of Kosovo, most of Albania was divided into a number of principalities under the control of native tribal chieftains, most of whom were subsequently forced into submission by the invading Turks. Some of these chieftains, however, were allowed their independence under Turkish suzerainty. One of the most noted of these was John Kastrioti of Kruje, a region northeast of Tirana, whose four sons were taken hostage by the sultan to be trained in the Ottoman service. The youngest of these, Gjergj, was destined to win fame throughout Europe and to be immortalized as the national hero of his country. Gjergj (b. 1403) soon won the sultan's favor, distinguished himself in the Turkish army, converted to Islam, and was bestowed the title of Skander Bey (Lord Alexander), which, in Albanian, became Skanderbeg or Skenderbey.

In 1443 Hungarian King Hunyadi routed at Nish the sultan's armies, in which Skanderbeg held command; Skanderbeg fled to his native land and seized from the Turks his father's fortress at Kruje. His defection and reconversion to Christianity and the creation in 1444 of the League of Albanian Princes, with himself as its head, enraged the Ottomans, who began a series of intense campaigns that lasted until Skanderbeg's natural death in 1468. In his wars against the Turks, Skanderbeg was aided by the kings of Naples and the popes, one of whom, Pope Nicholas V, named him Champion of Christiandom.

Skanderbeg's death did not end Albania's resistance to the Turks; however, they gradually extended their conquests in Albania and in time defeated both the local chieftains and the Venetians, who controlled some of the coastal towns. The Turkish occupation of the country resulted in a great exodus of Albanians to southern Italy and Sicily, where they preserved their language, customs, and Eastern Orthodox religion.

One of the most significant consequences of Ottoman rule of Albania was the conversion to Islam of over two-thirds of the population. As the political and economic basis of the Ottoman Empire was not nationality but religion, this conversion created a new group of Muslim Albanian bureaucrats, who not only ruled Albanian provinces for the sultans but also served in important posts as *pashas* (governors) in many parts of the empire. A number of them became *viziers* (prime ministers), and one, Mohammed Ali Pasha, at the beginning of the nineteenth century founded an Egyptian Dynasty that lasted until the 1950s.

Some of the Albanian beys and pashas, especially in the lowlands, became almost independent rulers of their principalities. One of these, Ali Pasha Tepelena, known in history as the Lion of Yannina, whose principality at the beginning of the nineteenth century consisted of the whole area from the Gulf of Arta to Montenegro, by 1803 had assumed absolute power and negotiated directly with Napoleon and the rulers of Great Britain and

Russia. The sultan, however, becoming alarmed at the damage Ali Pasha was doing to the unity of the empire, sent his armies to surround him in Yannina, where he was captured and decapitated in 1822.

Under the Turks, Albania remained in complete stagnation and, when the Turks were expelled from the Balkans in 1912, they left it in about the same condition they had found it. The Albanian highlanders, especially in the north, were never fully subjected, and their tribal organizations were left intact. Turkish suzerainty affected them only to the extent that it isolated them from the world. Thus, they preserved their medieval laws, traditions, and customs. As a result, Western civilization and development did not begin to penetrate Albania in any meaningful way until it became independent in 1912.

In the summer and fall of 1912, while Serbia, Bulgaria, Montenegro, and Greece, prodded by Russia, were waging war against Turkey, the Albanians staged a series of revolts and began to agitate for the creation of an autonomous and neutral Albania. Accordingly, a group of Albanian patriots, led by Ismail Qemal bey Vlora, a member of the Turkish Parliament, proclaimed Albania's independence at Vlore on November 28, 1912, and organized an Albanian provisional government. Supported by Austria and Italy, Albania's independence was recognized on December 12, 1912, by the London Conference of Ambassadors, but its boundaries were to be determined later. In March 1913 agreement was reached on the northern frontiers, assigning Shkoder to Albania but giving Kosovo and Metohija (Kosmet), inhabited then chiefly by Albanians, to Serbia. This frontier demarcation was very similar to the frontiers between Yugoslavia and Albania as they existed in 1970.

The boundaries in the south were more difficult to delineate because Greece laid claim to most of southern Albania, which the Greeks call northern Epirus. The Conference of Ambassadors appointed a special commission to draw the demarcation line on ethnographic bases and in December 1913 drafted the Protocol of Florence, which assigned the region to Albania. The 1913 boundaries in the south, like those in the north, were almost the same as those that existed between Greece and Albania in 1970. The Albania that emerged from the Conference of Ambassadors was a truncated one; as many Albanians were left out of the new state as were included in it.

The Conference of Ambassadors also drafted a constitution for the new state, which was proclaimed as an autonomous principality, sovereign, and under the guarantees of the Great Powers; created an International Control Commission to control the country's administration and budget; and selected as ruler the German Prince William of Wied. Prince William arrived in March 1914 but had to flee the country six months later because of the outbreak of World War I and the difficulties caused by the unruly feudal beys. As a consequence, Albania's independence came to an end, and for the next four years the country served as a battleground for the warring powers.

At the end of World War I Albania was occupied by the Allied armies, mostly Italian and French. The Secret Treaty of London, concluded in 1915 and published by the Russian Bolsheviks after the October 1917 Revolution, provided for the partition of nearly all Albania among Italy, Serbia, Montenegro, and Greece. Another accord, known as the Tittoni-Venizelos Agreement, concluded between Italy and Greece in 1919, also called for the dismemberment of Albania. At the 1919–20 Paris Peace Conference Greece laid claim to southern Albania; Serbia and Montenegro, to the northern part; and Italy, to the port of Vlore and surrounding areas. But President Woodrow Wilson's principle of self-determination and his personal insistence on the restoration of an independent Albania saved the country from partition. In the summer of 1920 an Albanian partisan army drove the Italians from Vlore, and the Italian government recognized Albania's independence.

From 1920 to 1924 there was political freedom in the country along with extreme political strife. A group of statesmen and politicians, mostly from the old Turkish bureaucracy, attempted to lay the foundation of a modern state, but there was a bitter struggle between the old conservative landlords and Western educated or inspired liberals. The landowners, led by Ahmet Zogu, advocated the continuance of feudal tenure and opposed social and economic reforms, especially agrarian reforms. The liberals, led by Bishop Fan S. Noli, a Harvard University graduate who had founded the Albanian Autocephalous Orthodox Church in Boston in 1908 and had returned to Albania in 1920, favored the establishment of a Western-type democracy. The country was torn by political struggles and rapid changes of government revealed considerable political instability.

In June 1924 the liberals staged a successful coup against the conservative landlords, forcing their leader, Ahmet Zogu, to flee to Yugoslavia, and formed a new government under Bishop Noli. But Noli was too radical to command the support of the disparate coalition that had ousted Zogu. Internally he proposed radical agrarian reforms, the purging and reduction of the bureaucracy, and the establishment of a truly democratic regime. In foreign affairs he extended recognition to the Soviet Union, a move that alienated some of his supporters at home and alarmed some neighboring states. As a consequence, Zogu, having secured foreign support, led an army from Yugoslavia and in December 1924 entered the capital city of Tirana and became ruler of the country. Bishop Noli and his closest supporters fled abroad; some eventually went to Moscow, and others fell under Communist influence in western capitals.

Zogu's rule in the 1925–39 period, first as President

King Zog I

Zogu and after September 1, 1928, as Zog I, king of the Albanians, brought political stability and developed a national political consciousness that had been unprecedented in Albanian history. To secure his position both internally and externally, he concluded in 1926 and 1927 bilateral treaties with Italy, providing for mutual support in maintaining the territorial status quo and establishing a defensive alliance between the two countries. These two treaties, however, assured Italian penetration of Albania, particularly in the military and economic spheres.

King Zog ruled as a moderate dictator, his monarchy being a combination of despotism and reform. He prohibited political parties but was lenient to his opponents unless they actually threatened to overthrow his rule, as happened in 1932, 1935, and 1937. But even during these open revolts, he showed a good deal of leniency and executed only a few ringleaders. He effected some substantial reforms both in the administration and in society, particularly outlawing the traditional vendetta and carrying of arms, of which the Albanians were very fond. The most significant contribution of Zog's fourteen-year rule, the longest since the time of Skanderbeg, was the development of a truly national consciousness and an identity of the people with the state, although not necessarily with the monarchy, and the gradual breakdown of the traditional tribal and clan systems.

In April 1938 Zog married Geraldine Apponyi, a Hungarian countess with an American mother. Italian foreign minister Count Ciano was the best man. On Ciano's return to Italy from the wedding, he proposed to his father-in-law, Benito Mussolini, Fascist dictator of Italy, the annexation of Albania. The following year, on April 7, 1939, Ciano's suggestion was consummated. Italian forces invaded Albania on that day, forcing Zog to flee the country, never to return. In the next few months rapid steps were taken to unite Albania with Italy under the crown of King Vittorio Emanuele III and to impose a regime similar to that of Fascist Italy. Albania as an independent state disappeared.

B
The Principality of Andorra

The geographical location of Andorra between France and Spain

An agreement (the Paréage) between the count of Foix (French) and the bishop of Seo de Urgel (Spanish) in 1278 to recognize each other as co-princes of the Andorran valleys gave the small state what has been its political form and territorial extent continuously to the present day. Over the years, the title on the French side passed to the kings of Navarre, then to the kings of France, and is now held by the presidents of France.

Napoleon declared Andorra a republic in 1806, but today the country is referred to as a principality.

In its mountain fastness, Andorra has existed outside the mainstream of the major historical events of Europe.

Earlier Bishops of Urgel—coprinces.

Andorra, located high in the Pyrenees between France and Spain, is one of Europe's smallest nations.

Most of Andorra's rugged terrain consists of gorges, narrow valleys, and defiles, surrounded by high mountain peaks rising over nine thousand feet (2,743 m.) above sea level.

It is said that Charlemagne drove the Moors from the territory that is now Andorra in 806, and local legend maintains that he personally thanked the mountaineers for their assistance to his armies. The Andorran national anthem says, "The great Charlemagne, my father, has delivered me from the Arabs. . . ."

In recent times, however, its thriving tourist industry has propelled it into the twentieth century.

Vestiges of its long history remain in the form of a number of twelfth-century Romanesque churches. Most notable among these are the Chapel of Sant Miquel d'Engolasters, in Les Escaldes, and the church in Santa Coloma. The countryside is also dotted with Romanesque bridges.

The president of France and the bishop of Seo de Urgel (Spain), as co-princes, are charged with the conduct of foreign affairs, defense, and the judicial system. Andorra pays annual tribute of nine hundred sixty francs ($196) to France and four hundred sixty pesetas ($6) to Spain. The co-princes are represented in Andorra by *veguers* (designated representatives) and *battles* (magistrates).

No formal constitution has been written for the country, although administrative statutes were passed in 1748 and 1763. A Plan of Reform, passed in 1866, established the present governmental system, which has evolved into a ruling General Council of twenty-four members (four from each of the six parishes—Andorra, Canillo, Encamp, La Massana, Ordino, and Sant Julià). Members of the council serve four-year terms, and half of the council

French President Georges Pompidou was the coprince from 1969 to 1974.

is elected every two years by the Andorran citizens in each parish. Women were granted equal suffrage in April 1970.

PRINCIPAL GOVERNMENT OFFICIALS (AS OF MAY 1981)

Co-prince—François Mitterrand, president of France
Co-prince—Juan Marti Alanis, bishop of Seo de Urgel, Spain

C

The Royal Dynasties of Bohemia

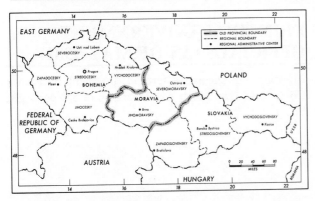

Czechoslovakia in its modern setting, but showing the territories of Bohemia, Moravia, and Slovakia

The Czechoslovakian Republic consists of Bohemia, Moravia and Silesia, Slovakia, and Ruthenia (Carpatho-Ukraine). In March 1939 a German protectorate was established over Bohemia and Moravia, as well as Slovakia, which had meanwhile declared its independence. Ruthenia was incorporated into Hungary. In 1945, after World War II, these territories were returned to Czechoslovakia, except for Ruthenia, which was ceded to Russia.

In its early history, the Slavs, dominated by the Cechove (Czechs) started to penetrate into Bohemia by the middle of the first century A.D. The East Slav leader, Mojmir I, began the consolidation of the Great Moravian Empire which, under Svatopluk (869–94), approximated what is now Czechoslovakia consisting of Saxony, southern Poland, and eastern Hungary (Pannonia). The empire was destroyed by the Magyars in 907. (Slovakia passed under Hungarian rule until 1918, when it became a part of Czechoslovakia.) The center of power in the area shifted to Bohemia when the Premyslid family united the tribes by the end of the tenth century.

In 1029 Moravia was attached to Bohemia, and Vratislav (Vaclav) II was made the first king in 1088. By the thirteenth century, under Ottakar II, the Premyslid Dynasty had taken control of most of Austria. Wences-

laus II was proclaimed king of Poland. In 1306, Wenceslaus III, king of Poland and Hungary, the only son of Wenceslaus II, was assassinated and the Premyslid Dynasty ended.

John of Luxemburg, who was married to Elizabeth (Eliska), the second daughter of Wenceslaus II, claimed the crown and this started the Luxemburg Dynasty, which lasted until 1526, when King Louis died while retreating from the Battle of Mohacs, August 29, 1526. The crown was then claimed by Archduke Ferdinand of Austria by virtue of the hereditary rights invested in his wife, Anne, King Louis's sister, and the Habsburg Dynasty ruled from then (1526) until 1918, when Bohemia became a part of Czechoslovakia.

King Svatopluk

King Vratislav I   *King Wenceslaus II*

THE ROYAL SOVEREIGNS OF THE DYNASTIES OF BOHEMIA

PREMYSLID DYNASTY

Reign	Title	Ruler	Birth	Death
871–894	Count	Borivoj I		
894–895	Count	Spithnjew I		
895–912	Duke	Spithnjew I		
912–926	Duke	Vratislav I		
926–928	Regent	Drahomire, von Stoder		
928–935	Duke	Wenceslaus (Wenzel, the Holy)		
935–967	Duke	Boleslaus I (Boleslav)		
967–999	Duke	Boleslaus II		
999–1003	Duke	Boleslaus III		
1003–1035	Duke	Vladivoj of Poland		
1035–1055	Duke	Bretislav I		
1055–1061	Duke	Spithnjew II		
1061–1092	Duke	Vratislav II (king, 1088)		
1092–1100	Duke	Bretislav II		
1100–1107	Duke	Borivoj II		
1107–1109	Duke	Swartopluk		
1109–1125	Duke	Ladislas I		
1125–1140	Duke	Sobjislaw		
1140–1158	Duke	Ladislas II		
1158–1173	King	Ladislas II		
1197–1230	King	Ottokar I		1230
1230–1253	King	Wenceslaus II (Wenzel)		1253
1253–1278	King	Ottokar II		1278
1278–1305	King	Wenceslaus II		1305
1305–1306	King	Wenceslaus III		1306
1307–1310	King	Henry		1335

LUXEMBURG DYNASTY

Reign	Title	Ruler	Birth	Death
1310–1346	King	John the Blind		1346
1346–1378	King	Charles		1378
1378–1419	King	Wenceslaus IV		1419
1419–1437	King	Sigismund of Hungary		1437
1437–1439	King	Albert of Austria	1397	1439
1440–1457	King	Ladislas Posthumus	1440	1457
1458–1471	King	George of Podebrad	1420	1471
1469–1471	Rival King	Matthias of Hungary	1440	1490
1471–1516	King	Ladislas II (Vladislav)	1456	1516
1516–1526	King	Louis	1506	1526
1526–1564	King	Ferdinand I of Austria	1503	1564
1619–1620	King	Frederick V of the Palatinate	1596	1632

The Principality of Liechtenstein

The geographical location of Liechtenstein between Switzerland and Austria

The Principality of Liechtenstein is located in central Europe between Switzerland and Austria, in the Alps mountain range which runs east and west through the southern half of Switzerland. One-third of the country lies in the upper Rhine Valley; the rest is mountainous.

Because of its strategic location on a north-south/east-west crossroads in central Europe, Liechtenstein has been permanently inhabited since the Neolithic age. Recorded inhabitants include the Celts, then the Romans, and later a Germanic tribe—the Alemanni—whose descendants now inhabit the principality. The

area became a direct fief of the Holy Roman Empire of the German nation in 1396.

The Imperial Principality of Liechtenstein was established in its present form in 1719 when the princely House of Liechtenstein, in order to maintain a seat in the Imperial Diet of the Holy Roman Empire, purchased the territory and gave its name to the principality. Liechtenstein was a member of the Confederation of the Rhine during the Napoleonic period and later became a member of the German Confederation until its dissolution in 1866.

Although it had been politically independent since 1815, Liechtenstein joined in a customs union with the Austro-Hungarian Empire in 1852. It abrogated this treaty with Austria in 1918. The principality remained neutral in both world wars.

Based on the constitution of October 1921, the Principality of Liechtenstein is a hereditary constitutional monarchy. The prince is head of the House of Liechtenstein and thereby chief of state. All legislation must have his concurrence; he is also empowered to dissolve the Diet (parliament).

The highest executive authority of the principality is a five-member Collegial Board (cabinet). Its chairman is the head of government (prime minister), who is appointed to this position by the prince after being proposed by the Diet from among the members of the majority party. The deputy head of government is also appointed by the prince after being proposed by the Diet. By tradition he is a member of the minority political party.

The three remaining members of the Collegial Board, called government councilors, are elected by the Diet and appointed by the prince.

The Diet is a unicameral body composed of fifteen members. They are elected by direct male suffrage for four-year terms. Women are not eligible to vote or run for office.

In 1977 Liechtenstein had an estimated population of

24,700, with an annual growth rate of about 2.3 percent. Although the population density for the country as a whole is more than 398 people per square mile, about one-fourth of the people live at Vaduz, the capital. Most of the remainder live in ten other communities in the Rhine Valley. The social structure of the principality is similar to that found in other modern industrialized Western communities of equal size, except for the survival of the aristocratic ruling family, the House of Liechtenstein.

Prince Francis Joseph II and Princess Georgina. Prince Francis Joseph II, a grandson of Emperor Francis Joseph of Austria-Hungary, became the ruler of Liechtenstein on July 26, 1938. He is the first head of a ruling family to live permanently in Vaduz in Liechtenstein's history as a sovereign state. The prince was seventy-four years of age in 1980.

August 12, 1962, the fiftieth anniversary of Liechtenstein, stamp honors the three rulers during the period. Left to right: *John II (1858–1929), Francis I (1929–38), and Francis Joseph II from 1938.*

THE SOVEREIGNS OF LIECHTENSTEIN

Reign	Title	Ruler
1699–1712	Prince	John Adam
1712–1718	Prince	Joseph Wenzel
1718–1721	Prince	Antony Florian
1721–1732	Prince	John Joseph
1732–1748	Prince	John Charles
1748–1772	Prince	Joseph Wenzel
1772–1781	Prince	Francis Joseph I
1781–1805	Prince	Alois Joseph I
1805–1836	Prince	John Joseph I
1836–1858	Prince	Alois Joseph II
1858–1929	Prince	John II
1929–1938	Prince	Francis I de Paula
1938–	Prince	Francis Joseph II

Stamps commemorating the marriage of Crown Prince Hans Adam von Liechtenstein and Countess Marie Aglae Kinsky, June 29, 1967

The Grand Duchy of Luxemburg

Luxemburg is geographically located with Belgium to her west, the Federal Republic of Germany to the east, and France to the south.

Luxemburg is located in Western Europe, bordered by France, the Federal Republic of Germany, and Belgium. The northern half of the country is largely a continuation of the Belgian Ardennes and is heavily forested and slightly mountainous. The Lorraine Plateau extends from France into the southern part of Luxemburg, creating an open, rolling countryside (average elevation—one thousand feet, or three hundred meters). The Our, Sure, and Moselle rivers form the north-south frontier between Luxemburg and Germany.

In 1815, after four hundred years of domination by various European nations, Luxemburg was made a grand duchy by the Congress of Vienna. It was granted political autonomy in 1839 under King William I of the Netherlands, who was also the grand duke of Luxem-

burg. The country considers its year of independence to be 1839.

By the Treaty of London in 1867, Luxemburg was recognized as an independent state and was guaranteed its perpetual neutrality. After being overrun by Germany in both world wars, Luxemburg formally abandoned neutrality in 1949 by becoming a charter member of NATO.

The present sovereign, Grande Duke Jean, succeeded his mother, Grand Duchess Charlotte, on November 12, 1964, when she voluntarily abdicated after a forty-five-year reign.

Luxemburg has a parliamentary form of government with a constitutional monarchy. Under the Constitution of 1868, as amended, the grand duke is the chief of state. Executive power is exercised by the grand duke and the Council of Government (cabinet), which consists of a president of the government (prime minister) and several other ministers. The prime minister is the leader of the political party or coalition of parties which has the most seats in the Parliament.

Legislative power is vested in the Chamber of Deputies, elected directly to five-year terms. A second body in the Parliament is the Council of State, largely composed of elder statesmen and appointed by the grand duke. It

John the Blind, count of Luxemburg, king of Bohemia, who fell in the Battle of Crecy on August 26, 1346, is considered by historians as the first recognized ruler of Luxemburg. He reigned from 1310 to 1346.

exercises some of the functions of an upper house but can be overridden by the Chamber of Deputies.

The law is codified, as in France and Belgium, and is a composite of local practice, legal tradition, and foreign systems (French, Belgian, and German). The apex of the judicial system is the Superior Court whose judges are appointed by the grand duke.

Under the Constitution of 1868, as amended, Luxemburg is a parliamentary democracy which for many years has been ruled by a combination of two of the three major parties: the Christian Socialists (PCS), the Socialists (POSL), and the Democrats (PD).

From the period immediately following World War I until 1974, the PCS had always been the dominant partner in governing coalitions. The PCS is Roman Catholic-oriented and is in many ways comparable to the Christian Democratic parties of other West European countries. It enjoys widely based popular support among farmers, conservative groups, and Catholic labor circles. It is relatively "internationalist" in outlook.

The royal crest; its motto is that of John the Blind's coat of arms: ich dien.

Grand-Duchess Josephine-Charlotte and Grand-Duke Jean. The ruler, grand-duke, Jean, was born on January 5, 1921, and succeeded his mother, Grand-Duchess Charlotte, in 1964.

Grand-Duke Jean (right) has a serious discussion with President Ronald Reagan in the White House in Washington, D.C. during an official visit to the United States in November, 1984. (Photograph by Bill Fitz-Patrick)

The Principality of Monaco

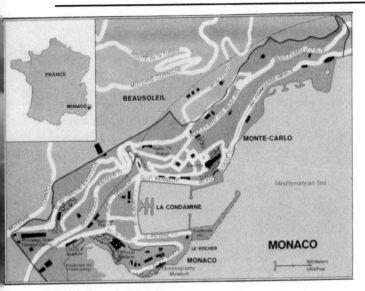

Detailed map of Monaco

The Principality of Monaco is the second smallest independent state in the world, after the Vatican City. It is located on the Mediterranean Sea nine miles (14 km.) from Nice, France, and is surrounded on three sides by France. Monaco is traditionally divided into three sections: Monaco-Ville, the old city situated on a rocky promontory extending into the Mediterranean; La Condamine, the section along the port; and Monte Carlo, the new city and principal residential and resort area. Fontvieille, the industrial area in La Condamine, is often considered a fourth section.

Monaco's population in 1975 was 25,000, with an annual growth rate of about 0.9 percent. Monaco-Ville has about 1,685 inhabitants.

Founded in 1215 as a colony of Genoa (Italy,) Monaco has been ruled by the House of Grimaldi since 1419, except when it fell under French rule during the years of the French Revolution and the First Empire. Designated a protectorate of Sardinia during 1815–60 by the Treaty of Vienna, Monaco's sovereignty was recognized by the Franco-Monegasque Treaty of 1861. The prince of Monaco was an absolute ruler until a constitution was promulgated in 1911.

On July 17, 1918, a treaty was signed providing for limited French protection over Monaco. The treaty established that Monacan policy would be aligned with French political, military, naval, and economic interests.

Prince Rainier III, the present ruler of Monaco, acceded to the throne following the death of his grandfather, Prince Louis II, in 1949. Prince Albert, the heir apparent, was born in 1958.

A new constitution, proclaimed on December 17,

A 1974 stamp commemorating the first twenty-five years of Prince Rainier III's reign. He succeeded his grandfather, Louis II, in 1949.

1949   1974

RAINIER III
PRINCE DE MONACO

A First Day cover commemorating the marriage of Prince Rainier III and the famous American movie star, Grace Patricia Kelly, April 19, 1956.

1962, abolished capital punishment and provided for female suffrage and the establishment of a Supreme Tribunal to guarantee fundamental liberties.

Monaco has been governed as a constitutional monarchy since 1911 with a prince as chief of state. The executive branch consists of a minister of state (head of government), assisted by a three-member Council of Government (cabinet). The minister of state (a French citizen traditionally appointed by the prince for a three-year term from among several senior French civil servants nominated by the French government) is responsible for foreign relations. As the representative of the prince, he also directs the executive services, commands the public police, and presides (with a casting vote) over the Council of Government. The three members of the latter body are responsible for finance and national economy, internal affairs, and public works and social affairs.

Under the 1962 constitution the prince shares his power with the unicameral National Council. The eighteen members of this legislative body are elected for five-year terms by universal adult suffrage from a list of names given to the voters. Should the prince decide to dissolve the National Council, new elections must be held within three months. Usually meeting twice annually, the council votes on the budget and endorses laws proposed by the Prince.

Ordinances passed by the National Council are debated in the Council of Government, as are the ministerial decrees signed by the minister of state. Once approved, the ordinances must be submitted to the prince within eighty days for his signature, which makes them legally enforceable. If he does not express opposition within ten days of submission, they become valid.

Judicial power is in the hands of the prince, but according to the constitution, he delegates full powers of exercise to the courts and the Supreme Tribunal, the highest judicial authority. The Supreme Tribunal is composed of five chief members and two assistant judges. Named by the prince on the basis of nominations by the National Council and other governmental bodies, the justices on the Supreme Tribunal constitute a court of last resort, resolve jurisdictional conflicts, and supply the National Council with interpretations on the constitutionality of proposed legislation. Monaco's legal system is based on French codes.

A stamp honoring Princess Grace, and one for the princess and family (February 1, 1965)

A sampling of former rulers of Monaco. Top, left to right: *Seigneur Charles II (1581–89), Prince Antoine I (1701–31).* Center, left to right: *Princess Louise-Hippolyte, daughter of Antoine I, (1731); Prince James I, husband of Louise-Hippolyte, (1731–33); and* bottom, left to right: *Prince Honore III, son of Louise-Hippolyte and James I (1733–95); Prince Albert I (1889–1922).*

Princess Grace, left, and her son, Prince Albert, right, pay a state visit to the United Nations Headquarters in New York City in 1978. UN Secretary-General Kurt Waldheim, center, is their official greeter.

EN HOMMAGE A

LA PRINCESSE GRACE

1929-1982

Monaco postage stamp commemorates the death of Princess Grace. She died as the result of an automobile accident on September 13, 1982.

Prince Rainier and the hereditary Prince Albert.

Christian Names
of the European Monarchs

English	Danish	Dutch	French	German	Italian	Spanish
Albert	Albrekt	Albert	Albert	Albrecht	Alberto	Alberto
Charles	Carl	Karel	Charles	Karl	Carlo	Carlos
George	Georg	Joris	Georges	Georg	Giorgio	Jorge
Edward	Edvard	Edward	Edouard	Eduard	Eduardo	Eduardo
Francis	Frans	Frans	Francois	Franz	Francesco	Francisco
Frederick	Frederik	Frederik	Frederic	Friedrich	Federico	Federigo
Henry	Henrik	Hendrik	Henri	Heinrich	Enrico	Enrique
James	Jacob	Jacob	Jacques	Jakob	Giacomo	Jaime
John	Hans	Johan	Jean	Johann	Giovanni	Juan
Louis	Ludvig	Lodewijk	Louis	Ludwig	Lodovivo	Luis
Paul	Paul	Paulus	Paul	Paul	Paolo	Pablo
Peter	Peter	Pieter	Pierre	Peter	Pietro	Pedro
Philip	Filip	Philip	Philippe	Philipp	Filippo	Filipe
William	Vilhjelm	Willem	Guillaume	Wilhelm	Guglielmo	Guillermo

Index

I

J

N

LIGHT FROM THE ANCIENT PAST

LIGHT FROM
THE ANCIENT PAST

The Archeological Background
of
Judaism and Christianity

By JACK FINEGAN

PRINCETON UNIVERSITY PRESS

MCMLIX

Printed in the United States of America
by Princeton University Press
Princeton, New Jersey

Preface

THE purpose of this book is to give a connected account of the archeological background of Judaism and Christianity. Within the last century and a half and largely within the past few decades, oriental archeology has pioneered a new past, in which are revealed more extensive vistas and higher cultures than hitherto were imagined. The account which can now be given of the rise of civilization in the Middle East, of the development of art, and of the formulation of ethical, philosophical, and religious ideas is of fascinating interest in itself. It is also of great significance for an understanding of Judaism and Christianity, both of which in their origin and earlier history were integral parts of that ancient world. To see that world come vividly and startlingly alive is to find biblical and early Christian history invested with a fresh sense of reality and interest. There are, moreover, many points at which biblical records and archeological discoveries are in direct contact, and increasingly in the later centuries there are many archeological remains which are primary historical monuments of Judaism and Christianity. A knowledge of these facts is now indispensable to all serious study of the Bible, and the proper utilization of the abundant new archeological materials may even be said to constitute one of the most important tasks in that study.

The presentation of this archeological background in the present book is in the form of a continuous account extending, in round numbers, from 5000 B.C. to A.D. 500. After an introduction dealing with the nature of archeological work in general, the narrative begins with the rise of civilization in the valley of the Tigris and Euphrates rivers where the origins of the people of Israel traditionally are located and where antecedents of their mythology and law are found. Then the development of culture in the valley of the

Nile is sketched, and the Exodus of the Israelites and their use of Egyptian materials in the Psalms and Proverbs are considered. Moving to Palestine, the "bridge" between these two ancient homes of empire, archeological findings are summarized, illuminating both Canaanite and Israelite times. Then the later Assyrian, Neo-Babylonian, and Persian empires are described, upon whose imperial policies the fate and future of the kingdoms of Israel and Judah depended. With the world at last under Roman domination, the cities of Palestine are pictured as they were in the time of Jesus, and afterward a glimpse is obtained of the chief places in which the work of the apostle Paul was done. In view of the great importance of the writings collected in the New Testament, a study is made of ancient writing materials and practices and of the transmission of the text to the present time. Then the Roman catacombs are investigated, together with their art and inscriptions, and a brief account is given of characteristic early Christian sarcophagi. Finally, the development of distinctive places of Christian assembly is indicated and the basilicas of Constantinian times are described—basilicas whose successors were the Byzantine churches of the East and the Romanesque and Gothic cathedrals of the West. With the clear emergence of the Christian community, centered in the place where the gospel of Jesus Christ is proclaimed, our story comes to an end.

In the earlier part of the narrative it is the broader background of the general history and civilization which is most illuminated by archeology and to which the major part of the portrayal is devoted. In the later part not only is the general history relatively simpler and more generally known, but there are also many more monuments of Judaism and Christianity themselves. Therefore in the course of the book a steadily diminishing amount of space is apportioned to the general history and a steadily increasing amount given to the specifically biblical and early Christian materials.

In order to give a more vivid sense of direct contact with the living past, frequent quotations are made from the ancient sources, and numerous photographs are presented of actual places and objects. Many of the sites are ones which I have visited and many of the objects are ones which I have studied in the museums of Chicago, Philadelphia, New York, London, Paris, Berlin, Rome, Cairo, and Jerusalem. An extensive literature has been consulted and all references cited, both ancient and modern, have been taken from personally used sources. The full title and date of each book are given upon its first appearance, with the exception of those works for which abbreviations are employed and which appear on pages xxxv-xxxvii. The maps and plans were prepared in detail by myself, and executed and lettered by Mr. William Lane Jones.

In the writing I thought often of Dean Jesse Cobb Caldwell of the College of the Bible, Drake University, who taught me the importance of history, and of Professor Dr. Hans Lietzmann of Friedrich-Wilhelms-Universität, Berlin, who instructed me in early Christian archeology, and I have dedicated the book to their memory. In the publication I was also very grateful to Mr. Datus C. Smith, Jr., former Director of Princeton University Press, for his deep understanding, constant interest, and many courtesies.

In the present second edition the structure of the book remains the same but the results of many new excavations and further studies are incorporated. Among other things there is reference to fresh work or publication relative to Jarmo, Matarrah, Samarra, Baghouz, Tepe Gawra, Eridu, Lagash, Nippur, Saqqara, Amarna, Kawa, Abu Usba, Yarmuk, Jericho, Abu Ghosh, Abu Matar, Khirbet el-Bitar, Hebron, Dotha, Nebo, Gilgal, Ai, Gibeon, Hazor, Megiddo, Ugarit, Shiloh, Tell en-Nasbeh, Shechem, Tirzah, Dibon, Nimrod, Herculaneum, and Rome; to new studies on the Habiru; to newly discovered documents including extensive Sumerian literature, the law codes of Ur-Nammu, Eshnunna, and Lipit-Ishtar, Egyptian execration texts, Babylonian chronicles, the Dead Sea scrolls, and the Nessana and other papyri; to new translations of ancient sources; and to recent researches in Egyptian, Assyrian, Babylonian, and biblical chronology. The literature dealt with extends up to January 1, 1959. Mention may also be made of my own articles on Christian Archaeology in *The Encyclopedia Americana*; on Baalbek, Babylon, Behistun Rock, Cuneiform, Jerusalem, Layard, Sir Austen Henry, Near Eastern Architecture, Nineveh, Persepolis, Petra, Ras Shamra, Tyre, and Ur in *Collier's Encyclopedia*; on Christian Archaeology in the *Twentieth Century Encyclopedia of Religious Knowledge, An Extension of the New Schaff-Herzog Encyclopedia of Religious Knowledge*; and on Achaia, Adramyttium, Adria, Agora, Amphipolis, Appian Way, Areopagus, Athens, Berea, Beroea, Cenchreae, Corinth, Dalmatia, Elymais, Ephesus, Fair Havens, Forum of Appius, Illyricum, Italy, Lasea, Macedonia, Melita, Neapolis, Nicopolis, Philippi, Puteoli, Rhegium, Spain, Syracuse, Thessalonica, and Three Taverns in the forthcoming *The Interpreter's Dictionary of the Bible*; and Research Abstracts in Archeology in *The Journal of Bible and Religion* in October 1947 and following years. For their kindness and efficiency in everything concerned with the publishing of the present revised edition it is a pleasure to thank Mr. Herbert S. Bailey, Jr., Director and Editor, and Miss Harriet Anderson of Princeton University Press.

Pacific School of Religion   Jack Finegan
Berkeley, California

Acknowledgments

IN addition to the acknowledgments made in the List of Illustrations, thanks are also due to the following for kind permission to make reproductions: to the American Academy of Arts and Sciences, Boston, for Figures 152 and 153; to the American Schools of Oriental Research, New Haven, for Figure 195; to the Biblioteca Apostolica Vaticana, Rome, for Figure 145; to the Trustees of the British Museum, London, for Figures 24, 46, 72, 74, 78, 90, 146, 147, and 149; to the University of Chicago Press for Figures 30, 40, and 43; to the Clarendon Press, Oxford, for Figures 64 and 148; to Les Éditions d'Art et d'Histoire, Paris, for Figure 82; to Éditions Albert Morancé, Paris, for Figures 42 and 49; to the Egypt Exploration Society, London, for Figures 39 and 141; to the Field Press (1930) Ltd., London, for Figures 68 and 69; to the President and Fellows of Harvard College, Cambridge, for Figure 114; to Arthur Upham Pope, Director of the Iranian Institute, New York, for Figure 87; to the Director of the Istanbul Arkeoloji Müzeleri Müdürlügü, Istanbul, for Figure 118; to Kirsopp Lake for Figure 148; to Kirsopp and Silva Lake for Figures 152 and 153; to Librairie Orientaliste Paul Geuthner, Paris, for Figure 21; to Librairie Hachette, Paris, for Figure 97; to Macmillan and Co. Ltd., London, for Figures 4, 5, and 6; to the New York Public Library for Figure 113; to Sir Humphrey Milford, Oxford University Press, Oxford, for Figures 60, 61, 62, 70, 141, 186, 190, and 193; to the Government of Palestine for Figures 190 and 193; to the Palestine Exploration Fund, London, for Figures 59 and 66; to Presses Universitaires de France, Paris, for Figure 150; to George Routledge and Sons Ltd., London, for Figure 35; to C. F. A. Schaeffer for Figures 60, 61, and 62; to the Service des Antiquités de l'Égypte, Cairo, for Figures 38 and 44; to George Steindorff for Figure 47; to Emery Walker Ltd., London, for Figure 143; and to the Trustees of the late Sir Henry Wellcome, owners of the copyright, for Figure 70. The following pictures are from books whose copyright is vested in the Alien Property Custodian, 1945, pursuant to law, and their reproduction is by permission of the Alien Property Custodian in the public interest under License No. JA-964: Figure 154, Copyright 1919 by Gesellschaft zur Förderung der Wissenschaft des Judentums, Berlin; Figure 151,

Copyright 1929 by Peter Hanstein, Bonn; Figure 76, Copyright 1938 by J. C. Hinrichs, Leipzig; Figures 84, 85, Copyright 1925 by J. C. Hinrichs, Leipzig; Figure 168, Copyright 1927 by Josef Kösel & Friedrich Pustet K.-G., Munich; Figures 41, 138, Copyright 1936 by Phaidon Verlag, Vienna; Figures 75, 134, Copyright 1925 by Propyläen-Verlag G.m.b.H., Berlin; Figures 156, 157, 158, 160, 161, 163, 164, Copyright 1933 by Verlag für Kunstwissenschaft G.m.b.H., Berlin-Friedenau; Figure 127, Copyright 1923 by Ernst Wasmuth A.G., Berlin. Because of the war and other circumstances, it was impossible to communicate with certain publishers and individuals, and for pictures used under such conditions appreciation is recorded here.

Thanks are likewise expressed to The Westminster Press, Philadelphia, for permission to derive various details of Plan 1 from G. Ernest Wright and Floyd V. Filson, eds., *The Westminster Historical Atlas to the Bible*, 1945, Pl. xvii; and to Princeton University Press for permission to quote from *Ancient Near Eastern Texts Relating to the Old Testament*, ed. James B. Pritchard, 2d ed. 1955.

Except where otherwise indicated, the scripture quotations are from the *Revised Standard Version of the Bible*, copyrighted 1946 and 1952 by the Division of Christian Education of the National Council of Churches, and used by permission. For permission to quote from *The Bible, An American Translation*, by J. M. Powis Smith and Edgar J. Goodspeed, acknowledgment is made to the University of Chicago Press.

Contents

List of Illustrations

LIST OF MAPS AND PLANS

MAPS

1. Mesopotamia
2. Egypt
3. Sinai, Transjordan, and Palestine
4. The Middle East
5. Palestine
6. The Mediterranean World

PLANS

1. Jerusalem
2. Ancient Rome
3. The Catacombs of Rome
4. The Churches of Rome

List of Abbreviations

AASOR   *Annual of the American Schools of Oriental Research.*

AB   *The Art Bulletin.*

ADAJ   *Annual of the Department of Antiquities of Jordan.*

AJA   *American Journal of Archaeology.*

AJP   *The American Journal of Philology.*

AJSL   *The American Journal of Semitic Languages and Literatures.*

AJT   *The American Journal of Theology.*

ANEA   James B. Pritchard, *The Ancient Near East: An Anthology of Texts and Pictures.* 1958.

ANEP   James B. Pritchard, *The Ancient Near East in Pictures Relating to the Old Testament.* 1954.

ANET   James B. Pritchard, ed., *Ancient Near Eastern Texts Relating to the Old Testament.* 2d ed. 1955.

ANF   Alexander Roberts and James Donaldson, eds., rev. by A. Cleveland Coxe, *The Ante-Nicene Fathers, Translations of the Writings of the Fathers down to A.D. 325.* 10 vols. 1885-87.

AO   *Archiv für Orientforschung.*

AP   *Archiv für Papyrusforschung.*

ARAB   Daniel David Luckenbill, *Ancient Records of Assyria and Babylonia.* 2 vols. 1926-27.

ARE   James Henry Breasted, *Ancient Records of Egypt.* 5 vols. 1906-07.

AS   *Assyriological Studies.* Oriental Institute.

ASBACH   Joseph C. Ayer, *A Source Book for Ancient Church History.* 1913.

ASV   *American Standard Version.*

ATR   *Anglican Theological Review.*

AZKK   *Die Antike, Zeitschrift für Kunst und Kultur des klassischen Altertums.*

BA   *The Biblical Archaeologist.*

BASOR   *Bulletin of the American Schools of Oriental Research.*

BDSM   William H. Brownlee, *The Dead Sea Manual of Discipline,* BASOR Supplementary Studies 10-12. 1951.

BDSS   Millar Burrows, *The Dead Sea Scrolls.* 1955.

BJRL   *Bulletin of the John Rylands Library, Manchester.*

BML   Millar Burrows, *More Light on the Dead Sea Scrolls.* 1958.

CAH   J. B. Bury, S. A. Cook, F. E. Adcock, M. P. Charlesworth and N. H. Baynes, eds., *The Cambridge Ancient History.* 12 vols. and 5 vols. of plates, 1923-39.

CALQ   Frank M. Cross, Jr., *The Ancient Library of Qumran and Modern Biblical Studies.* 1958.

CAP   R. H. Charles, ed., *The Apocrypha and Pseudepigrapha of the Old Testament in English with Introductions and Critical and Explanatory Notes to the Several Books.* 2 vols. 1913.

CBQ   *The Catholic Biblical Quarterly.*

CIG   *Corpus Inscriptionum Graecarum.* 1828-77.

DACL   *Dictionnaire d'archéologie chrétienne et de liturgie.* 1924ff.

DJD   *Discoveries in the Judaean Desert.* I, *Qumran Cave I,* by D. Barthélemy and J. T. Milik. 1955.

DLO   Adolf Deissmann, *Licht vom Osten, Das Neue Testament und die neuentdeckten Texte der hellenistisch-römischen Welt.* 4th ed. 1923.

DM   *The Mishnah Translated from the Hebrew with Introduction and Brief Explanatory Notes,* by Herbert Danby. 1933.

EB   *The Encyclopaedia Britannica.* 14th ed. 24 vols. 1929.

GBT   Lazarus Goldschmidt, *Der babylonische Talmud.* 9 vols. 1899-1935.

GCS   *Die griechischen christlichen*

	Schriftsteller der ersten Jahrhunderte.
GDSS	Theodor H. Gaster, *The Dead Sea Scriptures in English Translation.* 1956.
HDB	James Hastings, ed., *A Dictionary of the Bible.* 4 vols. 1898-1902.
HERE	James Hastings, ed., *Encyclopaedia of Religion and Ethics.* 12 vols. 1910-22.
HFDMM	W. H. P. Hatch, *Facsimiles and Descriptions of Minuscule Manuscripts of the New Testament.* 1951.
HJ	*The Hibbert Journal.*
HPUM	W. H. P. Hatch, *The Principal Uncial Manuscripts of the New Testament.* 1939.
HTR	*The Harvard Theological Review.*
HUCA	*Hebrew Union College Annual.*
ICC	*The International Critical Commentary.*
IEJ	*Israel Exploration Journal.*
JANT	M. R. James, *The Apocryphal New Testament.* 1942.
JAOS	*Journal of the American Oriental Society.*
JBL	*Journal of Biblical Literature.*
JBR	*The Journal of Bible and Religion.*
JCS	*Journal of Cuneiform Studies.*
JE	Isidore Singer, ed., *The Jewish Encyclopedia.* 12 vols. 1901-05.
JEA	*The Journal of Egyptian Archaeology.*
JHS	*The Journal of Hellenic Studies.*
JJS	*Journal of Jewish Studies.*
JNES	*Journal of Near Eastern Studies.*
JPOS	*The Journal of the Palestine Oriental Society.*
JQR	*The Jewish Quarterly Review.*
JR	*The Journal of Religion.*
JRAS	*The Journal of the Royal Asiatic Society.*
JSS	*Journal of Semitic Studies.*
JTS	*The Journal of Theological Studies.*
KAT	J. A. Knudtzon, *Die El-Amarna Tafeln.* 2 vols. 1908-15.

KFTS	Samuel N. Kramer, *From the Tablets of Sumer.* 1956.
KJV	*King James Version.*
KPGÄ	Friedrich K. Kienitz, *Die politische Geschichte Ägyptens vom 7. bis zum 4. Jahrhundert vor die Zeitwende.* 1953.
KRAC	Theodor Klauser, ed., *Reallexikon für Antike und Christentum, Sachwörterbuch zur Auseinandersetzung des Christentums mit der antiken Welt.* 1950ff.
LCL	*The Loeb Classical Library.*
LLP	Louise Ropes Loomis, *The Book of the Popes (Liber Pontificalis), I, To the Pontificate of Gregory I.* 1916.
LXX	The Septuagint. Henry Barclay Swete, ed., *The Old Testament in Greek according to the Septuagint.* I, 4th ed. 1909; II, 3d ed. 1907; III, 3d ed. 1905. Alfred Rahlfs, ed., *Septuaginta, id est Vetus Testamentum Graece iuxta LXX interpretes.* 2 vols. 1935. *Septuaginta, Vetus Testamentum Graecum auctoritate Societatis Litterarum Gottingensis editum.* 1931ff.
MMVGT	James H. Moulton and George Milligan, *The Vocabulary of the Greek Testament Illustrated from the Papyri and Other Non-Literary Sources.* 1949.
MPG	Jacques Paul Migne, *Patrologiae cursus completus. Series graeca.*
MPL	Jacques Paul Migne, *Patrologiae cursus completus. Series latina.*
MTAT	Samuel A. B. Mercer, *The Tell El-Amarna Tablets.* 2 vols. 1939.
NGM	*The National Geographic Magazine.*
NPNF	Philip Schaff, ed., *A Select Library of the Nicene and Post-Nicene Fathers,* First Series. 14 vols. 1886-89.
NPNFss	Philip Schaff and Henry Wace, eds., *A Select Library of Nicene and Post-Nicene Fathers of the Christian*

	Church, Second Series. 14 vols. 1890-1900.
NSH	Samuel M. Jackson, ed., *The New Schaff-Herzog Encyclopedia of Religious Knowledge.* 12 vols. 1908-12.
NTS	*New Testament Studies.*
OIC	*Oriental Institute Communications.*
OIP	*Oriental Institute Publications.*
OL	*Orientalistische Literaturzeitung.*
OP	*The Oxyrhynchus Papyri.*
PATD	Samuel B. Platner and Thomas Ashby, *A Topographical Dictionary of Ancient Rome.* 1929.
PBA	*Proceedings of the British Academy.*
PCAE	Richard A. Parker, *The Calendars of Ancient Egypt.* SAOC 26, 1950.
PCAM	Ann Louise Perkins, *The Comparative Archeology of Early Mesopotamia.* SAOC 25, 1949.
PDBC	Richard A. Parker and Waldo H. Dubberstein, *Babylonian Chronology 626 B.C.-A.D. 75.* 3d ed. 1956.
PEFA	*Palestine Exploration Fund Annual.*
PEFQS	*Palestine Exploration Fund Quarterly Statement.*
PEQ	*Palestine Exploration Quarterly.*
PWRE	Pauly-Wissowa, *Real-Encyclopädie der classischen Altertumswissenschaft.*
QDAP	*The Quarterly of the Department of Antiquities in Palestine.*
RAAO	*Revue d'assyriologie et d'archeologie orientale.*
RAC	*Rivista di archeologia cristiana.*
RB	*Revue Biblique.*
RBT	Michael L. Rodkinson, *New Edition of the Babylonian Talmud.* 10 (xx), vols. 1903, 1916.
RHR	*Revue de l'histoire des religions.*
RSV	*Revised Standard Version.*
SAOC	*Studies in Ancient Oriental Civilization.* Oriental Institute.
SBT	I. Epstein, ed., *The Babylonian Talmud* (Soncino Press). 1935ff.
SHJP	Emil Schürer, *A History of the Jewish People in the Time of Jesus Christ.* 5 vols. 1896.
SRK	Paul Styger, *Die römischen Katakomben, archäologische Forschungen über den Ursprung und die Bedeutung der altchristlichen Grabstätten.* 1933.
TL	*Theologische Literaturzeitung.*
TMN	Edwin R. Thiele, *The Mysterious Numbers of the Hebrew Kings.* 1951.
TU	*Texte und Untersuchungen zur Geschichte der altchristlichen Literatur.*
TZ	*Theologische Zeitschrift.*
UMB	*The University Museum Bulletin.*
VT	*Vetus Testamentum.*
WCCK	D. J. Wiseman, *Chronicles of Chaldaean Kings (626-556 B.C.) in the British Museum.* 1956.
ZA	*Zeitschrift für Assyriologie.*
ZÄS	*Zeitschrift für ägyptische Sprache und Altertumskunde.*
ZAW	*Zeitschrift für die alttestamentliche Wissenschaft.*
ZDPV	*Zeitschrift des Deutschen Palästina-Vereins.*
ZNW	*Zeitschrift für die neutestamentliche Wissenschaft und die Kunde der älteren Kirche.*
ZTK	*Zeitschrift für Theologie und Kirche.*

LIGHT FROM THE ANCIENT PAST

Introduction

THE ancient Greeks felt themselves to be very modern and hence had a word ἀρχαιολογία which signified the discussion of antiquities. From this term is derived the English word "archeology" which means the scientific study of the material remains of the past.

Archeological interest existed even long before the time of the Greeks. In the seventh century B.C., Ashurbanipal of Assyria was proud of his ability to decipher the writing on ancient tablets, and sent his scribes far and wide to collect copies of early records and documents for his wonderful library at Nineveh. Nabonidus, who ruled at Babylon in the sixth century B.C., made exploratory soundings in the age-old ziggurat which loomed up at Ur, read the foundation records of its earlier builders, and carefully carried out restorations, giving due credit to his ancient predecessors in his own inscriptions. The daughter of Nabonidus, sister of the famous Belshazzar, shared the interest of her father and maintained a small museum in which objects of interest from earlier times were kept.

Unfortunately the "collection" of antiquities was undertaken all too often by persons of less disinterestedness, and untold treasures have been lost to scientific archeology through the depredations of robbers. An early story of papyrus-hunting, for example, concerns Setna-Khaemuast, the fifth and favorite son of Ramses II. An account written probably in the reign of Ptolemy II tells how this young adventurer of the long ago braved the wrath of the spirits of the departed to enter the tomb of a certain prince. With this prince had been buried a magic roll of papyrus, whose possessor would know what is said by the birds as they fly and by the serpents as they crawl and would be able to enchant anything in heaven or earth. After incredible adventures Setna made away with the papyrus roll, only eventually to be driven to return it to the ghosts of the dead. Unfortunately the predecessors and successors of the illustrious Setna in the art of tomb-robbing have seldom been constrained by the powers of the spirit world to replace their spoils, and so modern archeologists all too frequently have found themselves anticipated by the unauthorized efforts of plunderers before whose greed and skill not even as mighty monuments as the pyramids were secure. A commission appointed by Ramses IX to examine into the condition of cemeteries reported in part as follows: "It was found that the thieves had violated them all, that they had torn their occupants away from their coffins and cases, had thrown them into the dust and had stolen all the funeral objects which had been given to them, as well as the gold and silver and the ornaments which were in their coffins." Among the tomb-robbers who rifled so many of the graves of the kings of Ur, special ignominy should attach to those workmen who in the very process of burying Lady Shub-ad managed to loot the grave of her previously deceased husband immediately below, hiding the hole they made in the brick vault by placing over it the lady's great clothes-chest.

In distinction from the foregoing, modern archeology may be said to have had its beginning in 1798, when nearly one hundred French scholars and artists accompanied Napoleon on his invasion of Egypt. They gazed with wonder upon the impressive monuments of that ancient land, wrote out systematic descriptions, copied texts and prepared watercolor illustrations.

Early in the nineteenth century Claudius James Rich, the resident of the East India Company at Baghdad, observed in the regions surrounding that place the mounds of ancient cities and found many inscriptions. This aroused widespread interest and when the French vice-consul at Mosul, Paul Émile Botta, found Sargon's palace at Khorsabad, the enthusiasm of a young Englishman, Austen Henry Layard, was stirred. Layard's excavations, begun in 1845, at Nimrod and notably at the mound of Kuyunjik, which was the site of ancient Nineveh, constitute the next great landmark in the history of modern archeology.

The honor of beginning the scientific study of the localities and antiquities of Palestine belonged to an American, Professor Edward Robinson, of Union Theological Seminary in New York City, who on travels through Palestine in 1838 and 1852 made extensive observations and notes. Thereafter the Palestine Exploration Fund was organized in London in 1865, and its first representative, Captain Charles Warren, made a series of sketch maps of the country and, on a second expedition, actually carried out excavations on the temple hill in Jerusalem.

The real archeological work thus initiated in Egypt, Babylonia, Assyria, and Palestine, has been continued and extended into related areas by a distinguished international succession of investigators, until modern archeology has become a true science, with most impressive results.

The work involved includes the excavation of far-flung sites, the discovery and decipherment of long-lost inscriptions and manuscripts, and the study of ancient monuments and objects of all kinds. The techniques of the science have been developed slowly through actual practice and experimentation. At first attention was naturally attracted by objects of large size and obvious impressiveness but now even the tiniest pieces of broken pottery are recognized as having their own important story to tell. Early digging sometimes was done without the requisite knowledge and skill to avoid destroying much of value, but today every step is taken with the greatest care and much attention is given to the recording and preservation of the resulting finds.

The difficulties which beset the work are various. The ancient sites may be hidden beneath modern towns or be in the possession of private persons whose interests are quite different from those of the archeologists. In the case of one famous site in Palestine, Tell el-Mutesellim (Fig. 57), the thirteen-acre area was found to be owned privately by no less than ninety separate individuals from whom it had to be leased or purchased. Unexpected discoveries of great value sometimes have provoked national jealousies and led to prolonged litigation concerning the respective rights of those concerned. Again, petty officials have presented formidable impediments to the work. Friction or discontent may arise among the laborers, while wandering dealers in antiquities sometimes lurk in the neighborhood to buy from the diggers anything which those workmen may manage to steal. Many times the work is done in regions where conditions are hazardous to health, and the malarial mosquito and other scourges have often prostrated archeological staffs. Not infrequently the sites have been in relatively lawless sections where foreigners penetrated only at risk; and in modern times as well as ancient, warfare has often raged across the Bible lands.

The object of investigation is often one of the ancient city-mounds which are so conspicuous a feature of the landscape in the Middle East.[1] Such a mound is usually known as a *tell*, the plural being *tulul*. This word, which occurs in ancient Babylonia and is still in use in modern Arabic, means high, and hence is applicable to a hill or mound.[2] These ancient mounds were built up through the centuries by the accumulation of the debris of the successive cities which occupied the site. The city's own rubbish collected constantly and filled up the streets, while after each time of destruction by war or fire the new city was rebuilt upon the ruins of the old. In Joshua 11:13 there is a picturesque allusion to this situation in the mention of "the cities that stood on mounds" (cf. also Jeremiah 30:18).

When such a *tell* is excavated today, the more recent remains are naturally found toward the top of the mound and the more ancient toward the bottom. Thus in digging from top to bottom one passes through the cultural layers in reverse sequence. While a test pit or trench may be useful as a preliminary survey, or may have to suffice when more extensive excavations cannot be attempted, more effective procedure calls for laying bare a considerable portion of the mound. This is the more necessary because the strata often are not nicely differentiated like the layers of a cake, but are intricately confused. A given stratum may bend down over the edge of the hill just as the town it represents followed the natural slopes or was built on artificial terraces. Hence it is important to clear an adequate area of each stratum and to record it in its proper order. This is known as stratigraphical excavation. Sometimes the entire mound is dug completely but it is regarded as preferable to leave at least a portion where future excavators may check the results.

The process of excavating a city-mound or other ancient site may be very laborious, involving the excavation and disposal of many

[1] The term Middle East is used here as including southwestern Asia and Egypt. The same region is also called the Near East. Following the latter usage, Harry W. Hazard, *Atlas of Islamic History* (1951), defines the Near East as extending from the western border of Egypt (25° E) to the eastern border of Iran (60° E), the Middle East as stretching from the western border of Afghanistan (60° E) to the eastern border of Burma (100° E), and the Far East as continuing from the eastern boundary of Burma (100° E) across China and Japan (150° E).

[2] Other Arabic words which are frequently encountered include *ain*, spring; *bahr*, lake or canal; *jebel*, mountain; *kalat*, castle; *khirbet*, ruin; *nahr*, river; *shatt*, river or canal; and *wadi*, watercourse or valley.

tons of dirt and debris. The approach to objects of value is made with all care, and not only the pick but also the knife and brush are employed. As the various walls and structures appear they are plotted precisely and all the objects which are found from day to day are recorded with the greatest exactitude. Detailed descriptions, drawings and photographs are prepared, and thus the archeologist's conclusions are based upon a comprehensive body of detailed information.[3]

While large numbers of records and documents have been among the finds brought to light in the course of excavations, many other inscriptions have been preserved on monuments above ground. This is notably the case in Egypt where a great body of historical inscriptions provides a major basis for the knowledge of ancient Egyptian history. The transcription of these records, which are slowly perishing under exposure to the elements, and their translation and publication are among the most important parts of the archeological enterprise. Whereas the copying was formerly done entirely by hand, later epigraphic expeditions have employed more advanced methods. A photograph is taken of the inscription, and this is compared directly with the original by an artist who pencils in any necessary additions and retraces the lines of the whole. The resultant drawing is transformed into a blueprint and it in turn is "proofread" in comparison with the original by an expert in the decipherment and interpretation of ancient inscriptions. Thus the final facsimile combines the accuracy of the camera, the skill of the artist, and the reading ability of the epigrapher.

A great variety of monuments and objects fall under the archeologist's scrutiny. They range in size from the massive pyramids to small bits of jewelry and tiny scraps of papyrus, but none is neglected. Among the modern instruments which have been found useful in the study of the ancient remains is the X-ray. When an Egyptian mummy is to be studied, the X-ray makes it possible, even before the wrappings are opened, to determine the exact position of things such as jewelry which were placed with it; it is even possible to determine facts such as the cause of the individual's death and his approximate age at the time.

While aerial photography was first practiced in connection with

[3] cf. W. F. Badè, *A Manual of Excavation in the Near East.* 1934; A. H. Detweiler, *Manual of Archaeological Surveying.* 1948; Kathleen M. Kenyon, *Beginning in Archaeology.* 1952; M. B. Cookson, *Photography for Archaeologists.* 1954.

archeological work by suspending a camera from a balloon, the employment of the airplane greatly expanded the possibilities in this field. In addition to recording the progress of excavations on the ground, this made possible swift and extensive explorations of unknown areas and pictorial documentation of important sites from the air.[4] Ancient contours invisible on the ground are often seen clearly in such pictures and, if it is desired to heighten the relief effects, stereoscopic photography may be employed.[5] Needless to say, aerial photographs are invaluable to later archeological work on the ground.

Thus through the application of highly scientific techniques and by the cooperative efforts of scholars in many lands, the shattered mosaic of the past is slowly being fitted together again. Some portion of the result will be recounted in the following pages.

[4] Erich F. Schmidt, *Flights over Ancient Cities of Iran.* Special Publication of the Oriental Institute, 1940.

[5] Arthur W. Judge, *Stereoscopic Photography.* 2d ed. 1935, p.284.

I

Mesopotamian Beginnings

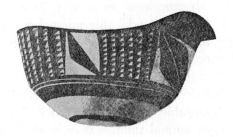

THE story begins in Mesopotamia. In the land which is now known as Iraq there flow two great rivers, the Tigris and the Euphrates. So distinctive is the geographical character which they impart to the region that the Greeks coined for it the picturesque name Mesopotamia, meaning "the land between the rivers." Strictly speaking this designation applies only to the upper part of the valley of the two rivers, which in similar fashion the Arabs today call al-Jazira or "the Island." In modern usage, however, the name Mesopotamia includes also the lower part of the valley and describes graphically the entire land.

The Tigris and the Euphrates take their rise in the northern mountains of Armenia where 10,000-foot peaks gather snow and rain sufficient to feed streams destined for the desert. As the Euphrates emerges from the mountains it is flowing in a southwesterly direction as if to empty into the Mediterranean, but it bends in a large circle southward and eastward, swinging toward the course of the Tigris River which is flowing down at the foot of the hills of Kurdistan. The two rivers move in gradually converging courses down across wide and undulating grassy plains which drop 1,000 feet between the foothills and a point somewhat above modern Baghdad. Watered by these large rivers, Lower Mesopotamia was probably made up at an early time of marsh, lagoon, and lake, even as much of it is yet today. Amidst the swamps and around them, more solid areas of land made possible the establishment of human habitation.[1]

[1] *Sumer.* 11 (1955), pp.5-13 (M. E. L. Mallowan), 15f. (Ralph S. Solecki), 88 (H. E. Wright).

While we do not know the earliest name which may have been applied to Lower Mesopotamia, by the time of the Third Dynasty of Ur the entire land was being designated as "Sumer and Akkad,"[2] Sumer being the southern region and Akkad the part farther up the rivers and nearer modern Baghdad. Later the Akkadian city of Bab-ilu became so prominent as to give its name to the entire region. Meaning "Gate of God," this name became Babel in the Hebrew language, and Babylon in Greek and Latin. Hence we now know Lower Mesopotamia best as Babylonia.

The alluvial silt of the Tigris and Euphrates doubtless built much of the plain of Babylonia, and the waters of the two rivers have always been indispensable to its productivity. The sun is blazing hot and the average annual rainfall is only six inches, but where the rivers run or irrigation canals are dug from them the soil is very fertile. Wheat, corn, barley, dates, figs, and pomegranates are grown. In ancient times an extensive system of canals irrigated the plain and it bore a dense population and was the home of great civilizations. In their inscriptions the kings of those days spoke often, and with justifiable pride, of their works in canal-building. Rim-Sin of Larsa "dug the canal of the plain, the canal of abundance, as far as the sea." Hammurabi of Babylon provided "permanent water of plenty" by a splendid canal to which he gave his own name, "Hammurabi-is-the-prosperity-of-the-folk." Sin-idinnam wrote, "Indeed I have provided waters of everlastingness, unceasing prosperity, for my land of Larsa."

But the onetime fertile gardenland became a vast desolation. The wonderful system of irrigation which the ancient empires had maintained gradually fell into disrepair and finally, with the coming of the Muslims in the seventh century A.D. and the Mongols in the thirteenth, into utter ruin. Under Turkish rule, which lasted until the British took Baghdad in 1917 and were succeeded by the national Iraq government in 1932, the land between the rivers became one of the most desolate areas on earth. Baghdad, which was founded in A.D. 762 and raised to splendor in the ninth century by Harun-al-Rashid, the famous Caliph of the *Arabian Nights*, shrank from a reputed onetime population of 2,000,000 to 300,000. Still today it is a mud-colored city on the banks of a mud-colored river. The slightest wind blows powdered mud as fine as talcum powder through the streets. Outside the city, roads of beaten mud, where every

[2] Samuel N. Kramer in IEJ 3 (1953), p.220 n.5; ANET p.159, etc.

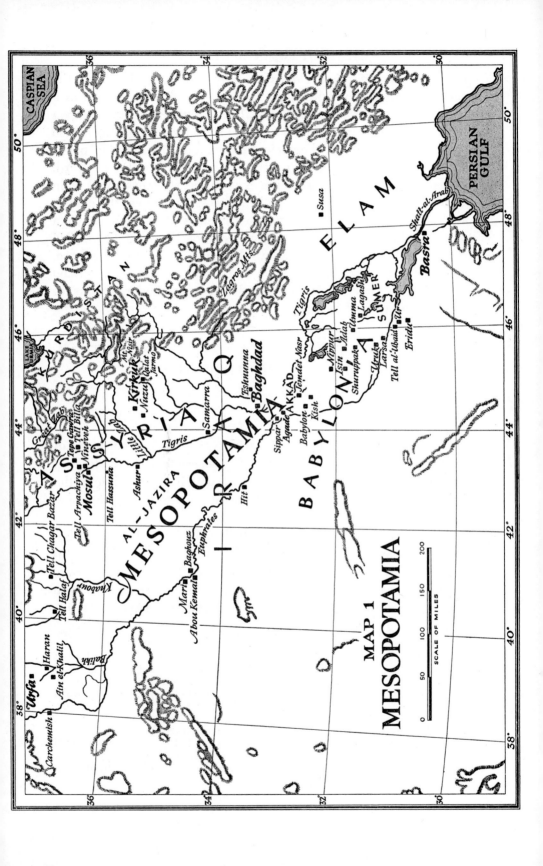

MAP 1

MESOPOTAMIA

passing horseman raises clouds of brown dust, lead among the cultivated areas. Beyond this the land stretches away, smooth as a table, brown and barren, to the sky. The city of Ur stood once upon the banks of the Euphrates but now the river has changed its course and from the summit of the ancient city-mound the fringe of palms on the river's bank is visible on the skyline twelve miles eastward. In all other directions, as far as the eye can see, stretches a vast plain of unprofitable sand. Shimmering heat waves dance over the monotonous waste, and mirages feign nonexistent waters. Here at Ur a tourist, disgruntled, wrote in the register of the mud hotel, "No wonder Abraham left; even Job would have!" But, as we shall see, in the time of Abraham the scene at Ur was far different, and no doubt it will once again become different as modern works of irrigation are carried forward.

1. THE NEOLITHIC, CHALCOLITHIC, AND LATE PREHISTORIC PERIODS,
c.5000-c.2800 B.C.[1]

EARLY VILLAGES

MESOPOTAMIA was the home of various peoples for thousands of years before the time of Abraham, and if we are to place the biblical patriarchs in their true setting we must sketch at least briefly the long historical development of which they were at least in some degree the heirs.

The earliest village settlements which have been discovered belong to the Neolithic Age and are in the northern part of Mesopotamia. One of these villages was found in 1948 at Qal'at Jarmo, thirty miles east of Kirkuk, by an expedition of the Oriental Institute of the University of Chicago, led by Robert J. Braidwood.[2] At this

---

[1] Most dates, it will be noted, are approximate rather than exact, and particularly in the earlier millenniums only the broadest chronological indications can be given. Recent discoveries have necessitated successive revisions in the early chronology of the Middle East, and in general the tendency has been toward the lowering of previously accepted dates. See Sidney Smith, *Alalakh and Chronology.* 1940, p.29; O. Neugebauer in JAOS 61 (1941), pp.58-61; Theophile J. Meek in JR 21 (1941), p.404 n.15; William F. Albright in BASOR 69 (Feb. 1938), pp.18-21; 77 (Feb. 1940), pp.25-30; 88 (Dec. 1942), pp.28-36; and in AJA 47 (1943), pp.491f. The dates given here are substantially those of Albright's revision in BASOR 88, p.32.

[2] F. Basmachi in *Sumer.* 4 (1948), pp.135f.; PCAM p.1; E. A. Speiser in NGM 99 (1951), p.46. A link between the last stage of man's life as a cave dweller and the first of his permanently established villages such as Jarmo, is provided by the dis-

site there were the remains of permanent habitations, showing that man had made the significant transition to settled life. Stone implements bore witness to a Neolithic culture.[3] No pottery was found, and it is probable that the art of making pottery vessels, subsequently so important, was not yet known. Crude clay statuettes represented the animals which had been domesticated, the goat, the sheep, the dog, and the pig. Cereals were ground between grinding stones, but the absence of stone hoes, such as appear at Tell Hassuna, suggests that the grains were not yet cultivated by human hand but simply gathered from wild growth. Primitive clay figurines of the mother goddess type attest the existence of religion or magic.

As to date, Jarmo may probably be assigned to a time not long after 5000 B.C. Confirmation of this figure has been given by an application of the Carbon 14 method of dating to snail shells from Jarmo, with a resultant date of 4756 B.C., plus or minus 320 years.[4]

TELL HASSUNA

Tell Hassuna is the name of a prehistoric site twenty-five miles south of Mosul, excavated in 1943 and 1944 by the Iraq Museum.[5] The first settlers at this place are known only from their flint or obsidian weapons and tools, and coarse pottery. Among the tools are stone axes with which they may have broken the ground in crude agriculture. A little later they had permanent adobe houses, soon numbering several rooms grouped around an open courtyard. Their pottery became much finer, and was adorned with incised or

---

covery in 1950-1951 by the American School of Oriental Research at Baghdad of a temporary open-air settlement of the Mesolithic Age at Karim Shahir, a little over a mile from Jarmo. Robert J. Braidwood in BASOR 124 (Dec. 1951), pp.12-18.

[3] Linda S. Braidwood in *Sumer.* 7 (1951), pp.105f.

[4] Robert J. Braidwood and Linda Braidwood in JNES 11 (1952), p.66; Willard F. Libby, *Radiocarbon Dating.* 2d ed. 1955, p.79. The Carbon 14 dating method has been developed by Willard F. Libby and J. R. Arnold at the Institute for Nuclear Studies of the University of Chicago. It depends upon the fact that in their exchange with the atmosphere, in the life process, all living things take in Carbon 14, which is an unstable or radioactive form of carbon with an atomic weight of 14. Upon the death of a living thing, this radiocarbon begins a long process of decay at a known rate. An ounce of it, for example, is reduced by disintegration to a half ounce in 5,500 years, this half is diminished to a quarter ounce in the next 5,500 years, and so on. Having determined experimentally the proportion of Carbon 14 in living matter, and knowing its "half-life" as just indicated, it is possible to ascertain the age of an ancient organic sample by the amount of Carbon 14 (measured by a radiation counter) it contains. With present techniques, the effective range of the method is about 20,000 years, with a year error in dating samples of 5 to 10 per cent. Donald Collier in BA 14 (1951), pp.25-28.

[5] AJA 48 (1944), p.371; Seton Lloyd and Fuad Safar in JNES 4 (1945), pp.255-289.

painted decorations. The development of agriculture is attested by the finding not only of more stone hand axes but also of flint-toothed sickles for reaping, and of large spherical clay grain bins sunk beneath the floors of the houses for storage. There were also flat rubbing-stones for grinding flour, and clay ovens for baking bread. Infant burials were found in pottery jars, and other jars, perhaps intended for water or food, were sometimes placed nearby. The bones of domesticated animals, the ox, the ass, and the sheep, were numerous. Beads and amulets reveal an interest in personal ornament; mother goddess figurines of clay suggest the religious or magical beliefs of the time. Such was the early farming community to which Levels i-v at Tell Hassuna bear witness. Since pottery was found at Hassuna but not at Jarmo, the settlement here was presumably somewhat later in date than that at Jarmo.

Another village which appears to have been approximately contemporary with Hassuna, although relatively poorer in its culture, was at Matarrah, about twenty miles south of Kirkuk. The excavations at this place were conducted by the Oriental Institute of the University of Chicago in 1948.[6]

Remains almost as early as those at Hassuna have been found at the famous site of Nineveh, the location of which is just across the Tigris from Mosul. A prehistoric sounding was conducted here in 1931-1932 by M. E. L. Mallowan on behalf of the British Museum.[7] A large pit was dug down ninety feet from one of the highest points on the mound to virgin soil. Underlying the later Assyrian levels a series of strata was penetrated, the lowest of which corresponded to the first settlement at Nineveh. Here were the evidences of a village which once existed on a low mound only slightly above the level of the plain. The huts of the people were represented by debris of decayed wood and ashes. Mingled with this were fragments of their handmade pottery, which was thick and coarse, poorly fired and unburnished. For the most part light gray in color, some of it was incised with deeply cut hatching, notches, and punctuations, these illustrating the earliest attempts of the potter at Nineveh to decorate his clay vessels. Elementary painted designs soon appear

[6] Robert J. Braidwood, Linda Braidwood, James G. Smith, and Charles Leslie in JNES 11 (1952), pp.1-75.

[7] M. E. L. Mallowan in *Annals of Archaeology and Anthropology, issued by the Institute of Archaeology, University of Liverpool.* 20 (1933), pp.127-177; and in *Proceedings of the First International Congress of Prehistoric and Protohistoric Sciences, London 1932.* 1934, pp.165-167.

also, and as time goes on become more common. While the very earliest level at Tell Hassuna probably precedes anything known from Nineveh, it may in general be said that the strata called Ninevite 1 and 2 are of antiquity comparable to Levels i-v at Tell Hassuna.

Yet other sites where some of the pottery appears to belong to this same period include the following: At Tell Arpachiya, north of Mosul, excavation penetrated to the tenth building level (tt 10), counting down from the top of the mound, and brought forth some incised and painted sherds resembling similarly decorated pottery at Nineveh; while in an outlying area one specimen was found just above virgin soil which was identical with the rough incised ware of Ninevite 1.[8] At Tell Chagar Bazar, a site located in the area drained by the Khabour river, Level 15 represented the first settlement on virgin soil and contained coarse pottery, with incised decoration, like that of Ninevite 1.[9] At Tell ej-Judeideh in the Plain of Antioch in Syria, excavation was carried down to Level xiv and incised ware comparable to that of the first level at Nineveh was found.[10] At Jericho in Palestine the oldest pottery appeared in Layer ix, and has been compared with that of Judeideh xiv and Hassuna i, sometimes even being regarded as slightly more primitive than the latter.[11]

The evidences of the culture here discussed thus extend from the Tigris to the Mediterranean, and reveal a village life the most characteristic marks of which are its pottery and its houses built of clay. The domestication of animals and the practice of agriculture provide the economic basis of the life of the society. Figurines and amulets attest the presence of religious and magical practices, and the burial of the dead with objects accompanying them suggests belief in an afterlife. Since the most distinctive objects of this culture were first found at Tell Hassuna, this is taken as the type site and the period is called the Hassuna period. Since no metal is found, we are still in the Neolithic Age.

A distinctive phase in the development of this culture seems to have been reached at Samarra. Samarra is on the Tigris north of Baghdad. Excavations were undertaken here in 1911-1913 by Ernst E.

---

[8] pcam p.10.   [9] pcam p.11.

[10] Robert J. Braidwood, *Mounds in the Plain of Antioch, an Archaeological Survey*, oip xlviii, 1937, pp.6f.; C. W. McEwan in aja 41 (1937), pp. 10f.

[11] G. Ernest Wright, *The Pottery of Palestine from the Earliest Times to the End of the Early Bronze Age*. 1937, pp.7-11, 107; pcam p.15.

Herzfeld with particular reference to Islamic ruins.[12] Underneath the pavements of the Islamic houses, however, was a five-foot layer of debris resting on virgin soil and consisting of badly preserved graves. In the graves was an abundance of painted pottery. The vessels included plates, dishes on high bases, flaring and hemispherical bowls, wide-mouthed pots, and squat jars. Mostly of medium thickness and often overfired, they were commonly provided with a slip as a base for the painting.[13] In the painted design there is an emphasis upon geometric motifs and a preference for straight lines rather than curves. The linear patterns are carried around the exterior surface of the vessels in continuous horizontal zones. Multiple parallel lines are used in many forms, and hatching, crosshatching, chevrons, zigzags, and meanders are very frequently found.[14]

Similar ware has been found at other places, including Baghouz, a site on the Middle Euphrates discovered and excavated by le Comte du Mesnil du Buisson in 1934-1936.[15] This has led some to surmise that Samarra should be recognized as marking a separate cultural phase,[16] but at present it seems best to consider it as simply representing the height of artistic achievement in the Hassuna period.[17]

TELL HALAF

The Neolithic Age, to which the early settlements just mentioned belong, was followed by the Chalcolithic or "copper-stone" Age when the peoples were moving out of the age of stone and into the times of the use of metal. In the Middle East this transition may have begun by around 4500 B.C. To the Chalcolithic Age belongs a new and notable culture which, like its more primitive predecessors, was centered in northern Mesopotamia. The first evidences of this culture were discovered at Tell Halaf. This site is in the northwest, near where the Beirut-Baghdad railway swings across the upper part of al-Jazira, and is on the Khabour, the only permanently

[12] Ernst E. Herzfeld, *Die Ausgrabungen von Samarra*, III, *Die Malereien von Samarra*. 1927, p. vii.

[13] In pottery-making the "slip" is liquid clay applied to the surface of the vessel as a decoration. It is fired, and serves also to receive whatever painting is done. J. L. Kelso and J. Palin Thorley in AASOR 21-22 (1941-43), p.106.

[14] Ernst E. Herzfeld, *Die Ausgrabungen von Samarra*, V, *Die vorgeschichtlichen Töpfereien von Samarra*. 1930.

[15] Le Comte du Mesnil du Buisson, *Baghouz, l'ancienne Corsôtê, le tell archaïque et la nécropole de l'âge du bronze*. 1948, pp.xii, 18-19.

[16] W. F. Albright in AJA 55 (1951), p.209.

[17] PCAM pp.5-8, 15; Charles Leslie in JNES 11 (1952), pp.57-66.

flowing tributary of the Euphrates in Mesopotamia. Remains of the same culture have also been found at Carchemish over 100 miles west of Tell Halaf, at Tell Chagar Bazar 50 miles to the east, and at Tepe Gawra and Tell Arpachiya 175 miles to the east.[18] From the type site this is called the Halaf period.

The first intimation that Tell Halaf was an ancient site came when native Chechens undertook to bury one of their dead on the hill and were frightened away upon digging up stone statues of animals with human heads. Baron Max von Oppenheim secured the secret from them in 1899 and worked at Tell Halaf in 1911-1913 and again in 1927 and 1929.[19] In the lowest levels were found the remains of a civilization which was much advanced over the life of the primitive Neolithic villages. The most distinctive product of this culture was its superb painted pottery. This was made by hand and among all the handmade wares of antiquity ranks as one of the best on both the technical and the artistic sides. Characteristically it is a fine, thin pottery covered with a smooth cream or buff slip on which are inimitable polychrome designs in black and orange-red paint. Many of the patterns are geometrical in character, while bird, animal and human representations also appear. Several fragments of this remarkable pottery are shown in Fig. 1. A genuine glaze paint was used, and the pottery was fired at an intense heat in closed kilns, which gave it a porcelain-like finish. Kilns of this type, making perfectly controlled temperatures possible, have been found in place at Carchemish, Tell Arpachiya, and Tepe Gawra.[20] Among the other technical developments of the time appears to have been the use of wheeled vehicles. On a painted vase found at Tell Halaf there is to be seen what, if its usual interpretation is correct, is the earliest known picture of a chariot. The chariot has great eight-spoked wheels and carries a man.[21]

Of the other northern sites representative of the Halaf period, Tepe Gawra may be chosen for description. "The Great Mound," as the name means, stands about fifteen miles northeast of Mosul and two miles east of Khorsabad. Beginning with a sounding in

[18] See e.g. M. E. L. Mallowan and J. Cruikshank Rose, *Prehistoric Assyria, The Excavations at Tall Arpachiyah 1933.* 1935, pp.17, 25, 104f.

[19] Max von Oppenheim, *Der Tell Halaf, Eine neue Kultur im ältesten Mesopotamien.* 1931; tr. *Tell Halaf, A New Culture in Oldest Mesopotamia.*

[20] See e.g. E. A. Speiser in BASOR 66 (Apr. 1937), pp.15f.; *The New York Times,* May 11, 1937, p.26.

[21] M. von Oppenheim, *Der Tell Halaf,* Pl. 51, No. 8, p.184.

1927 and continuing through seven more campaigns between 1931 and 1938, excavations were conducted here by the American Schools of Oriental Research and the University Museum of the University of Pennsylvania, with additional assistance from The Dropsie College, Philadelphia. The discoverer of Tepe Gawra and director of four of the eight expeditions which worked there was E. A. Speiser of the University of Pennsylvania.[22]

On the main mound excavation began by complete levels and was gradually restricted to smaller areas as greater depths were reached, Stratum xx being explored only by trenches. In addition, soundings were made in two regions at the foot of the mound on the southeast and northeast respectively, which are known as Area A, and Northeast Base. In Area A, Northeast Base, and Stratum xx the oldest pottery was found and was of the Halaf type. As at Tell Halaf the wares were usually thin and always very hard, having been fired at high temperatures. Often covered with a light-colored slip, the vessels were painted with geometrical and linear designs, and also with naturalistic patterns of birds, in colors of red, black, and brown.[23]

The sites thus far mentioned as characteristic of the Halaf period are all in the north or northwest, and it is believed that the original home of the Halaf culture is to be sought somewhere in the Mosul area.[24] At the same time settlement was also beginning in southern Mesopotamia.

ERIDU

The earliest site yet known in Lower Mesopotamia has been found at Tell Abu Shahrain, which is identified as the ancient city of Eridu. Interestingly enough, as will be noted later, this is the very city where the first antediluvian kingship is located by the Sumerian King List. Under the direction of Fuad Safar, excavations were conducted at Tell Abu Shahrain by the Department of Antiquities of the Iraq Government for three seasons between 1946 and 1949.[25]

The lowest levels, which probably represent a time not long after 4500 b.c., are characterized by a fine painted pottery. Shallow dishes, deep bowls, and tall goblets are among the most frequent

[22] E. A. Speiser, *Excavations at Tepe Gawra*, i, *Levels I-VIII*. 1935; and in NGM 99 (1951), pp.42f.; Arthur J. Tobler, *Excavations at Tepe Gawra*, ii, *Levels IX-XX*. 1950.
[23] Tobler, *Excavations at Tepe Gawra*, ii, pp.126-137.
[24] PCAM p.44.
[25] Naji al-Asil in *Sumer*. 3 (1947), p.3; 6 (1950), pp.3f., 27-33; Seton Lloyd and Fuad Safar in *Sumer*. 4 (1948), pp.115-125.

shapes found. The paint usually employed was chocolate-colored, sometimes red. Ornamental designs included checks, grids, cross-hatchings, and zigzag lines. While in the painting there is reminiscence of Tell Halaf and Samarra, in other respects this pottery is different. It appears immediately above virgin soil and continues upward through half a dozen successive levels of occupation, only then being supplanted by another kind of pottery already previously known from Tell al-'Ubaid. Whereas the 'Ubaid pottery and related objects had formerly been supposed to represent the earliest culture that had appeared in Lower Mesopotamia, the Eridu ware is now recognized as antecedent and as the indication of a distinct and prior cultural period in that area.

Also belonging to this early period were the ruins of a small shrine, ten feet square, built of sun-dried bricks, the first in a series of no less than fourteen prehistoric temples, one succeeding the other, which were found in the mound. In some of the higher levels the traces of huts were still discernible which had been made of reeds and plastered both inside and out with clay. Although the reeds had completely decayed, the impressions of their stems and leaves remained on the inner surfaces of the two layers of plaster. Such building with reeds may well have been the very first kind of construction practiced in the lower Mesopotamian marshes.

TELL AL-'UBAID

Tell al-'Ubaid (or el-Obeid) was once directly on the Euphrates, although the river has now shifted its course some distance away. In 1919 early ruins were found at this site by H. R. Hall, and in 1923-1924 C. Leonard Woolley directed the Joint Expedition of the British Museum and the University Museum of the University of Pennsylvania in important excavations.[26] This is the type site for the 'Ubaid period which must have begun around 4000 B.C. and is represented in finds in both southern and northern Mesopotamia.

The characteristic pottery found at Tell al-'Ubaid (Fig. 2) is a fine, pale greenish ware, painted with free geometrical designs in black or dark brown. It was made either entirely by hand or on a slow, hand-turned wheel. While animal motifs were rare in the decoration of the pottery, numerous animal and human figures, hand-modeled in clay, were found.

Like huts already mentioned at Eridu, 'Ubaid houses were built

---

[26] H. R. Hall and C. Leonard Woolley, *Ur Excavations*, I, *Al-'Ubaid*. 1927.

out of reeds plastered with mud. Building was also done with bricks
made of mud dried in the sun. The mud-plastered walls were sometimes decorated with most interesting mosaics made of small,
slender pencil-like cones of baked clay, the ends of which were left
plain, or painted red or black. This usage gave the wall an almost
waterproof protection and a permanent decoration, and was practiced for centuries.

Another village of the 'Ubaid period has been excavated at Telul
ath-Thalathat some forty miles west of Mosul. This work was done
by the Iraq-Iran Archaeological Expedition of Tokyo University
under the sponsorship of Prince Takahito Mikasa and others. Dwelling houses, pottery, and skeletal remains of the 'Ubaid period were
unearthed, while a larger building of the subsequent Uruk period
was believed to have been a very early temple.[27]

At Eridu on the northwest side of the mound a large cemetery
was found which belongs to the 'Ubaid period, as shown by much
pottery of the same kind as at Tell al-'Ubaid. There were about one
thousand graves here, built out of sun-dried bricks in the form of
oblong boxes. After the body was placed therein the box was filled
with earth and sealed with a covering of bricks. In many cases more
than one member of a family was buried in the same tomb, the
grave having been opened to permit the additional interment. The
pottery accompanying the dead was ordinarily placed near the
feet; where a second burial was introduced the vessels were put
near the head to avoid confusion with the previous deposit. One
unsealed grave contained the skeleton of a dog lying directly upon
that of a young boy.[28]

At Tepe Gawra the Strata from xix up to xii correspond with the
'Ubaid period. In Stratum xix were the poorly preserved ruins of a
temple, which was rebuilt in similar form in the next level above.
In Stratum xiii, which is perhaps to be dated around the close of
the fifth or beginning of the fourth millennium B.C., was an extraor-
dinarily impressive acropolis. Three monumental temple buildings
enclosed three sides of a large open court. All the temples had their
corners oriented to the cardinal points of the compass, and all were
ornamented with recessed niches on both the exterior and interior
surfaces of the walls. Built of sun-baked mud brick, the temples
were also plastered and at least in part painted. Entering the court

[27] Namio Egami in *Sumer.* 13 (1957), pp.5-11.
[28] Lloyd and Safar in *Sumer.* 4 (1948), pp.117-119.

the ancient worshiper saw on the right what the archeologists call the Eastern Shrine where traces of color suggest that the building was painted bright red; on the left the warm reddish-brown brick walls of the Northern Temple; and directly ahead the white-plastered façade and great niche of the Central Temple, the inner rooms and cult chamber of which were painted in reddish-purple. Architectural relationships suggest that the three buildings were erected in the order just named. The existence of this acropolis with its imposing places of worship, the construction of which would have been possible only through the combined efforts of a large community, witnesses to the social and religious development of the time.[29]

The 'Ubaid civilization was evidently related to a contemporaneous Iranian Highland culture which reached eastward across the plateau of Iran into Baluchistan, and it is closely associated with the findings in the lowest levels at Susa, known as Susa I.[30] The famous ancient site of Susa is in Persia, 150 miles north of the head of the Persian Gulf. Susa was explored by Dieulafoy, Houssaye, and Babin Expedition[31] sent out by the French government in 1884-1886, and in 1897 and following years was studied intensively by a series of expeditions under the direction of Jacques de Morgan and R. de Mecquenem, while more recently further work has been directed by G. Contenau and R. Ghirshman.[32] An aerial photograph of the site is shown in Fig. 3. On the principal elevation are the fortlike quarters of the French archeological expedition, while to the left is the modern village of Shush with the traditional "Tomb of Daniel."

Susa was founded about 4000 B.C. and was still a great city in the twelfth century A.D. Outside the earthen rampart of the mud village in which the earliest inhabitants lived were many graves. In them was found an abundance of fragile pottery, painted a glossy black, with decorations including geometrical patterns of triangles, rectangles, and zigzags, and human, animal, and plant designs reduced to almost geometrical forms. Galloping dogs, goats whose fore and

[29] E. A. Speiser in BASOR 65 (Feb. 1937), p.8; 66 (Apr. 1937), pp.3-9; and in *Asia*. 38 (1938), pp.542f.; Tobler, *Excavations at Tepe Gawra*, II, *Levels IX-XX*, pp.30-36, 43-47.

[30] Henri Frankfort, *Archaeology and the Sumerian Problem*. SAOC 4, 1932, p.29; Donald E. McCown, *The Comparative Stratigraphy of Early Iran*. SAOC 23, 1942, p.36 and Fig.13.

[31] M. A. Dieulafoy, *L'Acropole de Suse d'après les fouilles exécutées en 1884, 1885, 1886 sous les auspices du Musée du Louvre*. 1890.

[32] See M. Pézard and E. Pottier, *Les Antiquitiés de la Susiane*. Musée de Louvre, 1913; and the *Mémoires* of the French expeditions.

hindquarters are triangles and whose horns are sweeping semicircles, and rows of storks, whose bodies are large triangles and whose heads are small triangles, are among the conventionalized designs represented in the sophisticated art of Susa i.[33] Copper mirrors, beads of black and white limestone or imported turquoise, and little conical vases once containing green mineral paint for the eyelids, were also found. Among tools and weapons buried with the dead were stone-headed clubs and copper-headed tomahawks. Fragments of cloth also remain to indicate that these people had the art of making fine linen.

Beyond Persia lies Baluchistan, the bridge to India, where the Iranian Highland culture may even have come into contact with the culture of the Indus Valley. Baluchistan is now to a great extent desert, but many prehistoric sites have been discovered there which may be links between the civilizations of Mesopotamia and of the Indus Valley.[34] The prehistoric culture of the Indus Valley is known through the excavations at Mohenjo-daro, some 140 miles northeast of Karachi, and at other sites on the Five Streams of the Punjab. At Mohenjo-daro, "the Place of the Dead," there existed around the middle of the third millennium B.C. a planned city with broad streets, buildings made of fine brick, and an elaborate sanitary system including a bathroom in almost every house.[35]

The indications of early contact between Mesopotamia and India includes such facts as the following: In the Tell al-'Ubaid period the inhabitants of Mesopotamia were making beads out of lapis lazuli, an azure blue stone which comes from Central Asia, and amazonite, a green stone which is found only in Central India and Transbaikalia. Later, in the tombs of Ur, is found the little figure of a squatting monkey precisely similar to figures unearthed at Mohenjo-daro, while around 2500 B.C. at Tell Asmar other Indian animals—the elephant, rhinoceros, and gharial or fish-eating crocodile—appear on a seal of undoubted Indian workmanship.[36]

[33] J. de Morgan and R. de Mecquenem, *La Céramique peinte de Suse, Mémoires, Délégation en Perse.* xiii (1912); R. de Mecquenem, *Notes sur la céramique peinte archaïque en Perse, Mémoires,* xx (1928); G. Contenau in Arthur U. Pope, ed., *A Survey of Persian Art from Prehistoric Times to the Present.* 1938, i, pp.171f.; H. A. Groenewegen-Frankfort, *Arrest and Movement, An Essay on Space and Time in the Representational Art of the Ancient Near East.* 1951, pp.146f.

[34] Aurel Stein, *Archaeological Reconnaissances in Northwestern India and Southeastern Iran.* 1937; and in *A Survey of Persian Art.* i, p.168.

[35] John Marshall, ed., *Mohenjo-Daro and the Indus Civilization.* 3 vols. 1931; E. J. H. Mackay, *Further Excavations at Mohenjo-Daro.* 2 vols. 1937-38.

[36] Ernest Mackay, *The Indus Civilization.* 1935, pp.170, 191-193, 199. cf. 2d ed. rev. by Dorothy Mackay, *Early Indus Civilizations.* 1948.

URUK

The story of Mesopotamia is continued at Warka, which was ancient Erech or Uruk and is some thirty-five miles up the Euphrates Valley from Tell al-'Ubaid. This is the type site for the Uruk period which occupies much of the fourth millennium B.C. If the following Jemdet Nasr period be included along with the Uruk period this entire time may be called the Late Prehistoric period since it is the last before the Early Dynastic period which is the first historic age.[37]

In the excavation of Uruk by the Deutsche Orientgesellschaft[38] the most distinctive pottery found was a red ware, running from brick-red to plum-red in color. Black and gray wares were also found; they were baked in a kiln smothered down to make the smoke penetrate and color the clay. Both of these kinds of pottery were made on a genuine spinning potter's wheel, and they were highly polished but left unpainted.[39]

A small pavement of rough limestone blocks at Uruk is the oldest stone construction in Mesopotamia, and here, too, is found the first ziggurat. The Assyrian-Babylonian word *ziqquratu* comes from the verb *zaqaru* meaning "to be high, or raised up," and hence signifies the top of a mountain, or a staged tower. Such a tower provided a sort of artificial mountain in the flat Mesopotamian plain as a high place for a god whose shrine stood on its summit. From its first appearance here at Uruk, it was ever afterward the most characteristic feature of temple architecture in Mesopotamia, and the locations of more than two dozen such structures are known today.[40]

The Uruk ziggurat was simply a vast mass of clay stamped down hard and strengthened with layers of asphalt and unburnt bricks.

[37] At this point PCAM (p.97) introduces a new terminology and speaks of the Warka and Protoliterate periods, but Albrecht Goetze (in JCS 4 [1950], pp.77f.) favors retention of the scheme already internationally agreed upon of distinguishing the periods subsequent to the 'Ubaid period by the type sites and names of Uruk and Jemdet Nasr, and the latter system is followed here. In *Relative Chronologies in Old World Archeology*, ed. Robert W. Ehrich, 1954, p.46, Miss Perkins employs "Late Prehistoric" as the designation for the period between the 'Ubaid period and the Early Dynastic. For the successive early periods see also the chronological tables of Henri Frankfort, *The Birth of Civilization in the Near East*. 1951, p.112 (using the Warka and Protoliterate terminology), and of Perkins in *Relative Chronologies in Old World Archeology*, pp.52f. (using the sequence Hassuna, Halaf, 'Ubaid, Late Prehistoric, Early Dynastic).

[38] Julius Jordan, *Uruk-Warka nach den Ausgrabungen durch die Deutsche Orient-Gesellschaft*. 1928.

[39] T. J. Meek in Elihu Grant, ed., *The Haverford Symposium on Archaeology and the Bible*. 1938, p.164.

[40] Jean de Mecquenem in *Gazette des Beaux-Arts*. 6e période 18 (1937), pp.201-214; André Parrot, *Ziggurats et Tour de Babel*. 1949, pp.52-54; *The Tower of Babel*. 1955.

Rows of pottery jars were embedded in the upper edges to support them and prevent them from crumbling away. Facing outward, their white rims and dark interiors made a striking ornament. The ziggurat measured some 140 by 150 feet and stood about 30 feet high, its corners being oriented toward the points of the compass. On the summit was the actual shrine, oriented similarly, 65 feet long, 50 feet wide, and built about a long narrow court, 14 feet across, and entered by doors at either end and in the center of the southwest side. The outer walls were ornamented with vertical recesses, and this feature together with the system of orientation remained characteristic of later temples. The original whitewash was still preserved on the mud-brick walls, and hence the German archeologists applied to the shrine the name, *der weisse Tempel*, the White Temple. In similar fashion they named a second temple building, to whose walls a plum-red paint had been applied, the Red Temple. Yet another monumental structure was ornamented beautifully with three-colored mosaic work of clay cones in patterns of zigzags, triangles, and diamonds. This method of ornamentation already had been developed, it will be remembered, at Tell al-ʿUbaid, and the use of the hollow clay cones on the Uruk ziggurat was another adaptation of the same principle.

The most notable achievements of the Uruk culture, however, were the introduction of the cylinder seal and of script. In the White Temple mentioned above, two small square tablets of gypsum plaster were found which bore the impressions of cylinder seals. These are the first instances known of the use of cylinder seals, which appear to have been invented by the people of this period. Such a seal was made in the form of a small stone cylinder which left its impression not by being stamped upon a surface but by being rolled across it. The surface of the cylinder was engraved in intaglio, so that when the seal was used it yielded an image in which the design stood out in relief.[41] Such a cylinder seal is shown in Fig. 5 while the impression from the same seal appears in Fig. 6.

The origin of cylinder seals preceded the invention of writing, and at first they were used chiefly to safeguard possessions. A jar or package was sealed with clay, and while this was moist the cylinder was rolled over it. Since each cylinder bore a distinctive design, a permanent proof of personal ownership was left behind. Later, when writing had developed and letters, contracts, and other records were

[41] cf. Job 38:12-14; Albert E. Bailey, *Daily Life in Bible Times*. 1943, p.27.

inscribed upon clay tablets, these documents were conveniently legalized by similar seal impressions.

From their origin here in the fourth millennium B.C., cylinder seals continued in use until finally supplanted by the stamp seal in Persian times, thus having a demonstrable history of more than 3000 years. From Mesopotamia their manufacture and employment spread to peripheral regions as widely distant as India and Egypt. The decoration of the cylinder seals constituted Mesopotamia's most original contribution to art, and the influence of the seals was felt in all the other branches of decorative art as well.

The excellence of the seals upon their first appearance in the Uruk period is amazing. Vivid animal studies, ornamental heraldic compositions, abstract religious symbols, and narrative illustrations of ritual practice all are found. In Fig. 4 is shown the impression of a cylinder belonging to this period which was found at Tell Billa northeast of modern Mosul. The scene represented has not been explained fully but seems to be of a ritual character. At the left appears what may be a shrine, and it is approached by three men who are presumably bringing offerings. At the right is a boat which has plants at either end.

Only an intimation of later developments in the glyptic art may be given here. In the Early Dynastic period a new and distinctive style was achieved. Decoration rather than narration was emphasized. The subject was often reduced to a pattern of lines whose rhythmic recurrence formed a frieze of indefinite extent. The result was a decorative scheme such as a weaver or embroiderer might use, and hence this has been termed the "brocade" style. The long, slender cylinder shown in Fig. 5 comes from this period, and its impression reproduced in Fig. 6 is characteristic of the style just described. In this instance, the basis of the representation is nothing but two goats, one upright and one upside down, with a few additional strokes completing the design. In the time of Sargon and the Old Akkadian period another notable change in style took place, and the art of the seal reached perhaps its highest expression. The continuous frieze was supplanted by the heraldic group and the linear figures gave way to wholly modeled figures whose physical characteristics were emphasized realistically. At the center of the composition there was often a panel containing an inscription. A seal impression displaying these characteristic features of the Sargonid style is illustrated in Fig. 7. The bearded hero appears in various ways in Mesopotamian art but here seems to represent a spirit of water. In this capacity he is watering the buffaloes from a vase out of which flow two streams. The water and rock border at the bottom is in harmony with the same theme. The inscription in the panel names a certain scribe, Ibnisharrum, as the owner of the seal and dedicates it to Shargalisharri, king of Akkad.[42]

Returning now to Uruk and its culture, it may be noted that the introduction of the cylinder seal was soon followed by the emergence of writing, a momentous invention which must have taken place sometime in the middle of the fourth millennium B.C.[43] In the Red Temple at Uruk were found a number of thin, flat clay tablets inscribed in a crude pictographic script. This picture-writing represents the earliest stage of Babylonian writing known and is evidently the direct ancestor of cuneiform. The pictographs were gradually reduced for speed in drawing to arbitrary groups of lines and these developed into the wedge-shaped writing which we call cuneiform. As the tablets show, the writing material which was used in Mesopotamia from the beginning was clay into which the writing signs were pressed with a stylus whose point was formed into a three-sided prism. The clay tablet was held for writing in the left hand, or when larger in size was laid down flat, and the text was written in vertical columns running from left to right. The numerals found on these tablets show that a sexagesimal system of arithmetic, in which the computing was by sixties, was in most common use but that a decimal system was also employed.[44] Since the sexagesimal system was that of the Sumerians, soon to be mentioned, and since the tablets also refer to Sumerian gods such as Enlil, it is believed that the language of these earliest of written records is Sumerian.[45]

JEMDET NASR

Jemdet Nasr, a site in the Mesopotamian Valley not far from

[42] Richard A. Martin, *Ancient Seals of the Near East*. Field Museum of Natural History Anthropology Leaflet 34, 1940, No.5. For the basic discussion of the entire subject of cylinder seals see Henri Frankfort, *Cylinder Seals*. 1939. See also *Corpus of Ancient Near Eastern Seals in North American Collections, Edited for the Committee of Ancient Near Eastern Seals, A Project of the Iranian Institute, The Oriental Institute of the University of Chicago and the Yale Babylonian Collection*, I, *The Collection of the Pierpont Morgan Library*, ed. Edith Porada, Text, Plates (The Bollingen Series, XIV). 1948.

[43] This is the beginning of the Protoliterate period if this terminology is used. For the date around 3500 B.C. see Henri Frankfort, *The Art and Architecture of the Ancient Orient*. 1954, p.1.

[44] A. Falkenstein, *Archaische Texte aus Uruk*. 1940, pp.49,62.

[45] Frankfort, *The Birth of Civilization in the Near East*, p.50 n.1.

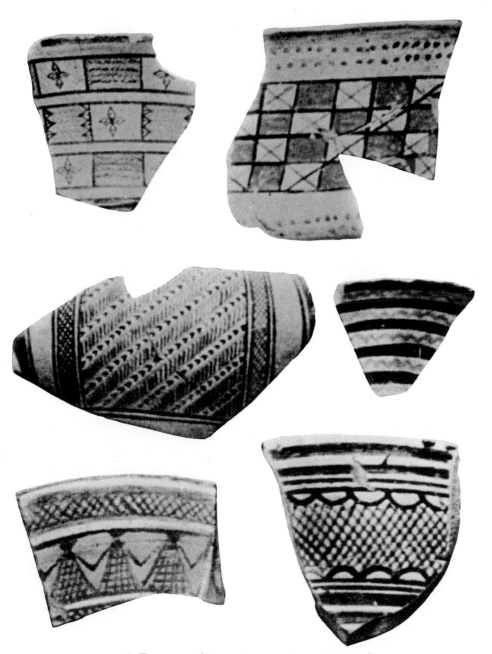

1. Fragments of Painted Pottery from Tell Halaf

2. Pottery from Tell al-'Ubaid

3. Air View of Susa

4. Impression of Cylinder Seal from the Uruk Period

5. Cylinder Seal from the
Early Dynastic Period

6. Impression of Cylinder Seal from the Early Dynastic Period

7. Impression of Cylinder Seal from the Old Akkadian Period

9. Tablet from Nippur with the Story of the Creation and the Flood

8. The Flood Stratum at Kish

11. An Early Sumerian Worshiper

10. Sumerian Statues of the Lord of Fertility and the Mother Goddess

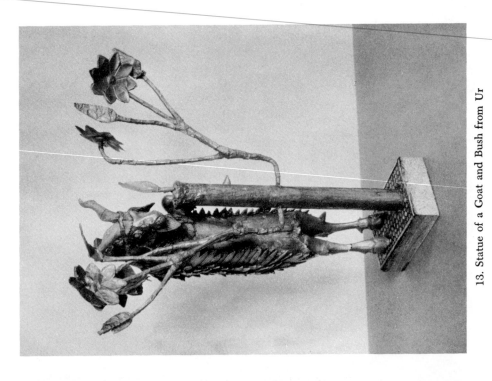

13. Statue of a Goat and Bush from Ur

12. The Headdress of Lady Shub-ad

15. Fluted Gold Bowl from the "Royal" Cemetery at Ur

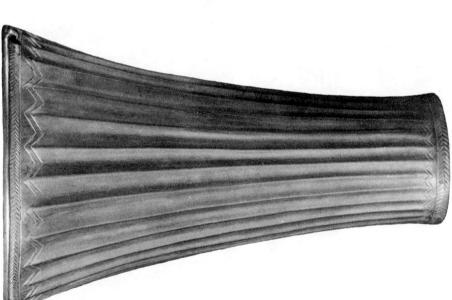

14. Fluted Gold Tumbler from the "Royal" Cemetery at Ur

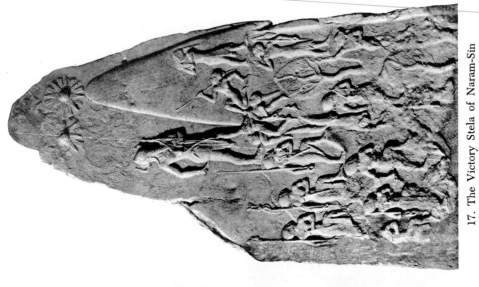

17. The Victory Stela of Naram-Sin

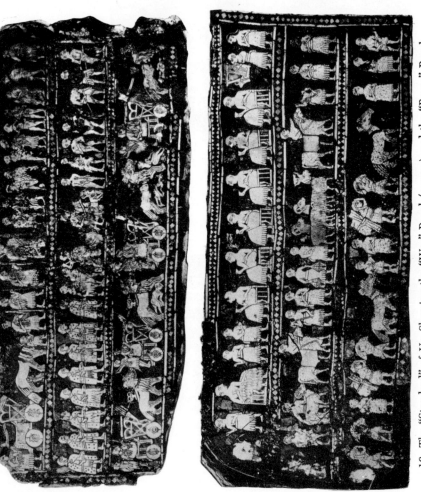

16. The "Standard" of Ur, Showing the "War" Panel (upper) and the "Peace" Panel

18. Statue of Gudea

20. The Stela of Ur-Nammu

19. The Ziggurat at Ur

22. A Business Contract from the Time
of Hammurabi

21. A Worshiper Carrying a Kid for Sacrifice

23. Hammurabi Standing before Shamash

24. The Fourth Tablet of the Epic of Creation

25. Camel and Rider from Tell Halaf

where Babylon was later to stand, may be taken as the type site for the last period in Mesopotamian prehistory.[46] The date of this period is probably around the end of the fourth or beginning of the third millennium B.C. The characteristic pottery at Jemdet Nasr is a painted ware featuring black and yellow on a deep red ground. Metal was employed more freely, and the first use of bronze indicates the beginning of the Bronze Age in Mesopotamia. Tablets were found written in a semipictographic script somewhat more advanced than that of the Uruk period.

Sculpture in stone was a noteworthy achievement of the people of the Jemdet Nasr period. Some of the finest examples come from levels at Uruk and Ur contemporary with Jemdet Nasr. At Uruk a block of basalt was found, carved in bas-relief with a hunting scene in which two bearded men are fighting three lions. At Ur the first example of sculpture in the round was discovered. It was the figure of a crouching boar, carved in steatite or soapstone, and executed in the style of a mature art. The conception is on the whole in terms of an abstract balance of mass, but the character of the animal is suggested realistically by the drawing back of the upper lip over the tusks.

During the Jemdet Nasr period the important cities of Shuruppak (Fara), Eshnunna (Tell Asmar), and Kish were founded. Shuruppak was perhaps eighty-five miles from Jemdet Nasr down the Mesopotamian Valley in the direction of Tell al-'Ubaid, Eshnunna was over fifty miles to the north, while Kish was nearer at hand, some fifteen miles southwest of Jemdet Nasr. All three of these cities will be mentioned again.

THE FLOOD

In a flat river valley such as that of the Tigris and Euphrates and in a region where torrential rains are known, it would be easily possible for great floods to take place. In excavations at a number of Mesopotamian sites, layers of clean clay have been found which could have been deposited by such floods. At the edge of the mound of Ur, C. Leonard Woolley dug down through an early cemetery located in what had once been the rubbish heap of the ancient city. Beneath the level of the graves the diggers continued to find the pottery and other objects of the earlier city, the pottery changing from Jemdet Nasr to Uruk to later 'Ubaid forms. Then they encountered a stratum of perfectly clean silt which the workmen took

[46] Ernest Mackay and Stephen Langdon, *Report on Excavations at Jemdet Nasr, Iraq.* 1931.

for the bottom of the original delta. When measurements showed that this was not the case, they dug on down. Beneath some eight to eleven feet of clean clay they came again upon rubbish full of stone implements and bits of hand-painted pottery such as were found in the earliest levels at Tell al-'Ubaid. This appeared to Woolley to represent a flood of great magnitude which must have inundated the whole valley although Ur itself was high enough that most of the city escaped.[47]

At Shuruppak there was a similar stratum some two feet thick but, whereas the Ur deposit came in the midst of the 'Ubaid period, this was at the end of the Jemdet Nasr period.[48] Likewise at Uruk there was a similar layer five feet in depth which marked the end of the Jemdet Nasr period.[49] Again at Kish there was a layer of sediment one and one-half feet in thickness but this was some distance above the Jemdet Nasr stratification and thus yet somewhat later in date.[50] A picture of this last "flood stratum" is shown in Fig. 8.

It is evident that if the several strata just described are actually flood deposits they still do not represent one and the same inundation since they occur at different points in the stratigraphic sequence. If it was one of these disasters in particular which provided the basis for the later accounts of the flood in Mesopotamian and biblical literature,[51] it might possibly have been that which is attested at Shuruppak and Uruk, or the one at Kish, since in the Sumerian King List, next to be discussed, it is indicated that Shuruppak was the last ruling city before the flood and Kish the seat of the first Sumerian dynasty after the flood.[52]

In the Early Dynastic period of which we shall soon speak the

---

[47] C. L. Woolley, *Ur of the Chaldees*. 1929, pp.22-29; *Excavations at Ur*. Third (corrected) impression 1955, pp.26-36; and in PEQ Jan.-June 1956, pp.17f. For a different interpretation see William A. Irwin in *Church History*. 15 (1946), pp.236f. Concerning this stratum W. F. Albright writes (in BASOR 146 [Apr. 1957], p.35): "Since it brought no change of culture, most archaeologists consider it as a deposit laid down by a river flood which was higher than ordinary, somewhere about the 35th century B.C. or even later."

[48] Erich F. Schmidt in *The Museum Journal*. 22 (1931), pp.200f.

[49] Julius Jordan in *Abhandlungen der preussischen Akademie der Wissenschaften*. 1929, p.20; V. Christian in AO 8 (1932), p.64.

[50] S. Langdon in JRAS 1930, p.603; L. C. Watelin, *Excavations at Kish IV 1925-1930*. 1934, pp.40-44.

[51] André Parrot, *The Flood and Noah's Ark*. 1955, pp.51f.

[52] Another theory is that the flood stories, which are so widespread in the ancient world, embody a memory of the presumably much more far-reaching inundations which came at the end of the last Ice Age, probably ten thousand years ago. Georges Contenau, *Everyday Life in Babylon and Assyria*. 1954, p.196.

Sumerians were dominant in Lower Mesopotamia. This folk, who called themselves "the black-headed people" and their land Sumer, were neither Semites nor Aryans and their language, in which many texts are now available, was neither Semitic nor Indo-European.[53] Since the pictographic writing found at Uruk, mentioned above, was probably Sumerian, these people must have been in Mesopotamia at least in the later part of the Uruk period. Some think that they were indeed the first settlers in Lower Mesopotamia, but a probably preferable theory supposes that the first civilization was established by Iranians from the East and Semites from the West, upon whom came the Sumerians perhaps early in the fourth millennium B.C.[54] An important cultural center of the Sumerians was Nippur, one hundred miles south of modern Baghdad and about midway between Kish and Shuruppak. Excavated first by the University of Pennsylvania in 1889 to 1900 and again since 1948 by a joint Oriental Institute-University Museum expedition under Donald E. McCown, this site has produced thousands of inscribed tablets and fragments which reveal how extensive was the Sumerian literature which was composed in the third and second millenniums B.C.[55]

The Sumerian King List is an interesting chronological list of early rulers, written not later than the middle of the famous Third Dynasty or Ur and probably in the slightly earlier reign of Utu-hegal of Uruk.[56] It is obvious that the list is not entirely dependable, since it ascribes reigns of the most exaggerated length to the earlier kings. It begins with the statement, "When kingship was lowered from heaven the kingship was in Eridu," and then continues with the names of the sovereigns who reigned before the flood. Eight such antediluvian kings are listed and it is stated that their rule centered in five different cities and lasted for 241,200 years. The last of the eight was Ubar-Tutu who, according to the list, reigned at Shuruppak

[53] Frankfort, *The Art and Architecture of the Ancient Orient*, p.235 n.2; André Parrot, *Discovering Buried Worlds.* 1955, p.72.

[54] Samuel N. Kramer in AJA 52 (1948), pp.156-164; KFTS pp.238-248.

[55] J. P. Peters, *Nippur, or Explorations on the Euphrates.* 2 vols. 1897; H. V. Hilprecht, *The Excavations in Assyria and Babylonia.* 1903, pp.289-568; KFTS p.277.

[56] The Weld-Blundell prism, giving an almost complete text of the King List, was published by S. Langdon, *Oxford Editions of Cuneiform Texts.* II (1923); cf. George A. Barton, *The Royal Inscriptions of Sumer and Akkad.* 1929, pp.346-355. A critical edition of the text, also making use of other tablets now available, is given by Thorkild Jacobsen, *The Sumerian King List*, AS 11, 1939. An excerpt of the King List is translated by A. Leo Oppenheim in ANET pp.265-267.

for 18,600 years. The complete outline of the antediluvian period, according to the cuneiform list, is as follows:

CITY	SOVEREIGN	LENGTH OF RULE
Eridu	Alulim	28,800 years
	Alalgar	36,000 "
Badtibira	Enmenlu-Anna	43,200 "
	Enmengal-Anna	28,800 "
	divine Dumuzi, a shepherd	36,000 "
Larak	Ensipazi-Anna	28,800 "
Sippar	Enmendur-Anna	21,000 "
Shuruppak	Ubar-Tutu	18,600 "
		241,200 years

A later form of the same list has long been known from the writings of Berossos, who was a priest of Marduk at Babylon under Antiochus I (281-261 B.C.). Berossos gives the names quite differently, and a further exaggeration of the length of reigns has taken place:

Alorus	36,000 years
Alaparos	10,800 "
Amelon	46,800 "
Ammenon	43,200 "
Megalaros	64,800 "
Daonos or Daos	36,000 "
Euedorachos	64,800 "
Amempsinos	36,000 "
Otiartes	28,800 "
Xisouthros	64,800 "
	432,000 years

Amelon and Ammenon may both be corruptions of the name Enmenlu-Anna, while Xisouthros, the hero of the flood, has been added, thus giving ten names in all. There may be some correspondence between this tradition of ten antediluvian kings, and the biblical record of ten patriarchs from Adam to Noah.[57] Then came the flood, apparently wiping out Shuruppak, after which sovereignty again was established from heaven, this time at Kish. The King List states:

> After the flood had swept thereover,
> when the kingship was lowered from heaven
> the kingship was in Kish.

[57] George A. Barton, *Archaeology and the Bible*, 7th ed. 1937, p.320.

After that the King List continues with the First Dynasty of Kish and with other dynasties which we shall mention later.

In addition to the brief allusion in the King List, the Sumerians had an extensive legend concerning a great flood. Like the King List, this legend also, at least in some of its versions, mentions Shuruppak as the particular city upon which the flood came. It is possible, however, that the traditions of other floods such as those at Ur and Kish may have contributed to the development of the story. An early version of this story appears on the fragment of a Sumerian tablet (Fig. 9) found at Nippur and now in the University Museum. It is inscribed on both sides, with three columns to the side.[58]

In the first column some deity is speaking who alludes to an earlier destruction of mankind and then tells how men and animals were created. A portion of this reads as follows:

> After Anu, Enlil, Enki, and Ninhursag[59]
> Had fashioned the black-headed people,
> Vegetation luxuriated from the earth,
> Animals, four-legged creatures of the plain, were
>   brought artfully into existence.

The second column relates how some deity founded five cities, these being the same as the five antediluvian cities in the King List, Eridu, Badtibira, Larak, Sippar, and Shuruppak. The deity assigned each city to the special care of a guardian god, and also established irrigation canals.

The third column finds some of the deities weeping over the decision which has evidently been reached to send a deluge upon earth. At that time, it is explained, Ziusudra (the Xisouthros of Berossos' list), whose name means "Life-day prolonged," was king and priest. Other references show that Ziusudra was the son of Ubar-Tutu (the Otiartes of Berossos), and ruled in Shuruppak. In his extremity Ziusudra sought guidance from such divine revelations as might come to him through dreams or the use of incantations. In the fourth column he is told to stand beside a wall where some deity will speak to him. In the revelation which now comes to him the full plan of the gods to destroy mankind by a flood is made known:

> Ziusudra, standing at its side, listened.
> "Stand by the wall at my left side . . .

---

[58] S. N. Kramer in ANET pp.42-44 (ANEA pp.28-30); and *Sumerian Mythology.* 1944, pp.97f.; S. Langdon, *Semitic Mythology.* 1931, pp.206-208.
[59] For these deities see below, p.45.

By the wall I will say a word to thee, take my word,
Give ear to my instruction:
By our . . . a flood will sweep over the cult-centers;
To destroy the seed of mankind . . .
Is the decision, the word of the assembly of the gods.

When column five in its broken form again continues the narrative, the terrific deluge has begun, and Ziusudra is riding it out in a great boat.

All the windstorms, exceedingly powerful, attacked as one,
At the same time, the flood sweeps over the cult-centers.
After, for seven days and seven nights,
The flood had swept over the land,
And the huge boat had been tossed about by the windstorms
    on the great waters,
Utu[60] came forth, who sheds light on heaven and earth.
Ziusudra opened a window of the huge boat,
The hero Utu brought his rays into the giant boat.
Ziusudra, the king,
Prostrated himself before Utu,
The king kills an ox, slaughters a sheep.

Thus the terrible storm came to an end, and as column six closes we read how Ziusudra received the gift of immortality and was transferred to live forever in the land of Dilmun.

Ziusudra, the king,
Prostrated himself before Anu and Enlil.
Anu and Enlil cherished Ziusudra,
Life like that of a god they give him,
Breath eternal like that of a god they bring down for him.
Then, Ziusudra the king,
The preserver of the name of vegetation and of the seed of
    mankind,
In the land of crossing, the land of Dilmun, the place where
    the sun rises, they caused to dwell.[61]

Such is the essential outline of the ancient Sumerian story of the flood as preserved in the fragment from Nippur. This story was

[60] The sun-god.

[61] Interpreting the last line as meaning the mountain-land which the sun crosses immediately upon rising in the east, Kramer suggests that the land of Dilmun was in southwestern Iran (BASOR 96 [Dec. 1944], pp.18-28). P. B. Cornwall (BASOR 103 [Oct. 1946], pp.3-11) identifies Dilmun with the island of Bahrein. He believes that the Sumerians came to Mesopotamia by way of the Persian Gulf and stopped on the way at Bahrein, the only place where a sheltered harbor and good fresh water were available. This would help to explain the sacred character which Dilmun assumed in Sumerian tradition.

ultimately incorporated in the famous epic of Gilgamesh and it is here that it is found in most detailed form. Composed in Akkadian, the Semitic language of the non-Sumerian inhabitants of Mesopotamia, probably by the beginning of the second millennium B.C., the Gilgamesh epic is known chiefly from texts preserved in the library of Ashurbanipal at Nineveh in the seventh century B.C. (p. 217), although some fragments have been found elsewhere.[62]

Ziusudra appears now in the Old Babylonian translation of his name as Utnapishtim, "Day of Life." Gilgamesh, a legendary king of Uruk, has a friend named Enkidu who is his faithful companion in adventures and difficulties. Enkidu dies and Gilgamesh expresses his bewilderment in these words:

> Enkidu, my younger friend, thou who chasedst
> The wild ass of the hills, the panther of the steppe!
> We who have conquered all things, scaled the mountains . . .
> What, now, is this sleep that has laid hold on thee?

In sadness and desperation Gilgamesh then undertakes a hazardous pilgrimage across untraversed mountains and the waters of death to find Utnapishtim, the immortal, and seek from him an answer to the question of death.

> For Enkidu, his friend, Gilgamesh
> Weeps bitterly, as he ranges over the steppe:
> "When I die, shall I not be like Enkidu? . . .
> Fearing death, I roam over the steppe.
> To Utnapishtim, Ubar-Tutu's son,
> I have taken the road to proceed in all haste.

On the way he is told by Shamash,

> The life thou pursuest thou shalt not find,

and from the barmaid, Siduri, he receives advice which Ecclesiastes (9:7-9) will echo:

---

[62] The text of the Assyrian version was published by R. Campbell Thompson, *The Epic of Gilgamish* (1930). The translation quoted here is that by E. A. Speiser in ANET pp.72-99 (ANEA, pp.40f.). Alexander Heidel, *The Gilgamesh Epic and Old Testament Parallels* (2d ed. 1949) gives a translation and full discussion of the relationships of the Gilgamesh epic and the Old Testament. See also Langdon, *Semitic Mythology*, pp.210-223; E. A. Wallis Budge, *The Babylonian Story of the Deluge and the Epic of Gilgamesh.* 1920; R. Campbell Thompson, *The Epic of Gilgamesh, A New Translation from a Collation of the Cuneiform Tablets in the British Museum rendered literally into English Hexameters.* 1928; William E. Leonard, *Gilgamesh, Epic of Old Babylonia, A Rendering in Free Rhythms.* 1934. A cuneiform tablet containing some forty lines of the epic has recently been discovered in the debris of the excavation of Megiddo (BA 18 [1955], p.44; PEQ May-Oct. 1955, p.104).

Gilgamesh, whither rovest thou?
The life thou pursuest thou shalt not find.
When the gods created mankind,
Death for mankind they set aside,
Life in their own hands retaining.
Thou, Gilgamesh, let full be thy belly,
Make thou merry by day and by night.
Of each day make thou a feast of rejoicing,
Day and night dance thou and play!
Let thy garments be sparkling fresh,
Thy head be washed; bathe thou in water.
Pay heed to the little one that holds on to thy hand,
Let thy spouse delight in thy bosom!
For this is the task of mankind![63]

The eternal question still agitates the mind of Gilgamesh, however, and drives him forward upon his quest.

How can I be silent? How can I be still?
My friend, whom I loved, has turned to clay!
Must I too, like him, lay me down,
Not to rise again for ever and ever?

Nevertheless, as Shamash and Siduri have warned him, he is doomed to eventual failure on his mission. Even though at last he reaches and converses with Utnapishtim and at the latter's direction obtains the plant of life, it is stolen from him by a serpent and he returns disconsolate.

It is in the eleventh tablet of this long epic which occupies twelve tablets that Utnapishtim explains his possession of immortality by relating to Gilgamesh the story of the flood. Utnapishtim begins:

Shuruppak—a city which thou knowest,
And which on Euphrates' banks is situate—
That city was ancient, as were the gods within it,
When their heart led the great gods to produce the flood.

The god Ea participates in the assembly of the gods, but reveals their plans to Utnapishtim through the wall of a reed hut.

Ninigiku-Ea[64] was also present with them;
Their words he repeats to the reed-hut:
"Reed-hut, reed-hut! Wall, wall!
Reed-hut, hearken! Wall, reflect!

[63] These two passages are found in an Old Babylonian version of the epic, which may date from around the time of Hammurabi. Bruno Meissner, *Mitteilungen der vorderasiatischen Gesellschaft*. 1902, Heft 1, p.9.

[64] Ea was the same as the Sumerian Enki, god of water and of wisdom.

Man of Shuruppak, son of Ubar-Tutu,
Tear down this house, build a ship!
Give up possessions, seek thou life.
Forswear worldly goods and keep the soul alive!
Aboard the ship take thou the seed of all living things.
The ship that thou shalt build,
Her dimensions shall be to measure.
Equal shall be her width and her length."

The ark which Utnapishtim obediently constructed was a huge cube, 120 cubits or nearly 200 feet on each side. It was divided into seven stories, each containing nine rooms. Onto the ship he loaded all the silver and gold and all the living things which he had, and embarked with his family and relatives. The appointed time came. At evening a frightful storm took place and the next morning a black thunder cloud advanced from the eastern horizon, darkening the entire land. Even the gods were terrified at the deluge and cowered like dogs against the wall of heaven, or sat dejected and weeping. The climax of the flood and the final grounding of the boat on Mount Nisir[65] is described vividly:

Six days and six nights
Blows the flood wind, as the south-storm sweeps the land.
When the seventh day arrived,
    The flood-carrying south-storm subsided in the battle,
Which it had fought like an army.
The sea grew quiet, the tempest was still, the flood ceased.
I looked at the weather: stillness had set in,
And all of mankind had returned to clay.
The landscape was as level as a flat roof.
I opened a hatch, and light fell upon my face.
Bowing low, I sat and wept,
Tears running down on my face.
I looked about for coast lines in the expanse of the sea:
In each of the fourteen regions
    There emerged a region-mountain.
On Mount Nisir the ship came to a halt.
Mount Nisir held the ship fast,
    Allowing no motion.

On the seventh day Utnapishtim sent forth a dove which came back because it could find no resting place. Likewise a swallow returned, but a raven which was sent out saw that the waters were diminishing

[65] Mount Nisir was probably in the mountains of Kurdistan east of the Tigris, and may be identified with modern Pir Omar Gudrun (E. A. Speiser in AASOR 8 [1926-27], pp.7, 17f.).

and did not come back. On top of the mountain peak Utnapishtim offered sacrifice to the gods, who smelled the sweet savor and collected about him like flies. Enlil was angry that anyone had escaped destruction in the flood, but Ea urged that it was not right to have endeavored to destroy the righteous together with the sinful. "On the sinner impose his sin," said Ea. Enlil, persuaded, took Utnapishtim by the hand and led him from the boat. With his wife, Utnapishtim knelt before Enlil while the god blessed them:

> Hitherto Utnapishtim has been but human.
> Henceforth Utnapishtim and his wife shall be like unto us gods.
> Utnapishtim shall reside far away, at the mouth of the rivers!

Such is the ancient flood story of Babylonia which, purified of its polytheistic elements, survived among the Israelites in two sources, now woven together into a single moving story in Genesis 6:5 to 9:17.

2. THE EARLY DYNASTIC PERIOD,
c.2800-c.2360 B.C.

AFTER the mention of the flood the Sumerian King List continues with a series of dynasties which may be summarized as follows:

NAME OF DYNASTY	NUMBER OF KINGS	YEARS OF REIGN
First Dynasty of Kish	23	24,510
First Dynasty of Uruk (E-Anna)	12	2,310
First Dynasty of Ur	4	177
Dynasty of Awan	3	356
Second Dynasty of Kish	8	3,195
Dynasty of Hamazi	1?	360?
Second Dynasty of Uruk	1?	60?
Second Dynasty of Ur	4	116
Dynasty of Adab	1	90
Dynasty of Mari	6	136
Third Dynasty of Kish	1 (queen)	100
Dynasty of Akshak	6	99
Fourth Dynasty of Kish	7	491
Third Dynasty of Uruk	1	25

Whereas the King List treats these dynasties as if they succeeded one another in regular order, it is probable that in actuality some of them were contemporary dynasties which ruled at the same time in various cities. Also it may be noted that in the case of the individual cities there is a tendency to start out with reigns of legendary length and work down to reigns of actual historical length. Evidently the compiler of the King List used as sources a collection of local lists from a number of cities, in most of which the earlier periods were treated with legendary exaggeration while the later times were recorded with historical accuracy. By adding all of these lists together in an uncritical fashion the author of our King List has arrived at a total of over 30,000 years, whereas in all probability the entire period covered by these dynasties was not much more than 500 years.

Among the rulers in the First Dynasty of Kish was Etana "a shepherd, the one who to heaven ascended." A very interesting legend came to be told concerning Etana, as is attested by representations on early Sumerian seals and by fragments of Babylonian and Assyrian literature. Seeking "the plant of birth," Etana rode high into the heavens on the back of an eagle but upon reaching such a height that even the sea could no longer be distinguished grew afraid and fell back to earth. This legend was eventually transferred to Alexander the Great, who was said to have ascended by riding in a basket attached to two great and hungry birds that were attracted upward by a piece of meat held upon a spear above their heads.[1] The next dynasty is described as centering at E-Anna, which was the temple precinct of Uruk. Twelve kings are said to have reigned here for 2,310 years. Among these kings was Gilgamesh, the hero of the great epic already described.

The surmise of contemporaneity or overlapping among the dynasties of the King List is confirmed in the case of the First Dynasty of Kish and the First Dynasty of Uruk by an interesting item of evidence outside the King List. This is a Sumerian poem which may be entitled "Gilgamesh and Agga." In the King List, Agga was the last king of the First Dynasty of Kish, and Gilgamesh the fifth ruler of the First Dynasty of Uruk. In the poem, recently translated, the two rulers are contemporaries. Although the tablets containing the poem were probably only written in the first half of the second millennium B.C., and Gilgamesh and Agga probably belong in the first quarter of the third millennium B.C., the events narrated sound authentic and the later author may be believed to have used trustworthy sources.

Most interesting also is the information provided by the "Gilgamesh and Agga" poem about Sumerian political organization. Among

[1] Langdon, *Semitic Mythology*, pp.166-174.

the numerous city-states of Sumer it is evident that Kish and Uruk were strong rivals, and it seems that at this time the former had issued some kind of ultimatum to the latter. Upon receipt of the threat from Agga, Gilgamesh put the matter before the elders of his city and they advised submission to Kish. Not satisfied with this decision, Gilgamesh presented the question to the men of his city, probably meaning the men bearing arms, and they chose to fight for their independence, which pleased Gilgamesh. Since the poem explicitly mentions "the convened assembly of the elders" (line 9), and "the convened assembly of the men" (line 24), there was evidently a sort of primitive democracy in the Sumerian city-state in which the king was advised by a "congress" of two "houses."[2]

TELL ASMAR

Archeologically it is possible to divide the Early Dynastic period into three successive subdivisions. This is largely on the basis of work at Tell Asmar. This site is in the area of the Diyala River fifty miles northeast of Baghdad, and was the ancient city of Eshnunna or Ashnunnak. Beginning in 1930 and continuing for a number of years, excavations were conducted here by Henri Frankfort and others on behalf of the Oriental Institute of the University of Chicago.[3] At the same time, Khafaje, a related site twenty miles east of Baghdad, was also explored with corroborative results. The earliest settlement at Tell Asmar took place in the Jemdet Nasr period and was attested by the typical polychrome pottery of that time. Above that, the subdivision which Frankfort calls Early Dynastic I represents the transition from Jemdet Nasr to later times, and is marked by the erection of the so-called Archaic Temple. In the next subdivision, Early Dynastic II, the culture of Tell Asmar reached the high point marked by the rebuilding of the Archaic Temple into the Square Temple, and by the remarkable hoard of statues found in this temple. The almost perfect preservation of these statues is evidently

---

[2] Thorkild Jacobsen in JNES 2 (1943), pp. 165f.; Samuel N. Kramer in AJA 53 (1949), pp. 1-18; KFTS pp. 26-31; cf. Geoffrey Evans in JAOS 78 (1958), pp. 1-11.

[3] Henri Frankfort, Thorkild Jacobsen, and Conrad Preusser, *Tell Asmar and Khafaje, The First Season's Work in Eshnunna 1930/31.* OIC 13, 1932; Henri Frankfort, *Tell Asmar, Khafaje and Khorsabad, Second Preliminary Report of the Iraq Expedition.* OIC 16, 1933; *Iraq Excavations of the Oriental Institute 1932/33, Third Preliminary Report of the Iraq Expedition.* OIC 17, 1934; *Oriental Institute Discoveries in Iraq, 1933/34, Fourth Preliminary Report of the Iraq Expedition.* OIC 19, 1935; *Progress of the Work of the Oriental Institute in Iraq, 1934/35, Fifth Preliminary Report of the Iraq Expedition.* OIC 20, 1936.

due to the fact that they had been taken out of service and hidden under the floor of the Square Temple. Two of these were idols representing Abu the chief god and lord of fertility, to whom the temple was dedicated, and his wife the mother goddess (Fig. 10). The statue of Abu is about thirty inches high and the god is shown with a full black beard, while his consort wears a one-piece cloak passing under the right arm and fastened together on the shoulder. These figures are of great interest both because they are the first Sumerian cult statues known and because of their fine workmanship, the statue of Abu in particular conveying an impression of extraordinary power. Another statue, shown in Fig. 11, represents a worshiper who is holding a cup, perhaps in connection with his participation in a feast of communion at the temple. Like the others, the figure is made of gypsum, the eyes have disks of black limestone set with bitumen into eyeballs cut from shell, and the dark wavy hair and full beard are reproduced with black pitch. It is indeed interesting to have so striking and naturalistic a representation of one of "the black-headed folk," as we have seen they called themselves, the Sumerians of the early third millennium B.C.[4] The subdivision Early Dynastic III at Tell Asmar corresponds with the time of the First Dynasty of Ur, and we may turn to that site next to study the culminating phase of this entire period.

THE FIRST DYNASTY OF UR

The information in the King List now agrees with contemporary inscriptions surviving until our day. The King List reads: "Uruk was smitten with weapons; its kingship to Ur was carried. In Ur Mes-Anne-pada became king and reigned 80 years; [A-Anne-pada, son of Mes-Anne-pada reigned . . . years;] Meskiag-Nanna, son of Mes-Anne-pada, became king and reigned 36 years; Elulu reigned 25 years; Balulu reigned 36 years. 4 kings reigned its 177 years. Ur was smitten with weapons."

At Tell al-ʿUbaid a tablet to the goddess Ninhursag was found, bearing the words "A-Anne-pada king of Ur, son of Mes-Anne-pada king of Ur, has built a temple for Ninhursag." This inscription not only verifies the name of Mes-Anne-pada as a ruler of Ur but also makes it possible to explain the one improbability which appears in the King List at this point, namely the ascription of the extraordi-

[4] Henri Frankfort, *Sculpture of the Third Millennium B.C. from Tell Asmar and Khafajah.* OIP XLIV, 1939.

narily long reign of eighty years to Mes-Anne-pada. It is of course not impossible that a king might inherit a throne in childhood and reign thereafter for eighty years. But Mes-Anne-pada was the founder of his dynasty which was established only by military victory over Uruk. He is not likely, therefore, to have been only a small child at the time, and the more mature a fighting man he was when he came to the throne the less apt he is to have had yet eighty years to reign. Now it appears, however, that in actuality he was followed in the kingship by a son with the very similar name of A-Anne-pada. Due no doubt to this similarity, the son's name dropped out of the King List. At the same time, the length of the son's reign probably was added to that of the father's, so that Mes-Anne-pada emerged with a reign of eighty years. The King List probably preserved correctly, therefore, the total number of years covered by the dynasty, but needs to be corrected by the addition of the name of A-Anne-pada as in brackets in the quotation just given, and by the distribution of the eighty years between the reigns of the two kings. Concerning A-Anne-pada it is of interest to note that another inscription is in existence in which he calls himself "the god A-Anne-pada."

The high culture which was achieved under the First Dynasty of Ur is shown by the famous "royal" cemetery discovered by C. Leonard Woolley at Ur. This is the burial area deep beneath which were found the evidences of the flood. Outside the walls of the primitive town which stood here after the flood, a great rubbish heap accumulated, into which the graves afterward were dug. The date of this cemetery is probably around 2500 B.C.[5]

The largest number of graves were those of common folk who were buried in rectangular pits, with the bodies wrapped in matting or put in coffins of wood, wickerwork, or clay. Often the first sign which showed the excavators that they were coming upon such a grave would be a paper-thin wavy line of white powder remaining from the edge of the reed-mat, or a few small vertical holes left in a line by the decay of the wooden staves which strengthened the sides of the coffin. Personal belongings and other items had been placed in the graves, including bracelets, necklaces, vanity cases, weapons, tools, food, and drink. The body always lay on its side, in the attitude of

---

[5] Woolley's date of c.3500-c.3200 B.C. (*Ur Excavations*, II, *The Royal Cemetery* [1934] p.223) was criticized by V. Müller in JAOS 55 (1935), pp.206-208; and by H. Frankfort in JRAS 1937, pp.332-341. For the chronological correlations pointing to the date given above see W. F. Albright in BASOR 88 (Dec. 1942), p.32; and in AJA 47 (1943), p.492.

one asleep, and the hands held close to the mouth a cup which probably once contained water. Thus kindly provisions were made for the dead.

The most remarkable graves were those which have become known as the "royal" tombs, although it is now believed by some scholars that they actually belonged not to royal persons but to priests and priestesses sacrificed in fertility rites.[6] The rooms and vaults of these tombs were built of brick and stone—and the stone must have been brought from at least thirty miles away in the higher desert.

In one tomb, which had already been plundered by grave-robbers, a cylinder seal remained to give the name of the deceased, A-bar-gi. Also overlooked against the wall was a silver model of a boat, which was of a type identical with that in use today on the marshes of the lower Euphrates.[7] Above this plundered vault was the untouched grave of a lady, these circumstances suggesting that those who conducted the latter burial were the ones who at the same time contrived to rob the lower tomb. The occupant of the new tomb was identified by a lapis lazuli cylinder as Lady Shub-ad, and her body lay upon the remains of a wooden bier, a gold cup near her hand. Her elaborate headdress was still in good order, and is shown in Fig. 12 upon a head copied from a Sumerian statuette. The headdress contained nine yards of gold band, and was accompanied by huge crescent-shaped earrings and a golden "Spanish comb" whose five points ended in gold flowers with lapis centers.[8]

In a great pit connecting with A-bar-gi's tomb were found the bodies of more than sixty people, while some twenty-five persons had been buried together with Lady Shub-ad. Other such "death-pits" were found, one containing the remains of as many as six men and sixty-eight women. Even chariots were driven down into these death-pits and fine treasures were placed in them. All these people and offerings have the appearance of sacrifices made in honor of the royal or sacred personage who was being buried, yet the indications are that the human victims went willingly to their deaths.

Some magnificent harps or lyres were found in these graves, decorated with heads of animals, including a bearded bull, a cow and a stag, and two statues were recovered each representing a goat

⁶ Sidney Smith in jras 1928, pp.862-868; Franz M. Th. Böhl in za Neue Folge 5 (39) 1930, pp. 83-98; H. Frankfort in *Iraq.* 1 (1934), p.12 n.3; and in jras 1937, pp.341f.; E. A. Speiser in *Antiquity.* 8 (1934), p.451.

⁷ anep Fig. 105.

⁸ For Woolley's reconstruction see *Ur Excavations*, ii, pp.85f., Pl. 128.

standing up in front of a bush from which it is perhaps eating the leaves (Fig. 13).[9]

Another tomb was identified by inscriptions as belonging to "Meskalam-dug, Hero of the Good Land." The body lay in a normal way on its right side, between the hands was a bowl of heavy gold, from a broad silver belt hung a dagger of gold and over the fragments of the skull was a helmet of beaten gold. The helmet was made in the form of a wig with the locks of hair hammered up in relief and the individual hairs engraved as delicate lines. Yet other examples of the work of the goldsmiths of Ur are shown in Figs. 14-15. Their achievement approached perfection.

In the largest of the stone-built tombs was found the so-called "Standard" of Ur. This was a wooden panel twenty-two inches long by nine inches high, with triangular end pieces, inlaid with mosaic work on both sides, and probably carried on a pole in processions. The wooden background had perished entirely but the tiny pieces of inlay kept their relative positions in the soil, and skillful work made possible the accurate restoration of the mosaics.

The two main panels of the Standard (Fig. 16) illustrate War and Peace respectively, there being in each case three rows filled with figures made of shell and set in a background of lapis lazuli. In the first row of the panel depicting War, stands the king, dismounted from his chariot and distinguished by his greater height, while soldiers bring before him naked captives with arms bound behind their backs. In the second row advances the phalanx of the royal army, the men wearing long cloaks and copper helmets, and carrying axes. Ahead of them are the light-armed infantry, without cloaks, and fighting with axes or short spears. In the third row are the chariots of the javelin throwers, drawn by animals which break into an excited gallop as they encounter the corpses strewn on the ground. Thus the ancient Sumerians anticipated the chariotry which other nations adopted later and the phalanx with which Alexander the Great won his victories. On the other side of the panel, Peace is illustrated with the king and royal family sitting at a feast, entertained by musicians, while servants bring food-supplies for the banquet and spoils captured from the enemy. The people wear the old-fashioned sheepskin kilts, with the upper part of the body left bare.

[9] Woolley (*Ur Excavations*, ii, p.266) draws an analogy with Genesis 22:13 but it is difficult to see any actual connection.

LAGASH

Another dynasty which flourished during the last phase of the Early Dynastic period was that founded about 2500 B.C. by Ur-Nanshe at Lagash (Telloh) some fifty miles north of Ur. Telloh has been excavated by French archeologists in twenty campaigns extending from 1877 to 1933.[10] Settled first in the 'Ubaid period, Lagash was only finally deserted in the second century B.C. The inscriptions of Ur-Nanshe make reference to extensive building of temples and digging of canals. His grandson, Eannatum, claims victories over Umma, Uruk, Ur, Akshak, Kish, and Mari, and was evidently, at least for a brief time, ruler of almost all Sumer. The battle of Eannatum against nearby Umma is depicted on the fragmentary Stela[11] of the Vultures, where his soldiers march in a close-packed phalanx with lances protruding from behind huge rectangular shields, and vultures bear heads and limbs away from the field of slaughter.[12]

The eighth ruler after Ur-Nanshe was Urukagina. When he assumed power, probably in the early twenty-fourth century B.C., the citizens of Lagash had fallen prey to the greed of their city officials. In a recently translated text, a contemporary historian of Lagash tells how the government inspectors seized boats, cattle, and fisheries. If a man obtained a divorce he had to pay the *ishakku,* or city governor, five shekels and the vizier one. If a perfumer made an oil preparation he paid the *ishakku* five shekels, the vizier one shekel, and the palace steward one shekel. Although the *ishakku* ruled nominally as the representative of the tutelary god of the city, Ningirsu, he had become so bold as to encroach upon the prerogatives of the priests and to appropriate the properties of the temple. "The oxen of the gods ploughed the *ishakku's* onion-patches; the onion and cucumber patches of the *ishakku* were located in the god's best fields." Even at the cemetery numerous officials extracted large contributions from the bereaved. Throughout the state, writes the historian: "There were the tax collectors." This was the situation which Urukagina undertook to correct. He removed the parasitic officials, eliminated or reduced the exactions upon the people, and stopped the exploitation of the poor by the rich. Now from one end of the land to the other: "There was no tax collector." Thus Uruk-

[10] André Parrot, *Tello, vingt campagnes de fouilles* (*1877-1933*). 1948.

[11] Stela or stele is a Greek word (στήλη) meaning an erect stone and is used in archeology for an ancient monument in the form of an upright stone slab.

[12] Parrot, *Tello,* pp. 95-101; ANEP Figs. 298-302.

agina "established the freedom" of the citizens of Lagash. And thus in the oldest known document of social reform the word "freedom" appears for the first time in recorded history.[13]

LUGALZAGGISI

In spite of the commendable reforms of Urukagina, it was only a few years until Lagash fell to its long-time northern rival, the city-state of Umma and to its ambitious ruler, the *ishakku* Lugalzaggisi. A chronicler who may be the same as the author of the reform document just cited, describes the plundering of Lagash and declares that it was not the sin of Urukagina which led to this disaster but the sin of Lugalzaggisi and of his personal deity, Nidaba, goddess of writing and wisdom.[14] In spite of this condemnation, Lugalzaggisi continued his rise in power, ultimately becoming king also of Uruk and Ur, and one of the most important figures in Sumerian history. His twenty-five-year reign constituted, according to the King List, the Third Dynasty of Uruk.

The extent of the dominion which he achieved is indicated in the following triumphal inscription from Nippur, in which Lugalzaggisi prayed Enlil, the wind-god, for the permanence of his reign:

"When Enlil king of the countries had granted to Lugalzaggisi the kingship of the land; had turned the eyes of the land toward him; had prostrated the countries at his feet: then did he make straight his path for him, from the Lower Sea, by Tigris and Euphrates, to the Upper Sea. From East to West Enlil nowhere allowed him a rival. Lugalzaggisi gave the countries to rest in peace; watered the land with water of joy. . . . Then made he Uruk to shine in sheen of countenance; skyward, like a bull's, upraised the head of Ur; Larsa, dear city of the sun-god, watered with waters of joy; nobly exalted Umma, dear city of Shara. . . . May Enlil king of the countries prefer my prayer before his dear father An. May he add life to my life; cause the country to rest at peace with me. Folk as numerous as scented herbs may he bestow on me with open hand; guide for me the flock of An;[15] look benevolently for me upon the land. Let the gods not change the good destiny that they have assigned to me. Shepherd, leader let me be forever!"[16]

The reference to the Upper Sea indicates that the armies of Lugal-

---

[13] Samuel N. Kramer in IEJ 3 (1953), pp.227-232; in *Archaeology.* 7 (1954), pp.145f.; KFTS pp.40-46. cf. W. v. Soden, *Herrscher im alten Orient.* 1954, pp.8-15.

[14] Kramer in IEJ 3 (1953), p.232 n.45.

[15] i.e. mankind.

[16] Patrick Carleton, *Buried Empires, The Earliest Civilizations of the Middle East.* 1939, p.118.

zaggisi marched as far west as the shores of the Mediterranean. So great had become the outreach of Sumerian power.

Extensive as it was at this time, the Sumerian kingdom was not permanent, and the more lasting contributions of this ancient people were in their literature and thought. Quotations have already been made from some of this literature which, as it is now known, was very extensive and included myths, epics, legends, law, historiography, hymns, proverbs, and letters. In form the Sumerian poetry, like that of the Old Testament, often exhibits the feature of parallelism, and the proverbs, like those of the Bible, are often couplets characterized by the synonymous or antithetical meaning of the two lines.[17] In its content the literature does not provide a systematic philosophy or theology, but it may be gathered that the Sumerians believed in a flat earth and a vaulted heaven above, this whole heaven-earth being surrounded by a boundless sea. In control of this universe was a pantheon of anthropomorphic but invisible and immortal beings who functioned as an assembly much like the earthly political "congress" we have already mentioned (p. 38). Of the hundreds of deities the most important were An or Anu, the heaven-god, whose main center of worship was Uruk; Enlil, the air-god, a beneficent, fatherly deity with a great temple in Nippur;[18] Enki, the water-god and god of wisdom; and Ninhursag, the mother-goddess. Other members of the pantheon were Nanna or Sin, the moon-god and son of Enlil; Utu, the sun-god, and Inanna, the queen of heaven, both the children of the moon-god. When the creating deities made the universe and ordered its affairs they did so simply by the utterance of their command. Thus the Sumerian thinkers enunciated the doctrine of the creative power of the divine word, a doctrine which was widely accepted thereafter throughout the Middle East.[19]

[17] Samuel N. Kramer in BASOR 122 (Apr. 1951), p.29. For Sumerian proverbs see Edmund I. Gordon, *Sumerian Proverbs, Glimpses of Everyday Life in Ancient Mesopotamia* (to be published); and in JAOS 77 (1957), pp.67-79; JCS 12 (1958), pp.1-21, 43-75.

[18] For the excavation of this temple see Donald McCown in UMB 16 (1951), pp.7-13.

[19] KFTS pp.71-96. On the thought world of the ancient Middle East in general see H. and H. A. Frankfort, John A. Wilson, Thorkild Jacobsen, and William A. Irwin, *The Intellectual Adventure of Ancient Man.* 1946.

3. THE OLD AKKADIAN PERIOD,
c.2360-c.2180 B.C.

MEANWHILE the strength of the Semitic peoples in Mesopotamia was increasing. They were distinguished from the Sumerians by their language which belonged to the great Semitic family of languages. The Akkadian, Assyrian, and Babylonian dialects constitute the older East Semitic branch of this family, while Hebrew, Aramaic, Phoenician, Syriac, Arabic, and Ethiopic are included in the West Semitic.

Semitic names had been appearing for some time in the King List. In the First Dynasty of Kish several of the names were definitely Semitic while the Third Dynasty of Kish consisted of a single ruler "Ku-Baba, a barmaid," whose own name was Sumerian but who bestowed a Semitic name upon her son, Puzur-Sin. The later kings of the Dynasty of Akshak and all the kings of the Fourth Dynasty of Kish bore Semitic names, and excavations both at Mari and at Nuzi show that there were lines of Semitic kings at those places.

In civilization, however, the Old Akkadian period was a continuation of the Sumerian. Indeed on through Babylonian and Assyrian times it is possible to speak simply of Mesopotamian civilization for, in spite of differences in language or political control, fundamental ideas such as those of government and law remain much the same and provide strongly unifying factors.[1]

SARGON

With Sargon a dynasty of Semitic-speaking kings attained supremacy in all Lower Mesopotamia. This man was of lowly origin. An inscription makes him say:

> Sargon, the mighty king, king of Agade, am I.
> My mother was a changeling, my father I knew not.
> The brothers of my father loved the hills.
> My city is Azupiranu, which is situated on the banks of the Euphrates.
> My changeling mother conceived me, in secret she bore me.
> She set me in a basket of rushes, with bitumen she sealed my lid.
> She cast me into the river which rose not over me.

[1] Thorkild Jacobsen in JAOS 59 (1939), pp.485-495; E. A. Speiser in JAOS Supplement 17 (1954), p.14.

The river bore me up and carried me to Akki, the drawer
of water.

Akki, the drawer of water lifted me out as he dipped his
ewer.

Akki, the drawer of water, took me as his son and reared
me.[2]

The story of the baby in the basket of rushes reminds one of the
similar story concerning Moses.

As the text just quoted states, Sargon ruled in the city of Agade or
Akkad. From it the narrow northern plain of Lower Mesopotamia
was also known as Akkad and its Semitic peoples were designated
as Akkadians. Sargon was able to overthrow the powerful Lugalzaggisi and conquer the entire region of Lower Mesopotamia. At
Ur he installed his own daughter as high-priestess of the moon-god
Nannar, the Sumerian Nanna or Sin. A historical inscription of
Sargon describes the victory over Lugalzaggisi in these words: "Sargon, king of Agade . . . defeated Uruk and tore down its wall; in the
battle with the inhabitants of Uruk he was victorious. Lugalzaggisi,
king of Uruk, he captured in this battle, he brought him in a dog
collar to the gate of Enlil."[3]

Eventually the dominion of Sargon was extended on eastward into
Elam and westward as far as Syria and the Mediterranean. An inscription of his gives recognition to "the god Dagan," the chief god
of the Semites of northern Syria, for the Syrian coast lands which
that deity gave him.[4] Thus Sargon became the most powerful monarch who had ever ruled in Mesopotamia.

A small but important city of the Old Akkadian period was Gasur,
the site of which is known now as Yorgan Tepa and is a dozen miles
southwest of modern Kirkuk. Excavations at this place have been
conducted through the cooperation of a number of institutions including the American School of Oriental Research at Baghdad, the
Iraq Museum, Harvard University, and the University Museum of the
University of Pennsylvania.[5] In the time of which we are speaking
the population of Gasur was overwhelmingly Semitic, but later the
city became an important center of the Hurrians at which time it

[2] E. A. Speiser in ANET p.119 (ANEA p.85); Hugo Gressmann, *Altorientalische
Texte und Bilder zum Alten Testament.* 1909, ɪ, p.79.

[3] A. Leo Oppenheim in ANET p.267.   [4] ANET p.268.

[5] Richard F. S. Starr, *Nuzi, Report on the Excavations at Yorgan Tepa near Kirkuk,
Iraq, conducted by Harvard University in conjunction with the American Schools of
Oriental Research and the University Museum of Philadelphia 1927-1931.* 2 vols.,
1937-39.

was known as Nuzi.[6] Many tablets have been found here which date from the Old Akkadian period and reveal the prosperity and extensive business activity of those days. Among the business records was an inscribed clay map, prepared perhaps to indicate the location of some estate, and ranking now as the oldest map ever discovered.[7] Other tablets show that buying and selling on the installment plan were practiced, and indicate that the commercial dealings of this one community extended over a very considerable portion of the far-flung empire of Sargon.[8]

The development of art in this period was notable and reached its climax under Sargon's grandson, the great ruler Naram-Sin, whose full title was, "The divine Naram-Sin, the mighty, god of Agade, king of the Four Quarters." His Victory Stela (Fig. 17), discovered by de Morgan at Susa and now in the Louvre at Paris, "is the most impressive and beautiful work of early western Asiatic art which we possess."[9] It celebrates his victorious campaign against the mountain-dwelling Lullubians. The scene is the wooded foothills of a mountain whose conical peak rises to the stars. The king's light-armed soldiers advance up the slope, carrying lances and standards. High in the hill above, from which the bodies of the slain are plunging, the king climbs inexorably upward. He is colossal in size, wearing the horned helmet of a god, and carrying war-axe and bow and arrow. His enemies fall beneath his feet, one with throat transfixed by an arrow. Yet another lifts his hands to beg for his life.

4. THE GUTIAN PERIOD, c.2180-c.2070 B.C.

BUT Naram-Sin's great empire, stretching from central Persia to the Mediterranean and from northeastern Arabia to the Taurus Mountains, lasted only through the reign of his son Shargalisharri. Thereafter the Gutians, a little-known Caucasian people from the eastern mountain country of Gutium overran Lower Mesopotamia.

[6] For the spelling of the name see E. A. Speiser in JAOS 75 (1955), pp.52-55.
[7] For a city map of Nippur made about 1500 B.C. see KFTS pp.271-275.
[8] Starr, *Nuzi.* I (1939), p.23; T. J. Meek, *Old Akkadian, Sumerian, and Cappadocian Texts from Nuzi* (Harvard Semitic Series, 10, 1935), p.xv.
[9] Heinrich Schäfer and Walter Andrae, *Die Kunst des alten Orients.* 1925, p.493.

5. THE NEO-SUMERIAN PERIOD, c.2070-c.1960 B.C.

GUDEA

IN THE YEARS when the power of the Gutians was declining, a remarkable Sumerian ruled as governor at Lagash and prepared the way for a renaissance of Sumerian power and culture. His name was Gudea and numerous statues have been found of him, one of which is shown in Fig. 18. Gudea is represented as wearing a turban in the fashion which became very popular in those days, and his face is clean-shaven, grave, and kindly.[1]

With true piety Gudea endeavored to be the shepherd of his people and the servant of the gods. Beseeching divine guidance, he prayed in the temple, "I have no mother; my pure mother thou art. I have no father; thou art my pure father." Through a dream it was revealed to him that he should restore Eninnu, "the House of Fifty [gods]," a Lagash temple first mentioned as early as the end of the Jemdet Nasr period.[2] "In the dream a man that shone like the heaven and was joyful like the earth—from the crown of his head he was a god; by his side was the divine black storm-bird as a companion; below and before him was a storm; on his right and left, lions were standing; he commanded to build his house; his meaning I did not understand." There also appeared in this dream a warrior who held a tablet of lapis lazuli in his hand which contained the plan of a temple. Eventually the goddess Nina made it clear to Gudea that the man at whose side was the storm-bird was the god Ningirsu who wished to command Gudea to build his temple Eninnu, and the warrior with the tablet in his hand was the god Nindub who was bringing the plan for the temple.

So Gudea proceeded at once to the task, himself laying the first brick. The work was very extensive, and Gudea's account mentions the bringing of cedar wood all the way from the Amanus Mountains in northern Syria,[3] a part of the same general range as the Lebanon from which Solomon was to cut cedar trees for the temple at Jerusalem (I Kings 5:6). At last the work was finished. "The holy temple rising from earth to heaven . . . shone in the brilliance of heaven with radiant light. . . . It illumined the country."[4]

[1] cf. Gaston Cros, *Nouvelles fouilles de Tello.* II (1911), Pl. I; Simon Harcourt-Smith, *Babylonian Art.* 1928, p.19.
[2] Carleton, *Buried Empires*, p.63.
[3] ANET pp.268f.
[4] Barton, *Royal Inscriptions of Sumer and Akkad*, pp.206-235.

THE THIRD DYNASTY OF UR

With the final downfall of the Gutians, the great Third Dynasty of Ur arose in splendor. Its first king was Ur-Nammu who took the new title "King of Sumer and Akkad," and whose mightiest work was the erection of a great ziggurat at Ur. The ziggurat which stood at Babylon in the days of Hammurabi and was known as Etemenanki, "the House of the Terrace-platform of Heaven and Earth,"[5] became more famous and was remembered in biblical tradition as the Tower of Babel, but the ziggurat at Ur is today the best preserved of all monuments of this type and therefore the best fitted to give a vivid impression of their character (Fig. 19).

As long ago as 1854, J. E. Taylor visited Ur (then only a ruined site known by the Arabs as al-Muqayyar, the Mound of Bitumen) and dug down into the corners of the great pile which dominated it. He found cuneiform cylinders of Nabonidus of Babylon (556-539 B.C.), stating that Nabonidus had there restored the ziggurat of Ur, begun by Ur-Nammu. The text reads: "Nabonidus king of Babylon . . . am I. E-lugal-malga-sidi, the ziggurat of E-gish-shir-gal in Ur, which Ur-Nammu, a king before me, had built but not completed, did Shulgi[6] his son finish. On the inscription of Ur-Nammu and of his son Shulgi saw I that Ur-Nammu had built but not completed that ziggurat and that Shulgi his son had finished the work. Now was that ziggurat old. Upon the ancient foundations whereon Ur-Nammu and his son Shulgi had built I made good the structure of that ziggurat, as in old times, with mortar and burnt brick. . . ."[7] Then Nabonidus concluded with a dedication to Nannar, lord of the gods of heaven and earth, and a prayer for the life of himself and of his son Belshazzar.

In 1918 Dr. H. R. Hall cleared part of one end of the mound but the complete excavation requiring the removal of thousands of tons of rubbish was first undertaken by C. L. Woolley in 1922-1923.[8] Ur-Nammu's structure probably was built on top of a smaller ziggurat which may have been as old as the time of Mes-Anne-pada. In its upper part the great artificial mountain clearly was the work of Nabonidus. The bulk of the construction, however, had been carried out by Ur-Nammu himself and his name and title were found

---

[5] W. F. Albright in AJA 48 (1944), p.305.

[6] The reading of the name, formerly given as Dungi, is uncertain. Thorkild Jacobsen in BASOR 102 (Apr. 1946), pp.16f.

[7] C. L. Woolley, *Abraham, Recent Discoveries and Hebrew Origins*. 1936, p.62.

[8] *Ur Excavations*, V, *The Ziggurat and Its Surroundings*. 1939.

stamped on the bricks. The tower was a solid mass of brickwork, 200 feet long, 150 feet wide, and some 70 feet high. The core was of un-baked brick, with a facing about eight feet thick of baked brick set in bitumen. The whole design was a masterpiece, the lines of the walls all being built on calculated curves to give the appearance of light-ness and strength, a principle used much later by the Greeks. Orig-inally the shrine of Nanna or Nannar, the moon-god, stood on the topmost stage and it is possible that the various terraces were covered with soil and irrigated so that the green of growing plants beautified the whole.[9]

Interestingly enough, we possess a contemporary record of the building of this ziggurat in the Stela of Ur-Nammu, a slab of white limestone nearly five feet across and ten feet high, recovered unfortu-nately only in fragments (Fig. 20). At the top the king stands in the attitude of prayer while from above come flying angels with vases out of which flow the streams of life. An inscription elsewhere enum-erates the canals dug by Ur-Nammu, and here he thanks the gods for the gift of life-bringing water. This is the earliest known represen-tation of an angel in art.[10] At least three panels of the stela are de-voted to the building of the ziggurat. In the first of these Ur-Nammu stands at the left in front of the goddess Ningal and again at the right before the god Nanna, receiving the command to build him a house. In the next panel the king is setting forth, bearing on his shoulder the tools of the architect and builder, compasses, mortar-basket, pick, and trowel, while in the third panel little remains but one of the ladders of the workmen which leaned against the side of the rising structure.

In the course of time other buildings were erected around the ziggurat, so that the entire sacred area was very extensive. One of these was the square temple known as the Gig-par-ku, which was dedicated to Ningal, the moon-goddess and wife of Nanna. The kitchen was an important part of the temple, since worship was by sacrifice and the cooked flesh of the sacrificial animal was shared among the god, the priests, and the worshipers. The temple in the Gig-par-ku was equipped with a well for water, fireplaces for boiling the water, a bitumen-covered brick table on which the carcass of the

[9] cf. Th. A. Busink, *Sumerische en Babylonische Tempelbouw.* 1940, p.69. For the use of bitumen in antiquity see R. J. Forbes, *Studies in Ancient Technology*, I, (1955), pp.1-120.
[10] C. L. Woolley, *The Development of Sumerian Art.* 1935, p.112.

victim was cut up, a flat-topped cooking range, and a domed bread oven.

Much business took place within the sacred area. As sacrifices, tithes and taxes were brought in, a receipt was given to each man. The temple scribe then made a notation for himself on a small clay tablet, and eventually these memoranda were incorporated in weekly, monthly, and yearly reports. Large numbers of such business tablets and ledgers have been found. Factories and workshops also were to be found there. One such establishment at Ur was a weaving factory which produced twelve sorts of woolen cloth. Tablets still give the names of the women weavers, the amount of rations allotted to them, the quantity of wool issued to each, and the amount of cloth manufactured. The temple area was also the home of the law court. Dublal-mah or "Great House of Tablets" was the name of the building at Ur from whose doorway the judges announced their findings and in whose store chambers the clay documents recording their decisions were kept.

In the ruins of Ur at about this time there are some twenty houses per acre. Assuming six to ten persons per house, there were 120 to 200 people per acre, the average figure of 160 being exactly the same as the population density in modern Damascus. Ur covered 150 acres, and it may therefore be estimated that the population was approximately 24,000 inhabitants.[11]

Recently a law code promulgated by Ur-Nammu has been found among the Sumerian texts in the Museum of the Ancient Orient at Istanbul. Dating as it does some three hundred years before Hammurabi, this is at present the oldest code of laws known. The text states that Ur-Nammu was selected by the god Nanna to rule over Ur and Sumer as his earthly representative. It tells how the king removed the dishonest "grabbers" of the livestock of the citizens, and established honest weights and measures. The king was concerned that "the orphan did not fall a prey to the wealthy," "the widow did not fall a prey to the powerful," and "the man of one shekel did not fall a prey to the man of one mina."[12] Of the actual laws which the code contained, only a few can now be restored and read, but they include statements of fines to be imposed upon the man who has caused certain injuries to another.[13]

[11] Henri Frankfort, *Kingship and the Gods, A Study of Ancient Near Eastern Religion as the Integration of Society and Nature*. An Oriental Institute Essay. 1948, p.396 n.23.

[12] 1 mina = 60 shekels.

[13] Samuel N. Kramer in *Archaeology*. 7 (1954), pp.143f.; KFTS pp.48-51. For

Ur-Nammu was succeeded by his son Shulgi, to whom Nabonidus referred as the completer of the ziggurat. Figurines of both Ur-Nammu and Shulgi have recently been discovered in foundation boxes unearthed at Nippur.[14] The latter ruler proclaimed himself "the divine Shulgi, god of his land," and his greatest monument was his own mortuary temple and sepulcher. Extant texts from several sites show that both within his own lifetime and afterward he was honored as a god with temples and offerings.[15] He was succeeded by his son Bur-Sin who was followed in turn by Gimil-Sin and then by Ibi-Sin.

6. THE ISIN-LARSA PERIOD,
c.1960-c.1830 B.C.

IT WAS in the days of Ibi-Sin that disaster came upon the Sumerians. The Elamites stormed down out of the hills, took Ibi-Sin captive and sacked the capital city of Ur. A later poet wrote in lamentation:

> O my city attacked and destroyed, my city attacked without
> cause,
> Behold the storm ordered in hate—its violence has not
> abated;
> O my house of Sin in Ur, bitter is thy destruction.[1]

Among the leaders of the invading Amorites were Ishbi-Irra from Mari, and Naplanum. These two settled respectively at Isin and Larsa. An Elamite ruler, Kirikiri, was established at Eshnunna.

Beginning with Ishbi-Irra, a series of sixteen kings held the throne of Isin for 225 years, or until Isin was conquered by Rim-Sin of Larsa in the year after Hammurabi became king of Babylon.[2] As will be shown later, the accession date of Hammurabi was probably about 1728 B.C., and thus the rule of Ishbi-Irra must have begun around 1952 B.C. After a thirty-three year reign, Ishbi-Irra was succeeded by Shu-ilishu who was on the throne for ten years, beginning about 1919 B.C. Contemporary with the latter was an early successor of Kirikiri at Eshnunna, namely Bilalama.

An important code of laws has recently been discovered which

Sumero-Akkadian law see now Adam Falkenstein, *Die neusumerischen Gerichtsurkunden*. 3 vols. 1956-57; cf. Edmond Sollberger in JCS 12 (1958), pp.105-107.

[14] Richard C. Haines in *Sumer*. 11 (1955), pp.107-109.

[15] T. Fish in BJRL 11 (1927).

[1] S. N. Kramer in ANET p. 461; *Lamentation Over the Destruction of Ur*. AS 12, 1940, p.57.

[2] F. R. Kraus in JCS 3 (1949), pp.13f., 26f.; Francis R. Steele in AJA 52 (1948), p.430.

may have been composed by the last-named king.[3] Written in the Akkadian language, the laws are recorded in two copies on two tablets which were excavated at Tell Abu Harmal near Baghdad by the Iraq Directorate of Antiquities and placed in the Iraq Museum. Tell Abu Harmal covers the ruins of a rural town which was a part of the kingdom of Eshnunna, and these are the laws of that kingdom.

The preamble of the code is very badly preserved but contains the statement that Tishpak, the chief god of Eshnunna, bestowed upon some ruler "the kingship over Eshnunna." Upon preliminary study it was thought that the name of king Bilalama was given at this point, but it is now recognized that the name of the king to whom reference is made is lost in a gap in the text, nevertheless it is still held that the code was composed at about the time of Bilalama and perhaps by that very king himself.[4]

The code itself extends through some sixty paragraphs of law, and then breaks off. The subjects on which legislation is enunciated include the price of commodities, the hire of wagons and boats, the wages of laborers, marriage, divorce and adultery, assault and battery, and the matter of responsibility for an ox which gores a man and a mad dog which bites a man. Typical form and sample subject matter of the laws may be seen in these two examples: "If the boatman is negligent and causes the sinking of the boat, he shall pay in full for everything the sinking of which he caused" (§5); "If an ox is known to gore habitually and the ward authorities have had the fact made known to its owner, but he does not have his ox dehorned, it gores a man and causes his death, then the owner of the ox shall pay two-thirds of a mina of silver" (§54).

Returning to Isin, the fifth king at that city was Lipit-Ishtar, who reigned for eleven years beginning about 1868 B.C. A code of laws which he promulgated has also recently become known.[5] Most of the tablets containing this code were excavated at Nippur by the University of Pennsylvania and are now in the University Museum. Although he was king of an Amorite dynasty, Lipit-Ishtar wrote his law code in the Sumerian language and probably derived many of

[3] Albrecht Goetze in *Sumer.* 4 (1948), pp.63-102; ANET pp.161-163 (ANEA pp.133f.); AASOR 31 (1951-52).
[4] Goetze in AASOR 31 (1951-52), p.20 n.18, p.22 n.24.
[5] Francis R. Steele in AJA 52 (1948), pp.425-450; and in *Archiv Orientální, Journal of the Czechoslovak Oriental Institute, Prague.* XVIII, No.1-2 (1950), pp.489-493; S. N. Kramer in ANET pp.159-161.

the laws from a Sumerian heritage running back to Ur-Nammu or earlier.

The laws of Lipit-Ishtar begin with a prologue in which the king states that Anu and Enlil, the leading Sumerian-Akkadian deities, had called him to the princeship of the land, and that in accordance with the word of Enlil he had established justice in Sumer and Akkad. The legal text proper, of which much less than half is preserved, contains some thirty-eight regulations. These deal with such subjects as boat hire, real estate, slaves, tax defaults, inheritance and marriage, and rented oxen. Typical form and sample subject matter of the laws may be seen in these two examples: "If a man cut down a tree in the garden of another man, he shall pay one-half mina of silver" (§10); "If a man rented an ox and damaged its eye, he shall pay one half of its price" (§35). In an epilogue Lipit-Ishtar refers to the fact that he "erected this stela," evidently that on which the code was originally inscribed, and calls down a blessing on those who do not damage it, and a curse on those who do.

The laws of Ur-Nammu, Eshnunna, and Lipit-Ishtar are the earliest such codes now known. Dating well before the famous Code of Hammurabi, they show the sort of materials which were drawn upon in the compilation of that later system of laws.

7. THE OLD BABYLONIAN PERIOD,
c.1830-c.1550 B.C.

No doubt it was the rivalry of the several city-states which now existed in lower Mesopotamia which made it possible for a little-known man with an Amorite name, Sumu-abu, to become master of an unimportant Akkadian city nine miles west of Kish and carve out a small kingdom for himself in that neighborhood. The name of the city was Bab-ilu or Babylon, and Sumu-abu became the founder of the First Dynasty of Babylon.

THE FIRST DYNASTY OF BABYLON

The struggles among the various city-states were long and complex, but eventually Babylon and Larsa faced each other as the two chief powers in lower Mesopotamia. At Larsa an Elamite, Kudur-Mabug, had placed his son Warad-Sin on the throne and he in turn was followed by his younger brother, Rim-Sin. At Babylon Sumu-abu had been followed by Sumu-la-el, Sabum, Apil-Sin, and Sin-muballit. Then Hammurabi came to the throne. When war broke out between Rim-Sin and Hammurabi the outstanding military genius of the latter soon became evident. Rim-Sin and his allies were defeated and Sumer passed into the hands of Hammurabi, Larsa becoming his southern administrative capital. Isin had been captured earlier and Eshnunna soon fell.[1] Mari, the city from which Ishbi-Irra had come, remained as a powerful rival on the northern frontier, athwart the route to the Mediterranean. In the thirty-second year of his reign Hammurabi conquered and partially destroyed this city, too, returning a very few years later to make the destruction complete. Thus was established in full power the Old Babylonian Kingdom.

MARI

Mari is of such importance historically and archeologically that a further word must be said about it at this point. The ancient city was on the Middle Euphrates and is represented today by Tell Hariri six or seven miles north of Abou Kemal. Excavations have been conducted there since 1933 by the *Musée du Louvre* under the leadership of André Parrot.[2] It is revealed that in the third millennium B.C. Mari was one of the most flourishing and brilliant cities of the Mesopotamian world. Among its public edifices were a temple of Ishtar and a ziggurat. Statuettes representing humble worshipers and dedicated to the goddess were found in the temple, and give a vivid picture of the devotion with which Ishtar was regarded. Near the ziggurat another very interesting small statue was found and is shown in Fig. 21. It represents a worshiper carrying in honor in his arms a kid which is doubtless intended for a sacrificial offering.

Most notable of all the buildings in Mari was the palace of the king. This was a tremendous structure covering more than fifteen acres. It contained not only the royal apartments but also admin-

[1] H. Frankfort, T. Jacobsen and Conrad Preusser, *Tell Asmar and Khafaje, The First Season's Work in Eshnunna 1930/31.* OIC 13, 1932, pp.38,41.

[2] A. Parrot in *Syria, Revue d'Art orientale et d'archéologie.* 16 (1935), pp.1-28; 17 (1936), pp.1-31; 18 (1937), pp.54-84; 19 (1938), pp.1-29; 20 (1939), pp.1-22; etc.; *Mari, une ville perdu.* 1935; George E. Mendenhall in BA 11 (1948), pp.1-19; A. Parrot, ed., *Studia Mariana.* 1950 (with bibliography to 1949); *Archives royales de Mari:* I, Georges Dossin, *Correspondance de Samši-Addu et de ses fils.* 1950; II, Charles-F. Jean, *Lettres diverses.* 1950; III, J.-R. Kupper, *Correspondance de Kibri-Dagan gouverneur de Tirqa.* 1950; Charles-F. Jean, *Six campagnes de fouilles à Mari, 1933-1939.* 1952; A. Leo Oppenheim in JNES 11 (1952), pp.129-139; A. Parrot, *Mari, documentation photographique de la mission archéologique de Mari.* 1953.

istrative offices and even a school for scribes. Furthermore it was adorned with great mural paintings, portions of which are still preserved. Among these were scenes of sacrifice, and a representation of the king of Mari receiving from Ishtar the staff and ring which were the emblems of his authority.[3] The palace bore the marks of two destructions which had been visited upon it in close succession, evidently corresponding to the two times when Mari fell to Hammurabi.

From the archives of the palace over 20,000 tablets were recovered, constituting a discovery of the greatest importance. A large number of these tablets represent diplomatic correspondence of the last king of Mari, Zimri-Lim, with his ambassadors and agents and with Hammurabi, king of Babylon, himself. Others date from the time of the predecessors of Zimri-Lim. The dynasty of kings ruling at Mari, it is now learned, had been dispossessed temporarily when Shamshi-Adad I of Assyria (p. 200) sent his son Yasmah-Adad to exercise power at Mari. Later Yasmah-Adad had to give way to Zimri-Lim, who was the legitimate heir to the throne. Zimri-Lim then ruled until Mari fell to Hammurabi in the thirty-second year of the latter's reign.[4] The proof given by the Mari documents that Hammurabi was a contemporary of Shamshi-Adad I casts important light on the long-discussed problem of the date of Hammurabi. From the Khorsabad list of Assyrian kings (p. 200 n.5), Shamshi-Adad I can be dated around 1748-1716 B.C. and a detailed examination of the intricate interrelationships leads to fixing the date of Hammurabi at around 1728-1686 B.C.[5]

[3] Parrot in *Syria*. 18 (1937), pp.325-354.
[4] Parrot, *Mari, une ville perdu*, 1935, pp.235f.
[5] François Thureau-Dangin in RAAO 36 (1939), pp.24f.; W. F. Albright in BASOR 88 (Dec. 1942), pp.28-36; and in AJA 47 (1943), p.492. The date given above for Shamshi-Adad I is that proposed by Albright and differs slightly from that at which A. Poebel arrived, namely 1726-1694 B.C. (JNES 1 [1942], p.285). Friedrich Schmidtke (*Der Aufbau der babylonischen Chronologie* [1952], p.46) puts Shamshi-Adad I at 1753-1721 B.C. and Hammurabi at 1730-1688 B.C. See also F. M. Th. Böhl, *King Hammurabi of Babylon in the Setting of His Time (About 1700 B.C.).* Mededeelingen der Koninklijke Nederlandsche Akademie van Wetenschappen, Afd. Letterkunde, Nieuwe Reeks, Deel 9, No. 10. 1946; M. B. Rowton in JNES 10 (1951), pp.184-204. Further confirmation of the so-called "low" date for Hammurabi has come from the radiocarbon test. In 1950 Donald E. McCown excavated the roof beam of a house at Nippur which, as shown by dated tablets, was built not later than the third year of Ibi-Sin. The radiocarbon date for this beam was 1993 B.C., plus or minus 106 years. Since Ibi-Sin lived about 250 years before Hammurabi, the result is strikingly close to the date given above for Hammurabi. See W. F. Libby in *Science*. 119, No.3083 (Jan. 1954), pp.135f. For arguments for a "high" date around 1900 B.C. see Benno Landsberger in JCS 8 (1954), pp.119f. According to the Mari texts Hammurabi was also a

THE CODE OF HAMMURABI

Hammurabi was not only a great military commander but also an outstanding administrator and law-giver. Relatively little remains today of the Babylon of his time, since the city was reconstructed almost entirely in the sixth century B.C. by Nabopolassar and Nebuchadnezzar, but in one quarter some dwelling houses from Hammurabi's day have been unearthed. The distinctive thing here is the new and planned way in which the streets are laid out in regular straight lines which intersect approximately at right angles. Many letters written by Hammurabi have also been found, revealing his close attention to all the details of his realm and illustrating the terse clarity with which he issued his instructions. But his greatest achievement was represented by his code of laws.[6]

Hammurabi named the second year of his reign the "year when he established justice," and eventually he set forth a compilation and codification of laws which continued in force in Babylonia for a thousand years. In 1901 a copy of this code was found by de Morgan at Susa where it had been carried off by the Elamites. The code was inscribed on a round-topped stela of black diorite, some six feet in height, which now is in the Louvre. At the top is a bas-relief (Fig. 23) showing Hammurabi standing before the enthroned sun-god Shamash, the patron of law and justice. The god wears a pointed headdress with horns, rays are to be seen upon his shoulders, and he holds a ring and staff, the insignia of royalty, in his right hand. Hammurabi, who stands before him to receive his kingly law-giving power,[7] wears a long robe with right arm and shoulder bare, and is shown with beard and clean-shaven upper lip.

---

contemporary of Yarim-Lim of Alalakh. For the excavation of this site and discussion of its chronology see Leonard Woolley, *Alalakh, An Account of the Excavations at Tell Atchana in the Hatay, 1937-1949.* 1955 (for Yarim-Lim see pp.91, 384, 389); see also articles by Albrecht Goetze and W. F. Albright in BASOR 146 (Apr. 1957), pp.20-26, 26-34; and Albrecht Goetze in JCS 11 (1957), pp.53-61, 63-73. The latest stratigraphic correlations by W. F. Albright (in BASOR 144 [Dec. 1956], pp.26-30) reaffirm an accession date for Hammurabi between c.1750 and c.1700. M. B. Rowton, however, distinguishes for the first regnal year of Hammurabi an ultra-high date c.1900, a high date in 1848, a middle date in 1792, and a low date in 1728, and himself now (in JNES 17 [1958], pp.97-111) favors the middle chronology with the reign of Hammurabi assigned to 1792-1750. For the low date see most recently F. Cornelius in JCS 12 (1958), pp.101-104.

[6] Robert F. Harper, *The Code of Hammurabi King of Babylon about 2250 B.C.* 1904; W. W. Davies, *The Codes of Hammurabi and Moses.* 1905; Albrecht Goetze in JAOS 69 (1949), pp.115-120; Theophile J. Meek in ANET pp.163-180 (ANEA pp.138f.); G. R. Driver and John C. Miles, *The Babylonian Laws.* 2 vols. 1952-55.

[7] T. Fish in E. I. J. Rosenthal, ed., *Judaism and Christianity.* III (1938), p.43.

Beneath, were carved fifty-one columns of text, most of which are still preserved, written in the Akkadian language in beautiful cuneiform characters. In a lengthy prologue it is stated that the gods "named me to promote the welfare of the people, me, Hammurabi, the devout, god-fearing prince, to cause justice to prevail in the land, to destroy the wicked and the evil, that the strong might not oppress the weak, to rise like the sun over the black-headed people,[8] and to light up the land." The prologue concludes: "When Marduk[9] commissioned me to guide the people aright, to direct the land, I established law and justice in the language of the land, thereby promoting the welfare of the people." A long epilogue reaffirms Hammurabi's desire "that the strong might not oppress the weak, that justice might be dealt the orphan and the widow," and says: "Let any oppressed man who has a cause come into the presence of the statue of me, the king of justice, and then read carefully my inscribed stela, and give heed to my precious words, and may my stela make the case clear to him; may he understand his cause; may he set his mind at ease! 'Hammurabi, the lord, who is like a real father to the people, bestirred himself for the word of Marduk, his lord . . . and he also ensured prosperity for the people forever, and led the land aright'—let him proclaim this, and let him pray with his whole heart for me!"

The law code itself included nearly three hundred paragraphs of legal provisions touching commercial, social, domestic, and moral life. Procedure in the law courts had to be taken very seriously for false accusation in a capital case was a ground for death (§3). Theft in certain cases, kidnaping, and house-breaking were punishable by death (§§6, 14, 21). In case of stealing at a fire, the thief was to be thrown into the fire (§25). Other laws dealt with the duties of soldiers (§§26-41), and regulated farm rentals (§§42ff.), deposits and debts (§§112ff.). Marriage was legal only when recorded in writing (§128) and the woman as well as the man had the right of divorce (§142). Death for both parties was the penalty in case of adultery between a man and another man's wife (§129), but a woman accused of adultery without proof might clear herself by swearing her innocence, or by the ordeal by water (§§131f.). This latter consisted of leaping into the sacred river where sinking was proof of guilt and floating of innocence. A married woman might hold property

---

[8] In late-Sumerian usage this term refers to men in general.
[9] The god of Babylon, biblical Merodach.

(§150). Inheritance and adoption were regulated (§§162-191). Laws covering assault and battery were based largely on the principle of equal retaliation, but with some complications because of the division of society into three classes, nobles, commoners, and slaves (§§195-214).[10] For example (§§200f.), "If a seignior has knocked out a tooth of a seignior of his own rank, they shall knock out his tooth. If he has knocked out a commoner's tooth, he shall pay one-third mina of silver." One very extreme application of the *lex talionis* was provided for (§§209f.): if under certain circumstances a man caused the death of another man's daughter, his own daughter was to be put to death. The fees of physicians were governed and in the case of an operation under which the patient died the doctor's hand might be cut off (§§215-225)! Likewise if a builder erected an unsafe house which fell upon its owner and killed him, he himself was liable to death (§229). River navigation (§§234-239), rental of cattle (§§242ff.), wages of laborers (§§257f.) and numerous other matters were covered in the code.

That this code was largely based upon earlier systems of Mesopotamian law has long been surmised and may now be demonstrated at least in part by comparison with the earlier codes already mentioned. Concern for the rights of orphan and widow was stated already in the Sumerian code of Ur-Nammu, even as it is also expressed in the epilogue of Hammurabi. Paragraphs 5 and 54 of the Akkadian Laws of Eshnunna, quoted above, correspond to sections 237 and 251 in the Hammurabi corpus: "If a man hire a boatman and a boat and freight it with grain, wool, oil, dates or any other kind of freight, and that boatman be careless and he sink the boat or wreck its cargo, the boatman shall replace the boat which he sank and whatever portion of the cargo he wrecked"; "If a man's bull have been wont to gore and they have made known to him his habit of goring, and he have not protected his horns or have not tied him up, and that bull gore the son of a man and bring about his death, he shall pay one-half mina of silver." Likewise paragraphs 10 and 35 in the Sumerian Code of Lipit-Ishtar, also quoted above, reappear as follows in paragraphs 59 and 247 of the Code of Hammurabi: "If a man cut down a tree in a man's orchard, without the consent of the owner of the orchard, he shall pay one-half mina of silver"; "If a man hire an

---

[10] *Awilum*, a noble or man of the higher class, a seignior; *mushkenum*, a commoner or man of the middle class (the modern Arabic *masqin* is derived from this ancient Babylonian term); and *wardum*, a slave.

ox and destroy its eye, he shall pay silver to the owner of the ox to the extent of one-half its value."

There are also not a few similarities between the Code of Hammurabi and the later laws of Israel which again suggest a relationship or common background. With points which have been mentioned above as included in the Hammurabi code may be compared the following Old Testament laws: According to Deuteronomy 19:18f. a false witness is to be punished with the penalty he had thought to bring upon the other man. Exodus 21:16 makes the stealing and selling of a man a capital offense, and Exodus 22:2 allows the killing of a thief breaking into a house. The biblical law of divorce in Deuteronomy 24:1 permits the man to put away his wife but does not extend the same right to her as the Hammurabi code did. Leviticus 20:10 and Deuteronomy 22:22 agree exactly with Hammurabi's code on the death penalty for both the man and the other man's wife in case of adultery. Exodus 21:23-25 and Deuteronomy 19:21 state vividly the same principle of retaliation upon which a number of Hammurabi's laws were based: "life for life, eye for eye, tooth for tooth, hand for hand, foot for foot, burning for burning, wound for wound, stripe for stripe." Note also how exactly Exodus 21:29 agrees in phrasing with paragraph 54 of the Laws of Eshnunna and paragraph 251 of the Code of Hammurabi, yet how much more severe the imposed penalty is, a fact which can be understood in the light of the higher value set upon human life in Israel than in Babylonia: "But if the ox has been accustomed to gore in the past, and its owner has been warned but has not kept it in, and it kills a man or a woman, the ox shall be stoned, and its owner also shall be put to death."

In addition to Hammurabi's famous code of laws a great many other written documents remain from the Old Babylonian period to attest the intense literary activity of those days. Thousands of letters show that a considerable part of the population was literate.[11] Extant texts indicate that a remarkable knowledge of medicine, botany, chemistry, geology, and mathematics had been attained.[12] A business document from the time of Hammurabi is shown in Fig.

[11] G. R. Driver, *Letters of the First Babylonian Dynasty*. Oxford Editions of Cuneiform Texts, 1942; T. Fish in BJRL 16 (1932), p.508.

[12] R. C. Thompson, *Assyrian Medical Texts*. 1923; *A Dictionary of Assyrian Chemistry and Geology*. 1936; O. Neugebauer, *Mathematische Keilschrift-Texte*. 1-3 (1935-37). For Babylonian and also Egyptian and Hellenistic mathematics and astronomy see O. Neugebauer, *The Exact Sciences in Antiquity*. 1952.

22. The tablet was found in the region of the Diyala River, and contains a contract concerning a loan of grain on which the borrower paid interest. The date formula on the tablet mentions the year when Shamshi-Adad I died. In the Old Babylonian period the story of the flood was reedited, as was the epic of creation.

THE EPIC OF CREATION

Like the legend of the flood so too an account of the creation was at least as ancient as the time of the Sumerians. The fragmentary tablet from Nippur which alluded to the creation as well as narrated the flood has already been mentioned (p. 31), likewise the general nature of the Sumerian conception of the universe has been indicated (p. 45). Here additional reference may be made to other texts, dating probably around 2000 B.C., in which the creation of man is described. As in one of the narratives of creation in the Old Testament man is formed "of dust from the ground" (Genesis 2:7), so in this Sumerian account he is fashioned out of clay. It was Nammu, the goddess of the primeval sea, who besought her son Enki, the water-god and god of wisdom, to "fashion servants of the gods." Thereupon Enki led forth a group of "fashioners," and said to Nammu:

> O my mother, the creature whose name you uttered, it exists,
>   Bind upon it the image of the gods;
> Mix the heart of the clay that is over the abyss,
> The good and princely fashioners will thicken the clay. . . .
> It is man. . . .[13]

But it was in the First Dynasty of Babylon that the account of the creation of the world was given the form in which it was to be told for the next thousand years and the form in which it is most familiar to us. The first tablets containing the Babylonian version of the creation were discovered at Nineveh in the ruins of the seventh century B.C. library of Ashurbanipal (p. 217), and other tablets and fragments of tablets of the epic have been found at Ashur, Kish, and Uruk. Those from Ashur belong to approximately 1000 B.C., while the remaining ones are probably from the sixth century B.C. and later. Despite the relatively late date of the extant tablets, it is almost certain that the epic was composed in substantially its present form in the days of Hammurabi. That was the time when Babylon rose

[13] Kramer, *Sumerian Mythology*, pp.37f., 69f.; KFTS pp.142f.

to political supremacy and when Marduk became the national god, and one purpose of the creation epic is to show the preeminence of Babylon over all other cities in the country and especially the supremacy of Marduk over all other Babylonian gods.

The epic, which is written on seven clay tablets and consists in all of about 1,000 lines, was known in Akkadian as *Enuma elish* from its two opening words ("When on high").[14] The account begins with the time when only the two divine principles, the mythical personalities Apsu and Tiamat, were in existence. These two represented the living, uncreated world-matter, Apsu being the primeval sweet-water ocean and Tiamat the primeval salt-water ocean.[15] It has usually been assumed that the Babylonians thought of Tiamat as a dragon or similar monster, but this is uncertain.[16] Tiamat is explicitly called a woman in the myth (Tablet II, line 111) and she and Apsu became the mother and father of the gods. Eventually the doings of these gods became so annoying to their parents that Apsu announced his intention of destroying them. The god Ea, however, perceived the plan and was able to fetter and slay Apsu. Then among the gods the real hero of the myth, Marduk the city-god of Babylon, was born. In the copy of the epic found at Ashur the name of Marduk was replaced by that of the Assyrian god, Ashur. On her side Tiamat created a host of gruesome monsters whose bodies were filled with poison instead of blood. One of her own offspring, Kingu, was exalted to be the supreme director of her forces. So much is related in the first tablet of the myth.

Tiamat now was ready to wage war against the gods and avenge Apsu. The gods were afraid when they learned their danger but

---

[14] Alexander Heidel, *The Babylonian Genesis, The Story of Creation.* 2d ed. 1951; E. A. Speiser in ANET pp.60-72. (ANEA pp.31f.). For comparison with Genesis 1 see also C. F. Whitley in JNES 17 (1958), pp.32-40.

[15] Jensen in Erich Ebeling and Bruno Meissner, eds., *Reallexikon der Assyriologie.* I (1928), p.123.

[16] A well-known Assyrian relief from Nimrod (E. A. Wallis Budge, *Assyrian Sculptures in the British Museum, Reign of Ashur-nasir-pal, 885-860 B.C.* 1914, Pl. XXXVII) has often been interpreted as representing the combat of Marduk with Tiamat. It shows a winged god striding forward against a fleeing monster which is half lion and half bird. But this relief comes from the temple of Ninurta and bears an inscription beginning with a prayer to Ninurta, and hence must represent this deity rather than Marduk. Moreover, the monster is a masculine creature of land and air, while Tiamat was a feminine water deity. On the other hand it is said in *Enuma elish* that "Tiamat opened her mouth to devour" Marduk, while there are other texts which refer to the tail of Tiamat, and these ways of speech may suggest the idea of a dragon. Heidel (*The Babylonian Genesis*, pp. 83-88) considers the evidence, and concludes with Jensen (in *Reallexikon der Assyriologie*, II, p.85, under "Chaos") that the picture of Tiamat as a dragon is "a pure figment of the imagination."

Marduk volunteered to be their champion. He asked that he should be made the highest god if he should vanquish Tiamat. This is narrated in Tablet II, and Tablet III tells how the gods assembled at a banquet for the council of war. In Tablet IV (Fig. 24) we find Marduk preparing for the struggle. He took bow, arrow, and club, and held lightning before his face. He made a net to enclose the body of Tiamat and raised up the hurricane as his mighty weapon. His chariot was the storm, drawn by four steeds named the Destructive, the Pitiless, the Trampler, and the Fleet. When he came before Tiamat, Marduk uttered his challenge, "Come thou forth alone and let us, me and thee, do single combat!" Then:

> Tiamat and Marduk, the wisest of the gods, advanced against one
>   another;
> They pressed on to single combat, they approached for battle.
> The lord spread out his net and enmeshed her;
> The evil wind, following after, he let loose in her face.
> When Tiamat opened her mouth to devour him,
> He drove in the evil wind, in order that she should not be able
>   to close her lips.
> The raging winds filled her belly;
> Her belly became distended, and she opened wide her mouth.
> He shot off an arrow, and it tore her interior;
> It cut through her inward parts, it split her heart.
> When he had subdued her, he destroyed her life;
> He cast down her carcass and stood upon it.

The helpers of Tiamat now attempted to flee, but were captured and cast into prison. Then Marduk returned to the corpse of Tiamat.

> The lord rested, examining her dead body,
> To divide the abortion and to create ingenious things therewith.
> He split her open like a mussel[17] into two parts;
> Half of her he set in place and formed the sky therewith as a
>   roof.

Next Marduk established the earth, which is represented as a great structure in the shape of a canopy over Apsu, and is poetically called Esharra. Then he determined the residences of the gods, Anu being caused to occupy the sky, Enlil the air, and Ea the waters underneath the earth. Here ends Tablet IV. Only a fragment of Tablet V remains, but it tells how Marduk set up the constellations which mark the days and months of the year, and caused the moon to shine forth, entrusting the night to her.

---

[17] Also translated "like a flat fish" (Barton, *Archaeology and the Bible*, p.288); "like a shellfish" (Speiser in ANET p.67 [ANEA pp.31f.]).

In Tablet VI the creation of man is described. In the assembly of the great gods the guilt for Tiamat's revolt was determined to belong to Kingu, the leader of her hosts. Thereupon, Kingu was slain, and when his arteries were cut open the gods fashioned mankind with his blood. The service of the gods was laid upon mankind, while the gods themselves molded bricks for a year and labored to construct Esagila, the large temple tower of Marduk at Babylon. Then the gods gathered at a festive banquet and joined in singing praises of Marduk. Finally, Marduk's advancement from chief god of Babylon to head of the entire pantheon is signified by the conferring upon him of fifty names which represent the power and attributes of the various Babylonian gods. This is the seventh and last tablet.

Obviously there are some interesting points of comparison between the account of creation given in *Enuma elish* and that in Genesis 1:1-2:3. Both refer to a watery chaos at the beginning of time, and the term *tehom* by which it is designated in Genesis 1:2 may go back to the same Semitic form from which the proper name Tiamat is derived. Genesis 1:7 speaks of a firmament placed to divide the waters beneath it from those above it. The word for firmament means literally "what is spread out" and corresponds in a much more refined way to the crude Babylonian idea of the half of Tiamat used by Marduk to construct the vault of heaven. The sequence of events in the creation also is the same in the two stories, in that the following happenings take place in the same order: the creation of the firmament, the creation of dry land, the creation of the luminaries, and the creation of man. Both accounts begin with the watery chaos and end with the gods or the Lord at rest.

On the whole, however, it must be recognized that the differences between *Enuma elish* and the Old Testament are far more important than the similarities. The Babylonian creation story is mythological and polytheistic while the accounts in Genesis are elevated and strictly monotheistic. Doubtless certain features of the biblical narrative of creation are derived from the Babylonian myth, or at least back of both Israelite and Babylonian thought are certain common sources. But the dignity and exaltation of the words of the Bible are unparalleled.

NUZI

Other materials which have an important relationship to biblical narratives are found in the tablets from Nuzi. In the second millennium B.C. this city (cf. p. 47) was a provincial center of the Hurrians. The latter were a people who seem to have come into Mesopotamia from the north in the second half of the third millennium and who became a dominant ethnic element throughout the Middle East during the second millennium B.C.[18] They were the biblical Horites (Genesis 14:6, etc.), but aside from the few references to them in the Old Testament have become known only through the archeological discoveries of the last decades.[19] At Nuzi thousands of clay tablets were found which had been written by Hurrian scribes in the Babylonian language but with the occasional employment of native Hurrian words. The bulk of these tablets date in the fifteenth century B.C. or just shortly after the Old Babylonian period. Since transactions of all kinds are recorded in them, much information is given concerning the life of the people.[20]

Among the customs and laws which the tablets reveal to have prevailed at Nuzi are many which cast light upon incidents recorded in the Bible and particularly upon events of the patriarchal age.[21] Adoption was frequent at Nuzi, and in particular childless couples often adopted a son who would care for them when they were old, bury them when they died, and be heir to their estate. It was specified however that if, after the adoption, they had a son of their own, the adopted son would have to give way to the real son as the chief heir. This provides a legal explanation for Genesis 15:2-4 where the heir of the childless Abraham is expected to be his slave Eliezer, until the promise is given that a son of his own will be born to become his heir.

Marriage contracts of Nuzi contained a provision obliging a childless wife to provide her husband with a handmaid who would bear children. This explains the action of Sarah in giving Hagar to Abraham (Genesis 16:1f.) and of Rachel in giving Bilhah to Jacob

[18] E. A. Speiser in AASOR 13 (1931-32), pp.13-54.

[19] W. F. Albright in L. G. Leary, ed., *From the Pyramids to Paul.* 1935, pp.9-13.

[20] For these texts including related ones from Kirkuk see C. J. Gadd in RAAO 23 (1926), pp.49-161; E. A. Speiser in AASOR 10 (1928-29), pp.1-73; Robert H. Pfeiffer and E. A. Speiser in AASOR 16 (1935-36); Cyrus H. Gordon in *Orientalia.* 5 (1936), pp.305-330; Edward Chiera, *Joint Expedition with the Iraq Museum at Nuzi.* 6 vols. 1927-39; *Harvard Semitic Series.* 5 (1929); 9 (1932); 12 (1942); cf. Cyrus H. Gordon in *Orientalia.* 7 (1938), p. 32 n.1; Francis R. Steele, *Nuzi Real Estate Transactions.* American Oriental Series 25. 1943; Ignace J. Gelb, Pierre M. Purves, and Allan A. MacRae, *Nuzi Personal Names.* OIP 57, 1943. For the seal impressions of Nuzi see Edith Porada in AASOR 24 (1944-45).

[21] Cyrus H. Gordon, *The Living Past.* 1941, pp.156-178; in BA 3 (1940), pp.1-12; and in JNES 13 (1954), pp.56-59.

(Genesis 30:1-3). According to the Nuzi documents the offspring of the handmaid could not be driven out, which shows that there was a legal basis for Abraham's apprehension over the expulsion of Hagar and her child (Genesis 21:11).

Another Nuzi tablet records a relationship between a man named Nashwi and his adopted son called Wullu, which is parallel in some ways to the relationship between Laban and Jacob (Genesis 29-31). Nashwi bestows his daughter upon Wullu, even as Laban promised a daughter to Jacob when he received him into his household. When Nashwi dies, Wullu is to be the heir. If Nashwi begets a son, however, Wullu must share the inheritance with that son, and only the latter shall take Nashwi's gods. Evidently the possession of the household idols implied the leadership of the family. Since Laban had sons of his own when Jacob departed for Canaan, they alone had the right to have their father's gods, and the theft of the teraphim by Rachel (Genesis 31:19, 30-35) was a serious offense.

It will be remembered that Laban searched Jacob's camp in vain for his stolen idols because "Rachel had taken the household gods and put them in the camel's saddle, and sat upon them" (Genesis 31:34). In this connection it is of interest to notice a stone slab sculptured in relief, which was found at Tell Halaf and is shown in Fig. 25. It probably dates from about the ninth century B.C.[22] It shows a camel, with a rider sitting on a saddle which looks very much like a square box, fastened on the animal by crosswise girths. Such a saddle would be exactly the kind in which Rachel could readily have hidden the household idols. Another Tell Halaf sculpture, it may be added, shows a six-winged goddess, the conception of which may have some connection with the description of the seraphim in the Bible (Isaiah 6:2).[23]

HARAN

Other links with patriarchal times appear in northwestern Mesopotamia. The town of Haran (Genesis 11:31f.) is still in existence on the Balikh River sixty miles west of Tell Halaf. Cuneiform sources

[22] E. Douglas Van Buren in OL 50 (1955), cols. 451-455; cf. Joseph P. Free in JNES 3 (1944), p.191. On the camel in ancient Mesopotamian art see also E. Douglas Van Buren, *The Fauna of Ancient Mesopotamia as Represented in Art.* Analecta Orientalia 18. 1939, pp.36f. For some possible early occurrences of the camel in Palestine see B. S. J. Isserlin in PEQ 1950, pp.50-53. For the earliest known reference to horseback riding, in Sumerian literature, see Edmund I. Gordon in JCS 12 (1958), p.19.
[23] Von Oppenheim, *Tell Halaf*, Pl. XXXII B.

make frequent references to Haran, and show that it was a flourishing city in the nineteenth and eighteenth centuries B.C. The city of Nahor, which was Rebekah's home (Genesis 24:10), is mentioned often in the Mari documents as Nakhur, and seems to have been below Haran in the valley of the Balikh. In the time of Hammurabi, both places were ruled by Amorite princes. It may be noted that Haran and Nahor were the name not only of towns but also of members of Abraham's family (Genesis 11:22-27), and the same situation prevails in relation to several other names, including Terah and Serug. Both were among the ancestors of Abraham, and both names appear as designations of towns near Haran.[24] So persistent is tradition in the East that present-day Muslims living in the neighborhood of Haran, particularly at Urfa and at Ain el-Khalil, still relate many legends concerning Abraham, whom they look upon as an Islamic saint. At Urfa, Nimrod is said to have fired glowing charcoal from a catapult against Abraham. Instead of burning the holy man, a pond arose where the charcoal fell, and the glowing bits of charcoal turned into fishes. To this day the fish are holy and not to be eaten. At Ain el-Khalil native Muslim peasants still declare themselves to be direct descendants of Father Abraham.[25] It is certain, therefore, particularly in view of the correspondence between the biblical indications and the archeological evidences, that the region of Haran was an important center in the life of the forefathers of the Israelite people.

THE HABIRU

In the time of the First Dynasty of Babylon, people called Habiru are known in Mesopotamia. A text from Babylon mentions the issue of clothing to Habiru soldiers,[26] a letter to Zimri-Lim of Mari speaks of two thousand Habiru soldiers who have assisted an enemy king in the Middle Euphrates region,[27] and another tablet from Mari refers to thirty Habiru who have come from a district north of Babylonia.[28] Many other texts dating mostly from the eighteenth to the twelfth centuries B.C. and coming from many places largely on the borders of Babylonia and Assyria also mention the Habiru. Although the Habiru are frequently described as foreigners it is also several times indicated that they have fixed places of abode and thus can-

---

[24] William F. Albright, *From the Stone Age to Christianity*. 2d ed. 1946, pp.179f.
[25] Von Oppenheim, *Tell Halaf*, pp.65f.
[26] Jean Bottéro, ed., *Le problème des Ḥabiru à la 4ᵉ rencontre assyriologique internationale*. Cahiers de la Société Asiatique 13. 1954, No.16, p.18.
[27] *ibid.*, No.18, pp.18f.   [28] *ibid.*, No.19, p.19.

not be considered as pure nomads. They find employment not only as soldiers but also as workers of many sorts and, particularly in texts from Nuzi, are found voluntarily entering into labor contracts some of which involve virtual enslavement. Individuals, however, are also found attaining to high positions. The grandfather of a fourteenth century North Syrian king, and himself the possessor of a city, was a Habiru; a man with the Kassite name Harbi-Shihu, active in the twelfth century at the court of Assyria and called by the king of Babylonia the actual ruler of Assyria, and a certain Kudurra, who was in the service of the king of Babylon in the eleventh century, were each designated as "the Habirean," perhaps meaning the descendant of a Habiru.[29]

Habiru are also mentioned frequently in the Tell el-Amarna tablets where they appear as marauding raiders in Syria and Palestine (p. 111). Likewise the name 'Apiru or 'Aperu is found in a number of Egyptian texts (pp. 119f.) and is doubtless to be identified with Habiru.

A form of the name similar to this Egyptian form is also found in cuneiform texts from Ras Shamra.[30] In both Egyptian and Ugaritic it is easy to explain how a foreign *b* was changed into *p*, but as far as known an *h* would have been preserved as such. Contrariwise a cuneiform *h* could represent a West-Semitic '.[31] Accordingly it is reasoned, the original form of the name may have been 'abiru. Since the root 'br means "to cross a boundary," the name can be explained as meaning "those who have crossed a boundary," that is, "immigrants."

In the Bible the name "Hebrew" is applied first to Abram[32] (Genesis 14:13) and after that to the children of Israel in Egypt (Genesis 39:14, etc., Exodus 1:15, etc.). Phonetically the word Hebrew ('ibri) corresponds very closely with 'Apiru or Habiru,[33] and thus may well have been applied originally to Abraham and to Israel in the sense of "immigrant." The Septuagint agrees with this understanding of the word when it translates it in Genesis 14:13 as ὁ περάτης, meaning "the one who passes through, the wanderer."

---

[29] *ibid.*, Nos.165, 166, p.131; Julius Lewy in HUCA 14 (1939), pp.618f.

[30] Moshe Greenberg, *The Ḫab/piru*. 1955, pp.11, 53, 78.

[31] Battiscombe Gunn and E. A. Speiser in AASOR 13 (1931-32), pp.38f.; J. W. Jack in PEQ 1940 pp. 99f.

[32] Abram (Genesis 11:27, 29, etc.) and Abraham (Genesis 17:5, etc.) are probably only variant spellings of essentially the same name.

[33] Speiser in AASOR 13 (1931-32), p.40.

Ultimately the word "Hebrew" became an ethnic designation for the people of Israel as it is in Judith 10:12, and for their language as it is in Jubilees 12:25-27, both books dating probably in the second century B.C.[34]

ABRAHAM

The migration of Abraham from Mesopotamia, in response to a divine call and promise (Genesis 12:1-3; cf. Hebrews 11:8-10), was regarded as the initial act of faith which made possible the unfolding of all the later history of his descendants. That Abraham's home was originally in Mesopotamia, and specifically at the cities of Ur and Haran, is indicated in several strands of Old Testament narrative. In Joshua 24:2 (E) the people of Israel are reminded of their polytheistic eastern ancestry in these words: "Your fathers lived of old beyond the Euphrates,[35] Terah, the father of Abraham and of Nahor; and they served other gods." Genesis 11:28-30; 12:1-4a, 6-9; cf. 15:7 (J) identifies the birthplace of Abraham with the city of Ur, and this tradition is echoed in a Levitical prayer of praise in Nehemiah 9:7: "Thou art the Lord, the God who didst choose Abram and bring him forth out of Ur of the Chaldees and give him the name Abraham."[36] Genesis 11:10-27, 31f.; 12:4b-5 (P)[37] likewise places the original home in Ur but indicates that the migration was first to Haran and then, after Terah's death at that place, on to Canaan. It has ordinarily been supposed that the Ur referred to in the foregoing citations was the well-known city in lower Mesopotamia already described (pp. 39-42, 50-52). In Genesis 24 (J), however, Abraham speaks of "my country" (v. 4) and "the land of my birth" (v. 7) and then sends his servant "to Mesopotamia, to the city of Nahor" (v. 10). Since Nahor was doubtless in northwestern

---

[34] For the Habiru see Mary F. Gray, "The Ḫâbirū-Hebrew Problem in the Light of the Source Material Available at Present," in HUCA 29 (1958), pp.135-202.

[35] For "the River" (ASV) as a frequent designation of the Euphrates see HDB IV p.287.

[36] In Genesis 11:28 (J), 31 (P); 15:7 (J), and Nehemiah 9:7 the LXX (ed. Swete, I, pp.18f., 23) reads "the land of the Chaldees" instead of "Ur of the Chaldees," but even so the reference is to the same general area, for the home of the Chaldeans was in lower Babylonia. Strictly speaking, the words "of the Chaldees" are an anachronism. The Chaldeans were a Semitic people who first came into southern Babylonia around 1000 B.C. as far as we can tell, and eventually established the Neo-Babylonian or Chaldean empire. It was, of course, quite natural for the biblical writers to apply to the city or land the appellation customary in their own day.

[37] For the abbreviations, E, J, and P, which are commonly used to distinguish hypothetical source documents in the Old Testament see Robert H. Pfeiffer, *Introduction to the Old Testament*. 5th ed. 1941, pp.139f.

Mesopotamia the question has been raised whether Abraham's original home should not be sought in that region rather than in lower Mesopotamia. An Akkadian tablet from Ugarit has now become known in which the Hittite king, Hattusilis III (c.1275-c.1250 B.C.; cf. below p. 199), writes to the king of Ugarit, Niqmepa' by name, about the status of merchants of Hattusilis who are trading in Ugarit. These traders are called "merchant men, citizens of the city of Ura." Since the name Ura could easily become Ur in Hebrew, this may attest the existence of another city of Ur and one presumably somewhere in the northwest. That this city could be "Ur of the Chaldees" would require that there had been Chaldeans in the northwest as well as in lower Mesopotamia (see above p. 70 n. 36), and that this was the case is attested by Xenophon (c.400 B.C.) who mentions the Chaldeans as blocking the way to Armenia and as neighbors of the Armenians.[38]

If we seek for indications in the Bible as to the date of Abraham's residence in Mesopotamia, we find it necessary to consider a complex series of chronological notations, most of which are from priestly sources. In some cases they bear not only on the date of Abraham but also on the date of the Exodus, a problem to which attention must be given later.

Priestly notices in Genesis 12:4b; 21:5; 25:26 and 47:9 give a total of 215 years for the period from Abraham's coming into Canaan to Jacob's going down into Egypt. As to the length of time the children of Israel (Jacob) were in the land of Egypt there are two traditions. The first represents this period as covering 430 years, or in round numbers 400 years. The precise figure of 430 years is given in the Hebrew text of Exodus 12:40f. (P), "The time that the people of Israel dwelt in Egypt was four hundred and thirty years." The round number, 400 years, is used in Genesis 15:13 in both the Hebrew and the Septuagint,[39] and is also found in Acts 7:6. Josephus, likewise, in two passages, represents the Israelites as having been in Egypt for 400 years.[40] The second tradition as to the length of time the Israelites were in Egypt appears in the Septuagint version of Exodus

---

[38] Xenophon, *Anabasis.* IV, iii, 4; cf. v, v, 17; *Cyropaedia.* III, i, 34. The "land of the Chaldeans" referred to in Isaiah 23:13 may also have been in the northwest. For the text cited above from Ugarit and for the suggestion that Abraham should be thought of as a merchant prince like the Hittite merchants of this text, see Cyrus H. Gordon in JNES 17 (1958), pp.28-31.

[39] Genesis 15 is largely J and E, but v.13 may be by a later hand.

[40] Josephus (A.D. c.37-c.95), *Antiquities.* II, ix, 1; *War* v, ix, 4 (tr. H. St. J. Thackeray and Ralph Marcus, LCL [1926-], IV, p.253; III, p.321).

12:40 which reads, "The time that the people of Israel dwelt in Egypt and in the land of Canaan was four hundred and thirty years."[41] Since, as we have seen, the patriarchs were in Canaan for 215 years, this would allow the Israelites only 215 years in Egypt. The statement in Galatians 3:17 evidently was based upon the Septuagint text, for it likewise makes 430 years cover the entire period from the call of Abraham to the Exodus and the giving of the law. Josephus also follows this tradition in one passage where he says of the Israelites, "They left Egypt . . . 430 years after the coming of our forefather Abraham to Canaan, Jacob's migration to Egypt having taken place 215 years later."[42]

It may be held that the standard Hebrew text of Exodus 12:40 is more reliable than the reading in the Septuagint. The affirmation of the following verse 41 that at the end of 430 years, "on that very day," the people went out of Egypt, seems more impressive if it is the anniversary of the beginning of their life in Egypt that is so marked.

On the other hand, Genesis 15:16 (E) says that the Exodus will take place "in the fourth generation," and priestly genealogies in Exodus 6:16-20 and Numbers 26:57-59 make Moses the great-great-grandson of Jacob, and in Joshua 7:1 list Achan, a contemporary of Joshua, as the great-great-great-grandson of Jacob. While the biblical word "generation" is a broad term and may simply mean all the people living at a given time, as in Exodus 1:6, four such groups of contemporaries in general, and a series of four descendants in particular, would surely be much more likely to cover only a span of something like 215 years than of 430.

If, then, we accept the Hebrew text we find that the patriarchs were 215 years in Canaan and the Israelites 430 years in Egypt. Abraham would have entered Canaan, accordingly, 645 years before the Exodus. But if we take the Septuagint text, the entry of Abraham into Canaan would have been only 430 years before the Exodus.

As we shall see in the next chapter the most probable date for the Exodus is either around the middle of the fifteenth century B.C. or toward the middle of the thirteenth century B.C., the latter date appearing definitely preferable. Taking the more probable latter date and adding 645 years we arrive at approximately 1900 B.C. for Abraham's entry into Canaan; adding 430 years we get a date shortly after 1700 B.C.

[41] Some MSS read 435 years (LXX ed. Swete, I, p.128).
[42] *Ant.* II, xv, 2.

The date around 1900 B.C. would mean that Abraham left Mesopotamia in the troubled period of the Elamite and Amorite invasions, which may be judged a likely time for a family to depart from its old home. The date near 1700 B.C., on the other hand, would make Abraham a contemporary of Hammurabi (1728-1686 B.C.) and as far as chronology is concerned would allow an identification of that famous king with "Amraphel king of Shinar" in Genesis 14:1, an identification which while much debated would not be impossible if Am-mu-ra-bi (Hammurabi) were erroneously read as Am-mu-ra-pil (Amraphel).[43]

It is also of interest to find that names very similar to "Abraham" occur at a slightly later time in Babylonia. A clay tablet from the reign of Ammizaduga, tenth king of the First Dynasty of Babylon, deals with the hiring of an ox by a certain Abarama son of Awel-Ishtar. Other similar documents deal with a field leased by Abamrama.[44] While the reference is of course not to Abraham the son of Terah, the name is essentially the same.

Certainly the patriarchal stories fit with thorough congruity and often with surprising relevance of detail into the historical setting of life in Mesopotamia during the first half of the second millennium B.C. Likewise, as we have seen, other portions of the Old Testament reflect intimate connections with both the mythology and the law of Mesopotamia. It may well have been Abraham himself who carried with him upon his historic migration some of the stories and the laws which his descendants were to raise to so high a level and to pass on to the world. If Abraham did come from Mesopotamia sometime in the early second millennium B.C., it is necessary to revise the picture sometimes painted of him as a primitive nomad accustomed only to the open spaces of the desert, and to recognize that at least to some extent he must have been the heir of a complex and age-old civilization.

[43] *Recueil Édouard Dhorme, études bibliques et orientales.* 1951, pp.262, 265; and see pp.191-272 for Abraham in the setting of history.

[44] Barton, *Archaeology and the Bible*, pp.344f.

II

The Panorama of Egypt

WHEN Hecataeus of Miletus called Egypt "the gift of the river" he characterized the land accurately.[1] Similarly an ancient Egyptian oracle said that all the land watered by the Nile in its course was Egypt, and all who dwelt lower down than the city Elephantine and drank of that river's water were Egyptians.[2] The Nile River upon which Egypt depended for existence was believed by Ptolemy (second century A.D.) to take its rise in farthest Africa at the foot of "the Mountains of the Moon."[3] The ancient geographer was almost correct. In 1888 Henry Stanley for the first time caught sight of a snow-clad mountain towering into the sky at the very Equator. Almost always veiled in mist and clouds and literally invisible, it is small wonder that hitherto it had been known only by rumor. Stanley gave the mountain a new and appropriate name, Ruwenzori, "The Rain-Maker." Early in the twentieth century a mountaineering expedition led by the Duke of the Abruzzi climbed to the 16,791-foot summit of the range and proved that the Nile does rise in the Mountains of the Moon. Their snows and rains drain down to the east and pour into the waters of the lakes, Victoria,

[1] See Arrian (A.D. c.96-c.180), *Anabasis of Alexander*. v, vi, 5. tr. E. Iliff Robson, LCL (1929-33) II, p.23. Hecataeus lived in the sixth or fifth century B.C. The epigram was quoted later by Herodotus (c.484-425 B.C.) II, 5. tr. A. D. Godley, LCL (1920-24) I, p.281, and then repeatedly by Strabo (c.63 B.C.-after A.D. 21), *Geography*. I, ii, 23, 29; XII, ii, 4 (tr. H. L. Jones, LCL [1917-32] I, pp.111,131; v, p.357). cf. William A. Heidel in *American Academy of Arts and Sciences Memoirs*. XVIII, 2 (1935), p.61.

[2] Herodotus II, 18.

[3] *Geography*. IV, 8. ed. Edward L. Stevenson. 1932, p.109.

Albert, and Edward, which in turn are the sources of the famous river of Egypt.[4]

From the Equator to the shores of the Mediterranean is 2,450 miles in a direct line and thither the Nile flows in an estimated 4,000 miles of windings, the "greatest single stream on earth," traversing almost one-tenth of the earth's circumference.[5] At Khartoum the White Nile (Bahr el-Abyad), as the upper part of the main river is known, is joined by a tributary, the Blue Nile (Bahr el-Azraq), which descends from the mountains of Ethiopia. One hundred forty miles farther north the only other tributary, the Atbara, flows in from the east. The almost daily tropical rains of the Equator provide the White Nile with a constant volume of water, sufficient to carry it through the thousand miles of rainless Egypt. Ethiopia, on the other hand, has both a dry and a rainy season. During the latter a great flood of turbid water pours down the "Blue" Nile. This accounts for the annual inundation which from time immemorial irrigated and fertilized the lower Nile Valley. As Herodotus said: "The river rises of itself, waters the fields, and then sinks back again; thereupon each man sows his field . . . and waits for the harvest."[6] Herodotus foresaw that the gradual rise in the level of the land would lessen the effectiveness of this natural irrigation system and expressed anxiety for the future of Egypt when it would be neither inundated by the river nor watered by rain—little dreaming of the enormous dam at Aswan which today is capable of giving Egypt a greater cultivable area than it had in the days of the Pharaohs.

Between Khartoum and Aswan there are six cataracts, where the Nile flows over granite ridges. This region was that of ancient Nubia. From the First Cataract at Aswan, which was ancient Elephantine, on down to Memphis, near modern Cairo, is a distance of 500 miles and was known as the land of Upper Egypt. The last 100 miles from Memphis to the Mediterranean, in which the Nile spreads out into the Delta, constituted Lower Egypt. In Nubia and Upper Egypt the valley of the Nile is but a narrow ribbon of green, rarely more than a dozen miles across and strictly bounded on either side by the cliffs and shelves of the desert. In the Delta, however, the fertile land forms a great triangle, traversed by the various mouths of the Nile, of which the most important are the Rosetta and the Damietta.

[4] James Ramsey Ullman, *High Conquest*. 1941, p.152.
[5] Emil Ludwig, *The Nile*. 1937, p.vii.
[6] II, 14.

The archeological situation in Egypt differs somewhat from that in Mesopotamia. Many of Egypt's monumental structures were built of stone, which was naturally far more enduring than the mud brick of Babylonia. In numerous instances pyramids, obelisks, temples, and other works still stand beneath the sky, relatively well preserved, massive and impressive. Immediately upon the beginning of modern archeological investigations, therefore, extensive materials were at hand, and the publications regarding Egyptian monuments issued by the scholars who accompanied Napoleon (p. 4),[7] by Ippolito Rosellini,[8] Jean François Champollion,[9] Karl Richard Lepsius,[10] Auguste Mariette,[11] and others, made them known to the world at an early date. To the objects already visible above ground in Egypt have now been added, of course, all the many things which have been discovered in actual excavations, which range from bits of prehistoric pottery to the fabulous treasures of Tutankhamun's tomb.

Probably the most important features of many of the temples and other monuments still standing in Egypt were the inscriptions which appeared on their walls and sides. To a remarkable degree these had endured the ravages of time, yet could not but grow dimmer and less legible as the years went on. It was one of the most urgent tasks in Egyptian archeology, therefore, to make a comprehensive survey of all such records as could be found, and to copy and translate them as accurately as possible. To this undertaking indefatigable labors were devoted by James Henry Breasted (1865-1935), America's eminent Egyptologist and founder of the Oriental Institute of the University of Chicago. He traveled throughout Egypt, sailing on the Nile, climbing the cliffs on the edge of the desert, entering temples and tombs, seeking out every place where historical documents might have survived.[12] To copy, translate, and edit the inscriptions which he found was a task of over a decade, but the resultant publication of the *Ancient Records of Egypt* (5 volumes, 1906-1907) made available a standard compilation of historical sources extending from the First Dynasty to the Persian conquest of Egypt.

In the arrangement of these and other Egyptian materials within

---

[7] *Description de l'Égypte, ou Recueil des observations et des recherches qui ont été faites en Égypte pendant l'expédition de l'armée française, publié par les ordres de sa majesté l'empereur Napoléon le Grand.* 21 vols. 1809-28.

[8] *I Monumenti dell'Egitto e della Nubia.* 9 vols. 1832-44.

[9] *Monuments de l'Égypte et de la Nubie.* 4 vols. 1835-45.

[10] *Denkmäler aus Ägypten und Äthiopien.* 12 vols. 1849-56.

[11] *Voyage dans la Haute-Égypte.* 2 vols. 2d ed. 1893.

[12] Charles Breasted, *Pioneer to the Past.* 1943, p.78.

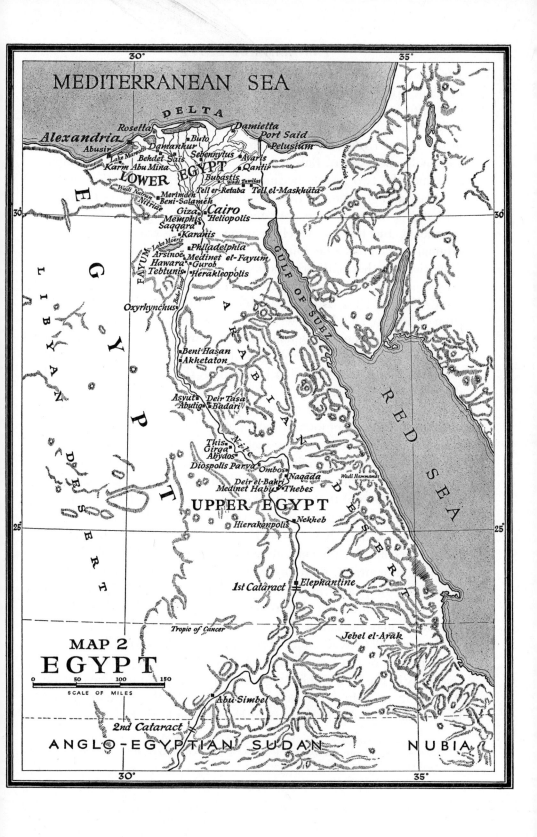

MEDITERRANEAN SEA

DELTA

Rosetta
Damietta
Port Said
Alexandria
Pelusium
Abusir
Damanhur
Behdet
Sais
Buto
Sebennytus
Karm Abu Mina
Avaris
Qantir
LOWER EGYPT
Bubastis
Wadi Tumilat
Merimdeh
Tell er-Retaba
Tell el-Maskhuta
Beni-Salameh
Wadi Natrun
Nitrite
Giza
Cairo
Memphis
Heliopolis
Saqqara
Karanis
Philadelphia
Lake Moeris
Arsinoë
Medinet el-Fayum
FAYUM
Hawara
Gurob
Tebtunis
Bahr Yusef
Herakleopolis

Oxyrhynchus

Beni Hasan
Akhetaton

Asyut
Deir Tasa
Abutig
Badari

This
Girga
Nile
Abydos
Diospolis Parva
Ombos
Deir el-Bahri
Naqada
Medinet Habu
Thebes
Wadi Hammamat

UPPER EGYPT

Hierakonpolis
Nekheb

1st Cataract
Elephantine

Tropic of Cancer
Jebel el-Arak

MAP 2
EGYPT

0   50   100   150
SCALE OF MILES

Abu Simbel

2nd Cataract
ANGLO-EGYPTIAN SUDAN
NUBIA

LIBYAN DESERT
EGYPT
ARABIAN DESERT
GULF OF SUEZ
RED SEA
Wadi el-Arish

a framework of consecutive dynasties, all modern historians are dependent upon an ancient predecessor. This was an Egyptian priest and writer named Manetho who lived under Ptolemy II Philadelphus (285-246 B.C.). Manetho was born at Sebennytus (now Samannud) in the Delta. Eventually he rose to be high priest in the temple at Heliopolis. Berossos of Babylon (p. 30) was practically a contemporary, and the two priests became rivals in the proclamation of the antiquity and greatness of their respective lands. Manetho's *Egyptian History*,[13] with which we are concerned here, is preserved only in fragments, the text of which is often corrupt. Excerpts from the original work are to be found in Josephus, and Manetho's lists of dynasties together with brief notes on important kings or events are preserved in the *Chronicle* (A.D. c.221) of Sextus Julius Africanus, the *Chronicon* (A.D. 326) of Eusebius, and the history of the world from Adam to Diocletian written by George Syncellus about A.D. 800. With all of these fragments collected and arranged in order[14] it is possible to gain a reasonably good view of Manetho's outline, and the usual division of Egyptian history into thirty dynasties is based directly upon his work.

Throughout the period covered by these thirty successive houses of rulers, life in Egypt manifested a notable continuity which was interrupted but not destroyed by such an event as the Hyksos invasion. While the narrow Nile Valley was by no means isolated from the rest of the ancient world, it offered its inhabitants sufficient protection to render incursions of that sort infrequent. Also, in the character of the people there was a trait of tenacity which may have been exaggerated in the remark that they "could learn but not forget,"[15] but which helps to account for the amazing persistence of many things in Egyptian life. In contrast, therefore, with the changing kingdoms which complicate the scene in Mesopotamia, the drama of Egypt has a linear quality somewhat akin to that of the land itself which, omitting the Delta, may be said to have but one dimension—length.[16]

The immediate availability of a large body of historical documents, the existence of the framework provided by Manetho, and the relative unity of the land and homogeneity of the happenings, have made it possible to reduce archeological findings to the form of actual history more quickly in the case of Egypt than in that of some other

[13] Αἰγυπτιακὰ ὑπομνήματα.   [14] *Manetho*, tr. W. G. Waddell. LCL. 1940.
[15] George Foot Moore, *History of Religions*. I (rev. ed. 1920), p.148.
[16] Barton, *Archaeology and the Bible*, p.3.

lands. In telling the archeological story of Egypt, therefore, we can follow an historical outline which has already been formulated with considerable definiteness. Before coming to the First Dynasty, however, it is necessary to mention those earlier vistas in Egyptian life which were too remote to be known even to Manetho but which have reappeared within the horizon of our knowledge, thanks to the investigations of modern archeology.

1. THE NEOLITHIC, CHALCOLITHIC, AND PREDYNASTIC PERIODS,
c.5000-c.2900 B.C.[1]

As IN Mesopotamia so too in Egypt, we may note that Neolithic settlements were in existence by probably c.5000 B.C. The culture of this early time is known from discoveries at Deir Tasa opposite Abutig in Middle Egypt,[2] in the Fayum,[3] and at Merimdeh Beni-Salameh[4] west of the Rosetta branch of the Nile.

A Chalcolithic culture of perhaps the middle of the fifth millennium B.C. appears at Badari, twenty miles south of Asyut on the east bank of the Nile, where the people already had knowledge of copper. The Badarians were distinguished for their fine pottery and were accustomed to grind green malachite on slate palettes to use for eye-paint. This is an excellent germicide, still used by Africans, and particularly effective when spread around the eyes as a protection from flies. In their burials the Badarian dead were laid down as if sleeping, and food offerings as well as other objects were placed in the graves with them.[5]

Akin to the Badarians were the succeeding Amratians, who belong perhaps to the beginning of the fourth millennium B.C., and with whom the so-called Predynastic period properly begins. Known first

---

[1] For the dates in Egyptian prehistory see William C. Hayes, *The Scepter of Egypt, A Background for the Study of the Egyptian Antiquities in The Metropolitan Museum of Art*, Part I: *From the Earliest Times to the End of the Middle Kingdom*. 1953, p.8; cf. Helene J. Kantor in Ehrich, ed., *Relative Chronologies in Old World Archeology*, p.16; Robert-P. Charles in JNES 16 (1957), pp.240-253; and for the Egyptian calendar see the Appendix of the present book.

[2] Guy Brunton in *Antiquity, A Quarterly Review of Archaeology*. 3 (1929), pp.456-467.

[3] Gertrude Caton-Thompson and E. W. Gardner, *The Desert Fayum*. 2 vols. 1934.

[4] V. Gordon Childe, *New Light on the Most Ancient East*. 1935, pp.58-61; Hermann Ranke in JAOS 59 (1939) No.4, Supplement p.8.

[5] Guy Brunton and Gertrude Caton-Thompson, *The Badarian Civilization*. 1928, pp.20-42.

from el-Amreh not far from Abydos, their village sites and cemeteries have been found throughout Upper Egypt from Badari to Lower Nubia. The Amratians, it is thought, may have been organized as totemic clans. Copper was used, and boats made out of bundles of papyrus lashed together facilitated travel on the Nile. The dead were buried, doubled up, in shallow oval pits and accompanied by food, ornaments, and weapons. Statuettes of women and of servants bearing water-pots on their heads also were placed in the graves, perhaps as substitutes of magical efficacy for the living wives and attendants who in earlier times were sent to the grave with their master. Representations of men and animals on the pottery in the grave were also probably intended to be of magical help to the deceased.[6]

While the Amratian culture was focused in Upper Egypt, the Gerzean had its center at Gerzeh and other Nile Valley sites in the latitude of the Fayum. From there in Middle Predynastic times, perhaps around the middle of the fourth millennium, the Gerzean culture spread into and came to dominate Upper Egypt as well. Among the characteristic objects of Gerzean times are wavy-handled jars,[7] pear-shaped maces, vessels of clay or stone in the shape of animals, and amulets representing the bull, the cow, the toad, the fly, and the falcon.

The villages were becoming towns and each seems to have recognized an animal or plant as its totem. On decorated pots there are figures of ships which bear totemic standards on their masts. Thus was emerging that structure of society which is known in historic times when the Egyptians lived in independent districts, each designated by a banner or ensign representing an animal or plant. These regional divisions, of which eventually there were twenty-two in Upper Egypt and twenty in the Delta, later were called "nomes" by the Greeks.

Gerzean graves were oblong trenches, on one side of which a ledge accommodated the ever more numerous offerings. Burial places of the rich were lined with mud bricks, and one such has been discovered at the site of Hierakonpolis in which the walls were adorned

[6] Brunton in *Antiquity*. 3 (1929), p.460; Childe, *New Light on the Most Ancient East*, pp.69-74.

[7] It was the progressive degeneration of the wavy-ledges which once served as handholds on these jars into mere decorative marks that provided W. M. Flinders Petrie with his clue for the development of "sequence dating" for the Predynastic period (*Diospolis Parva*. 1901, pp.28-30; *Prehistoric Egypt*. 1920, pp.3f.).

with a mural painting.[8] Thus the vase-paintings of Amratian times now find a place on the walls of the tomb, where Egyptian paintings are so well known and so important in all later years. The comparative splendor of the tomb just mentioned is an indication, also, of the rise of kingship which led at last to the unification of the land.[9]

Two powerful states came into existence first, one in Upper Egypt, the other in Lower Egypt or the Delta. The capital of southern or Upper Egypt was at Ombos on the left bank of the Nile, near the modern town of Naqada. Its king wore a tall white helmet as a crown, and the symbol of the kingdom was a plant not identified botanically but usually called the lotus. The capital of northern or Lower Egypt was at Behdet, near modern Damanhur and Alexandria. The king's crown here was a red wickerwork diadem, and the kingdom's symbol was the papyrus which grew so abundantly in the swamps and marshes of the Delta. These plants which were the symbols of the two lands are represented on two columns still standing at Karnak (Fig. 26), the lotus of Upper Egypt being at the right and the papyrus of Lower Egypt at the left. Although Egypt ultimately became one united land, the remembrance of the two kingdoms always persisted. The ruler of all Egypt bore the title "King of Upper Egypt and Lower Egypt" and wore a crown which combined the tall helmet of Upper Egypt and the wickerwork diadem of Lower Egypt. The symbol of the united land was a device in which the lotus and the papyrus were knotted together (p. 85).[10] Even in the Old Testament the Hebrew name for Egypt remained literally "the two Egypts."[11]

The earliest Egyptian annals begin with the names of kings in this Predynastic period. Herodotus remarked that "the Egyptians . . . who dwell in the cultivated country are the most careful of all men to preserve the memory of the past, and none whom I have questioned have so many chronicles."[12] As early as the Fifth Dynasty historical records were inscribed on slabs of stone, fragments of which still survive and constitute early annals in "the history of history."[13] One of these fragments is the famous Palermo Stone, shown in Fig. 27. It is a small piece of hard black diorite, about 17

[8] J. E. Quibell, *Hierakonpolis.* II (1902), pp.20f.
[9] Childe, *New Light on the Most Ancient East*, pp.86-100.
[10] E. A. Wallis Budge, *The Gods of the Egyptians.* 1904, II, pp.42-48.
[11] Genesis 15:18, etc.
[12] II, 77.
[13] James T. Shotwell, *The History of History.* I. 1939, p.79.

inches high, 9½ inches wide, and 2½ inches thick. At the top is a simple row of oblong spaces containing hieroglyphic signs. The clue to their meaning is given by the lower section of each oblong space where a figure wearing a red crown and holding a flail appears. This is the sign for the king of Lower Egypt and consequently each symbol in the space above must be the name of a ruler of the Lower Kingdom. Some nine of these names can still be read, and lost portions of the stone doubtless contained more names for Lower Egypt and a list for Upper Egypt too. As a matter of fact, on a Cairo fragment of the annals some Predynastic kings appear wearing the double crown of Lower and Upper Egypt combined.[14]

This occurrence of the double crown and the domination of Upper Egypt by the Gerzean culture which originated in the Delta, have suggested the hypothesis that a temporary unification of the two lands was accomplished during the Middle Predynastic period. If such a unification did take place it must have been the work of conquerors from the Delta who were able to establish their supremacy also in Upper Egypt. If there was such a union, however, it did not endure, and the Late Predynastic period saw the two lands broken apart again and warring against each other. At this time the capital of Upper Egypt was at Nekheb, a site which later was known as Eileithyiaspolis and is the modern Elkab; and the royal residence was just across the river at Nekhen, which later was called Hierakonpolis. The capital of Lower Egypt was at Buto, with the royal residence in a suburb called Pe. Finally a king of Upper Egypt conquered the Delta and united the two Egypts permanently in a single kingdom under one central rule.[15]

2. THE PROTODYNASTIC PERIOD
(FIRST AND SECOND DYNASTIES), c.2900-c.2700 B.C.[1]

MENES

ACCORDING to Manetho the first king of permanently united Egypt was Menes. The statement of the ancient historian as he introduces

[14] James Henry Breasted, ARE I, §§76-167; and in *Bulletin de l'Institut Français d'Archéologie Orientale*. 30 (1930-31), pp.709-724.

[15] A. Moret, *The Nile and Egyptian Civilization*. 1927, pp.101-113; A. Scharff, *Grundzüge der Ägyptischen Vorgeschichte*. 1927, pp.46-49; Ranke in JAOS 59 (1939) No.4, Supplement, pp.14f.

[1] For the dates see Albright in BASOR 88 (Dec. 1942), p.32, with correlations with Mesopotamian and other Middle Eastern chronologies; cf. Meek in JR 21 (1941),

the First Dynasty runs as follows: "The first royal house numbers eight kings, the first of whom Menes of This reigned for 62 years. He was carried off by a hippopotamus and perished."[2] The native city of Menes was This, not far from the great bend of the Nile below Thebes, near where the modern town of Girga stands. This was the capital of the nome of the same name, and was the seat of both the First and Second Dynasties, which took from it their customary designation as the Thinite dynasties.

Since This was situated far south in Upper Egypt, the new ruler of all the Egyptians also built a fortress three hundred miles to the north, at the apex of the Delta and on the border of the two lands. Herodotus says that the site was gained by building a dam to divert the Nile.[3] In reference to the White Kingdom whose victorious power it represented, the new city was known as "White Wall." From the Sixth Dynasty on it bore the name Men-nefru-Mire or Menfe, from which is derived the familiar Greek name, Memphis.[4]

The cemetery of the Thinite kings was in the desert not far from This and near the site of Abydos. As a result of excavations carried out here in 1899 and following by W. M. Flinders Petrie, the tombs of most of these kings have been discovered.[5] They were in the form of underground pits lined with brick walls, and originally roofed with timber and matting. In the more elaborate examples the burial chamber proper was a wooden hall in the center of the larger pit, surrounded by smaller chambers to hold the offerings. Smaller tombs for the king's servants were ranged about the structure. In the Second Dynasty vaults of brick took the place of the original wooden ceilings for the tombs. In turn a more elaborate superstructure was developed, consisting of a great rectangle of brickwork with slop-

---

p.404 n.16. See also tables of Egyptian chronology in George Steindorff and Keith C. Seele, *When Egypt Ruled the East*. 2d ed. rev. by Keith C. Seele. 1957, pp.274f.; John A. Wilson, *The Burden of Egypt*. 1951, pp.vii-viii; and Hayes, *The Scepter of Egypt*, I, pp.34, 58, etc. Steindorff and Seele, and Hayes place the beginning of the First Dynasty around 3200 B.C., Wilson around 3100 B.C. A radiocarbon test has given a measure of confirmation to the date c.2900 B.C. in that a piece of wood from a beam in the tomb at Saqqara of Hemaka, a vizier of the First Dynasty, has been dated at 2933 B.C., but there is a possible margin of error of 200 years either way. G. E. Wright in BA 14 (1951), p.31.

[2] *Manetho*, tr. Waddell, pp.27-29.

[3] II, 99.

[4] J. H. Breasted, *A History of Egypt*. 1909, p.37. Memphis is mentioned frequently in the Old Testament (Hosea 9:6; Isaiah 19:13; Jeremiah 2:16; 44:1; 46:14, 19; Ezekiel 30:13, 16), the Hebrew name being Noph, which is perhaps a corruption of the middle part of the ancient Egyptian name.

[5] Petrie, *The Royal Tombs of the First Dynasty*. 1900; *The Royal Tombs of the Earliest Dynasties*. 1901.

ing sides, distinctive recesses, and a flat top. To this type of tomb it is customary now to apply the Arabic name *mastaba*, meaning platform or bench.

Like so many of the burial places of ancient Egypt, the royal tombs at Abydos had already been plundered by robbers. Enough of their contents remained, however, to show that with the mummies a profusion of jewelry, stone vases, copper vessels, and other objects had been buried. Also the names of a number of the kings were found, including Narmer, Aha, Zer, and others. These are the "Horus titles" or names of the kings as earthly representatives of the god Horus, rather than their personal names which were used by Manetho. Identifications are not certain, therefore, but it is probable that Narmer is the king who was called Menes by Manetho, and who was founder of the First Dynasty.

The finest monument of Narmer which we possess is a slate palette found at Hierakonpolis and shown in Fig. 28. The palette is like those on which the Egyptians had long ground eye-paint, but is of a very large size as befitted a great king. On the obverse side (right) the king and priests walk in triumphal procession while the long necks of two monsters are curved to form a circular recess where the cosmetics may be ground. On the reverse stands the tall figure of the king who lifts a heavy mace with pear-shaped head of white stone to crush the skull of his enemy whom he grasps by the hair. Upon the king's head is the tall, white, helmet-like crown of Upper Egypt, while a long animal tail hangs from the back of his belt. The latter probably was an ancient North African badge of chieftaincy but it remains henceforth a regular attribute of the Egyptian kingship. Behind the king is his servant, carrying the king's sandals and a water-pot or oil-jar. Around the king's belt and also at the top of the palette are heads of Hathor, the cow-goddess. At one side is a very early example of Egyptian hieroglyphics, or writing in picture form. A falcon, as symbol of the king, holds a length of rope which is attached to a man's head. The head is connected with an area of ground out of which grow six papyrus stalks, representing the marshes of Lower Egypt. Below is a single-barbed harpoon head and a rectangle which is the sign of a lake. The entire pictograph means that the falcon king led captive the people of the Harpoon Lake in Lower Egypt. At the top of the palette, between the heads of Hathor, is the name of the king, Narmer.[6]

[6] Quibell, *Hierakonpolis*. I (1900), p.10.

Other First Dynasty tombs have been excavated recently at Saqqara near Memphis, which are even larger and more elaborate than the ones at Abydos. This discovery has led to the suggestion that the early kings of the then recently united Upper and Lower Egypt may each have had two tombs, one in the south and another in the north. In this case the Abydos tombs could have been their cenotaphs, those at Saqqara their actual burial places. Tomb 3504 at Saqqara is dated to the reign of King Wadjy, fourth monarch of the First Dynasty, and contains a large burial chamber surrounded by magazines for storing the food and other things needed by the deceased in the world beyond. Around three sides of the tomb are also small graves which may have been for retainers sacrificed to accompany the king in death. Striking too is a bench surrounding this tomb structure on which were once probably more than three hundred bulls' heads modeled in clay with real horns attached. Tomb 3505, dating to the reign of King Ka-a, last ruler of the dynasty, was even larger and in general design provides a prototype of the pyramid complex of later times with the funerary temple on the north side of the tomb.[7]

Lines two and three of the Palermo Stone (Fig. 27) give annals from the time of the First Dynasty, although the fragment as we have it does not include the beginning of that dynasty. As compared with the bare list of names of the Predynastic kings the record now is fuller, and an entire oblong is devoted to each year of a king's reign, the dividing lines curling over at the top being the hieroglyphic signs for palms, and signifying years. The name of the king is given in the long horizontal space above the yearly records, as may be seen above rows 3 and 4. The vertical line extending up through the horizontal space near the right end of row 2 marks the termination of a reign. The oblong immediately to the right shows six new moons, a sun, and seven strokes, thus indicating six months and seven days which is some detail as to the time when this reign ceased. Continuing to read from right to left, the next oblong gives the date of the new king's accession, the fourth month and thirteenth day, ten being represented by two strokes joined at the top. When a king came to the throne a feast was celebrated called "Union of the Two Lands," and by it the king's first year was characterized and named. This designation appears in the same oblong in the form of the lotus and papyrus tied together. The measurements in the little rectangles

---

[7] Walter B. Emery in *Archaeology.* 8 (1955), pp.2-9.

below, giving a number of cubits, palms, and fingers, may have registered the height of the Nile inundation that year.

In the early years and reigns most of the events noted are but names of religious feasts. Lines 4 and 5 are devoted to the Second Dynasty, and here we come upon a mention of the "fourth occurrence of the numbering," a reference to a regular census or inventory of some sort. With line 6 and the Third Dynasty the annal becomes yet more detailed and the yearly sections are necessarily much larger. Here there is reference to the building of ships of some size, and the bringing by sea of cedar wood, probably from Lebanon. A double palace was erected whose double name recalled the old kingdoms of South and North: "Exalted-is-the-White-Crown-of-Snefru-upon-the-Southern-Gate. Exalted-is-the-Red-Crown-of-Snefru-upon-the-Northern-Gate." Most of the record of the Fourth Dynasty is missing, but the lines on the back of the Palermo Stone carry the annals on down into the Fifth Dynasty.

Before continuing the narrative into later eras it should be indicated that already in the late Predynastic and early Protodynastic periods Egypt was in contact with the environing world. Indeed the period of about 3000 B.C. constituted the first great epoch of international commerce. This will be remembered as the Jemdet Nasr period in Mesopotamia, and there are definite evidences of Mesopotamian influence in Egypt at the time. In the painted tomb at Hierakonpolis already mentioned a boat is depicted which is very different from the usual papyrus boats of Egypt but is similar to those represented in Mesopotamia. At Jebel el-Arak a carved ivory knife-handle has been found which not only shows another such foreign-type boat but also reveals a scene whose Mesopotamian character is even more unmistakable. In the latter a hero is shown in combat with two lions which rise against him from either side. Not only is the grouping typically Mesopotamian but the man himself is pictured in Asiatic style with full beard and long robe.[8] Mesopotamian cylinder seals of the Jemdet Nasr period have also been found in Egypt, and the development of Egyptian cylinder seals was a result of original impact from the land of the Two Rivers.[9] Likewise the sudden appearance in Egypt of an advanced technique and style in the erection of recessed brick buildings evidently was

[8] Georges Bénédite in *Académie des inscriptions et belles-lettres, Commission de la fondation Eugène Piot, Monuments et mémoires.* 22 (1916), pp.1-34; René Dussaud in *Syria.* 16 (1935), pp.320-323.

[9] Frankfort, *Cylinder Seals*, pp.292-300.

based upon knowledge of architectural achievements in Mesopotamia which had reached a similar level at this time. These facts show that Mesopotamian influences were a stimulus in Egypt during some of the most formative phases of that land's development.[10]

3. THE OLD KINGDOM (THIRD TO SIXTH DYNASTIES), c.2700-c.2200 B.C.

THE Third to Sixth Dynasties constitute the time of the Old Kingdom or the Pyramid Age, the first great culminating point of Egyptian civilization. Under the rule of Djoser, first king of the Third Dynasty, the remarkable Imhotep attained renown as priest, magician, author of wise proverbs, physician, and architect. For his king, Imhotep undertook the construction of a royal mausoleum of a style more impressive than any hitherto known. Starting with a lofty *mastaba* of stone, and superimposing five successive shells upon it, he built the famous "step pyramid" at Saqqara, a terraced monument 190 feet high, the earliest large structure of stone known in history. From this there developed the great pyramids which have been in all succeeding centuries a wonder of the world.

THE PYRAMIDS

Of all the pyramids[1] the greatest (Fig. 29) was built by Khufu, second king of the Fourth Dynasty. Upon a square base covering some thirteen acres, he heaped up 2,300,000 blocks of yellowish limestone, each weighing on the average two and one-half tons, until the whole pyramid towered originally 481 feet into the sky. According to Herodotus, laborers toiled on the monument in groups of 100,000 men, each group for three months at a time. Ten years were required to make the road whereon the stones were dragged and twenty years more for the pyramid itself. Like a good tourist Herodotus reports that it was written on the pyramid how much was spent on onions and garlic for the workmen and says, "to my sure remembrance the interpreter when he read me the writing said that sixteen hundred talents of silver had been paid."[2] The stonework was done

---

[10] A. Scharff in ZÄS 71 (1935), pp.89-106; H. Frankfort in AJSL 58 (Jan.-Oct. 1941), pp. 329-358; and *The Birth of Civilization in the Near East*, pp. 100-111; Helene J. Kantor in JNES 3 (1944), pp.110-136; and in Ehrich, ed., *Relative Chronologies in Old World Archeology*, pp.5-8.

[1] I. E. S. Edwards, *The Pyramids of Egypt*. 1947.   [2] II, 124f.

with a precision involving seams of one ten-thousandth of an inch, and the entire exterior was covered with an exquisitely fitted casing of fine white limestone. Such is "the earliest and most impressive witness surviving from the ancient world, to the final emergence of organized society from prehistoric chaos and local conflict, thus coming for the first time completely under the power of a far-reaching and comprehensive centralization effected by one controlling mind."[3]

Khafre, the successor of Khufu, built the even more spectacular Second Pyramid of Giza. Its present height is 447½ feet, only 1½ feet less than the present height of the Great Pyramid, while its base is smaller, each side of the base now measuring 690½ feet as compared with 746 feet on the Great Pyramid. The angle of the sides of the Second Pyramid (52° 20′) is therefore steeper than that of the Great Pyramid (51° 50′) while the upper one-fourth of the slopes still retains the original casing of smooth limestone and granite slabs.[4] Khafre himself is represented in the head of the great Sphinx which stands to the east of the Second Pyramid. The body of the Sphinx is that of a couchant lion, but the head is that of the king, wearing the usual cloth headdress and with the uraeus or deadly cobra coiled on his forehead. This serpent was symbol of the kingship and coiled itself upon the king's brow to destroy his enemies as once it had annihilated the adversaries of the sun-god Re. The Sphinx was carved out of a spur of natural rock and built up with blocks of stone at the same time that the pyramid of Khafre was built or soon after. The monument was gradually half-buried by the ever-drifting sands of the desert but was excavated by Thutmose IV and again by modern Egyptian archeologists in 1926-1927 and 1936-1946.[5]

Kings of the Fifth and Sixth Dynasties built a number of smaller pyramids at Saqqara. On the walls of the inner passages and chambers of these monuments they caused inscriptions to be carved which are known as the Pyramid Texts.[6] Since in some cases they reflect conditions prior even to the union of Upper and Lower Egypt, many of these texts must be much earlier than the time of their

[3] J. H. Breasted, *A History of the Ancient Egyptians.* 1903, p. 110.

[4] This is the pyramid from which Rand Herron, member of the 1932 mountaineering expedition to Nanga Parbat, fell to his death. Ullman, *High Conquest,* p.194.

[5] Selim Hassan, *The Sphinx, Its History in the Light of Recent Excavations.* 1949. See pp.88-91 for the date in the reign of Khafre.

[6] Samuel A. B. Mercer, *The Pyramid Texts in Translation and Commentary.* 4 vols. 1952; John A. Wilson in ANET pp.32f.

recording in the pyramids and may be supposed to have existed previously, written on papyrus or potsherds. Their theme is the prospect of a glorious hereafter for the deceased king in the presence of the sun-god. Frequently their form is that of couplets which display parallelism in the arrangement of words and thought.

The composing of proverbs was also practiced by the early Egyptians. Imhotep was famous in this regard as we have noted, and so were Kagemni and Hardedef. Of all the sages, however, the best known is Ptahhotep, who was grand vizier under a king of the Fifth Dynasty. His proverbs take the form of instructions to his son and have to do particularly with behavior that is fitting on the part of a state official. "Let not thy heart be puffed-up because of thy knowledge," said the father to the son, "be not confident because thou art a wise man. Take counsel with the ignorant as well as the wise. . . . Good speech is more hidden than the emerald, but it may be found with maidservants at the grindstones." "Wrongdoing has never brought its undertaking into port," he warned, "but the strength of justice is that it lasts." Having given such advice and much more, he admonished gently: "How good it is when a son accepts what his father says!"[7]

4. FIRST INTERMEDIATE PERIOD
(SEVENTH TO ELEVENTH DYNASTIES), c.2200-c.1991 B.C.

As THE glory of the Old Kingdom faded, there ensued a period of disintegration and chaos when weak kings were unable to maintain a strong, central government. Manetho's Seventh and Eighth Dynasties which continued to rule weakly at Memphis, and the Ninth and Tenth Dynasties which arose at Herakleopolis (seventy-seven miles south of Cairo), are included in this Intermediate period. The disturbances and upset conditions which were experienced are reflected in "The Admonitions of Ipuwer."

"Why really, the land spins around as a potter's wheel does. . . . The nomes are destroyed. Barbarians from outside have come to Egypt. . . . Laughter has disappeared. . . . It has come to a point where the land is despoiled of kingship by a few irresponsible men. . . . The owners of

---

[7] John A. Wilson in ANET pp.412-414; cf. T. Eric Peet, *A Comparative Study of the Literatures of Egypt, Palestine, and Mesopotamia.* 1931, pp.101-103; Adolf Erman, *The Literature of the Ancient Egyptians.* 1927, p.60.

robes are now in rags. But he who never wove for himself is now the owner of fine linen."[1]

Ipuwer hoped however for the coming of an ideal king whom he described in the following words: "It shall come that he brings coolness upon the heart. Men shall say: 'He is the herdsman of all men. Evil is not in his heart. Though his herds may be small, still he has spent the day caring for them.'"[2] Such is one of the earliest expressions of the Messianic hope in history.

Another burdened writer of the same period wistfully longed for death itself as a glad release:

> Death is in my eyes today
> As when a sick man becomes whole,
> As the walking abroad after illness.
>
> Death is in my eyes today
> Like the desire of a man to see his home
> When he hath passed many years in captivity.[3]

In the Eleventh Dynasty the Intefs and Mentuhoteps were able at least partially to restore order and to reestablish a centralized state. Their place of rule was at Thebes, a city which was situated on the Nile 440 miles above Memphis, and which was destined later to become Egypt's greatest capital.[4]

5. THE MIDDLE KINGDOM
(TWELFTH DYNASTY), c.1991-c.1786 B.C.[1]

WITH the Twelfth Dynasty which was inaugurated by Amenemhet I, Egypt entered the second great period of its history, the Middle Kingdom. The kings of this dynasty were native Thebans but they

[1] John A. Wilson in ANET pp.441f.; cf. Peet, *A Comparative Study of the Literatures of Egypt, Palestine, and Mesopotamia*, p.118; cf. Josephine Mayer and Tom Prideaux, *Never to Die, the Egyptians in Their Own Words*. 1938, p. 68.

[2] Wilson in ANET p.443; cf. Breasted, *The Dawn of Conscience*, p.198.

[3] Peet, *A Comparative Study of the Literatures of Egypt, Palestine, and Mesopotamia*, pp.116f.; John A. Wilson in ANET p.407; R. O. Faulkner in JEA 42 (1956), pp.21-40.

[4] The Egyptian name for the town was Weset or more briefly Newt, "the city," whence is derived the biblical No (Jeremiah 46:25; Ezekiel 30:14-16) or No-Amon (Nahum 3:8), "city" or "city of Amun." The Greeks called it Thebes (Θῆβαι) and also Diospolis (Διόσπολις), meaning "city of Zeus" (Amun), or Diospolis Magna in distinction from Diospolis Parva or Hou. The modern villages at this site are Luxor and Karnak.

[1] H. E. Winlock, *The Rise and Fall of the Middle Kingdom in Thebes*. 1947, p.91. Hayes (*The Scepter of Egypt*. I, pp.150, 170, 340) treats the Eleventh Dynasty as

27. The Palermo Stone

26. The Plants that Were the Symbols of Upper and Lower Egypt

28. Cast of the Slate Palette of King Narmer

29. The Great Pyramid at Giza as Seen from the Summit of the Second Pyramid

31. Statue of Queen Hatshepsut

30. A Semite with his Donkey, as Painted in the Tomb of Khnumhotep II

32. The Terraced Temple of Hatshepsut at Deir el-Bahri

34. Thutmose III

33. Statue of Senenmut and Nefrure

35. The Obelisk of Thutmose III now in New York City

36. Bricklayers at Work, a Painting in the Tomb of Rekhmire

37. The Judgment Scene in the Papyrus of Ani

39. Amenhotep II, Standing under the Protection of the Cow-Goddess, Hathor

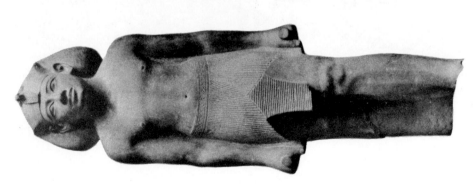

38. Statue of Amenhotep II

40. Syrians Bringing Tribute

41. Head of Amenhotep III

42. The Colonnade of Amenhotep III at Luxor
(with Pylon of Ramses II in the Background)

43. Fowling in the Marshes

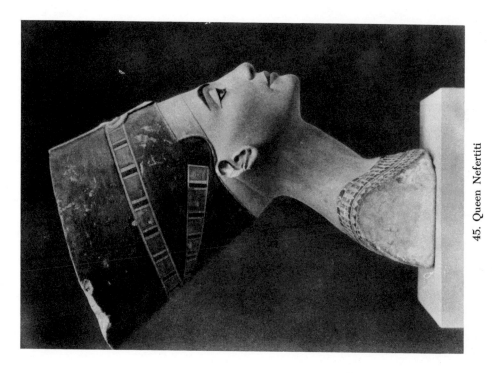

45. Queen Nefertiti

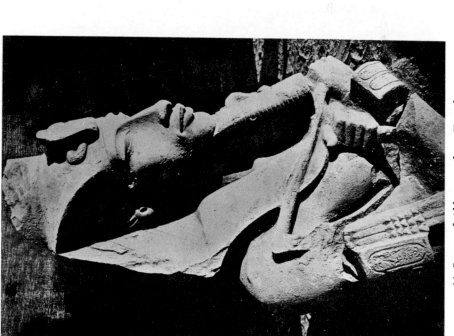

44. Statue of Akhenaton from Karnak

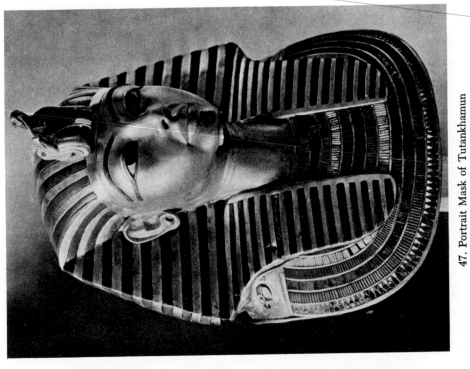

47. Portrait Mask of Tutankhamun

46. Obverse of Tell el-Amarna Tablet with Letter
from Rib-Addi to Amenhotep III

49. The Hypostyle Hall in the Temple at Karnak

48. Haremhab as a Royal Scribe, before his
Accession as King

51. The Victory Stela of Merneptah

50. Statue of Ramses II at Abu Simbel

53. Temple Relief of Ramses III at Medinet Habu

52. Philistine Prisoners Being Led into the Presence of Ramses III

55. The Rosetta Stone

54. Israelite Captives of Sheshonk I

ruled chiefly from capitals in Memphis and in the Fayum. Their house endured for over two hundred years, and their accomplishments included the conquest of Nubia to the Second Cataract,[1a] the connecting of the Nile with the Red Sea by canal, and the development of mining in Sinai into a permanent industry. The art and architecture of the age were characterized by refinement. Feminine jewelry was made with unsurpassed beauty of design and microscopic accuracy of execution. A "literature of entertainment" arose for the first time, including such stories as "Baufra's Tale" and "The Eloquent Peasant."[2] In the Fifth and Sixth Dynasties the Pyramid Texts (p. 88) had described a future life to be enjoyed by the king, but now in the Middle Kingdom others besides kings could anticipate the privilege of being buried with texts at hand to guide and protect them in the after-life. These texts were written on the inside of the coffin of the deceased, hence are known as the Coffin Texts.

If Abraham's migration to Palestine and subsequent visit to Egypt[3] (p. 72) fell in the neighborhood of 1900 B.C. then he was in Egypt in the days of the Middle Kingdom; if it was around 1700 B.C. then it was in the Second Intermediate period. Abraham does not figure in Egyptian records of the time, the earliest occurrence of his name being when Pharaoh Sheshonk I (tenth century B.C.) records capturing a place in Palestine called "The Field of Abram" (p. 126).[4] But it is interesting to have such tangible evidence of communication between Egypt and Palestine and Syria in these very days as appears in the following account.

THE TALE OF SINUHE

When Amenemhet I died, his son, Senusert (or Sesostris) I, was campaigning in the western Delta against the Libyans. Word of the

---

marking the beginning of the Middle Kingdom, and the Thirteenth and Fourteenth Dynasties as representing its decline and fall. For the chronology of the Twelfth Dynasty see William F. Edgerton in JNES 1 (1942), pp.307-314, with revisions by PCAE p.69. Several coregencies are involved and the probable dates of the rulers are: Amenemhet I, 1991-1962; Senusert I, 1971-1928; Amenemhet II, 1929-1895; Senusert II, 1897-1879; Senusert III, 1878-1843; Amenemhet III, 1842-1797; Amenemhet IV, 1798-1790; Sebeknefrure, 1789-1786.

[1a] For an Egyptian fortress at Buhen just north of the Second Cataract see *Archaeology.* 11 (1958), pp.215f.

[2] W. M. F. Petrie, *Egyptian Tales.* First Series, 2d ed. 1899, pp.16-22,61-80.

[3] Genesis 12:10-13:1 (J). Genesis 20:1-17 (E) corrects the unfavorable impression created by the story of Sarah in Pharaoh's harem, by transferring the situation to King Abimelech's court at Gerar, and changing many of the details.

[4] ARE IV, §715.

old king's death was dispatched to the son who, upon receiving it, kept the news secret and returned at once to the capital to establish himself firmly as king before any pretender could precede him. This was quite in accord with the spirit of instructions which Amenemhet had given his son earlier. The old king, whose life had been attempted by assassins, had advised:

"Hold thyself apart from those subordinate to thee, lest that should happen to whose terrors no attention has been given. . . . Fill not thy heart with a brother, nor know a friend. Create not for thyself intimates—there is no fulfilment thereby. Even when thou sleepest, guard thy heart thyself, because no man has adherents in the day of distress."[5]

With Senusert I in the field was a noble of high rank, named Sinuhe. Accidentally overhearing the message about Amenemhet's death, he fled the country immediately for political reasons and returned only in his old age and upon the pardon of Senusert. The story of his adventures as he fled overland to Syria is related in "The Tale of Sinuhe." Hiding in the bushes and fields, he passed the Egyptian frontier fort at night. In the desert he grew faint with thirst and his throat was hot with the taste of death but he was rescued at last by an Asiatic sheikh. Eventually he came through Qedem, meaning the East generally, and arrived in Upper Retenu, Retenu being the usual Egyptian name for Syria and Palestine.[6] Here he settled in a "good land," which he describes in language similar to that later applied to Palestine in the Old Testament (Exodus 3:8; Deuteronomy 8:8; etc.):

"Figs were in it, and grapes. It had more wine than water. Plentiful was its honey, abundant its olives. Every kind of fruit was on its trees. Barley was there, and emmer. There was no limit to any kind of cattle."[7]

THE TOMB OF KHNUMHOTEP III

In the days of Senusert II, fourth king of the Twelfth Dynasty, a powerful noble, Khnumhotep III, lived at Beni Hasan, 168 miles above Cairo. In his tomb a famous scene still depicts a visit paid him by a group of thirty-seven Asiatics of the desert, bringing gifts

[5] John A. Wilson in ANET p.418; cf. ARE I, §479.
[6] Steindorff and Seele, *When Egypt Ruled the East*, p.47. The same area was also called Khor (Khuru, Kharu), from the Hurrians or Horites, and Palestine was known as Djahi. The region north of the Lebanon was Amor (Amurru), and the land at the upper reaches of the Euphrates was Nahrin (Naharin). On Egyptian influence in Palestine in the time of the Middle Kingdom, see John A. Wilson in AJSL 58 (1941), pp.225-236.
[7] John A. Wilson in ANET p.19 (ANEA p.5); cf. ARE I, §496.

and desiring trade.[8] The men have thick black hair which falls to the neck, and their beards are pointed. They wear long cloaks and carry spears, bows, and throw-sticks. The accompanying inscription reads, "The arrival, bringing eye-paint, which 37 Asiatics brought to him." The leader of the group is labeled "the Ruler of a Foreign Country," and his name is given as Ibsha. A date is appended, the sixth year of Senusert II, or about 1892 B.C.[9] One portion of this very interesting painting is reproduced in Fig. 30. We see a black-bearded nomad walking behind his donkey to the accompaniment of music which he makes upon a lyre. The man carries a water-skin upon his back, while on the donkey's gay saddle-cloth are tied other objects including a spear and throw-stick.

By the end of the Middle Kingdom period, it is clear that the Asiatic peoples had become a threat to Egypt. Numerous broken pottery bowls have been found, dating probably from the reign of Senusert III or later, on which are inscriptions expressing curses against the enemies of the king. It is probable that these were used in magical procedures where the smashing of the inscribed bowl was intended to break the power of the enemy named on it. In these execration texts, as the inscriptions are called, the most prominently named foes are Asiatic rulers. It is very interesting to find that among the places mentioned is Aushamem, which is probably Jerusalem. The names of two rulers of Aushamem are given, Iyqa-'ammu, a Semitic name, and Setj-'anu.[10]

6. SECOND INTERMEDIATE PERIOD
(THIRTEENTH TO SEVENTEENTH DYNASTIES),
c.1786-c.1570 B.C.

IN THE days which followed, native Egyptian power disintegrated more and more and the land fell eventually under rule by foreigners. The Thirteenth and Fourteenth Dynasties were made up of numerous petty kings, some of whom probably ruled contemporaneously. Already in the Thirteenth Dynasty several of the kings bear Semitic names.[1] There is also a papyrus in the Brooklyn Museum, dated in the first and second regnal years of the Thirteenth Dynasty ruler

---

[8] P. E. Newberry, *Beni Hasan.* I (1893), Pl. xxx; ANEP No.3 (ANEA No.2).
[9] ANET p.229; ARE I, p.281, d.
[10] ANEP No.593 (ANEA No.153); ANET p.329.
[1] Hayes, *The Scepter of Egypt*, I, p.351.

Sebek-hotep III, about 1740 B.C., which lists ninety-five slaves, thirty-seven of whom are labeled as "male Asiatic" or "female Asiatic." Nearly thirty of the names are Northwest-Semitic, and one is virtually the same as that of Shiprah, one of the Israelite midwives in Exodus 1:15.[2]

THE HYKSOS

In the Fifteenth and Sixteenth Dynasties the rulers of much of Egypt were the Hyksos. The coming of the Hyksos is described by Manetho in a passage preserved in Josephus. Referring to Tutimaeus, who probably was a king of the Thirteenth Dynasty, Manetho says: "In his reign, for what cause I know not, a blast of God smote us; and unexpectedly, from the regions of the East, invaders of obscure race marched in confidence of victory against our land. By main force they easily seized it without striking a blow; and having overpowered the rulers of the land, they then burned our cities ruthlessly, razed to the ground the temples of the gods, and treated all the natives with a cruel hostility. . . . Finally, they appointed as king one of their number whose name was Salitis."[3] Manetho states further that Salitis ruled from Memphis and that he also rebuilt as a powerful stronghold "a city very favourably situated on the east of the Bubastite branch of the Nile, and called Auaris." The branch of the Nile referred to is the one farthest east, and the city of Auaris or Avaris doubtless is to be identified with Tanis, near the modern fishing village of San el-Hagar. Manetho also explains that the name Hyksos means " 'king-shepherds': for *hyk* in the sacred language means 'king,' and *sos* in common speech is 'shepherd' or 'shepherds': hence the compound word 'Hyksos.' " It is probable, however, that this is only a late popular etymology and that the name actually was derived from Egyptian words meaning "rulers of foreign lands."[4] In the Eighteenth Dynasty Queen Hatshepsut refers to repairs which she made of damage done by the Hyksos:

> I have restored that which was ruins,
> I have raised up that which was unfinished,
> Since the Asiatics were in the midst of Avaris of the Northland,
> And the barbarians were in the midst of them.[5]

[2] W. F. Albright in JAOS 74 (1954), pp.222-233.

[3] *Manetho*, tr. Waddell, pp.79-81; Josephus, *Against Apion*. I, 14.

[4] Adolf Erman and Hermann Grapow, *Wörterbuch der ägyptischen Sprache*. III (1929), p.171, 29.

[5] ARE II, §303.

It is probable that the Hyksos were well established in Egypt by around 1700 B.C. and that they ruled for about a century and a half.[6] The foreigners may have been of mixed stock but the preponderant element among them seems to have been Semitic.[7] As a matter of fact, Josephus identified the Hyksos with the children of Israel. He introduced his quotations from Manetho concerning the Hyksos as statements "about us," that is about the Jewish people, and described "the so-called shepherds" as "our ancestors."[8] His purpose in this identification was that he might adduce the testimony of Manetho as proving the antiquity of the Jews. While it is hardly possible to believe from the biblical records that the Israelites played any such role of conquest and domination in Egypt as did the Hyksos, nevertheless there is probably this much truth in the tradition of Josephus, that the people of Israel were in Egypt at the same time as the Hyksos. This fact could account for the representation found in Josephus, and it is antecedently probable that the Israelites would find a friendly reception in Egypt at a time when the country was under rulers who were themselves of Semitic descent.[9]

While Manetho states that Salitis ruled in Upper as well as Lower Egypt, it is evident that the center of Hyksos power was in the eastern Delta. In Upper Egypt native princes reasserted themselves, and Seventeenth Dynasty kings were rivals of the later Hyksos. At last war broke out between Sekenenre, ruling at Thebes, and Apophis, Hyksos king at Avaris. A folk tale concerning the start of the war, found in a Nineteenth Dynasty papyrus, tells that Sekenenre had a hippopotamus pool in Thebes and the bellowing of the hippopotami was such that King Apophis sent a complaint from Avaris that he could not get any sleep day or night.[10] A more realistic testimony to the outbreak of conflict between the native Egyptians and the

[6] A stela from Tanis commemorates the four hundredth anniversary of that city which was observed probably in the reign of Haremhab (c.1340-c.1303), and thus a time shortly before 1700 B.C. is indicated for the foundation of Tanis. See Kurt Sethe in zäs 65 (1930), pp.85-89. Winlock (*The Rise and Fall of the Middle Kingdom in Thebes*, pp. 97-99) follows the Turin Papyrus in assigning 108 years to their reign, and lists the Hyksos kings with approximate dates as follows: (1) Salatis or Salitis (perhaps really a title, "the Sultan"), 1675-1662; (2) Bnon or Beon, 1662-1654; (3) Apachnan, 1654-1644; (4) Khian (also called Iannas or Staan), 1644-1604; (5) Assis or Archles, 1604-1600; (6) Apopi or Apophis, 1600-1567. See also Z. Mayani, *Les Hyksos et le Monde de la Bible.* 1956.

[7] R. M. Engberg, *The Hyksos Reconsidered.* 1939, pp.9,49.

[8] *Against Apion.* i, 14, 16.

[9] cf. J. Leibovitch in iej 3 (1953), pp.99-112.

[10] Erman, *The Literature of the Ancient Egyptians*, p.166.

foreigners may be found in the mummy of Sekenenre, which shows three terrible wounds in the head.[11]

The sons of Sekenenre, Kamose and Ahmose, continued the struggle against the Hyksos. It fell to Ahmose to drive out the invaders completely. He took Avaris and then pursued the fleeing Hyksos as far as Palestine. There they made a last stand at Sharuhen (cf. Joshua 19:6) but after a six-year siege Ahmose destroyed this stronghold too. Of these happenings we can read a direct account in the biography of one of Ahmose's naval officers.[12]

Another stronghold in Palestine which was occupied by the Hyksos during the time of their conquest of Egypt was at Tell el-'Ajjul, the "Mound of the Little Calf," four miles southwest of modern Gaza. In excavation at this site, which he identified with ancient Gaza, Flinders Petrie found numerous objects used by the Hyksos including gold jewelry, and bronze daggers, toggle-pins, and horse-bits. There was also evidence which seemed to indicate the practice of horse sacrifice.[13]

Whereas Josephus thought that the expulsion of the Hyksos was identical with the exodus of the children of Israel, it is most probable that the latter still continued to live in Egypt at this time. It is of interest to note that after the expulsion of the Hyksos most of the Egyptian lands and fields, apart from the properties attached to the temples, are found in the possession of the Pharaoh. This is a situation similar to that described in Genesis 47:13-26 as having been instituted by Joseph in time of famine.[14]

7. THE NEW KINGDOM
(EIGHTEENTH TO TWENTIETH DYNASTIES),
c.1570-c.1090 B.C.

THE EIGHTEENTH DYNASTY

AHMOSE is usually regarded as the first king of the Eighteenth Dynasty, which was destined to become probably the most brilliant age in all Egyptian history. The horse and chariot became known to the Egyptians during the Hyksos period, and the use of chariotry now

[11] Steindorff and Seele, *When Egypt Ruled the East*, pp.28f., Fig. 7.
[12] ARE II, §§1-16.
[13] Flinders Petrie, *Ancient Gaza, Tell El Ajjul*. 5 vols. 1931-52.
[14] Steindorff and Seele, *When Egypt Ruled the East*, p.88.

facilitated far-flung conquests. An empire soon was to be built which reached from the Fourth Cataract of the Nile to beyond the Euphrates.

HATSHEPSUT

About 1546 B.C. Ahmose was succeeded by his son Amenhotep I, and then (c.1525 B.C.) by his daughter's husband, Thutmose I, who campaigned successfully in Nubia and as far as the Euphrates.[1] The only living child of Thutmose I and his queen was a daughter, the remarkable Hatshepsut (Fig. 31), "the first great woman in history of whom we are informed."[2] Legally, Hatshepsut was the only heir to the throne, yet could not actually reign as "king" but could only convey the crown to her husband by marriage. Thutmose I also had a son who was born by one of his secondary wives. In order to secure the throne for this son, he was married to his half-sister, Hatshepsut, and reigned as Thutmose II. The only son of Thutmose II was born to him by a harem girl and was still a boy when his father died. As Thutmose III (c.1490-c.1436 B.C.) he ruled nominally with Hatshepsut, but actually this powerful and brilliant woman now took full control of the government (c.1486-c.1468 B.C.). She had herself proclaimed "king" and appears in a scene representing this proclamation dressed in king's costume and wearing the double crown of Upper and Lower Egypt.[3] As the court official Ineni remarked in his biography, "The God's Wife, Hatshepsut, settled the affairs of the Two Lands according to her own plans. Egypt was made to labor with bowed head for her."[4]

---

[1] For the dates see Ludwig Borchardt, *Die Mittel zur zeitlichen Festlegung von Punkten der ägyptischen Geschichte und ihre Anwendung.* 1935, pp.87, 116-128; W. F. Edgerton in AJSL 53 (1936-37), pp.188-197; and now M. B. Rowton in JEA 34 (1948), pp.57-74; and in BASOR 126 (Apr. 1952), p.22. From the data of Manetho, from Assyrian and Hittite synchronisms, and from astronomical calculation of the date of a new moon mentioned in the fifty-second year of Ramses II, Rowton has placed the accession of Ramses II in 1290 B.C. (JEA 34 [1948], p.69; cf. W. F. Albright in BASOR 130 [Apr. 1953], p.7). Other dates in the Eighteenth and Nineteenth Dynasties are reckoned backward and forward from this date. See also W. F. Albright in BASOR 118 (Apr. 1950), p. 19; Albrecht Goetze in BASOR 127 (Oct. 1952), p.24; Richard A. Parker in JNES 16 (1957), pp.39-43.

While in the Old Kingdom the regnal year of a king was considered as coinciding with the civil calendar year, from the New Kingdom to the beginning of the Saite period it was reckoned from the actual accession of the king (see also below p.128 n.24). For the Egyptian calendar see the Appendix.

[2] Breasted, *A History of the Ancient Egyptians*, p.217.

[3] ARE II, §231.

[4] ARE II, §341. For the complicated succession of rulers at this time see W. F. Edgerton, *The Thutmosid Succession.* SAOC 8 (1933), pp.41f.

Part of that labor was directed toward the construction of what remains Hatshepsut's most impressive memorial, her mortuary temple (Fig. 32). This temple rises against the face of an imposing cliff at Deir el-Bahri, near Thebes. It was a beautiful structure of white limestone, built in colonnaded terraces from the plain to the cliff, deep within which the tomb itself was to be found. A major sea expedition to Punt, on the Somali coast, brought back the myrrh trees with which its terraces were planted. Another undertaking on behalf of Hatshepsut was the erection of two great obelisks at Karnak, in a hall built earlier by the queen's father, Thutmose I. The enormous granite shafts were quarried at Aswan and brought down the river on a huge barge drawn by a fleet of galleys. One of these still stands in its place and is the most striking of all known obelisks as well as the largest one now in Egypt. It is 97½ feet high, contains 180 cubic yards of granite, and weighs 700,000 pounds. The obelisks were crowned with pyramidions of polished metal and an inscription said concerning them, "Their height pierces to heaven, illuminating the Two Lands like the sun disk. Never was done the like since the beginning."[5]

These great works were carried out for Hatshepsut by the architect Senenmut, her favorite noble to whom she also entrusted the education of her eldest daughter, Princess Nefrure.[6] Senenmut is represented in the statue shown in Fig. 33 holding the little Nefrure protectingly wrapped in his mantle.

THUTMOSE III

After the great queen Hatshepsut was no more, Thutmose III (Fig. 34) reigned as Pharaoh alone (from c.1468 B.C.). "Pharaoh," it may be explained, is the Hebrew form of the Egyptian title "The Great House," which was pronounced something like *per-o*. Originally a designation of the palace, it was commonly used as the official title of the king from the Eighteenth Dynasty on. Upon emerging as sole ruler, the long-suppressed energies of Pharaoh Thutmose III burst forth in furious activity. He expressed his resentment at having been kept so long in a minor position by hacking out the figure and the name of Hatshepsut wherever these appeared on monuments throughout Egypt. Then he led his armies into battle in Palestine and Syria. His grandfather, Thutmose I, had begun the subjection

[5] ARE II, §305.   [6] ARE II, §§345-347.

of Asiatic provinces for Egypt but among those peoples there was now general revolt. The inhabitants of Palestine, Coelesyria, and the coastal plain were Semitic tribes called Canaanites, while the Hyksos also remained there after having been driven out of Egypt. A confederation of these peoples was organized against Egypt and the enemies of the Pharaoh were in control of the strong fortress of Megiddo, commanding the road from Egypt to the Euphrates. Thutmose III acted swiftly and surprised his opponents by approaching through a narrow pass in the Carmel ridge. Battle was joined upon the plain of Esdraelon. "His majesty went forth in a chariot of electrum, arrayed in his weapons of war. . . . His majesty prevailed against them at the head of his army, and when they saw his majesty prevailing against them they fled headlong to Megiddo in fear, abandoning their horses and their chariots of gold and silver."[7] Although the Egyptian troops tarried for a time with the spoils, Megiddo soon was besieged and taken.

In sixteen further campaigns during the next eighteen summers, Thutmose the Great[8] established the absolute power of Egypt as far as the Euphrates.[9] "Never before in history had a single brain wielded the resources of so great a nation and wrought them into such centralized, permanent, and at the same time mobile efficiency."[10] In a Hymn of Victory, Amen-Re the god of Thebes was made to address him:

> I have given to thee might and victory against all countries,
> I have set thy fame, even the fear of thee, in all lands,
> Thy terror as far as the four pillars of heaven. . . .
> I have felled thine enemies beneath thy sandals.[11]

Coming home each fall from his campaigns, Thutmose III carried out large-scale building projects. Much work was done in enlargement and beautification of the temple of Amun which had stood at

[7] ARE II, §430.

[8] His full name was "Horus: Mighty Bull, Appearing in Thebes; the Two Ladies: Enduring of Kingship; the Horus of Gold: Splendid of Diadems; the King of Upper and Lower Egypt: Enduring of Form Is Re [Menkheperre]; the Son of Re: Thoth Is Born [Thutmose]." The last of these names was the one given him at birth, the others were adopted upon accession to the throne and indicated that the king was the embodiment of the various gods named, such as the Two Ladies who were the tutelary goddesses of Upper and Lower Egypt. So mighty was the name of Thutmose III that for centuries his praenomen Menkheperre was inscribed on amulets as a good-luck charm.

[9] ARE II, §478.

[10] Breasted, *A History of the Ancient Egyptians*, p.242.

[11] ARE II, §656.

Karnak since the days of the Middle Kingdom[12] and to which many different Pharaohs both before and after Thutmose III made contributions. On the walls of one of the temple's corridors which he built were inscribed the annals of his seventeen military campaigns, from which quotations have just been made. At Karnak and elsewhere he erected great obelisks which have been set up now in places as far distant as Constantinople, the Lateran, London, and New York (Fig. 35).[13] Concluding a list of his building works an inscription of Thutmose III said, "He did more than any king who has been since the beginning."[14]

THE TOMB OF REKHMIRE

Many of the building operations of Thutmose III were supervised by his vizier, Rekhmire. The vizier was a sort of prime minister and grand steward who exercised powers as extensive as those ascribed to Joseph in the Old Testament. All administrative business passed through his hands, and he was also a judge and a superintendent of public works. While there was a time beginning in the Fifth Dynasty when the office was hereditary, later it was bestowed by the king upon a noble of his own choosing. One vizier exercised authority over all Egypt until the time of Thutmose III when two appointments were made, one for Upper and one for Lower Egypt. Rekhmire is well known to us from his tomb near Thebes which is covered with scenes and inscriptions depicting and narrating his career. In one of these pictures Rekhmire leans on his staff and inspects stonecutters, sculptors, brickmakers, and builders who toil before him. A portion of this painting, showing the labor of the bricklayers, is reproduced in Fig. 36. The making of bricks in ancient Egypt was a process which involved breaking up the Nile mud with mattocks, moistening it with water, and then mixing it with sand and chopped straw (cf. Exodus 5:6-19). After that it was formed in molds and taken out and baked in the sun. Among the makers and layers of bricks pictured in Rekhmire's tomb are Asiatic foreigners, and the accompanying inscription refers to the "captives brought by his majesty for the works of the temple of Amun." The bricklayers are quoted as saying, "He supplies us with bread, beer, and every good sort," while the taskmaster says to the builders, "The rod is in my hand; be not idle."[15]

[12] ARE I, §§421, 484.
[13] ARE II, §§623-636; cf. George A. Zabriskie in *The New York Historical Society Quarterly Bulletin.* 24 (1940), pp.103-112.
[14] ARE II, §158.
[15] P. E. Newberry, *The Life of Rekhmara.* 1900, p.38; ARE II, §§758f.; Norman de

THE PAPYRUS OF ANI

Some glimpse of Theban religious beliefs in the middle of the Eighteenth Dynasty may be had from the Papyrus of Ani.[16] This papyrus is our finest copy of what is known collectively by the name, "The Egyptian Book of the Dead." The texts which were written in the pyramids of the kings of the Fifth and Sixth Dynasties (p. 88), and the instructions and charms which were inscribed on the interior of coffins in the Middle Kingdom (p. 91), had grown now to be a whole collection of religious compositions relating to the after-life. Written more or less fully on larger or smaller papyrus rolls, everyone might have such a book placed with him in the tomb. The beautiful Papyrus of Ani is no less than seventy-eight feet long and one foot three inches wide. Chapter 125 is the most important and probably the most ancient part. An illustration of this chapter in the Papyrus of Ani (Fig. 37) shows Ani, followed by his wife Tutu, bowing humbly in the great Hall of Judgment. In the middle is the balance, operated by the jackal-headed Anubis. On the left scalepan is Ani's heart, represented by an Egyptian hieroglyph looking much like a tiny vase, while in the other is a feather symbolizing truth or righteousness. The god of Destiny stands beneath the beam of the balance and two goddesses of Birth are between the scale and Ani. The soul of Ani in the shape of a human-headed hawk hovers at the end of the beam. On the other side stands the ibis-headed god Thoth, performing his function as scribe and recording with pen and writing palette the verdict of the weighing. Behind him is Amemit, the Devourer of the Dead, a monster with the head of a crocodile, the body of a lion, and the hindquarters of a hippopotamus. If Ani's heart is proved unjust by the weighing it will be devoured by this monster, and Ani's hope of immortality will be lost. On the left is written Ani's prayer to his heart not to betray him, above is a panel of twelve gods as judges, and at the right is the sentence of acquittal.

In the text of Chapter 125 the deceased recites a great repudiation of sins in which forty-two sins are denied before forty-two judges. Each judge has a specific crime to consider and the deceased addresses him by name and denies ever having committed that crime:

Garis Davies, *Paintings from the Tomb of Rekh-mi-Rē' at Thebes* (Publications of the Metropolitan Museum of Art, Egyptian Expedition, x). 1935; *The Tomb of Rekh-mi-Rē' at Thebes* (Publications of the Metropolitan Museum of Art, Egyptian Expedition, xi). 2 vols. 1943; ANEP No.115; cf. Charles F. Nims in BA 13 (1950), pp.22-28.

[16] E. A. Wallis Budge, *The Papyrus of Ani.* 1913.

"O Swallower-of-Shadows . . . I have not robbed." "O Dangerous-of-Face . . . I have not killed men." "O Breaker-of-Bones . . . I have not told lies." Other denials of sins include: "I have not added to the weight of the balance; I have not been contentious; I have not committed adultery; I have not been unresponsive to a matter of justice; I have not been quarrelsome; I have not done evil." In a concluding address to the gods the deceased affirms his moral worthiness, here making positive as well as negative statements: "Behold me—I have come to you without sin, without guilt, without evil. . . . I have done that which men said and that with which gods are content. I have satisfied a god with that which he desires. I have given bread to the hungry, water to the thirsty, clothing to the naked, and a ferry-boat to him who was marooned. I have provided divine offerings for the gods and mortuary offerings for the dead. So rescue me, you; protect me, you. Ye will not make report against me in the presence of the great god. I am one pure of mouth and pure of hands. . . ."[17] Having been justified in the hour of judgment, the deceased is led by Horus into the presence of Osiris, where he is welcomed to the joys of paradise. Although the Book of the Dead in most of its parts and in most of its use was a book of magical charms, it reveals a perception of the truth that happiness after death is dependent upon the ethical quality of earthly life.[18]

AMENHOTEP II

Thutmose III died around 1436 B.C. and was followed upon the throne by his son who ruled as Amenhotep II. Since the latter had at least a twenty-six year reign,[19] his dates must be approximately 1436-1410 B.C., although it may be that he was coregent with his father for a year or so. A statue of this king is shown in Fig. 38, and another interesting representation of him appears in Fig. 39, where he stands beneath the protecting head of the cow-goddess Hathor, a deity fervently worshiped by the sovereigns of the Eighteenth Dynasty. Even in his youth Amenhotep II distinguished himself for strength and valor. In rowing, in horsemanship, and in archery he was unsurpassed. A stela recently discovered near the great Sphinx

[17] John A. Wilson in ANET pp.34-36.
[18] H. Frankfort (*Ancient Egyptian Religion*. 1948, pp.118f.) doubts that the protestation of sinlessness in the Book of the Dead has much ethical significance.
[19] Rowton in BASOR 126 (Apr. 1952), p.22 n.9.

at Giza narrates various exploits of the young prince, among them the following:

"And he came also and did the following, which I wish to call to your attention. He entered his northern garden and found set up for him four targets of Asiatic copper of a span [three inches] in their thickness and with twenty cubits [nearly thirty-five feet] between one pole and its fellow. Then his majesty appeared in a chariot like Montu [the god of war] in his power. He seized his bow and grasped four arrows at once. He rode northward, shooting at them [the targets] like Montu in his regalia. His arrows came forth from the back of [one of] them while he attacked another. And that is a thing, indeed, which had never been done nor even heard of in story: that an arrow shot at a target of copper came forth from it and dropped to the earth, excepting [at the hand of] the king, rich of glory, whom Amun has strengthened, . . . Okheprure [Amenhotep II], heroic like Montu."[20]

When the great warrior's mummy was found in 1898 in the Valley of the Kings at Thebes,[21] his famous bow, which he boasted no other man could draw, was still beside him. It bore the inscription, "Smiter of the Cave-dwellers, overthrower of Kush, hacking up their cities— the Great Wall of Egypt, Protector of his soldiers."[22]

Amenhotep II was followed by his son Thutmose IV (c.1410- c.1400). From his time an interesting wall painting survives in the tomb of Sebekhotep at Thebes (Fig. 40). It depicts the arrival of Syrian ambassadors bearing tribute to the Egyptian court. The foremost figures are kneeling and raising their arms in reverence to the sovereign. The faces of the men are bearded, and the shawls which are wound round their bodies from the waist downward are an interesting feature of their costumes.[23]

AMENHOTEP III

The son and successor of Thutmose IV was Amenhotep III who reigned from around 1400 B.C. to around 1364 B.C. Sometimes called "The Magnificent," he was Pharaoh as the empire attained its greatest splendor and Eighteenth Dynasty art reached its zenith. In sculpture, the work of a master is to be seen in the head (Fig. 41) of a gigantic granite statue of the king which once must have stood in

[20] Steindorff and Seele, *When Egypt Ruled the East*, pp.68f.

[21] Thutmose I was the first to have his royal tomb excavated in this secluded valley deep among the western cliffs at Thebes, which became the cemetery of the Eighteenth, Nineteenth, and Twentieth Dynasties.

[22] NGM 43 (Jan.-June 1923), p.488.

[23] cf. James B. Pritchard in BASOR 122 (Apr. 1951), pp.36-41.

his own funerary temple near Thebes. The famous "Colossi of Memnon," each seventy feet high and weighing seven hundred tons, also were statues of Amenhotep III. It was in Roman times that the northern colossus was believed to be a statue of Memnon, who greeted his mother Eos (Aurora), goddess of the dawn, with a sweet and plaintive note when she appeared in the morning. This musical phenomenon is mentioned somewhat skeptically by Strabo[24] and described with complete credulity by Philostratus (A.D. c.170-c.245) in connection with the visit of Apollonius and Damis to the statue: "When the sun's rays fell upon the statue, and this happened exactly at dawn, they could not restrain their admiration; for the lips spoke immediately the sun's ray touched them, and the eyes seemed to stand out and gleam against the light."[25]

In architecture the achievements of the time may be illustrated by the great colonnade of Amenhotep III at Luxor (Fig. 42), while in painting the excellence of the work done may be seen in a superb fowling scene from the Theban tomb of Nebamun (Fig. 43). Nebamun, the "scribe who keeps account of the grain," is depicted "taking recreation, seeing pleasant things, and occupying himself with the craft of the Marsh-goddess," as the accompanying inscription states. Accompanied by his wife and little daughter, Nebamun stands upon his light papyrus skiff which is pressing among the lotuses and water-weeds. Three herons are held as decoys, while Nebamun is about to launch his throw-stick at a covey of pintail ducks, geese, and other fowl rising from a clump of papyrus. A cat, which already has retrieved three birds, sits precariously upon a few papyrus-stems, while delicately drawn butterflies enhance the gaiety of the scene.

AMENHOTEP IV (AKHENATON)

Amenhotep IV (c.1370-c.1353 B.C.) was first coregent with his father, Amenhotep III, who was very ill in his old age, and then successor to him. Even before the father died there were ominous rumblings of revolt and invasion in Palestine, Syria, and the north, but the son's greatness was to lie not in the field of military exploit but in the realm of religious thought. Characterized by his portraits (Fig. 44)[26] as an idealist, an artist, and almost a fanatic, Amenhotep

---

[24] *Geography.* XVII, i, 46.

[25] *The Life of Apollonius of Tyana.* VI, 4. tr. F. C. Conybeare. LCL (1912) II, p.15.

[26] The statues and the mummy of the king indicate that he suffered from an abdominal deformity. M. A. Murray, *Egyptian Sculpture.* 1930, p.135.

IV allowed the empire of his fathers to break apart while he devoted himself to contemplation. Yet so lofty were the ideals which he cherished and so exalted the philosophy which he developed that he has been called "the first *individual* in human history."[27]

The religion which Amenhotep IV introduced was a solar monotheism. The sun always was a dominant fact in the Nile Valley and already had been frequently identified as a god and even the supreme god. According to one belief, the sun was the eye of Horus, the falcon-god, who represented the sky; according to another idea he was a calf, born each day of the cow-goddess of the sky, Hathor. Again the sun was a scarabaeus, rolling the solar globe across the sky; or a mariner traversing the sky in a boat, and returning in the night to the east by a subterranean river. At Heliopolis, near Memphis, the sun was worshiped under the name of Re. The priests here, who have been called "the first religious thinkers in Egypt,"[28] taught that Re, or Re-Harakhti ("Re-Horus of the Horizon"), was the greatest of all gods. This was the religion of state in the Fifth Dynasty, and was still highly influential. At Thebes, Amun (or Amen), who originally had been a ram-headed god of life or reproduction, was exalted to the position of chief god of the Egyptian world empire. He, too, was connected with the sun, and, united with Re, became the great sun-god Amen-Re, bearing the title, "the father of the gods, the fashioner of men, the creator of cattle, the lord of all being." With Thebes as the capital of the empire, the magnificent temples of Amun at Karnak and Luxor were the center of the state cult and were presided over by a chief priest who claimed to stand at the head of all the priesthoods in the land.

In the exaltation of Re or Amun or Amen-Re to the supreme place in the Egyptian pantheon there was obviously a tendency toward monotheism. Yet the theoretical monotheism of the priests was in most cases accommodated in practice to the practical polytheism of the people. All the other gods were retained in subordinate positions as helpers or as names or forms of the sun-god. Likewise the sun-god himself continued to be represented in all manner of animal and human forms. Amun was connected with the ram, and Re with the falcon, the lion, the cat, and the crocodile. A familiar representation of Re was as a man with a falcon's head, on top of which was the

[27] Breasted, *A History of the Ancient Egyptians*, p.265.
[28] Moore, *History of Religions*. I, p.152.

solar disk. Amen-Re appeared as a man wearing on his head a disk surmounted by tall ostrich plumes.

Amenhotep IV now endeavored to go all the way in establishing an exclusive solar monotheism as Egypt's religion. An ancient but hitherto neglected name of the solar disk was Aton. Under this name the worship of the sun might be set free from its mythological connections and exalted into a purer monotheism. This Amenhotep IV undertook to accomplish. Changing his own name from Amenhotep, "Amun Is Satisfied," to Akhenaton, "He Who Is Beneficial to Aton," the king boldly ousted the powerful priesthood of Amun, suppressed the public worship of Amun, and chiseled the very name of Amun and the other old gods from the monuments throughout the land. Then saying farewell to Thebes, the ancient center of Amun worship, he sailed three hundred miles down the Nile to found on an unoccupied site a completely new center for the worship of Aton. The site chosen was where the cliffs retreat from the east side of the river to enclose a plain some three miles wide and five long. At this place Akhenaton built his holy city, devoted to the service of the one god, and named Akhetaton, "Horizon of Aton."[29] Here the king took up his own residence and established the new capital of Egypt. In the sanctuary of the god no idol represented Aton, but only a sun disk from which long rays issued, each ending in a hand, often holding out the hieroglyphic sign for "life," and thus suggesting the celestial power which reached down into the affairs of men.

In the limestone cliffs surrounding the plain of Tell el-Amarna, as Akhetaton's site is now known, are cut a series of tombs of Akhenaton's nobles. Inscriptions in them contain the hymns of the Aton faith. In the great hymn of praise from the tomb of Eye, which may well have been composed by the king himself, the universal and eternal god is hailed in words echoed centuries later by the 104th Psalm:

> Thou appearest beautifully on the horizon of heaven,
> Thou living Aton, the beginning of life!
> When thou art risen on the eastern horizon,
> Thou hast filled every land with thy beauty.

[29] *The City of Akhenaten*, I, *Excavations of 1921 and 1922 at el-'Amarneh*, by T. Eric Peet and C. Leonard Woolley. 1923; II, *The North Suburb and the Desert Altars, The Excavations at Tell el-Amarna during the Seasons 1926-1932*, by H. Frankfort and J. D. S. Pendlebury. 1933; III, *The Central City and the Official Quarters, The Excavations at Tell el-Amarna during the Seasons 1926-1927 and 1931-1936*, by J. D. S. Pendlebury. 2 vols. 1951. Memoirs of the Egypt Exploration Society, XXXVIII, XL, XLIV; J. D. S. Pendlebury, *Tell el-Amarna*. 1935.

Thou art gracious, great, glistening, and high over every land;
Thy rays encompass the lands to the limit of all that thou hast made.
Though thou art far away, thy rays are on earth;
Though thou art in their faces, no one knows thy going.

When thou settest in the western horizon,
The land is in darkness, in the manner of death.[30]
They sleep in a room, with heads wrapped up.
Every lion is come forth from his den;[31]
All creeping things, they sting.
Darkness is a shroud, and the earth is in stillness,
For he who made them rests in his horizon.
At daybreak, when thou arisest on the horizon,
When thou shinest as the Aton by day,
Thou drivest away the darkness and givest thy rays.
The Two Lands are in festivity every day,
Awake and standing upon their feet,
For thou hast raised them up.
Washing their bodies, taking their clothing,
Their arms are raised in praise at thy appearance.
All the world, they do their work.[32]

How manifold it is, what thou hast made!
They are hidden from the face of man.
O sole god, like whom there is no other!
Thou didst create the world according to thy desire,
Whilst thou wert alone.[33]

Thou settest every man in his place,
Thou suppliest their necessities:
Everyone has his food, and his time of life is reckoned.[34]
Their tongues are separate in speech,
And their natures as well;
Their skins are distinguished,
As thou distinguishest the foreign peoples.

How effective they are, thy plans, O lord of eternity!
Thou makest the seasons in order to rear all that thou hast made,
The winter to cool them,
And the heat that they may taste thee.
Thou madest millions of forms of thyself alone.
Cities, towns, fields, road, and river—
Every eye beholds thee over against them,
For thou art the Aton of the day over the earth.
Thou art in my heart.[35]

[30] cf. Psalm 104:20.   [31] cf. Psalm 104:21.   [32] cf. Psalm 104:22f.
[33] cf. Psalm 104:24.   [34] cf. Psalm 104:27.
[35] John A. Wilson in ANET pp.369-371; cf. Breasted, *The Dawn of Conscience,* pp.281-286. Wilson (*ibid.,* and *The Burden of Egypt,* pp.223-229) points out that while Akhenaton and his family worshiped the sole god Aton, his court still wor-

Thus the king felt that although the darkness fell and men slept, his god was still present in his heart. The life-giving power and fatherly kindness of Aton filled the whole world, he believed. He said, "Thou art the mother and the father of all that thou hast made."[36]

Under the influence of this reformation, art showed an even greater delight than before in lovely natural designs of animals, birds, reeds, and plants, and whereas the Pharaoh had always hitherto been depicted in a conventionalized pose of august immobility, Akhenaton allowed himself to be represented in an entirely informal way, often appearing together with his famously beautiful wife, Queen Nefertiti (Fig. 45), and four little daughters.

It is a pathetic fact that Akhenaton did not combine with his great religious insight any corresponding genius for administration and statesmanship. The days of his concentration upon religious reform were days of disintegration of the Egyptian empire. At home resentment and disorder prevailed, abroad in Asia the possessions of the empire were slipping away.

THE TELL EL-AMARNA TABLETS

The state of affairs abroad is very evident in the Tell el-Amarna letters, a group of clay tablets found accidentally by an Egyptian

---

shiped Akhenaton himself, and most Egyptians remained ignorant of or opposed to the new faith, therefore the significance of this so-called "monotheism" should not be overestimated. He also doubts that the faith of Akhenaton could have been influential in the development of the monotheism of Moses, because it does not appear how it could have been transmitted from the one to the other, and because Atonism lacks the ethical content of Israelite monotheism. See also H. H. Rowley in ZAW 69 (1957), pp.9f. On the other hand it is surely the case that Akhenaton desired to convert others to the cult which he cherished (Frankfort, *Ancient Egyptian Religion*, p.3), and that the sun was specially connected with justice in Egypt and elsewhere in the Middle East (Frankfort, *Kingship and the Gods*, pp.157f.). Leslie A. White (in JAOS 68 [1948], pp.91-114) has attacked the supposition that Akhenaton was a religious genius at all by endeavoring to show that he originated virtually nothing and that the stirring events of his reign can be accounted for as a part of a general process of cultural change. If the tendencies toward the emergence of such a religion were as widespread as this argument assumes, however, it is difficult to see why the reformation of Akhenaton was as ephemeral as it actually was. W. F. Albright thinks it probable that there was some indirect connection between the cult of Akhenaton and the monotheism of Moses. See his *The Biblical Period* (reprinted from Louis Finkelstein, ed., *The Jews, Their History, Culture and Religion*. 1949). 1950, p.9. On the problem of Akhenaton see also R. Engelbach in *Annales du Service des Antiquités de l'Egypte*. 40 (1940), pp.135-185; Rudolf Anthes in JAOS 72 (1952), Supplement 14.

[36] Breasted, *The Dawn of Conscience*, p.288.

peasant woman at Tell el-Amarna. Written in cuneiform, they represent correspondence from vassal princes and governors in Syria and Palestine with Amenhotep III and with Akhenaton. Although many of the details of the letters remain obscure, it is clear that Syria and Palestine were seething with intrigue within and were under attack from without, while adequate help to maintain Egyptian sovereignty was not forthcoming. Rib-Addi, governor at Gubla or Byblus, twenty miles north of Beirut, wrote more than fifty times to Amenhotep III and Akhenaton, the following letter (Fig. 46) probably having been addressed to Amenhotep III:

> Rib-Addi to the king. . . .
> At the feet of my lord, my sun,
> seven times and seven times I fall down. . . .
> The king has let his faithful city
> go out of his hand. . . .
> They have formed a conspiracy with one another,
> and thus have I great fear that there is no man to rescue me
> out of their hand. Like birds that
> lie in a net
> so am I in
> Gubla. Why dost thou hold thyself back in respect to thy land?
> Behold, thus have I written to the palace,
> but thou hast paid no attention to my word. . . .
> May the king care for his land. . . .
> What shall I do in
> my solitude? Behold, thus I ask day
> and night.[37]

The governor of a city in northern Syria wrote in similar appeal to Akhenaton:

> To the king of the land of Egypt, our lord. . . .
> At the feet of the lord we fall down. . . .
> Now for twenty years we have been sending to the king, our
>   lord, . . .
> But now Tunip,
> thy city, weeps,
> and her tears are running,
> and there is no help for us.
> We have been sending to the king, the lord, the king of the land
>   of Egypt,
> for twenty years;

[37] C. Bezold and E. A. W. Budge, *The Tell el-Amarna Tablets in the British Museum.* 1892, No.12; KAT No.74 = MTAT No.74. See also translations of the Amarna Letters by W. F. Albright in ANET pp.483-490 (ANEA pp.262f.).

but not one word
has come to us from our lord.[38]

In Jerusalem, Abdi-Hiba (sometimes Abdi-Heba) was governor,
and he wrote repeatedly to Akhenaton, asking for Egyptian troops
and stating that unless they were sent the entire country would be
lost to Egypt.[39] His letters customarily begin with some salutation of
the greatest deference like this:

> To the king, my lord, say.
> Thus saith Abdi-Hiba, thy servant:
> At the feet of the king, my lord,
> seven times and seven times I fall down. . . .[40]

Then he proceeds, as in the following letter, to protest vehemently
his own loyalty and to beg urgently for help:

> What have I done to the king, my lord?
> They slander me
> to the king, the lord: "Abdi-Heba
> has become faithless to the king, his lord."
> Behold, neither my father
> nor my mother has put me
> in this place.
> The mighty hand of the king
> has led me into the house of my father.
> Why should I practice
> mischief against the king, the lord?
> As long as the king, my lord, lives
> I will say to the deputy of the king, my lord:
> "Why do you love
> the Habiru, and hate
> the regents?" But therefore
> am I slandered before the king, my lord.
> Because I say: "The lands of the king,
> my lord, are lost," therefore
> am I slandered to the king, my lord. . . .
> So let the king, the lord, care for his land. . . .
> Let the king turn his attention to the archers
> so that archers of the king,
> my lord, will go forth. No lands of the king remain.
> The Habiru plunder all lands of the king.
> If archers are here
> this year, then the lands of the king,

---

[38] KAT No.59 = MTAT No.59.

[39] H. Winckler, *Keilinschriftliches Textbuch zum Alten Testament.* 3d ed. 1909,
pp.4-13.

[40] KAT No.285 = MTAT No.285.

the lord, will remain; but if archers are not here,
then the lands of the king, my lord, are lost.
To the scribe of the king, my lord, thus saith Abdi-Heba,
thy servant: Bring words,
plainly, before the king, my lord: All the lands
of the king, my lord, are going to ruin.[41]

Other letters of Abdi-Hiba include the following passages:

Verily, this land of Urusalim,
neither my father nor my mother has
given it to me; the mighty hand of the king
gave it to me. . . .
Verily, the king has set his name
upon the land of Urusalim for ever.
Therefore he cannot abandon
the lands of Urusalim.[42]

Let the king care for his land.
The land of the king will be lost. All of it
will be taken from me; there is hostility to me. . . .
But now
the Habiru are taking
the cities of the king. . . .
If there are no archers
this year, then let the king
send a deputy that he may take me
to himself together with my brothers and we
die with the king, our lord.[43]

Behold, Milkilim and Tagi
the deed which they have done is this:
After they have taken Rubuda,
they seek now to take Urusalim. . . .
Shall we then let Urusalim go? . . .
I am very humbly thy servant.[44]

The name Habiru, which figures prominently in the letters of
Abdi-Hiba, is the same as that previously discussed (pp. 68f.) in its
occurrence in Mesopotamian texts, and doubtless the same as the
word 'Apiru soon to be mentioned in Egyptian inscriptions. Since it
probably means, "those who have crossed a boundary," and in the
Tell el-Amarna letters describes those who are assaulting Palestinian
cities, it could well be applied to the children of Israel in their
conquest of Palestine. The date of the latter conquest was, however,

[41] KAT No.286 = MTAT No.286. [42] KAT No.287 = MTAT No.287.
[43] KAT No.288 = MTAT No.288. [44] KAT No.289 = MTAT No.289.

probably later than the time of the Tell el-Amarna letters; thus the Israelites were indeed Habiru or "Hebrews," but probably not the same group as these Habiru.

Not even the religious reformation of Akhenaton was permanently successful. Having no son of his own, Akhenaton was followed on the throne, after a period of confusion, by his son-in-law Tutankhaton (c.1353-c.1344). He, abandoning the new religion and the new capital, returned to Thebes and Amun worship. His own name was changed back from "Beautiful in Life Is Aton" to Tutankhamun, "Beautiful in Life Is Amun," and the name of Amun was inscribed again on Egypt's monuments. Tutankhamun's reign was not otherwise of great significance and the young king died at the early age of about eighteen. His prominence in the mind of the modern world is due to the circumstance that of all the royal tombs in the Valley of the Kings, his was the first to be found unplundered and intact. Howard Carter's discovery of the tomb in 1922 revealed that the young Pharaoh had gone to his grave amidst an almost unbelievable splendor of golden coffins, thrones, and jewels.[45]

For a single example out of this wealth of precious objects we show in Fig. 47 the portrait mask from the head of the king's mummy. This is made of beaten and burnished gold, and the headdress and collar are inlaid with opaque glass of many colors in imitation of semi-precious stones. On the forehead are the royal insignia of vulture and serpent. The mask represents Tutankhamun as he appeared at the time of his death, and it was fashioned by the goldsmiths within the relatively brief period before his burial took place. It is a beautiful portrait, and when the actual face of the mummy was exposed it was seen to be a faithful and accurate representation of the young king.[46]

Tutankhamun was followed briefly by Eye (c.1344-c.1340), but soon the government was taken over by a general named Haremhab (c.1340-c.1303), who prepared the way for the Nineteenth Dynasty and another great period of imperial glory.[47] The statue shown in Fig. 48 represents Haremhab as a royal scribe before his accession as king. He sits cross-legged on the floor, holding on his lap a papy-

[45] Howard Carter, *The Tomb of Tut-ankh-Amen*. 2 vols. 1923-27; C. Breasted, *Pioneer to the Past*, pp.327-373.

[46] Edward D. Ross, *The Art of Egypt through the Ages*. 1931, pp.43f.

[47] Haremhab has often been listed as the first king of the Nineteenth Dynasty but may better be considered as the last of the Eighteenth. cf. Keith C. Seele in JNES 4 (1945), pp.234-239.

rus roll which contains a hymn to Thoth, patron god of scribes. Haremhab was a man of real administrative ability and he gave the kingdom an efficient reorganization. His practical legislation for the abolition of abuses survives as one of the important edicts of ancient Egypt. "Behold," said the king, "his majesty spent the whole time seeking the welfare of Egypt."[48] He was also kind to foreigners and a scene in his tomb shows him receiving fugitive Asiatics who come begging a home in Egypt, as they say, "after the manner of your fathers' fathers since the beginning."[49]

THE NINETEENTH DYNASTY

Since he had no son of his own, Haremhab was followed by the son of one of his distinguished army officers. This man, already of an advanced age upon accession to the throne, ruled briefly as Ramses I (c.1303-c.1302), and then was succeeded by his son Seti I (c.1302-c.1290).

Word of the disturbed conditions abroad fell now upon the ear of a man disposed to attempt action. "One came to say to his majesty: . . . 'They have taken to cursing and quarreling, each of them slaying his neighbor, and they disregard the laws of the palace.' The heart of his majesty was glad on account of it. Lo, as for the Good God, he rejoices to begin battle."[50] Henceforth the inscriptions of Seti I speak of campaigns in Palestine and Syria, Pekanan[51] ("the Canaan"),[52] Retenu,[53] and Kadesh[54] being among the places mentioned. One inscription said of his return to Egypt, "His majesty arrived from the countries . . . when he had desolated Retenu and slain their chiefs, causing the Asiatics to say: 'See this! He is like a flame when it goes forth and no water is brought.' "[55]

RAMSES II

Actually "the Asiatics" were not as fearful of Egyptian power as Seti I liked to believe, and his successor, Ramses II (c.1290-c.1224), had to battle throughout the sixty-seven years of his reign against them. Although his only victory in the famous Kadesh-on-the-Orontes battle with the Hittites was that of escaping complete destruction, the personal heroism of Ramses II was depicted proudly in numerous Egyptian scenes. Eventually Ramses II signed a "good

[48] ARE III, §50. [49] ARE III, §10. [50] ARE III, §101.
[51] *Pe* is the article. [52] ARE III, §88. [53] ARE III, §§103, 111, etc.
[54] ARE III, §141. [55] ARE III, §139.

treaty of peace and of brotherhood" with the king of the Hittites, which left southern Syria and all of Palestine in the possession of Egypt but relinquished northern Syria and Amurru to the Hittites. This is the earliest extant treaty of international nonaggression. It was sealed by the marriage of Ramses II and a daughter of the Hittite king.

While the military successes of Ramses II in Asia were not as glorious as he might have wished, the magnitude of the king's building enterprises left nothing to be desired. These included the erection of his own mortuary temple at Thebes, known as the Ramesseum, the making of additions to the Luxor temple, and the completion of the enormous hypostyle hall of the Karnak temple (Fig. 49). In the hypostyle hall, 134 tremendous columns, the tallest sixty-nine feet in height, supported the roof of a room which was part of the largest temple ever erected by man, while six acres of painted relief sculpture decorated the interior of the hall.[56] At Abu Simbel, between the First and Second Cataracts of the Nile, Ramses II hewed a complete temple in the sandstone cliff above the Nile and carved four colossal sixty-five-foot statues of himself from the rock before it. The upper part of one of these statues is shown in Fig. 50. An ear on the statue measures over three feet in height, yet, enormous as the statues are, they are fine portraits.

While the old capital of Thebes with its great temple of Amun continued to be esteemed most highly, the political center of gravity shifted somewhat in these times to the Delta which was nearer to the Asiatic portions of the Egyptian empire. Early in the Nineteenth Dynasty the seat of government was actually transferred from Thebes to the Delta. The capital city which was built there was called Per-Ramses, "House of Ramses," or more fully Per-Ramses Meri-Amun, "House of Ramses-beloved-of-Amun," and is mentioned in various Egyptian texts.[57] This is surely the same as the city named Raamses in Exodus 1:11.

This capital may have been at Tanis in the northeastern Delta, near modern San el-Hagar, where the Hyksos had their capital of Avaris. Tanis has been excavated by Pierre Montet.[58] The city was evidently forsaken after the expulsion of the Hyksos, but was reestablished by Seti I and enlarged and beautified by Ramses II.

[56] NGM 80 (July-Dec. 1941), p.513.

[57] ANET pp.199, 470f.

[58] P. Montet, *Les nouvelles fouilles de Tanis 1929-1932.* 1933; *Le Drame d'Avaris.* 1941; *Tanis, douze années de fouilles dans une capitale oubliée du delta égyptien.* 1942.

Extensive temple ruins were found there, together with many statues, sphinxes, and stelae, bearing the name of Ramses II and his successors. On the basis of the excavations, Montet maintains strongly that Tanis is the ancient Raamses, an identification proposed by Brugsch as long ago as 1872.[59]

Another possible identification is with Qantir, some twelve miles south of Tanis. This site was excavated by Mahmud Hamza.[60] The ruins of a large palace were found, and also the remains of a factory which made the striking glazed tiles and glazed statues with which the royal residence was adorned. Furthermore there were five ostraca discovered which actually bore the name Per-Ramses. In accordance with these finds, Hamza, believed that this was the ancient Raamses, and has been supported by William C. Hayes and Père Couroyer.[61]

Since there was a palace at Qantir and a temple complex at Tanis, a reconciliation of the alternative identifications may be effected by supposing that the former was essentially the residential site and the latter the place of worship, both being included in fact in a single large area which all together comprised the Delta capital of Ramses II.[62]

Ramses II also built or rebuilt a city the ruins of which have been found at Tell er-Retaba in the Wadi Tumilat, and which was probably known as Pi-Tum, "House of the god Tum," and appears in Exodus 1:11 as Pithom.[63]

THE MERNEPTAH STELA

The great Pharaohs of the past had fought campaigns to extend the empire, but those who followed Ramses II had to struggle to preserve it. Merneptah (c.1224-c.1214), the son and successor of

[59] H. Brugsch in zäs 10 (1872), p.18; P. Montet in RB 39 (1930), pp.15-28. This conclusion has also been accepted by Alan H. Gardiner (in JEA 19 [1933], pp.122-128), who previously favored an identification with Pelusium. According to Exodus 12:37; 13:20, Raamses was two days' journey from the edge of the wilderness. This agrees exactly with the location of Tanis, whereas Pelusium is itself on the edge of the wilderness. The possible locations of Etham (Exodus 13:20) and the sites in Exodus 14:2 are discussed by H. Cazelles in RB 62 (1955), pp.321-364.

[60] Hamza in *Annales du service des antiquités de l'Égypte.* 30 (1930), pp.31-68.

[61] Hamza, *op.cit.*, p.65; William C. Hayes, *Glazed Tiles from a Palace of Ramesses II at Kantir.* The Metropolitan Museum of Art Papers, 3. 1937; B. Couroyer in RB 53 (1946), pp.75-98.

[62] Albrecht Alt in *Festschrift für Friedrich Zucker.* 1954, pp.3-13. The distance of twelve miles between the two sites is not greater than the distance between remaining boundary stones marking out the sacred area where Akhenaton built his city of Akhetaton (*ibid.*, p.12 n.19).

[63] The earlier identification of Pithom with Tell el-Maskhuta, a site eight and one-half miles farther east, has been abandoned. Albright, *From the Stone Age to Christianity*, p.194.

Ramses II, already was advanced in years when he came to the throne. He fought valiantly against Libyans and Mediterranean peoples who were pushing into the western Delta, and also campaigned in Palestine. In the fifth year of his reign (about 1220 B.C.) Merneptah took a large black granite stela set up by Amenhotep III and carved an inscription of victory on it. This stela was found in Merneptah's mortuary temple at Thebes and is shown in Fig. 51. At the top is a double representation of the god Amun and the king. Behind the king on the left stands the goddess Mut, wife of Amun, and behind the king on the right is the moon-god Khonsu, son of Amun and Mut. Below are twenty-eight closely packed lines of inscription, celebrating the triumph over the Libyans and concluding with a strophe in which other defeated foreigners are listed, notably including Israel. This closing portion of the inscription reads as follows:

> The princes are prostrate, saying: "Mercy!"[64]
> Not one raises his head among the Nine Bows.
>
> Desolation is for Tehenu;[65] Hatti[66] is pacified;
> Plundered is the Canaan with every evil;
>
> Carried off is Ashkelon; seized upon is Gezer;
> Yanoam[67] is made as that which does not exist;
>
> Israel is laid waste, his seed is not;
> Hurru[68] is become a widow for Egypt!
>
> All lands together, they are pacified;
> Everyone who was restless, he has been bound
> by the King of Upper and Lower Egypt, Merneptah,
> given life like Re every day.[69]

The foregoing passage is worthy of special attention since it is the only mention in any Egyptian inscription of the name of Israel. In contrast with other names such as Hatti which are written with the determinative indicating a country, Israel is written with the determinative of people, which presumably shows that they were not yet a settled people. The statement that the people Israel "is laid waste, his seed is not," is a conventional way of describing any defeated and plundered foe. The description of Hurru or Syria,

---

[64] The Canaanite word *shalam*, meaning "Peace!" is used.
[65] Libya.   [66] The land of the Hittites.
[67] A town in northern Palestine.   [68] Kharu or Syria.
[69] John A. Wilson in ANET p.378 (ANEA pp.231f.); W. F. Albright in BASOR 74 (Apr. 1939), pp.21f.; ARE III, §617.

doubtless including Palestine, as "a widow for Egypt" means that the land is without a husband, in other words without a protector and helpless against Egypt. Thus Israel is clearly listed among other strong and dangerous peoples in the west of Palestine upon whom Merneptah has inflicted defeat. The stela proves, therefore, that Israel was in western Palestine by around 1220 B.C. and provides a convenient point at which to pause to discuss the Exodus.

THE DATE OF THE EXODUS

There are two chief theories as to when the Exodus of the Israelites from Egypt took place.[70] The first is based upon a perhaps late notation in I Kings 6:1 which states that Solomon began building the temple in the fourth year of his reign and the 480th[71] year after the Exodus from Egypt. The division of the kingdom under Rehoboam and Jeroboam is probably to be dated in 931/930 B.C.,[72] and since Solomon is said to have reigned for forty years (I Kings 11:42) his first year must have been about 970/969 B.C. The fourth year of his reign was accordingly 967/966 B.C., and if this was the 480th year after the departure from Egypt the Exodus must have taken place around 1446 B.C.

The date just mentioned falls within the last few years of the reign of Thutmose III (d. c.1436 B.C.), and if accepted would lead us to consider him as the Pharaoh of the Exodus. The picture of Thutmose III as the oppressor of the Israelites would be quite credible, since we know that he was a great builder and employed Asiatic captives on

---

[70] cf. W. M. F. Petrie, *Palestine and Israel.* 1934, pp.54-58.

[71] The figure is given as 440 instead of 480 in the LXX (ed. Swete, I, p.684).

[72] Edwin R. Thiele in JNES 3 (1944), pp.147, 184; TMN pp.54f.; and in *Vetus Testamentum.* 4 (1954), pp.187-191. The fixed point from which this reckoning is made is the battle of Qarqar, the date of which is established as 853 B.C. by Assyrian records (see below, p.204). If between the disruption and this point, the reigns of the kings of Judah were recorded in terms of the accession-year system, and those of the kings of Israel according to the nonaccession-year system, the intervening period was 78 years in length, which gives the indicated date for the division of the kingdom. Joachim Begrich (*Die Chronologie der Könige von Israel und Juda und die Quellen des Rahmens der Königsbücher.* 1929, p.155) places the division of the kingdom in 926 B.C. W. F. Albright (in BASOR 100 [Dec. 1945], pp.16-22; and in *Interpretation.* 6 [1952], pp.101-103) puts it in 922 B.C. The last date, with a correlative of 959 B.C. for the founding of Solomon's temple, has been supported by M. B. Rowton (in BASOR 119 [Oct. 1950], pp.20-22) from evidence in the king list of Tyre as cited by Josephus from Menander of Ephesus. Dealing with the same materials, however, J. Liver (in IEJ 3 [1953], pp.113-122) accepts the date of 825 B.C. for the foundation of Carthage as given by Pompeius Trogus (rather than 814 B.C. as stated by Timaeus), puts the beginning of the reign of Hiram of Tyre in 979/978 B.C., and arrives at the date of 968/967 for the commencement of work on the temple, and 931/930 for the separation of the kingdoms.

his construction projects (p. 100). Ahmose who expelled the Hyksos might have been the "new king over Egypt, who did not know Joseph" mentioned in Exodus 1:8, and Hatshepsut might even have been the "Pharaoh's daughter" of Exodus 2:5-10. Allowing the traditional forty years in the wilderness (Exodus 16:35; Numbers 14:33; Deuteronomy 2:7; Joshua 5:6; etc.), the Israelites would have arrived in Palestine shortly before 1400 B.C. and might be identified with the Habiru who were pressing into the land at that time (pp. 111f.).[73] Furthermore we know that there was a city at Jericho around 1400-1350 B.C. which could have been taken by Joshua and, as the excavations at that site now stand, we do not know if there was a city there a century later (p. 159).

Attractive as is the hypothesis just outlined, it must be recognized that there are serious objections to it. The identification of the Habiru of the Amarna letters with the biblical Hebrews is improbable, since the frantic correspondence of Abdi-Hiba indicates that Jerusalem was in imminent danger of serious conquest, and that city does not seem to have been a major objective of Joshua and was only permanently conquered in the time of David (II Samuel 5:6f.). Other evidence, moreover, both in Transjordan (p. 153) and in Palestine (p. 166) requires a date considerably later than around 1400 B.C. for the coming of the Israelites to Canaan. As for the original entry of the Israelites into Egypt, if we reckon backward from an Exodus around 1446 and allow for a sojourn of 430 years in accordance with Exodus 12:40 (pp. 71f) we arrive at a date around 1875 B.C. This is nearly two centuries before the establishment of the Hyksos in Egypt, however, in whose time it seems historically probable that the Israelites first entered that land (p. 95). Furthermore, while Thutmose III carried out large building projects, those activities centered as far as we know in Upper Egypt, and it was not until the Nineteenth Dynasty that the Pharaohs resided in the Delta and directed major attention to building operations there. But it was in the Delta that the Israelites are said to have lived and worked. This brings us to the second and more probable hypothesis as to the date of the Exodus.

The basis of the theory now to be considered is the statement in Exodus 1:11 that the Israelites "built for Pharaoh store-cities, Pithom and Raamses." Raamses can hardly be other than Per-Ramses, the

---

[73] cf. J. W. Jack, *The Date of the Exodus*. 1925.

"House of Ramses [II]," which has been identified with Tanis-Qantir (p. 114). Since Tanis was the Avaris of the Hyksos and was abandoned and allowed to fall into ruins after their expulsion (c.1570 B.C.) and was only reestablished by Seti I (c.1302-c.1290), it is not likely that any large construction activities were being conducted in this vicinity in the years just before 1446 B.C. But in the days of Seti I and Ramses II the Israelites could have toiled in construction work at Raamses and also at Pithom. The only other explanation of Exodus 1:11 would be to say that the Israelites labored at these places at some far earlier time, presumably back in the Hyksos period, and that the use of the name Raamses is an anachronism.

Unless we are to regard Exodus 1:11 as an erroneous or anachronistic statement, we must conclude that Ramses II was the Pharaoh under whom the oppression of the Israelites reached its climax. This is in harmony with our knowledge of his vast building activities and particularly with the fact that he resided in the Delta and devoted the opening years of his reign largely to building operations at Tanis. The general impression given by the book of Exodus is that the Israelites were settled not far from Pharaoh's court, and in Psalm 78:12, 43 they are definitely said to have lived "in the land of Egypt, in the fields of Zoan." Zoan is the Hebrew name for Tanis, as the rendering in the Septuagint shows,[74] and thus we have a picture of the Israelites as living in the vicinity of Tanis at a time when Pharaoh's court was there. This situation is fulfilled in the time of Ramses II but not in the earlier days of Thutmose III.

In connection with the presence of the children of Israel in Egypt it is also of interest to note that a number of Egyptian texts dating from the fifteenth century to the twelfth mention the 'Apiru, a name which we have seen (p. 69) to be phonetically very similar to Hebrew. The oldest are inscriptions accompanying two Theban tomb paintings which identify as 'Apiru men shown at work pressing out grapes.[75] Amenhotep II gives a list of captives which begins with 127 princes of Retenu, that is Syria-Palestine, and includes 3,600 'Apiru.[76] Two papyri of the reign of Ramses II give instructions for the distribution of grain to the 'Apiru as well as the men of the army who were engaged in the transport of stone for a pylon the

[74] LXX, ed. Swete, II, pp.315,317.
[75] Georges Posener in Bottéro, *Le problème des Ḥabiru à la 4e rencontre assyriologique internationale*, Nos.181,182, p.166.
[76] *ibid.*, No.183, p.167; cf. ANET p.247.

Pharaoh was erecting.[77] A papyrus of Ramses III records the gift of over 2,000 persons to be the property of the temple of Re at Heliopolis, among them Asiatic warriors, 'Apiru, and "people settled who are in this place."[78] Again, an inscription from the Wadi Hammamat in Upper Egypt from the time of Ramses IV mentions 8,000 workmen sent to the quarries in that vicinity and lists among them 800 'Apiru.[79] Thus the use of "immigrants" in Egyptian labor forces is attested not only for this period in general but also precisely in the reign of Ramses II.

If we now try to date the Exodus more exactly, we may suppose that the children of Israel were first employed at Tanis by Seti I (c.1302-c.1290) and then had their burdens yet further increased by Ramses II (c.1290-c.1224) to the point of driving them to attempt their escape. During this time Moses was born, grew up, lived in the wilderness, and returned to Egypt, as recounted in Exodus 2-3, thus the reign of Ramses II must have been fairly well advanced by the time of the departure of the enslaved people. Since the Israelites must also have arrived in Palestine and penetrated to the place where Merneptah met them by about 1220 B.C., there is hardly time for them still to have wandered in the wilderness for a full forty years (Exodus 16:35, etc.), but this figure may have been a conventional round number for what was actually a somewhat briefer time.

If, then, the children of Israel made their way from Egypt to Palestine sometime around the middle of the thirteenth century B.C. and had previously dwelt in Egypt for 430 years, their original entry there must have been soon after 1700 B.C. This is not long after the Hyksos established themselves in Egypt, which seems a likely time for another Semitic group to enter there. If the sojourn in Egypt was for only 215 years, then the entry would have been about the middle of the fifteenth century B.C., perhaps in the reign of Thutmose III (c.1490-c.1436 B.C.), which may seem a less likely time, yet withal a time when the presence of Asiatics in the land is otherwise attested (p. 100).

The chief objection to this second theory of an Exodus in the thirteenth century is that it is out of harmony with the 480 years mentioned in I Kings 6:1, an explicit statement which some feel provides the fundamental datum in the entire problem.[80] This is often

[77] *ibid.*, Nos.187,188, p.169f.   [78] *ibid.*, No.189, p.170; cf. ANET p.261.
[79] *ibid.*, No.190, pp.170f.
[80] Merrill F. Unger, *Archeology and the Old Testament.* 1954, p.141.

regarded, however, as a late addition to the text, and may bear the marks of an artificial reckoning in that it amounts to twelve generations of forty years each. Another suggestion is that the 480 years may refer to the time when an earlier group, perhaps Judah and associated tribes, entered Palestine from the south, this being separate from and prior to the coming of the Joseph tribes under Moses and Joshua, although in tradition the two events were ultimately combined into one.[81] It must be admitted that no single theory as to the date of the Exodus is conclusive, but best justice seems done to the evidence now available if we conclude that the main movement of the Israelites from Egypt to Palestine took place toward the middle of the thirteenth century B.C.

THE TWENTIETH DYNASTY

After the death of Merneptah there ensued a state of confusion in which several kings followed each other in swift succession and even a Syrian prince seized the rule.[82] About 1197 B.C. a certain Setnakht "set in order the entire land, which had been rebellious,"[83] and as the founder of the Twentieth Dynasty left a stable throne for his son, Ramses III.

RAMSES III

Like his predecessors, Ramses III (c.1195-c.1164) had to fight to defend the frontiers of Egypt against invaders who pressed in from the west and the north. Among these enemies were those known as the "peoples of the sea," who included the so-called Peleste. Some of the Peleste settled on the Palestinian coast and became the Philistines of the Bible. In honor of his success in repelling the invaders, Ramses III erected a large temple to Amun at a point on the western plain of Thebes now called Medinet Habu and adorned its walls with a vast record of his achievements. The earliest known representation of a salt-water naval battle is here,[84] and also realistic representations of the Philistines who had been taken captive. Two of these Philistine prisoners are shown in Fig. 52 being led by an Egyptian officer into the presence of the Pharaoh. The unusual manacles which are made in the form of a fish and suspended from

---

[81] H. H. Rowley, *From Joseph to Joshua* (The Schweich Lectures of the British Academy 1948). 1950, pp.139f.,147f.

[82] ARE IV, §398.

[83] ARE IV, §399.

[84] ARE IV, §69; Harold H. Nelson in JNES 2 (1943), pp.40-55.

the prisoner's neck by a cord are characteristic of this period. In connection with the flight of other enemies, Ramses III expressed himself poetically as the song of Deborah (Judges 5:20) was to do: "The stars of the *seshed*-constellation were frightful in pursuit of them, while the land of Egypt was glad and rejoiced at the sight of his valor: Ramses III."[85] The sovereign himself is depicted (Fig. 53) at Medinet Habu in heroic size, with the falcon sun-god hovering with wings protectingly outspread above his head, reminding us of the figure of speech which the Israelites were to use—"the shadow of thy wings" (Psalms 17:8; 36:7; 57:1; 63:7; cf. Malachi 4:2).

Since Ramses III records the building of a temple of Amun in Pekanan and lists nine towns of Khuru which belonged to the same god,[86] it is evident that Palestine and Syria still belonged to Egypt at this time. After this, however, there is no further record by the Pharaohs of the possession of Asiatic territory, and the days of Egyptian empire were over. A series of kings, still bearing the name of Ramses which had once been so great, ruled weakly at home and enjoyed little prestige abroad. Court documents attest a series of robberies in which most of the royal tombs at Thebes were ransacked,[87] and "The Report of Wenamon" shows the humiliating treatment to which an Egyptian envoy could be subjected in Syria where Egyptian armies once had marched in triumph.[88]

8. THE DECLINE
(TWENTY-FIRST TO THIRTIETH DYNASTIES),
c.1090-332 B.C.

WITH the Twenty-first Dynasty the decline of Egypt had set in fully. The Pharaohs ruled feebly at Tanis in the Delta while the high priest of Amun at Thebes was virtually king of Upper Egypt. The intact tomb of the second king of this dynasty, Psusennes I, was discovered in 1939-1940 at Tanis. The king was buried in a funerary chamber of pink granite and in a series of sarcophagi, the outermost one of which likewise was made of pink granite. The second sarcophagus was sculptured out of black granite in the likeness of the king while the third and fourth were made of silver and of silver overlaid with gold respectively. The other treasures found in the tomb constituted

---

[85] John A. Wilson in *Medinet Habu Studies 1928/29*. OIC 7, 1930, p.27.
[86] ARE IV, §§219, 384.   [87] ARE IV, §§499-556.   [88] ARE IV, §§557-591.

one of the richest discoveries ever made in Egypt, and included a necklace of lapis lazuli and gold which weighed more than seventy-two pounds.[1]

AMENEMOPET

In these days a certain wise man named Amenemopet was moved to profounder reflections. In a way reminiscent of Ptahhotep (p. 89), he offered sound advice to his son on honesty, integrity, self-control, and kindliness. The dominant ideal which he held up was that of the truly tranquil man whom he contrasted with the hot-headed man in a figure of two trees:

> As for the heated man of a temple,
> He is like a tree growing in the open.
> In the completion of a moment comes its loss of foliage,
> And its end is reached in the shipyards;
> Or it is floated far from its place,
> And the flame is its burial shroud.
>
> But the truly silent man holds himself apart.
> He is like a tree growing in a garden.
> It flourishes and doubles its yield;
> It stands before its lord.
> Its fruit is sweet; its shade is pleasant;
> And its end is reached in the garden.
>
> (VI,1-12)[2]

By reliance on the god, Amenemopet taught that man could attain this tranquility of mind and consequent freedom from overanxiety.

> Do not spend the night fearful of the morrow.
> At daybreak what is the morrow like?
> Man knows not what the morrow is like.
>
> God is always in his success,
> Whereas man is in his failure;
> One thing are the words which men say,
> Another is that which the god does.
>
> There is no success in the hand of the god,
> But there is no failure before him.
> If he[3] pushes himself to seek success,
> In the completion of a moment he damages it.

[1] *The New York Times.* 1940: Feb. 20, p.23; Mar. 6, p.20; May 4, p.6; Montet, *Tanis, douze années de fouilles,* pp.112-123.

[2] John A. Wilson in ANET p.422 (ANEA pp.237f.); cf. F. Ll. Griffith in JEA 12 (1926), p.202.

[3] i.e. a man.

Be steadfast in thy heart, make firm thy breast.
Steer not with thy tongue alone.
If the tongue of a man be the rudder of a boat,
The All-Lord is its pilot.

(xix,11-17,22 - xx,6)[4]

The Wisdom of Amenemopet must have been known to the Israelite people, for it seems to be reflected, or even translated, at a number of points in the Old Testament.[5] Both Jeremiah (17:5-8) and Psalm 1 may reflect Amenemopet's striking picture of the two trees, while freely edited translations from other parts of the Wisdom of Amenemopet are thought to be recognizable in the book of Proverbs. Here are two probable parallels:

AMENEMOPET	PROVERBS
Better is poverty in the hand of the god Than riches in a storehouse;	Better is a little with the fear of the Lord than great treasure and trouble with it.
Better is bread, when the heart is happy, Than riches with sorrow. (ix,5-8)	Better is a dinner of herbs where love is than a fatted ox and hatred with it. (15:16f.)
Better is bread, when the heart is happy, Than riches with sorrow. (xvi,13f.)	Better is a dry morsel with quiet than a house full of feasting with strife. (17:1)

Especially does Proverbs 22:17-24:22 seem to be based upon the Wisdom of Amenemopet. This may be seen in the following passages.

AMENEMOPET	PROVERBS
Give thy ears, hear what is said, Give thy heart to understand them. To put them in thy heart is worth while, But it is damaging to him who neglects them. (iii,9-12)	Incline your ear, and hear the words of the wise, and apply your mind to my knowledge; for it will be pleasant if you keep them within you, if all of them are ready on your lips. (22:17f.)
Do not associate to thyself the heated man, Nor visit him for conversation. (xi,13f.)	Make no friendship with a man given to anger, nor go with a wrathful man. (22:24)

---

[4] ANET pp.423f. (ANEA p.238); cf. Peet, *A Comparative Study of the Literatures of Egypt, Palestine, and Mesopotamia*, pp.110f.
[5] H. Grimme in OL 28 (1925), cols. 59-62; D. C. Simpson in JEA 12 (1926), pp.232-239.

AMENEMOPET	PROVERBS
As for the scribe who is experienced in his office,	Do you see a man skilful in his work?
He will find himself worthy to be a courtier.	he will stand before kings.
(xxvii,16f.)	(22:29)

Do not strain to seek an excess. . . .	Do not toil to acquire wealth. . . .
If riches are brought to thee by robbery,	
They will not spend the night with thee. . . .	
They have made themselves wings like geese	For suddenly it takes to itself wings,
And are flown away to the heavens.	flying like an eagle toward heaven.
(ix,14-x,5)	(23:4f.)

Do not carry off the landmark at the boundaries of the arable land. . . .	Do not remove an ancient landmark
Nor encroach upon the boundaries of a widow.	or enter the fields of the fatherless.
(vii,12,15)	(23:10)

At one point the phrasing of the wise advice may be traced all the way back to Ptahhotep. He had said: "If thou art one of those sitting at the table of one greater than thyself, take what he may give, when it is set before thy nose. Thou shouldst gaze at what is before thee. Do not pierce him with many stares. . . . Let thy face be cast down until he addresses thee, and thou shouldst speak only when he addresses thee."[6] This counsel from the days of the Fifth Dynasty was echoed by Amenemopet and finally adopted by Proverbs.

AMENEMOPET	PROVERBS
Do not eat bread before a noble,	When you sit down to eat with a ruler,
Nor lay on thy mouth at first.	
If thou art satisfied with false chewings,	observe carefully what is before you;
They are a pastime for thy spittle.	and put a knife to your throat
Look at the cup which is before thee,	if you are a man given to appetite.
	Do not desire his delicacies
And let it serve thy needs.	for they are deceptive food.
(xxiii,13-18)	(23:1-3)[7]

[6] ANET p.412 (ANEA p.234).

[7] ANET pp.421-424 (ANEA pp.237f.); cf. Breasted, *The Dawn of Conscience*, pp.372-378.

SHESHONK I

The Twenty-second Dynasty was founded when a soldier from a Libyan family at Herakleopolis seized the royal authority and proclaimed himself Pharaoh. This new king, Sheshonk I (c.945-c.924 B.C.),[8] ruled from a residence at Bubastis (called Pi-beseth in Ezekiel 30:17) in the eastern Delta, and was strong enough to invade Palestine in the fifth year of Rehoboam of Judah (I Kings 14:25, where he is called Shishak). This Palestinian campaign was memorialized in a relief after the style of the earlier Pharaohs on a wall at Karnak. A portion of the relief is shown in Fig. 54 where the god Amun leads forward by cords rows of Asiatic captives, doubtless Israelites. On the entire relief no less than 156 captives are represented, each of whom symbolizes a different Palestinian town which Sheshonk I claims to have taken. In each case the name of the town is enclosed in an oval marked out beneath the head and shoulders of the captive. Of the names which can still be read and identified geographically, many are found in the Old Testament. These include Rabbith, Taanach, Shunem, Beth-shean, Rehob, Hapharaim, Gibeon, Beth-horon, Ajalon, Megiddo, Socoh, and Arad. This is also the list which includes "The Field of Abram" (p. 91).[9] In 1938-1939 the intact burial chamber of Sheshonk I was discovered at Tanis, the body of the king being splendidly arrayed, with a gold mask over his face, and enclosed in a coffin of electrum.[10]

The dynasty founded by Sheshonk I endured for some two centuries, although the country was organized in an essentially feudal way, and Upper Egypt was divided into two principalities dominated respectively by Herakleopolis (called Hanes in Isaiah 30:4)[11] and Thebes. The Twenty-third and Twenty-fourth Dynasties which followed were short and feeble, and Isaiah was quite correct in his description (Chapter 19) of the divided and hopeless state of Egypt at that time.

THE KUSHITE PERIOD

Meanwhile strong native rulers had arisen at Napata near the Fourth Cataract in the region which the Egyptians called Kush.

---

[8] Manetho (tr. Waddell, p.159) gives 21 years for the reign of Shesonk I. The date given above is that of Breasted (*A History of Egypt*, p.600); Albright (in BASOR 130 [Apr. 1953], p.7) suggests 935-914 B.C. If 931/930 B.C. was the accession year of Rehoboam, the fifth year of Rehoboam, in which Sheshonk I invaded Palestine, would have been 926/925 (TMN p.56; cf. Breasted, *op.cit.*, p.529).

[9] ARE IV, §§712-716. [10] AJA 44 (1940), p.145.

[11] ARE IV, §790.

One of these, named Kashta, pushed into Thebes, and his successor, Piankhi, conquered all of Egypt as is recorded on a stela of pink granite found at Napata.[12] Piankhi was followed upon the throne by his brother, Shabako, and then by two sons in turn, Shebitko, and Taharqo. The last three are listed by Manetho, who calls them Ethiopians, as comprising the Twenty-fifth Dynasty of Egypt.[13]

The tombs of these Kushite kings have been found in the vicinity of Napata,[14] and a temple built by Taharqo has been excavated among other ruins at Kawa near the Third Cataract.[15] There were several inscriptions of Taharqo in this temple, and they have provided data for a fresh study of the chronology of Taharqo and his predecessors, with the following results established as probable: Piankhi became king in 740 B.C. and invaded Egypt in 720. Shabako began to reign in 708 B.C. Shebitko was associated with Shabako in 699 B.C. and became sole ruler in 697. Taharqo, born in 709 B.C., was associated with Shebitko in 689 and became sole ruler in 684.[16]

In the days of these kings the power of Assyria was being extended more and more threateningly in the direction of Egypt. According to II Kings 19:9 Taharqo, who is there called "Tirhakah king of Ethiopia," went out to fight against Sennacherib when the latter was campaigning against Hezekiah (see below p. 212). In 671 B.C. Esarhaddon invaded Egypt and destroyed Memphis, while Taharqo only escaped by the loss of family and property.[17] Although Esarhaddon claimed the conquest of Egypt, Upper Egypt, and Kush, Taharqo soon asserted himself again, and Ashurbanipal led the Assyrian armies back into Egypt in 667 B.C. The inscriptions of Ashurbanipal tell how Taharqo was driven from Memphis and from Thebes, and how "the night of death overtook him," a decease which probably took place in 664 B.C.[18] Then Tanutamun (664-654/653), whom Ashurbanipal calls Urdamane and describes as a son of Shabako.

[12] ARE IV, §§816-883.
[13] tr. Waddell, pp.167-169.
[14] G. A. Reisner in JEA 9 (1923), pp.34-77; Dows Dunham in AJA 50 (1946), pp.378-388.
[15] M. F. Laming Macadam, *The Temples of Kawa*, II, *History and Archaeology of the Site* (Oxford University Excavations in Nubia), Text. 1955, pp.61-113.
[16] Macadam, *The Temples of Kawa*, I, *The Inscriptions*, Text. 1949, pp.18f.; cf. W. F. Albright in BASOR 130 (Apr. 1953), p.11, who alters Macadam's figures slightly. The names of these kings were formerly read as Shabaka, Shabataka, and Taharka; in Manetho they are Sabacon (Σαβάκων), Sebichos (Σεβιχώς), and Tarcus (Τάρκος); for the spelling used above see Macadam, *op.cit.*, p.124 n.1.
[17] ARAB II, §§580, 710; J. M. A. Janssen in *Biblica*. 34 (1953), pp.37f.
[18] ARAB II, §§901, 906; Janssen, *op.cit.*, pp.38f.

took the throne.[19] He made Thebes his stronghold, and went out to challenge the Assyrians. Ashurbanipal defeated him, pursued him to Thebes and, probably in 663 B.C., "conquered this city completely, smashed it as if by floodstorm."[20] "Thebes that sat by the Nile" with "Ethiopia . . . her strength" (Nahum 3:8f.) was fallen and the Kushite rule of Egypt soon came to its end.

THE SAITE PERIOD

Yet a brief period of restoration was at hand. At Saïs in the Delta native princes had cooperated with the Assyrians and, when the Kushites were eliminated, these rulers had opportunity to rise in influence. According to Manetho there were nine of these kings of Saïs who constituted the Twenty-sixth Dynasty, a dynasty which this authority probably reckoned as extending from the Assyrian invasion in 671 B.C. to the Persian invasion in 525.[21] Stephinates and Nechepsos, the first two in Manetho's list, are otherwise unknown and were probably only insignificant local rulers.[22] The next name is Necho I, and he was probably considered the founder of the dynasty. Beginning with his successor, Psamtik I, the kings are also known from Egyptian inscriptions, the data in which provide material for calculating their probable respective dates.[23] It was Psamtik I (663-610 B.C.)[24] who, evidently by taking advantage of the preoccupation of the Assyrians in their struggles with Babylon and Elam, was able to establish the Saite rule throughout Egypt in freedom from foreign domination.[25] With the renewal of centralized government, peace and prosperity were restored in considerable measure to Egypt. There was a revival of the more ancient Egyptian art and culture; and relations were entered into with the rising country of Greece. Probably at about the end of his reign there was a new

[19] The reign of Tanutamun is not included in Manetho's list. Political events of the time are recorded on a stela of Tanutamun which was discovered at Napata (ARE IV, §§919-934).

[20] ANET p.297; ARAB II, §906; Janssen, *op.cit.*, pp.39f.; cf. below pp.215f.

[21] tr. Waddell, pp. 169-173; cf. Rowton in JEA 34 (1948), pp.60-62.

[22] "Ammeris the Ethiopian" heads the list in some versions and may have been Tanutamun.

[23] KPGÄ pp.154-157.

[24] Psamtik I did not actually die until in 609 B.C. but this fraction of a year was counted as a part of the first year of his successor, thus now in the Saite period the years of a king's reign were again (cf. above p.97 n.) considered as coinciding with the years of the civil calendar, that is, the entire calendar year in which a king took the throne was reckoned as the first year of his reign. See ARE IV, §§959, 975, 984. By the Saite period the civil calendar had regressed sufficiently that in 663 B.C. the Egyptian year began on February 5, and in 525 B.C. on January 2. See KPGÄ p.157.

[25] KPGÄ p.16.

threat, however, when the Scythians marched against Egypt. Herodotus describes this, and tells how Psamtik I met them in Palestine and with gifts and prayers persuaded them not to come further.[26]

NECHO II

Psamtik I was succeeded by his son, Necho II (609-595 B.C.). The last king of Assyria, Ashur-uballit II, was now hard pressed by the Babylonians in western Mesopotamia, and Egypt evidently still considered itself on the side of the Assyrians against the so rapidly rising Babylonians. A cuneiform text known as the Babylonian chronicle (B.M. 21901; cf. p. 218) states that in the sixteenth year (610/609 B.C.) of Nabopolassar this king marched against Ashur-uballit II, who had established his throne in Haran. In Arahsamnu, the eighth month, or November, 610 B.C., the Babylonians were joined by the Manda-hordes, probably the Scythians, and successfully drove Ashur-uballit II out of Haran. In Addaru, the twelfth month, or February/March, 609 B.C., the Babylonians and Scythians returned to their own countries. Following that, in what (although it is not so specified by the Babylonian chronicle) was obviously the seventeenth year of Nabopolassar, for a period extending from Duzu, the fourth month, to Ululu, the sixth month, that is from June/July to August/September of 609 B.C., Ashur-uballit II and "a large army of Egypt" undertook to reconquer Haran.[27] Since we read in II Kings 23:29 that "Pharaoh Neco king of Egypt went up to the king of Assyria to the river Euphrates," and in the parallel account in II Chronicles 35:21 that he went in "haste," we may conclude that the references in the Babylonian chronicle and in the Old Testament are to the same event, and that Necho II made this expedition with the purpose of giving assistance to Ashur-uballit II. Accordingly, too, the attempt of King Josiah described in the Old Testament (II Kings 23:29f.; II Chronicles 35:20-24) to halt Necho II may be explained as an endeavor to keep this potential aid from reaching Assyria, the power which had been such a terrible enemy of Judah; and the death of Josiah on the plain of Megiddo may be dated shortly before the month Duzu in the seventeenth year of Nabopolassar, that is shortly before June/July 609 B.C.[28]

[26] I, 105.

[27] tr. A. Leo Oppenheim in ANET p.305 (ANEA p.202); cf. C. J. Gadd, *The Fall of Nineveh*. 1923, p.41; ARAB II, §1183. For the principles of Babylonian chronology see the Appendix of the present book.

[28] Hayim Tadmor in JNES 15 (1956), pp.228f. For the previously held theory that it was on a second campaign of Necho II in 608 B.C. that Josiah died, see M. B. Rowton in JNES 10 (1951), pp.128-130.

According to the Babylonian chronicle Ashur-uballit II and his Egyptian supporters did not succeed in taking Haran and afterward "they retired."[29] Perhaps it was then that Necho II captured Gaza, an event mentioned by Herodotus[30] as taking place after the battle of Megiddo, and probably also referred to in Jeremiah 47:1.[31] In spite of failure at Haran the expedition of Necho II had evidently taken all of Syria, and Egyptian forces held the important city of Carchemish for several years. This is shown by two recently published Babylonian texts of the British Museum (B.M. 22047 and B.M. 21946) which constitute a continuation of the Babylonian chronicle. The one text (B.M. 22047) records a successful attack by the army of Egypt upon the Babylonian garrison in the city of Kimuhu on the Euphrates which took place in the twentieth year of Nabopolassar, 606/605 B.C.[32] The other, which will be cited below (pp. 220f.), tells of the final and for the Egyptians disastrous battle which was fought at Carchemish. Here in 605 B.C. the Egyptian army was decisively defeated by the Babylonians under the command of Nebuchadnezzar.

Henceforth Necho II confined his attention to Egypt. II Kings 24:7 states: "And the king of Egypt did not come again out of his land, for the king of Babylon had taken all that belonged to the king of Egypt from the Brook of Egypt[33] to the river Euphrates." Dying in 594 B.C., Necho II was followed by his son, Psamtik II (594-589 B.C.), who continued to avoid military endeavor in Asia and campaigned instead, as Herodotus[34] states, in Ethiopia, perhaps in this case meaning Lower Nubia.[35]

On February 8, 588 B.C.[36] Psamtik II died and was followed on the throne by his son Apries (588-570 B.C.), who is called Hophra in Jeremiah 44:30.[37] Not far from this time Nebuchadnezzar began the

[29] tr. Albright in JBL 51 (1932), p.87 n.33.   [30] II, 159.

[31] If Necho II came down at this time from Haran his invasion of Philistia would have been "out of the north" as Jeremiah 47:2 says. Another interpretation makes Jeremiah 47:2-7 refer to the Scythians. See A. Malamat in IEJ 1 (1950-51), pp.154-159.

[32] WCCK p.67.

[33] This watercourse which marked the border of Egypt was probably the Wadi el-'Arish, between Gaza and Pelusium.

[34] II, 161.   [35] KPGÄ pp.128f.

[36] A stela of Enekhnesneferibre, daughter of Psamtik II, records the death of the Pharaoh: "Year 7, first month of the first season, day 23, went forth this Good God, Lord of the Two Lands, Psamtik II to heaven" (ARE IV, §988E). In 588 B.C. the Egyptian year began on January 17; the twenty-third day of the first month of the first season was February 8.

[37] The name appears as Wahibpre in Egyptian, 'Απρίης in Herodotus (II, 161), and Οὐαφρις in Manetho (tr. Waddell, p.170).

final siege of Jerusalem.[38] The predecessors of Apries had abandoned attempts at warfare in Asia, but the new Pharaoh now reversed this policy and boldly undertook to challenge Nebuchadnezzar. According to Herodotus[39] Apries sent the Egyptian fleet against Phoenicia, which would threaten Nebuchadnezzar's line of connection with his homeland, and according to the Old Testament (Jeremiah 37:5, 7, 11) he led the Egyptian army directly into Palestine where Nebuchadnezzar had to lift the siege of Jerusalem temporarily to meet this doubtless unexpected challenge. In Phoenicia Egyptian influence must have been reestablished with some success, since for many years after that the city of Tyre was found holding out against forces of Nebuchadnezzar (Ezekiel 26:1-28:19; 29:18), but in Palestine Apries was evidently unable to accomplish his purpose and must have been driven back into Egypt, since the Babylonian army soon returned to Jerusalem to complete its task of destruction there.

Egypt still offered refuge to those who feared the Babylonians, however, and some time after the fall of Jerusalem the remnant of Judah fled thither, taking with them the prophet Jeremiah (II Kings 25:22-26; Jeremiah 43:4-7). Jeremiah (43:8-13; 46:13-25) and also Ezekiel (29-32) often expressed the expectation that Nebuchadnezzar would invade Egypt, but the opportunity for this action did not come until in the time of the next Egyptian king.

The failure of the policies of Apries must have led to the unrest which marked the end of his reign. In 569 B.C. a rival king, whom Herodotus[40] pictures as a very common man who was backed by the army, challenged Apries and drove him from the throne. This was Amasis,[41] who came from a town called Siuph in the province of Saïs[42] and who reigned from 569 to 527 B.C. Civil war between the new king and the deposed one was probably still in progress and probably provided the favorable occasion at the time when Nebuchadnezzar made some kind of move against Egypt. A fragmentary cuneiform inscription states that in his own thirty-seventh year, that is in 568/567 B.C., Nebuchadnezzar fought against the troops

---

[38] The final siege of Jerusalem began probably on January 15, 588 B.C., or January 4, 587, either just before or within less than a year after Apries came to the throne. The date is discussed in the Appendix (p.594) where some preference is given to January 4, 587, the date correlative with final destruction of Jerusalem in 586.

[39] II, 161.

[40] II, 162, 172-174.

[41] The name is Ἄμασις in Herodotus, Ἄμωσις in Manetho (tr. Waddell, pp.170-172).

[42] Herodotus II, 172.

of "(Ama)su, of Egypt."[43] The same occasion may be referred to when Josephus relates that Nebuchadnezzar "invaded Egypt in order to subdue it, and, having killed the king who was then reigning and appointed another, he again took captive the Jews who were in the country and carried them to Babylon."[44] It is true that Josephus places this event in the twenty-third year of Nebuchadnezzar, or 582/581 B.C., but that date is in the midst of the reign of Apries and the reference to the elimination of one king and establishment of another looks much more like the time when Apries was being driven from his throne by Amasis.

Whatever the exact action of Nebuchadnezzar at this time, the power of the Babylonians must have been made sufficiently plain to Egypt, for throughout the long reign of Amasis there is no further record of conflict between his kingdom and that of Nebuchadnezzar and his successors. In this period of peace Egypt enjoyed a prosperity which Herodotus, presumably with exaggeration, says was marked by the existence of no less than twenty thousand inhabited cities in the country.[45]

In the latter part of his reign Amasis witnessed the rise of Cyrus the Great of Persia. Even as in his time Necho II took the side of Assyria against the rising power of Chaldea, so now Amasis entered into an alliance which bound Egypt, Lydia, and Babylonia together against the threat which was coming from Persia.[46] This was in vain, however, since in spite of whatever aid Egypt was able to give,[47] both Croesus of Lydia and Nabunaid of Babylon were swiftly overcome by Cyrus (in 546 and 539 B.C.).

Egypt presumably could expect attack soon, but as it transpired Cyrus was occupied with fighting on his northeastern front and died there in the summer of 530 B.C. The son of Cyrus, Cambyses II (529-522 B.C.), was not long in turning toward the Egyptian objective, but by the time his troops reached Egypt, as Herodotus[48] relates, Amasis was no longer alive, having died after a reign of forty-four years and been succeeded by his son Psamtik III. The death of Amasis must have been near the end of 526 B.C. and, since Manetho[49] gives Psamtik III a reign of six months, the defeat of the latter by the

---

[43] ANET p.308 (ANEA p.205); cf. Sidney Smith in CAH III, p.304.

[44] *Ant.* x, 182.   [45] II, 177.   [46] Herodotus I, 77.

[47] Xenophon (c.430-c.355 B.C.), *Cyropaedia.* VI, ii, 10. tr. Walter Miller, LCL (1914) II, p.155, speaks of 120,000 Egyptians coming to fight on the side of Croesus, but Herodotus (I, 77) gives no impression of actualized assistance in such magnitude.

[48] III, 10.   [49] tr. Waddell, p.171.

Persians must have ensued in the spring of 525. The decisive and for Egypt disastrous battle was fought at Pelusium in the eastern Delta and, when it was finished, Egypt belonged to the empire of the Persians.

Cambyses himself appears in the list of Manetho[50] as the first king of the Twenty-seventh Egyptian Dynasty, and the date of his accession to the Egyptian throne is correctly given in the same source as the fifth year of his kingship over the Persians, that is 525 B.C. Henceforward, throughout the Twenty-seventh to Thirtieth Dynasties, Egypt was under Persian rule, although sometimes local kings exercised authority under Persian domination. In 332 B.C. Egypt was conquered by Alexander the Great. After his death (323 B.C.) the land came under the rule of the Ptolemies until the death of Cleopatra (30 B.C.) when it became a Roman province under Octavian.

THE ROSETTA STONE

In 196 B.C. while Alexander's successors were ruling Egypt, the priests at Memphis composed a decree honoring King Ptolemy V Epiphanes (c.203-c.181 B.C.) for numerous benefits which he had conferred upon the temples of Egypt. This decree was ordered engraved on a tablet in three forms, "in the sacred writing, in the native script and in Greek letters." The "sacred writing" was the ancient picture-writing of Egypt which only the priests then understood, and which the Greeks called *hieroglyphics*, literally "sacred carvings."[51] The "native script" was what the Greeks called *demotic* meaning "common," or "popular," and was a new and simplified form of the Egyptian language and writing that had come into use some hundreds of years before. It was the Greek language which was to provide the clue for the decipherment of the inscription.

A stone inscribed with this decree (Fig. 55) was found in 1798 by an officer of Napoleon's expedition at Rosetta (Rashid) near the westernmost mouth of the Nile. The Greek text at the bottom of the Rosetta Stone was read easily and scholars at once took up the challenge to solve the problem of the two Egyptian scripts above. Silvestre de Sacy of France and J. D. Akerblad of Sweden successfully studied the demotic text on the monument, identifying the Greek personal names which it contains—Ptolemy, Berenike, and Arsinoë.

[50] tr. Waddell, p.175.
[51] When hieroglyphics were written on papyrus with a brush-pen, a bolder and more cursive form of writing developed, to which the Greek name *hieratic*, or "priestly," was applied.

Thomas Young of England was then able to identify the name of Ptolemy in the hieroglyphic portion, where groups of signs enclosed in oval frames (called "cartouches") had already been thought to be kings' names. Finally the young French scholar Jean François Champollion (1790-1832) was able to demonstrate the true nature of the hieroglyphic system of writing, to formulate an Egyptian grammar and dictionary, and to read numerous Egyptian texts. Thus the key was found which unlocked the doors to a knowledge of ancient Egypt.[52]

MOSES AND THE CHILDREN OF ISRAEL

In conclusion we may say that Egypt has afforded us no direct evidence of the sojourn of the Israelites, but it has revealed much which makes that sojourn and the Exodus which followed entirely credible. There are many connections between life in Egypt as known from archeology and the details of the biblical narrative at this point.[53] It was not uncommon for Asiatic people to find refuge in Egypt nor for them to be set at heavy labor on the great building projects of the Pharaohs. Without doubt the children of Israel were in Egypt in the days of the Hyksos, and their oppression and Exodus probably fell under Ramses II. The very name of Moses is clearly Egyptian, being the Egyptian word *mose* meaning "is born." Names like Amenmose ("Amun Is Born") and Thutmose ("Thoth Is Born") were familiar, and it may be presumed that Moses originally bore some fuller name of which only the "Mose" continued in current usage.[54]

In Egypt it has also been possible to trace ideas of the overshadowing care of God, and of ethical demands on earthly life. Actual passages from the wisdom literature of Egypt appear to have been taken over by Israelite writers. Thus the psalms, wisdom books, and prophetic works of Israel exhibit connections with Egyptian literature just as the mythology and law of the Old Testament are related to that of Babylonia.[55]

---

[52] E. A. Wallis Budge, *The Rosetta Stone in the British Museum.* 1929; H. Hartleben, *Champollion, sein Leben und sein Werk.* 2 vols. 1906.

[53] G. Ernest Wright, *Biblical Archaeology.* 1957, pp.53f.; Jozef M. A. Janssen in *Jaarbericht No.14 van het Vooraziatisch-Egyptisch Genootschap Ex Oriente Lux.* 1955-56, pp.63-72. Greta Hort in zaw 69 (1957), pp.84-103; 70 (1958), pp.48-59.

[54] cf. J. Gwyn Griffiths in jnes 12 (1953), pp.225-231.

[55] cf. J. M. P. Smith in ajsl 49 (1933), pp.172-184; William S. Smith in jbr 19 (1951), pp.12-15.

III

Penetrating the Past in Palestine

THE land of Palestine derives its name from the Philistines (Peleste) who settled along the southern coast in the twelfth century B.C. (p. 121). The area where they settled became known as Philistia (Joel 3:4, etc.) and from that in turn came the Greek name Palestine.[1] Josephus refers to the territory which extends from Gaza to Egypt and says that the Greeks call that area Palestine.[2] Herodotus even uses the name to include Phoenicia as well. Referring to the northern part of the coast where the Phoenicians settled, he says, "that part of Syria and as much of it as reaches to Egypt, is all called Palestine."[3] Elsewhere he speaks of "the part of Syria called Palestine,"[4] and "the Palestine part of Syria."[5] The Romans in their turn called the land *Palaestina* and from that came the English name Palestine.

The older name of the land was Canaan. This name is found frequently in the Bible (Genesis 11:31, etc.), in Egyptian texts of the Nineteenth Dynasty and later,[6] and in the Amarna letters.[7] According to Genesis 10:19 Canaanite territory extended from Gaza to Sidon. In the Amarna letters, for example in a letter of Abimilki of Tyre, the name Canaan applies to the Phoenician coast as far north as Ugarit.[8]

In the Akkadian of the Amarna letters and also in Hurrian[9] the form of the name is Kinahhi. Since there is also a common noun *kinahhu* in Hurrian which means "purple," it seems probable that the original meaning was "land of the purple," probably referring to the purple dye made from the murex shellfish found on the coast. Since the name Phoenicia comes from Greek φοῖνιξ, also meaning

[1] ἡ Παλαιστίνη. [2] *Ant.* I, vi, 2. [3] VII, 89.
[4] I, 105. [5] II, 106.
[6] ANET pp.258,261,264,378,478; and cf. above pp.113,116.
[7] KAT No.8 = MTAT No.8, lines 15, 17, 25; etc.
[8] KAT No.151 = MTAT No.151, line 50. [9] ANET p.352.

"purple," the original reference of the name to that region is substantiated. From Phoenicia then the name was evidently extended to include the whole region between the Jordan and the Mediterranean.[10]

The land east of the Jordan was simply called "beyond the Jordan," or "the other side of the Jordan" (Genesis 50:10; Numbers 32:19, etc.), even as it is still known as Transjordan.

Syria, of which as Herodotus said Palestine is a part, includes the entire area of fertile land, bounded by the desert on the east and south, the sea on the west, and extending to the Taurus Mountains on the north. The name Syria was derived by the Greeks from Assyria, but whereas it was at first applicable to the entire Assyrian Empire from the Caucasus to the Levant, it shrank finally to the limits just stated.

Palestine proper, meaning the country west of the Jordan and running from Dan in the north to Beersheba in the south (cf. Judges 20:1, etc.), is 150 miles in length and averages something like 40 miles in breadth. In comparison with the 6,000 square miles of Palestine proper, Transjordan, running east to the desert, comprises some 4,000 square miles.

Between the sea and the desert the land of Palestine and Transjordan may be conceived as lying in four parallel strips running north and south.[11] First, along the coast is the maritime plain, of which the most famous portion is the Plain of Sharon between Mount Carmel and Joppa. Secondly, a rugged series of hills runs through the interior and may be known as the central range. This line of hills descends from the mountains of Lebanon far to the north. Between Galilee and Samaria a spur of the range runs out to the Mediterranean and terminates in 1,810-foot Mount Carmel, to the north of which lies the Plain of Esdraelon. In Judea the range attains an average elevation of 2,400 feet, a high point a few miles north of Jerusalem being 3,317 feet in elevation, Jerusalem itself 2,593 feet, and Bethlehem 2,550 feet. On the western border between Judea and Philistia the high central range drops toward the maritime plain in a region of low hills

[10] Sabatino Moscati, *I predecessori d'Israele*. 1956, pp.42-74; and in JBR 24 (1956), pp.247-249.

[11] For Bible geography see George Adam Smith, *The Historical Geography of the Holy Land*. 25th ed. 1931; Félix Marie Abel, *Géographie de la Palestine*. 2 vols. 1933-38; Denis Baly, *The Geography of the Bible*. 1957. For Bible atlases see G. Ernest Wright and Floyd V. Filson, *The Westminster Historical Atlas to the Bible*. rev. ed. 1956; L. H. Grollenberg, *Atlas of the Bible*, tr. Joyce M. H. Reid and H. H. Rowley. 1956; Emil G. Kraeling, *Rand McNally Bible Atlas*. 1956.

called the Shephelah or "lowland" (Joshua 15:33, etc.). On the southern frontier of Judea the range breaks down and spreads out in the area known as the Negeb, sometimes translated "the South" (ASV), but literally meaning the Dry or Parched Land (Genesis 13:1, etc.).

On its eastern side the central range drops quickly to the Jordan Valley, whose great depression constitutes the third of the four parallel bands in which the country may be seen to lie. The Jordan River has sources at Banias and elsewhere in the north in the neighborhood of 9,100-foot-high Mount Hermon, where snow and rain provide ample water. Soon it flows through Lake Huleh, where the valley is about 230 feet above sea level. Next, the river flows through the Sea of Galilee, about 695 feet below the level of the sea, and then follows an ever-deepening valley until it terminates in the Dead Sea about 1,290 feet below sea level. As will be explained more fully in Chapter v, this profound depression represents a geological rift which runs on down along the Wadi el-Arabah to the Gulf of Aqabah and through the Red Sea into Africa. Beyond the Jordan and towering some 4,400 feet above the Dead Sea is an eastern range of barren hills which constitutes the fourth of the parallel bands and beyond which is the desert.

The lower valley of the Jordan is subtropical, but the greater part of Palestine lies one or two thousand feet above the level of the sea and enjoys a temperate climate. The year is divided into a dry season and a rainy season, the rains coming from the end of October to the middle of April. During the rainy or winter season, snow is not uncommon in the hills.

Of all the geographical facts that may be adduced about Palestine, the most significant is that it constitutes a "bridge" connecting Mesopotamia and Egypt. With the sea on the one hand and the desert on the other, Palestine was the natural and only highroad between those two great homes of empire, the valley of the Tigris and Euphrates, and the valley of the Nile. Palestine's history was connected intimately, therefore, with that of its powerful neighbors, and it was the fate of the land at most times to be a dependency, a buffer state, or a battleground.

A land as often invaded as Palestine, and as perennially dominated by various foreign powers, cannot display an historical development of such homogeneity and directness as was manifest in Egypt. Nor do we find in Palestine, at such ancient periods as in both Egypt and

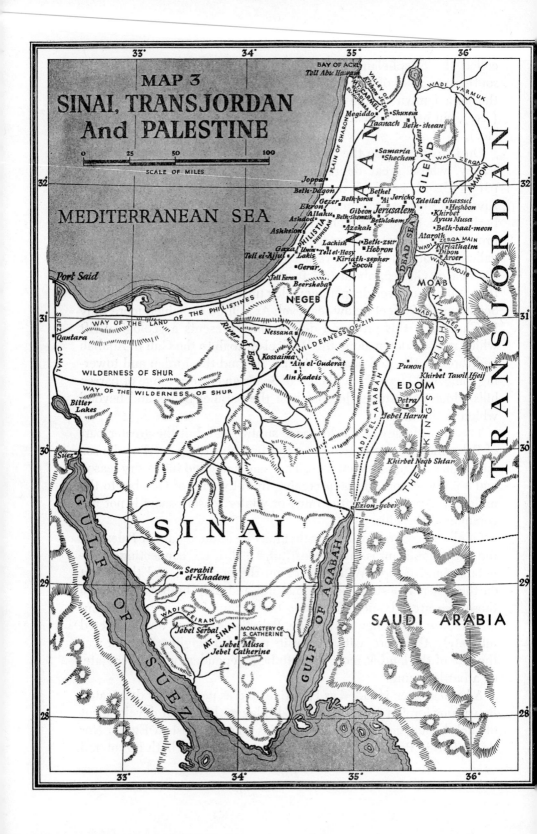

MAP 3
SINAI, TRANSJORDAN
And PALESTINE

0   25   50   100
SCALE OF MILES

MEDITERRANEAN SEA

BAY OF ACRE
Tell Abu Hawam
VALLEY OF JEZREEL
MT. CARMEL
EL-KISHON
KISHON RIVER
WADI YARMUK
Megiddo • Shunem
Taanach • Beth-shean
Samaria
• Shechem
GILEAD
WADI ZERQA
AMMON

CANAAN

Joppa•
Beth-Dagon •
Gezer • Bethel
Ekron • • Ai • Jericho
Altaku• Gibeon Jerusalem
Ashdod • Beth-shemesh
Ashkelon • Bethlehem
PHILISTIA Azekah
SHEPHELAH
Lachish • Beth-zur
Gaza• Umm • • Hebron
Tell el-'Ajjul • Lakis • Tell el-Hesy
• Kiriath-sepher
Gerar• • Socoh
Tell Fara •
Beersheba•

Teleilat Ghassul
• Heshbon
• Khirbet
Ayun Musa
• Beth-baal-meon
Ataroth
ZERQA MAIN
WADI • Kiriathaim
• Dibon
• Aroer
WADI MOJIB

DEAD SEA

MOAB

WADI HESA

Port Said

NEGEB

WAY OF THE LAND OF THE PHILISTINES

Qantara•

River of Egypt

Nessana •

WILDERNESS OF ZIN

WADI EL-ARABAH

Kossaima•
•Ain el-Guderat
Ain Kadeis•

• Punon
Khirbet Tawil Ifjeij

EDOM

Petra•
•Jebel Harun

THE KING'S HIGHWAY

WILDERNESS OF SHUR

WAY OF THE WILDERNESS OF SHUR

Bitter
Lakes

SUEZ CANAL

Suez•

•Khirbet Neqb Shtar

TRANSJORDAN

Ezion-geber•

SINAI

• Serabit
el-Khadem

SAUDI ARABIA

WADI FIRAN
Jebel Serbal•
MONASTERY OF
S. CATHERINE
MT. SINAI
Jebel Musa
Jebel Catherine

GULF OF SUEZ

GULF OF AQABAH

56. Jericho

57. Tell el-Mutesellim, the Site of Megiddo (Armageddon)

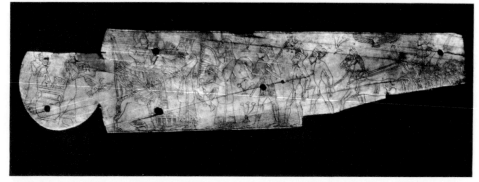

58. Ivory Plaque of the Prince of Megiddo

59. Standing Stones at Gezer

61. Ras Shamra Stela with the God Baal

60. Ras Shamra Stela with the God El

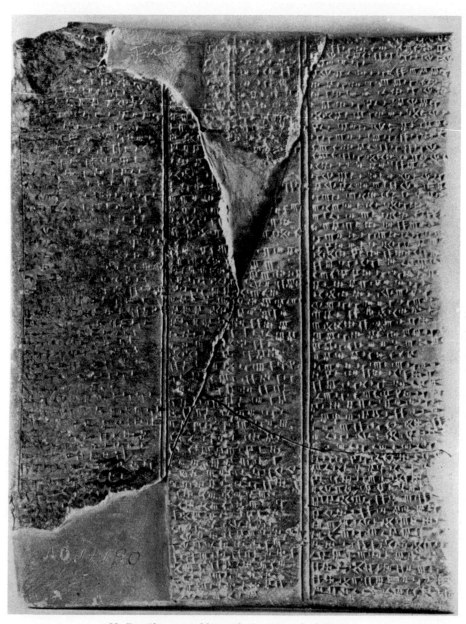

62. Ras Shamra Tablet with the Legend of Keret

64. The Sacred Rock beneath the Dome of the Rock

63. The Dome of the Rock

65. The Great Stables at Megiddo

66. Ivory Medallion with the Child Horus

68. The Siloam Tunnel

67. Cast of the Moabite Stone

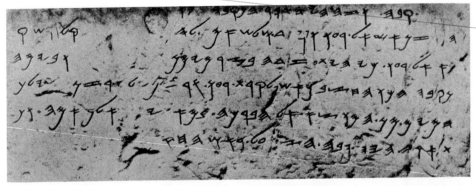

69. The Siloam Inscription

70. One of the Lachish Letters

Mesopotamia, powerful rulers and well established dynasties whose records survive to show the course of events. It is only in the time of the Israelite kings, and then chiefly because of the records preserved in the Bible, that a relatively precise historical framework can be established.

For the earlier Palestinian times we can speak only in terms of broad archeological periods, and it is customary to refer to the Stone, Chalcolithic, Bronze, and Iron Ages and their respective subdivisions. It will be desirable, therefore, first to sketch briefly the salient characteristics of these successive periods, and then to deal more fully with the archeological discoveries which relate particularly to biblical times and happenings.

1. THE ARCHEOLOGICAL PERIODS IN PALESTINE

THE STONE AGE, UP TO c.4500 B.C.

THE traces of the presence of man in Palestine go back into the earliest periods of human life. The famous "Galilee skull" which was found by F. Turville-Petre in 1925 in the "robbers' cave" near the Sea of Galilee, and the fossil human remains which were excavated by Theodore D. McCown in 1932 in the Wadi el-Mughara or "valley of the cave" at Mount Carmel, belong to the Paleolithic or Early Stone Age and represent a primitive type of humanity akin to the Neanderthal, which is commonly dated from 50,000 to 100,000 years ago.[1]

Other discoveries in the Wadi el-Mughara reveal a Mesolithic or Middle Stone Age culture whose people had learned to grow wheat and to carve statuettes and were in the habit of buying their dead, laying the body on its side with legs drawn up and sometimes leaving ornaments with it. To this culture the name Natufian is given, and its date is supposed to have been around 8000 B.C.[2]

In the Neolithic or Late Stone Age man had learned to shape and polish his stone implements, and during the period pottery was made for the first time in Palestine. Mugharet Abu Usba, a cave on Mount

---

[1] Arthur Keith, *New Discoveries relating to the Antiquity of Man.* 1931, pp.173-198; Theodore D. McCown and Arthur Keith, *The Stone Age of Mount Carmel,* II, *The Fossil Human Remains from the Levalloiso-Mousterian.* 1939; J. Philip Hyatt in JBR 12 (1944), pp.232-236.

[2] Dorothy A. E. Garrod and D. M. A. Bate, *The Stone Age of Mount Carmel,* I, *Excavations at the Wady el-Mughara.* 1937; W. F. Albright, *The Archaeology of Palestine.* 1949, pp.59-61.

Carmel, has preserved the sickle blades and pottery fragments of a people whose culture may have been derived from the Natufian but was definitely in advance of it and clearly belongs to the Neolithic period. This may be called the Usbian culture, and a date around 7500 B.C. has been suggested for it.[3]

At a prehistoric village close to Sha'ar ha-Golan and near where the Yarmuk River flows into the Jordan, over three thousand flint implements were unearthed, including arrowheads, axes, and other tools for hunting and for agriculture. The accompanying pottery was coarse, but decorated with triangular and zigzag lines and short parallel strokes. To this culture the name Yarmukian is given, and a date around 7000 B.C. has been suggested.[4]

At Jericho in the excavations conducted in 1930-1936 by John Garstang of the University of Liverpool, levels of the Neolithic period were reached and it was discovered that there had been a phase here with pottery and an earlier phase without pottery.[5] When the excavation of Jericho was resumed in 1952 and following years under Kathleen M. Kenyon of the British School of Archaeology in Jerusalem, one of the chief aims was to explore further in the Neolithic levels and it is in fact in the pre-pottery Neolithic that the most important discoveries have thus far been made.[6]

It has been found that the pre-pottery Neolithic town extended over an area of more than seven acres, and that its debris is more than forty feet in depth, indicating a very long occupation in this period. As a matter of fact it is now known that there were at least two distinct phases in the pre-pottery period. In the earlier of these two phases dwellings were built of elongated oval bricks which most characteristically have a pointed section on account of which the excavators describe them as "hog-backed." The rooms were generally circular and sunk somewhat beneath the surrounding level, with sloping entrance passages leading to them. The walls incline inwards which may indicate that the rooms were domed, and there are traces of timber or wattling which suggest that the roofs were made of

[3] M. Stekelis and G. Haas in IEJ 2 (1952), pp.15-47.

[4] M. Stekelis in IEJ 1 (1950-51), pp.1-19.

[5] Immanuel Ben-Dor in *Annals of Archaeology and Anthropology, issued by the Institute of Archaeology, University of Liverpool.* 23 (1936), pp.77-90.

[6] Kathleen M. Kenyon in PEQ 1952, pp.72f.; 1953, pp.83-88; 1954, pp.47-55; 1955, pp.109-112; 1956, pp.69-77; 1957, pp.101-107; and in *Scientific American.* 190 (1954), pp.76-82; Kathleen M. Kenyon and A. Douglas Tushingham in NGM 104 (1953), pp.853-870; A. Douglas Tushingham in BA 16 (1953), pp.50-55; 17 (1954), pp.98-102; Kathleen M. Kenyon, *Digging Up Jericho.* 1957.

plastered branches. It would not be difficult to think, therefore, that here were settlers only recently removed from nomadism who were endeavoring to reproduce in more permanent material the round tents to which they had been accustomed. Already in this earlier phase the town was defended by a strong stone wall with a ditch cut out of the solid rock in front of it and, at least at one point, an imposing tower behind it.[7]

In the later phase of the pre-pottery Neolithic, which is separated from the earlier by a distinct break in the stratigraphy, bricks of a different kind are used which the excavators describe as thumb-impressed and of a flattened-cigar shape. The houses now have rectangular rooms with wide entrances and, most characteristically, the walls and floors are covered with highly burnished plaster. In some of the houses rush mats had also been used on the floors, and these survived as a thin white film which showed the grain of the rushes and the curve of the coils. Most remarkable of all were a number of portrait skulls. These were actual human skulls on which the features of the face had been modeled in plaster. The eyes were inset with shell, with slits to represent the pupils. It is surmised that these may have been the heads of important leaders or venerated ancestors.[8]

Radiocarbon tests have been made of material from both the "plastered-floor" and the "hog-backed brick" phases of pre-pottery Neolithic Jericho, and have given dates around 5850 and around 6800 B.C. respectively, hence the beginnings of settlement at Jericho must have been as early as the beginning of the seventh millennium B.C.[9]

Even as the two phases of the pre-pottery Neolithic were separated by a clear stratigraphic break, so too there was a plain demarcation between the pre-pottery and the pottery levels at Jericho. There was a period of erosion and quarrying and then after that the first debris containing pottery is found. The pottery includes both coarse ware mixed with straw and finer vessels decorated with geometric designs, and both sorts appear together from the first. The architecture is also again different in this time, and the bricks have a distinctive bun-shaped or plano-convex form.[10]

Since the finest decorated pottery appears from the first at Jericho,

[7] Kenyon in PEQ 1956, pp.69-72.
[8] Kenyon in PEQ 1953, pp.86f.; 1954, pp.48f.; 1955, pp.110f.; 1956, pp.72-74.
[9] Kenyon in PEQ 1956, pp.74-76; 1957, p.105.
[10] Kenyon in PEQ 1953, pp.84f.

the making of pottery must have begun at other places and been introduced at Jericho by those who were already familiar with it, and we have already noted that at Mugharet Abu Usba and Sha‘ar ha-Golan pottery was made at what seem to be very early times. Also at Abu Ghosh, ten miles west of Jerusalem, finely polished axes, hatchets, sickles, and other stone objects attest the existence of a small community whose chief occupations were tilling and harvesting, and there pottery was found which is very similar to that found at Jericho.[11]

While Jericho shows the existence of relatively excellent accommodations for human life, it is probable that during the Stone Age many people still lived in caves even as some inhabitants of Palestine have done until modern times. At Gezer a number of caves in which people of the Stone Age dwelt were explored by R. A. S. Macalister.[12] Some of these were natural, some had been enlarged, and others had been cut out of the soft limestone. In size they varied from eighteen to forty feet in diameter and the roofs were usually very low, the entrance in most cases being through a hole in the roof. Rude drawings on the walls show an animal among reeds, shot by an arrow, and a man plowing with a pair of oxen or buffaloes. At Jerusalem under ancient Zion there is a large natural cave which originally was entered through a sort of rock funnel. Those who dwelt in it lived at one end and buried their dead at the other, while a rough pit in the floor served as the place where pottery was made.[13]

Across in Transjordan we find prehistoric rock-drawings, including representations of the ox and the ibex, which probably come from the Middle Stone Age,[14] and also menhirs and dolmens, which quite likely date from the Late Stone Age. The latter are megalithic monuments in which huge stones are placed in an upright position as monoliths or arranged to form a chamber covered by a flat capstone. These are believed to have been burial monuments in most cases and to have belonged to pastoral peoples who ranged across these regions.[15]

[11] Jean Perrot in *Syria*. 29 (1952), pp.119-145; cf. in IEJ 2 (1952), pp.73-81.

[12] Macalister, *The Excavation of Gezer*. I (1912), pp.72-152.

[13] J. Garrow Duncan, *Digging Up Biblical History*. 1931, I, pp.14-17.

[14] Nelson Glueck, *The Other Side of the Jordan*. 1940, pp.45-49. For Stone Age exploration in Jordan see also F. E. Zeuner in PEQ 1957, pp.17-54.

[15] Albright, *From the Stone Age to Christianity*, pp.95f.; Edwin C. Broome, Jr., in JBL 59 (1940), pp.479-497.

THE CHALCOLITHIC AGE, c.4500-c.3000 B.C.

As in the countries hitherto studied, so also in Palestine the Stone Age was followed by a period in which flint still was used extensively but in which copper also was employed. This was the Chalcolithic period to which it will be remembered the cultures of Tell Halaf in Mesopotamia (p. 16) and Badari in Egypt (p. 79) belonged. As in the neighboring lands, the first appearance of copper in Palestine was probably about 4500 B.C.

At Jericho Level VIII in the Garstang excavations is considered to belong to the Early Chalcolithic period, perhaps toward the end of the fifth millennium.[16]

In recent investigation at Tell Abu Matar near Beersheba many copper objects were found along with flint implements, handmade pottery, and human and animal figurines. Four levels of occupation were recognized, the first two of which were remarkable for the subterranean dwellings which were used. These were dug around the summit of a hill, connected in groups by tunnels, and entered by shafts or galleries. In Level IV there were rectangular houses built of brick or earth on foundations of stone. In this last stage the culture of Tell Abu Matar was similar to the Ghassulian, next to be mentioned.[17]

The Ghassulian culture takes its name from the site of its first discovery, Teleilat Ghassul, just north of the Dead Sea and not far from Jericho. The pottery of this period was improved in technique and more varied in form, simple painted designs being common. At Teleilat Ghassul the houses were made of mud brick and the plastered inner surfaces of some were adorned with amazing mural paintings. Among the frescoes which survive are intricate and elaborate geometric patterns, figures now almost destroyed but apparently representing a seated god and goddess, and a well-preserved painting of a bird executed in a most naturalistic and lifelike way.[18] In date the Ghassulian culture is considered to represent the Middle Chalcolithic period and to fall in the first half of the fourth millennium, corresponding approximately to the time of the Amratian culture in Egypt and that of 'Ubaid in Mesopotamia.[19]

[16] Albright, *The Archaeology of Palestine*, pp.65f.

[17] J. Perrot in IEJ 5 (1955), pp.17-40, 73-84, 167-189; and in *Syria*. 34 (1957), pp.1-38.

[18] *Teleilât Ghassûl, compte rendu des fouilles de l'Institut Biblique Pontifical.* I, 1929-1932, by Alexis Mallon, Robert Koeppel, and René Neuville. 1934; II, 1932-1936, by Robert Koeppel. 1940; cf. Nelson Glueck in BASOR 97 (Feb. 1945), pp.10f.

[19] Albright, *The Archaeology of Palestine*, p.66.

Probably a little later than the latest level at Teleilat Ghassul are the remains, including stone buildings and good pottery, found at Khirbet el-Bitar near Beersheba. A Carbon 14 analysis of charcoal from a sealed pit, probably a granary, at Khirbet el-Bitar yielded a date of 3325 B.C. with a margin of error of 150 years in either direction.[20] At Jericho, also, there are tombs which belong to about this time, that is to the Late Chalcolithic period. A piece of burned wood from one of these has given a date, by the radiocarbon method, of 3260 B.C. plus or minus 110 years.[21]

The first clay lamps in Palestine also belong to the fourth millennium B.C. and are simply small bowls with the wick laid over the edge. Later, by the Hyksos period, the rim is pinched together at one place to make a groove to hold the wick.

THE EARLY BRONZE AGE, c.3000-c.2000 B.C.

By somewhere around 3000 B.C. metal had displaced stone as the dominant material for tools and weapons in Palestine and the Bronze Age was ushered in. It is customary to divide this era into three periods of which the Early Bronze Age is dated from around 3000 to around 2000 B.C. This corresponds approximately to the Early Dynastic period in Sumer and the succeeding empire of Sargon in Akkad and to the time of the first half-dozen or more dynasties in Egypt. As far as material culture is concerned, Palestine at this time was but an outlying and destitute part of Syria, and nothing like the magnificence of the First Dynasty of Ur or of the Pyramid Age is to be found. The cities were often on low hills and fortified with strong walls, but their buildings were usually constructed rather crudely as compared with the architecture of Mesopotamia and Egypt. The pottery likewise is poorer than that of the neighboring lands, although made in some cases with considerable excellence. No writing has been found as yet in the Early Bronze Age in Palestine proper, but at Byblus on the Syrian coast a number of syllabic inscriptions on copper have been discovered which date probably from the late third millennium B.C.[22]

The earliest sanctuaries which have been discovered in Palestine belong to this age and include examples at Megiddo, Jericho, and Ai. In the case of the temple at Ai there were two main rooms, the first

[20] M. Dothan in IEJ 3 (1953), pp.262f.; 6 (1956), pp.112-114.
[21] Kenyon in PEQ 1954, p.67; 1955, p.113.
[22] W. F. Albright in *The Haverford Symposium on Archaeology and the Bible*, p.13.

of which was approached by a ramp, and contained ledges perhaps for the purpose of holding offerings. Through a narrow door access was gained to the inner room, where behind a partition stood the altar. Bones of birds, fowls, and lambs were found in the ashes on the ground.[23]

Since a number of the cities known to have been founded in the Early Bronze Age, such as Ai and Beth-shemesh, have names which are probably or certainly Semitic, it is indicated that there were Semitic-speaking peoples in Palestine in this period.[24]

In Transjordan an important civilization flourished between the twenty-third and twentieth centuries B.C. A long line of settlements existed along the main north-south track through central Transjordan and the fertile plateau lands of the country were employed for agriculture.[25]

THE MIDDLE BRONZE AGE, c.2000-c.1500 B.C.

The Middle Bronze Age is dated in Palestine from around 2000 to around 1500 B.C. and includes, according to our reckoning, the time of Abraham's migration as well as the period of Hammurabi and his predecessors and successors in Mesopotamia and the time of the Hyksos invasion of Egypt. The Hyksos must have moved through Palestine and Transjordan on their way into Egypt, and after their expulsion from that land they remained in Palestine at least until the time of Thutmose III. Their presence in Palestine is indicated by the appearance of a new type of fortification, namely great rectangular camps surrounded by massive sloping ramparts of packed earth, and doubtless used to shelter the horses and chariots which were introduced into Palestine as well as Egypt at this time.

According to the Old Testament Amorites were already in Palestine when Abraham came (Genesis 14:13) as well as later when the children of Israel invaded the land (Amos 2:9). The word Amorite is evidently related to Sumerian Martu and Akkadian Amurru which, in the first place, simply meant "West." Thus in the same passage in which Gudea tells of bringing cedar wood from Mount Amanus which was in northern Syria (cf. above p. 49), he also speaks of

---

[23] Millar Burrows, *What Mean These Stones?* 1941, p.200.

[24] Moscati, *I predecessori d'Israele*, pp.28-40; and in JBR 24 (1956), pp.246f.

[25] Nelson Glueck, *The Other Side of the Jordan*, pp.114-125; and in BASOR 122 (Apr. 1951), pp.14-18. See AASOR XIV, pp.1-113, XV, XVIII-XIX, XXV-XXVIII, for Glueck's *Explorations in Eastern Palestine*. I (1934), II (1935), III (1939), IV, Part I, Text, Part II, Pottery Notes and Plates (1951).

obtaining great blocks of alabaster from the mountains of Martu,[26] doubtless meaning the West and referring to some region not far from that of Amanus. In the Amarna letters Amurru is definitely a geographical district in Syria and also a political state, ruled at the time by Abdi-Ashirta.[27] Thus it seems probable that a term which at first simply meant the West in general, later became the designation of a specific political region in the West, and from that came to be applied in the form Amorite to the peoples of Syria and Palestine.[28]

There must also have been Hittites in Palestine during the Middle Bronze Age. In Genesis 23, Hebron is described as in possession of the Hittites at the time when Abraham purchased the cave of Machpelah there as a burial place. The traditional site of this famous cave is in a large enclosure at Hebron known as the Haram el-Khalil, Arabic *khalil* meaning "friend" and referring to Abraham under this designation which is familiar in the Bible and the Qur'an.[29] From the nature of its stonework the wall of this enclosure was probably built by Herod the Great. Within is a church, probably originally of Byzantine date, rebuilt by the Crusaders, and finally remade into a mosque. Since the entrance to the cave is within the mosque, it is quite inaccessible to research.[30] The legal code of the ancient Hittites has been found at Boghazköy in Asia Minor, capital of the Hittite Empire from 1800 to 1200 B.C., and a comparison of its regulations about real estate with Genesis 23 shows that the biblical account corresponds accurately with Hittite law and custom.[31]

In Ezekiel 16:3,45 Jerusalem is described as a Canaanite city founded and built by a combination of the Amorites and Hittites: "Your origin and your birth are of the land of the Canaanites; your father was an Amorite, and your mother a Hittite."

An important city of the time of the patriarchs was Gerar (Genesis 20-21, 26). The Valley of Gerar is probably the present Wadi esh-Shari'ah, between Beersheba and Gaza, and Gerar may be identified with Tell Abu Hureira, a site on the edge of that wadi where abundant sherds of the Middle Bronze Age have been found.[32]

---

[26] ANET p.269.   [27] KAT No.60 = MTAT No.60, line 8.

[28] Moscati, *I predecessori d'Israele*, pp.79f.,104f.,125f.; and in JBR 24 (1956), pp.249-252.

[29] II Chronicles 20:7; Isaiah 41:8; James 2:23; Qur'an 4:125.

[30] L. H. Vincent and E. J. H. Mackay, *Hébron, le Ḥaram el-Khalîl, sépulture des patriarches.* 2 vols. 1923; Eric F. F. Bishop in JBR 16 (1948), pp.94-99; C. F. Arden-Close in PEQ 1951, pp.69-77.

[31] Manfred R. Lehmann in BASOR 129 (Feb. 1953), pp.15-18.

[32] Y. Aharoni in IEJ 6 (1956), pp.26-32.

In general the cities of the Middle Bronze Age were powerfully fortified—walls, towers, and moats being employed. Some of the walls were constructed in a type of masonry known as Cyclopean which employed huge irregularly shaped blocks of stone and filled the spaces between them with small stones. The potter's wheel, which had been introduced in the Early Bronze Age, was in general use, and good pottery is characteristic of the time.

We know a Canaanite shrine of this period which stood on the slope of Mount Gerizim above Shechem, and consisted of a small central court surrounded on all four sides by chambers. Also three buildings were found at Megiddo which are to be dated around 1900 B.C. and probably were used for sacred purposes. In each of these a porch with end walls gave access to a single large room, off which in at least two instances a smaller room opened. The three buildings stood in connection with a circular structure ascended by a flight of steps, which evidently was a sacrificial altar of unique form.[33]

It must also have been in the Middle Bronze Age that the catastrophic destruction of Sodom and Gomorrah (Genesis 19:24-28) took place. A careful survey of the literary, geological, and archeological evidence points to the conclusion that the infamous "cities of the valley" (Genesis 19:29) were in the area which now is submerged beneath the slowly rising waters of the southern part of the Dead Sea, and that their ruin was accomplished by a great earthquake, probably accompanied by explosions, lightning, ignition of natural gas, and general conflagration.[34]

In the Negeb in cultivable valleys and along routes of travel there were many settlements in the first part of the Middle Bronze Age, as has been shown by recent archeological exploration.[35] Here, however, as also in Transjordan, about 1900 B.C. there was a break in sedentary occupation as the people for some reason ceased living in towns and returned to nomadic life. Not until the Iron Age, about 1200 B.C., was there again extensive settlement in the Negeb and Transjordan.[36]

The city of Dothan figures in this period in the story of Joseph (Genesis 37:17) and is also listed by Thutmose III among places

[33] Gordon Loud in *The Illustrated London News*. Nov. 25, 1939, p.794.
[34] J. Penrose Harland in BA 5 (1942), pp.17-32; 6 (1943), pp.41-54.
[35] Nelson Glueck in BASOR 131 (Oct. 1953), pp.6-15; 137 (Feb. 1955), pp.10-22; 138 (Apr. 1955), pp.7-29; 142 (Apr. 1956), pp. 17-35; and in BA 18 (1955), pp.2-9.
[36] Glueck in BA 18 (1955), p.9; BASOR 142 (Apr. 1956), p.21.

he captured.[37] It is identified with Tell Dotha sixty miles north of Jerusalem. Excavations conducted there since 1953 by Professor Joseph P. Free of Wheaton College have revealed eleven levels of successive occupation from Early Bronze to Iron II. Middle Bronze Age pottery attests the existence of the city in the patriarchal period and the time of Joseph. The skeleton of a child, accompanied by Middle Bronze pottery, was found under the corner of a stone wall and raises the question whether this was a foundation sacrifice.[38]

Toward the end of the Middle Bronze Age pottery was being decorated much more frequently with geometric designs and with pictures of birds, fishes, and animals. Particularly notable was the work of an unknown vase-painter of about the sixteenth century whose products were found by Flinders Petrie at Tell el-'Ajjul a few miles from Gaza, and whose animal paintings were executed in a sensitive and beautiful way.[39]

Down in the peninsula of Sinai a number of inscriptions have been found which are probably to be dated at the end of the Middle or beginning of the Late Bronze Age, about 1500 B.C. These are written on monuments and rocks at Serabit el-Khadem, only about fifty miles from the traditional site of Mount Sinai. They were discovered in 1904-1905 by Flinders Petrie, have been published by Alan H. Gardiner and T. Eric Peet, and were restudied in 1948 by W. F. Albright as a member of the University of California African Expedition.[40]

In distinction from the properly so-called Sinaitic inscriptions which consist of a large number of Nabatean inscriptions dating from the first several centuries A.D. these are known as the proto-Sinaitic inscriptions. The script seems to be founded upon Egyptian hieroglyphic, but is actually alphabetic in character. There are ancient turquoise mines in this region which were worked by the Egyptians, and the inscriptions are thought to have been written by Semitic people whose home was in Egypt, perhaps around Tanis, who were laborers in the Egyptian mines. The inscriptions contain appeals to deities and overseers to provide offerings on behalf of

[37] ANET p.242.
[38] Joseph P. Free in BASOR 131 (Oct. 1953), pp.16-20; 135 (Oct. 1954), pp.14-20; 139 (Oct. 1955), pp.3-9; BA 19 (1956), pp.43-48.
[39] W. F. Albright in AJSL 55 (1938), pp.337-359; W. A. Heurtley in QDAP 8 (1939), pp.21-37.
[40] Petrie, *Researches in Sinai*. 1906, pp.129-132; Gardiner and Peet, *The Inscriptions of Sinai*, 2d ed. rev. by Jaroslav Černý. 2 vols. 1952-55; Albright in BASOR 109 (Feb. 1948), pp.5-20; 110 (Apr. 1948), pp.6-22.

deceased persons. The script is now considered to be "normal alphabetic Canaanite" of this period,[41] containing most of the letters later found in Hebrew and Phoenician, out of which ultimately grew the Greek, Latin, and English alphabets.[42]

THE LATE BRONZE AGE, c.1500-c.1200 B.C.

The Late Bronze Age in Palestine covers the years from around 1500 to around 1200 B.C. and corresponds to the days of the Kassites in Babylonia and the Hittites at Boghazköy and the time of Thutmose III, Amenhotep IV, and Ramses II in Egypt. One of the interesting discoveries belonging to this period is that of an actual potter's workshop, which was found in a cave at Lachish (Tell ed-Duweir). The workshop still contained the stone seat on which the potter sat, a limestone pivot on which no doubt the potter's wheel turned, and sherds, pebbles, shells, and a bone point, all of which had been used for smoothing, burnishing, and incising the vessels.[43]

Mycenaean pottery also was imported into Palestine by sea at this time. Excavations in 1932-1933 at Tell Abu Hawam, near modern Haifa, have shown that between 1400 and 1200 B.C. this place probably was an important port for the reception of such wares.[44]

IRON I, c.1200-c.900 B.C.

The beginning of the Iron Age in Palestine is dated around 1200 B.C. Iron was known before this, as is shown by a steel battle-axe of about 1400 B.C. found at Ras Shamra, but it took the place of bronze only gradually.[45] As far as the Israelites were concerned, the Philistines managed to maintain a monopoly of the importing and forging of iron until the reign of Saul (I Samuel 13:19-22).[46] It is interesting to note that in stating the charge made by the Philistines for sharpening plowshares and mattocks I Samuel 13:21 uses the word pim (RSV). At one time quite unknown, this word has been found on small stone weights in Palestine. The name of the weight was evidently the expression of a price, as was the case also with the shekel.[47]

[41] Albright in BASOR 110 (Apr. 1948), pp.13,22.
[42] Martin Sprengling, *The Alphabet, Its Rise and Development from the Sinai Inscriptions*. OIC 12, 1931; John W. Flight in *The Haverford Symposium on Archaeology and the Bible*, pp.115-118; David Diringer, *The Alphabet*. 1948, pp.199-202; G. R. Driver, *Semitic Writing*. rev. ed. 1954, pp.94-98,140-144,194f.
[43] Burrows, *What Mean These Stones?* p.163.
[44] R. W. Hamilton in QDAP 3 (1934), pp.74-80; 4 (1935), pp.1-69.
[45] Burrows, *What Mean These Stones?* p.158.
[46] W. F. Albright in AASOR 4 (1922-23), p.17.
[47] E. J. Pilcher in PEFQS 1914, p.99.

It is customary to divide the Iron Age into three periods of which the first is from around 1200 to around 900 B.C. This is known as Iron I. This period includes the time when Tiglath-pileser I was beginning to raise Assyria toward world power and when the kings of the Twentieth and Twenty-first Dynasties were allowing Egypt to slip into decline.

IRON II, c.900-c.600 B.C.

The second period is Iron II around 900 to around 600 B.C. In these years the world trembled before the power of Assyria, and Palestine felt the tramp of the armies of Shalmaneser III, Sargon II, and Sennacherib, while the continuing decline of Egyptian power was only slightly relieved by the exploits of such kings as Sheshonk I and Taharqo.

IRON III, c.600-c.300 B.C.

The third period is Iron III and is dated from around 600 to around 300 B.C. During these centuries the New Babylonian and Persian Empires followed each other swiftly on the stage of world history, while Egypt enjoyed a brief renaissance under Psamtik I and his successors and then bowed to Persian power. But before the close of the period all the world was ruled by Alexander the Great.[48]

2. EXCAVATIONS AND DISCOVERIES RELATING TO ISRAELITE TIMES

THE COMING OF THE ISRAELITES

IF OUR earlier reckoning (p. 120) was correct it was not far from the middle of the thirteenth century B.C. or near the beginning of the Iron Age that the children of Israel came into the promised land. Is any light cast upon their coming by archeological evidences in Transjordan and Palestine?

To some extent we can trace the probable course of the Israelites in their journey from Egypt to Palestine. The name of the wilderness and the mount where the law was given was Sinai according to J (Exodus 19:18, 20, etc.) and P (Exodus 19:1, etc.; Numbers 10:12;

[48] The later archeological periods in Palestine are the Hellenistic (c.300-63 B.C.), Roman (63 B.C.-A.D. 323), Byzantine (323-636), Arabic (636-1517), and Turkish (1517-1918). For tables of archeological periods in Palestine with more detailed subdivisions and, in some cases, slightly varying dates, see Glueck, *Explorations in Eastern Palestine*, IV, i, p. XIX; G. E. Wright in BA 15 (1952), p. 18 n.1. For new subdivisions in the Iron Age see Y. Aharoni and Ruth Amiran in IEJ 8 (1958), pp.171-184.

33:16) although in other sources (Exodus 3:1; 33:6 [E]; Deuteronomy 1:2, 6, 19; 4:10, etc.) "the mountain of God" is called Horeb. At least since Byzantine times Christian tradition has placed the giving of the law somewhere in the lofty granite range of Sinai in the south central part of the peninsula of Sinai (cf. p. 434), and this tradition may well be correct. The range of Sinai is an impressive mass of mountains, dominated by three peaks, all of which might be enclosed within a circle twenty-five miles in diameter. The three peaks are known today as Jebel Serbal (6,759 feet), Jebel Musa or "Mountain of Moses" (7,519 feet) and Jebel Catherine (Katerina) (8,551 feet), the latter two being side by side and the first named farther distant. Geologically speaking, the crystalline masses of these mountains appear to have loomed up here practically unchanged since the oldest times. Encircled by the desert, their towering cliffs, stupendous precipices, and magnificent summits form a wild and imposing scene.[1]

From the wilderness of Sinai the Israelites journeyed by many stages to Ezion-geber (Numbers 33:16-35 [P]). Ezion-geber probably is to be identified with Tell Kheleifeh at the head of the Gulf of Aqabah, which is the site where Solomon later built a port city and factory town (p. 181). As far as is known from excavations there, no city existed at Tell Kheleifeh at the time of the Exodus, but what is meant is that the Israelites stopped at the place where the city later was established.[2]

From Ezion-geber the Israelites came to Kadesh or Kadesh-barnea in the wilderness of Zin (Numbers 20:1; 33:36f.; Deuteronomy 1:19) and apparently made their headquarters there for some considerable time.[3] Miriam died and was buried there (Numbers 20:1b) and from there the spies were sent to view the promised land (Numbers 13:21-26; Deuteronomy 1:19-25). The wilderness of Zin has been explored by C. Leonard Woolley and T. E. Lawrence and the probable location of Kadesh-barnea discussed in the light of their ex-

[1] F. E. Hoskins in NGM 20 (1909), pp.1021f.; Karl Baedeker, *Palestine and Syria*. 5th ed. 1912, pp.196,206,208.

[2] Ezion-geber is connected with Elath in Deuteronomy 2:8 and is said to be beside Eloth in I Kings 9:26. The exact connection between the two is obscure but perhaps in its later history Ezion-geber was called Elath or Eloth.

[3] According to Numbers 20:14 (JE) they still were encamped at Kadesh in their fortieth year, just previous to making the circuit of Edom. Deuteronomy 1:46 says that they "abode in Kadesh many days" but seems to imply that they spent the last thirty-eight years of their wanderings in compassing Mount Seir and coming to the brook Zered (Deuteronomy 2:1, 14). The total of forty years may, however, be a conventional figure.

periences. Largely because of the similarity of names, Kadesh-barnea has been traditionally identified with Ain Kadeis. But Woolley and Lawrence found Ain Kadeis only an obscure water-hole, "too small to water the flocks of other than the few poor families who live near it, and . . . too remote from all roads to come to the notice of such Arab guides as live at any distance." They think, however, that the Israelites may have come upon the valley of Kadeis first and have extended its name to the whole district as far as Kossaima. This larger area would have been a very likely place for the Israelites to abide. The Kossaima Plain is relatively extensive and fertile, and enjoys the proximity of a strong though not easily found spring known as Ain el-Guderat, "The Spring of the Earthenware Kettles." Strategically, this district agrees well with what is known of Kadesh-barnea, for roads run out to north, south, east, and west. The road to the south runs to Elath or Ezion-geber. The Darb el-Shur or "Way of the Wilderness of Shur" runs westward directly to Egypt and may have accentuated the longings for a return thither (cf. Numbers 14:4). Northward the same road runs to Hebron, whither the men went to spy out the land. Eastward other roads lead into the Wadi el-Arabah, the great valley which runs from the Gulf of Aqabah to the Dead Sea, and to Jebel Harun, the traditional Mount Hor, "by the border of the land of Edom," where Aaron died (Numbers 20: 22-29; 33:38f.).[4] In the Wadi el-Arabah it has been possible to identify one of the points mentioned in the route of the Exodus, namely Punon (Numbers 33:42f.). The Arabs, who cannot pronounce the letter "P" and change it into either "B" or "F," still call the place Feinan.[5]

From Kadesh, Moses sent messengers to the king of Edom requesting permission for the Israelites to pass through the land: "Thus says your brother Israel . . . here we are in Kadesh, a city on the edge of your territory. Now let us pass through your land. . . . We will go along the King's Highway, we will not turn aside to the right hand or to the left, until we have passed through your territory" (Numbers 20:14, 16f.). These words presuppose that at that time a strong kingdom existed in Edom and that the land was traversed by the "king's highway." As we have noted (p. 145) there was a flourishing civilization in Transjordan in the Early Bronze Age. A main central highway ran from north to south through the land at that time

4 Woolley and Lawrence, *The Wilderness of Zin.* 1936, pp.70-88.
5 Glueck, *The Other Side of the Jordan*, p.27.

and is clearly traceable by the ruins of sites dated from the twenty-third to the twentieth centuries B.C. This was probably the line along which the eastern kings of Genesis 14 moved when they pushed the length of Transjordan and as far as El-paran, which may have been on the north shore of the Gulf of Aqabah. The same route was followed by the famous Trajan highway built by the Romans in the first part of the second century A.D. The Roman road was paved all the way from Aqabah to Bosrah and many sections of it still are comparatively intact. It was divided into two lanes with the middle line and the sides marked by raised stones. The modern highway constructed by the Government of Transjordan follows the old Roman road almost exactly. Thus the "king's highway" has a history from before the twentieth century B.C. to the twentieth century A.D.

But the Early Bronze Age civilization of Transjordan disappeared about 1900 B.C. (p. 147) and from then until upon the eve of the Iron Age there is a gap in the history of permanent sedentary occupation in that land. Not until the beginning of the thirteenth century did a new agricultural civilization appear belonging to the Edomites, Moabites, Ammonites, and Amorites.[6] Therefore the situation presupposed in Numbers 20:14-17 did not exist before the thirteenth century B.C. but did prevail from that time on exactly as reflected in the Bible. If the Israelites had come through southern Transjordan at any time within the preceding 600 years they would have found neither the Edomite nor the Moabite kingdoms in existence and only scattered nomads would have disputed their passage. But coming sometime in the thirteenth century as we have reason for believing they did, they found their way blocked at the outset by the well organized and well fortified kingdom of Edom. The high, comparatively fertile, and well watered plateau of Edom drops off precipitously on the south. At Khirbet Neqb Shtar on the southwestern corner of the plateau, at Khirbet Tawil Ifjeij on the eastern side, and at a series of other strategic points, the frontiers were guarded by fortresses whose ruins still are impressive. Many of them were so well located that their sites serve as major triangulation points for modern government surveys.

Thus when the ruler of Edom refused permission for the Israelites to traverse the land by the "king's highway" it became necessary for

---

[6] *ibid.*, pp.125-147; and in BA 10 (1947), pp.77-84. Discovery of a Middle Bronze Age tomb at Amman (G. Lankester Harding in PEFA 6 [1953], pp.14-26) may, however, require modification of the theory of the long interval in permanent settlement in Transjordan. See Olga Tufnell in PEQ 1958, p.150.

them to make their weary way around through the wilderness. It is written that when "they journeyed . . . to compass the land of Edom, . . . the soul of the people was much discouraged because of the way" (Numbers 21:4, ASV).

North of Edom was Moab. The boundary between the two countries was the Wadi Hesa, which runs into the lower corner of the Dead Sea. It is known in the Bible as the valley of Zered or the brook Zered, and the arrival of the Israelites at it is mentioned in Numbers 21:12. Moab stretched eastward from the Dead Sea to the desert and extended northward to the Wadi Mojib which is the biblical river Arnon. Like Edom, Moab was strongly fortified at strategic sites on the borders and in the interior. Therefore the Israelites had to continue to march "in the wilderness which is opposite Moab, toward the sunrise" (Numbers 21:11) until they reached "the other side of the Arnon" (Numbers 21:13). Beyond the Arnon (Wadi Mojib) lay the land of Gilead which was the territory of the Amorites. The king of the Amorites was Sihon, who had taken or retaken land from Moab and made Heshbon his capital city. From the River Arnon his land extended north to the River Jabbok (Judges 11:22) which is now the Wadi Zerqa. This wadi runs east from the Jordan and then turns south. The latter portion of the Wadi Zerqa, running approximately north and south, constituted the eastern border of Sihon's territory, beyond which was the kingdom of Ammon. North of the east-west stretch of the River Jabbok was the territory of King Og, which extended to the Wadi Yarmuk, not far below the Sea of Galilee. While the Israelites had laboriously to make the circuit of Edom and Moab they were able successfully to challenge Sihon and Og in battle and so to arrive at the Jordan Valley opposite Jericho (Numbers 21:21-35; 22:1; Deuteronomy 2:26-3:11).[7] Incidentally, Balaam who figures in the story at this point (Numbers 22:2-24:25) seems to have been a typical Babylonian diviner, and has been shown from parallels in Mesopotamian ritual to have proceeded with what was at the time quite an approved ceremony of divination.[8]

---

[7] In view of our date for these events at the end of the Late Bronze Age and near the beginning of the Iron Age it is interesting to note that King Og is reported to have had a bedstead of iron (Deuteronomy 3:11). The term is believed by some, however, to refer instead to a sarcophagus made of black basalt which has an iron content of about 20 per cent. S. R. Driver in ICC, *Deuteronomy*. 1895, pp.53f.

[8] Samuel Daiches in *Hilprecht Anniversary Volume*. 1909, pp.60-70; cf. W. F. Albright in JBL 63 (1944), p.231 n.141.

From the top of Pisgah (Deuteronomy 3:27), which was presumably a part of Mount Nebo (Deuteronomy 34:1), Moses looked upon the promised land and then died and was buried in the valley in the land of Moab (Deuteronomy 34:6). Mount Nebo is probably the present Jebel Neba, and Pisgah may be a lower and western summit of the same mountain now called Ras es-Siaghah. From these heights a very fine view is obtained of western Palestine. A steep trail leads down from the mount to the Ayun Musa or "Springs of Moses," overlooking which are the ruins of a fortress, the Khirbet Ayun Musa, that may have been in existence in the time of Moses.[9] There are also ruins not far away now known as Khirbet el-Mekhayyat which may be identified with the town of Nebo (Numbers 32:3, etc.),[10] while on the mountain itself are the remains of a Byzantine church.[11]

The Jordan River was crossed by the children of Israel at a point which is described in Joshua 3:16 as "opposite Jericho," which has traditionally been identified with the present ford known as el-Maghtas or el-Hajleh,[12] some two miles south of the Allenby Bridge. The crossing seems to have been made in the spring when the river was out of its banks (Joshua 3:15), but it is stated that at this particular time "the waters coming down from above stood and rose up in a heap far off, at Adam" (Joshua 3:16), and so the people went over on dry ground. The city of Adam may be identified with Tell ed-Damiyeh, some fifteen miles up the river. There are limestone cliffs there which could have been shaken into the river by an earthquake to dam it for a time completely. Such an event is reported to have shut off the flow of the Jordan for more than twenty hours as recently as 1927.[13]

GILGAL

After the crossing of the Jordan the Israelites camped in Gilgal (Joshua 5:9f.). The location of Gilgal has been difficult to establish although it was clearly in the vicinity of Jericho which has long

[9] Glueck, *The Other Side of the Jordan*, pp.143f.

[10] Sylvester J. Saller and Bellarmino Bagatti, *The Town of Nebo (Khirbet el-Mekhayyat), With a Brief Survey of Other Ancient Christian Monuments in Transjordan.* 1949.

[11] Sylvester J. Saller, *The Memorial of Moses on Mount Nebo.* 2 vols. 1941.

[12] Kraeling, *Rand McNally Bible Atlas*, p.134. This is also the traditional place of the baptism of Jesus (cf. below p.301).

[13] John Garstang, *Joshua Judges, The Foundations of Bible History.* 1931, pp.136f.; Kraeling, *Rand McNally Bible Atlas*, p.133.

been identified with Tell es-Sultan. The site has been sought both at en-Nitleh, three miles south of Tell es-Sultan, and at Khirbet el-Mefjir, one and one-quarter miles northeast of the same tell. Josephus states that the Israelites, after crossing the Jordan, went on fifty stadia and then pitched camp ten stadia from Jericho.[14] The location of en-Nitleh, twenty-six stadia from Tell es-Sultan, is not in harmony with these data, but the place of Khirbet el-Mefjir agrees almost exactly. Reckoning a Roman stadium at 607 feet, Khirbet el-Mefjir is 10.87 stadia from Tell es-Sultan, and fifty stadia from the el-Maghtas ford. In excavation at en-Nitleh in 1950 by James L. Kelso no remains earlier than the fourth century A.D. were found, but in soundings in one of several small tells at Khirbet el-Mefjir in 1955 by James Muilenburg many sherds were found indicating settlement there in the Iron I and Iron II periods. Therefore it seems probable that Gilgal was at or near Khirbet el-Mefjir.[15]

JERICHO

The chief city of strategic importance commanding the entrance to Canaan from the east was Jericho. As already indicated, the mound which represents the Old Testament site is now known as Tell es-Sultan. It rises above an oasis and a spring called Ain es-Sultan, which is the most abundant water supply in the vicinity. In the background the hills of the western highlands rise very sharply, and only a mile away the bold, 1,500-foot-high ridge called Jebel Kuruntul casts its shadow upon the city in the early afternoon. These were "the hills" to which Joshua's spies fled from Rahab's house (Joshua 2:22). Forbidding as the western barrier appears, it is actually cut by gorges which give access to the interior plateau of Palestine. Jericho's strategic significance lay in the fact that it guarded these passes.

The excavation of Jericho was first attempted by Professor Ernst Sellin and the Deutsche Orientgesellschaft in 1907-1909,[16] and was continued by Professor John Garstang in 1930-1936.[17] A portion of the mound as it appeared in the latter excavations is shown in the

[14] *Ant.* v, i, 4.
[15] Muilenburg in BASOR 140 (Dec. 1955), pp.11-27.
[16] Ernst Sellin and Carl Watzinger, *Jericho.* 1913.
[17] J. Garstang in *Annals of Archaeology and Anthropology, issued by the Institute of Archaeology, University of Liverpool.* 19 (1932), pp.3-22; 20 (1933), pp.3-42; 21 (1934), pp.99-136; 22 (1935), pp.143-168; 23 (1936), pp.67-76; J. and J. B. E. Garstang, *The Story of Jericho.* 1940.

foreground of Fig. 56, while in the background is the nearby oasis. Again, beginning in 1952, further excavations have been conducted by Kathleen M. Kenyon of the British School of Archaeology in Jerusalem.[18]

The remarkable discoveries in the Neolithic period have already been noted (pp. 140f.), and the existence of the city in Chalcolithic times as well (p. 143). In the Early Bronze Age Jericho was an important walled city which must have been attacked often by nomads trying to force their way into Palestine from the desert. The wall which defended the city was built of flat mud bricks on a foundation of rough stones, and Miss Kenyon found that it had been broken down and rebuilt no less than seventeen times. The tumbled bricks of its first collapse probably indicate destruction by an earthquake. On the last occasion it was still being reconstructed with marks of haste when it was burned in a great conflagration. This destruction may have been at the hands of invading Amorites at about 2100 B.C.[19]

Above the burned wall was a layer of silt with pottery of a new kind, and then scanty architectural remains. This suggests that the newcomers were nomads who at first did little more than camp on the site, and only later began to build poor houses for themselves. Tombs of this intermediate period were surprisingly large, however, and contained pots, daggers, and javelins. On a rock face in the shaft of one of these were several graffiti or rudely scratched drawings. Several show horned animals, probably goats, some of which seem to be browsing on trees, while two drawings represent men who hold square shields in their left hands and long shafts, evidently javelins, in the right. Presumably these picture the very nomads who brought the Early Bronze Age civilization of Jericho to an end.[20]

By probably about 1900 B.C. well-built houses and strong city walls are found again at Jericho. Not only the architecture but also the pottery, weapons, and burial customs indicate the arrival of a new people of a more advanced culture. In this period, which occupied most of the Middle Bronze Age, Jericho grew to the greatest size it ever attained. The defensive system was of a new sort with a

[18] Kenyon in PEQ 1952, pp.62-82; 1953, pp.81-95; 1954; pp.45-63; 1955, pp.108-117; 1956, pp.67-82; and in *Scientific American.* 190 (1954), pp.76-82; Kenyon and A. Douglas Tushingham in NGM 104 (1953), pp.853-870; A. Douglas Tushingham in BA 16 (1953), pp.46-67; 17 (1954), pp.98-104.

[19] PEQ 1952, pp.64-70; 1953, pp.88-90; 1954, pp.55f.; 1955, pp.114f.; 1956, p.77. For the destruction of the first wall by earthquake see PEQ 1952, pp.64,68.

[20] PEQ 1954, pp.56-58; 1956, p.78.

sloping ramp, commonly called a glacis, at the base of the city wall, presumably for defense against the chariotry which the Hyksos introduced at this time. Three phases of construction are distinguished: in the first two the steep ramp was covered with plaster; in the third there was also a stone revetment with mud-brick parapet at the foot of the slope.[21]

In the cemetery area at Jericho a number of Middle Bronze Age tombs have been explored, among them one group in particular, dating probably in the seventeenth century B.C., in which the objects placed with the deceased were in an amazing state of preservation. Almost perfectly intact although very fragile were wooden tables and stools, bowls and boxes, many with bone inlay, and baskets with toilet articles such as wooden combs and little boxes. There were also fragments of textiles, remains of rush mats, and many pottery vessels. Pomegranates and raisins were still recognizable, roast meat was preserved, and within some of the human skulls the desiccated brain was found, its convolutions plainly to be seen. In an endeavor to account for such remarkable preservation of organic material, F. E. Zeuner sampled the air in one tomb and found the concentration of carbon dioxide to be ten times as great as in the atmosphere outside. Since Jericho lies on a series of faults on the western side of the Jordan Valley and must have experienced a great many earthquakes, it is possible that natural gas came up through the faults and collected in the tombs to produce the result noted.[22]

Middle Bronze Age houses and storerooms, many of the latter containing jars full of corn, were found on the east side of the tell by both Professor Garstang and Miss Kenyon. The latest of these structures were destroyed by fire, and it is supposed that this was at a date shortly before the middle of the sixteenth century B.C. when the Egyptians expelled the Hyksos and reasserted their authority in Palestine.[23]

After this destruction at the end of the Middle Bronze Age, Jericho must have been rebuilt and again occupied during the Late Bronze Age, but according to the present understanding of the tell very little now remains there from this latter period. Just under the surface of the tell on the east side were the foundations of a wall together with a small patch of floor. On the floor was a small oven,

[21] PEQ 1952, pp.70f.; 1954, pp.58-60; 1956, pp.79f.

[22] Kenyon in PEQ 1952, p.74; 1953, pp.93f.; 1954, pp.62f.; 1955, p.116; 1956, p.81; Zeuner in PEQ 1955, pp.118-128.

[23] Kenyon in PEQ 1954, p.61; 1955, p.116; 1956, p.81.

and beside it a juglet of fourteenth century date.[24] Some other Late Bronze Age pottery was found by Garstang, and Kenyon dates it between 1400 and somewhat after 1350 B.C.[25] Otherwise whatever city stood at Jericho in the Late Bronze Age has, as far as present knowledge goes, simply disappeared in what Miss Kenyon calls the "tremendous denudation" of the upper strata of the tell.[26] In the areas excavated there is a gap in the remains until in the Iron Age when some materials, probably of the seventh century B.C., are found.[27] There is now, therefore, virtually no evidence at the site by which to try to determine at what date Joshua might have taken Jericho. There was a city there in the fourteenth century but since almost all of it has disappeared there could also have been a thirteenth century city which is completely lost.[28] If the walls of such a city did collapse before Joshua's forces it remains possible that an earthquake was the agency[29] since the geological situation of the city is conducive to such occurrences and, as we have noted, the first wall of the Early Bronze Age appears to have fallen by that very cause.

While much-to-be-desired evidence is therefore lacking at Jericho, in the case of the cities of Bethel, Lachish, Debir, and Hazor, we have evidence of their destruction within the thirteenth century B.C., which is in agreement with the hypothesis that the Israelite conquest was in progress at that time. These cities will be among those next to be considered.

AI AND BETHEL

The capture of Ai is described in Joshua chapters 7-8. Ai is identified with et-Tell, a site thirteen miles west and somewhat north of Jericho, and 3,200 feet higher in the hill country. The place was excavated between 1933 and 1935 by Mme. Judith Marquet-Krause and the remains of an important city of the Early Bronze Age were uncovered. This city was completely destroyed and abandoned about 2200 B.C., and the site was not occupied again except by a brief village settlement sometime between 1200 and 1000 B.C.[30] At the

---

[24] PEQ 1954, p.61.   [25] PEQ 1951, pp.120,133.   [26] PEQ 1952, p.71.
[27] PEQ 1952, p.71; 1953, p.91.
[28] PEQ 1954, p.61; cf. ADAJ 3 (1956), p.75. Although she points to this possibility, Kathleen Kenyon thinks it more probable that the latest Bronze Age occupation was in the third quarter of the fourteenth century and that it was at this time that Jericho fell to Joshua (*Digging Up Jericho*, pp.262f.).
[29] Garstang, *Joshua Judges, The Foundations of Bible History*, pp.144f., 404.
[30] Marquet-Krause, *Les fouilles de 'Ay (et-Tell) 1933-1935.* 2 vols. 1949. W. F. Albright in AJA 40 (1936), p.158; and in BASOR 118 (Apr. 1950), p.31.

time of the Israelite conquest, therefore, no city existed at this place. As a matter of fact, the Hebrew name Ai means "the Ruin."

The most probable explanation of the difficulty at this point lies in a confusion between Ai and Bethel. The site of the latter city is less than one and one-half miles distant from Ai, and is known now as Beitin. Excavations were conducted here by joint expeditions of the American School of Oriental Research in Jerusalem and the Pittsburgh-Xenia Theological Seminary under W. F. Albright in 1934 and under James L. Kelso in 1954 and following.[31] Bethel was found to have been occupied first after the destruction of the Early Bronze Age city of Ai and to have existed as a well-built town in the Middle and Late Bronze Ages. Sometime in the thirteenth century B.C. the city was consumed by a tremendous conflagration which left behind a solid mass of burned brick, ashes, and charred debris. There can be little doubt but that this destruction represents the conquest of the city by the children of Israel. In the Iron I period the town was rebuilt, presumably by the Israelites, and in a rude fashion as compared with the earlier city. In the sixth century B.C. Bethel was again destroyed by fire, probably by the Chaldeans, and afterward reoccupied in the Persian and Hellenistic periods.

It may be noted that in the book of Joshua no account is given of the capture of Bethel while, on the other hand, in the probably older account of Judges 1 the taking of Bethel by the house of Joseph is narrated (vv. 22-25) but nothing is said of Ai. Therefore it may be supposed that at a later date the tradition of the sack of Bethel was attached, erroneously but naturally, to the nearby and impressive ruins of Ai.[32]

GIBEON

Through the well-known stratagem of its emissaries related in Joshua 9, the city of Gibeon made peace with Israel. The location of this "great city," as it is called in Joshua 10:2, was at a place eight miles northwest of Jerusalem still known as el-Jib. Excavations were begun here in 1956 by the University Museum of the University of Pennsylvania, the Church Divinity School of the Pacific, and the American Schools of Oriental Research, under the direction of

[31] W. F. Albright in BASOR 56 (Dec. 1934), pp.2-15; James L. Kelso in BA 19 (1956), pp.36-43; BASOR 137 (Feb. 1955), pp.5-10; 151 (Oct. 1958), pp.3-8.

[32] W. F. Albright in BASOR 74 (Apr. 1939), pp.15-17; G. E. Wright in BA 3 (1940), p.36. For the valley of Achor (Joshua 7:24, etc.) see Frank M. Cross, Jr., and J. T. Milik in BASOR 142 (Apr. 1956), pp.5-17.

Professor James B. Pritchard of the Church Divinity School of the Pacific.

In the portions first explored of the large tell evidences were found of occupation in the Early and Middle Bronze Ages and again in Iron I and II. Some walls of the Iron I period were found together with three grain pits, and the great city wall of Iron II was partially traced. A sloping rock tunnel was cleared which probably belonged to the Iron II period. This led down ninety-six steps to a pool, into which through another tunnel the waters of a spring were led, thus providing safe access for the inhabitants of the city to their water supply. Elsewhere on the tell there was an enormous pool, thirty-six feet in diameter, and more than thirty feet deep, with a spiral staircase around the side. This, built perhaps around 1200 B.C., may have been the "pool of Gibeon" of II Samuel 2:13. In the debris which filled the pool were three jar handles bearing the name Gibeon in Hebrew characters of the eighth century B.C.; thus the identification of the site seems positive.[33]

LACHISH

One of the next cities to fall to the Israelites was Lachish as is told in Joshua 10:31f. The site of Lachish was sought first at Umm Lakis and then at Tell el-Hesy,[34] but finally was identified at Tell ed-Duweir.[35] Excavations were begun here by the Wellcome-Marston Archaeological Expedition in 1933, the work being directed by J. L. Starkey until his murder by brigands January 10, 1938, and continued thereafter by Charles H. Inge and Lankester Harding. It was found that the site had been occupied by a cave dwellers' settlement in the Early Bronze Age and thereafter by a whole series of cities. The city with which we are concerned at this point is the Lachish of the Late Bronze Age which was standing when the Israelites came.

One of the important features of Lachish at this time was the temple, which probably was constructed in its earliest form in the first part of the fifteenth century B.C. and was rebuilt at least twice thereafter.[36] The temple had walls of stone plastered with lime,

[33] James B. Pritchard in BA 19 (1956), pp.65-75; UMB 21 (1957), pp.3-26; 22 (1958), pp.12-24. The identification is questioned by Karl Elliger in ZDPV 73 (1957), pp.125-132.

[34] W. M. F. Petrie, Tell el-Hesy (Lachish). 1891; F. J. Bliss, A Mound of Many Cities. 1894.

[35] W. F. Albright in ZAW 6 (1929), p.3.

[36] Olga Tufnell, C. H. Inge, and L. Harding, Lachish II (Tell ed Duweir), The Fosse Temple. 1940.

the floor was of hard clay, and the roof was supported by wooden columns. A small vestibule gave access to the sanctuary proper, where there was a raised shrine on top of which presumably the cult statue or statues stood. At the base of the shrine was a small hearth, beside it was a pottery stand to hold a bowl for libation, and nearby was a niche for lamps. Benches running around three sides of the room provided a place for the laying of offerings, for the storage of which there were also a large bin and a back storeroom. Around the shrine and in the rubbish pits connected with the building were large quantities of bones of sheep, oxen, and other animals. Most of the bones were from the right foreleg, which corresponds to the prescription for sacrifice in Leviticus 7:32.[37]

One of the lion-hunt scarabs of Amenhotep III, commemorating his feat of killing 102 lions with his own hand during the first ten years of his reign, was found at Lachish and the continuation of Egyptian dominance until in the thirteenth century was indicated by the presence of a scarab of Ramses II. But the most important discovery for the fixing of the date when the Late Bronze Age city was destroyed, was that of a broken bowl on which had been written in Egyptian and apparently by an Egyptian tax collector a record of certain wheat deliveries. All of these were dated in the "year four" of a certain Pharaoh. The character of the script points to the time of Merneptah, and it is believed almost certain that he is the Pharaoh in question. The "year four," therefore, is to be referred to his reign and is equivalent to about 1221 B.C. Since the fragments of the bowl were found, all together, in the debris of the burned city, the bowl was doubtless broken at the very time when the city fell. The destruction of Lachish thus must have taken place just about 1221 B.C. and doubtless was the work of the Israelites just as it is stated in the Old Testament.[38]

There must also be mentioned the discovery, in the Late Bronze Age temple at Lachish, of a bowl and a jar on which were inscriptions written in an early type of Canaanite script. This script is identical with that of the proto-Sinaitic inscriptions found at Serabit

[37] G. Ernest Wright points out that such similarity between early Canaanite ritual and late priestly legislation in the Old Testament tends to support the claim that the substance of much of the ritual contained in the priestly document is very old and reflects practices of the Solomonic temple perhaps ultimately borrowed from the Canaanites (AJA 45 [1941], p.634).

[38] W. F. Albright in BASOR 68 (Dec. 1937), pp.23f.; 74 (Apr. 1939), pp.20-22; 132 (Dec. 1953), p.46; Raymond S. Haupert in BA 1 (1938), p.26.

el-Khadem (pp. 148f.). Other specimens of similar script also have come to light in Middle and Late Bronze Age levels at such Palestinian sites as Shechem (see below), Gezer, Tell el-Hesy, and Bethshemesh. The Lachish inscriptions together with these others constitute very important connecting links between the proto-Sinaitic and the earliest known Phoenician forms of the alphabet.[39]

DEBIR

Debir, earlier known as Kiriath-sepher, was another city taken by the Israelites (Joshua 10:38f.; 15:15-17; Judges 1:11-13). Kiriath-sepher is believed to be the mound now called Tell Beit Mirsim, thirteen miles southwest of Hebron. The excavation of Tell Beit Mirsim was carried out in 1926 and following years by a joint expedition of the Pittsburgh-Xenia Theological Seminary and the American School of Oriental Research at Jerusalem under the leadership of Melvin G. Kyle and William F. Albright.[40] A beautiful royal scarab of Amenhotep III was found which doubtless was used by the Egyptian official at Kiriath-sepher. This is clear evidence that in the reign of Amenhotep III Egypt was still in power here and the Israelites had not yet taken possession of the land. At the end of the Late Bronze Age there is a great burned layer and above it are Israelite remains. Thus the evidences here, too, point to the arrival of the Israelites and the destruction of the Canaanite city shortly before 1200 B.C.[41]

Among the interesting discoveries made at Tell Beit Mirsim was a household stela showing a Canaanite serpent goddess. She appears as a woman clad in a long robe and with a large snake coiling around her. Exactly the same kind of representation was found on a small limestone plaque at Shechem (Balatah) in 1934 by Dr. H. Steckeweh. This plaque also carried an inscription written in the early alphabetic script of Canaan.[42]

---

[39] Tufnell, Inge, and Harding, *Lachish II (Tell ed Duweir), The Fosse Temple*, pp.47-57; W. F. Albright in BASOR 58 (Apr. 1935), pp.28f.; 63 (Oct. 1936), pp.8-12; S. Yeivin in PEQ 1937, pp.180-193; Chester C. McCown, *The Ladder of Progress in Palestine*. 1943, pp.100-117.

[40] Albright in ZAW 6 (1929), pp.1-17; and in AASOR 12 (1930-31); 13 (1931-32), pp.55-128; 17 (1936-37); 21-22 (1941-43); M. G. Kyle, *Excavating Kirjath-Sepher's Ten Cities*. 1934.

[41] Kyle, *Excavating Kirjath-Sepher's Ten Cities*, p.192; Albright in AASOR 17 (1936-37), p.79.

[42] Albright in AASOR 17 (1936-37), Pls. 21a, 22; pp.42f.

HAZOR

In Joshua 11 a great victory of Joshua over a coalition of kings at the waters of Merom is described, after which it is stated (11:10-13) that he turned back and took the city of Hazor, the head of all those kingdoms, and burned it with fire. The prominence of Hazor is confirmed by its appearance in other ancient sources including the Egyptian execration texts of the nineteenth century[43] and the Amarna letters of the fourteenth century B.C.[44] The ancient city has been identified with Tell el-Qedah in the plain of Huleh, some five miles southwest of Lake Huleh and nine miles north of the Sea of Galilee. The site comprises a more-or-less oval-shaped tell nearly 2,000 feet in length and, north of this mound, a very large rectangular plateau about 2,300 feet wide and 3,300 feet long. On the west side this plateau was fortified by a wall of beaten earth which still stands over forty-five feet high, and on the other naturally steep sides there was also a protective glacis. The latter area was called a "camp enclosure" by John Garstang, who made soundings there in 1928. Because he found no Mycenaean pottery which otherwise occurs in northern Palestine about 1400-1200 B.C.,[45] Garstang concluded that Hazor must have been destroyed about 1400 B.C., the same date he gave for the fall of Jericho.[46]

Beginning in 1955 excavations have been conducted at Hazor by the Hebrew University—James A. de Rothschild Expedition under the direction of Yigael Yadin.[47] Several areas have been excavated on the tell and on the rectangular plateau. Area A on the tell was penetrated through four levels of occupation of the Iron II period. Uppermost were the remains of a small town of the end of the eighth and beginning of the seventh centuries B.C.; beneath that a city destroyed by fire in the second half of the eighth century, probably by Tiglath-pileser III in 732 B.C.; then a city with pottery of the ninth and eighth centuries; and a town constructed perhaps in the time of Ahab in the third quarter of the ninth century. Area B on

---

[43] ANET p.329 n.8.

[44] KAT Nos.148,227,228 = MTAT Nos.148,227,228; MTAT No.256a.

[45] cf. above p.149; Hamilton in QDAP 4 (1935), p.11.

[46] Garstang, *Joshua Judges, The Foundations of Bible History*, pp.184f., 382f., cf. 146.

[47] Yadin in BA 19 (1956), pp.2-11; IEJ 6 (1956), pp.120-125; 7 (1957), pp.118-123; *Archaeology.* 10 (1957), pp.83-92; BA 20 (1957), pp.34-47; 21 (1958), pp.30-47; *The James A. de Rothschild Expedition at Hazor, Hazor I, An Account of the First Season of Excavations, 1955.* 1958; cf. W. F. Albright in BASOR 150 (Apr. 1958), pp.21-25; Yadin in IEJ 8 (1958), pp.1-14.

the highest point of the tell at the west was defended with a series of citadels which were traced down from the Hellenistic period to about the ninth century B.C.

The areas explored on the rectangular plateau showed that, at least at these points, this was not just a camp enclosure but a city with well-constructed houses and drainage systems. In Area C four strata were explored. Stratum I, completely uncovered, had dwellings with rooms opening onto a cobbled courtyard, and on the floors was Mycenaean as well as locally-made pottery. The stratum, in which two phases were recognized, was dated by the Mycenaean pottery to the Late Bronze Age and the thirteenth century B.C. Strata II, III, and IV, explored by trench, revealed earlier settlements of the Late and Middle Bronze Ages, as far back as the Hyksos period. Nearby, at the foot of the beaten-earth wall, were two temples, one above the other, of the Late Bronze Age, the upper of the same date as the lower phase of the dwellings. In Areas D and E there were also dwellings, cisterns, and tombs, which confirmed the picture of the rectangular plateau as containing a series of cities dating back to the Hyksos period and coming to an end in the thirteenth century B.C. A small jar fragment of the thirteenth century from Area D has two letters of the proto-Sinaitic alphabet; the script is like that on the Lachish bowl of about the same date (p. 162).

Hazor was thus in existence at the time which seems most probable for the Israelite invasion, the middle of the thirteenth century B.C. With its very large area, justifying an estimate of 40,000 inhabitants, it must have been a place of great prominence exactly as represented in the book of Joshua. Since the last city on the rectangular plateau was probably destroyed in the second half of the thirteenth century, it may well be that it was at the hands of Joshua that it fell, although of that specific fact there is, at least as yet, no actual proof.

Yet another city occupied by the Israelites was Beth-zur, according to Joshua 15:58, although no description of its capture is given. Excavation was inaugurated at this site in 1931 and resumed in 1957.[48] The city was formidably fortified in the Middle Bronze Age but was evidently abandoned during the fourteenth and thirteenth centuries and only reoccupied at the beginning of the Iron Age, or around 1200 B.C. Also mentioned in Joshua 15:27 is the city of Beth-

[48] O. R. Sellers, *The Citadel of Beth-zur*. 1933; and in BA 21 (1958), pp.71-76; Robert W. Funk in BASOR 150 (Apr. 1958), pp.8-20.

pelet. Petrie believed that he found Beth-pelet at Tell Fara, south-east of Gaza,[49] but Albright thinks that this is more probably ancient Sharuhen.[50]

In the case, therefore, of at least some cities which the Israelites are said in the Bible to have captured, notably including Bethel, Lachish, Debir, and Hazor, there is evidence upon the site of destruction of the city at the end of the Late Bronze Age or shortly before 1200 B.C. The identification of this event with the conquest by the children of Israel seems very probable.

It is significant, also, to note that at the beginning of the Iron Age the houses and fortifications of Palestine are considerably poorer than before. Likewise the pottery shows in general a great deterioration in quality, and is little ornamental. This sudden drop in the cultural level fits well with the invasion of the Israelites from the desert, any cultivation of the arts among whom would have suffered during the long years in the wilderness. The characteristic city walls as built by the Israelites were only five, six, or seven feet in width. Perhaps because with their looser patriarchal form of society there was no systematic coercion of the individual and it was not possible to make the people submit to the prolonged and difficult labor of constructing a massive city wall.[51] It is also of interest to note how, as may be seen very clearly at Bethel for example, in the earlier city levels there are many Canaanite cult objects, but at the point believed to represent the Israelite conquest these suddenly disappear, presumably in accordance with the avoidance of idols enjoined upon the children of Israel.[52]

Viewed in its entirety the work of Joshua was evidently very successful and it could be said in Joshua 11:23 that he "took the whole land"; yet the conquest was neither easy nor swift, and it is stated that "Joshua made war a long time with all those kings" (Joshua 11:18). Even after the death of Joshua the individual tribes doubtless had to make many more conquests as they settled down in the land, as is described in Judges 1. In some cases places once overcome may have had to be retaken as, for example, Debir which was smitten by Joshua and all Israel according to Joshua 10:38f. and then captured for the tribe of Judah by Othniel according to Joshua 15:15-17 and Judges 1:11-13. Likewise additional places may have been taken at

[49] W. M. F. Petrie, *Beth-pelet I* (*Tell Fara*). 1930.
[50] W. F. Albright, *The Archaeology of Palestine and the Bible.* 2d ed. 1933, p.53.
[51] *ibid.,* p.102.
[52] Kelso in BA 19 (1956), p.40.

this time and then again lost as, for example, Jerusalem which was burned by the men of Judah according to Judges 1:8 but only finally taken for permanent control by the Israelites in the time of David (p. 177).[53]

There may also have been yet other cities which were too strong to be taken at all at this time, or where at any rate the native inhabitants were not dispossessed. Listed in Judges 1 among cities where the inhabitants were not driven out are a number of well-known and powerfully fortified places including Beth-shean, Taanach, Megiddo (Judges 1:27), Gezer (Judges 1:29), and Beth-shemesh (Judges 1:33). From discoveries at these sites we may learn more of the culture of the land into the midst of which the Israelites had come.

BETH-SHEAN

Beth-shean, also known as Beth-shan or Beisan, and later the Hellenistic city of Scythopolis, is identified with the imposing mound Tell el-Husn above the Jordan in the Valley of Jezreel. Excavations have been conducted on the site by the University Museum of the University of Pennsylvania under the leadership of Clarence S. Fisher, Alan Rowe, and G. M. Fitzgerald.[54] The Canaanite city here was found to have been fortified with double walls, and the inner and outer walls were connected with cross walls which formed small rooms. The fortifications included a strong tower, built with large unbaked bricks on a foundation of basalt blocks. Beth-shean was occupied by Egyptian garrisons down at least to the time of Ramses III. An Egyptian stela of Seti I (c.1302-c.1290 B.C.) was found there which refers to the 'Apiru of some mountain district with a Semitic name.[55]

No less than four Canaanite temples have been excavated at Beth-shean: one, of the seventh city level which is ascribed to the thirteenth century B.C.; another, of the sixth level which dates in the twelfth and early eleventh centuries; and two of the fifth level belonging to the eleventh and tenth centuries. Since the last two temples continued in use until approximately the tenth century it has been suggested that the Southern Temple may have been the Temple of Dagon of I Chronicles 10:10, and the Northern Temple may have been the House of Ashtaroth of I Samuel 31:10.

[53] G. Ernest Wright in JNES 5 (1946), pp.105-114.
[54] Alan Rowe, *The Topography and History of Beth-shan.* 1930.
[55] W. F. Albright in BASOR 125 (Feb. 1952), pp.24-32.

Serpents played an important part in the cult here too (cf. p. 163) and plaques with serpents and shrine-houses with serpents on them were found in the temples.[56]

TAANACH

Taanach still bears the name Tell Taanak and attracted the attention of Professor Ernst Sellin of Vienna on a visit to Palestine as early as 1899. His excavations there in 1902 and 1903 were the first to be carried out in northern Palestine.[57] Taanach was found to have been fortified with stone walls built in the so-called Cyclopean style of masonry (p. 147), and the remains of a fourteenth century B.C. palace of a local king were uncovered. Tablets unearthed at Taanach contain the interesting expression, "If the finger of Ashirat points," which is interpreted as meaning that oracles were given in the name of a goddess Ashirat, who probably is the same as the goddess Asherat known from Ras Shamra (p. 173). The Asherim mentioned in the Old Testament may have been wooden symbols, perhaps trees or poles, of this goddess (Exodus 34:13; Deuteronomy 16:21; I Kings 14:23; II Kings 17:10; 18:4; 23:14), while she herself probably is referred to in other passages (Judges 3:7; I Kings 15:13; 18:19; II Kings 21:7; 23:4, 6, 7).[58] Later brick houses whose ruins were found at Taanach may represent the eventual Israelite settlement there.[59] In a building which may have been a private house of Israelite times was found a terra-cotta incense altar possibly used by some of the Israelites in worship.[60]

MEGIDDO

Commanding the best pass from the Mediterranean coastal plain to the Valley of Esdraelon and on north to Galilee and Damascus, Megiddo always has been a point of great strategic importance. This was where Thutmose III met the Asiatics (p. 99) and where Josiah was slain by Necho (p. 129). It was through the same pass

[56] Alan Rowe, *The Four Canaanite Temples of Beth-shan.* i (1940); G. E. Wright in AJA 45 (1941), pp.483-485.

[57] E. Sellin, *Tell Ta 'annek.* 1904.

[58] Burrows, *What Mean These Stones?* p.231. Numerous nude female figurines have been found in most Palestinian excavations of the second and first millenniums B.C., and it is probable that they are representations of Asherah or of other similar Canaanite goddesses such as Ashtart or Anat. See James B. Pritchard, *Palestinian Figurines in Relation to Certain Goddesses Known through Literature.* 1943; G. E. Wright in JBL 63 (1944), pp.426-430; P. J. Riis in *Berytus.* 9 (1949), pp.69-90.

[59] Duncan, *Digging Up Biblical History.* i, p.181.

[60] Barton, *Archaeology and the Bible*, p.221.

that Allenby's cavalry surprised the Turkish armies in 1918,[61] and it is here that the book of Revelation expects the climactic battle "on the great day of God the Almighty" (16:14, 16).

The modern name of the site of Megiddo is Tell el-Mutesellim (Fig. 57), and Dr. G. Schumacher of the Deutsche Orientgesellschaft first drove an exploratory trench into it in 1903-1905.[62] Large-scale systematic horizontal clearance of the site was begun by the Oriental Institute of the University of Chicago under the direction of Clarence S. Fisher in 1925 and continued in succeeding years by P. L. O. Guy and by Gordon Loud.[63] It appears that in the Early Bronze Age, Megiddo was surrounded by a massive city wall, originally some thirteen feet thick and later strengthened to twice that thickness. A mud brick wall and gate of about 1800 B.C. are known, and the present indications are that the Canaanite city was destroyed near the end of the twelfth century, while the Israelite occupation, represented for example by the mud brick wall of Level V, began about a half century later.

In 1937 Gordon Loud explored the palace of the princes who ruled at Megiddo as vassals of the Pharaohs of Egypt. The palace showed five building periods, running from the sixteenth into the twelfth century B.C., and the fifth palace had a subterranean treasury in which a wonderful find of more than two hundred carved and incised ivories was made. One of these was an ivory pen case belonging to an Egyptian who bore the title, "Royal Envoy to every Foreign Country." It is to be dated just after 1200 B.C. since it carries the cartouche of Ramses III. Another is an ivory plaque which shows the prince of Megiddo probably celebrating a victory (Fig. 58). At the right he drives naked captives before his chariot. At the left he sits upon his sphinx-sided throne and drinks from a bowl while a musician, "a David of his court," plays upon the harp. At the extreme left is a large jar, with animal heads.[64]

61 It is a well-known fact that Allenby depended chiefly upon the Bible and upon *The Historical Geography of the Holy Land* by George Adam Smith for information concerning the topography of Palestine. cf. David S. Cairns in *Religion in Life*. 11 (1942), pp.532f.

62 G. Schumacher and C. Steuernagel, *Tell El-Mutesellim*. 1908.

63 Robert S. Lamon and Geoffrey M. Shipton, *Megiddo I, Seasons of 1925-34*. OIP XLII, 1939; Gordon Loud, ed., *Megiddo II, Seasons of 1935-39*. OIP LXII, 2 vols. 1948; Robert M. Engberg in BA 3 (1940), pp.41-51; 4 (1941), pp.11-16; G. E. Wright in BA 13 (1950), pp.28-46.

64 Loud, *The Megiddo Ivories*. 1939; C. de Mertzenfeld in *Syria*. 19 (1938), pp.345-354. On the ivory trade, in which the Phoenicians were active, see Richard D. Barnett in *Archaeology*. 9 (1956), pp.87-97.

GEZER

The site of Gezer was identified at Tell Jezer by Professor Clermont-Ganneau in the nineteenth century, and the city was excavated for the Palestine Exploration Fund by Professor R. A. S. Macalister in 1902-1908.[65] Gezer is well situated on the lower slope of hills above the maritime plain to guard the western frontier. Cave dwellers lived here at an early time in natural rock caverns, and apparently practiced the cremation of their dead. In the Early Bronze Age several of the caves were used for interments as the inhabitants gradually shifted to homes on the rock surface above.[66] Later the city was fortified with a brick wall, and still later with a thirteen-foot-thick stone wall. After the destruction of the latter, its materials were employed in the construction of what is now known as the outer wall, fourteen feet thick and enclosing an area of twenty-seven acres. One hundred and twenty feet below the present surface of the ground and ninety-four feet below the surface of the rock is a spring in a cave to which a tunnel was cut to enable the people of the city to obtain water in time of siege.

In the northern part of the city and above one of the caves in which early burials were made is a row of standing stones (Fig. 59) which have elicited much interest. Originally the series consisted of ten rough stone pillars varying in height from five to ten feet, and standing in a slightly curved line from north to south. At the time of discovery one was fallen and two were broken off at the bottom, but the remainder still stood upright. At a point near the middle of the row and just to one side was a stone base with a rectangular depression in which doubtless yet another stela once stood. The area containing these standing stones has been regarded as of cultic significance and interpreted as a Canaanite "high place,"[67] but it now appears more probable that the pillars were simply memorial stones of the kings of the city.[68]

BETH-SHEMESH

Beth-shemesh, now known as Ain Shems or Tell er-Rumeileh, and lying southeast of Gezer in the Shephelah, was the next site after Gezer whose excavation was undertaken by the Palestine Explora-

---

[65] Macalister, *The Excavation of Gezer*. 3 vols. 1912.
[66] G. E. Wright in PEQ 1937, pp.67-78.
[67] R. A. S. Macalister, *Bible Side-Lights from the Mound of Gezer*. 1906, pp.57-65.
[68] Carl Watzinger, *Denkmäler Palästinas*. I (1933), pp.63f. On the search for "high places" of Israelite times, see C. C. McCown in JBL 69 (1950), pp.205-219.

tion Fund. The work was directed by Dr. Duncan Mackenzie during the years 1911-1912 and was the last Palestinian excavation just before the First World War.[69] Further excavations were carried out in 1928 and following by Professor Elihu Grant of Haverford College.[70] It appears that the site was occupied by a series of cities between 2000 and 600 B.C., final destruction having probably come from the army of Nebuchadnezzar II of Babylon. Fine pottery, weapons, jewelry and scarabs were uncovered from the late Canaanite and early Israelite periods and further illustration of Canaanite religion appeared in a plaque with a serpent goddess.

RAS SHAMRA

The insights which Palestinian archeology has been giving as to Canaanitish culture and religion have been greatly supplemented by recent discoveries in Syria, particularly at Ras Shamra. This is a site on the northern coast of Syria, opposite the island of Cyprus, which was discovered almost by chance in 1929 and studied since that date in a series of campaigns conducted by C. F. A. Schaeffer.[71] The site was already occupied in the Neolithic Age, to which time the plain pottery of the lowest level belongs.[72] As early as the second millennium B.C. the city is called by the name Ugarit and it is mentioned in Egyptian inscriptions, in the Tell el-Amarna letters, and in Hittite documents. In the days of the Twelfth Dynasty, Egyptian influence was strong, as is shown by the finding of a statue of the wife of Senusert II and two sphinxes sent by Amenemhet III. In the fifteenth and fourteenth centuries Ugarit flourished greatly but was overwhelmed by an earthquake about the middle of the fourteenth century (c.1360 B.C.). After the earthquake the city again prospered, being first under the dominance of the Hittites but coming again

[69] R. A. S. Macalister, *A Century of Excavation in Palestine*. 1930, p.69.

[70] E. Grant, *Beth Shemesh* (1929); *Ain Shems Excavations*. 5 vols. 1931-39.

[71] C. F. A. Schaeffer in *Syria*. 10 (1929), pp.285-297; 12 (1931), pp.1-14; 13 (1932), pp.1-27; 14 (1933), pp.93-127; 15 (1934), pp.105-131; 16 (1935), pp.141-176; 17 (1936), pp.105-149; 18 (1937), pp.125-154; 19 (1938), pp.193-255,313-334; 20 (1939), pp.277-292; 28 (1951), pp.1-21; etc.; *The Cuneiform Texts of Ras Shamra-Ugarit*. 1939; *Ugaritica, études relatives aux découvertes de Ras Shamra*. Première série, 1939; *Ugaritica II, nouvelles études relatives aux découvertes de Ras Shamra*. 1949; *Stratigraphie comparée et chronologie de l'Asie occidentale (IIIe et IIe millénaires)*. 1948, pp.8-39; Johannes Friedrich, *Ras Schamra, Ein Überblick über Funde und Forschungen*. Der Alte Orient 33, 1/2, 1933; W. F. Albright in AJA 54 (1950), p.164. And see now the publications of the *Mission de Ras Shamra*, ed. by C. F. A. Schaeffer, including VI, *Le palais royal d'Ugarit*, III, *Textes accadiens et hourrites des archives est, ouest et centrales*. 2 vols. 1955.

[72] Schaeffer, *Ugaritica*, Première série, pp.3-8; T. H. Gaster in *Antiquity*. 13 (1939), p.306.

under Egyptian authority with Ramses II. Toward the close of the thirteenth or beginning of the twelfth century the city suffered invasion from the peoples of the north and from the sea, and after the twelfth century Ugarit ceased to exist.

The discovery of greatest importance at Ras Shamra was that of documents in a library which had been housed in a building situated between the city's two great temples, one dedicated to Baal and the other to Dagon. Hundreds of clay tablets were uncovered, dating from the fifteenth and early fourteenth centuries, and bearing texts in a cuneiform alphabet which is the earliest known alphabet written with wedge-shaped signs. The language was recognized by Professor H. Bauer of the University of Halle to be of Semitic origin and its decipherment was finally accomplished by Bauer and the French scholars É. Dhorme and C. Virolleaud. Known as Ugaritic, this language is closely related both to biblical Hebrew and to Phoenician. Most of the Ras Shamra texts are poetic in form, and the Ugaritic poetry exhibits exactly the same characteristic feature of parallelism as does Hebrew poetry. This may be seen in an example such as the following:

> The heavens rain oil
> The wadies run with honey.[73]

The majority of the documents under consideration are in the nature of mythological poems concerning Canaanite gods and heroes, but some of the texts deal with other subjects including even the treatment of sick and infirm horses. Incidentally, one of the remedies mentioned in this "veterinary manual" is a sort of pressed fig-cake which is similar to what Isaiah ordered for Hezekiah's boil (II Kings 20:1-8). The early Canaanitish beliefs which are reflected in the religious and mythological texts are of the greatest interest, and the discussion of them and their evident relationship with many of the religious beliefs and practices reflected in the Old Testament has already elicited an extensive literature.[74] The supreme god is known

[73] Cyrus H. Gordon, *The Loves and Wars of Baal and Anat and Other Poems from Ugarit.* 1943, pp.xi,10.

[74] Charles Virolleaud in *Antiquity.* 5 (1931), pp.405-414; William C. Graham in JR 14 (1934), pp.306-329; Walter G. Williams in AJSL 51 (1934-35), pp.233-246; J. W. Jack, *The Ras Shamra Tablets, Their Bearing on the Old Testament.* 1935; Ditlef Nielsen, *Ras Šamra Mythologie und biblische Theologie.* Abhandlungen für die Kunde des Morgenlandes, Deutsche morgenländische Gesellschaft. 21 (1936), No.4; René Dussaud, *Les découvertes de Ras Shamra (Ugarit) et l'Ancien Testament.* 2d ed. 1941; Samuel H. Hooke, *The Origins of Early Semitic Ritual.* 1938, pp.28-38; J. Philip Hyatt in BA 2 (1939), pp.2-8; John H. Patton, *Canaanite Parallels in the Book*

as El, a name by which God is called in the Old Testament.[75] On a stela found at Ras Shamra the god El is shown seated upon a throne with the king of Ugarit presenting an offering before him (Fig. 60). The god is represented as mature in age and paternal and majestic in appearance. The wife of El is Asherat-of-the-Sea, the counselor of the gods, and their son is the god Baal. Baal is a god of the rain and storm and is represented on a Ras Shamra stela brandishing a mace in his right hand and holding in his left hand a stylized thunderbolt ending in a spear-head (Fig. 61). One of his titles is "Zabul [Prince], Lord of the Earth," and this doubtless has survived in the name of the god Baal-zebub in II Kings (1:2, etc.) and of Beelzebub in the New Testament (Mark 3:22, etc.). Asherat probably is to be identified with Asherah in the Old Testament (p. 168), and Baal of course figures prominently there. Asherat is mentioned regularly after Baal in the Ras Shamra texts and the similar and close connection of the two is likewise reflected in I Kings 18:19 and II Kings 23:4.[76] Among the adventures related of Baal in the Ras Shamra tablets is a conflict with Lotan, "the nimble serpent . . . the sinuous serpent, the mighty one with seven heads." Lotan is the same as the Hebrew Leviathan that is described in similar terms in Isaiah 27:1 (cf. Job 26:12f.).

Baal or Aliyan Baal figures prominently in the mythology made known by the Ras Shamra tablets. Aliyan represents the growth of plants, and fights against Mot, the god of the dried-up summer soil, but is slain by him. Thereupon the goddess Anat, the sister and lover of Aliyan, goes in search of him, recovers his body and slays his enemy, Mot. Aliyan is then brought back to life and placed on Mot's throne so that he may ensure the revival of vegetation in another season.[77]

An interesting legend is written on four large tablets found at Ras Shamra, one of which is shown in Fig. 62. This is the Legend of

---

of Psalms. 1944; H. L. Ginsberg in BA 8 (1945), pp.41-58; Robert de Langhe, Les textes de Ras Shamra-Ugarit et leurs rapports avec le milieu biblique de l'Ancien Testament. 2 vols. 1945; Julian Obermann, Ugaritic Mythology, A Study of Its Leading Motifs. 1948; Cyrus H. Gordon, Ugaritic Literature. 1949; Theodor H. Gaster, Thespis, Ritual, Myth and Drama in the Ancient Near East. 1950, pp.113-313; Arvid S. Kapelrud, Baal in the Ras Shamra Texts. 1952; Marvin H. Pope, El in the Ugaritic Texts. 1955.

[75] Genesis 33:20, and frequently in the plural of majesty, Elohim.

[76] H. Bauer in ZAW 10 (1933), p.89. For a seventeenth century B.C. temple at Nahariyah, twelve miles north of Haifa, probably dedicated to Asherat, see M. Dothan in IEJ 6 (1956), pp.14-25.

[77] W. F. Albright, Archaeology and the Religion of Israel. 1942, pp.84-90.

Keret and tells of the time when El entrusted Keret with the command of "the army of the Negeb."

One rite is mentioned in the Ras Shamra texts in which the seething of a kid in milk is prescribed as an item in the magical technique for producing the early rains. This procedure is practically what the Israelites are forbidden to carry out, in Exodus 23:19; 34:26. A wise hero Daniel is mentioned who is identified by some with the Daniel spoken of in Ezekiel 14:14. Such biblical words occur as "anoint" from which "Messiah" is derived, and also the expression for "bring good tidings." The *rpem* or *rpum* are mentioned frequently, these probably being the same as the Old Testment *rephaim*, the "shades" or inhabitants of the world of the dead (Job 26:5, etc.).

Such are a few of the glimpses given us by the Ras Shamra tablets of the religion which prevailed among the Canaanites of Ugarit at a time only shortly before the period when the Israelites entered Palestine. This religion was polytheistic, mythological, and ritualistic, and was centered to a large degree in interest in the fertility of the soil. When the children of Israel came in contact with this environment they evidently adopted some of the customs and beliefs of their neighbors, but through the leadership of the prophets were able to rise superior to the grosser features of the Canaanite fertility religion.

SHILOH

According to Joshua 18:1 the Israelites under Joshua set up their tent of meeting at Shiloh, and in the days of the judges this place remained the central sanctuary of Israel where an annual festival was held (Judges 21:19). In the time of Eli and during the early years of Samuel the tabernacle and ark were still at Shiloh (I Samuel 1:9; 2:22; 3:3), but when the Philistines defeated the Israelites and took the ark they probably destroyed Shiloh too. This is suggested by the fact that when the ark was returned it was not brought back to Shiloh but taken to Beth-shemesh (I Samuel 6:12) and afterward to Kiriath-jearim (I Samuel 7:1f.). Furthermore in the time of Jeremiah, although Shiloh was again inhabited (Jeremiah 41:5), it is evident that the memory and the marks of a great destruction of that place were still vivid. The prophet stated the Lord's message in these words: "Go now to my place that was in Shiloh, where I made my name dwell at first, and see what I did to it for the wickedness of my people Israel" (Jeremiah 7:12; cf. 26:6).

174

Shiloh has been identified with Tell Seilun, about ten miles north of Bethel (cf. Judges 21:19), and this site was studied and partially excavated in 1926 and 1929 by a Danish expedition under the leadership of Hans Kjaer. It is clear that the city was inhabited and flourishing in the twelfth and early eleventh centuries B.C., and also that it was destroyed by conflagration at a time around 1050 B.C., after which it remained deserted for several centuries. That this destruction was that visited upon Shiloh by the Philistines seems beyond doubt.[78]

TELL EN-NASBEH

A town which was probably settled by the Israelites in the time of the judges, and which is of the greater interest because it has been so thoroughly excavated and studied, was at Tell en-Nasbeh, eight miles north of Jerusalem. The excavations were conducted by Professor William F. Badè of Pacific School of Religion in a series of five expeditions from 1926 to 1935, and after the death of Dr. Badè the publication of the results was carried out by Professor Chester C. McCown of the same institution with the assistance of several others.[79]

The first occupation of Tell en-Nasbeh was at least as early as the Early Bronze Age in the third millennium B.C. A number of caves and tombs in the limestone rock of the hill contained the pottery, implements, ornaments, and skeletons of some of the inhabitants of this time. Then in Iron I, probably in the twelfth century B.C., a small town was founded on the same hill, the settlers presumably being the Israelites. The wall which first protected this settlement was a comparatively thin one, perhaps a yard thick, built of rubble. By the end of Iron I, around 900 B.C., a new and very powerful city wall was built. It was half a mile in circumference and enclosed an area of eight acres. Made of large, roughly-shaped stones laid in clay mortar, it had an average thickness of over thirteen feet. Still standing in places to a height of twenty-five feet, it was probably at one time thirty-five or forty feet high, and was strengthened with nine

[78] Hans Kjaer in JPOS 10 (1930), pp.87-174; *The Excavation of Shiloh 1929.* 1930; Albright, *Archaeology and the Religion of Israel,* pp.103f.

[79] *Tell en-Naṣbeh, Excavated under the Direction of the Late William Frederic Badè,* I, *Archaeological and Historical Results,* by C. C. McCown, with contributions by James Muilenburg, J. C. Wampler, Dietrich von Bothmer, and Margaret Harrison; II, *The Pottery,* by J. C. Wampler, with a chapter by C. C. McCown. 1947. See also C. C. McCown, *The Ladder of Progress in Palestine.* 1943, pp.209-214; W. F. Albright in JPOS 3 (1923), pp.110-121; and in AASOR 4 (1922-23), pp.90-111; G. E. Wright in BA 10 (1947), pp.69-77; James Muilenburg in *Studia Theologica.* 8 (1955), pp.25-42.

or ten rectangular towers. At the northeast side of the city the ends of the wall were caused to overlap, and in the thirty-foot space between them the great city gate was set. Inside the gate were guard rooms, and on the outside the court was lined with stone benches. This was the place where many of the business and legal transactions of an ancient Middle Eastern city were conducted, as the Old Testament indicates with its frequent references to events which transpired "in the gate" (Deuteronomy 22:14; Ruth 4:11; II Samuel 19:8; etc.).

Occupation continued at Tell en-Nasbeh down to Hellenistic times, although from the fifth century on the population was greatly reduced and the once powerfully fortified city became only a small, defenceless village. Dating probably from the later pre-exilic period, over eighty stamp impressions on jar handles were found at Tell en-Nasbeh with the inscription *lemelekh,* meaning "belonging to the king," which suggests that it designated royal property. Perhaps the contents of the jars were to go to the king as taxes. Such *lemelekh* stamps have also been found at other sites in the southern kingdom and were doubtless used widely there before the exile. Since no such stamps were found at Bethel, three miles to the north, this is taken as evidence that at this time Tell en-Nasbeh belonged to the southern kingdom, with the boundary line running between this city and Bethel. Twenty-eight stamps were found, probably postexilic in date, with an inscription the three Hebrew letters of which have been read as either *m ṣ h* or *m ṣ p.* A bronze fragment, with part of a cuneiform inscription, dating perhaps around the seventh century B.C., indicates some contact with the East. Most interesting of all, for the possible Old Testament relationship which will be indicated in the next paragraph, is the seal found in a tomb at Tell en-Nasbeh with a Hebrew inscription reading, "Ya'azanyahu, servant of the king."

The foregoing archeological history of Tell en-Nasbeh has many points which support an identification of this site with the ancient Mizpah, a city which was prominent in the time of Samuel (I Samuel 7:5, etc.), and after the destruction of Jerusalem was the residence of Gedaliah, whom Nebuchadnezzar made governor of Judah. The powerful wall which was such a conspicuous feature of the city may have been built by King Asa of Judah, who is known to have fortified Mizpah against the northern tribes (I Kings 15:22; II Chronicles 16:6). If the stamp impressions mentioned above are read *m ṣ p*, the vocalization could be Miṣpah and would support the identification. The Ya'azanyahu of the seal inscription could be the Jaazaniah mentioned in II Kings 25:23 and Jeremiah 40:8, who was a captain of forces and who came to Mizpah to pay his respects to Gedaliah. Perhaps he died at Tell en-Nasbeh and was buried in the tomb where his seal was found.

There are, however, possible objections to the identification of Tell en-Nasbeh with Mizpah. It may be said that if Asa built these walls as a military measure against the north it is strange that the gate was placed to face the north. It is not certain that the stamp inscriptions should be read *m ṣ p*; if the letters are really *m ṣ h* no connection with Mizpah is apparent. At all events one example of the same inscription was also known from Jericho, and three more have now been discovered at Gibeon.[80] It has also been proposed to identify Tell en-Nasbeh with some ancient place other than Mizpah, possibly Ataroth-addar or Beeroth. The Arabic place name, Khirbet 'Attarah, doubtless derived from Ataroth, is attached to a site not far south of Tell en-Nasbeh. The ruins at this site are not older than the Roman period, and it could be supposed that after Tell en-Nasbeh was abandoned its name was transferred to this new town which arose not far away. Also it has been suggested that Mizpah itself could have been at Nebi Samwil, a site about four miles southwest of Tell en-Nasbeh with a commanding view appropriate to a place called Mizpah or "watchtower." Named for the "prophet Samuel," Nebi Samwil is held in Arab tradition as the burial place of Samuel. Although excavation has not been possible, potsherds have been collected on the surface showing that a village of Israelite date did once exist here. In view of these facts, identification of Tell en-Nasbeh with Mizpah is not positive although it may be regarded as probable.

JERUSALEM

Jerusalem was captured by the Israelites under David and made the capital of the kingdom (II Samuel 5:6-10; I Chronicles 11:4-9). The city has a strategic location of exceptional strength. Its site is a rocky plateau with two promontories running south from it. Between these two rocky ridges is the valley el-Wad, which in Roman times was known as the Tyropeon. On the east is the valley of the

[80] Pritchard in UMB 21 (1957), p.21. N. Avigad (in IEJ 8 [1958], pp.113-119) reads the inscription as *moṣah* and thinks it refers to the Mozah of Joshua 18:26, from which town products might have come to Tell en-Nasbeh.

Kidron, and on the south and west the valley of Hinnom. Two springs provide water. One, an intermittent spring known as Gihon (now Ain Sitti Maryam or "Fountain of the Virgin"), is at the foot of the eastern hill in the Kidron Valley. The other, known as En-rogel (now Bir Aiyub or "Job's Well") is farther distant, at the point where the valleys of Kidron and Hinnom join, and beneath the hill where the modern village of Silwan (Siloah) stands.[81] An interesting discovery in connection with the Gihon spring was made by Charles Warren in the earliest explorations at Jerusalem by the Palestine Exploration Fund. He found that the early inhabitants of Jerusalem had made a rock-cut passage, similar to the ones we have mentioned at Gibeon and Gezer (pp. 161, 170), to enable them to secure water from the spring without going outside the city walls. From the cave in which the Gihon spring empties,[82] a horizontal tunnel was driven back into the hill, some thirty-six feet west and twenty-five feet north. This led the spring waters back into an old cave, which thus served as a reservoir. Running up from this was a vertical shaft perhaps forty feet high, at the top of which was a platform on which the women could stand to lower and lift their water vessels. From this a sloping passage ran on up to open within the city walls. This probably constituted the water system which was in use by the Jebusites who occupied Jerusalem through the period of the Judges (Judges 19:10f.) and in the time of David. The account of David's capture of the city includes the words (II Samuel 5:8), "Whoever would smite the Jebusites, let him get up the water shaft," which makes it seem likely that access to the city was first gained when Joab (I Chronicles 11:6) penetrated this tunnel.[83]

Thus "the stronghold of Zion," as the city of the Jebusites was called, became "the city of David" (II Samuel 5:7, 9), and the capital of the Israelite nation. It is quite certain that Zion was the lower eastern hill at Jerusalem and that David's city was situated on the portion of the hill known as Ophel or "hump" (II Chronicles

[81] Baedeker, *Palestine and Syria*, pp.83f.

[82] Actually its source is a great crack in the rock at the bottom of the valley, at the eastern end of which a wall was built by some of the earliest inhabitants of the place which compels the water to flow into the cave rather than emptying into the valley.

[83] Macalister, *A Century of Excavation in Palestine*, pp.173-178; and in CAH III, p.343. The meaning of the Hebrew word translated "water course" or "water shaft" in II Samuel 5:8 is debatable. Duncan (*Digging Up Biblical History*, I, p.15) thinks it refers to the funnel entrance from within the city to a large cave which also has an eastern exit in the hill above the Gihon spring. For another explanation of the matter see Hans J. Stoebe in ZDPV 73 (1957), pp.73-99.

27:3, etc.) above the Virgin's Spring.[84] Excavations at Zion have revealed a strong stone wall which was broken through violently, and it may be that this is the breach made by David in his assault on the city. Behind the breach a lighter wall was built which perhaps was put there by David as a temporary barricade, and may have been the work referred to in II Samuel 5:9. Above the breach a fortress tower was finally built, which filled the gap in the wall and used the fallen stones of the breach as a foundation. This may have been the "Millo" which was built by Solomon (I Kings 9:15, 24; 11:27).[85]

Solomon may also have included the western hill inside "the wall around Jerusalem" which he constructed (I Kings 3:1; cf. 9:15). In early excavations on the western hill, walls were found which may have been the work of Solomon. The most famous building of Solomon, of course, was the temple, which he began to construct in the fourth year of his reign (I Kings 6:1). According to II Chronicles 3:1 this was on Mount Moriah at a place where Ornan (or Araunah) the Jebusite had had a threshing floor. The threshing floor had been purchased earlier by David for the erection of an altar at the time of pestilence (II Samuel 24:15-25). Moriah is also named in Genesis 22:2 as the place where Abraham went to offer Isaac.

The site lies today within the sacred enclosure of the Muslims known as the Haram esh-Sherif, "the Noble Sanctuary." The most striking natural feature is a great outcropping of rock some fifty-eight feet long, fifty-one feet broad, and four to six and one-half feet high. This is known as es-Sakhra or the Sacred Rock, and today is covered by a structure called the Qubbet es-Sakhra ("Dome of the Rock"). The Dome of the Rock is shown in Fig. 63 and in Fig. 64 we look down from within the balcony of the Dome upon the sacred rock enclosed as it now is by a wooden screen. Evidently the rock was used as an altar in very ancient times, since channels can still be traced on it; they may have conducted the blood of the sacrificial

[84] George Adam Smith, *Jerusalem*. 1908, I, pp.134f.,161f.; II, p.39. Josephus (*War.* v, iv, 1; *Ant.* VII, iii, 2) and later tradition erroneously located the city of David on the western hill and this error is preserved in modern names like that of "David's Tower" near the Jaffa Gate which probably actually stands on the base of Herod's Tower of Phasael.

[85] If Millo was built first by Solomon, its mention in II Samuel 5:9 must be regarded as meaning that David built from the point where later Millo stood. On the other hand, Solomon's work might have been that of rebuilding an earlier structure, known already in David's time as Millo.

animals to an opening and on down to a cavity below. The rock itself most likely served as Araunah's threshing floor, since presumably the strongest breeze for the threshing was found on it. Therefore David's altar probably was erected on the very rock.[86] On the other hand, it is possible to suppose that the relatively large and level area directly east of the rock provided a better surface for the work of threshing, and became the site of the altar. In the latter and somewhat less probable case it was the Holy of Holies which eventually arose over the sacred rock itself.[87]

The building of the temple required seven years, while thirteen years were spent by Solomon in the building of his own palace (I Kings 6:38; 7:1). Phoenician craftsmen and workers were supplied for these enterprises by Hiram of Tyre (I Kings 5:1-12) and doubtless the work was of a character unusually imposing in Palestine. The buildings are described in detail in the Old Testament[88] but, save for the great ancient rock, almost everything connected with them has been lost to us. Nevertheless it is possible to draw upon archeological knowledge of the architecture of the time at other places and, combining this with the biblical data, to make a reconstruction of Solomon's temple which has at least good grounds for a claim to authenticity.[89]

THE STABLES AT MEGIDDO

Solomon is also known to have rebuilt the city of Megiddo (I Kings 9:15). In view of the king's well-known interest in horses and chariots (I Kings 10:26-29; II Chronicles 1:14-17) it was a matter of great interest to discover extensive stables in the excavation of Megiddo.

[86] A. T. Olmstead, *Jesus in the Light of History*. 1942, p.85; G. Dalman, *Neue Petra-Forschungen und Der heilige Felsen von Jerusalem*. 1912, pp.133-145; Floyd V. Filson in BA 7 (1944), p.81.

[87] F. J. Hollis, *The Archaeology of Herod's Temple, with a Commentary on the Tractate "Middoth."* 1934, pp.84-86,99; Hans Schmidt, *Der Heilige Fels in Jerusalem*. 1933, pp.26,55. The supposition encounters the difficulty that the rock was larger (58 by 51 feet) than the Holy of Holies (20 cubits long and 20 cubits wide, according to I Kings 6:20), and at any rate could not have been enclosed within the room. cf. below p.326.

[88] I Kings 6:1-7:51; II Chronicles 3:1-5:1. Ezekiel's vision of the future temple (40:1-44:3) probably was based on his memories of the first temple before its destruction in 586 B.C. cf. Watzinger, *Denkmäler Palästinas*. I, pp.88-95. A description of Solomon's temple, in which the biblical account is amplified somewhat, is given by Josephus, *Ant.* VIII, iii.

[89] G. Ernest Wright in BA 4 (1941), pp.17-31; 7 (1944), pp.73-77; Paul L. Garber in BA 14 (1951), pp.1-24; and in *Archaeology*. 5 (1952), pp.165-172. For the entire history of the temple see now André Parrot, *The Temple of Jerusalem*. 1955. On Old Testament Jerusalem in general see J. Simons, *Jerusalem in the Old Testament*. 1952; L.-H. Vincent and M.-A. Steve, *Jérusalem de l'Ancien Testament*. 2 vols. 1954.

A photograph of them is shown in Fig. 65. It is evident that they were composed of units built on a standard plan. Stone pillars, with holes in their corners, separated the horses and served as hitching-posts. Stone mangers were provided, and the ground on which the horses stood was paved with rough stones to prevent hoofs from slipping.

The date of these stables has not been determined with certainty, and it is believed by some that they were the work of the warrior king Ahab (cf. p. 205) rather than of Solomon.[90] The most authoritative study of the chronology of Megiddo, however, places Stratum IV in which the stables were found, at least partly within the reign of Solomon, and it remains probable that these famous structures really belonged to that king.[91]

EZION-GEBER

In I Kings 9:26 (cf. 9:27f.; 10:11, 22) it is recorded that Solomon furthermore built a fleet of ships at Ezion-geber, beside Eloth, on the shore of the Red Sea. This seaport city of the king has been discovered and excavated at Tell Kheleifeh at the head of the Gulf of Aqabah (cf. p. 151).[92] The city was built on a carefully chosen and hitherto unoccupied site, according to plans which had been worked out in advance. The site selected was between the hills of Edom on the east and the hills of Palestine on the west, where the north winds blow most steadily and strongly down the center of the Wadi el-Arabah. This was because Ezion-geber was to be not only a seaport but also an important industrial city. An elaborate complex of industrial plants, devoted to the smelting and refining of copper and iron and the manufacturing of metal articles for markets at home and abroad, was uncovered there. The furnace rooms were set at an angle carefully calculated to get the full benefit of the winds from the north and to utilize these to furnish the draft for the fires. Ezion-geber was able to draw upon the important mineral deposits which are found in the Wadi el-Arabah all the way from the Gulf of Aqabah to the Dead Sea, and a series of mining centers of Solomon's time is known where these ores were dug and subjected to an initial smelting process. The mines of the Wadi el-Arabah were probably used first

[90] J. W. Crowfoot in PEQ 1940, pp. 143-147.

[91] W. F. Albright in AJA 44 (1940), pp.546-550; and in AASOR 21-22 (1941-43), p.2 n.1; Robert M. Engberg in BA 4 (1941), pp.12f.; G. E. Wright in BA 13 (1950), p.44.

[92] Glueck, *The Other Side of the Jordan*, pp.50-113; and in NGM 85 (Jan.-June 1944), pp.233-256.

by the Kenites, whose name means "smiths,"[93] and the related Keniz-zites, from whom in turn the Edomites learned mining and metal-lurgy. When David subjugated the Edomites (II Samuel 8:13f.; I Kings 11:15f.; I Chronicles 18:11f.) he may well have continued to exploit these mines, but it was Solomon who had the ability and power to put the mining industry in the Wadi el-Arabah on a truly national scale. Ezion-geber still belonged to the domain of Judah in the days of King Jotham, and a signet seal ring inscribed with the name of the latter was found there in the stratum belonging to the eighth century B.C.[94] In connection with the statement in I Kings 9:28 that Solomon's fleet went to Ophir and brought gold from there, much interest attaches to a potsherd of the eighth century B.C. recently discovered at Tell Qasile near Jaffa on which is the inscription: "Gold of Ophir for Beth-horon: 30 shekels."[95] Ophir, it is now suggested, may have been (S)uppara, near Bombay, India, since in some Indian dialects the initial "S" disappears.[96]

THE GEZER CALENDAR

In Canaan itself agriculture, of course, always remained far more important than industry. A side light on Palestinian agriculture comes from the Gezer calendar. This is a small limestone tablet, about four inches long and three inches wide, which was found at Gezer and comes probably from a time around 925 B.C. It seems to be simply a schoolboy's exercise, but it contains a list of the various months and the agricultural work done in them. Written in good biblical Hebrew, it reads:

> His two months are (olive) harvest,
> His two months are planting (grain),
> His two months are late planting;
> His month is hoeing up of flax,
> His month is harvest of barley,
> His month is harvest and feasting;
> His two months are vine-tending,
> His month is summer fruit.[97]

[93] A. H. Sayce in HDB II, p.834. [94] AJA 45 (1941), p.117.
[95] B. Maisler in IEJ 1 (1950-51), pp.209f.
[96] R. D. Barnett in *The Manchester Guardian Weekly*. Vol. 71, No.19, Nov. 4, 1954, p.15; and in *Archaeology*. 9 (1956), p.92. The Greeks credited Hippalus in the first century A.D. with the discovery of the seasonal monsoons and the opening of a direct sea route to India, but even if it was unknown to the Greeks there must have been commerce by others on the Indian Ocean and even utilization of the monsoon winds long before that. See Gus W. Van Beek in JAOS 78 (1958), p.147.
[97] W. F. Albright in ANET p.320 (ANEA pp.209f.); cf. BASOR 92 (Dec. 1943), pp.16-20; Sabatino Moscati, *L'epigrafia ebraica antica 1935-1950*. 1951, pp.8-26.

In view of the oppression which the peasantry endured at the hands of Solomon and which contributed to the division of the kingdom after his death, some interest attaches to an inscription on an Aramean stela of King Kilamuwa which reads: "Before the former kings the Muskabim [peasant farmers] crawled like dogs, but I [Kilamuwa] was a father to one, a mother to another."[98]

Unfortunately Rehoboam was not as wise as this Kilamuwa and, about 931/930 B.C.,[99] the great kingdom of Solomon broke into two parts (I Kings 12:1-20). Jeroboam, a political exile in Egypt in Solomon's time (I Kings 12:2), returned to lead the revolt of the northern tribes. Egypt itself, which had entered into an alliance with Solomon (I Kings 3:1), now took advantage of the divided and weakened kingdom, and invaded Palestine. Shishak (Sheshonk I), founder of the Twenty-second Dynasty, plundered Jerusalem in the fifth year of King Rehoboam (I Kings 14:25f.) and also conquered other cities both in Judah and Israel, a record of which exploits was duly inscribed at Karnak (p. 126). Among the cities mentioned in the Karnak inscription was Megiddo, and in the excavation of Megiddo a fragment of a stela of Shishak was found.[100]

SHECHEM

Jeroboam I made his residence first at Shechem (I Kings 12:25), which is probably the same as Tell Balatah east of modern Nablus. German expeditions under E. Sellin, G. Welter, and H. Steckeweh worked here between 1913 and 1934, but did not obtain clear results chronologically. Excavations were begun here in 1956 and 1957 by Drew University, McCormick Theological Seminary, and the American Schools of Oriental Research, under the direction of G. Ernest Wright.[101] The site was evidently settled as early as the Chalcolithic period and again in the Bronze Age. The city probably reached its height in the Middle Bronze Age and the time of the Hyksos, and there is evidence of its destruction about the middle of the sixteenth century B.C., perhaps when the Egyptians took the place from the Hyksos. After that it was again an important site in the Late Bronze

---

[98] Duncan, *Digging Up Biblical History.* II, p.132.

[99] For the date of the division of the kingdom see above p.117 n.72, and for the dates of the kings of Israel and Judah see TMN p.283.

[100] R. S. Lamon and G. M. Shipton, *Megiddo I, Seasons of 1925-34, Strata I-V.* 1939, p.61.

[101] Eduard Nielsen, *Shechem, A Traditio-Historical Investigation.* 1955; G. Ernest Wright in BASOR 144 (Dec. 1956), pp.9-20; Walter Harrelson, Bernhard W. Anderson, and G. Ernest Wright in BA 20 (1957), pp.1-32; G. Ernest Wright in BASOR 148 (Dec. 1957), pp.11-28; H. C. Kee and L. E. Toombs in BA 20 (1957), pp.82-105.

Age and in the Iron Age down to the eighth century. As far as presently known evidence goes, the place was then uninhabited for several centuries but was again a large city in the Hellenistic period from the end of the fourth to the end of the second century B.C. Features of the city were the powerful wall of the Middle Bronze Age, with its large East Gate, and an extensive temple of the Late Bronze Age which may have been the "house of Baal-berith" of Judges 9:4.

TIRZAH

After Shechem Jeroboam I resided at Tirzah, as we learn almost incidentally from I Kings 14:17, and this place remained the capital of northern Israel until the time of Omri. In the Song of Solomon 6:4 Tirzah ranks with Jerusalem as a standard of beauty, a reference which would seem to belong to a time when Tirzah was a flourishing place. When Omri, formerly commander of the army, was made king of Israel he besieged and took Tirzah and reigned there for six years until he transferred the capital to Samaria (I Kings 16:17, 23). Tirzah has been tentatively identified with Tell el-Far'ah, a large mound some seven miles northeast of Nablus, and excavations have been made here since 1946 by the Dominican Biblical School at Jerusalem under the direction of R. de Vaux.[102]

Tell el-Far'ah was occupied in the Chalcolithic, Bronze, and Iron Ages. In the Iron Age the excavators distinguish four periods which correspond very well with the biblical history of Tirzah. Period 1, that of Level III in the tell, is marked by well-built houses and abundant pottery. This period probably extended from the end of the eleventh to the beginning of the ninth century B.C., and the end of the period could very well coincide with the taking of Tirzah by Omri at the beginning of his reign in 885/884 B.C.[103] Periods 2 and 3 belong to an intermediate level in the tell. In Period 2 building work of considerable magnitude was begun but left unfinished. This could be work Omri started at Tirzah before moving to Samaria. Period 3 has only poor and limited remains, which could reflect a virtual transfer of the population to Samaria when Omri made the move thither. Period 4, that of Level II in the tell, has excellent buildings again, and could correspond to the time of Israel's prosperity in the eighth century under Jehoash and Jeroboam II. Finally Level

---

[102] R. de Vaux and A.-M. Steve in RB 54 (1947), pp.394-433,573-589; 55 (1948), pp.544-580; 56 (1949), pp.102-138; R. de Vaux in RB 58 (1951), pp.393-430,566-590; 59 (1952), pp.551-583; 62 (1955), pp.541-589; 64 (1957), pp.552-580.

[103] TMN p.60.

II comes to an end at a time which is probably that of the Assyrian invasion of 725/724-723/722,[104] and in Level I above this it is Assyrian pottery which is prominent.[105]

SAMARIA

It was evidently in his sixth year (880/879 B.C.) that Omri moved the capital of northern Israel from Tirzah to Samaria (I Kings 16:24). The hill of Samaria, probably meaning "Watch-Mountain," rises three or four hundred feet above the valley and provided a strong strategic site for the fortified city which Omri built. Excavations were carried out at Samaria in 1908-1910 by Harvard University under the leadership of G. A. Reisner, C. S. Fisher, and D. G. Lyon,[106] and this work was continued in 1931-1933 under the direction of J. W. Crowfoot in a joint expedition in which Harvard University, the Hebrew University in Jerusalem, the Palestine Exploration Fund, the British Academy, and the British School of Archaeology in Jerusalem participated. In 1935 further work was done by the three last-named institutions.[107]

The stratigraphy of Israelite times was clarified by the last excavations, and the following sequence of levels and dates is now recognized:[108] Levels I and II, 880-850 B.C., the time of the Omri-Ahab Dynasty; Level III, 850-800 B.C., including the time of Jehu who made a great slaughter there (II Kings 10:17); Levels IV-VI, 800-722 B.C., the period of the city's greatest prosperity; and Level VII, after the Assyrian conquest in 722 B.C. The correlation between this sequence and that which was arrived at for Tell el-Far'ah is extremely interesting. At Tell el-Far'ah Period 1 and Level III came to an end prior to the first Israelite occupation of Samaria, and Period 2 with its incompleted buildings probably immediately preceded Level I at Samaria. Levels I, II, and III at Samaria correspond to Period 3 or

---

[104] TMN p.128.

[105] de Vaux in RB 62 (1955), pp.587f.; and in PEQ 1956, pp.125-140; cf. W. F. Albright in JPOS 11 (1931), pp.241-251; and see also *Asiatische Studien.* 1/2 (1947), p.78; BA 12 (1949), pp.66-68.

[106] Reisner, Fisher, and Lyon, *Harvard Excavations at Samaria 1908-1910.* 2 vols. 1924.

[107] J. W. Crowfoot, Kathleen M. Kenyon, and E. L. Sukenik, *The Buildings at Samaria.* 1942; *Samaria-Sebaste, Reports of the Work of the Joint Expedition in 1931-1933 and of the British Expedition in 1935;* cf. W. F. Albright in BASOR 150 (Apr. 1958), pp.21-25.

[108] Kathleen M. Kenyon as cited by de Vaux in RB 62 (1955), p. 587. Note that these strata are numbered from the lower toward the upper, while at Tell el-Far'ah the numbering of levels was from the upper toward the lower.

the rest of the intermediate period at Tell el-Far'ah. Levels IV-VI at Samaria agree in their signs of prosperity with Period 4, Level II, at Tell el-Far'ah, while at the end of this period both cities share a common ruin, doubtless that of the Assyrian invasion. Thus the findings at the two sites agree well with the biblical history of Tirzah and Samaria.

In their work at Samaria Omri and Ahab evidently leveled the top of the hill, banked its sides, and built inner and outer walls with geometrical precision around the summit. Later walls were built on the middle terraces and also on the lower slopes of the hill, thus rendering the city exceedingly well fortified. These walls constitute a graphic commentary on the two sieges which Samaria underwent, the first when the city held out against the Syrians to the terrible lengths described in II Kings 6:24-30, and the second when Samaria withstood the mighty Assyrians for so long before succumbing (II Kings 17:5). The city has also been found to have been provided with a number of large cisterns which were very important in time of siege since there was no natural water supply.

The Israelite kings built their palaces within the walls on the western brow of the hill. The first palace was relatively simple but served as a core for later and more splendid structures. The palace which first was ascribed to Ahab, but perhaps belonged to Jeroboam II instead, was built from large blocks of limestone, and boasted a strong rectangular tower and an extensive outer court. At the north end of the palace courtyard was a cemented water pool, which may even have been the "pool of Samaria" in which the bloodstained chariot of Ahab was washed (I Kings 22:38).

It is probably from the time of the reign of Jeroboam II in the first part of the eighth century that the famous Samaritan ostraca come.[109] These are potsherds with writing on them, which were found in a storehouse in one of the palaces. They contain notes or accounts of oil and wine received as royal revenue for the king. A typical one reads:

> In the tenth year.
> To Gaddiyau.
> From Azah.
> Abi-ba'al 2
> Ahaz   2
> Sheba   1
> Meriba'al 1

[109] J. W. Jack, *Samaria in Ahab's Time.* 1929, pp.37-105; McCown, *The Ladder of Progress in Palestine*, p.199; W. F. Albright in ANET p.321 (ANEA p.211).

In this case Gaddiyau was the steward of the treasury to whom the wine was sent, Azah the name of the village or district, and the other names those of the peasant farmers who paid their taxes in the form of so many jars of wine. The stewards frequently have names which are used also in the Bible, such as Ahinoam, Gamar (Gomer), and Nimshi. Too, the senders of contributions often have biblical names, as do Ahaz, Sheba, and Meribaal in the ostracon quoted above. The name Meribaal and many other names compounded with Baal testify to the prevalence of Baal-worship. It will be remembered that Meribbaal is the name borne by Jonathan's son, for which Mephibosheth (*bosheth* meaning "shame") later was substituted when it came to be felt wrong to use the title Baal (lord) in connection with the God of Israel.[110] On the other hand many of the names have *Yahu* as an element, thus suggesting that the divine name Yahweh was often used in personal names at this time. The ostraca also mention over twenty place-names in the northern kingdom, six of which—Abiezer, Helek, Shechem, Shemida, Noah, and Hoglah—appear as names of clans in the Old Testament (Joshua 17:2; Numbers 26:30-33). Two more of the ostraca may be quoted since they provide a commentary on Amos 6:6:

> In the tenth year.
> From Abiezer to Shemariyo.
> A jar of old wine.
> To Ish-Ba'al [?].
> A jar of old wine.
> From Tetel.
>
> In the tenth year. From Azzah.
> To Gaddiyo. A jar of fine
> oil.

The old wine or "pure clarified wine," and the fine oil used probably for anointing the body, which are specified here, are exactly the things whose use by the luxurious and selfish rich people of Samaria is mentioned and condemned by the prophet.[111]

In view of the similar denunciation by Amos (6:4, 3:15) of the "beds of ivory" and "houses of ivory" of the rich people of Samaria and the mention in I Kings 22:39 of the "ivory house" which Ahab (874/873-853 B.C.) built, it is of much interest that numerous ivories were found in the excavation of Samaria. These are mostly in the

---

[110] I Chronicles 8:34; 9:40; II Samuel 4:4; 9:6, 10, etc.; cf. HDB II, pp.501f.
[111] René Dussaud in *Syria.* 7 (1926), pp.9-29.

form of plaques or small panels in relief and presumably were once attached to furniture and inlaid in wall paneling. The subjects depicted in the ivories include lotus, lilies, papyrus, palmettes, lions, bulls, deer, winged figures in human form, sphinxes, and figures of Egyptian gods such as Isis and Horus. A richly decorated ivory medallion in relief showing the infant Horus sitting upon a lotus, holding a flail in the right hand and raising the forefinger of the left hand to his lips in typical gesture, is shown in Fig. 66. This and other subjects as well as the technique of execution of the ivories indicate that Egyptian influence was strong in Palestine at this time.[112]

THE MOABITE STONE

In the days of Ahab the kingdom of Moab was tributary to Israel and sent annual payments of "a hundred thousand lambs, and the wool of a hundred thousand rams," but "when Ahab died . . . the king of Moab rebelled against the king of Israel" (II Kings 3:4f.). Ahab's immediate successor Ahaziah reigned but briefly and it was Jehoram who went out to do battle with Mesha king of Moab. In the midst of the battle Mesha offered his oldest son as a burnt offering upon the wall and "there came great wrath upon Israel" (II Kings 3:27).

A contemporary record of the relations between Israel and Moab exists in the famous Moabite Stone (Fig. 67). It was erected, with a long inscription by King Mesha at the Moabite capital of Dibon (the present Dhiban), north of the Arnon. Reports of its existence came to the French scholar Clermont-Ganneau in Jerusalem, and a Prussian traveler, the Reverend F. A. Klein, saw it for the first time in 1868. A squeeze[113] was taken of it, but before the stone itself could be obtained it was broken into pieces by the Arabs. Finally two large fragments and eighteen small pieces were recovered and a restoration and reconstruction was made and the monument placed in the Louvre.[114] In the inscription Mesha says in part:

"I am Mesha, son of Chemosh. . . , king of Moab, the Dibonite—my father had reigned over Moab thirty years, and I reigned after my father,—who made this high place for Chemosh in Qarhoh . . . because he saved me from all the kings and caused me to triumph over all my adversaries. As for Omri, king of Israel, he humbled Moab many years, for

---

[112] J. W. and Grace M. Crowfoot, *Early Ivories from Samaria.* 1938.

[113] A squeeze is a facsimile impression made by forcing a plastic substance into the depressions.

[114] C. S. Clermont-Ganneau, *La Stèle de Mésa.* 1887.

Chemosh was angry at his land. And his son followed him and he also said, 'I will humble Moab.' In my time he spoke thus, but I have triumphed over him and over his house, while Israel hath perished for ever! Now Omri had occupied the land of Medeba, and Israel had dwelt there in his time and half the time of his son, forty years; but Chemosh dwelt there in my time."[115]

Obviously there are differences between this and II Kings 3:4-27 and it is not certain whether the two accounts relate to the same or different campaigns. According to the Bible the total reigns of Omri and his son Ahab amounted to only thirty-four years,[116] but Mesha's "forty years" could be a round number. Also he claims that "Israel perished for ever" in the days of Ahab, while it was under Jehoram that Israel suffered the defeat which is probably referred to in the cryptic statement of II Kings 3:27. In general it is evident that on each side the writers selected that part of the history of the two lands to record which was most pleasing to them. Also it is noteworthy that Israel ascribed its victory to the Lord (II Kings 3:18) while Mesha thanked his god Chemosh for his. In the entire inscription the following places are mentioned which are also named in the Bible: the Arnon (Numbers 21:13, etc.; Deuteronomy 2:24; 3:16, etc.), Aroer (Joshua 13:16), Ataroth (Numbers 32:34), Baal-meon or Beth-baal-meon (Joshua 13:17; Numbers 32:38), Beth-bamoth (Bamoth-baal, Joshua 13:17), Beth-diblathaim (Jeremiah 48:22), Bezer (Joshua 20:8), Dibon (Numbers 32:34; Joshua 13:17; Isaiah 15:2), Horonaim (Isaiah 15:5), Jahaz (Joshua 13:18; Isaiah 15:4), Kerioth (Jeremiah 48:24), Kiriathaim (Joshua 13:19; Jeremiah 48:23), Medeba (Madeba, Joshua 13:9, 16; Isaiah 15:2), and Nebo (Numbers 32:38; Deuteronomy 34:1; Isaiah 15:2).

DIBON

Excavations have been conducted at Dhiban since 1950-1951 by the American School of Oriental Research in Jerusalem. The remains of four or five city walls have been brought to light, together with a square tower, and a number of buildings. Pottery ranges from Early Bronze to Early Arabic, but there is almost none of Middle and Late Bronze Age date, thus confirming to that extent the conclusion that Transjordan largely reverted to nomadism during those periods. In the Moabite Stone Mesha states that he said to all the

[115] W. F. Albright in ANET pp.320f. (ANEA p.209f.); G. A. Cooke, A Text-Book of North-Semitic Inscriptions. 1903, pp.1-14.

[116] I Kings 16:23—Omri, 12 years; 16:29—Ahab, 22 years.

people of Qarhoh (which may have been the name of Dibon for a time), "Let each of you make a cistern for himself in his house!" and it is therefore of interest that at Dhiban nearly one hundred cisterns have already been catalogued. A small fragment of another inscribed stela has also been found there, probably, like the Moabite Stone, dating from the ninth century B.C.[117]

THE SILOAM TUNNEL

In 722 B.C. Samaria fell to Assyria. In 701 B.C. Sennacherib of Assyria invaded Palestine and besieged Jerusalem itself. Hezekiah was king of Judah at this time, and he seems to have taken a far-sighted measure to strengthen the city against siege. II Kings 20:20 states that "he made the pool, and the conduit and brought water into the city." The same achievement is narrated in II Chronicles 32:30: "This same Hezekiah closed the upper outlet of the waters of Gihon and directed them down to the west side of the city of David." Thus the attackers were deprived of water at the same time that the besieged city was assured of an unfailing supply. "Why should the kings of Assyria come and find much water?" they asked as they stopped the waters that were outside the city (II Chronicles 32:2-4).

It will be remembered (p. 178) that Jerusalem's main source of fresh water was the Gihon spring, outside the city wall on the edge of the Kidron Valley, and that the Jebusites had somewhat difficult access to these waters through a vertical shaft and connecting tunnel. The entire system of tunnels related to the Gihon spring was cleared by Captain Parker in 1909-1911 and studied, measured, and photographed by Father Vincent at that time.[118] The Jebusite water system was found to have been walled off near the cave at the foot of the vertical shaft, and from this point a new rock tunnel was cut west and southwest for around 1,777 feet to empty into the Pool of Siloam (Ain Silwan). The ancient wall of Jerusalem used to cross the Tyropeon Valley just below this point, so at that time this pool was within the walls and safe from attackers in time of siege. It is natural to conclude that the cutting of this tunnel was the work of Hezekiah as referred to in II Kings 20:20 and II Chronicles 32:30.

Another tunnel also remains which runs south from the spring of Gihon near the outside edge of the rock and probably emptied into

[117] F. V. Winnett in BASOR 125 (Feb. 1952), pp.7-20; Roland E. Murphy in BASOR 125 (Feb. 1952), pp.20-23; A. Douglas Tushingham in BASOR 133 (Feb. 1954), pp.6-26.

[118] H. Vincent, *Jerusalem sous terre.* 1911.

the old Pool of Siloam or a similar reservoir within the city. It may be that this tunnel was cut by one of the earlier kings, perhaps David or Solomon, and afterward repaired by Hezekiah. This would provide a possible explanation of the difficult passage in which Isaiah (22:11) reproaches Hezekiah: "You made a reservoir between the two walls for the water of the old pool. But you did not look to him who did it, or have regard for him who planned it long ago." This would mean that Hezekiah took the entire credit for the conduit to himself, and also failed to follow David's example in faithfulness to God. Even if this is the correct explanation of its character, this tunnel must have proved insufficient, for ultimately it was supplanted by the more efficient tunnel cut right back through the heart of the rock and identified with Hezekiah's work as described in II Kings and II Chronicles.[119]

The great tunnel of Hezekiah was excavated in the solid rock with wedge, hammer, and pick, and the marks of the expertly wielded pickaxes are still to be seen on the walls. The excavators worked from both ends, and after many windings and turnings met in the middle. The average height of the tunnel is about six feet, but later cutting has made it much higher at the Siloam end. A photograph of the tunnel at the point where the workers met is shown in Fig. 68. On the right wall of the tunnel, about nineteen feet in from the Siloam entrance, an inscription was discovered in 1880 by a boy who had been wading in the pool. This inscription (Fig. 69) was later cut out and placed in the Museum of the Ancient Orient at Istanbul. It is translated as follows:

". . . when the tunnel was driven through. And this was the way in which it was cut through:—While . . . were still . . . axes, each man toward his fellow, and while there were still three cubits to be cut through, there was heard the voice of a man calling to his fellow, for there was an overlap in the rock on the right and on the left. And when the tunnel was driven through, the quarrymen hewed the rock, each man toward his fellow, axe against axe; and the water flowed from the spring toward the reservoir for 1,200 cubits, and the height of the rock above the heads of the quarrymen was 100 cubits."[120]

Such was the conclusion of a truly notable engineering feat.

[119] Duncan, *Digging Up Biblical History.* II, pp.126f., 201-215.

[120] W. F. Albright in ANET p.321 (ANEA p.212); A. H. Sayce, *Records of the Past.* New Series, I, pp.168-175; Gesenius-Kautzsch, *Hebrew Grammar.* ed. Collins and Cowley, 1898, p. xix; Cooke, *A Text-Book of North-Semitic Inscriptions*, pp.15-17; David Diringer, *Le iscrizioni antico-ebraiche palestinesi.* 1934, pp.81-102; Hans J. Stoebe in ZDPV 71 (1955), pp.124-140. The Hebrew cubit was probably about seventeen and one-half inches, and for simplicity may be taken as one and a half feet.

THE LACHISH LETTERS

Although Jerusalem was wonderfully delivered from Sennacherib as Isaiah promised (Isaiah 36-37; II Kings 19:20, 32-36; II Chronicles 32:20-22), its downfall came at last. In succession to the Assyrians, the Neo-Babylonian Empire dominated western Asia. When King Jehoiakim of Judah ventured to rebel, he and his son Jehoiachin who succeeded him were punished speedily by the invasion of Judah and the taking of Jerusalem in 597 B.C. (II Kings 24:1-17). Zedekiah was installed at Jerusalem as puppet king and when he, too, broke faith with his Babylonian master the city's final doom was sealed, Nebuchadnezzar II advanced for the last time upon Judah, and after an eighteen-month siege Jerusalem fell (586 B.C.), its walls were broken down, its houses and great temple burned with fire, and its people, save for the very poorest of the land, carried into exile (II Kings 25:1-12).

Jeremiah the prophet lived through these terrible events and in the introduction to one of the prophecies which he addressed to Zedekiah there is a striking reference to the time "when the army of the king of Babylon was fighting against Jerusalem and against all the cities of Judah that were left, Lachish and Azekah; for these were the only fortified cities of Judah that remained" (Jeremiah 34:7). Both of these cities have been excavated. Azekah is identified with Tell Zakariya in the Shephelah. It was excavated in 1898 by Dr. Frederick J. Bliss of the Palestine Exploration Fund and revealed a strong inner citadel fortified with eight large towers. This may have been built by Rehoboam, who is reported to have fortified this city, as well as Lachish (II Chronicles 11:9).[121]

The identification of Lachish with Tell ed-Duweir and the excavations at this site have already been mentioned (pp. 161f.) with particular reference to the city of the Late Bronze Age and its destruction presumably by the incoming Israelites. This devastation marked the end of Level VI as the strata are counted downward from the top by the excavators. In the succeeding Iron Age[122] Lachish was fortified with a great brick wall twenty feet thick around the summit of the mound and a revetment of stone and brick about fifty feet below on the slope of the mound. The initial building of these defenses may reasonably be attributed to Rehoboam after the division of the kingdom (II Chronicles 11:9). In his time Sennacherib

---

[121] Macalister, *A Century of Excavation in Palestine*, pp.55f.
[122] Olga Tufnell, *Lachish III (Tell ed-Duweir), The Iron Age*. 2 vols. 1953.

(704-681 B.C.) captured Lachish and took booty from it, as is mentioned in an inscription and pictured in a relief of the Assyrian king (p. 214). A large pit tomb at Tell ed-Duweir with the jumbled remains of 1,500 human bodies may represent the clearance of the city after this conquest, since the pottery which is mingled with the bones is probably of the eighth or early seventh century B.C.[123] Levels V, IV, and III are not yet clearly distinguishable for lack of sufficiently extensive excavation, but it is plain that Level III came to an end with the burning of the city and the overthrow of its walls. Amidst the debris of this destruction the city of Level II arose. The wall was repaired hastily with whatever material was available, the palace was not yet rebuilt. Then Level II also experienced a violent end. So intense was the fire in which the city perished that masonry was melted into a liquid stream of white and red which flowed down over the lower wall where charred heaps of burned timber still remain. While some think that a greater time must have intervened between the end of Level III and of Level II, it seems very probable that the two destructions mark the coming of Nebuchadnezzar in 597 and again in 588 B.C.[124]

Of great interest was a discovery made by J. L. Starkey in 1935. In a small room, believed to be the guard room, adjoining the outer gate of the city of Lachish and lying buried in the burned layer of charcoal and ashes which represented the last destruction of the city mentioned just above, were eighteen ostraca with Hebrew writing in the ancient Phoenician script.[125] Almost all of them were dispatches or letters which had been written by a certain Hoshaiah, who was at some military outpost, to a man named Yaosh, who must have been a high commanding officer at Lachish. At the time of writing the final siege of Jerusalem and Lachish was probably beginning, and Azekah may even have fallen already, since one of the letters (No. IV) says, "We are watching for the fire-signals of Lachish according to all the signs which my lord arranged, for we no longer can see the signals of Azekah."[126] Lachish itself appears to have

---

[123] G. Ernest Wright in BA 18 (1955), p.13 n.1.

[124] W. F. Albright in BASOR 132 (Dec. 1953), p.46; Briggs W. Buchanan in AJA 58 (1954), pp.335f.; G. Ernest Wright in BA 18 (1955), pp.14f.; Herbert G. May in JBL 75 (1956), p.343.

[125] Harry Torczyner, *Lachish I (Tell ed Duweir), The Lachish Letters*. 1938; W. F. Albright in BASOR 70 (Apr. 1938), pp. 11-17; and in ANET pp.321f. Three additional ostraca, bringing the total number up to twenty-one, were found in the last campaign at Lachish in 1938 (BASOR 80 [Dec. 1940], pp. 11-13; 82 [Apr. 1941], p.24).

[126] Frank M. Cross, Jr., in BASOR 144 (Dec. 1956), p. 25; cf. W. F. Albright in ANET p.322.

held out at least until after the autumn olive harvest since many carbonized olive stones were found in the embers of the burned city.

One of the letters (No. III) reads as follows:

"Thy servant Hoshaiah hath sent to inform my lord Yaosh: May Yahweh cause my lord to hear tidings of peace! And now thou hast sent a letter, but my lord did not enlighten thy servant concerning the letter which thou didst send to thy servant yesterday evening, though the heart of thy servant hath been sick since thou didst write to thy servant. And as for what my lord said, 'Dost thou not understand?—call a scribe!', as Yahweh liveth no one hath ever undertaken to call a scribe for me; and as for any scribe who might have come to me, truly I did not call him nor would I give anything at all for him!

"And it hath been reported to thy servant, saying, 'The commander of the host, Coniah son of Elnathan, hath come down in order to go into Egypt; and unto Hodaviah son of Ahijah and his men hath he sent to obtain . . . from him.'

"And as for the letter of Tobiah, servant of the king, which came to Shallum son of Jaddua through the prophet, saying, 'Beware!', thy servant hath sent it to my lord."[127]

Hoshaiah is a biblical name and appears in Jeremiah 42:1 and Nehemiah 12:32. God is referred to by the four letters *Yhwh*, which are the consonants of the name Yahweh and in this and other of the letters many of the men's names have Yahweh endings. The prophet who is mentioned in this letter has been believed by some to be Jeremiah himself,[128] but this is not necessarily or even probably true.[129]

Another of the Lachish letters (No. VI) is illustrated in Fig. 70 and translated as follows:

"To my lord Yaosh: May Yahweh cause my lord to see this season in good health! Who is thy servant but a dog that my lord hath sent the letter of the king and the letters of the princes, saying, 'Pray, read them!' And behold the words of the princes are not good, but to weaken our hands and to slacken the hands of the men who are informed about them. . . . And now my lord, wilt thou not write to them saying, 'Why do ye thus even in Jerusalem? Behold unto the king and unto his house are ye doing this thing!' And, as Yahweh thy God liveth, truly since thy servant read the letters there hath been no peace for thy servant. . . ."[130]

The mention in this letter of words which are weakening the hands of the people, reminds us again of Jeremiah against whom it

---

[127] W. F. Albright in ANET p.322; cf. in BASOR 82 (Apr. 1941), pp.20f.
[128] J. W. Jack in PEQ 1938, pp.165-187.
[129] Gordon, *The Living Past*, p.189.
[130] W. F. Albright in ANET p.322; and in BASOR 82 (Apr. 1941), pp.22f.

was charged: "he is weakening the hands of the soldiers who are left in this city, and the hands of all the people, by speaking such words to them" (Jeremiah 38:4). In the letter, however, the discouraging words appear to have come from princes rather than from a prophet, and so Jeremiah is probably not referred to here either. Nevertheless, despite the enigmatical language of the letters we can discern conditions very comparable to those which are known from the biblical records to have prevailed at this time.

It was also of interest to find at Lachish a clay seal, the back of which still showed the mark of the fibers of the papyrus document to which it had been affixed, and on which was the inscription, "The property of Gedaliah who is over the house." This is the same name as that of the man who was made governor of Judah by Nebuchadnezzar after 586 B.C. (II Kings 25:22; Jeremiah 40:5f.; 41:2) and his title "who is over the house" is elsewhere known in the Old Testament (Isaiah 22:15; 36:3).[131]

The ravages of the conquest of Palestine by Nebuchadnezzar were very terrible. The land was devastated and laid waste, and the best of the population was carried off into captivity. From this awful time Judah did not recover for two or three hundred years. The exiles were allowed to return to their homeland at last but the population remained small and poor, while the temple which Zerubbabel rebuilt was as nothing in the eyes of those who had seen it in its former glory (Haggai 2:3). This pitiful state of affairs is reflected only too clearly in the archeological realm by the paucity of important materials. We know that the small Jewish state stamped official jar handles and also silver coins with the legend Yehud, that is "Judah,"[132] but it is not until in the Hellenistic period (c.300-63 B.C.) that solidly constructed buildings and abundant pottery again appear. Even then the archeological monuments thus far discovered in Palestine are relatively scant.[133]

[131] PEFQs 1935, pp.195f.
[132] E. L. Sukenik in JPOS 14 (1934), pp.178-184.
[133] For daily life in Old Testament Palestine see E. W. Heaton, *Everyday Life in Old Testament Times*. 1956.

IV

Empires of Western Asia: Assyria, Chaldea and Persia

I N ITS later Old Testament days the fate of the Israelite people was connected closely, as we have just seen, with the great powers to the north and east.

1. THE KASSITES, c.1650-c.1175 B.C.

THE beginnings of civilization in the valley of the Tigris and Euphrates have already been traced and Mesopotamia has been described as it was in the time of Abraham and of Hammurabi (Chapter I). In the days that followed, the entire northern boundary of the Fertile Crescent felt the pressure of advancing Indo-European hordes[1] and the kings who came after Hammurabi on the throne of Babylon had to struggle against Kassites from the eastern mountains and Hittites from the west. Samsuiluna, Hammurabi's immediate successor, repelled a wholesale invasion of Kassites but the latter continued to make a peaceful penetration of the country, and for almost 150 years Kassite names appear in Babylonian business documents as laborers, harvesters, and hostlers. Finally the Kassites attained power and established a dynasty which ruled in Babylon for half a millennium. On the whole the Kassite period is obscure historically but it is thought that the main outlines of the social order as established by Hammurabi continued to exist. It is known that the horse, which was a divine symbol to the Kassites, became common in Babylonia only after their entry.[2]

[1] Albrecht Götze, *Hethiter, Churriter und Assyrer*. 1936, p.27.
[2] George G. Cameron, *History of Early Iran*. 1936, pp.89-95.

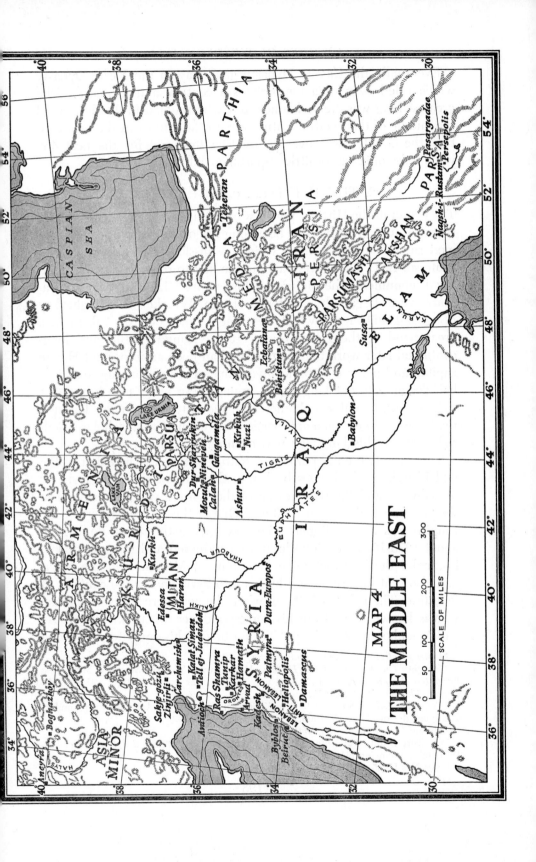

MAP 4

THE MIDDLE EAST

SCALE OF MILES

50   100   200   300

Eventually the Kassite Dynasty gave way to the Pashe Dynasty which ruled Babylonia for perhaps a century and a quarter. The greatest king was Nebuchadnezzar I who reigned probably around the middle of the twelfth century B.C. In the middle of the next century the country was overrun by Elamites, and for the next 450 years Babylonia was of little importance politically.

2. THE HITTITES, c.1900-c.1200 B.C.[1]

THE center of the Hittites' power was in Asia Minor, where an empire that was once great but had been long forgotten was rediscovered by modern archeology. William Wright, a missionary at Damascus, and Professor A. H. Sayce were among the first to reconstruct from scattered monuments the picture of this empire.[2] Then in 1906 excavations were begun by Professor Hugo Winckler at Boghazköy (Boghaz-keui), a site which lies ninety miles east of Ankara in a great bend of the Halys River.[3] It was found in this and long-continued later work that Boghazköy had been an important Hittite capital, and many clay tablets were unearthed containing texts in a half-dozen different languages. Among these were a large number written with cuneiform characters in the Hittite language. Through the labors of many men and particularly of the Czech scholar Friedrich Hrozný this language was eventually deciphered.[4]

There are two chief periods of Hittite power, the first that of the Old Kingdom which goes back into the time of the First Dynasty of Babylon, and the second that of the Empire which flourished in the years around 1460 to 1200 B.C.[5] One of the greatest rulers of the Empire was Suppiluliumas who was on the throne at Boghazköy about 1375-1335 B.C. Suppiluliumas conquered and incorporated in his realm the Mesopotamian kingdoms of Mitanni and the Hurri and also sent his armies southward into Syria and to the confines of Palestine. The ruler of Mitanni whom he conquered was Tushratta, who is known to us from his correspondence with Amenhotep III and Amenhotep IV of Egypt.[6] Tushratta gave his daughter Taduhepa

---

[1] Götze, *Hethiter, Churriter und Assyrer*, p.80.

[2] Wright, *The Empire of the Hittites*. 1884; Sayce, *The Hittites, The Story of a Forgotten Empire*. rev. ed. 1925. See now O. R. Gurney, *The Hittites*. 1952; C. W. Ceram, *The Secret of the Hittites*. 1956.

[3] Winckler, *Die im Sommer 1906 in Kleinasien ausgeführten Ausgrabungen*. Sonderabzug aus der OL, Dec. 15, 1906.

[4] Hrozný, *Die Sprache der Hethiter*. 1917.

[5] cf. Kurt Bittel, *Die Ruinen von Boğazköy, der Hauptstadt des Hethiterreiches*. 1937, table following p.102.

[6] KAT Nos.17-25, 27-29 = MTAT Nos.17-25, 27-29.

to be the wife of Amenhotep III. Suppiluliumas also corresponded with Amenhotep IV, whom he called Huria, and the following is one of the letters which has been preserved:

> Thus hath Suppiluliumas, the great king,
> king of Hatti-land, to Huria,
> king of Egypt, my brother, spoken:
> I am well. With thee may it be well.
> With thy wives, thy sons, thy house, thy warriors, thy chariots,
> and in thy land, may it be very well.
>
> Now, thou, my brother, hast ascended the throne of thy father,
> and, just as thy father and I
> mutually requested presents,
> so wilt also thou and I now be mutually
> good friends.[7]

So great, indeed, was the influence of Suppiluliumas that a queen of Egypt, probably Ankhesenamun, daughter of Akhenaton and widow of Tutankhamun, wrote and asked for one of his sons to be her husband. The son was actually sent but was killed in Egypt, probably at the instigation of Eye who became the next Pharaoh.[8]

Suppiluliumas was succeeded by his son, Arnuwandas III, and then by the latter's brother, Mursilis II. His son and successor was Muwatallis who reigned about 1306-1282 B.C. The rivalry with Egypt now reached its climax in the famous battle of Kadesh on the Orontes. Here in the fifth year of Ramses II (1286 B.C.) Muwatallis routed the Egyptian forces, although the fact that the Pharaoh himself managed to escape with his life enabled him afterward to boast of the encounter. The brother of Muwatallis and second king after him was Hattusilis III (c.1275-c.1250 B.C.), who signed a nonaggression pact with Ramses II in the twenty-first year of the latter's reign. The agreement was confirmed by the marriage of a daughter of Hattusilis to Ramses II (p. 114).

By this time, however, both the Hittites and the Egyptians were greatly weakened and around 1200 B.C. the Hittite Empire reached its end.[9] The "Hittite City," as Boghazköy was called, fell, and such Hittite kingdoms as continued to exist at Carchemish, Zinjirli (Senjirli), Sakje-gözü (Sakjegeuzi), Hamath, and other places were relatively small and impotent, although Hittite cultural influence is

---

[7] KAT No.41 = MTAT No.41.

[8] Gurney, *The Hittites*, p.31.

[9] K. Bittel and R. Naumann, *Boğazköy*. 1938, p.5.

traced until in the first century A.D. in the Kingdom of Commagene.[10] Thus the old balance of power was destroyed and Assyria's opportunity had come to emerge in international affairs as the dominant world power.

3. ASSYRIAN BEGINNINGS, c.3000-c.1700 B.C.

THE homeland of Assyria was in the northeast corner of the Fertile Crescent where the Tigris River flows southward across the plains, and the mountains of Kurdistan loom up in the background. The country has a length of about 350 miles and a width of from 200 to 300 miles, with a total area of some 75,000 square miles or somewhat smaller, for example, than the state of Nebraska. In contrast with stoneless Babylonia, Assyria was supplied abundantly with limestone, alabaster, and, in the Kurdistan hills, marble.[1]

The city which gave its name to the country and empire, even as it took its own name from the national god, was Ashur.[2] It was located strategically on a low bluff on the right bank of the Tigris at a place now called Qalat Sharqat. After some earlier digging done there by Layard, Rassam, and Place, Ashur was excavated in 1903-1914 by a German expedition under the direction of Walter Andrae.[3] It appears that the site was occcupied from the early part of the third millennium B.C., while the earliest literary references to the city of Ashur occur in texts which were found at Nuzi and which date from the Old Akkadian period.[4]

Under Shamshi-Adad I (c.1748-c.1716 B.C.)[5] Assyria enjoyed a

---

[10] Ceram, *The Secret of the Hittites*, pp.213, 260. For the excavation of the temple-tomb of Antiochus I of Commagene (c.69-34 B.C.) at Nemrud Dagh see Theresa Goell in BASOR 147 (Oct. 1957), pp.4-22.

[1] Morris Jastrow, *The Civilization of Babylonia and Assyria.* 1915, p.6.

[2] A. T. Olmstead, *History of Assyria.* 1923, p.1.

[3] Andrae, *Das wiedererstandene Assur.* 1938.

[4] Meek, *Old Akkadian, Sumerian and Cappadocian Texts from Nuzi*, p.xi.

[5] The dates of the kings are based now upon a list of Assyrian rulers discovered in the palace of Sargon III at Khorsabad by the Oriental Institute of the University of Chicago in 1932-33 and published by A. Poebel in JNES 1 (1942), pp.247-306,460-492; 2 (1943), pp.56-90. From the thirty-third king on, not only the names but also the lengths of reign are given. Albright's revision of Poebel's date for Shamshi-Adad I is that which is given here (cf. p.57 n.5). In contrast with the Sumerians and early Babylonians, who designated individual years by naming them after important events which had just transpired, the Assyrians selected a high official each year, often even the king himself, to be known as the *limmu* and to give his name to the year. Lists of these limmus or eponyms were kept (see for example ARAB II, §§1194-1198), and provide important materials for chronology along with the king lists. Since in connection with Bur-Sagale, eponym in the tenth year of Ashur-dan III, an eclipse of the sun is mentioned, and since this has been identified with an astronomically computed eclipse which took place on June 15, 763 B.C., a fixed point is won from which other chronological calculations are made (TMN pp.44f.).

period of independence and Ashur began to be a great city, well fortified and with a fine temple to house its god.[6]

4. THE ASSYRIAN KINGDOM, c.1700-c.1100 B.C.

As THE First Dynasty of Babylon declined the power of Assyria increased. Doubtless there was also stimulus at this time from the present of the Hurrians, whose important city of Nuzi has already been mentioned (p. 66).

Some light is cast on the life of this period by the Assyrian laws which were discovered at Ashur. The Babylonian code, or a body of laws of closely related character, was still the law of the land. However, in cases where the Babylonian code was inadequate to Assyrian requirements and customs or in need of amendment to suit Assyrian conditions, further regulations were necessary and these are represented by the laws just mentioned.[1] Of interest also is an Assyrian text of this time found at Susa which contains a collection of dream-omens, showing how dreams were interpreted as indications of events to come.[2]

In the days of Suppiluliumas of the Hittites and Amenhotep IV of Egypt, Ashur-uballit I, "Ashur-has-given-life" (c.1362-c.1327) was king of Assyria. Among the Tell el-Amarna tablets are letters which he addressed to Amenhotep IV. In one he wrote:

> To the king of Egypt,
> say.
> Thus saith Ashur-uballit, king of Assyria:
> With thee, thy house, thy wives,
> thy chariots, and thy chief men
> may it be well!

In another he told of the gifts he was sending:

> A beautiful royal chariot, with my span,
> and two white horses, with my span, also
> one chariot without a span, and one seal of beautiful lapis lazuli.

But he expected gifts in return:

> If thou art very friendly disposed,
> then send much gold.[3]

---

[6] ARAB I, §43A.

[1] G. R. Driver and J. C. Miles, *The Assyrian Laws*. 1935, pp.14f.

[2] A. Leo Oppenheim, *The Interpretation of Dreams in the Ancient Near East, With a Translation of an Assyrian Dream-Book*. Transactions of the American Philosophical Society. New Series, Vol. 46, Pt. 3, 1956.

[3] KAT Nos.15f. = MTAT Nos.15f.

His proud assumption of equality with the Egyptian Pharaoh was not entirely unjustified, for Ashur-uballit I was one of the men who by conquest and political strategy began to make the kingdom of Assyria into the great Assyrian Empire.

5. THE ASSYRIAN EMPIRE, c.1100-633 B.C.

WITH Tukulti-apil-Esharra I, better known as Tiglath-pileser I (c.1114-c.1076), we enter the period that may properly be called that of the Assyrian Empire. This was the time described above (pp. 199f.) when the stage was clearly set for the emergence of Assyria as the greatest power in the Middle East. Amidst the confusion of small, hostile states which had taken the place of the old balance of power, Tiglath-pileser I was able to extend the conquests of Assyria westward to the Mediterranean Sea and northward to the region of Lake Van. Now, too, for the first time in Assyrian history, detailed annals are available describing many of the campaigns in which Tiglath-pileser I strove for the mastery of the world.[1] He said: "Ashur and the great gods, who have made my kingdom great, and who have bestowed might and power as a gift, commanded that I should extend the boundary of their land, and they entrusted to my hand their mighty weapons, the storm of battle. Lands, mountains, cities, and princes, the enemies of Ashur, I have brought under my sway, and have subdued their territories. . . . Unto Assyria I added land, unto her peoples, peoples. I enlarged the frontier of my land, and all of their lands I brought under my sway."[2]

ASHUR-NASIR-PAL II

The next two centuries, however, were ones of relative darkness for Assyria, and it remained for Ashur-nasir-pal II (883-859)[3] to make Assyria the ruthless fighting machine whose calculated frightfulness was the terror of its enemies. The merciless cruelty of his campaigns is the constant boast of Ashur-nasir-pal II:

"I stormed the mountain peaks and took them. In the midst of the mighty mountain I slaughtered them, with their blood I dyed the mountain red like wool. With the rest of them I darkened the gullies and preci-

[1] A. T. Olmstead, *Assyrian Historiography*. The University of Missouri Studies, Social Science Series, III, 1. 1916, p. 10.

[2] ARAB I, §219.

[3] The dates are cited now according to the accession-year system which is explained in the Appendix. Thus 859 B.C. is the last year of Ashur-nasir-pal II and the accession year of Shalmaneser III, while 858 is the first regnal year of Shalmaneser III.

pices of the mountains. I carried off their spoil and their possessions. The heads of their warriors I cut off, and I formed them into a pillar over against their city, their young men and their maidens I burned in the fire."

"I built a pillar over against the city gate, and I flayed all the chief men who had revolted, and I covered the pillar with their skins; some I walled up within the pillar, some I impaled upon the pillar on stakes, and others I bound to stakes round about the pillar; many within the border of my own land I flayed, and I spread their skins upon the walls; and I cut off the limbs of the officers, of the royal officers who had rebelled."[4]

The quotations just given are typical of many more which can be read in the annals of this king. The final edition of these annals was inscribed on the pavement slabs of the entrance to the temple of Ninurta at Calah. It was characteristic of some of the most energetic rulers of Assyria to move the royal residence to a new center, and the already ancient and ruined city of Calah (cf. Genesis 10:11) was that chosen by Ashur-nasir-pal II for his new capital. Calah is now represented by the mound of Nimrod and that is where the young Englishman, Austen Henry Layard, began his Assyrian excavations in 1845. At the very outset the palace of Ashur-nasir-pal II was uncovered. When the first colossal winged man-headed lion (Fig. 71) which guarded the palace entrance came into view the Arab chief cried, "This is not the work of men's hands, but of those infidel giants of whom the prophet (peace be with him!) has said that they were higher than the tallest date-tree. This is one of the idols which Noah (peace be with him!) cursed before the Flood."[5] In a small temple near by, a statue of Ashur-nasir-pal II, about half life-size, was found which is the only perfect statue in the round of an Assyrian king that is extant. This statue is shown in Fig. 72. The king holds in each hand a symbol of sovereignty, that in the right hand resembling an Egyptian scepter and that in the left is a mace. On the breast are eight lines of inscription, giving the king's name and titles and stating that he had conquered the whole region from the Tigris to Mount Lebanon and the Great Sea, meaning the Mediterranean.

A century after Layard terminated his work at Nimrod, the British School of Archaeology in Iraq undertook further excavations at the same site. These were conducted in 1949 and 1950 by M. E. L. Mallowan. Work centered again to a considerable extent on the great

---

[4] ARAB I, §§447, 443.

[5] Frederic Kenyon, *The Bible and Archaeology*. 1940, p.38; Seton Lloyd, *Foundations in the Dust*. 1947, pp.94-143.

palace of Ashur-nasir-pal II. Some of the sculptured wall reliefs which had been exposed and then reburied by Layard were again uncovered and recorded by photography. Also a new southeastern wing of the palace was found and excavated. Inscriptions with dates in the reign of Sargon II were found here, and also fine carved ivory pieces which had probably once adorned the royal furniture. Another palace was found too, bricks in which were inscribed with the name and titles of Shalmaneser III. In two rooms of this palace, over one hundred clay tablets were found, dating for the most part from the reign of Tiglath-pileser III. These suggest that this building was an administrative headquarters, for they contain government and military archives, records of loans and contracts, lists of individual possessions, and lists of personal names. In one contract it is stated that if either party infringes the agreement, "his eldest son he shall burn before Sin and his eldest daughter before. . . ."[6]

SHALMANESER III

The ruthless Assyrian fighting machine which Ashur-nasir-pal II had developed was directed by his son Shulmanu-ashared III or Shalmaneser III (858-824) in repeated campaigns against Syria and Palestine. "In my first year of reign," states Shalmaneser III, "I crossed the Euphrates at its flood. To the shore of the sea of the setting sun I advanced. I washed my weapons in the sea."[7] A few years later a great battle was fought at Qarqar (Karkar) on the Orontes River against a formidable Syrian coalition of twelve kings. The "Monolith Inscription" of Shalmaneser III, which came to the British Museum from Kurkh, records the military activities of the king up to his sixth year, and in the annals of the sixth year includes a description of this battle. The date of the battle of Qarqar is therefore 853 B.C.[8] Among the allied leaders who opposed Shalmaneser III, Hadadezer of Damascus is named first. Then Irhuleni of Hamath is mentioned, and in third place stands "Ahab, the Israelite."[9] While the Bible does not mention this incident, the Assyrian inscription

---

[6] M. E. L. Mallowan in *Sumer*. 6 (1950), pp.101f.; 7 (1951), pp.49-54; Donald J. Wiseman in *Sumer*. 6 (1950), p.103; 7 (1951), pp.55-57.

[7] ARAB I, §558.

[8] Military campaigns were usually launched in the spring, after the winter rains, and since the record in the Monolith Inscription (ARAB I, §610; ANET p.278 [ANEA p.188]) states that Shalmaneser III left Nineveh on the fourteenth day of Aiaru and crossed the Euphrates at its flood, it is probable that the battle of Qarqar took place in the summer of 853 B.C.

[9] ARAB I, §611; ANET p.279 (ANEA p.188).

testifies to the prominence of Ahab among the rulers of the time. The inscription gives statistics on the fighting forces involved and describes Ahab as commanding 2,000 chariots and 10,000 soldiers. In chariotry, Ahab's forces were much larger than those of any other king, Hadadezer being credited with 1,200 and Irhuleni with 700. The mention of Ahab is of importance also in giving an entirely independent confirmation of the fact that this king was on the throne of Israel just before the middle of the ninth century B.C. In this battle Shalmaneser III claimed an overwhelming triumph in which he made the blood of his enemies flow down the valleys and scattered their corpses far and wide, yet the fact that he avoided Syria thereafter for several years may mean that the victory was not as decisive as his boasts would indicate.

On one of the later campaigns of Shalmaneser III, Jehu of Israel paid heavy tribute to him. This is known to us from the famous Black Obelisk which Layard found in 1846 in the palace of Shalmaneser at Nimrod.[10] This is a four-sided pillar of black limestone six and one-half feet in height with five rows of roughly executed bas-reliefs extending around it and with texts between and below them. The inscriptions record the military achievements of Shalmaneser III from the first thirty-one years of his reign and the reliefs illustrate the payment of tribute from five different regions. A reproduction of the Black Obelisk is seen in Fig. 73 where, on the front of the monument in the second row of reliefs, Jehu is actually pictured kneeling before Shalmaneser III. The Assyrian king accompanied by two attendants, one of whom holds a sun-shade above him, stands proudly, with the symbols of Ashur and Ishtar in the field above. At his feet kneels Jehu in all humility. The Israelite king is shown with a short, rounded beard and wears a soft cap on his head. He is clothed in a sleeveless jacket and long fringed skirt with girdle. Following him come Israelites in long robes, carrying precious metals and other tribute. The inscription reads: "The tribute of Jehu, son of Omri; I received from him silver, gold, a golden bowl, a golden vase with pointed bottom, golden tumblers, golden buckets, tin, a staff for a king, and wooden [word unknown]."[11] Another inscription preserves a fragment of the annals of Shalmaneser III, in which he also refers to the taking

---

[10] A. H. Layard, *Nineveh and Its Remains.* 1849, I, p.282. The Black Obelisk was nearly lost at sea when the sailing ship on which it was being transported to England came close to foundering in a great storm in the Indian Ocean. C. J. Gadd, *The Stones of Assyria.* 1936, p.48.

[11] ANET p.281 (ANEA p.192); ARAB I, §590.

of tribute from Jehu, son of Omri, and dates this event in the eighteenth year of his reign. The date was, therefore, 841 B.C.[12]

Shalmaneser III liked to call himself "the mighty king, king of the universe, the king without a rival, the autocrat, the powerful one of the four regions of the world, who shatters the might of the princes of the whole world, who has smashed all of his foes like pots,"[13] but despite his boasts, he died amidst revolts with which his son Shamshi-Adad V (823-811) had to contend. Shamshi-Adad V, Sammuramat or Semiramis the famous queen, and her son Adad-nirari III (810-783), were fairly successful in maintaining the power of Assyria but under Shalmaneser IV (782-773), Ashur-dan III (772-755), and Ashur-nirari V (754-745) came decline.

TIGLATH-PILESER III

Then the throne was usurped by a great warrior and statesman who took the famous name of Tiglath-pileser (p. 202). Tiglath-pileser III (744-727), a sculptured representation of whose head is shown in Fig. 74, brought the moribund Assyrian Empire back to vigorous life. He carried out conquests to the east and west and in Babylon itself was recognized as king. There they called him Pulu, and it is by a form of this name, Pul, that he is referred to in II Kings 15:19 and I Chronicles 5:26.[14] In one of his inscriptions Tiglath-pileser III mentions receiving tribute from a number of kings, among whom he names Azriau from Iuda, probably meaning King Azariah of Judah.[15] In another he speaks of taking tribute from Menahem of Samaria,[16] doubtless the event mentioned in the Old

---

[12] ANET p.280 (ANEA p.192); ARAB I, §672. Ahab fought against Shalmaneser III at Qarqar in 853 B.C., and Jehu paid tribute to the same king in 841 B.C. Between Ahab and Jehu the rulers of Israel were Ahaziah and Joram, who are credited with reigns of two years and twelve years respectively in I Kings 22:51 and II Kings 3:1. By the nonaccession-year system these two reigns would actually total twelve years, which is the time between Qarqar and the paying of tribute by Jehu. Therefore the death of Ahab at Ramoth-gilead (I Kings 22:3, 35) must have taken place in 853 B.C. soon after Qarqar, and the accession of Jehu have been in 841 B.C. TMN pp.48-53,62.

[13] ARAB I, §674.

[14] I Chronicles 5:26 should probably be translated: "So the God of Israel stirred up the spirit of Pul king of Assyria, even the spirit of Tiglath-pilneser king of Assyria" (TMN p.77).

[15] ANET p.282 (ANEA p.193); ARAB I, §770. This reference belongs to the third year of the reign of Tiglath-pileser III; since he departed from the traditional system of counting regnal years and included his accession year (745 B.C.), his third year was 743 B.C. A. Poebel in JNES 2 (1943), p.89 n.23.

[16] ANET p.283 (ANEA p.194); ARAB I, §772. The year is unknown. W. F. Albright (in BASOR 100 [Dec. 1945], pp.18,21) puts it in 738 B.C.; Thiele (TMN pp.75-98) in 743 B.C.

Testament (II Kings 15:19). Another text which probably refers to the same Israelite king reads: "[As for Menahem I] overwhelmed him . . . and he . . . fled like a bird, alone. . . . I returned him to his place . . . gold, silver, linen garments with multicolored trimmings . . . I received from him."[17]

A few years later, as is related in II Kings 16:5-9, Pekah of Israel and Rezin of Damascus allied themselves against Assyria and also attacked Ahaz of Judah, evidently to try to force him to join the coalition too. Ahaz appealed to Tiglath-pileser III for help, and the Assyrian king moved again into the west. In Israel he took captive many of the people and deported them to Assyria, while Pekah was slain by conspiracy and Hoshea made ruler in his place. This is told in II Kings 15:29f. and I Chronicles 5:26, and there is a corresponding record in the inscriptions of Tiglath-pileser III: "Bit Humria [Israel] . . . all its inhabitants and their possessions I led to Assyria. They overthrew their king Paqaha [Pekah] and I placed Ausi' [Hoshea] as king over them. I received from them 10 talents of gold, 1,000 talents of silver as their tribute and brought them to Assyria."[18] Bit Humria or House of Omri had been the usual Assyrian designation for the land of Israel since the days of King Omri more than one hundred years before. That such a ruthless deportation of peoples, doubtless in order to prevent future rebellions, was a usual feature of Tiglath-pileser's policy we know from other of his inscriptions. Elsewhere he says, for example: "[I deported] 30,300 inhabitants from their cities and settled them in the province of the town. . . . 1,223 inhabitants I settled in the province of the Ullaba country."[19]

In Syria Tiglath-pileser III attacked Damascus and killed Rezin (II Kings 16:9). This event is probably referred to in another inscription of Tiglath-pileser III where he speaks of the defeat inflicted upon Rezin (Rezin) in a campaign which may be dated according to the eponym lists in 732 B.C.[20] This was, accordingly, also the date of the deportation in Northern Israel and of the change in rule from Pekah to Hoshea.

In Damascus Ahaz also presented himself before Tiglath-pileser

[17] ANET pp.283f. (ANEA pp.194f.); ARAB I, §815. The year to which this text refers is also unknown.

[18] ANET p.284 (ANEA p.194); ARAB I, §816.

[19] ANET p.283 (ANEA p.193); ARAB I, §770.

[20] ANET p.283 (ANEA p.194); ARAB I, §779; cf. TMN pp.90,106,121; Albright in BASOR 100 (Dec. 1945), p.22 n.26.

III (II Kings 16:10), and this event is no doubt referred to in another text of Tiglath-pileser III where he lists "Iauhazi of Judah" among those from whom he received tribute.[21] The fact that he calls the king by this name shows that Ahaz was probably an abbreviated form of Jehoahaz.

SHALMANESER V

The son and successor of Tiglath-pileser III was Shalmaneser V (726-722). In his time, Hoshea ventured to rebel against Assyria, whereupon Shalmaneser V laid siege to the Israelite capital. According to II Kings 18:9f., Samaria was thus besieged for three years, beginning with the seventh year of King Hoshea and ending with the fall of the city in the ninth year of Hoshea. If the accession of Hoshea was in the summer or later in 732 B.C., as the records of Tiglath-pileser III mentioned above make probable, his first full year of reign began in Nisan 731 B.C. The seventh regnal year of Hoshea was then that from Nisan 725 to Nisan 724 B.C., and his ninth year that from Nisan 723 to Nisan 722 B.C. If the fall of Samaria is placed at the latest possible point allowed by these data it was in the spring of 722 B.C., and this was still within the reign of Shalmaneser V. A Babylonian chronicle written in the twenty-second year of King Darius, 500 B.C., and covering Assyrian and Babylonian history from Tiglath-pileser III to Ashurbanipal, states that the death of Shalmaneser V was in the month Tebetu and the accession of his successor, Sargon, on the twelfth day of the same month, this being late in December, 722 B.C. This Babylonian chronicle also records as the noteworthy event of Shalmaneser's reign that he destroyed the city of Shamarain, which may be identified with Samaria. This evidence, therefore, suggests that the fall of Samaria should be attributed to Shalamaneser V and placed in the fighting season of 722 B.C.,[22] that is sometime between spring and autumn of that year.

SARGON II

Sharrukin II or Sargon II came to the throne at the time described in the preceding paragraph and enjoyed a reign of seventeen years (721-705). He bore a name which appears once before in the Khorsa-

21 ANET p.282 (ANEA p.193); ARAB I, §801.

22 Babylonian Chronicle I, 27-31; Hugo Winckler, Keilinschriftliches Textbuch zum Alten Testament. 2d ed. 1903, p.61; cf. A. T. Olmstead, Western Asia in the Days of Sargon of Assyria, 722-705 B.C. 1908, p.45 n.9; History of Assyria, p. 205; TMN pp.122-128. It should be noted that some wish to read the word in question in the Babylonian chronicle as Shabarain instead of Shamarain and to identify it with

bad King List[23] somewhat earlier than Shamshi-Adad I, a name which was also famous from the exploits of the yet earlier Sargon of Agade (p. 46). According to one record he was a brother of Shalmaneser V.[24] Sargon is mentioned in Isaiah 20:1 in connection with his capture of Ashdod,[25] and for a long time this was the only place in extant literature where his name was known. In 1843 the French consular agent at Mosul, Paul Émile Botta, began to dig at Khorsabad (Dur-Sharrukin) and discovered the palace of Sargon II. Sargon had made his capital successively at Ashur, Calah, and Nineveh, and then finally here at this place. He called the new capital after himself, Dur-Sharrukin or Sargonsburg, but eventually the ruin was ascribed to a Sasanid hero, Khosroes, and called Khorsabad, "town of Khosroes." The large palace which Botta discovered and which has been reexplored more intensively in recent years by the Oriental Institute of the University of Chicago, was built by Sargon II in the closing years of his reign and was adorned on the walls with texts describing the events of his kingship.[26]

In his Khorsabad inscriptions known as Annals, Sargon II claims the taking of Samaria as his own accomplishment. The text is fragmentary at this point but is reconstructed and translated as follows: "At the begi[nning of my royal rule, I . . . the town of the Sama]rians [I besieged, conquered] . . . [for the god . . . who le]t me achieve this my triumph. . . . I led away as prisoners [27,290 inhabitants of it] and [equipped] from among [them soldiers to man] 50 chariots for my royal corps. . . . [The town I] re[built] better than it was before and [settled] therein people from countries which [I] myself [had con]quered. I placed an officer of mine as governor over them and imposed upon them tribute as is customary for Assyrian citizens."[27] Again in Sargon's so-called Display Inscriptions at Khorsabad there is this record which presumably, like the foregoing, refers to the beginning of his reign: "I besieged and conquered Samaria, led away as booty 27,290 inhabitants of it. I formed from among them a contingent of 50 chariots and made remaining inhabitants assume

---

some other city than Samaria, but this is little probable (A. T. Olmstead in AJSL 21 [1904-5], pp.180f.). For the conclusion that Samaria was taken by Shalmaneser V see now Hayim Tadmor in JCS 12 (1958), pp.22-40.

[23] Poebel in JNES 2 (1943), p.86. [24] ibid., p.89 n.26.

[25] cf. ANET p.286 (ANEA p.197); ARAB II, §30; Tadmor in JCS 12 (1958), pp.83f.

[26] Gordon Loud, Khorsabad I, Excavations in the Palace and at a City Gate. OIP XXXVIII, 1936; G. Loud and Charles B. Altman, Khorsabad II, The Citadel and the Town. OIP XL, 1938.

[27] ANET p.284 (ANEA p.195); ARAB II, §4; cf. A. G. Lie, The Inscriptions of Sargon II, Part I, The Annals. 1929, p.5.

their social positions. I installed over them an officer of mine and imposed upon them the tribute of the former king."[28]

If these statements comprise the authentic record of the fall of Samaria, then that city must have been captured at the earliest in the accession year of Sargon II, that is sometime after late December, 722 B.C., hence probably in 721 B.C. This is, however, in conflict with the data which indicate that Samaria was taken by Shalmaneser V. If Samaria fell in the summer or fall of 722 B.C. it was only a few months until the death of Shalmaneser V in December of that year, and this may have made it easy for Sargon II, in inscriptions written late in his reign, to claim for his own glory the conquest which was actually accomplished by his predecessor. Furthermore, in the few months before his death Shalmaneser V may have but barely begun the deportation of the people of Samaria and the actual carrying out of this deportation may have actually been the work of Sargon II, as the latter says.[29]

An alabaster relief from Khorsabad gives us an impressive picture of the kind of fighting man Sargon II could send into action (Fig. 75). Carrying bow and arrow, short sword and short club, this powerfully muscled warrior stands in calm confidence, a symbol of the overwhelming military might of Assyria. Yet sometimes even the Assyrians faced enemies against which the bowsman could not avail and terrible plagues of locusts devastated the land as they did in Judah in the days of Joel. An enameled tile painting (Fig. 76) from the time of Sargon II shows some great man of Assyria standing in front of the all-seeing sun-god Shamash to ask for deliverance from a plague of locusts, or possibly to give thanks for the deliverance which has already taken place. The theme of his prayer is made unmistakable by the representation of the locust above his head.

SENNACHERIB

Sargon II fell in battle and was succeeded by his son, Sin-ahhe-eriba or Sennacherib (704-681). The capital of Sennacherib was the famous city of Nineveh on the east bank of the Tigris, across

[28] ANET pp.284f. (ANEA pp.195f.); ARAB II, §55; cf. A. T. Olmstead in AJSL 47 (1930-31), pp.262f.

[29] Tadmor in JCS 12 (1958), pp.37f. It has also been thought that Sargon II might have participated in the taking of Samaria along with his brother, Shalmaneser V, but prior to his own accession to the kingship, and in this connection it is pointed out that II Kings 18:9f. says that Shalmaneser besieged Samaria but that "they" (ASV) took it. The use of the word "they" could allow for the association of Sargon with Shalmaneser at the end of the siege; on the other hand it may be simply a reference to the Assyrian army in the plural. See TMN p.124.

from where the modern city of Mosul now stands. Sennacherib planned the fortifications of this city, gave it a system of water-works, restored its temples and built its most magnificent palaces. The ancient city is represented by two large mounds known as Kuyunjik and Nebi Yunus, the latter being so named because it is the site of the reputed tomb of the prophet Jonah. In 1820 Claudius James Rich, the British resident at Baghdad, visited Mosul. Although he died of cholera the next year, the posthumous publication in 1836 of his *Narrative of a Residence in Koordistan* awakened much interest in the possibilities of archeological work in Assyria. In 1842 Paul Émile Botta was sent to Mosul by the French government as consular agent. He made brief and unsuccessful attempts to dig at Nebi Yunus and Kuyunjik before transferring his efforts to Khorsabad where he made the brilliant discovery mentioned above (p. 209). He was followed in work both at Khorsabad and at Kuyunjik by Victor Place. Austen Henry Layard, the English archeologist, concerned himself first with Nimrod, as we have seen (p. 203), but also did some digging at Kuyunjik and in 1847 discovered there the great palace of Sennacherib. During Layard's second expedition, which lasted from 1849 to 1851, this palace was largely unearthed. No less than seventy-one rooms were found, and it was computed that the palace had contained approximately 9,880 feet of walls lined with sculptured slabs.[30]

Early in the reign of Sennacherib, Hezekiah of Judah revolted against Assyria and in 701 B.C. the Assyrian king moved west and south. The campaign is described in the annals of Sennacherib which were recorded on clay cylinders or "prisms." The final edition of these annals appears on the Taylor Prism of the British Museum and in an even better copy on a prism now in the Oriental Institute of the University of Chicago (Fig. 77). The prism is hexagonal in form, and the middle column in the photograph contains the reference to Hezekiah quoted below.

Sennacherib names Sidon, Beth-Dagon, Joppa, and other cities as having fallen before him and tells of his victory in a great battle fought in the neighborhood of the city of Altaku or Eltekeh[31] in which the Palestinian forces were assisted by Egyptian bowmen and chariotry. Then Sennacherib continues:

[30] Layard, *Nineveh and Its Remains*. 1849; *Discoveries among the Ruins of Nineveh and Babylon*. 1875; *The Monuments of Nineveh*. 1853; *A Second Series of the Monuments of Nineveh*. 1853; André Parrot, *Nineveh and the Old Testament*. 1955.

[31] Probably the same city mentioned in Joshua 19:44; 21:23 (HDB I, p.698).

"As to Hezekiah, the Jew, he did not submit to my yoke, I laid siege to 46 of his strong cities, walled forts and to the countless small villages in their vicinity, and conquered them by means of well-stamped earth-ramps, and battering-rams brought thus near to the walls combined with the attack by foot soldiers, using mines, breeches as well as sapper work. I drove out of them 200,150 people, young and old, male and female, horses, mules, donkeys, camels, big and small cattle beyond counting, and considered them booty. Himself I made a prisoner in Jerusalem, his royal residence, like a bird in a cage. I surrounded him with earthwork in order to molest those who were leaving his city's gate. His towns which I had plundered, I took away from his country and gave them over to Mitinti, king of Ashdod, Padi, king of Ekron, and Sillibel, king of Gaza. Thus I reduced his country, but I still increased the tribute and the presents due to me as his overlord which I imposed later upon him beyond the former tribute, to be delivered annually. Hezekiah himself, whom the terror-inspiring splendor of my lordship had overwhelmed and whose irregular and elite troops which he had brought into Jerusalem, his royal residence, in order to strengthen it, had deserted him, did send me, later, to Nineveh, my lordly city, together with 30 talents of gold, 800 talents of silver, precious stones, antimony, large cuts of red stone, couches inlaid with ivory, chairs inlaid with ivory, elephant-hides, ebony-wood, box-wood and all kinds of valuable treasures, his own daughters, concubines, male and female musicians. In order to deliver the tribute and to do obeisance as a slave he sent his personal messenger."[32]

Presumably this inscription refers to the same invasion that is described in II Kings 18:13-19:37; II Chronicles 32:1-22; Isaiah 36:1-37:38. In comparing the Old Testament account with Sennacherib's record we note that Hezekiah's tribute is placed at 30 talents of gold in both sources but at only 300 talents of silver in II Kings 18:14 as compared with 800 talents of silver which the Assyrian king claims to have received.

In II Kings 19:9 = Isaiah 37:9 it is stated that "Tirhakah king of Ethiopia" came out to fight against Sennacherib. In 701 B.C. a Kushite dynasty, commonly called "Ethiopian," was indeed ruling Egypt, but according to the chronology given above (p. 127) King Taharqo, who is the biblical Tirhakah, was first associated with his predecessor Shebitko in 689 B.C. and was sole ruler only from 684 on. To account for this discrepancy it has previously been suggested that while Taharqo was not yet king in 701 B.C. he might have been a military commander under his uncle Shabako and as such have fought

---

[32] ANET p.288; ARAB II, §240. Like other Assyrian campaigns, this one was no doubt launched in the spring and the date of the siege of Jerusalem was summer, 701 B.C. According to II Kings 18:13; Isaiah 36:1 this was the fourteenth year of Hezekiah. cf. TMN pp.101,110; Albright in BASOR 100 (Dec. 1945), p.22 n.28.

against Sennacherib.[33] According to the present chronology, however, not even this would have been possible, since Taharqo was probably only born in 709 B.C. and was yet much too young. Therefore strength is given to the alternative hypothesis which had also already been advanced, namely that Sennacherib made a second invasion of Palestine after Taharqo was actually ruling as king, that is after 689 or 684, and before his own death in 681 B.C. In this case we might consider II Kings 18:13-19:8 as describing Sennacherib's first invasion when Hezekiah paid heavy tribute, and II Kings 19:9-37 with its mention of Tirhakah as king as referring to Sennacherib's second campaign. Some support is gained for this view if II Kings 19:37 is interpreted as giving the impression that Sennacherib's death ensued shortly after his return from the disaster at Jerusalem. It is true that such a second and later Palestinian campaign on the part of Sennacherib cannot be verified in his own annals but inscriptions referring to the last eight years of his reign are lacking.

At all events we must acknowledge that Sennacherib says nothing of the disaster which overwhelmed his armies at Jerusalem according to II Kings 19:35f. = Isaiah 37:36f. In view of the general note of boasting which pervades the inscriptions of the Assyrian kings, however, it is hardly to be expected that Sennacherib would record such a defeat. Perhaps the fact that he claims to have shut up Hezekiah in Jerusalem "like a bird in a cage," but does not claim to have taken the city, is evidence that he did suffer discomfiture there. Incidentally, the Old Testament account finds support in a somewhat enigmatic story recorded by Herodotus and running as follows:

"The next king was the priest of Hephaestus, whose name was Sethos. He despised and took no account of the warrior Egyptians, thinking he would never need them; besides otherwise dishonouring them, he took away the chosen lands which had been given to them, twelve fields to each man, in the reign of former kings. So presently came king Sanacharib against Egypt, with a great host of Arabians and Assyrians; and the warrior Egyptians would not march against him. The priest, in this quandary, went into the temple shrine and there bewailed to the god's image the peril which threatened him. In his lamentation he fell asleep, and dreamt that he saw the god standing over him and bidding him take courage, for he should suffer no ill by encountering the host of Arabia: 'Myself,' said the god, 'will send you champions.' So he trusted the vision, and encamped at Pelusium with such Egyptians as would follow him, for here is the road into Egypt; and none of the warriors would go with him,

[33] ARE IV, §892; L. L. Honor, *Sennacherib's Invasion of Palestine.* 1926, p.34 n.112.

but only hucksters and artificers and traders. Their enemies too came thither, and one night a multitude of field-mice swarmed over the Assyrian camp and devoured their quivers and their bows and the handles of their shields likewise, insomuch that they fled the next day unarmed and many fell. And at this day a stone statue of the Egyptian king stands in Hephaestus' temple, with a mouse in his hand and an inscription to this effect: 'Look on me, and fear the gods.' "[34]

The mention of mice may well indicate that it was plague which struck Sennacherib's army, since mice are a Greek symbol of pestilence and since rats are carriers of the plague. Perhaps this is the real explanation of the disaster referred to in II Kings 19:35 as a smiting of the army by an angel of the Lord, for plague and disease elsewhere in the Bible are regarded as a smiting by an angel of God (II Samuel 24:15-17; Acts 12:23).[35]

In Fig. 78 we see a portion of a frieze illustrating one of Sennacherib's wars in the west. His soldiers are advancing to the attack in relentless procession. At the left are auxiliaries in crested helmets, carrying round shields and long spears, and wearing knee-coverings. In the center are spearsmen of a different type and in front are slingers. Another sculpture (Fig. 79) shows Sennacherib seated upon his throne before the captured city of Lachish (cf. II Kings 18:14, 17; 19:8, etc.) and receiving the spoils of the city to the accompaniment of the torture of hapless prisoners.[36] The inscription states: "Sennacherib, king of the world, king of Assyria, sat upon a throne and passed in review the booty taken from Lachish."[37]

ESARHADDON

Sennacherib was assassinated in 681 B.C. He had named his favorite son Ashur-aha-iddina or Esarhaddon to be his successor, although the latter was not the eldest son. The other sons, hoping to gain the kingship, slew Sennacherib their father, but Esarhaddon swiftly attacked the rebels and secured the crown.[38] The most important achievements of Esarhaddon's reign (680-669) were the restoration of the city of Babylon, which had been destroyed by his father, and

[34] II, 141.

[35] Samuel I. Feigin has pointed out that Assyrian omen texts speak of the outbreak of the *shibu* fever in an army as foreshadowing victory for the enemy. See William A. Irwin in JNES 9 (1950), p.123.

[36] Layard, *Discoveries among the Ruins of Nineveh and Babylon*, pp.126-128; R. D. Barnett in IEJ 8 (1958), pp.161-164.

[37] ANET p.288; ARAB II, §489.

[38] ANET pp.288f.; ARAB II, §§500-506.

the defeat of Taharqo, now upon the throne of Egypt, at whose border Sennacherib had been turned back.

The victory over Taharqo was commemorated with a victory stela (Fig. 80) set up at Zinjirli in northern Syria, and discovered in 1888 by a German expedition. It shows the king with a mace in his left hand, and in his right a cup from which he has poured a libation to the gods symbolized at the top of the stela. From the left hand extend ropes which pass through the lips of the two figures at his feet. The kneeling figure is doubtless Taharqo, represented with strongly marked Negroid features. His hands are lifted in supplication, and both hands and feet are shackled. The other figure, standing, may be Ba'alu of Tyre, although the inscription does not claim his surrender. The inscription says concerning the conquest of Egypt: "I fought daily, without interruption, very bloody battles against Tirhakah, king of Egypt and Ethiopia, the one accursed by all the great gods. Five times I hit him with the point of my arrows inflicting wounds from which he should not recover, and then I laid siege to Memphis, his royal residence, and conquered it in half a day by means of mines, breaches and assault ladders; I destroyed it, tore down its walls and burnt it down.[39] Proudly Esarhaddon says of himself, "I am powerful, I am all powerful, I am a hero, I am gigantic, I am colossal," and for the first time an Assyrian ruler takes the new title, "King of the kings of Egypt."[40]

ASHURBANIPAL

Taharqo may have been wounded grievously, but he survived to fight again, while Esarhaddon died on his next march toward Egypt. Esarhaddon was succeeded by his son Ashurbanipal (668-633), the great king who was called Osnappar in the Old Testament (Ezra 4:10) and Sardanapalus by the Greeks. Ashurbanipal campaigned in Egypt, defeating both Taharqo and Tanutamun and taking both Memphis and Thebes (pp. 127f.). Concerning the triumphs in Egypt, the defeat of Taharqo and of Tanutamun, whom he calls Urdamane, and the plundering of Thebes, Ashurbanipal wrote:

"In my first campaign I marched against Egypt and Ethiopia. . . . Tirhakah, king of Egypt and Nubia, heard in Memphis of the coming of my expedition and he called up his warriors for a decisive battle against me. . . . I defeated the battle-experienced soldiers of his army in a great open battle. . . . He left Memphis and fled, to save his life, into the town

[39] ANET p.293; ARAB II, §580. [40] ARAB II, §§577, 583.

of Thebes. This town too I seized and led my army into it to repose there. . . . The terror of the sacred weapon of Ashur, my lord, overcame Tirhakah where he had taken refuge and he was never heard of again. Afterwards Urdamane, son of Shabako, sat down on the throne of his kingdom. He made Thebes and Heliopolis his fortresses and assembled his armed might. He called up his battle-experienced soldiers to attack my troops, and the Assyrians stationed in Memphis. . . .

"In my second campaign I marched directly against Egypt and Nubia. Urdamane . . . left Memphis and fled into Thebes to save his life. . . . I followed Urdamane and went as far as Thebes, his fortress. He saw my mighty battle array approaching, left Thebes and fled to Kipkipi. . . . I, myself, conquered this town completely. From Thebes I carried away booty, heavy and beyond counting: silver, gold, precious stones, his entire personal possessions, linen garments with multicolored trimmings, fine horses, certain inhabitants, male and female. I pulled two high obelisks, cast of shining bronze, the weight of which was 2,500 talents, standing at the door of the temple, out of their bases and took them to Assyria. Thus I carried off from Thebes heavy booty, beyond counting. I made Egypt and Nubia feel my weapons bitterly and celebrated my triumph. With full hands and safely, I returned to Nineveh, the city where I exercise my rule."[41]

Ashurbanipal's wars were numerous and his conduct often ruthlessly cruel, yet he is remembered most of all for his culture. The paradox of his culture and his cruelty is well represented in the relief which shows him at a banquet in the royal pleasure garden with his queen Ashur-sharrat (Fig. 81). The scene is one of peaceful beauty until it is noted that the head of the leader of the Elamites, whom Ashurbanipal has just conquered, hangs like ghastly fruit from the coniferous tree at the left.

In his inscriptions Ashurbanipal refers frequently to the education which he received in the days of his youth and to his intellectual as well as military and sporting achievements.

"I, Ashurbanipal, learned the wisdom of Nabu,[42] the entire art of writing on clay tablets. . . . I learned to shoot the bow, to ride, to drive and to seize the reins.

"I received the revelation of the wise Adapa, the hidden treasure of the art of writing. . . . I considered the heavens with the learned masters. . . . I read the beautiful clay tablets from Sumer and the obscure Akkadian writing which is hard to master. I had my joy in the reading of inscriptions

41 ANET pp.294f.; ARAB II, §§770-778; Arthur C. Piepkorn, *Historical Prism Inscriptions of Ashurbanipal.* I (AS 5), 1933, pp.39-41.

42 The patron god of the art of writing. (A. H. Sayce in HDB III, pp.501f.).

on stone from the time before the flood. . . . The following were my daily activities: I mounted my horse, I rode joyfully . . . I held the bow . . . I drove my chariot, holding the reins like a charioteer. I made the wheels go round. . . . At the same time I learned royal decorum and walked in kingly ways."[43]

The interest of Ashurbanipal in education resulted ultimately in the establishment of a great royal library. In the Temple of Nabu at Nineveh one library had already been in existence at least since the time of Sargon II, but the collection of Ashurbanipal was to surpass all others in size and importance. He sent scribes throughout Assyria and Babylonia with authority to copy and translate the writings they found, and tens of thousands of clay tablets were brought together, containing historical, scientific, and religious literature, official dispatches and archives, business documents and letters. Ashurbanipal's royal palace containing this library was discovered in 1853 by Hormuzd Rassam, the brother of the British vice-consul at Mosul, who was continuing Layard's work at Kuyunjik.

Among the tablets which Rassam unearthed and sent to the British Museum were the ones which were later found to contain Assyrian copies of the Babylonian flood and creation stories (pp. 33, 62). The identification and decipherment of these particular tablets was the work of George Smith, then a young assistant in the British Museum. In 1872, while engaged in the sorting and classification of the Kuyunjik tablets, he noticed pieces containing portions of mythical stories. "Commencing a steady search among these fragments," Smith afterward related, "I soon found half of a curious tablet which had evidently contained originally six columns. . . . On looking down the third column, my eye caught the statement that the ship rested on the mountains of Nizir, followed by the account of the sending forth of the dove, and its finding no resting-place and returning. I saw at once that I had here discovered a portion at least of the Chaldean account of the Deluge."[44]

In the royal palace were also found the magnificent reliefs of the lion hunts of Ashurbanipal, one section of which is reproduced in Fig. 82. With their close attention to animal forms, their thrilling realism and unmistakable atmosphere of the excitement of the chase, these sculptures represent the climax of Assyrian art.

[43] Maximilian Streck, *Assurbanipal und die letzten assyrischen Könige bis zum Untergang Ninevehs.* 1916, ii, pp.5,255,257.

[44] R. C. Thompson, *A Century of Exploration at Nineveh.* 1929, p.49. Quoted by permission of the publishers, Luzac and Co., London.

6. THE DECLINE AND FALL OF ASSYRIA,
633-612 B.C.

FOLLOWING Ashurbanipal with Assyria at the height of its glory, three undistinguished rulers, Ashur-etil-ilani, Sin-shum-lishir, and Sin-shar-ishkun occupied the throne, and then the end came with startling suddenness and Assyrian civilization was snuffed out.

For the story of Nineveh's fall and the end of the Assyrian Empire, we can now turn to a contemporary record of events. Assyrian records are largely lacking during the last twenty-five years before the end, perhaps because the kings were reluctant to record their reverses, but a Babylonian clay tablet which chronicles the fall of Nineveh has been discovered and is in the British Museum.[1] This Babylonian chronicle, known as B.M. 21901, is inscribed with a summary of the chief events in years ten to seventeen of the reign of Nabopolassar, king of Babylon. Nabu-apal-usur, or Nabopolassar in the Greek form of the name, was a Chaldean. The Chaldeans, whom Jeremiah (5:15) called "an ancient nation," were a Semitic people who entered Babylonia around 1000 B.C.[2] They stirred up disaffection against Assyrian rule of Babylonia, and in the days of Sargon II one of their chiefs, Merodach-baladan (II Kings 20:12; Isaiah 39:1), was able to rule Babylon for a time. The persistent rebelliousness of Babylon was finally punished by Sennacherib, who destroyed the city completely. Esarhaddon restored Babylon, hoping to gain the support of the south, and when he died left Ashurbanipal's younger brother, Shamash-shum-ukin, as king of Babylon. After the rebellion and death of Shamash-shum-ukin, Ashurbanipal was himself king of Babylon. But when he died, Nabopolassar, a Chaldean and a descendant of Merodach-baladan, seized the kingship of Babylon and established an independent Chaldean or New Babylonian empire.

Another British Museum tablet from Babylon recently published (B.M. 25127), gives the date of the accession of Nabopolassar to the throne of Babylon: "On the twenty-sixth day of the month of Arahsamnu, Nabopolassar sat upon the throne in Babylon. This was the 'beginning of reign' of Nabopolassar."[3] The reference is to the

---

[1] C. J. Gadd, *The Fall of Nineveh*. 1923; ARAB II, §§1166-1186; ANET pp.303-305 (ANEA p.202).
[2] Olmstead, *History of Assyria*, p.250.
[3] WCCK pp.50f.

72. Ashur-nasir-pal II

71. Man-headed Lion from the Palace of Ashur-nasir-pal II

74. Head of Tiglath-pileser III

73. Cast of the Black Obelisk of Shalmaneser III

77. The Prism of Sennacherib

76. An Assyrian Prays to Shamash Concerning a Plague of Locusts

75. A Warrior of Sargon II

78. The Army of Sennacherib Advances to the Attack

79. Sennacherib at Lachish

80. The Zinjirli Stela of Esarhaddon

81. Victory Banquet of Ashurbanipal and his Queen

82. Ashurbanipal on the Lion Hunt

83. The Ruins of Babylon

84. Enameled Lion from the Processional Street in Babylon

85. Enameled Bricks from the Throne Room of Nebuchadnezzar II

86. The Cyrus Cylinder

87. Relief from the Palace of Cyrus at Pasargadae

88. The Tomb of Cyrus the Great

89. The Rock of Behistun

90. Darius Triumphs over the Rebels

91. The Rock-hewn Tomb of Darius I the Great

92. The Palace of Darius (Tachara) at Persepolis

94. Standing Columns of the Hall of Xerxes (Apadana) at Persepolis

93. Tripylon Relief at Persepolis Showing Darius I and Xerxes

95. Relief from the Apadana Stairway at Persepolis

96. Eastern Portal of the Gate of Xerxes at Persepolis

97. Enameled Brick Panels from Susa Showing Spearmen of the Achaemenid Period

year 626 B.C. and the date would be November 23;[4] his ensuing twenty-one years of reign were 625-605 B.C.[5]

It was in the fourteenth year of Nabopolassar, according to the Babylonian chronicle first mentioned above (B.M. 21901),[6] that Nineveh fell, and this date was accordingly 612 B.C. In the destruction of Nineveh Nabopolassar of Babylon was joined by Cyaxares the Mede (p. 231) and by the king of the Scythians. As a matter of fact, the Median king was the most important figure in the enterprise. He had begun operations against Nineveh a few years earlier, and although he did not take the capital at that time he did capture the city of Ashur. In 613 B.C. the siege of Nineveh seems to have been lifted, and this may have been due to a Scythian attack upon the Medes, which is mentioned by Herodotus.[7] But in 612 B.C. the Babylonians, Medes, and Scythians all combined for the final and successful attack upon the Assyrian capital. The siege lasted from Simanu to Abu, that is from May/June to July/August, but eventually Nineveh fell and its last king, Sin-shar-ishkun, died. Yet one more man, a certain Ashur-uballit II (611-608), reigned for a few years as king of Assyria in the western city of Haran, but this last capital of a great empire soon was also taken by its enemies. Nineveh the Great had fallen. The destruction predicted by Zephaniah (2:13-15) had taken place. As he saw the end come Nahum cried (3:1-3):

> Woe to the city, bloody throughout,
> Full of lies and booty!
> Prey ceases not.
> The crack of the whip, and the noise of the rumbling wheel,
> And the galloping horse, and the jolting chariot;
> The charging horseman, and the flashing sword,
> And the glittering spear, and a multitude of slain,
> And a mass of bodies, and no end to the corpses!
> They stumble over the corpses![8]

The spoils were divided equally, the Medes taking the regions east and north of the Tigris, and the king of Babylon taking those to the

---

[4] PDBC p.27. A temple record at Sippar recognizes Nabopolassar as king two months earlier, this city evidently having become independent of Assyria before Babylon (WCCK pp.7,93).

[5] For most of the dates in the remainder of this chapter see PDBC; and cf. Dubberstein in JNES 3 (1944), pp.38-42. See also the Appendix of the present book.

[6] ANET p.304 (ANEA p.202); ARAB II, §§1177f.

[7] I,103-106.

[8] *An American Translation.*

west and south of that natural dividing line.[9] The agreement was sealed by the marriage of Amytis, daughter of Cyaxares's son Astyages, to Nebuchadnezzar II, son of Nabopolassar.

7. THE NEW BABYLONIAN EMPIRE, 612-539 B.C.

NEBUCHADNEZZAR II

It has already been noted (p. 129) that Pharaoh Necho II made an attempt to assist the Assyrians and resist the rising power of the New Babylonian Empire, but that the Egyptians were finally defeated by Nebuchadnezzar at Carchemish in 605 B.C. This decisive battle is mentioned in Jeremiah 46:2 where it is stated that Pharaoh Necho was defeated at Carchemish by Nebuchadrezzar[1] king of Babylon in the fourth year of Jehoiakim king of Judah. Berossos as quoted by Josephus[2] also narrates the event and provides the further details that Nebuchadnezzar was sent as commander of the Babylonian army by his father King Nabopolassar, and after the victory learned that his father had just died and so hastened home to ascend the throne himself.

This information is now confirmed by a newly published text from Babylon in the British Museum (B.M. 21946), which covers events from the twenty-first year of Nabopolassar to the eleventh year of Nebuchadnezzar, that is from 605 to 594 B.C. It begins as follows, the king of Akkad mentioned at the outset being Nabopolassar:

"In the twenty-first year the king of Akkad stayed in his own land, Nebuchadrezzar his eldest son, the crown-prince, mustered the Babylonian army and took command of his troops; he marched to Carchemish which is on the bank of the Euphrates, and crossed the river to go against the Egyptian army which lay in Carchemish. . . . He accomplished their defeat and to non-existence beat them. As for the rest of the Egyptian army which had escaped from the defeat so quickly that no weapon had reached them, in the district of Hamath the Babylonian troops overtook and defeated them so that not a single man escaped to his own country. At that time Nebuchadrezzar conquered the whole area of the Hatti-

[9] George Stephen Goodspeed, *A History of the Babylonians and Assyrians.* 1902, p.333.
[1] In Babylonian the king's name is Nabu-kudurri-usur and means "Nabu protect the border." Jeremiah (21:2, etc.) and Ezekiel (26:7, etc.), both contemporary prophets, render the name Nebuchadrezzar; it is given as Nebuchadnezzar in part of Jeremiah (27:6, etc.), and in II Kings (24:1, etc.), Chronicles (I 6:15; II 36:6, etc.), Ezra (1:7, etc.), Nehemiah (7:6), Esther (2:6), and Daniel (1:1, etc.). The former rendering is closer to the original, the latter more familiar.
[2] *Against Apion.* I, 19; *Ant.* x, xi, 1.

country. For twenty-one years Nabopolassar had been king of Babylon. On the 8th of the month of Abu he died; in the month of Ululu Nebuchadrezzar returned to Babylon and on the first day of the month of Ululu he sat on the royal throne in Babylon."[3]

It is certain, therefore, that the battle of Carchemish took place in 605 B.C. The exact month is not given but it had to be between Nisanu when the twenty-first year of Nabopolassar began and Abu when the king died; perhaps Simanu (May/June) is a reasonable guess.[4] Precise dates are stated for the death of Nabopolassar and the accession of Nebuchadnezzar; they are equivalent respectively to August 15 and September 7, 605 B.C.

After the battle of Carchemish, according to the same Babylonian text, Nebuchadnezzar took all of "the Hatti-country." In the record of the seventh year, which will be quoted below, "the Hatti-land" includes "the city of Judah," therefore this term must be used as a general designation for Syria-Palestine.[5] As our text continues with the record of Nebuchadnezzar's reign it states that in his first year (604/603 B.C.) he returned to the West:

"In the first year of Nebuchadrezzar in the month of Simanu he mustered his army and went to the Hatti-territory, he marched about unopposed in the Hatti-territory until the month of Kislimu. All the kings of the Hatti-land came before him and he received their heavy tribute."[6]

Jehoiakim king of Judah had been put on the throne by Necho II (II Kings 23:34), but after the defeat of the Pharaoh at Carchemish fell necessarily under the power of Nebuchadnezzar. His submission is recorded in II Kings 24:1, and if he was one of "the kings of the Hatti-land" just mentioned in the Babylonian text, this was in 604/603 B.C.

In his second and in his third years Nebuchadnezzar went back to the Hatti-land, and in his fourth year (601/600 B.C.) he marched to Egypt. An open battle was fought with the Egyptians and the Babylonian chronicle honestly reports that each side inflicted great havoc on the other, and that Nebuchadnezzar and his troops "turned back and returned to Babylon."[7] This virtual defeat, as it appears to have been, of the Babylonians may well have been what encouraged Jehoiakim to the act of rebellion against Nebuchadnezzar which is recorded in II Kings 24:1. It is there stated that this was

[3] WCCK pp.67-69.   [4] WCCK p.25.
[5] cf. J. Philip Hyatt in JBL 75 (1956), p.280.
[6] WCCK p.69.   [7] WCCK p.71.

after Jehoiakim had been servant to the Babylonian king for three years, which would probably indicate this very year of 601/600 B.C.[8]

"In the fifth year the king of Akkad stayed in his own land and gathered together his chariots and horses in great numbers," the Babylonian text continues.[9] In the sixth and seventh years he marched again to the Hatti-land. The purpose of Nebuchadnezzar now undoubtedly included punishment of the defection of Judah and re-establishment of his control there, and in the record of the seventh year we are told explicitly of attack upon "the city of Judah" which must mean Jerusalem:

"In the seventh year, the month of Kislimu, the king of Akkad mustered his troops, marched to the Hatti-land, and encamped against [i.e. besieged] the city of Judah and on the second day of the month of Addaru he seized the city and captured the king. He appointed there a king of his own choice, received its heavy tribute and sent them to Babylon."[10]

The seventh year of Nebuchadnezzar began on the first day of Nisanu, 598 B.C. The month of Kislimu when he marched to Hatti-land and besieged Jerusalem began on December 18, 598 B.C. The second day of Addaru when he seized the city and captured the king was March 16, 597 B.C. Thus the Babylonian record has provided the exact date of the first fall of Jerusalem. The name of the king of Judah captured by Nebuchadnezzar is not given in the Babylonian source but from the biblical record it is evident that it was Jehoiachin (II Kings 24:12). The "king of his own choice," whom Nebuchadnezzar then put on the throne at Jerusalem is also not named in the Babylonian chronicle but must have been Jehoiachin's uncle, Mattaniah, whose name was changed to Zedekiah according to II Kings 24:17 and II Chronicles 36:10.[11]

Even though Zedekiah was installed in the kingship of Judah as vassal of Nebuchadnezzar, the time came when he too ventured to rebel against his Babylonian master. Thereupon Nebuchadnezzar came back again to besiege Jerusalem. While the Babylonian tablet (B.M. 21946) which has supplied such valuable information about the first fall of Jerusalem reports several succeeding expeditions of Nebuchadnezzar to the Hatti-land it terminates with the eleventh year (594/593 B.C.) of the Babylonian king and does not extend far enough to chronicle the final fall of Jerusalem. According to II Kings

[8] The three years of submission were 604/603, 603/602, 602/601.
[9] WCCK p.71.   [10] WCCK p.73.
[11] He is called the brother of Jehoiachin in the passage in II Chronicles.

25:2, 8 and Jeremiah 52:5, 12 the final destruction of the city was in the eleventh year of King Zedekiah and the nineteenth year of King Nebuchadnezzar. If this date is given in terms of the accession-year system and the regnal year beginning in Nisan, it indicates 586 B.C. According to II Kings 25:8 it was on the seventh day of the fifth month that the city was destroyed; according to Jeremiah 52:12 it was on the tenth day of the same month. In 586 B.C. these days corresponded to August 14 and 17.[12]

The Babylonian tablets just discussed, which have added so much to our knowledge of the relations of Nabopolassar and Nebuchadnezzar with Syria, Palestine, and Egypt, show that the kings of the New Babylonian Empire were much engaged in military activities. According to the record they provide for the twenty-three years from 616 to 594 B.C., the Babylonian army was called out twenty-one times in seventeen different years.[13] We also know from Josephus[14] that Nebuchadnezzar conducted a thirteen-year siege of Tyre; and another inscription has already been cited (pp. 131f.) which tells of a battle against King Amasis of Egypt as late as the thirty-seventh year of Nebuchadnezzar. Another inscription describes his conquests in general terms: "In exalted trust in him [Marduk] distant countries, remote mountains from the upper sea [Mediterranean] to the lower sea [Persian Gulf], steep paths, blockaded roads, where the step is impeded, where was no footing, difficult roads, desert paths, I traversed, and the disobedient I destroyed; I captured the enemies, established justice in the lands; the people I exalted; the bad and evil I separated from the people."[15]

Concerning Babylon itself and its splendor under Nebuchadnezzar II much is known. Many of the king's inscriptions deal with his

---

[12] That two different days are given might possibly correspond with the beginning and the completion of the final destruction. For the rabbinic tradition to this effect see below p.328 n.4. For the chronology in the light of the Babylonian chronicles see David N. Freedman in BA 19 (1956), pp.56f.; W. F. Albright in BASOR 143 (1956), pp.31f.; Edwin R. Thiele in BASOR 143 (Oct. 1956), pp.22-27; Hayim Tadmor in JNES 15 (1956), pp.226-230; A. Malamat in IEJ 6 (1956), pp.246-256; J. Philip Hyatt in JBL 75 (1956), pp.275-284; and see also the Appendix in this book.

[13] WCCK p.95.

[14] *Against Apion.* I, 21 (quoting "the Phoenician record"); *Ant.* x, xi, 1 (citing a certain Philostratus, author of a *History of Phoenicia*). The statement in *Against Apion* puts the beginning of the siege in the seventh year of Nebuchadnezzar (598 B.C.), but it has been surmised that this is a corruption from the seventeenth year (588 B.C.). Ezekiel's prophecy (chapters 26-28) against Tyre, which is probably connected with Nebuchadnezzar's siege, is dated (26:1) in the eleventh year, doubtless meaning the eleventh year of the exile of Jehoiachin.

[15] Barton, *Archaeology and the Bible*, p.478.

extensive building operations, and his capital city was excavated thoroughly by the Deutsche Orientgesellschaft under the direction of Robert Koldewey from 1899 onward.[16] Nebuchadnezzar's work included the design and construction of a vast system of fortifications, and the building of streets, canals, temples, and palaces. The king could well have uttered the words which are put in his mouth in Daniel 4:30, "Is not this great Babylon, which I have built by my mighty power as a royal residence and for the glory of my majesty?"

A general view of the tremendous complex of ruins that is Babylon today is shown in Fig. 83. Most prominent is the Ishtar Gate, a double gate leading through the double wall of fortifications and adorned with rows of bulls and dragons in enameled, colored brick.[17] The gate gave access to the city's processional street whose walls were lined with enameled lions like the one shown in Fig. 84. The throne room in the palace of Nebuchadnezzar II likewise was adorned with enameled bricks in patterns such as are shown in Fig. 85. In the temple area the most conspicuous structure was the ziggurat which Nebuchadnezzar rebuilt (cf. p. 50). Only the ground plan now remains but Herodotus says that it rose to a height of eight stages, with an ascent to the top running spirally around the successive towers.[18] Not far away was Esagila ("House whose Top is Lofty"), the temple of Marduk or Bel, which the king also restored, a tremendous pile, built with step-backs like a skyscraper in a modern city. Most famous of all Nebuchadnezzar's works at Babylon were the hanging gardens which the king built in terraces to compensate his Median queen for the absence of her beloved mountains, and which were known to the Greeks as constituting one of the seven wonders of the world. The gardens can no longer be identified with any certainty. The ruins of a series of vaulted rooms found near the Ishtar Gate were believed by the excavators to represent their substructure, but now appear more probably to have been a part of some other important public building, perhaps a distribution depot for the royal storehouses.

Thus Nebuchadnezzar II was interested in construction as well as destruction, and under his rule the arts of civilization flourished.

[16] Koldewey, *Das wieder erstehende Babylon.* 4th ed. 1925; Oscar Reuther, *Die Innenstadt von Babylon (Merkes).* 2 vols. 1926.

[17] R. Koldewey, *Das Ischtar-Tor in Babylon.* 1918.

[18] I, 181. For a reconstruction of the Tower of Babel according to a description on a cuneiform tablet of the third century B.C. see E. Unger, *Assyrische und babylonische Kunst.* 1927, Fig. 104. See also Parrot, *The Tower of Babel.*

The typical Babylonian gentleman, as described by Herodotus little more than a century later, was obviously a man of culture: "For clothing, they wear a linen tunic, reaching to the feet; over this the Babylonian puts on another tunic, of wool, and wraps himself in a white mantle; he wears the shoes of his country, which are like Boeotian sandals. Their hair is worn long, and covered by caps; the whole body is perfumed. Every man has a seal and a carven staff, and on every staff is some image, such as that of an apple or a rose or a lily or an eagle: no one carries a staff without a device."[19]

The inscriptions of Nebuchadnezzar also express lofty sentiments in religion:

> O eternal prince! Lord of all being!
> As for the king whom thou lovest, and
> Whose name thou hast proclaimed
> As was pleasing to thee,
> Do thou lead aright his life,
> Guide him in a straight path.
> I am the prince, obedient to thee,
> The creature of thy hand;
> Thou hast created me, and
> With dominion over all people
> Thou hast entrusted me.
> According to thy grace, O Lord,
> Which thou dost bestow on
> All people,
> Cause me to love thy supreme dominion,
> And create in my heart
> The worship of thy god-head,
> And grant whatever is pleasing to thee,
> Because thou hast fashioned my life.[20]

THE CAPTIVITY OF JEHOIACHIN

Amidst the splendors of Babylon, however, our greatest interest lies in the inquiry as to whether any traces of the Jewish exiles remain. A discovery of much importance to the biblical archeologist makes it possible to give an affirmative answer to this question.[21] In the ruins of the vaulted building near the Ishtar Gate which was mentioned just above, some three hundred cuneiform tablets were un-

---

[19] I, 195; cf. Ezekiel 23:14f. For the daily life in general of the period 700-530 B.C. see Georges Contenau, *Everyday Life in Babylon and Assyria.* 1954.

[20] Goodspeed, *A History of the Babylonians and Assyrians*, p.348.

[21] Ernst F. Weidner in *Mélanges Syriens offerts a Monsieur René Dussaud.* II, 1939, pp.923-927; W. F. Albright in BA 5 (1942), pp.49-55; Oppenheim in ANET p.308; D. Winton Thomas in PEQ 1950, pp.5-8.

earthed. Upon study these have been found to date from between 595 and 570 B.C., and to contain lists of rations such as barley and oil paid to craftsmen and captives who lived in and near Babylon at that time. Among the recipients of these rations are persons from Egypt, Philistia, Phoenicia, Asia Minor, Elam, Media, Persia, and Judah. The Jews who are mentioned include some with such biblical names as Gaddiel, Semachiah, and Shelemiah, the last named being called a "gardener." But the name of most sigificance to us is none other than that of Yaukin, king of Judah, with whom also five royal princes are listed.

The name of this king is written in several ways on the tablets, but clearly was pronounced something like "Yow-keen." The same name had already been found stamped on some jar handles in Palestine and had been recognized as an abbreviated form of Jehoiachin. On the tablets from Babylon, Yaukin is explicitly called "king of the land of Yahud." Yahud is simply a shortened form of the name of Judah such as is perfectly familiar in the time after the exile (cf. p. 195). Since the date of the tablets in general corresponds to the time when the first Jewish exiles were in Babylon, and since one of the documents which mentions Yaukin is specifically dated in 592 B.C., there can be little doubt that the reference is to the biblical Jehoiachin himself, who at that time was residing with his family in the land of his banishment.

Immediately after the name of Yaukin, the tablets three times refer to his five sons who are described as in the hands of an attendant with the Jewish name of Kenaiah. Doubtless several or all of these young sons lived to be included in the list of seven sons of Jehoiachin (Jeconiah) given in I Chronicles 3:17f., where Shealtiel is named as the oldest (cf. Matthew 1:12; Luke 3:27).

It is evident from these tablets that the Babylonians themselves continued to regard Jehoiachin as the legitimate claimant to the throne of Judah, although they did not see fit to restore him to actual rule. At this time he seems to have been free, moreover, to move about in the city, as is suggested by the distribution of rations to him. Presumably it was only at a later date, therefore, that he was cast into the prison out of which in the thirty-seventh year of his captivity we find him being lifted up and restored to favorable and even preferential treatment (II Kings 25:27-30).

In view of this understanding of Jehoiachin's position in Babylon, the dating of events by Jewish writers according to the years of his captivity is thoroughly understandable. He was the lawful but exiled king of Judah. Since his actual rulership had been terminated by the Babylonians, events could hardly be dated by the years of his reign but they could be stated in terms of the years of his exile. Such a mention of his thirty-seventh year is found in II Kings 25:27 and Jeremiah 52:31, while in Ezekiel there is a series of such dates (1:2; 8:1; etc.) which evidently have the same reference and run from the fifth to the twenty-seventh year.[22]

In connection with the exile Ezekiel mentions the river Chebar a number of times (1:1, etc.). This was probably a large canal called Kabaru which came out of the Euphrates above Babylon and flowed past Nippur before it entered the Euphrates again. There are references to it in business documents found at Nippur, written in the time of Artaxerxes I.[23]

NABUNAID AND BELSHAZZAR

The New Babylonian empire was also destined to fall, and the decline came rapidly. Nebuchadnezzar II was followed on the throne by his son Amel-Marduk (561-560), the Evil-merodach of II Kings 25:27. This man was soon slain by his brother-in-law, Nergal-shar-usur (Neriglisar). The latter ruled but four years (559-556) and his son, Labashi-Marduk (Laborosoardoch), was on the throne only a few months (556) when conspirators made away with him. One of the conspirators, a Babylonian noble named Nabunaid (Nabonidus), then ruled (555-539) as the last king of New Babylonia.[24]

In practice, however, Nabunaid shared the kingship with his own oldest son Belshazzar. Belshazzar is named as the crown prince in Babylonian inscriptions,[25] and in the so-called Verse Account of Nabunaid we read the following statement concerning Nabunaid:

> He entrusted the 'Camp' to his oldest son, the first-born,
> The troops everywhere in the country he ordered under his command.
>
> He let everything go, entrusted the kingship to him
> And, himself, he started out for a long journey,
> The military forces of Akkad marching with him;
> He turned towards Tema deep in the west.

[22] For discussion of these dates see the Appendix.

[23] W. F. Albright in JBL 51 (1932), p.100; G. A. Cooke, *The Book of Ezekiel.* ICC, 1937, I, p.4; Herbert G. May in IB 6, p.68.

[24] cf. Berossos quoted by Josephus, *Against Apion.* I, 20.

[25] ANET p.309 n.5.

He started out the expedition on a path leading to a
    distant region. When he arrived there,
He killed in battle the prince of Tema,
Slaughtered the flocks of those who dwell in the city
    as well as in the countryside,
And he, himself, took his residence in Tema, the forces
    of Akkad were also stationed there.

He made the town beautiful, built there his palace
Like the palace in Babylon, he also built walls
For the fortifications of the town and. . . .
He surrounded the town with sentinels. . . .[26]

This passage states plainly that before Nabunaid started on an expedition to Tema he divided the rule of the empire between himself and his son and entrusted actual kingship to Belshazzar. Then he undertook the distant campaign which was probably in Arabia, conquered Tema, established his residence there, and built that city with the glory of Babylon. Likewise the Nabunaid chronicle contains the following statements concerning King Nabunaid:

"Seventh year: The king stayed in Tema, the crown prince, his officials and his army were in Akkad. . . .
"Ninth year: Nabunaid, the king, stayed in Tema; the crown prince, the officials and the army were in Akkad. . . .
"Tenth year: The king stayed in Tema; the crown prince, his officials and his army were in Akkad. . . .
"Eleventh year: The king stayed in Tema; the crown prince, the officials and his army were in Akkad."[27]

Each of these initial statements for the seventh, ninth, tenth, and eleventh years of the king is supplemented by this comment: "The king did not come to Babylon for the ceremonies of the month Nisanu, Nabu did not come to Babylon, Bel did not go out from Esagila in procession, the festival of the New Year was omitted." This means that during the years mentioned Nabunaid was in Tema and Belshazzar was in Babylon and that owing to the absence of Nabunaid the usual New Year's festival was not observed. Since, therefore, Belshazzar actually exercised the co-regency at Babylon and may well have continued to do so unto the end, the book of Daniel (5:30) is not wrong in representing him as the last king of Babylon.[28]

---

[26] ANET pp.313f.   [27] ANET pp.305f. (ANEA p.203).
[28] R. P. Dougherty, *Nabonidus and Belshazzar.* 1929, pp.105-200. Julius Lewy (in HUCA 19 [1945-46], pp.434-450) thinks that the stay of Nabunaid at Tema began in the fourth year of his reign and lasted at least until the eleventh year. He suggests

THE FALL OF BABYLON

In the seventeenth year of King Nabunaid, Babylon fell to Cyrus the Persian. The Nabunaid chronicle gives exact dates. In the month of Tashritu on the fourteenth day, October 10, 539 B.C., the Persian forces took Sippar; on the sixteenth day, October 12, "the army of Cyrus entered Babylon without battle"; and in the month of Arahsamnu, on the third day, October 29, Cyrus himself came into the city.[29]

The fall of Babylon is narrated not only in the Nabunaid chronicle but also in the inscription on the famous cylinder of Cyrus (Fig. 86). The latter reads in part as follows:

"Marduk . . . scanned and looked through all the countries, searching for a righteous ruler. . . . He pronounced the name of Cyrus, king of Anshan, declared him to be the ruler of all the world. . . . He made him set out on the road to Babylon, going at his side like a real friend. His widespread troops—their number, like that of the water of a river, could not be established—strolled along, their weapons packed away. Without any battle, he made him enter his town Babylon, sparing Babylon any calamity. He delivered into his hands Nabunaid, the king who did not worship him."[30]

If Cyrus claimed to be sent by Marduk, the Second Isaiah felt that the conqueror was anointed by the Lord himself for the task of releasing the Jewish exiles and returning them to their home (Isaiah 45:1; cf. 44:28). The spirit of Cyrus' decree of release which is quoted in the Old Testament (II Chronicles 36:23; Ezra 1:2-4) is confirmed by the Cyrus cylinder, where the king relates that he allowed the captives to return to their various countries and rebuild their temples:

---

that Nabunaid transferred his residence to this place because it was an ancient center of worship of the moon-god, Sin, to whom he was devoted above Marduk and all other gods. In Daniel 5:18 Nebuchadnezzar is named as the father of Belshazzar, instead of Nabunaid. It has been surmised that Belshazzar was a grandson of Nebuchadnezzar, who might then be referred to, after Semitic usage, as his father. It is also possible that, in Jewish tradition, Babylonian legends were transferred to Nebuchadnezzar which originally had to do with Nabunaid. This would be understandable inasmuch as it was Nebuchadnezzar rather than Nabunaid who figured prominently in Jewish history and was a great enemy of the Jewish people. Thus the story of how Nebuchadnezzar went mad and was driven forth from men to dwell for seven years with the beasts of the field (Daniel 4) might reflect the stay of Nabunaid in the wilderness at Tema for about that same length of time, as it was viewed by the priests of Marduk at Babylon. See Wolfram von Soden in ZAW 53 (1935), pp.84,86f.

[29] ANET p.306 (ANEA p.203); PDBC pp.13,29.

[30] ANET pp.315f. (ANEA p.206); cf. Robert W. Rogers, *Cuneiform Parallels to the Old Testament*. 1912, p.381; *A Guide to the Babylonian and Assyrian Antiquities, British Museum*. 3d ed. 1922, p.144.

"As to the region from . . . as far as Ashur and Susa, Agade, Eshnunna, the towns Zamban, Me-Turnu, Der as well as the region of the Gutians, I returned to these sacred cities on the other side of the Tigris, the sanctuaries of which have been ruins for a long time, the images which used to live therein and established for them permanent sanctuaries. I also gathered all their former inhabitants and returned to them their habitations. Furthermore, I resettled upon the command of Marduk, the great lord, all the gods of Sumer and Akkad whom Nabunaid has brought into Babylon to the anger of the lord of the gods, unharmed, in their former chapels, the places which make them happy.

"May all the gods whom I have resettled in their sacred cities ask daily Bel and Nabu for a long life for me and may they recommend me to him; to Marduk, my lord, they may say this: 'Cyrus, the king who worships you, and Cambyses, his son. . .' . . . all of them I settled in a peaceful place. . . ."[31]

8. THE PERSIAN EMPIRE, 539-331 B.C.

CYRUS THE GREAT, who conquered Babylon in 539 B.C. and reigned there from 538 to 530, was the founder of the Persian Empire. In order to understand his place in history it is necessary to indicate briefly the earlier happenings in the land of Persia.

THE EARLIER HISTORY OF PERSIA

The homeland of Persia was the western and larger part of the Iranian plateau, which stretches from the Indus on the east to the Tigris and Euphrates on the west. It is a high, arid plateau overlooked by vast barren mountain ranges. The native name of the land, and the name to which the Persian government officially returned in 1935, is Iran. This name, Airyana or Iran, means "the [land] of the Aryans,"[1] and refers to the Aryan-speaking people who settled on the highland. Before the Aryans came, aboriginal Caspians had lived on the plateau and perhaps were the first people to develop agriculture and metallurgy. Then, around 1500 B.C., the Aryans entered the country.[2]

The two Aryan tribes which were to attain the greatest importance were the Amadai or Medes and the people from the land of Parsua (west of Lake Urmia) or Persians. Both are mentioned for the first time in annals of Shalmaneser III concerning Assyrian campaigns

---

[31] ANET p.316. For the "substantial historicity" of the edict of Cyrus as given in the Old Testament cf. W. F. Albright in BA 9 (1946), p.7. See also Kurt Galling in ZDPV 70 (1954), p.7.

[1] Old Persian, *Aryanam khshathram*; Middle Persian, *Eran*. Ernst Herzfeld and Arthur Keith in *A Survey of Persian Art*. I, p.42 n.1.

[2] Ernst Herzfeld, *Archaeological History of Iran*. 1935, p.8.

in the region of the Caspian plateau.[3] The Medes occupied the north-western part of the country, now Iraq-i-ajam, with their capital at Hagmatana, known later as Ecbatana and now as Hamadan. According to Herodotus[4] Ecbatana was founded by "a clever man called Deioces" who for the first time united the nomadic Median tribes into one nation and ruled as king. Deioces was succeeded by his son Phraortes, as Herodotus further states, and he in turn by his son Cyaxares. Cyaxares (or Uvakhshatra) we have already seen cooperating with Nabopolassar in the overthrow of Nineveh in 612 B.C. (p. 219).

The Persians moved on southward and settled not far from the Elamite land Anzan or Anshan in a region to which they gave the name Parsamash or Parsumash in memory of their old homeland of Parsua. By about 700 B.C. their leader was Hakhamanish or Achaemenes whose name was preserved by the later Persian kings. Around 675 to around 640 B.C. Teispes was king of Parsumash, and he was able to extend the Persian holdings to include a region east of Anshan and north of what we call the Persian Gulf. This area became known as Parsa or Persian land. Teispes divided his empire between his two sons, Ariaramna (c.640-c.615) receiving Parsa and Kurash or Cyrus I (c.640-c.600) receiving Parsumash.

In the land of Elam, it may be explained, a series of kingdoms had been in existence for many centuries but mostly under domination by Mesopotamian rulers from Sargon (p. 46) to the Kassites. In the first quarter of the twelfth century Kutir-Nahhunte of Elam ended Kassite control and established a true Elamite Empire but by the middle of the century Elam succumbed again to Nebuchadnezzar I. Elam enjoyed other periods of dominance but finally about 646 B.C. was destroyed and depopulated by the Assyrians.[5] Thus it was possible for the Persians to acquire much Elamite territory and we find Kanbujiya or Cambyses I (c.600-c.559), the successor of Cyrus I, bearing the title "king of the city Anshan."

Up to this time the Persians had been under the domination of the Medes. Nominally Cambyses I was a king in his own right, yet actually he was subordinate to the Median king Astyages (p. 220) to whose daughter Mandane he was married. The subserviency was not to last much longer. The son of Cambyses I and Mandane was Cyrus the Great.[6]

---

[3] ARAB I, §581. [4] I, 96-103.
[5] René Grousset in *A Survey of Persian Art.* I, pp.61,64.
[6] Herodotus. I, 107-130.

CYRUS II THE GREAT

Cyrus II came to the throne of Anshan around 559 B.C., and Astyages soon recognized that revolt was intended. Astyages therefore marched against Cyrus, but the Median army rebelled and Cyrus was able to proceed to Ecbatana, the capital of his former master, in triumph. Parsa henceforth was the first ranking satrapy in the entire land, Media the second, and Elam the third. The sovereignty of the Persians was definitely established although the Medes continued to have equal honor with the Persians and foreigners spoke of either "the Persians and the Medes" (Esther 1:19) or "the Medes and Persians" (Daniel 5:28, etc.).[7]

Cyrus II extended his conquests swiftly and far. He challenged Croesus, the famously rich king of Lydia, who held sway as far eastward as the Halys River, and defeated him (546 B.C.). Finally he completed his task by conquering Babylon itself (539 B.C.) as we have already seen. Thus was established the mighty Persian Empire in which Judea for the next two centuries remained a province. The new king wrote proudly: "I am Cyrus, king of the world, great king, legitimate king, king of Babylon, king of Sumer and Akkad, king of the four rims of the earth, son of Cambyses, great king, king of Anshan, grandson of Cyrus, great king, king of Anshan, descendant of Teispes, great king, king of Anshan, of a family which always exercised kingship."[8]

Throughout his extensive campaigns, and in contrast with other ancient oriental conquerors, Cyrus always was humane. The lives of Astyages and Croesus were spared and each was allotted a royal train. Babylon was not destroyed but its people won over by his mercy and the Jews were reestablished in their homeland as we have seen.

Cyrus made his capital at Pasargadae in the land of Parsa. Here he built a palace on whose ruins the repeated inscription is still to be read, "I, Cyrus, the king, the Achaemenid."[9] The royal buildings seem to have formed a group consisting of scattered individual pavilions set amidst gardens, and surrounded by a masonry wall some thirteen feet in thickness.[10] The carving shown in Fig. 87 adorned a doorway at Pasargadae and is our earliest extant Persian relief. The

[7] Cameron, *History of Early Iran*, pp.179-226.
[8] ANET p.316.
[9] E. Herzfeld, *Archaeologische Mitteilungen aus Iran.* I (1929-30), p.10.
[10] Friedrich Wachtsmuth in *A Survey of Persian Art.* I, p.309.

strange four-winged genius is believed by some to represent the deified Cyrus.

Nine years after the surrender of Babylon, Cyrus marched eastward to meet enemies and was killed in battle (530 B.C.). His body was brought back to Pasargadae and buried in a tomb which still exists and which consists of only a single small room on a foundation course of six steps (Fig. 88). Arrian (A.D. c.96-c.180) describes the tomb as follows: "The tomb itself was built, at the base, with stones cut square and raised into rectangular form. Above, there was a chamber with a stone roof and with a door leading into it so narrow that with difficulty, and after great trouble, one man, and he a small one, could enter. And in the chamber was placed a golden sarcophagus, in which Cyrus' body had been buried."[11] Plutarch (A.D. c.46-c.120) says that the tomb had this inscription: "O, man, whosoever thou art and whencesoever thou comest, for I know that thou wilt come, I am Cyrus, and I won for the Persians their empire. Do not, therefore, begrudge me this little earth which covers my body."[12]

CAMBYSES II

Cyrus was followed on the throne by his son Cambyses II (529-522) who defeated the Egyptians at Pelusium (pp. 132f.) and added Egypt to the Persian dominions. The Persian Empire was now the greatest the world had even seen. Not long after his Egyptian victories, however, Cambyses went mad and committed suicide. The new empire nearly broke up in the confusion which followed. Gaumata, a Magian, declared himself to be Smerdis, the younger brother of Cambyses (who actually had been murdered), and seized the throne. Also national kings of Babylonia, Media, Armenia, and other provinces which had been annexed by Cyrus, attempted to break away.

DARIUS I THE GREAT

It was an Achaemenid prince of a younger line, Daryavaush or Darius I the Great (521-486), son of Hystaspes,[13] who saved the empire. The name of the father of Darius, Hystaspes or Vishtaspa, is the same as that of the traditional royal convert and patron of Zoroaster. The traditional dates for Zoroaster (c.660-c.583) are too early to allow for the identification of the father of Darius with the patron of the prophet, however, and either it must be supposed that

[11] *Anabasis of Alexander.* VI, xxix, 5. tr. E. I. Robson, LCL (1929-33) II, p.197.
[12] *Life of Alexander.* LXIX, 2. tr. B. Perrin, LCL (1914-26) VII, p.417. cf. below p.244.
[13] Herodotus. I, 209.

the latter was an earlier Vishtaspa or else the date of Zoroaster's birth must be brought down to a later date, perhaps around 570 B.C.[14] At any rate it is well known that Darius I was a zealous worshiper of Ahura Mazda, the god preached by Zoroaster, and so were Xerxes and Artaxerxes as well.

In the Old Testament the appearance of the prophet Haggai in Jerusalem is dated (Haggai 1:1) on the first day of the sixth month of the second year of Darius, which would be August 29, 520 B.C.; and the first sermon of Zechariah is placed (Zechariah 1:1) in the eighth month of the same year or in October/November 520 B.C. Likewise the completion of the rebuilt Jewish temple is dated on the third day of the month Adar in the sixth year of Darius (Ezra 6:15), or March 12, 515 B.C.[15]

THE ROCK OF BEHISTUN

Returning now to the rebellion with which Darius I was confronted, it may be said that the new king acted swiftly. Gaumata was defeated, seized and killed, and the various provincial uprisings were suppressed. An impressive memorial of the victory over the rebels was left on the famous Rock of Behistun. This great rock looms up above a spring-fed pool of water on the old caravan-road from Ecbatana to Babylon. The rock is really the last peak (3,800 feet high) of a long narrow range of mountains which skirts the plain of Karmanshah on the east. The name by which we customarily refer to it is derived from the small village of Bisitun or Behistun which is now located at its foot. High upon the face of the rock, perhaps five hundred feet above the level of the plain, Darius I carved a large relief panel and accompanied it with many columns of inscription (Fig. 89).[16] The scene represents the king receiving the submission of the rebels. At the left (Fig. 90) we see the life-sized figure of Darius I, accompanied by two attendants. The king's left foot is placed upon the prostrate form of Gaumata, the leading rebel. In his left hand the king grasps a bow while he lifts his right hand toward the winged disk with anthropomorphic head which is the symbol of Ahura Mazda. Behind Gaumata is a procession of rebel leaders, roped together by their necks. The last one, Skunkha the

---

[14] Herzfeld, *Archaeologische Mitteilungen aus Iran.* II (1930), p.47; cf. A. T. Olmstead, *History of the Persian Empire* [*Achaemenid Period*]. 1948, pp.102f.

[15] cf. Peter R. Ackroyd in JNES 17 (1958), pp.13-27.

[16] cf. E. Herzfeld, *Am Tor von Asien, Felsendenkmale aus Irans Heldenzeit.* 1920, Pl. IX.

Scythian, wearing a high pointed cap, was a later addition to the group. Beside and beneath the sculptured panel are many columns of inscription relating how Darius gained the crown and put down the rebellion. The inscription is composed in three languages, Old Persian, Elamite, and Akkadian (formerly known as Old Persian, Susian, and Babylonian), all written in cuneiform characters. Copies of the inscription were also circulated in distant provinces of the Persian Empire, as is known from the discovery of an Aramaic version of it among papyri at Elephantine in Upper Egypt (p. 239).

The great carving at Behistun was indestructible and unconcealable and hence early became known to travelers in that region. The Arabian geographical writer Ibn Hawkal, who was born at Mosul in the tenth century A.D., described it and supposed that the scene represented "a schoolhouse, with the master and the boys; further in the schoolmaster's hand is an instrument like a strap wherewith to beat."[17] In the early nineteenth century another traveler saw the monument and thought that the winged figure of Ahura Mazda was a cross, and that Darius and his officers and prisoners were the Twelve Apostles![18]

Then in 1835 and following, Henry C. Rawlinson, a British official in the Middle East, made the difficult climb up to the inscription and made copies and squeezes. He said, "The climbing of the rock to arrive at the inscriptions, if not positively dangerous, is a feat at any rate which an antiquary alone could be expected to undertake."[19] Fresh copies were made from the original in 1904 by L. W. King and R. Campbell Thompson, who were sent out by the British Museum,[20] a new photograph of the monument was published in 1943 by George G. Cameron of the Oriental Institute of the University of Chicago (see Fig. 89), and further study of the inscriptions was made by Dr. Cameron in 1948.[21]

Efforts had already been made to read cuneiform, or wedge-shaped writing, particularly by G. F. Grotefend of Germany who was able to identify in other inscriptions the names of Darius and his son Xerxes as well as the title "King of Kings." Rawlinson was finally

[17] G. LeStrange, The Lands of the Eastern Caliphate. 1905, p.187.

[18] E. A. W. Budge, The Rise and Progress of Assyriology. 1925, p.30.

[19] A. V. W. Jackson in JAOS 24 (1903), p.81.

[20] King and Thompson, The Sculptures and Inscription of Darius the Great on the Rock of Behistun in Persia. 1907.

[21] Cameron in JNES 2 (1943), pp.115f. and Pl. II; in NGM 98 (1950), pp.825-844; and in JCS 5 (1951), pp.47-54. See also Roland G. Kent in JCS 5 (1951), pp.55-57; W. C. Benedict and Elizabeth von Voigtlander in JCS 10 (1956), pp.1-10.

able to decipher the Persian part of the Behistun inscription and this victory at last led to the reading of the other two languages.[22] Such was the Rosetta Stone of cuneiform decipherment.

Darius I not only dealt effectively with the rebellion which he faced at the beginning of his reign but also continued to rule well the far-flung Persian territories. Indeed his genius lay most of all in the field of administration, and one of his outstanding achievements was the completion of the organization of the empire into twenty satrapies.[23] Furthermore, he undertook extensive works of construction which ranged from the digging of a canal from the Nile to the Red Sea,[24] to the erection of a new capital at Persepolis (p. 241).

Despite the fact that in so many ways Darius I deserved the title "the Great," which has been given him, the closing years of his reign saw the outbreak of the Greco-Persian wars which were to be disastrous for Persia. This conflict grew ultimately out of the fact that the conquests of Cyrus in Asia Minor had included Greek colonies, but the wars now were begun by the Greeks themselves. During the reign of Darius I, Persian armies suffered defeat at Marathon (491 B.C.) and again a few years after his death the Persian fleet was beaten at Salamis (480 B.C.). Thereafter the future belonged to Europe instead of Asia.

NAQSH-I-RUSTAM

Darius I died in 486 B.C. and was buried in a rock-hewn tomb at Naqsh-i-Rustam (Fig. 91) a few miles northeast of Persepolis.[25] The name of this place means "Pictures of Rustam," for the rock sculptures have been associated by the local inhabitants with the legendary Persian hero, Rustam. The tomb of Darius bears trilingual inscriptions which give the king's own account of his achievements and of his character. His words include the following: "Says Darius the king: By the favor of Ahuramazda I am of such a sort that I am a friend to right, I am not a friend to wrong; it is not my desire that the weak man should have wrong done to him by the mighty; nor is that my desire, that the mighty man should have wrong done to him by the weak."[26]

[22] Henry C. Rawlinson, *The Persian Cuneiform Inscription at Behistun.* 1846.
[23] CAH IV, pp.194f.
[24] Roland G. Kent in JNES 1 (1942), pp.415-421.
[25] cf. E. Herzfeld and F. Sarre, *Iranische Felsreliefs.* 1910, Pl. IV.
[26] Roland G. Kent in JNES 4 (1945), pp.39-52.

Similar tombs were later cut from the same cliff for the three successors of Darius—Xerxes, Artaxerxes I, and Darius II—and are to the right and to the left of the tomb of Darius. These tombs do not appear in Fig. 91. The carving which is seen in the lower left hand corner of the illustration is a yet later representation of the Sasanian king Shapur I (A.D. 241-272) receiving the submission of the Emperor Valerian. Not far away and facing the cliff of the royal tombs is a strange structure of stone to which the name Ka'bah-i-Zardusht ("Square [Tomb] of Zoroaster") has been attached. It is thought perhaps to have been a Zoroastrian fire temple, and may later have served as the shrine where the Sasanian kings were crowned and the crown jewels were kept.

XERXES

Darius was followed on the throne of Persia by his son Khshayarsha or Xerxes (485-465 B.C.). An important historical inscription of Xerxes discovered at Persepolis lists the numerous subject nations over which he ruled, tells of uprisings with which he had to contend at the time of his accession to the throne, and reveals his devotion to the worship of Ahura Mazda. This record reads as follows:

"Ahuramazda is the great god who gave us this earth, who gave us that sky, who gave us mankind, who gave to his worshipers prosperity, who made Xerxes, the king, rule the multitudes as only king, give alone orders to the other kings.

"I am Xerxes, the great king, the only king, the king of all countries which speak all kinds of languages, the king of this entire big and far-reaching earth,—the son of king Darius, the Achaemenian, a Persian, son of a Persian, an Aryan of Aryan descent.

"Thus speaks king Xerxes: These are the countries—in addition to Persia—over which I am king under the 'shadow' of Ahuramazda, over which I hold sway, which are bringing their tribute to me—whatever is commanded them by me, that they do and they abide by my laws—: Media, Elam, Arachosia, Urartu (Armenia), Drangiana, Parthia, Haria, Bactria, Sogdia, Chorasmia, Babylonia, Assyria, Sattagydia, Sardis, Egypt, the Ionians who live on the salty sea and those who live beyond the salty sea, Maka, Arabia, Gandara, India, Cappadocia, Da'an, the Amyrgian Cimmerians, the Cimmerians wearing pointed caps, the Skudra, the Akupish, Libya, Banneshu (Carians) and Kush.

"Thus speaks king Xerxes: After I became king, there were some among these countries the names of which are written above, which revolted but I crushed these countries, after Ahuramazda had given me his support, under the 'shadow' of Ahuramazda, and I put them again into their former political status. Furthermore, there were among these countries some which performed religious service to the 'Evil Gods' (Daivas), but under the 'shadow' of Ahuramazda I destroyed these temples of the 'Evil Gods' and proclaimed as follows: 'You must not perform religious service to the 'Evil Gods' any more!' Wherever formerly religious service was performed to the 'Evil Gods,' I, myself, performed a religious service to Ahuramazda and the *arta* (cosmic order) reverently. Furthermore, there were other things which were done in a bad way, and these too I made in the correct way.

"All these things which I did, I performed under the 'shadow' of Ahuramazda and Ahuramazda gave me his support until I had accomplished everything.

"Whosoever you are, in future days who thinks as follows: 'May I be prosperous in this life and blessed after my death!'—do live according to this law which Ahuramazda has promulgated: 'Perform religious service only for Ahuramazda and the *arta* reverently.' A man who lives according to this law which Ahuramazda has promulgated, and who performs religious service only to Ahuramazda and the *arta* reverently, will be prosperous while he is alive and—when dead—he will become blessed.

"Thus speaks king Xerxes: May Ahuramazda protect me, my family and these countries from all evil. This I do ask of Ahuramazda and this Ahuramazda may grant me!"[27]

Xerxes is no doubt the Ahasuerus[28] who is mentioned in Ezra 4:6 between Darius and Artaxerxes and who also figures prominently in the book of Esther (1:1, etc.).

ARTAXERXES I

The successor of Xerxes was Artakhshathra or Artaxerxes I Longimanus (464-424 B.C.). According to Nehemiah 2:1 the request of Nehemiah to visit Jerusalem was made in the month Nisan in the twentieth year of Artaxerxes; assuming, as is probable, that the reference is to Artaxerxes I, the date indicated is in April/May, 445 B.C.

General confirmation of a date around this time for Nehemiah is found in the Elephantine papyri, which belong toward the end of this same century and mention by name two persons connected in the Old Testament with Nehemiah. Both are named in a letter which is dated in the seventeenth year of King Darius II, 408 B.C.[29]

[27] ANET pp.316f.; Erich F. Schmidt, *The Treasury of Persepolis and Other Discoveries in the Homeland of the Achaemenians.* OIC 21, 1939, pp.14f.

[28] The Hebrew אחשורוש represents the Persian Khshayarsha of which the Greek form is Xerxes. In Esther the LXX (ed. Swete, II, p.755) renders the name as Artaxerxes and is followed in this by Josephus (*Ant.* XI, vi) who names Artaxerxes I as king in the days of Esther.

[29] ANET p.492. The equation of the date with 408 B.C. supposes that Egyptian custom was followed and the accession year of Darius was counted as his first regnal year.

One is Sanballat who is mentioned in connection with reference to his two sons, Delaiah and Shelemiah; the other is Johanan who is spoken of as high priest in Jerusalem. Sanballat was the leading opponent of Nehemiah (Nehemiah 2:19, etc.). Johanan was grandson of Eliashib (Nehemiah 12:23) who was high priest when Nehemiah came to Jerusalem (Nehemiah 3:1).

In Ezra 7:1, 8, it is stated that Ezra came to Jerusalem in the seventh year of Artaxerxes. If this means Artaxerxes I the date was 458 B.C. and Ezra preceded Nehemiah. Since Jehohanan the son of Eliashib is mentioned in connection with the work of Ezra (Ezra 10:6), however, it seems probable that Ezra followed Nehemiah. In this case Ezra's mission may have fallen under Artaxerxes II, the seventh year of whose reign was 398 B.C.[30]

THE ELEPHANTINE PAPYRI

The Elephantine papyri referred to above give us an interesting glimpse of one of the outlying regions of the Persian empire at this time. These documents were discovered in 1903 on the island of Elephantine at the First Cataract in Egypt.[31] They date from toward the end of the fifth century B.C. and come from a Jewish military colony which was settled here. The papyri are written in Aramaic, which was the language of diplomacy and of trade throughout western Asia in the Persian period, and which was gradually replacing Hebrew as the everyday tongue of the Jewish people not only abroad but also at home in Palestine.

The contents of the Elephantine papyri are varied, ranging from the copy of the Behistun inscription of Darius mentioned above (p. 235), to such a document as a Jewish marriage contract. In one letter, dated about 419 B.C., the Jews of Elephantine are instructed by the authority of the Persian government to celebrate the Passover according to the official practice of the Jerusalem temple as embodied in the priestly code (Exodus 12:1-20). Again we learn that there was a Jewish temple at Elephantine which had just been sacked in an anti-Jewish pogrom of around 411 B.C. As their national God, the Jews of this colony worshiped Yahweh, whom they referred

---

[30] Albright, *The Archaeology of Palestine and the Bible*, pp.169f.; R. H. Pfeiffer, *Introduction to the Old Testament*. 1941, pp.819f.,827; Norman H. Snaith in ZAW 63 (1951), pp.53-66; H. H. Rowley, *The Servant of the Lord and Other Essays on the Old Testament*. 1952, pp.131-159; and in BJRL 38 (1955), pp.166-198.

[31] E. Sachau, *Aramäische Papyrus und Ostraka aus einer jüdischen Militär-Kolonie zu Elephantine*. 2 vols. 1911; A. Ungnad, *Aramäische Papyrus aus Elephantine*. 1911; A. Cowley, *Aramaic Papyri of the Fifth Century B.C.* 1923.

to by the name Yahu. Also three other divine names appear, Eshem-bethel, Herem-bethel, and 'Anath-bethel or 'Anath-Yahu. These usually have been interpreted as polytheistic borrowings on the part of the Elephantine Jews from their pagan surroundings. It is possible, however, that they represent hypostatized aspects of Yahweh under the respective titles, "Name of the House of God," "Sacredness of the House of God," and "Sign of the House of God."[32]

Other papyri from Elephantine, which have only recently become known and been published by the Brooklyn Museum, show that the temple was rebuilt after its destruction, and contain mention of Yahu as "the god who dwells in Yeb[33] the fortress," much as Psalm 135:21 speaks of Yahweh as the one "who dwells in Jerusalem." The new papyri also show that Egypt was still under the authority of Persia in the first years of the reign of Artaxerxes II.[34]

As both the Elephantine papyri and the biblical records show, the Persian kings took an interest in the welfare and religious life of their subjects. Despite some exceptions, it may be said in general that the Achaemenids exercised a more liberal rule than any other oriental despots of the ancient world. They manifested a great capacity for administration and adhered to relatively high ethical conceptions. Under their sway peace was maintained throughout the Orient for approximately two centuries. The different civilizations which fell under their dominion were allowed to continue in existence, and the various religions were tolerated. Instead of sudden, random exactions of tribute, systematic taxation was introduced and with it civil progress was supported in many ways. Roads were repaired carefully, agriculture was protected, and justice was administered systematically and well. The attitude of the Jews is significant in this regard, for we find them, although still a subject people, displaying an appreciation of their Achaemenid masters which contrasts strongly with their resentment against all of their other conquerors, Egyptian, Assyrian, Chaldean, Seleucid, and Roman.[35]

[32] Albright, *From the Stone Age to Christianity*, p.286.
[33] The Egyptian name of Elephantine.
[34] Emil G. Kraeling, *The Brooklyn Museum Aramaic Papyri, New Documents of the Fifth Century B.C. from the Jewish Colony at Elephantine.* 1953; and in BA 15 (1952), pp.50-67. Fourteen of the new papyri bear dates, and for the evidence they provide concerning the Jewish calendar in use at this time at Elephantine see S. H. Horn and L. H. Wood in JNES 13 (1954), pp.1-20.
[35] René Grousset in *A Survey of Persian Art.* I, pp.66f.

PERSEPOLIS

The most impressive evidence of the height which Persian culture attained is to be found in the ruins of Persepolis.[36] This was the place to which Darius I transferred the main capital of Persia from Pasargadae (pp. 232, 236), and it remained from that time on the chief home of the Achaemenian dynasty. Archeological excavations have been conducted at Persepolis by the Oriental Institute of the University of Chicago under the direction of Ernst Herzfeld in 1931-1934 and of Erich F. Schmidt in 1935-1939. The location of the new capital was some twenty-five miles southwest of Pasargadae, on a spur of what is now known as the Kuh-i-Rahmat or "Mountain of Mercy," overlooking the plain now called Marv Dasht.

Persepolis was surrounded by a triple fortification system with one row of towers and walls running over the crest of the mountain itself. The chief buildings were erected upon a large, roughly rectangular, terrace. Here stood the palace of Darius, known as the Tachara (Fig. 92). It had an entrance hall opening across the entire width of the building, and a main hall some fifty feet square. It was adorned with relief sculptures which are still well preserved, and bears the repeated inscription, "I am Darius, great king, king of kings, king of lands, son of Hystaspes, the Achaemenid, who constructed this palace.[37]

A building known today as the Tripylon probably was the first reception hall of Persepolis. In its stairway reliefs, rows of dignitaries are shown ascending, and on its eastern gate jambs Darius I is shown on the throne, with Xerxes, the crown prince, standing behind him (Fig. 93). The later and greater audience halls at Persepolis were the so-called Apadana, begun by Darius I and completed by Xerxes, and the Hall of One Hundred Columns started by Xerxes and finished by Artaxerxes I. The Apadana or Hall of Xerxes was a huge room approximately 195 feet square and surrounded by vestibules on three sides. The wooden roof was supported by seventy-two stone columns of which thirteen still stand. Several of these are shown in their classic beauty in Fig. 94. The building stood upon an elevated platform which was ascended by two monumental sculptured stairways. Of these the northern one has always been partially exposed

[36] For Persepolis see now Erich F. Schmidt, *Persepolis*, i, *Structures, Reliefs, Inscriptions*. oip 68, 1953; ii, *Contents of the Treasury and Other Discoveries*. oip 69, 1957.

[37] F. H. Weissbach, *Die Keilinschriften der Achämeniden*. 1911, pp.80f.

and is badly weathered, but the eastern was discovered and excavated first by Professor Herzfeld. The reliefs on the latter are very well preserved and show the opposite side of the same procession which is sculptured on the northern stairway. The chief figures are those of envoys from twenty-three subject nations who are bringing New Year's gifts to the Persian emperor. A portion of these reliefs is illustrated in Fig. 95. In the upper panel we see Parthians bringing vessels and leading a camel, in the center are Gandarans from the region of Afghanistan with a humped bull, shields and lances, and in the lower panel are Bactrians with gold vessels and another camel. The reliefs are regarded as the greatest monument of Achaemenian art, and the rhythmical arrangement of the figures in the procession and the excellent delineation of the animal forms are particularly noteworthy.[38]

The central unit of the Hall of One Hundred Columns was even more immense than that of the Apadana, being a room over 229 feet square. The roof was once supported by one hundred columns, the northern portico was flanked by huge stone bulls, and eight stone gateways were ornamented with throne scenes and representations of the king's combat with demons.

Another impressive structure on the royal terrace was the Gate of Xerxes, which stood above the stairway leading up from the plain. As in the Assyrian palaces, colossal bulls guarded the entrances of this gate. Those on the eastern side, shown in Fig. 96, are human headed, bearded, and crowned. The accompanying inscription reads, "King Xerxes says: By the grace of Ahura Mazda I constructed this gateway called All-Countries."[39]

Other buildings at Persepolis include the Harem of Darius and Xerxes, the residence of Xerxes known as the Hadish, a badly weathered palace which may have been begun by Xerxes and completed by Artaxerxes I, and the royal treasury which contains fine reliefs of Darius and Xerxes like those on the Tripylon.

ECBATANA AND SUSA

Both Ecbatana and Susa were also important centers of the Persian Empire, the former serving as a summer residence of the kings and the latter as a winter capital. Ecbatana, as we have seen (p. 231), was the former Median capital. Polybius (c.208-c.126 B.C.) says that

[38] Stanley Casson in *A Survey of Persian Art*. I, p.349.
[39] Weissbach, *Die Keilinschriften der Achämeniden*, pp.108f.

the citadel of the city was strongly fortified, and he gives a description of the palace of the Persian kings in which he says that "the woodwork was all of cedar and cypress, but no part of it was left exposed, and the rafters, the compartments of the ceiling, and the columns in the porticoes and colonnades were plated with either silver or gold, and all the tiles were silver."[40] Little now remains of the ancient city, but an inscription has been found there in which Artaxerxes II Mnemon (404-359) celebrated the erection of a palace.[41]

Susa became a part of the Achaemenid empire when Cyrus took Babylon and all of its provinces. The city is called Shushan in the Old Testament (Nehemiah 1:1; Esther 1:2, etc.; Daniel 8:2; ASV), just as the people there today call it Shush (p. 21) which was probably the ancient name. The greatest monument of Persian Susa is the royal palace which was begun by Darius I and enlarged and further beautified by the later kings.[42] The foundation of the building was commemorated by Darius I in an inscription in which he tells of bringing materials for its decoration from afar, including columns of stone from a town called Aphrodisias of Ogia, cedar wood from Lebanon, silver from Egypt, gold from Bactria, and ivory from India.[43]

The outline of the palace can still be traced by some rows of bricks, and bits of brick and lime remain from the pavements. The main plan included three courts of varying size, surrounded by large halls and apartments, while a great hypostyle hall stood nearby. The walls were of sun-dried brick covered with whitewash on the inside, and the paving was coated throughout with polished red ochre.

Panels of beautifully colored glazed bricks, which served in the same role as tapestries, constituted the most notable feature in the decoration of the palace. Many of the designs were executed in relief, and included winged bulls, winged griffins, and the famous spearmen of the guard—of whom two are shown in Fig. 97. Most of the extant examples of this type of decoration at Susa come probably from the reign of Artaxerxes II Mnemon, mentioned above.[44]

The splendid capitals of the Achaemenid kings were destined to

[40] *The Histories.* x, xxvii, 10. tr. W. R. Paton, LCL (1922-27) IV, p.167.

[41] Georges Perrot and Charles Chipiez, *Histoire de l'art dans l'antiquité.* v (1890), p.501; Oscar Reuther in Gunther Wasmuth, ed., *Lexikon der Baukunst.* II (1930), p.328.

[42] R. de Mecquenem in *A Survey of Persian Art.* I, pp.321-326.

[43] J. M. Unvala in *A Survey of Persian Art.* I, p.339.

[44] Stanley Casson in *A Survey of Persian Art.* I, p.351.

be looted and destroyed by Alexander the Great. Following Arta-
xerxes I the Persian throne was occupied by Darius II (423-405 B.C.),
Artaxerxes II Mnemon (404-359), Artaxerxes III Ochus (358-338),
Arses (337-336), and Darius III (335-331).[45] Then came the end.

9. ALEXANDER THE GREAT, 336-323 B.C.

IN 331 B.C. Alexander the Great[1] invaded Persia after having made
himself master of the entire eastern Mediterranean world including
Egypt. Beyond the Tigris by the village of Gaugamela, Alexander
met and defeated the armies of Darius III. Then he advanced to
Susa, Persepolis, and Ecbatana, at each of which places he seized
fabulous treasures. At Persepolis, according to Plutarch, ten thousand
pairs of mules and five thousand camels were required to carry away
the loot.[2] There at the main capital, with three thousand of his soldiers occupying the royal terrace, Alexander sealed the conquest of
Persia by putting to the torch the palaces which symbolized the
power of the Achaemenids.

In 324 B.C. the youthful conqueror of the world returned from
India and stopped to visit the tomb of Cyrus at Pasargadae, which
he found already despoiled. The man who had committed the outrage was slain, and Plutarch adds that the sight of the inscription
on the tomb (p. 233) "deeply affected Alexander, who was reminded
of the uncertainty and mutability of life."[3] If this is true, Alexander's
forebodings were not unfounded, for he died not long after (323
B.C.) at the early age of thirty-three.

10. THE SUCCESSORS OF ALEXANDER, 323-30 B.C.

AFTER the death of Alexander the Great, his empire fell to his generals who are known as the Diadochi or "Successors." In Egypt,
Ptolemy I Soter I (323-285), son of Lagus, carried on the government at first for Philip Arrhidaeus, the feeble-minded half-brother
of Alexander the Great, and Alexander (II), the young son of Alexander the Great and then for the latter alone after Philip Arrhidaeus

---

[45] It was in the reign of either Artaxerxes II or Artaxerxes III that a rebellion of
the Jews was put down with great severity by the king's general Bagoses (Josephus,
Ant. XI, vii, 1).

[1] For new discoveries at Pella in Macedon, birthplace and capital of Alexander
the Great, see Photios Petsas in *Archaeology.* 11 (1958), pp.246-254.

[2] *Life of Alexander.* XXXVII, 2.   [3] *ibid.*, LXIX, 3.

was killed around 317. About 310 Alexander II was killed and Ptolemy assumed the title of king. His successors, the dynasty of the Ptolemies or the Lagidae, ruled Egypt until it became a Roman province in 30 B.C.[1] In the eastern provinces, Seleucus I Nicator (312-281) emerged eventually as master. He took Babylon and began his official reign in Syria in the autumn of 312. The founding of the Seleucid Kingdom was taken as the beginning of the Seleucid era, a chronological system which was long used in western Asia and among the scattered Jews.[2] The successors of Seleucus I, comprising the Seleucid Dynasty, continued to rule Syria until Pompey made it a Roman province in 64 B.C.[3]

As far as Judea was concerned, the land was ruled for a time by the Ptolemies, but around 198 B.C. was taken by Antiochus III and made a part of Syria, where the Seleucids had established their capital at Antioch. In general the rule of the Ptolemies was favorable to the

[1] The kings who followed the first Ptolemy, with their approximate dates, were: Ptolemy II Philadelphus (285-246), Ptolemy III Euergetes I (246-222), Ptolemy IV Philopator (222-203), Ptolemy V Epiphanes (203-181), Ptolemy VI Philometor (181-146), Ptolemy VII Eupator, Ptolemy VIII Neos Philopator, Ptolemy IX Euergetes II (Physkon), Ptolemy X Soter II (Lathyrus), Ptolemy XI Alexander I, Ptolemy XII Alexander II, Ptolemy XIII Neos Dionysos (Auletes) (80-51), Ptolemy XIV (51-47), Ptolemy XV (47-45), Ptolemy XVI Caesar or Caesarion (45-44). Cleopatra became queen jointly with Ptolemy XIV and dominated the closing part of this period until her death in 30 B.C. George Steindorff in Karl Baedeker, *Egypt and the Sudan.* 8th ed. 1929, pp.cxi-cxiii.

[2] The Seleucid era began in the Macedonian calendar with October 7, 312 B.C., and in the Babylonian with April 3, 311 B.C. PDBC p.20; cf. Wilhelm Kubitschek, *Grundriss der antiken Zeitrechnung* (in Walter Otto, ed., *Handbuch der Altertumswissenschaft.* I, 7 [1928]), p.70.

[3] The kings who followed Seleucus I, with their approximate dates, were: Antiochus I Soter (281-261), Antiochus II Theos (261-246), Seleucus II Callinicus (246-225), Seleucus III Soter (225-223), Antiochus III the Great (223-187), Seleucus IV Philopator (187-175), Antiochus IV Epiphanes (175-164), Antiochus V Eupator (164-162), Demetrius I Soter (162-150), Alexander I Balas (150-145), Demetrius II Nicator (145-139/38, 129-125), Antiochus VI Epiphanes (145-142/41), Antiochus VII Sidetes (139/38-129), Alexander II Zabinas (128-123), Antiochus VIII Grypus and Cleopatra Thea (125-121), Seleucus V (125), Antiochus VIII Grypus (121-96), Antiochus IX Cyzicenus (115-95), Seleucus VI Epiphanes Nicator (96-95), Antiochus X Eusebes Philopator (95-83), Demetrius III Eucaerus Philopator Soter (95-88), Antiochus XI Philadelphus (92), Philippus I Philadelphus (92-83), Antiochus XII Dionysus (87-84), Tigranes of Armenia (83-69), Antiochus XIII Asiaticus (69-64), Philippus II (65-64).

When the Seleucids neglected their Iranian possessions in favor of their Syrian territory, Persia fell into the power of the Parthians, an Iranian people whose leader Arsaces (c.250-c.248 B.C.) founded the Arsacid Dynasty which endured from c.250 B.C. to A.D. c.229. The Parthian Empire was overthrown by Ardashir I (the name is the modern form of Artaxerxes), who ruled A.D. c.224-241. He was the descendant of Sasan, and thus the Sasanian or Neo-Persian Empire was established which endured until the victory of the Arabs in A.D. 651. There is a list of the Parthian kings in PDBC p. 24, and Eduard Meyer gives a list of the Sasanid kings in EB XVII, p.583.

Jews, and Ptolemy II Philadelphus is remembered favorably for having encouraged the beginning of work by the Seventy at Alexandria on the famous Greek version of the Old Testament. The Seleucids, however, soon laid a heavy hand upon the Jews and the persecution by Antiochus IV Epiphanes (c.168 B.C.) led to the Maccabean war and the temporary freedom of Judea. This independence lasted until Jerusalem fell to Pompey (63 B.C.) and Palestine passed under the sway of Roman power.

V

The Holy Land in the Time of Jesus

1. THE RISE OF ROME AND THE ROMAN EMPIRE,
c.753 B.C.-A.D. 476

IN EARLY Christian times the Mediterranean world was ruled by
Rome. Stone Age remains in the neighborhood of Rome attest
the great antiquity of human settlement in that vicinity. The
actual founding of the city was supposed, according to Roman traditions, to have occurred in 753 B.C., and that date was taken as the
initial point in the usual chronological system which reckoned *ab
urbe condita*, from the founded city.[1]

The early kings gave way in 509 B.C., according to the traditional
chronology, to a republican form of government which endured until 27 B.C. Rome was the natural center of the Mediterranean, and her
supremacy in the West was established indisputably by the defeat
of Hannibal of Carthage in the battle of Zama in 202 B.C. In the East,
Greece and western Asia Minor were conquered by the middle and
end respectively of the second century B.C., but it remained for the

---

[1] In the A.U.C. era the year was originally reckoned as beginning with a festival which
fell on April 21, but writers usually refer to the year as beginning when the consuls
took office and, from A.U.C. 601 on, this was generally January 1. In the Julian calendar,
of course, the year began on January 1. For the Roman and Christian calendars see
Walter F. Wislicenus, *Der Kalender in gemeinverständlicher Darstellung*. 1905; Hans
Lietzmann, *Zeitrechnung der römischen Kaiserzeit, des Mittelalters und der Neuzeit
für die Jahre 1-2000 nach Christus*. 1934. For a table of parallel years of the Greek,
Seleucid, Roman, and Christian eras see SHJP I, ii, pp.393-398.

Roman general Pompey (106-48 B.C.), whose bust is shown in Fig. 98, to close the circle of empire around the eastern end of the Mediterranean.

The opposition to Rome in the East was headed by King Mithradates VI Eupator of Pontus, member of a dynasty which belonged to the highest Persian nobility, who warred with the Romans in Asia Minor for twenty-five years, and by his son-in-law King Tigranes of Armenia, member of a dynasty founded by Artaxias, a general of Antiochus III. Tigranes was for a time the most powerful ruler in western Asia, and used Antioch in Syria as one of his residential cities. The defeat of Mithradates and Tigranes by Pompey led to the consolidation of Roman power in the eastern Mediterranean, to the establishment of Syria as a Roman province, and to the inclusion of Palestine in the empire (cf. p. 246).

While Pompey was winning the East, Gaius Julius Caesar (c.102-44 B.C.) was rising to political importance in Rome. For a time the two men shared power, then faced each other in civil war. Pompey was defeated at Pharsalus in 48 B.C. and afterward was murdered in Egypt, whither he fled for refuge, while the last of his forces were crushed at Munda in Spain in 45 B.C. Thereafter Caesar was undisputed master of the Roman world, a glory which he enjoyed for only a brief six months before being assassinated on March 15, 44 B.C.

Two relatives of Julius Caesar were then the chief claimants to his empire. The first was Marcus Antonius, commonly called Mark Antony, who was related on his mother's side to Julius Caesar, and who was consul with Caesar in 44 B.C. The second was Gaius Octavius, whose grandmother was Caesar's sister, and who was adopted and made heir by Caesar, thereby acquiring the designation of Gaius Julius Caesar Octavianus. Associating himself with Cleopatra, the heiress of the Ptolemies in Egypt, Mark Antony was dominant in the East, while Octavian appropriated Italy and the West. The final trial of strength between the two rivals came in the naval battle of Actium (September 2, 31 B.C.), where Antony was decisively defeated. In the following year Alexandria was taken and Antony and Cleopatra committed suicide.

From 31 B.C. on, Octavian was the real master of the empire, and two years later the restoration of peace was marked by the closing of the doors of the temple of Janus for the first time in two hundred years. In recognition of Octavian's distinguished services to the state, the Roman Senate in 27 B.C. conferred upon him the title Augustus,

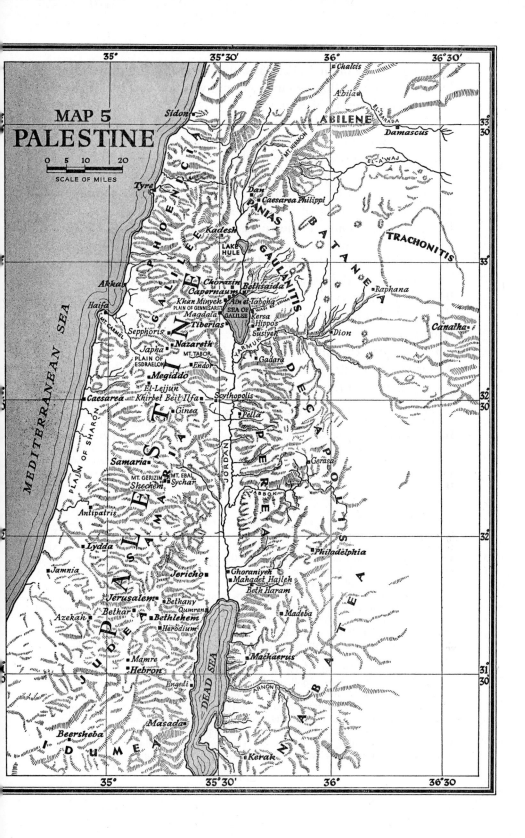

MAP 5
PALESTINE

SCALE OF MILES
0 5 10 20

■ Chalcis

Abila

ABILENE

Sidon

Damascus

EL BARADA

MT. HERMON

EL A'WAJ

P H O E N I C I A

Tyre

■ *Dan*
■ *Caesarea Philippi*

PANIAS

BATANEA

TRACHONITIS

Kadesh

LAKE
HULE

G A U L A N I T I S

Akka

MEDITERRANEAN SEA

Haifa

MT. CARMEL

■ *Chorazin*
■ *Capernaum*
■ *Bethsaida*

Khan Minyeh
Ain et Tabgha
PLAIN OF GENNESARET
■ *Magdala*
SEA OF GALILEE

Kersa
■ *Raphana*

G A L I L E E

WADI EL YARMUK

Sepphoris
■ *Tiberias*
Hippos
Susiyeh

■ *Dion*

Canatha ■

Japha
■ *Nazareth*
MT. TABOR
■ *Endor*

Gadara

YARMUK

PLAIN OF ESDRAELON

■ *Megiddo*

D

El-Lejjun

Caesarea ■
Khirbet Beit Ilfa ■
Scythopolis

E

Ginea ■

■ *Pella*

C

Gerasa

PLAIN OF SHARON

Samaria ■

MT. GERIZIM   MT. EBAL
Shechem ■ ■ *Sychar*

S A M A R I A

A

JORDAN

P

O

L

■ *Antipatris*

I

Lydda ■

S

■ *Philadelphia*

Jamnia ■

Jericho ■
■ *Ghoraniyeh*
■ *Mahadet Hajleh*
Beth Haram

Jerusalem ■
■ *Bethany*
■ *Qumran*

Bethar ■
Azekah ■
■ *Bethlehem*
■ *Herodium*
■ *Madeba*

J U D A E A

N

■ *Mamre*
■ *Hebron*

■ *Machaerus*

Engedi

A

ARNON

DEAD SEA

B

Masada ■

A

Beersheba ■

T

I D U M E A

E

A

■ *Kerak*

meaning august or majestic. This appellation of dignity was borne by him as the first Roman emperor, and was adopted by all the later Caesars or emperors of Rome.

Under the rule of Augustus (d. A.D. 14) and his successors, for two centuries the Mediterranean world as a whole enjoyed an internal peace, the *Pax Romana,* which it never before had had and which for so long a period it has never since possessed. The author of this outstanding achievement is portrayed in the statue shown in Fig. 99. This work of a master sculptor[2] was found near Prima Porta north of Rome in the ruins of the villa of Livia, the wife of Augustus; the statue is now in the Vatican. The emperor is represented in the prime of manhood and at the height of his power, and his features are delicate and refined. On his breastplate is carved in relief an allegory of empire. Beneath Caelus, the Sky, drives Sol, the Sun, in his four-horse chariot—symbol of the new order in all its splendor.

In the New Testament the birth of Jesus is dated in the reign of Augustus (Luke 2:1)[3] and the beginning of the public ministry of Jesus is placed in the reign of Tiberius (Luke 3:1).[4] The latter was

---

[2] Gerhart Rodenwaldt in AZKK 13 (1937), pp.160-163.

[3] In A.D. 533 the Roman monk Dionysius Exiguus suggested counting years no longer from the founding of Rome (cf. above p.247 n.1) but rather from the birth of Christ. Clement of Alexandria (A.D. c.200) stated (*Stromata.* I, xxi, 147; ANF II, p.333): "And our Lord was born in the twenty-eighth year, when first the census was ordered to be taken in the reign of Augustus." Octavian became emperor and received the title Augustus on January 16, A.U.C. 727. Counting A.U.C. 727 as his first year, his twenty-eighth year was A.U.C. 754, and this was taken as the year A.D. 1. Augustus died August 19, A.D. 14 (A.U.C. 767), having reigned forty-one years. Clement of Alexandria, however, in a paragraph preceding the quotation given above, attributed to him a reign of forty-six years, four months, and one day. Counting back exactly that far from August 19, A.D. 14 would bring one to a starting point of April 18, 33 B.C. Reckoned from that initial point, the twenty-eighth year of Augustus began on April 18, 6 B.C. At all events it is clear that Dionysius Exiguus was not entirely correct in the year selected for the beginning of the Christian era.

[4] Luke gives the date as "in the fifteenth year of the reign of Tiberius Caesar." The more usual method of dating in this period was by indicating the honors accorded to the emperor and specifying the number of times he was invested with the tribunician power, designated consul, and acclaimed imperator (Carl H. Kraeling in ATR 24 [1942], p.344). When tribunician years were not stated, it was usually the custom in the first century A.D. to count the years of an emperor's reign from the death of his predecessor or the day on which he himself began to rule (W. M. Ramsay, *Was Christ Born at Bethlehem?* 1898, pp.133, 202). Augustus died August 19, A.D. 14; Tiberius was formally proclaimed emperor within less than one month on September 17 (H. Dessau, ed., *Prosopographia Imperii Romani.* II [1897], No. 150, pp.182f.; M. Cary, et al., eds., *The Oxford Classical Dictionary.* 1949, pp.906f.). The first year of Tiberius began, accordingly, on August 19 or September 17, A.D. 14, and his fifteenth year began at the same time in A.D. 28. The appearing of John the Baptist and the inauguration of the public work of Jesus may be dated, therefore, with considerable

the successor of Augustus, and reigned from A.D. 14 to 37. The marble head of Tiberius shown in Fig. 100 is in the Boston Museum of Fine Arts, and portrays him as yet a lad with fresh and pleasing features.[5]

probability in the fall of A.D. 28. For other ways of reckoning see Werner Foerster, *Neutestamentliche Zeitgeschichte*, II, *Das römische Weltreich zur Zeit des Neuen Testaments*. 1956, p.268, n.37.

[5] The successors of Augustus and Tiberius in the Julio-Claudian line were Gaius (A.D. 37-41), generally known as Caligula, Claudius (41-54), and Nero (54-68). In 68 Galba, Otho, and Vitellius all claimed the throne, but the final winner in the struggle was Vespasian (69-79). The Flavian Dynasty which he founded included also Titus (79-81) and Domitian (81-96). The rulers who followed belonged to the house of Nerva and included Nerva (96-98), Trajan (98-117), and Hadrian (117-138). Then the Antonines came to the throne, including Antoninus Pius (138-161), Marcus Aurelius (161-180), and Commodus (180-192). The Severan house embraced Septimus Severus (193-211), Caracalla (211-217), Elagabalus (218-222), and Severus Alexander (222-235). The succeeding military emperors were Maximinus Thrax (235-238), Gordian III (238-244), Philip the Arab (244-249), Decius (249-251), Gallus (251-253), Valerian (253-260), and Gallienus (260-268). After Gallienus was murdered, Claudius II reigned briefly (268-270), but it remained for Aurelian (270-275) to restore unity. He was followed by Tacitus (275), Probus (276-282), Carus (282), Carinus and Numerian (283), and Diocletian (284-305). Diocletian reorganized the empire in 286 by entrusting the West to his friend Maximian while he retained the East for himself. This arrangement was modified further in 292 when the two Augusti each recognized a Caesar as a subordinate colleague. Thus Galerius Caesar was associated with Diocletian Augustus in the East and Constantius Chlorus Caesar with Maximian Augustus in the West. Diocletian and Maximian abdicated in 305, leaving Galerius and Constantius Chlorus as Augusti in control of the empire. Galerius was able to secure the promotion to the rank of Caesar of his faithful servant Flavius Valerius Severus and of his nephew Daia Maximinus, hoping thus on the death of Constantius Chlorus to become the sole master of the empire. Constantius Chlorus died in 306, but his soldiers continued to be loyal to Constantine, son of Constantius Chlorus and Helena. Maximian now reassumed the dignity which he had relinquished in 305, and with his son Maxentius brought the number of Roman rulers to six. In the struggle that followed, Maximian was killed in 310, and Maxentius was defeated by Constantine at the decisive battle of the Milvian bridge outside Rome in 312. Meanwhile in the East Licinius had become co-regent with Galerius and, upon the latter's death in 311, succeeded him on the throne. Constantine and Licinius now (313-323) exercised authority jointly as colleagues in the West and the East respectively, and Licinius married the sister of Constantine. The two rulers warred however in 314 and again in 323. In the second conflict Licinius was defeated, and in 324 was executed at Constantine's command. Thus Constantine the Great emerged as sole ruler of the Roman Empire (323-337). After Constantine, his three sons divided the empire, but Constantine II (337-340) died in civil war against his brother Constans (337-350) and the latter was slain by the usurper Magnentius. The remaining son Constantius (337-361) had received the East, and now upon defeating Magnentius again united the whole empire under one authority. He was followed by Julian the Apostate (361-363), and Jovian (363-364). In 364 the empire was divided again, Valentinian I (364-375) taking the West and Valens (364-378) the East. The later emperors in the West were Gratian (367-383) and Valentinian II (375-392), Theodosius I (394-395), Honorius (395-423), Joannes (424), Valentinian III (425-455), Maximus (455), Avitus (455-456), Majorian (457-461), Libius Severus (461-465), Anthemius (467-472), Olybrius (472), Glycerius (473), Julius Nepos (473-475), and Romulus Augustulus (475-476). The last named king was deposed by the Teutonic invaders in 476 and replaced by Odoacer as the first barbarian ruler of Italy. Thus the Roman Empire in the West came to an end. In the East the emperors who

In connection with the birth and the public appearance of Jesus, Luke not only refers to the Roman emperors Augustus and Tiberius, but also gives more detailed mention of a number of lesser governors and officials. The passages (Luke 2:1f.; 3:1f.) are as follows:

"In those days a decree went out from Caesar Augustus that all the world should be enrolled. This was the first enrollment, when Quirinius was governor of Syria.

"In the fifteenth year of the reign of Tiberius Caesar, Pontius Pilate being governor of Judea, and Herod being tetrarch of Galilee, and his brother Philip tetrarch of the region of Ituraea and Trachoritis, and Lysanias tetrarch of Abilene, in the high-priesthood of Annas and Caiaphas, the word of God came to John the son of Zechariah."

Elsewhere Luke dates the promise of the birth of John the Baptist "in the days of Herod, king of Judea" (1:5), and Matthew places the birth of Jesus "in the days of Herod the king" (2:1), this Herod being identified (2:22) as the father of Archelaus.[6] In order to explain these references to Syrian and Palestinian authorities and to give an understanding of the inner political situation in Palestine in the time

---

followed Valens included Theodosius I the Great (379-395), who also ruled the West for a time, Arcadius (395-408), Theodosius II (408-450), Marcian (450-457), Leo I (457-474), Leo II (474), Zeno (474-491), Anastasius I (491-518), Justin I (518-527), Justinian I the Great (527-565), and a long line of further rulers who occupied the throne until Constantinople fell to the Crusaders in 1204 and became the seat of a Latin Empire. On the Roman emperors and Christianity see Ethelbert Stauffer, *Christ and the Caesars, Historical Sketches.* 1955.

[6] Since Herod died in 4 B.C. the birth of Jesus must have been at least that early, and Matthew 2:16 suggests that it may have been as much as two years before that. The date of Herod's reign is fixed by the following facts. Josephus (*Ant.* XVII, viii, 1; *War.* I, xxxiii, 8) tells of the death of Herod and says that at that time he had reigned thirty-seven years. He died shortly before a Passover (*Ant.* XVII, ix, 3; *War.* II, i, 3), and not long before his death there was an eclipse of the moon (*Ant.* XVII, vi, 4). This is the only eclipse of moon or sun mentioned by Josephus in any of his writings (William Whiston, *The Works of Flavius Josephus*, p.514 n.), and must be the lunar eclipse which was seen in Palestine on the night of March 12/13, 4 B.C., no such phenomenon having taken place there in 3 or 2 B.C. It is also known that Archelaus was deposed in A.U.C. 759 in the tenth year of his reign, which leads back to A.U.C. 750 or 4 B.C. for his accession and the death of his father (SHJP I, i, p.465 n.165). Thus Herod died in the spring of 4 B.C. and his thirty-seven year reign was 40-4 B.C. In 7 B.C. there was a triple conjunction of Jupiter and Saturn, a phenomenon which occurs once in 805 years and was observed by Johannes Kepler in A.D. 1603. The planets passed each other on May 29, September 29, and December 4, 7 B.C., and in 6 B.C. Mars moved past them too, in February of that year forming with them a triangle in the evening sky, a configuration known as a massing of the planets. These unusual astronomical happenings took place in Pisces, the sign of the zodiac which ancient astrologers called the House of the Hebrews, and it has been thought that this was the "star" which the wise men saw. See the pamphlets, *The Star of Bethlehem*, published by the Adler Planetarium, Chicago; and *The Christmas Star*, published by the Morrison Planetarium, California Academy of Sciences, San Francisco.

of Jesus, it is necessary now to tell briefly a complex and fascinating story which has its beginnings in the days of the Maccabean War.

2. THE TIME OF THE MACCABEES, c.168-63 B.C.

It was an old priest Mattathias and his five sons who led the revolt against Antiochus IV Epiphanes (p. 246).[1] Of these sons, Judas, called Maccabeus, or the Hammer (165-161 B.C.), became the great general and gave his name to the struggle, while his brother Simon eventually ruled (142-135) as prince and high priest over a small independent kingdom. The dynasty thus founded was known as the Hasmonean, from Asamoneus the father of Mattathias.[2] In the succession of rulers Simon was followed by his son John Hyrcanus (135-104), and his grandson Aristobulus I (104-103), who assumed the title of king. Under the latter's brother, Alexander Janneus (103-76), the Jewish kingdom attained its greatest extent, reaching to limits practically the same as those of the kingdom of David. The title of king was stamped proudly in Hebrew and Greek upon the coins of Alexander Janneus.

But the sons of Janneus, Hyrcanus II and Aristobulus II, quarreled for the throne and both appealed to the Romans for help. Pompey had already (64 B.C.) made Syria a Roman province and was near at hand in Damascus. When Aristobulus lost the confidence of the Romans and his adherents entrenched themselves in the temple, Pompey besieged Jerusalem. The city fell after three months (63 B.C.) and Pompey outraged the Jews by entering the Holy of Holies. Aristobulus II was taken prisoner to Rome, and the elder brother, Hyrcanus II (63-40 B.C.), was established as high priest and ethnarch. From that time on the Jews were subject to the Romans.[3]

3. PALESTINE UNDER HERODIAN AND ROMAN RULE, 63 B.C.-A.D. 70

When Pompey was defeated and Julius Caesar was established as master in Rome, Hyrcanus II and his friend Antipater, the Idumean,

---

[1] The history of the Maccabean struggle is narrated in a generally trustworthy way in I Maccabees. For the history from here on through the wars with Rome see Robert H. Pfeiffer, *History of New Testament Times with an Introduction to the Apocrypha.* 1949.

[2] Josephus, *War.* i, i, 3.

[3] *ibid.*, i, vii, 4; *Ant.* xiv, iv. For Palestine in the Roman period see G. M. Fitz-Gerald in PEQ 1956, pp.38-48.

attached themselves to Caesar's party and rendered him such services as to secure for Judea freedom both from taxes and from the obligation of military service. Antipater, who already, it seems, had attained the position of procurator of Judea,[1] was confirmed in this office by Caesar. He soon appointed his two sons, Phasael and Herod, governors of Jerusalem and Galilee respectively.

Phasael ended his life by suicide when Antigonus (40-37 B.C.), son of Aristobulus II and last of the Hasmonean rulers, captured Jerusalem with Parthian help. For Herod there was a greater future. In Rome he gained the favor of Mark Antony and Octavian, who at that time divided the Roman world between themselves, and was given by the Senate the rank of king of Judea (40 B.C.). By 37 B.C. Herod was able to besiege and take Jerusalem. Antigonus was beheaded by the Romans, and Herod assumed the Jewish crown, meanwhile having strengthened his claim by marrying the Hasmonean princess, Mariamne. When Mark Antony was defeated and Octavian emerged as the sole emperor of the Roman Empire, Herod knew how to continue in his favor and even to gain by imperial favor the doubling of his own territory.

HEROD THE GREAT

Herod "the Great"[2] ruled for thirty-seven years (40-4 B.C.) with much energy and success, but was always hated by the Jews as a half-foreigner[3] and a friend of the Romans. Moreover, he had little real interest in Judaism and was instrumental in spreading Greek culture throughout the land. The love of Herod for pagan civilization was reflected in most of his numerous building activities.[4] Temples dedicated to pagan gods and emperor worship, halls and theaters in the Greek style, palaces, castles, and baths were constructed throughout the land. On the site of ancient Samaria he built a new city, named Sebaste, in honor of the Emperor Augustus.[5] On the coast, on the site of the ancient Straton's Tower, he built a new city and port which he named Caesarea and which later was to be the capital of the country.

[1] *Ant.* XIV, viii, 1.

[2] This title is applied once to Herod by Josephus, *Ant.* XVIII, v, 4. See now Stewart Perowne, *The Life and Times of Herod the Great.* 1956.

[3] As an Idumean he was called a "half-Jew" by Josephus, *Ant.* XIV, xv, 2. The Idumeans, or Edomites, living in southern Palestine had been conquered and compelled to accept Judaism by John Hyrcanus (*Ant.* XIII, ix, 1).

[4] *War.* I, xxi.

[5] The Latin title Augustus was rendered in Greek by Σεβαστός. cf. Dio Cassius (A.D. c.150-c.235), *Roman History.* LIII, xvi, 8. tr. E. Cary, LCL (1914-27), VI, p.235.

But the most magnificent single piece of building done by Herod was carried out in strict conformity with Jewish principles. This was the restoration of the temple in Jerusalem,[6] which was begun in 20/19 B.C. Only priests were allowed to build the temple proper, and Herod himself refrained from entering the inner temple, whose precincts should be trodden by none but priests. The temple proper was built in one year and six months, but other building work was long continued, and was finished only in the time of the procurator Albinus (A.D. 62-64), a few years before the temple's final destruction.

THE SONS OF HEROD

A few days before his death in 4 B.C., the aged Herod rewrote his will providing for the division of his kingdom among his sons. Of the various sons of Herod's ten legal marriages several had perished in intrigues or had been put to death by their father's orders, including Alexander and Aristobulus, the sons of Mariamne (who also was slain), and Antipater, who was executed five days before Herod died. Three younger sons were to inherit the kingdom. Philip, the son of Cleopatra of Jerusalem, became tetrarch of Gaulanitis, Trachonitis, Batanea, and Panias (Paneas), regions north and east of the Sea of Galilee and mostly inhabited by pagans.[7] Over this territory Philip reigned well for nearly forty years (4 B.C.-A.D. 34). At the sources of the Jordan he rebuilt the city of Panias and gave it the name Caesarea in honor of the emperor.[8] To distinguish it from Caesarea on the coast[9] it was called Caesarea Philippi (Matthew 16:13; Mark 8:27). Also he raised the village of Bethsaida, which was situated at the lake of Gennesareth, to the dignity of a city, both by the number of inhabitants it contained and by its size, and named it Julias after the daughter of the emperor.[10]

Herod Antipas, the younger son of Malthace, became tetrarch of Galilee and Perea (4 B.C.-A.D. 39). He built a splendid capital for himself at a beautiful site in the western shore of the Sea of Galilee, and named it Tiberias in honor of Tiberius who was then on the Roman throne. Antipas brought trouble upon himself through put-

---

[6] *War.* I, xxi, 1; *Ant.* xv, xi.

[7] *War.* I, xxxiii, 8; *Ant.* xvII, viii, 1.

[8] *War.* II, ix, 1; *Ant.* xvIII, ii, 1.

[9] For coastal Caesarea, founded by Herod the Great in 22 B.C., see A. Reifenberg in IEJ 1 (1950-51), pp.20-32.

[10] *Ant.* xvIII, ii, 1; cf. *War.* II, ix, 1. Julias was the daughter of Augustus, but was banished in 2 B.C. Since Philip hardly would have named a city for her after that event, Julias must have been built before 2 B.C.

ting away his first wife, the daughter of King Aretas of Nabatea, to marry Herodias, whom he alienated from his half-brother, Herod.[11] Thereafter Antipas was defeated in war by Aretas, and when he sought the king's title from Caligula was banished instead to Lyons in Gaul, whither Herodias followed him.

Archelaus, the older son of Malthace, received the principal part of Herod's territory—Judea, Samaria, and Idumea—and was intended by Herod to have the title of king but actually was given only that of ethnarch (4 B.C.-A.D. 6). Insurrection was spreading throughout the land, however, and the rule of Archelaus was violent and incompetent. When he was deposed and banished to Vienne in Gaul in A.D. 6, his territory was put directly under Roman rule.[12]

THE PROCURATORS AND LEGATES

Authority over the former dominions of Archelaus was placed in the hands of a governor of the equestrian order, whose title was that of procurator, and who could receive help in case of need from the legate who governed the province of Syria.[13] The residence of the

[11] Herodias was a granddaughter of Herod the Great, her father being Aristobulus, the son of Mariamne, who was executed in 7 B.C. Mark 6:17; Matthew 14:3 (contrast Luke 3:19) call Herodias the wife of Philip, meaning doubtless the tetrarch of Trachonitis. Josephus (*Ant.* XVIII, v, 4) states that Herodias was married to Herod, the son of Herod the Great and the second Mariamne, the high priest's daughter. Also Josephus says that Herodias' daughter, Salome, was married to Philip, the tetrarch of Trachonitis. The relationships may have been confused in the Gospels, or it is barely possible that this Herod bore the surname Philip.

[12] *War.* II, viii, 1; *Ant.* XVII, xiii; XVIII, i, 1.

[13] In 27 B.C. Augustus divided the provinces of the Roman Empire into imperial and senatorial. (1) The imperial provinces, which the emperor continued to hold, were those which were most difficult to manage and which required the presence of a strong military force. They in turn were divided, with the exception of some which were administered by simple knights, into two classes: those administered by men who had been consuls, and those administered by men who had been praetors. The governors were nominated by the emperor, were directly responsible to him, and held office for a term the length of which depended on the emperor's pleasure. The governors of both consular and praetorian provinces were called *legati Augusti* (or *Caesaris*) *pro praetore.* (2) The provinces which were given over to the senate were those which did not require the presence of an army but only of a small garrison sufficient for the purpose of maintaining order. They were also divided into those administered by men who had been consuls and those administered by men who had been praetors. The governors of the senatorial provinces were appointed for a year at a time, were responsible to the senate, and were called proconsuls. (3) Certain other possessions were regarded as domains of the emperor and were placed under governors of the equestrian order responsible to the emperor. Their title was that of praefect or procurator, and the title procurator soon became the prevailing one. Judea thus belonged to the third and more exceptional class of provinces. Dio, *Roman History.* LIII, xii-xv; Strabo, *Geography.* XVII, iii, 25.

procurator was at Caesarea, but on occasions when special oversight was necessary he would live for a time in Jerusalem.

The first procurator of Judea was Coponius (probably A.D. 6-9), and his immediate successors were Marcus Ambivius (probably A.D. 9-12), Annius Rufus (probably A.D. 12-15), Valerius Gratus (A.D. 15-26), Pontius Pilate (A.D. 26-36), Marcellus (A.D. 36-37), and Marullus (A.D. 37-41).[14]

Of them all the most famous and perhaps the most ruthless was Pontius Pilate. Pilate was appointed to office through Sejanus, the anti-Semitic prime minister of Tiberius, and he gave offense to the Jews in many ways. His soldiers carried into the Holy City standards bearing the likeness of the emperor, which violated Jewish principles and provoked a determined and successful protest. Again, he took money from the temple treasury to build an aqueduct to Jerusalem, and mercilessly beat down the crowds which gathered to make petition against this act. Later he put inscribed shields in Herod's palace, which were taken down only when the Jews appealed to Tiberius. Yet another and otherwise unknown act of violence is referred to in Luke 13:1, where Pilate is said to have mingled the blood of certain Galileans with that of their animal sacrifices. Finally he slaughtered and imprisoned a multitude of Samaritans who had gathered at Mount Gerizim to search for some sacred vessels which were believed to have been buried there since the time of Moses. The Samaritans complained to Vitellius, the legate in Syria, and Pilate was replaced by Marcellus. Agrippa I charged against Pilate, according to a letter quoted by Philo, "corruptibility, violence, robberies, ill-treatment of the people, grievances, continuous executions without even the form of a trial, endless and intolerable cruelties," yet it must be admitted that the position of a Roman governor in Judea was very difficult, and no doubt it was to Pilate's credit that he retained office for as long as ten years.[15]

Of the Lysanias who is mentioned by Luke (3:1) as tetrarch of Abilene, little is known. The capital of the tetrarchy was at Abila, not far from Damascus, and an inscription of the time of Tiberius has been found there naming Lysanias as tetrarch.[16]

---

[14] For a tabulation of dated coins struck by the procurators from Coponius to Antonius Felix, including examples from the second to the sixth years of Pontius Pilate, A.D. 27/28 to 31/32, see A. Kindler in IEJ 6 (1956), pp.54-57; cf. Florence A. Banks, *Coins of Bible Days*. 1955.

[15] Josephus, *Ant.* XVIII, iii, 1f.; iv, 1f.; *War.* II, ix, 2-4; Philo (c.20 B.C.-A.D. c.54), *Legatio ad Gaium.* 38. ed. L. Cohn and P. Wendland VI (1915), p.210.

[16] CIG III, No.4521. This younger Lysanias to whom Luke refers and who undoubt-

The legates who ruled Syria at the end of the old era and the beginning of the new are usually listed as follows: M. Titius, 10-9 B.C.; C. Sentius Saturninus, 9-6 B.C.; P. Quinctilius Varus, 6-4 B.C.; P. Sulpicius Quirinius, 3-2 B.C. (?); C. Caesar, 1 B.C.-A.D. 4 (?); L. Volusius Saturninus, A.D. 4-5; P. Sulpicius Quirinius, A.D. 6-7. It must be admitted, however, that there are considerable gaps in the evidence upon which this list is based.[17]

Luke's reference (2:2) to the census that was taken at the time of the birth of Jesus, which was the first enrollment made when Quirinius was governor of Syria, constitutes a difficult problem. Josephus writes concerning Quirinius: "Now Cyrenius, a Roman senator, and one who had gone through other magistracies, and had passed through them till he had been consul, and one who, on other accounts, was of great dignity, came at this time into Syria, with a few others, being sent by Caesar to be a judge of that nation, and to take an account of their substance. Coponius also, a man of the equestrian order, was sent together with him, to have the supreme power over the Jews."[18] Tacitus (A.D. c.55-c.117) describes the public funeral Tiberius requested for Quirinius, and tells briefly of his life.[19] He says that Quirinius was born at Lanuvium, and that he won a consulate under Augustus. A little later he earned the insignia of triumph by capturing the strongholds of the Homanadensians beyond the Cilician frontier. Again he was appointed as adviser to Caius Caesar during the latter's command in Armenia.

Known dates of events mentioned in the foregoing passages are the consulship of Quirinius in 12 B.C., his going with C. Caesar to Armenia in A.D. 3, and his death and public funeral in A.D. 21. His governorship of Syria can also be fixed as beginning in about A.D. 6 by the fact that he took that office, as Josephus says, at the same time that Coponius went to Judea as procurator. Josephus also informs us that the taxings conducted by Quirinius while governor of Syria were made in the thirty-seventh year of Caesar's victory over Antony at Actium.[20] Since that battle took place on September 2, A.U.C. 723 or 31 B.C., the year indicated is that beginning Septem-

---

edly existed, is not to be confused with an older Lysanias who ruled at nearby Chalcis, 40-36 B.C.

[17] SHJP I, i, pp.350-357; E. Honigmann in PWRE, Zweite Reihe, IV, ii (1932), col. 1629; Erich Klostermann, *Das Lukasevangelium* (Handbuch zum Neuen Testament. 5 [2d ed. 1929]), p.33.

[18] *Ant.* XVIII, i, 1.

[19] *Annals.* III, 48. tr. J. Jackson, LCL (1931-37), II, pp.597-599.

[20] *Ant.* XVIII, ii, 1.

ber 2, A.D. 6. A census held in A.D. 6/7 is, of course, too late to be brought into connection with the birth of Jesus.

The fact, however, that Luke speaks of the census at the time of the birth of Jesus as the "first" which was made when Quirinius was governor, may suggest that the census attested above was a second one by that governor. The circumstance that Quirinius conducted the war against the Homanadensians, as stated by Tacitus, suggests that he was already at that earlier time in an official position, perhaps even governor, in Syria, inasmuch as that war was probably conducted from the province of Syria. That one man might hold the same governorship twice is proved by an inscription found in A.D. 1764 near Tibur (Tivoli) and placed in the Lateran Museum, which mentions a person who governed Syria twice as legate of Augustus.[21] Some have wished to refer this to Quirinius himself, but since the name is missing in the inscription it cannot be demonstrated. The exact date of the Homanadensian war is also uncertain. Finding an apparent gap in the list of Syrian legates in 3-2 B.C., Schürer concluded that Quirinius was governor there at that time and in that position conducted the war.[22] It may be, however, that the war with the Homanadensians was as much earlier as 10-7 B.C. (cf. below p. 344 n.37), for it is argued that their opposition must certainly have been broken by 6 B.C. when the net of Roman roads was laid out in the province of Galatia.[23] If a gap could be found in the list of Syrian legates at that time it might be supposed that Quirinius was governor then,[24] even as Schürer by the same logic assigned him to a hypothetical place in 3-2 B.C. Or we may think, as W. M. Ramsay suggested,[25] that Quirinius was at that time a special officer sent out by Augustus to conduct the war against the Homanadensians and to see after other foreign relations of the province of Syria. In this position he might also have been responsible for the census in Palestine, which he probably could not have started until the war was over in 7 B.C. Conditions in Palestine, a land normally difficult for the Romans to deal with, might have delayed the census even beyond that, say to 6 B.C. That two Roman officials could exercise administrative authority in the same province at the same time is shown by a statement of Josephus in which he speaks of "Saturninus and Volumnius,

---

[21] SHJP I, i, p.354 n.25.   [22] SHJP I, i, pp.351f.
[23] Groag in PWRE, Zweite Reihe, IV, i (1931), col. 831.
[24] Egbert C. Hudson in JNES 15 (1956), pp.106f.
[25] Ramsay, *Was Christ Born at Bethlehem?* p.238.

the presidents of Syria."[26] Perhaps Quirinius was associated with Saturninus for a time in a similar way. If that were the case we would understand why Tertullian said that the census at the time of the birth of Jesus was "taken in Judea by Sentius Saturninus."[27]

One other inscription may be mentioned which deals with the career of a Roman officer, Q. Aemilius Secundus, who served under Quirinius when the latter was governor of Syria. Here Quirinius is called legate of Syria, and it is stated that by his orders Aemilius Secundus carried out a census of Apameia, where 117,000 citizens were enumerated.[28] While this may well have to do with the Syrian census of A.D. 6/7 rather than the hypothetical earlier census of Quirinius, it is still of interest in connection with the complex question which we have discussed.

As to the taking of such an enrollment in general, it is known from discoveries among the Egyptian papyri that a Roman census was taken in Egypt, and therefore perhaps also throughout the empire, regularly every fourteen years. Many actual census returns have been found, and they use the very same word (ἀπογραφή) which Luke 2:2 uses for the "enrollment." The earliest definitely dated example is from A.D. 34,[29] then there is one from A.D. 48,[30] another from A.D. 62,[31] and from then on there are numerous examples extending to A.D. 202 and attesting the fourteen year period.[32] Another such return, although now without a date, is believed to have been written in A.D. 20,[33] and yet another is thought to belong to A.D. 34, or 20, or possibly even 6.[34]

That A.D. 6 was a census year we have also seen already from the reference considered above from Josephus. Fourteen years before this would be the year 9 B.C. While actual returns have not been found for this date, there are poll tax lists for even earlier dates and they were presumably connected with some kind of census. It is a reasonable supposition, therefore, that the periodic enrollment was instituted by Augustus in 9 B.C.[35] There is reason to think the actual taking of a census came in the year following that in which the order

---

[26] *Ant.* XVI, x, 8. [27] *Against Marcion.* IV, 19; ANF III, p.378.
[28] Ramsay, *Was Christ Born at Bethlehem?* pp.151, 274. The inscription was at one time considered a forgery but is now accepted as genuine (John E. Sandys, ed., *A Companion to Latin Studies.* 3d ed. 1921, p.763).
[29] MMVGT pp.59f. s.v. ἀπογραφή. [30] OP II, No.255.
[31] OP II, p.207. [32] *ibid.* [33] OP II, No.254.
[34] OP II, No.256.
[35] Bernard P. Grenfell and Arthur S. Hunt in OP II, pp.209-211.

for it was given,[36] in which case 8 B.C. would be indicated here, and other reasons have already been given why if this census were taken in Palestine by Quirinius it might have been delayed to 7 or 6 B.C. when it would still fulfill the condition of Tertullian's statement in coming under Saturninus.

The papyri also attest the practice of going to one's own home place for enrollment. An edict of A.D. 104 says: "Since the enrollment by household[37] is approaching, it is necessary to command all who for any reason are out of their own districts to return to their own home, in order to perform the usual business of the taxation. . . ."[38] Also in a late third century letter a writer asks his sister to endeavor to enroll for him but to let him know in case that is impossible so he may come and do it himself:

"To my sister, lady Dionysia, from Pathermouthis, greeting. As you sent me word on account of the enrollment (τῆς ἀπογραφῆς) about enrolling yourselves, since I cannot come, see whether you can enroll us. Do not then neglect to enroll us, me and Patas; but if you learn that you cannot enroll us, reply to me and I will come. Find out also about the collection of the poll tax, and if they are hurrying on with the collection of the poll tax, pay it and I will send you the money; and if you pay the poll tax, get the receipt. Do not neglect this, my sister, and write to me about the enrollment, whether you have done it or not, and reply to me and I will come and enroll myself. I pray for your lasting health."[39]

Thus the situation presupposed in Luke 2:3 seems entirely plausible.[40]

When Philip died in A.D. 34 his tetrarchy was for a few years included in the province of Syria, then in A.D. 37 was given by Caligula, together with the title of king, to the brother of Herodias, Herod Agrippa I. In A.D. 39 the tetrarchy of Herod Antipas was added, and in A.D. 41 Claudius gave him also what had been the ethnarchy of Archelaus, so that from then until he died in A.D. 44 Herod Agrippa I ruled almost as extensive a kingdom as his grandfather Herod the Great.[41] In his time the emperor Caligula ordered a statue of himself erected in the Temple at Jerusalem. The order reached the legate of Syria, Publius Petronius, in the winter of 39/40,

[36] W. M. Ramsay, *The Bearing of Recent Discovery on the Trustworthiness of the New Testament.* 1915, p.255.
[37] τῆς κατ᾽ οἰ[κίαν ἀπογραφῆς].   [38] DLO p.231.   [39] OP VIII, No.1157.
[40] For further discussion of this problem see Lily R. Taylor in AJP 54 (1933), pp.120-133.
[41] Acts 12:20-23; *Ant.* XIX, viii, 2; Eusebius, *Church History.* II, x. tr. Arthur Cushman McGiffert, NPNFSS 1, pp.111f.

but he delayed the matter as much as he could and Agrippa I begged Caligula not to perform the outrage. Caligula agreed not to desecrate the Temple but still wanted emperor worship altars erected outside Jerusalem, and only his death on January 24, A.D. 41, ended the threat.

Upon the death of Herod Agrippa I his kingdom was reorganized by Claudius into a Roman province (A.D. 44-66), although some portions of the country, including the former tetrarchy of Philip and parts of Galilee and Perea, were after a time given to his son, Agrippa II (A.D. 50-100).[42] The procurators who now governed the land were Cuspius Fadus (A.D. 44-c.46), Tiberius Alexander (c.46-48), Ventidius Cumanus (48-52), Antonius Felix (52-60), Porcius Festus (60-62), Albinus (62-64), and Gessius Florus (64-66), and their cumulative cruelties drove the Jews to the great war (A.D. 66-73) which was climaxed with the destruction of Jerusalem in A.D. 70.

THE HIGH PRIESTS

Our brief outline of the history suggested by Luke's references may be completed by noting that from the time of Herod the Great to the destruction of Jerusalem, twenty-eight high priests exercised spiritual authority in Palestine.[43] The two to whom Luke (3:2) refers are

---

[42] In A.D. 50 Agrippa II received the kingdom of Chalcis in the Lebanon which had been ruled by his uncle, a grandson of Herod the Great, Herod of Chalcis (A.D. 41-48), and with it the right which Herod of Chalcis had obtained from Claudius of nominating the high priest and overseeing the Temple and its treasury. Also after the death of her husband, Bernice, second wife of Herod of Chalcis and sister of Agrippa II, lived with Agrippa II (cf. Acts 25:13, etc.). In A.D. 53 Agrippa II gave up the kingdom of Chalcis and in its place received from Claudius the former tetrarchy of Philip, while under Nero parts of Galilee and Perea were also given to him. Josephus (*War.* II, xiv, 4) dates the beginning of the great Jewish war in the seventeenth year of Agrippa and the twelfth year of Nero, A.D. 66 (SHJP I, ii, p.193 n.5; but see also S. Zeitlin in JQR 41 [1950-51], pp.243f.). In the war Agrippa II sided with the Romans and after it received additions to his kingdom over which he continued to reign until he died in A.D. 100. Then his territory was no doubt incorporated in the province of Syria.

[43] *Ant.* xx, x. The collation of Josephus' various notices of them gives the following list of twenty-eight names (SHJP II, i, pp.197-202): Appointed by Herod (37-4 B.C.): Ananel (37-36 B.C.), Aristobulus (35 B.C.), Jesus the son of Phabes, Simon (father-in-law of Herod the Great), Matthias (5-4 B.C.); Joseph, Joazar (4 B.C.); appointed by Archelaus (4 B.C.-A.D. 6): Eleazar, Jesus the son of Sie; appointed by Quirinius (A.D. 6): Annas or Ananos (A.D. 6-15), *Ant.* xviii, ii, 1f.; Luke 3:2; John 18:13, 24; Acts 4:6; appointed by Valerius Gratus (A.D. 15-26): Ishmael (A.D. c.15-c.16), Eleazar the son of Annas (A.D. c.16-c.17), Simon the son of Kamithos (A.D. c.17-c.18), Joseph called Caiaphas, the son-in-law of Annas (A.D. c.18-36), *Ant.* xviii, ii, 2; iv, 3; Matthew 26:3, 57; Luke 3:2; John 11:49; 18:13f., 24, 28; Acts 4:6; appointed by Vitellius (A.D. 35-39): Jonathan the son of Annas (A.D. 36-37), Theophilos the son of Annas (A.D. 37-40); appointed by Agrippa I (A.D. 41-44): Simon Kantheras, Matthias

Annas and Caiaphas. While Annas was actually high priest only in A.D. 6-15, he continued to be a dominant influence in the days when his sons Eleazar, Jonathan, Theophilus, Matthias, and Ananos, and his son-in-law Caiaphas (A.D. 18-36) held that position.

As appears in Mark 14:55 where "the chief priests and the whole council (συνέδριον) sought testimony against Jesus," the high priests were prominent in the Sanhedrin or supreme court of the Jews. In that body there were also leaders like the famous pair of teachers, Hillel (d. A.D. c.10) and Shammai, and the presidency of the Sanhedrin continued in the family of the former for generations.[44]

4. THE DEAD SEA SCROLLS AND THE QUMRAN COMMUNITY

REMARKABLE and widely heralded discoveries in recent years in the vicinity of the Dead Sea have brought to light the evidences of a community, together with the remains of some of its literature, which probably existed in the first and second centuries B.C. and only came to an end at the time of the great Jewish war in the first century A.D. These finds are therefore an important part of our material for a knowledge of what was happening in Palestine just before, during, and for a few decades after the lifetime of Jesus.

THE GEOLOGY OF THE DEAD SEA REGION

The region of the Dead Sea is of unusual interest geographically and geologically. The geography of Palestine has been outlined in Chapter III, and at this point a brief description of the geology, par-

the son of Annas (A.D. c.43), Elionaios; appointed by Herod of Chalcis (A.D. 44-48): Joseph, Ananias (A.D. c.47-c.59), *Ant.* xx, v, 2; vi, 2; ix, 2-4; *War.* II, xii, 6; xvii, 6, 9; Acts 23:2; 24:1; appointed by Agrippa II (A.D. 50-100): Ishmael (A.D. c.59-c.61), Joseph Kabi (A.D. 61-62), Ananos the son of Annas or Ananos (A.D. 62 for only three months), Jesus the son of Damnaios (A.D. c.62-c.63), Jesus the son of Gamaliel (A.D. c.63-c.65), Matthias the son of Theophilus; appointed by the people during the war (A.D. 67-68): Phannias.

[44] According to the Talmud (*Shabbath.* 15a; SBT p.63) the leadership of the father-and-son succession of Hillel, Simeon I, Gamaliel I, and Simeon II covered the one hundred years prior to the destruction of the Temple. Gamaliel I the Elder, as the grandson of Hillel is called, worked in the second third of the first century A.D. and is probably mentioned in Acts 5:34 and 22:3. Simeon II ben Gamaliel I was president of the Sanhedrin in the last two decades before the destruction of Jerusalem. Gamaliel II or Gamaliel of Jabneh (Jamnia), as he is called to distinguish him from his grandfather Gamaliel I, was head of the Jews in Palestine about A.D. 80-116, and may have been the first to whom was given the title of *nasi* or "prince," later replaced by "patriarch" (JE V, p.560).

ticularly with reference to the immediate region around the Dead
Sea, may be given which will help to show the nature of the area
the Qumran community was in.

The outer covering of this planet is made up of stratified rock
formations perhaps fifty miles thick. The upper layers which contain
distinctive fossils are classified within three time units known as eras:
Paleozoic, meaning "pertaining to ancient life" (trilobites to rep-
tiles), beginning an estimated 500,000,000 years ago; Mesozoic, "pertaining to middle life" (mammals to dinosaurs), beginning 200,000,-
000 years ago; and Cenozoic, "pertaining to recent life" (horses to
man), beginning 70,000,000 years ago. The rocks in the several eras
are divided into systems and the name of the system also serves as
the name of the time unit or period in which the system was formed.
In the Paleozoic era the systems and periods run from the Cambrian
up to the Permian; in the Mesozoic they are the Triassic, Jurassic,
and Cretaceous; and in the Cenozoic era the system and period are
both called Cenozoic. The systems in turn are divided into series of
rocks each with its corresponding epoch of time. Thus the Cretaceous
includes the Cenomanian and Senonian in Palestine, and the Cenozoic includes the Eocene, Miocene, Pliocene, and Pleistocene.[1]

In that part of the world with which we are concerned, at a very
early time, long before the Cambrian period, a great block of granite
was pushed up to the surface of the sea. This was essentially what
we now know as Arabia. What we call Palestine was the coastland
where this land mass met the adjacent sea. This ancient sea, which
lay in the Mediterranean-Turkey-Iran area, has been named Tethys[2]
by the geologists, and our Mediterranean Sea is what now remains
of it.

The land mass just described was from time to time raised or lowered. In general this movement had two effects with which we are
concerned. For one thing, as the land mass was lifted or lowered the
sea was pushed back or allowed to encroach farther inland. Much
of the time it reached to about where the Jordan Valley now is. It

[1] The Pleistocene epoch, when "most of the new" or present-day animals were in
existence, corresponds approximately to the Ice Age in climate and to the Paleolithic
Age in culture. It began perhaps 1,000,000 years ago and lasted until the Holocene
when "all of the new" fauna were known. The Holocene, beginning 10,000 years ago,
includes the Mesolithic, Neolithic, Chalcolithic, Bronze, and Iron Ages. For the divisions of geologic time see Chester R. Longwell and Richard F. Flint, *Introduction to
Physical Geology.* 1955, pp.54f.
[2] Tethys was the wife of Oceanus.

was the deposits of the sea which formed the limestones and chalks of western Palestine, while the desert sandstones of Transjordan were formed where the land was dry.

Also, in the course of the lifting and lowering, the great crystalline block of granite, which was too rigid to bend, was itself at last actually broken and one part was pushed up and the other down. This made a deep rift which runs from north to south in Palestine along the line where the Jordan River now flows and on down through the Dead Sea, the Wadi Arabah, and the Gulf of Aqabah. In the extreme south the granite mass was pushed up so high that it can still be seen in the mountains around Aqabah.

Tracing now what happened in particular in succeeding periods, in the Paleozoic era and the Cambrian period a dark limestone was laid down upon the underlying granite platform. This limestone extends well to the east of the Jordan and may be seen in places where the valleys of Transjordan cut deeply into the earth.

As the Cambrian sea retreated there ensued in Transjordan a long period of desert conditions during which the colorful Nubian sandstone was formed which can be seen, for example, in the cliffs at the famous city of Petra.

In the Mesozoic era and the Cretaceous period the sea again extended over much of the land, and in this time most of the Palestinian rocks were formed. The Cenomanian series of rocks laid down in this period are limestones. These were deposited in greatest thickness in northern and central Palestine west of the Jordan where they are one thousand to two thousand feet thick. Since the limestone is usually quite hard it tends to stand up in mountains and hills and often forms deep gorges and steep cliffs. Being porous, the rock absorbs rain and pays it out in springs, and it also becomes dotted with caves. It is these limestones which form the central highlands of Palestine and also the cliffs on the west side of the Dead Sea.

Later in the Cretaceous period the Senonian rocks were deposited. In contrast with the relatively hard Cenomanian limestones, these rocks are often a soft chalk. Being easily eroded the chalk wears away into smooth and rounded hills and forms valleys which provide passes among the harder formations. It is the Senonian chalk which forms the Wilderness of Judea, which lies to the west of the Dead Sea and the lower Jordan Valley. This rock is extremely porous and with only two inches of rain in the year the result in this region is a most arid wasteland of desert hills and valleys.

In the Cenozoic era and period, the Eocene, Miocene, and Pliocene epochs were a time of mountain building. While the greatest
ranges were pushed up in Iran and Anatolia, Palestine felt what has
been called the "ground swell" from this activity. Not only was the
underlying rock platform broken to make the great Rift Valley but
also a whole series of faults was produced which run parallel to the
valley and also off at angles from it. A main fault line is near Qumran
and Jericho and accounts for the earthquakes which have left such
marked evidences at both places.

On the whole, Palestine tended to be lifted up out of the sea at
this time. By the end of the Eocene epoch Judea, Samaria, and eastern Galilee were probably dry land, and the waters which remained
in the depression between western Palestine and Transjordan formed
a large inland sea with its shore somewhat near Bethlehem. By the
Pliocene epoch Mount Carmel was beginning to appear above the
coastal sea, but the inland sea was being lowered as renewed faulting
in that area pushed the valley floor down.

In the Pleistocene epoch there was much volcanic action on both
sides of the Rift Valley in the north and also in the southern part of
the plateau to the east; and at the same time there were also some
sedimentary rocks laid down in the valley as well as on the Coast
Plain. In this epoch the large inland sea was reduced to several separated basins. Calling them by the names of places now well known,
they were from north to south the Huleh basin, the Tiberias-Beisan
basin, the Jordan-Dead Sea basin, and the Aqabah basin. The Huleh
basin and the Tiberias-Beisan basin were joined together at first,
but in the middle of the epoch were separated by a dam of basalt
which poured across the valley south of the present Lake Huleh.

The Pleistocene was the time of the Ice Age, and in Palestine this
meant very heavy rains. The resultant floods produced a large salt
lake which encompassed both the Tiberias-Beisan basin and the
Jordan-Dead Sea basin and extended some distance south of the
present Dead Sea. The deposits of this lake are to be seen in the gray
marls of the Jordan Valley and the Dead Sea. At the same time the
gravels were washed down which form the alluvium in the Jordan
Valley and the mouths of the wadis which lead into the Rift.

In the last part of the Pleistocene epoch the rains diminished, the
large salt-water lake shrank to become the fresh-water Sea of Galilee
and the heavily mineralized Dead Sea, the Jordan River cut its immediate valley below the level of the marls the larger lake had left,

and the tributary wadis carved their valleys deeper. Thus, during the past fifty thousand years, the great Rift Valley took on its present appearance.

So it was that in the time with which we are concerned the people of Qumran settled in a region where long before the Senonian chalk had produced a forbidding wilderness relatively isolated from the rest of Palestine, and where the wadis, cutting down through the Cenomanian limestone and through the marl, had made gorges and cliffs in whose steep walls were the caves which were to preserve the literature of a remarkable community.[3]

QUMRAN CAVE 1

Wadi Qumran is about seven miles south of Jericho and reaches the shore of the Dead Sea at a point some distance north of a spring known as Ain Feshkha. On a marl plateau beside the Wadi and between the Sea on the east and the limestone cliffs on the west is an ancient ruin, long known, called Khirbet Qumran. Farther south another valley, a continuation of the Kidron at Jerusalem, known here as Wadi en-Nar, descends to the Sea. Clinging to its steep walls is the Mar Saba Monastery, and some four miles to the northeast is another ancient ruin, Khirbet Mird. Yet farther south, a dozen miles below Qumran, is Wadi Murabba'at.[4] Throughout the area the hills are dotted with caves. It was in one of these, a cave in the limestone cliffs less than half a mile north of Khirbet Qumran, that the first find was made. This cave is hidden near the center of the cliffs in Fig. 101.

In 1945 a Bedouin of the Ta'amireh tribe by the name of Muhammad al-Di'b was seeking a lost goat in this region. Noticing a cave he threw stones into it and heard something breaking. Going down into the cave he found pottery jars which he broke open. In one of these was some rolled leather with writing on it. This material he took to his home and kept for two years, then took to a dealer in

[3] For the geology here summarized see Denis Baly, *The Geography of the Bible.* 1957, pp.14-26.

[4] For the enormous literature on the Dead Sea Scrolls and the Qumran community see Christoph Burchard, *Bibliographie zu den Handschriften vom toten Meer* (Beihefte zur ZAW 76). 1957. Other bibliographies are to be found in H. H. Rowley, *The Zadokite Fragments and the Dead Sea Scrolls.* 1952, pp.89-125; J. van der Ploeg in *Jaarbericht ex Oriente Lux.* 14 (1955-56), pp.85-116; BDSS pp.419-435; Charles T. Fritsch, *The Qumrān Community, Its History and Scrolls.* 1956, pp. 131-141; BML pp.411-424. And see now the *Revue de Qumran.* 1- (1958-).

antiquities at Bethlehem.[5] These were the now-famous scrolls from Qumran Cave 1, and finally in that year, 1947, they came in part into the possession of the Syrian Orthodox Monastery of St. Mark in Jerusalem, from which they were brought to the American School of Oriental Research in Jerusalem for study and were eventually purchased for the State of Israel; and in part into the possession of the Hebrew University in Jerusalem.

For convenient reference to these and the many other manuscripts and fragments that have been found, a system of abbreviations has been internationally adopted.[6] First, the material on which the writing is found is indicated, no sign meaning leather, p standing for papyrus, cu for copper, and o for ostracon. Second, the place of discovery is shown, 1Q, for example, meaning the cave mentioned above, Cave 1 at Qumran. Third, the contents of the document are shown. Biblical and apocryphal books are designated with customary abbreviations. Commentaries are indicated with the letter p standing for *pesher* or commentary. New works are marked with a letter corresponding to the first letter of their Hebrew title as known or as supposed. Thus the work commonly called the Manual of Discipline is designated 1QS, the S standing for the word סרק (*serek*) meaning the "Order" or "Rule" of the community; and The War of the Sons of Light with the Sons of Darkness is 1QM from מלחמה (*milḥamah*) meaning "War."

The scrolls referred to above as coming to the American Schools of Oriental Research were the following: The Isaiah scroll (1QIs^a)[7] is a virtually complete copy of the book of Isaiah. It is written on a roll of parchment twenty-four feet in length and about ten inches high. Having been sealed in its container and left in a place where the climate is similar to that of the Fayum and Upper Egypt, the state of preservation is very good. The writing fills fifty-four columns with an average of thirty lines to the column. The text is substantially the same as the later standard Masoretic text.[8] This scroll is shown in Fig. 102. The bottom line in the not entirely visible right-hand column is the beginning of Isaiah chapter 40.

---

[5] For Muhammad al-Di'b's own story of the scroll discovery see William H. Brownlee in JNES 16 (1957), pp.236-239; and see also the somewhat different account in DJD I, p. 5.

[6] DJD I, pp.46-48.

[7] *The Dead Sea Scrolls of St. Mark's Monastery*, I, *The Isaiah Manuscript and the Habakkuk Commentary*, ed. Millar Burrows. 1950.

[8] The Masora is the early tradition as to the correct text of the Hebrew Scriptures, the Masoretes were the scribes who dealt with these studies. Caspar Levias in JE VIII, pp.365-371.

The Habakkuk Commentary (1QpHab)[9] contains the first two chapters of the book of Habakkuk with a commentary accompanying the text. This roll has suffered more disintegration than the preceding one and is broken off all along the bottom edge with the loss of several lines of text. As it now exists the roll is over four and one-half feet long and less than six inches high. The first fragment of this scroll, containing portions of columns 1 and 2, is shown in Fig. 103.

The Manual of Discipline or Rule of the Community (1QS)[10] is the name now commonly given to a book which contains liturgical and disciplinary instructions for the order of people who lived at Qumran. It is written on a parchment roll over six feet long and about nine inches high. Column 10 in this manuscript is reproduced in Fig. 104.

A fourth document the American Schools of Oriental Research found in too bad condition to be able to unroll. From a broken-off piece which contained the name of Lamech it was surmised, incorrectly, that this might be an otherwise lost apocryphal book of Lamech. Since the acquisition of these scrolls for Israel, this work too has been unrolled, and it is found that it is an Aramaic version of several chapters of the book of Genesis with additional stories and legends woven around the lives of the patriarchs. The roll is about nine feet long and twelve inches high, and the work is now known as a Genesis Apocryphon (1QApoc).[11]

The rolls which were acquired at the outset by Hebrew University included the following: A second copy of the book of Isaiah (1QIs[b])[12] is badly disintegrated but contains at least portions of a number of the chapters of the book and is most nearly complete from chapter 38 on to the end. The text is close to that of the Masoretic tradition.

A scroll which the editors call The War of the Sons of Light with the Sons of Darkness (1QM)[13] describes the conflict which is to

[9] *The Dead Sea Scrolls of St. Mark's Monastery*, I, *The Isaiah Manuscript and the Habakkuk Commentary*; tr. BDSS pp. 365-370; GDSS pp.249-256.

[10] *The Dead Sea Scrolls of St. Mark's Monastery*, II, Fascicle 2, *Plates and Transcription of the Manual of Discipline*, ed. Millar Burrows. 1951; tr. BDSM; BDSS pp.371-389; GDSS pp.39-60, 115-122; P. Wernberg-Møller, *The Manual of Discipline Translated and Annotated With an Introduction* (J. van der Ploeg, ed., Studies on the Texts of the Desert of Judah, I). 1957.

[11] Nahman Avigad and Yigael Yadin, *A Genesis Apocryphon, A Scroll from the Wilderness of Judaea, Description and Contents of the Scroll, Facsimiles, Transcription and Translation of Columns II, XIX-XXII*; cf. N. Avigad in BA 19 (1956), pp.22-24; detached fragments (1Q20) in DJD I, pp.86f.; tr. BML pp.387-393.

[12] *The Dead Sea Scrolls of the Hebrew University*, ed. E. L. Sukenik. 1955.

[13] *ibid.*; tr. GDSS pp.281-301; and selections in BDSS pp.390-399.

break out between the tribes of Israel and their enemies, the Kittim. The document details the equipment of the troops, outlines their battle formations and tactics, gives the prayers of the priests prior to battle, and closes with the hymn of thanksgiving which celebrates the victory. The roll, over nine feet long and six inches wide, was well preserved and even its original outer leather wrapping was still with it.

The scroll of Thanksgiving Psalms or Hodayot (1QH)[14] was received in three separate leaves of leather and about seventy detached fragments, but was once a connected roll about six feet long and thirteen inches high with about thirty-nine lines of writing in each of a dozen columns. This is a collection of hymns, composed in a style similar to the Psalms of the Bible, in which the writer gives thanks for the acts of kindness which God has done.

Since the three scrolls just described were acquired originally by Hebrew University, and since those handled by the American Schools of Oriental Research were later purchased for Israel, it is anticipated that they will be brought together in a projected Shrine of the Book at Hebrew University.[15]

Certain other fragments from Cave 1 have come into circulation through various channels. Portions of the book of Daniel are contained on three small pieces of leather (1Q71, 72), each two or three inches wide and four or five inches high. They include the point in Daniel 2:4 where the language changes from Hebrew to Aramaic, and also contain the names Shadrach, Meshach, and Abednego. The text is substantially the same as the Masoretic.[16] Two larger pieces contain two columns of writing which seem to belong to the Manual of Discipline. The text (1QSa)[17] begins, "This is the rule . . . ," and contains information about admission to the sessions of the community and to its common meal.

In 1949 Cave 1 was excavated by R. de Vaux, Director of the École Biblique in Jerusalem, and G. Lankester Harding, Director of the Department of Antiquities of Jordan. A great many fragments of pottery were recovered, enough to piece together into more than forty jars such as those in which the manuscripts were found, about two feet high and ten inches in diameter.[18] One of the jars from the

[14] ibid.; tr. GDSS pp.123-202; and selections in BDSS pp.400-415.
[15] Avigad in BA 19 (1956), pp.22f.; Yigael Yadin, *The Message of the Scrolls.* 1957, pp.39-52.
[16] BA 12 (1949), p.33; DJD I, pp.150-152.
[17] DJD I, pp.108-118; tr. GDSS pp.307-310.
[18] DJD I, pp.8-17.

cave is shown in Fig. 105.[19] Also many pieces of linen cloth were found, which had doubtless been used to wrap the scrolls since in at least one case cloth was still adhering to a piece of scroll.[20] In addition there were hundreds of fragments of manuscripts, many very tiny, most on leather, a few on papyrus, most in Hebrew, some in Aramaic. Represented are texts of Genesis, Exodus, Leviticus, Deuteronomy, Judges, Samuel, Ezekiel, and Psalms; commentaries on Psalms, Micah, and Zephaniah; apocryphal books including the book of Jubilees, and the Testament of Levi; books of discipline, of liturgy, and of hymns; and pieces as yet unidentified.[21]

THE DATE OF THE MANUSCRIPTS

Prior to the Qumran discovery the oldest known manuscript with an Old Testament text was the Nash Papyrus.[22] This papyrus, which is in the Cambridge University Library, contains the Ten Commandments and the Shema (Deuteronomy 6:4ff.). On the basis of comparison with Aramaic papyri and ostraca from Egypt on the one hand, and with Herodian inscriptions on the other, it has been dated in the Maccabean period, that is between 165 and 37 B.C.[23] When the first Isaiah scroll was first brought to the American School of Oriental Research in Jerusalem, John C. Trever compared it with a photograph of the Nash Papyrus and noted a striking similarity of script.[24] W. F. Albright supported this observation and dated the newly found scrolls in the second and first centuries B.C.,[25] while Solomon A. Birnbaum made an independent approach to the problem and arrived at similar results.[26] An intense discussion of the entire subject ensued and every possible dating of the scrolls was explored. Solomon Zeitlin thought they could not date before the Middle Ages and might even be a hoax.[27] The original paleographical

[19] cf. Carl H. Kraeling in BASOR 125 (Feb. 1952), pp.5-7.

[20] DJD I, pp.18-38.   [21] DJD I, pp.49-155.

[22] Stanley A. Cook in *Proceedings of the Society of Biblical Archaeology.* 25 (1903), pp.34-56; Norbert Peters, *Die älteste Abschrift der zehn Gebote, der Papyrus Nash.* 1905.

[23] W. F. Albright in JBL 56 (1937), pp.145-176.

[24] Trever in BA 11 (1948), pp.46f.

[25] Albright in BASOR 115 (Oct. 1949), pp.10-19.

[26] Birnbaum in BASOR 115 (Oct. 1949), pp.20-22; and in BASOR Supplementary Studies 13-14. 1952.

[27] Concerning the Habakkuk Commentary, for example, he argued (in JQR 39 [1948-49], pp.236f.) that it was axiomatic that the Jews did not write commentaries on the prophetic books in the period prior to A.D. 70. See also his other articles in JQR, and *The Dead Sea Scrolls and Modern Scholarship* (JQR Monograph Series, 3). 1956.

conclusions have been supported, however, by other types of evidence soon to be mentioned, and there seems to be no doubt that these are genuine documents of remarkable antiquity. On primarily paleographic grounds the first Isaiah scroll may probably be put about 150 B.C., and the various manuscripts from Cave 1 and other similar caves of the Qumran area yet to be described may be assigned to three periods, Archaic, c.200-c.150 B.C., Hasmonean, c.150-c.30 B.C., and Herodian, c.30 B.C.-A.D. 70.[28] If the Isaiah scroll was written in the second century B.C., it is approximately one thousand years older than the oldest previously known Hebrew manuscripts of the Old Testament, such as Oriental Codex 4445 in the British Museum containing the Pentateuch and written probably about A.D. 820-850, and the St. Petersburg Codex of the Latter Prophets dated in A.D. 916.[29]

The pieces of linen cloth which were with the manuscripts in Cave 1 have also been studied.[30] The linen seems to have been a local Palestinian product. Some of the cloth had fringes and corded edges, and blue lines and rectangles showed that decorative designs were made. The cloth seems to have been used both for scroll wrappers and for jar covers. The employment of cloth wrappers for leather scrolls accords with references in the Mishnah where there is mention of scroll wrappers of linen[31] and with ornamentation.[32] In 1950 some of the linen cloth from Cave 1 was subjected to the Carbon 14 test and it was found that the flax of which it was made had ceased to grow 1,917 years before, that is in A.D. 33. There is a margin of error in the test of plus or minus 200 years, however, therefore the limits are actually between 167 B.C. and A.D. 233.[33] If the flax was cut and the linen made around the median date of A.D. 33, presumably the scrolls were wrapped and sealed in their jars sometime later in the first century. At all events the Carbon 14 date is at least in broad agreement with the paleographic conclusions.

[28] Frank M. Cross, Jr. in JBL 74 (1955), pp.148 n.3, 164. For the available examples of early Hebrew writing see S. A. Birnbaum, *The Hebrew Scripts.* 1954-. For a table of the letters of the Hebrew alphabet as written in the scrolls see Sukenik, ed., *The Dead Sea Scrolls of the Hebrew University*, p.40.

[29] Christian D. Ginsburg, *Introduction to the Massoretico-Critical Edition of the Hebrew Bible.* 1897, pp.469-476.

[30] Louisa Bellinger in BASOR 118 (Apr. 1950), pp.9-11; G. M. Crowfoot in PEQ 1951, pp.5-31; and in DJD I, pp.18-38.

[31] *Kil'ayim.* IX, 3; DM p.38.

[32] *Kelim.* XXVIII, 4; DM p.646; SBT p.134.

[33] ADAJ 1 (1951), p.6.

The pottery from Cave 1 also gave an indication of the date of the manuscripts which were with it. Two intact jars said to have come from the cave were sold by the Bedouins to Professor E. L. Sukenik at Hebrew University and, when the cave was excavated, the mass of potsherds recovered was found to represent the same type of pottery. This pottery was judged to belong to the end of the Hellenistic period in the first century B.C., while some additional pieces were recognized as Roman and thought to belong to the second or third century A.D.[34] When Khirbet Qumran was excavated both types of pottery were found, and the coins also discovered there showed that the Roman ware itself belonged to the first century A.D. and before the destruction of Jerusalem in A.D. 70.[35]

KHIRBET QUMRAN

The ruins known as Khirbet Qumran were explored by Charles Clermont-Ganneau in 1873-1874 and he called attention to the adjacent cemetery of a thousand or so tombs.[36] After the discovery of the manuscripts in the nearby cave, interest turned to the ruins again, and in 1951, 1953, 1954, 1955, and 1956 de Vaux and Harding excavated there.[37] A photograph of the site is shown in Fig. 106.

The main building was a large rectangular structure about 100 by 120 feet in size. At its northwest corner stood a massive two-story stone tower evidently intended for defense. In the southwest corner were a court and several large rooms. A low bench around the four sides of one room suggested a place of assembly. Fragments from an upper story room in this area fitted together to make a plaster table and bench, and when two Roman period inkwells were found, one of copper and one of terra cotta, it was seen that this must have been a scriptorium, doubtless the very place where many of the Dead Sea Scrolls were copied.

In the center of the building was a court and to the north and northeast of it were various rooms, one containing several fireplaces. In the southeast section were a lavatory, a workshop with iron implements, and two pools, one small and one large. The large pool was entered by fourteen steps with four guiding lanes on the upper

---

[34] *The Dead Sea Scrolls of the Hebrew University*, ed. Sukenik, p.20.

[35] James L. Kelso in JBL 74 (1955), pp.141f.

[36] Clermont-Ganneau, *Archaeological Researches in Palestine during the Years 1873-1874*. II (1896), pp.14-16.

[37] R. de Vaux in RB 60 (1953), pp.83-106; 61 (1954), pp.206-236; James L. Kelso in JBL 74 (1955), pp.141-146; Fritsch, *The Qumrān Community, Its History and Scrolls*, pp.1-25.

steps. There were also many other pools and reservoirs in and around the building, perhaps as many as forty in all.[38] The water for them was brought by a stone aqueduct from natural reservoirs at the base of the cliffs not far from Khirbet Qumran.

In an extension of the main building to the south was a large room, twenty-two feet long, which may have been used for a communal meal since a smaller room adjoining it was found to contain more than one thousand bowls stacked against the wall.

Near the ruins is a cemetery which, as Clermont-Ganneau observed, contains around one thousand tombs. Laid out in orderly arrangement, these are simple graves in which the bodies were protected with a layer of stones or bricks. The bodies lie supine, feet to the north. Lack of jewelry or pottery indicates the simplicity of the interment, but potsherds in the earth fill show that the cemetery is of the same age as the nearby ruins. According to what is known thus far, the main cemetery contains only adult male skeletons, but there are remains of women and children in smaller burial areas adjoining it.[39]

In the ruins of Khirbet Qumran some 750 coins were found and, together with the pottery and the evidences of architectural changes in the building, these provide clues for a reconstruction of the history of the site.

Even before the periods in which we are here interested there was an occupation, probably in the eighth and seventh centuries B.C., by the Israelites. It is also thought that Khirbet Qumran was the 'Ir-Hammelah or City of Salt of Joshua 15:62.[40]

The original building which we described above was probably erected in the reign of John Hyrcanus (135-104 B.C.), since many coins of this ruler were found. Likewise coins of Antigonus (40-37 B.C.), the last Hasmonean ruler, show that this period of occupation continued until the end of Hasmonean times. In the reign of Herod the Great, however, the place may have been abandoned, since but a single one of this king's coins was found. Such an abandonment could have been due at least in part to an earthquake. There are

---

[38] Since reservoirs with steps leading down into them are familiar in Palestine, many of these pools were no doubt simply intended for water storage, yet some may have been used for ablutions, while Ain Feshkha and the Jordan River also provided relatively nearby and abundant waters for washings and baptisms (CALQ pp.49f.).

[39] R. de Vaux in RB 63 (1956), pp.569-572.

[40] Martin Noth in ZDPV 71 (1955), pp.111-123.

evidences of such a disaster in discernible damage in the great tower and in a large diagonal crack running down through the steps into the large pool, and these may well be recognized as marks of the severe earthquake which Josephus says struck Judea in the seventh year of Herod, 31 B.C.[41]

The coins also suggest that the building was reoccupied under Herod's son Archelaus (4 B.C.-A.D. 6), when it was enlarged and the great tower strengthened, and that occupation continued until in the early part of the Jewish war. Arrowheads of iron and a layer of burnt ash attest the military conquest and the conflagration which then befell the place. Josephus states that in the spring of A.D. 68 Vespasian set out with his army from Caesarea to finish the conquest of Palestine and on the second day of the month Daisios reached and took Jericho whose inhabitants had already fled to the hill country.[42] It may readily be assumed therefore that it was at this very time, June, A.D. 68,[43] that the Roman army also took Qumran, and the presence of coins from Caesarea in the ruins confirms this conclusion.[43a]

Afterward Vespasian returned to Caesarea but left a garrison at Jericho,[44] and it was also by way of Jericho that Legion X came up to Jerusalem when Titus mustered his forces for the final attack upon the Judean capital in the spring of A.D. 70.[45] That the Tenth Legion had contact with Qumran is shown by one coin found there marked with an "X." From other coins and from modifications in the Qumran building evidently intended to make it into a barracks it seems that Roman troops were quartered there until about the end of the first century A.D.

Again during the second revolt (A.D. 132-135), Jewish forces occupied Qumran briefly. After that there were only temporary encampments attested by a few Byzantine and Arab coins.

[41] *Ant.* xv, v, 2; *War.* i, xix, 3. Since Josephus equates the date with the battle of Actium (31 B.C.) he must have reckoned 37 B.C. when Herod took Jerusalem as the first year of his reign. For other reasons why the community may have left Qumran under Herod the Great see Charles T. Fritsch in JBL 74 (1955), pp. 173-181.

[42] *War.* iv, viii, 1-2.

[43] For the months see PDBC p.24.

[43a] Perhaps the Qumran community was allied at this time with the Zealots who led the rebellion against Rome (H. H. Rowley in BJRL 40 [1957-58], p.144). For a theory which identifies the Qumran group with the Zealots see Cecil Roth in *Commentary.* 24 (1957), pp.317-324; and for the supposition that Simeon ben Kosiba was an Essene see L. E. Toombs in NTS 4 (1957), pp.65-71.

[44] *War.* iv, ix, 1.

[45] *War.* v, i, 6; ii, 3.

The periods just described may therefore be outlined as follows:[46]

Period I.	Construction under John Hyrcanus, 135-104 B.C.
	Earthquake
Abandonment	
Period II.	Restoration under Archelaus, 4 B.C.-A.D. 6
	Destruction, June, A.D. 68
Period III.	Military occupation, A.D. 68-c.100
Abandonment	
	Occupation during the Second Revolt, A.D. 132-135
Final Abandonment	

Thus it was from the time of John Hyrcanus near the end of the second century B.C. to the time of the great Jewish war and in particular the spring of A.D. 68, with an interruption in the time of Herod the Great, that Khirbet Qumran was occupied by the group with which we are concerned. Since the arrangements of the building we have described had to do with assemblage and ablution, with cooking, eating, and writing, rather than with residence, it seems probable that this was a community center and that the people must be thought of as having actually dwelt in the neighboring caves and perhaps also in tents and other less permanent structures. Soundings made at Ain Feshkha in 1956 by R. de Vaux also show remains at that site contemporary with Khirbet Qumran.[47] Therefore the entire occupation at this time must be pictured as extending over a very considerable area, with Khirbet Qumran doubtless representing the center of the whole settlement.

OTHER QUMRAN CAVES

In 1952 it became known that the Bedouins had found more manuscripts in another cave near the one where the original discovery had been made. Thereupon the École Biblique, the Palestine Archaeological Museum, and the American School of Oriental Research in Jerusalem joined in an expedition under Père de Vaux and William L. Reed to explore the Qumran area more thoroughly.[48] In a distance of about five miles from north to south thirty-nine

---

[46] De Vaux in RB 61 (1954), p.234.

[47] De Vaux in RB 63 (1956), pp.576f.

[48] R. de Vaux in RB 60 (1953), pp.540-561; William L. Reed in BASOR 135 (Oct. 1954), pp.8-13.

caves and crevices were found which contained pottery and other objects, the pottery being of the same sort already known from Cave 1 and Khirbet Qumran. Two caves had written material. One of these was that which the Bedouins had already found and which they had cleared so completely that only two small fragments of manuscripts remained in it. This cave, which was only about three hundred feet from the cave of the original discovery, is now known as 2Q. All together there came from it fragments of Exodus, Leviticus, Numbers, Deuteronomy, Ruth, Psalms, Jeremiah, and Jubilees, and also fragments of perhaps forty nonbiblical books including a liturgical document in Aramaic. The other cave (3Q) was over a mile north of Khirbet Qumran. In it were fragments of a dozen manuscripts including a few lines of Isaiah and, surprisingly enough, two copper rolls inscribed in Hebrew characters. Preliminary study had to be based on the letters which showed through on the back,[49] but the document was finally opened by cutting.[50] This was done in England in 1956 and then the rolls were returned to the Jordan Museum in Amman. Actually there were three strips of copper riveted together to form a document nearly eight feet long and one foot high. The script probably belongs to about the middle of the first century A.D. Listed are the hiding places, such as in cisterns, pools, and tombs, all over Palestine, of some sixty caches of treasure, mostly silver and gold, totaling over two hundred tons in weight. The language is colloquial, and it has been suggested that this is simply a compilation of traditional folklore concerning legendary ancient treasures. On the other hand it is notable that the text is inscribed in such a permanent way, and it may be that it is a genuine list of the treasures hidden away in their time of peril by the Essene communities, an order which had many goods even though its individual members were pledged to poverty.[51]

Later in 1952 the Bedouins found Caves 4, 5, and 6, all not far from Khirbet Qumran. Caves 5 (5Q) and 6 (6Q) had relatively few fragments of manuscripts, but Cave 4 (4Q) provided a discovery of scope exceeding that of the original Cave 1. This cave, which is in the same marl terrace on which Khirbet Qumran lies, is shown in Fig. 107. No less than tens of thousands of manuscript fragments were found here and acquired by the Palestine Archaeological Mu-

---

[49] K. G. Kuhn in RB 61 (1954), pp.193-205.

[50] J. T. Milik in BA 19 (1956), pp.60-64; H. Wright Baker in BJRL 39 (1956-57), pp.45-56.

[51] A. Dupont-Sommer in RHR 151 (1957), pp.22-36.

seum. A very great labor was involved in the ensuing endeavor to assemble such pieces as belonged together and to identify the books represented. By 1956 approximately 330 manuscripts had been identified, about ninety of them of biblical books.[52] Every book of the Hebrew Old Testament is represented excepted Esther. Most nearly complete is a copy of Samuel (4Q Samᵃ), the fragments of which represent forty-seven out of an original total of fifty-seven columns of text. This is written on leather to which later a backing of papyrus was added. The script appears to belong to the first century B.C. The text is not like the Masoretic as in the case of scrolls mentioned above, but rather is so much like the Septuagint that it must be in general the kind of Hebrew text upon which that translation was based.[53] There are also thirteen manuscripts of Deuteronomy, twelve of Isaiah, ten of Psalms, seven of part or all of the Book of the Twelve Prophets, and five of books of the Pentateuch. As in the case of the book of Samuel just mentioned, the text of the other historical books is like that of the Septuagint. In the Pentateuch some of the manuscripts resemble the Septuagint, some the Masoretic text, and some the Old Samaritan recension. An example of the last is a copy of Exodus (4QExᵃ), a scroll of about the same size as the first Isaiah scroll (1QIsᵃ) containing sections from Exodus 6:25 to 37:15.[54] In the case of at least one of the Isaiah manuscripts from Cave 4 the text conforms closely to the Masoretic.[55] Of interest also are fragments of Ecclesiastes (4QQohᵃ) written in a beautiful Hebrew script of about 150 B.C., which show that at least by this date this book was accepted in the Qumran community.[56]

In the Cave 4 manuscripts there are also fragments of apocryphal books, of commentaries on Isaiah, Malachi, and Psalms, and of liturgical texts, and a page of *testimonia* (4Q Testimonia) or Old Testament texts expressing the Messianic hope (p.288 n.87). In addition, as study progresses on this extensive if fragmentary material, undoubtedly many more books will become known.

[52] Frank M. Cross, Jr., in BASOR 141 (Feb. 1956), pp.9-13.

[53] Frank M. Cross, Jr., in BASOR 132 (Dec. 1953), pp.15-26.

[54] Patrick W. Skehan in JBL 74 (1955), pp.182-187. The Samaritan Pentateuch has been edited by A. von Gall, *Der hebräische Pentateuch der Samaritaner*. 5 vols. 1914-18. It varies from the Masoretic text in about 6,000 cases, in 1,900 of which it agrees with the Septuagint. While many of the variants are evidently due to accidental or intentional changes, some of them, particularly those in agreement with the LXX, appear to represent good tradition. Pfeiffer, *Introduction to the Old Testament*, pp.101-104.

[55] James Muilenburg in BASOR 135 (Oct. 1954), pp.28-32; cf. Patrick W. Skehan in CBC 17 (1955), pp.158-163.

[56] James Muilenburg in BASOR 135 (Oct. 1954), pp.20-28.

Likewise other discoveries continue to be made in the Qumran region, and in 1956 unofficial reports told of the finding of important manuscripts, comparable to those of Cave 1, in Cave 11 (11Q) somewhat over half a mile north of Cave 1. These are now said to include copies of Leviticus and Psalms, an apocalyptic description of the New Jerusalem, and an Aramaic targum of the book of Job.[57] As the manuscripts and fragments come in they are brought together in the Palestine Archaeological Museum in Jerusalem and studied with painstaking care.

Outside of the immediate Qumran district but still in the general area west of the Dead Sea other finds have been made, notably in Wadi Murabba'at and at Khirbet Mird, but at both places most of the manuscripts are of later date than those of Qumran.

WADI MURABBA'AT

In Wadi Murabba'at four large caves were found by the Bedouins and were excavated by an expedition of the Jordan Department of Antiquities, the École Biblique in Jerusalem, and the Palestine Archaeological Museum in 1952.[58] As was shown by the pottery the caves had been occupied in the Chalcolithic, Bronze, and Iron Ages, and there were great quantities of potsherds from the Roman period, in particular the second century A.D. Caves I and II, the largest ones, each over 150 feet long and fifteen feet high and wide, contained manuscripts, with the majority of these in Cave II. Except for a Hebrew papyrus of the sixth century B.C. containing a list of names and numbers, most of the documents come from the second century A.D. There are fragments of Genesis, Exodus, Deuteronomy, and Isaiah, with a text identical with the Masoretic. There are cursive Aramaic, and Greek business documents, frequently with dates. And there are several Hebrew letters on papyrus, including two written by Simeon ben Kosiba. This is none other than the leader of the Second Revolt (A.D. 132-135), whose name was changed by Akiba to Bar Kokhba. Thus these caves must have been used as a hideaway of the revolutionists in their bitter struggle. In one of the ben Kosiba letters there is mention of certain Galileans who seem to be staying apart from the conflict, and it has been suggested that these could have been Christians.[59] Since in the Qumran manuscripts there was

[57] *Time.* April 15, 1957, p.60; CALQ pp.25f.
[58] G. Lankester Harding in PEQ 1952, pp.104-109; Frank M. Cross, Jr. in BA 17 (1954), pp.8-12; Fritsch, *The Qumrân Community, Its History and Scrolls*, pp.51-59.
[59] J. T. Milik in RB 60 (1953), pp.276-294.

yet much deviation from the Masoretic text, but the Wadi Murab-ba'at fragments are identical with it, it may be concluded with some probability that the standardization of this text took place between the First and Second Revolts, that is between A.D. 70 and 135.[60]

KHIRBET MIRD

In 1952 the Bedouins brought in manuscripts from the Wadi en-Nar region, and in 1953 an expedition of the University of Louvain found that the source was Khirbet Mird. This ruin is identified as the fortress Hyrcania which was used by the Hasmoneans and re-built by Herod the Great. The manuscripts include papyri from the early Islamic period; fragments of Greek codices, written in uncial letters, of the Wisdom of Solomon, Mark, John, and Acts, from the fifth to the eighth centuries; and Syriac fragments of Joshua, Mat-thew, Luke, Acts, and Colossians.[61]

THE ESSENES

Who were the people who, beginning in the second century B.C., had their center at Khirbet Qumran and who, shortly before disaster befell them in A.D. 68, deposited in the nearby caves their valuable manuscripts?

In a short passage in his *Jewish Antiquities*[62] and a longer section in the *Jewish War*[63] Josephus describes the Essenes as the third philosophical sect among the Jews after the Pharisees and the Sad-ducees, and in the *Life* he states that he himself had taken training with all three groups.[64] The Essenes, he says, live simply and have their property in common, with officers elected to look after the in-terests of the community. They settle in various towns. They clothe themselves in white, and do not discard their garments until they are entirely worn out. They pray before sunrise, labor till the fifth hour, then bathe in cold water. After this purification they assemble for a common meal, before and after which a priest says grace. Laboring after that until evening, they again sup in like manner. They display an extraordinary interest in the writings of the ancients. One desiring to join the order is proved for a year, then allowed to share in the waters of purification, but tested yet two years more

[60] Joachim Jeremias in ZAW 67 (1955), pp.289-290; Moshe Greenberg in JAOS 76 (1956), pp.157-167.
[61] J. T. Milik in RB 60 (1953), pp.526f.; Fritsch, *The Qumrān Community, Its History and Scrolls*, pp.50f.
[62] *Ant.* XVIII, i, 5.   [63] *War.* II, viii, 2-13.   [64] *Life.* 2.

before being admitted and allowed to take the common food. In doctrine the Essenes teach that souls are immortal, and when set free from the prison of the body will mount upward with joy. The Essenes disdain marriage but adopt children to raise in their own teachings; one order, however, allows marriage.

Philo[65] also tells about the Essenes at some length. They are, he says, more than four thousand in number. Their name is a variation of the word "holiness."[66] Some of them labor on the land and others pursue crafts of all peaceful sorts. They denounce slavery and abstain from oaths. They study particularly the ethical part of the laws of their fathers, and use allegory in their philosophy. They dwell together in communities and have a single treasury, common disbursements, and common meals. Characterized as they are by frugality, simple living, contentment, humility, love of men, and the spirit of fellowship, they are indeed "athletes of virtue."

Pliny[67] too writes briefly of the Essenes. He speaks of them as a "solitary tribe" who are located "on the west side of the Dead Sea, but out of range of the noxious exhalations of the coast," and who are remarkable for having no women, no money, and only palm trees for company. "Lying below the Essenes," Pliny continues, "was formerly the town of Engedi," and "next comes Masada." If "lying below" means "south of" then Pliny has listed the Essene center, Engedi, and Masada in order from north to south.

The Essenes, therefore, were a communal order with an important center on the west side of the Dead Sea. The location of this center north of Engedi, which is about half way down the west coast, can agree perfectly with the Qumran area in general and Khirbet Qumran in particular. Khirbet Qumran was a community center with special arrangements for ablutions, for communal eating, and for the copying of books. The Qumran manuscripts are copies of scriptural and other books including a rule of the order in which also ablutions and communal eating are prescribed. The correspondence of location and of attested practice at Qumran with the descriptions of Pliny, Philo, and Josephus make probable the identification of the community at Qumran as a group of Essenes,[68] or at least a

[65] *Every Good Man is Free.* 75-91. tr. F. H. Colson, LCL IX (1941), pp.53-63.

[66] Philo uses the word ὁσιότης. In Aramaic the word for "holy" is *hese*, and this may indeed be the source of the name. A. Dupont-Sommer, *The Dead Sea Scrolls*. tr. E. Margaret Rowley. 1950, pp.86f.

[67] *Natural History.* v, xv.

[68] A. Dupont-Sommer, *The Jewish Sect of Qumran and the Essenes.* tr. R. D. Barnett. 1954; H. H. Rowley, *The Zadokite Fragments and the Dead Sea Scrolls.*

group related to that movement. While the Essenes were also to be found in other places in Palestine, the relatively elaborate character of the main building at Qumran and the extent of the library even make it possible to suppose that at the time this was a headquarters for the entire movement.[69]

THE ZADOKITE DOCUMENT

There is also some connection between the discoveries at Qumran and two manuscripts which were found in 1896 in the *genizah* or storeroom of a medieval synagogue in Cairo.[70] Manuscript A, as the first of these is designated, consists of eight leaves copied probably in the tenth century A.D. Manuscript B is a single leaf, with a portion of the same work, probably copied in the eleventh or twelfth century. The entire work comprises two writings, the Admonition (pages I-VIII = chapters 1-9), and the Laws (pages IX-XVI = chapters 10-20), and is commonly known in its entirety as the Cairo Document of the Damascus Covenanters (CD), although a simpler name is the Zadokite Document. The reasons for the two names will be obvious in what follows. There is also a fragment of the same work (6QD) which was found in Cave 6 at Qumran.[71]

In this work we are told about a group of Jews who took thought of their trespasses and came to realize that they were "guilty men." After they had groped their way for some time, God raised up for them "a teacher of righteousness."[72] This group came forth "from Israel and Aaron," that is, from the laity and the priesthood (page 1, lines 5-11 = chapter 1, verses 5-7).[73] The priests, and possibly the en-

---

1952, pp.78f.; *The Dead Sea Scrolls and Their Significance.* 1955, p.20; and in TZ 13 (1957), pp.530-540.

[69] GDSS pp.2,328.

[70] S. Schechter, *Documents of Jewish Sectaries, I, Fragments of a Zadokite Work Edited from Hebrew Manuscripts in the Cairo Genizah Collection now in the Possession of the University Library, Cambridge, and Provided with an English Translation, Introduction and Notes.* 1910; CAP II, pp.785-834; Solomon Zeitlin, *The Zadokite Fragments, Facsimile of the Manuscripts in the Cairo Genizah Collection in the Possession of the University Library, Cambridge, England* (JQR Monograph Series, 1). 1952; Chaim Rabin, *The Zadokite Documents.* 1954; GDSS pp.61-85.

[71] Maurice Baillet in RB 63 (1956), pp.513-523.

[72] CALQ pp.95-119 identifies the teacher of righteousness with a Zadokite priest of Hasidic sympathies who probably began his ministry late in the reign of Jonathan (160-142 B.C.) and was persecuted by Simon (142-135 B.C.) who appears as "the wicked priest" in the Qumran literature. Rowley (in BJRL 40 [1957-58], pp.114-146) places the teacher of righteousness and the wicked priest in the time of Antiochus IV Epiphanes (175-164 B.C.) and the Maccabean uprising.

[73] tr. Rabin, *The Zadokite Documents*, p.2; cf. GDSS p.61.

98. Pompey

99. Caesar Augustus

100. The Young Tiberius

101. The Site of Cave 1 at Qumran

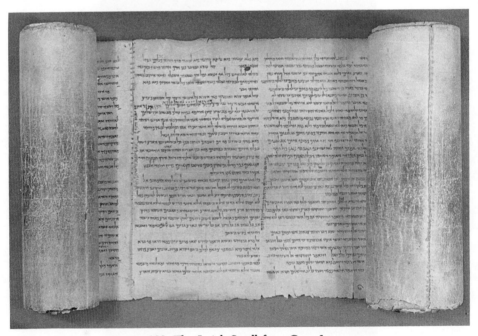

102. The Isaiah Scroll from Cave 1

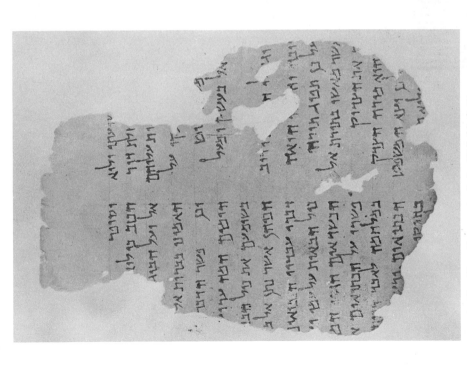

103. The First Fragment of the Habakkuk Commentary

104. Column Ten of the Manual of Discipline

105. A Jar from Cave 1

106. Khirbet Qumran as Seen from Cave 4

107. Cave 4 at Qumran

108. A Palestinian Shepherd with his Sheep

109. The Jordan River

110. Plowing on the Hills above the Sea of Galilee

111. The Synagogue at Capernaum

112. The Synagogue Inscription of Theodotus

113. A Portion of the "Fourth Map of Asia" in Ptolemy's *Geography*

114. Herod's Towers at the West Gate of Samaria

115. The Garden of Gethsemane

116. Jerusalem from the Air

118. Warning Inscription from Herod's Temple

117. The Wailing Wall

119. Titus, the Conqueror of the Jews

120. Relief on the Arch of Titus at Rome

tire group, are called "sons of Zadok" (iv, 3 = 6:1), the reference being to the leading priestly family of the time of David (II Samuel 8:17), who were designated as the only legitimate priests in the future Temple in the vision of Ezekiel (40:46, etc.).[74]

This group entered into a solemn agreement to keep away from evil men, not to rob the poor, to keep the Sabbath in every detail, to love each man his brother, and to keep away from all uncleanness, these and yet other items of the compact being "according to the findings of the members of the 'new covenant' in the land of Damascus" (vi, 15 - vii [xix], 4 = 8:12-20).

The mention of Damascus at this and other points in the document has been taken to show that the group actually migrated to Damascus, but it may be that the geography is purely figurative, meaning that the residence of the group in the desert was a fulfillment of the prophecy of Amos (5:27) that the people would go "into exile beyond Damascus." Likewise a reference to 390 years (i, 5-6 = 1:5) is probably based on the 390 days of Ezekiel 4:5 and thus may have symbolic significance rather than being a clue for exact dating of the origin of the group.[75]

In its references to the "new covenant," the "sons of Zadok," and the "teacher of righteousness," and at a great many more points as well, this document (CD) agrees in language and ideas with the Qumran Manual of Discipline (1QS).[76] Because of these agreements, and also because an actual fragment of this work (6QD) was found at Qumran, the Zadokite Document may be taken as representing at least the same general movement as that of the community at Qumran. Since it speaks, however, of "the order (*serek*) of the meeting of the cities" (xii, 19 = 15:1) as well as of "the order of the meeting of the camps" (xii, 22-23 = 15:4), it seems to be concerned with groups established in urban places as well as more remote regions like Qumran, thus hardly represents the latter place alone. In the same connection the statement of Josephus that the Essenes settle in various towns may be recalled. Likewise there are variations in details of organization and life as reflected in the Zadokite Document and in the Manual of Discipline.[77]

[74] GDSS pp.4,333.

[75] Isaac Rabinowitz in JBL 73 (1954), pp.11-35; GDSS pp.4,24; Norman Walker in JBL 76 (1957), pp.57f.

[76] William H. Brownlee in BA 13 (1950), pp.50-54; P. Wernberg-Møller in JSS 1 1956), pp.110-128.

[77] Fritsch, *The Qumrān Community, Its History and Scrolls*, pp.79-86.

THE COMMUNITY OF THE COVENANT

In the damaged line with which our text begins, the Manual of Discipline (1QS) is speaking, according to the probable reconstruction, about living in "the order (*serek*) of the community (יחד, *yahad*)" (I, 1).[78] The members of this community are described as in a "covenant (*berith*) of friendship" (I, 8), and the requirement is stated that they shall bring all their property into the community (I, 12). The priests, Levites, and people who belong are arranged in groups of thousands, hundreds, fifties, and tens (II, 19-21). No one may be admitted who is unwilling to enter the covenant and prefers to walk in his own "stubbornness of heart" (II, 25-26). A person of such iniquity cannot be sanctified by any washing:

> He cannot purify himself by atonement,
> Nor cleanse himself with water-for-impurity,
> Nor sanctify himself with seas or rivers,
> Nor cleanse himself with any water for washing! (III, 4-5).

The wicked may not, therefore, enter the water in which the holy men of the community purify themselves, for no one can be cleansed unless he has truly turned from his wickedness (v, 13). Those who have done so, however, are united together and form "a holy congregation (עדה, *'edah*)" (v, 20).

Even a group of the smallest allowable size, that is of ten men, may constitute a local unit of the order if one among them is a priest (VI, 3-4). Concerning their meals it is ordered that "they shall eat communally," and "when they arrange the table to eat, or the wine to drink, the priest shall first stretch out his hand to invoke a blessing" (VI, 2, 4-5). There must also never cease to be a man who expounds the Torah day and night, therefore the members must keep awake, no doubt in shifts, a third of all nights of the year for study and worship (VI, 6-8), this requirement presumably being intended to secure a literal fulfillment of Joshua 1:8 and Psalm 1:2.

When the community meets in public assembly, the "session of the many (רבים, *rabbim*)," as it is called, is presided over by a supervisor (מבקר, *mebaqqer*) or overseer (פקיד, *paqid*), these probably being two titles for the same officer (VI, 8, 12, 14).[79] One who wishes to join the community must be examined by the overseer and subsequently by "the many." During his first year the candidate must not touch "the purity" of the many, which presumably means that

---

[78] tr. BDSM p.6.
[79] BDSM p.25 n.24,27. See also Ralph Marcus in JBL 75 (1956), pp.298-302.

he must not participate in the purificatory rites of the group, and he is also not allowed to share in the common property. During his second year he still may not touch the drink of the many, presumably meaning that he may not join in the common meals. Only after successful completion of the entire two-year period, and after a final examination by the overseer, may he become a full member (VI, 13-23).

In connection with the admission of candidates, the enforcement of discipline, and the maintenance of high standards in the community, mention is also made of a council (עֵצָה, 'eṣah).[80] This body is made up of fifteen men, twelve laymen and three priests, "who are perfect in all that is revealed of the whole Torah" (VIII, 1).

In the Zadokite Document (CD) the community has four classes, priests, Levites, and people, as mentioned in the Manual of Discipline, and also proselytes (XIV, 3-4 = 17:2-3). In agreement with the Manual, the arrangement is by thousands, hundreds, fifties, and tens, ten men sufficing to form a group providing there is a priest among them (XIII, 1-2 = 15:4-5). As in the Manual of Discipline so in the Zadokite Document the supervisor (mebaqqer) has to do with the admission of members to the community (XIII, 11-13 = 16:4-6; XV, 7-11 = 19:8-12), and he is also the spiritual guide of his congregation. The description of his duties employs scriptural allusions and draws particularly upon the idea of the shepherd in Ezekiel 34:12, 16. "He shall instruct the many in the works of God," it is ordered, "and make them consider his wonderful mighty deeds. And he shall recount before them the events of eternity. . . . And he shall take pity upon them like a father upon his sons, and shall bring back all them that have strayed of them . . . like a shepherd his flock" (XIII, 7-9 = 16:1-3). In addition to the supervisor of the individual "camp" there is also a "supervisor (mebaqqer) over all the camps," and it is required that he "shall be from thirty to fifty years old, one that has acquired mastery in every secret of men and in every language" (XIV, 8-10 = 17:6).

Fewer details are given by the Zadokite Document than by the Manual of Discipline concerning the requirements for entrance to the group, and it does not appear that such a lengthy probation is required. "With regard to everyone who turns from his corrupt way: on the day that he speaks to the supervisor (mebaqqer) of the many,

[80] Like the Greek βουλή by which it is often translated in the Septuagint (Deuteronomy 32:28, etc.), the Hebrew word means both "council" and "counsel."

they shall muster him with the oath of the covenant" (xv, 7-8 = 19:7-8). But the secret rulings of the order may not be divulged to the newly admitted one until he has passed the examination of the supervisor (xv, 10-11 = 19:10). It also does not seem that all property has to be turned over to the community, as in the Manual of Discipline, but rather that the member must give at least two days' wages each month to the supervisor and the judges who will use it for the poor and needy (xiv, 13-16 = 18:1-6). Marriage is also evidently allowed, since those who dwell in the "camps" are said to "take wives" and "beget children" (vii, 7 = 9:1).

The judges of the community, according to the Zadokite Document, are a group of ten men, four from the tribe of Levi and Aaron, that is priests, and six of Israel, that is laymen (x, 4-6 = 11:1-2), this court resembling the council of the Manual of Discipline but being somewhat different from it in makeup. The "assembly" (קהל, *qahal*) of the community is sometimes referred to (xii, 6 = 14:6; xiv, 18 = 18:6), the Hebrew word being the same as that commonly used in the Old Testament for the "assembly" (RSV) or "congregation" (KJV) of the whole people of Israel (Leviticus 4:14; Deuteronomy 31:30; etc.).

The communal meal is not mentioned in the Zadokite Document, due perhaps to the fact that the text is fragmentary, but purification with water is referred to and it is ordered: "Let no man bathe in water that is dirty or less than the quantity that covers up a man" (x, 11-12 = 12:1).

For the teaching of the community a long passage in the Manual of Discipline (iii, 13-iv, 26) is of special interest. "From the God of knowledge," it is affirmed at the outset, "exists all that is and will be." Then it is explained that God created man to have dominion over the world, "and assigned him two spirits by which to walk until the season of His visitation." These two are "the spirits of truth and perversion," or "the spirits of light and darkness." The prince of lights rules over the sons of righteousness and they walk in the ways of light; the angel of darkness rules over the sons of perversion and they walk in the ways of darkness. God made both spirits, but he delights forever in the spirit of light and has hated forever the spirit of darkness. Until now the two spirits "strive within man's heart," but in his wisdom God "has appointed an end to the existence of perversity," and "at the season of visitation, he will destroy it for ever." Such a doctrine of the conflict of light and darkness and the ultimate conquest of the latter is reminiscent of the teachings of Zoroastrianism, and the influence of Iranian dualism may be recognizable here.[81]

The War of the Sons of Light with the Sons of Darkness (1QM) is also concerned with this great conflict and describes the final battles in which the struggle will reach its climax. According to this writing, the climactic period of warfare will last for forty years (II, 6).[82] This may be the same period of about forty years which the Zadokite Document (CD) says will elapse from the time that the teacher of the community is gathered in or dies until the time when all the men of war are consumed who go with the man of falsehood (xx [MS. B], 14-15 = 9:39). This man of falsehood or man of lies is also referred to in the Habakkuk Commentary (1QpHab II, 1), and is evidently the "Antichrist" of the last days.[83]

At this time of "visitation" there will also come, according to the Zadokite Document, "the Messiah of Aaron and Israel" (VII [XIX], 21 = 9:10; XII, 23-XIII, 1 = 15:4). This Messiah who "shall arise from Aaron and from Israel" (xx [MS. B], 1 = 9:29) will bring to an end the old "epoch of wickedness" (XII, 23 = 15:4) and inaugurate the future age. In a small fragment recovered in the excavation of Cave 1 and sometimes known as The New Covenant (1Q34bis),[84] this new age is called the "epoch of favor" (II, 5). In a two-column fragment from the same source which has been called a Manual of Discipline for the Future Congregation of Israel (1QSa),[85] an "order" (*serek*) is set forth for the whole congregation (*'edah*) of Israel when, at the end of time, they live together in obedience to the ordinances of the sons of Zadok, the man who in the midst of inquity kept the covenant of God in order to make atonement (כפר, *kaphar*) for the land (I, 1-3). When this community of the future comes together for common deliberation, the priest as chief of the entire congregation comes first and then, in case he is present among them, the Messiah, that is presumably their anointed king,[86] takes his place, after that all the others in carefully determined grades. If they meet for a common meal, no one is to put his hand to bread or wine before

---

[81] Dupont-Sommer, *The Jewish Sect of Qumran and the Essenes*, pp.118-130; Karl G. Kuhn in ZTK 49 (1952), pp.296-316.

[82] GDSS pp.283, 315 n.10.

[83] GDSS p.103 n.41.

[84] DJD I, pp.152-155; tr. GDSS pp.311f.

[85] DJD I, pp.108-118; tr. GDSS pp.307-310; cf. H. Neil Richardson in JBL 76 (1957), pp.108-122.

[86] GDSS pp.278f.

the priest. It is the priest who must first pronounce the blessing over the bread and wine and stretch out his hand to the bread. Then the Messiah of Israel[87] puts his hand to the bread and after that the members of the congregation say the blessing. Such is the common meal of the community in the blessed future age (II, 11-22).

RELATIONSHIPS WITH EARLY CHRISTIANITY

It will have become evident that not a few points in the life and teachings of the community we have been describing suggest comparison with early Christianity. The extent and significance of the similarities have been judged variously by various investigators. One holds that the people of Qumran were Jewish Christians and the teacher of righteousness was Jesus himself,[88] but alone the chronology we have indicated above will not support this identification. Another thinks that the teacher of righteousness was crucified and held a place in the sect much the same as that of Jesus in Christianity,[89] but while a fragmentary Commentary on Nahum from Cave 4 (4QpNah) mentions a "Lion of Wrath" "who used to hang men up alive" (6-7) there is no proof that the teacher of righteousness was his victim.[90] Again it is held that so much in the Qumran community and its leader anticipated the work of Jesus that the latter was, at least in many regards, a veritable "reincarnation" of the teacher of

---

[87] The explicit designation of this leader as the "Messiah of Israel" suggests that the priest was the "Messiah of Aaron." Thus the future community would be presided over by two "anointed ones," one priestly and sacerdotal, the other lay and royal. This is in agreement with 1QS IX, 11 which speaks of "the Messiahs [plural] of Aaron and Israel." See Karl G. Kuhn in NTS 1 (1954-55), pp.168-179. A leaf from Cave 4 at Qumran (4QTestimonia) contains several Old Testament passages which were evidently used as *testimonia* or texts to express the Messianic expectations of the community. The citations are in succession Deuteronomy 18:18 (combined with 5:25-29), the announcement of the coming of the prophet like Moses; Numbers 24:15-17, the prophecy of Balaam about the star out of Jacob; and Deuteronomy 33:8-11, the blessing of Levi. It would appear that these were intended to refer respectively to the coming prophet (cf. Acts 3:22), the Davidic king (cf. Justin, *Dialogue with Trypho*. 106; and possibly Revelation 22:16), and the priestly Messiah (cf. *The Testament of Levi*. 18:2-14), so all of these personages figured in the expectations for the future. See DJD I, pp.121f.; F. F. Bruce in NTS 2 (1955-56), pp.179f.

[88] J. L. Teicher in JJS 5 (1954), pp.53f.

[89] J. M. Allegro in JBL 75 (1956), pp.89-95; and *The Dead Sea Scrolls and the Origins of Christianity*. No date, pp.99f.

[90] H. H. Rowley in JBL 75 (1956), pp.190f. GDSS pp.5, 333 even suggests that "teacher of righteousness" may have been the title not just of the founder of the community but of each of a series of its leaders, so that no single individual is necessarily indicated.

righteousness;[91] while on the other hand it is felt that the more the Qumran literature and the New Testament are compared the more skeptical one must become as to any direct contacts between the two.[92]

The judgment that will be expressed here, and briefly illustrated, is that the Qumran and related discoveries provide important information on a part of the background of early Christianity. The organization of the community of the covenant, as we have noted it above, manifests similarities with the organization of the early Christian church. The emphasis upon "community" (yaḥad) makes one think of the "fellowship" (κοινωνία) of the Jerusalem church (Acts 2:42), and both at Qumran and Jerusalem there was actual community of property. The word "congregation" ('edah) is that usually translated συναγωνή, "synagogue" in the Septuagint,[93] and this word is used for the Christian assembly in James 2:2. The "many" (rabbim) of the Qumran community are designated by a word (rab) to which in the Septuagint the term πλῆθος, "multitude," often corresponds,[94] and the latter word is used for the Christian group in Acts 6:2, 5; 15:12, 30.[95] The word "assembly" (qahal), used in the Zadokite Document, is usually translated by ἐκκλησία in the Septuagint,[96] and this is the word for "church" in the New Testament.

The "council" ('eṣah) of the community is designated by a word related to Greek συνέδριον;[97] in the New Testament this refers to local judicial councils of the Jews (Matthew 10:17) or to the supreme court, the Sanhedrin (Matthew 26:59); but Ignatius uses the Greek word for the assembly or council of the apostles to which he likens the elders of the church.[98] The make-up of this council in the Manual of Discipline, with its twelve laymen and three priests, at least makes one think of "the twelve" in the Jerusalem church (Acts 6:2), and of the three who were considered "pillars" (Galatians 2:9).

[91] Dupont-Sommer, The Jewish Sect of Qumran and the Essenes, pp.160f.; cf. Edmund Wilson, The Scrolls from the Dead Sea. 1955, pp.112f.

[92] Geoffrey Graystone, The Dead Sea Scrolls and the Originality of Christ. 1956.

[93] Exodus 12:3, etc. Edwin Hatch and Henry A. Redpath, A Concordance to the Septuagint and the Other Greek Versions of the Old Testament (Including the Apocryphal Books). 1892-1906, p.1309.

[94] Genesis 16:10, etc.

[95] Note the varying translations of the word in these passages in the Revised Standard Version: body, multitude, assembly, congregation.

[96] Deuteronomy 31:30, etc.   [97] GDSS p.332.

[98] To the Magnesians. VI, 1. ANF I, p.61; O. de Gebhardt, A. Harnack, and T. Zahn, Patrum Apostolicorum Opera. 1900, p.94.

Perhaps the most interesting of the possible antecedents to features of early church organization is the office of the supervisor (*mebaqqer*) or overseer (*paqid*). The two titles seem to have about the same meaning and the latter, *paqid*, is translated in the Septuagint by ἐπίσκοπος (Judges 9:28; Nehemiah 11:9, 14, 22). In the New Testament the same Greek word appears in the Revised Standard Version as "guardian" (Acts 20:28; I Peter 2:25) and "bishop" (Philippians 1:1; I Timothy 3:2; Titus 1:7).

The practices in the Qumran community of ablution and communal eating make one think of baptism and the breaking of bread in the early church (Acts 2:41f.). As the Greek word (βαπτίζω) signifies, the baptism of the church was an immersion, and we have noted the requirement of the Zadokite Document that ablution be in a quantity of water sufficient to cover a man. Likewise the insistence of the Manual of Discipline that the water is effective for cleansing only if the person has truly turned from his wickedness, is in agreement with the connection between baptism and repentance emphasized by both John the Baptist (Mark 1:4, etc.) and early Christianity (Acts 2:38, etc.). The baptism of John and of the church was an initial act performed once rather than a repeated washing like the ablutions of the community of the covenant, yet in this community also where, as we have seen, ablution was so closely connected with repentance and sanctification, it may well be that there was an initial bath at the time of admission. Again, as seen in the accounts of the Last Supper (Mark 14:22-25, etc.), the elements of the common meal of the disciples of Jesus were bread and wine, and the partaking was preceded by a blessing, just as in the covenant community. Likewise the common meal of the disciples of Jesus as also that of the community at Qumran expressed an eschatological anticipation of the Messianic banquet (Mark 14:25; I Corinthians 12:26). Yet the Christian records also connect the observance with the Passover (Mark 14:12, etc.), which was not the case at Qumran as far as we know.[99]

In its teachings it has been noted that the community of the covenant spoke of a conflict of light and darkness and looked forward to the final victory of the light. While this doctrine comes from a dualistic background, probably Iranian, it has been brought into harmony with Jewish monotheism by the explicit statement that God

[99] CALQ pp.177f. For further comparison between the Manual of Discipline and the Jerusalem church see Sherman E. Johnson in ZAW 66 (1954), pp.106-120.

made both the spirit of light and truth, and the spirit of darkness and perversion. Furthermore the teaching does not lead to extreme asceticism or libertinism, as Gnostic dualism often did, but is closely bound up with ethical ideals which belong to the Jewish tradition. The doctrine is accordingly much in line with the ethical dualism which is found in the New Testament, particularly in the Gospel according to John. For example, both the Manual of Discipline and the Gospel of John speak on the one hand of walking in the darkness (1QS III, 21; John 8:12; 12:35), and on the other hand of being "sons of light" (1QS I, 9; III, 24-25; John 12:36).[100]

Connections may be discerned also with the Letter of James. The otherwise enigmatical statement in James 4:5, "Do ye think that the scripture saith in vain, The spirit that dwelleth in us lusteth to envy?" (KJV) does not seem to refer to any passage in the canonical Old Testament but might be citing such a writing as the Manual of Discipline which says that "to the spirit of perversion belong greediness . . . wickedness and falsehood, pride and haughtiness of heart, lying and deceit, cruelty and gross impiety, quick temper and abundant folly and proud jealousy" (IV, 9-10). Likewise we have noted that it is James who uses the word "synagogue" (συναγωγή) for the Christian "assembly" (James 2:2), this being equivalent to 'edah or "congregation" as commonly used for the community of the covenant in the Dead Sea Scrolls.[101]

Likewise there is possible relationship between the Manual of Discipline and the thought of Paul. Near the end of our copy of the Manual of Discipline are these two remarkable passages:

For as for me, my justification belongs to God;
And in His hand is the perfection of my way. (XI, 2)

In His compassion He has brought me near,
And in His dependable mercy He will bring my justification.
In His steadfast righteousness He has justified me
And in His great goodness He will pardon [or, atone for] all
    my iniquities;
And in His righteousness He will cleanse me from man's impurity
And from the sin of the children of men. (XI, 13-15)

[100] Karl G. Kuhn in ZTK 47 (1950), pp.209f.; Lucetta Mowry in BA 17 (1954), pp.78-97; W. F. Albright in W. D. Davies and D. Daube, eds., The Background of the New Testament and Its Eschatology, Studies in Honour of Charles H. Dodd. 1956, pp.167-171. The evidence now available suggests that John is no longer to be regarded as the most Hellenistic but rather, at least in some respects, the most Jewish of the Gospels (CALQ pp.161f.).
[101] GDSS pp.15-17.

When the writer speaks here of God's "righteousness" he uses the word צדק (sedeq), which is regularly translated by δικαιοσύνη in the Septuagint,[102] and is the Greek word so frequently used by Paul (Romans 1:17, etc.). For "justification" the writer of the Manual of Discipline uses משפט (mishpaṭ) (xi, 2), and when he says, "He has justified me," this is expressed with a verbal form of the same root, שפטני (shepaṭni) (xi, 14). In the Septuagint mishpaṭ is frequently translated by κρίσις generally meaning "justice,"[103] but in Leviticus 24:22 it is rendered δικαίωσις with the sense of "law," and in Isaiah 61:8 it is translated δικαιοσύνη in the sense of "justice." When Paul, on the other hand, speaks of "justification" he uses the noun δικαίωσις (Romans 4:25; 5:18), and when he speaks of being "justified" he uses the verb δικαιόω (Romans 2:13, etc.), thus employing terms which are of the same root with the word "righteousness" (δικαιοσύνη) itself. In the Manual of Discipline however, the words ṣedeq and mishpaṭ are practically of the same meaning, therefore the passages just quoted may still be considered rudimentary expressions of the doctrine of justification which was later developed so fully by Paul.[104]

Finally, the fact that the Qumran community was looking for the time when God would renew his covenant with them (1Q34bis II, 6) and when the Messiah would be in their midst (1QSa II, 20), links this congregation with the early church which was also a community of eschatological hope. But it was the faith of the church that the new covenant had now actually been established by Jesus (I Corinthians 11:25) whom it knew as the Christ (Mark 8:29). He was himself the expected prophet (Acts 3:22), priest (Hebrews 9:11f.), and king (John 1:49).[105]

That Jesus himself had direct contact with the Qumran community is not indicated, since at his baptism he "came from Nazareth of Galilee" (Mark 1:9).[105a] That John the Baptist could have had contact with this or another such group is suggested by the fact that, although he was born in "a city of Judah" (Luke 1:39), he was "in

---

[102] Leviticus 19:15, etc. [103] Genesis 18:19, etc.

[104] Sherman E. Johnson in HTR 48 (1955), pp.160-165.

[105] Bruce in NTS 2 (1955-56), p.180. For further discussion of the Messianic ideas at Qumran see William H. Brownlee in NTS 3 (1956), pp.12-30; and for possible identification of the Messiah with the Suffering Servant see William H. Brownlee in BASOR 132 (Dec. 1953), pp.8-15; 135 (Oct. 1954), pp.33-38. For theological conceptions in the Dead Sea Scrolls see Matthew Black in Svensk Exegetisk Årsbok. 18-19 (1953-54), pp.72-97.

[105a] See now Ethelbert Stauffer, Jesus und die Wüstengemeinde am Toten Meer. 1957.

the wilderness," that is presumably the general area west of the Dead Sea, "till the day of his manifestation to Israel" (Luke 1:80). That he even grew up in an Essene community is a possible surmise in view of the statement of Josephus that the non-marrying Essenes adopted other children to raise in their teachings.[106]

If John the Baptist had been in contact with the community of the covenant, the influence of that community could have been carried on into the early church through disciples of John who became followers of Jesus (John 1:35-37). Also, Acts 6:7 states that many priests accepted the Christian faith and, as we have seen, there were many priests in the community of the covenant, so it is at least possible that members of that community went directly into the group of followers of Jesus. Likely as it seems that some such contacts existed, even if they did not it is probable that "diffusion of ideas" from the various communities in Palestine which belonged to the movement now best known from Qumran could account for the influence attested by such evidence of relationship as has been cited.[107]

THE CALENDAR AT QUMRAN

A further topic of specialized interest with regard to the Dead Sea Scrolls is suggested by their emphasis upon times, seasons, and the calendar. The Manual of Discipline (1QS) describes the members of the covenant as desiring to walk before God "perfectly in all things that are revealed according to their appointed seasons" (I, 8-9; III, 10). They are also "not to advance their times, nor to lag behind any of their seasons" (I, 14-15). Likewise the duties of the council of fifteen include "the proper reckoning of the time" (VIII, 4),[108] while the wise man is admonished "to walk . . . according to the proper reckoning of every time," "to do God's will according to all that has been revealed for any time at that time, and to study all the wisdom found with reference to the times" (IX, 12-13).

Again in the latter part of our copy of the same Manual there is a long poem in which it is told how the devout worshiper blesses God at different times and seasons. The section with which we are concerned begins as follows (IX, 26-X, 1):

---

106 William H. Brownlee in *Interpretation.* 9 (1955), p.73.

107 J. Philip Hyatt in JBL 76 (1957), p.11. For further discussion of the relationships between the Qumran texts and early Christianity see Oscar Cullmann in JBL 74 (1955), pp.213-226; Sherman E. Johnson, *Jesus in His Homeland.* 1957, pp.23-67; Krister Stendahl, ed., *The Scrolls and the New Testament.* 1957.

108 Another translation, however, is simply, "in conduct appropriate to every occasion" (GDSS p.55).

> With an offering of the lips he shall bless Him
> During the periods which Aleph ordained:
> At the beginning of the dominion of light with its circuit;
> And at its withdrawal to the habitation of its ordinance.

Aleph is the first letter of the Hebrew word for God (אלהים, *'Elo-him*) and is probably used here as a somewhat mysterious abbreviation for God. The "beginning of the dominion of light" is evidently dawn, and it may be recalled that Josephus said the Essenes prayed before sunrise. The word "circuit" (תקופתו, *tequfato*) is the same that is used in Psalm 19:6[109] for the circuit of the sun. The "withdrawal" of the light is likewise the sunset, and the word (אסף, *'aṣaph*) is the same that is also used in the Old Testament for the setting of moon (Isaiah 60:20) and stars (Joel 2:10). Thus sunrise and sunset were taken account of by the community as times of worship.

After this the poem mentions the time "when luminaries shine from the abode of holiness" (x, 2-3). The word "luminaries" (מאורות, *me'orot*) is the same as that translated "lights" in Genesis 1:14, and the "abode of holiness" (זבול קודש, *zebul qodesh*) is the same as the "holy habitation" of God in Isaiah 63:15. According to Genesis 1:14 the "lights" serve "for signs and for seasons and for days and years," and the Qumran community undoubtedly looked to the heavenly bodies for the marking out of periods of time.

Using the same word "seasons" (מועדים, *mo'adim*) as is in Genesis 1:14, the poem next speaks of "the coming together of seasons to the days of a new moon" (x, 3). This probably means in effect, "whenever the days and nights add up to a month,"[110] and indicates concern with this unit of time.

Following this the characters Mem and Nun are introduced into the poem (x, 4). As seemed probable in the case of the Aleph above (x, 1), there was doubtless also an esoteric meaning attaching to these letters. Mem, it may be noted, is the first letter of the word "luminaries" and also of the word "seasons." As it lends itself readily to doing, the letter Nun is written in the manuscript in a form which looks like a simple key, and the text reads, "the sign Nun is for the unlocking of His eternal mercies, at the beginnings of seasons in every period that will be" (x, 4-5). Together Aleph, Mem, and Nun form the word Amen, and it seems probable that this acrostic is intended. A possible allusion contained in it would be to Isaiah 65:16

---

[109] Verse 7 in the Hebrew text.   [110] BDSM p.39 n.13.

where it is said that "he who blesses himself in the land shall bless himself by the God of Amen,"[111] while the probable relationship to the calendar will be explained below (p. 587).

Having spoken of days and months the poem refers also to times "at the beginnings of years and at the completion of their terms" (x, 6). In this connection there is mention of how the seasons are joined to each other, namely "the season of reaping to the season of summer-fruit, the season of sowing to the season of green herbage" (x, 7), this manner of speech being reminiscent of the Gezer calendar (p. 182). Then the poem speaks of the adding together of "seasons of years to their weeks, and the beginning of their weeks to a season of release" (x, 7-8). The week of years must refer to the provision found in Leviticus 25:1-7 according to which the children of Israel are to sow their fields for six years but in the seventh year to allow the land "a sabbath of solemn rest"; and the season of release must be the "year of jubilee" of Leviticus 25:8-55 when, after seven "weeks" of seven years, in the fiftieth year they are to proclaim liberty throughout the land and each return to his property and to his family.

The Zadokite Document (cd) reveals a similar interest in times and seasons and shows that the covenant community believed that it was faithful to the divine laws in these regards whereas all the rest of Israel had erred (iii, 12-16 = 5:1-3): "But with them that held fast to the commandments of God who were left over of them, God established His covenant with Israel even until eternity, by revealing to them hidden things concerning which all Israel had gone astray. His holy sabbaths and His glorious appointed times, His righteous testimonies and His true ways and the requirements of His desire, which man shall do and live thereby, these He laid open before them; and they digged a well for much water, and he that despises it shall not live."

Over against the failure of Israel otherwise, it was the undertaking of those who entered the covenant "to keep the sabbath day according to its exact rules and the appointed days and the fast-day according to the finding of the members of the new covenant in the land of Damascus" (vi, 18-19 = 8:15). The "appointed days" must be those of the various religious festivals of the year. The "fast-day" (יום התענית, *yom ha-ta'anit*), although only designated with the

---

[111] See the margin of the asv, and cf. II Corinthians 1:20; Revelation 3:14. bdsm p.38 n.2.

same general word for fasting which occurs in Ezra 9:5, is no doubt the most solemn fast of the year, the Day of Atonement (הכפרים יום‎, *yom ha-kippurim*), described in Leviticus 16 and 23:26-32, and in Acts 27:9 also called simply "the fast" (ἡ νηστεία).

Again, even as the Manual of Discipline referred to the "season of release" which must be the year of jubilee, so the Zadokite Fragment says that "the exact statement of the epochs of Israel's blindness" can be learned "in the Book of the Divisions of Times into Their Jubilees and Weeks" (XVI, 2-4 = 20:1). This seems plainly enough to be a reference to the writing commonly called the Book of Jubilees, the prologue of which begins: "This is the history of the division of the days of the law and of the testimony, of the events of the years, of their (year) weeks, of their Jubilees throughout all the years of the world."[112] Since two fragments of the book of Jubilees were found in Cave 1 at Qumran (1QJub = 1Q17 and 18), it is evident that the work was used by this community.[113]

In the Habakkuk Commentary (1QpHab) there is reference to the observance by the community of the day of atonement (*yom ha-kippurim*), and it is stated that "the wicked priest," an enemy for whom various identifications have been proposed, chose that very occasion to appear among them in order "to confound them and to make them stumble on the day of fasting, their Sabbath of rest" (XI, 6-8, commenting on Habakkuk 2:15).[114] That the wicked priest could break in upon the community on this solemn occasion would suggest that they were celebrating the fast on a day other than that which he himself recognized, and thus again it is indicated that the Qumran group was separated from other Jews by its calendar of festivals and fasts.[115]

The foregoing references suggest, then, that the Qumran community had its own religious calendar and that this was similar to the calendar of the book of Jubilees. This has now been confirmed by the discovery, announced in 1956 by J. T. Milik, in Cave 4 at Qumran of an actual liturgical calendar. The fragments on which this is contained appear to belong, paleographically, to the first part of the first century A.D. The calendar gives the dates of service in rotation of the priestly families and the dates of the religious festivals. These dates are always stated in terms of days of the week and sometimes

[112] CAP II, p.11.
[113] DJD I, pp.82-84.
[114] BDSS p.370; cf. GDSS pp.255, 268f.
[115] See S. Talmon in *Biblica*. 32 (1951), pp.549-563.

in days of the month. The liturgical days fall regularly on Wednesday, Friday, and Sunday. The passover is celebrated on Tuesday evening. The offering of the sheaf of first fruits (Leviticus 23:11) falls on the twenty-sixth day of the first month, a Sunday. The New Year begins on the first day of the seventh month, a Wednesday. The day of atonement, the tenth day of the seventh month (Leviticus 16:29), comes on Friday. The feast of tabernacles, the fifteenth day of the seventh month (Leviticus 23:34), is on Wednesday. Occasionally in the case of historical rather than liturgical dates, these are expressed in terms of Babylonian month names. This suggests that a calendar derived from Babylonia was in common use for everyday purposes, but that the other calendar which was presumably more ancient was adhered to for liturgical purposes.[116]

5. SACRED WAYS AND SITES

"HERE everything is historical," is the way Dr. Gustaf Dalman always answered the question as to whether this or that place in Palestine was historical.[1] As one seeks to follow the steps of Jesus in Palestine it is often the country itself rather than any specific object which speaks most clearly. Its hills, lakes, and rivers, its sky, sun, and springtime flowers, must be much the same as they were in Jesus' day. Also in many ways, at least until very recent times, the life of the people, their villages, activities, and customs, have remained little changed. One has seen the women at the village well, the sower going forth to sow, and the shepherd leading his sheep, exactly as it is said in John 10:4, "He goes before them, and the sheep follow him" (Fig. 108).[2] But it is also possible to make many positive identifications of places of New Testament significance and to discover many tangible remains from the Palestinian world in which Jesus walked.

BETHLEHEM

Bethlehem may be mentioned as early as in the Amarna letters.[3] The town is about six miles south and slightly west of Jerusalem, in the hill country of Judea. It is situated on the two summits and in-

[116] A. Jaubert in vt 7 (1957), pp.60f. See the Appendix of the present book for further discussion of the calendars.

[1] Dalman, *Sacred Sites and Ways*. 1935, p.13.

[2] See A. C. Bouquet, *Everyday Life in New Testament Times*. 1953; Eric F. F. Bishop, *Jesus of Palestine: The Local Background to the Gospel Documents*. 1955.

[3] ANET p.489 and n.21.

termediate saddle of a ridge some 2,500 feet in elevation. The terraced hillsides and fertile valleys justify the name which means "House of Bread." As of the year 1955 the Government of Jordan reported the population of the subdistrict of Bethlehem as 60,430. From the point of view of the Bible the greatness of Bethlehem lies in the fact that it was the city of David and the birthplace of Jesus Christ (I Samuel 16:4-13; Matthew 2:1; Luke 2:4).

Three and one-half miles southeast of Bethlehem are the remains of the Herodium. This was a stronghold of Herod the Great, which he erected on an unusual, conical, and artificially heightened hill. Two hundred steps of polished stones once led up to the circular towers of the fort on the summit, which contained richly furnished apartments for the king.[4] Here, at his desert watch-tower, Herod the Great at last was buried.[5] Today the hill is known as Frank Mountain and still has on its summit the ruins of Herod's towers.

Yet much farther southeast, on the western bank of the Dead Sea, was Masada, the "Mountain Stronghold." On a rock which rose high and steep on all sides, was a fortress which had existed from the time of Jonathan the high priest and had been fortified anew in the greatest strength by Herod the Great.[6] This was the very last stronghold of the Jews to fall to the Romans in the great war. Here the Sicarii[7] under Eleazar held out during a prolonged siege. When hope was gone, the besieged put one another to death rather than fall into the hands of their enemies. The fortress, blazing in flames, and containing only the multitude of the slain, was entered by the Romans in April, A.D. 73.[8]

NAZARETH

Nazareth lies high on a sharp slope in the Galilean hills. Its altitude is about 1,150 feet. From the summit above the village one looks south across the extensive plain of Esdraelon, west to Mount Carmel on the Mediterranean coast, east to nearby Mount Tabor,[9] and far north to snow-capped Mount Hermon (Psalm 89:12):

[4] War. I, xiii, 8; xxi, 10; Ant. xiv, xiii, 9; xv, ix, 4.

[5] War. I, xxxiii, 9; Ant. xvii, viii, 3.

[6] War. vii, viii, 3. A. Reifenberg, Ancient Hebrew Arts. 1950, pp.90f.; M. Avi-Yonah, N. Avigad, Y. Aharoni, I. Dunayevsky, S. Gutman, and L. Kadman in iej 7 (1957), pp.1-65.

[7] These fanatical patriots received their name from the short daggers (sicae) which they carried (War. ii, xiii, 3; Ant. xx, viii, 10).

[8] War. vii, ix.

[9] The Gospel according to the Hebrews made Mount Tabor the mountain of Temptation (jant p.2), while in the fourth century A.D. it was believed to be the mount of the Transfiguration and in the sixth century three churches were built on its summit in memory of the three tabernacles (Mark 9:5 = Matthew 17:4 = Luke 9:33).

The north and the south, thou hast created them:
Tabor and Hermon joyously praise thy name.

As of the year 1955 the Government of Israel reported the population of Nazareth as 22,000. Stores, blacksmith shops where the sickles
characteristic of Nazareth are made, and carpenter shops open directly on the steep and narrow streets. Behind the present Greek
Church of the Annunciation is a spring which is the only source of
water in the village. A conduit carries this water farther down the
hill to a place which since A.D. 1100 has been called Mary's Spring
(Ain Maryam). Even as the mother of Jesus must once have visited
the spring for water, so the women of Nazareth come to the same
source today with their water pitchers balanced gracefully on their
heads. The synagogue in which Jesus spoke (Luke 4:16), like other
Jewish synagogues of the first century, was probably destroyed in
the great Jewish war, and only replaced in the second or third century. The Church of the United Greeks has usually been held to
mark the site of the ancient synagogue, but the place indicated by
the Orthodox Greeks, where the Church of the Forty Martyrs was,
has recently been held to be more likely.[10] There was also a basilica
in Nazareth in Crusader and Byzantine times, and recent investigation in this area has disclosed traces of a pre-Byzantine church wall.
There are several caves at the same place, one traditionally identified as the cave of the annunciation, and Iron II potsherds found
in them prove that there was occupation at Nazareth as early as
600 B.C.[11]

An inscription said to have come from Nazareth was brought to
Paris in 1878 and is in the Bibliothèque Nationale. Although the
significance and even genuineness of the text are still under discussion, the date seems to be not later than the first half of the first
century A.D., possibly in the reign of Tiberius. The inscription is
headed "Ordinance of Caesar" and has to do with the inviolability
of tombs. It expresses the imperial wish that one guilty of violation of sepulture be condemned to death. As far as is known such a
provision was not a regular feature of contemporary Roman law.
Accordingly it has even been suggested that this may represent
a rescript of Tiberius which came in answer to a report from Pilate
which included mention of the rumor (Matthew 28:13) that the
disciples of Jesus stole his body from the tomb. At any rate the

[10] Clemens Kopp in JPOS 20 (1946), pp.29-42.
[11] CBQ 18 (1956), p.42.

fact that such a law could be stated makes more unlikely than ever the supposition that the disciples could have perpetrated such a theft.[11a]

Nazareth is now on the main highway which runs north and south through Palestine and stands also at the junction of that road with the branch which runs west to Haifa. Anciently the caravan road from Damascus to Egypt crossed the plain of Jezreel some six miles south of Nazareth, as does the Damascus-Haifa railroad of today, while a branch road to Akka passed at the same distance north of Nazareth. Also the main road from Sepphoris to Jerusalem ran south directly through Nazareth, while a branch from it ran through Japha to join the Damascus-Egypt road by way of Megiddo or Legio (el-Lejjun). Yet a third route south led from Nazareth through Endor and by way of Jericho to Jerusalem. Thus Nazareth was by no means a small out-of-the-way place hidden in a corner of the land, but was on or near important thoroughfares carrying extensive traffic.

Japha, only one and one-half miles southwest of Nazareth, was an important village at that time and Sepphoris, or Zippori, Galilee's largest city, was but three miles distant to the north. Neither Japha[12] nor Sepphoris is mentioned in the New Testament, but Josephus refers to both places frequently. Japha was one of the strongholds of the country. On one occasion it was occupied by Josephus that he might guard from there the roads of Galilee to the south,[13] and another time it stoutly resisted the armies of Trajan.[14] The remains of a synagogue of the Roman period have been found there.[15]

Sepphoris was "the largest city in Galilee."[16] In the time of Alexander Janneus it was so strong that his enemy, Ptolemy Lathyrus, was unable to conquer it.[17] A royal palace was established there in the days of Herod the Great, and in the insurrection which followed his death the revolutionary leader Judas made Sepphoris a main center of rebellion.[18] Then Varus came with the Syrian legions and, assisted by Aretas, took Sepphoris, made its inhabitants slaves and burned the city.[19] Herod Antipas walled the city and rebuilt it so

[11a] See J. Carcopino in *Revue Historique*. 167 (1931), pp.34f.; Jacques Zeiller in *Recherches de Science Religieuse*. 1931, pp.570-576; J. H. Oliver in *Classical Philology*. 49 (1954), pp.180-182; and for the hypothesis of a reply from Tiberius to Pilate, Ethelbert Stauffer, *Jesus, Gestalt und Geschichte*. 1957, p.111.

[12] It was the Japhia of Joshua 19:12.　　[13] *Life of Josephus*. 52, cf. 45.
[14] *War*. III, vii, 31.
[15] L. H. Vincent in RB 30 (1921), pp.434-438.
[16] *Life*. 45.　　　　　　　　　　　　[17] *Ant*. XIII, xii, 5.
[18] *Ant*. XVII, x, 5.　　　　　　　　　[19] *Ant*. XVII, x, 9.

splendidly that it became the ornament of all Galilee.[20] It probably was Galilee's capital until the founding of Tiberias. Having learned from its earlier experience the futility of revolution against Rome, Sepphoris did not join in the uprising of A.D. 66, and, by taking a stand for peace with the Romans, received a Roman garrison for its protection.[21] The remains of a fort and of a theater, both probably built by Herod Antipas, were unearthed at Sepphoris in 1931 by an expedition of the University of Michigan.[22]

Thus Jesus grew to manhood in a village which was close to some of the most stirring events of those times.[23]

THE JORDAN

The Jordan River, in the vicinity of which John the Baptist preached and in which Jesus was baptized, flows down through a flat, semi-desert valley, but the river itself is lined with rich foliage (Fig. 109). Locusts and wild honey (cf. Matthew 3:4) are still found and used on occasion by the Bedouins for food. The place where John baptized is called Bethany beyond the Jordan in John 1:28. A variant reading is the name Bethabara,[24] which was preferred by Origen (d. A.D. c.254) in his commentary on this passage.[25] Since Bethabara means "House of the Ford" it may have been a descriptive term for the same place. In that case, as the two designations suggest, Bethany beyond Jordan was probably on the far side of the river, but near a ford which would be a likely place for baptism. Since early centuries church tradition has located Bethabara near the ford called el-Hajleh where the main roads from Judea to southern Perea and from Jerusalem to Beth Haram cross the Jordan. John is also said to have baptized at Aenon near Salim (John 3:23). The name Aenon means "springs," and church tradition has pointed to a place of springs, six miles south of Scythopolis, as the site. The location is again near a main thoroughfare running up the Jordan Valley.[26]

[20] *Ant.* XVIII, ii, 1.

[21] *War.* II, xviii, 11; III, ii, 4; iv, 1; *Life.* 8,22,25,45,65,67,74.

[22] Leroy Waterman, *Preliminary Report of the University of Michigan Excavations at Sepphoris, Palestine, in 1931.* 1937, pp.28f.

[23] cf. S. J. Case, *Jesus, A New Biography.* 1927, pp.202-212.

[24] ASV margin.

[25] Origen, *Commentary on John.* VI, 24 (ANF IX, p.370); cf. Baedeker, *Palestine and Syria*, p.131.

[26] Carl H. Kraeling, *John the Baptist.* 1951, pp.8-10. See also Pierson Parker in JBL 74 (1955), pp.257-261. For the Jordan River in general see Nelson Glueck, *The River Jordan, Being an Illustrated Account of Earth's Most Storied River.* 1946.

THE SEA OF GALILEE

When Jesus left Nazareth and dwelt in Capernaum (Matthew 4:13) he left the highlands and took up his abode on the shores of a lake[27] lying some 696 feet below sea level. For the most part high plateaus surround the lake and slope steeply down to it. Viewed from the heights in the springtime, the Galilean lake seems the most beautiful place in Palestine, its blue surface set in the green frame of the hills. Flowers are then profuse and the radiant Syrian sunlight floods everything. One understands how Professor Adolf Deissmann could say in his *Licht vom Osten* that when a beam of the eastern sun falls into the darkness of a room "it begins to dawn, to glitter and to move; the one beam seems to double itself, to multiply itself ten-fold," and one appreciates his admonition, "Take then this single beam with you, as your own, beyond the Alps to your study: if you have ancient texts to decipher, the beam will make stone and potsherds speak . . . and, if the honor is vouchsafed you to study the holy Scriptures, the beam will awaken for you apostles and evangelists, will show you, yet more luminous than before, the sacred figure of the Savior from the East, to whose worship and discipleship the church is pledged."[28]

Narrow strips of land along the lake are very fertile, but back up on the stony hills cultivation is difficult and everything which has no deep roots withers beneath the blazing sun of summer. Fig. 110 which shows present-day plowing being done on these hills might almost serve as an illustration of the "rocky ground" in Jesus' parable of the soils (Mark 4:5 = Matthew 13:5 = Luke 8:6).

In visiting the chief sites on the Sea of Galilee, the pilgrim both in ancient and in modern times arrives at them most naturally in the order, Tiberias, Magdala, Capernaum, and Bethsaida.[29]

TIBERIAS

Josephus says that the capital city, Tiberias, which Herod Antipas built (p. 255), was on the lake of Gennesaret in the best part of Galilee.[30] Since Josephus mentions Tiberias just following his notice

[27] It was called "The Sea of Galilee" (Matthew 4:18; 15:29; Mark 1:16; 7:31; John 6:1); "The Sea of Tiberias" (John 6:1; 21:1); "The Lake of Gennesaret" (Luke 5:1); "The Water of Gennesaret" (I Maccabees 11:67); and "The Lake of Chennereth" (Eusebius, *Onomasticon* see under *Chennereth*, Χενερέθ, ed. Joannes Clericus. 1707, p.55).

[28] DLO p.v. tr. Jack Finegan.

[29] This was the route of the pilgrim Theodosius, A.D. c.530 (P. Geyer, *Itinera Hierosolymitana*. 1898, pp.137f.), cf. Petrus diaconus (Geyer, p.112) and Arculf (Geyer, p.273).

[30] *Ant.* xviii, ii, 3.

of the coming of Pontius Pilate as procurator of Judea, it has been held that the city was built around A.D. 26. Evidence from coins and other data, however, suggests that the city was founded in A.D. 18, the year in which the Emperor Tiberius, for whom it was named, celebrated his sixtieth birthday and the twentieth anniversary of his holding of the *tribunica potestas*.[31] Josephus also relates that Herod Antipas had to remove many sepulchers in order to make room for his city. This kept strict Jews from settling there at first, and therefore the tetrarch had to secure inhabitants by bringing in foreigners and beggars. After the fall of Jerusalem, however, Tiberias became a chief seat of Jewish learning and in the second century the Sanhedrin, which had been moved from Jerusalem to Jamnia and then to Sepphoris, was established there. Despite its undoubted importance and magnificence at the time, Tiberias is mentioned only once in the New Testament (John 6:23).[32] Today the Arabs call the town Tabariya, and some ruins of the ancient city and its castle are still to be seen.

MAGDALA

Magdala was three miles north of Tiberias, at the southern end of the Plain of Ginnesar or Gennesaret, and is known today as Mejdel. This is doubtless the place from which Mary Magdalene (Matthew 27:56, etc.) came, and if Magadan (Matthew 15:39) and Dalmanutha (Mark 8:10) are to be traced to Magdal and Magdal Nuna or Nunaiya ("Magdal of fish") then they can be identified with the same place. If this is the city which Josephus called by its Greek name Tarichaeae, it had a population of 40,000 in his day.[33]

CAPERNAUM

The city on the lake which was of most importance in the ministry of Jesus was Capernaum. Insofar as Jesus had any fixed headquarters during his ministry in Galilee they were at Capernaum. The Gospels frequently mention his presence there[34] and Matthew calls it "his own city" (9:1; cf. Mark 2:1). Special reference is made to his teaching there on the sabbath day in the synagogue (Mark 1:21 = Luke 4:31), a building which was erected for the Jews by a sympathetic and generous Roman centurion (Luke 7:5). Finally Jesus pro-

[31] M. Avi-Yonah in IEJ 1 (1950-51), pp.160-169.
[32] John also (6:1; 21:1) calls the Sea of Galilee the Sea of Tiberias.
[33] *War.* II, xxi, 4.
[34] Matthew 8:5 = Luke 7:1; Matthew 4:13; 17:24; Mark 2:1; 9:33; Luke 4:23.

nounced a terrible woe against the city for its refusal to repent (Matthew 11:23 = Luke 10:15).

The site of Capernaum is doubtless that known today as Tell Hum,[35] where the most extensive ruins on the northwestern side of the lake are to be found. This location agrees with the geographical implications of an incident in which Josephus, suffering an accident near the Jordan and the city of Julias, was carried back to Capernaum for safety.[36] The other site whose identification with Capernaum has been considered seriously is Khan Minyeh, farther south along the shore beyond the springs known as Ain et-Tabgha and anciently called "Seven Springs."[37] But when the pilgrim Theodosius (A.D. c.530) came from Magdala to Capernaum he reached "Seven Springs" before arriving at Capernaum.[38] This he would have done if Capernaum were at Tell Hum but not if it were at Khan Minyeh.

The most important ruin at Capernaum is that of its famous synagogue.[39] This was explored by German archeologists and then excavated and restored (Fig. 111) by members of the Franciscan order on whose property the ruins stand. The synagogue was an imposing structure, built of white limestone, facing southward toward the lake and toward Jerusalem. In general, ancient synagogues in Palestine were built with this orientation toward Jerusalem, which in the case of those in northern Palestine was toward the south. This corresponded with the practice of offering prayer toward Jerusalem, which is reflected both in the Old Testament (I Kings 8:38, 44, 48; Daniel 6:10) and in rabbinical teaching, according to which Rabbi Hanna said to Rabbi Ashi, "Ye who are located on the north side of Palestine must recite your prayers towards the south (so that you shall face Jerusalem)."[40]

On the side toward the lake the Capernaum synagogue had three doors and a large window. The interior was more than seventy feet long and fifty feet wide, with a colonnade built around the three sides other than that at the entrance. Above was an upper floor, probably intended for women. There was also a colonnaded court

---

[35] The name may come from the fact that in later centuries the Jews made pilgrimages there to visit the grave of the prophet Nahum, or Rabbi Tanhum (Tanchuma).

[36] *Life.* 72.

[37] The present name is a corruption of the Greek Heptapegon (ἑπτάπηγον i.e. Χωρίον), "seven springs."

[38] Geyer, *Itinera Hierosolymitana*, p.138.

[39] H. Kohl and C. Watzinger, *Antike Synagogen in Galiläa.* 1916, pp.4-41; E. L. Sukenik, *Ancient Synagogues in Palestine and Greece.* 1934, pp.7-21.

[40] *Baba Bathra.* 25b (RBT 7 [v,xiii], p.77).

on the eastern side. Individual parts of the synagogue were gifts from various persons, and one fragment of a pillar still carries an inscription with the name of its donor, Zebida bar Jochanan, which is practically "Zebedee the son of John."

Ornamentation of the synagogue included figures of palm trees, vines, eagles, lions, centaurs, and boys carrying garlands. The attitude of the Jews toward such pictorial representations of living beings has varied greatly. Sometimes the letter of the law in Exodus 20:4 and Deuteronomy 5:8 was held to absolutely prohibit all such representations. The strenuous opposition of the Jews to the acts of Pilate in bringing standards with the likeness of the emperor into Jerusalem and in placing even inscribed shields in Herod's palace has already been noted (p. 257). Also in 4 B.C. the Jews at Jerusalem pulled down the golden eagle which Herod had put on the temple,[41] and in A.D. 66 Josephus was instructed to press for the destruction of the palace of Herod Antipas at Tiberias because it contained representations of animals.[42] In this connection Josephus expressly says that Jewish law forbade the making of such figures. But again the law was held to prohibit only the making of images for purposes of worship, and in this case animal and human motifs could be employed with perfect propriety. R. Eleazar b. R. Zadok, for example, who was well acquainted with Jerusalem before its destruction, said, "In Jerusalem there were faces of all creatures except men." Obviously the Capernaum synagogue represents in its decoration the more liberal policy.[43]

The synagogue at Tell Hum has been believed to belong to the time before A.D. 70,[44] but is more probably to be dated around A.D. 200 or later, since all the earlier Jewish synagogues appear to have been destroyed by Titus during the Jewish war and by Hadrian after the second century rebellion of Bar Kokhba.[45] Even so it is probable that the Capernaum synagogue stands on the site and follows the plan of an earlier synagogue or of earlier synagogues, and therefore may be safely regarded as a reconstruction of the one in which Jesus himself taught.

A number of other synagogues have been found in Galilee, but probably none of them is earlier than the third century A.D., while

[41] *War.* I, xxxiii, 2f.; *Ant.* XVII, vi, 2.   [42] *Life.* 12.
[43] Sukenik, *Ancient Synagogues*, pp.61-64.
[44] B. Meistermann, *Capharnaüm et Bethsaïde.* 1921, p.289; and *Guide to the Holy Land.* 1923, p.552; G. Orfali, *Capharnaüm et ses Ruines.* 1922, pp.74-86.
[45] Kohl and Watzinger, *Antike Synagogen in Galiläa*, p.218.

the famous synagogue of Beth Alpha, near Khirbet Beit Ilfa in the Valley of Jezreel, with its remarkable mosaic floor, belongs to the sixth century.[46]

An interesting inscription (Fig. 112) was discovered at Jerusalem, however, which undoubtedly is to be dated before A.D. 70.[47] It records the building of a synagogue to a certain Theodotus, whose family had had the honor of holding the office of ruler of the synagogue for three generations. Indeed the cornerstone had been laid already by the father and the grandfather of Theodotus, together with the elders (presbyters) of the synagogue and Simonides who doubtless had given some special gift toward the building. The enterprise, as Theodotus carried it to completion, included not only the erection of the synagogue proper but also the construction of a guest house and apartments for pilgrims from afar, together with arrangements for water for the ritual washings. The inscription reads: "Theodotus, son of Vettenos, priest and ruler of the synagogue,[48] son of a ruler of the synagogue, grandson of a ruler of the synagogue, built the synagogue for the reading of the law and for the teaching of the commandments;[49] furthermore, the hospice and the chambers, and the water installation for lodging of needy strangers. The foundation stone thereof had been laid by his fathers, and the elders, and Simonides."

CHORAZIN AND BETHSAIDA

Linked with Capernaum in the memorable woe which Jesus pronounced (Matthew 11:21-23 = Luke 10:13-15), and therefore presumably in the same general area, were two other cities, Chorazin and Bethsaida. Slightly less than two miles away in the hills above Tell Hum is a site called Kerazeh which doubtless is to be identified with ancient Chorazin. Again, the most impressive feature of the ruins is a synagogue, which was richly ornamented with sculptures showing animals, centaurs fighting with lions, and representations of grape-gathering and grape-pressing.[50]

The Bethsaida of the New Testament was probably the Bethsaida which Philip rebuilt and renamed Julias (p. 255). This city was just east of the Jordan near where the river flows into the Sea of Galilee,[51]

---

[46] E. L. Sukenik, *The Ancient Synagogue of Beth Alpha*. 1932.

[47] DLO pp.379f.; cf. Herbert G. May in BA 7 (1944), p.11.

[48] cf. Mark 5:35, etc.   [49] cf. Luke 4:16-21; Acts 13:15.

[50] Kohl and Watzinger, *Antike Synagogen*, pp.41-58; Sukenik, *Ancient Synagogues*, pp.21-24.

[51] Josephus describes Julias as being "in lower Gaulanitis" (*War*. II, ix, 1) and says that "below the town of Julias" the river Jordan "cuts across the Lake of Gennesar" (*War*. III, x, 7; cf. *Life*. 72).

and has usually been identified with et-Tell, a mound about one mile north of the lake. Some think that Bethsaida and Julias always remained distinct and that the village of Bethsaida itself may be represented by the site called Khirbet el-'Araj near the lakeshore.[52] These places are only a few miles distant from Capernaum across the lake, and Bethsaida might even be regarded loosely as belonging to Galilee. This would account for John's reference (12:21) to "Bethsaida in Galilee." Ptolemy also reckoned that Julias belonged to Galilee,[53] and in a similar way mention was sometimes made of "Judea beyond the Jordan."[54]

CAESAREA PHILIPPI

It was in the neighborhood of Philip's other city, Caesarea (p. 255), that Peter's confession was made (Mark 8:27 = Matthew 16:13). Caesarea Philippi was some distance north of the Sea of Galilee on a plateau at the southern foothills of Mount Hermon. At this place a strong stream of water issues from a cave (Mugharet Ras en-Neba) in the hillside and is a main source of the river Jordan. Although the cave is filled now with fallen stone, it was described impressively by Josephus: "At this spot a mountain rears its summit to an immense height aloft; at the base of the cliff is an opening into an overgrown cavern; within this, plunging down to an immeasurable depth, is a yawning chasm, enclosing a volume of still water, the bottom of which no sounding-line has been found long enough to reach."[55] The cave was sacred to Pan and hence the place originally bore the name Panias (modern Banias). Herod the Great adorned the site with "a most beautiful temple of the whitest stone," dedicated to Caesar Augustus, and Philip transformed the place into a town of some size.

THE DECAPOLIS

The "Decapolis" which is mentioned on two or three occasions in the Gospels (Matthew 4:25; Mark 5:20; 7:31) was a kind of confederacy, at first consisting of ten towns, as the name suggests.

[52] Kraeling, *Rand McNally Bible Atlas*, pp.388f.
[53] *Geography*. v, 15. ed. Stevenson, p.128.
[54] Matthew 19:1. The fact that Luke 9:10 speaks of Jesus and the disciples going "apart to a city called Bethsaida" while in the Marcan parallel at the close of the section (6:45) the disciples are sent "to the other side, to Bethsaida" has led to the hypothesis that there was a second Bethsaida on the western side of the lake, but it is probable instead that there is confusion in the topographical references at this point. cf. C. C. McCown in JPOS 10 (1930), pp.32-58. The extreme skepticism of *Formgeschichte* concerning *Situationsangaben* (Rudolf Bultmann, *Die Geschichte der synoptischen Tradition*. 2d ed. 1931, pp.67-69, 257f.,355,365,379f.,389f.), however, would lead one to expect such confusions far oftener than they actually occur.
[55] *War*. I, xxi, 3; *Ant*. xv, x, 3.

These were Hellenistic towns which had been subjugated by Alexander Janneus and then set free from Jewish authority by Pompey. Thereafter they were subject to the legate of Syria but enjoyed a considerable degree of autonomy. According to Pliny (A.D. 23-79) the ten cities which comprised the league were Damascus, Philadelphia, Raphana, Scythopolis, Gadara, Hippo, Dion, Pella, Galasa, and Canatha.[56] Ptolemy, a portion of whose map of Palestine and Syria is reproduced in Fig. 113, lists eighteen "towns in Coelesyria and Decapolis": Heliopolis, Abila which is called Lysinia, Saana, Ina, Damascus, Samulis, Abida, Hippus, Capitolias, Gadara, Adra, Scythopolis, Gerasa, Pella, Dium, Gadora, Philadelphia, Canatha.[57]

Scythopolis was at the point where the plain of Esdraelon joins the valley of the Jordan. This was the site of Old Testament Beth-shean (p. 167), the name of which survives in the designation of the present-day village at that place as Beisan. A large stone amphitheater still remains there from the time of the Hellenistic city. Aside from Scythopolis, all of the towns of the Decapolis lay in the country east of the Jordan. Hippos (Kalat el-Husn),[58] Dion, Raphana, and Canatha (Kanawat) were east of the Sea of Galilee. Gadara is identified with the ruins of Umm Qeis, some five miles southeast of the Sea of Galilee, beyond the river Yarmuk. The ruins of the city's theater, cut out of the black rock, are still to be seen.

Gerasa lay yet farther south, some fifty miles from the Sea of Galilee, on one of the tributaries of the Jabbok. The site is known today as Jerash. Excavations conducted at Gerasa by Yale University and the British School of Archaeology in Jerusalem in 1928-1930 and by Yale University and the American Schools of Oriental Research in 1930-1931 and 1933-1934, have revealed that in the early centuries of the Christian era Gerasa was one of the most brilliant cities of Transjordan. The city was adorned with fine colonnaded streets, a circular forum, and beautiful temples and theaters. South of the city an impressive triumphal arch carried an inscription welcoming Hadrian on his visit to Gerasa in A.D. 130,[59] and most of the architectural remains are somewhat later than the New Testament period.

In Mark's narrative of the demoniac, and the swine which rushed into the sea, the scene is laid in "the country of the Gerasenes" (Mark

[56] *Natural History.* v, 16. tr. H. Rackham, LCL (1938-), II, p.277.

[57] *Geography.* v, 14. ed. Stevenson, p.127.

[58] Hippos was the Susitha of the rabbis, and the latter name survives in Susiyeh, a little distance to the southeast.

[59] C. H. Kraeling, ed., *Gerasa, City of the Decapolis.* 1938, p.401, Inscr. No.58.

5:1 = Luke 8:26). The reference, however, can hardly be to Gerasa, which was so far distant. Matthew (8:28) states that it was in "the country of the Gadarenes," and the reference to Gadara may be correct if that city's territory can be supposed to have extended to the shores of the lake. Otherwise, however, there is no evidence that Gadara's territory crossed the Yarmuk. According to some texts, Luke (8:26, 37, RSV margin) spoke of "the country of the Gergesenes," and this makes it possible to suppose that somewhere on "the other side of the sea" (Mark 5:1 = Matthew 8:28; cf. Luke 8:26) there was a place called Gergesa, in whose vicinity the event took place. It has been suggested that this Gergesa is represented by the present Kersa, a small place on the eastern shore just below the Wadi es-Semak. In this neighborhood the hills do plunge steeply to the lake, as is presupposed in the Gospel narrative (Mark 5:13 = Matthew 8:32 = Luke 8:33).

Pella (Fahl) was midway between Gadara and Gerasa, across the Jordan somewhat south of Scythopolis. Pella was the city to which the Christians fled from Jerusalem in A.D. 68 and again in A.D. 135. Philadelphia lay south of Gerasa and was the southernmost of the cities of the Decapolis. Formerly it was known as Amman,[60] having been the chief city of the Ammonites. It was the Rabbah of the Old Testament (Deuteronomy 3:11; Joshua 13:25; II Samuel 11:1, etc.). The Hellenistic city at this site was built by Ptolemy II Philadelphus, and named for him. Both at Pella and at Philadelphia extensive ruins are still to be seen.

SAMARIA

The direct route from Galilee to Jerusalem ran through the land of Samaria, and Josephus says that it was the custom of the Galileans, when they came to the Holy City at the festivals, to journey through the country of the Samaritans.[61] By that route, which was the shortest and quickest, one could reach Jerusalem in three days' time.[62] Journeys by Jesus through the country of the Samaritans are noted in Luke 9:52 and John 4:4 (cf. Luke 17:11).

When the city of Samaria fell to the Assyrians, 27,290 of its people were carried off captive (p. 209). Doubtless these constituted the flower of the population, and those who remained behind were the poorest people. Then "the king of Assyria brought people from Babylon, Cuthah, Avva, Hamath, and Sephar-vaim, and placed them in

[60] Eusebius, *Onomasticon*, see under *Amman*, Ἀμμάν. ed. Clericus, p.15.
[61] *Ant.* xx, vi, 1.   [62] *Life.* 52.

the cities of Samaria" (II Kings 17:24) to take the place of those who had been deported. The descendants of the remnant of Israelites and the newly introduced foreigners constituted a mixed race which was looked upon with suspicion by the exiles who returned to Jerusalem. Any participation by the Samaritans in the rebuilding of the temple was spurned by the Jews (Ezra 4:3; Nehemiah 2:20), and Nehemiah expelled from Jerusalem the grandson of Eliashib, the high priest, because he was married to the daughter of Sanballat the Samaritan leader (Nehemiah 13:28). Eliashib's grandson was probably the Manasseh under whom the Samaritans set up their own rival priesthood and built their own temple on Mount Gerizim.[63]

The breach between the two groups was never healed. During the weak rule of the high priest Onias II (d. c.198 B.C.) the Samaritans carried off Jews into slavery,[64] and later John Hyrcanus made an expedition into Samaria and destroyed the Gerizim temple (c.128 B.C.).[65] In the time of unrest after the deposition of Archelaus (A.D. 6) the Samaritans defiled the Jerusalem temple by throwing in dead men's bodies at night.[66] Later a number of Galilean pilgrims were killed at Ginea (Jenin) as they started to cross Samaria on their way to Jerusalem. Thereupon a virtual civil war broke out which had to be appealed to Claudius Caesar (A.D. 51).[67]

The metropolis and chief center of the Samaritans was at Shechem,[68] between Mounts Gerizim and Ebal and on the most direct route from Galilee to Jerusalem. It was rebuilt as Flavia Neapolis in A.D. 72, and is today the village of Nablus, still inhabited by the remnant of the Samaritans. The village of Sychar which figures in John 4:5 has sometimes been identified with Shechem itself but is more probably to be found in the present-day village of Askar at the southeastern foot of Mount Ebal.[69]

"Jacob's Well" (John 4:6) is believed to be the well beside the main road, one and three-quarters miles southeast of Nablus and three-quarters of a mile southwest of Askar, but there are other wells in the neighborhood. This well, however, is near the crossing of the main north-south road with an important road running from the

---

[63] Josephus (*Ant.* xi, vii-viii) would make Manasseh the great-grandson of Eliashib, and place the schism in the time of Alexander the Great and Jaddua the high priest (332 B.C.), but that is probably one hundred years too late.

[64] *Ant.* xii, iv, 1.   [65] *Ant.* xiii, ix, 1; x, 2.   [66] *Ant.* xviii, ii, 2.
[67] *Ant.* xx, vi; *War.* ii, xii.   [68] *Ant.* xi, viii, 6.
[69] Walter Bauer, *Das Johannesevangelium* (*Handbuch zum neuen Testament.* 6 [3d ed. 1933]), p.66.

Jordan to the Mediterranean, and has been pointed to as Jacob's well by church tradition steadily since ancient times. From the well one looks directly up at the 3,000-foot summit of Mount Gerizim, concerning which the Samaritan woman said, "Our fathers worshipped on this mountain" (John 4:20).

The ancient city of Samaria itself was at this time a Hellenistic rather than a Samaritan city. Alexander the Great planted Macedonian colonists there (331 B.C.), and after many vicissitudes the city was bestowed upon Herod the Great by Augustus.[70] Herod rebuilt and greatly enlarged Samaria, honoring the Emperor Augustus both with the city's new name, Sebaste (p. 254), and with its temple dedicated to him.[71] This temple, which has been excavated, was approached by a massive stairway leading up to a large platform surrounded by pillars, behind which was the temple itself. At the foot of the stairway was an altar, near which the excavators found a fallen statue of Augustus.[72] Particularly impressive were the strong fortifications which Herod the Great erected at Samaria. An example of his work is to be seen in the great round towers flanking the west gate and shown in Fig. 114.[73]

In the early months of the Jewish revolt (A.D. 66) Sebaste was captured and burned by the rebels. Afterward, in the time about A.D. 180 to 230, Sebaste enjoyed a period of prosperity and was adorned with fine classical buildings, a columned street, and a Corinthian stadium.[74] In later times the Christian world was interested in Sebaste chiefly because it was supposed to be the place where John the Baptist was buried. Two shrines were dedicated to him here. One was at an old family burial place which dates probably from the second or third century and is in the eastern end of the city under the present mosque. It was identified as the tomb of John at least by the time of Julian the Apostate, for in an anti-Christian riot which took place at Sebaste during his reign the pagans demolished the tomb and scattered the ashes. The second memorial to the Baptist was at a high place south of the summit of the hill, where Herodias was supposed to have hidden John's head, and where eventually a Christian basilica was built.[75]

[70] *Ant.* xv, vii, 3; *War.* I, xx, 3.   [71] *Ant.* xv, viii, 5; *War.* I, xxi, 2.

[72] Reisner, Fisher, and Lyon, *Harvard Excavations at Samaria.* I, pp.48-50; Crowfoot, Kenyon, and Sukenik, *The Buildings at Samaria*, pp.123-127.

[73] Watzinger, *Denkmäler Palästinas.* II (1935), p.52; Crowfoot, Kenyon, and Sukenik, *The Buildings at Samaria*, pp.39-41.

[74] Crowfoot, Kenyon, and Sukenik, *The Buildings at Samaria*, pp.35-37.

[75] *ibid.*, pp.37-39.

PEREA

If one did not wish to pass through Samaria, two other routes were possible from Galilee to Jerusalem. A western road ran down the coastal plain in the territory of the city of Caesarea, and then roads ascended to Jerusalem from east of Antipatris and from Lydda. Or one could take an eastern route by following down the valley of the Jordan River. From Capernaum such a route led through Tiberias and on south past Scythopolis, where there was a regularly used ford across the Jordan. Or it was possible to go around the eastern side of the lake and come south in the neighborhood of Hippos, Gadara, and Pella.

Beyond Pella one entered Perea proper. This land, Galilee, and Judea, were reckoned by the Jews as the three Jewish provinces, for Samaria was excluded from such dignity.[76] Josephus says that the length of Perea was from Pella to Machaerus,[77] that is from the Jabbok to the Arnon, and the breadth from Gerasa and Philadelphia to the Jordan,[78] although sometimes the name Perea was used loosely to include the region on north to the Yarmuk.[79] The actual name "Perea" is not used in the Gospels, where the usual designation for this country is "beyond the Jordan" (Mark 3:8 = Matthew 4:25, etc.).

Mark seems to indicate that the Perean route was taken by Jesus on his last journey to Jerusalem. He came "beyond the Jordan" (Mark 10:1 = Matthew 19:1), went "on the way, going up to Jerusalem" (Mark 10:32 = Matthew 20:17), and arrived at last at Jericho (Mark 10:46 = Luke 18:35; cf. Matthew 20:29). Opposite Jericho the Jordan was forded regularly either at Ghoraniyeh (Roraniyeh) or at el-Hajleh (p. 301).

JERICHO

Jericho itself, in New Testament times, had spread out beyond the hill on which the Old Testament city stood. The celebrated palm and balsam district of Jericho was given by Antony to Cleopatra,[80]

---

[76] *Baba Bathra.* III, 2 (RBT 7, p.100), "There are three lands concerning the law of *hazakah*: The land of Judea, the land on the other side of the Jordan, and of Galilee."

[77] Machaerus was a fortress on a mountain east of the Dead Sea. Alexander Janneus was the first to fortify the place, and Herod greatly enlarged and strengthened it, also building there a magnificent palace (*War.* VII, vi, 2). From Herod the Great it passed into the hands of Herod Antipas together with Perea in which it was situated. It was here, according to Josephus (*Ant.* XVIII, v, 5) that Herod Antipas imprisoned and beheaded John the Baptist (cf. Mark 6:17-29 = Matthew 14:3-12 = Luke 3:19f.).

[78] *War.* III, iii, 3.

[79] *War.* IV, vii, 3, calls Gadara, which was near the Yarmuk, the capital of Perea.

[80] *War.* I, xviii, 5.

but restored to Herod the Great by Augustus.[81] Here Herod built a citadel called Cyprus,[82] a theater,[83] an amphitheater,[84] and a hippodrome in which he planned to have the leading Jews murdered at the moment of his own death so that he would not lack for mourning.[85] The palace at Jericho in which Herod died afterward was burned down by Simon, a former slave of the king's, and then magnificently rebuilt by Archelaus.[86]

A portion of the Jericho of these times has been excavated by the American School of Oriental Research in Jerusalem and the Pittsburgh-Xenia Theological Seminary. This work was begun in 1950 under the direction of James L. Kelso.[87] The ruins investigated are at a site now known as Tulul Abu el-'Alayiq one mile west of modern Jericho at the place where the Wadi Qelt opens into the Jordan Valley. This is where the ancient Roman road entered the wadi to climb from the valley of the Jordan to the city of Jerusalem. There are ancient remains here on both sides of the wadi. The excavations on the south side uncovered an Arabic fortress of the eighth or ninth century; then a Roman structure of concrete masonry forming part of an elaborate civic center built probably by Herod Archelaus or possibly by Hadrian; below that, Herodian masonry; and below that, a Hellenistic tower constructed probably in the second century B.C. during the struggle between the Maccabees and the Seleucids. At the foot of the tell was a grand façade along the wadi. As in the case also of the Roman structure mentioned above, the masonry of the façade was lined with small, square-faced, pyramidal stones which give the impression of a net (*reticulum*), this type of work being known as *opus reticulatum*. The façade also was ornamented with semicircular benches and numerous niches. Flower pots found on the benches suggest that these provided a terraced garden, although they could also have been seats in an outdoor theater. The supposition that not a little of this work is to be attributed to Archelaus is strengthened by the finding of a number of coins of this ruler.

[81] *Ant.* xv, vii, 3; *War.* i, xx, 3.   [82] *Ant.* xvi, v, 2; *War.* i, xxi, 4, 9.
[83] *Ant.* xvii, vi, 3.   [84] *Ant.* xvii, viii, 2; *War.* i, xxxiii, 8.
[85] *Ant.* xvii, vi, 5; *War.* i, xxxiii, 6.   [86] *Ant.* xvii, x, 6; xiii, 1.
[87] James L. Kelso in basor 120 (Dec. 1950), pp.11-22; in ba 14 (1951), pp.34-43; and in ngm 100 (1951), pp.825-844; James B. Pritchard in basor 123 (Oct. 1951), pp.8-17; James L. Kelso and Dimitri C. Baramki, *Excavations at New Testament Jericho and Khirbet en-Nitla.* aasor 29-30. 1955; James B. Pritchard, Sherman E. Johnson, and George C. Miles, *The Excavation at Herodian Jericho, 1951.* aasor 32-33. 1958. For other Roman settlements in the *Regio Iericho* see Lucetta Mowry in ba 15 (1952), pp.26-42; and cf. M. Avi-Yonah, *Map of Roman Palestine.* 1940, pp.26f.

Soundings in the tell on the north side of the wadi have shown that a brick fortress and two stone buildings existed there. The architecture is so typical of what was already known at such places as Rome, Pompeii, and Tivoli, that the excavators say one might think a section of Rome itself had been miraculously transported on a magic carpet from the banks of the Tiber to the banks of the Wadi Qelt. Such was the winter capital of Judea in the time of the Herods, the New Testament city of Jericho.

FROM JERICHO TO JERUSALEM

From Jericho to Jerusalem (cf. Luke 10:30) is a distance of some seventeen miles. Approaching the Holy City, the Jericho road swings over the shoulder of the Mount of Olives. From the summit of the Mount of Olives one can look back across the entire eastern countryside of Judea. A tawny wilderness of hills drops away to the white Jordan Valley with its ribbon of green vegetation, and to the dull blue surface of the Dead Sea, some 1,290 feet below sea level, with the high wall of the mountains of Moab in the background. The arrival of Jesus and his disciples is introduced with the words: "And when they drew near to Jerusalem, to Bethphage and Bethany, at the Mount of Olives. . . ." (Mark 11:1 = Matthew 21:1 = Luke 19:29). The exact location of Bethphage is unknown, but references to Beth Page in rabbinic literature point to its close connection with Jerusalem.[88] Bethany was doubtless on the east side of the Mount of Olives in the vicinity of the present village of el-Azariyeh, whose Arabic name preserves the tradition of the connection of Lazarus with Bethany (John 11:1).[89]

Gethsemane was apparently on the western slope of the Mount of Olives, just across the brook Kidron from the city of Jerusalem (Mark 14:26, 32 = Matthew 26:30, 36 = Luke 22:39; John 18:1). The precise location of the "enclosed piece of ground" (Mark 14:32 = Matthew 26:36, ASV margin) that was Gethsemane can hardly be determined now with certainty, since Josephus states that during the siege of Jerusalem Titus cut down all the trees and desolated the pleasant gardens for many miles round about Jerusalem.[90] The location of the beautiful little "Garden of Gethsemane" (Fig. 115) which

---

[88] Dalman, *Sacred Sites and Ways*, p.252.

[89] The "tomb of Lazarus" has been shown at this place at least from the time of the Bordeaux Pilgrim, A.D. 333 (*Itinerary from Bordeaux to Jerusalem*, tr. A. Stewart, Palestine Pilgrims' Text Society. 1887, p.25). Even if it is not genuine, its location doubtless corresponded with accurate knowledge of the position of Bethany.

[90] *War.* v, xii, 4; vi, i, 1.

belongs to the Franciscans corresponds very well to the general probabilities in the situation, however, and at least we can be certain that it was somewhere on the slope of this very hill that Jesus prayed.

JERUSALEM

From the western "descent" (Luke 19:37) of the Mount of Olives one looks directly across the Kidron Valley upon the Holy City. The city lies upon hills, 2,500 feet above sea level, yet in a sort of basin surrounded by somewhat higher ground. At the present time the city of Jerusalem is divided between the states of Jordan and Israel. As of the year 1955 the Government of Jordan reported a population of 92,658 in the sub-district of Jerusalem, and the Government of Israel reported for their side 146,000 inhabitants. The present city is built largely to the northwest of the ancient city, but it is possible nevertheless to recover a fairly accurate picture of the city of Jesus' time.

The site of Jerusalem (cf. pp.177f.) is a quadrilateral plateau, marked out on the east by the valley of the brook Kidron (II Samuel 15:23, etc.; John 18:1),[91] now known as the Wadi Sitti Maryam or "Valley of St. Mary," and on the west and south by the Valley of Hinnom (Wadi er-Rababi).[92] The steep walls of these valleys provided the city with naturally strong defenses on their respective sides but left the north and northwest sides vulnerable. The situation of Jerusalem is shown clearly in the aerial photograph reproduced in Fig. 116. In the immediate foreground are the slopes of the Mount of Olives and the Valley of the Kidron, at the left is the Valley of Hinnom, and at the right are the new northern suburbs. The prominent open area within the city walls is the Haram esh-Sherif where formerly the temple stood.

Within the city area there was a secondary valley, the Tyropeon,[93] which runs southward parallel to the Kidron Valley. Jerusalem has been destroyed and rebuilt so repeatedly that over much of the an-

[91] Eusebius, *Onomasticon*, see under *Cedron*, Κεδρών. ed. Clericus, p.52.

[92] The name Valley of Jehoshaphat (cf. Joel 3:2, 12) has been applied to both the Valley of the Kidron and the Valley of Hinnom. The Bordeaux Pilgrim, A.D. 333 (tr. Stewart, p.24), said, "Also as one goes from Jerusalem to the gate which is to the eastward, in order to ascend the Mount of Olives, is the valley called that of Josaphat," thus evidently referring to the Kidron Valley. Eusebius, however, states that this name was applied to the Valley of Hinnom (*Onomasticon*, see under Vallis Ennom, Φάραγξ 'Εννόμ. ed. Clericus, p.157).

[93] Josephus (*War.* v, iv, 1) called it "the Valley of the Cheesemakers" (Φάραγξ τῶν τυροποιῶν) and it is from this designation that the name Tyropeon is derived.

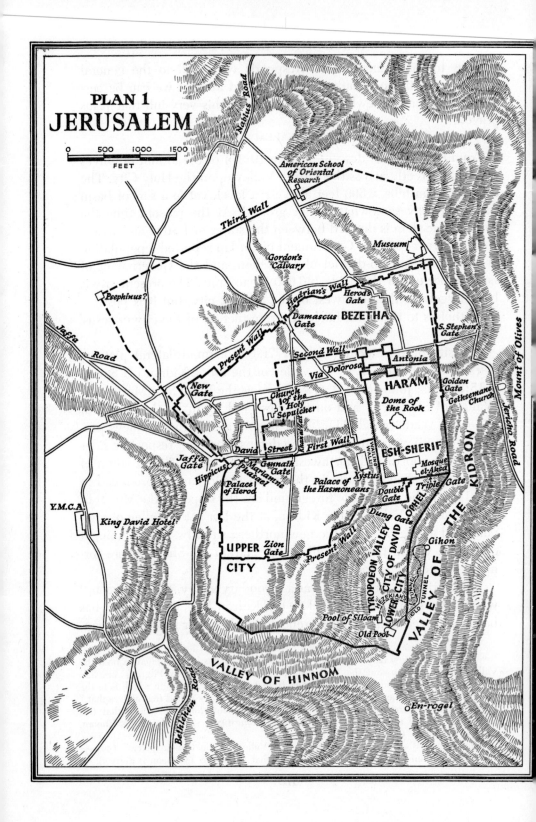

PLAN 1
JERUSALEM

0   500   1000   1500
FEET

Nablus Road

Third Wall

American School
of Oriental
Research

Museum

Gordon's
Calvary

Psephinus?

Hadrian's Wall   Herod's
Gate

Damascus   BEZETHA
Gate

S. Stephen's
Gate

Jaffa

Road

Present Wall

Second Wall

Via Dolorosa

Antonia

New
Gate

Church
of the
Holy
Sepulcher

HARAM

Dome
of the
Rock

Golden
Gate

Gethsemane
Church

David   Street   First Wall

ESH-SHERIF

Jaffa
Gate

Gennath
Gate

Palace of   Xystus
the Hasmoneans

Mosque
el-Aksa

Hippicus   Mariamne
Phasael

Double   Triple Gate
Gate

Palace
of Herod

Dung Gate

Y.M.C.A.

King David Hotel

OPHEL

UPPER   Zion
Gate

CITY

Present Wall

TYROPOEON VALLEY

CITY OF DAVID

Gihon

VALLEY OF THE KIDRON

Mount of Olives

Jericho Road

OLD TUNNEL

HEZEKIAH'S   LOWER CITY

Pool of Siloam

Old Pool

VALLEY OF HINNOM

Bethlehem Road

En-rogel

cient city forty to seventy feet of debris has accumulated, and the
Tyropeon Valley today is largely filled up and remains only as a
shallow depression called el-Wad. Formerly, however, it divided
Jerusalem into two clearly defined parts. The broader and higher
hill on the western side of the Tyropeon Valley was the site of the
Upper City, which Josephus called the Upper Market. The lower
eastern hill, which sloped down from the Temple area, was called
Acra and was the site of the Lower City.[94] The Temple area itself
was the "third hill" of Josephus, and northward of the Temple was
the "fourth hill," where the growing city was spreading out. This last
and newest part was called, according to Josephus, Bezetha (probably meaning "House of Olives") and also New Town.

In his description of Jerusalem, Josephus mentions three walls
which were in existence in his time.[95] Of these, two had been restored
by permission of Julius Caesar[96] and hence encompassed the city in
the days of Jesus, while the third was begun by Herod Agrippa I. The
latter desisted from finishing this wall, fearing that Claudius suspected him of intention to rebel, and the third wall was only completed by the Jews between A.D. 66 and 70. The first and most ancient
wall ran from the side of the Temple area west to the three imposing
towers named Hippicus, Phasael, and Mariamne. From there the wall
ran south and then east along the edge of the Valley of Hinnom.
Then it ran north and northeast, past the Pool of Siloam, and joined
the Temple area at its southeast corner. From there the old wall was
the same as the outer wall of the Temple. It ran north along the hill
high above the Kidron Valley, and then, beyond the "Golden Gate,"
swung west to Antonia, the fortress which overlooked the Temple
area at its northwest corner. From there it ran south along the western side of the Temple area to the point from which we described its
beginning. The line of this wall from the Temple to Herod's citadel
was probably just south of and parallel to the present David and
Temple Streets, which are in the very heart of the modern city. The
southern reaches of the wall as we have described it are now south
of the present city wall and in less densely inhabited areas where

[94] *War.* v, iv, 1. According to Josephus' description, the Acra originally was higher
than the Temple area and separated from it by a broad valley. The Hasmoneans cut
down the height of Acra and filled in the intervening valley. Whether or not this
tradition as to the earlier situation is correct, the hill doubtless was lower and the
valley filled up in the time of Josephus, for he would have seen these facts with his
own eyes. Josephus' error in locating the stronghold of David on the western instead
of the eastern hill has already been noted (p.179 n.84).

[95] *War.* v, iv, 2.   [96] *Ant.* xiv, x, 5.

some excavation has been possible. Portions of the south and east walls and of the gates at the southwest and southeast corners of the ancient city have been uncovered.

"The second wall started," according to Josephus, "from the gate in the first wall which they called Gennath, and, enclosing only the northern district of the town, went up as far as Antonia." This wall apparently started north from the First Wall at a point some distance east of Herod's three great towers, for if the junction of the Second Wall had been at Hippicus, Phasael, and Mariamne these surely would have been mentioned instead of the otherwise never-mentioned Gate of Gennath, or Garden Gate. The latter gate was therefore presumably in the First Wall somewhere east of Hippicus, Phasael, and Mariamne.[97] In this case the Second Wall may have swung north just east of the present Church of the Holy Sepulcher, and then have turned eastward and run to Antonia. If this is a correct interpretation, the Second Wall was some distance inside the present northern wall of Jerusalem, which swings west far outside the Church of the Holy Sepulcher and runs east at a considerable distance north of the Temple area. As a matter of fact it is indicated now that the present north wall of Jerusalem corresponds to the north wall of the Roman colony of Aelia Capitolina founded by Hadrian in the second century (p.329).

If the foregoing interpretation is correct, the site of the present Church of the Holy Sepulcher (p.527) was in the time of Jesus outside the wall of Jerusalem, as the New Testament requires when it states that Jesus was crucified "outside the gate" (Hebrews 13: 12). The Church of the Holy Sepulcher is, of course, far inside the present northern city wall, and if that wall were to be identified with the Second Wall of Josephus then it would be necessary to seek the site of the crucifixion outside of it. It is far more probable,

[97] Dalman, *Sacred Sites and Ways*, p.375. A. T. Olmstead (*Jesus in the Light of History*, p.73 and Plan of Jerusalem) places the Gate of Gennath and the beginning of the Second Wall at the Tower of Hippicus. But immediately after stating that the second wall took its beginning at the Gate of Gennath, Josephus says that "The third [wall] began at the tower Hippicus" (*War.* v, iv, 2), which makes it improbable that the Gate of Gennath and the Tower of Hippicus were at the same point. Olmstead (pp.72,239) agrees, however, that the course of the Second Wall was such that the present site of the Church of the Holy Sepulcher lay in the time of Jesus outside the city wall. Against this view see N. P. Clarke in PEQ 1944, pp.201f. For some wall fragments which probably belong to the Second Wall and indicate a course for it such as I describe, and for the firm conclusion that the Second Wall did leave the site of the Church of the Holy Sepulcher outside the Jerusalem of Jesus' time see now André Parrot, *Golgotha and the Church of the Holy Sepulchre*. 1957, pp.21-23.

however, that the Second Wall ran inside the present location of the Church of the Holy Sepulcher and that the line of the present northern city wall only represents the wall built long after the time of Jesus by Hadrian. It is not necessary, therefore, to turn to a hill north of the present city wall known as "Gordon's Calvary" as the site of the crucifixion. The latter identification was suggested in 1842 by Otto Thenius, a German pastor from Dresden, to whom the hill in question seemed to have the appearance of a skull (cf. Mark 15:22 = Matthew 27:33 = Luke 23:33; John 19:17). Forty years later this view was adopted by General Charles G. Gordon and since has enjoyed a wide popular acceptance, the hill in question continuing to be known by Gordon's name.[98] A nearby rock-hewn tomb, known as the "Garden Tomb," may be as late as the third or fourth century A.D.

The Third Wall, which was built by Herod Agrippa I more than a decade after the death of Jesus, had its beginning, according to Josephus, at the familiar tower of Hippicus. Evidently it ran far north and then east, for it enclosed Bezetha, the newly-built part of the city north of the tower of Antonia and the Temple area, into which the city's increasing population had been overflowing, and which hitherto had been quite unprotected by a city wall. Finally it ran south or southeast and joined the Old or First Wall at the Valley of Kidron, that is at the northeast corner of the Temple area. The line of the present northern wall of Jerusalem would seem to fulfill these conditions, but discoveries have shown that Agrippa's "Third Wall" must have stood yet considerably farther north. Explorations carried out by Professors E. L. Sukenik and L. A. Mayer of the Hebrew University at Jerusalem traced considerable sections of a wall which ran north to a point near the present Swedish School, then east to the American School of Oriental Research, and finally southeast toward the Temple area.[99] A tower of this wall was found beneath the tennis court of the American School of Oriental Research in 1940,[100] and certain other portions of it were also found later.[101] Since these remains fit the description of Josephus, and since there was no "Fourth Wall" as far as we know, doubtless this was the Third Wall built by Agrippa.

[98] Palästinajahrbuch des deutschen evangelischen Instituts für Altertumswissenschaft des heiligen Landes zu Jerusalem. 9 (1913), pp.100f.; Bertha S. Vester, Our Jerusalem, An American Family in the Holy City, 1881-1949. 1950, p.97.
[99] Sukenik and Mayer, The Third Wall of Jerusalem. 1930.
[100] BASOR 83 (Oct. 1941), pp.5-7.   [101] BASOR 89 (Feb. 1943), pp.18-21.

Josephus described the towers Hippicus, Phasael, and Mariamne as "for magnitude, beauty and strength without their equal in the world."[102] In reality Hippicus was 80 cubits (120 feet),[103] Phasael 90 cubits (135 feet), and Mariamne 50 cubits (75 feet) in height. The bases were of solid masonry and above were rooms, battlements, and turrets. The three towers were named respectively for Herod's friend Hippicus, his brother Phasael (p.254), and his wife Mariamne whom he murdered (p.255). The towers doubtless stood in the neighborhood of the present Jaffa Gate, Hippicus and Phasael probably being represented by the northwest and northeast towers respectively of the present citadel (cf. p.179 n.84).

Herod's palace adjoined the three towers.[104] It was entirely walled about, to a height of 30 cubits (45 feet), the walls on the north and west being the same as the old city walls. Josephus professed his inability to describe it for its magnificence, but alluded to its "immense banqueting-halls and bedchambers for a hundred guests," and its grounds with canals and groves of various trees. In the days of the Roman procurators this building became their residence and seat of government when in Jerusalem,[105] which would suggest an identification of the Praetorium of Pilate (Mark 15:16) with Herod's former palace. Later tradition, however, located the Praetorium in the fortress Antonia. This fortress, which stood at the northwest corner of the Temple area, was rebuilt by Herod the Great and renamed Antonia in honor of Mark Antony, who at that time was still in power in the East.[106] It stood on a precipice nearly seventy-five feet high, and had four strong towers, themselves seventy-five or one hundred feet high, at its four corners. Within, it was fitted up with the magnificence of a palace, and Josephus says a Roman cohort was always stationed there.[107]

The central court of the Castle of Antonia has been excavated and underneath the so-called Ecce Homo arch which may belong to the time of Herod Agrippa I,[108] an earlier pavement has been brought to light consisting of huge slabs of stone three feet square and a foot or more thick. If Pilate was residing at the Castle of Antonia at the time

---

[102] *War.* v, iv, 3.

[103] The ordinary cubit was approximately 17½ inches, but there was also a royal or sacred cubit of about 20½ inches. For simplicity the figures above take the cubit as 1½ feet.

[104] *War.* v, iv, 4.   [105] *War.* ii, xiv, 8; xv, 5.

[106] *Ant.* xv, viii, 5; xi, 4; Tacitus (A.D. c.55-c.117), *Histories. v*, 11. tr. C. H. Moore, LCL (1925-31) ii, p.195.

[107] *War.* v, v, 8.   [108] Watzinger, *Denkmäler Palästinas.* ii, pp.57f.

when Jesus was brought before him, as he might well have been in order to be in close proximity to the Temple at the Passover season, then Antonia was the "Praetorium" and this courtyard pavement may have been the very Pavement that was called Gabbatha (John 19:13).[109] In that event the traditional Via Dolorosa[110] or "Way of Sorrows" which runs from here to the Church of the Holy Sepulcher may preserve the true general direction of the last journey of Jesus from the Judgment Hall to Golgotha.

At the eastern side of the Upper City and overlooking the Temple area across from its southwestern corner was a building that had been the palace of the Hasmoneans.[111] From it Herod Agrippa II enjoyed looking down into the Temple and observing what was done there. The priests obstructed his view by building a high wall which, when the affair was appealed to Nero, was allowed to stand.[112] On the lower slopes of the western hill, between Agrippa's palace and the Temple area, was the Xystus, apparently a sort of open-air gymnasium. From here a viaduct led across the Tyropeon and thus gave direct connection between the Upper City and the Temple area.[113] Remnants of the arches of two ancient bridges communicating between the Upper City and the Temple may still be recognized at the western wall of the Temple area. One, near the southwestern corner of the Temple area, is known as Robinson's Arch, and the other farther to the north, as Wilson's Arch.[114]

North of the Temple area, in the vicinity of the Church of Saint Anne, was the probable location of the Pool of Bethesda (John 5:2). Two cisterns found here gave the clue which led to further excavation, and the outlines of a large double pool have now been traced. The area occupied was over five thousand square yards in extent, and numerous fragments of columns and capitals show that fine balustrades and galleries surrounded the pools. Since these are in Roman style, and since a Hebrew graffito found there proves that the buildings were older than the time of Hadrian, it may be sup-

[109] Millar Burrows in BA 1 (1938), pp.17f.; Soeur Marie Aline de Sion, *La forteresse Antonia à Jérusalem et la question du Prétoire.* 1956.

[110] The first pilgrim to speak of treading "the way on which Christ walked carrying the Cross," and to describe its stations, was the preaching friar Ricoldus de Monte Crucis who visited Jerusalem in A.D. 1294. J. C. M. Laurent, *Peregrinatores Medii Aevi Quatuor.* 2d ed. 1873, p.112.

[111] Perhaps this is where Herod Antipas resided when in Jerusalem (Luke 23:7).

[112] *Ant.* xx, viii, 11.

[113] *War.* ii, xvi, 3; vi, vi, 2.

[114] Charles W. Wilson and R. E. Warren, *The Recovery of Jerusalem.* 1871, pp.58, 72-85.

posed that this impressive establishment was due to Herod the Great and was constructed in connection with his work on the Temple. The pools lay in a side-valley of the Kidron Valley, and were well situated to collect rain water. Perhaps some feature of the canals and conduits connected with the pools was responsible for the troubling of the water referred to in John 5:7. Since Jerusalem did not have too abundant water, it may be surmised that the Pool of Bethesda was utilized for many Christian baptisms, both in the first century and after. In the fifth century a Byzantine church was built at this place, some of the remains of which are still in evidence. Because of the perennial shortage of water at Jerusalem it may also be assumed as probable that conquerors of the city would not destroy its cisterns and pools, hence that the Pool of Bethesda was preserved and that the early Christian traditions about it were well founded.[115]

THE TEMPLE

The Temple itself was naturally the chief center of interest in Jerusalem. The Herodian temple[116] is described by Josephus[117] and also by the tractate Middoth ("Measurements"), which belongs to the second century A.D. and is to be found in the division Kodashim ("Holiness") of the Mishnah and the Babylonian Talmud.[118] These are the chief written sources which are available for the archeologist who endeavors to recover a picture of the Temple in the time of Jesus. In general they are good guides, but there is a tendency on the part of Josephus toward vagueness and exaggeration, and on the part of the author of Middoth toward ignoring things which were distinctively heathen.[119]

"In the fifteenth year of his reign," relates Josephus, Herod "restored the Temple and by erecting new foundation-walls enlarged

---

[115] Joachim Jeremias, *Die Wiederentdeckung von Bethesda.* 1949; cf. A. M. Schneider in *Beiträge zur biblischen Landes- und Altertumskunde.* 68 (1951), p.282. The feature of the troubling of the water has led some to identify the Pool of Bethesda with the Pool of Siloam, since the intermittent Gihon spring empties into the latter and could have produced the phenomenon. John 9:7, however, mentions the Pool of Siloam as a separate place, and therefore the hypothesis is unlikely.

[116] cf. above pp.179f. for the First Temple of Solomon, and p.195 for the Second Temple of Zerubbabel. For the entire history of the Temple see Parrot, *The Temple of Jerusalem.*

[117] *Ant.* xv, xi; *War.* v, v; cf. *Against Apion.* i, 22, where Josephus gives a quotation descriptive of the Temple from Hecataeus of Abdera (c.300 B.C.).

[118] DM pp.589-598; GBT IX, pp.675-689; SBT pp.1-38; cf. JE VIII, pp.545f.

[119] Hollis, *The Archaeology of Herod's Temple, with a Commentary on the Tractate 'Middoth,'* p.105.

the surrounding area to double its former extent."[120] This increase in the area available for the Temple and its courts must have been accomplished by building up the hill itself. Today there is to be seen underneath the southeastern corner of the Haram esh-Sherif an extensive system of vaults popularly known as "Solomon's Stables." In their present form these probably were constructed at a date later than that of Herod. They preserve, however, ancient materials and traces of old work which may indicate the kind of efforts Herod made to build up a larger court for the Temple. At its outermost "pinnacle" (cf. Matthew 4:5 = Luke 4:9), the Temple enclosure was lifted 170 feet above the gorge of the Kidron until, as Josephus said, "one who looked down grew dizzy."[121]

The limits of the Temple area as established by Herod the Great probably were the same as the present limits of the Haram esh-Sherif on the east, south, and west. On the north, however, the area now has been extended considerably farther than the limits of Herod's day. The Noble Sanctuary now includes part of the place where the Castle of Antonia then stood, and also extends over the fillings of what was then a ravine running diagonally into the Kidron Valley.[122] The northern limit in Herod's time was probably along a line joining the east wall at a point not far north of the present Golden Gate.

Whereas Solomon had built a wall on the east side of the sanctuary area but left the other sides exposed,[123] Herod the Great completed the enclosure of the Temple hill with lofty walls on all sides. Remains of the typical Herodian masonry, which employed very large stones carefully fitted together, still are to be seen in portions of the wall around the Haram esh-Sherif, notably including the "Wailing Wall" (Fig. 117). Above ground this wall probably has been reconstructed and the stones are not fitted together as carefully now as they were formerly, but otherwise it must appear much as it did in New Testament times. The nine lowest courses of stone consist of huge blocks, as was characteristic of Herodian masonry, the largest one being sixteen and one-half feet long and thirteen feet wide. Above are fifteen courses of smaller stones. The practice of the Jews, to lament the destruction of the Temple, is attested as long ago as

[120] *War.* I, xxi, 1.
[121] *Ant.* xv, xi, 5.
[122] Today the measurements of the area, outside the walls, are south side 929 feet, north side, 1,041 feet, east side 1,556 feet, west side 1,596 feet.
[123] *War.* v, v, 1.

the time of the Bordeaux Pilgrim (A.D. 333). He mentions two statues of Hadrian which had been erected at the place where the Temple stood and says that "not far from the statues there is a perforated stone, to which the Jews come every year and anoint it, bewail themselves with groans, rend their garments, and so depart."[124] What is meant by the "perforated stone" is uncertain but it may have been the sacred Rock (p.179) itself. Today it is the Herodian wall just described which is the wailing place of the Jews.

The outer court of the Temple area[125] was entered on the west by four gates, according to Josephus,[126] two of which were doubtless at the points indicated by Robinson's Arch and Wilson's Arch. Gates on the other sides are mentioned in the tractate Middoth. On the south were the two gates of "Chuldah,"[127] whose location is probably represented by the Double Gate and Triple Gate now walled up in the southern wall of the Temple area at a point some thirty-five feet below the present level of the Haram.[128] Ramps probably led from these gates up to the level of the court. On the east was the Shushan Gate, which probably was somewhat south of the present Golden Gate, a structure of the fourth or fifth century.[129] This is the gate which has been blocked up since A.D. 810 by the Arabs who fear that one day a conqueror will enter by it.[130] Finally, on the north was one gate, called Todi,[131] while in the northwest there were also steps to the Tower of Antonia. These last were the steps that the chief captain together with the soldiers and centurions "ran down" into the Temple on the occasion of the riot over Paul, and from which the apostle made his address to the people (Acts 21:32, 40).

[124] tr. Stewart, p.22.

[125] In the Gospels, "the temple" (τὸ ἱερόν) ordinarily means the entire area (Mark 11:11; 13:1, 3, etc.), although occasionally it refers to some particular part. "The sanctuary" (ὁ ναός) was the temple edifice itself, including the Holy Place and the Holy of Holies with the veil between them (Mark 15:38, etc.).

[126] *Ant.* xv, xi, 5; *Middoth.* i, 3 mentions only one, perhaps the principal one, on the west, named "Qiponos."

[127] Josephus says only (*Ant.* xv, xi, 5), "the fourth front of the temple, which was southward, had indeed itself gates in its middle."

[128] The "Single Gate" in the same wall is believed to be much later.

[129] This has been thought to be the Gate Beautiful of Acts 3:2, 10, ὡραία ("beautiful") having been taken over as *aurea* ("golden") in Latin, but more probably the Beautiful Gate was the one at the east entrance to the court of the women, which was distinguished by folding doors of Corinthian brass (*War.* v, v, 3).

[130] cf. Ezekiel 44:1f., which says that the east gate of the sanctuary should be shut because by it the Lord had entered in. For the traditions about this gate see Julian Morgenstern in HUCA 6 (1929), pp.1-37; 21 (1948), pp.459f.

[131] Josephus refers to it incidentally in *War.* vi, iv, 1.

Upon entering the outer court one found its walls lined with porticoes, or cloisters of double rows of marble columns, roofed with carved cedar. The east porticoes were said by Josephus to be the work of Solomon, and probably did at least survive from some earlier time, for they were in need of repair in the time of Herod Agrippa II.[132] This was probably the Solomon's Porch of the New Testament (John 10:23; Acts 3:11; 5:12). On the south, where the el-Aqsa mosque now is, were the royal porticoes, or Stoa Basilica, with 162 columns, each of such size that three men could just reach around it. These were arranged in four rows which formed three aisles.

Since even Gentiles were allowed access to this outer court, it is commonly designated the Court of the Gentiles. Within it was an inner court, set apart by a stone partition, beyond which none but Jews might pass. This was described by Josephus as follows: "Proceeding . . . toward the second court of the Temple, one found it surrounded by a stone balustrade, three cubits [about four and one-half feet] high and of exquisite workmanship; in this at regular intervals stood slabs giving warning, some in Greek, others in Latin characters, of the law of purification, to wit, that no foreigner was permitted to enter the holy place, for so the second enclosure of the Temple was called."[133] One of these stone slabs of warning was found at Jerusalem by M. Clermont-Ganneau in 1871 and is now in the Museum of the Ancient Orient at Istanbul, while part of another such inscription was discovered more recently.[134] The first-mentioned inscription is shown in Fig. 118. It is carved in a limestone block some twenty-three inches high, thirty-four inches long, and fifteen inches thick. The letters are over one and one-half inches in height. The inscription reads: "No foreigner[135] may enter within the balustrade and enclosure around the Sanctuary. Whoever is caught will render himself liable to the death penalty which will inevitably follow." In Acts 21:28f. Paul apparently was believed to have taken Trophimus beyond this barrier, and there may also be a side ref-

---

[132] *Ant.* xx, ix, 7.

[133] *War.* v, v, 2; cf. vi, ii, 4; *Ant.* xv, xi, 5. This is probably the same wall that is called the Soreg in *Middoth.* ii, 3, although the Soreg is described as only "ten handbreadths in height." Since in the Hebrew system one handbreadth equaled one-sixth of a cubit this would have been just about thirty inches in height. Perhaps there was at first only a low stone barrier on which the warning tablets were erected, and later the higher and exquisitely worked stone trellis was added which Josephus describes.

[134] QDAP 6 (1938), pp.1-3.

[135] The same word appears in Luke 17:18.

erence to it in Ephesians 2:14 where Paul speaks of "the dividing wall of hostility."

Within the wall beyond which Gentiles could not go were several courts together with their walls, gates, and terraces. The Women's Court represented the limit beyond which women might not go.[136] Farther on was the Court of Israel or Men's Court, and then the Court of the Priests.[137] In the Priests' Court and in front of the temple edifice itself was the altar upon which sacrifices and burnt-offerings were made.[138] It is not certain whether the altar stood upon the sacred Rock (es-Sakhra) or in front of it, but the former seems more probable (p.180).

The sanctuary or temple edifice itself stood within this inmost court and was approached by a flight of twelve steps.[139] It was built of white stones, to each of which Josephus assigns the enormous size of approximately thirty-five feet by twelve feet by eighteen feet.[140] In front its height and its breadth were equal, each being one hundred cubits (nearly 150 feet) according to Josephus, and it was covered all over with gold (cf. Matthew 23:16), so that it reflected the rising sun with fiery splendor.[141] Within, it was divided into two parts, the first of which was the Holy Place (cf. Exodus 26:33). In the Holy Place were the seven-armed lampstand, the table of showbread and the altar of incense. The second and most sacred part of the sanctuary was the Holy of Holies. "The innermost recess measured twenty cubits," says Josephus, "and was screened in like manner from the outer portion by a veil. In this stood nothing whatever: unapproachable, inviolable, invisible to all, it was called the Holy of Holy."[142] It was entered only once a year by the high priest on the Day of Atonement.[143]

The orientation of the Temple edifice was toward the east,[144] as was in accordance with general oriental practice, and the Holy of

---

[136] *War.* v, v, 2; *Ant.* xv, xi, 5; *Middoth.* ii, 5.

[137] *Middoth.* ii, 7. [138] *Ant.* xv, xi, 5.

[139] *War.* v, v, 4. [140] *Ant.* xv, xi, 3. [141] *War.* v, v, 4f.

[142] *War.* v, v, 5; cf. Tacitus (*Hist.* v, 9) who says that after Pompey's conquest of Jerusalem and entry into the Temple (63 B.C.) "it was a matter of common knowledge that there were no representations of the gods within, but that the place was empty and the secret shrine contained nothing."

[143] Leviticus 16; *Tract Yomah.* RBT 3 (vi), pp.72f.

[144] cf. *The Letter of Aristeas.* 88. tr. H. St. J. Thackeray (1917), p.41: "The Temple looks towards the east, and its back is turned westwards." Precise measurements indicate that the east wall of the enclosure runs slightly toward the northwest, and is exactly at right angles to the line of direction between the sacred Rock and the summit of the Mount of Olives. But the eastern boundary of the "Platform of the Rock" runs due north and south and the inner courts and temple edifice probably had their eastern lines parallel with this.

Holies arose above or more probably, as we have seen (p.180), behind the ancient and sacred Rock.

The entire appearance of Herod's Temple must have been very impressive. Even Tacitus described it as "a temple of immense wealth,"[145] and the exclamation of one of the disciples of Jesus is recorded in the Gospels, "Look, Teacher, what wonderful stones and what wonderful buildings!" (Mark 13:1). Indeed the city as a whole must have presented the incoming visitor with a magnificent panorama. The Mount of Olives then as now would have provided the best point of view. From it one would have seen the Temple directly in the foreground, where the Dome now rises over the sacred Rock. Surrounded by sumptuous colonnades, its courts rose one within the other and each higher than the last to the inner sanctuary itself, whose marble and golden façade gleamed and glittered "like a snow-clad mountain."[146] At the northwestern corner of the Temple arose the powerful mass of the fortress Antonia, and beyond it, outside the wall, extended the villas of the northern suburb. To the south an uninterrupted sequence of houses and palaces fell away to the Pool of Siloam at the foot of the hill of Ophel. In the background on the western hill were ranged other populous quarters, crowned on the horizon by the imposing silhouette of Herod's Palace and Towers. "At no period of its history could the Sanctuary and City have presented a more inspiring aspect. The rhythm and harmony of Graeco-Roman art, so beautifully rendered against the oriental sky, restrained the louder tendencies of Herod himself, while infusing order and taste into the traditional chaos of the city."[147] The pride of the rabbis was not unjustified when they said, "He who has not seen Jerusalem in its beauty, has not seen a beautiful great city in his whole life; and who has not seen the building of the Second [i.e. Herod's] Temple, has not seen a handsome building in his life."[148]

6. THE LATER HISTORY OF JERUSALEM

But when the disciples were amazed at the splendor of the Temple, Jesus said, "Do you see these great buildings? There will not be left here one stone upon another, that will not be thrown down" (Mark 13:2 = Matthew 24:2 = Luke 21:6). His prophecy was fulfilled

---

[145] *Hist.* v, 8. [146] *War.* v, v, 6.

[147] J. Garstang in J. A. Hammerton, ed., *Wonders of the Past.* 1937, p.584.

[148] *Tract Succah.* v, 2. RBT 4 (VII), p.77; cf. *Baba Bathra.* I, 1. RBT 7, p.6, "It was said that he who had not seen the new Temple of Herod had not in all his life, seen a fine building."

swiftly. In A.D. 66, less than forty years after the death of Jesus,[1] the Jewish war broke out, an "utterly hopeless, and therefore unreasonable and disastrous struggle."[2] In A.D. 70, shortly before the Passover, Titus[3] (Fig. 119) and the Roman armies surrounded Jerusalem. A long and terrible siege ensued. Battering rams hammered against the walls, earthworks surrounded the city, and when the starving poor people slipped out to look for food the Romans caught and crucified them in sight of the city. Finally late in the summer Jerusalem fell, its beautiful temple was burned, and its people were slaughtered indiscriminately.[4] The city was razed to the ground and when Titus departed only Herod's towers—Hippicus, Phasael, and Mariamne—and a portion of the wall were left standing.

[1] According to John 19:14 the crucifixion was on the day of Preparation for the Passover, which doubtless means the fourteenth of Nisan, when the paschal lamb was slain. In agreement with this, Paul declares, "Christ, our paschal lamb, has been sacrificed" (I Corinthians 5:7); and a Baraitha or tradition of the Tannaitic period (A.D. 10-220) preserved in tractate Sanhedrin 43a in the Babylonian Talmud states, "On the eve of the Passover Yeshu was hanged" (SBT p.281; Morris Goldstein, *Jesus in the Jewish Tradition.* 1950, p.22). All four Gospels also place the crucifixion on a Friday, that day being followed by the sabbath and it by the first day of the week. The chronological problem, therefore, is to ascertain in what year, in the range of years which comes in question, the fourteenth day of Nisan fell on a Friday. By astronomical calculation this was the case in A.D. 30 and 33. In A.D. 30 Nisan 14 was Friday, April 7; in A.D. 33 it was Friday, April 3. If Jesus was baptized and began his public work in the autumn, A.D. 28 (see above p.250 n.4), crucifixion in A.D. 30 would mean a total ministry of about a year and a half, which is as much as the Synoptic record requires; crucifixion in A.D. 33 would mean a total of about four and a half years, which is enough to include the data of the Fourth Gospel. Perhaps John covers the entire ministry, the Synoptics only the latter and most critical part (Ethelbert Stauffer, *Jesus, Gestalt und Geschichte* [1957], pp.16f.). For the astronomical chronology see George Ogg, *The Chronology of the Public Ministry of Jesus.* 1940, pp.261-277; Johnston M. Cheney, "In What Year the Crucifixion?" paper read at annual meeting of the Society of Biblical Literature and Exegesis held at the Southern Baptist Theological Seminary, Louisville, Ky., Dec. 30-31, 1957. See also C. C. Torrey in JBL 50 (1931), pp.226-241; J. K. Fotheringham in JTS 35 (1934), pp.146-162; A. T. Olmstead in ATR 24 (1942), pp.1-26; and *Jesus in the Light of History.* 1942, pp.279-281; C. H. Kraeling in ATR 24 (1942), pp.336f.; T. J. Meek in JNES 2 (1943), pp.124f.; and articles in JQR 42 (1951-52), pp.37-44 (Percy Heawood), pp.45-50 (S. Zeitlin), pp.237-250 (Torrey), and pp.251-260 (Zeitlin). And see the Appendix in the present book.

[2] SHJP I, ii, p.209.

[3] The war against the Jews was begun by Vespasian but when he assumed the throne at Rome in A.D. 69 his son Titus took over the command of the Roman army in the Jewish war. Eventually Titus himself became emperor (A.D. 79-81).

[4] Rabbinic tradition (*Taanith.* IV. RBT 4 [VIII], pp.80,86f.) held that Herod's Temple was destroyed on the ninth day of Ab, even as the First Temple had been before it. II Kings 25:8f. and Jeremiah 52:12f. were interpreted by them as meaning that Nebuchadnezzar's men entered the Temple on the seventh day, ate and did damage in it also on the eighth and ninth and set it on fire toward the evening of the ninth, after which it continued to burn all day on the tenth. Josephus (*War.* VI, iv, 5) represents the same tradition that the Temple was burned by the Romans on the identical day that it was formerly burned by the king of Babylon, although he specifies the tenth instead of the ninth day of Lous or Ab. The month of Ab corresponded to our July-August.

328

In Rome the following year Titus celebrated his triumph, together with his father Vespasian. The triumphal procession was adorned by seven hundred of the most handsome Jewish prisoners and by abundant spoils of war. Speaking of the spoils, Josephus said, "Conspicuous above all stood out those captured in the temple at Jerusalem. These consisted of a golden table, many talents in weight, and a lampstand, likewise made of gold. . . . After these, and last of all the spoils, was carried a copy of the Jewish Law."[5] On the Arch of Titus, which was completed and dedicated *divo Tito*, "to the deified Titus,"[6] only after the death of the emperor (A.D. 81), was carved a representation of this event. It is in the form of a bas-relief (Fig. 120) on the passage of the arcade and shows a part of the triumphal procession. Roman soldiers, without weapons and crowned with laurels, are carrying the sacred furniture which was captured in the Temple. This included the seven-armed lampstand[7] and the table of showbread upon which the sacred trumpets are resting. Tablets fastened on staves are also to be seen, but the Law or Pentateuch mentioned by Josephus does not appear. In the relief on the other side of the passage Titus is shown, crowned by Victory, standing in a car drawn by four horses and conducted by a woman representing the city of Rome. In the relief under the vault the conqueror of the Jews appears once again, sitting on an eagle. The arch and the relief can be seen to this day in the city of Rome, a melancholy memorial to the Temple that is no more. The tradition still prevails there that no Jew ever passed beneath the arch.[8]

The Jewish national state and its central religious organization were now destroyed.[9] Judea was henceforth a Roman province separate from Syria and ruled directly by Roman governors residing at Caesarea. At Jerusalem, which had been razed to the ground, the Emperor Hadrian (A.D. 117-138) founded a new heathen city named Aelia Capitolina.[10] This provoked one more fanatical and useless

---

[5] *War.* VII, v, 5.   [6] M. da Firenze, *Itinerarium Urbis Romae.* 1931, p.141.

[7] Maximilian Kon (in PEQ 1950, pp.25-30) has shown that the seven-armed lampstand on the Titus Arch is a faithful representation of the Menorah in the Jerusalem Temple, even to the animal ornamentation on the base which shows the very kind of dragon which is explicitly allowed by the Talmud.

[8] JE XII, p.164.

[9] The Sanhedrin was superseded by the Bet Din, a court of much less political power (JE III, p.114), and the daily sacrifice was no more. Even the Jewish temple-tax was paid into the temple of Jupiter Capitolinus (p.371) in Rome (*War.* VII, vi, 6). But the Law still existed and the study of it was pursued more zealously than ever. The most notable center of rabbinical scholarship at this time was at Jamnia (p.303).

[10] *Colonia Aelia Capitolina.* It was called Aelia after Hadrian's family name, and Capitolina after the Capitoline Jupiter. cf. Ptolemy, *Geography.* v, 15. ed. Stevenson, p.128: "Hierosolyma which now is called Aelia Capitolia."

rebellion. It flamed out when Tineius Rufus was governor of Judea (A.D. 132). It was led by Bar Kokhba, "Son of a Star," in whom Rabbi Akiba saw the Messianic fulfillment of the prophecy in Numbers 24:17. The suppression of the rebellion was only completed by Julius Severus, who was sent to Judea from his governorship in Britain for that task. Bethar,[11] the last stronghold of Bar Kokhba and his followers, fell to Julius Severus in A.D. 135, and the final struggle of the Jews to regain independence was over.[12]

With the suppression of the rebellion, Hadrian, who was devoted to the erection of magnificent buildings and cities, was free to proceed energetically with the building of Aelia Capitolina. A Roman legion had continued to be garrisoned here since the time of Titus, and Greeks were now introduced in lieu of the Jews who were forbidden to enter the territory under pain of death. The city was divided into seven quarters, and many fine public edifices were built or rebuilt, including two baths, a theater, and the hippodrome. Two chief sanctuaries were established. On the site of the former Jewish temple of the Lord, a temple of Jupiter Capitolinus was erected.[13] In it Jupiter, Juno, and Minerva were represented and probably there was also a statue of Hadrian himself, while in the court in front of the temple there was a statue of the emperor on horseback. On the place where, according to Christian tradition, the sepulcher of Christ had been, a high terrace was constructed and a sanctuary of Venus (Aphrodite) erected.[14] On coins of the time it is represented as a round building with a dome. Within was a marble statue of the goddess.[15]

In A.D. 325 Jerusalem was made a Christian city by Constantine. The city was captured by the Neo-Persians under Khosroes II in A.D. 614, by the Arab Caliph Omar in A.D. 638, and by the Seljuk Turks in A.D. 1072. The crusader Godfrey de Bouillon took the city in A.D. 1099 and it was the seat of the Latin kingdom of Jerusalem until A.D. 1187, when it fell to Saladin. It was taken by the Ottoman Turks in A.D. 1517 and was entered by General Sir E. H. Allenby in December, 1917. In 1949 the Old City became a part of the Kingdom of Jordan, and the New City was made the capital of the State of Israel.

[11] Or Beth-ther. Probably the modern Bettir, some five miles southwest of Jerusalem. The rabbis said that like the Temple it too fell on the ninth of Ab (*Taanith.* IV; cf. p.328 n.4).

[12] Eusebius, *Ch. Hist.* IV, vi; Dio, *Roman History.* LXIX, 12-14.

[13] Dio, *Roman History.* LXIX, 12.

[14] Eusebius, *Life of Constantine.* III, 26 (NPNFSS I, p.527).

[15] Watzinger, *Denkmäler Palästinas.* II, pp.79f.

VI

Following Paul the Traveler

1. THE DECLINE AND DISAPPEARANCE
OF JEWISH CHRISTIANITY

IT WOULD be of much interest if any monuments were to be found of the early Jewish Christian Church which had its center in Jerusalem. In 1945 a chamber tomb was discovered and excavated near the Talpioth suburb south of Jerusalem beside the road to Bethlehem, in which were some fourteen ossuaries, rectangular stone chests for the bones of the dead. A coin of Agrippa I and pottery of late Hellenistic and early Roman style indicate a date around the middle of the first century A.D. and almost certainly before A.D. 70. Three ossuaries have Hebrew inscriptions which have been read as the names Simeon Barsaba, Miriam daughter of Simeon, and Mattathias in an abbreviated form. Two ossuaries have Greek inscriptions reading Ἰησοῦς ἰού and Ἰησοῦς ἀλώθ, and on the last burial chest a rough cross, like a plus sign, is marked on each of the four sides. It has been suggested that this was the tomb of a Jewish family of Barsabbas, some of the members of which became early followers of Jesus, and the inscriptions naming Jesus have been interpreted as lamentations for the death of the founder of Christianity, ἰού being taken as the interjection of grief in classical Greek, ἀλώθ being derived from a possible Hebrew and Aramaic root meaning "to wail" or "to lament," and the plus marks being regarded as the Christian sign of the cross. On this basis it has been suggested that these may be "the earliest records of Christianity in existence."[1] Another interpretation reads the inscriptions as meaning, "Jesus, help," and "Jesus, let (him who rests here) arise,"[2] and this would also definitely connect them with early Christianity.

On the other hand, it may be that the inscriptions have nothing to do with Christianity but are simply Jewish.[3] The occurrence of the name Jesus is not unusual since it is found in at least seven other ossuary inscriptions of that time. It is possible that Ἰησοῦς ἰού means "Jesus, son of Jehu" (since ἰού is a normal transcription of the name Jehu in the Greek Old Testament[4]), or "Jesus, son of Eias" (taking ἰού as the genitive of Ἰας, a name attested in an Egyptian papyrus of the fourth century A.D.); and that Ἰησοῦς ἀλώθ means either "Jesus the Aloes" (explaining this as a nickname from the Hebrew name for the aloe plant), or "Jesus, son of Aloth" (since ἀλώθ appears as a personal name in a papyrus from the Fayum); and thus the references would be to persons other than the founder of Christianity. As for the cross signs, rather than regarding them as Christian symbols, one suggestion is that, since they appear on the sides of an ossuary otherwise marked only with the name on the top, they were simply intended to show to anyone viewing the receptacle from the side that it was already in use.[5] Another suggestion is that these were magical marks of protection.[6] Yet again it has been observed that in early Hebrew script the last letter of the Hebrew alphabet, Taw, was written with a cross sign either upright + or lying on its side ×. The word Taw also means "mark" or "sign," and occurs in Ezekiel 9:4 where those who are faithful to the Law of the Lord are marked with this sign on their foreheads to protect them from judgment. Thus it might be that the cross sign was used on some Jewish graves to signify that the one buried there was a follower of the Law and would be protected by the Lord in the judgment.[7] In view of these alternative explanations, therefore, it remains uncertain whether the Talpioth ossuaries are to be considered as monuments of early Jewish Christianity.

[1] E. L. Sukenik in AJA 51 (1947), pp.351-365.

[2] Berndt Gustafsson in NTS 3 (1956), pp.65-69.

[3] Carl H. Kraeling in BA 9 (1946), pp.16-20; J. Simons in *Jaarbericht No. 11 van het vooraziatisch-egyptisch Genootschap Ex Oriente Lux* (1949-50), pp.74-78.

[4] e.g. I Kings 16:1, LXX ed. Rahlfs, I, p.672.

[5] Harold R. Willoughby in JBL 68 (1949), pp.61-65.

[6] Edwin R. Goodenough, *Jewish Symbols in the Greco-Roman Period.* I (1953), pp.130-132.

[7] Erich Dinkler in ZTK 48 (1951), pp.148-172.

Recently another ancient cemetery has been discovered by chance on the Mount of Olives. This is in the vicinity of the Franciscan chapel known as *Dominus flevit* which marks the traditional place where Jesus wept over Jerusalem (Luke 19:41), and the tombs have been investigated by P. Bellarmino Bagatti.[8] It is indicated that this burial place was in use in the first century A.D. as well as later in the third and fourth centuries. Some thirty-six ossuaries were found which doubtless belong to the early period since the use of such burial chests is believed to have ceased in the second century A.D. These also have inscriptions, and a number of names are found which occur in the Gospels, Jairus, Martha, Mary, Salome, and Simon Bar-Jonah. On an ossuary bearing the name of "Judah the proselyte of Tyre" there is a monogram composed of the Greek characters Chi and Rho which, being the first two letters of the name Christ, are at least at a later date a well-recognized Christian symbol, the so-called Constantinian monogram (p.469 n.19). Another monogram combines the letters Iota, Chi, and Beta, which could stand for Ἰησοῦς Χριστὸς Βασιλεύς, "Jesus Christ King." And finally there is a carefully drawn cross, analogous to the marks at Talpioth. Again therefore, although alternative explanations may be preferable, the possibility is raised that these remains represent the early Jewish Christian community at Jerusalem.

At any rate the fate of Jewish Christianity was sealed with the fall of Jerusalem in A.D. 70. Already the church at Jerusalem had seen Stephen stoned (Acts 7:59), James the son of Zebedee beheaded (Acts 12:2), and James the brother of the Lord thrown from the pinnacle of the Temple, stoned and beaten to death with a club.[9] Then at the time of the Jewish war a revelation was received by the church to leave Jerusalem and migrate to Pella in Transjordan (p.309).[10] This was a Gentile city, hated by the Jews and laid waste by them at the beginning of the war,[11] but it offered refuge to the Christians. Jewish Christianity survived here for a time, as did different kinds of Jewish sects which also, for various reasons, had taken refuge east of the Jordan, and Christian bishops of Pella are mentioned as late as the fifth and six centuries A.D.[12] But the land east of the Jordan was apart from the main streams in which the history of

[8] RB 61 (1954), pp.568-570.
[9] Eusebius, *Ch. Hist.* II, xxiii.
[10] *Ch. Hist.* III, v, 2f.
[11] Josephus, *War.* II, xviii, 1.
[12] M. LeQuien, *Oriens Christianus.* (1740) III, pp.698f.

the future was to flow. In the isolation of its lonely deserts Jewish Christianity sank quietly into oblivion.[13]

2. THE WORK OF PAUL

THE wider world was to be won by that true and universal Christianity which found no room for distinctions of Jew or Greek but saw all as one in Christ Jesus (Galatians 3:28). It was Paul who recognized most clearly this universal character of Christianity and labored most effectively to put it into practice by launching a world-wide mission.

TARSUS

To follow the footsteps of Paul one must go far afield from Palestine. Tarsus of Cilicia is named in the book of Acts (9:11; 21:39; 22:3; cf. 9:30; 11:25) as the home of Paul. Tarsus was a meeting place of East and West. The two chief trade routes from the East, one coming from the Euphrates over the Amanus Pass and the other coming from Antioch by the Syrian Gates, united fifty miles east of Tarsus and entered the city as a single road. This road then ran northward toward the mountain wall of the Taurus thirty miles away. The road over these mountains is seventy or eighty miles in length. The actual pass, one hundred yards in length, is known as the Cilician Gates,[1] and is a place where dark cliffs narrow to a mere slit, at the bottom of which is a torrent. Engineering work done here, probably as long ago as 1000 B.C., opened the way to central Asia Minor and the West.

Tarsus itself was situated in the Cilician Plain. The "cold and swift" Cydnus River[2] flowed directly through the heart of the city, entered some miles beyond it a lake called Rhegma, and flowed on to the Mediterranean ten miles away. Shipping came at that time all the way up the river to the city,[3] and thus it was an important port as well as a center on the land route.

The history of Tarsus goes back to Hittite times, and the city is mentioned on the Black Obelisk of Shalmaneser III as one of the cities captured by him.[4] Xenophon (c.400 B.C.) found Tarsus "a

---

[13] Karl Pieper, *Die Kirche Palästinas bis zum Jahre 135.* 1938, p.58.
[1] Pliny, *Natural History.* v, 22.
[2] Strabo, *Geography.* xiv, v, 12; cf. Plutarch, *Life of Alexander.* xix.
[3] Plutarch, *Life of Antony.* xxvi.
[4] ARAB I, §583.

large and prosperous city,"[5] and II Maccabees 4:30f. mentions an insurrection there which Antiochus IV Epiphanes hastened to quiet (c.170 B.C.). In the time of the Seleucids, Tarsus became strongly Hellenized, and in 64 B.C. Pompey made Cilicia a Roman province with Tarsus as the residence of the Roman governor. From the time of Antony and Augustus on it was a free city, densely populated and wealthy. Tarsus was also an intellectual center with a famed university. Strabo said, "The people at Tarsus have devoted themselves so eagerly, not only to philosophy, but also to the whole round of education in general, that they have surpassed Athens, Alexandria, or any other place that can be named where there have been schools and lectures of philosophers."[6] The most famous philosopher of Tarsus was the Stoic, Athenodorus, who was the teacher of the Emperor Augustus. Also Aratus, the Alexandrian poet of the third century B.C. whose *Phaenomena* was quoted by Paul at Athens according to Acts 17:28, was a native of Soli in Cilicia and was doubtless studied with pride in the schools of Tarsus.[7]

The ancient and splendid city of Paul is represented by the modern Tersoos, with 39,622 inhabitants according to the Turkish census of 1955. Beneath the grounds of the American Tarsus College there are enormous vaults which may have belonged to the hippodrome of Roman times, and at the southeastern edge of the town is the large mound of Gözlü Kule where excavations were conducted, beginning in 1934, by Bryn Mawr College.[8] A native factory of about the middle of the second century A.D. was unearthed. Apparently it had catered to the needs of the hippodrome and the theater, for it made terra-cotta figures of victorious charioteers and horsemen, lamps representing chariot races and gladiatorial combats, and theatrical masks. Here and elsewhere in the digging numerous representations of deities came to light, including Artemis, Athena, Apollo, Serapis, Isis, Aphrodite, Zeus, and Hermes. In the lower levels of the mound the excavators penetrated to remains of Hittite and Babylonian times.

Another link with the past is the trade of tent-making which is still carried on, as it was in the time of Paul (Acts 18:3). Goats

[5] *Anabasis.* I, ii, 23. tr. C. L. Brownson, LCL (1921-22) I, p.263.

[6] *Geography.* XIV, v, 13.

[7] Henri Metzger, *St. Paul's Journeys in the Greek Orient.* 1955, pp.47f.; cf. Henry J. Cadbury, *The Book of Acts in History.* 1955, pp.46, 48.

[8] Hetty Goldman in AJA 39 (1935), pp.526-549; 41 (1937), pp.262-286; and *Excavations at Gözlü Kule, Tarsus,* I, *The Hellenistic and Roman Periods, Text, Plates.* 1950.

living on the Taurus Mountains where the snow lies until May, grow magnificent coats whose hair has long been famous for strength and durability. This is spun into thread and woven into a tough fabric which anciently was known from the name of the province as *cilicium*. This fabric, in turn, is made into tents and other necessities.

DAMASCUS

The conversion of Paul to the faith which once he persecuted is intimately connected with the city of Damascus (Galatians 1:17; II Corinthians 11:32; Acts 9:1-25; 22:5-16; 26:12-20). Damascus lies in a fertile plain east of the Anti-Lebanon range, with snowy Mount Hermon filling the western horizon. The river el-Barada, "the Cool," runs through the heart of the city, while el-A'waj descends from the eastern slopes of Mount Hermon to water the southeastern plain. The Barada is doubtless the Abanah and the A'waj may be the Pharpar of II Kings 5:12, which Naaman thought "better than all the waters of Israel." So fertile is the oasis in which Damascus stands that the Arabian poets compared it with Paradise. The scene is indeed one of beauty with the white roofs, the domes, and the minarets of the city standing out against the green of the environing orchards.

Damascus is mentioned in Genesis (14:15; 15:2) as a city which was in existence in the days of Abraham, and in the fifteenth century B.C. was one of the places controlled by Thutmose III. After Alexander the Great, Damascus was possessed first by the Ptolemies and then by the Seleucids. Around 85 B.C. Antiochus XII was killed in the battle with the king of the Nabateans, and Damascus came under the control of the latter.[9] The Nabateans were a people who had established themselves beyond the Dead Sea in the district of Petra,[10] the ancient home of the Edomites, and the Nabatean king who conquered Antiochus XII was Aretas III (c.85-c.60 B.C.). In 64 B.C. Damascus was taken by the Romans under Metellus,[11] and thenceforward presumably belonged to the Roman province of Syria which was constituted soon afterward. At the time when Paul fled from Damascus, however, the city is stated to have been under a governor of Aretas the king (II Corinthians 11:32). This must have been the Nabatean king, Aretas IV, whose original name was Aeneas

[9] Josephus, *Ant.* XIII, xv, 1f.; *War.* I, iv, 7f.

[10] For Petra see William H. Morton in BA 19 (1956), pp.25-36; Peter J. Parr in PEQ 1957, pp.5-16.

[11] *Ant.* XIV, ii, 3; *War.* I, vi, 2.

and who reigned from 9 B.C. to A.D. 40. He is also known to us for his defeat of Herod Antipas in revenge for the divorce of his daughter by the latter (pp.255f.). Apparently, therefore, Damascus had been returned to the control of Aretas IV at the time to which II Corinthians refers. Some confirmation of this fact may be seen in the coins of Damascus, on which the image of Tiberius appears down to A.D. 34. Then in the time of Caligula (A.D. 37-41) and Claudius (A.D. 41-54) no Damascus coins are known which have the image of the Roman emperor. But coins of Nero begin again in A.D. 62. In the interval Damascus may have belonged to the Nabatean king.[12]

According to the census of 1952, Damascus had a population of 345,237. The East Gate (Bab esh-Sherqi) of the city probably dates from Roman times. It was a threefold archway, but two of the three arches are now walled up. The street which runs directly west from this gate through the city is still called Derb el-Mustaqim ("Straight Street") or Suq et-Tawileh ("Long Bazaar") and probably preserves the line of "the street called Straight" of Acts 9:11 (Fig. 121).

ANTIOCH

The Syrian city of Antioch, which is now in Turkey and is called Antakya, played an important part in early Christian history. It was there that "the disciples were for the first time called Christians" (Acts 11:26), and it was from there that Paul and Barnabas were sent out for wider missionary work (Acts 13:1-3).

Antioch lies on the Orontes River, about twenty miles from the Mediterranean, at the foot of Mount Silpius. Much information concerning the history and topography of the city is to be derived from the *Chronicle* of John Malalas (A.D. c.491-c.578), a Byzantine monk who was born and spent most of his life in Antioch. He relates that Seleucus I Nicator wished to build many cities and made a beginning at the sea of Syria. On the seashore at the trading place of Pieria he founded a city which he called Seleucia after his own name. Then "he built Antioch after the name of his son, Antiochus, surnamed Soter." John Malalas also says that Seleucus planted cypresses in Heraclea, which is now called Daphne, and states that "this same city was built outside a grove by the temple of Athena."[13]

Under Antiochus I Soter, Antioch became the capital of the west-

---

[12] SHJP I, ii, pp.357f.
[13] Matthew Spinka, *Chronicle of John Malalas, Books VIII-XVIII, translated from the Church Slavonic.* (1940) VIII, i-ii (pp.13-15).

ern part of the Seleucid Empire. This king also added a second quarter to the city on its eastern side. Later a third quarter was built by Seleucus II Callinicus on an island in the river; and a fourth was built by Antiochus IV Epiphanes on the slopes of Mount Silpius. Strabo says, "Antiocheia is . . . a Tetrapolis, since it consists of four parts; and each of the four settlements is fortified both by a common wall and by a wall of its own."[14]

Antioch fell into the hands of Tigranes of Armenia around 83 B.C., but about twenty years later was taken from him by the Romans and made a free city and the capital of the Roman province of Syria. It was further beautified by the Roman emperors, including Augustus and Tiberius, and Herod the Great paved one of its broad streets and erected colonnades along it.[15] Perhaps this was in appreciation of the very good relations which existed there between the Gentiles and the Jewish inhabitants, for in Antioch Jews were accorded the right of citizenship and "privileges equal to those of the Macedonians and Greeks who were the inhabitants."[16]

Josephus called Antioch the third city of the Roman Empire, only Rome and Alexandria taking precedence.[17] The city was known as "the Beautiful,"[18] but the reputation of its moral life was not good and Juvenal (A.D. c.60-c.140) described the flooding of Rome with the superstition and immorality of the East as a flowing of the Orontes into the Tiber.[19]

The present city of Antakya, with 37,484 inhabitants according to the census of 1955, covers only a fraction of the area of the ancient city and there is therefore excellent opportunity for archeological work. Excavations have been conducted here beginning in 1932 by Princeton University with the cooperation of the Baltimore Museum of Art, the Worcester Art Museum, and the Musées Nationaux de France.[20]

The island on which one of the principal districts of the city was

[14] *Geography.* xvi, ii, 4.
[15] Josephus, *War.* i, xxi, 11; *Ant.* xvi, v, 3.
[16] *Ant.* xii, iii, 1.   [17] *War.* iii, ii, 4.
[18] Athenaeus (end of 2d cent. A.D.), *The Deipnosophists.* i, 20. tr. B. Gulick, LCL (1927-41) i, p.87; cf. the oration in praise of Antioch delivered probably in A.D. 360 by Libanius, a native of that city (Leo Hugi, *Der Antiochikos des Libanios* [1919]).
[19] *Satire.* iii, 62. tr. G. G. Ramsay, LCL (1918), p.37.
[20] *Antioch on-the-Orontes, Publications of the Committee for the Excavation of Antioch and Its Vicinity.* i, *The Excavations of 1932*, ed. G. W. Elderkin. 1934; ii, *The Excavations 1933-1936*, ed. Richard Stillwell. 1938; iii, *The Excavations 1937-39*, ed. R. Stillwell. 1941; iv, 1, *Ceramics and Islamic Coins*, ed. Frederick O. Waagé. 1948.

built had disappeared from sight with the silting up of one of the channels of the Orontes, but in the excavations it was found again, and the wall which Justinian threw around the city in the sixth century was traced. Two ancient cemeteries of the second century A.D. were discovered, and the acropolis of the city was found to be on Mount Stauris instead of on Mount Silpius as was formerly supposed. The location was plotted of the two principal streets of the city, which had been famous in antiquity for their colonnades. The circus, which was one of the largest and most important in the Roman Empire, was found and excavated. It is believed to have been erected originally in the first century B.C. Other discoveries included baths, Roman villas, and a Byzantine stadium belonging to the fifth and sixth centuries.

Commanding the lower Orontes and looming above the sea south of the Gulf of Alexandretta is the mountain called Musa Dagh. The major portion of Antioch's seaport city, Seleucia Pieria, was built on a long, sloping spur of this mountain, and the city's walls ran on down to enclose the harbor, an area which now is largely marshland. Among the structures studied at Seleucia Pieria were the market gate, houses, the Doric temple of Hellenistic times, and the memorial church which will be referred to later along with the church at Kaoussie also near Antioch (pp.539-542).

The suburb of Daphne was on a plateau lying four or five miles southwest of Antioch and rising more than three hundred feet above the average level of the city. There are springs on the plateau, and the system of aqueducts by which their waters were carried to Antioch has been traced and studied. Beautiful pleasure villas were at Daphne, and there was a fine theater which was built in a splendid natural bowl formed by encircling hillsides on the slope of the plateau overlooking the valley of the Orontes. The theater was constructed probably around the end of the first century A.D.

Many sculptured pieces have been found, but doubtless the most spectacular finds at Antioch and its suburbs have been the numerous floor mosaics, many of which have been uncovered fortuitously or by the operation of natural forces. These extend in date from around A.D. 100 to the sixth century, and provide an unequaled wealth of material for the study of Greco-Roman mosaic art. One mosaic, which decorated the floor of the triclinium of a house belonging to the end of the first century A.D., portrays the judgment of Paris, and a drinking contest between Heracles and Dionysus, with the latter the victor. Other subjects include Oceanus and Thalassa in the midst of the fishes of the sea, landscapes, and hunting scenes, and an illustrated calendar in which the months of the year are personified as little figures carrying fruits and other symbols of the months.[21]

CYPRUS

The destination of Paul and Barnabas, when they were first sent out by the church at Antioch, was nearby Cyprus (Acts 13:4), one of the largest islands in the Mediterranean. The first appearance of Cyprus in history is when it was captured by Thutmose III of Egypt.[22] Later the island was colonized by the Phoenicians and the Greeks. About 58 B.C. it was taken from Ptolemy Auletes by Rome and later made a separate province.[23] In 22 B.C. it was transferred to the senate, and its governor therefore had the title of proconsul (cf. p.256 n.13). Acts 13:7 names a certain Sergius Paulus as proconsul when Paul came, and an inscription of the year A.D. 55 has been found at Paphos with the words "in the time of the proconsul Paulus."[24]

THE CITIES OF GALATIA

From Cyprus, Paul and Barnabas went to the mainland of Asia Minor. According to Acts (13:14, 51; 14:6) they preached there in Antioch of Pisidia, Iconium of Phrygia, and Lystra and Derbe of Lycaonia.

Pisidian Antioch[25] was another of the some sixteen Antiochs

[21] In connection with Antioch, the so-called "Chalice of Antioch" must be mentioned which is reported to have been found by natives at or near this city. It consists of an inner plain silver cup held in an outer openwork gilded shell and set on a solid silver base. The openwork holder is decorated with vines, birds, and animals, and twelve seated human figures. The last are divided into two groups, in each of which five persons are placed about one central figure. Evidently the central figure in each of the two groups is Christ and the others are his apostles. A first century date has been advocated vigorously for this remarkable object, with the additional suggestion that the inner cup is nothing other than the Holy Grail (Gustavus A. Eisen, *The Great Chalice of Antioch.* 1933), but on the other hand the authenticity of the chalice has been called in question (C. R. Morey in *Art Studies, Medieval, Renaissance and Modern* 3 [1925], pp.73-80), and the most that can be said is that it may be a piece of early Christian silver from the fourth or fifth century (H. Harvard Arnason in BA 4 [1941], pp.49-64; 5 [1942], pp.10-16).

[22] ARE II, §§493, 511 (Isy = Cyprus). [23] Strabo, *Geography.* XIV, vi, 6.

[24] Stephen L. Caiger, *Archaeology and the New Testament.* 1939, p.119.

[25] Ptolemy, *Geography.* v, 4. ed. Stevenson, p.116: *Antiochia Pisidiae.* Strabo, *Geography.* XII, viii, 14 (cf. XII, vi, 4): Ἀντιόχεια ἡ πρὸς Πισιδίᾳ καλουμένη. For the designation see William M. Calder, ed., *Monumenta Asiae Minoris Antiqua*, VII, *Monuments from Eastern Phrygia.* 1956, p.xi.

founded by Seleucus I Nicator, and it was made a free city by the Romans about 189 B.C. and a Roman colony by Augustus before 11 B.C. Antioch was in the extreme northeast of the district of Pisidia and on the frontier of the district of Phrygia. The Pisidians and the Phrygians were peoples of less high civilization but Antioch itself was a thoroughly Hellenized and Romanized city.

The site of Antioch was on the lower slopes of a majestic mountain now called Sultan Dagh, and on the right bank of the Anthius River. The place was discovered in 1833 by Francis V. J. Arundell, British chaplain at Smyrna, and is near the modern Turkish town of Yalovach. The ruins show that Antioch was a strongly fortified city, and the remains of the Roman aqueduct which brought water from the foothills of the Sultan Dagh still are to be seen.[26] The principal temple was dedicated to the god Men and was studied by William Ramsay just before the First World War. The great altar and many engraved tablets were uncovered, and the underlying soil was found to be full of the bones of sacrificial animals. An inscription was found which referred to a "Lucius Sergius Paullus the younger," whom Ramsay believed to be the son of Sergius Paulus, proconsul of Cyprus.[27]

Later, more intensive excavations were conducted by the University of Michigan,[28] and the most important remains of the Roman city founded by Augustus were brought to light. The city enjoyed two fine squares, the upper known as the Augusta Platea or Square of Augustus and the lower as the Tiberia Platea or Square of Tiberius. The two were connected by a broad flight of steps, at the top of which stood the three triumphal archways of the propylaea erected in honor of Augustus. The archways were adorned with many relief sculptures and probably were once surmounted with statues in the round as well. The reliefs in the spandrels of the arches portrayed captive Pisidians and commemorated the victories of Augustus on land, while a frieze with Poseidon, Tritons, dolphins, and other marine symbols celebrated his triumphs at sea, especially at Actium.

On the Square of Augustus stood the great temple, which was not Hellenistic as Ramsay believed but also belonged to the age of Augustus. A wonderful frieze of bulls' heads adorned the temple,

[26] W. M. Ramsay, *The Cities of St. Paul.* 1907. Plate facing p.252.

[27] W. M. Ramsay, *The Bearing of Recent Discovery on the Trustworthiness of the New Testament.* 4th ed. 1920, pp.150f.; Egbert C. Hudson in JNES 15 (1956), pp.103-107.

[28] David M. Robinson in AJA 28 (1924), pp.435-444.

the heads being connected by garlands of leaves and all kinds of fruits realistically rendered. The bull's head was the symbol of Men, who was the local god upon whom the prosperity of agriculture was believed to depend. As the god who bestowed all blessings upon the people, it was not difficult also to identify him with the Roman emperor Augustus.

Both the architecture and the sculpture of these first century structures were very impressive. "Nowhere else in the Roman empire has yet been discovered a better combination of superb realistic sculpture with excellent solid architecture in excellent vertical and horizontal rhythm," says David M. Robinson. "Greek refinement and restraint seem here to be combined with Roman luxuriance, Greek simplicity with Roman complexity, Greek beauty with Roman realism and massiveness."[29]

Another monumental structure at Pisidian Antioch was a triple gateway built into the city wall. It bore an inscription, in bronze letters which are preserved, of G(aius) Jul(ius) Asp(er), consul in A.D. 212, and was adorned with sculptures, but of a quality inferior to those of the propylaea and the temple. Other discoveries included numerous terra-cotta pipes through which the spring water brought by the aqueduct was distributed throughout the city; playing-boards, incised with circles and rectangles, where the Romans spent their idle hours in various games; and a Latin edict of Domitian's praetorian legate L. Antistius Rusticus which prescribed measures for preventing profiteering, controlling the price of grain after a severe winter and ensuring sufficient seed for the next season. Also there was a Christian basilica at Antioch which was more than two hundred feet long, and which dates, according to an inscription, in the time of Optimus, who was bishop of Antioch in the last quarter of the fourth century.

Iconium was sixty miles distant from Antioch to the southeast, on the frontier between Phrygia and Lycaonia. Therefore it was sometimes considered as the last city of Phrygia,[30] and was sometimes spoken of as belonging to the neighboring district of Lycaonia.[31] In Acts 14:6 it is regarded as belonging to Phrygia, for it is implied that in fleeing from Iconium to Lystra and Derbe Paul went from Phrygia to Lycaonia.[32]

[29] Robinson in AB 9 (1926-27), p.6.
[30] Xenophon, *Anabasis.* I, ii, 19.   [31] Strabo, *Geography.* XII, vi, 1.
[32] W. M. Ramsay, *A Historical Commentary on St. Paul's Epistle to the Galatians.* 1900, p.215.

The ancient Iconium is now known as Konia or Konya, and is a relatively modern Turkish city with 93,125 inhabitants according to the census of 1955. It is in a plain watered by streams from the Pisidian mountains, and nearby are twin conical hills known as the peaks of St. Philip and St. Thecla. Thecla was the young woman of Iconium who was associated with the apostle Paul in the apocryphal Acts of Paul. The latter is the work which contains the famous description of Paul as "a man of little stature, thin-haired upon the head, crooked in the legs, of good state of body, with eyebrows joining, and nose somewhat hooked, full of grace: for sometimes he appeared like a man, and sometimes he had the face of an angel."[33]

Lystra and Derbe were in the region of Lycaonia, and in the first century the common people still spoke the native Lycaonian language as is indicated in Acts 14:11. Lystra was some twenty-five miles from Iconium, and its site was discovered in 1885 by J. R. Sitlington Sterrett. It was identified by an altar still standing in its original position. This was a stone, about three and one-half feet high and twelve inches thick, with a clearly cut Latin inscription (Fig. 122). The inscription gave the usual Roman spelling of the city's name, Lustra, and indicated that it was a Roman colony.[34]

Derbe was presumably farther east and south in the same district, and has been thought to be represented by the large mound of Gudelisin, which was also first observed by Professor Sterrett.[35] In 1956, however, there was found at Kerti Hüyük, a mound more than thirty miles east and somewhat north of Gudelisin, an inscription dated in A.D. 157 which contains a dedication by the council and assembly of the people of Derbe, and which makes it probable that Derbe was located at this site.[35a]

In New Testament times all four of these cities—Antioch, Iconium,

---

[33] JANT p.273.

[34] Sterrett, *An Epigraphical Journey in Asia Minor.* 1888; Ramsay, *A Historical Commentary on St. Paul's Epistle to the Galatians*, p.224.

[35] Ramsay, *The Cities of St. Paul*, p.452 n.18. The location on our Map 6 corresponds to this identification.

[35a] . . . .] δερβητῶν ἡ βουλὴ κ-

αἰ ὁ δ]ῆμος . . . .

M. Ballance in *Anatolian Studies.* 7 (1957), pp. 147-151. For δερβήτης as the designation of an inhabitant of Derbe see Strabo, *Geography.* xii, vi, 3. In view of the distance from Lystra to the new site for Derbe, it may be noted that Acts 14:20 does not require that Paul and Barnabas went all the way from the one place to the other in one day, rather it is simply stated that on the morrow they went forth from Lystra toward (εἰς) Derbe, that is to go on the trip to Derbe.

Lystra, and Derbe—were included in the Roman province of Galatia. The Roman province took its name from the smaller northern district of Galatia proper which it included. This ethnographical district of Galatia proper was named from three Gallic tribes which entered Asia Minor around 278-277 B.C. and settled permanently in this region. In 64 B.C. they became a client state of the Roman Empire, and in the following years were able to extend their territory to include the whole center of Asia Minor. Amyntas, their last native king, ruled over Galatia, Phrygia-towards-Pisidia, Pisidia, Lycaonia, and part of Pamphylia.[36] Upon the death of Amyntas in 25 B.C. this kingdom was bequeathed to the Romans,[37] and became the Roman province of Galatia. The new province at first included the entire kingdom of Amyntas, but it was somewhat reduced in size in 20 B.C.[38] Thereafter, however, it continued to comprise Galatia proper, Pisidia, and western Lycaonia.[39] Thus Antioch, Iconium, Lystra and Derbe were all within the boundaries of the Roman province of Galatia.[40]

Paul's letter addressed "to the churches of Galatia" (Galatians 1:2) presumably went, therefore, to the churches of Antioch, Iconium, Lystra, and Derbe, which he himself had founded. To address them as "churches of Galatia," meaning the Roman province of Galatia, was entirely correct.[41] Those who insist on confining the word "Galatia" to its strict ethnographical meaning, on the other hand, believe that the letter was intended for otherwise unknown Christian churches in north Galatia proper.[42] This is less probable, and the first time that the existence of a Christian congregation at Ancyra is even

[36] CAH p.69.

[37] King Amyntas was taken prisoner and put to death by the brigand tribes of the Taurus known as Homanadenses. Augustus ultimately avenged the death of his subject king by sending out Publius Sulpicius Quirinius as consul to "pacify" the Homanadensians, which was done with characteristically cruel Roman thoroughness perhaps in the years 10-7 B.C. This was the Quirinius who was also governor of Syria (pp.258f.). CAH X, pp.271f.

[38] Eastern Lycaonia, together with Cilicia Tracheia, was transferred to the rule of the king of Cappadocia.

[39] CAH X, p.261.

[40] Ramsay, The Cities of St. Paul, pp.262f., 343, 401. For Paul's journeys in this region see also T. R. S. Broughton in Quantulacumque, Studies Presented to Kirsopp Lake by Pupils, Colleagues, and Friends, ed. by Robert P. Casey, Silva Lake, and Agnes K. Lake. 1937, pp.131-138.

[41] Ramsay, A Historical Commentary on St. Paul's Epistle to the Galatians; and in HDB II, pp.81-89; Edgar J. Goodspeed, The Story of the New Testament. 1916, p.9; Frederic Rendall in The Expositor's Greek Testament. III, p.128.

[42] Paul W. Schmiedel in T. K. Cheyne and J. Sutherland Black, eds., Encyclopaedia Biblica. 1899-1903, cols. 1592-1616; James Moffatt, An Introduction to the Literature of the New Testament. 3d ed. 1918, pp.90-101; and in EB IX, p.972.

mentioned is in A.D. 192.[43] Ancyra was the chief city of north Galatia and the capital of the entire province. The real greatness of this place dated from the time when Constantinople became the Roman metropolis and the location of Ancyra gave it a lasting importance. Today it is the modern Angora or Ankara, the capital of Turkey. Its most important monument is the Augusteum, a white marble temple which the council of the three Galatian tribes erected to Rome and Augustus during the lifetime of Augustus. On its walls is carved a long inscription in Latin and Greek narrating the public life and work of the emperor. The original which is now lost was composed in a dignified style by Augustus himself and was completed in A.D. 14, to be engraved on bronze tablets in front of his mausoleum in Rome. Fragments of other copies of the same text have been found also at Pisidian Antioch and at Apollonia.[44]

EPHESUS

Ephesus was the city of Asia Minor where Paul worked for the longest time (Acts 19:1-20:1). The earliest inhabitants of Ephesus were of Asiatic origin, and early in the first millennium B.C. the Ionian Greeks settled there. In the sixth century B.C. the city fell to Croesus of Lydia and then to Cyrus of Persia. Around 334 B.C. Ephesus came under the control of Alexander the Great, and later was held by the Seleucids of Syria. When the Romans defeated Antiochus III the Great in 190 B.C. they handed over Ephesus to Eumenes II (197-159 B.C.), king of Pergamum. It was Eumenes II who built the great Altar of Zeus at Pergamum which was reconstructed so splendidly in the Berlin Museum. This great structure was erected in celebration of the victory of Eumenes over the Gauls around 180 B.C. and is adorned with a frieze of magnificent sculptures depicting the combat of gods and giants. The remains of the Temple of Rome and Augustus have also been discovered at Pergamum. This temple was founded in 29 B.C. and was the first in the empire to be dedicated to the cult of Roman emperor worship, with which Christianity was to come into such serious conflict. Either the Altar of Zeus or the Temple of Rome and Augustus was probably the "Satan's throne" of Revelation 2:13.[45]

[43] EB I, p.893.

[44] Res Gestae Divi Augusti. tr. F. W. Shipley, LCL (1924).

[45] Altertümer von Pergamon. 10 vols. 1912-37; Hans Erich Stier, Aus der Welt des Pergamonaltars. 1932; Heinz Kähler, Pergamon. 1949; Arnold Schober, Die Kunst von Pergamon. 1951.

In 133 B.C. the last king of Pergamum, Attalus III Philometor, bequeathed Ephesus, together with the rest of the Pergamenian kingdom, to the Romans and thereafter it continued subject to them. At first Pergamum remained the capital of the Roman province of Asia, but eventually this honor passed to Ephesus. Whether it had become the capital in the time of Paul is uncertain. At any rate Ephesus was "the largest emporium in Asia this side of the Taurus,"[46] and ranked along with Antioch in Syria and Alexandria in Egypt as one of the three great cities of the eastern Mediterranean. This prominence it owed very largely to its favorable geographical location, for it was on the main line of communication between Rome and the Orient in general. The city was situated within three miles of the sea, on the left bank of the river Cayster. At that time this river was navigable as far up as the city, although attention was required to keep the city harbor and the channel of the Cayster free from silt. A breakwater was built under the Pergamenian king Attalus Philadelphus (159-138 B.C.), with the intention of contributing to this end but unfortunately it had the opposite result and made the harbor shallower. Around A.D. 65 the governor of Asia took further measures to improve the connection between harbor and sea.[47] In later centuries the engineering work necessary to maintain the harbor was neglected, and now the mouth of the river has been silted up badly and the harbor reduced to a marsh.

From Ephesus, the Cayster Valley offered the shortest route to Pisidian Antioch and the East. The way was relatively steep, but nevertheless was often preferred by travelers on foot because of its shorter distance. This could have been the route taken by Paul in Acts 19:1. The alternative was the longer but more level route on which the heavier traffic moved, which crossed a six-hundred-foot pass to the south of Ephesus and then followed the Meander and Lycus Valleys eastward by Laodicea even as the modern railroad does.[48]

The railroad station nearest to the site of Ephesus today is the small village of Ayasoluk, or Seljuk as the Turks call it. Ayasoluk is a corruption of Agios Theologos, as St. John "the Theologian" was

[46] Strabo, *Geography*. XIV, i, 24.
[47] Tacitus, *Annals*. XVI, 23. tr. J. Jackson, LCL (1931-37) IV, p.373.
[48] For Laodicea and neighboring cities, and the Lycus Valley, see Sherman E. Johnson in BA 13 (1950), pp.1-18. And for conditions involved in visiting Pauline sites from Syrian Antioch to Ephesus, and the cities of the Revelation, as they prevailed at the date of the article, see Robert North in CBQ 18 (1956), pp.30-35.

122. Inscription at Lystra

121. Straight Street in Damascus

123. The Theater at Ephesus

124. Air View of Philippi

125. The Temple of Zeus, with the Acropolis in the Background

126. The Altar to Unknown Gods at Pergamum

127. Ruins of the Temple of Apollo at Corinth, with Acrocorinth in the Background

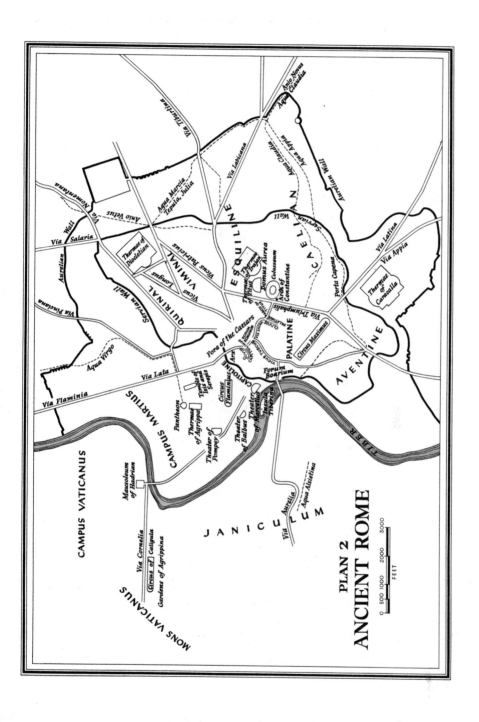

PLAN 2
ANCIENT ROME

0 500 1000 2000 3000
FEET

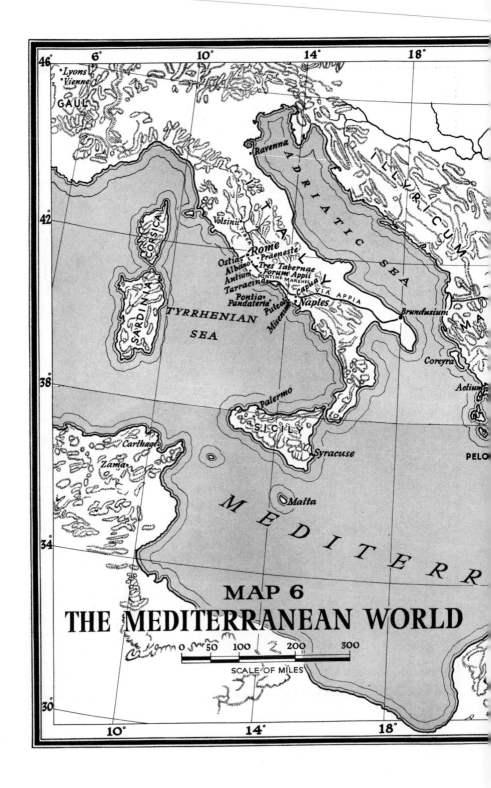

MAP 6
THE MEDITERRANEAN WORLD

0 50 100   200   300

SCALE OF MILES

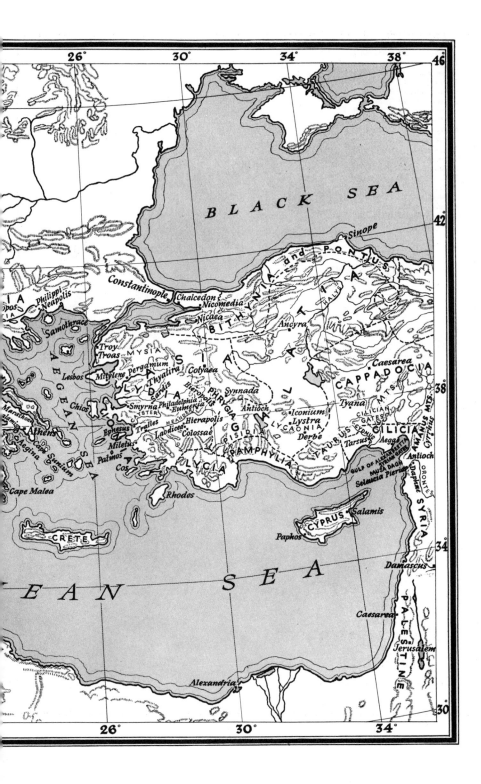

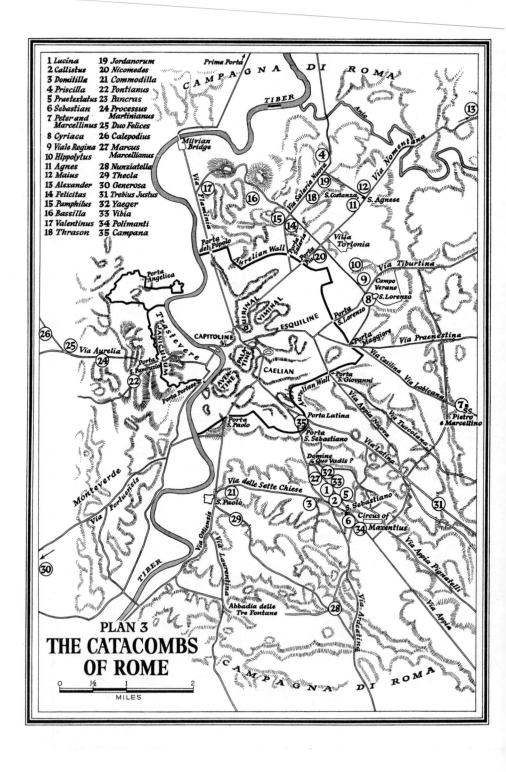

1 Lucina	19 Jordanorum
2 Callistus	20 Nicomedes
3 Domitilla	21 Commodilla
4 Priscilla	22 Pontianus
5 Praetextatus	23 Pancras
6 Sebastian	24 Processus
7 Peter and	Martinianus
Marcellinus	25 Duo Felices
8 Cyriaca	26 Calepodius
9 Viale Regina	27 Marcus
10 Hippolytus	Marcellianus
11 Agnes	28 Nunziatella
12 Maius	29 Thecla
13 Alexander	30 Generosa
14 Felicitas	31 Trebius Justus
15 Pamphilus	32 Yaeger
16 Bassilla	33 Vibia
17 Valentinus	34 Polimanti
18 Thrason	35 Campana

PLAN 3

THE CATACOMBS
OF ROME

0 ½ 1 2
MILES

128. The Agora at Corinth

129. Nero

130. The Appian Way and the Claudian Aqueduct

131. Caricature of the Crucifixion

132. The Roman Forum

133. The Pyramid of Cestius and the Gate of St. Paul

called, to whom Justinian dedicated here a fine church.[49] The houses of Ayasoluk mostly are made of stones brought from the ruins of Ephesus, a mile or two away to the southwest.

Ephesus was particularly famous for the worship of Artemis and the Artemision or temple of this goddess was accounted one of the seven wonders of the ancient world. The goddess originally had been a Lydian deity of character similar to the Phrygian Cybele and the Phoenician Astarte. The Greek colonists in Ephesus identified her with their own Artemis, who was known to the Romans as Diana. The first systematic exploration of Ephesus was carried out by the English architect, J. T. Wood, whose chief purpose was to find the famous temple of Artemis. The search was begun on May 2, 1863, and after the most persistent endeavor the temple wall was discovered on May 2, 1869. The clue which led to the discovery was a Roman inscription which was found in the course of clearing the theater and which dates in the time of Trajan, that is about fifty years after the time of Paul. This inscription described a number of gold and silver images of Artemis (cf. Acts 19:24), weighing from three to seven pounds each, which were to be presented to the goddess and placed in her temple. According to the inscription, an endowment was provided for the care and cleaning of the images, and instruction given that when they were carried from the temple to the theater for the birthday anniversary of the goddess the procession was to enter the city by the Magnesian Gate and leave it afterward by the Coressian Gate. By finding the site of the two city gates mentioned and then following the road from the Magnesian Gate, Wood finally discovered the temple, which stood more than a mile northeast of the city proper.[50]

Wood continued his work until 1874, and in 1904-1905 further excavations were made and the entire history of the temple studied by David G. Hogarth on behalf of the British Museum.[51] In the meantime in 1896 the Austrian Archaeological Institute began its thorough and long-continued excavations at Ephesus, the results of which have appeared in a series of impressive publications.[52]

[49] Procopius (A.D. c.490-c.562), *Buildings*. v, i, 4-6. tr. H. B. Dewing, LCL VII (1940), pp.317-319.

[50] J. T. Wood, *Modern Discoveries on the Site of Ancient Ephesus*. 1890, pp.37-41, 84.

[51] Hogarth, *Excavations at Ephesus, The Archaic Artemisia*. 1908; and in EB VIII, pp.641-644.

[52] *Forschungen in Ephesos, veröffentlicht vom Österreichischen archaeologischen Institute*. 5 vols. 1906-44. For the excavations as resumed in 1954 see L. Vanden

It is believed that the earliest beginnings of the Artemision go back to a time around the end of the eighth century B.C. At that time only a small shrine was in existence, being little more than an enclosure containing a platform, a sacred tree, and an altar, and perhaps later a wooden image. In the centuries immediately following this shrine was reconstructed at least twice. Later these primitive structures were replaced by a much larger and more splendid temple which was probably begun about 550 B.C., and to which Croesus, the famous king of Lydia, contributed some beautiful columns.[53] The building work continued for 120 years,[54] and the final dedication was around 430 B.C. Herodotus speaks of this temple as standing in his day, and tradition has it that it was burned in 356 B.C. on the night in which Alexander the Great was born.

This temple, in turn, was succeeded by what is known as the Hellenistic temple, the plans for which were drawn by Dinocrates, the famous architect of Alexandria. This structure was begun probably before 350 B.C. and work was continuing on it when Alexander came to Ephesus in 334 B.C. and offered to pay the cost of its completion. It stood on a large platform nearly 240 wide and over 400 feet long. The temple itself was 180 feet wide and 360 feet long and boasted more than one hundred columns over fifty-five feet high. This Hellenistic temple endured until A.D. 262, when it was sacked and burned by the Goths. The altar foundations have been discovered, behind which no doubt stood the statue of the goddess. The roof was covered with large white marble tiles, and the building was adorned with sculpture, painting, and gold. The cry, "Great is Artemis of the Ephesians" (Acts 19:28, 34) was fully justified, therefore, by what we know of the external splendor of the cult center.[55]

Berghe and H. F. Mussche, *Bibliographie analytique de l'Assyriologie et de l'archéologie du Proche-Orient*, I, A, *L'Archéologie 1954-1955*, p.23.

[53] Herodotus. I, 92; A. S. Murray in JHS 10 (1889), p.9.

[54] Pliny, *Natural History*. XXXVI, 14.

[55] cf. W. M. Ramsay, *The Church in the Roman Empire before A.D. 170*. 1912, pp.135-139. Referring to the seven wonders of the ancient world ([1] the wall of Babylon; [2] the statue of Zeus at Olympia; [3] the hanging gardens of Babylon; [4] the pyramids; [5] the temple of Artemis at Ephesus; [6] the Colossus of Rhodes; [7] the Mausoleum of Halicarnassus), Antipater of Sidon (first century B.C.) praised the temple of Artemis as supreme among them all: "I have set eyes on the wall of lofty Babylon on which is a road for chariots, and the statue of Zeus by the Alpheus, and the hanging gardens, and the colossus of the Sun, and the huge labor of the high pyramids, and the vast tomb of Mausolus; but when I saw the house of Artemis that mounted to the clouds, those other marvels lost their brilliancy, and I said, 'Lo, apart from Olympus, the Sun never looked on aught so grand.'" *The Greek Anthology*. IX, 58. tr. W. R. Paton, LCL III (1948), p.31.

Yet today the site of the temple of Diana which was built originally on marshy soil[56] has become but a stagnant pond, inhabited by myriads of frogs, and is permanently flooded.

The theater of Ephesus is also of special interest as having been the scene of the tumult which was aroused by the work of Paul (Acts 19:29). The site of the theater, which is shown in Fig. 123, was in the hollow of a hill from which one looked out over the busiest parts of the city. The theater had an imposing façade with aediculae and niches and was adorned with fine statuary. While the existing remains represent a reconstruction carried out after the period of Paul, the plan of the structure is probably essentially the same as that of the apostle's time.

Another important feature of ancient Ephesus was the agora or marketplace. This was a great rectangular, colonnaded area entered by magnificent gateways and surrounded by halls and chambers. Nearby was the library, built with fine columns and with its walls recessed with niches for bookcases. Other buildings which have been excavated include gymnasia, baths, and burial monuments. One of the city's finest streets ran directly from the theater to the river harbor, being nearly one-half mile long and about thirty-five feet wide, and lined with halls on either side. Also at the harbor there were monumental gateways.

Later Christian times are represented not only by the remains of Justinian's Church of St. John already mentioned (p.347), but also by the very interesting ruins of the double Church of the Virgin Mary, where the Council of Ephesus was held in A.D. 431. This church was built probably around A.D. 350 on the foundations of a pagan building more than eight hundred feet long, probably a school, which had been destroyed in the preceding century. There is an extensive Christian catacomb at Ephesus, too, which dates from the fifth and sixth centuries, and is connected with the legend of the Seven Sleepers of Ephesus. According to the story, these were seven Christian youths at Ephesus who took refuge in a cave outside the city during the persecution under Decius (A.D. 250). By the emperor's command they were sealed up in the cave, but instead of perishing they fell into a sleep from which they were awakened nearly two hundred years later when some stones happened to be removed from the entrance. Thereupon the youths reaffirmed their

[56] Pliny, *Natural History*. xxxvi, 14.

Christian faith before Theodosius II (A.D. 408-450) and Bishop Maximus, and then died.

PHILIPPI

After making the memorable crossing from Troas to what we now know as Europe, Paul preached in Philippi, the first city of that district of Macedonia and a Roman colony (Acts 16:12). This city was founded in the middle of the fourth century B.C. by Philip of Macedon. "In earlier times Philippi was called Crenides," says Strabo, "and was only a small settlement, but it was enlarged after the defeat of Brutus and Cassius."[57] This Battle of Philippi took place in 42 B.C. and to celebrate their victory Antony and Octavian made the city a Roman colony, its name, Colonia Julia Philippensis, honoring the victory of the cause of Julius Caesar. The first citizens appear to have been veterans of this battle, and after the Battle of Actium in 31 B.C. dispossessed adherents of the defeated Antony also were settled here. The victory of Augustus over Antony and Cleopatra was commemorated by the additional title Augusta, so that the full name of the city became Colonia Augusta Julia Philippensis.

The territory of the colony included Neapolis (the modern Kavalla), the seaport at which Paul landed (Acts 16:11), some nine miles distant on the coast. From Neapolis the Via Egnatia, the main overland route from Asia to Rome, ran over Mount Symbolum and directly into Philippi where it passed the whole length of the city's forum, and where the marks of wagon and chariot wheels can still be seen scored to a depth of three and four inches.

The once proud Roman colony is known today as Felibedjik, or "Little Philippi," and its ruins cover many acres of ground (Fig. 124). Excavations were conducted here between 1914 and 1938 by the École Française d'Athènes, which have provided much information concerning the city.[58] The forum, which has been uncovered completely, was a rectangular area over 300 feet long and 150 feet wide. It was entered through five porticoes on three sides, and had

[57] *Geography.* VII, fr. 41.
[58] *Bulletin de correspondance hellénique.* 44 (1920), pp.406f.; 45 (1921), pp.543-547; 46 (1922), pp.527-531; 47 (1923), pp.534-536; 48 (1924), p.501; 49 (1925), p.462; 52 (1928), pp.492f.; 54 (1930), pp.502-506; 55 (1931), pp.499-502; 57 (1933), pp.279-285; 58 (1934), pp.257-261; 59 (1935), pp.285-291; 60 (1936), pp.478-480; 61 (1937), pp.463-468; 62 (1938), pp.1-3; Paul Collart, *Philippes ville de Macédoine depuis ses origines jusqu'à la fin de l'époque romaine.* 2 vols. 1937; Paul Lemerle, *Philippes et la Macedoine orientale a l'époque chretienne et byzantine.* 1945.

on its north side a rectangular podium to which steps gave access on both sides. This was evidently the tribunal from which orators spoke and magistrates dispensed justice. The forum was overlooked by temples at either end, and otherwise surrounded with public buildings. Most of these ruins date from a rebuilding in the second century, but it is probable that the plan of the forum was not radically different in Paul's day. Incidentally, the Roman rain-gutters are so well preserved that they still carry off water.

Other features of Philippi which have been studied by the French archeologists include the acropolis, the Roman baths, the theater dating originally perhaps from the fourth century B.C. and rebuilt in the second century A.D., and the Christian churches whose ruins belong to a much later date.

While most of the extant remains at Philippi belong to a period considerably after that of Paul, one important structure has been identified which is believed to date from the time of the apostle and even to figure in the account of his work given in Acts. This is a colonial archway whose ruins are to the west of the city. It probably was constructed at the time the Roman colony of Philippi was established, and it served to symbolize the dignity and privileges of the city. Also, it may have marked the line of the pomerium within which foreign deities were not permitted. As the Via Egnatia left Philippi and headed west it ran beneath this arch and then, at a distance of a little over one mile from the city, it crossed the river Ganga or Gangites.[59] It seems natural to conclude, therefore, that the "gate" mentioned in Acts 16:13 was this very archway, that the Jews met beyond it because this was required by law, and that the "riverside" where Paul spoke to the assembled women was on the edge of the Gangites.[60]

THESSALONICA

From Philippi Paul proceeded to Thessalonica, seventy miles distant along the Via Egnatia. According to Strabo, this city was founded by Cassander (c.315 B.C.) and named after his wife Thessalonica, the sister of Alexander the Great.[61] Because of its support of Antony and Octavian in the Battle of Philippi, it was rewarded by

[59] Appian (2d cent. A.D.), *Roman History, The Civil Wars.* IV, xiii, 106. tr. Horace White, LCL (1912-13) IV, p.319; Hirschfeld in PWRE I (1894), col. 2191.
[60] Collart, *Philippes ville de Macédoine*, pp.319-322, 458-460.
[61] *Geography.* VII, fr. 21.

being made a free city (*civitas libera*). In the time of Strabo, Thessalonica was the most populous city in Macedonia.[62]

Thessalonica is now the modern city of Salonika and an important seaport. In 1951 the population of the city proper was estimated at 217,049. The place enjoys a picturesque location at the head of the Gulf of Salonika and has mountains piled behind it. The course of the Via Egnatia is still represented by the main street of the city on which there also stands the Arch of Galerius (A.D. 305-311). At its western entrance to the city, the Via Egnatia was spanned until 1876 by another Roman arch called the Vardar Gate. This was of special interest since it carried an inscription, now in the British Museum, beginning, "In the time of the Politarchs. . . ." It is probably to be dated somewhere between 30 B.C. and A.D. 143, while several other Thessalonian inscriptions, including one definitely dated in the reign of Augustus, also mention Politarchs. This is of importance since in the Greek of Acts 17:6 the rulers of Thessalonica are called Politarchs. The term is otherwise unknown in extant Greek literature, but Luke's accuracy in the matter is entirely vindicated by the inscriptions.[63]

ATHENS

When Paul came to Athens (Acts 17:15) he was in one of the world's most famous centers of philosophy, architecture, and art, a city in whose ruins are still to be seen today some of the most beautiful things ever made by man. Systematic study of the topography of ancient Athens was begun in the seventeenth century by the French consuls Giraud and Chataignier and by the Capuchin monks, while toward the end of the century descriptions of Greece and Athens were published by the French physician Jacques Spon[64] and the Englishman George Wheeler.[65] The most important studies of the next century were made by James Stuart and Nicholas Revett, who spent three years at Athens (1751-1754) and published four large volumes on *The Antiquities of Athens* (3d ed. 1885). In the nineteenth century the work of W. M. Leake introduced the period of modern research.[66] The scientific investigations of modern times, in which Greek archeologists and the Greek government as well as

[62] *Geography.* VII, vii, 4.
[63] Ernest DeWitt Burton in AJT 2 (1898), pp.598-632.
[64] *Voyage d'Italie, de Dalmatie, de Grèce et du Levant.* 1678.
[65] *Journey into Greece.* 1682.
[66] *The Topography of Athens.* 2d ed. 1841.

at least six foreign archeological schools have participated, have made available a wealth of information concerning ancient Athens. Although the multitudinous details cannot be considered here, it is of much interest to be able to glimpse, little dimmed by time, the beauty of "the city of the violet crown," in which the culture of the ancient world reached its greatest height and where the apostle Paul once stood though but briefly.

The remarkable and precipitous rocky hill (512 feet high) known as the Acropolis was occupied by man as early as Neolithic times. In the seventh century B.C. the city of Athens emerged from obscurity and in the wars with Persia after 500 B.C. became the natural leader of Greece. Under the administration of Pericles around 443-429 B.C. Athens reached its golden age. The friend of Pericles, the sculptor Phidias (d. c.432 B.C.), superintended the adornment of the city with a magnificent array of temples, public buildings, and works of art. From the spoils of Marathon, Phidias made a colossal bronze statue of Athena Promachos, the goddess who fights in front, which was erected on the Acropolis and towered so high that mariners rounding the promontory of Sunium could see the sunlight flashing on her spear and helmet.[67] Then the incomparable Parthenon was built and a great gold and ivory statue of Athena by Phidias erected within (c.438 B.C.). Later came the completion of the stately entrance, the Propylaea, and of the beautiful temples, the Erechtheum and the shrine of Athena Nike, the goddess of victory. Of the Parthenon-crowned Acropolis J. P. Mahaffy wrote, "There is no ruin all the world over which combines so much striking beauty, so distinct a type, so vast a volume of history, so great a pageant of immortal memories. . . . All the Old World's culture culminated in Greece—all Greece in Athens—all Athens in its Acropolis—all the Acropolis in the Parthenon."[68]

Along the southern base of the Acropolis ran the colonnaded precinct of Asclepius, the god of healing. Just to the east and partly hollowed out from the declivity of the Acropolis was the lovely Theater of Dionysus. The earlier wooden structures of this theater were replaced by stone under the administration of Lycurgus around 337-323 B.C. Farther east was the Odeum of Pericles where musical contests were held, and beyond was the small circular Monument of

[67] Pausanias, *Description of Greece.* i, xxviii, 2. tr. W. H. S. Jones, LCL (1918-35) i, p.147.

[68] *Rambles and Studies in Greece.* 1878, p.83. For the buildings of the Acropolis see Nicolas Balanos, *Les monuments de l'Acropole, relèvement et conservation.* 1936.

Lysicrates, dedicated about 335 B.C. Southeast of the Acropolis stood the colossal temple of Olympian Zeus (Fig. 125). Measuring 354 feet by 135 feet at its base and towering to a height of over ninety feet, this was the largest temple in Greece and one of the largest in the ancient world. Begun by the Athenian ruler Pisistratus about 530 B.C., it stood unfinished for several centuries. Then the work was resumed by Antiochus IV Epiphanes, king of Syria, who employed the Roman architect Cossutius on the project. Even then the temple was not finished entirely, and it remained for the Emperor Hadrian to complete certain details, probably including the interior colonnades and the roof. For the most part the extant remains probably represent the work of Cossutius.[69]

After the sacred precinct of the Acropolis, the most important part of ancient Athens was the agora or marketplace which was the center of the city's civic and commercial life. According to the book of Acts (17:17) it was "in the agora" as well as in the Jewish synagogue that Paul "argued . . . every day with those who chanced to be there." The agora was some distance to the north of the west end of the Acropolis and covered a large area. The western portion of this region is recognized as having been the Hellenic agora, while the space to the east represents an enlargement of the marketplace probably financed by Julius Caesar and Augustus and hence known as the Roman agora. Early agora excavations were conducted by the Greek Archaeological Society, and by the German Archaeological Institute under Professor Wilhelm Dörpfeld. Then between 1931 and 1940 very large-scale excavations, which involved the moving of around 250,000 tons of earth, were undertaken in the western or specifically Greek section of the agora by the American School of Classical Studies at Athens under the leadership of T. Leslie Shear.[70]

On the eastern side of the Greek agora stood a colonnaded portico known as the Stoa of Attalos, which, together with the near-by so-called Stoa of the Giants, had been uncovered by the Greek Archaeological Society. Along the south side ran two large parallel stoas and on the west were a number of important buildings all of which have been unearthed by the American archeologists. The structures excavated on the west side of the agora include from north to south the

[69] Charles H. Weller, *Athens and Its Monuments*. 1924, pp.161-165.
[70] Shear in *Hesperia*. 2 (1933), pp.96-109, 451-474; 4 (1935), pp.311-339, 340-370; 5 (1936), pp.1-42; 6 (1937), pp.333-381; 7 (1938), pp.311-362; 8 (1939), pp.201-246; 9 (1940), pp.261-307; 10 (1941), pp.1-8. For Paul in the agora see Suzanne Halstead in *Quantulacumque*, pp.139-143.

Stoa of Zeus Eleutherios, the last name having been applied to Zeus because he delivered the Athenians from the Persian menace; the Temple of Apollo Patroos (the Father); the Sanctuary of the Mother of the Gods; the Bouleuterion, where the Athenian Council of Five Hundred assembled; and the circular Tholos, where the executive sections of the Council were maintained. Other buildings found in the agora are the Temple of Ares, the Odeum or Music Hall in which poets and musicians contended for prizes, and the Library dedicated to Trajan and located just south of the Stoa of Attalos.

Overlooking the agora from the west is the hill called Kolonos Agoraios, on which are the well preserved ruins of a temple now identified as that of Hephaistos, the god of fire and metal-working. To the east in the region of the Roman agora are the ruins of numerous shops and arcades, and just beyond is the Horologium popularly called the Tower of the Winds. The latter was an octagonal marble structure with sun dials on the exterior and probably a water-clock on the inside. It served as a public timepiece for the city of Athens and therefore was near the chief trading center. Like the Roman agora, the Horologium was probably constructed in the second half of the first century B.C.[71]

In view of the address by Paul reported in Acts 17:22-31, special interest attaches to the Areopagus. Areopagus or Hill of Ares is the name of a bare, rocky hill, about 377 feet high, immediately northwest of the Acropolis and separated from it by a narrow declivity now largely filled in. Steps cut in the rock lead to the top where rough, rock-hewn benches, forming three sides of a square, can still be seen. In ancient times this was the meeting place of the Areopagus court. This court or council was composed of city fathers and in early times had supreme authority in both political and religious matters. In the time of Pericles the council became largely a criminal court, but in Roman times was charged again with the care of religion and of education. From its place of assembly the court itself was called the Areopagus, and in Acts 17:34 we find one of its members referred to as an Areopagite. The word Areopagus in Acts 17:19, 22 might be interpreted, therefore, either as referring to the hill or (v. 19 ASV margin) to the court. In either case, however, it remains probable that the place of Paul's speech was on this hill, since it was the customary meeting place of the court.[72]

[71] Henry S. Robinson in AJA 47 (1943), pp.291-305.
[72] Walther Judeich, *Topographie von Athen* (in Walter Otto, ed., *Handbuch der Altertumswissenschaft.* III, ii, 2, 2d ed. 1931), p.299; Oscar Broneer in BA 21 (1958), p.27 n.4.

It is true that the Areopagus court seems to have met at times in the Stoa Basileios or Royal Stoa, and if this happened to be the case when Paul was in Athens then the place of his address would have to be sought in this stoa. The stoa in question is identified by some with the already mentioned Stoa of Zeus Eleutherios at the northwest corner of the agora as now excavated,[73] but is believed by others to have lain yet farther north. The point cannot be decided at present since the excavations did not reach the northern limits of the agora. As a matter of fact, work in this northern region may be long delayed because of the presence of an important modern street and also of a railway line.[74]

In his Areopagus address Paul is reported (Acts 17:23) to have referred to an altar with the inscription, "To an unknown god," or "To the unknown god."[75] Not far from the time when Paul was in Athens, the city was visited by Apollonius of Tyana. This remarkable wandering Neo-Pythagorean philosopher, whose career parallels that of Paul's in some regards, was born at Tyana in Cappadocia, around the beginning of the Christian era, and died at Ephesus, probably in A.D. 98. After studying in Tarsus and in the temple of Asclepius at Aegae on the Gulf of Iskanderun, he traveled into all parts of the known world, at one time enduring trial and imprisonment in Rome. The last ten years of his life were spent in Greece. The biography of Apollonius was written by Flavius Philostratus (A.D. c.170-c.245) at the request of Julia Domna, the wife of the Emperor Severus, but not published until after her death in A.D. 217. Philostratus was able to draw upon a collection of letters by Apollonius and upon a travel journal by the Assyrian Damis, the disciple and companion of Apollonius. Nevertheless he added large amounts of legendary and miraculous material so that the *Life* resembles an historical novel. The biography is of interest to us, however, because it contains a remark of Apollonius to the effect that it is a proof of wisdom "to speak well of all the gods, especially at Athens, where altars are set up in honour even of unknown gods."[76]

[73] Homer A. Thompson in *Hesperia*. 6 (1937), pp.5-77. Wilhelm Dörpfeld (*Alt-Athen und seine Agora* [Heft 2, 1939], pp.146-167) thinks that the Stoa Basileios was the building immediately south of the Stoa of Zeus which the Americans called the Temple of Apollo Patroos.

[74] T. Leslie Shear in *Hesperia*. 4 (1935), p.354; 6 (1937), p.360.

[75] The article is absent in the Greek, but since this is common in inscriptions, either translation is permissible.

[76] ἀγνώστων δαιμόνων βωμοί. Philostratus, *The Life of Apollonius of Tyana*. VI, 3. tr. F. C. Conybeare, LCL (1912) II, p.13.

Another remarkable traveler who visited Athens at a somewhat later date than Apollonius was the geographer Pausanias. Born in Lydia, he had already traveled in Palestine and Egypt before he came to Greece. He visited Athens in the period between A.D. 143 and 159 and then devoted the first thirty chapters of his *Description of Greece* to an extensive and accurate topographical account of Athens as he saw it. He says that on the road from the Phaleron Bay harbor to the city he had noticed "altars of the gods named Unknown, and of heroes,"[77] and also mentions "an altar of Unknown Gods"[78] at Olympia.

Although no such altar now remains at Athens, a comparable one was discovered in 1909 at Pergamum in the sacred precincts of the temple of Demeter (Fig. 126). A corner of the stone is broken and a portion of the inscription is lost but it is probably to be read:

> To unknown gods,
> Capito,
> torch-bearer.[79]

A somewhat similar altar stands on the Palatine Hill at Rome and dates from about 100 B.C. Its inscription begins, *Sei deo sei deivae sac[rum]*, "Sacred to a god or goddess."[80]

After the time of Paul the Emperor Hadrian (A.D. 117-138) added to the city of Athens with lavish benefactions. About A.D. 143 a wealthy Roman resident, Herodes Atticus, rebuilt the old stadium, making it into an immense marble structure which would accommodate 44,000 spectators. The same man also later built a theater at the southwestern base of the Acropolis, known as the Odeum, in memory of his wife. In Byzantine times Athens sank into the position of a provincial town and was robbed of many of its works of art. The Athena Promachos and the Athena Parthenos were taken away to adorn Constantinople, and other spoliation took place when the church of Hagia Sophia was rebuilt in the sixth century. The Parthe-

---

[77] βωμοὶ δὲ θεῶν τε ὀνομαζομένων ᾿Αγνώστων καὶ ἡρώων. I, i, 4.

[78] ᾿Αγνώστων θεῶν βωμός. V, xiv, 8.

[79] Adolf Deissmann, *Paul*. tr. William E. Wilson. 2d ed. 1926, pp.288-291.

[80] Hammerton, *Wonders of the Past*. I, p.524. Although it is possible to give exact literary and epigraphic attestation only to the plural form "to unknown gods," it would have been quite possible even in a polytheistic environment for someone to have felt a sense of gratitude "to *an* unknown god." Therefore it is unnecessary to argue with E. Norden (*Agnostos Theos* [1913], p.121) that the author of the Areopagus address first changed the plural form to the singular in order to obtain the text for a monotheistic sermon.

non, the Erechtheum, and other temples, however, were converted into Christian churches and thus preserved throughout the Middle Ages. When the Acropolis was taken by the Turks in 1458 the Parthenon was transformed into a mosque, and a minaret was built at its southwestern corner. The Turkish commandant used the Propylaea as a residence and employed the Erechtheum for his harem. In 1687 the Venetians bombarded the Acropolis where the Turks were entrenched, and a bomb from a mortar struck the Parthenon and blew up a powder magazine in it, damaging the building severely.[81] The Turks remained in possession of the Acropolis until 1833, when Athens became the capital of the independent kingdom of Greece. At that time it was only a village of 5,000 inhabitants, but in 1951 the population of Athens proper was estimated at 565,084.

Eventually philosophers like Justin Martyr (A.D. c.100-c.165) were to recognize that in Christ the true Word had become manifest, only fragments of which had been laid hold of by the search and speculation of Socrates and the other thinkers of the past, and thus the Greek tradition was to be brought into relation to the Christian message.[82] But the sophisticated Athenians (cf. Acts 17:21) of Paul's time gave little serious attention to his message,[83] and Paul apparently went on soon to Corinth, convinced that "the wisdom of this world is folly with God" (I Corinthians 3:19), and seeking hearers to whom the foolishness of the preaching would seem a wisdom greater than that of men (cf. I Corinthians 1:21, 25).

CORINTH

In going from Athens to Corinth (Acts 18:1) Paul was moving from the intellectual center of Greece to its most splendid commercial city. Whereas Athens was situated on the Greek mainland near the southern end of the great plain of Attica, Corinth was just across the narrow isthmus which connects central Greece with the Peloponnesus. This isthmus was a natural meeting place for trade from East and West. Ships from Asia Minor, Syria, and Egypt put in to the

[81] Theodor E. Mommsen in AJA 45 (1941), pp.544-556.

[82] *Apology.* II, 10 (ANF I, p.191); cf. Paul Elmer More, *Christ the Word.* 1927, pp.9-11.

[83] Compared with the wealth of evidence concerning pagan Athens, there are few traces of the Christian community in this city during the first five centuries, the chief material being simple epitaphs from humble tombstones, dating perhaps in the fourth century and later. See John S. Creaghan and A. E. Raubitschek, *Early Christian Epitaphs from Athens.* 1947.

port of Cenchreae (cf. Romans 16:1) on the eastern side of the isthmus, while those of Italy, Sicily, and Spain docked at Lechaeum, the harbor on the western side. The distance between these two ports was less than ten miles, and while the cargoes of the larger vessels were transshipped, the smaller boats were hauled across bodily on a sort of tramway. Otherwise, the circumnavigation of stormy Cape Malea,[84] requiring a detour of two hundred miles, was necessary. Naturally enough the desirability of cutting a canal across the isthmus was recognized by many men including Alexander the Great, Julius Caesar, and Nero. In A.D. 66 Nero went so far as to dig the first dirt of such a canal with a golden spade, and to set at the task of excavating it six thousand young Jews recently captured by Vespasian in the Jewish War which had just begun. But this and all the other similar projects of antiquity were abandoned[85] and it was not until A.D. 1881-1893 that the present canal was cut. This canal runs straight across the isthmus at its narrowest point and is four miles in length. It is crossed by the 170-foot-high iron bridge of the Athens and Corinth railway. Situated but one and one-half miles south of this isthmus and commanding the ports on either side of it, the city of Corinth obviously was destined for commercial greatness. Pindar called the Isthmus of Corinth "the bridge of the sea,"[86] and Strabo summed up the situation accurately when he said, "Corinth is called 'wealthy' because of its commerce, since it is situated on the Isthmus and is master of two harbors, of which the one leads straight to Asia, and the other to Italy; and it makes easy the exchange of merchandise from both countries that are so far distant from each other."[87]

The site of Corinth was occupied as anciently as in the Neolithic and Chalcolithic ages,[88] and in Greek mythology the city was the home of Medea, Sisyphus, and Bellerophon. From early times the distinctive cult associated with Corinth was that of the worship of Aphrodite. In the eighth and seventh centuries B.C. Corinth estab-

---

[84] cf. Strabo, *Geography*. VIII, vi, 20: "But when you double Malea, forget your home."

[85] Philostratus (*Life of Apollonius*. IV, 24) records the report that Nero stopped the work of cutting the canal "because Egyptian men of science explained to him the nature of the seas, and declared that the sea above Lechaeum would flood and obliterate the island of Aegina."

[86] Pindar (c.522-c.448 B.C.), *The Nemean Odes*. VI, 40. tr. John Sandys, LCL (1915), p.373.

[87] *Geography*. VIII, vi, 20.

[88] John G. O'Neill, *Ancient Corinth, with a Topographical Sketch of the Corinthia*, Part I, *From the Earliest Times to 404 B.C.* 1930, pp.60f.; Saul S. Weinberg in *Hesperia*. 6 (1937), pp.487-524.

lished colonies at Syracuse and Corcyra, and under the tyrants Cypselus (c.657-c.629 B.C.) and Periander (c.629-c.585 B.C.) rose to great prominence and prosperity. She dominated extensive trade routes, and Corinthian bronze and pottery were exported widely over the Mediterranean. About 146 B.C. Corinth warred with Rome and upon defeat was completely destroyed, probably because of commercial jealousy. The inhabitants were sold into slavery and for one hundred years the site of the city lay desolate. Then in 46 B.C. Julius Caesar refounded the city as the Colonia Laus Julia Corinthiensis, and peopled it with Italian freedmen and dispossessed Greeks.[89] Its commercial prosperity was recovered rapidly, and Augustus made Corinth the capital of Achaia and seat of its proconsul (cf. Acts 18:12). After the time of Paul, Hadrian beautified the city with public works. In the Middle Ages it continued to be a flourishing place until captured by the Sicilians in 1406 and the Turks in 1458. In 1858 the ancient city suffered a terrible earthquake and the survivors built New Corinth on a new site three and one-half miles northeast of the old city. This city, too, was almost wholly destroyed by earthquake in 1928, but was rebuilt and thereafter attained a population of some 10,000.

The excavation of ancient Corinth has been conducted over a period of many years, beginning in 1896, by the American School of Classical Studies at Athens.[90] The city spreads out over two terraces, one about one hundred feet higher than the other, while in the southwestern background a towering mountain, Acrocorinth,[91] rises 1,500

[89] Strabo, *Geography*. VIII, iv, 8; vi, 23; XVII, iii, 15.

[90] See AJA 34 (1930), pp.403-454; 37 (1933), pp.554-572; 39 (1935), pp.53-75; 40 (1936), pp.21-45, 466-484; 41 (1937), pp.539-552; 42 (1938), pp.362-370; 43 (1939), pp.255-267, 592-600; O. Broneer in BA 14 (1951), pp.78-96; and various volumes of *Corinth, Results of Excavations Conducted by the American School of Classical Studies at Athens*, including I, 1, Harold N. Fowler and Richard Stillwell, *Introduction, Topography, Architecture*. 1932; I, 2, R. Stillwell, Robert L. Scranton, and Sarah E. Freeman, *Architecture*. 1941; I, 3, R. L. Scranton, *Monuments in the Lower Agora and North of the Archaic Temple*. 1951; II, R. Stillwell, *The Theatre*. 1952; III, 1, Carl W. Blegen, R. Stillwell, Oscar Broneer, and Alfred R. Bellinger, *Acrocorinth, Excavations in 1926*. 1930; III, 2, Rhys Carpenter and Antoine Bon, *The Defenses of Acrocorinth and the Lower Town*. 1936; IV, 1, Ida Thallon-Hill and Lida S. King, *Decorated Architectural Terracottas*. 1929; IV, 2, O. Broneer, *Terracotta Lamps*. 1930; V, T. Leslie Shear, *The Roman Villa*. 1930; VI, Katharine M. Edwards, *Coins 1896-1929*. 1933; VII, 1, Saul S. Weinberg, *The Geometric and Orientalizing Pottery*. 1943; VIII, 1, Benjamin D. Meritt, *Greek Inscriptions 1896-1927*. 1931; VIII, 2, Allen B. West, *Latin Inscriptions 1896-1926*. 1931; IX, Franklin P. Johnson, *Sculpture 1896-1923*. 1931; X, O. Broneer, *The Odeum*. 1932; XI, Charles H. Morgan II, *The Byzantine Pottery*. 1942; XIV, Carl Roebuck, *The Asklepieion and Lerna*. 1951; XV, 1, Agnes N. Stillwell, *The Potters' Quarter*. 1948.

[91] Strabo, *Geography*. VIII, iv, 8; vi, 21.

feet above the city and 1,886 feet above the sea. In the center of the city was a large agora or marketplace, surrounded with colonnades and monuments. On the north side the road from Lechaeum entered the agora through a stately gateway or propylaea. Just east of this was the famous fountain of Pirene, and from the southern side of the marketplace the road to Cenchreae departed. West of the Lechaeum road and north of the marketplace, on a low hill was the temple of Apollo. It was built probably in the sixth century B.C.,[92] and seven of its fine Doric columns still stand. A corner of this temple is shown in Fig. 127, with Acrocorinth looming in the background. Some distance away to the northwest was the theater of Corinth, built in the Greek period and repaired under the Romans. On the summit of Acrocorinth was a temple of Aphrodite.

Among the shops opening onto the agora at Corinth were ones which had clearly been used for the sale of meat and other foodstuffs. Interestingly enough, each was provided with a well connecting with a subterranean channel through which flowed fresh water. Evidently this arrangement provided the shops not only with a source of water but also with a means of cooling perishable products.[93] An inscription found there, belonging to the last years of Augustus or to the reign of Tiberius, calls one of these shops a "market," using in the Latin exactly the same word which Paul employs in the Greek in I Corinthians 10:25.[94] Another Corinth inscription mentions a certain Erastus who may very well be identified with the Erastus named as a friend of Paul's in Romans 16:23, II Timothy 4:20, and Acts 19:22.[95]

On the Lechaeum road in Corinth, at the foot of the marble steps leading to the propylaea, a stone was found in 1898 which once formed the lintel over a doorway. It bears an inscription in Greek and although the stone is broken at the right and damaged at the left the inscription clearly reads "Synagogue of the Hebrews."[96] The inscription is usually dated somewhere between 100 B.C. and A.D. 200.[97] Consequently it may once have stood over the entrance to the synagogue in which Paul preached (Acts 18:4), or have marked a

[92] Benjamin Powell in AJA 9 (1905), pp.44-63; Saul S. Weinberg in *Hesperia.* 8 (1939), pp.191-199.
[93] Oscar Broneer in *The Lutheran Companion.* Nov. 12, 1942, p.1306.
[94] Macellum, μάκελλον. H. J. Cadbury in JBL 53 (1934), pp.134-141; Gerhard Kittel, ed., *Theologisches Wörterbuch zum Neuen Testament.* (1933-), IV, pp.373f.
[95] H. J. Cadbury (in JBL 50 [1931], pp.42-58) questions the identification, but see C. C. McCown in AJA 50 (1946), p. 426.
[96] First published by Benjamin Powell in AJA 7 (1903), pp.60f.
[97] DLO p.12 n.8.

later building on the same site. The letters, which are two and one-half to three and one-half inches high, are poorly cut and suggest that the synagogue was not wealthy. This would accord with Paul's characterization of the Corinthian Christians in his letter to them (I Corinthians 1:26). Since the stone is of considerable weight it may be presumed that it was found not far from the place where the synagogue stood, and if this is correct then the synagogue was on or near the road to Lechaeum and not far from the marketplace. The west side of the Lechaeum road was lined with colonnades and shops close under the hill where the temple of Apollo stood, and the more probable location of the synagogue was therefore on the east side of the street. This area was in the main a residential district, as the many remaining house walls indicate, and consequently the house of Titus Justus could easily have been "next door" (Acts 18:7).

In the agora one of the prominent features is an elevated platform which once served as an outdoor speaker's platform. It is mentioned in an inscription by the Latin name *rostra* which is the equivalent of the Greek word by which the "judgment-seat" (ASV) or "tribunal" (RSV)[98] at Corinth is referred to in Acts 18:12-17, and is doubtless to be identified with the very place where Paul stood before Gallio. In the photograph reproduced in Fig. 128 the marketplace is viewed from the east and the ruins of the rostra appear to the left of the center of the picture. In the distance at the extreme left are the slopes of Acrocorinth and at the right is the temple of Apollo.

The Gallio who was proconsul of Achaia when Paul was in Corinth (Acts 18:12) was the elder brother of the philosopher Seneca and is mentioned by Tacitus[99] and Dio Cassius.[100] An important inscription has been found which makes it possible to date Gallio's arrival in Corinth as proconsul quite accurately. It was discovered at Delphi, which was on the other side of the Gulf of Corinth some six miles inland. The inscription begins: "Tiberius Claudius Caesar Augustus Germanicus, Pontifex Maximus, of tribunican authority for the 12th time, imperator the 26th time, father of the country, consul for the 5th time, honorable, greets the city of the Delphians." The emperor then goes on to say that he has long been well disposed to the city of Delphi, and that he has observed the religious ceremonies of the Pythian Apollo that were held there. The actual business with which

[98] τὸ βῆμα.
[99] *Annals.* xv, 73.
[100] *Roman History.* LXI, xxxv, 2.

the communication deals is lost in the broken places in the inscription, but it is possible to make out further along the words, "as Lucius Junius Gallio, my friend, and the proconsul of Achaia wrote. . . ." This inscription therefore provides testimony to the fact that Gallio did serve as proconsul of Achaia. Furthermore, at the time the emperor's letter was written to Delphi, Gallio had evidently been in office long enough to have given Claudius information of importance concerning the Delphians. Since the reference to the 12th tribunican year and the 26th imperatorship of Claudius dates this communication between January and August of the year A.D. 52, Gallio must have arrived in Corinth not later than the year 51. Dio Cassius reports a decree of Claudius that new officials should start for their provinces by the first day of June,[101] and therefore Gallio must have entered upon his proconsulship in Corinth in the summer, probably around July 1, in A.D. 51. The impression given by the book of Acts is that Gallio had arrived in Corinth only shortly before the time when the Jews brought Paul into his presence. Since at that time the apostle had been in the city a year and six months (Acts 18:11), we can date Paul's arrival in Corinth with considerable confidence at the beginning of the year 50.[102]

ROME

Already upon his last visit to Achaia Paul was purposing to go to Rome (Romans 15:23-28; Acts 19:21). That intention was achieved, though hardly in the way he might have wished, when the apostle was taken to Rome as a prisoner in the charge of Julius the centurion (Acts 27:1; 28:16). After the sea voyage, on which he suffered shipwreck,[103] Paul landed finally at Puteoli (Acts 28:13), the modern Puzzuoli, on the northern shore of the Bay of Naples.

Fifteen miles east of Puteoli was the town of Herculaneum, lying at the foot of the volcano Vesuvius, by which it was to be destroyed in A.D. 79. A discovery was made at Herculaneum in 1938 which may have connection with early Christianity and with Paul. In an upper

---

[101] *Roman History.* LVII, xiv, 5.

[102] Deissmann, *Paul*, pp.265-283; cf. Lemerle, *Philippes et la Macedoine orientale a l'époque chretienne et byzantine*, pp.18f.

[103] For the shipwreck voyage see Edwin Smith in Tom Davin, ed., *The Rudder Treasury*. 1953, pp.55-66, who reckons that a ship hove-to and drifting before the northeaster (Acts 27:14), would make about thirty-six miles in twenty-four hours, or 477 miles in thirteen and one-quarter days, which agrees almost exactly with a measured distance of 476.4 miles from a point under the lee of Clauda to the entrance of St. Paul's Bay on Malta.

room of the so-called "Bicentenary House" a stucco wall panel was found which contained a somewhat irregular depression roughly in the form of a Latin cross. There were nail holes in this depression and also elsewhere in the panel. On the floor beneath was a piece of wooden furniture. It seemed possible that a wooden cross had once been affixed to the wall at this point and then been torn off and a wooden covering nailed over the area. Likewise the piece of furniture might have been a sort of altar. If this is the correct interpretation of the evidence, then the room may have been a small chapel used by some early Christian or Christians and the use of the cross may even reflect the preaching of the cross by Paul (cf. I Corinthians 1:18, etc.) during his seven-day stay at nearby Puteoli. The removal of the cross and the covering over of the panel containing its impression could have been done by the Christians themselves in a time of persecution such as that by Nero in A.D. 64.[104] On the other hand, the irregularity of the cross-shaped depression and the many nail marks scattered over the area lead some to advance the alternative explanation that it was simply some practical object, such as a wall cabinet, which was anchored to the wall at this place and upon removal left these marks.[105]

At Pompeii, twenty-five miles east of Puteoli, a rudely scrawled inscription was found on the wall of a room, which may have contained a disparaging remark about Christians. This graffito is in Latin characters, and the word *Christianos* seems unmistakable. Otherwise the text is difficult to interpret. It has been suggested that it is actually in the Aramaic language, although transliterated in Latin letters, and on that basis the whole sentence has been translated: "A strange mind has driven A. and he has pressed in among the Christians who make a man a prisoner as a laughingstock." In that case the inscription might have been an expression of pagan opinion of Christian missionary work, and this might have been the very room in which some early Christian missionary of about the time of Paul taught. On this basis the text has been called the first known non-Christian reference to Christians. At all events the date of the inscription must be before A.D. 79 since, like Herculaneum, Pompeii was destroyed at that time.[106]

[104] Amadeo Maiuri in *Rendiconti della Pontificia Accademia Romana di Archeologia.* 15 (1939), pp.193-218; cf. William L. Holladay in JBR 19 (1951), pp.16-19; Parrot, *Golgotha and the Church of the Holy Sepulchre*, p.117.

[105] L. de Bruyne in RAC 21 (1945), pp.281-309; Erich Dinkler in ZTK 48 (1951), pp.158f.

[106] H. Leclercq in DACL VI, cols. 1482-1484; W. R. Newbold in AJA 30 (1926), pp.291-295; A. T. Olmstead in JNES 1 (1942), p.41.

From Puteoli Paul presumably went on to Capua, twenty miles away, to reach the Via Appia, the main highway to Rome. "The worn and well-known track of Appia, queen of the long roads," as this highway was described by Statius (A.D. c.45-c.96),[107] was built from Rome to Capua by the censor Appius Claudius Caecus in about 312 B.C. and was later extended until by around 244 B.C. it reached Brundisium (modern Brindisi), the important harbor 350 miles away on the southeastern coast. From Capua it was 132 miles to Rome. At Tarracina (modern Terracina) the Via Appia touched the coast, then ran for the final fifty-six miles almost as straight as an arrow across the Pontine Marshes and the Alban Hills to Rome. The Forum Appii or Market of Appius (Acts 28:15), where the first of "the brethren" met Paul, was a post station forty-three miles from Rome, and is mentioned by Horace (65-8 B.C.) as the usual halt at the end of the first day's journey from Rome.[108] Tres Tabernae or Three Taverns (Acts 28:15) was a village nearly ten miles farther on toward Rome, and is mentioned by Cicero (106-43 B.C.) as the point where a branch road from Antium joined the Appian Way.[109]

Rome itself, with Nero (Fig. 129) then on the throne (A.D. 54-68), was at that time approaching the height of its imperial greatness, and Martial (A.D. c.40-c.102) was soon to hail the proud capital of the world as "Rome, goddess of earth and of the nations, that has no peer and no second."[110] We shall seek to gain a swift glimpse of the city as it was when Paul entered it, in the midst of Nero's reign and before the great fire of A.D. 64. For the purpose of such an inquiry there is available an immense wealth of notices in ancient literature, inscriptions, and archeological monuments, all of which have been the object of intensive study by scholars of many nations, by the Roman Catholic Church, and by the Italian government.

Nearing Rome, the Via Appia crossed what is known as the Campagna di Roma, the low plain surrounding the city. Nearby ran the great aqueduct Claudia which was completed by the Emperor Claudius in A.D. 50 (Fig. 130). The water which it brought from more than forty miles away was carried across the Campagna on arches 110 feet high, the remains of which are yet very impressive.[111]

[107] *Silvae.* II, ii, 12. tr. J. H. Mozley, LCL (1928) I, p.97.
[108] I, v, 3-6. tr. H. R. Fairclough, LCL (1926), p.65.
[109] *Letters to Atticus.* II, xii. tr. E. O. Winstedt, LCL (1913-19) I, p.143.
[110] *Terrarum dea gentiumque Roma,*
    Cui par est nihil et nihil secundum.
Epigrams. XII, viii, 1f. tr. W. C. A. Ker, LCL (1925-27) II, p.325.
[111] cf. Pliny, *Natural History.* XXXVI, xxiv.

This was but one of eight or nine conduits and aqueducts which at that time brought water to Rome from distant springs and rivers.[112] Of them Sextus Julius Frontinus, their keeper at the close of the first century A.D., remarked, "With such an array of indispensable structures carrying so many waters, compare, if you will, the idle Pyramids or the useless though famous works of the Greeks!"[113]

On the Campagna, the Via Appia began to penetrate the suburbs of the city. The plain was dotted with houses, gardens, and magnificent villas. Nearing the city the houses naturally became closer together and smaller in size. Deep within the city of the first century A.D. was the old Servian Wall, through which the Via Appia entered by the Porta Capena. This ancient wall is named for King Servius Tullius (c.578-c.534 B.C.) but was actually built by order of the republican Senate between 378 and 352 B.C. After the Punic Wars of the third and second centuries B.C. it was allowed to fall into decay and the city spread far beyond its limits. Some portions of it still exist, and the remains of the Porta Capena have been found near where the Via di San Gregorio now unites with the Via di Porta San Sebastiano. In the third century A.D. the approach of the barbarians led to the building of a new wall. It was begun by the Emperor Aurelian (A.D. 270-275) and completed by the Emperor Probus (A.D. 276-282). Restored by later emperors and popes, the Aurelian Wall still surrounds the city on the left bank of the Tiber. The wall on the right bank of the Tiber dates mainly from the time of Pope Urban VIII (1623-1644).[114]

The main part of the city, which was attained when one reached the Porta Capena, was built upon a famous group of seven hills (cf. Revelation 17:9), past which the Tiber River sweeps in three great

[112] (1) The first, the Appia, was constructed about 312 B.C. by Appius Claudius Caecus, who also built the Via Appia. It was a ten-mile covered tunnel from springs east of the city. (2) The Anio Vetus, built around 272 B.C., brought water 41 miles from the river Anio in the Apennines. (3) The Marcia was built about 145 B.C. by Marcius the praetor. It was 58 miles long, the last seven miles being on arches high enough to carry the flow to the summit of the Capitol. (4) The Tepula of around 127 B.C. was small and short. (5) The Julia and (6) the Virgo were built by Agrippa in 33 B.C. and 20 B.C. respectively. (7) The Alsietina was constructed by Augustus. (8) The Claudia was started by Caligula in A.D. 36 and finished by Claudius. An archway of the Claudia was made by Aurelian into one of the gates of his city wall, and is now the Porta Maggiore. (9) The Anio Novus also was begun by Caligula but only completed in A.D. 86. Esther B. Van Deman, *The Building of the Roman Aqueducts.* 1934; Thomas Ashby, *The Aqueducts of Ancient Rome.* 1935.

[113] *The Aqueducts of Rome.* I, 16. tr. C. E. Bennett, LCL (1925), pp.357-359.

[114] I. A. Richmond, *The City Wall of Imperial Rome.* 1930; G. Säflund, *Le mura di Roma reppublicana.* 1932.

curves. Standing at the Porta Capena, the Aventine hill was on the left, the Caelian on the right, and the Palatine directly ahead. Beyond the Palatine was the Capitoline, which rises near the inner curve of the Tiber and the island in the river. Ranged north of the Caelian hill were the Esquiline, Viminal, and Quirinal hills. The plain west of the Quirinal and enclosed in the outward curve of the Tiber was the Campus Martius. Across the Tiber, on its right or western bank, was the commanding height of the hill of Janiculum, and beyond it at the northwestern end of Rome the Ager Vaticanus or Vatican district. The latter included a low eminence known as Mons Vaticanus and a plain beside the river called the Campus Vaticanus.

The Via Appia and the other highroads which led into Rome, such as the Via Ostiensis and Via Latina on the south, the Via Labicana and Via Tiburtina on the east, and the Via Nomentana, Via Salaria, Via Pinciana, and Via Flaminia on the north, were good thoroughfares, fifteen to twenty feet in width. In many cases these highways continued directly into the heart of the city in the form of fine avenues, and frequently the streets of modern Rome follow their lines exactly. The Via Flaminia, for example, which was constructed by the Roman statesman Caius Flaminius Nepos about 200 B.C., continued as the Via Lata directly to the foot of the Capitoline hill. It is represented by the splendid central avenue of modern Rome, the Corso Umberto Primo, beneath which at a depth of fifteen or twenty feet the lava paving blocks of the ancient street are still found.[115]

Within the old Republican Wall and on the Seven Hills, however, many of the streets were narrow, steep, and crooked. They were usually called *vici*, as for example the Vicus Longus and the Vicus Patricius. In cases where they made steep ascents and descents they were frequently known as *clivi*, as for example the Clivus Capitolinus and the Clivus Palatinus. It was required that they be at least nine and one-half feet wide to allow for projecting balconies. In many parts of the inner city they formed an inextricably tangled labyrinth. It was said that if they could have been straightened out and laid end to end they would have reached for more than sixty miles.[116] They were often defiled by refuse and were quite unlighted by night. By day they were jammed with pedestrians, horsemen, litters, and carrying chairs, and by night they were filled with the noise of trans-

[115] Rodolfo Lanciani, *Ancient and Modern Rome.* 1925, p.145.
[116] Pliny, *Natural History.* III, ix, 67.

port carts of all sorts, such wheeled vehicles being permitted within the city only between dusk and dawn.[117]

In the residential districts the dwellings were of two chief types. The *domus* was the home of the wealthy. It spread out horizontally in a series of halls, and had its doors and windows opening on its interior courts. The *insula* was the residence of the masses. It was an apartment house, filling a square or block, and rising vertically to surprising heights. Augustus found it necessary to place a limit of seventy feet on the height of structures on the public streets,[118] but this still allowed apartment houses of three, four, five, and six stories to be common. In external appearance these apartment houses, the finest of which were adorned with balconies and brightened with window gardens, would have seemed quite modern. Their conveniences within were strictly limited, however. Light and heat were inadequate. Water from the aqueducts seems to have been conveyed only to the ground floors, which alone were connected with Rome's excellent network of sewers.[119] Often, too, builders and landlords sought to increase their profits by cheap construction and poor repair even though the lives of the renters were imperiled by the frequent collapses of the buildings which ensued. In his satire on life at Rome Juvenal cried, "Who at cool Praeneste, or at Volsinii amid its leafy hills, was ever afraid of his house tumbling down? . . . But here we inhabit a city propped up for the most part by slats: for that is how the landlord patches up the cracks in the old wall, bidding the inmates sleep at ease under a roof ready to tumble about their ears."[120]

Thus Rome was a teeming metropolitan center at the time when Paul came to it. The population of the city in the first century A.D. has usually been estimated at about 1,200,000, or substantially the same as the modern population which in January 1939 was 1,284,600. In 1941, however, the discovery of an inscription at Ostia was announced with statistics indicating that in A.D. 14, the year in which Tiberius began to reign, the city of Rome had a population of 4,100,-000 inhabitants.[121] Statistics from 250 years after the time of Paul

---

[117] A. Grenier in Ch. Daremberg and Edmond Saglio, eds., *Dictionnaire des antiquités grecques et romaines d'après les textes et les monuments.* (1877-1919), v, cols.861-863.

[118] Strabo, *Geography.* v, iii, 7.

[119] The central collector for the system of sewers was the Cloaca Maxima, the mouth of which still can be seen opening into the Tiber, and which was in use until very recently. Pliny, *Natural History.* xxxvi, xxiv.

[120] *Satire.* iii, 190-196.   [121] AJA 45 (1941), p.438.

list 1,797 *domus* and 46,602 *insulae,* or blocks of apartment houses, in the city.[122]

The great city was fortunate in the possession of many parks and gardens. It has been calculated that one-eighth of the total area of the city was given over to parks and open spaces, whereas in modern London, for example, only one-tenth of the total area is so used.[123] In the Campus Martius numerous garden porticoes were to be found, many of which had been built by Augustus and his wealthy friends. These were large parallelograms of green enclosed by a colonnade. For the enjoyment of the public, the twelve largest of these porticoes protected an area of 28,000 square yards from sun and rain. Under such shelter it was possible to walk all the way from the Forum Boarium, which was between the Palatine hill and the Tiber, to the opposite end of the city where Hadrian's mausoleum was built. There were imperial gardens also in the Vatican district. The elder Agrippina, the wife of Germanicus (15 B.C.-A.D. 19), possessed a villa on the north slope of the Janiculum, and her son Caligula built his famous Circus in the plain beneath. To the east were the gardens of Domitia, Nero's aunt. After her death the entire district became a single domain, known as Horti Neronis or Nero's Gardens.

The buildings erected for purposes of amusement and recreation were among the most impressive structures in Rome. These included not only circuses but also theaters, amphitheaters, and baths, which were frequented avidly by a populace whose leisure time included no less than 159 holidays in the year. Ninety-three of these holidays were devoted to games and performances held at public expense.[124] The games par excellence at Rome in the time of Paul were the chariot races of the circus.[125] The characteristic plan of the circus was a long rectangle rounded off at one end into a semicircle, and with a low wall called the spina or "backbone" running lengthwise in the center. Of them all the Circus Maximus[126] was the oldest and largest. It was situated in the hollow between the Aventine and the Palatine, and Paul must have seen it soon after passing through the Porta

[122] These figures are from the *Regionaries,* which are two descriptions of Rome, one called the *Curiosum* and the other the *Notitia,* and both deriving from a lost original which probably was compiled in the reign of Constantine between A.D. 312 and 315. Jérôme Carcopino, *Daily Life in Ancient Rome.* 1940, pp.23,287f.

[123] A. G. Mackinnon, *The Rome of Saint Paul.* 1930, p.168.

[124] Carcopino, *Daily Life in Ancient Rome,* p.205.

[125] cf. Juvenal, *Satire.* x, 77-81, "The public has long since cast off its cares; the people . . . now . . . longs eagerly for just two things—Bread and Circuses!"

[126] PATD pp.114-120.

Capena. This circus had been used for centuries, but was greatly enlarged and improved by Caesar in 46 B.C., and later was adorned with the obelisk of Ramses II which Augustus brought from Heliopolis and which today is to be seen in the Piazza del Popolo. The Circus was 1,800 feet in length and seated 150,000 spectators.[127] After enlargements by Nero it seated 250,000.[128] The walls of the Circus Maximus have now disappeared almost entirely, but the form is still distinctly traceable. The Circus Flaminius[129] was built about 221 B.C. by the censor Caius Flaminius Nepos who also constructed the Via Flaminia (p.367). It stood on the site of the present Palazzo Caetani, and was 1,300 feet in length. The Circus of Caligula[130] (A.D. 37-41) was built on the west side of the Tiber in the Ager Vaticanus as was mentioned above (p.369). It was intended as a private course for chariot racing and was relatively small in size, being about six hundred feet long. On the spina Caligula erected an obelisk which he brought from Heliopolis, this being a monolith of red granite without hieroglyphics. The circus in the Vatican was a favorite place for the sports and orgies of Claudius (A.D. 41-54) and Nero (A.D. 54-68), and is often known as the Circus of Nero.

The theaters to which Romans went at that time to enjoy plays included the Theater of Pompey (55 B.C.) seating about 10,000,[131] the Theater of Balbus (13 B.C.) seating around 7,700,[132] and the yet well preserved Theater of Marcellus (11 B.C.) accommodating some 14,000.[133]

The chief development of the amphitheater, to whose cruel spectacles the Romans became so addicted, came after the time of Paul. One permanent amphitheater had been built in the southern part of the Campus Martius in 29 B.C., and was standing when Paul came to Rome.[134] The great Flavian amphitheater or Colosseum[135] in which the gladiators were to be sent to their work of mutual massacre and the Christians were to be thrown to the wild beasts, was not yet built. It was first begun by Vespasian, on a site which had formerly been occupied by an artificial lake at Nero's palace (p.372), and was completed by Titus and decorated by Domitian. A tremendous elliptical structure, measuring nearly one-third of a mile in circumference and built of hard travertine stone, the Colosseum has survived the cen-

---

[127] Dionysius of Halicarnassus (c.54-c.7 B.C.), *Roman Antiquities.* III, lxviii, 2f. tr. E. Cary, LCL (1937-) II, pp.241-243.
[128] Pliny, *Natural History.* XXXVI, xxiv.   [129] PATD pp.111-113.
[130] PATD pp.113f.,370f.   [131] PATD pp.515-517.   [132] PATD p.513.
[133] PATD pp.513-515.   [134] PATD p.11.   [135] PATD pp.6-11.

turies to loom up still in Rome in gloomy grandeur. In its midst now rises a cross, in memory of the Christian martyrs who died there and in silent protest against the barbarism which cost so many lives before the spirit of Christianity abolished it.[136]

More in accord with the Greek spirit, although a distinctively Roman development, were the *thermae* or baths. These were public institutions where the ideal of "a sound mind in a sound body"[137] was cherished and where gymnasium, bath, and library provided for exercise, cleanliness, and culture. In 33 B.C. when Augustus' son-in-law Agrippa was aedile there were already 170 public baths in Rome, and by Pliny's time he found them to be so numerous that he gave up trying to count them.[138] Remains of the Thermae which Agrippa built during his aedileship are still to be seen in the Campus Martius,[139] which is where the Thermae of Nero[140] also were erected. The most famous baths and those whose ruins are most impressive today, however, were built after the time of Paul. These included the Thermae of Titus[141] now destroyed, the Thermae of Trajan[142] on the Esquiline just southeast of the present church of San Pietro in Vincoli, the magnificent Thermae of Caracalla[143] on the Via Appia outside the Porta Capena, the extensive Thermae of Diocletian[144] which loom up so impressively as one emerges from the railway station in Rome and which today house the National Roman Museum, the Church of Saint Mary of the Angels, and the Oratory of Saint Bernard, and the Thermae of Constantine[145] on the Quirinal.

In the very midst of the city were the Capitoline and Palatine hills, with the Forum lying in the valley between. The outstanding feature of the Capitoline hill was the great temple of Jupiter[146] on the southwestern summit. This temple was originally built by Tarquinius Superbus, the last of the kings, and was dedicated in 509 B.C., the first year of the Republic. It was burned down in 83 B.C., rebuilt,

---

[136] Carcopino, *Daily Life in Ancient Rome*, pp.244-247. Gladiatorial combats were stopped by the Emperor Honorius in A.D. 404 (Theodoret, *Ecclesiastical History*. v, 26 [NPNFSS III, p.151]).

[137] Juvenal, *Satire*. x, 356.   [138] *Natural History*. XXXVI, xxiv.

[139] Karl Baedeker, *Rome and Central Italy*. 16th ed. 1930, p.280.

[140] cf. Martial, *Epigrams*. VII, xxxiv, 4f.:
What was worse than Nero?
What is better than Nero's warm baths?

[141] PATD pp.533f.   [142] PATD pp.534-536.

[143] PATD pp.520-524. They were begun by Septimus Severus in A.D. 206, inaugurated by Antoninus Caracalla before being finished, and finally completed by Severus Alexander between 222 and 235.

[144] PATD pp.527-530.   [145] PATD pp.525f.   [146] PATD pp.297-302.

burned again in A.D. 69, and finally reconstructed most splendidly by Domitian. The marble fragments which have been found in excavation of its ruins are probably from the time of Domitian, but even in Paul's time the temple of the chief god of the Romans must have been very impressive. The northern summit of the Capitoline hill was the citadel (Arx) of early Rome and the site later of the temple of Juno Moneta (the Warner). The Arx and north slope of the Capitol are occupied now by the enormous Monument of Victor Emmanuel II, while the site of the temple of Juno is taken by the church of Santa Maria in Aracoeli. On the side of the Capitoline, commanding the Forum, was the Tabularium, erected after the fire of 83 B.C. to provide a fireproof hall of records for the state. It was probably the first attempt at such a building which was to be absolutely impervious to the accidents of the elements, and its walls are well preserved although much rebuilt in the Palazzo del Senatore, which is the modern council chamber of Rome.

The Palatine hill was the residence of the Roman emperor. Augustus, Tiberius, and Caligula all built there until the imperial palace covered a large part of the hill. The house of Livia, the wife of Augustus, still remains on the hill, its walls containing excellent murals. Also the substructures of the palace of Tiberius (Domus Tiberiana) are to be seen occupying a large part of the northwest corner of the Palatine. The ruins which are in the center of the hill are usually called the Domus Augustiana but actually are mostly a reconstruction by Domitian. These structures now appear as great masses of brickwork with arched roofs, but in Paul's day they were splendidly encased in marble and presented a magnificent appearance.[147] The Palatine itself could not content the extravagant Nero, however, and so he built a palace extending from the Palatine to the Esquiline, northeast of where the Colosseum now stands. Shortly after its completion this building was burned in the great fire of A.D. 64 and upon being rebuilt received the name Golden House (Domus Aurea). Suetonius described it as follows: "Its vestibule was large enough to contain a colossal statue of the emperor a hundred and twenty feet high; and it was so extensive that it had a triple colonnade a mile long. There was a pond too, like a sea, surrounded with buildings to represent cities, besides tracts of country, varied by tilled fields, vineyards, pastures, and woods, with great numbers

---

[147] Augustus boasted of Rome that "he had found it built of brick and left it in marble." Suetonius (A.D. c.100), *Augustus.* 28. tr. J. C. Rolfe, LCL (1914) I, p.167.

of wild and domestic animals. In the rest of the house all parts were overlaid with gold and adorned with gems and mother-of-pearl."[148]

On the southwest side of the Palatine, near the Circus Maximus, was a building now known as the Paedagogium, which probably belonged to the offices of the imperial palace. Some of its rooms are thought to have been used as prisons. The walls are still covered with rudely scratched drawings and inscriptions. One of these drawings, which was discovered by Garrucci in 1856 and is now in the Museo Kircheriano in Rome, is the famous "caricature of the crucifixion" (Fig. 131). This crude graffito shows a man's body with an ass's head, on a cross. The feet are supported on a platform and the outstretched arms fastened to the transverse bar of the cross. To the left is a smaller figure of a boy or young man with one hand raised in an attitude of adoration. The inscription reads, "Alexamenos worships his god." Presumably this represents the mockery to which some young Christian in the imperial palace was subjected. This graffito is to be dated perhaps 150 years after Paul was in Rome, or at the beginning of the third century, but it shows vividly how the word of the cross was foolishness to many (I Corinthians 1:18).

The Palatine was the site not only of the imperial palace but also of at least two important temples. One was the Temple of Apollo, which was erected by Augustus, and whose identification among the ruins on the Palatine is now difficult. The other was the Temple of the Magna Mater, or Cybele, the great mother deity of the Phrygians. This goddess, in the form of a meteoric stone, was brought to Rome in response to an oracle in 204 B.C. when Hannibal was threatening the city.[149] Another temple where an imported oriental religion was already entrenched in Rome was that of Isis and Serapis. The sanctuary of these Egyptian gods was on the Campus Martius not far from the famous Pantheon,[150] and was erected probably about A.D. 39. It was a vast structure, the central part being 420 feet long, and approached by a long colonnaded court lined with lions and sphinxes. The site of the temple is now occupied by part of the Church of

---

[148] *Nero*, 31.

[149] Livy (59 B.C.-A.D. 17), *History of Rome*. XXIX, 10-14. tr. Cyrus Edmonds, *Bohn's Classical Library*. III (1878), pp.1244-1250; cf. Samuel Dill, *Roman Society from Nero to Marcus Aurelius*. 1925, p.548.

[150] The best preserved ancient edifice in Rome today, the Pantheon ("all-holy"), originally was built by Agrippa, the son-in-law of Augustus, and was given its present circular form and beautiful dome by Hadrian. It was made into the church Sancta Maria ad Martyres in A.D. 609 when twenty-eight wagonloads of the bones of the martyrs were brought there from the catacombs, and is now known as Santa Maria Rotonda.

Sant' Ignazio, a section of the Collegio Romano, the apse of the Church of Santa Maria sopra Minerva, and the Via del Piè di Marmo. The famous sculptures of the Nile (now in the Vatican Museum) and the Tiber (now in the Louvre in Paris) probably belonged to this temple, as did several obelisks including those now in front of the Pantheon (Piazza della Rotonda), Santa Maria sopra Minerva (Piazza della Minerva), and the Railway Station (Piazza delle Terme).

If Julius the centurion led Paul the prisoner directly to the Forum, the party would have skirted the eastern edge of the Palatine and then have begun to tread the Via Sacra at the point where the Arch of Constantine later was built and now stands. From there the Via Sacra ascended to the summit of the Velia, a low hill running across between the Palatine and Esquiline where the Arch of Titus was to be erected not many years afterward (p.329), and then traversed the great Forum area along its longitudinal axis from southeast to northwest. In front of where the Basilica of Constantine later was to stand the street was lined with the elegant shops of goldsmiths, bronze-workers, jewelers, and dealers in oriental pearls. Beyond were the Palace of the Vestal Virgins (Atrium Vestae) with many of its walls and a few of its statues remaining today, the Temple of Vesta (Aedes Vestae) in which the sacred fire was kept ever alight, and the Regia, an office building with historical lists of the Roman magistrates carved on its marble walls (Fasti Consulares). Then came the Triumphal Arch of Augustus (19 B.C.), of which only the foundations now exist, and on its left the Temple of Castor and Pollux and on its right the Temple of Julius Caesar. The temple to the twin gods, Castor and Pollux, is the most prominent ruin in the Forum today, and if, as is probable, the three beautiful columns which are still standing belong to a reconstruction in the reign of Augustus,[151] they were seen by the eyes of the apostle Paul. The Templum Divi Juli, of which only the concrete substructures now remain, was erected by Augustus to the deified Julius Caesar and dedicated in 29 B.C. Thus the worship of the deceased emperor was established in Rome in the same year in which in the province of Asia the worship of the living emperor was instituted (p.345). By the time Paul was in Rome a temple to Augustus had also been erected there. This Templum Divi Augusti was founded by Tiberius and completed by Caligula, later (after Nero's fire) being restored magnificently by Domitian. It has

[151] Baedeker, *Rome and Central Italy*, p.331.

often been identified with ruins lying south of the Temple of Castor and Pollux on the Vicus Tuscus, but this is uncertain. Later than the time of Paul but of interest because of the excellent preservation of its portico is the Temple of Faustina not far northeast of the Temple of Julius Caesar and now incorporated in the church of San Lorenzo in Miranda. It was dedicated by Antoninus Pius in A.D. 141 to his deified wife, the elder Faustina, and then was given an additional dedication to the emperor himself after his own death. Ten beautiful columns of the portico are still standing, and above them is the inscription, the first line of which was added after the death of Antoninus:

> "To the deified Antoninus and
> to the deified Faustina by the decree of the Senate."[152]

Finally one reached the Forum Romanum proper, the center of the ancient city and in Paul's day the center of the world. New fora had already been erected in the larger plain to the north, the Forum Julium, begun by Caesar and completed by Augustus, and the Forum of Augustus; and yet others would be constructed, the Forum of Vespasian, the Forum Transitorium begun by Domitian and finished by Nerva, and the magnificent Forum of Trajan with Trajan's marvelous Column, which still stands.[153] But nothing could replace the original Forum in the affections of the city, and the glorious traditions connected with it were commemorated with columns, statues, bronzes, marbles, and other works of art. Just to the northwest of the Forum, beyond the rostra or orators' platform and near where the Arch of Severus (A.D. 203) now stands, was the Umbilicus Urbis Romae, the ideal center of the city. Just to the southwest of the Forum, near the Arch of Tiberius (A.D. 16) and in front of the Temple of Saturn, was the Miliarium Aureum, a gilded column erected by Augustus and giving the names and distances of the chief towns to which highroads radiated from Rome. These included points no less distant than Londinium (ancient London) on the west and Jerusalem on the east. When Paul, the world-minded, reached here he

---

[152] *Divo Antonio et*
 divae Faustinae ex S.C.
The initials S.C. are the customary abbreviation for *Senatus consulto*.

[153] The Column is adorned with a spiral frieze over 650 feet in length, depicting military campaigns of Trajan. The emperor's ashes were deposited in the base upon his death in A.D. 117. His bronze statue which once stood on the summit, was replaced by a statue of Saint Peter in the sixteenth century.

had indeed reached the center from which the gospel he preached might spread to the uttermost parts of the earth.

A general view of this central part of ancient Rome is shown in Fig. 132. The eight columns standing in the left foreground belong to the Temple of Saturn which was dedicated originally around 497 B.C. and restored about 44 B.C. Beside and below them is the Forum Romanum proper and glimpsed through the last two of the eight columns is the portico of the Temple of Faustina. Beyond the trees in the right foreground and only partially hidden by them are the three columns of the Temple of Castor and Pollux. Just to the left of these columns and much farther beyond them is the Arch of Titus, while on the horizon appears the Colosseum.

On either side of the Forum stood great basilicas, or quadrangular courts surrounded by colonnades and containing court chambers and public shops. On the north was the Basilica Aemilia, built originally around 179 B.C. by the censors Aemilius Lepidus and Fulvius Nobilior and reconstructed about 54 B.C. by Aemilius Paullus. In the latter year on the other side of the Forum, Julius Caesar began the Basilica Julia, which he dedicated in 46 B.C. although it was not altogether completed until A.D. 12. Both of these vast and splendid structures, of which extensive remains are yet to be seen, are of interest in connection with Paul. It was probably within the colonnaded courts of the Basilica Julia that Paul eventually heard the sentence of death pronounced upon him. It was from the Basilica of Aemilius Paullus that the Roman prefect Probianus in A.D. 386 took twenty-four beautiful columns of Phrygian marble to adorn the Church of Saint Paul which was being erected outside the walls of the city—an event of which the condemned prisoner little could have dreamed.[154]

A short distance northwest of the Forum Romanum and beneath the present church of San Giuseppe de' Falegnami is the prison known as the Carcer Mamertinus. Built in the side of the Capitoline hill, it has an upper vaulted chamber, and a lower chamber or dungeon originally accessible only through a hole in its ceiling. The lower chamber was probably an old springhouse and hence was called Tullianum from the early Latin word *tullius*, meaning "spring." This was where noted prisoners like Jugurtha, the Catilinarian conspirators, and Vercingetorix were kept before execution. In telling of the execution of Catiline's confederates, the Roman historian Sal-

154 Mackinnon, *The Rome of Saint Paul*, pp.33f.; Dorothy M. Robathan, *The Monuments of Ancient Rome*. 1950, pp.64-70.

lust (86-34 B.C.) describes the Tullianum almost exactly as it now exists: "In the prison . . . there is a place called the Tullianum, about twelve feet below the surface of the ground. It is enclosed on all sides by walls, and above it is a chamber with a vaulted roof of stone. Neglect, darkness, and stench make it hideous and fearsome to behold."[155]

3. THE MARTYRDOM OF PAUL AND PETER

ACCORDING to tradition which goes back at least to the fifth century, the Mamertine prison is the place where both Paul and Peter were confined before their execution under Nero.[1] Whether this is correct or not is difficult to determine, but the fact seems certain that the two great apostles suffered martyrdom in Rome under Nero.[2] In the case of Paul, the last statement of the book of Acts is that he lived two whole years in his own hired dwelling in Rome, preaching freely to all who came to him (Acts 28:30f.). Whether his martyrdom followed at the close of these two years, as the further silence of Acts might seem to imply,[3] cannot now be said with certainty. Perhaps he was set free at the expiration of that period and enabled to achieve his cherished purpose of preaching in Spain (Romans 15:24, 28), before eventually suffering death in Rome.[4] In the case of Peter there is a veiled reference to his death in John 21:18: "when you are old, you will stretch out your hands, and another will gird you and carry you where you do not wish to go."

Then, before the end of the first century we find a writer at Rome referring at some length to the impressive example set by Peter and

---

[155] *The War with Catiline.* LV, 3f. tr. J. C. Rolfe, LCL (1921), p.115.

[1] A. S. Barnes, *The Martyrdom of St. Peter and St. Paul.* 1933, p.67.

[2] For arguments that Peter never went to Rome but died in Jerusalem in A.D. 44 see Donald F. Robinson in JBL 64 (1945), pp.255-267; and Warren M. Smaltz in JBL 71 (1952), pp.211-216.

[3] cf. B. W. Bacon (in AJT 22 [1918], p.15), "But as to Paul the reader is *not* really left in ignorance. His fate *is* made known, but made known with that chaste reticence which the Greek poets employ when they only report through others the tragedies enacted behind the scenes. In the great Farewell Discourse of Acts 20:17-38 the martyr takes his leave. In Acts 28:17-31 the tragedy itself is veiled behind the triumph of the cause."

[4] I Clement 5, which is quoted more fully just below, gives support to this view for it speaks of Paul as "having come to the farthest bounds of the West," which to one writing in Rome as Clement did surely would have meant Spain. The Muratorian Fragment (middle of the 2d century A.D.) also refers to "the departure of Paul from the city (i.e. Rome) on his journey to Spain" (ASBACH p.118).

Paul in their martyrdom. The passage is to be found in a letter which Clement, the bishop of Rome (A.D. c.88-c.97), wrote to the Corinthians around A.D. 95. Since there was disharmony in the Corinthian church which had its roots in envy and jealousy, Clement pictured the evil results which had followed upon such attitudes both in ancient and in recent times. As a recent illustration, he cited the persecution and martyrdom of Peter and Paul. Clement said:[5]

"But to leave the ancient examples, let us come to the champions who lived nearest our times; let us take the noble examples of our generation. On account of jealousy and envy the greatest and most righteous pillars of the church were persecuted, and contended even unto death. Let us set before our eyes the good Apostles: Peter, who on account of unrighteous jealousy endured not one nor two, but many sufferings, and so having borne his testimony, went to his deserved place of glory. On account of jealousy and strife Paul pointed out the prize of endurance. After he had been seven times in bonds, had been driven into exile, had been stoned, had been a preacher in the East and in the West, he received the noble reward of his faith; having taught righteousness unto the whole world, and having come to the farthest bounds of the West, and having borne witness before rulers, he thus departed from the world and went unto the holy place, having become a notable pattern of patient endurance."

Clement then proceeded immediately to group with Peter and Paul a large number of Christians, including both men and women, who were persecuted fiendishly and put to death:

"Unto these men who lived lives of holiness was gathered a vast multitude of the elect, who by many indignities and tortures, being the victims of jealousy, set the finest examples among us. On account of jealousy women, when they had been persecuted as Danaïds and Dircae,[6] and had suffered cruel and unholy insults, safely reached the goal in the race of faith and received a noble reward, feeble though they were in body."

That is an unmistakable reference to the persecution of the Christians at Rome by Nero, as it is more fully known to us through the Roman historian Tacitus (A.D. c.55-c.117). Although Tacitus was not an eyewitness of the persecution, he had very good opportunities for obtaining accurate information and his account is regarded as entirely trustworthy. In the fifteenth book of his *Annals* he tells of the terrible conflagration which broke out at Rome on the eighteenth day of July in the year 64. Raging for six days and driven by the

[5] I Clement, 5f. (ASBACH pp.7f.).

[6] That is, they were forced to play the part of the daughters of Danaüs who, according to Greek mythology, suffered in the underworld, and of Dirce who was tied by the hair to a wild bull and dragged to death.

wind, the fire swept irresistibly through the labyrinth of Roman streets and when finally it was stopped only four of the city's fourteen districts were standing entire.[7] Whether the fire started accidentally or was set deliberately by Nero,[8] public suspicion turned upon the emperor as its instigator. Thereupon Nero cast the blame upon the hated Christians and subjected them to the most atrocious tortures. This persecution is described vividly by Tacitus:

"Nero put in his own place as culprits, and punished with most ingenious cruelty, men whom the common people hated for their shameful crimes and called Christians. Christ, from whom the name was derived, had been put to death in the reign of Tiberius by the procurator Pontius Pilate. The deadly superstition, having been checked for awhile, began to break out again, not only throughout Judea, where this mischief first arose, but also at Rome, where from all sides all things scandalous and shameful meet and become fashionable. Therefore, at the beginning, some were seized who made confessions; then, on their information, a vast multitude was convicted, not so much of arson as of hatred of the human race. And they were not only put to death, but subjected to insults, in that they were either dressed up in the skins of wild beasts and perished by the cruel mangling of dogs, or else put on crosses to be set on fire, and, as day declined, to be burned, being used as light by night. Nero had thrown open his gardens for that spectacle, and gave a circus play, mingling with the people dressed in a charioteer's costume or driving in a chariot. From this arose, however, toward men who were, indeed, criminals and deserving extreme penalties, sympathy, on the ground that they were destroyed not for the public good, but to satisfy the cruelty of an individual."[9]

This description by Tacitus agrees remarkably well with the intimations of Clement's letter and fills out the details of the indignities and tortures heaped upon the Christians at Nero's circus play. Both accounts evidently refer to the same events, and the close agreement between Tacitus and Clement is strong reason for regarding the year 64 as the date of the death of the two great apostles.

Around A.D. 200 Tertullian likewise refers to the death of Peter and Paul as having taken place at Rome under Nero and correctly interprets John 21:18 as a reference to Peter's crucifixion: "At Rome Nero was the first who stained with blood the rising faith. Then is Peter girt by another, when he is made fast to the cross. Then does

---

[7] Tacitus, *Annals.* xv, 38, 40.

[8] Suetonius (*Nero*, 38) states that the city was set on fire openly by Nero, who pretended to be disgusted with the ugliness of Rome's old buildings and the narrow and crooked streets.

[9] *Annals.* xv, 44.

Paul obtain a birth suited to Roman citizenship, when in Rome he springs to life again ennobled by martyrdom."[10] On another occasion Tertullian incidentally indicates the manner of both martyrdoms by comparing the death of Peter to that of Jesus and the death of Paul to that of John the Baptist:[11] "How happy is its church, on which apostles poured forth all their doctrine along with their blood! Where Peter endures a passion like his Lord's![12] where Paul wins his crown in a death like John's!"[13]

Also Eusebius relates in his *Church History* that Peter and Paul suffered martyrdom at about the same time in Rome under Nero. The *Church History* was published in A.D. 326, but Eusebius derived his information in this regard from authorities who had lived much earlier. He cites Caius, who probably lived in Rome in the time of Pope Zephyrinus about A.D. 199-217, and Dionysius, who was bishop of Corinth at the same time that Soter was bishop of Rome around A.D. 166-174. The entire passage, with the quotations from the two earlier sources, is as follows:[14]

[10] *Scorpiace.* 15 (ANF III, p.648).

[11] *On Prescription against Heretics.* 36 (ANF III, p.260).

[12] The martyrdom of Peter is narrated with apocryphal elaboration in the Acts of Peter (JANT pp.333f.), which is probably to be dated around A.D. 200-220. In this work is found the famous and beautiful "*Domine quo vadis?*" legend, according to which Peter was warned to leave Rome and went forth but met Jesus coming into the city. "And as he went forth out of the city, he saw the Lord entering into Rome. And when he saw him, he said: Lord whither goest thou here? And the Lord said unto him: I go into Rome to be crucified. And Peter said unto him: Lord, art thou being crucified again? He said unto him: Yea, Peter, I am being crucified again. And Peter came to himself: and having beheld the Lord ascending up into heaven, he returned to Rome, rejoicing, and glorifying the Lord, for that he said: I am being crucified: the which was about to befall Peter." When Peter was crucified he insisted that it should be "with the head downward and not otherwise" and so it was done. Eusebius also states, on the authority of Origen, that Peter was crucified head-downward (see below, n.14).

[13] Mark 6:27. That Paul should have been put to death by the sword was to be expected since he was a Roman citizen (Acts 16:37; 22:27f.; 23:27). Both crucifixion and condemnation *ad bestias* appear to have been methods of execution usually reserved for persons of lower standing than Roman citizens. D. W. Riddle (*Paul, Man of Conflict.* 1940, pp.140f.) suggests the possibility that Paul was thrown to the wild beasts, since Ignatius (A.D. c.110-c.117) who was to die that way (Romans 4. ANF I, p.75) said that he wanted to "be found in (*literally* under) the footsteps of Paul" (Ephesians 12. ANF I, p.55). Ignatius, however, well may have been referring simply to the fact of martyrdom, since in another place he hopes that by fighting with beasts at Rome he "may indeed become the disciple of Jesus" (Ephesians 1 [ANF I, p.49]). Riddle regards the ascription of Roman citizenship to Paul by Acts as a tendentious and therefore unreliable statement, but that Saul who bore the eminent Roman cognomen Paul actually was a Roman citizen is entirely probable.

[14] *Ch. Hist.* II, xxv; cf. III, i, where Eusebius says, "Peter appears to have preached in Pontus, Galatia, Bithynia, Cappadocia, and Asia to the Jews of the dispersion. And at last, having come to Rome, he was crucified head-downwards; for he had requested

"When the government of Nero was now firmly established, he began to plunge into unholy pursuits, and armed himself even against the religion of the God of the universe. . . . He was the first of the emperors who showed himself an enemy of the divine religion. The Roman Tertullian is likewise a witness of this. He writes as follows: 'Examine your records. There you will find that Nero was the first that persecuted this doctrine, particularly then when after subduing all the east, he exercised his cruelty against all at Rome. We glory in having such a man the leader in our punishment. For whoever knows him can understand that nothing was condemned by Nero unless it was something of great excellence.' Thus publicly announcing himself as the first among God's chief enemies, he was led on to the slaughter of the apostles. It is, therefore, recorded that Paul was beheaded in Rome itself, and that Peter likewise was crucified under Nero. This account of Peter and Paul is substantiated by the fact that their names are preserved in the cemeteries of that place even to the present day. It is confirmed likewise by Caius, a member of the Church, who arose under Zephyrinus, bishop of Rome. He, in a published disputation with Proclus, the leader of the Phrygian heresy, speaks as follows concerning the places where the sacred corpses of the aforesaid apostles are laid: 'But I can show the trophies of the apostles. For if you will go to the Vatican or to the Ostian way, you will find the trophies of those who laid the foundations of this church.' And that they both suffered martyrdom at the same time is stated by Dionysius, bishop of Corinth, in his epistle to the Romans, in the following words: 'You have thus by such an admonition bound together the planting of Peter and of Paul at Rome and Corinth. For both of them planted and likewise taught us in our Corinth.[15] And they taught together in like manner in Italy, and suffered martyrdom at the same time.' "[16]

This passage in Eusebius is of particular interest because of the quotation which it contains from Caius. As a presbyter in the Roman

---

that he might suffer in this way. What do we need to say concerning Paul, who preached the Gospel of Christ from Jerusalem to Illyricum, and afterwards suffered martyrdom in Rome under Nero? These facts are related by Origen in the third volume of his Commentary on Genesis."

[15] The mention of a "Cephas" party at Corinth in I Corinthians 1:12 makes it probable that Peter did work there as Dionysius states.

[16] "At the same time" (κατὰ τὸν αὐτὸν καιρόν. ed. E. Schwartz, *Kleine Ausgabe*. 3d ed. 1922, p.73), allows some margin and does not necessarily imply on the very same day. In his *Chronicon* (ed. Scaliger. 1606, p.192, cf. p.162) Eusebius places the deaths of Peter and Paul together in the fourteenth year of Nero, which would be A.D. 67-68. But in the very same connection Eusebius describes Nero's persecution of the Christians in Rome and assigns it likewise to Nero's fourteenth year. It must be concluded, therefore, that Eusebius made an error as to the date of the Neronian persecution, which is definitely known to have taken place in the summer of A.D. 64. It should be noted that a date around A.D. 67 for the martyrdom of Peter and Paul does have the support of a statement by Jerome that Seneca (c.4 B.C.-A.D. 65) died two years before the apostles (Orazio Marucchi, *Pietro e Paolo a Roma*. 4th ed. 1934, p.21), but since this involves separating their death by several years from the fire and persecution of A.D. 64 it seems less probable.

church at the beginning of the third century, he was involved in a disputation with Proclus, the leader of the sect of the Montanists. As is evident from a later passage in the *Church History*, Proclus had supported his position by an appeal to the existence of the tombs of Philip and his four daughters at Hierapolis in Asia.[17] This latter passage reads: "And in the Dialogue of Caius which we mentioned a little above, Proclus, against whom he directed his disputation, in agreement with what has been quoted, speaks thus concerning the death of Philip and his daughters: 'After him there were four prophetesses, the daughters of Philip, at Hierapolis in Asia. Their tomb is there and the tomb of their father.' "[18]

Over against the claims of Proclus, Caius appealed to the existence in Rome of the glorious last resting places of Peter and Paul, who had taught there and laid the foundations of the Roman church. "But," said he in reply to Proclus, "I can show the trophies of the apostles.[19] For if you will go to the Vatican or to the Ostian Way, you will find the trophies of those who laid the foundations of this church." The Greek word "trophy" which is used here, originally meant the memorial of a victory which was raised on the field of battle. Thus, for example, the armor or weapons of the defeated enemy might be fixed to a tree or upright post, with an accompanying inscription and dedication. In similar fashion when a Christian hero fell on the field of martyrdom, a marker at that place or above his grave might appropriately enough be referred to as a "trophy." Since Proclus had appealed, on his side, to the existence of the tomb of the apostle Philip at Hierapolis, Caius in answering him must have been using the word "trophies" to refer to grave-monuments at the last resting places of the two famous martyrs in Rome.

The Vatican, to which Caius pointed as the place of the tomb of Peter, was the Ager Vaticanus, where "Nero's Circus" and "Nero's Gardens" were (pp.369f.), and where so many other Christians also perished in Nero's frightful exhibition of cruelty (p.379). There on the outskirts of Nero's Circus, as near as possible to the place of his triumph in death, was the grave of Peter. According to the first chapter of the Liber Pontificalis[20] the exact location was

[17] A city about five miles north of Laodicea, and mentioned in Colossians 4:13.

[18] *Ch. Hist.* III, xxxi.

[19] *Ch. Hist.* II, xxv, 7: ἐγὼ δὲ τὰ τρόπαια τῶν ἀποστόλων ἔχω δεῖξαι. ed. Schwartz, p.73.

[20] The Liber Pontificalis is a series of biographies of the popes and was compiled in the text in which we have it in the seventh century from earlier papal annals. While

between the Via Aurelia and the Via Triumphalis, near a temple of Cybele which by popular error was later called a shrine of Apollo.

The Ostian Way, to which Caius referred as the place of the tomb of Paul, was the ancient Via Ostiensis. This road led from Rome to the port city of Ostia, some fourteen miles distant at the mouth of the Tiber.[21] It departed from the southern side of Rome at a point some distance west of the Via Appia by which Paul had first entered the city. As Paul was led forth to die his eyes must have fallen upon one monument which still stands today upon the Via Ostiense. This is the Pyramid of Cestius at the present Porta San Paolo (Fig. 133). It was a tomb which was erected in Egyptian pyramidal form for a certain Caius Cestius Epulo who died before 12 B.C. One hundred and sixteen feet high and covered with marble slabs, the pyramid was enclosed by Aurelian within his city wall but extricated in 1660 by Pope Alexander VII, and looms up today exactly as it did when Paul passed. The last resting place of the great apostle was some one and one-quarter miles farther out the Via Ostiensis.[22]

Thus, as Caius is witness, the graves of Peter and of Paul at the Vatican and on the Ostian Way respectively, were perfectly well-known martyr-memorials in Rome around A.D. 200. Nor could these graves have been recent inventions of pious credulity as if they first had been arbitrarily "discovered" say around A.D. 170. By that time the Christian custom of burial in the catacombs was fully established, and if one had wished to invent the graves of Peter and of

---

a considerable part is obviously legendary it also contains much valuable historical material. Louis Duchesne, *Le liber pontificalis, texte, introduction et commentaire.* 2 vols. 1886-92; LLP pp.ix-x.

[21] The city derived its name from the *ostium* or mouth of the river.

[22] The place of Paul's execution is believed to have been yet another one and one-quarter miles out on the Via Laurentina at the Abbey of the Three Fountains (Abbadia delle Tre Fontane). There are three springs here which anciently were known as the Aquae Salviae, and according to the apocryphal Acts of Peter and Paul (R. A. Lipsius and M. Bonnet, *Acta Apostolorum Apocrypha.* I [1891], p.214) Paul was beheaded at a place of this name and under a pine tree. The late legend that when the apostle's head struck the earth it bounced three times and at each place one of the springs welled forth, is of course as worthless as the other story that when his head was struck off, milk came forth (Carl Schmidt, ed., *Praxeis Paulou: Acta Pauli.* 1936, pp.68f.). But the location of the execution at this place also has the authority of Pope Gregory I the Great (A.D. 590-604) and may be not incorrect. The old abbey which stood here was virtually abandoned for a long time owing to malaria but around 1867 was entrusted to French Trappist monks. It is an interesting fact that when the Trappists were doing some digging in connection with one of their buildings in 1875 they unearthed a mass of coins of Nero together with several fossilized pine-cones. R. Lanciani, *Wanderings through Ancient Roman Churches.* 1924, p.169.

Paul it would have been most natural to place them in or near some of these recognized Christian cemeteries where undisturbed veneration of the holy places would have been possible. Instead both graves are remote from all Christian cemeteries and in fact lie amidst pagan cemeteries of the first and second centuries. This fact has been established by excavations which have revealed pagan burial places in the immediate neighborhood of the graves of both Peter and Paul. No one would have "invented" the holy graves in such unholy surroundings.[23]

In the light of history it is eminently fitting that Peter's grave should be hard by Nero's Circus to proclaim that the tyrant's triumph was transient but the apostle's was everlasting. And it is likewise appropriate that Paul who had traveled so far for Christ should be buried at last beside a highway as if to signify that his strong heart was still eager for the preaching of the gospel in distant places. Both graves are truly trophies of victory.

[23] Hans Lietzmann, *Petrus und Paulus in Rom.* 2d ed. 1927, pp.246f.; and cf. below pp.515f.

VII

Manuscripts Found in the Sand

A S EXTENSIVELY as Paul himself traveled, his letters traveled even farther. Occasionally his correspondence was addressed to cities and churches where his face had never been seen (cf. Colossians 2:1), and some of his letters were passed on from one church to another (Colossians 4:16). Moreover, within twenty-five years after his death, copies of his letters appear to have been gathered from the various churches to which he had sent them, and published as a collection.[1] From A.D. 90 on these collected letters of Paul were known widely, and their language and ideas were reflected frequently in other Christian writings.[2] In II Peter 3:16 this collection is referred to and is already regarded as "scripture."

In this manner the letters of Paul were preserved to become known down through the centuries and around the world. The influence of a single one of them, that to the Romans, for example, has been nothing less than world-transforming. The conversion of Augustine came when he took up "the volume of the Apostles" and read Romans 13:13-14.[3] The sudden enlightenment of Martin Luther

---

[1] E. J. Goodspeed (*Christianity Goes to Press*. 1940, pp.49-62) thinks that the collection was made first at Ephesus, possibly by Onesimus, who had been the slave of Philemon and around A.D. 110 became bishop of Ephesus.

[2] A. E. Barnett (*Paul Becomes a Literary Influence*. 1940) finds that Pauline influence was strong in I Peter, Hebrews, I Clement, the Johannine writings, Ignatius, and Polycarp; that it subsided, perhaps due to an anti-Marcionite reaction, in James, Jude, Hermas, Barnabas, the Didache, II Clement, the Martyrdom of Polycarp, and the Apology of Aristides; and that it revived again in II Peter, Tatian's Address to the Greeks, Justin, Melito, Athenagoras, and the Pastoral Epistles.

[3] *Confessions*. VIII, 12 (NPNF I, p.127).

came when he was reading the epistle to the Romans in his monastery cell. The decisive experience in the life of John Wesley came from hearing Luther's preface to the Commentary on Romans read in a little meeting in Aldersgate Street, London. Twentieth century theology has been influenced by the endeavor of Karl Barth to see modern life through the lens of Paul's conception of faith, and the writing by Barth of his first book on *The Epistle to the Romans*.[4] Certainly this single writing of Paul's has been a *Schicksalsbrief*, a "letter of destiny," in the history of Christianity.

Many other writings were also produced in the early Christian community and, of these, four Gospels, the book of Acts, and various other letters and books were eventually joined together with the letters attributed to Paul to constitute the canonical New Testament.[5] The discovery and study of ancient copies of all of these documents is part of the work of archeology,[6] and through such research we may come closer to the original text of the New Testament. In what follows something will be told of the nature of this work, and special reference will be made to manuscripts of the letters of Paul since these are recognized as providing the best place to begin the study of the New Testament text.[7] First, however, we must notice the writing materials and practices of the early Christian centuries.

1. WRITING MATERIALS AND PRACTICES
IN THE ANCIENT WORLD

In addition to the stone and clay which, as we have seen, were so abundantly used to write on particularly in Egypt and Mesopotamia respectively,[1] two other materials were widely used in the ancient world, namely papyrus and leather.

PAPYRUS

In the Mediterranean world of the first century A.D. it was undoubtedly papyrus which was the most commonly employed mate-

[4] *Der Römerbrief*. 1919. tr. Edwyn C. Hoskyns, 1933.

[5] For early lists of the canon see F. W. Grosheide, ed., *Some Early Lists of the Books of the New Testament* (Textus Minores, 1). 1948.

[6] Kenneth W. Clark in BASOR 122 (Apr. 1951), pp.7-9.

[7] Hans Lietzmann, *Einführung in die Textgeschichte der Paulusbriefe* (in *An die Römer, Handbuch zum neuen Testament*. 8 [4th ed. 1933]), p.1.

[1] Reference has also already been made to the early development of writing in Mesopotamia (p.26), Egypt (p.84), and Sinai-Palestine (pp.148f.).

rial, even as it is the term from which the modern word "paper" is derived.[2] It in turn took its name from the plant from which it was made. This was a reed or sedge called papyrus[3] which grew abundantly in Egypt and was also found in adjoining lands.[4] The papyrus plant appears frequently in Egyptian art, from the earliest times. A particularly delightful example is the wall painting representing a wildcat in a papyrus thicket (Fig. 134) from the famous tomb of Khnumhotep (Twelfth Dynasty) at Beni Hasan (pp.92f.). Another scene, in the tomb of Puyemre (Eighteenth Dynasty), shows the papyrus plant being harvested and split for papermaking (Fig. 135).

The process of making writing material from the papyrus plant has been described, although not with complete clarity, by Pliny in his *Natural History:*[5]

"Papyrus grows either in the marshes of Egypt, or in the sluggish waters of the river Nile, when they have overflowed and are lying stagnant, in pools that do not exceed a couple of cubits [about three feet] in depth. The root lies obliquely, and is about the thickness of one's arm; the section of the stalk is triangular, and it tapers gracefully upwards towards the extremity, being not more than ten cubits [about fifteen feet] at most in height. . . .[6]

"Paper is made from the papyrus, by splitting it with a needle into very thin leaves, due care being taken that they should be as broad as possible. That of the first quality is taken from the center of the plant, and so in regular succession, according to the order of division. . . .

"All these various kinds of paper are made upon a table, moistened with Nile water; a liquid which, when in a muddy state, has the peculiar qualities of glue. This table being first inclined, the leaves of papyrus are laid upon it lengthwise, as long, indeed, as the papyrus will admit of, the jagged edges being cut off at either end; after which a cross layer is placed over it, . . . When this is done, the leaves are pressed together, and then dried in the sun; after which they are united to one another, the best sheets being always taken first, and the inferior ones added afterwards. There are never more than twenty of these sheets to a roll."

In other words, single sheets of paper were made out of thin vertical and horizontal strips of papyrus glued together, and a number of such sheets were glued together, side by side, to form a con-

---

[2] Greek, πάπυρος; Latin, *papyrus*; German, *Papier*; French, *papier*; English, *paper*.

[3] Linnaeus, *Cyperus papyrus*.

[4] Strabo, *Geography*. xvii, i, 15. The plant now is practically extinct in Lower Egypt, but is found in Nubia, Ethiopia, at Syracuse in Sicily, and at Lake Huleh in Palestine (for the last place see Walter C. Lowdermilk, *Palestine Land of Promise.* 1944, p.145).

[5] xiii, 11f.

[6] cf. Theophrastus (c.372-c.287 b.c.), *Enquiry into Plants.* iv, viii, 3. tr. A. Hort, lcl (1916) i, pp.347-349.

tinuous roll. They could also, as we shall see, be used in the form of a codex.

Even as Egypt was the place in which the papyrus plant grew most abundantly, so it was in Egypt that papyrus probably first came into use as a writing material. The representation of scribes writing on papyrus is found in Egyptian art from very ancient times. The statuette of a scribe shown in Fig. 137 comes from the Third Dynasty and may be the earliest such figure that has even been found. The scribe is seated cross-legged and holds upon his lap a roll of papyrus. The unrolled portion of the papyrus is grasped by the left hand and the free end of the roll lying across the lap is held down by the right hand which is in a position to write. The expression upon the face is that of one waiting to take dictation. Similar examples are to be found in the statue of Henka the scribe (Fourth Dynasty) in the Berlin Museum, in that of the Scribe Accroupi (Fifth Dynasty) in the Louvre at Paris, and in that of Haremhab (Eighteenth-Nineteenth Dynasties) already mentioned (pp.112f., Fig. 48). Another interesting representation is that of the limestone relief carving from the Eighteenth Dynasty shown in Fig. 138. Here four scribes are standing and bending forward attentively, each with his papyrus roll and pen.

The oldest actual specimen of a papyrus manuscript yet discovered dates from the Fifth Dynasty,[7] and from that ancient time papyrus continued in use on down through the Greek and Roman periods and well into the days after the occupation of Egypt by the Arabs in A.D. 641. Extant papyri are written not only in the language of ancient Egypt, but also in Greek,[8] Latin,[9] Hebrew,[10] Aramaic,[11]

[7] F. G. Kenyon, *The Palaeography of Greek Papyri.* 1899, p.14. The statement of the Roman antiquarian, Varro (c.116-c.27 B.C.), which is quoted by Pliny (*Natural History.* XIII, 11) that the use of papyrus for writing was discovered first in the time of Alexander the Great is entirely incorrect and was doubted by Pliny himself (XIII, 13).

[8] Greek was the official language of Egypt from the founding of the Ptolemaic Dynasty until the Arab invasion, and by far the largest number of extant papyri are written in Greek.

[9] Latin was used chiefly for military and legal business and in private correspondence between Roman officials, and papyri written in this language are not numerous.

[10] Hebrew papyri are rare in Egypt. The Nash Papyrus, already mentioned (p.27) as containing the Ten Commandments and the Shema (Deuteronomy 6:4ff.) and written probably in the second or first century B.C., was found in Egypt (W. F. Albright in JBL 56 [1937], p.145 n.2).

[11] The best known Aramaic papyri are those from Elephantine which have already been mentioned (pp.239f). On Aramaic in general see Raymond A. Bowman in JNES 7 (1948), pp.65-90.

Coptic,[12] and Arabic.[13] Thus, this amazing writing material was in continuous and demonstrable use in Egypt for a period of three or four thousand years.[14]

From Egypt the use of papyrus spread to many other lands. Its use in Palestine at least as early as the sixth century B.C. was already proved by the finding at Lachish of a clay seal of Gedaliah with the impression on its back of the papyrus document to which it had originally been attached (p.195), and is now further shown by the discovery in Cave II at Wadi Murabba'at of an actual Hebrew papyrus believed to have been written in the sixth century (p.279). Among the Qumran manuscripts there are various papyrus fragments inscribed in Hebrew, Aramaic, and Greek.[15] At Masada, the Dead Sea fortress destroyed in the war with the Romans in A.D. 73, a small piece of papyrus has been found with traces of Hebrew writing.[16] And at Nessana in the Negeb important though relatively late papyri have been unearthed (pp.429f.). Since in much of Palestine the dampness of the climate is not conducive to the preservation of papyrus, it is probable that it was used even earlier and more widely than we are now able to demonstrate. In Mesopotamia the use of papyrus is attested by fragments of this material which were discovered at Dura-Europos and which date in the third century B.C.[17]

Among the Greeks papyrus was in use at least in the fifth century B.C.[18] and probably much earlier. In the century and a half after the birth of Christ it was the usual writing material, and it continued to be employed as late as the sixth and seventh centuries A.D. The Romans were using papyrus in the third century B.C. and continued to employ it until the seventh century A.D. Thus, as Caspar René Gregory has said of the period in which the New Testament was written, papyrus "was the common writing material, the paper, of that day, whether at Alexandria or at Antioch or at Rome. If a man put a handbill up at Rome, he wrote it on a big piece of coarse

[12] The Copts were the native Egyptians, descended from the ancient inhabitants of the land, and large numbers of Coptic papyri have been found.

[13] C. H. Becker, *Papyri Schott-Reinhardt*. I (1906). After the Arab conquest Greek continued for some time to be employed officially alongside Arabic and then gradually died out.

[14] Wilhelm Schubart, *Das alte Ägypten und seine Papyrus*. 1921, p.6.

[15] DJD I, pp.47,148f.,155.

[16] IEJ 7 (1957), p.60.

[17] C. B. Welles in *Münchener Beiträge zur Papyrusforschung und antiken Rechtsgeschichte*. 19 (1934), pp.379-399.

[18] Herodotus. v, 58.

papyrus. If he wrote a delicate note to his wife or his mother, he wrote it on a little piece of fine papyrus. Papyrus was their paper."[19]

LEATHER, PARCHMENT, AND VELLUM

Leather, parchment, and vellum were also used as writing material. In Egypt the use of leather is attested, for example, by the fact that the victory of Thutmose III at Megiddo "was recorded upon a roll of leather in the temple of Amun."[20] According to Herodotus,[21] the Greeks of Ionia had formerly, when papyrus was scarce, written on the skins of goats and sheep, a custom which was continued by the barbarians in his own day. The Jews employed leather for writing from an early time.[22] When Jeremiah dictated his prophecies to his secretary Baruch (Jeremiah 36:4), they may have been written upon a roll of leather, since King Jehoiakim later used a knife to cut the roll in pieces when he wanted to burn it (Jeremiah 36:23).[23] In the Talmud we find that the Law was written upon the skins of animals,[24] and this doubtless reflects an ancient tradition. The Letter of Aristeas and Josephus state that the copy of the Law which was sent from Jerusalem to Egypt for the making of the Septuagint translation was written on leather skins ($\delta\iota\phi\theta\acute{\epsilon}\rho\alpha\iota$).[25] Most of the Dead Sea Scrolls were written on leather and parchment.[26]

When skins are given a special treatment to prepare them for writing, the material is known as parchment. Whereas leather is tanned, parchment is made by soaking the skin in limewater, scraping off the hair on the one side and the flesh on the other, stretching and drying in a frame, and rubbing with chalk and pumice stone, thus producing a fine material capable of receiving writing on both sides. The skins of sheep, goats, and other animals are used for parchment, but the finest kind of all is prepared from calfskins. This is properly called

---

[19] *Canon and Text of the New Testament.* 1907, p.317.

[20] ARE II, §433.

[21] v, 58. For other ancient references see G. R. Driver, *Semitic Writing.* rev. ed. 1954, pp.81f. See also R. J. Forbes, *Studies in Ancient Technology.* v (1957), pp.1-77.

[22] L. Löw, *Graphische Requisiten und Erzeugnisse bei den Juden.* (1870-71) I, p.114.

[23] The knife employed was a "scribe's knife" (LXX [ed. Swete, III, p.328], $\tau\hat{\wp}$ $\xi\upsilon\rho\hat{\wp}$ $\tau o\hat{\upsilon}$ $\gamma\rho\alpha\mu\mu\alpha\tau\acute{\epsilon}\omega s$), such as a scribe used for making erasures on leather. On the other hand it can be held that the king would have been more apt to throw papyrus than leather into the fire in his brazier to burn.

[24] *Makkoth.* 11a. SBT p.71.

[25] *Letter of Aristeas.* 3, 176. ed. H. G. Meecham. 1935, pp.5,25,174; Josephus, *Ant.* XII, ii, 11.

[26] Sukenik, *The Dead Sea Scrolls of the Hebrew University,* p.25.

"vellum,"[27] but the name vellum is now used also less discriminatingly to include the other kinds of skins as well, when prepared with particular care to receive writing. The chief marks of vellum are its semitransparent fineness and the striking beauty of its polish.[28]

The Latin expression for parchment was *membrana,* while the Greeks continued to employ the term διφθέρα, meaning leather, or borrowed the word μεμβράνα from the Romans. The word περγαμηνή, *pergamena,* or "parchment,"[29] appears first in an edict of Diocletian in A.D. 301, and apparently is derived from the city of Pergamum in Asia Minor. According to Pliny,[30] Varro stated that parchment was invented at Pergamum. His story was that rivalry existed between King Eumenes II (197-159 B.C.) of Pergamum and King Ptolemy of Egypt over their respective libraries. Since Ptolemy feared that the library at Pergamum might come to surpass the library of Alexandria, he endeavored to retard the literary progress of the rival city by prohibiting the export of papyrus from Egypt. Consequently, the people of Pergamum were driven to the invention of parchment. This account can hardly be historical, but it is doubtless true that a high quality of parchment was developed at Pergamum and that the city was famous for its manufacture and export.[31]

The statement of Herodotus already cited that it was the barbarians who wrote on the skins of goats and sheep, suggests that in the Mediterranean world in general parchment was not at that time as much used as papyrus. In the first century B.C. Roman writers make occasional references to parchment,[32] but it still appears to have been generally regarded as inferior to papyrus. Likewise in the first century A.D. Quintillian (A.D. c.35-c.100), for example, mentions the use of parchment notebooks in the law courts, but himself preferred to write on wax tablets rather than parchment because the latter, "although of assistance to the eye, delays the hand and interrupts the stream of thought owing to the frequency with which the pen has to be supplied with ink."[33] In an interesting passage in II Timothy 4:13 a request is made for the bringing of "the books,

[27] French, *vélin;* from Latin *vitellus,* diminutive of *vitulus,* a calf.
[28] G. Peignot, *Essai sur l'histoire du parchemin et du vélin.* 1812, p.28.
[29] cf. German, *Pergament;* French, *parchemin.*
[30] *Natural History.* xiii, 21.
[31] Theodor Birt, *Kritik und Hermeneutik nebst Abriss des antiken Buchwesens* (*Handbuch der klassischen Altertumswissenschaft.* 1913), p.280.
[32] Cicero, *Letters to Atticus.* xiii, xxiv; Horace ii, iii, 2.
[33] *Institutio Oratoria.* x, iii, 31. tr. H. E. Butler, LCL (1921-22), iv, p.109.

and above all the parchments" (τὰ βιβλία, μάλιστα τὰς μεμβράνας).[34]
The "books" would have been in the first instance papyrus rolls,
while the "parchments" could have been vellum rolls of the Old
Testament, although it is also possible that both the papyrus and
the parchment were yet to be written on.[35] A fragment now in the
British Museum shows that an oration of Demosthenes was copied
on vellum, probably in the second century A.D.,[36] while a vellum
fragment of Tatian's Diatessaron has been found at Dura-Europos,
a town which was destroyed about A.D. 256.[37] There are also some
vellum fragments of the *Iliad*[38] and the *Odyssey*[39] which are believed
to have been written at least by around A.D. 300.

THE ROLL

Even as there were two chief writing materials in the early centuries of the Christian era, papyrus and parchment, so also there
were two chief forms in which written documents were prepared,
the roll and the codex.

In Pliny's description of the manufacture of papyrus already
quoted (p.387), it may be remembered that this author said papyrus was made in sheets and the sheets were united to one another
to make a roll. The single sheet[40] could, of course, be made in a
variety of sizes, and papyri are extant which vary in size from less
than two inches to over fifteen inches. A sheet of average size probably ran about nine to eleven inches in height and six to nine inches
in width. For a brief letter or other document a single such sheet
might suffice, and New Testament writings such as Philemon and
II and III John probably each occupied a single sheet.[41] For a
longer writing, as Pliny shows, the sheets were glued together to

[34] cf. F. F. Bruce, *The Books and the Parchments, Some Chapters on the Transmission of the Bible.* 1950.

[35] Mackinnon (*The Rome of St. Paul*, pp.87,146) thinks that Paul's mention of
parchment implies that he used this material for his own letters which he knew to
be of permanent value, but the "occasional" character of Paul's correspondence may
make this supposition open to question.

[36] Kenyon, *The Palaeography of Greek Papyri*, p.113.

[37] C. H. Kraeling, *A Greek Fragment of Tatian's Diatessaron from Dura.* 1935.

[38] E. M. Thompson, *An Introduction to Greek and Latin Palaeography.* 1912,
pp.198f., 201.

[39] A. S. Hunt, *Catalogue of the Greek Papyri in the John Rylands Library.* I (1911),
p.91.

[40] The sheet was called a κόλλημα because the strips of papyrus of which it was
made up were glued together (κολλᾶν). Papyrus which was prepared for writing but
not yet written upon was called χάρτης as in II John 12. HPUM p.6 n.29, 30.

[41] F. G. Kenyon, *Books and Readers in Ancient Greece and Rome.* 1932, pp.49f.

form an extended strip and this was rolled up for convenience in handling.

When Pliny said that a papyrus roll never consisted of more than twenty of these sheets, he must have been referring to the length of the papyrus rolls as they were customarily placed on the market. With individual sheets not usually running over nine inches in width, a roll such as Pliny refers to, composed of twenty sheets, would have attained a length of fifteen feet at the maximum. Of course if the work of an individual writer did not extend to this length he could cut off a portion, or if it was of greater length he could glue a second roll onto the first. A normal Greek literary roll probably did not exceed thirty-five feet, but Egyptian ceremonial copies of the Book of the Dead were often fifty or one hundred feet in length. The longest papyrus known is a panegyrical chronicle of the reign of Ramses II called the Harris Papyrus, which is 133 feet in length and seventeen inches in height.[42] An average roll in New Testament times, however, would have been probably thirty or thirty-five feet in length, and when rolled up upon itself would have appeared as a cylinder perhaps ten inches in height and one or one and one-half inches in diameter. A book such as the Gospel according to Luke would have filled an ordinary papyrus roll thirty-one or thirty-two feet long, while the book of Acts by the same author would have required a second such roll, and it has been surmised that this is one of the reasons why Luke-Acts was issued in two volumes (Acts 1:1). Likewise if Paul's ten collected church letters (including Philemon) were issued in this form they would probably have filled two papyrus rolls. The papyrus roll (Greenfield Papyrus) shown in Fig. 136 is considerably larger than the average since it measures nineteen inches in height. Other and smaller rolls both open and sealed are shown in Fig. 139.

A sheet or roll of papyrus was ordinarily written on only one side, that where the papyrus fibers ran in the horizontal direction naturally being preferable and being used for the front or right side which is known as the *recto* in speaking of a manuscript. The other side or *verso*, meaning reverse or left, where in the case of a papyrus sheet the component strips were running vertically, could also be used, however, and a roll written on both front and back is called an opisthograph. It is a book of this sort which is described in Revelation 5:1, "a scroll written within and on the back, sealed with seven

[42] ARE IV, §§151-412.

seals." The text was written in a column or series of columns (σελίδες), each of which was usually two or three inches wide. In the case of a roll, these columns were not correlated with the sheets of papyrus and the writing frequently ran over the juncture of two sheets. Except in the more elegant books the margins were not large and the columns were close together.

It is obvious that the roll form could also be used with leather or parchment as well as with papyrus, and in the Dead Sea Scrolls we have seen numerous examples of Old Testament and also of non-canonical writings in this form.[43]

How widely used the roll form and the papyrus material were is shown by the fact that the ordinary Greek word for "book" etymologically meant a papyrus scroll. The fibrous part of the papyrus plant (πάπυρος) from which paper was made was known as βύβλος or βίβλος, and this word, preferably in the form βίβλος and indeed most frequently in the diminutive form βιβλίον, was the usual word for "book."[44] These words may be seen in their ordinary Greek usage, for example, in Herodotus[45] where Egyptian priests recite from a book (βύβλος) the names of their kings, and in Aristotle[46] where this author refers to his book (βιβλίον) on meteorology, and in each case it was presumably a papyrus roll which was meant. Although etymologically the word implied papyrus it was also used for a written roll of leather or parchment, as may be seen in Luke 4:17 where "the book (βιβλίον) of the prophet Isaiah" must have been, in accordance with ordinary Jewish usage and as illustrated almost contemporaneously at Qumran, a leather scroll. Also in the passage already cited (pp.391f.), II Timothy 4:13, where request is made to bring "the books, and above all the parchments" (τὰ βιβλία, μάλιστα τὰς μεμβράνας), the manner of expression makes it seem that the word βιβλία is inclusive of the parchments as well as of the papyri. Likewise although βιβλίον usually referred to a roll it could presumably be used for a book or written document even in some other form. Thus the paper (βυβλίον) sealed up in a fish of which Herodotus[47] tells, and the certificate (βιβλίον) of divorce mentioned in Matthew 19:7 = Mark 10:4 might not necessarily have been in the form of rolls.

[43] For the roll form in the Old Testament cf. Psalm 40:7; Ezekiel 2:9; Zechariah 5:1.

[44] In Latin the word for a book in the form of a scroll was *volumen*, from the verb *volvere*, "to roll."

[45] II, 100.   [46] *On Plants.* II, ii, 1.   [47] I, 123.

As seen in the quotation from II Timothy 4:13, the plural of βιβλίον is βιβλία. In I Maccabees 12:9 the plural word occurs in the phrase τὰ βιβλία τὰ ἅγια, "the holy books," no doubt referring to books of the Old Testament. In II Clement 14:2 it is stated that "the books and the apostles" (τὰ βιβλία καὶ οἱ ἀπόστολοι) show that the church is not of the present but from the beginning or from above (ἄνωθεν), and here again τὰ βιβλία certainly refers to holy books, perhaps to ones of the Old Testament (with οἱ ἀπόστολοι referring to New Testament books), or perhaps even to ones of the New Testament. Thus τὰ βιβλία, that is "the books" par excellence, came to be the name for the scriptures. In Latin the word was *biblia* and eventually this plural noun came to be regarded as singular and so the name "Bible" emerged.

THE CODEX

The other chief form of book was the codex. In spite of how widely and long it was used, the roll was after all a relatively inconvenient form. The reader had to employ both hands, unrolling with one hand and rolling up with the other as the reading proceeded. Moreover, there was no simple way to give a reference to a specific passage within a longer roll, and to find a given section might necessitate unrolling the scroll to the very end. Consequently it was inevitable and desirable that the roll should be superseded by a more readily usable form of book. This was found in the codex, where the leaves of the manuscript were fastened together as in a modern book.

The Latin word *caudex* or *codex* meant originally the trunk of a tree, and then a block of wood split up into leaves or tablets.[48] It was possible to write on such a leaf directly, or to cover it with wax and thereby to have a readily erasable writing surface. There is reference to writing on tablets, presumably of wood, in Isaiah 8:1; 30:8; and Luke 1:63. In Rome these wooden tablets, used either plain or with a covering of wax, were known as *tabellae*, and there are actual examples of them extant from Pompeii with dates corresponding to A.D. 53 and 55.[49] When several of these were bound together a convenient notebook was produced which was commonly called a *pugillaris* (sc. *libellus*), literally a "fist (book)," or a handbook. From this point it was an easy step to employ leaves of papyrus or parchment instead of wood, and when this was done the flexibility and utility of the codex form of book were greatly improved. Thus finally the

[48] George Milligan, *The New Testament and Its Transmission.* 1932, p.15.
[49] David Diringer, *The Hand-Produced Book.* 1953, p.33.

word "codex" could designate any leaf book, whether of papyrus, parchment, or other material.

In the centuries just before and after the turn of the era, the Dead Sea Scrolls show us that the roll was the prevailing form for Jewish writings, and at the same time the same was true for works of literature in the pagan world. According to a recent enumeration, 476 non-Christian literary papyrus manuscripts have been found in Egypt dating from the second century A.D., and of these 465 or more than 97 per cent are in the form of the roll.[50] But already at least in the first century A.D. the codex was also being used even for pagan literature. In about A.D. 85 the Latin writer Martial composed a number of verses to accompany presents such as the Romans gave to their friends at the Saturnalia. Found in Book XIV of his Epigrams, these poems contain references to what we may call "pocket editions" in the form of parchment (*membrana*) codices of Homer, Virgil, Cicero, and Livy. Concerning a parchment codex edition of Virgil (*Vergilius in membranis*), Martial remarks on how much such a small parchment book would hold.[51] Similarly he recommends a parchment codex of Cicero (*Cicero in membranis*) as a handy traveling companion.[52]

Interestingly enough, particularly in Christian circles the codex seems to have been specially favored and used from a very early date. From the second century A.D., when 97 per cent of the non-Christian literary papyri were in the roll form, we have by recent enumeration eight Christian biblical papyri and all of these are in the form of the codex. In the entire period extending to shortly after the end of the fourth century, we have 111 biblical manuscripts or fragments from Egypt, of which 99 are codices.[53] Some of the New Testament papyri will be listed a little later in this chapter and it will be seen that almost all of them are from codices. Likewise the great parchment manuscripts of the fourth century and onward, Codex Vaticanus, Codex Sinaiticus, and so on, are, as these names indicate, in the same form.

Since the examples we are fortunate enough to possess will hardly

[50] C. H. Roberts in PBA 40 (1954), p.184; cf. C. C. McCown in BA 6 (1943), p.27.

[51] XIV, 186.

[52] XIV, 188. In itself the word *membrana* simply means skin prepared for writing, or parchment, and it can be used of parchment rolls, but in most cases where it appears in classical Latin it is in a context which requires or permits the meaning of notebook or codex (Roberts in PBA 40 [1954], p. 174).

[53] C. C. McCown in HTR 34 (1941), pp.219-250; Roberts in PBA 40 (1954), pp.185-191.

have been the first of their kind, it appears very possible that the codex was used for Christian books even in the first century A.D. at which time, as we have seen from Martial, this form of book was definitely available. The correspondence of the books of Luke and Acts to the length of an ordinary papyrus roll each, has already been noted (p.393) as a possible indication that these works were composed in that form. There is a possible intimation, on the other hand, that the Gospel according to Mark might have been written originally in a codex in the fact that its original ending seems to be missing and could have been lost by wear and tear: in a codex the last leaf is most likely to suffer damage; in a roll the destruction is most apt to be at the beginning. Like the numerous papyrus communications now known from the everyday life of the ancient world and to be illustrated later in this chapter, it may be supposed that the letters of Paul were written originally on papyrus, Philemon on a single sheet, longer letters on rolls. When Paul's letters were collected, however, probably in the latter part of the first century, the codex form was available and, since the purpose of the collection was to make it possible to consult these writings and this could be done much more readily in a codex than in a roll, the collection may well have been made in that form,[54] even as our oldest copy of the collection, namely $\mathfrak{p}^{46}$, is a codex.

By the fourth century A.D. both the codex form and the parchment material were in supreme use for New Testament and biblical manuscripts. In A.D. 332 the Emperor Constantine instructed Eusebius to have fifty parchment manuscripts of the Bible prepared for the churches in his new capital, Constantinople. The letter of the emperor to Eusebius read in part: "I have thought it expedient to instruct your Prudence to order fifty copies of the sacred Scriptures, the provision and use of which you know to be most needful for the instruction of the Church, to be written on prepared parchment in a legible manner, and in a convenient, portable form, by professional transcribers thoroughly practiced in their art."[55]

"Such were the emperor's commands," reports Eusebius, "which were followed by the immediate execution of the work itself, which we sent him in magnificent and elaborately bound volumes of a threefold and fourfold form."[56] The expression "threefold and fourfold" (τρισσὰ καὶ τετρασσά) probably means "having three columns

---

[54] G. Zuntz, *The Text of the Epistles.* 1953, p.15.

[55] *Life of Constantine.* IV, 36 (πεντήκοντα σωμάτια ἐν διφθέραις).

[56] *ibid.,* IV, 37.

and four columns" and indicates that the pages were written respectively in three columns and in four columns.[57] Furthermore, two great vellum codices of the Bible, dating probably about the middle of the fourth century A.D., are still extant, Codex Vaticanus and Codex Sinaiticus. Although the probability seems to be that they were copied in Egypt and thus would hardly have been among the manuscripts ordered by Constantine, it is interesting to find that they have three and four columns of writing per page respectively. We also learn that about the middle of the same century the famous library of Origen (d. A.D. c.254) and Pamphilus (d. A.D. 309) at Caesarea had fallen into decay and was restored by two priests, Acacius and Euzoius, who replaced what were probably damaged papyrus rolls with copies written on parchment (*in membranis*) and presumably in codices.[58] From this time on, parchment or vellum remained the chief writing material until the general establishment of the use of paper in the fourteenth century; and the codex was retained permanently as the prevailing form of books.

Like modern books the ancient codices were bound in quires. A sheet of papyrus was folded once in the middle, thus forming two leaves or folios[59] of equal size. By fastening together a number of such two-leaf quires a codex was made. Or a more extensive quire could be made by laying a larger number of sheets one upon another, these forming, when folded, a correspondingly larger number of leaves. In the case of $\mathfrak{p}^{46}$ fifty-two sheets of papyrus were laid together, recto side on top, and the whole pile was folded in the middle to make 104 folios. The bulk of so many sheets folded together in such a single-quire book made difficulty, however, in that the middle pages were pushed out and might even have to be trimmed at the edge of the book, thus reducing the area of the inner pages. Accordingly the multiple-quire book was ultimately the preferred form. Also instead of laying the sheets of a quire all with the recto side on top, it was often the custom to place alternately uppermost the recto and the verso, so that when the book was opened a recto page would face a recto page, and a verso a verso. If the same principle was followed in the quires of a parchment or vellum codex, the flesh side of each sheet was laid upon the flesh side of another, and the hair side upon a hair side, so that when the book was opened the pages

[57] J. H. Ropes in F. J. Foakes Jackson and Kirsopp Lake, *The Beginnings of Christianity*, Part I, *The Acts of the Apostles*. III (1926), p.xxxvii.

[58] Jerome, *Epistle*. 34 (141); MPL XXII, col. 448; cf. F. G. Kenyon in HDB IV, p.947.

[59] From Latin *folium*, leaf.

which faced each other were of similar kind. In order to guide the writing, lines were drawn on the hair side with a sharp instrument and allowed to show through on the flesh side.

The adoption of the codex also led gradually to a change in the style of columns employed. In the roll form of book it had been convenient to write in narrow columns of short lines, and the first great vellum manuscripts, especially Codex Sinaiticus, reflect their inheritance from the roll in the narrow columns of writing which they use. With the codex it became desirable to write in wider columns of longer lines, and eventually the prevailing practice was that of having only one or two columns on each page.[60]

PEN AND INK

Writing was done with pen and ink. In a room at Qumran which was evidently the scriptorium of the community centered at that place, there were long, narrow writing tables, and in the debris two actual inkwells were found, one of bronze and the other of terra cotta, one still containing some dried ink.[61] In the New Testament pen and ink are mentioned in III John 13, and ink also in II John 12 and II Corinthians 3:3.[62] The Greek word for pen is κάλαμος which also means reed, and a pen of this sort was made from a thoroughly dried reed stalk, the end of which was sharpened to a point and split into two parts. The word for ink is μέλαν which also means "black." Two kinds of ink were in common use, one made from lampblack, gum, and water, and the other from nutgalls, green vitriol, and water. The former was very black and unfading, the latter turned in the course of time into a handsome rusty brown color.[63]

STYLES OF HANDWRITING

In the Roman period manuscripts of a literary character were generally written in a relatively handsome, regular "bookhand," while other documents and letters were often written in a nonliterary script of "cursive" type. In the latter case the letters were characterized by their roundness and relative continuity of formation, the pen being carried on to some extent from one character to another. The literary

---

[60] HPUM pp.17-19; McCown in HTR 34 (1941), p.228.

[61] R. de Vaux in RB 61 (1954), p.212 Pls. ixa, xb. On the book trade in the Roman empire see Felix Reichmann in *The Library Quarterly.* 8 (1938), pp.40-76.

[62] In the Old Testament the pen is mentioned in Jeremiah 8:8 and Psalm 45:1; and ink in Jeremiah 36:18. See Driver, *Semitic Writing*, pp.84-86.

[63] HPUM pp.13-15.

and nonliterary scripts were sometimes used side by side, and their forms also varied a great deal from one period to another, occasionally almost approximating one another and again diverging widely. The appearance of any given manuscript depended, of course, largely upon the skill and neatness of the individual or individuals who wrote it, and at all times there was both poor writing and good.[64]

Writings such as those of Paul, which have every appearance of genuine letters rather than literary productions, were probably written originally in the nonliterary script. These letters, however, were often dictated to Christian helpers who, since they rendered this service for Paul, were probably practiced in the art of penmanship. The use of such secretarial assistants is shown in Romans 16:22 where the scribe interjects, "I Tertius, the writer of this letter, greet you in the Lord," and is also indicated by Paul's custom of adding the closing part of the letter in his own handwriting (II Thessalonians 3:17). In Galatians 6:11 Paul refers to his own writing as being with "large letters." This probably means that as a man more accustomed to manual labor (cf. I Thessalonians 2:9; Acts 18:3) than to the fine art of penmanship, Paul made relatively large, stiff, square characters which contrasted with the flowing cursive script of his scribe. It may be presumed, therefore, that the main body of a Pauline letter was written originally in a relatively careful and practiced hand of the nonliterary type. When the New Testament writings came to be regarded as literature, however, they were naturally copied in the literary bookhand. This style of handwriting developed into the handsome form which is found in the vellum codices and to which the term "uncial" is customarily applied. "Uncial characters" are mentioned by Jerome[65] (A.D. c.340-420) in connection with elegant manuscripts of his time, and since the Latin word *uncia* means "the twelfth part" it is thought that an uncial character may have been one occupying about one-twelfth of a line.[66] This would fit the case of Codex Sinaiticus, for example, where there are approximately twelve letters per line. The New Testament codices from the fourth to the ninth centuries were written in uncial characters.

The uncial style of writing was quite slow and cumbersome, however, and the need was felt for a script which could be written

---

[64] H. Idris Bell in EB XVII, p.97; Wilhelm Schubart, *Griechische Palaeographie* (in Walter Otto, ed., *Handbuch der Altertumswissenschaft.* I, iv, 1. 1925), p.19.

[65] *Preface to Job* (NPNFSS VI, p.492).

[66] HPUM p.22 n.5.

more easily and swiftly and yet be of sufficient legibility and beauty to be employed appropriately for literary and sacred writings. The rapid nonliterary cursive script which we met with in Roman times had continued in use in various forms during the Byzantine period (A.D. c.300-c.650) but did not have the dignity demanded by the Bible and works of literature. From it there was developed, however, a truly calligraphic script which could still be written at a relatively high speed. This is known as minuscule script and is characterized by smaller, differently formed letters, many of which are connected without the raising of the pen. Coming into use in the ninth century, the minuscule hand gradually superseded the uncial characters and thereafter was never supplanted but continued in use as long as books were copied by hand. Thus, numerically speaking, the great mass of New Testament manuscripts are minuscules.[67]

By careful study of these various styles of handwriting and the many intermediate changes of form which they underwent, paleographers are able to establish at least approximate dates for manuscripts upon the basis of the character of the writing which they display.[68]

PUNCTUATION

In the first century, manuscripts were usually written practically without punctuation and with the words following each other in an unbroken succession of letters, as if one should begin to copy Paul's Letter to the Romans in the English in this manner:

PAULASERVANTOFJESUSCHRISTCALLEDTO

BEANAPOSTLESEPARATEDUNTOTHEGOSPE

LOFGODWHICHHEPROMISEDAFORETHROU

GHHISPROPHETSINTHEHOLYSCRIPTURES

Those who were accustomed to such writing could read it rapidly, but even so the possibility of error and misunderstanding was present owing to the absence of punctuation and the lack of division between words. There was, therefore, a gradual increase in the employment of punctuation marks and other aids to the reader.

In the second century papyrus fragment of the Gospel according to John designated as $\mathfrak{p}^{52}$ the words sometimes appear to be slightly

---

[67] F. G. Kenyon, *Handbook to the Textual Criticism of the New Testament.* 2d ed. 1912, p.124; and see HFDMM.

[68] cf. Thompson, *An Introduction to Greek and Latin Palaeography*, pp.144-147; and see C. H. Roberts, *Greek Literary Hands 350 B.C.-A.D. 400.* 1956.

separated, but there is still no punctuation, although a dieresis is placed over the initial letter Iota. In the Chester Beatty Papyrus of the Letters of Paul ($\mathfrak{p}^{46}$) there are occasional slight intervals between words to mark pauses in sense, initial Iota and Upsilon are marked with a dieresis, and Greek breathings and accents are employed. Also a single point is occasionally used to mark a division in the text. Such use of a point or dot became more frequent in later centuries and high, middle, and low points were differentiated to indicate respectively what would now be signified by a period, a comma, and a semicolon. Eventually a comma proper, a colon, and a question mark written like a modern semicolon, as well as some other marks came to be employed.

Brief headings to the various books are found as early as the Chester Beatty Papyrus of Paul's Letters ($\mathfrak{p}^{46}$), where there are also subscriptions giving the number of stichoi ($\sigma\tau\iota\chi o\iota$) contained, the latter being standard lines probably of a standard number of letters or syllables used in the measurement of the length of a manuscript.[69] Later the superscriptions and subscriptions of the New Testament books were expanded to contain more data of a traditional character concerning their origin.

To facilitate reference the pages of a codex and also the columns of a scroll could be numbered as may be seen, for example, in $\mathfrak{p}^{46}$ and $\mathfrak{p}^{13}$ respectively.[70] The convenience of the readers was served further by the making of divisions in the text. In $\mathfrak{p}^{64}$ (p.418), fragmentary though it is, there is evidence that the text was divided into sections. In Codex Vaticanus the Gospels are divided into a large

---

[69] Charles Graux in *Revue de Philologie.* 2 (1878), pp.97-143; J. Rendel Harris, *Stichometry.* 1893; and in NSH XI, pp.91-94; Jack Finegan in HTR 49 (1956), pp.97-101.

[70] The letters of the Greek alphabet were used for numerals as follows:

Alpha	a'	1	Omicron	o'	70
Beta	β'	2	Pi	π'	80
Gamma	γ'	3	Koppa	φ'	90
Delta	δ'	4	Rho	ρ'	100
Epsilon	ϵ'	5	Sigma	σ'	200
Vau	F'	6	Tau	τ'	300
Zeta	ζ'	7	Upsilon	v'	400
Eta	η'	8	Phi	ϕ'	500
Theta	θ'	9	Chi	χ'	600
Iota	ι'	10	Psi	ψ'	700
Kappa	κ'	20	Omega	ω'	800
Lambda	λ'	30	Sampi	$\mathfrak{z}'$	900
Mu	μ'	40		a	1,000
Nu	ν'	50		$'$	etc.
Xi	ξ'	60			

number of sections and Paul's letters are divided into chapters which are numbered continuously throughout as if all the letters formed one book. In Codex Alexandrinus there are also chapters (κεφάλαια) with summary headings (τίτλοι) describing their contents.[71] On the basis of earlier work by Ammonius of Alexandria, Eusebius of Caesarea divided the Gospels into sections (the "Ammonian Sections") and prepared tables (the "Eusebian Canons") of parallel and independent passages,[72] while the so-called "Euthalian Apparatus" supplied tables of chapters, tables of Old Testament quotations, and other introductory materials for Acts and the Epistles.[73] The system of chapter divisions now found in the New Testament was the work of Cardinal Hugo de S. Caro in 1238, while the modern verses were introduced by Robert Étienne (Stephanus) in 1551.

NOMINA SACRA

Another interesting feature of the biblical manuscripts is the employment of abbreviations for the sacred names (*nomina sacra*) and for certain other words. Instead of writing the name in full, the scribe would save time and space by writing only a few of the letters, usually the first and last, and drawing a line above them thus:

K̄C̄	X̄C̄ X̄P̄C̄	ΠNA̅
κύριος	χριστός	πνεῦμα
Lord	Christ	Spirit

Θ̄C̄	Π̄P̄ Π̄H̄P̄	A̅N̅C̅ A̅N̅O̅C̅
θεός	πατήρ	ἄνθρωπος
God	Father	man

Ī̄C̄ Ī̄H̄C̄ Ī̄H̄	Ȳ̄C̄	C̄T̄C̄ C̄P̄C̄ C̄T̄P̄C̄
Ἰησοῦς	υἱός	σταυρός
Jesus	Son	cross

Π̄P̄O̅Φ̅A̅C̅
προφήτας
prophets

Such abbreviations appear in the fragments of an unknown Gospel dating probably around the middle of the second century A.D.

[71] Kirsopp Lake, *The Text of the New Testament.* 6th ed. rev. by Silva New, 1928, pp.55f.

[72] These tables as well as the letter of Eusebius to Carpian in which he describes the plan of his work are printed regularly in the preface to Nestle's *Novum Testamentum Graece.* 16th ed. 1936.

[73] Ernst von Dobschütz in NSH IV, p.215.

(p.413), in $\mathfrak{p}^{64}$ of the latter part of the second century (p.417f.), in $\mathfrak{p}^{46}$ (p.420) and $\mathfrak{p}^{66}$ (p.425) both of around A.D. 200, and in many other manuscripts down to the latest times.[74] It is probable that the practice of making contractions of this type was borrowed by the Christians from the Jews. When the Jews translated the Tetragrammaton YHWH into Greek they represented the holy name by Lord or God, written in the abbreviated forms shown above. The Christians naturally adopted this practice and extended it to the specifically Christian names and to other words as well.[75]

2. THE MODERN DISCOVERY
OF ANCIENT PAPYRI

Now we may turn to the story of the actual recovery of ancient manuscripts, and first of all those written on papyrus. The first papyri to reach Europe, so far as is known, were one Greek and two Latin fragments which were given to the library at Basel about the end of the sixteenth century by the theologian Johann Jakob Grynaeus. In 1752 the charred remains of a library of Greek philosophical works were found in the ruins of Herculaneum, and in 1778 an unknown European dealer in antiquities purchased a papyrus roll from Egyptians who had already burned fifty other ancient rolls because they enjoyed the aromatic odor![1] Since that first discovery Egypt has proved to be an almost inexhaustible storehouse of ancient papyri. In its dry climate and buried beneath its drifted sands the fragile papyri have resisted the ravages of time as effectively, and endured as indestructibly, as the pyramids.

During the nineteenth century an increasing number of papyri found their way to the museums of Europe, as the *fellahin* of Egypt awakened to the fact that they could obtain money for these ancient fragments. Many papyri were found accidentally by persons digging

[74] Gregory, *Canon and Text of the New Testament*, p.335. No sacred names appear on the tiny second century fragment of the Gospel according to John (p.417; Fig. 142), so it cannot be told whether abbreviations were employed in this manuscript. The earliest literary attestation of the abbreviation IH for the name of Jesus appears around A.D. 130 in the *Letter of Barnabas* (9 [ANF I, p.143]).

[75] Ludwig Traube, *Nomina Sacra, Versuch einer Geschichte der christlichen Kürzung.* 1907, p.31. Gunnar Rudberg (in *Skrifter utgifna af Kungl. Humanistiska Vetenskaps-Samfundet i Uppsala.* 17 [1915], No. 3) proposes the less plausible theory that the practice was taken over from the use of short forms of the names of the Roman emperors.

[1] DLO p.23; Ulrich Wilcken, *Die griechischen Papyrusurkunden*, p.10.

in the ancient mounds for *sebakh,* or nitrous earth which is used for fertilizer. Others were unearthed by Egyptian antique dealers and also by illicit plunderers. In 1877 a great mass of papyri was discovered in the site of Arsinoë, which earlier was Crocodilopolis, in the Fayum, but probably half of it was lost through carelessness.[2]

Before the end of the nineteenth century, however, the Fayum became the scene of truly scientific and highly rewarding work in the recovery of papyri. This district, in which such important finds have been made, is a sunken oasis in the Libyan desert west of the Nile, its capital, Medinet el-Fayum, being about eighty miles south-south-west of Cairo. In ancient times the famous Lake of Moeris[3] occupied a large part of this depression and still is represented by the Birket Qarun. The Egyptian name for this lake was *Shei,* "the lake," and later *Piom,* "the sea," whence the name Fayum is derived. The capital and most important city of the district was situated on this lake, and was a center of worship of the crocodile god, Sebek. The city was known to the Greeks as Crocodilopolis, or Arsinoë,[4] and its ruins are represented by mounds north of the present capital, Medinet el-Fayum. There were other towns and villages in the district, and just south of the oasis was the important city of Oxyrhynchus, the modern Behnesa. It was only about ten miles from the Nile, and on the chief canal (Bahr Yusef) which brought water to the Fayum. In ancient times Oxyrhynchus was the capital of the Oxyrhynchite nome, and in the fourth and fifth centuries A.D. was famous for the number of its churches and monasteries, Christianity apparently having found a place there at a relatively early date.

In the winter of 1889-1890, Professor Flinders Petrie excavated a Ptolemaic cemetery at Gurob, near the mouth of the Fayum, and found a quantity of papyrus manuscripts which had been used as cartonnage in making the inner coffins of mummies. Professor Petrie, of course, fully realized the value of such finds and patiently recovered from their unusual place of preservation all the papyri possible. Then, in the winter of 1895-1896, the Egypt Exploration Fund sent out under the leadership of Drs. B. P. Grenfell, A. S. Hunt, and D. G. Hogarth the first expedition definitely undertaken for the discovery of papyri. The work which was done that year, and continued by

---

[2] James Baikie, *Egyptian Papyri and Papyrus Hunting.* 1925, pp.230f.

[3] Herodotus. II, 149; Strabo, *Geography.* xvii, i, 35.

[4] Strabo, *Geography.* xvii, i, 38.

Grenfell and Hunt during a number of subsequent seasons, was amazingly successful.[5]

At Tebtunis papyri were found in a resting place even stranger than the human mummy cases at Gurob. Here, there was a crocodile cemetery in which sacred crocodiles had been buried ceremonially. One after another of the mummified crocodiles was turned up, until finally a workman, who was hoping for far better finds, in disgust smashed one of the burials in pieces. It broke open, revealing that the crocodile had been wrapped in the same kind of papyrus cartonnage as the Gurob mummies, and in several instances papyrus rolls were found stuffed into the animals' mouths or other cavities in their bodies.

Oxyrhynchus was no doubt the most rewarding site of all, and the publication of the papyri from this one place has filled a whole series of volumes.[6] In what follows, Oxyrhynchus papyri will be cited a number of times. All together, Grenfell and Hunt recovered from the sands of Egypt many thousands of manuscripts and fragments of papyrus, while other workers who followed them have made many important additions to the vast mass of material now available for papyrological research.

EARLY PAPYRUS LETTERS

Since much of the New Testament and particularly the part connected with the name of Paul was written in the form of letters, it will be of special interest to notice the numerous pagan letters on papyrus which we have from about the same time. On June 17, 1 B.C., an Egyptian laborer Hilarion, who had gone to Alexandria to work, wrote a short letter to his wife Alis, who had remained at home in Oxyrhynchus. The letter (Fig. 140) sounds amazingly modern at most points, yet reflects the pagan custom of exposure of children. It reads:

"Hilarion to Alis his sister, heartiest greetings, and to my lady Berous and to Apollonarion. Know that we are still even now in Alexandria. Do not worry if when all the others return I remain in Alexandria. I beg and beseech of you to take care of the little child. And as soon as we receive wages I will send them to you. If—good luck to you!—you bear a child, if it is a boy, let it live; if it is a girl, expose it. You told Aphrodisias, 'Do not forget me.' How can I forget you? I beg you, therefore, not to worry."[7]

---

[5] Grenfell, Hunt, and Hogarth, *Fayum Towns and Their Papyri.* 1900.

[6] op 1898ff. For Oxyrhynchus in Roman times see E. G. Turner in JEA 38 (1952), pp.78-93.

[7] op IV, No.744; Wilhelm Schubart, *Ein Jahrtausend am Nil.* 2d ed. 1923, pp.65f.; DLO pp.134-136.

At the bottom is the date, "In the 29th year of Caesar, Pauni 23," corresponding to June 17, 1 B.C.,[8] and on the back side is the address: "Hilarion to Alis, deliver." The greeting of Alis as "sister" may be only a tender form of address but perhaps is to be taken literally since marriages of brother and sister were not uncommon in Egypt. Berous, who is courteously called "lady"[9] may have been the mother of Alis, and Apollonarion perhaps was the child of Alis and Hilarion. On the whole the letter is written rather crudely and contains a number of grammatical errors, such as the use of the accusative when the dative is required,[10] which are not shown in the translation above.

On September 13, A.D. 50, an Egyptian olive planter named Mystarion sent a letter to a chief priest named Stotoëtis in order to introduce a certain Blastus who was to perform an errand and return quickly:

"Mystarion to his own Stotoëtis many greetings. I have sent unto you[11] my Blastus for forked sticks for my olive-gardens. See then that you do not stay him. For you know how I need him every hour.
"Farewell
"In the year 11 of Tiberius Claudius Caesar Augustus Germanicus Imperator in the month Sebastos 15."[12]

The address was written on the back: "To Stotoëtis, chief priest, at the island. . . ." This note was penned at the very time when the first of Paul's letters were being written and is an example of letters of introduction such as Paul himself mentions and writes (I Corinthians 16:3; II Corinthians 3:1; Romans 16:1). But the letter of Mystarion is of special interest because the closing "Farewell" and the lengthy date are written in a hand different from the careful scribal hand in which the body of the letter and the address on the back are penned. Evidently Mystarion himself took the pen at the close to add a final personal touch, just as Paul said he did in every letter (II Thessalonians 3:17; cf. Galatians 6:11; I Corinthians 16:21; Colossians 4:18).

The timeless woes of human life are reflected poignantly in a tiny[13]

---

[8] For the months see the table in George Milligan, *Selections from the Greek Papyri*. 1910, p.xviii.

[9] The same polite form of address is found in II John 1 and 5.

[10] In line 8 of the Greek text.

[11] The grammar is exactly the same as in I Corinthians 4:17 and similar passages.

[12] Fritz Krebs, *Ägyptische Urkunden aus den Königlichen Museen zu Berlin, Griechische Urkunden*. I, No.37; DLO pp.136-139.

[13] The actual size of the papyrus is about three inches square.

second century letter from Irene to Philo and Taonnophris, a married couple who have lost a son in death. Irene, who is evidently a friend of the sorrowing mother (since the latter is named before the father in the salutation), and who has already gone through the experience of losing her own loved one, Didymas, writes to the bereaved parents as follows:

"Irene to Taonnophris and Philo, good cheer.

"I am as much in grief and weep over the blessed one as I wept for Didymas. And everything that was fitting I did and so did all of mine, Epaphroditus and Thermuthion and Philion and Apollonius and Plantas. But truly there is nothing anyone can do in the face of such things. Do you therefore comfort one another.

"Farewell. Athyr 1."[14]

The letter is addressed on the back, "To Taonnophris and Philo."[15]

In the second century a young man named Apion from the small Egyptian town of Philadelphia in the Fayum entered the Roman navy and sailed to Misenum, the naval harbor near Naples. When the voyage became stormy and dangerous Apion was in peril but he prayed to the lord Serapis and was delivered. Upon reaching port he received three pieces of gold as pay, was given a new Roman name, Antonis Maximus, in keeping with his new Roman service, and was assigned to the company Athenonica. Like a modern youth in the service he had his picture made in his new uniform to send home, and then he wrote the following letter to his father:

"Apion to Epimachus his father and lord, many greetings. Before all things I pray that you are in health and that you prosper and fare well continually together with my sister and her daughter and my brother. I thank the lord Serapis that, when I was in peril in the sea, he saved me immediately. When I came to Miseni[16] I received as journey-money from the Caesar three pieces of gold. And it is well with me. I beseech you therefore, my lord father, to write me a little letter, firstly of your health, secondly of that of my brother and sister, thirdly that I may look upon your handwriting with reverence, because you have taught me well and I therefore hope to advance rapidly, if the gods will. Salute Capito much and my brother and sister and Serenilla and my friends. I am sending you by Euctemon a little picture of me. Moreover my name is Antonis[17] Maximus. Fare you well, I pray.

"Centuria Athenonica."[18]

---

[14] The date is equivalent to October 28.

[15] OP I, No.115; Milligan, *Selections from the Greek Papyri*, pp.95f.; DLO pp.143-145.

[16] This is the plural form of the name of the harbor generally called Misenum.

[17] Antonis is a short form of the name Antonius.

[18] Paul Viereck, *Ägyptische Urkunden aus den Königlichen Museen zu Berlin.* II, No.423; DLO pp.145-150.

The companions of Apion wanted him to include their greetings and since there still was room along the side of the papyrus sheet Apion added: "There salute you Serenus the son of Agathus Daemon, and . . . the son of . . . and Turbo the son of Gallonius and D . . . nas the son of. . . ." The letter was to go by military post to the garrison of the Apamenians in Egypt and through the office of the paymaster of that company be forwarded to the father. This address was written on the back, "To Philadelphia for Epimachus from Apion his son," with the instruction, "Give this to the first cohort of the Apamenians to Julianus . . . the Liblarios, from Apion so that he may send it to Epimachus his father." The lines of address and instruction were divided in the middle by two heavy X-marks which indicate the place for tying up the letter.

Not only does the letter of Apion sound as if it could have been written in the twentieth century instead of the second, but it contains a number of expressions similar to ones found in New Testament letters. "I pray that you are in health" is the same polite and standard formula of greeting that appears in III John 2. Apion's word of thanks to the lord Serapis, the Egyptian god whose worship was widespread throughout the Roman Empire, reminds one of Paul's almost constant habit of beginning his letters with thanks to God (I Thessalonians 1:2; II Thessalonians 1:3; I Corinthians 1:4; Romans 1:8; Philippians 1:3; Colossians 1:3; Philemon 4; cf. Ephesians 1:3,16). The phrase "in peril in the sea" is nearly identical with Paul's words in II Corinthians 11:26, although the Roman soldier's grammar is not quite as excellent as Paul's. Likewise "Salute Capito much" is very similar to the form of greeting in I Corinthians 16:19.

Interestingly enough we have a second letter from the same Apion to his sister, written probably years later when his father was dead and he himself had children of his own.[19]

Also filled with human interest is another second century letter, which a prodigal son wrote to his mother. Addressed on the back, "To . . . his mother from Antonius Longus her son," the pathetic epistle reads:

"Antonis Longus to Nilus his mother many greetings. Continually I pray for your health. Supplication on your behalf I direct each day to the lord Serapis. I wish you to know that I had no hope that you would come up to the metropolis. On this account neither did I enter into the city. But

[19] Krebs, *Ägyptische Urkunden aus den Königlichen Museen zu Berlin.* II, No.632; DLO pp.150-153.

I was ashamed to come to Karanis,[20] because I am going about in rags. I write to you that I am naked. I beseech you, mother, be reconciled to me. But I know what I have brought upon myself. Punished I have been every way. I know that I have sinned. I hear from Postumus[21] who met you in the Arsinoïte nome, and unseasonably related all to you. Do you not know that I would rather be a cripple than be conscious that I am still owing anyone an obol? . . . come yourself . . . I have heard that . . . I beseech you . . . I almost . . . I beseech you . . . I will . . . not . . . do otherwise."[22]

Not only is the grammar here similar to that of the New Testament at several points, including the expressions, "I wish you to know" (cf. Philippians 1:12) and "I beseech you" (Philemon 10, etc.), but the youth himself was almost a living example of the lost son in the parable told by Jesus.

Many other letters and documents of all sorts could be cited from these very same times, including a letter saying "Do not lose heart about the rent, for you will certainly get it,"[23] a letter regarding funeral expenses, a boy's letter, an invitation to dinner, a public notice, a contract of apprenticeship, a report of a lawsuit, a marriage contract, a deed of divorce, a deed of adoption, a warrant for arrest, a tax receipt, a census return, a lease of a perfumery business, a will, a magical incantation, and many others.[24] But already it is clear that the papyri have provided much information about the daily and amazingly modern life of the ancient world, as well as affording the possibility of fresh comparisons with the writings of the New Testament.

The longer papyrus letters generally have an opening address or greeting, a thanksgiving and prayer, special contents, and closing salutations and valediction. These are exactly the main features which in a more elaborate form are found in the letters of Paul.[25] Also the language of the papyri is in many ways similar to that of the New Testament. In both grammar and vocabulary there are

[20] A village in the Fayum, and probably the home of the writer.

[21] The reading of the name is not certain.

[22] Krebs, Ägyptische Urkunden aus den Königlichen Museen zu Berlin. III, No.846; Milligan, Selections from the Greek Papyri, pp.93-95; DLO pp.153-158.

[23] C. M. Cobern, The New Archaeological Discoveries and their Bearing upon the New Testament and upon the Life and Times of the Primitive Church. 9th ed. 1929, pp.93f.

[24] See Milligan, Selections from the Greek Papyri; A. S. Hunt and C. C. Edgar, Select Papyri. 2 vols. LCL (1932-34); E. J. Goodspeed and E. C. Colwell, A Greek Papyrus Reader. 1935.

[25] G. Milligan, The New Testament Documents, their Origin and Early History. 1913, p.93.

134. Wildcat in a Papyrus Thicket

135. Gathering and Splitting Papyrus for Papermaking

136. Papyrus Roll before Opening

137. Statuette of an Early Egyptian Scribe

138. Four Scribes with Pens and Rolls

139. Papyrus Rolls Open and Sealed

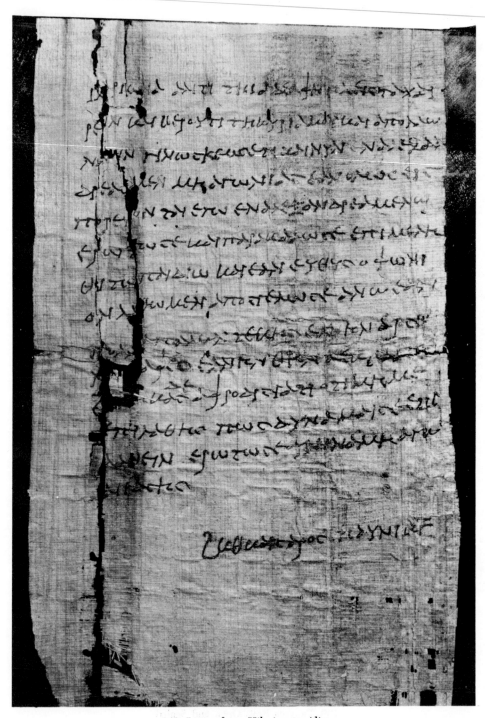

140. Letter from Hilarion to Alis

141. The Sayings of Jesus Found at Oxyrhynchus

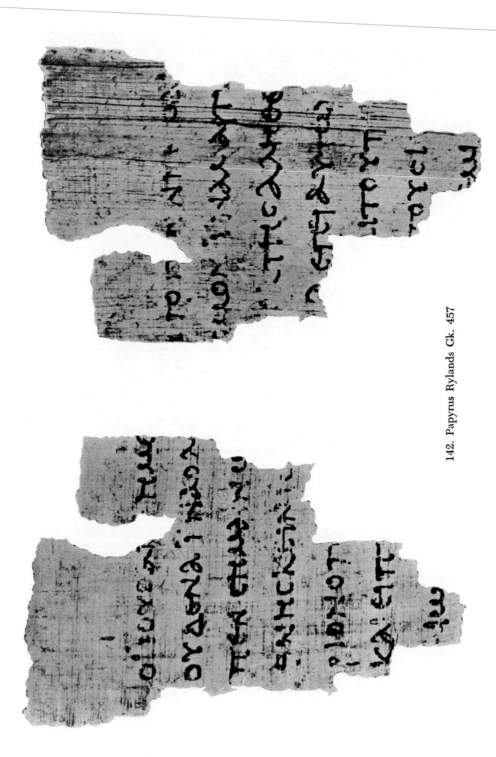

142. Papyrus Rylands Gk. 457

143. A Page from the Chester Beatty Papyrus of Paul's Letters

144. A Papyrus Fragment with the Opening of Paul's Letter to the Romans

ᾱ ✝   ✝   ✝

145

ΠΑΥΛΟϹΔΟΥΛΟϹΧΥΙΥ
ΚΛΗΤΟϹΑΠΟϹΤΟΛΟϹ
ΑΦΩΡΙϹΜΕΝΟϹΕΙϹΕΥ
ΑΓΓΕΛΙΟΝΘΥΟΠΡΟΕΠΗΓ
ΓΕΙΛΑΤΟΔΙΑΤΩΝΠΡΟ
ΦΗΤΩΝΑΥΤΟΥΕΝΓΡΑ
ΦΑΙϹΑΓΙΑΙϹΠΕΡΙΤΟΥ
ΥΙΟΥΑΥΤΟΥΤΟΥΓΕΝ
ΜΕΝΟΥΕΚϹΠΕΡΜΑΤΟϹ
ΔΑΥΕΙΔΚΑΤΑϹΑΡΚΑΤΟΥ
ΟΡΙϹΘΕΝΤΟϹΥΙΟΥΘΥ
ΕΝΔΥΝΑΜΕΙΚΑΤΑΠΝΕΥ
ΜΑΑΓΙΩϹΥΝΗϹΕΞΑΝΑ
ϹΤΑϹΕΩϹΝΕΚΡΩΝΙΥΧΥ
ΤΟΥΚΥΗΜΩΝΔΙΟΥΕΛΑ
ΒΟΜΕΝΧΑΡΙΝΚΑΙΑΠΟ
ϹΤΟΛΗΝΕΙϹΥΠΑΚΟΗΝ
ΠΙϹΤΕΩϹΕΝΠΑϹΙΝΤΟΙϹ
ΕΘΝΕϹΙΝΥΠΕΡΤΟΥΟΝΟ
ΜΑΤΟϹΑΥΤΟΥΕΝΟΙϹ
ΕϹΤΕΚΑΙΥΜΕΙϹΚΛΗΤΟΙ
ΙΥΧΥΠΑϹΙΤΟΙϹΟΥϹΙΝ
ΕΝΡΩΜΗΑΓΑΠΗΤΟΙϹΘΥ
ΚΛΗΤΟΙϹΑΓΙΟΙϹΧΑΡΙϹ
ΥΜΙΝΚΑΙΕΙΡΗΝΗΑΠΟθΥ
ΠΑΤΡΟϹΗΜΩΝΚΑΙΚΥΙΥ
ΧΥ ΠΡΩΤΟΝΜΕΝΕΥΧΑ
ΡΙϹΤΩΤΩΘΩΜΟΥΔΙΑ
ΙΥΧΥΠΕΡΙΠΑΝΤΩΝΥΜ
ΟΤΙΗΠΙϹΤΙϹΥΜΩΝΚΑ
ΤΑΓΓΕΛΛΕΤΑΙΕΝΟΛΩΤ
ΚΟϹΜΩΜΑΡΤΥϹΓΑΡΜΟΥ
ΕϹΤΙΝΟΘϹΩΛΑΤΡΕΥ
ΕΝΤΩΠΝΕΥΜΑΤΙΜΟΥ
ΕΝΤΩΕΥΑΓΓΕΛΙΩΤΟΥ
ΥΙΟΥΑΥΤΟΥΩϹΑΔΙΑΛΕ
ΙΠΤΩϹΜΝΕΙΑΝΥΜΩΝ
ΠΟΙΟΥΜΑΙΠΑΝΤΟΤΕ
ΕΠΙΤΩΝΠΡΟϹΕΥΧΩΝ
ΜΟΥΔΕΟΜΕΝΟϹΕΙΠΩϹ
ΗΔΗΠΟΤΕΕΥΟΔΩΘΗϹ
ΜΑΙΕΝΤΩΘΕΛΗΜΑΤΙ

ΤΟΥΘΥΕΛΘΕΙΝΠΡΟϹΥ
ΜΑϹΕΠΙΠΟΘΩΓΑΡΙΔΕ
ΥΜΑϹΙΝΑΤΙΜΕΤΑΔΩ
ΧΑΡΙϹΜΑΥΜΙΝΠΝΕΥΜΑ
ΤΙΚΟΝΕΙϹΤΟϹΤΗΡΙΧΘΗ
ΝΑΙΥΜΑϹΤΟΥΤΟΔΕΕ
ϹΤΙΝϹΥΝΠΑΡΑΚΛΗΘΗ
ΝΑΙΕΝΥΜΙΝΔΙΑΤΗϹΕΝ
ΑΛΛΗΛΟΙϹΠΙϹΤΕΩϹΥ
ΜΩΝΤΕΚΑΙΕΜΟΥΕΓΩ
ΛΥΔΕΥΜΑϹΑΓΝΟΕΙΝΑ
ΔΕΛΦΟΙΟΤΙΠΟΛΛΑΚΙϹ
ΠΡΟΕΘΕΜΗΝΕΛΘΕΙΝΠ
ΥΜΑϹΚΑΙΕΚΩΛΥΘΗΝΑ
ΧΡΙΤΟΥΔΕΥΡΟΙΝΑΤΙΝΑ
ΚΑΡΠΟΝϹΧΩΚΑΙΕΝΥΜ
ΚΑΘΩϹΚΑΙΕΝΤΟΙϹΛΟΙ
ΠΟΙϹΕΘΝΕϹΙΝΕΛΛΗϹΙ
ΤΕΚΑΙΒΑΡΒΑΡΟΙϹϹΟΦ
ΤΕΚΑΙΑΝΟΗΤΟΙϹΟΦ
ΛΕΤΗϹΕΙΜΙΟΥΤΩϹΤ
ΚΑΤΕΜΕΠΡΟΘΥΜΟΝΚ
ΥΜΙΝΤΟΙϹΕΝΡΩΜΗΕΥ
ΑΓΓΕΛΙϹΑϹΘΑΙΟΥΓΑΡ
ΠΑΙϹΧΥΝΟΜΑΙΤΟΕΥΑ
ΓΕΛΙΟΝΔΥΝΑΜΙϹΓΑΡΘΥ
ΕϹΤΙΝΕΙϹϹΩΤΗΡΙΑΝ
ΠΑΝΤΙΤΩΠΙϹΤΕΥΟΝ
ΤΙΙΟΥΔΑΙΩΤΕΚΑΙΕΛΛΗ
ΝΙΔΙΚΑΙΟϹΥΝΗΓΑΡΘΥ
ΕΝΑΥΤΩΑΠΟΚΑΛΥΠ
ΤΑΙΕΚΠΙϹΤΕΩϹΕΙϹΠΙ
ϹΤΙΝΚΑΘΩϹΓΕΓΡΑΠΤΑ
ΟΔΕΔΙΚΑΙΟϹΕΚΠΙϹΤΕ
ΩϹΖΗϹΕΤΑΙ ΑΠΟΚΑΛΥ
ΠΤΕΤΑΙΓΑΡΟΡΓΗΘΥΑ
ΠΟΥΡΑΝΟΥΕΠΙΠΑϹΑΝ
ΑϹΕΒΕΙΑΝΚΑΙΑΔΙΚΙΑΝ
ΑΝΘΡΩΠΩΝΤΩΝΤΗΝ
ΑΛΗΘΕΙΑΝΕΝΑΔΙΚΙΑ
ΚΑΤΕΧΟΝΤΩΝΔΙΟΤΙ
ΤΟΓΝΩϹΤΟΝΤΟΥΘΥ

ΦΑΝΕΡΟΝΕϹΤΙΝΕΝΑΥ
ΤΟΙϹΟΘϹΓΑΡΑΥΤΟΙϹε
ΦΑΝΕΡΩϹΕΝ ΤΑΓΑΡΑΟ
ΡΑΤΑΑΥΤΟΥΑΠΟΚΤΙ
ϹΕΩϹΚΟϹΜΟΥΤΟΙϹΠΟΙ
ΗΜΑϹΙΝΝΟΟΥΜΕΝΑΚΑ
ΘΟΡΑΤΑΙΗΤΕΑΙΔΙΟϹΑΥ
ΤΟΥΔΥΝΑΜΙϹΚΑΙΘΕΙΟ
ΤΗϹΕΙϹΤΟΕΙΝΑΙΑΥΤΟΥϹ
ΑΝΑΠΟΛΟΓΗΤΟΥϹΔΙΟ
ΤΙΓΝΟΝΤΕϹΤΟΝΘΝΕΔΥ
ΧΩϹΘΝΕΔΟΞΑϹΑΝΗΕΥ
ΧΑΡΙϹΤΗϹΑΝΑΛΛΕΜΑ
ΤΑΙΩΘΗϹΑΝΕΝΤΟΙϹΔΙΑ
ΛΟΓΙϹΜΟΙϹΑΥΤΩΝΚΑΙ
εϹΚΟΤΙϹΘΗΗΑϹΥΝΕΤ
ΑΥΤΩΝΚΑΡΔΙΑΦΑϹΚΟΝ
ΤΕϹΕΙΝΑΙϹΟΦΟΙΕΝΩ
ΡΑΝΘΗϹΑΝΚΑΙΗΛΛΑΞ
ΤΗΝΔΟΞΑΝΤΟΥΑΦΘΑΡ
ΤΟΥΘΥΕΝΟΜΟΙΩΜΑΤΙ
ΕΙΚΟΝΟϹΦΘΑΡΤΟΥΑΝ
ΘΡΩΠΟΥΚΑΙΠΕΤΕΙΝΩ
ΚΑΙΤΕΤΡΑΠΟΔΩΝΚΑΙ
ΕΡΠΕΤΩΝ ΔΙΟΠΑΡΕ
ΔΩΚΕΝΑΥΤΟΥϹΟΘϹΕΝ
ΤΑΙϹΕΠΙΘΥΜΙΑΙϹΤΩΝ
ΚΑΡΔΙΩΝΑΥΤΩΝΕΙϹ
ΑΚΑΘΑΡϹΙΑΝΤΟΥΑΤΙ
ΜΑΖΕϹΘΑΙΤΑϹΩΜΑΤΑ
ΑΥΤΩΝΕΝΑΥΤΟΙϹΟΙ
ΝΕϹΜΕΤΗΛΛΑΞΑΝΤΗ
ΑΛΗΘΕΙΑΝΤΟΥΘΥΕΝΤ
ΨΕΥΔΕΙΚΑΙΕϹΕΒΑϹΘΗ
ϹΑΝΚΑΙΕΛΑΤΡΕΥϹΑΝΤΗΚΤΙ
ϹΕΙΠΑΡΑΤΟΝΚΤΙϹΑΝΤΑ
ΟϹΕϹΤΙΝΕΥΛΟΓΗΤΟϹ
ΕΙϹΤΟΥϹΑΙΩΝΑϹΑΜΗΝ
ΔΙΑΤΟΥΤΟΠΑΡΕΔΩΚΕΝ
ΑΥΤΟΥϹΟΘϹΕΙϹΠΑΘΗ
ΛΕΚΑΙΑΥΤΩΝΜΕΤΕΛΛΑ

145. The First Page of the Letter to the Romans in Codex Vaticanus

146. The Monastery of Saint Catherine at Mount Sinai

147. The Appearance of Codex Sinaiticus before Binding

148. The First Page of the Letter to the Romans in Codex Sinaiticus

149. The First Page of the Letter to the Romans in Codex Alexandrinus

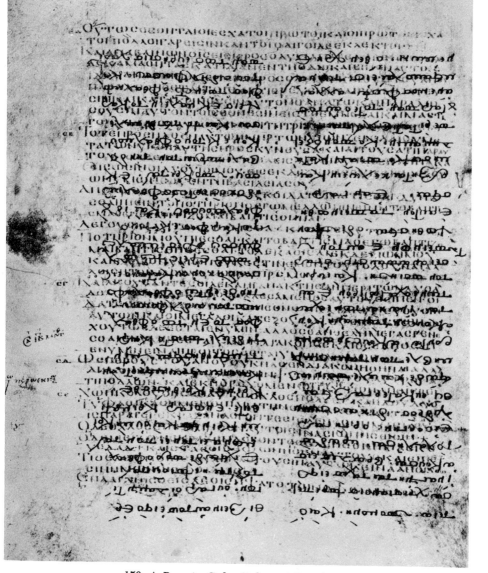

150. A Page in Codex Ephraemi Rescriptus

151. A Double Page in Codex Claromontanus

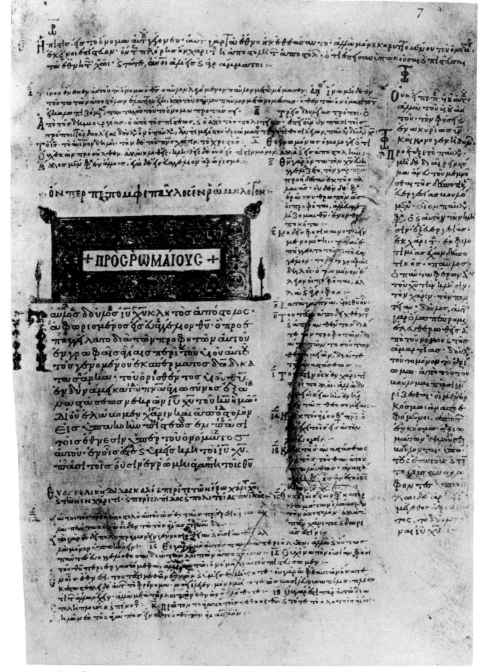

152. The First Page of Romans in a Minuscule Manuscript Written in A.D. 1045

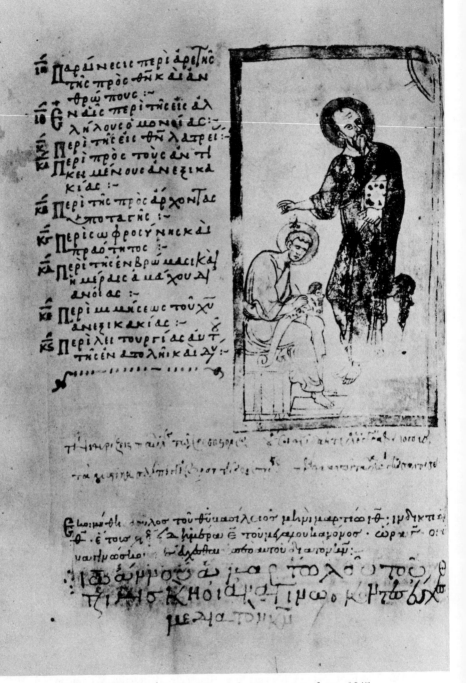

153. An Illustration in the Minuscule Manuscript of A.D. 1045

many differences between the Greek of the New Testament and classical Greek. All together the New Testament language is doubtless influenced in part by the Hebrew and Aramaic of Palestine and the Old Testament, in part by the Greek of the Septuagint translation, and in part by the *Koine* or Common Greek then widely used in the Mediterranean world. This relatively simpler Greek is found in a literary variety in writers of the time like Strabo and Josephus, and in a nonliterary form in the papyri of which we have been speaking. The similarity of the New Testament language with that of the papyri was first recognized by Adolf Deissmann, Privatdozent at Marburg and later Professor of New Testament at Friedrich-Wilhelms-Universität at Berlin. Through his work and that of others much material has been collected from the papyri to illustrate the contemporary usage and meaning of words which occur in the New Testament.[26]

EARLY CHRISTIAN PAPYRI

Not only documents of everyday life in general but also ones recognizably related to the Christian faith have been recovered from the sands of the past. Apart from manuscripts of the canonical New Testament to be described in the next section, these discoveries include such writings as the following.

On January 11, 1897, Grenfell and Hunt began to dig in the rubbish mounds of ancient Oxyrhynchus, and on the second day unearthed a tattered papyrus leaf, nearly four by six inches in size, of which the verso is shown in Fig. 141.[27] In the upper right-hand corner of the verso was a numeral which was clearly a page number and showed that this leaf had been a part of a papyrus codex. In the case of this particular leaf the verso had been uppermost in the codex. The first indication of the character of the contents of the leaf came with the recognition of the word κάρφος, or "mote," which at once reminded Dr. Hunt of Jesus' saying concerning the mote and the beam (Matthew 7:3-5 = Luke 6:41f.). When the entire fragment was read it was found that it actually did contain a series of sayings of Jesus as follows:

". . . and then shalt thou see clearly to cast out the mote that is in thy brother's eye.

[26] See MMVGT. For the Koine, Semitic, and Christian elements in the language of the New Testament and the individual characteristics of the several books see Bruce M. Metzger in IB VII, pp.43-59.

[27] Grenfell and Hunt, *Sayings of Our Lord.* 1897; OP I, No.1; cf. Leon E. Wright in JBL 65 (1946), pp.175-183.

"Jesus saith, Except ye fast to the world, ye shall in no wise find the kingdom of God; and except you make the sabbath a real sabbath, ye shall not see the Father.

"Jesus saith, I stood in the midst of the world, and in the flesh was I seen of them, and I found all men drunken, and none found I athirst among them, and my soul grieveth over the sons of men, because they are blind in their heart, and see not.

". . . poverty.

"[Jesus saith,] Wherever there are two, they are not without God, and wherever there is one alone, I say, I am with him. Raise the stone, and there thou shalt find me, cleave the wood, and there am I.

"Jesus saith, A prophet is not acceptable in his own country, neither doth a physician work cures upon them that know him.

"Jesus saith, A city built upon the top of a high hill and established, can neither fall nor be hid.

"Jesus saith, Thou hearest with one ear [but the other ear thou hast closed]."

This papyrus is probably to be dated in the third century A.D., and shows the kind of collection of Jesus' sayings that was being read by Christians in Egypt at that time. A second fragment containing sayings of Jesus was found by Grenfell and Hunt at Oxyrhynchus in 1903.[28] It was a piece of a papyrus roll, which was probably written slightly later in the third century than the fragment first found. In it the words of Jesus have lost yet more of their original freshness and simplicity, and have taken on still more of the complexity of the later age.

In a large group of papyri purchased for the John Rylands Library in Manchester, England, by J. Rendel Harris in 1917 was a part of a double leaf of a papyrus codex, written in a hand of probably the fourth century A.D., which contained verses from different parts of the Septuagint.[29] Two other fragments belonging to the same codex are in Oslo. The Old Testament texts used include portions of the "Messianic" passages in the fifty-second and fifty-third chapters of Isaiah, and in general are such as could be applied to Christ and Christianity.[30] It is believed, therefore, that the work represented by these surviving fragments originally comprised a collection of "pro-

[28] Grenfell, L. W. Drexel, and Hunt, *New Sayings of Jesus and Fragment of a Lost Gospel.* 1904.

[29] C. H. Roberts, *Two Biblical Papyri in the John Rylands Library, Manchester.* 1936, pp.47-62.

[30] The combined texts contain quotations from the following verses: Isaiah 42:3f.; 66:18f.; 52:15; 53:1-3, 6f., 11f.; Genesis 26:13f.; II Chronicles 1:12; Deuteronomy 29:8 (9), 11 (12).

phetic" passages from the Old Testament which were used as witnesses to the truth of Christianity.[31]

In another collection of papyri purchased from a dealer around 1935 were two imperfect leaves and a scrap of a third from a papyrus codex dating probably not later than the middle of the second century. Now designated as Papyrus Egerton 2, these fragments contain an account of four different incidents in the life of Jesus, namely a dispute with the rulers of the people who attempt to stone him, the healing of a leper, a question about paying dues to kings, and a miracle of some sort on the bank of the Jordan. The document is believed to depend upon sources other than the canonical Gospels, and perhaps to have been intended for private use by individual Christians. It may be noted that the writer employed abbreviations for Lord, God, Jesus, prophets, as shown on p. 403, and some other words.[32]

In 1946 an accidental discovery at the ancient Sheneset-Chenoboskion in the region of Nag Hammadi thirty-two miles north of Luxor brought to light thirteen papyrus codices, all remarkably well preserved, nine with leather covers still about them.[33] They were all written in Coptic, most in the Upper Egyptian dialect called Sahidic, and are probably to be dated between the middle of the third and the middle of the fourth century A.D. Most or all are believed to rest on Greek originals. The thirteen codices contain some forty-four different treatises including literature of the nature of gospels, epistles, apocalypses, and prayers, and discussions of cosmogony and dogmatics. In some cases the material purports to be what was divulged by Jesus to his disciples during his ministry or after his resurrection,

---

[31] Such works are otherwise known, as for example in the collection of *Testimonies against the Jews* made by Cyprian about A.D. 248, and consisting of extensive quotations from the Old Testament arranged under various headings (*Treatise.* XII. ANF V, pp.507-557). J. Rendel Harris even believed that such an assemblage of "testimonies" directed against the Jews was the first Christian book to be written and that its influence could be traced throughout the New Testament as well as in the church fathers (J. R. Harris and V. Burch, *Testimonies.* 2 vols. 1916-20; cf. D. Plooij in *Verhandelingen der Koninklijke Akademie van Wetenschappen te Amsterdam, Afdeeling Letterkunde, Nieuwe Reeks Deel.* XXXII, 2 [1932]). We now know that collections of texts expressive of Messianic hope were made among the Jews too, since a page of *testimonia* was found in Cave 4 at Qumran (see above p.278).

[32] H. Idris Bell and T. C. Skeat, *Fragments of an Unknown Gospel and Other Early Christian Papyri.* 1935, pp.1-41; H. Idris Bell, *Recent Discoveries of Biblical Papyri.* 1937, pp.17-20; Goro Mayeda, *Das Leben-Jesu-Fragment Papyrus Egerton 2 und seine Stellung in der urchristlichen Literaturgeschichte.* 1946; Bruce M. Metzger in JBL 68 (1949), pp.73-75; Sherman E. Johnson in JNES 5 (1946), p.46.

[33] Victor R. Gold in BA 15 (1952), pp.70-88.

and all of it is intended for those initiated in the doctrines of the sect to which the literature belonged, evidently a group of Egyptian Gnostics. As an example of what is contained, one of the works is the Apocryphon or Secret Book of John. Three copies were found at Chenoboskion and another was already known in the fifth century Berlin Coptic Codex 8502.[34] The contents of the book are supposed to have been given by Jesus to John on the Mount of Olives with a warning to reveal these things only to those who are worthy. In brief the teaching is that the true God, the highest being in the world of light, created various divine beings, among them Barbelo the image of the invisible One, and Sophia or Wisdom. The latter had an evil son, Yaldabaoth, who is the God of the Old Testament and the creator of this world. Since it is the constant endeavor of Yaldabaoth to keep the divine spark which is in man from returning to the world of light from whence it came, it was necessary for Christ to come into the world and bring the knowledge of the truth through which those who are able to receive it can be delivered. This truth, it is evident, is of the sort contained in this book and taught by the Gnostics. In his work *Against Heresies*,[35] Irenaeus (A.D. c.180) describes Gnostics who were evidently akin to those represented at Chenoboskion since they too recognized Barbelo as a high divine being, and after outlining their teachings the Christian apologist says, "Such are the falsehoods which these people invent."[36]

3. NEW TESTAMENT MANUSCRIPTS

LIKE the documents of which we have just been telling, the oldest known copies of any parts of the New Testament are written upon papyrus, and after that come the parchment or vellum manuscripts, first those written in uncial letters and then those in minuscule script. There are so many of these documents all together that some kind of brief designation and also of comprehensive listing is necessary.

[34] This papyrus, which contains not only the Apocryphon of John, but also the Gospel of Mary, and the Wisdom of Jesus Christ, is edited by Walter C. Till, *Die gnostischen Schriften des koptischen Papyrus Berolinensis 8502* (TU 60). 1955.

[35] I, xxix. ANF I, pp.353f.

[36] Another Coptic manuscript which contains Gnostic texts is the Codex Jung, a papyrus of probably the fourth century A.D. It contains a copy of the Gospel of Truth, probably the work of that title attributed by Irenaeus (*Against Heresies*. III, xi, 9) to the Gnostics who followed Valentinus. See Henri-Charles Puech, Gilles Quispel, and W. C. van Unnik, *The Jung Codex*. 1955; Michel Malinine, H.-C. Puech, and G. Quispel, *Evangelium Veritatis*. 1956; cf. R. McL. Wilson in NTS 3 (1957), pp.236-243; Floyd V. Filson in BA 20 (1957), pp.76-78.

In 1751-1752 Johann Jakob Wettstein published in Amsterdam a critical edition of the Greek New Testament,[1] in the prolegomena of which he listed by letters of the alphabet and by numbers some 125 manuscripts. Beginning with the uncial manuscripts available at that time, A was Codex Alexandrinus, B Codex Vaticanus, C Codex Ephraemi Syri rescriptus, and so on. Continuing with the available minuscule manuscripts, these were numbered 1, 2, 3, and so on.

In the latter part of the nineteenth century Constantine Tischendorf (1815-1874) published his *Novum Testamentum Graece*.[2] Having discovered Codex Sinaiticus and having a very high regard for its importance, Tischendorf put it at the head of his list of manuscripts, labeling it with the first letter of the Hebrew alphabet, Aleph. The number of uncials known also extended now beyond the letter Z, and Tischendorf continued his list with capital letters of the Greek alphabet, Γ, Δ, Θ, and so on.

Like Wettstein and Tischendorf, in the first volume of his *Textkritik des Neuen Testaments*, published in 1900, Caspar René Gregory listed the uncials by capital letters and the minuscules by numbers. The letter Aleph was still used for Codex Sinaiticus, but it was noted that some wished to avoid the introduction of a Hebrew letter in the series and proposed alternatively to employ here the letter S.[3] Even by using letters from the Hebrew, Latin, and Greek alphabets, however, there was a limit to how many manuscripts could be so designated, and accordingly in the third volume of the *Textkritik*, published in 1909,[4] Gregory employed another system in which the uncial manuscripts were designated by numbers. To distinguish these numbers from those used for the minuscule manuscripts they were preceded by **0** and printed in boldface type. Although the familiar letter designations were still used for the earlier known uncials, these manuscripts were also included in the new system and so Codex Sinaiticus was shown as ℵ or **01**, Codex Alexandrinus as A or **02**, Codex Vaticanus as B or **03**, Codex Ephraemi Syri rescriptus as C or **04**, and so on. The numbers ran at that time to **0165**. After the uncials Gregory listed the papyri, of which fourteen were then

---

[1] Ἡ Καινὴ Διαθήκη. 2 vols.   [2] Editio octava critica maior. 2 vols. 1869-72.

[3] *Textkritik des Neuen Testaments*, I, p.122. S is used instead of ℵ for Codex Sinaiticus by Hans Lietzmann, *Einführung in die Textgeschichte der Paulusbriefe*, p.6, by Burton H. Throckmorton, Jr., ed., *Gospel Parallels, A Synopsis of the First Three Gospels*. 2d ed. 1957, p.viii, and by others (cf. Merrill M. Parvis in JR 27 [1947], p.216), and is used in the present book. Otherwise S designates the relatively unimportant Vatican manuscript Gr. 354.

[4] cf. also his *Die griechischen Handschriften des Neuen Testaments*. 1908.

known. For these he used an Old German $\mathfrak{p}$ with a superior number, thus $\mathfrak{p}^1$, $\mathfrak{p}^2$, and so on. The minuscules in turn ran at this time from 1 to 2304. Lectionaries were designated with numbers preceded by a small letter l, thus l 3, l 707, and the like. When these and also the versions such as Syriac, Armenian, and Latin translations were included, Gregory's catalogue must have included over four thousand items.

The work of Gregory in assigning numbers and listing manuscripts was continued by Ernst von Dobschütz, and hundreds of manuscripts more were added to the catalogue.[5] By the time installment IV of his list was published in 1933, without including versions in other languages the total of the Greek manuscripts was approximately 4,230. Upon the death of von Dobschütz in 1934 the *Kirchenväter Kommission der Preussischen Akademie der Wissenschaften* entrusted the same responsibility to Walther Eltester, and more recently the list has been continued by Kurt Aland.[6]

In the meantime, Hermann Freiherr von Soden (1852-1914) undertook to make an entirely new listing and new assignment of numbers.[7] In this system, Codex Vaticanus became δ1, Codex Sinaiticus δ2, Codex Ephraemi Syri rescriptus δ3, Codex Alexandrinus δ4, and so on. In spite of the large volume of the work he did, the system of von Soden was not most widely accepted.

With several systems of identification thus in existence, it is useful to have a concordance of the several listings.[8] In practice the earlier known uncials are still usually cited by the letters as found in Tischendorf and in the first volume of Gregory's *Textkritik*; the later known uncials and the minuscules by their respective series of numbers as listed by Gregory, von Dobschütz, Eltester, and Aland; and the papyri by the $\mathfrak{p}$ series of the same authorities. In 1957 in Aland's continuation list VI the papyri extended to $\mathfrak{p}^{68}$, the uncials to **0241**, the minuscules to 2533, and the lectionaries to l 1838, making a total of 4,680 items.[9]

---

[5] E. von Dobschütz in ZNW 23 (1924), pp.248-264; 25 (1926), pp.299-306; 26 (1927), p.96; 27 (1928), pp.216-222; 32 (1933), pp.185-206; cf. J. Schmid in ZNW 34 (1935), pp.308f.; 39 (1940), pp.241f.

[6] Hans Lietzmann in ZNW 35 (1936), p.309. K. Aland in ZNW 45 (1954), pp.179-217; 48 (1957), pp.141-191; cf. in TL 82 (1957), col. 167 n.11.

[7] *Die Schriften des Neuen Testaments.* Teil I, 2d ed. 1911; Teil II, 1913.

[8] Benedikt Kraft, *Die Zeichen für die wichtigeren Handschriften des griechischen Neuen Testaments.* 3d ed. 1955.

[9] K. Aland in TL 82 (1957), col. 161 n.3; and in ZNW 48 (1957), pp.141-191.

PAPYRI

As has already been stated the earliest known copies of any portions of the New Testament are papyrus fragments and manuscripts.[10] The oldest of these belong to the second century, and at present the very earliest that is known is a tiny piece of papyrus leaf with a small portion of the Gospel according to John. This was discovered in 1935 in the John Rylands Library in Manchester, England, among papyri acquired in Egypt in 1920 by B. P. Grenfell.[11] In that library the fragment is catalogued as Papyrus Rylands Gk. 457, and in the international listing it is $\mathfrak{p}^{52}$. The actual size of the papyrus, shown somewhat enlarged in Fig. 142, is 3.5 by 2.3 inches. The recto is at the left, the verso at the right. The recto contains John 18:31-33, the verso John 18:37-38, and thus the fragment is almost certainly from a codex. According to its style of handwriting the papyrus is dated in the first half of the second century A.D., probably about A.D. 125. As far as it goes the text agrees with Codex Vaticanus, Codex Sinaiticus, and Codex Ephraemi Syri rescriptus.[12] In comparison with the relatively irregular handwriting in an everyday papyrus such as the Letter from Hilarion to Alis (Fig. 140), the writing in $\mathfrak{p}^{52}$ seems like a rather carefully executed literary script. There is no punctuation, although the dieresis is placed over initial Iota, and the words appear to be slightly separated. No *nomina sacra* appear, so it cannot be established whether abbreviations were employed.

Our second oldest manuscript, as presently known, is $\mathfrak{p}^{64}$.[13] This consists of three small fragments of a codex leaf, purchased in Luxor in 1901 and preserved in the Library of Magdalen College at Oxford. The handwriting is regarded as an early predecessor of the later uncial script, and the date is believed to be in the latter part of the second century. The writing is in two columns to the page, and on the verso and recto are contained parts of Matthew 26:7, 10, 14-15, 22-23, 31, 32-33. *Nomina sacra* in abbreviated form are found

[10] For the papyri see also Georg Maldfeld in ZNW 42 (1949), pp.228-253; 43 (1950-51), pp.260f.; Kurt Aland in ZNW 45 (1954), p.187; and in NTS 3 (1957), pp.261-286.

[11] C. H. Roberts, *An Unpublished Fragment of the Fourth Gospel in the John Rylands Library*. 1935. For the date of the fragment cf. Roberts in BJRL 36 (1953), p.98; Kurt Aland in TL 82 (1957), col. 162.

[12] Textual affinities of the papyri are given by Maldfeld in ZNW 42 (1949), pp.239, 242-253; and by Kraft, *Die Zeichen für die wichtigeren Handschriften des griechischen Neuen Testaments*, pp.48f.

[13] Colin Roberts in HTR 46 (1953), pp.233-237; Aland in TL 82 (1957), col. 164.

in verses 23 and 31, the line above the abbreviations not being visible because of damage to the papyrus but presumably having once stood there. In verse 31 the first letter of the word αὐτοῖς ("to them") projects into the left margin. The line which is marked in this way is the first complete line of the section of texts which begins, "Then Jesus said to them," and this same section division is also recognized in Codex Alexandrinus; therefore the section divisions used in the latter codex must have originated at least as early as the present papyrus. In verse 14 "twelve" is written with a numerical symbol (ι]β) rather than with the word; in verse 22 the damaged text probably read "to say one after another to him," which is a unique word order; and in verse 32 Galilee is misspelled (γαλεγλαιαν); thus the text, brief as it is, shows how variations entered.

Coming to the end of the second century or the beginning of the third, say about A.D. 200 as the date is usually given, we find two papyrus manuscripts which are still relatively very early and are also, in contrast with the tiny fragments thus far mentioned, of very considerable extent, thus are extremely important documents. These are 𝔭⁴⁶ and 𝔭⁶⁶, and will be described next.

𝔭⁴⁶ is one of a group of papyrus manuscripts which became known in 1931. These were found and marketed by diggers and dealers in Egypt, and the greater part of the collection was purchased by Mr. A. Chester Beatty, an American living then in London and now in Dublin, while some portions of the find were acquired by the University of Michigan and by other individuals. The entire assemblage comprises no less than eleven codices, which date from the second to the fourth century and presumably represent the library of some early Christian church. The codices contain portions of nine Old Testament and fifteen New Testament books as well as the Book of Enoch and a homily by Melito of Sardis. The part of the collection with which we are concerned at this point is a codex of the letters of Paul. It is designated as 𝔭⁴⁶, and is believed to date around A.D. 200.[14] This means that it is 150 years older than the major manuscripts such as Codex Vaticanus upon which we have otherwise previously been dependent for the text of Paul's letters, and that it is removed from the time of the origin of the Pauline collection by little more than a century and from the time of the composition of the originals by 150 years in round numbers.

Eighty-six leaves of this notable codex survive, of which thirty

[14] U. Wilcken in AP 11 (1935), p.113.

belong to the University of Michigan and the remainder to Mr. Beatty.[15] Seven leaves are missing at the beginning, which implies that an equal number are lost at the end, while four other leaves near the beginning and end also are missing. Thus the original codex must have consisted of 104 leaves. It was formed by laying fifty-two sheets of papyrus one upon another, each having the recto side uppermost, and then folding the entire stack in the middle.[16] None of the extant leaves is preserved perfectly, but most of them have lost only a few lines at the bottom. The maximum size of the present leaves is approximately nine by six inches, and the original column of writing was normally around eight inches high by four and three-quarters inches wide.

The codex contains the letters of Paul in the following order: Romans, Hebrews, I and II Corinthians, Ephesians, Galatians, Philippians, Colossians, I Thessalonians. The last leaf which is extant contains the conclusion of I Thessalonians, but, as was pointed out just above, seven leaves have been lost from the end of the codex. Of these the first two doubtless contained II Thessalonians, with which book the codex seems to have closed. It is believed that the remaining five leaves were left blank, for ten more leaves instead of five would have been required if I and II Timothy, Titus, and Philemon had been included.[17] If this is true, then it appears that at this time the standard Pauline collection included his church letters but not the four letters to individual persons, although a small letter like Philemon might have been included. The place of Hebrews immediately following Romans is almost unique but is in agreement with Egyptian opinion which at that time ascribed Hebrews to Paul.[18] At the same time the Muratorian Canon, representing the usage of Rome about A.D. 200, does not include Hebrews among Paul's letters,[19] and the doubt of its Pauline authorship relegated it

[15] The entire manuscript is edited by Frederic G. Kenyon, *The Chester Beatty Biblical Papyri*. Fasciculus III. Text 1934, Supplement Text 1936, Supplement Plates 1937. See also H. A. Sanders, *A Third Century Papyrus Codex of the Epistles of Paul*. 1935; cf. Ernest C. Colwell in JR 16 (1936), pp.96-98.

[16] Consequently in the first half of the manuscript the verso side of the leaf precedes the recto, and in the second half the recto precedes the verso. The change comes at folio 53.

[17] Frederic Kenyon, *Our Bible and the Ancient Manuscripts*. 1958, p.188 n.1.

[18] Clement of Alexandria (A.D. c.200) said that Hebrews was the work of Paul (Eusebius, *Ch. Hist.* VI, xiv) and repeatedly quoted it as Pauline (e.g. *Stromata*. IV, 16, 20 [ANF II, pp.427f., 432]).

[19] *The Muratorian Fragment* (ASBACH p.119); E. J. Goodspeed, *The Formation of the New Testament*. 1926, pp.187f.

afterward to a place following II Thessalonians,[20] and finally, when the Pastorals and Philemon were accepted fully, to a place on the borderland between the Pauline epistles and James. Aside from the inclusion of Hebrews, and also the reversal of the order of Galatians and Ephesians, the Chester Beatty Papyrus lists Paul's church letters in exactly the order which became accepted generally and is used now in our printed Bibles. The principle of arrangement seems to be in the order of length, with letters which have the same address placed together.

Since the first seven leaves of the manuscript have been lost, Romans 1:1-5:17 is missing. Folio 8 contains Romans 5:17-6:14 but more than half of the leaf is broken away. Folios 9 and 10 again are missing, but beginning with folio 11 (Romans 8:15ff.) the remainder of Romans is substantially preserved. Folio 11 verso, containing Romans 8:15-25, is reproduced in Fig. 143. The text is broken away slightly at the left, but the missing words or portions of words are easily restored. At the bottom of the page four lines have been lost. The scribe wrote a large, flowing hand of calligraphic character, with the individual letters upright and square in formation and well spaced. Another hand put in the page numeration, the Greek letter κ at the top of this page being equivalent to number 20. Probably this latter hand is responsible also for the rather thick oblique stroke above the line which marks the ends of clauses as in lines 3, 5, 8, 10, 15, 20, and 22. The original scribe occasionally used a high dot for punctuation, as in line 3, and generally marked initial Upsilon and Iota with a dieresis, as in lines 1, 5, 11, and 23.[21] The scribe also abbreviated some words including the sacred names.

The text of this page reads as follows, the translation and punctuation being made in the style of the American Standard Version for convenience in comparison.

> Ye received the spirit of adoption, whereby we cry,
> Abba, Father. The Spirit itself beareth witness with
> our spirit, that we are children of God: and if children,
> then heirs of God and joint-heirs with Christ;
> if so be that we suffer, that we may be glorified with him. For
> I reckon that the sufferings of this present time are not worthy
> to be compared with the glory which shall

[20] This is the position it has in Codex Sinaiticus. Hebrews also follows Thessalonians in the present arrangement of Codex Vaticanus, but the paragraph numbers indicate that in an older division of this manuscript Hebrews stood between Galatians and Ephesians. Gregory, *Canon and Text of the New Testament*, pp.336, 344.
[21] Medial Iota also has the dieresis in line 9.

be revealed to us-ward. For the earnest expectation
of the creation waiteth for the revealing of the sons
of God. For the creation was subjected to vanity,
not of its own will but by reason of him who
subjected it, in hope that the creation itself also shall be delivered from the bondage of
corruption into the liberty of the glory of the
children of God. For we know that the whole creation
groaneth and travaileth in pain together until now.
And not only so, but we who have
the first-fruits of the Spirit also ourselves groan within ourselves, waiting for the redemption
of our body. For in hope were we saved:
but hope that is seen is not hope:
for who hopeth for that which he seeth? But if we hope for
that which we see not, then do we with patience wait for it.

Even a rapid reading of the above passage indicates that the
Chester Beatty Papyrus of the Letters of Paul presents substantially the same text with which we are familiar in the best modern
versions of the Bible. Indeed this very fact is the most significant
thing about the manuscript. Here is our oldest copy of Paul's letters,
and it emphatically confirms the accuracy and soundness of the
general textual tradition.[22]

When manuscripts are copied many times, however, mistakes and
alterations both unintentional and intentional creep in. Intentional
alterations which are found include the simplification of a difficult
passage, the addition of a lacking word or a desired quotation, and
even changes made for dogmatic reasons. Far more frequent are
unintentional alterations, which include writing a word once when
it should be repeated, writing a word twice when it should appear
only once, omitting a word or line when the eye skips to a second
word or line ending similarly, and other errors of like kind. It is
not surprising that such mistakes occurred in the laborious copying
by hand of ancient manuscripts, for the same types of errors are
perfectly familiar to modern stenographers, and even appear in
printed books whose proofs have been carefully examined and re-
examined. Thus, an edition of the English Bible printed in 1653
omitted the word "not" in I Corinthians 6:9 and made the passage
read, "Or know ye not that the unrighteous shall inherit the kingdom of God?" The famous "Printer's Bible" gave Psalm 119:161 in

[22] Hans Lietzmann, *Zur Würdigung des Chester-Beatty-Papyrus der Paulusbriefe*
(*Sitzungsbericht der Preussischen Akademie der Wissenschaften Phil.-Hist. Kl. 1934.*
xxv), pp.3f.

the form "Printers have persecuted me without a cause" instead of "Princes have persecuted me without a cause," and an edition printed in 1717 became known as the "Vinegar Bible" because it misprinted "Vinegar" for "Vineyard" in the headline to the twentieth chapter of Luke. It is no wonder, therefore, that Irenaeus (A.D. c.180) thought it necessary to add the following note at the close of one of his writings: "I adjure thee who mayest copy this book, by our Lord Jesus Christ, and by his glorious advent when he comes to judge the living and the dead, to compare what thou shalt write, and correct it carefully by this manuscript, and also to write this adjuration, and place it in the copy."[23]

Rufinus (A.D. c.345-c.410) included an even longer adjuration and entreaty in the prologue to his translation of Origen's *De Principiis*:

"And, verily, in the presence of God the Father, and of the Son, and of the Holy Spirit, I adjure and beseech every one, who may either transcribe or read these books, by his belief in the kingdom to come, by the mystery of the resurrection from the dead, and by that everlasting fire prepared for the devil and his angels, that, as he would not possess for an eternal inheritance that place where there is weeping and gnashing of teeth, and where their fire is not quenched and their worm dieth not, he add nothing to Scripture, and take nothing away from it, and make no insertion or alteration, but that he compare his transcript with the copies from which he made it, and make the emendations and distinctions according to the letter, and not have his manuscript incorrect or indistinct, lest the difficulty of ascertaining the sense, from the indistinctness of the copy, should cause greater difficulties to the readers."[24]

And in his Preface to the Vulgate Translation of the Four Gospels (A.D. 383), Jerome spoke of "the mistakes introduced by inaccurate translators, and the blundering alterations of confident but ignorant critics, and further, all that has been inserted or altered by sleepy copyists."[25]

As a very early manuscript, the Chester Beatty Papyrus of Paul's letters is free from many alterations which appear in later codices. An instance of this may be seen in line 12 of the page reproduced in Fig. 143. Here in Romans 8:20f. it is probable that Paul wrote exactly as the papyrus reads, "by reason of him who subjected it, in hope that[26] the creation itself also shall be delivered. . . ." Codex Vaticanus, Codex Alexandrinus, and Codex Ephraemi rescriptus all

---

[23] Irenaeus, *On the Ogdoad*; quoted by Eusebius, *Ch. Hist.* v, xx.
[24] ANF IV, p.238; cf. Revelation 22:18f.
[25] NPNFSS VI, p.488.   [26] ἐφ' ἐλπίδι ὅτι.

agree that this is the correct reading. But in Codex Sinaiticus, Codex
Claromontanus, and Codex Boernerianus a slight alteration is found
whereby the sentence is made to read, "by reason of him who subjected it, in hope, because[27] the creation itself also shall be delivered. . . ." At many other points also the Chester Beatty Papyrus
clearly preserves what Paul wrote originally. In Romans 6:8 he
wrote, "But if we died with Christ, we believe that we shall also
live with him." Later scribes changed the last word "him" into
"the Christ" in order to remove any possible ambiguity, but the
papyrus preserves the original "him."[28] In Romans 9:31 Paul wrote
"but Israel, following after a law of righteousness, did not arrive
at the law,"[29] just as the papyrus has it. But some scribe thought
that Paul should have used the same phrase in both parts of his
sentence, and so changed the conclusion to read "did not arrive at
the law of righteousness,"[30] and this appears in the mass of the
later manuscripts. In Romans 10:15 Paul wrote, "How beautiful are
the feet of them that bring glad tidings of good things!" and that
is the way the Chester Beatty Papyrus has it.[31] This was a quotation,
however, from Isaiah 52:7 and later manuscripts added from the
Septuagint, "How beautiful are the feet of them that bring glad
tidings of peace,[32] of them that bring glad tidings of good things."

In a number of instances, however, alterations have already crept
into the text of the Chester Beatty Papyrus. Examples may be seen
in lines 17-20 and 22 of the page illustrated in Fig. 143. In Romans
8:23 Paul wrote originally, "but also ourselves, who have the first-
fruits of the Spirit, we also ourselves groan within ourselves, waiting
for the adoption, the redemption of our body."[33] This was an involved and complicated sentence, as many of Paul's sentences are.
In the papyrus the first "also ourselves" was omitted and so was
the word "adoption" with the result that the sentence emerged in
simplified form but with Paul's tumultuous manner of speech and
richness of thought considerably modified: "but we who have the
first-fruits of the Spirit also ourselves groan within ourselves, waiting
for the redemption of our body." Codex Claromontanus and Codex
Boernerianus later did the same as the papyrus in the omission of

---

[27] ἐφ' ἐλπίδι διότι.

[28] αὐτῷ 𝔭⁴⁶ SABC sa bo; τῷ Χριστῷ DG Latt.

[29] νόμον 𝔭⁴⁶ SAB sa bo DG.   [30] νόμον δικαιοσύνης Latt Koine.

[31] 𝔭⁴⁶ SABC sa bo.   [32] + τῶν εὐαγγελιζομένων εἰρήνην DG Latt.

[33] ἀλλὰ καὶ αὐτοὶ τὴν ἀπαρχὴν τοῦ πνεύματος ἔχοντες ἡμεῖς καὶ αὐτοὶ ἐν ἑαυτοῖς στενά-
ζομεν υἱοθεσίαν ἀπεκδεχόμενοι, τὴν ἀπολύτρωσιν τοῦ σώματος ἡμῶν SAC.

the word "adoption," but handled the first part of the sentence differently: "but also ourselves, who have the first-fruits of the Spirit, ourselves groan within ourselves, waiting for the redemption of our body." Codex Vaticanus, on the other hand, did nothing but omit the original "we."

In Romans 8:24 the Chester Beatty Papyrus again seems to have slightly changed and simplified an originally more complex Pauline sentence. The papyrus reads, "for who hopeth for that which he seeth?"[34] Other forms in which the sentence is found are: "for what a man seeth, why doth he hope for?"[35] "for what a man seeth, why doth he yet hope for?"[36] "for who yet waiteth for that which he seeth?"[37] and "for what a man seeth, why doth he yet wait for?"[38] Of these the last is probably the original form since it is more probable that a scribe would change the verb "wait for" into "hope for" which appears so frequently in the rest of the passage, than that someone would invent the new expression "wait for."

Elsewhere in the papyrus appear errors, changes in words, and attempted corrections. For example there is a grammatical error in Romans 6:13 made through carelessness,[39] a word changed in 9:27 to make a quotation agree more exactly with the Septuagint,[40] and an omission of two words in 11:17 in order to simplify Paul's grammar where three genitives follow one another in unbroken succession.[41]

As the preceding examples have shown and as may also be seen by detailed study of the entire papyrus, p^{46} agrees most often with the manuscripts of the Alexandrian family, sABC, but also not infrequently with those of the Western family, including D and G.[42] As a very early codex it is free from many alterations which appear in later manuscripts, yet it also shows how changes and errors had already been introduced. Doubtless this papyrus is typical of many other codices which were in existence in the second and third cen-

---

[34] ὃ γὰρ βλέπει τίς ἐλπίζει p^{46} B.

[35] ὃ γὰρ βλέπει τις, τί ἐλπίζει DG Latt.

[36] ὃ γὰρ βλέπει τις, τί καὶ ἐλπίζει C Koine.

[37] ὃ γὰρ βλέπει τις καὶ ὑπομένει S.

[38] ὃ γὰρ βλέπει τις, τί καὶ ὑπομένει A.

[39] ζῶντες p^{46} DG instead of ζῶντας.

[40] κατάλιμμα p^{46} DG instead of ὑπόλειμμα SAB.

[41] τῆς ῥίζης τῆς πιότητος τῆς ἐλαίας ("of the root of the fatness of the olive tree") SBC; "of the root" is omitted by p^{46} DG; another attempt to make the sentence more readable is represented by the addition of "and" in A Koine, "of the root and of the fatness of the olive tree."

[42] Kenyon, *The Chester Beatty Biblical Papyri*, Fasciculus III Supplement Text, pp.xv-xvii. (These terms are explained later in this chapter: Alexandrian, p.432, Western p.441, and Caesarean, p.446.)

turies A.D., no two of which were exactly alike and in each of which numerous variations were to be found.

𝔭⁶⁶ is a codex which is in the Bibliothek Bodmer in Geneva where it is known as Papyrus Bodmer II.[43] Upon its publication in 1956 it was recognized to be of significance comparable to 𝔭⁴⁶ upon grounds of both age and extent. As to its date, a time around A.D. 200 is probable and some think that it may be even somewhat earlier. As to its extent, the codex preserves for us approximately two-thirds of the Gospel according to John. There is an unwritten leaf at the outset which provides a front cover. Beginning with the first written page, the pages are numbered. They run consecutively from page α′ (page 1) to page λδ′ (page 34) which ends in the eleventh verse of the sixth chapter of John; then pages 35-38 are missing; and after that the manuscript continues from page λθ′ (page 39), beginning in the thirty-fifth verse of chapter six, to page ρη′ (page 108), ending with the twenty-sixth verse of the fourteenth chapter of the Gospel. Except for the two missing leaves (pages 35-38), the intact character of this part of the manuscript is amazing. The leaves are nearly rectangular and quite small, being about five and one-half inches wide and a little over six inches high. Individually the leaves are so well preserved that there are rarely more than a few letters missing on a page. In addition to this part of the manuscript, however, there are said to be portions of the balance of the codex which still await publication which are extremely fragmentary.

The handwriting of 𝔭⁶⁶ is an excellent, upright, regular, quadratic literary script. There is rudimentary punctuation with a high point at the end of sentences and a double point at the end of sections. The dieresis is used frequently over Iota and Upsilon. The words θεός, Ἰησοῦς, κύριος, and Χριστός are always abbreviated, and so also sometimes are ἄνθρωπος, πατήρ, πνεῦμα, and υἱός. There are numerous errors in the manuscript, but most of these have been corrected, many of the corrections perhaps having been made by the scribe himself during the course of his work. This, it has been thought, may suggest that the manuscript was written by a commercial copyist. As to the text, in fashion similar to 𝔭⁴⁶, there are many variants and

[43] Victor Martin, *Papyrus Bodmer II, Evangile de Jean, chap. 1-14* (Bibliotheca Bodmeriana v). 1956; cf. Georg Maldfeld in NTS 3 (1956-57), pp.79-81; K. Aland in TL 82 (1957), cols. 161-184; and in NTS 3 (1956-57), pp.280-284; J. Ramsey Michaels in *The Bible Translator.* 7 (1956), pp.150-154; Floyd V. Filson in BA 20 (1957), pp.54-63; M.-E. Boismard in RB 64 (1957), pp.363-398; C. K. Barrett in *The Expository Times.* 68 (1956-57), pp.174-177.

the manuscript does not agree consistently with any of the major texts established later. John 5:4 and John 7:53-8:11 are omitted, passages which other manuscript evidence had already suggested were not a part of the Gospel according to John in its original form.[44]

Continuing now on into the third century A.D. we may note the following papyri. $\mathfrak{p}^{45}$ is another of the Chester Beatty Papyri, with a fragment of the same manuscript in the Österreichische National-bibliothek in Vienna.[45] There are thirty leaves of this codex, often poorly preserved, and the content extends, with many gaps, from the twentieth chapter of Matthew to the seventeenth chapter of Acts. The date is probably in the early part of the third century. The text is mixed, being mainly Caesarean in Mark but Alexandrian and Western in the other parts.

$\mathfrak{p}^{53}$ is the designation of two fragments at the University of Michigan of a codex which probably like the foregoing one also contained the four Gospels and the book of Acts, since the extant portions have most of the verses of Matthew 26:29-40 and Acts 9:33-10:1.[46] The date is probably about the middle of the third century. The text shows agreements with the Alexandrian, Western, and Caesarean families of manuscripts.

$\mathfrak{p}^{37}$ is a codex leaf at the University of Michigan with Matthew 26:19-52.[47] It was probably written in the second half of the third century, and the text has resemblances to the Caesarean. $\mathfrak{p}^{5}$ designates two Oxyrhynchus papyri in the British Museum which came from the same codex and contain parts of John 1, 16, and 20.[48] They were probably written in the second half of the third century, and the text resembles the Alexandrian and the Western. $\mathfrak{p}^{22}$ is also a papyrus from Oxyrhynchus and is in the University Library at Glasgow.[49] In this case the copy was a roll rather than a codex, and parts of two columns are preserved with portions of John 15 and 16. The date is probably toward the end of the third century; the text often agrees with S but sometimes also with D.

---

[44] John 5:4 is found in AG but is omitted in SBCD. John 7:53-8:11 is found in D but is omitted in SABC (A and C are actually imperfect at this point but calculation of space shows that they cannot have contained the passage; see Marcus Dods in *The Expositor's Greek Testament*. I, p.770).

[45] Frederic G. Kenyon, *The Chester Beatty Biblical Papyri*. Fasciculus II, *The Gospels and Acts*, Text 1933, Plates 1934.

[46] Henry A. Sanders in *Quantulacumque*, pp.151-161.

[47] Henry A. Sanders in HTR 19 (1926), pp.215-226; HPUM Pl. XIII.

[48] OP II, No.208; XV, No.1781; HPUM Pl. VIII.

[49] OP X, No.1228; HPUM Pl. VII.

𝔭²⁷ designates two fragments of a codex leaf from Oxyrhynchus, now in the Cambridge University Library, with portions of Romans 8 and 9.[50] The date is probably in the third century. The text agrees generally with B, and there are some readings like the Western text. 𝔭⁴⁹ is a codex leaf in three pieces in the possession of Yale University.[51] It contains Ephesians 4:16-29 and 4:31-5:13, and was probably written in the third century. The text shows agreements with B and 𝔭⁴⁶. 𝔭³² is a codex leaf in the John Rylands Library with Titus 1:11-15 on the recto and Titus 2:3-8 on the verso.[52] The date is in the third century; the text agrees with S and also with Western manuscripts. 𝔭³⁰ is two leaves of a codex from Oxyrhynchus, now in the Bibliothèque Universitaire in Ghent, containing I Thessalonians 4:12 to II Thessalonians 1:2 with breaks.[53] Page numbers 207 and 208 are preserved, and if the codex contained Paul's collected letters the usual order from Romans to I Thessalonians would exactly account for the preceding 206 pages. The date is probably late in the third century. The text shows agreements with the Alexandrian manuscripts but also divergences.

𝔭⁴⁷ is another part of the Chester Beatty Papyri and consists of ten leaves of a codex containing Revelation 9:10-17:2.[54] The date is probably in the latter part of the third century. The text agrees generally with A, C, and S.

Belonging to the third or fourth century is 𝔭¹, a codex leaf found at Oxyrhynchus only a day or two after the first discovery of the sayings of Jesus (OP No. 1; see above pp.411f.) and in nearly the same place.[55] Now at the University of Pennsylvania, it contains most of Matthew 1:1-20. The text is similar to S and B.

Continuing on in the fourth century we note the following papyri. 𝔭⁴ designates four fragmentary codex leaves in the Bibliothèque Nationale in Paris which are from a lectionary (1943) and contain portions of the first six chapters of Luke.[56] The date is fourth century, and the text is Alexandrian. 𝔭²⁸ is a codex leaf from Oxyrhynchus, now in the Palestine Institute of Archeology at Pacific School of Religion, with John 6:8-12, 17-22.[57] The date is the early or middle fourth century; the text agrees with B. 𝔭⁵⁰ is two codex leaves at Yale

---

[50] OP XI, No.1355. [51] Maldfeld in ZNW 42 (1949), p.250.

[52] HPUM Pl. III (where it is numbered 𝔭³¹).

[53] OP XIII, No.1598.

[54] Kenyon, *The Chester Beatty Biblical Papyri.* Fasciculus III. Text 1934; Plates 1936.

[55] OP I, No.2; HPUM Pl. XI. [56] RB 47 (1938), pp.5-22.

[57] OP XIII, No.1596.

University, containing Acts 8:26-32 and 10:26-31.[58] The date is fourth century; the text agrees mostly with B.

𝔭[13] is a portion of a papyrus roll from Oxyrhynchus, now in the British Museum, with an unusually interesting history.[59] The roll was written originally in the third century A.D. as an epitome in Latin of the history of Rome by Livy.[60] Probably in the first half of the fourth century the back (verso) of the roll was used to copy at least part of the New Testament. The extant portion contains eleven broad columns with parts of Hebrews 2-5 and 10-12. The columns are numbered at the top, the preserved numbers being 47-50, 63-65, and 67-69; thus some other part of the New Testament presumably occupied the preceding part of the roll. The text tends generally to agree with B, but also has agreements with D.

𝔭[10] (Fig. 144) is an individual leaf from Oxyrhynchus, now in the Semitic Museum at Harvard University.[61] At the top, Romans 1:1-7 is copied in eleven lines of rough, large letters. There are several mistakes in spelling and part of verse six is left out. From the carelessness of the copying and the rudeness of the uncial letters, Grenfell and Hunt thought that this was a schoolboy's exercise. At the bottom of the leaf are two lines of cursive writing, and Adolf Deissmann suggested that the entire leaf might have served as an amulet for the Aurelios Paulos who is named there.[62] The cursive writing is such as occurs in the first half of the fourth century, and the papyrus was actually found tied up with a contract dated in A.D. 316, so an early fourth century date is confirmed. In the copying the following divine names are all abbreviated: Christ Jesus (line 1), God (lines 2, 9, 10), Son (line 3), Son of God (line 5), Spirit (line 5), Jesus Christ (lines 6, 8), Lord (line 6), Father (line 10) and Lord Christ Jesus (lines 10-11). The text is mainly Alexandrian. In verse 1, 𝔭[10] and Codex Vaticanus are the chief witnesses for the characteristic Pauline "Christ Jesus" (instead of "Jesus Christ") in verse 1, while 𝔭[10] is quite alone in the same order in verse 7 (lines 10-11) and in reading "the name of Jesus Christ" instead of "his name" in verse 5 (line 8).

𝔭[15] is a codex leaf from Oxyrhynchus, now in Cairo, containing I Corinthians 7:18-8:4.[63] Written also in a good-sized uncial hand, the date of the papyrus is probably in the second half of the fourth century. With some exceptions, the text agrees with BSA.

[58] Carl H. Kraeling in *Quantulacumque*, pp.163-172.   [59] OP IV, No.657.
[60] OP IV, No.668.   [61] OP II, No.209.   [62] DLO p.203 n.4.   [63] OP VII, No.1008.

Moving on into the fifth century A.D., we note these examples: $\mathfrak{p}^{21}$ is a fragmentary codex leaf from Oxyrhynchus, now in Muhlenberg College, Allentown, Pennsylvania.[64] It contains several verses of the twelfth chapter of Matthew. The rather large uncials point to a date in the fifth century. Textually there are agreements with D and with a corrector of S. $\mathfrak{p}^{11}$, now in Leningrad, consists of six or seven fragments which probably came from a papyrus codex but were later used for some kind of a book cover.[65] They contain parts of I Corinthians 1-2 and 6-7. The date is probably fifth century, and the text is Alexandrian.

In the sixth century we note these papyri: $\mathfrak{p}^{3}$ is a fragment of a lectionary (1 348), now in the Österreichische Nationalbibliothek, Vienna, with Luke 7:36-45; 10:38-42.[66] The date is sixth century, and the text is Alexandrian. $\mathfrak{p}^{36}$ is two codex leaves, now in the Bibliotheca Laurenziana in Florence, containing John 3:14-18, 31-32.[67] The date is probably sixth century; the text is Alexandrian and Western.

Coming to the end of the sixth or beginning of the seventh century we find such a papyrus as $\mathfrak{p}^{44}$. This is three leaves of a codex, now in the Metropolitan Museum of Art, New York City, with portions of Matthew 17, 18, and 25, and John 9, 10, and 12.[68] The text is Alexandrian, agreeing particularly with B. $\mathfrak{p}^{35}$ is probably to be dated sometime in the seventh century. This is a codex leaf, now in the Bibliotheca Laurenziana in Florence, which contains Matthew 25:12-15, 20-22.[69] The text is Alexandrian and Western.

Finally toward the end of the seventh century we find several fairly extensive papyri which have only recently been published. These were found at Nessana in the Negeb in southern Palestine by the Colt Archaeological Expedition, under H. Dunscombe Colt, which worked at this place in 1936 and 1937. Nessana was a stopping point on the caravan route from Aqabah to Gaza, was fortified as early as the second century B.C., flourished in the sixth and seventh centuries A.D., and is the location of a small settlement named 'Auja-el-Hafir at the present time. The papyri found here had been buried in the collapse of a room annexed to a small church. Since southern Palestine is relatively dry, and since the church was on the top of a hill where such rain as fell ran off rapidly, conditions were fairly favorable for the preservation of the papyri. All together

---

[64] OP X, No.1227.
[66] *ibid*., pp.242f.   [67] *ibid*., p.247.
[65] Maldfeld in ZNW 42 (1949), p.244.
[68] *ibid*., p.249.   [69] *ibid*., p.247.

there were found not only the New Testament papyri about to be mentioned but also a copy of the apocryphal correspondence between Abgar and Christ, a version of the legend of St. George, a portion of the Twelve Chapters on Faith ascribed, perhaps incorrectly, to Gregory Thaumaturgus, and classical, legal, and nonliterary documents. These are now in New York University.[70]

The New Testament papyri from Nessana are $\mathfrak{p}^{59}$, $\mathfrak{p}^{60}$, and $\mathfrak{p}^{61}$. $\mathfrak{p}^{59}$ and $\mathfrak{p}^{60}$ are probably from the latter part of the seventh century, $\mathfrak{p}^{61}$ is slightly later, either at the end of the seventh or the beginning of the eighth century. $\mathfrak{p}^{59}$ consists of fourteen leaves, two complete, the others fragmentary, with parts of John 1, 11, 12, 17, 18, and 21. $\mathfrak{p}^{60}$ is made up of twenty consecutive leaves, half or two-thirds intact, with text extending from John 16:29 to 19:26. $\mathfrak{p}^{61}$ consists of seven fragmentary leaves with small portions of Romans, I Corinthians, Philippians, Colossians, I Thessalonians, Titus, and Philemon. Since, as far as can be determined, these books stood in the order just given, it appears likely that the complete codex contained the entire Pauline collection and in the usual order. Determination of the character of the text of the Nessana papyri awaits further study.

Such are some representative and interesting examples of the papyri of the New Testament. While many are only fragments, they doubtless give us a more realistic impression of how many of the New Testament writings appeared originally than do the relatively elegant vellum manuscripts of which we shall soon speak. Including all of the more than sixty papyri thus far known, only seven out of the twenty-seven books of the New Testament are not represented, namely I and II Timothy, and I and II Peter, II and III John, and Jude.[71] All together also the known papyri contain a good 50 per cent of the entire New Testament text, and in the case of the Gospel according to John they preserve 88 per cent of it.[72] Naturally the individual papyri must be individually evaluated as to age and text form.[73]

In the analysis above of a section of $\mathfrak{p}^{46}$ it was seen that on the whole the text of this papyrus was very good and agreed frequently with the oldest parchments such as Codex Vaticanus, Codex Sinaiticus, and Codex Alexandrinus, but that it also contained readings

---

[70] *Excavations at Nessana*, II, *Literary Papyri*, by Lionel Casson and Ernest L. Hettich. 1950. For the *Non-Literary Papyri* see Vol. III by Casper J. Kraemer, Jr. 1958.

[71] Maldfeld in ZNW 42 (1949), p.239.

[72] Maldfeld in NTS 3 (1956), p.80.

[73] Kurt Aland in *Forschungen und Fortschritte*. 31 (1957), p.51.

which seemed to be errors and changes from what Paul probably wrote originally. Likewise the other papyri cited from the second and third centuries usually manifested texts of a mixed character. In the fourth and later centuries, however, we have observed many papyri the text of which is much more strictly Alexandrian. This suggests that the very existence of many different copies of New Testament writings in the second and third centuries, each with its own variants, led to the desire for a better text and that, probably in the fourth century, a more nearly standard text was wrought out. This hypothesis will be referred to again in what follows.

PARCHMENTS

We turn next to early copies of the New Testament, or portions of the New Testament, written on parchment or vellum. The earliest of these presently known belong probably to the third century A.D. and thus are about a century later in date than the earliest known New Testament papyri. By the fourth century, as we have seen (pp.397f.), parchment became the chief material for New Testament manuscripts although, as we have also just seen, copies on papyrus are also found for yet a number of centuries.

As far as known at the present time, the oldest parchment containing New Testament material is **0212**, a fragment in the possession of Yale University.[74] It is a little over three and one-half by four inches in size, and may have been part of a scroll rather than a codex. The fifteen lines of writing which are preserved provide a text in which the four Gospels are woven together to make a single narrative in the manner of the well-known Diatessaron. The material contained is Matthew 27:56-57; Mark 15:40, 42, 43; Luke 23:49-51, 54; John 19:38. The date is probably in the first half of the third century.

The next oldest parchment and the first with text which is directly from a New Testament book as known in the regular canon is **0220**.[75] This is a fragment obtained in Cairo in 1950 by Dr. Leland C. Wyman of Jamaica Plain, Massachusetts, and said to have come from Fustat, northeast of Old Cairo and near the site of the Roman fortress of Babylon. It is about three and one-half by four and one-half inches in size and contains Romans 4:23-5:3 on the recto and Romans 5:8-13 on the verso. The writing suggests a date in the latter part of the

[74] Aland in ZNW 45 (1954), p.188; and in TL 82 (1957), cols. 161f.
[75] William H. P. Hatch in HTR 45 (1952), pp.79-85.

third century. As far as it goes the text is mostly like the Alexandrian, although it is no doubt pre-Hesychian. There is an important reading in 5:1 where the indicative ἔχομεν is found instead of the subjunctive ἔχωμεν which is in BSACD^p and other manuscripts. This confirms the conclusion already drawn on grounds of the context that Paul meant to affirm that "we have peace," rather than to exhort, "let us have peace."[76]

THE ALEXANDRIAN TEXT

We come now to the theory already suggested, that the existence in the second and third centuries of many different manuscripts with many different readings led to the desire to obtain a more nearly standardized text, freed from as many as possible of these changes and errors. The hypothesis is that in the fourth century the scholars at Alexandria brought together a number of the better manuscripts, such as the Chester Beatty Papyri, and endeavored to strike out their variants and thus arrive at a good average text.[77] At any rate the next few manuscripts to be mentioned form a sort of family whose text well might have arisen in this very way. In each of these several manuscripts there are still individual corrections, changes, and errors, but the group has such decided similarities that it is commonly referred to as representing the Egyptian or Alexandrian text. Since this characteristic text may go back to the Egyptian bishop and martyr Hesychius (d. A.D. c.311),[78] whose work on the text of the Gospels is mentioned by Jerome,[79] it is also called the Hesychian recension (𝔥). Four great vellum Bibles, written in uncial characters, constitute the chief witnesses to the Egyptian text. These are Codex Vaticanus, Codex Sinaiticus, Codex Alexandrinus,[80] and Codex Ephraemi Syri rescriptus.

CODEX VATICANUS

Codex Vaticanus, designated as B or **03**, is a fine parchment codex containing almost the entire Greek Bible. It was already in the possession of the Vatican Library at Rome before the first catalogue of

76 Lietzmann, *An die Römer*, p.58.

77 Lietzmann, *Zur Würdigung des Chester-Beatty-Papyrus der Paulusbriefe*, p.10.

78 Eusebius, *Ch. Hist.* VIII, xiii.

79 Preface to the Vulgate Translation of the Four Gospels, addressed to Pope Damasus, A.D. 383 (NPNFSS VI, p.488); cf. Lietzmann, *Einführung in die Textgeschichte der Paulusbriefe*, p.13.

80 It must be noted, however, that while the text of Codex Alexandrinus is Alexandrian in the letters of Paul it is Byzantine in the Gospels.

that library was made in 1475. Napoleon carried the manuscript to Paris as a prize of war, and it remained there from 1809 until it was returned to Rome in 1815. While at Paris the manuscript was studied by Leonhard Hug, a Roman Catholic professor from Tübingen, and its great age and true value were recognized for the first time. In 1843 Constantine Tischendorf was able to study the manuscript in Rome, but only under very restricted circumstances, and full and accurate knowledge was not available to the scholars of the world until a complete photographic facsimile was published in Rome in 1889-1890.

The codex must have originally contained about 820 leaves, of which 759 are preserved, 142 of these belonging to the New Testament. Each leaf measures about ten and one-half by ten inches, and there are three columns of text to the page with forty-two lines to a column. The writing is in perfectly simple and unadorned uncials, smaller letters sometimes being crowded in at the ends of lines. The words are written continuously without separation. There is almost no punctuation, although initial Iota and Upsilon are marked with a dieresis and sacred names are abbreviated. Old Testament quotations are marked with a horizontal caret (>). One scribe copied the entire New Testament, although a different scribe wrote the Old Testament. Two correctors have made corrections in the manuscript, one being almost contemporary with the original scribes, and the other being as late as the tenth or eleventh century. The later corrector retraced the pale letters, omitting only the letters and words which he believed to be incorrect, and also added the breathings and accents. The style of handwriting and almost complete absence of ornamentation indicate a date for Codex Vaticanus in the middle of the fourth century A.D., and the place of writing may have been in Alexandria.[81]

As far as the letters of Paul are concerned, then, in this manuscript we have a copy which was made, in round numbers, only 150 years later than the Chester Beatty Papyrus and three hundred years after the originals. The opening page of Paul's Letter to the Romans, with its simple title, "To the Romans," is reproduced in Fig. 145.

CODEX SINAITICUS

Codex Sinaiticus (‭א‬, S, or **01**)[82] derives its name from Mount Sinai

---

[81] Lake, *The Text of the New Testament*, pp.14f.
[82] For the designation cf. above p.415.

where it was found in the Monastery of Saint Catherine (Fig. 146). The traditional region of Mount Sinai (cf. p.151) was one of the places sought out by hermits and anchorites upon the inception of the Christian monastic movement in the third and fourth centuries. These hermits settled in the caves of Jebel Serbal, and eventually churches and convents were built in the neighboring valley of Pharan (now the Wadi Feiran), which became the seat of the Bishop of Pharan. Other hermits established themselves twenty-five miles away at a place where a bush was shown as the Burning Bush of Exodus 3:2-4. This was in a desolate valley of nearly four thousand feet altitude at the foot of Jebel Musa and nearby Jebel Catherine. It is believed that St. Helena built a church here to enshrine the Burning Bush and also a tower of refuge for the hermits who were under attack by Arab raids. Such interest on the part of Helena is not improbable since we know that she visited Jerusalem about A.D. 327 and was interested in the erection of churches in the Holy Land (p.532). About A.D. 460 the region was visited by the Spanish nun and pilgrim Etheria. She was received at a certain monastery and energetically climbed various mountains including a middle one to which the name of Sinai was especially attached, but whether this was at Jebel Serbal or Jebel Musa is difficult to make out. Her travel journal reads:

"We reached the mountain late on the sabbath, and arriving at a certain monastery, the monks who dwelt there received us very kindly, showing us every kindness; there is also a church and a priest there. We stayed there that night, and early on the Lord's Day, together with the priest and the monks who dwelt there, we began the ascent of the mountains one by one. These mountains are ascended with infinite toil, for you cannot go up gently by a spiral track, as we say snail-shell wise, but you climb straight up the whole way, as if up a wall, and you must come straight down each mountain until you reach the very foot of the middle one, which is specially called Sinai."[83]

In A.D. 530, since the attacks of the Arabs were continuing, the Emperor Justinian built a massive wall around St. Helena's church and tower. At about this time the Church of the Burning Bush was rebuilt on a larger scale and renamed the Church of the Transfiguration. When the settlement at Pharan broke up under Arab raids the Bishop of Pharan took refuge in the Monastery of the Burning Bush, and after A.D. 630 his successors had the title of Bishop of Sinai. The

[83] The Pilgrimage of Etheria. tr. M. L. McClure and C. L. Feltoe in Translations of Christian Literature. Series III Liturgical Texts, pp.3f.

Archbishop of Sinai now resides in Cairo. Saint Catherine, by whose name the Monastery of the Burning Bush later became known, was a martyr in Alexandria under the Roman ruler Maximinus (A.D. 305-313). According to legend her body was transported by angels to Mount Sinai, where some five centuries later her bones were discovered and where, at least in part, they are still preserved. Curiously enough, the monastery enclosure now includes also a mosque with a square minaret which rises beside the bell tower of the church. The story told concerning this is that centuries ago a Turkish general was marching against the monastery with troops which were thirsting for the conquest. He was met by a deputation of monks and dissuaded from his purpose, but fearing that his troops could not be restrained, he advised the hasty erection of the mosque. When the troops arrived the minaret appeared beside the church tower, and the Muslims spared the place where it appeared that their Prophet was known.[84]

Such is the story of the famous monastery in which one of the greatest manuscript discoveries of all time was made. The discoverer was the unrivaled critic and decipherer of ancient manuscripts, Dr. Constantine Tischendorf. He told the story of the great discovery in his own words as follows:

"It was at the foot of Mount Sinai, in the Convent of St. Catherine, that I discovered the pearl of all my researches. In visiting the library of the monastery, in the month of May, 1844, I perceived in the middle of the great hall a large and wide basket full of old parchments; and the librarian, who was a man of information, told me that two heaps of paper like these, mouldered by time, had been already committed to the flames. What was my surprise to find amid this heap of papers a considerable number of sheets of a copy of the Old Testament in Greek, which seemed to me to be one of the most ancient that I had ever seen. The authorities of the convent allowed me to possess myself of a third of these parchments, or about forty-three sheets, all the more readily as they were destined for the fire."[85]

Tischendorf was allowed to take the forty-three leaves to Leipzig where he edited them under the title *Codex Friderico Augustanus* (1846) in acknowledgment of the patronage of the king of Saxony. In 1853 Tischendorf returned to Sinai but could find nothing more of

[84] H. V. Morton, *Through Lands of the Bible*. 1938, p.347.
[85] *Codex Sinaiticus, the Ancient Biblical Manuscript now in the British Museum, Tischendorf's Story and Argument Related by Himself*. 8th ed. 1934, pp.23f. The quotations from this book are made by permission of the Lutterworth Press, Redhill, Surrey, England.

the manuscript. Once again in 1859 he came back, this time with the approval of the emperor of Russia for systematic researches in the East, but still there was no trace of the great treasure. He was on the point of leaving when the steward of the convent invited him to his cell. Tischendorf relates that the monk "took down from the corner of the room a bulky kind of volume, wrapped up in a red cloth, and laid it before me. I unrolled the cover, and discovered, to my great surprise, not only those very fragments which, fifteen years before, I had taken out of the basket, but also other parts of the Old Testament, the New Testament complete, and, in addition, the Epistle of Barnabas and a part of the Pastor of Hermas."[86]

After complex transactions it became possible for Tischendorf to place the great manuscript in the hands of the emperor of Russia and for himself to prepare a facsimile edition of it. Payment of some $6,750 was made to the monks by the emperor for the manuscript. Acclaim came to Tischendorf from throughout the Christian world for his notable discovery. Relating the recognitions which he received, Tischendorf said:

"The two most celebrated universities of England, Cambridge and Oxford, desired to show me honour by conferring on me their highest academic degree. 'I would rather,' said an old man—himself of the highest distinction for learning—'I would rather have discovered this Sinaitic manuscript than the Koh-i-noor of the Queen of England.'

"But that which I think more highly of than all these flattering distinctions is the fact that Providence has given to our age, in which attacks on Christianity are so common, the Sinaitic Bible, to be to us a full and clear light as to what is the real text of God's Word written, and to assist us in defending the truth by establishing its authentic form."[87]

Codex Sinaiticus remained in Leningrad until it was purchased from the Soviet government by the British Museum for some $500,000. When the valuable manuscript arrived at the British Museum December 27, 1933, its appearance was still much as when Tischendorf first saw it at Sinai, a large pile of loose quires and leaves, lacking both beginning and end and having no covers or binding (Fig. 147). It has been carefully bound by the British Museum in two volumes, Old Testament and New Testament.

Whereas originally the Sinaitic manuscript probably had at least 730 leaves, only 390 (including those at Leipzig) remain today— 242 in the Old Testament and 148 in the New Testament. The leaves

[86] *ibid.*, p.26.   [87] *ibid.*, pp.31f.

are about fifteen inches high by thirteen and one-half or fourteen inches broad, and the text is written in four columns to the page, with forty-eight lines to the column. The words are written continuously without separation and there are no accents or breathings, although high and middle points and colon are used for punctuation, initial Iota and Upsilon have the dieresis and sacred names are abbreviated. The codex was written by three scribes, known as A, B, and D, of whom Scribe A wrote almost all of the New Testament. The three hands are very much alike, but they show individual peculiarities, particularly in the matter of spelling; it is largely on the basis of spelling that the three are differentiated. Many corrections have been made in the manuscript not only by the original scribes but also by a series of correctors from the fourth to the twelfth century.[88] No less than 14,800 places are enumerated in Tischendorf's edition where some alteration has been made to the text.[89] The dignified simplicity of the elegant capital letters in which the manuscript was originally written is comparable to that of Codex Vaticanus, and both manuscripts were probably written at about the same time around A.D. 350, the Vatican manuscript being perhaps a little the older of the two.[90] The place where the Codex Sinaiticus was written is uncertain but at least there is nothing to contradict an Egyptian origin although Caesarea or Palestine are also regarded as possibilities. Since Codex Vaticanus and Codex Sinaiticus are written in three and four columns respectively it has sometimes been believed that they are two of the fifty vellum Bibles ordered by Constantine from Eusebius of Caesarea in A.D. 332 but, as we have already noted (p.398), there are also arguments against this supposition. The first page of Paul's Letter to the Romans in Codex Sinaiticus is shown in Fig. 148.[91]

[88] H. J. M. Milne and T. C. Skeat, *Scribes and Correctors of the Codex Sinaiticus.* 1938, pp.22f., 40-50.

[89] Milne and Skeat, *The Codex Sinaiticus and the Codex Alexandrinus.* 1938, p.19.

[90] Schubart, *Griechische Palaeographie,* p.155.

[91] In 1949-1950 a Mount Sinai Expedition, for which Kenneth W. Clark was general editor, surveyed 3,300 manuscripts in six languages in the Monastery of Saint Catherine at Mount Sinai and copied more than 1,600 of them on microfilm. These include over five hundred manuscripts of biblical text in five languages, 175 of them of Greek New Testament text. The oldest Greek text is a seventh-century lectionary with readings from the Gospels and Letters of Paul. The same expedition also studied 2,400 manuscripts in eleven languages in the library of the Patriarchate of the Greek Orthodox Church at Jerusalem, and yet others in the library of the Armenian Patriarchate at Jerusalem. Over one thousand of these manuscripts were photographed on microfilm, including 270 biblical texts, ninety of the Gospels in Greek. A complete New Testament in Greek, written in the eleventh century and not previously noted

CODEX ALEXANDRINUS

Codex Alexandrinus (A or **02**) was given by Cyril Lucar, patriarch of Constantinople, to Sir Thomas Roe, the English ambassador to the Sublime Porte, to be presented to the king of England, and is first mentioned in a letter by Roe dated January 20, 1624 (i.e. January 30, 1625) as "an autographall bible intire, written by the hand of Tecla the protomartyr of the Greekes, that liued in the tyme of St. Paul; and he doth auerr yt to be true and authenticall, of his owne writing, and the greatest antiquitye of the Greeke church."[92] The codex arrived in England in 1628 and was placed in the Royal Library, which in 1757 was incorporated in the British Museum.

Cyril Lucar had been patriarch of Alexandria before assuming the same position in Constantinople in 1620, and probably brought the codex with him from Alexandria when he came to Constantinople. The earlier Alexandrian location of the manuscript is also indicated by an Arabic note written at the bottom of the first page of Genesis: "Made an inalienable gift to the Patriarchal Cell in the City of Alexandria. Whosoever shall remove it thence shall be accursed and cut off. Written by Athanasius the humble."

This Athanasius who calls himself "the humble" was probably the Melchite patriarch who died in A.D. 1308. Another Arabic note of the thirteenth or fourteenth century is written at the back of the Table of Books and gives the tradition alluded to in Sir Thomas Roe's letter that the manuscript was written by the martyr Thecla, but this is probably only a legend. The close connection of the codex with Alexandria makes it probable that that city was its place of origin. In point of time Codex Alexandrinus was presumably somewhat later than the Vatican and Sinaitic manuscripts, generally being ascribed to the first half of the fifth century.[93]

The manuscript originally contained perhaps 820 leaves, of which 773 are extant, 630 in the Old Testament, and 143 in the New Testament. The vellum leaves measure approximately twelve and five-eighths by ten and three-eighths inches. The quires were of eight leaves, numbered in Greek characters in the center of the top margin

---

by outside scholars, was found. The microfilms are in the Library of Congress. See Kenneth W. Clark in BA 16 (1953), pp.22-43; *Checklist of Manuscripts in St. Catherine's Monastery, Mount Sinai.* 1952; *Checklist of Manuscripts in the Libraries of the Greek and Armenian Patriarchates in Jerusalem.* 1953; Aziz Suryal Atiya, *The Arabic Manuscripts of Mount Sinai.* 1955.

[92] Milne and Skeat, *The Codex Sinaiticus and the Codex Alexandrinus*, p.28.

[93] *ibid.*, p.31.

of each first page. A fourteenth century Arabic numeration is written in the lower outer corner of the verso of the leaves, while Patrick
Young, librarian to Charles I, made the modern ink foliation and
chapter notation. The text is written in two columns per page with
from forty-six to fifty-two lines to the column. The words are written
continuously without separation and there are no accents and only
rare breathings. High and middle points are used, initial Iota and
Upsilon have the dieresis, sacred names are abbreviated, and Old
Testament quotations are marked.

While in general this manuscript still has the air of simplicity
which is characteristic of the oldest uncials, a small amount of ornamentation has been introduced. At the beginning of each book a
few lines are written in red, and the paragraphs are marked by
larger letters set in the margin. It is not necessarily the first letter
of the first word of the new paragraph which is thus enlarged.
Rather, the new paragraph begins in the line wherever it may happen to fall, and then the first letter which strikes the next line is
placed in the margin. Also, there are panel-shaped tailpieces or colo-
phons at the end of the various books. Two scribes are distinguishable in the Old Testament, and the first of these seems also to be
responsible for the New Testament, except perhaps in Luke 1 to
I Corinthians 10:8 where a smoother, lighter hand may indicate
the work of yet a third scribe.[94] There are also many corrections,
but most of them are of an early date. The appearance of the opening page of Romans in Codex Alexandrinus is shown in Fig. 149.

CODEX EPHRAEMI SYRI RESCRIPTUS

Codex Ephraemi Syri rescriptus (C or **04**) was in the possession
of Cardinal Ridolfi of Florence, a member of the de' Medici family,
in the sixteenth century, and later in the same century through
Catherine de' Medici, wife of Henry II of France, was brought to
Paris, where it is now in the Bibliothèque Nationale.

The codex is what is technically known as a palimpsest, or rewritten manuscript. Originally it was written in the fifth century as a
manuscript of the Greek Bible. In the twelfth century, when vellum
was scarce, the original writing was erased and many of the sheets
were used over again to receive a Greek translation of the discourses
of Ephraem Syrus, the latter having been a prominent theologian
of the Syrian church in the fourth century A.D. The underlying

---

[94] *ibid.*, p.32.

writing was not destroyed entirely, however, although it did appear impossible that it could ever be read again. Several attempts to make it out, including one in which chemical reagents were employed, had failed or met with very limited success, when the task was undertaken by Tischendorf. In 1840 the man who was to study the Vatican manuscript in 1843 and to discover the Sinaitic treasure in 1844 had just habilitated as a Privatdozent in the theological faculty at Leipzig. During 1841-1842 he attempted the decipherment of the famous palimpsest and was able in 1843 to publish a complete edition of the New Testament.[95] Today it has been found possible to use ultra-violet rays to read such manuscripts, but this device was not available to Tischendorf.

Only 209 leaves remain of the original codex, but of these 145 are in the New Testament and they contain portions of every New Testament book except II Thessalonians and II John. The leaves measure twelve and one-half by nine and one-half inches and the text is written in a single column of forty to forty-six lines to the page. The words are written continuously without separation and there are no accents or breathings but high and middle points are employed. Two correctors, perhaps of the sixth and of the ninth centuries respectively, have worked on the manuscript, the second of whom inserted a cross after the high point. The original writing is generally believed to belong to the fifth century, and perhaps to be a little later than Codex Alexandrinus. A page from Codex Ephraemi rescriptus (Matthew 20:16-34) is shown in Fig. 150.

Such are the four great uncial manuscripts which, together with the Sahidic (sa) and Bohairic (bo) versions,[96] and church fathers like Clement of Alexandria and Origen, are the chief witnesses to the Alexandrian text.[97] With this type of text the Chester Beatty Papyrus of Paul's letters is most often in agreement,[98] as is shown in the examples cited above (p.424), although sometimes the papyrus goes its own way and sometimes agrees with the Western

[95] C. Tischendorf, *Codex Ephraemi Syri rescriptus sive fragmenta Novi Testamenti.* 1843.

[96] These are third and fourth century translations into the native Egyptian language known as Coptic, Sahidic being the dialect spoken in Upper Egypt and Bohairic that spoken in Lower Egypt. For the early New Testament versions see Arthur Vööbus, *Early Versions of the New Testament* (Papers of the Estonian Theological Society in Exile, 6). 1954.

[97] It has already been noted (p.432 n.80) that in the Gospels the text of Codex Alexandrinus is Byzantine.

[98] The preponderance of agreement is with B and next with SAC. Kenyon, *The Chester Beatty Biblical Papyri.* Fasc. iii. Suppl. Text, pp.xvi-xvii.

text. On the whole the Alexandrian text is the best and most dependable which we have, but nevertheless it has to be compared constantly with as many other early manuscripts as possible.

THE WESTERN TEXT

Even as the manuscripts just described seem to represent a text which probably originated in Egypt, so other groups of manuscripts may be recognized which represent texts which prevailed in other areas. The Western text (𝔐) is represented by several manuscripts now to be described which are written in both Greek and Latin, by the Old Latin versions, and by quotations in Latin church writers such as Cyprian. The fact that these authorities are all from the West suggests that this text originated there, perhaps in North Africa, and if this is the case the customary naming of the text as "Western" may be taken in the natural geographical sense of the word. Some think, however, that it originated in some other place, perhaps Asia Minor, and if this should be correct then "Western" would have to be understood as a technical rather than a geographical designation. Since some of the Western manuscripts such as W and k perhaps come from Africa, and some such as D and a from Europe, it is possible to speak of African and European branches of the text.[99]

CODEX BEZAE

Codex Bezae (D or 05),[100] one of the bilingual manuscripts just referred to, was given to the University of Cambridge in 1581 by Calvin's friend and successor at Geneva, Theodore Beza, who said that the manuscript had been found in 1562 in the monastery of Irenaeus at Lyons. It is believed to have been written in the fifth or sixth century. The manuscript now has 406 leaves and probably originally had at least 510. The pages measure about ten by eight inches in size, and each page has only a single column of writing, Greek on the left-hand page which is the place of honor, Latin on the right-hand page. The lines are short sense-lines, which make it more easily possible to keep the Greek and Latin parallel, and the Greek uncial letters are shaped somewhat like the Latin letters. The words are not separated and there are no accents or breathings on

---

[99] See *An Introduction to the Study of the New Testament*, by A. H. McNeile, 2d ed. rev. by C. S. C. Williams. 1953, pp.378, 441.

[100] *Codex Bezae Cantabrigiensis Quattuor Evangelia et Actus Apostolorum complectens Graece et Latine Sumptibus Academiae phototypice repraesentatus.* 1899; cf. HPUM Pl. XXII.

the Greek. Initial Iota and Upsilon are marked with the dieresis, and there is some punctuation. Sacred names are abbreviated. A number of correctors, from the sixth century to the twelfth, have made corrections in both the Greek and the Latin. The manuscript contains the four Gospels in the order, Matthew, John, Luke, and Mark, and the book of Acts. Also just ahead of the book of Acts the Latin has III John 11-15, which suggests that once the codex also contained the Catholic Epistles.

CODEX CLAROMONTANUS

Codex Claromontanus (D^p or **06**)[101] is a sixth century vellum manuscript of the letters of Paul (including Hebrews, added at the end), which was acquired between 1565 and 1582 by Theodore Beza, who stated that it was found in the monastery at Clermont in Beauvais. In 1656 the codex was purchased by Louis XIV, and it is now in the Bibliothèque Nationale, Paris. The manuscript comprises 533 leaves, each measuring nine and three-quarters by seven and three-quarters inches and having wide margins. The Greek text is written in a single column on the left-hand page and the corresponding Latin on the right-hand. There are twenty-one lines to the page, the lines being divided according to pauses in the sense and the first letter of a new section being thrust into the margin. The words are written continuously without separation and there is no punctuation. Initial Iota and Upsilon have the dieresis, but the accents and breathings have been added by one of the numerous later correctors. The first three lines of each letter are written in red, and so are the quotations from the Old Testament. The Greek and Latin columns of the manuscript do not always agree, and the Latin translation was not just made from this Greek text but doubtless is one of the Latin translations already in existence before Jerome. A double page from this manuscript (Romans 16:23-27) is shown in Fig. 151.

Codex Augiensis (F^p or **010**) was once in the monastery of Reichenau on an island in the Lake of Constance, and in 1786 was presented to the Library of Trinity College, Cambridge.[102] The manuscript consists of 136 leaves of vellum, and contains the Pauline letters including Hebrews. Each page has two columns of text, Greek in the inner column, the Latin of the Vulgate in the outer column. Hebrews

---

[101] C. Tischendorf, *Codex Claromontanus sive Epistulae Pauli omnes Graece et Latine.* 1852.
[102] HPUM Pl. L.

follows Philemon and is preserved only in the Latin. The date is probably in the ninth century.

Codex Boernerianus (G^P or **012**) came into the possession of Professor Christian Friedrich Börner in 1705 and is now in the Royal Library at Dresden.[103] It also is a bilingual manuscript, but in this case the Latin is written interlinearly above the Greek. It contains the Pauline letters, not including Hebrews. The date is also probably in the ninth century.

The Washington Codex (W or **032**) was purchased by Mr. Charles L. Freer in 1906 from an Arab dealer at Gizeh and is in the Freer Gallery of Art in Washington, D.C.[104] This is a Greek manuscript, and was written probably in the fifth century. It contains the four Gospels in the Western order, Matthew, John, Luke, and Mark, and has a Western text in Mark 1:1-5:30. The rest of Mark, however, may be Caesarean; Luke 1:1-8:12 is mainly Alexandrian; and the rest of Luke and Matthew are Byzantine. Thus the entire manuscript contains a remarkable variety of text types.

The Old Latin manuscripts are designated by small italicized letters and are often referred to collectively as the Itala, this being abbreviated as "it." Examples of the manuscripts are: Codex Bobbiensis (*k*), written probably in Africa not later than A.D. 400, once belonged to the monastery of Bobbio in North Italy and is now in Turin; it contains Mark 8-16 and Matthew 1-15, and the text is almost identical with the quotations of Cyprian. Codex Vercellensis (*a*) is preserved in the cathedral at Vercelli in North Italy, and is traditionally said to have been written by Eusebius, the bishop of Vercelli who was martyred in A.D. 371; it contains the four Gospels, with breaks, in the Western order, Matthew, John, Luke, and Mark, and at least in Luke is practically identical with the text regularly cited by Jerome.[105] For the letters of Paul, Old Latin texts are found in two commentaries, one preserved in the works of Ambrose (A.D. c.340-397) but written by an unknown author of the time of Pope Damasus (A.D. 366-384), and the other written by Pelagius (c.400).[106] A revision of the Old Latin versions was carried out by Jerome at

---

[103] *Der Codex Boernerianus der Briefe des Apostels Paulus . . . in Lichtdruck Nachgebildet.* 1909.

[104] Henry A. Sanders, *The New Testament Manuscripts in the Freer Collection.* 2 vols. 1912-18; HPUM Pl. XXI.

[105] *An Introduction to the Study of the New Testament,* by McNeile, rev. by Williams, pp.391, 393f.; *The Text and Canon of the New Testament,* by Alexander Souter, 2d ed. rev. by C. S. C. Williams. 1954, pp.34f., 38.

[106] Lietzmann, *Einführung in die Textgeschichte der Paulusbriefe,* p.9.

the suggestion of Damasus, the Gospels being published in A.D. 383 and the rest of the Bible in 405. This is known as the Vulgate (vg). Also, as already mentioned, Latin church writers such as Cyprian (A.D. c.200-258) are witnesses to the Old Latin text. They are sometimes referred to by the abbreviation Latt.[107]

The Western type of text is very old and was the basis for Marcion's revision before A.D. 150.[108] Nevertheless, when judged by inner criteria, it is found to contain numerous alterations. Quotations are supplemented according to the Septuagint, corrections are made which result in a smoother style or clearer sense, and unintentional alterations are introduced through mistakes in copying. In general the Western text is characterized by many interpolations, and hence was regarded by Westcott and Hort as of greatest weight in its omissions. That is, its omissions are not omissions so much as non-interpolations.

THE EASTERN TEXT

An Eastern text may also be recognized and, just as the Western text has two branches, African and European, so this has two forms, namely the Old Syriac, sometimes also called the Antiochene, and the Caesarean.[109]

THE OLD SYRIAC TEXT

The Old Syriac has agreements with the Western text and used to be considered a part of it, but now is often treated as an independent text. It is represented by two manuscripts. The Sinaitic Syriac (sy[s]) is a manuscript in the Monastery of Saint Catherine at Mount Sinai, and was discovered there in 1892 by Mrs. A. S. Lewis and Mrs. M. D. Gibson.[110] It is a palimpsest or rewritten manuscript. The upper writing is a Syriac treatise dated in A.D. 778; the text underneath is that of the four Gospels in the usual order, and was probably written not later than the early fifth century. The Curetonian Syriac (sy[c]) was brought in 1842 from the Convent of St. Mary Deipara in the Nitrian desert west of Cairo to the British Museum and was there recognized in 1847 and published in 1858 by William Cureton. It contains portions of the four Gospels in the unusual order, Matthew, Mark, John, and Luke, and was probably written

[107] *ibid.*, p.10.　　　　　　　　　　[108] *ibid.*, p.14.
[109] *An Introduction to the Study of the New Testament,* by McNeile, rev. by Williams, p.378.
[110] cf. R. V. G. Tasker in HTR 41 (1948), p.74.

in the middle of the fifth century.[111] Although these manuscripts are relatively late, the Old Syriac text which they preserve is probably much older, and it has been held that it was originally a translation made about A.D. 200 of the Greek text of the Gospels current at that time at Antioch.[112]

The Syrians called this version the *Evangelion da-Mepharreshe*, meaning the "Gospel of the Separated Ones," to distinguished it from the Diatessaron of Tatian which they spoke of as the *Evangelion da-Mehallete* or "Gospel of the Mixed Ones." The latter was a harmony of the four Gospels arranged in one narrative, a work which Tatian, the disciple of Justin Martyr, may have made in Greek[113] at Rome and then brought with him when he returned in about A.D. 173 to the East, where it was soon translated into Syriac.[114] The Greek text underlying the Diatessaron was closely related to that of Codex Bezae (D) and the Old Latin, therefore since the Diatessaron was probably known by those who made the *Evangelion da-Mepharreshe* it may be the influence of the Diatessaron which accounts for Western readings found in the Old Syriac.[115]

It was probably in order to displace the Diatessaron and provide a standard text of the separate four Gospels that Rabbula, the bishop of Edessa from A.D. 411 to 435, made a revision of the Old Syriac. This, if the hypothesis just stated is correct, accounts for the origin of the Peshitta, the "Simple" version which thereafter was supreme in the Syrian churches. The Peshitta also contained the other New Testament books, except that II and III John, II Peter, Jude, and Revelation were not included, and its text agrees with the Byzantine.[116] Two more revisions were also made, intended to make the Syriac render the Greek more literally, one in A.D. 508 by Philoxenus, bishop of Mabug or Hierapolis in eastern Syria, which is extant only in the books lacking in the Peshitta, namely II and III John, II Peter, Jude, and Revelation; and the other in A.D. 616-617 by Thomas of Heraclea or Harkel in Mesopotamia. There is also a Palestinian Syriac version, as it is called, known from various lectionaries and frag-

[111] F. Crawford Burkitt, *Evangelion da-Mepharreshe*. 2 vols. 1904.

[112] *ibid.*, II, pp.5f., 209.

[113] A Greek fragment of the Diatessaron found at Dura-Europos has already been mentioned (p.392).

[114] cf. J. Hamlyn Hill, *The Earliest Life of Christ Ever Compiled from the Four Gospels, Being the Diatessaron of Tatian [circ. A.D. 160], Literally Translated from the Arabic Version and Containing the Four Gospels Woven into One Story.* 1894.

[115] Burkitt, *Evangelion da-Mepharreshe*, II, pp.5f., 206, 210.

[116] *The Text and Canon of the New Testament*, by Souter, rev. by Williams, pp.55f.

ments, whose language is a Western Aramaic that is believed to be much like the Aramaic spoken in Galilee in the time of Jesus, but the version itself is probably a translation from Greek, perhaps made at Antioch, and not older than the sixth century.[117]

Of the Peshitta version there are several hundred manuscripts. One of these is the Yonan Codex. This takes its name from the Yonan family of a Christian community near Lake Urmia in Azerbaijan, is in the possession of Mr. Norman Yonan of Washington, D.C., and in 1955 was on loan to the Library of Congress for exhibition. The codex contains 227 leaves and extends from Matthew to Hebrews. The text appears to be that of the standard Peshitta Syriac, and the writing to be of the seventh century at the earliest.[118]

THE CAESAREAN TEXT

Some other manuscripts have been believed to form a recognizable group which might have centered around Caesarea. The Koridethi Codex (Θ or **038**) once belonged to a monastery at Koridethi at the eastern end of the Black Sea, was discovered in 1853 in the Caucasus, and was finally placed in the Georgian Museum at Tiflis.[119] It contains the four Gospels in the usual order, and has been assigned to a date from the seventh to the ninth century. The so-called Lake Group or Family 1, also designated λ, is a group of minuscules which was identified by Kirsopp Lake and which includes the manuscripts numbered 1, 118, 131, and 209. Codex 1, which heads the group, is in the University Library at Basel and is dated in the tenth to twelfth centuries.[120] While this manuscript contains Acts, the Catholic Epistles, and the Pauline letters including Hebrews, as well as the four Gospels, it is only the Gospels which have the Caesarean text, while the other books are Western. The Ferrar Group or Family 13, also designated ϕ, includes the minuscules 13, 69, 124, and 346, which were edited by W. H. Ferrar and T. K. Abbott, and others which were added to the group later. Codex 13, which heads the group, is in the Bibliothèque Nationale at Paris.[121] It contains the four Gospels and was probably written in the twelfth or thirteenth century.

The reason for connecting the text represented by the foregoing manuscripts with Caesarea is that Origen, who came from Alexandria to Caesarea in A.D. 231, seems to have used this text at the latter

[117] F. C. Burkitt in JTS 2 (1901), pp.174-185.
[118] Bruce M. Metzger in *The Christian Century.* Feb. 22, 1956, pp.234-236.
[119] HPUM Pl. XLIV. [120] HFDMM Pl. LX.
[121] HFDMM Pl. LXVII.

place.[122] Two other manuscripts already mentioned, however, also have at least in part a "Caesarean" text, namely $\mathfrak{p}^{45}$ (p.426) which is mainly Caesarean in Mark, and W (p.443) which is Caesarean in Mark 5:31-16:20. Since $\mathfrak{p}^{45}$ was found in Egypt, and since Origen may in fact have used a "Caesarean" text in Alexandria as well as at Caesarea,[123] it is possible that this text originated in Egypt. It may also be that the entire text is not as clear-cut and homogeneous as sometimes supposed.[124]

THE BYZANTINE OR KOINE TEXT

If the foregoing textual families have been rightly recognized there were then, broadly speaking, an Alexandrian text, a Western text with manuscripts both from Africa and Europe, and an Eastern text with both Syriac and Caesarean manuscripts.[125] There was, however, yet another revision of the New Testament text, and the purpose of this seems to have been to make the text as full and smooth as possible. Even as the Alexandrian text may have been the work of Hesychius, so this one may have been carried out by Lucian, a presbyter of the church at Antioch and a martyr at Nicomedia under Maximinus in A.D. 312. The reason for pointing to him is that both Eusebius[126] and Jerome[127] speak of his learning and Jerome says that even in his time there were copies of the Scriptures which bore the name of Lucian. That Antioch was the place where this text arose is rendered likely by the fact that the Syrian Peshitta of the next century has a very similar text. From Antioch, if this is where it originated, the text under discussion spread to Constantinople and became the text generally accepted throughout the Byzantine church. For this reason it is known as the Byzantine text, or the Koine (𝕶), that is the Common text.

As has already been mentioned, the Byzantine text is found in Codex Alexandrinus in the Gospels (see above p.432 n.80), and in the Washington Codex in Matthew and most of Luke (p.443). For the letters of Paul it is represented by three ninth century uncial manuscripts, Codex Angelicus (L or **020**), Codex Porphyrianus (P or **025**), and Codex Mosquensis (K or **018**). Likewise this text is

---

[122] Burnett H. Streeter, *The Four Gospels.* 1925, pp.92-102.

[123] Kirsopp Lake, Robert P. Blake, and Silva New in HTR 21 (1928), pp.207-404.

[124] *An Introduction to the Study of the New Testament,* by McNeile, rev. by Williams, p.389.

[125] *ibid.,* pp.378f.   [126] *Ch. Hist.* VIII, xiii, 2; IX, vi, 3.

[127] *Lives of Illustrious Men.* 77. NPNFSS III, p.378.

found in most of the other late uncials and in the great mass of minuscules. The minuscule manuscripts (cf. p.401) are scattered in many different libraries, and extend in date from the ninth to the sixteenth century. In some cases the manuscripts bear dates, and as far as known the oldest definitely dated one is Codex 461. This is in the Public Library in Leningrad, contains the four Gospels, and was written in A.D. 835.[128] The second oldest dated minuscule has only recently became known and bears the number 2500. It was written in A.D. 891, and is in the Akademiebibliothek in Leningrad.[129] A sample page of yet another of the many minuscules is shown in Fig. 152. This manuscript is in Paris where it is known as Cod. Gr. 223.[130] It contains the Pauline letters and Acts with commentary, and is dated in the year 1045. On another page of the same manuscript is an illustration showing the apostle Paul dictating to his secretary (Fig. 153).

In addition, the Byzantine text is found in the Peshitta (p.445) and Gothic versions,[131] and the writings of church fathers such as Chrysostom (A.D. c.390), Basil of Caesarea in Cappadocia (d. A.D. 380), and Ephraem Syrus (d. A.D. 373).

The Koine is now clearly recognized as a late and secondary text. Interpolations and corrections are numerous in it. Often it combines Alexandrian and Western readings and thus retains them both. For example in Romans 1:29 the Alexandrian text reads "wickedness, covetousness, maliciousness," although these three words stand in different order in different manuscripts.[132] The Western text changed "wickedness" into "fornication," these two words having a very similar appearance in the Greek.[133] The Byzantine text then combined the Alexandrian and Western readings and the result was a list including "fornication, wickedness, covetousness, maliciousness."[134]

THE DEPENDABILITY OF THE NEW TESTAMENT TEXT

At first, European translations of the New Testament were based

[128] HFDMM Pl. I.

[129] Aland in TL 82 (1957), col. 162; and in ZNW 48 (1957), pp.141, 161.

[130] Kirsopp and Silva Lake, *Monumenta Palaeographica Vetera*, First Series, *Dated Greek Minuscule Manuscripts to the Year 1200*, IV, *Manuscripts in Paris*. Part I (1935), Pl. 267.

[131] A translation by Bishop Ulfilas, A.D. c.350.

[132] πονηρίᾳ πλεονεξίᾳ κακίᾳ B; πονηρίᾳ κακίᾳ πλεονεξίᾳ SA; κακίᾳ πονηρίᾳ πλεονεξίᾳ C bo sa.

[133] κακίᾳ πορνείᾳ πλεονεξίᾳ DG.

[134] πορνείᾳ πονηρίᾳ πλεονεξίᾳ κακίᾳ L; πορνείᾳ πονηρίᾳ κακίᾳ πλεονεξίᾳ Peshitta. Lietzmann, *An die Römer*, pp.13, 35.

simply upon the Latin Vulgate. Then men sought to go back to the Greek text, but only manuscripts of the less accurate Byzantine type were available. This was still the case when the Authorized Version was made under King James (1611), for the value of Codex Vaticanus was not yet realized at that time nor was Codex Sinaiticus even discovered. The scholars who have made the American Standard Version and the Revised Standard Version have had the advantage of the use of these and many other important manuscripts, and therefore these translations are more accurate than former ones could be. But every scrap of biblical parchment or papyrus recovered from the sands of the past adds to the vast amount of material available for the work of textual criticism, and the task of painstaking comparison of all the witnesses to the original text is an unending labor.[135]

The total number of New Testament manuscripts is very impressive. As we have already seen (p.416), even without counting the versions in other languages, the listed Greek papyri, uncials, minuscules, and lectionaries now total 4,680, and of these it may roughly be estimated that over two thousand contain the text of the Gospels, over seven hundred the text of Paul.[136] No other Greek book has anything like this amount of testimony to its text. It is true that there are numerous textual variations among these different New Testament manuscripts, but the majority of them are of a relatively minor character, as has appeared in the examples given in this chapter. As a matter of fact, it has been estimated that there are substantial variations in hardly more than a thousandth part of the entire text.[137]

The close relationship in time between the oldest New Testament manuscripts and the original texts is also nothing less than amazing. The proximity of the Chester Beatty Papyrus of the letters of Paul to the time when the apostle wrote those letters, and of Papyrus Bodmer II to the time when the Gospel according to John must have been written, and for that matter the closeness of Codex Vaticanus and Codex Sinaiticus to the period of the composition of the New Testament, can be appreciated properly only by contrast with most of the rest of the literature of the Greco-Roman world. For our knowledge of the writings of most of the classical authors we are dependent upon manuscripts the oldest of which belong to a time between

[135] Merrill M. Parvis and Allen P. Wikgren, *New Testament Manuscript Studies, The Materials and the Making of a Critical Apparatus.* 1950.
[136] Kenneth W. Clark in BA 16 (1953), p.42.
[137] Gregory, *Canon and Text of the New Testament*, p.528.

the ninth and eleventh centuries A.D., or in other words are a thousand years removed from their originals.[138] Thus it is that the certainty with which the text of the New Testament is established exceeds that of any other ancient book. The words which the New Testament writers addressed to their world and time have crossed the further miles and centuries to us substantially unchanged in form and certainly undiminished in power.

[138] Hans Lietzmann in *Die Antike, Zeitschrift für Kunst und Kultur des klassischen Altertums.* 11 (1935), pp.142-146.

VIII

Exploring the Catacombs and Studying the Sarcophagi

Less than one hundred years after Paul wrote his Letter to the Romans, or by the middle of the second century A.D., the Christians of Rome are known to us through their remarkable places of burial, the catacombs.

Cremation was the normal practice of pagan Rome in the first century A.D.,[1] and the cinerary urns were placed in the niches of vaults constructed for this purpose and known as columbaria. Not until the time of Hadrian (A.D. 117-138) did cremation give way to inhumation among the pagan population of Rome. Then their interments were made in and beneath the columbaria and also in sarcophagi. But from the first the Christians seem to have avoided the burning of the bodies of the deceased, and no trace of early Christian cremation has been found. Rather, the first Christians followed the practice of the Jews who were living in Rome and buried their dead in underground sepulchral chambers and galleries.

1. THE CHARACTER OF THE CATACOMBS

The development of such subterranean burial places was specially favored at Rome by the underlying geological formation. The great plain surrounding the city is composed of materials of volcanic

[1] A. D. Nock in HTR 25 (1932), p.232.

origin. There is sand (*pozzolana*), there is stone (*tufa litoide*), and there is granular tufa (*tufa granolare*). The sand is too soft to permit excavations unless the walls are faced with brick, and the stone is so hard that it is quarried for building purposes, but the granular tufa is relatively easy to cut, yet is strong and holds up satisfactorily. Also, it is porous and drains well. The existence of this tufa facilitated the digging of the catacombs.[1] The actual excavation was done by a sort of guild of workers known as *fossores* or "diggers." Their title appears in inscriptions on their own tombs in the catacombs and they are depicted in the wall paintings, holding pick and spade, the tools of the trade.[2]

The characteristic form of a catacomb is that of a network of interconnected corridors and chambers containing burial niches in the walls. The corridors are usually approximately three feet in width and have a normal height of a little over six feet. This corresponds to a man's height, with a bit of additional room for the *fossor* to swing his pick. In their simplest form the graves were square-cornered, horizontal recesses, known as *loculi*, cut in the walls of the galleries and chambers. The corpses were laid here wound in wrappings, in accordance with Jewish custom, and the openings were closed with bricks or marble slabs. A more elaborate form of grave was that known as an *arcosolium*, where a semicircular recess was cut in the wall, and the body was placed in a coffin-like space closed from above by a horizontal slab.

When additional space was needed for more graves the corridor was often deepened. By digging the floor of the gallery some three feet deeper two more rows of graves could be accommodated, and this process was sometimes continued until there were as many as a dozen tiers of graves one below the other. As a moment's consideration of the work involved will indicate, this was an entirely feasible procedure, but to have attempted to *heighten* the corridor would have necessitated extremely awkward manipulation of pick and shovel. Thus in such corridors the highest graves are normally the oldest and the lowest are the newest. Also entire second, third, or more stories of galleries and chambers often were laid out. While the uppermost corridors are some twenty or twenty-five feet below the surface of the earth, the lowest may be forty or fifty feet deeper.

[1] cf. G. de Angelis D'Ossat, *La Geologia delle Catacombe Romane*. 1938-.
[2] L. von Sybel, *Christliche Antike, Einführung in die altchristliche Kunst*. I (1906), p.102.

The oldest catacombs seem to have been excavated within privately owned and therefore relatively small and limited areas and thus characteristically assumed a sort of gridiron pattern. When later catacombs were excavated in more extensive properties owned by the church, their corridors branched out and out almost endlessly. Whereas at first sight the catacombs now appear to be inextricably tangled networks, an appreciation of the process of their excavation enables the scientific investigator to retrace the course of their development and understand their earlier forms.

2. THE REDISCOVERY OF THE CATACOMBS

THE rediscovery of the catacombs at Rome dates from 1578 when some workmen accidentally happened upon one of the long-lost subterranean cemeteries. The pioneer investigation of the catacombs was undertaken by Antonio Bosio, who devoted thirty-six years to the task, and whose *Roma Sotterranea* was published in 1632, three years after his own death. Not until the nineteenth century was Bosio's work worthily resumed, most notably by Giovanni Battista de Rossi (d. 1894).[1] He was assisted by his brother, Michele Stefano de Rossi, who had the knowledge of a geologist and an engineer, and was followed in the work by his pupils, Josef Wilpert[2] and Orazio Marucchi.[3] More recently Professor Paul Styger[4] has applied the most rigorously scientific techniques to a fresh investigation of the catacombs, with results necessitating many revisions of the earlier conclusions.

3. THE JEWISH CATACOMBS

BEFORE proceeding to describe the oldest and most important Christian catacombs, a word should be said about the Jewish catacombs. It was noted above that the Christians were probably following a Jewish custom in adopting catacombs for burial places, and some half-dozen ancient Jewish cemeteries of this sort have been found in Rome.

[1] *La Roma Sotterranea Cristiana.* 1864-77.
[2] *Die Malereien der Katakomben Roms.* 1903.
[3] *Le Catacombe Romane, opera postuma.* 1932.
[4] SRK.

The beginnings of the Jewish community in Rome, like those of the later Christian community, are little known. In 161 B.C. an embassy of Judas Maccabeus came to Rome seeking assurances of support in the struggle against the Seleucids, and in 139 B.C. Simon, the last of the sons of Mattathias, renewed relations with Rome and obtained ratification of a treaty between Rome and the now independent Jewish state. In the same year that the embassy of Simon was received in honor by the Roman Senate and sent away with the promise of friendship, Hispalus, the praetor peregrinus, who was the magistrate having jurisdiction in cases involving foreigners, banished the Chaldeans and the Jews from Rome and Italy within a period of ten days. But the Jews returned, and in the first half of the first century A.D. the Jewish population of Rome is estimated at about twenty thousand.[1]

It was always the custom of the Jews to practice inhumation, and in Palestine many graves were hewn in the native rock.[2] At Rome the soft tufa formation made it easily possible to dig more extensive corridors and halls to receive the graves. The oldest catacomb of the Jews now known was discovered by Bosio in 1602 but was lost to knowledge again and rediscovered only in 1904. The other Jewish catacombs have also become known only since the middle of the nineteenth century and later. The oldest Jewish catacomb just mentioned lies near Monteverde, before the Porta Portese in Trastevere, and burials were probably begun there in the first century A.D.[3] One of the inscriptions of this catacomb, probably belonging to the second century, is shown in Fig. 154. It reads, simply and pathetically, "Here lies Leontia, 20 years old." The seven-armed lampstand is a characteristic mark in all the Jewish catacombs.

Two other Jewish catacombs are on the Via Appia before the Porta San Sebastiano, one in the Vigna Randanini and the other in the Vigna Cimarra. A fourth is on the Via Appia Pignatelli, a fifth under the Via Labicana east of the Esquiline, and the sixth, most recently discovered, is in the Villa Torlonia (onetime residence of Benito Mussolini), before the Porta Pia in the northeast part of the city.

[1] Hermann Vogelstein, *Rome* (1940. tr. from rev. ed. of *Geschichte der 'uden in Rom*), pp.9f., 17.

[2] For the remarkable Jewish catacombs at Beth She'arim in Galilee, dating from the second to the fourth century A.D., see N. Avigad in *Archaeology*. 8 (1955), pp.236-244; 10 (1957), pp.266-269; and in IEJ 5 (1955), pp.205-239; 7 (1957), pp.73-92, 239-255.

[3] N. Müller, *Die jüdische Katakombe am Monteverde zu Rom, der älteste bisher bekannt gewordene jüdische Friedhof des Abendlandes*. 1912, p.120.

Numerous rooms in the catacomb of the Villa Torlonia are adorned with paintings, and as usual the ruling motif is the seven-armed lampstand. One of the frescoes is reproduced in Fig. 155. On the right is the scroll of the Law, on the left the ethrog, and in the middle the seven-armed lampstand. The scroll of the Law is rolled around a rod whose knobs are indicated by heavy points. A small triangular piece of parchment is to be seen above at the right. In reality this was glued to the roll and contained the title of the work. The perspective is primitive and shows both ends of the roll at once. The ethrog is a citron, which was used along with the lulab or festive palm branch in the Feast of Tabernacles, and hence was a symbol of Judaism.[4] The seven-armed lampstand likewise was a notable symbol of the Jewish religion. The prototype was the golden lampstand in the temple at Jerusalem which Titus carried off in triumph (p.329) but similar lampstands burned also in the synagogues and in the homes of the Jews at the reading of the Law and at other religious ceremonies. So instead of seeking in the symbol of the seven-armed lampstand some mysterious astral-eschatological significance as certain scholars have done, it is correct to interpret it far more simply. Wherever it appears it signifies, "Here a Jew worships his God," and when it is found upon graves it means, "He was a faithful Jew."[5]

4. THE CHRISTIAN CATACOMBS

THE great development of catacombs, however, was carried out by the Christians. Michele Stefano de Rossi estimated that the catacombs known in 1867 covered a surface area of 615 acres and, basing his calculations upon the average development of the galleries under a given area, he computed that the total length of their corridors was over five hundred miles.[1] Today thirty-five or more separate Christian catacombs are known at Rome (see Plan 3). They are for the most part in a circle outside the city, some three miles from its center, the reason being that Roman law prohibited burial or cremation within the walls and forbade dwelling in the neighborhood of a sepulchral monument. Like the pagan tombs which were built along

[4] This was in accordance with Leviticus 23:40, the citron being held to be "the fruit of goodly trees" (cf. JE v, pp.261f.).

[5] Hermann W. Beyer and Hans Lietzmann, *Die jüdische Katakombe der Villa Torlonia in Rom.* 1930, p.18.

[1] Karl Baedeker, *Central Italy and Rome.* 15th ed. 1909, p.453.

all the public roads leading out from Rome, so the catacombs also were chiefly on the main roads like the Via Appia and others.

According to Professor Styger's researches into their origins, the oldest of the catacombs belong to a time around the middle of the second century.[2] Although no Christian catacombs earlier than this have been found, it is possible that such did exist. The catacombs of the middle of the second century manifest a fully developed system of construction which not only reflects Jewish models but suggests that the Christians themselves had learned by actual experience in earlier excavations. If such earlier catacombs did exist they of course had to be outside the Wall of Servius, but could still have been considerably nearer the center of the city than the later ones were. The city was growing rapidly at that time and seldom, if ever, was there more building done here than in the first half of the second century, particularly in the reign of Hadrian. The areas of suburban extension on all sides are clearly shown by the line which the Aurelian Wall had to follow in A.D. 270-275. This rapid suburban development must constantly have pushed the burial zone farther out from the center of the city to where it is represented by the now known catacombs. If there were earlier catacombs it may be that they had to be abandoned and were destroyed as the city grew. The four oldest catacombs now known are those of Lucina, Callistus, Domitilla, and Priscilla, all of which belonged originally to the middle of the second century.

THE CRYPTS OF LUCINA

On the edge of the Via Appia, a little more than a mile outside the Porta San Sebastiano, are the impressive remains of a tomb which probably belonged to some prominent Roman of the first century. Connected with the monument was a piece of ground beneath which, at about the end of Hadrian's reign (A.D. 117-138), a Christian cemetery was excavated. Whether the owner of the tomb had himself become a Christian, or simply had allowed his Christian slaves and freedmen to make their burials on his property, remains unknown. The first excavation consisted of entrance steps leading down to a long passageway about six feet in height, from which two other passageways branched off. From this earliest period only empty loculi remain, perhaps fifty in number.

A decade or two later the subterranean cemetery was extended

[2] SRK p.319.

by the digging of steps to a passageway at a deeper level and also by the excavation of several chambers opening off from the original passageways. Paintings, datable to about the middle of the second century,[3] remain in some of these chambers. The finest is the ceiling painting in the chamber known as "Y" (Fig. 156), in which the motifs in part are still those of classical Roman interior decoration. The field is divided by lines into circles and sections, while the figures are represented in an almost statuary way and with an exaggerated thinness. The representations include little winged persons, women with arms uplifted in prayer, and the Good Shepherd who carries a lamb upon his shoulders. In the center stands Daniel between two lions.

Toward the end of the second century additional room was gained in the cemetery by deepening the passageways, and early in the third century other extensive work was done on a series of galleries at a lower level. At about the end of the third century, the remains of Pope Cornelius, who had died in exile in 253, were buried in one of the chambers. Later accounts state that this was done by a certain Saint Lucina (p.458), but since several persons of the same name are mentioned in sixth century legends it is difficult to establish for certain any historical facts concerning the woman whose name the area has come to bear.[4]

THE CATACOMB OF CALLISTUS

Somewhat farther back in the same field in which the Crypts of Lucina were located, another Christian cemetery was begun at about the middle of the second century. The area in which it was excavated may have belonged to the church by purchase or gift. Two main corridors, each entered by its own steps, were driven lengthwise along the two longer sides of this area. Later these were connected at the far end of the field by a cross corridor, and additional cross galleries began to give the whole a sort of gridiron plan. At first the place was known simply as Coemeterium or "sleeping chamber," which was the name generally applied by the early Christians to their burial places. Pope Zephyrinus (c.198-c.217) placed the cemetery under

[3] Here and elsewhere in this chapter the dates that are given for the Christian catacombs at Rome and also for their paintings, are those of Styger. The paintings are dated somewhat later by Fritz Wirth who believes that no Christian catacomb paintings in Rome are earlier than the third century A.D. (*Römische Wandmalerei vom Untergang Pompejis bis ans Ende des dritten Jahrhunderts.* 1934, p.226). Wirth ascribes the ceiling painting in the Lucina catacomb which is mentioned in the text above, to a time around A.D. 220 (*ibid.*, pp.168f.).

[4] SRK pp.21-33.

the administration of Callistus, who at that time was a priest and was to become the next pope (c.217-c.222). This is narrated by Hippolytus, who states that Zephyrinus entrusted Callistus with the management of the clergy and "appointed him over the cemetery."[5] A notable extension of the cemetery was carried out under the leadership of Callistus, and thereafter the catacomb retained his name although he had not been its founder nor was buried there himself. The old passageways were deepened at this time, new cross corridors were made, and a number of larger burial chambers were excavated.

Of these the most important was a large double chamber which became a burial place for the Roman popes and hence is known as the Crypt of the Popes (Fig. 157). Up to this time most of the popes had been buried, like Peter himself, in the Vatican. The Liber Pontificalis lists fourteen men who headed the Roman church between Peter and Zephyrinus and indicates burial at the Vatican for all but two of them. The two exceptions are Clement I, who is said to have been buried in Greece, and Alexander who is stated to have been buried on the Via Nomentana. Otherwise the typical statement concerning each of these popes is, "He also was buried near the body of the blessed Peter in the Vatican." But for Zephyrinus and his successors the burial notices in the Liber Pontificalis run as follows:

> Zephyrinus (d. c.217) "He also was buried in his own cemetery near the cemetery of Calistus on the Via Appia."
> Callistus I (d. c.222) "in the cemetery of Calipodius on the Via Aurelia at the third milestone"
> Urbanus I (d. 230) "in the cemetery of Pretextatus on the Via Appia"
> Pontianus (d. 235) "in the cemetery of Calistus on the Via Appia"
> Anteros (d. 236) "in the cemetery of Calistus on the Via Appia"
> Fabianus (d. 250) "in the cemetery of Calistus on the Via Appia"
> Cornelius (d. 253) "And his body was taken up at night by the blessed Lucina and the clergy and was buried in a crypt in her own garden, near the cemetery of Calistus on the Via Appia."
> Lucius (d. 254) "in the cemetery of Calistus on the Via Appia"
> Stephen I (d. 257) "in the cemetery of Calistus on the Via Appia"
> Xystus II (d. 258) "in the cemetery of Calistus on the Via Appia"
> Dionysius (d. 268) "in the cemetery of Calistus on the Via Appia"
> Felix I (d. 274) in the cemetery of Callistus (according to earlier lists)[6]

---

[5] *The Refutation of All Heresies (Philosophumena).* IX, vii (ANF V, p.130).
[6] LLP p.33 n.1; SRK p.48.

Eutychianus (d. 283) "in the cemetery of Calistus on the Via
    Appia"

Gaius (d. 296) "in the cemetery of Calistus on the Via Appia"

Marcellinus (d. 304) "on the Via Salaria in the cemetery of
    Priscilla"

Marcellus (d. 309) "in the cemetery of Priscilla on the Via
    Salaria"

Eusebius (d. c.310) "in the cemetery of Calistus on the Via
    Appia"

Miltiades (d. 314) "in the cemetery of Calistus on the Via Appia"

Sylvester (d. 335) "in the cemetery of Priscilla on the Via Salaria,
    three miles from the city of Rome."

Of these popes who are stated by the Liber Pontificalis to have
been buried "in the cemetery of Calistus," at least some found their
last resting place in the simple niches of the double chamber under
consideration. This is certain for Pontianus, Anteros, Fabianus,
Lucius, and Eutychianus, whose grave inscriptions have been found
there and who are mentioned in prayers scratched on the walls by
pious visitors of ancient times, and it is probable for Stephen I, Xystus
II, Dionysius, and Felix I, although their actual epitaphs are now lost.
Several of these popes were martyrs, including Xystus II who perished on August 6, 258 in Valerian's persecution, when he and four
deacons were taken by surprise in the catacomb and killed.

The papal crypt was enlarged in later times, and the wall between
the two halves of the double chamber gave way to two simple marble columns, but the original plan is still clearly recognizable. Pope
Damasus (366-384), who everywhere was zealous to honor the
martyrs, placed one of his monumental inscriptions here. As is well
known, these inscriptions were composed in poetic style by Damasus,
lettered by his secretary and artist Furius Dionysius Filocalus, and
placed in a large number of Rome's most venerated tombs. While
most of the originals have perished, the text of many of them is preserved in copies which were made by pilgrims.[7] The marble slab
which bore the inscription of Damasus in the crypt of the popes
was broken into over one hundred fragments, but has been restored
and replaced in its original location as may be seen in Fig. 157. The
inscription reads: "Here if you inquire, lies crowded together a
throng of the righteous, the venerable tombs hold the bodies of the
saints, their lofty spirits the palace of heaven took to itself. Here the

[7] C. M. Kaufmann, Handbuch der altchristlichen Epigraphik. 1917, pp.338-365.

companions of Xystus who bore trophies from the enemy; here a number of the leaders who ministered at the altars of Christ; here is placed the priest who lived in long peace; here the holy confessors whom Greece sent; here young men and boys, old men and their pure descendants, who chose to keep their virgin modesty. Here, I confess, I Damasus wished to deposit my body, but I feared to disturb the holy ashes of the righteous."[8]

It was probably in the fourth century that the further chamber beyond the Crypt of the Popes was excavated; it is known as the Tomb of Cecilia. By the middle of that century it was adorned with marble and mosaic work. Having been damaged perhaps at the time of the Goths (410) and Vandals (455), it was restored toward the end of the fifth century and some of the mosaics were replaced by paintings. The name of the chamber is connected with Saint Cecilia, whose remains are said to have been discovered by Pope Paschal I (817-824). She is represented, along with Pope Urban (222-230) and with Christ, in the frescoes of the main wall, which are dated by their style in the ninth century. At the same time pilgrims have scratched on the walls their appeals to the famous martyr and saint. Definite information concerning Saint Cecilia is no longer available, however, since the existing late fifth century account of her life is full of contradictions and improbabilities, and the date of her martyrdom is unknown.

Under the administration of Callistus the entire cemetery increased greatly in size, many of the common Christians of Rome as well as the clergy and martyrs no doubt now being buried there. On the other side of the main corridor from the papal crypt, three large chambers were excavated in the time of Callistus, and to these yet three more were later added. The six chambers have received the name of Sacrament Chapels since, when first discovered, their frescoes were believed to be symbolical representations of the sacraments of baptism, the Eucharist, confirmation, and confession.[9] Actually, it is probable that these chambers served not only as burial places but also as rooms in which the survivors held meals in honor of the deceased. Therefore they were adorned especially with numerous paintings for which place was found on the ceilings and on the walls between the graves. The paintings of the first chamber are now destroyed almost

[8] Walter Lowrie, *Monuments of the Early Church.* 1901, pp.74f.
[9] J. Wilpert, *Die Malereien der Sacramentskapellen in der Katakombe des hl. Callistus.* 1897.

completely, but those which remain in the other rooms include the following subjects: the Fossor, the Woman with Arms Uplifted in Prayer, the Shepherd, a Meal Participated in by Seven Persons, Abraham's Sacrifice of Isaac, Moses' Miracle of Bringing Water from the Rock, Jonah, the Baptism of Jesus, the Healing of the Paralytic, and the Resurrection of Lazarus.

The first three chambers are believed to belong to the time of Callistus, and the style of the paintings which remain in them is in agreement with a date at the beginning of the third century. In the middle of the second century the classical tradition still prevailed and tall figures stood in statuary repose, with all details carefully worked out, but here the forms are relatively coarse, the faces are but masks, and details, such as the number of fingers, are neglected.[10]

THE CATACOMB OF DOMITILLA

The Catacomb of Domitilla is some distance from that of Callistus on the Via delle Sette Chiese where anciently ran the Via Ardeatina. It has been known as Coemeterium Domitillae at least since the seventh century and doubtless since its origin. The Domitilla whose name it preserves was probably the Flavia Domitilla who is described in Dio's *Roman History* as a relative of the Emperor Domitian and wife of the consul Flavius Clemens. In A.D. 95 both she and her husband were condemned on account of "atheism" and inclination toward Judaism, these being familiar charges against the early Christians, and while he was beheaded she was banished to the island of Pandateria in the Tyrrhenian Sea. Dio's statement is: "And the same year Domitian slew, along with many others, Flavius Clemens the consul, although he was a cousin and had to wife Flavia Domitilla, who was also a relative of the emperor's. The charge brought against them both was that of atheism, a charge on which many others who drifted into Jewish ways were condemned. Some of these were put to death, and the rest were at least deprived of their property. Domitilla was merely banished in Pandateria."[11]

Substantially the same account is recorded by Eusebius, although he probably is wrong in calling Domitilla the niece instead of the wife of Flavius Clemens. He also names a different but nearby island, Pontia, as the place of Domitilla's exile, and explicitly describes her

---

[10] SRK pp.34-62; cf. G. B. de Rossi, *La Roma Sotterranea Cristiana.* II (1867); E. Josi, *Il Cimiterio di Callisto.* 1933.
[11] *Rom. Hist.* LXVII, xiv, 1f.

as a Christian although he does not mention Flavius Clemens as also having been a Christian martyr. The statement of Eusebius is: "In the fifteenth year of Domitian Flavia Domitilla, daughter of a sister of Flavius Clemens, who at that time was one of the consuls of Rome, was exiled with many others to the island of Pontia in consequence of testimony borne to Christ."[12] Jerome also tells how at the end of the fourth century the widow Paula visited "the island of Pontia ennobled long since as the place of exile of the illustrious lady Flavia Domitilla who under the Emperor Domitian was banished because she confessed herself a Christian," and saw "the cells in which this lady passed the period of her long martyrdom."[13]

It does not appear, however, that the catacomb was constructed in the time of Domitilla herself. Without doubt this area of ground belonged to her, and two heathen inscriptions were found near by which indicated that burials had been made there by the permission of Flavia Domitilla. Evidently she had made a gift of her property or a portion of it for burial purposes, and since the burials there were pagan she must not yet have been converted to Christianity. The pagan possessors of the property developed it into an extensive place of burial. This is indicated by the ruins of columbaria and of an enclosing wall which still exist there, and it is probable that pagan burials continued to be made until around A.D. 140. Up to this time it is extremely unlikely that a Christian catacomb would have been excavated beneath ground while pagan rites and ceremonies were conducted overhead. Meanwhile the area continued to be known by the name of Domitilla. Then shortly before the middle of the second century the owners of the property appear to have accepted Christianity. At any rate the pagan burials ceased above ground and beneath the surface a Christian catacomb came into existence. Whose name should it bear if not that of the earlier owner of the property, Flavia Domitilla, who now long since had become a Christian and a glorious martyr?

The origin of the Christian cemetery only shortly before the middle of the second century is indicated not only by the continuation of pagan burials above ground until about that date, but also by the oldest frescoes in the catacomb itself. These are comparable in style to those in the crypts of Lucina and like them evidently belong to a time near the middle of the second century. They are to be found in

---

[12] *Ch. Hist.* III, xviii.
[13] *Letter 108 to Eustochium* (NPNFSS VI, p.197).

a region of the catacomb which is generally known as the Hypogeum of the Flavians. This name was given because of the belief that the catacomb was established sometime in the relatively quiet period between Nero and Domitian and was the burial place of members of the Flavian house. This was the view presented originally by G. B. de Rossi, but no Flavian inscriptions have been discovered in the Hypogeum, and Professor Paul Styger finds no historical argument which justifies the first century date.[14]

Another portion of the catacomb whose origins probably go back to the same period at the middle of the second century as the Hypogeum of the Flavians, is the so-called Region of the Aurelians. This area is relatively distinct and is marked by corridors of unusual height. Evidently its owners limited themselves to their own definite area and kept digging their passageways deeper as more burial space was required.

Between these two regions is yet a smaller area where a third group of the owners of the property made their burials. It is a subterranean room containing a number of burial places in the floor and two niches designed to receive sarcophagi. One sarcophagus still remains *in situ*, and De Rossi saw a second of similar type standing there when the place was first discovered in 1854, but the latter has since been purloined. The sarcophagus which remains is of the tub-shaped kind, adorned with rippled marks and lions' heads, which is ascribed to the time of the Antonines in the middle of the second century. Since there is nothing distinctively Christian about this sarcophagus and since Roman custom did change to inhumation in the immediately preceding time of Hadrian, it is possible that it was a pagan who was buried here. But even if that is the case, the subterranean room must have become a Christian burial place very soon afterward, that is around the middle of the century, when the portions of the same property on either side were so employed, for Christians and pagans would not have shared an almost common cemetery. Later the upper part of this subterranean room was destroyed by the building of a basilica directly above it. This was the Basilica of Saint Petronilla, which was in use from the fifth to the eighth centuries, and the area which we have described beneath it is known as the Hypogeum under the Basilica.

The hypothesis that the property of Domitilla was made available to a group of pagans for a burial ground in the first century, and that

[14] SRK p.78.

about the middle of the second century their heirs accepted Christianity and established the three underground burial places just described, is substantiated by the inscriptions found in the debris in these regions. These are both Christian and pagan in character, and it is presumable that the heathen inscriptions belonged originally to the heathen burial area within the enclosing wall above ground. The older Flavian inscriptions are almost entirely pagan, but the inscriptions from the time of the Antonines are not only pagan but also frequently Christian. It was, therefore, at this time that Christianity was being accepted by those to whom the former property of Domitilla belonged.

Two other areas of the cemetery of Domitilla have often been regarded as of great antiquity, but more recent research places them at the end of the third century or in the fourth century. These are the region with the painted chamber at the foot of the great stairway by the Tor Marancia, and the region of the grave of Ampliatus.[15] These sections are outside the old wall which surrounded the original pagan burial area, and eventually many other areas were excavated in yet other directions also. Evidently in its later development the catacomb could be extended quite freely and was not limited to a precisely defined area. Thus there developed in the fourth century a vast system of subterranean galleries and rooms, connecting with the three most ancient regions and branching off in all directions. To the entire mighty complex the name of Domitilla continued to belong.[16]

THE CATACOMB OF PRISCILLA

The Catacomb of Priscilla is on the other side of Rome from the catacombs thus far described, on the Via Salaria Nuova. Its extent and complexity surpass anything met hitherto, but three chief component parts of the entire cemetery can be clearly distinguished. Evidently these three areas originally were separate, privately owned burial places.

The first is the so-called Hypogeum of the Acilians, which was excavated and studied by De Rossi in 1880, and which lies beneath the Basilica di San Silvestro. It has been believed that this was the burial place of Manius Acilius Glabrio who was consul in the year 91, and in 95 was condemned to death by Domitian on account of Christian

---

[15] P. Testini (in RAC 28 [1952], pp.77-117) claims a date in the middle of the second century A.D. for the crypt of Ampliatus.

[16] SRK pp.63-99.

faith at the same time that Domitilla was exiled and Titus Flavius Clemens was executed. No trace of his grave has been found, however, and on the contrary the style of the oldest painting here is that of the middle of the second century. The Priscilla whose name the entire catacomb preserves may well have been a member of the same senatorial family. The catacomb bore her name at least from the fifth century and probably from the beginning. A third century inscription found in the debris mentions a certain Priscilla in connection with a Manius Acilius, both of whom are called "most illustrious." Perhaps the connection of the original Priscilla with this catacomb is comparable to that of Domitilla with the cemetery previously considered.

The Hypogeum is entered by a subterranean stairway, which leads to a wide corridor running first to the northwest and then to the southwest. This corridor originally was vaulted, and traces of the paintings which adorned its walls still remain. The schematic division of field by red, green, and brown lines and the classical elegance of birds and flowers which are still recognizable in these paintings indicate a date around the middle of the second century. In later years the Hypogeum was extended to include a number of further passageways and rooms.

The stairway which leads down to the Hypogeum also gives access to a complex of corridors in a near-by area. These are laid out on a regular plan of the gridiron type as in Lucina and Callistus, and probably also belong to the middle of the second century. While in the Hypogeum there are sarcophagus niches for relatively well-to-do persons, the corridors here have only simple loculi and presumably served for the poor. On the graves were marked the anchor, the palm, and the dove.

A second major area of the catacomb likewise belongs in its origin to the middle of the second century. This is known as the Region of the Cryptoporticus and includes the famous Cappella Greca. Here again a common entrance gives access on the one hand to a large hall with chambers and niches for rich graves and on the other hand to an unadorned corridor whose simple arcosolia and loculi were for the poor. The most important and best preserved room is the so-called Cappella Greca (Fig. 158) which opens off from the large hall just mentioned. The "Greek Chapel" is a relatively small room around the sides of which runs a masonry bench with two simple graves underneath it. It has been believed that this room was intended for the celebration of the Eucharist in solemn church assembly, but since not more than ten people could find comfortable seats in it at once it may have served only for the holding of meals in honor of the dead. A neighboring room, which has a water drain of lead piping, has been interpreted wrongly as a baptistery,[17] but was probably the place where these meals were prepared.

The Cappella Greca is adorned with the greatest series of early Christian paintings which is preserved in any single room of the catacombs. In general the elegance of the tall, statuary figures, the conscientious reproduction of the features, the exact treatment of the garments, and the plastic handling of light and shade represent a style comparable to that in the oldest paintings of the Crypts of Lucina on the Via Appia and of the Hypogeum of the Flavians on the Via Ardeatina and indicate a date around the middle of the second century. This date is confirmed by the coiffure of the half-veiled woman in the painting of the meal scene which will be mentioned in a moment. She wears the braid of hair on the crown of the head in the same way as that worn by the Empress Faustina, wife of Antoninus Pius (138-161), as seen on some well-known coins bearing her likeness, while the daughter, Faustina Junior, wife of Marcus Aurelius (161-180) changed the style.

On the wall at the end of the chamber is painted a meal scene, showing seven persons provided with fish and baskets full of bread to eat (Fig. 159). Elsewhere in the chamber are a number of biblical scenes, including Noah in the Ark, Abraham's Sacrifice, the Miracle of the Water in the Wilderness, the Three Youths in the Fiery Furnace, Daniel between the Lions, the Story of Susanna, the Adoration of the Magi, the Healing of the Paralytic, and the Resurrection of Lazarus.

The painting of the Resurrection of Lazarus is now almost effaced but it is still possible to recognize that on one side is depicted a small building containing a mummy and, on the other, the sister of Lazarus standing with arms upraised. In the middle Christ is shown, facing toward the tomb and with the right hand uplifted in a gesture of speech. He is represented in the Roman type, and is dressed in tunic

---

[17] If the drain pipe had been shut off water could have stood in this room only to a depth of about four inches. Moreover, it is unlikely that the Roman Christians were baptized in the catacombs at all. The *Teaching of the Twelve Apostles* (7 [ANF VII, p.379]), written about the beginning of the second century, calls for baptism in running water, and at Rome this was probably in the Tiber where, according to Tertullian (*On Baptism.* 4 [ANF III, p.671]), Peter himself baptized.

and pallium, the left hand holding the garment. He is youthful and beardless, with short hair and large eyes. The left portion of this picture, showing Christ in the center and the sister of Lazarus at the left, is reproduced in Fig. 160. Although it is now only barely recognizable, this picture is of great interest since it is the oldest representation of Jesus that is preserved anywhere.

In part the Region of the Cryptoporticus lies in an area where there had been a sand quarry. The third major region of the Catacomb of Priscilla arose in farther reaches of this abandoned quarry whose subterranean galleries could be readily employed to receive Christian graves. In general this part of the cemetery (Fig. 161) is simple and little adorned and appears to have served largely for the burial of the poorer Christians. A date around the end of the second or beginning of the third century is probable for the origin of this burial place. Some of the graves have bricks with which they were originally closed, still remaining in place, and stamps on these indicate a time under the Severan house of emperors.

In the neighborhood of some stamped bricks of this date, and at the end of one of the quarry galleries there are a number of badly damaged paintings. They are grouped around the highest loculus on the right wall of the corridor and all were produced at the same time. On the ceiling in painted stucco relief are two shepherds with lambs, represented amidst olive trees. One of these pictures, with the Good Shepherd standing between two lambs and carrying another on his shoulders, is reproduced in Fig. 163. To the right, on the ceiling, is a painting (Fig. 162) showing a mother, seated and holding her child, and with a star above her head. Standing beside her is a man dressed in a pallium, holding a roll in his left hand and pointing upward with his right hand. This is believed to be a representation of Isaiah prophesying the birth of the Messiah (Isaiah 7:14), with the fulfillment of the prophecy indicated at the same time in the Madonna. On the wall of the corridor to the left of the loculus are three figures of the deceased, a man, a woman, and a child, with uplifted arms, while at the right is another standing figure of a man together with traces of a feminine figure.

When compared first with the earliest frescoes in Lucina and Domitilla, and then with the later ones in the Callistus chambers, these are clearly seen to be comparable to the latter. The tall, elegant form of the figures in the paintings of classical style does not appear here. Rather the figures are relatively heavy and executed without close attention to detail. A date at the end of the second or beginning of the third century is probable. Thus of the three main areas of the catacomb the two older arose about the middle of the second century, while the newer was established at the end of the second century or beginning of the third. All three evidently were at first private property. Around the middle of the third century they appear to have been used no more. Then, approximately in the time of Constantine, they again came into use, this time as church property, and were connected with one another and further extended.[18]

THE CATACOMB OF PRAETEXTATUS

On an ancient road to the left of the Via Appia and not far from the cemetery of Callistus lies a catacomb which preserves the name of an otherwise unknown founder, Praetextatus. Of the eight distinct areas which are recognizable within the entire complex, the first is known as the Region of the Scala maggiore. It is characterized by the large stairway leading down to a long corridor, with which are connected two chambers and seven branch corridors. The main chamber is adorned with frescoes which represent the scene at Jacob's Well, the Healing of the Woman with an Issue of Blood, the Resurrection of Lazarus, and another incident which may be an illustration of Similitude VIII in the Shepherd of Hermas. The style of these paintings seems to be midway between that of the oldest frescoes in Lucina, Domitilla, and Priscilla, and the early third century paintings in Callistus, and a date toward the end of the second century is indicated. The first excavation probably was done a decade or so before the time of the paintings.

A second area is called the Spelunca Magna in the pilgrim itineraries of the eighth century. This means literally "large cave" but the pilgrims used *spelunca* practically as a synonym for "cemetery." A long corridor some six and one-half feet in height was later deepened to more than eleven feet and elegant burial chambers were established on either side of it. The original excavation here belongs to the middle of the third century, while the later chambers, including the so-called crypt of Januarius, are dated by the style of their frescoes in the middle of the fourth century.

Adjoining the Spelunca Magna is a third area which is designated as the Region Cocorum from a graffito which seems to refer to a col-

18 srk pp.100-145.

lective burial place of cooks and bakers. The frequently encountered abbreviation of *Christos* known as the Christ-monogram or the Constantinian monogram probably indicates a fourth century date.[19] At the foot of the entrance to the Spelunca Magna a stairway leads to a fourth area at a lower level, whose numerous chambers likewise seem to belong to the middle of the fourth century. A few steps from the entrance to the Spelunca Magna is another stairway which leads down to a system of subterranean corridors which is laid out in an unusually orderly fashion. This is the Region of the Scala minore and constitutes the fifth area of the cemetery. It belongs to the fourth century.

The sixth area is excavated at an intermediate level and still bears dates from the year A.D. 384. Also to the late fourth century belongs the seventh area which lies beneath the Via Appia Pignatelli. Its corridors are crowded with loculi of the poorest appearance. The eighth region is that where the great arcosolium grave of Celerina was found, with its late fourth century paintings representing the story of Susanna and portraying saints including Liberius and Xystus II.

Thus in the catacomb of Praetextatus the origins of the Region of the Scala maggiore go back into the late second century and of the Spelunca Magna into the middle of the third. The other complexes which were connected with these regions later, belong to the fourth century.[20]

THE CATACOMB OF SEBASTIAN

The cemetery of Sebastian is in a valley on the Via Appia. This depression was so marked as to give to the region the name Catacumbas, "by the hollow." The Emperor Maxentius (A.D. 306-312) built a circus near by, and a notice in the Roman city calendar of A.D. 354 which states that this circus was built *in catacumbas*, meaning "in the place which is called Catacumbas," is the earliest appearance of the term. The Christian cemetery at this place originally was known, therefore, as Coemeterium Catacumbas, and only later re-

---

[19] This is the symbol (☧) which Constantine is said to have seen in a dream or vision, and to have inscribed on the shields of his soldiers or to have fashioned as a labarum or imperial standard, before his victory at the Milvian bridge (p.251 n.5), and which appears thereafter with frequency on his coins and those of his sons, and in Christian inscriptions. Lactantius (A.D. c.260-c.325), *Of the Manner in Which the Persecutors Died.* 44 (ANF VII, p.318); Eusebius, *Life of Constantine.* I, 28-31; Max Sulzberger in *Byzantion, Revue Internationale des Études Byzantines.* 2 (1925), pp.393-448. For a possible earlier occurrence of a similar symbol see above p.333.

[20] SRK pp.146-174.

ceived the name of Saint Sebastian. By a natural misunderstanding the name "catacombs" now has come to be applied generally to all subterranean burial places of the early Christians throughout Rome and elsewhere in Italy and other lands.

Excavations begun here in 1915 beneath the Church of San Sebastiano have led to the most significant discoveries. At the lowest level to which the digging penetrated, a heathen necropolis was unearthed. No less than sixteen pagan columbaria were found in the precincts of the basilica alone. These were rectangular brick structures dating, according to the style of their inscriptions, stucco paintings and mosaics, in the first and second centuries. Their walls held niches for the urns of cremation. As the custom changed to inhumation, burials were made in the earth beneath, with clay pipes leading down through the floor into the graves for the usual oblations of wine. At the beginning of the second century, three two-story mausoleums were built near by. One of these was constructed to accommodate urns for ashes but the other two were intended exclusively for inhumation. When the first one came into the possession of a certain M. Clodius Hermes, who is known from an inscription at the door, he had the niches for the urns walled in and new frescoes painted. These showed a deceased person being led by Hermes, the conductor of souls, into the presence of Hades, the ruler of the underworld. In the course of the second century the necropolis grew also through the building of assembly rooms for holding meals in memory of the dead. Nowhere at this lowest level was any trace of a Christian monument found. The necropolis was exclusively pagan.

Then the property came into the possession of Christians. Perhaps this was by purchase or gift, but more probably the owners themselves were converted to Christianity at this time. At any rate, about the middle of the third century the heathen necropolis was entirely filled in, rooms for Christian use were built above it, and a Christian catacomb came into existence beneath ground. The level at which the Christian rooms were found in the excavations was above that of the pagan necropolis but still some six feet beneath the floor of the church. The first room now called the Triclia, was supported at the back against an old basalt wall, which probably was the enclosing wall of the heathen necropolis, and at one end rested upon the first century columbaria. At the front, on the slope of the hill, pillars supported a roof and provided an open loggia. Masonry benches ran around the sides of the room. At one corner was a small spring, in the slime of whose drain were found remains of food, bones of fish, chicken, and hare, and bits of broken glass. A fresco showed a bright garden scene, with a reed hedge, vine leaves, and fluttering birds.

The most important discovery was that of the numerous graffiti which had been scratched on the walls of the room by those who visited it (Fig. 164). A great part of the wall with these rough inscriptions is still preserved in its original position, while broken pieces lay on the floor and could be pieced together again. The graffiti are written in both Greek and Latin and in capital as well as in cursive letters. Most of them are short prayers to Paul and Peter for remembrance and intercession, like the following:

> PAULE ET PETRE PETITE
> PRO VICTORE

> PAUL AND PETER PRAY
> FOR VICTOR

Others mention *refrigeria* or "refreshments" in honor of the apostles. These were meals held according to ancient custom at famous graves in remembrance of venerated saints. One such inscription reads:

> PETRO ET PAULO
> TOMIUS COELIUS
> REFRIGERIUM FECI

> TO PETER AND PAUL
> I TOMIUS COELIUS
> MADE A REFRIGERIUM

In all, the names of the two great apostles are scratched on the wall more than one hundred times.[21] A second room was of somewhat similar character, and also had the names of the apostles, *Petre Paule*, scratched at least once on a brick column.

The style of the painting and the paleographical character of the graffiti point to a date around the middle of the third century for the origin of these rooms. Since not a single visitor scratched on the wall a so-called Constantinian monogram, such as is met at every turn on fourth century monuments, the Triclia cannot have continued in use long after the year 313. Soon after this date, and certainly within the first half of the fourth century, the two rooms, as well as other

[21] As far as the order of the two names is concerned, they are written "Paul and Peter" or "Peter and Paul" without any apparent preference. Lanciani, *Wanderings through Ancient Roman Churches*, p.89.

buildings on this part of the hill, were largely destroyed as the site was leveled up for the building there of a great three-aisled church, the "Basilica of the Apostles." Since the technique of the construction of its walls is similar to that of the nearby Circus of Maxentius (306-312), the basilica must belong to Constantinian times.

The character of the rooms which were frequented so eagerly from the middle of the third to the early part of the fourth century, and which then disappeared so completely beneath the basilica until their recent discovery, is indubitable. They constituted a memorial gathering place, where the Christians honored the memory of Paul and Peter. In the so-called Triclia, common meals were held in remembrance of the two great apostles and the visitors scratched innumerable prayers to them on the walls.[22]

All the evidence points, therefore, to the fact that at this time the bones of Peter and of Paul actually rested here. This is confirmed by an inscription of Pope Damasus I, who as we know was eager to adorn the graves of the martyrs with precious marbles and poetic inscriptions composed by himself. While the original of the inscription in question has perished, it is known from several medieval manuscripts and from a partial thirteenth century copy which stands in the Church of Saint Sebastian, presumably in its original place. This is near the entrance to the crypt of Sebastian, which as we shall see was in the immediate vicinity of the resting place of Peter and Paul. The inscription reads:

> Hic habitasse prium sanctos cognoscere debes,
> Nomina quisque Petri pariter Paulique requiris,
> Discipulos Oriens misit, quod sponte fatemur—
> Sanguinis ob meritum, Christumque per astra secuti
> Aetherios petiere sinus regnaque piorum—
> Roma suos potius meruit defendere cives.
> Haec Damasus vestras referat nova sidera laudes.

> You should know that the saints formerly dwelt here, if you are seeking the names of Peter and Paul. The Orient sent the disciples, as we freely admit, but on account of their bloody martyrdom—they followed Christ through the stars and reached the heavenly bosom and the realm of the pious—Rome rather has won the right to claim them as citizens. This Damasus records to your praise, ye new stars.[23]

[22] SRK pp.331-345.
[23] Lietzmann, *Petrus und Paulus in Rom*, pp.145f.; Walter Lowrie, *SS. Peter and Paul in Rome*. 1940, pp.87f. A misunderstanding of this inscription appears to have

The inscription of Damasus is in complete agreement with the evidence of the graffiti in the Triclia. Writing in the latter half of the fourth century, Damasus declares that Peter and Paul "formerly dwelt here," which is a poetic way of saying "were formerly buried here." At a time from the middle of the third to the early part of the fourth century, Christians came here in numbers to hold meals in honor of Paul and Peter and to scratch prayers to the two great saints on the walls.

We have seen already that around A.D. 200 Caius pointed to the graves of Peter and of Paul at the Vatican and on the Ostian Way respectively as well-known martyr memorials, and we have concluded that the tradition of the apostles' original interment near the respective places of their martyrdoms is entirely trustworthy (p. 384). It must be concluded, therefore, that at the middle of the third century their remains were transferred temporarily to the Via Appia. As a matter of fact there is further evidence that this was the case. This evidence is to be found in the fourth century Church Calendar for the City of Rome. The latter document constituted a sort of yearbook for the inhabitants of Rome, which was edited in A.D. 354 by Furius Dionysius Filocalus, the calligrapher who later was in the service of Pope Damasus and carried out the making of the latter's poetical inscriptions in honor of the martyrs.[24] The portion of the Calendar with which we are concerned is the Depositio Martyrum. This is a list of the dates of the various festivals which were held in honor of the martyrs during the church year, together with an indication of the places where these observances were celebrated. The notation for June 29 reads:

III KAL. IUL.   Petri in Catacumbas
et Pauli Ostense Tusco et Basso cons.[25]

A more complete and correct text of the same notice is found in the Martyrologium Hieronymianum as follows:

Romae Via Aurelia natale[26] sanctorum apostolorum
Petri et Pauli, Petri in Vaticano, Pauli vero
in via Ostensi, utrumque in Catacumbas, passi
sub Nerone, Basso et Tusco consulibus.

---

given rise to the fifth century legend of an attempt by men from the Orient to carry off the bodies of Peter and Paul (Lipsius and Bonnet, Acta Apostolorum Apocrypha, I, pp.220f.).

[24] J. P. Kirsch, Aus den römischen Katakomben. 1926, p.15.

[25] Hans Lietzmann, ed., The Three Oldest Martyrologies. 1904, p.4.

[26] It is the "birthday" of the heavenly life of the saints that is celebrated.

Thus, according to sources from the middle of the fourth century, at that time the church festivals in honor of the martyrdom of Peter and Paul were celebrated at three different places. The festival in honor of Peter was held at the Vatican, that in remembrance of Paul on the Ostian Way, and a celebration in honor of both of them was held in Catacumbas. What is signified by "Basso et Tusco consulibus"? This is the consular date indicating the year 258. In that year Valerian's brief but terrible persecution of the Christians was raging, when, among other acts of violence which were committed, on August 6 Pope Xystus II and four deacons were taken by surprise in a catacomb and killed (p.459). We conclude naturally that fear was felt for the safety of the bones of the two great apostles hitherto resting at their relatively exposed locations in the Vatican district and on the Ostian Way, and that on June 29, 258, they were transferred to the greater safety of the subterranean cemetery *ad Catacumbas*. When the brief persecution was over, the remains of the two apostles were returned to rest permanently in their original graves at the Vatican and on the Ostian Way where later, under Constantine, the churches of Saint Peter and Saint Paul were built. But the names of Peter and Paul continued to be remembered *in Catacumbas* as well as *in Vaticano* and *in via Ostensi*. Such is at least a possible hypothesis to account for the evidence presented above.[27]

The honoring of Paul and Peter *ad Catacumbas* greatly accelerated the development of an extensive Christian cemetery at this place. Many of the faithful wished to find their last rest in proximity to the spot thus hallowed by the two great saints. So there developed a vast network of subterranean corridors and chambers, constituting one of Rome's largest catacombs. Wide areas of these subterranean complexes continued to be visited by pilgrims throughout the Middle Ages as in the case of no other catacomb, but today a great part is filled up and forgotten beneath the surrounding hills. In corridors

---

[27] Lietzmann, *Petrus und Paulus in Rom*, p.126; cf. Kirsch, *Aus den römischen Katakomben*, p.36; Lowrie, SS. *Peter and Paul in Rome*, pp.91f. Styger believes that if not both of the apostles at least Peter originally was buried on the Via Appia and only later interred near the place of his martyrdom. But he is then able to give no more convincing explanation of the reference to the year 258 in the Calendar of Filocalus than that it signifies that the two apostles began to be honored *in Catacumbas* around the middle of the third century (SRK p.346). Why not until then if one or both were buried here in A.D. 64, and why is the precise year 258 specified? See also below (p.515) for an item of evidence at the Vatican held by some to indicate that the bones of Peter remained permanently at the Vatican from the time of their original burial there. And see H. Chadwick in JTS 8 (1957), pp.31-52 for alternative explanations of the origin of the memorial *ad Catacumbas*.

156. Painting on the Ceiling of Chamber "Y" in the Crypts of Lucina

154. Inscription and Seven-armed Lampstand in the Jewish Catacomb at Monteverde

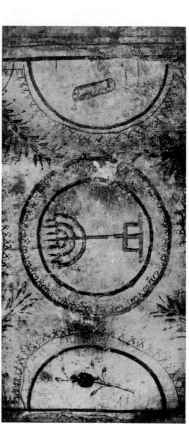

155. Fresco in the Jewish Catacomb of Villa Torlonia

157. The Crypt of the Popes in the Catacomb of Callistus

158. The Cappella Greca in the Catacomb of Priscilla

159. The Meal Scene in the Cappella Greca

160. The Oldest Picture of Christ, a Fresco in the Cappella Greca

161. Burial Niches in the Catacomb of Priscilla

162. The Prophet and the Madonna

163. The Good Shepherd as Painted in the Catacomb of Priscilla

164. Graffiti Invoking Peter and Paul

165. Grave Inscription of Licinia Amias

166. The Deceased Offering Prayer in the Garden of Paradise,
a Painting in the Catacomb of Callistus

167. Statuette of the Good Shepherd   168. Noah in the Ark, a Painting in the Catacomb
of Peter and Marcellinus

169. Wall Paintings in the Catacomb of Domitilla

171. Portrait of Paul in the Catacomb of San Gennaro in Naples

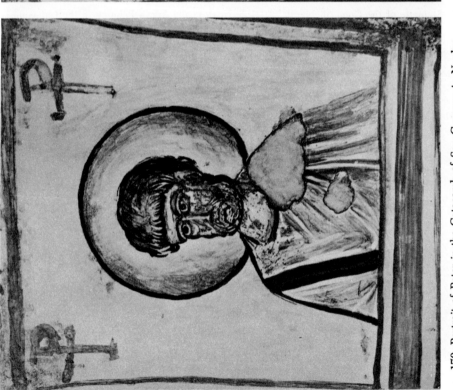

170. Portrait of Peter in the Catacomb of San Gennaro in Naples

172. Early Christian Sarcophagus of the "Philosopher" Type

173. Sarcophagus with the Story of Jonah

174. Sarcophagus of the Latin Frieze Type

175. A "City-Gate" Sarcophagus

176. A "Bethesda" Sarcophagus

177. The Sarcophagus of Junius Bassus

so long trampled by pilgrim feet it is not to be expected that many monuments should remain and as a matter of fact only a few traces of frescoes are to be seen and a few inscriptions with dates in the latter part of the fourth century.

The name by which the entire catacomb is known is that of Sebastian, the saint and martyr. The Roman city calendar of A.D. 354 lists the festival *Sebastiani in Catacumbas* on the date XIII KAL. FEB. or January 10.[28] According to the fifth century *Acts of Saint Sebastian* he was shot with arrows in the Colosseum as a victim of the great persecution by Diocletian and then was buried *ad Catacumbas in initio cryptae iuxta vestigia apostolorum*, "at Catacumbas in the entrance of the crypt near the vestiges of the apostles."[29] Actually the present crypt of Sebastian is found in immediate proximity to the memorial of the apostles at the entrance to the catacomb. The grave was originally in the wall of a simple corridor, and later the opposite wall was removed to provide more room for the numerous visitors. Probably in the time of Constantine, a basilica was built above ground. It was known as the Church of the Apostles and later as the Church of Saint Sebastian.[30] The martyr's grave continued to be accessible by steep steps leading down from within the church. At the beginning of the fifth century two priests, Proclinus and Ursus, rebuilt the crypt of Sebastian, giving it strong brick walls and a new monumental entrance, as well as placing the holy relics in an altar at the same place where the original grave had been.[31]

THE CATACOMB OF PETER AND MARCELLINUS

The Catacomb of Peter and Marcellinus lies on the Via Casilina, as the ancient Via Labicana now is known, and is one of the most extensive complexes of subterranean Rome. It is also notable since no other cemetery possesses so many chambers adorned with frescoes. Before it received the name of Peter and Marcellinus it was known simply by a place-designation as Inter duas Lauros, "Between the two Laurels" (p.522). Three great stairways lead down to as many regions, which were originally independent of one another but developed so extensively as eventually to interconnect. The first stairway led down from the Via Labicana at right angles to the main

[28] Lietzmann, ed., *The Three Oldest Martyrologies*, p.4.
[29] Lietzmann, *Petrus und Paulus in Rom*, p.169.
[30] San Sebastiano was rebuilt in the form it has today in 1612.
[31] SRK pp.177-184; cf. F. Farnari, S. Sebastiano *"extra moenia."* 1934.

corridor, from which side corridors ran off at regular intervals. Several chambers were excavated in connection with these corridors, and the paintings in the first of them are in the style of the fourth century.

The last corridor attained special significance when the remains of two martyrs (Peter, an exorcist, and Marcellinus, a priest[32]) were interred there in simple wall graves. This took place perhaps in the time of the peace of the church, since at the time of their death under Diocletian in A.D. 304 the two martyrs were buried at the place of their beheading on the Via Cornelia. Since many persons now wished to find a last resting place in the catacomb near the revered saints, numerous burial chambers were laid out in the vicinity. They are adorned with paintings in the style of the advanced fourth century. The excavation in the immediate neighborhood became so extensive that a small, subterranean basilica had to be built for the protection of the graves of the martyrs. Later a Constantinian basilica was built above ground and became the center of a cemetery lying in the open air.

The second stairway led down to another extensive region with numerous chambers. The paintings here belong to the fourth century and include frequent representations of a meal scene. The third stairway gave access to yet a third region of more limited extent. Its most important chamber contains a fresco of the advanced fourth century. Thus this catacomb appears to have undergone its most important development during the later years of that century.[33]

5. THE ART OF THE CATACOMBS

IN DESCRIBING the above Roman catacombs some of the more important paintings on their walls have been mentioned. A brief summary of the development of Christian art in the catacombs can now be given. In the first place, early Christian art did not hesitate to borrow from representations already familiar in pagan art. Christianity was not hostile to ancient culture except where faith or moral principles were endangered. Just as Clement of Alexandria around A.D. 200 held that a Christian should not employ for his signet ring any idolatrous, warlike, or licentious symbol but rather such seals as

[32] Not to be confused with Pope Marcellinus (296-304), who also died later in the same year in the persecution of Diocletian and was buried in the cemetery of Priscilla on the Via Salaria.

[33] SRK pp.198-205.

a dove, a fish, a ship, a lyre, or an anchor,[1] so too the artists of the catacombs freely employed such figures in a decorative way and even gave some of them deeper Christian meaning. The little winged persons, which we noted in the Crypts of Lucina (p.457) and which are known as Erotes or Amoretti, might have seemed less acceptable since actually they came from pagan tombs where they had represented departed souls. But such signification had long since been forgotten and they were employed in a purely decorative way and without offense to Christian taste, along with butterflies, birds, and flowers.

Other representations were interpreted to convey deeper Christian meanings. The fish had already appeared in pagan art, but the Christians soon discovered that in the Greek language the five letters constituting the word "fish" were the initial letters of the phrase "Jesus Christ, the Son of God, the Saviour."[2] Writing about A.D. 200 *On Baptism*, Tertullian said, "But we, little fishes, after the example of our FISH Jesus Christ, are born in water,"[3] while Augustine (A.D. c.425) said that in the word fish "Christ is mystically understood, because he was able to live, that is, to exist, without sin in the abyss of this mortality as in the depth of waters."[4] Thus the fish might stand symbolically for the name of Christ. In the catacomb of Priscilla there is an inscription reading "ALEXANDER IN," after which a fish is shown, completing the phrase "Alexander in Christ."[5] Or fishes might stand for the Christians themselves. A grave inscription of Licinia Amias from around A.D. 200 (Fig. 165) has the word "Fish" followed by "of the living," which must mean "Jesus Christ, the Son of God, the Saviour of the living," and is adorned with two fishes, which may represent the Christians who are "the living."[6] The initials D.M. which appear on this inscription stand for *Dis Manibus*, meaning "To the spirits of the world of the dead."[7] These initials appeared regularly on pagan graves, and were frequently employed by Christians simply as a conventional form and without further thought of their original meaning.

---

[1] *The Instructor.* III, 11 (ANF II, p.285).

[2] ΙΧΘΥΣ—Ἰησοῦς Χριστὸς Θεοῦ Υἱὸς Σωτήρ.

[3] *On Bapt.* I (ANF III, p.669).

[4] *The City of God.* XVIII, 23 (NPNF II, p.373).

[5] Orazio Marucchi, *The Evidence of the Catacombs for the Doctrines and Organization of the Primitive Church.* 1929, p.32.

[6] F. J. Dölger, *Ichthys, das Fischsymbol in frühchristlicher Zeit.* I (1910), pp.159-177.

[7] René Cagnat, *Cours d'épigraphie latine.* 4th ed. 1914, p.424.

The representations of a woman with arms uplifted in prayer and of a shepherd with a lamb on his shoulders were also familiar in Hellenistic art. But these figures recur with great frequency in the Christian art of the catacombs from this time on and are invested with special significance. The woman with hands lifted up in prayer is known as an orant[8] and reflects the Hellenistic tendency to personify abstract ideas.[9] Here in the catacombs the orant becomes a distinctive Christian figure, a personification of prayer for salvation and a symbol of Christian devotion. Since such figures occasionally are shown amidst the garden of paradise, and have the names of the departed written nearby, it is clear that they might also be regarded as symbolical representations of the deceased who offer prayer to God in the blessedness of heaven (Fig. 166).[10]

The sight of a shepherd carrying a sheep on his shoulders is familiar in the Middle East today, and the representation of a subject of this type is found not only in Greco-Roman times as for example in Hermes Criophorus, the protector of flocks who carries a ram on his shoulders, but also much more anciently. In Assyria and Syria, reliefs have been found from the eighth and tenth centuries B.C. which portray a man bearing a gazelle upon his shoulders, while the statue from Mari of a man carrying a kid in his arms is as early as the third millennium B.C. (p.56, Fig. 21). These older figures, to be sure, represent worshipers bringing animals for sacrifice, but at least by the time of the ram-bearing Hermes of Greece and perhaps much earlier the thought of the Good Shepherd was introduced.[11] In Christian art the type was conceived anew and filled with Christian meaning.[12] The Good Shepherd now is none other than Christ himself (John 10:11) who carries the lost sheep back to the fold (Luke 15:5f.). The particular appropriateness of such a picture in the catacombs is seen in the conception preserved in a later Latin liturgy: "Lord, let these who are asleep, when they are redeemed from death, freed from guilt, reconciled to the Father, and brought home on the shoulders of the Good Shepherd, enjoy everlasting blessedness in the

[8] C. M. Kaufmann, *Handbuch der christlichen Archäologie.* 3d ed. 1922, p.272.

[9] Charles R. Morey, *Early Christian Art.* 1942, p.63.

[10] H. Leclercq in DACL II, col. 2472.

[11] A. Parrot in *Mélanges Syriens offerts a Monsieur René Dussaud.* I (1939), pp.171-182; G. Ernest Wright in BA 2 (1939), pp.44-48; also for prehistoric antecedents in Egypt see Valentine Muller in JNES 3 (1944), pp.87-90.

[12] Pierre Maranget, *Jésus-Christ dans les peintures des catacombes.* 1932, p.41; J. Wilpert, *Principienfragen der christlichen Archäologie.* 1889, p.15.

train of the eternal king and in the company of the saints."[13] The famous marble statuette of the Good Shepherd (Fig. 167), usually dated in the third century and now in the Lateran Museum in Rome, also once may have stood in a cemeterial crypt. It shows the Shepherd as a young and beardless man whose curly hair falls upon his shoulders. He wears a tucked-up tunic and high stockings, and has a basket slung on a strap. He carries the lost sheep gently on his shoulders holding its front feet in one hand and the rear feet in the other.[14]

The juxtaposition of the orant and the Good Shepherd is found as early as in the painting in the Lucina crypt (p.457; Fig. 156) and recurs frequently thereafter in Christian art. The significance of placing these two symbols in connection with each other is unmistakable. The Christian prayer for deliverance in time of need and death is answered by the Good Shepherd who carries the soul safely home to its fatherland in paradise.[15]

The famous inscription of Abercius[16] casts light on the place held by the Shepherd and the Fish in Christian thought at the end of the second century. Abercius was a Christian of Hieropolis,[17] a small town in Phrygia between Eumenia and Synnada, who at the age of seventy-two composed an epitaph relating his visit to Rome and return by way of Syria and Mesopotamia. He said:

"I, a citizen of an elect city, in my lifetime have erected this monument, to have where to place my body when time shall require it.

"My name is Abercius, a disciple of the holy Shepherd who feeds his sheep upon the hills and plains, whose eyes are large and all-seeing, who taught me the sure learning of life, and sent me to Rome to see the imperial majesty and the queen clad in a golden robe and with golden shoes. There I saw a people who had the gleaming seal. I saw also the plains of Syria and all cities, Nisibis, beyond the Euphrates. Everywhere I had a companion, for Paul sat in the chariot with me; everywhere Faith was my guide, and gave me everywhere for food the Fish from the spring, the great, the pure, which the spotless Virgin caught and ever puts before the friends to eat; she has also delicious wine, and she offers wine mixed with water together with bread. I, Abercius, dictated this to

[13] Hans Lietzmann, *Geschichte de alten Kirche.* II (1936), p.138.

[14] O. Marucchi, *I Monumenti del Museo Cristiano Pio-Lateranense riprodotti in atlante di XCVI tavole, con testo illustrativo.* 1910, p.13.

[15] cf. Cyprian (A.D. c.200-258), *Treatise VII On the Mortality.* 26 (ANF v, p.475): "We regard paradise as our country."

[16] Dölger, *Ichthys.* II (1922), pp.454-507; *Die Eucharistie nach Inschriften frühchristlicher Zeit.* 1922, pp.10-42.

[17] He is probably to be identified with the Avircius Marcellus to whom an anti-Montanist work was dedicated in that region around A.D. 183 (Eusebius, *Ch. Hist.* v, xvi, 3).

be written in my presence, and in fact in the seventy-second year of my life. Let every fellow believer who understands this pray for Abercius.

"No man may lay another in my grave; but if it be done, he must pay to the Roman treasury two thousand gold pieces, and to my dear native city Hieropolis a thousand gold pieces."

The language of Abercius is poetic but he expects fellow Christians to understand. Rome is referred to as "the imperial majesty and the queen clad in a golden robe," in fashion somewhat similar to the symbolism employed in Revelation (17:3-5, 9, 18). The Christians are the people with the "gleaming seal." Abercius had Paul for a companion in the sense that he carried the Pauline letters with him. Even so he describes Christ now as the great Shepherd who cares for his flock upon the hills and plains, and again as the Fish from the spring, caught by the holy Virgin. He says that the Virgin places the Fish before the friends to eat, and offers them wine and bread. The inner meaning of this last language is that the Christians everywhere partake of Christ in the observance of the Lord's Supper. It will be remembered that meal scenes are frequently represented in the catacombs with fish and bread, and sometimes wine, for food. It is not certain whether these scenes depict the meals that were held in honor of the dead, as was also done in pagan custom,[18] or represent the Lord's Supper itself. Perhaps the loaves and fishes reflect the Feeding of the Five Thousand, which was regarded as the prototype of the Lord's Supper because of the interpretation given to it in John 6:54, "He who eats my flesh and drinks my blood has eternal life, and I will raise him up at the last day."[19] At any rate the words of Abercius, combining the Fish with the bread and wine, give some support to the interpretation of the meal scenes of the catacombs in a eucharistic sense.

In the second place, not only pagan but also Jewish art seems to have made its contribution to the Christian art of the catacombs. Some seven Old Testament scenes appear repeatedly among the oldest paintings in Lucina, Domitilla and Priscilla (middle of the second century), and Callistus and Praetextatus (end of the second and beginning of the third century). These seven subjects are: Noah in the Ark, Abraham's Sacrifice of Isaac, Moses' Miracle of Water in the Wilderness, the Story of Jonah, the Three Youths in the Fiery Furnace, Daniel in the Lions' Den, and, from the Old Testament

---

[18] Morey, *Early Christian Art,* p.64.
[19] Lietzmann, *Geschichte der alten Kirche.* II, p.141.

Apocrypha, the Story of Susanna.[20] It is now known that the Jews used paintings and other artistic representations in their catacombs (p.455) and synagogues (p.497f.) and some of those that have been found reveal the same subjects that appear in the Christian catacombs at Rome. In the synagogue at Dura one of the wall paintings depicts Abraham's Sacrifice of Isaac, in a third-century Palestinian synagogue the floor mosaic shows Daniel between the Lions, and around A.D. 200 the city of Apamea in Phrygia, under the influence of the Jews who lived there, stamped on some of its coins the same type of portrayal of Noah in the Ark that is familiar in the Christian catacombs. Thus it is probable that at least some of the Christian representations of Old Testament events were taken over from the realm of Jewish art.[21]

In the third place, the Christian artists went on to develop their own representations of New Testament subjects. Perhaps this was done first for the decoration of the walls of Christian houses and cult-rooms,[22] and from there the paintings were copied in the catacombs. At any rate some half-dozen New Testament scenes appear repeatedly in the oldest Roman catacombs. These are: the Visit of the Magi, the Baptism of Jesus, the Healing of the Paralytic, the Healing of the Woman with an Issue of Blood, the Samaritan Woman at the Well, and the Resurrection of Lazarus.[23]

These thirteen scenes which have now been mentioned—seven from the Old Testament and six from the New Testament—not only appear frequently in the five oldest Christian cemeteries at Rome but also are repeated over and over again in all the later catacombs. The Old Testament picture of Noah in the Ark reproduced in Fig. 168 is from the Catacomb of Peter and Marcellinus, while the paintings in Fig. 169 are from the Catacomb of Domitilla and include three of the New Testament scenes, the Raising of Lazarus, the Coming of the Magi, and the Walking of the Paralytic with his Bed, as well as a representation of the Bringing of Water from the Rock. Ultra-symbolic interpretations have been advanced for all these subjects, but actually their leading motif is the simple theme of deliverance. As the early Christians faced tribulation and death, their courage was increased by the remembrance of God's mighty deeds in

[20] SRK p.356.
[21] Lietzmann, *Geschichte der alten Kirche.* II, p.140. See also Heinz-Ludwig Hempel in ZAW 69 (1957), pp.103-131.
[22] cf. the house church at Dura, see below pp.499f.
[23] SRK p.356.

the past on behalf of his children. The wonderful deliverances which had taken place were types of the resurrection to which Christian faith looked forward with confidence. This conception which shines through the earliest art of the catacombs is preserved also in written sources. Thus, for example, in the *Constitutions of the Holy Apostles*, a work belonging probably to the fourth century, the author urges that martyrdom be faced with equanimity because of the certainty of the resurrection, and says: "Now he that brought Jonah in the space of three days, alive and unhurt, out of the belly of the whale, and the three children out of the furnace of Babylon, and Daniel out of the mouth of the lions, does not lack power to raise us up also."[24] Even so, in the prayer for a departing soul which is still in use today in the Roman Catholic Church the words are found: "Deliver, O Lord! the soul of Thy servant, as Thou didst deliver Noah in the flood . . . Isaac from the sacrificing hand of his father . . . Daniel from the lions' den . . . the three children from the fiery furnace . . . Susanna from her false accusers."[25]

From the time of Constantine and the peace of the church on, a large number of other subjects are found among the paintings in the catacombs. More than sixty new scenes appear, including pictures from the Old Testament like those of Job, Adam and Eve, and Moses before Pharaoh; representations from the Gospels like the Annunciation to Mary, the Entry into Jerusalem, and the Women at the Tomb; events from the book of Acts like the Sin of Ananias and Sapphira, and the Raising of Tabitha; and stories from the New Testament Apocrypha like Peter's Miracle of the Water (p.488), and the Healing of Petronilla. In contrast to the constantly repeated thirteen scenes of older times, these new subjects appear far less frequently, over half of them being found but a single time. It is probable that they were copied from the new paintings and mosaics which were being developed to adorn the numerous new churches of Constantinian times.[26]

6. THE INSCRIPTIONS IN THE CATACOMBS

AN additional word should be said about the inscriptions in the catacombs. In the Jewish catacombs at Rome most of the inscriptions

---

[24] v, i, 7 (ANF VII, p.440).

[25] P. Griffith, compiler, *The Priest's New Ritual, revised in accord with the latest Vatican Edition of the Roman Ritual.* 1939, pp.138-140.

[26] SRK pp.357-360.

are in Greek and some in Latin. Inscriptions in Hebrew are rare, except for the single word Shalom, meaning peace or rest. Very frequently found are the Greek words, "May his [or her] sleep be in peace."[1]

The Christian inscriptions are also more often in Greek than in Latin and thus may indicate the humble and foreign extraction of those on whose graves they are written.[2] The following are typical inscriptions in the Christian catacombs:

> Victorina, in peace and in Christ.
> Julia, in peace with the saints.
> Thou wilt live in God.
> Mayest thou live in the Lord Jesus.
> Mayest thou live in the Holy Spirit.
> Thou wilt live forever.
> May God give thee life.

An epitaph on the grave of a little child reads:

> To Paul, my son, in peace. May the spirit of all the saints receive thee. He lived two years.

Some inscriptions refer to the life beyond as a *refrigerium* or refreshment:

> May God refresh thy spirit.

Some contain a prayer on behalf of the departed one:

> Demetris and Leontia, to their daughter, Sirita. Jesu, be mindful of our child.

Others request the prayers of the departed:

> In thy prayers pray for us, for we know that thou dwellest in Christ.[3]

Not only paintings and inscriptions are found in the catacombs but also many small objects which were left at the graves. These include lamps, pitchers, vases, plates, and the interesting "gold-glasses" within whose glass bottoms medallions made of gold leaf were sealed.[4]

---

[1] G. M. Bevan, *Early Christians of Rome, their Words and Pictures.* 1927, p.24.

[2] Morey, *Early Christian Art*, p.60.

[3] Bevan, *Early Christians of Rome, their Words and Pictures*, pp.28-32.

[4] Oskar Beyer, *Die Katakombenwelt, Grundriss, Ursprung und Idee der Kunst in der römischen Christengemeinde.* 1927, pp.106-112. For glass in antiquity see R. J. Forbes, *Studies in Ancient Technology.* v (1957), pp.110-231.

7. CATACOMBS IN OTHER CITIES AND LANDS

NUMEROUS catacombs are to be found elsewhere in Italy and in other places including Sicily, Malta, North Africa, Egypt, and Palestine.[1] As a single example we may mention the catacombs at Naples. Six early Christian catacombs exist here whose origins are in the second and third centuries and whose use continued for many centuries thereafter. They are adorned with many paintings, and the development of their art is traceable through several periods. In the first period, in the second and third centuries, it may be seen clearly that the Christian art has arisen out of the decorative painting of the ancient world. Flowers, birds, and leaping animals such as antelopes and panthers are represented, while also such a biblical subject as that of Adam and Eve makes its appearance. In the second period, in the fourth century, the influence of the Roman catacomb art is felt strongly, and the painters at Naples copied Roman models to represent the Story of Jonah, Moses Striking Water from the Rock, and other familiar subjects. Only in the third period, from the fifth to the eighth centuries, did the Christian art of Naples achieve independent significance and attain its high point. Examples of the portraits characteristic of this period may be seen in two fifth century paintings of Peter and Paul. The two apostles are decidedly different in type, Peter (Fig. 170) with his broader face, curling hair, and short beard, and Paul (Fig. 171) with his bald head, lofty brow, long nose, and straight beard. Peter's expression is distrustful or almost sullen, and may reflect the influence of monasticism, while in the companion picture of Paul a Christian thinker and philosopher is depicted.[2]

8. THE LATER HISTORY OF THE ROMAN CATACOMBS

A BRIEF word may be said concerning the later history of the catacombs at Rome. During the third century the persecuted Christians frequently sought refuge in the catacombs and many even suffered martyrdom within them.[1] In that century and the next the venera-

---

[1] See Leclercq in DACL II, cols. 2442-2450.

[2] Hans Achelis, *Die Katakomben von Neapel.* 1936.

[1] In his edict of A.D. 257, Valerian forbade the Christians to hold assemblies or to enter into the catacombs (Eusebius, *Ch. Hist.* VII, xi, 10) but in A.D. 261 Gallienus again allowed the Christians to use their places of worship inclusive of the cemeteries (*Ch. Hist.* VII, xiii).

tion of the martyrs who were buried in the catacombs became very important and we have already noted (pp.459f., 472) the contributions of Pope Damasus to the beautification of the crypts now so eagerly visited by pilgrims. With the peace of the church under Constantine it became possible to build cemeterial churches above the catacombs and to erect other churches elsewhere. From this time on it became gradually customary to bury the dead no longer in the subterranean rooms of the catacombs but in graves and sarcophagi in and around these churches. As the burials in surface cemeteries became more and more numerous, the catacombs fell into disuse. With the sack of Rome by Alaric in A.D. 410, interments in them ceased entirely. The tombs of the martyrs were still visited after that and kept in repair, but other sections of the catacombs were neglected and often became inaccessible. When the Goths besieged Rome in 537 and the Lombards in 755 the catacombs suffered much destruction and the crypts of the martyrs were damaged badly. The popes of the eighth and ninth centuries found it necessary to bring the bones of the martyrs from their graves in the catacombs to safer resting places in the churches inside the city. Where there are basilicas still standing outside the city today, however, these churches were always kept in use and the remains of the martyrs buried there did not have to be removed.[2] But after the remains of the martyrs were removed from the crypts at the catacombs, the catacombs fell into complete ruin. Their entrances were choked with dirt, the grass of the Campagna covered them, and their very existence was forgotten until their accidental rediscovery in 1578.

9. EARLY CHRISTIAN SARCOPHAGI

OCCASIONALLY in the catacombs and far more frequently in and around the churches above ground there are found the sculptured stone coffins which are known as sarcophagi.[1] These constitute relatively elaborate tombs and reflect the existence of a wealthier group of believers than some of the poor who buried their dead in the humble niches of the catacombs.[2]

The employment of sarcophagi for pagan burials has already been

[2] Kirsch, *Aus den römischen Katakomben*, pp.10-12.
[1] James C. Stout in *Papers of the American Society of Church History*. Second series. 8 (1928), pp.1-15.
[2] Morey, *Early Christian Art*, p.67.

alluded to (pp. 451, 463), and it may be presumed that when Christians first began to use such tombs they were procured directly from the workshops of those who served the population as a whole. In such cases the sarcophagi would not exhibit any marks distinctive of Christianity, but would be adorned like the pagan coffins with lines, animal heads, scenes from the sea and the chase, and other subjects. Themes repugnant to Christian principles, of course, would be avoided in the selection of the sarcophagi.[3]

SARCOPHAGI OF THE THIRD CENTURY

But the time soon came when Christianity developed its own plastic art, and sculptured sarcophagi appear which are unmistakably Christian productions. According to the researches of Friedrich Gerke, the oldest of these are to be dated around the middle of the third century A.D.[4] It was probably at about this time, and particularly under the influence of the philosopher Plotinus who worked in Rome from 244 until 270, that a distinctive type of pagan sarcophagus arose in whose sculptures the deceased was represented in the role of a philosopher with his book.[5] When, therefore, a number of Christian sarcophagi display this very theme, it is a natural conclusion that they are to be dated at about the same time. In the case of the latter productions, however, the orant and the Good Shepherd are characteristically added in the sculptures to show that the content of the true philosophy is the Christian message of immortality.

A Christian sarcophagus of the "philosopher" type, which was found in the Via Salaria in Rome and now is in the Lateran Museum, is shown in Fig. 172. This sarcophagus is of the tub-shaped kind and is adorned at the corners with figures of rams. Two trees serve to divide the sculptures on the front into three groups. At the left sits the deceased man in the guise of a philosopher accompanied by two friends. At the right is his wife, with whom are two companions. Of these, however, the one in front appears as an orant who gazes toward the Good Shepherd in the center. The Shepherd in turn looks toward the orant, and in this unmistakable juxtaposition of the two figures the motif familiar in the catacombs (p.479) appears again.[6] The

[3] O. Marucchi, *Manual of Christian Archaeology*. tr. from 4th Italian edition by Hubert Vecchierello, 1935, pp.330f.

[4] F. Gerke, *Die christlichen Sarkophage der vorkonstantinischen Zeit*. 1940, p.316.

[5] Gerhart Rodenwaldt in *Jahrbuch des Deutschen Archäologischen Instituts*. 51 (1936), pp.101-105.

[6] The heads of both the orant and the Good Shepherd are modern restorations, but

prayer for deliverance from death is answered by the Good Shepherd. This theme holds the place of focal importance in the composition and toward this central truth of Christian philosophy the attention of the believers is directed.[7]

In the latter part of the third century another distinctive type of Christian sarcophagus makes its appearance. General symbolism here gives way to specifically biblical composition. The motif in the sculptures is still that of deliverance from death, but the idea now is conveyed through the portrayal of events from the Bible. Obviously the influence of the art of the catacombs continues to be effective, and the stories which are represented include such familiar ones as those of Jonah, Daniel, and the Fiery Furnace.

Of the prominent class of sarcophagi which portray the history of Jonah, an outstanding example now in the Lateran Museum is shown in Fig. 173. Against a unified background of sea and rocky coast, the story of Jonah is unfolded in three consecutive parts. At the left Jonah is being cast out of the ship and received into the mouth of the sea monster. In the scene immediately adjacent the sea monster is shown again, throwing up Jonah on the rocks of the coast. The picture is enlivened at this point with representations of the flora and fauna of the seacoast, including reeds and trees, the snail, the lizard, the crab, and the heron. An angler is drawing a fish from the ocean, and a shepherd is seen with his sheep before a massive sheep stall. The third part of the dramatic history of Jonah is represented just above the seacoast, where Jonah rests beneath the shade of the gourd. Although most of the front of the sarcophagus is occupied by this detailed and extensive portrayal of the story of Jonah, some room remains in which other biblical subjects are introduced. On a bit of open sea between the monster and the coast, Noah floats in his ark, and in an upper panel we see from left to right the Resurrection of Lazarus, the Water Miracle of Moses, and what is probably yet a further scene from the life of Moses.[8]

SARCOPHAGI OF THE FOURTH CENTURY
THE LATIN FRIEZE STYLE

The greatest number of early Christian sarcophagi belong to the fourth century, and in this period it is possible clearly to distinguish

---

sufficient traces of the original heads remain to show clearly that they were represented as gazing at each other.

[7] Gerke, *Die christlichen Sarkophage der vorkonstantinischen Zeit*, pp.246-299.

[8] *ibid.*, pp.38-46.

two main groups among them, namely those of the frieze type and those of the columnar style. In the case of the frieze group the entire front of the sarcophagus is occupied with a continuous series of figures. Such a style of arrangement was customary in the pagan sarcophagus art of the Latin West during the second and third centuries and doubtless provided the pattern for the Christian sculptors. The Christian sarcophagi display a basic difference, however, in that the façade is made to carry not a single unified representation but a halfdozen or more separate scenes crowded together in undivided succession. The purpose clearly is to tell as many stories as possible in the space at hand. The subjects chosen are largely biblical scenes such as were already represented in conveniently abbreviated form in the art of the catacombs.[9]

A sarcophagus executed in the Latin frieze style and now in the Lateran Museum is shown in Fig. 174. Placed side by side upon its front are the representations of no less than nine different events. At the left is the Fall of Man, with Adam and Eve standing on either side of the tree and the Lord laying his hand on Adam's shoulder. Continuing to the right we see the Miracle of the Wine at Cana, the Healing of the Blind, and a Resurrection scene which may represent one of the miracles of Christ or Ezekiel's vision of the valley of dry bones (Ezekiel 37:1-14). In the center Christ is prophesying the Denial of Peter, at whose feet the symbolic cock appears. Farther to the right we find the Healing of the Paralytic, the Sacrifice of Isaac, the Arrest of Peter, and Peter Smiting the Rock to bring water to baptize his jailers. The last scene is similar to that of Moses' Miracle of Water in the Wilderness, but is believed to be derived from some apocryphal incident in the life of Peter.

THE ASIATIC COLUMNAR STYLE

In contrast with the crowded and indiscriminate arrangement of the sculptures of the Latin frieze sarcophagi, a far more orderly composition is exhibited by the so-called columnar sarcophagi. The latter are characterized by the placing of the various figures in an architectural framework which is usually made up of columns and arches. This type of arrangement is known in the pagan sarcophagi of the second and third centuries, and seems to have originated in Asia Minor. The Christian sarcophagi of the columnar group are regarded, therefore, as standing under the direct influence of this

[9] Alexander C. Soper in AB 19 (1937), pp.148-202.

Asiatic style, and it is believed that many of them, although made in the West, were executed by Asiatic artisans.[10]

Since the columnar sarcophagi constitute a numerous group, the general style may be illustrated by two examples in each of which a characteristic modification appears. Fig. 175 shows a sarcophagus which was discovered in the foundation of St. Peter's Church in Rome and is now in the Louvre. Its Asiatic style is unmistakable, and in this case the columns and arches are so arranged as to give the appearance of a series of city-gates. Sarcophagi of this type commonly are spoken of as belonging to the "city-gate" group.[11] We see that in the present case the entire front of the sarcophagus is given over to a single scene, that of the Mission of the Apostles. Christ stands upon the mount, surrounded by the Twelve, and with the two donors of the sarcophagus represented as small figures at his feet. While many of the heads were broken and have been restored, that of Christ is original and shows him as bearded. Christ is giving the scroll of the new law to Peter, who carries a jeweled cross and heads the apostles from the right. Paul occupies the corresponding position on the left.

The sarcophagus shown in Fig. 176, and now in the Lateran Museum, displays the architectural features of the Asiatic style and by virtue of the appearance of the gate of Jerusalem at the extreme right is allied with the "city-gate" sarcophagi. A special modification occurs here, however, in the introduction, near the center, of a double-register scene portraying the Healing of the Paralytic at the Pool of Bethesda. In the lower register, the paralytic lies upon his bed; in the upper, at the command of Christ, he walks away with his bed upon his back. Sarcophagi having this central scene as an identifying feature are commonly designated as belonging to the "Bethesda" type.[12] The other representations which appear on the sarcophagus illustrated include at the left the Healing of Two Blind Men, and the Healing of the Woman with an Issue of Blood, and at the right the Triumphal Entry of Christ into Jerusalem.

THE SARCOPHAGUS OF JUNIUS BASSUS

The influence of the eastern tradition in the West led in many cases to a mingling of the Asiatic and the Latin styles, and some of

[10] Marion Lawrence in AB 13 (1931), pp.535f.; 14 (1932), pp.103-185.
[11] *ibid.*, 10 (Sept. 1927-June 1928), pp.1-45.
[12] *ibid.*, 14 (1932), p.121.

the resultant productions were very fine. For a single example we may turn to the sarcophagus of Junius Bassus (Fig. 177), which is believed to have been the work of a Latin artist using various Asiatic models.[13] This magnificent stone coffin, which was found in the Church of St. Peter in 1595, was the tomb of a prefect of Rome who died in A.D. 359. This is indicated by the following inscription upon the sarcophagus: "Junius Bassus, a most illustrious man, who lived forty-two years and two months, and when he was in office as prefect of the city and after he had received baptism went to God on the 25th day of August in the year in which Eusebius and Hypatius were consuls." On the top of the sarcophagus may be scenes from the life of Junius Bassus, which are now difficult to make out, on the ends are representations from ancient nature mythology, but on the front are wholly Christian scenes. Here there are two rows of sculptures, each row in turn being divided by columns into niches in which the various scenes are found. In the upper row the scenes are from left to right (1) Abraham's Sacrifice, (2) the Arrest of Peter, (3) Christ Enthroned above Caelus[14] and bestowing upon Peter and Paul their missions, and (4-5) Christ Led before Pilate. In the lower row are (1) Job, (2) Adam and Eve, (3) Christ's Entry into Jerusalem, (4) Daniel between the Lions,[15] and (5) Paul Led to Execution. In between, in the spandrels of the lower colonnade, lambs play the parts in scenes representing the Three Hebrews in the Fiery Furnace, Peter's Miracle of Water, the Baptism of Christ, the Multiplication of Loaves and Fishes, Moses Receiving the Law, and the Resurrection of Lazarus. The plan of the main sculptures is clear if we may consider that when they were carried out the niches of Abraham and Paul became reversed. Thinking of Abraham as belonging to the lower register we find there a series of Old Testament scenes, with Christ in the center, riding triumphantly through the world of human sin and suffering. Placing Paul in the upper series, we have there the theme of the passion in which Christ is followed in death by his two apostles. On the right, Christ walks slowly between two soldiers toward the judgment place, while Pilate sits upon the magistrate's chair and a servant prepares to pour the water for the symbolic washing of his hands. On the left, Peter stands between two soldiers, calmly

[13] *ibid.*, 14 (1932), p.133.

[14] The god who in Roman art spreads out the veil of the sky, as on the breastplate of Augustus (cf. Fig. 99 and p.250).

[15] The figure of Daniel in the middle is a modern restoration. The lions are accompanied by men holding rods.

awaiting the end, and Paul, in the other niche, bows his head as the officer draws the sword while reeds indicate the marshes of the Tiber where his execution was fulfilled. In the center the heavenly Christ is upon his throne of eternal victory and over the entire sarcophagus there is a calm peace, the peace which the early Christians wished for their deceased when they carved the words *in pace*.[16]

[16] Friedrich Gerke, *Der Sarkophag des Junius Bassus*. 1936.

IX

The Story of Ancient Churches

THE meeting places of the early Christians were in private homes. At Jerusalem the first disciples, being Jews, continued for a time to frequent the Temple (cf. Acts 3:1), but it was doomed to destruction in A.D. 70. In the Gentile world Paul at first went regularly to the synagogue to preach, but Christianity could not remain long within its confines (cf. Acts 13:5,14,45f., etc.). Having, therefore, no other meeting place of their own, the disciples perforce assembled in private houses. Wherever some Christian had the room and desire to invite his fellow believers to gather in his home for worship, there a "house church" arose.

The use of private homes for Christian assemblage is reflected clearly in various New Testament passages. An upper room in a private house in Jerusalem was used by Jesus and the twelve for the Last Supper (Mark 14:15), and the apostles later stayed in an upstairs room (Acts 1:13) in that city, while the house of Mary the mother of John Mark was a place where they gathered for prayer (Acts 12:12). Even so it is said that Saul "laid waste the church, and entering house after house, he dragged off men and women and committed them to prison" (Acts 8:3). When he himself as a Christian preacher was ejected from a synagogue, he frequently went to private homes instead. Paul's experience at Corinth may well have been typical of that which happened at many other places. He preached in the synagogue every Sabbath but his assertion that Jesus was the Christ met with contradiction and abuse, so finally he left the synagogue "and went to the house of a man named Titius Justus, a worshiper of God; his house was next door to the synagogue" (Acts 18:7). At Philippi, Lydia, who as a seller of purple may have been relatively well-to-do, made her house available for Paul and perhaps also for Christian meetings (Acts 16:14f.). At Troas the Christian gathering took place in an upper chamber (Acts 20:8), and at Caesarea the house of Philip the evangelist may have been the Christian center (Acts 21:8). At Rome Paul lived in his own rented house, and preached in it (Acts 28:30f.).

The references in Paul's letters are even more explicit. "Aquila and Prisca, together with the church in their house, send you hearty greetings" (I Corinthians 16:19). "Greet Prisca and Aquila . . . also the church in their house" (Romans 16:3, 5; cf. 14f.). "Give my greetings . . . to Nympha and the church in her house" (Colossians 4:15). "Paul . . . to Philemon . . . and the church in your house" (Philemon 1f.).

Eusebius mentions a tradition that up to the time of Hadrian's siege there existed in Jerusalem a very large Christian church which was constructed by the Jews.[1] Nothing else is known about this church, but it may have been a large assembly room in the house where the heads of the church lived.[2] In the account of the *Martyrdom of Justin Martyr* (d. A.D. c.165) it is related that Rusticus, the prefect of Rome, asked Justin in what place he had his followers assemble, and Justin replied that he lived with a certain Martinus, and that those who wished came there to him to hear his teaching.[3] Similarly, in the *Recognitions of Clement*[4] it is narrated that when Peter was in Tripoli large numbers of people wished to hear him preach. Upon his asking where there was a suitable place for discussion, a certain Maro offered his house saying, "I have a very spacious hall which can hold more than five hundred men, and there is also a garden within the house." "Then Peter said: 'Show me the hall, or the garden.' And when he had seen the hall, he went in to see the garden also; and suddenly the whole multitude, as if some one had called them, rushed into the house, and thence broke through into

---

[1] *Demonstratio Evangelica.* III, v, 108. ed. G. Dindorf, *Eusebii Caesariensis Opera.* (1867) III, p.188.

[2] J. W. Crowfoot, *Early Churches in Palestine.* 1941, p.1.

[3] *Martyrdom.* 2 (ANF I, p.305).

[4] A fictional work of the early fourth century, probably based upon an earlier and lost Clement romance of A.D. c.260, which describes a journey of Clement of Rome to Palestine where he met and talked at length with Peter and marvelously had his own long lost parents and brothers restored to him (hence the name, *Recognitions*). E. J. Goodspeed, *A History of Early Christian Literature.* 1942, p.127.

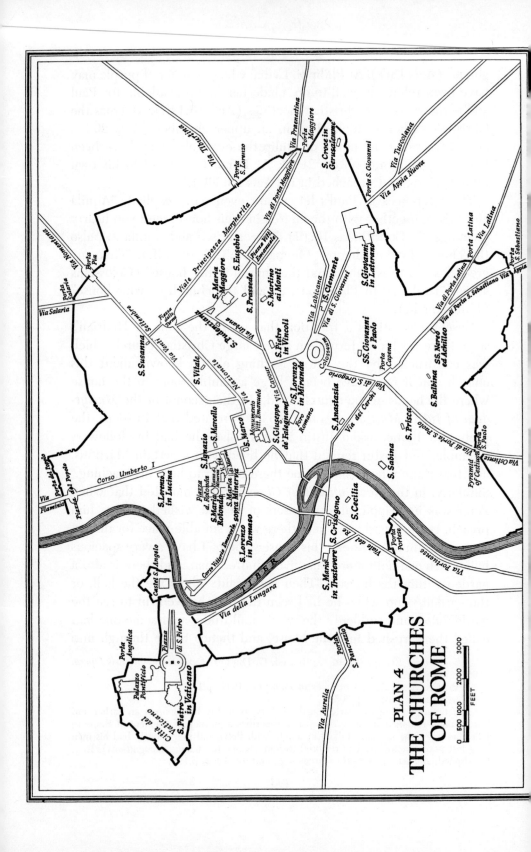

PLAN 4
THE CHURCHES
OF ROME

the garden where Peter was already standing, selecting a fit place for discussion."[5]

At this time we also hear of private houses set aside entirely for the work of the church. When Peter was in Antioch, according to the *Recognitions of Clement,* more than ten thousand men were baptized within seven days and thereupon "Theophilus, who was more exalted than all the men of power in that city, with all eagerness of desire consecrated the great palace of his house under the name of a church, and a chair was placed in it for the Apostle Peter by all the people; and the whole multitude assembled daily to hear the word."[6]

It is clear, therefore, that the earliest gathering places of the Christians were in private houses. Having no temple or synagogue of their own, they naturally made use of available rooms in their own homes. When concealment was necessary, as in time of persecution, such meeting places were inconspicuous and relatively secret. When conditions warranted, parts or even the whole of such residences might be dedicated entirely to church use and equipped and adorned for this purpose. Such were the meeting places of the early Christians, as we may reconstruct the situation from literary references.

1. DURA-EUROPOS

IT IS of great interest, therefore, that such an actual house church of the early Christians has now been discovered.[1] We must tell the story of it in some detail. The city of Dura-Europos lies in the Syrian desert on an immemorial caravan route beside the Euphrates. Here, on the site of an earlier settlement known by the Aramaic name of Dura, there was established around 300 B.C. a Seleucid fortress. This took place in the early part of the reign of Seleucus I Nicator, and although the colony was actually established by the king's governor general, Nicanor, Seleucus Nicator was regarded as the founder. Hence the place was renamed Europos after Europos in Macedon, the native city of Seleucus. In the second half of the second century B.C. Dura-Europos became a part of the Parthian Empire and in the years of Partho-Roman peace rose to be an important agricul-

---

[5] *Rec.* IV, 6 (ANF VIII, p.136).   [6] *Rec.* X, 71 (ANF VIII, p.210).

[1] We have already mentioned (p.364) the place at Pompeii where a Christian missionary may have preached, and the upper room at Herculaneum which may possibly have been a small Christian chapel.

tural and caravan city. Although it remained a Parthian city at this time, the prestige of Rome was high in Dura; also the influence of the famous city of Palmyra[2] nearly 150 miles to the west, situated in an oasis in the Syrian desert, was strongly felt. In the second century A.D. there was war between Parthia and Rome, and Dura was taken by the Romans and made a part of the province of Syria. The ancient fortress received a Roman garrison in A.D. 167 and was maintained as an important stronghold on the Euphrates frontier of the Roman Empire.

Yet the end was not far distant. It came in the third century when the Sasanian kings took the offensive against the Roman Empire. The troops of Ardashir (224-241) nearly captured Dura-Europos in A.D. 238, and the final siege came soon after 256. The exact date of the fall of Dura is unknown but it was probably just after the famous battle of Edessa (between 258 and 260), where the Roman emperor Valerian was taken prisoner (p.237) by the Sasanian king Shapur I (241-272). Dura was probably occupied for a short time by the Persians and then abandoned. It reverted swiftly to the desert, and on the expedition in which he was to die fighting against Shapur II (310-379) the Emperor Julian (361-363) hunted lions among its ruins. It was reserved for modern archeologists to rescue the city from oblivion.[3]

The first intimation of what might be waiting beneath the desert sand came by chance in 1921. The British army was operating against the Arabs, and in the course of digging trenches in the ruins of Dura some notable temple paintings came to light.[4] From 1928 on, a series of archeological expeditions was conducted at Dura by Yale University and the French Academy of Inscriptions and Letters under the general supervision of M. I. Rostovtzeff.[5] The house church with which we are concerned here was found in the season of 1931-1932, and the Jewish synagogue which also is to be mentioned came to light in 1932-1933.

[2] Palmyra is the Greek and Latin name of the city which is called Tadmar in the inscriptions of Tiglath-pileser I (ARAB I, §§287, 308). It is mentioned in II Chronicles 8:4 where Solomon is said to have built "Tadmor in the wilderness." But this passage is evidently based upon I Kings 9:18 which says that Solomon built "Tamar in the wilderness," a city in Judah (Ezekiel 47:19; 48:28). The Chronicler may have altered the name to Tadmor to increase the extent of Solomon's kingdom and heighten the glory of his achievements.

[3] M. I. Rostovtzeff, *Dura-Europos and its Art*. 1938, pp.10-30.

[4] J. H. Breasted, *Oriental Forerunners of Byzantine Painting, First-Century Wall Paintings from the Fortress of Dura on the Middle Euphrates*. 1924.

[5] Rostovtzeff, ed., *The Excavations at Dura-Europos*. 1929-.

THE SYNAGOGUE

As a striking air view (Fig. 178) made in 1932 shows, the city was surrounded by a wall against which the desert sand is now heaped heavily. The main gate of the city was on the west side where the wall faces the desert (at the left side of the photograph). A little distance north of this gate, with the city wall at its back and a street in front, was the synagogue.[6] This building was originally a private residence, and may have served as an informal synagogue even before being rebuilt. Later it was enlarged and made into a formal house of worship, this being under the presbytership of Samuel the priest, as an inscription states, and "in the year 556 which is the second year of Philip Caesar." The date is given in the Seleucid era (p.245) and corresponds to A.D. 245. Some years later this building was replaced by a new synagogue, which seems to have been opened for services in about 253, although at that time it was not yet entirely finished. The completion of the synagogue probably was in 255, when the frescoes were added. This was only a very few years before the destruction of Dura.[7]

One entered the synagogue through a courtyard on the east and came into a room of approximately twenty-five by forty feet in size, along the walls of which were benches for the worshipers. The orientation was toward the west, and in the middle of the west wall was a niche where the Ark of the Law was placed during the services. The walls were adorned from top to bottom with paintings, many of which are well preserved and have been removed to Damascus. Around the niche just mentioned are a representation of the shrine in which the Law was kept, a seven-branched lampstand, an ethrog and lulab on the left, and a picture of Abraham's Sacrifice of Isaac on the right. Abraham stands with his back to the viewer, holding a knife in his right hand. Isaac is bound on the altar, but a hand symbolizes the intervention of God and a ram is waiting by the bush behind Abraham. Other wall paintings include scenes from the life of Moses, the Exodus, the Return of the Ark, Ezekiel's Vision of the Valley of Dry Bones, the Story of Job, and other subjects. These subjects seem to have been chosen to illustrate from a variety of incidents the covenant relationship between God and his people as

[6] A. R. Bellinger, F. E. Brown, A. Perkins, and C. B. Welles, *The Excavations at Dura-Europos conducted by Yale University and the French Academy of Inscriptions and Letters.* Final Report VIII, Part I, *The Synagogue,* by Carl H. Kraeling with contributions by C. C. Torrey, C. B. Welles, and B. Geiger. 1956.

[7] AJA 47 (1943), p.335.

it was established with Abraham and as it was yet to be fulfilled in a future messianic era.[8]

The painting of the Return of the Ark (I Samuel 5f.) shows five lords of the Philistines sending away the ark upon a cart drawn by two oxen, while the Philistine temple stands in the background (Fig. 179). Strewn upon the ground are holy vessels, musical instruments, and the broken images not of Dagon but of the principal Palmyrene gods which were worshiped in Dura.[9] In the picture of the story of Job one of the friends rides to visit the afflicted man, and it is at first surprising to note that the friend is represented in kingly splendor. The explanation is found in a midrash which evidently was familiar to the Jews of Dura and which states explicitly that the three friends of Job were kings. A careful comparison of the Vision of Ezekiel, the Finding of Moses, and the Visit to Job in these paintings, and in corresponding miniature paintings in later Christian illustrated manuscripts, has shown that both must go back to an earlier and common Jewish source.[10] Thus again the dependence of early Christian art upon Jewish art is suggested.

THE CHRISTIAN CHURCH

The Christian church was on the same street as the synagogue but to the south of the main city gate. Like the synagogue, it had once been a private house. Probably this house belonged to a citizen of some means and standing for it was somewhat larger than the average home at Dura. Otherwise, however, it conformed in its original plan exactly to the customary arrangement of a private residence at Dura. From the street one entered by a little vestibule which turned into an inner paved court. Around this court was a series of rooms, while a covered stairway led to the flat roof which

---

[8] Kraeling, *The Synagogue* (*The Excavations at Dura-Europos*, Final Report VIII, Part I), p.357. Rachel Wischnitzer (*The Messianic Theme in the Paintings of the Dura Synagogue*. 1948) interprets the paintings as animated by the messianic idea of return, restoration, and salvation, and thinks that the Jews of Dura considered themselves descendants of the Lost Ten Tribes. See also Comte du Mesnil du Buisson in *L'Illustration*. 185 (July 1933), pp.454-457; Marcel Aubert in *Gazette des Beaux-Arts*. 6e période. 20 (1938), pp.1-24; Sukenik, *Ancient Synagogues in Palestine and Greece*, pp.82-85; Jacob Leveen, *The Hebrew Bible in Art* (The Schweich Lectures of the British Academy, 1939). 1944, pp.22-65; James A. Fischer in CBQ 17 (1955), pp.189-195; Kurt Weitzmann in AJA 61 (1957), pp.89f.

[9] Comte du Mesnil du Buisson in *Gazette des Beaux-Arts*. 6e période. 14 (1935 2e semestre), pp.25-203; Lietzmann, *Geschichte der alten Kirche*. II, pp.35f. For the temple of the Palmyrene gods in Dura cf. Otto Eissfeldt in *Der Alte Orient*. 40 (1941), pp.134-139.

[10] Gitta Wodtke in ZNW 34 (1935), pp.51-62.

was over fifteen feet high. When the house was being built, or soon afterward, someone pressed into the plaster a graffito which supplies the date of the building, the year A.D. 232-233.

One of the rooms in the house was used, probably from the first, as a Christian chapel. A few years later two other rooms were thrown together to provide a larger meeting place, accommodating about one hundred people and having an elevated rostrum at one end for the speaker. From this time on the larger part of the build-ing, or perhaps all of it, was employed openly and entirely as a church.[11] Of its Christian use there can be no doubt. Three graffiti read, "One God in heaven," "Remind Christ of Proclus among your-selves" (TON XN IN YMEIN MNHCKECΘ[E . . .]OKΛOY), and "Remind Christ of the humble Siseos" (TON XPIC[12] MNHCKETE CICEON TON TAΠINON), the two latter being requests that Proclus and Siseos should be remembered by the congregation in prayer. The greatest interest attaches to the small room known as the chapel. At its west end is a niche set against the wall with an arched roof resting on pillars. This contains a sunken receptacle which may have been a baptismal font.[13] Like the baptistery in the later church at Kaoussie (pp.540f.), this was too small to have permitted the prac-tice of immersion, and if it was really a baptistery it must be as-sumed that the rite was performed by affusion. Since the more general custom among the early Christians was that of immersion,[14] other explanations have been sought such as that this was the tomb of a martyr.[15]

The chapel was decorated with wall paintings in a fashion very similar to that of the synagogue.[16] At the back of the niche just men-tioned are two paintings, the lower depicting Adam and Eve, the upper showing the Good Shepherd. Adam and Eve stand with the tree between them as in similar representations in the West. The

---

[11] *Preliminary Report of Fifth Season of Work October 1931-March 1932 of the Excavations at Dura-Europos conducted by Yale University and the French Academy of Inscriptions and Letters*, pp.237-252 "The Christian Church" by C. Hopkins.

[12] The abbreviation XPIC is unusual (*Preliminary Report of Fifth Season of Work*, p.285), but for a parallel see M. Avi-Yonah, *Abbreviations in Greek Inscriptions* (*The Near East, 200 B.C.-A.D. 1100*) in QDAP Supplement to vol. 9 (1940), p.112.

[13] C. Hopkins in *Preliminary Report of Fifth Season of Work*, pp.249-252; Ros-tovtzeff, *Dura-Europos and its Art*, p.131.

[14] cf. Tertullian, *On Baptism. 7* (ANF III, p.672); Kenneth Scott Latourette, *A History of the Expansion of Christianity.* I (1937), p.259.

[15] P. V. C. Baur in *Preliminary Report of Fifth Season of Work*, p.255.

[16] *Preliminary Report of Fifth Season of Work*, pp.254-283 "The Paintings in the Christian Chapel" by P. V. C. Baur.

Good Shepherd carries a huge ram on his shoulders in the manner with which we are familiar, but whereas in Rome he usually stands in a symmetrical composition between his sheep, here he stands behind his flock. The placing of these two scenes together evidently is meant to show that through Adam came death but through Christ came salvation.

The south wall of the chapel is broken by two doors which give access to the room. Between these two doors and under an arched niche is a painting of David and Goliath, the two characters being identified by their names which are written on in Greek. Goliath is misspelled Golitha. While this scene could be regarded as representing the familiar theme of deliverance (cf. I Samuel 17:37), it does not otherwise occur frequently in early Christian art. At the west end of the same wall the Samaritan woman is shown grasping a rope with both hands to raise a pail from the mouth of a well. Doubtless for lack of space the figure of Christ does not appear. The coiffure of the Samaritan woman is like that of Julia Soaemias who was killed at the same time as her son Elagabalus in A.D. 222, and confirms a date early in the third century for these paintings. In the upper register on the same wall was another scene now so badly damaged that only the traces of a garden can be recognized.

The pictures on the north wall were placed most conspicuously opposite the two entrances to the chapel. In the lower register is a scene showing a structure which has been called a huge sarcophagus and beside which are at least three women. This has been interpreted as a representation of the women at the sepulcher of Christ (cf. Mark 16:1).[17] The coiffure of the two women whose heads still appear in the painting is the same as that used by Julia Mamaea and Orbiana, the mother and wife respectively of the Emperor Severus Alexander (222-235). In the upper register on the north wall are two scenes. On the right is the Miracle of the Lake (Matthew 14:24-31). In a ship which is plowing through the water are seated several men. They look out to sea with gestures of astonishment at two figures walking on the water. Peter is sinking. Christ is walking toward him with outstretched hand which Peter is about to grasp. Christ is clad in a tunic, but the head and shoulders of the figure are destroyed. The figure of Peter, who is shown

---

[17] It has also been suggested that the same painting may have been continued on the east wall of the room, and that it may have portrayed the parable of the Wise and Foolish Virgins (Joseph Pijoan in AB 19 [1937], pp.592-595).

with beard and thick curly hair, is well preserved and of much interest since it is the earliest representation of that apostle now known.

To the left of the foregoing scene and with no line of demarcation, is the picture (Fig. 180) of the Healing of the Paralytic (Mark 2:1-12). The sick man lies at full length on his left side on a small bed. The bed has a coverlet with red fringes and the man is dressed in a yellow tunic outlined in brown. Above the bed stands Jesus, clothed in tunic and mantle, and in the act of reaching out his right hand toward the paralytic. The second act in the drama is shown at one side. The sick man, now healed, is walking away. He has turned his bed upside down and is carrying it upon his back, holding it by the crisscross lacing. In the West the Healing of the Paralytic is a subject frequently employed, as we have seen (p.481), but the first part of the scene with Christ standing over the bed is usually omitted and only the sequel shown in which the man walks away with his bed. Also in the West the bed is carried with its legs hanging down. The illustration at Dura is of special interest because the picture of Christ is one of the two oldest such representations now known. The almost destroyed painting of Christ in the Catacomb of Priscilla at Rome (pp.466f. and Fig. 160) probably belongs, as we have seen, to the middle of the second century. The painting at Dura is dated even more definitely in the first part of the third century. In both pictures Christ is shown as a young and beardless man with short hair and wearing the ordinary costume of the day. These and similar portrayals are the earliest type of Christ as far as is now known in early Christian art.[18] Later in the third century Christ appears still as youthful but with long, curly hair, and from the fourth century on the more familiar bearded type appears.[19]

Such was the gathering place of the Christians in Dura and similar to this, doubtless, were many other house churches throughout the Roman Empire during the early centuries of Christianity's life.

2. EARLY CHURCHES AT ROME

AT THE same time that the Christians of Dura were meeting in the house church just described, many Christians in Rome were assem-

[18] cf. L. von Sybel, *Christliche Antike.* I, pp.225, 229, 233.

[19] On the representation of Christ in early Christian art see Johannes Kollwitz, *Das Christusbild des dritten Jahrhunderts.* 1953; and in KRAC III, cols. 1-24.

bling in private buildings which had been transferred to the church for the purpose of public worship. In Rome almost all of these later disappeared beneath new buildings by which they were replaced, but for centuries each of these churches continued to be designated by the name or *titulus* of its former owner and founder. For this reason they are called "title churches." Of the twenty-five churches which are known to have had this designation, eighteen are earlier than Constantine and the majority of these probably go back at least as far as to the middle of the third century or to around the time of the Dura house church.[1]

SAN CLEMENTE

As an example of one of these title churches in Rome we may turn to San Clemente, which according to tradition was built on the site originally occupied by the house of Clement I who suffered martyrdom around A.D. 100. San Clemente is now on the modern Via di San Giovanni, running from the Colosseum to the Lateran, but once stood in the middle of an *insula* or block of buildings, fronting on a public road and with more distant streets on the other three sides. From the Via di San Giovanni one descends a few steps to the level of the present church. This is a structure which was consecrated in 1108 by Pope Paschal II and has been restored frequently since. It is a building oriented on an east-west axis, with a nave ending in a semicircular apse, and flanked by two side aisles likewise terminating in apses. In front is an atrium of oblong shape, surrounded by colonnaded porticoes.

Beneath this church Prior Mulhooly (d.1880) discovered in 1852 a second and older basilica. Like the church above, it was divided by rows of columns into a nave and two aisles. The nave ended in an apse, and in front of the church was an atrium. This lower church was a grander structure than the building afterward superimposed, its nave being as wide as the upper church's nave and right aisle combined. This lower church was probably constructed around A.D. 390.

In turn, beneath this church are the remains of still older Roman buildings. The Roman structure under the main section of the lower church was a rectangular edifice, constructed of heavy tufa blocks, and probably was a part of some public building. It is believed to date from the end of the first or beginning of the second century.

[1] Lietzmann, *Geschichte der alten Kirche.* ii, p.256.

Behind this public building and separated from it only by a narrow passage, a large private house was built. The latter is to be dated probably not before the middle of the second century. At a later time, perhaps in the second quarter of the third century, the inner courtyard of this house was transformed into a Mithraeum, or chapel in which Mithras was worshiped.[2]

In approximately the third quarter of the third century, a new brick house was erected above the tufa edifice. It was a large building and contained an extensive hall on the ground floor. This hall was divided by rows of supports in a longitudinal direction, and opened in a series of wide apertures on both sides onto the exterior level. Later this last house was transformed into the existing lower basilica, in which a portion of the adjoining building, where the Mithraeum had been, was also incorporated. This rebuilding involved piercing the west wall of the house with the large hall and constructing an apse which projected into the neighboring house, adding a narthex and atrium at the east end, and erecting two rows of columns in the interior, thus making a nave and two aisles.

The complicated architectural history just outlined is of much interest because it enables us to show clearly that the fourth-century basilica of San Clemente was preceded by a third-century house in which there was a large ground-floor hall appropriate for public gatherings. It is very probable, therefore, that the third-century building was the meeting place of the Christian community before the lower basilica came into being. Whether the house and hall were constructed by the Christians from the very beginning or only purchased by them to serve as a place of meeting, remains uncertain. But at any rate in this hall, which evidently was arranged for relatively large Christian gatherings, we see an important transitional stage between the simple homes in which the earlier believers met and the large basilicas in which the later Christians were privileged to worship.[3]

[2] At Ostia, the remains of seven such Mithraea have been found (Baedeker, *Rome.* 16th ed., p.540).

[3] Richard Krautheimer, *Corpus Basilicarum Christianarum Romae.* I, 2 (1937), pp.117-136; E. Junyent, *Il titolo di San Clemente in Roma.* 1932, p.23, Fig. 1; Louis Nolan, *The Basilica of San Clemente in Rome.* 4th ed. 1934.

3. YEARS OF PERSECUTION AND
YEARS OF PEACE

IN THE same period in which the hall church just described was in use in Rome, many other buildings were probably being erected throughout the empire for Christian assembly. Christianity underwent bitter persecutions in the time of Decius (A.D. 250) and Valerian (A.D. 257-258), but in A.D. 261 the Emperor Gallienus granted toleration in an edict which permitted the Christians again to use their places of worship and their cemeteries and provided that no one should molest them.[1] The final and terrible persecution of Diocletian (A.D. 303) was yet to come, but in the more than forty years intervening Christianity attracted great masses of people, and for their accommodation in services of worship it was necessary to erect buildings specifically planned as churches. This situation is explicitly indicated by Eusebius in the following words: "But how can anyone describe those vast assemblies, and the multitude that crowded together in every city, and the famous gatherings in the houses of prayer; by reason of which not being satisfied with the ancient buildings they erected from the foundation large churches in all the cities?"[2] In connection with an isolated case of martyrdom which took place at this same time, Eusebius incidentally mentions "the church" at Caesarea.[3]

DIOCLETIAN

Over these churches which sprang up during the relatively peaceful last four decades of the third century, a devastating storm was soon to break. This was the great persecution of Diocletian, who ruled in the East as Augustus, Galerius Caesar being his subordinate colleague and Nicomedia his capital. It was largely at the instigation of Galerius that the blow was planned. At dawn on February 23, 303, officers appeared before the Christian church in Nicomedia. The gates were forced open, the church pillaged and the Bibles burned. The church was situated on rising ground within view of the imperial palace where Diocletian and Galerius were standing, watching. Galerius wished to have the building set on fire, but Diocletian feared that the fire might spread to other parts of the city, so

---

[1] Eusebius, *Ch. Hist.* vii, xiii (cf. above p.484 n.1).
[2] *Ch. Hist.* viii, i, 5.
[3] *Ch. Hist.* vii, xv, 4.

the Praetorian Guards were sent with axes and other instruments of iron, "and having been let loose everywhere, they in a few hours levelled that very lofty edifice to the ground."[4] On the next day an edict went out which was published everywhere. It not only deprived the Christians of all legal rights and called for the burning of the Scriptures but also commanded that the churches should be levelled to the ground.[5] Eusebius was living in Caesarea at this time and gives an eyewitness account of the persecution as it was carried out in Palestine. "We saw with our own eyes the houses of prayer thrown down to the very foundations,"[6] he says, and goes on to tell of the burning of Bibles and the torturing and slaying of martyrs.[7]

How many churches were destroyed before Galerius terminated the persecutions with an edict signed on his deathbed we do not know. Doubtless they were many. If, perchance, some did not fall before the storm they were ultimately replaced by later structures so that they, too, disappeared from sight. Of all the church buildings whose existence we infer in the latter years of the third century, scarcely a trace now survives.[8]

CONSTANTINE

It is first from the time of the Emperor Constantine and the true peace of the church that abundant and material evidence remains concerning early Christian churches. When Constantine and his eastern colleague, Licinius, issued the Edict of Milan in A.D. 313, full legal standing was granted to Christianity, and all confiscated church buildings and properties were returned. The churches which had been destroyed were now rebuilt and new ones were erected, all on a grander scale than had been known hitherto. "We saw," says Eusebius, "every place which shortly before had been desolated by the impieties of the tyrants reviving as if from a long and death-fraught pestilence, and temples again rising from their foundations

---

[4] This account is given by Lactantius, who was a teacher of rhetoric in Nicomedia at this time and therefore an eyewitness. It is found in his book entitled *Of the Manner in Which the Persecutors Died* (12), in which he shows the evil end to which all of the emperors came, from Nero on, who persecuted the Christians.

[5] Lactantius, *Of the Manner in Which the Persecutors Died*. 13; Eusebius, *Ch. Hist.* viii, ii, 4 = *Martyrs of Palestine*, Intro.

[6] *Ch. Hist.* viii, ii, 1.

[7] *Martyrs of Palestine* (a separate work, later appended to Bk. viii of the *Church History*).

[8] Lietzmann, *Geschichte der alten Kirche*. iii (1938), p.43.

to an immense height, and receiving a splendor far greater than that of the old ones which had been destroyed."[9]

THE CATHEDRAL AT TYRE

On the rubbish-covered site of an earlier church at Tyre, a new and elegant cathedral was erected, at the dedication of which around A.D. 316 Eusebius himself delivered an oration. From this address we can gain some idea of the church. The area in which it stood was enclosed by a wall and the main entrance was through a vestibule on the east. Between the outer entrance and the church building proper was a colonnaded court open to the sky with a fountain in the middle. Triple doors gave access to the church itself, which was paved with marble and roofed with cedar. Adjacent to the church were additional rooms and buildings, probably including a baptistery.[10]

THE "BASILICA"

The church at Tyre was evidently built on the plan characteristic of most of the great churches of the fourth and fifth centuries and to which the name basilica is given. The word "basilica" refers literally to a kingly hall,[11] and was therefore applied to a building of grandeur, but came to have a meaning almost as broad as our simple word, hall. Greek and Roman law courts, markets, and meeting halls all were occasionally known by this term basilica (cf. p.376).[12] But the private houses of the Greeks and Romans[13] and the synagogues of the Jews[14] also often exhibited the rectangular, colonnaded form which is the chief characteristic of the basilica and, as we have seen, it is most probably out of such backgrounds that Christian meeting places were developed.[15]

In its most distinctive Christian development the basilica had some or all of the following features. It might stand, as at Tyre, in an area surrounded by a wall or *peribolos*. Also as at Tyre, the entrance was often through a colonnaded court or *atrium*, which

---

[9] *Ch. Hist.* x, ii, 1.
[10] *Ch. Hist.* x, iv, 37-45.　[11] βασιλική i.e. στοά.
[12] Sartell Prentice, *The Heritage of the Cathedral.* 1936, pp.19-28.
[13] Lowrie, *Monuments of the Early Church*, pp.97-101.
[14] Kohl and Watzinger, *Antike Synagogen in Galiläa*, p.219.
[15] For the basilica see H. Leclercq in DACL II, cols. 525-602; E. Langlotz and Fr. W. Deichmann in KRAC I, cols. 1225-1259; *Kunst-Chronik* (Zentralinstitut für Kunstgeschichte). 4 (1951), pp.97-121; L. H. Vincent in *Quantulacumque*, pp.55-70; J. G. Davies, *The Origin and Development of Early Christian Church Architecture.* 1953; cf. H. R. Willoughby in *Religion in Life.* Summer 1953, pp.473-475.

178. Air View of Dura-Europos

179. The Ark Reclaimed from the Philistines

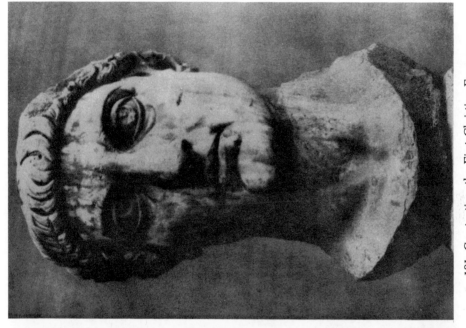

181. Constantine, the First Christian Emperor

180. The Healing of the Paralytic

182. San Pietro in Vaticano, Rome

183. Canopy over the Altar, San Pietro

184. San Paolo fuori le Mura, Rome

185. San Paolo fuori le Mura, Interior

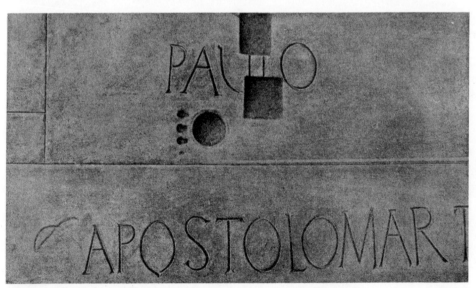

186. The Marble Slab over the Tomb of Paul

187. Apse Mosaic in Santa Pudenziana

188. The Taking of Jericho

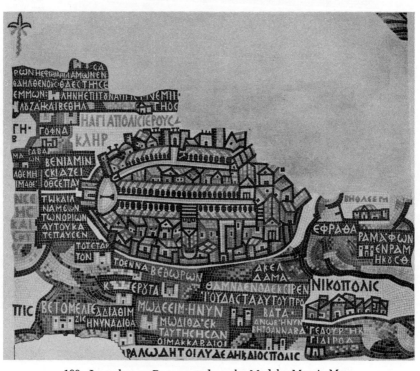

189. Jerusalem as Represented on the Madeba Mosaic Map

190. The Church of the Holy Sepulcher, Jerusalem

191. The Church of the Nativity, Bethlehem

192. Interior of the Church of the Nativity

193. Early Mosaic in the Church of the Nativity

195. Mosaic in the Church of the Prophets,
Apostles and Martyrs at Gerasa

194. Mosaic in the Church of the Loaves
and Fishes at et-Tabgha

196. Air View of the Ruins of the Church at Kaoussie

197. Ruins of the Martyrion at Seleucia Pieria

198. Mosaic in the Martyrion at Seleucia Pieria

199. The West Door of the Church of St. Simeon Stylites

201. A Flask of St. Menas

202. The Baptistery at the Church of St. Menas

200. The Crypt in the Church of St. Menas

203. The Church of Hagia Sophia at Istanbul

204. Interior of Hagia Sophia

protected the worshipers from the noise of the streets and contained the fountain (*cantharus*) where the hands were washed symbolically before entering.[16] The basilica proper was a long, rectangular hall, which might be entered through a vestibule or *narthex*. The main, longitudinal area within the basilica was known as the *nave*, a word probably derived from the Latin word for ship (*navis*), to which the church was often likened. On each side of the nave were one or two rows of columns, which formed side aisles. These aisles had relatively low roofs, while the roof of the nave was much higher. The part of the nave which rises clear of the lower roofs of the side aisles is known as the *clerestory* and its walls were pierced with windows for lighting the central part of the basilica's interior. The nave and aisles were the parts occupied by the laity, and movable seats or benches were presumably provided for them here. At its far end the nave opened into the *apse*, which was a semicircular recess, usually covered by a half dome. Between the nave and apse there might be a *transept* or cross aisle. If the latter projected beyond the side aisles it gave the church the form of a cross. The great arch above the half dome of the apse is known as the triumphal arch, and where there was a transept another triumphal arch might separate it from the nave. The part of the church formed by the transept and apse was reserved for the clergy and might be called the *presbyterium*. Low screens sometimes separated it from the rest of the church. They were known in Latin as *cancelli* and later the presbyterium itself was called the *chancel*. There might also be a row of columns standing in front of the presbyterium for adornment. The altar, usually a relatively simple table of wood or stone, stood in the center of the transept or in the apse. If the church was built above the grave of a martyr the altar if possible was placed directly above the holy tomb, and in case this lay at some depth beneath the ground was connected with it by a vertical shaft. To the chamber around the tomb, and the shaft connecting it with the altar, the name *confessio* is applied. The altar might be further dignified by a *ciborium*, or roof erected over it on four columns. The clergy sat behind the altar, on benches running around the wall of the semicircular apse. In the center and raised above the presbyters' seats was the *cathedra*, or official chair in which the bishop sat and from which he preached.[17] An *ambon*

---

[16] Lowrie, *Monuments of the Early Church*, p.179.

[17] The famous statue of Hippolytus (d. after A.D. 235), which was probably made

or pulpit in the nave was used for the scripture reading, and sometimes the sermon was preached from it, too, in order for the speaker
to be nearer the people. The baptistery was usually a small, separate
building in the center of which was a round or octagonal pool (*fons*
or *piscina*), entered by a flight of steps, for the act of immersion.[18]
Other structures, too, might be grouped around the church, including chapels, hospices, baths, hospitals, or schools.

In exterior appearance the basilica ordinarily was very plain,
although it was decorated occasionally with mosaic on the façade
or, as in Syria, was developed impressively with single and double
towers. Within, however, the basilica was often richly adorned. A
marble incrustation (*opus sectile*) was frequently applied to the
lower portion of the walls, while on the upper walls of the nave,
on the triumphal arch, and in the half dome of the apse were often
placed the most beautiful representations in mosaic. This was fitting,
since the essential purpose of the basilica was fulfilled in its interior.
There the congregation felt itself a unity, and the thoughts of all
were led forward to the place where the Lord's table stood and
where the gospel was preached.

A mention of such a basilica and a description of the worship
of the Christians within it, is found in the *Apostolic Constitutions*,
written about A.D. 380. It compares the church to a ship and reads
in part as follows:

"Let the building be long, with its head to the east,[19] with its vestries
on both sides at the east end, and so it will be like a ship. In the middle
let the bishop's throne be placed, and on each side of him let the presbytery sit down; and let the deacons stand near at hand, with closely girt
garments, for they are like the mariners and managers of the ship. In
accordance with their arrangement, let the laity sit on the other side,
with all quietness and good order. And let the women sit by themselves,
they also keeping silence. In the middle, let the reader stand upon some
high place: let him read the books of Moses . . . and the Epistles of Paul
. . . and the Gospels. . . . In the next place, let the presbyters one by one,
not all together, exhort the people, and the bishop in the last place, as
being the commander. Let the porters stand at the entrances of the men
and give heed to them, while the deaconesses stand at those of the

---

soon after his death and is now in the Lateran Museum, shows this Roman church
leader seated upon such a chair.

[18] H. Leclercq in DACL II, cols. 382-469; F. W. Deichmann in KRAC I, cols. 1157-
1167.

[19] This rule calling for the orientation of the apse toward the east, was frequently
but by no means always followed.

women, like shipmen. . . . But if anyone be found sitting out of his place, let him be rebuked by the deacon, as a manager of the foreship, and removed into the place proper for him; for the church is not only like a ship, but also like a sheepfold. For as the shepherds place all the brute creatures distinctly . . . so is it to be in the church. Let the young men sit by themselves, if there be a place for them, but if not let them stand upright. Let those already advanced in years sit in order and let the children stand beside their mothers and fathers. Let the younger women also sit by themselves if there be a place for them but if not let them stand behind the elder women. Let those women who are married and have children be placed by themselves, while the virgins and the widows and the elderwomen stand or sit before all the rest. Let the deacon be the disposer of the places, that every one of those that comes in may go to his proper place and not sit at the entrance. In like manner let the deacon oversee the people that nobody may whisper nor slumber nor laugh nor nod, for all ought in the church to stand wisely and soberly and attentively, having their attention fixed upon the word of the Lord. After this, let all rise up with one consent and looking towards the east, after the catechumens and penitents are gone out, pray to God eastward. . . . As to the deacons, after the prayer is over, let some of them attend upon the oblation of the eucharist, ministering to the Lord's body with fear. Let others of them watch the multitude and keep them silent. But let that deacon who is at the high priest's hand say to the people, Let no one have any quarrel against another; let no one come in hypocrisy. Then let the men give the men, and the women give the women, the Lord's kiss. . . . After this let the deacon pray for the whole church, for the whole world. . . . Let the bishop pray for the people. . . . After this let the sacrifice follow, the people standing and praying silently; and when the oblation has been made, let every rank by itself partake of the Lord's body and precious blood in order, and approach with reverence and holy fear, as to the body of their king. Let the women approach with their heads covered, as is becoming the order of women; but let the door be watched, lest any unbeliever, or one not yet initiated, come in."[20]

4. CHURCHES IN ROME

THE BASILICAS OF CONSTANTINE

THE most famous basilicas of the fourth century were built by Constantine, who after his victory over Licinius and the death of the latter in A.D. 324 and until his own death in A.D. 337 was sole ruler of the Roman Empire. His political and military position was so secure that he could personally devote much time and interest to

[20] II, 57 (ANF VII, pp.421f.); cf. E. H. Short, *A History of Religious Architecture.* 1936, p.65.

religious matters, including the building of great churches. A letter which he directed at this time to all the bishops in the various provinces has been preserved by Eusebius in which the emperor urged "all to be zealous in their attention to the buildings of the churches, and either to repair or enlarge those which at present exist, or, in cases of necessity, to erect new ones."[1] The bishops were authorized to request whatever was needful for the work from the provincial governors, to whom corresponding instructions were sent. "In every province," states Eusebius, "he [Constantine] raised new churches on a far more imposing scale than those which had existed before his time."[2] The personal appearance of this benefactor of early Christianity is seen in Fig. 181, this being the head of a colossal statue which once stood in the Basilica of Constantine in the Roman Forum.

A list of the churches which Constantine erected in Rome is given in the Liber Pontificalis. This list forms a part of the biography of Sylvester who was pope (314-335) at the time of Constantine's reign. Since Sylvester was the thirty-fourth Head of the Roman Church, his biography constitutes Chapter 34 of the Liber Pontificalis. While the text of the Liber Pontificalis dates from the seventh century (p.382 n.20), the notices which are numerous from the time of Sylvester on, concerning churches built or repaired and gifts offered for them, must often have been copied directly from memoranda and records in the papal archives. In particular the list of Constantine's churches and donations gives evidence of genuineness although there is some corruption in the text, as for example where the proper names occasionally become unintelligible.[3]

SAN PIETRO IN VATICANO

The holiest sites upon which churches could be erected at Rome were the graves of Peter and Paul, and the Liber Pontificalis records that Constantine founded basilicas at both of these places. The location of the graves at the Vatican and on the Ostian Way has been discussed already, and also the probable temporary transfer of the remains to Catacumbas in A.D. 258 (pp.382-384, 471-474). When peace came to the church, suitable memorials could be erected in

---

[1] *Life of Constantine.* II, 46.

[2] *ibid.*, III, 47. For the materials in Eusebius relative to the church buildings of Constantine see Ludwig Voelkl in RAC 29 (1953), pp.49-66.

[3] LLP pp.xvii-xviii.

the form of fine basilicas. Concerning the first of these two buildings the Liber Pontificalis records:

"At the same time Constantine Augustus built by the request of Silvester, the bishop, the basilica of blessed Peter, the apostle, in the shrine of Apollo, and laid there the coffin with the body of the holy Peter; the coffin itself he enclosed on all sides with bronze, which is unchangeable: at the head 5 feet, at the feet 5 feet, at the right side 5 feet, at the left side 5 feet, underneath 5 feet and overhead 5 feet: thus he enclosed the body of blessed Peter, the apostle, and laid it away.

"And above he set porphyry columns for adornment and other spiral columns which he brought from Greece.

"He made also a vaulted roof in the basilica, gleaming with polished gold, and over the body of the blessed Peter, above the bronze which enclosed it, he set a cross of purest gold weighing 150 lbs. . . . and upon it were inscribed these words: 'CONSTANTINE AUGUSTUS AND HELENA AUGUSTA THIS HOUSE SHINING WITH LIKE ROYAL SPLENDOR A COURT SURROUNDS,' inscribed in enamelled letters upon the cross."

A list follows of the precious vessels and revenues which Constantine bestowed upon the church.[4]

Constantine's basilica stood until it was destroyed by the popes of the Renaissance to make way for the present Church of St. Peter. In those intervening centuries it was altered somewhat and much added to, but seems basically to have preserved its original structure. Thus, while little now remains of Constantine's original church its essential character can be surmised from sketches and descriptions of the building as it stood in the Middle Ages. A flight of steps led up to a propylaeum which gave access to a large atrium. This court was surrounded by colonnades and had a fountain in the center. The basilica was entered by five doors and divided into nave and two aisles on either side. The columns in the church had been taken from ancient monuments and their bases, shafts, and capitals were varied in size and style. The Constantinian origin of the building was shown plainly when the apse was finally demolished, for the emperor's stamp was on its bricks. The mosaic which at that time still was on the triumphal arch, showing Constantine offering a model of the church to Christ, probably also dated from the original basilica.[5] On the arch, Constantine's inscription addressed to Christ read: "Because, led by thee, the world rises triumphant to the stars, Constantine, victorious, built this hall for thee."[6]

[4] LLP pp.53f.
[5] A. L. Frothingham, *The Monuments of Christian Rome.* 1908, pp.25-27.
[6] E. Diehl, *Inscriptiones latinae christianae veteres.* I (1925), No.1752.

In the course of the fourth and fifth centuries a baptistery was added in the right arm of the transept, the atrium was paved, a mosaic was placed on the façade[7] and the church was connected with Hadrian's mausoleum and bridge by an arcaded boulevard. Many subsidiary buildings grew up around the basilica and eventually an entire suburb surrounded it. In the barbarian invasions Alaric king of the Goths (410) and Genseric king of the Vandals (455) ordered that the Church of St. Peter should be spared, and it also escaped damage in the siege by the Lombards (756). But in the Saracen invasion in 846 it suffered damage and, after that, Pope Leo IV (847-855) built for its protection the so-called Leonine Wall around the basilica and the Vatican hill.

By the time of Pope Nicholas V (1447-1455) Constantine's basilica was leaning badly to one side and generally falling into ruin. It was decided that the old church would have to be torn down and a new one built upon its site. The new structure was designed by Bramante and the first stone laid in 1506. The work was carried forward in following years under the direction of Raphael (1514) and Michelangelo (1546). Dedication was in 1626.

As it stands today the Basilica di San Pietro in Vaticano is the largest church in the world. Its interior is 609 feet in length and its area is about 163,200 square feet. The great dome, which is its crowning glory, is 138 feet in diameter and rises to a height of 405 feet. At an early time the subterranean tomb of Peter was made inaccessible to protect it from marauders and when the old basilica was demolished and the new one built the tomb was not molested. Bramante's plan, indeed, called for moving the tomb in order to give the new church a different orientation, but Pope Julius II (1503-1513) refused to allow this to be done. In 1594, when the present high altar was being built by Pope Clement VIII, it is said that the bottom of the shaft leading to the grave was laid open but that the pope immediately ordered the opening to be filled up again.[8] Through one unblocked place, Hartmann Grisar is said to have caught a glimpse, in 1895, of an ancient marble slab, then broken in half, but presumably still in place over the tomb.[9]

---

[7] Repair or decoration of the basilica by Leo I (440-461) is mentioned in the Liber Pontificalis (see below p.517) and the mosaic on the façade is known to have borne a dedicatory inscription concerning a restoration by the praetorian prefect Marinianus and his wife Anastasia at Leo's request.

[8] LLP p.53 n.3.

[9] E. Pucci in EB XXIII, p.5.

In front of the church, in the center of the piazza, stands the great obelisk which Caligula brought from Heliopolis to adorn the *spina* of his Circus. The presumed original location of the obelisk in the Circus is still marked by a stone in the small Piazza del Circo Neroniano, just south of St. Peter's. The obelisk was moved to its present site by Xystus V in 1586. The two semicircular colonnades which now beautify the sides of the elliptical piazza were erected by Bernini in 1657-1663 (Fig. 182).

Bernini also designed (1633) the imposing *baldacchino* or bronze canopy which rises to a height of 95 feet over the high altar in St. Peter's. It will be remembered (p.511) that above the tomb of Peter, Constantine set porphyry columns and other spiral columns. Apparently the porphyry columns supported the ciborium above the altar, while the spiral columns formed a colonnade separating the *confessio* from the nave. Several of the spiral columns still exist, some now adorning the upper niches in the four huge piers that support the dome of St. Peter's, and one being preserved in the side chapel known as the Cappella della Pieta. These served Bernini as models for the great gilded spiral columns which support the present ciborium over the high altar (Fig. 183).

In 1940 by the command of Pope Pius XII excavations were undertaken beneath the Church of St. Peter and continued for ten years.[10] Beneath the main part of the church and under its crypts was found a double row of mausoleums, part of the cemetery of a well-to-do class of people. Almost all of the mausoleums were originally vaulted, but most of the vaults were destroyed in the building of Constantine's basilica, the walls of which were set down right in the midst of this cemetery. While the mausoleums were in use mainly from around A.D. 100 to the fourth century, the region was certainly a place of burial even before A.D. 100 as was shown by the ossuaries in which bones from preceding tombs were collected. It is also clear that the cemetery was of pagan origin, although there are a few

[10] B. M. Apollonj Ghetti, A. Ferrua, E. Josi, E. Kirschbaum, L. Kaas, and C. Serafini, *Esplorazioni sotto la Confessione di San Pietro in Vaticano, eseguite negli anni 1940-1949.* 2 vols. 1951; Roger T. O'Callaghan in BA 12 (1949), pp.1-23; 16 (1953), pp.70-87; L. E. Hudec in JBR 20 (1952), pp.13-18; Oscar Cullmann, *Petrus, Jünger, Apostel, Märtyrer.* 1952, pp.152-169; Armin von Gerkan in ZNW 44 (1952/53), pp.196-205; J. Gwyn Griffiths in HJ 55 (1956-57), pp.140-149, 285f.; Jocelyn Toynbee in HJ 55 (1956-57), pp.284f.; Jocelyn Toynbee and John Ward Perkins, *The Shrine of St. Peter and the Vatican Excavations.* 1956; Theodor Klauser, *Die römische Petrustradition im Lichte der neuen Ausgrabungen unter der Peterskirche.* 1956; cf. J. M. C. Toynbee in AJA 62 (1958), pp.126-129.

Christian burials toward the latter part of the time of its use. In the case of one mausoleum, although all the sarcophagi it contained probably belonged to one family, the earliest revealed motifs from an Egyptian cult, a later one showed a Dionysian scene, and the latest had Christian motifs. In the area directly beneath the high altar of the church above, was an open area where no mausoleums were ever built. There were burials here, however, one tomb having a tile stamped with a date in the time of Vespasian (A.D. 69-79). Yet these burials left free one particular spot. Across the edge of this spot a red-colored wall was built at about A.D. 160. The date is determined by the bricks of a drainage channel connected with the wall, on several of which are the names of Aurelius Caesar and his wife Faustina Augusta. Since the reference is to Marcus Aurelius before he became emperor (161-180), the date stated above is indicated. In this wall are what the excavators describe as three niches, one above the other. The lowest is very roughly finished, the two above form a sort of shrine which was marked by two marble columns standing on a travertine base and supporting a slab of travertine fixed into the red wall. In loose earth under the lowest niche were some human bones, but since with them were also coins of the second and third centuries it is difficult to assume that these are the remains of Peter. But the date of the niche with its columns seems well established at around A.D. 160, and since this was the exact spot around which Constantine's basilica as well as the present church were built, it would seem probable that this niche is the very "trophy" mentioned by Caius about A.D. 200.[11]

No remains of the Circus of Nero were found in these excavations, making untenable the former supposition that the basilica of Constantine was in part built directly upon the walls of that structure.[12]

[11] If the "trophy" was built about A.D. 160 it would probably have been under Anicetus (c.154-c.165), but of this the Liber Pontificalis says nothing (LLP pp.15f.), attributing the building and adorning of "the sepulchral monument of the blessed Peter" to Anacletus instead (LLP p.9), the successor of Clement. It has been suggested that the desire to assign a greater antiquity to events helped produce the probable confusion between the two names in the later tradition (O'Callaghan in BA 16 [1953], pp.80f.).

[12] It is still possible that the circus occupied this location just south of St. Peter's, as the former location of the obelisk (see above p.513) suggests, but in this case the circus must have been a rather simple structure architecturally, perhaps built mostly of wood which perished in the course of time. See Gavin Townend in AJA 62 (1958), pp.216-218. Cullmann (Petrus, pp.165f.) thinks that the niches found in the excavations are indeed the "trophy" of Caius, but suggests that the spot thus marked was not that of the grave but of the place of martyrdom of Peter. Since that place, however, was presumably within the Circus of Nero, the suggestion seems unlikely.

But in a mausoleum at the eastern end of the double row of excavated mausoleums, was an extremely important inscription. Here
was recorded part of the will and testament of a certain C. Popilius
Heraclea, whose estate was bequeathed to his heirs with the understanding that his mausoleum was to be erected *in Vaticano ad Cir-
cum juxta monumentum Ulpii Narcisii*, "in the Vatican near the
Circus beside the monument of Ulpius Narcissus." This is proof that
the famous circus, without doubt that of Caligula and of Nero, was
near at hand.

In another of the mausoleums, that of the Valerii, there was recently found the drawing of the head of an old man, represented as
bald, furrowed of brow, and with pointed beard. The accompanying
inscription has been read as, *Petrus roga Christus Iesus pro sanctis
hominibus Chrestianis ad corpus tuum sepultis*, meaning "Peter, pray
Christ Jesus for the holy Christian men buried near your body."
Since the drawing and inscription had been partly covered by a wall
belonging to Constantine's basilica, they must be earlier than the
erection of that church and may date from around A.D. 280. It is held
by some that this makes unlikely the theory of a temporary removal
of the bones of Peter to the cemetery *ad Catacumbas*, but if as we
have surmised they were brought back to the Vatican as soon as
Valerian's brief persecution was terminated this would not be a difficulty.[13]

The excavations, then, have shown that Nero's Circus was definitely in this region, have revealed a sort of simple shrine which
may have been the "trophy" mentioned by Caius, have brought to
light an inscription which, if properly read, attests early belief that
Peter was buried in the vicinity, and have given much knowledge
of the pagan cemetery which Constantine had to invade for the
construction of his basilica. All of these facts support the belief that
the tomb of the apostle Peter was indeed at this place.[14]

[13] O'Callaghan in BA 16 (1953), pp.82f.; Toynbee and Perkins, *The Shrine of
St. Peter and the Vatican Excavations*, p.14.

[14] On the slope of the Janiculum hill in Rome is the Church of San Pietro in Mon-
torio, and in the court of the adjoining convent is the Tempietto, a small circular
building erected about 1500 from plans by Bramante, which is also said to mark the
place of the martyrdom of Peter. The probable explanation of this variant tradition
is as follows. In some of the accounts of the death of Peter it was stated that the
place was *inter duas metas*. The *meta* was the turning post at each end of the *spina*
in a circus, and this meant that Peter was crucified midway between the two turning
posts, that is at the middle of the *spina*. *Meta* also means pyramid, however, and in
Rome two pyramids were conspicuous, that in the Vatican district by the Church of
Santa Maria Traspontina, called Meta Romuli, and the pyramid of Cestius by the

SAN PAOLO FUORI LE MURA

The Liber Pontificalis states that the basilica over the grave of Paul, now known as San Paolo fuori le Mura, was also founded by Constantine. One manuscript, however, adds the name of his son, the Emperor Constantius (337-361), who probably carried this church to completion. The statement in the Liber Pontificalis is: "At the same time Constantine Augustus and Lord Constantius Augustus built the basilica of blessed Paul, the apostle, at the bidding of Silvester the bishop, and laid his body away there in bronze and enclosed it, as he did the body of the blessed Peter. . . . Moreover he placed a golden cross over the tomb of blessed Paul, the apostle, weighing 150 lbs." Gifts and revenues devoted to the church also are listed, as in the case of the basilica of St. Peter.[15]

The Constantinian basilica of St. Paul was only a small structure. This seems surprising in comparison with the large church built in honor of Peter, but the explanation is to be found in the character of the available site. The grave of Paul lay between the Via Ostiensis and another small paved street, the Via Valentiniana, which joined it at a sharp angle somewhat to the south. Only the area in the angle between these two streets was available for the basilica, unless the streets were to be destroyed. Also, the site was unfavorable because it stood far distant from the city residences of most of the Christians and because it was in a low-lying area frequently overflowed by the Tiber River. Nevertheless the basilica was erected here. Certainly the location was not invented, but only accepted because it was the actual place of Paul's grave.[16]

In 384 the three emperors, Valentinian II, Theodosius I the Great, and his son Arcadius, issued a decree which moved the inconvenient side street far enough away so that space was gained to accommodate a truly monumental church, and in 386 a letter to Sallust, the prefect of Rome, ordered the construction of the new basilica. The work was completed under the Emperor Honorius (395-423) the

---

Porta San Paolo, known as Meta Remi. So this spot on the Janiculum was chosen because it was midway between the pyramid of Romulus and the pyramid of Remus! These relationships may be seen plainly on the *Forma Urbis Romae Imperatorum Aetate*, delineaverunt Iosephus Lugli et Italus Gismondi (Istituto Geografico de Agostini-Novara). 1949; cf. Rodolfo Lanciani, *Pagan and Christian Rome*. 1892, p.128; Arthur S. Barnes, *St. Peter in Rome and His Tomb on the Vatican Hill*. 1900, p.97.

[15] LLP pp.57f.

[16] Lietzmann, *Petrus und Paulus in Rom*, pp.220f.

younger son of Theodosius, and dedicated by Pope Siricius (384-399), the latter's name and the date 390 still existing on a column of the church.[17] The orientation of the new structure was the reverse of the old, so that the main entrance was from the bank of the Tiber and the apse faced to the east. The church extended across the disused Via Valentiniana and was so much greater than the Constantinian basilica that its transept alone was larger than the entire old church. It was so arranged, however, that the grave of Paul was not changed and the altar and *confessio* remained on their original site.

The basilica of the three emperors stood until destroyed by a great fire in 1823. It was probably damaged by Genseric and the Vandals in 455 and may have been struck by lightning about the same time, since the Liber Pontificalis says that the roof was rebuilt "after the fire from God" by Pope Leo I the Great (440-461): "He replaced all the consecrated silver vessels in all the parish churches after the Vandal devastation. . . . He repaired the basilica of blessed Peter,[18] the apostle, and restored the vaulting of blessed Paul after the fire from God."[19]

Pope Symmachus (498-514) is credited with extensive works of restoration and beautification: "Also in the church of blessed Paul, the apostle, he rebuilt the apse of the basilica, which was falling into ruin, and he embellished it with a picture behind the confession and he made a vaulting and a transept; and over the confession he erected a silver image of the Saviour and the 12 apostles, which weighed 120 lbs.; and before the doors of the basilica he rebuilt steps into the atrium and a fountain; and behind the apse he brought down water and built there a bath from the foundation."[20] Although the Lombards devastated the environs of Rome during the siege of 756, they spared St. Paul's. The Saracens did more damage and may even have rifled the tomb of the apostle Paul. Afterward Pope John VIII (872-882) followed the example of Leo IV at the Vatican (p.512) and surrounded the basilica of St. Paul and the suburb that had grown up around it with a strong battlemented wall. He called the suburb Johannipolis.

Immediately after the terrible fire of 1823, Leo XII began the work of building a new church. The transept of the modern struc-

[17] Frothingham, *Monuments of Christian Rome*, p.48.
[18] Another text reads, "He made the vaulting and decorated the basilica of blessed Peter."
[19] LLP p.100.
[20] LLP p.121.

ture was consecrated in 1840 and the entire church in 1854. The square forecourt, lined with granite columns, was added in 1890-1929. In plan and dimensions the new basilica closely followed its predecessor. The main entrance is by the western façade (Fig. 184), which faces toward the Tiber, and the interior is arranged with nave, double aisles, and transept. Eighty columns of polished gray granite support the ceiling of the nave, which is coffered instead of being open as formerly. The large dimensions of the interior, 394 feet in length and 75 feet in height, and the rich ornamentation combine to produce a very imposing effect (Fig. 185).

The mosaics on the triumphal arch of the basilica of the three emperors were executed in 440-461 by order of the Empress Galla Placidia, sister of the Emperor Honorius, but were damaged badly in the great fire, and the present mosaics are an entirely modern restoration. The mosaic inscription states that the basilica was begun by Theodosius and finished by Honorius and that it was restored and decorated by Placidia under Pope Leo. The mosaics in the apse date from around 1218 and also had to be restored completely after the fire.

When the present church was being constructed there was seen at the bottom of the shaft under the high altar a marble slab with an inscription in letters characteristic of the time of Constantine: PAULO APOSTOLO MARTYRI (Fig. 186). The circular hole seen in the slab was the *billicum* or opening of a little well which led into the tomb, through which it was customary to lower objects to touch the coffin beneath. The two square holes may have been connected with some obscure medieval ceremony.[21]

While all too little from Constantinian and earlier times now remains at the sites of the churches of Paul and Peter, the chain of archeological evidence is such that the last resting places of the two great apostles may confidently be sought beneath the extensive hall of the three emperors and the soaring dome of Bramante and Michelangelo.

SAN GIOVANNI IN LATERANO

In addition to the basilicas of Peter and Paul, five more churches were built in Rome by Constantine. As a matter of fact, in the Liber Pontificalis one of these stands at the head of the list of all the basilicas erected by Constantine, being mentioned even before St. Peter's and St. Paul's. This is "the Constantinian basilica" as the

---

[21] Barnes, *Martyrdom of St. Peter and St. Paul*, p.148.

Liber Pontificalis calls it,[22] or St. John Lateran (San Giovanni in Laterano) as it is now known. A palace belonging to the senator Plautius Lateranus was confiscated by Nero and thus became imperial property. A portion of it was given by the Emperor Maximian (286-305) to his daughter Fausta, who was married to Constantine in 307. Fausta lived there until she was put to death in 326, and the place became known as the Domus Faustae, or House of Fausta. In 313 a church council under Pope Miltiades met "in the house of Fausta in the Lateran,"[23] and after Fausta's death Constantine gave the palace to Pope Sylvester I as a residence. It continued to be the official residence of the popes for nearly a thousand years. It was burned down in 1308 and the present Palazzo del Laterano was not erected until 1586. In 1843 Gregory XVI made this palace into the Museum Gregorianum Lateranense.

According to tradition, the basilica which Constantine built at the Lateran was dedicated in 324. It was destroyed by an earthquake and reerected by Pope Sergius III (904-911), at that time being dedicated to John the Baptist. After being burned down twice in the fourteenth century it was rebuilt by Urban V (1362-1370) and Gregory XI (1370-1378) and repeatedly altered and modernized at various later times. The interior appears today chiefly in the form given to it by Borromini in the seventeenth century, and the principal façade is the work of Alessandro Galilei in the eighteenth century. Many important church councils have been held here and, as the papal cathedral, the basilica bears the inscription "the mother and head of all the churches of the city and the world." But of the building of Constantine nothing remains.[24]

SANTA CROCE IN GERUSALEMME

"At the same time," continues the Liber Pontificalis after recording the founding of St. Peter's and St. Paul's, "Constantine Augustus constructed a basilica in the Sessorian palace, where he also placed and enclosed in gold and jewels some of the wood of the holy cross of our Lord Jesus Christ, and he dedicated the church under the name by which it is called even to this day, Hierusalem."[25] The Sessorian palace was the residence of Constantine's mother, the Em-

---

[22] LLP p.47.

[23] LLP p.47 n.1.

[24] The Altar of the Sacrament in the south transept of the present church has four antique columns of gilded bronze which are said to have belonged to the original basilica. Baedeker, *Rome*, p.384.

[25] LLP p.58.

press Helena, and two inscriptions in her honor have been discovered there. While Helena's pilgrimage to the Holy Land is a well known fact, Eusebius says nothing of her discovery of the actual cross of Christ[26] and the accounts of that happening given about the middle of the fifth century by Socrates[27] and Sozomen[28] are certainly legendary in character. The existence of the cross and the sending of pieces of its wood throughout the world were believed in, however, by Cyril of Jerusalem around A.D. 348.[29] It is evident, therefore, that the Sessorian palace hall was transformed into a basilica and named in honor of the discovery of the cross at Jerusalem. The present church, Santa Croce in Gerusalemme, has been rebuilt and restored but still shows traces of once having been a private hall.

SANT'AGNESE FUORI LE MURA

"At the same time," continues the Liber Pontificalis concerning Constantine, "he built the basilica of the holy martyr Agnes at the request of Constantia,[30] his daughter, and a baptistery in the same place, where both his sister, Constantia, and the daughter of Augustus were baptized by Silvester the bishop."[31] St. Agnes was a famous martyr who is mentioned by Jerome[32] and whose place of burial was outside the city on the Via Nomentana, where the catacomb is located which now bears her name. The basilica which Constantine erected in honor of St. Agnes was carried beneath the level of the ground in order to bring its altar immediately over the holy tomb. Rebuilt by Pope Honorius I (625-638) and restored again in the fifteenth and nineteenth centuries, the present Church of St. Agnes outside the Walls (Sant'Agnese fuori le Mura) still lies at a low level, being reached by a descending stairway of forty-five steps, and still retains many characteristics of an early Christian basilica.

SANTA COSTANZA

Nearby is a circular, domed building which is known now as the Church of Santa Costanza. No doubt it represents the baptistery mentioned by the Liber Pontificalis in connection with the basilica

[26] *Life of Constantine.* III, 26, 42.
[27] *Church History.* I, 17 (NPNFSS II, p.21).
[28] *Church History.* II, 1 (NPNFSS II, p.258).
[29] *Catechetical Lectures.* IV, 10; X, 19; XIII, 4 (NPNFSS VII, pp.21,63,83).
[30] Actually the name of Constantine's daughter was Constantina, while his sister was named Constantia.
[31] LLP p.60.
[32] *Letter 130 to Demetrias.* 5 (NPNFSS VI, p.262).

of Agnes, although its original character seems to have been that of a mausoleum. Probably it was used later as a baptistery, the font perhaps having been located in the central space under the dome. The funerary character of the building is shown by the niches in the wall intended to receive sarcophagi, and by the one sarcophagus actually found here and now kept in the Vatican Museum. In the sixteenth century Vincenzo Cartari mentions a ship of Dionysus, executed in mosaic, which was to be seen in the Church of Sant' Agnese "and in what once was a temple of Bacchus," by the latter doubtless meaning Santa Costanza. This suggests that the structure was originally built as a pagan mausoleum, and that the Christian elements are later additions. It has been suggested that it was commissioned by Constantine as an imperial family mausoleum, perhaps as early as A.D. 312 immediately after his victory over Maxentius.[33] In A.D. 354 Constantine's elder daughter, Constantina, died and was buried here. Six years later the younger daughter, Helena, wife of Julian the Apostate, also died and her body was sent to Rome, as the Roman historian Ammianus Marcellinus (c.330-c.395) relates, to be buried on the Via Nomentana where her sister Constantina already lay.[34]

In the low vault of the circular aisle which runs around the interior of Santa Costanza are fine fourth century mosaics in the Roman antique tradition. These include naturalistic representations of flowers, fruit, birds, and sheep, and an interesting vintage scene in which cupids pluck the grapes, carry them to vats, and trample out the juice.[35]

SAN LORENZO FUORI LE MURA

The Liber Pontificalis continues: "At the same time Constantine Augustus built the basilica of blessed Lawrence, the martyr, on the Via Tiburtina in the Ager Veranus over the buried crypt, and he made stairs of ascent and of descent to the body of the holy martyr Lawrence. In that place he erected an apse and adorned it with porphyry and the spot over the tomb he enclosed with silver and beautified it with railings of purest silver, which weighed 1000 lbs."[36] Lawrence was the famous martyr who was put to death over a slow fire in the Valerian persecution of 258. The Constantinian

[33] Karl Lehmann in AB 37 (1955), pp.193-196.
[34] XXI, 1, 5. tr. J. C. Rolfe, LCL (1935-39) II, p.93.
[35] E. W. Anthony, *A History of Mosaics.* 1935, p.63; H. H. Powers, *The Art of Mosaic.* 1938, p.79.
[36] LLP pp.61f.

basilica was located so that the altar came over the martyr's crypt to which a stairway gave access. The passage in the Liber Pontificalis is specially interesting since it is one of the earliest descriptions of such a *confessio*.

In 578 Pope Pelagius II rebuilt the church, his work evidently being thorough since the Liber Pontificalis says that "he built from its foundations a basilica over the body of blessed Lawrence."[37] He is also responsible for the mosaic which in restored form is still to be seen on the arch, with Christ in the center, Peter, Lawrence, and Pelagius (with a model of the basilica) on his right side, Paul, Stephen, and Hippolytus on his left, and the cities of Jerusalem and Bethlehem beneath. These are the earliest mosaics in Rome to show Byzantine influence, Christ being seated on the globe of the world as in San Vitale at Ravenna, and Peter being placed in accordance with Byzantine tradition at Christ's right side instead of at the left as was the Roman tradition from the fourth to the thirteenth century.

A complete reorientation and remodeling of this church took place under Honorius III (1216-1227). He turned the nave into a choir with a crypt beneath it, added the present nave at a level ten feet higher on the opposite side of the triumphal arch, thus leaving the mosaics of Pelagius facing the choir, and transferred the entrance to the opposite end of the church. The present San Lorenzo in Agro Verano,[38] or San Lorenzo fuori le Mura, is therefore a basilica far different from that originally built by Constantine.[39]

SANTI PIETRO E MARCELLINO

"At the same time Constantine Augustus built a basilica to the blessed martyrs Marcellinus, the priest, and Peter, the exorcist, at Inter duas Lauros; also a mausoleum where his mother, Helena Augusta, was buried on the Via Lavicana, at the 3rd milestone."[40] The catacomb which still bears the name of these two martyrs has been mentioned (pp.475f.) but the basilica which Constantine built in their honor has disappeared completely. The remains of the octagonal, domed mausoleum of Constantine's mother still stand, however, and the huge porphyry sarcophagus which was found here is

---

[37] LLP p.168.

[38] The Campo Verano is now the chief cemetery of modern Rome.

[39] For recent excavation at San Lorenzo see W. Frankl, E. Josi, and R. Krautheimer in RAC 26 (1950), pp.9-50; L. E. Hudec in JBR 20 (1952), pp.136-138; R. Krautheimer in *Archaeological Newsletter* (Archaeological Institute of America). 11 (Feb. 28, 1949), pp.85-87.

[40] LLP p.63.

preserved in the Vatican Museum near the sarcophagus from the mausoleum of Constantina. A small church called Santi Pietro e Marcellino has been fitted up in the mausoleum of Helena, which otherwise now is known as the Torre Pignattára. The latter name comes from the *pignatte* or earthenware vessels which were used in the construction of the vaulting for the sake of lightness, as was customary in the late imperial period.

This completes the list of churches erected in Rome by Constantine as given by the Liber Pontificalis. Outside of Rome the same source ascribes to him the building of basilicas at Ostia, Albano, Capua, and Naples,[41] but does not mention the ones he founded in more distant places like Palestine. Before turning to some of the basilicas erected by Constantine in lands outside of Italy a few other Roman churches will be mentioned briefly.

THE "TITLE CHURCHES"

At this time the so-called "title churches" (p.502) formed the majority of the Roman churches and provided the basis of administrative organization, since they were the seats of the presbyters. The priests were divided among the title churches and had responsibility for the corresponding sections of the Roman church members, namely those who lived in that part of the city. The cardinal priests are still assigned to these churches and are titularly in charge of them.[42] By the fifth century the list of title churches numbered twenty-five and included those known today as Santi Giovanni e Paolo, San Clemente, Santi Pietro e Marcellino, San Pietro in Vincoli, San Martino ai Monti, Santa Prassede, Santa Pudenziana, Sant' Eusebio, San Vitale, Santa Susanna, San Marcello, San Lorenzo in Lucina, San Lorenzo in Damaso, San Marco, Sant' Anastasia, Santi Nereo ed Achilleo, Santa Balbina, Santa Sabina, Santa Prisca, Santa Maria in Trastevere, Santa Cecilia, and San Crisogono, as well as the churches of Xysti, of Aemilianae, and of Cyriaci whose identifications are not certain.[43] Of the foregoing, San Clemente and Santi Pietro e Marcellino have already been noted; and of the remainder we shall discuss only Santa Pudenziana and Santa Sabina.

[41] LLP pp.66f.,69f.
[42] J. P. Kirsch, *Die römischen Titelkirchen.* 1918, p.1.
[43] These churches are listed by Frothingham (*Monuments of Christian Rome*, pp.39f.) according to the fourteen *regiones* of ancient Rome.

SANTA PUDENZIANA

The church of Santa Pudenziana is mentioned in an epitaph of
A.D. 384 and was rebuilt by Pope Siricius (384-399) who changed it
from a hall church into a three-aisled basilica. The date of its original
founding is unknown but tradition ascribes it to Pius I (c.142-c.154).
To his biography as given by the Liber Pontificalis the following
sentences are added in certain eleventh century manuscripts: "He
by request of the blessed Praxedis dedicated a church in the baths
of Novatus in the Vicus Patricius[44] to the honor of her sister, the holy
Pudentiana, where also he offered many gifts and frequently he ministered, offering sacrifice to the Lord. Moreover he erected a font of
baptism and with his own hand he blessed and dedicated it and many
who gathered to the faith he baptized in the name of the Trinity."[45]
Pudentiana and Praxedis[46] were the daughters of Pudens, but
whether he is to be identified with the Pudens of II Timothy 4:21
is questionable.

Santa Pudenziana is most famous for the mosaic in its apse which
probably dates from the time of Pope Siricius. The mosaic was restored somewhat at the end of the eighth century under Pope Hadrian I (772-795) and was heavily trimmed around the curved margin when the apse was narrowed in 1588. Also a portion of the lower
part was removed later by the erection of the *baldacchino* and in
1831 the right side was largely done over. Nevertheless it remains
the earliest and most beautiful apse mosaic in existence and is characterized by a solemn and triumphant grandeur (Fig. 187). In the
center Christ arrayed in a tunic of gold is seated upon a throne and
holds an open book in his hand bearing the inscription "The Lord,
Guardian of the Church of Pudentiana." Originally the twelve tunic-
clothed apostles were to be seen on either side of Christ, but the
outermost figure on each side was lost when the apse was narrowed.
Peter stands at the right[47] and Paul[48] at the left. Behind each of
the two great apostles stands a woman clothed in gold, holding over
his head a laurel crown. These women are believed to represent the
Jewish Church (Ecclesia ex Circumcisione) and the Gentile Church
(Ecclesia ex Gentibus) respectively. The background is formed by

[44] The Vicus Patricius was near the modern Via Urbana, on which Santa Pudenziana now is located.

[45] LLP p.15 n.3.

[46] To whom the church of Santa Prassede is dedicated.

[47] That is, at the right as seen by the viewer, or at the left hand of Christ. This was
the position which was customary in the Roman tradition (p.522).

[48] The opening words of Matthew appear on the open book in Paul's hand but the
inscription is a modern restoration.

a portico above which in the center looms the rock of Calvary, surmounted by a great jeweled cross.[49] At the right appears a structure which is probably to be identified with the Church of the Nativity at Bethlehem, while the one at the left probably represents the Church of the Holy Sepulcher in Jerusalem. Above in the clouds are the winged symbols of the four evangelists, now appearing for one of the earliest times in art: the man (angel), lion, ox, and eagle (cf. Ezekiel 10:14; Revelation 4:7) representing respectively Matthew, Mark, Luke, and John.[50]

SANTA SABINA

The church of Santa Sabina was erected by the priest Peter under the pontificate of Celestine I (422-432) as is evident from the dedicatory *titulus* inscription in mosaic which still is in place over the door of the entrance wall. The church was restored in the thirteenth, fifteenth, sixteenth, and twentieth centuries, but with its twenty-four marble columns and open roof the essential structure is still that of an early Christian basilica. Originally, however, it was almost entirely covered within with mosaics, of which all are now lost except the mosaic inscription over the door. On either side of the mosaic inscription is the figure of a woman, the one at the left being shown as a woman of Palestine and labeled Ecclesia ex Circumcisione and the one at the right being represented as a Roman matron and labeled Ecclesia ex Gentibus.[51]

Santa Sabina is most famous for its great cypress doors whose carvings also belong to the time of the origin of the church around 430. Of their original twenty-eight panels only eighteen are left. Eight large panels give scenes from the life of Moses and other Old Testament subjects, while ten small ones are mostly devoted to scenes of the passion of Christ and his appearances after the resurrection. It is thought that the original plan of the door provided a parallelism between the events of the Old Testament and those of the New.[52] The crucifixion appears for perhaps the first time in Christian art.[53]

[49] The style of the cross seems later than that of the rest of the composition and it may be due to Hadrian's restoration.

[50] Anthony, *A History of Mosaics*, pp.66-68; cf. Thomas Albert Stafford, *Christian Symbolism in the Evangelical Churches*. 1942, p.101; Marguerite van Berchem and Étienne Clouzot, *Mosaïques chrétiennes du IVme au Xme siècle*. 1924, pp.11-58.

[51] Anthony, *A History of Mosaics*, p.76.

[52] Morey, *Early Christian Art*, p.138; cf. E. H. Kantorowicz in AB 26 (1944), pp.207-231.

[53] Lowrie, *Monuments of the Early Church*, p.273.

SANTA MARIA MAGGIORE

Our survey of some of the most interesting early Christian churches in Rome may be concluded with mention of Santa Maria Maggiore, which is neither a Constantinian basilica nor a title church but the largest of the eighty churches in the city dedicated to the Virgin, being exceeded in size only by St. Peter's, St. Paul's, and St. John Lateran. It was built by Pope Liberius (352-366), who probably remodeled an already existing palace, and sometimes was known as the Basilica Liberiana. The Liber Pontificalis states in the biography of this pontiff: "He built the basilica of his own name near the Macellum of Libia."[54] The latter is equivalent to "the market of Livia." This basilica was rebuilt by Xystus III (432-440), concerning whom the Liber Pontificalis says, "He built the basilica of the holy Mary, which was called by the ancients the basilica of Liberius, near the Macellum of Lybia."[55]

Santa Maria Maggiore is most famous for its glorious mosaics. Those of the triumphal arch go back to Xystus III, whose inscription still may be read on them: XYSTUS EPISCOPUS PLEBI DEI, "Bishop Xystus to the People of God."[56] The mosaics of the nave, like its ancient marble columns, may go back to Liberius but more probably also belong to the period of Xystus III.[57]

Of the forty-two original panels of nave mosaics, twenty-seven remain. These give a remarkable series of Old Testament pictures of which the Taking of Jericho is shown in Fig. 188. The procession of the ark and trumpeters is shown in the lower panel of the picture, and in the upper the Israelite warriors surround the city whose walls already are falling down. In antique perspective, the man and building which actually are within the city are shown on top of the walls. On the triumphal arch in Santa Maria Maggiore are beautiful scenes relating to the infancy of Christ.

5. CHURCHES IN PALESTINE

THE most sacred sites in all the world on which to erect Christian churches of course were to be found in the Holy Land. Concerning the basilicas which Constantine and his family erected there, we

---

[54] LLP p.77.   [55] LLP p.94.

[56] A. Schuchert, S. *Maria Maggiore zu Rom.* I, *Die Gründungsgeschichte der Basilika und die ursprüngliche Apsisanlage.* 1939, p.55.

[57] Morey, *Early Christian Art*, p.146; Anthony, *A History of Mosaics*, p.76.

are informed by Eusebius, whose writings are substantially contemporary.[1]

THE CHURCH OF THE HOLY SEPULCHER

For nearly two hundred years a pagan sanctuary (p.330) had stood over the sepulcher of Christ at Jerusalem. But at the command of Constantine this temple and its idols were thrown down and the polluted surface soil carried away. In the course of this work the tomb of Christ came to light again and the emperor forthwith wrote to Macarius, the bishop of Jerusalem, instructing him to erect there at imperial expense a basilica[2] which should surpass in beauty all others everywhere.[3] This church was dedicated in A.D. 335 and is described in considerable detail by Eusebius.[4] Following his description in reverse order, we find that the propylaea or main entrances opened off from the middle of the chief market street of the city, and "afforded to passers-by on the outside a view of the interior which could not fail to inspire astonishment." Beyond and several feet above the level of the street was the first court or atrium which was entered by three doorways, surrounded by porticoes, and left open to the sky. Passing through this one came to the basilica proper, later called the Martyrium, to which access was gained by three doors at the eastern end. Its walls were made of accurately fitted stones, while the roof was covered with lead as a protection against the winter rains. Within, the church was floored with marble slabs of various colors and on each side of the nave were double aisles with galleries above. The ceiling was finished with sculptured panel work like a great sea, "and, being overlaid throughout with the purest gold, caused the entire building to glitter as it were with rays of light." The crowning part of the basilica was what Eusebius calls the Hemisphere. This was at the western end and rose to the very summit of the church, being encircled by twelve columns whose capitals were adorned with large silver bowls presented by the emperor himself.

[1] cf. Paul Mickley, *Die Konstantin-Kirchen im Heiligen Lande, Eusebius-Texte übersetzt und erläutert.* 1923. *The Life of Constantine*, in which much of the relevant material is found, was finished after the death of Constantine (337), since it records that event (IV, 64), but cannot have been written much later, since Eusebius himself died in 340.

[2] Constantine's express designation of the building as a "basilica" is the first appearance of this term in literature in reference to a Christian church (Watzinger, *Denkmäler Palästinas.* II, pp.117f.).

[3] Eusebius, *Life of Constantine.* III, 26-32.

[4] *ibid.*, III, 33-40; cf. J. G. Davies in AJA 61 (1957), pp.171-173.

Beyond the basilica was a second atrium or open court. This was paved with finely polished stone and enclosed with colonnades on three sides. Yet farther to the west was the rock tomb itself. As the place where once the angel had announced the resurrection, this was the chief part of the entire work and was "beautified with rare columns and profusely enriched with the most splendid decorations of every kind." So much is related by Eusebius.

A brief description of the site and church is given also in the itinerary of the famous Bordeaux Pilgrim who visited Jerusalem in A.D. 333. It reads: "On the left hand[5] is the little hill of Golgotha where the Lord was crucified. About a stone's throw from thence is a vault wherein his body was laid, and rose again on the third day. There, at present, by the command of the Emperor Constantine, has been built a basilica, that is to say, a church of wondrous beauty, having at the side reservoirs from which water is raised, and a bath behind in which infants are baptized."[6]

It is evident from these passages that Constantine's architects sought to develop a plan which would be related to two chief points, the rock of Calvary and the tomb itself. The structures which they built were axially on a line which ran from east to west between the market street and the site of the tomb. This left the rock of Calvary just to the south of the main axis. Therefore the second court was colonnaded on three sides, as Eusebius described it, but left open on the south to face directly upon the rock of Calvary. This rock was probably brought to a regular shape by quarrying away superfluous portions of its slopes, and stood in the open air, surrounded by a grille and rising twelve or fifteen feet above the ground. West of the rock of Calvary there was a dip in the ground and then a rise. In the upward slope, "about a stone's throw" from Calvary, was the rock-cut tomb which had been the sepulcher of Christ. Here, too, unimportant portions of the rock round about appear to have been cut away and the sepulcher left standing up prominently from a rock floor. The sacred monument then was enclosed by a round, domed building with a circle of columns on the inside. In the middle stood the tomb itself, probably surrounded by a grille and covered

[5] The description is given from the point of view of one "walking towards the gate of Neapolis." Flavia Neapolis (now corrupted into Nabulus or Nablus) was the name given to the ancient city of Shechem in honor of the Flavian emperor Vespasian, when it was rebuilt after his conquest of the country (p.310). The Gate of Neapolis was therefore in the north wall of Jerusalem.

[6] *The Bordeaux Pilgrim.* tr. Stewart, pp.23f.; cf. R. W. Hamilton in PEQ 1952, pp.83-90.

with a pointed roof. This building became known as the Anastasis because it commemorated the place of the resurrection. Somewhere near at hand must have been the baptistery mentioned by the Bordeaux Pilgrim.[7]

Of these Constantinian structures only a few fragmentary portions remain today. They include a part of the wall of the first court, now embodied in the Russian and Coptic buildings at this place, and a segment of the outer wall of the Anastasis which still forms a part of the wall of the present Rotunda above the sepulcher. Perhaps also the lower courses of masonry in the present chapel of St. John just south of the Rotunda once belonged to the Constantinian baptistery.

Our knowledge of the original Church of the Holy Sepulcher rests primarily, therefore, upon the contemporary accounts of Eusebius and the Bordeaux Pilgrim and upon the fragments of Constantinian masonry which still stand. Confirmation of the general picture which we have drawn is to be found in the writings of Cyril of Jerusalem. Cyril was probably born around A.D. 315 and seems to have grown up in or near the city of which later he was bishop. About A.D. 348 he delivered a famous series of catechetical lectures in the Constantinian basilica itself. In the course of these he referred repeatedly to Golgotha or Calvary, speaking of it sometimes as near the place in which he and his listeners were assembled,[8] and sometimes as standing up above them in their sight.[9] Again he asked his hearers if they saw the spot of Golgotha, and they answered with a shout of praise.[10] A second group of lectures for those newly baptized was held in the "Holy Place of the Resurrection" or the Anastasis itself.[11]

In addition we have one or two very important representations of the Church of the Holy Sepulcher in early Christian art. The fourth century mosaic in the apse of Santa Pudenziana in Rome (Fig. 187; pp.524f.), portrays Christ seated in front of a great rock surmounted by a tall jeweled cross. It is probable that this scene is based upon one of the ceremonies at Jerusalem in which the bishop sat upon a throne in front of the rock of Calvary, surrounded by the deacons. The arcade in the background may then depict the second atrium itself and the buildings at the left be the Anastasis and other structures of Constantine.[12] The other representation of the church is in

---

[7] E. T. Richmond in W. Harvey, *Church of the Holy Sepulchre, Jerusalem.* 1935, p.vi; Crowfoot, *Early Churches in Palestine,* pp.19f.

[8] *Catechetical Lecture.* xiii, 4 (NPNFSS vii, p.83).

[9] *ibid.,* x, 19.   [10] *ibid.,* xiii, 23.   [11] *ibid.,* xviii, 33.

[12] Crowfoot, *Early Churches in Palestine,* p.19.

the famous mosaic map at Madeba.[13] Madeba is an ancient site across the Jordan and some fifty miles south of Gerasa. About 1880 it was occupied by Christians from Kerak, who in the course of building operations uncovered a number of churches and floor mosaics. One of the mosaics, dating from the end of the sixth century, gives a map of Palestine. On this map the sea is shown in deep green, plains in light brown, and mountains in dark brown, while place locations are named in Greek letters. Portions of the mosaic are destroyed, but the Jerusalem area is well preserved (Fig. 189) and the city is shown in such detail that even individual buildings can be distinguished. Jerusalem appears as a large oval, with its chief, colonnaded street running from north to south through the heart of the city. On the entire map the directions are recognizable without any doubt, since the street just mentioned parallels the course of the Jordan River and the Dead Sea seen in the distance. The basic outline of the Christian city is still that of Hadrian's colony. At the north end of the main street (left side in our reproduction) is the gate from which the Roman road led to Neapolis and Caesarea. Remains of this gate still exist beneath the present Damascus Gate in Jerusalem. Behind it the mosaic shows an open place and a memorial column on which once stood a statue of Hadrian. The colonnaded street ran through the city to the Roman gate at the south. This was called the middle market street by Eusebius and is identical with the present Khan al-Zeit. A row of columns has been found which probably represents a late Byzantine reconstruction of the western colonnade of this street. The mosaic shows a second colonnaded street running from the plaza at the north gate diagonally to the northwest corner of the temple area and then parallel to the west wall of the temple. The city must have had a main east-west street also but only small, short streets running in this direction are shown on the map. The interior of the city is filled with churchly buildings. Most prominent is the Church of the Holy Sepulcher at a point perpendicular to the middle of the chief market street. The mosaic clearly shows the flights of steps leading up to the first atrium, the three entrance doors, the roof of the basilica, and the dome of the Anastasis.[14]

Not long after the time when the Madeba mosaic map was made, the Constantinian Church of the Holy Sepulcher was destroyed by the Persians. This took place in A.D. 614, and afterward Modestus,

[13] Roger T. O'Callaghan in *Dictionnaire de la Bible*, Supplement, Pt. xxvi, cols. 627-704; Victor R. Gold in BA 21 (1958), pp.50-71.
[14] Watzinger, *Denkmäler Palästinas*. II, pp.81f.

who was patriarch, carried out a reconstruction in far simpler style but on the same general lines as those of Constantine's work. Thereafter many vicissitudes were in store, including earthquake, fire, pillage, and general neglect. In 935 a mosque was built on the site of the atrium of the church, and in 1009 the church itself was destroyed by the Fatimid Caliph al-Hakim but later rebuilt by the Byzantine emperor Constantine IX Monomachus (1042-1054). The Crusaders, who captured Jerusalem in 1099, found Constantine Monomachus's timber-domed rotunda above the Holy Sepulcher, the tomb itself being surrounded by a circular colonnade of columns and piers. To the east was the court, with the rock of Calvary on its southern side standing to the height "of a lance." Constantine's basilica was in ruins, but its crypt, known by the name of St. Helena, still existed. The Crusaders designed and built a church which covered beneath its roof both the rock of Calvary and the court which formerly adjoined it. This church was connected with the rotunda by a triumphal arch, and with the crypt of St. Helena, now made into a chapel, by a stairway. The basilica of the Crusaders still stands, although eight centuries of neglect have damaged it badly. Constantine Monomachus's dome over the Anastasis was repaired around 1719, then destroyed by fire in 1808. Thereafter the Greeks were authorized by Sultan Mahmud II to repair the church, and they constructed certain walls which obscured the interior arrangement of the rotunda, built a new edicule over the sepulcher, replaced the doors of the main entrance by new ones, and erected a new dome which lasted for about fifty years. The latter was again rebuilt in 1863-1868, but in recent times the general condition of the whole church has become so questionable as to demand a thoroughgoing investigation of its structural weaknesses and a comprehensive plan for works of restoration and preservation.[15]

Thus the handiwork of man over a period of more than nineteen centuries is represented by the existing Church of the Holy Sepulcher. The earliest examples are the traces of the original sepulcher that still survive, as well as another ancient rock tomb still to be seen in the western part of the rotunda, just south of the present Jacobite Chapel. The most recent are the works of repair carried out in the twentieth century. The history and traditions of the centuries are such that we may with confidence seek beneath the roof

[15] William Harvey, *Church of the Holy Sepulchre, Jerusalem, Structural Survey, Final Report.* 1935, pp.vii-xv.

of this structure the true place of Golgotha and the sepulcher of Christ.[16]

A photograph of the main south front of the church is shown in Fig. 190. On the left of the open court are several chapels, including the chapel of St. John, and the bell tower which was built about 1170. The façade of the church is divided into two stories and there are two doors with corresponding windows above. One of the portals is now walled up, as are many of the windows of the church. This is the main entrance and leads directly ahead into the western end of the south aisle of the Crusaders' church which, as will be remembered, was located where the second atrium was in Constantinian times. The chapel of St. Helena, where once Constantine's basilica stood, is descended to by steps leading out from the eastern end of this church. The dome which appears prominently in this picture rises above the western part of the Crusaders' church, while the large dome of the rotunda of the sepulcher is hidden behind the bell tower.

THE CHURCH OF THE NATIVITY

At Bethlehem the Church of the Nativity was built under the leadership of Helena, the mother of Constantine. Not long before her death, which occurred around A.D. 327 at the age of eighty years, this venerable lady visited the Holy Land in person. Eusebius tells how she dedicated a church "at the grotto which had been the scene of the Saviour's birth," and explains, "For he who was 'God with us' had submitted to be born even in a cave of the earth, and the place of his nativity was called Bethlehem by the Hebrews." The sacred cave was beautified with all possible splendor, and the emperor joined his mother in costly offerings.[17]

While the gospel narrative of the birth of Jesus relates only that Mary "laid him in a manger, because there was no place for them in the inn" (Luke 2:7), it is not surprising that this should have been in a cave, since until modern times caves have frequently been employed in Palestine to house both animals and men. The cave is mentioned between A.D. 155 and 160 by Justin Martyr, who says: "when the child was born in Bethlehem, since Joseph could not find a lodging in that village, he took up his quarters in a certain cave near the

---

[16] Joachim Jeremias in ΑΓΓΕΛΟΣ, *Archiv für neutestamentliche Zeitgeschichte und Kulturkunde*. 1926, p.33; H. T. F. Duckworth, *The Church of the Holy Sepulchre*. 1922, p.11; André Parrot, *Golgotha and the Church of the Holy Sepulchre*. 1957.

[17] Eusebius, *Life of Constantine*. III, 41-43; cf. Socrates, *Ch. Hist.* I, 17; Sozomen, *Ch. Hist.* II, 2.

village."[18] Again in A.D. 246-248, Origen writes: "Corresponding to the narrative in the Gospel regarding his birth, there is shown at Bethlehem the cave where he was born, and the manger in the cave where he was wrapped in swaddling clothes. And this sight is greatly talked of in surrounding places, even among the enemies of the faith, it being said that in this cave was born that Jesus who is worshipped and reverenced by the Christians."[19]

As a matter of fact, this cave was evidently identified as the birthplace of Christ long before the time of Hadrian, for that emperor defiled it with pagan worship just as he did the site of the Holy Sepulcher in Jerusalem. This is related by Jerome, who himself lived at Bethlehem from 386 until his death in 420:[20]

"From the time of Hadrian to the reign of Constantine—a period of about one hundred and eighty years—the spot which had witnessed the resurrection was occupied by a figure of Jupiter; while on the rock where the cross had stood, a marble statue of Venus was set up by the heathen and became an object of worship. The original persecutors, indeed, supposed that by polluting our holy places they would deprive us of our faith in the passion and in the resurrection. Even my own Bethlehem, as it now is, that most venerable spot in the whole world of which the psalmist sings: 'the truth hath sprung out of the earth,'[21] was overshadowed by a grove of Tammuz, that is of Adonis; and in the very cave where the infant Christ had uttered his earliest cry lamentation was made for the paramour of Venus."[22]

The church which was erected over this sacred site by Helena and Constantine is mentioned in A.D. 333 by the Bordeaux Pilgrim. Speaking of Bethlehem, he says, "There a basilica has been built by order of Constantine."[23] Under the Emperor Justinian (527-565), the original Constantinian basilica was demolished and a larger church constructed. This fact is stated in a document written at the beginning of the tenth century by Eutychius, the patriarch of Alexandria. Eutychius says that the Emperor Justinian ordered his legate to pull down the church at Bethlehem, which was a small building, and to

---

[18] *Dialogue with Trypho.* 78 (ANF I, p.237).

[19] *Against Celsus.* I, 51 (ANF IV, p.418).

[20] *Letter 58 to Paulinus.* 3 (NPNFSS VI, p.120).

[21] Psalm 85:11.

[22] Tammuz was the Mesopotamian god who died and rose annually with the death and rebirth of vegetation. He is here identified with the Greek Adonis, the lover of Venus (Aphrodite). The lamentations of the goddess over his tragic death and descent to the underworld were echoed in the liturgical wailings of his worshipers (cf. Ezekiel 8:14). Frankfort, *Kingship and the Gods,* pp.286-294; T. G. Pinches in HERE XII, pp.187-191.

[23] *The Bordeaux Pilgrim.* tr. Stewart, p.27.

erect another of such size and beauty that not even the temple at Jerusalem might vie with it in beauty. The legate arrived, had the church at Bethlehem destroyed, and built the church as it stands now. When he had finished his work he returned to the emperor, who proceeded to question him as to the way in which he had carried out his commands. But when he described the building the emperor became very angry. "I gave you money," he said, "and you have pocketed it all, but the building you have erected is badly put together, the church is quite dark, and the result is not at all what I intended or according to the plan I told you to follow." And straightway he ordered him to be punished.[24]

Justinian's church, much dilapidated, still stands in Bethlehem. It was spared by the Persians in 614, because they saw on the exterior a mosaic of the adoration of the Magi in which the latter were clothed in Persian dress. The Muslims held the church in veneration and it escaped the general destruction of Palestinian churches ordered in 1009 by the Fatimid Caliph al-Hakim. Baldwin I was crowned king here at Christmas in 1101, and during the period of the Latin kingdom (twelfth century) the church was invested with splendid mosaic decoration. Since that time, however, earthquake, fire, and neglect have reduced it to a sad state of deterioration.[25]

The Church of the Nativity is on the promontory upon which the southeastern part of the town of Bethlehem is now built. The western front and principal entrance of the church are shown in Fig. 191. The large open area paved with stone is where the atrium of the Constantinian basilica must have been. A modern graveyard now encroaches from the north and the buildings of the Armenian Convent project prominently at the right. The narthex was formerly entered through three doors, but these have now been blocked save for a small low rectangular opening in the central door, which remains as the chief public entrance. Within (Fig. 192)[26] the nave is still flanked by Justinian's columns, which form double aisles on either side. Beneath the central area where the transept crosses the main axis of the church, and descended to by steps on either side of the chancel, is the grotto of the Nativity.

The church as described hitherto is essentially that of Justinian. Is anything known of the Constantinian basilica? In 1934 Mr. Wil-

---

[24] *Annales.* MPG 111 (1863), col. 1070, 159f.

[25] E. T. Richmond in William Harvey, *Structural Survey of the Church of the Nativity, Bethlehem.* 1935, pp.v-xv.

[26] The cross wall shown at the head of the nave in this photograph has now been removed.

liam Harvey discovered the remains of the church of Helena and Constantine beneath the floor of the present church. Only limited excavations were possible, but the essential nature of the original church was determined.[27] The general plan was similar to that of the Church of the Holy Sepulcher. As at Jerusalem the structures were set out axially, but in this case ran from west to east. First there was the atrium. Then three doors gave access to the basilica at its western end. The north and south walls of the basilica stood on the same lines as the existing side walls of the present church, and the interior was divided practically as now into nave and four aisles. At its eastern end the basilica connected directly with an octagonal building which stood above the subterranean cave of the Nativity. Steps arranged on an octagonal plan surrounded the circular mouth of a shaft about twelve feet across, through which it was possible to look down into the grotto itself. The roof of the cave was broken through to make this view possible from the Octagon above.

The floors of the aisles, the nave, and the passage around the shrine in the Octagon, were paved with patterned mosaics. Considerable fragments of these remain, and being probably of Constantinian time are the earliest floor mosaics which have been found in a Palestinian church. Since they were to be trodden underfoot no religious scenes were represented, but geometrical designs, swastikas, acanthus leaves, flowers, fruits, and birds constituted the decorations. A small panel on the north side of the Octagon where no one ordinarily would walk, had the Greek word "Fish" (IXΘYC) in the center (Fig. 193).

An almost contemporary picture of this church is probably to be seen in the apse mosaic of Santa Pudenziana, Rome (Fig. 187). Whereas Jerusalem appears at our left in the mosaic, Bethlehem is seen at our right. In the extreme corner is a high entranceway, to the left of which a long low building represents the atrium of the Church of the Nativity. Adjoining this is a somewhat taller building which is the basilica and immediately to the left of it is the yet loftier Octagon.

THE CHURCH ON THE MOUNT OF OLIVES

Yet another Palestinian church was founded by Helena and likewise enriched by Constantine. The statement of Eusebius concerning

---

[27] W. Harvey, *Structural Survey of the Church of the Nativity, Bethlehem*, pp.20-30; and in PEFQS 1936, pp.28-32; E. T. Richmond in QDAP 6 (1938), pp.63-66; Crowfoot, *Early Churches in Palestine*, pp.22-30, 119-121.

it is: "And further, the mother of the emperor raised a stately structure on the Mount of Olives also, in memory of his ascent to heaven who is the Saviour of mankind, erecting a sacred church and temple on the very summit of the mount. And indeed authentic history informs us that in this very cave the Saviour imparted his secret revelations to his disciples. And here also the emperor testified his reverence for the King of kings, by diverse and costly offerings."[28] The Bordeaux Pilgrim writes: "From thence you ascend to the Mount of Olives, where before the Passion, the Lord taught his disciples. There by the orders of Constantine a basilica of wondrous beauty has been built."[29]

Evidently the basilica was built near the place on the Mount of Olives where fourth century tradition believed the ascension had taken place (cf. Acts 1:9, 12) and directly over a cave in which it was said Jesus had taught his disciples. The Bordeaux Pilgrim says that these teachings were delivered before the Passion, and perhaps the discourse on the last things was in mind which was described in the gospels as given on the Mount of Olives (Mark 13:3 = Matthew 24:3). Eusebius, however, speaks of the teachings as "secret revelations" which makes one think of the apocryphal teachings which Christ was supposed to have given on the Mount of Olives in the period between the resurrection and the ascension.[30]

However confused some of these traditions may have been, it is certain that a Constantinian basilica did stand over a cave on the Mount of Olives directly across from the Holy City and just south of the summit of the ridge of the Mount. Since the name of the Mount of Olives was Eleona ('Ελαιών, Luke 21:37), the basilica was known as "the church of Eleona," or simply Eleona for short. Although hardly more than a few stones of its walls and small patches of its mosaic floor have survived, the Dominicans have been able to trace the ground plan from the foundation trenches cut in the solid rock, and to establish a very probable reconstruction of its original character.[31]

---

[28] *Life of Constantine.* iii, 43.

[29] Tr. Stewart, pp.24f.

[30] See e.g. *The Gospel of Bartholomew.* 4:1 (JANT p.173); and above p. 414.

[31] Hugues Vincent and F. M. Abel, *Jérusalem, recherches de topographie, d'archéologie et d'histoire.* ii (1914), pp.337-360,383f. A different reconstruction and a later date have been proposed by E. Weigand (in ZDPV 46 [1923], pp.212-220) and Watzinger (*Denkmäler Palästinas.* ii, p.127), but probably are not to be accepted (see Crowfoot, *Early Churches in Palestine,* pp.30-34; Vincent in RB 21 [1924], pp.310f.; 45 [1936], p.419; 64 [1957], pp.48-71).

According to these investigations, it appears that one approached the basilica through a fine portico with six columns, which gave access to a colonnaded atrium under which was a large cistern. At the farther end of the atrium several steps led up to the level of the basilica itself. The length of the basilica proper was about one hundred feet, this being a little longer than the one at Bethlehem and probably a little shorter than the one in front of the Anastasis. It was divided by two rows of columns into a nave and two side aisles, and the nave terminated in a semicircular apse, on the north side of which was an additional small chamber. The famous cave itself, which was transformed into a crypt, lay beneath the eastern end of the nave and the apse.

The church was destroyed by the Persians in 614, somewhat restored by Modestus, and finally quite ruined. During the Middle Ages two chapels were built on the site, one called the Pater to mark the place where Jesus was supposed to have taught the Pater Noster or Lord's Prayer, and the other named the Credo to commemorate the place where the Apostles were said to have written the Creed. These were destroyed also, and the present Church of the Creed and Church of the Lord's Prayer date only from 1868 when the site was purchased by the Princesse de la Tour d'Auvergne. The east end of the Constantinian basilica and the cave crypt lie directly under the second of these present-day structures.

THE CHURCH AT MAMRE

Not only Constantine's mother, Helena, but also his mother-in-law, Eutropia, joined him in interest in the erection of churches in the Holy Land. Eutropia visited the famous oaks of Mamre (Genesis 18:1) and found the place defiled by heathen idols and sacrifices. When she informed Constantine of the situation the emperor straightway wrote a letter, preserved in full by Eusebius, to Macarius of Jerusalem and the other bishops in Palestine, informing them of his desire that the pagan altar should be demolished and replaced by a church.[32] At this place, which is nearly two miles north of Hebron on the east side of the road to Jerusalem,[33] there is a large enclosure now known as the Haram Ramet el-Khalil. Part of the walls seem to date from the time of Herod and part from the time of Hadrian. Within the enclosure at the east side are the ruins of a church which

[32] *Life of Constantine.* III, 51-53.
[33] Sozomen, *Ch. Hist.* II, 4.

has been excavated by Father Mader. It was a small basilica with a long narthex and the apse "inscribed," or built within the rectangle of the church. While the church was restored, perhaps by Modestus, the present ruins doubtless represent the site and plan of the Constantinian basilica.[34]

THE CHURCH OF THE LOAVES AND FISHES
AT ET-TABGHA

Many other churches were built in Palestine during the following centuries, but to them only the briefest allusion here is possible. Most of them were basilical in plan, long buildings with a nave and two aisles. The finest floor mosaics are in the Church of the Loaves and Fishes at et-Tabgha (p.304), the place where fourth century tradition located the feeding of the five thousand (Mark 6:30-44). This church was built above an earlier small chapel on the same site and must be at least as late as the end of the fourth or beginning of the fifth century. The best preserved mosaic is that in the left or north transept (Fig. 194), with its wonderful pictures of birds and plants. Amidst lotus, papyrus, and other plants, ducks are nestling, cormorants flapping their wings, and a flamingo is fighting with a snake.[35]

THE CHURCHES OF GERASA

The Palestinian city of Roman times whose ruins are best preserved today is Gerasa (p.308) in Transjordan. This city was rebuilt in the second century A.D., shattered by earthquakes in the eighth, and left deserted for most of the next thousand years. A number of early Christian churches have been investigated there. The first is known as the cathedral and is a three-aisled basilica with an inscribed apse. It faced upon a paved court in the middle of which was a fountain reported to run with wine annually on the anniversary of the miracle at Cana in Galilee. The church and the miracle are referred to in A.D. 375 by Epiphanius, bishop of Constantia (Salamis) in Cyprus, and the excavators date the church around A.D. 365.[36] In 494 a second basilica, dedicated to the martyr Theodore, was founded on the other side of the fountain court, and with the addition of a baptistery block,

[34] A. E. Mader in RAC 6 (1929), pp.249-312; and in RB 39 (1930), pp.84-117; and *Mambre, Die Ergebnisse der Ausgrabungen im heiligen Bezirk Haram Râmet el-Halîl in Südpalästina 1926-1932.* 2 vols., 1957.

[35] A. M. Schneider, *Die Brotvermehrungskirche von et-ṭâbġa am Genesarethsee und ihre Mosaiken.* 1934.

[36] Kraeling, ed., *Gerasa, City of the Decapolis*, pp.212-219.

baths, and other structures the Christian precinct became a very impressive complex. The baptistery comprised three rooms, in the middle one of which was the baptismal pool. The candidate went down into the pool by four steps and left by steps on the other side.[37] Yet other churches at Gerasa include: the one dedicated to the Prophets, Apostles, and Martyrs, which was built (464-465) in the form of a Latin cross and contains interesting floor mosaics (Fig. 195); the basilica built by a certain Procopius (526-527); the round church of St. John the Baptist with the basilicas of St. George and SS. Cosmas and Damianus on either side of it (529-533); the Synagogue which was rebuilt as a church (530-531); the basilica of SS. Peter and Paul (c.540); the Propylaea church (565); and the basilica containing the name of Bishop Genesius (611).

6. CHURCHES IN SYRIA

THE work of Constantine in the erection of churches was also extended to Syria, according to Eusebius. At Heliopolis (Baalbek), a city whose hitherto exclusively pagan character is emphasized by Eusebius and attested by its world famous ruins of temples and altars, the emperor built "a church of great size and magnificence," and at the same time made arrangements concerning its clergy and provision for the necessities of the poor.[1] At Antioch likewise he erected another church which was "of unparalleled size and beauty." "The entire building," Eusebius continues, "was encompassed by an enclosure of great extent, within which the church itself rose to a vast elevation, being of an octagonal form, and surrounded on all sides by many chambers, courts, and upper and lower apartments; the whole richly adorned with a profusion of gold, brass, and other materials of the most costly kind."[2]

THE CHURCH OF ST. BABYLAS AT KAOUSSIE

While we are dependent upon Eusebius for our knowledge of the Constantinian church at Antioch, excavations in the vicinity of that important site have disclosed two other important early Christian churches. The first of these was found to the north of the city, on the

[37] J. Barbee Robertson in *The College of the Bible Quarterly.* 33 (1956), pp.12-20.
[1] *Life of Constantine.* III, 58. For Baalbek see Theodor Wiegand, *Baalbek, Ergebnisse der Ausgrabungen und Untersuchungen in den Jahren 1898 bis 1905.* 4 vols. 1921-25.
[2] *Life of Constantine.* III, 50.

way to the village of Kaoussie, on the right bank of the Orontes River.[3] As may be seen in the air view in Fig. 196, the plan of the church is essentially that of a cross with four equal arms oriented to the four points of the compass. While the walls have been destroyed their foundations remain, together with extensive portions of the mosaics with which the floors were adorned, and thus a good idea of the original structure can be obtained.

The four radiating arms or naves of the church are almost equal in their dimensions, each being about thirty-six feet wide and eighty-two feet long. Of the mosaics with which their floors were covered, those in the north, west, and south naves display a similar pattern of continuous geometric designs. Each of these three floor mosaics is accompanied by an inscription containing substantially the same statement. The one in the north nave reads, "In the time of our most holy bishop Flavian,[4] and in the time of the most pious Eusebius the steward and presbyter, Dorys the presbyter in fulfillment of a vow completed the mosaic of this hall too. In the month of March of the year 435 [A.D. 387]." The mosaics in the east nave are of a different character, being divided into large areas each with its own style of decoration including triangles, circles, and other figures. Any inscription which was here unfortunately is lost.

From all four of the naves attention clearly was directed toward the center of the church. Here the four halls opened into a central room which was about fifty-five feet square. Above, the roofs of the naves abutted upon the presumably yet higher roof of this room. In the center of the room was a raised platform, and beneath the floor were two tombs. One was a tomb of bricks, the other was like a monolithic sarcophagus with a horizontal division in the middle so that it could accommodate two bodies.

The *simple et grandiose* plan of this church, as its excavators call it, was not seriously altered by later additions. Among the smaller structures which were annexed to the main halls the most important was a baptistery. This was entered from the north nave through a hall designated by a mosaic inscription as a Pistikon (ΠΕΙCΤΙΚΟΥ), perhaps the place where the catechumen recited the confession of faith before being baptized. The inscription is dated under Theodotus who was bishop of Antioch in A.D. 420-429. In the baptistery the baptismal basin was large enough to receive the candidate into

---

[3] Jean Lassus in *Antioch on-the-Orontes. II: The Excavations 1933-1936*, pp.5-44.
[4] Flavian was bishop of Antioch in A.D. 381-404 (NSH IV, p.327).

the water but not large enough to provide for his immersion, so the ceremony must have been carried out by affusion.

As the inscription of Dorys shows, the mosaics which he placed in the main church were completed in A.D. 387. An interesting bit of history enables us with considerable probability to date the original construction of the church a few years earlier and to identify its name.[5] Babylas, bishop of Antioch, suffered martyrdom in A.D. 250 under Decius. His remains presumably were interred first at Antioch, afterward were transferred to Daphne, and finally were brought back to Antioch. In a discourse concerning Babylas, Chrysostom[6] refers to the return of the body to Antioch, and says, "You indeed gave him back to the band of fellow enthusiasts; but the grace of God did not suffer him to remain there forever, but again removed him beyond the river, so that much of the countryside was filled with the sweet odor of the martyr." In connection with this burial of the saint beyond the river, Chrysostom continues, "And he was not destined when he went there to remain alone, but he soon received a neighbor and fellow lodger (γείτονα καὶ ὁμόσκηνον), one of similar life; and he had shared the same office with him."

This second person, Chrysostom says, had been responsible for the construction of the church in which the martyr and he himself were buried. While the church was being built, he had visited it every day and even participated in the actual labor of its erection. This must have been Meletius, the bishop of Antioch, who died in Constantinople in A.D. 381 during the meeting of the ecumenical council over which he presided, and whose remains, according to Sozomen, "were . . . conveyed to Antioch, and deposited near the tomb of Babylas the martyr."[7] Meletius therefore seems to have been buried at Antioch about A.D. 381 in a church in the construction of which he had been instrumental and in a tomb which was in immediate proximity to the interred martyr Babylas. Since Meletius had a stormy career and was most secure in his position as bishop of Antioch in about A.D. 379 and following, it is probable that he began the construction of the church only within the year or so preceding his death.

The identification of the church at Kaoussie with the one which figures in the foregoing account is most probable. Since its main

---

[5] Glanville Downey in *Antioch on-the-Orontes. II: The Excavations 1933-1936*, pp.45-48.

[6] *De Sancto Hieromartyre Babyla.* 3 (MPG 50 [1859], col. 533).

[7] Sozomen, *Ch. Hist.* VII, 10; cf. NSH VII, p.288.

floor mosaics were completed in A.D. 387, the church itself could very well have been built about A.D. 380 by Meletius. In the center of the church, moreover, was a sarcophagus which had once received two bodies. Very possibly this was the place where Babylas received as a "neighbor and fellow lodger" the man who had held the same office that he had, namely Meletius the bishop of Antioch. If these coordinations between the history as known from literary sources and the material findings revealed in the excavations are correct, the church at Kaoussie was constructed and received the remains of the famous martyr Babylas about A.D. 380; Meletius, the builder, was buried there in 381; and the adornment with many of its fine mosaics followed in 387. Its proper name is the Church of St. Babylas.

THE MARTYRION AT SELEUCIA PIERIA

The second church newly discovered in the same vicinity is at Seleucia Pieria, the seaport of Antioch. It seems to have been a memorial church, and commonly is referred to as the Martyrion.[8] According to the style of its mosaics and architecture it is dated tentatively in the last quarter of the fifth century A.D. It is believed to have been destroyed by earthquakes in A.D. 526 and 528 and to have been rebuilt soon after that time.

In its original plan the structure comprised a central quatrefoil, with an ambulatory around it, and a chancel projecting on the east side. The outlines of the quatrefoil and ambulatory appear clearly in Fig. 197, which is a view of the ruins looking north.

The floor of the ambulatory was adorned with a rich mosaic pavement which undoubtedly belonged to the first construction of the building. A portion of the mosaic in the north ambulatory is shown in its original place in Fig. 198. The border is of the type known as rinceau, and shows a continuous stalk of grapevine running in regular undulations, together with bunches of grapes, birds, and fowls. The main field represents a veritable paradise of natural wild life, and shows animals, birds, trees, flowers, and bits of landscape. Among the animals identified by the excavators are a lonely giraffe, a zebra startled by a large crane, inquisitive horses, fleet gazelles, a childishly irritable elephant, ferocious lions, sheep, goats, a hyena, and other beasts. The birds in the field and border include an eagle flapping its wings, a gallinule scratching its head, peacocks,

[8] W. A. Campbell in *Antioch on-the-Orontes. III: The Excavations 1937-1939*, pp.35-54.

flamingoes, cranes, ducks, and geese. Pomegranate, pear, fir, and pine trees, date palms, plants, and flowers add to the beauty of the scene.

The Martyrion was also adorned with an important series of sculptured marble revetments. The fragments recovered fall into two groups, one of which is composed of incised drawings believed to date in the fifth century, the other made up of low plastic reliefs thought to belong to the end of the fifth century or first half of the sixth. The bas-reliefs represent Old Testament subjects exclusively, including Daniel, Moses before the Burning Bush, Samson Fighting with a Lion, and others. The incised reliefs show not only Old Testament scenes such as Joseph in Prison, and Saul Fighting the Amalekites, but also New Testament pictures including the Adoration of the Magi, the Rich Man and Lazarus, the Feeding of the Multitude, and various scenes of healing, and furthermore include figures like Constantine and St. Simeon Stylites. Thus these reliefs include a very comprehensive selection of themes and afford a glimpse of the richness of Christian iconography at this time.[9]

THE CHURCH OF ST. SIMEON STYLITES

In the interior of Syria there were many early Christian churches which were lost to knowledge until, in the second half of the nineteenth century, a number of them were rediscovered and described by the Marquis de Vogüé.[10] More intensive studies have been made since by American and German scholars.[11] The churches date in the time from the fourth to the seventh centuries. On the whole it may be said that it was characteristic of the architecture revealed here to retain the basic form of the basilica but to place a new emphasis upon the development and decoration of the exterior. Single and double towers were employed to achieve an impressive façade, which was often adorned further with an open loggia above a broadly arched entrance.

Of all the Syrian churches the greatest was that of Qalat Siman, the

---

[9] Kurt Weitzmann in Antioch on-the-Orontes. III: The Excavations 1937-1939, pp.135-149; Harold R. Willoughby in JBL 69 (1950), pp.129-136.

[10] C. J. Melchior de Vogüé, Syrie Centrale. 2 vols. 1865-77.

[11] The Publications of an American Archaeological Expedition to Syria in 1899-1900. II: Architecture and Other Arts, by Howard Crosby Butler. 1903; Publications of the Princeton Archaeological Expeditions to Syria in 1904-5 and 1909. II: Architecture. A. Southern Syria. 1919, B. Northern Syria. 1920, by H. C. Butler; H. C. Butler, Early Churches in Syria, Fourth to Seventh Centuries. ed. E. Baldwin Smith, 1929; Hermann W. Beyer, Der syrische Kirchenbau. 1925.

Church of St. Simeon Stylites,[12] which was on a hilly plateau some forty miles northeast of Antioch. Simeon, in whose honor it was built, was born in northern Syria around A.D. 390, and became the first and most famous saint to practice living on top of a pillar. At the age of thirty and after having experimented with numerous other austerities, he built a pillar six feet high and made his home on its summit. He increased the height of the pillar gradually until after ten years it was sixty feet high. Here, protected from falling as we may suppose by a railing and possibly reached by a ladder up which his disciples brought his food, he lived without ever coming down until his death in 459.

The church built in memory of the saint is believed to have been erected shortly after his death, probably between A.D. 460 and 490. The extensive and impressive ruins of this structure which still stand (Fig. 199) provide a good indication of its character. The ground plan was similar to that of the Church of St. Babylas at Kaoussie, in that four rectangular halls were arranged to radiate from a central area, thus forming a cross. In St. Simeon's church the focal point of interest was the column on which the saint had dwelt. This pillar, a piece of which remains today, was left standing in its original position and the memorial edifice was built around it. Each of the four halls which extended out from this center was divided by columns into a nave and two side aisles, and the eastern hall ended in a magnificent triple apse. The central area where the four arms of the cross met was arranged as an octagon and, according to the latest research, was roofed with a soaring wooden cupola or dome.[13]

Hitherto it has been widely believed that the central octagon was left as an unroofed court open to the sky. The chief support for this opinion is a passage in which the church historian Evagrius (b. A.D. c.536) describes the edifice as he saw it upon a visit to the site around A.D. 560. He writes: "The temple is constructed in the form of a cross, adorned with colonnades on the four sides. Opposite the

[12] De Vogüé, *Syrie Centrale*, pp.141-152 and Planches 139-148; Butler in *The Publications of an American Archaeological Expedition to Syria in 1899-1900.* II, pp.184-190; in *Publications of the Princeton Archaeological Expeditions to Syria in 1904-5 and 1909. II: B.*, pp.261-284; and in *Early Churches in Syria, Fourth to Seventh Centuries*, pp.97-110; Beyer, *Der syrische Kirchenbau*, pp.60-71; Daniel Krencker, *Die Wallfahrtskirche des Simeon Stylites in Kal'at Sim'ân I Bericht über Untersuchungen und Grabungen im Frühjahr 1938 ausgeführt im Auftrag des Deutschen Archäologischen Instituts* (*Abhandlungen der Preussischen Akademie der Wissenschaften.* 1938. Phil.-hist. Kl. 4 [1939]).

[13] Krencker, *Die Wallfahrtskirche des Simeon Stylites in Kal'at Sim'ân.* I, pp.20f.

colonnades are arranged handsome columns of polished stone, sustaining a roof of considerable elevation; while the center is occupied by an unroofed court of the most excellent workmanship, where stands the pillar, of forty cubits, on which the incarnate angel upon earth spent his heavenly life."[14] Since Evagrius explicitly describes the central area as an unroofed or open air court (αὐλὴ ὑπαιθρίος), this must be accepted as the state of the church at the time of his visit. The probability is, however, not that it had been built that way originally, but that by the time Evagrius came the dome had been destroyed by fire or earthquake. When it proved too difficult to rebuild, the central room was left from that time on as an open court.

In the year 979 some further building work was done at Qalat Siman, as is indicated by an inscription which was found written in Greek and in Syrian. The Syrian form of the inscription gives the date in the Seleucid era as 1290, which refers to the year extending from October 7, 978, to October 6, 979. The Greek inscription actually uses the Christian era (κατὰ $\overline{X[\nu]}$), a system of reckoning which in this time occurs but seldom.[15]

Around Qalat Siman were grouped monasteries, and at the foot of the western hill was a town whose ruins show what elaborate accommodations were necessary to care for the large numbers of pilgrims who for centuries came to the place made memorable by the saint whom Evagrius called an "aerial martyr."[16]

7. CHURCHES IN EGYPT

THE CHURCH OF ST. MENAS

For a single example of early Christian churches in Egypt we turn to the remarkable ruined city of St. Menas, Karm Abu Mina, the "vineyard of Menas." According to the legendary lives of this saint, he was an Egyptian born of Christian parents in answer to a prayer of the mother addressed to an ikon of the Virgin. Since a voice seemed to answer this prayer with "Amen," the child was named Amen, or Menas. Growing up, he became a soldier and was on duty at Cotyaea in Phrygia when Diocletian's persecution broke out. Here, around

[14] *Church History.* I, 14 (*Bohn's Ecclesiastical Library.* 1854, pp.275f.).

[15] A slightly earlier example from the year 834 (ἀπὸ δὲ Χριστο[ῦ] ἔτους ω[λ]δ) is found in CIG IV, No.8680.

[16] *Church History.* I, 13.

A.D. 295, Menas bravely confessed his faith in Christ and suffered martyrdom. When his fellow soldiers were sent back from Phrygia to the Mareotis district in Egypt they took his corpse with them. They were threatened en route by terrible sea monsters, but fire went forth from the corpse and drove the creatures back. Arriving safely in Egypt, they buried the body of Menas beside the Lake of Mareotis where he had been born. When the troops were moved again they placed the bones of the saint on a camel to carry with them, but the camel refused to move. When another camel did likewise, it was interpreted as a sign and the bones were interred permanently at the place where the camels had stood. The grave would have been forgotten, save that one day a sick sheep drank from the nearby spring and was miraculously healed. Other wonderful healings, not only of animals but also of men, began to take place, and so many pilgrims were attracted there that a church was built above the martyr's tomb and an entire pilgrim city sprang up. Almost everyone who came carried away in a little flask some of the water from the spring or some oil from the lamp which hung in the church and burned day and night. Wherever the water or oil was carried miraculous healings took place.[1]

As remarkable as are the legends attaching to the name of St. Menas, almost more remarkable still are the actual churches and city which were built at his grave, lost for nearly one thousand years, and rediscovered at the beginning of the twentieth century. The Lake of Mareotis dried up in the Middle Ages and, although during the siege of Alexandria in 1801 the British cut through the dunes at Abusir and let in the sea, the ruins of the city of St. Menas lie now in a barren wilderness. The site, which is thirty miles or more southwest of Alexandria, was rediscovered and excavated by Carl Maria Kaufmann in 1905-1907.[2]

The Burial Church of St. Menas seems to have been consecrated under the Emperor Theodosius I the Great (379-395) although the first building work above the martyr's grave may have been done by Athanasius (c.298-373) with the help and interest of Constantine himself. The Burial Church was a basilica, 125 feet long and 74 feet

---

[1] For a reference to the custom, doubtless based originally upon James 5:14, of taking home oil from the lamps at church to anoint the sick, see Chrysostom, *Homilies on Matthew*. xxxii, 9 (NPNF x, p.217).

[2] C. M. Kaufmann, *Die Ausgrabung der Menasheiligtümer in der Mareotiswüste*. 1906; *Zweiter Bericht über die Ausgrabung der Menasheiligtümer in der Mareotiswüste*. 1907; *Die Menasstadt*. 1910; *Die heilige Stadt der Wüste*. 4th ed. 1924; Leclercq in DACL xi, cols. 324-397.

wide, with nave and aisles each terminating in an apse. It was so arranged that the altar came directly above the martyr's crypt which lay some twenty-six feet below. Not only did this *confessio* enable the holy tomb to be viewed from the room above but also there was provided a great marble stairway at one side which led directly down into the crypt. On the wall opposite the point at which the stairway enters the crypt the place can still be seen where a large marble plate was once affixed, doubtless bearing the famous representation of Menas with two camels bowing down to him. A photograph of the crypt is shown in Fig. 200. The picture is taken from a little chapel on the west of the crypt and looks toward the cryptoporticus which was built later to connect with the basilica of Arcadius. The recess which once held the Menas relief is on the south wall at the immediate right and is approximately three-quarters life size. While this relief no longer exists, it doubtless was the prototype of the picture of Menas between the camels which is stamped on so many of the flasks which were carried away from here by pilgrims. One of these flasks is shown in Fig. 201.

The basilica just described was oriented from west to east. Under the Emperor Arcadius (395-408), in order to accommodate the increasing masses of people a much larger basilica was built on at the eastern end of the first church. A large transept, 164 feet long and 66 feet wide gave the latter structure the form of a cross. At the same time a monumental baptistery church was erected at the western end of the first church. This was a square structure, which was turned into an octagon by the niches in the corners. In the center of its marble pavement was the deep marble tank, entered by steps from each side, in which the immersions were conducted (Fig. 202).

Notably under the eastern Emperor Zeno (474-491) this place developed into a great pilgrim city, and yet other basilicas, baths, and guesthouses were erected. Also there was a flourishing pottery industry which produced lamps, statuettes, plates, vases, and flasks for the pilgrims. Eventually came decline. In the seventh and eighth centuries, the Melchites and Jacobites[3] contended for possession of the sanctuary and in the ninth century a Melchite architect was permitted to carry away the church's marble pillars. Later in the

[3] The Melchites were Egyptian Christians who accepted the decrees of the Council of Chalcedon (A.D. 451) which were directed against the Jacobites and others. The Jacobites took their name from Jacob Baradai, bishop of Edessa (d. 578), the reorganizer of Syrian Monophysitism.

ninth century the place was despoiled by the Muslims and thereafter it became the prey of marauding Bedouins. The Church of St. Menas was seen around A.D. 1000 by an anonymous Arab traveler, but from then until its rediscovery by Kaufmann in 1905 it remained lost beneath the sands of the Mareotic Desert.

8. CHURCHES IN CONSTANTINOPLE

AFTER the defeat and death of Licinius (324), Constantine lived almost continuously in the East and in A.D. 330 officially founded his new capital, Constantinople, which formerly had been the city of Byzantium.[1] New Rome, as Constantinople was also called, was intended to be a wholly Christian city and therefore was adorned not only with a hippodrome, baths, fountains, and porticoes, but also with numerous houses of prayer and memorials of martyrs. A little distance away on the Bosporus was a sanctuary of the Archangel Michael.[2]

THE CHURCH OF ALL THE APOSTLES

At least two churches were founded by Constantine within the city.[3] One of these was dedicated to All the Apostles and intended by Constantine to be his own last resting place.[4] According to Eusebius, the building was carried to a vast height and had a great dome. From foundation to roof it was encased with slabs of various colored marbles while the roof was of brass adorned with gold.[5] This church was reconstructed by Justinian the Great (527-565),[6] but upon the fall of Constantinople to the Turks in 1453 was torn

[1] In Nicomedia of Bithynia, which had served as capital and under Diocletian had been the chief city of the East, Constantine erected a magnificent and stately church as "a memorial of his victory over his own enemies and the adversaries of God" (Eusebius, *Life of Constantine.* III, 50).

[2] Sozomen, *Ch. Hist.* II, 3; Eusebius, *Life of Constantine.* III, 48.

[3] That Constantine later gave encouragement at least toward the building of yet other churches is indicated by his letter to Eusebius (*Life of Constantine.* IV, 36), in which the emperor mentions the need for an increased number of churches in Constantinople to accommodate the growing mass of Christians, and places an order for fifty fine copies of the Bible to be placed in these churches (cf. p.397).

[4] Eusebius, *Life of Constantine.* IV, 70; Socrates, *Ch. Hist.* I, 40.

[5] *Life of Constantine.* IV, 58-60.

[6] Procopius, *Buildings.* I, iv, 9-16. Procopius stated (*ibid.,* I, iv, 19) that the church was built by the Emperor Constantius but the explanation of this difference from Eusebius is doubtless that it was begun by Constantine and completed after his death by his son.

down and replaced by the Mosque of Sultan Mohammed II the Conqueror.[7] The Church of All the Apostles was resembled closely by Justinian's Church of St. John at Ephesus[8] and also is believed to have served as a model for St. Mark's at Venice.

THE CHURCH OF ST. EIRENE

The second church had already been in existence as a Christian sanctuary in the old town of Byzantium, but was considerably enlarged and adorned by Constantine. He dedicated it to holy peace —Eirene—in honor of the peace which he had brought to the world after eighteen years of civil war.[9] In this Constantine followed the example of Augustus who likewise had symbolized the calm and quiet he brought to a torn world by the dedication of an altar at Rome, the Ara Pacis, to the imperial peace. Constantine's church stood for two centuries and then was burned to the ground in the fire of A.D. 532. It was restored by Justinian the Great,[10] but again damaged by fire in 564 and seriously injured by the violent earthquake of 740. The church still stands but has been used by the Turks as an armory and a museum. The present walls of the main body of the building probably date from the new structure erected by Justinian after 532, and the narthex and some other portions represent the same emperor's repairs after 564. The apse and upper part of the church including the dome probably belong to the reconstruction after the earthquake and may have been carried out by the Emperor Leo III the Isaurian (717-740) or by his son and successor Constantine V Copronymus (740-775).[11]

The essential plan of St. Eirene as it now exists is that of the basilica, with atrium, narthex, nave, side aisles, and apse. But a great dome is placed above the nave, even as Eusebius mentioned a dome as a prominent feature of the lost Church of All the Apostles. The combination of a domed superstructure with the earlier ground plan of the basilica became the characteristic theme of Byzantine church buildings. The culminating example of the domed basilica type was to appear in Justinian's church of Hagia Sophia in Constantinople.

[7] A. Van Millingen, *Byzantine Churches in Constantinople*. 1912, pp.3,175; Ernest Mamboury, *Constantinople*. 1925, p.355.
[8] Procopius, *Buildings*. v, i, 6.   [9] Socrates, *Ch. Hist.* i, 16; ii, 16.
[10] Procopius, *Buildings*. i, ii, 13.
[11] Walter S. George, *The Church of Saint Eirene at Constantinople*. 1912; Van Millingen, *Byzantine Churches in Constantinople*, pp.101f.

THE CHURCH OF HAGIA SOPHIA

The first foundations of the famous Church of Hagia Sophia,[12] or "Holy Wisdom," are believed by some to have been laid by Constantine,[13] but the church historian Socrates states only that it was built by Constantine's son and successor, Constantius II (337-361) and consecrated in A.D. 360.[14] It was known as "The Great Church"[15] and was dedicated to the Immortal Wisdom of Christ. The structure of Constantius was of the basilican type, with atrium, narthex, and nave flanked by side aisles marked off with rows of columns. Its roof was of wood, except for the half dome of the apse. This church was burned to the ground in A.D. 404, restored, and again burned down in A.D. 532. Then it was rebuilt in magnificence by Justinian, with Anthemius of Tralles and Isidorus of Miletus as his master builders. Dedication was in A.D. 537. Earthquake damage in 553 and 557 was repaired by Justinian and the dome somewhat raised by Isidorus the younger nephew of the other Isidorus. Since that time the Great Church has survived the vicissitudes of the centuries, little changed. The huge exterior buttresses were added by the Emperor Andronicus II Palaeologus (1282-1328), and the four minarets were erected after the Muslims made the church into "the great mosque of Hagia Sophia" (Fig. 203). In 1931 the Turkish Government issued an order enabling the Byzantine Institute to begin to lay bare and study the ancient mosaics with which the church was adorned.[16] In 1934 the use of the building for a mosque was terminated and it was announced that it would be preserved henceforth as a museum and monument of Byzantine art.

A contemporary description of Hagia Sophia as it appeared in the time of Justinian was given by Procopius of Caesarea, who wrote extensively concerning that emperor's reign and particularly his

[12] Alfons Maria Schneider, *Die Hagia Sophia zu Konstantinopel*; Emerson H. Swift, *Hagia Sophia*. 1940; William Emerson and Robert L. Van Nice in AJA 47 (1943), pp.403-436.

[13] A. Van Millingen, *Byzantine Constantinople*. 1899, p.36.

[14] *Ch. Hist.* II, 16,43.

[15] Procopius, *Buildings*. I, i, 66. This title was sometimes applied to include both Hagia Sophia and St. Eirene, which stood close together and were regarded as forming one sanctuary.

[16] Thomas Whittemore, *The Mosaics of St. Sophia at Istanbul, Preliminary Report on the First Year's Work, 1931-1932, The Mosaics of the Narthex*. 1933; *Second Preliminary Report, Work Done in 1933 and 1934, The Mosaics of the Southern Vestibule*. 1936; *Third Preliminary Report, Work Done in 1935-1938, The Imperial Portraits of the South Gallery*. 1942; and in AJA 42 (1938), pp.219-226; 46 (1942), pp.169-171 and Plates I-X; cf. Harold R. Willoughby in Massey H. Shepherd, Jr., and Sherman E. Johnson, eds., *Munera Studiosa*. 1946, pp.124f.

widespread and notable building achievements.[17] "The church," wrote Procopius, "has become a spectacle of marvellous beauty, overwhelming to those who see it, but to those who know it by hearsay altogether incredible. For it soars to a height to match the sky, and as if surging up from amongst the other buildings it stands on high and looks down upon the remainder of the city."[18] Impressive as was the exterior of the Great Church, the interior (Fig. 204) was more wonderful still. It was adorned with many colored marbles and bathed with an abundance of light until the visitor "might imagine that he had come upon a meadow with its flowers in full bloom."[19] The crowning glory was the huge golden dome which seemed not to rest upon solid masonry but to hang suspended from heaven.[20] In its misty vastness the Spirit of God seemed to descend, and whoever entered to pray felt "that He cannot be far away, but must especially love to dwell in this place which He has chosen."[21] Such was the culminating achievement in the Byzantine development of the basilica.

The mysticism of the East was matched by the aspiration of the West. In the West the path of future development led through the modifications of Romanesque style[22] to the Gothic,[23] whose soaring loftiness is the soul's upward reach toward God. But basic to both Gothic and Byzantine adaptations was the essential structural form and meaning of the early Christian basilica which they preserved. This was the place where was preached the gospel of Jesus Christ.

---

[17] The treatise on the *Buildings* of Justinian was published in 560 or soon thereafter.

[18] *Buildings.* I, i, 27. [19] *Buildings.* I, i, 59.

[20] *Buildings.* I, i, 46. [21] *Buildings.* I, i, 61.

[22] Romanesque means Roman-like and describes the architectural style which prevailed in the West from the fall of Rome (A.D. 476) down to the rise of Gothic. Here the basic basilican idea was modified chiefly through the increasing use of the rounded arch.

[23] Gothic architecture, which developed in Western Europe after A.D. 1100, was an outgrowth of Romanesque but particularly characterized by the use of the pointed arch.

Appendix

The Principles of the Calendar and the Problems of Biblical Chronology

1. THE UNITS OF TIME

THE chief units in the reckoning of time for calendrical purposes are the day, week, month, and year, while the year is also divided into seasons and the day into hours or other parts. Revelation 9:15 mentions the units, hour, day, month, and year; and Galatians 4:10 speaks of days, months, seasons, and years. There are some indications, to be noted in what follows, which suggest that recognition of the day, week, month, and year was based first upon climatic and agricultural factors; later these units of time were associated with the celestial bodies.

THE DAY

In the Sumerian and Akkadian languages the word for "day" also means "wind." Likewise in the Song of Solomon 2:17 and 4:6 it is said that "the day breathes" or literally that it blows. It has been suggested, therefore, that it was first of all the daily land and sea breezes of the Mesopotamian and Palestinian coastlands which called attention to this time unit long before there was systematic observation of the sun.[1]

The rising and setting of the sun and the alternation of light and darkness were also very obvious facts of nature, however, and these too must have been recognized very early as marking out the day. In Hebrew the word for day is יוֹם (*yom*). This is used to designate the day in the sense of daytime as distinct from nighttime as, for example, in Genesis 1:5 where "God called the light Day." It is also used for day in the sense of the complete cycle which includes both the daytime and the nighttime as, for example, in Genesis 1:5: "And there was evening and there was morning, one day." In Greek the corresponding word ἡμέρα is used for the daytime as, for example, in Matthew 4:2 where Jesus fasted for "forty days and forty nights."

[1] Hildegard and Julius Lewy in HUCA 17 (1942-43), pp.5f.

For the complete cycle of light and darkness there is a word, νυχ-θήμερον, which combines "night" (νύξ) and "day" (ἡμέρα) in one term. This is used in II Corinthians 11:25 where it is translated "a night and a day." Usually, however, the "day" which includes the nighttime and the daytime is simply designated with the word ἡμέρα and the context makes plain what is meant as, for example, in John 2:12 or Acts 9:19 where the several "days" are certainly several successive periods each comprising daytime and nighttime.

A "day" in the sense of a complete period of light and darkness might be reckoned as beginning with the coming of the light or with the coming of the darkness, as well as of course theoretically at any other point in the daily cycle, midnight now being used as that point. In Egypt the day probably began at dawn,[2] in Mesopotamia it began in the evening.[3] In the Old Testament the earlier practice seems to have been to consider that the day began in the morning. In Genesis 19:34, for example, the "morrow" (ASV) or "next day" (RSV) clearly begins with the morning after the preceding night. The later practice was to count the day as beginning in the evening. In Leviticus 23:27 it is stated that the day of atonement is to be observed on the tenth day of the seventh month; in verse 32 it is said that the observance is to be "on the ninth day of the month beginning at evening, from evening to evening." These last words can hardly be intended to change the actual date of the fast; rather they appear to be an addition which simply defines what the tenth day of the month was at a time when the day had come to be reckoned as beginning in the evening: the tenth day of the month is the day which begins on the evening of the ninth and continues until the following evening. In making the shift from a morning reckoning to an evening reckoning, the "day" was therefore in fact moved back so that it began a half day earlier than had been the case previously.[4]

In the New Testament in the Synoptic Gospels and Acts the day seems usually to be considered as beginning in the morning. Mark 11:11 states that Jesus entered Jerusalem, went into the temple, and when he had looked at everything, since it was "now eventide" (ASV) or "already late" (RSV), went out to Bethany with the twelve; verse 12 continues the narrative and tells that on the "morrow" (ASV) or the "following day" (RSV) they came back to the city. It is evident

[2] PCAE p.10.   [3] PDBC p.26.
[4] Julian Morgenstern in HUCA 10 (1935), pp.15-28; 20 (1947), pp.34-38.

that the new day has begun with the morning following the preceding evening. Likewise Matthew 28:1, Mark 16:1f., and Luke 23:56-24:1 all picture the first day of the week beginning with the dawn following the preceding sabbath. And Acts 4:3, for an example in that book, tells how Peter and John were put in custody "until the morrow, for it was already evening," thus clearly indicating that the new day would begin the next morning. On the other hand, Mark 1:32 = Luke 4:40 seems to picture the sabbath (Mark 1:21 = Luke 4:31) as coming to an end at sunset, at which time the people of Capernaum were free to bring the sick to Jesus. Likewise in the Gospel according to John the day seems to be reckoned as beginning in the evening. In John 20:1 Mary Magdalene comes to the tomb while it is still dark, yet it is already "on the first day of the week," hence the new day must have already begun. It is evident that this reckoning of the day as beginning with the preceding evening corresponds with the late Old Testament usage described in the preceding paragraph, and it may be assumed that this was the standard custom of the Jews in New Testament times as since. It has been suggested that the other usage, namely that of counting the day as beginning with the morning, is a continuation of the earlier Old Testament practice also already described, and that this usage was maintained in parts of Galilee and was followed by Jesus and the early disciples, which would account for its appearing so frequently in the Synoptic Gospels and Acts.[5]

The coming of light and the coming of darkness are of course gradual events, and it is therefore to periods of transition which are not necessarily sharply defined that the terms "morning" and "evening," as also "dawn" (e.g. Judges 19:25f.) and "twilight" (e.g. I Samuel 30:17), refer. For a more precise line of demarcation between one day and the next the time of sunrise or of sunset could be taken, and we have seen probable examples of such usage in Mark 16:2 and Mark 1:32 respectively. Or the determination could be made in terms of the intensity of the light or the completeness of the darkness. For example, it was held by the Jewish rabbis that Deuteronomy 6:4-7 required the recitation of the Shema in the evening and in the morning, and in the Talmud there is found an extended dis-

---

[5] Julian Morgenstern in *Crozer Quarterly*. 26 (1949), pp.232-240. It may be noted that the Greeks reckoned the day from sunset to sunset, and the Romans began the day at midnight. James Gow, *A Companion to School Classics*. 3d ed. 1891, pp.78, 147; and in Leonard Whibley, ed., *A Companion to Greek Studies*. 3d ed. 1916, p.589.

cussion of exactly what times are thereby intended. The recital could begin in the morning, it was declared, as soon as one could distinguish between blue and white (or between blue and green, as another rabbi taught), and it must be finished before sunrise.[6] As for the evening, Nehemiah 4:21 was cited, where work went on "till the stars came out," and from that analogy it was shown that the appearance of the stars was the sign that the day had ended and the recital could begin.[7] Thus in the morning it was either the dawning light or the following sunrise, and in the evening it was either the sunset or the ensuing nightfall when the stars became visible, that provided the line of demarcation.[8]

Parts of the day were described at an early time in terms of the customary occupation then performed as, for example, the "time for the animals to be gathered together" (Genesis 29:7), or "the time when women go out to draw water" (Genesis 24:11). The nighttime was divided into watches. Lamentations 2:19 speaks of "the beginning of the watches," Judges 7:19 mentions "the middle watch," and Exodus 14:24 and I Samuel 11:11 refer to "the morning watch." The rabbis debated whether there were three watches or four;[9] and Mark 13:35 names four: evening, midnight, cockcrow, and morning. The daytime had recognizable periods such as "the heat of the day" (Genesis 18:1) and "the cool of the day" (Genesis 3:8), and was also divided broadly into morning, noon, and evening (Psalm 55:17). A division of the daytime into three parts, and of the nighttime into three parts, is mentioned in Jubilees 49:10, 12.[10]

The word "hour" (שָׁעָה, *sha'ah*) occurs several times in Daniel (3:6, etc.) in Aramaic, and is common in later Hebrew. In Daniel it still denotes simply a short period of time and the phrase "the same hour" (ASV) may properly be translated "immediately" (RSV). In Greek the corresponding word is ὥρα, and it too is used for an inexactly defined period of time, as for example in John 5:35 where πρὸς ὥραν is translated "for a while."

In Mesopotamia the entire day was divided into twelve periods of what we would call two hours each.[11] Herodotus[12] refers to these

---

[6] *Berakoth.* I, 2; DM p.2.   [7] *Berakoth.* 2b; SBT p.3.

[8] As the line between one day and the next, nightfall was later defined even more precisely as the moment when three stars of the second magnitude become visible. Michael Friedländer in JE III, p.501.

[9] *Berakoth.* 3a-b; SBT pp.5-8.

[10] CAP II, p.80.

[11] Contenau, *Everyday Life in Babylon and Assyria*, p.11.

[12] II, 109.

"twelve divisions (μέρεα) of the day," and observes that the Greeks learned of them from the Babylonians. Among the Greeks themselves the day and the night were each divided into twelve hours.[13] These hours naturally varied in length depending upon the time of year and were known as ὧραι καιρικαί. For scientific purposes, an hour of standard length was used, the entire day (νυχθήμερον) being divided into twenty-four periods of equal length. The astronomer Hipparchus (c.150 B.C.) speaks of these "equinoctial hours" (ὧραι ἰσημεριναί),[14] as he calls them, and Ptolemy[15] also distinguishes between ordinary and equinoctial hours.

In order to measure the hours there were available for the time when the sun was shining the sunclock (πόλος) and the sundial (γνώμων), which are mentioned by Herodotus in the passage cited just above with the statement that they came from Babylonia. The same principle of measurement by the shadow of the sun was of course also known in Egypt, where the obelisks were evidently used for astronomical measurements.[16] For the measurement of time during the darkness as well as the light, there was the water clock (κλεψύδρα), which is mentioned by Aristotle[17] and others.

The division of the day into twelve hours appears in John 11:9 where it is asked, "Are there not twelve hours in the day?" Likewise in Matthew 20:1-12 the householder goes to hire laborers early in the morning, and again at the third, sixth, ninth, and eleventh hours, and the last ones have only one hour to work before the end of the day. If an average daytime lasting from six a.m. to six p.m. was taken as the basis, then the third hour was nine o'clock in the morning, and so on.

In the Talmud[18] there is a discussion in connection with the testimony of witnesses of the extent of reasonable error in a man's estimate of what hour it is, and it is noted that "in the sixth hour the sun stands in the meridian."

Among the parts of the day the "evening" was of special importance. We have already seen how the regularly used day in later Jewish times began in the evening rather than in the morning, and

---

13 Gow, A Companion to School Classics, p.79.

14 Hipparchus II, iv, 5. ed. C. Manitius, 1894, p.184.

15 Tetrabiblos. 76. tr. F. E. Robbins, LCL (1948), pp.165-167.

16 Henry N. Russell, Raymond S. Dugan, and John Q. Stewart, Astronomy, A Revision of Young's Manual of Astronomy, I, The Solar System. rev. ed. 1945, p.78.

17 Athenian Constitution. LXVII, 2. tr. H. Rackham, LCL (1952), p.187. cf. Sontheimer in PWRE Zweite Reihe, IV, ii, cols. 2017-2018.

18 Pesaḥim. 11b-12b; SBT pp.51-56.

how either the sunset or the appearing of the stars was taken as the exact time of its beginning. The evening was also important because of the sacrifices which were made at that time, and in this connection there was discussion of exactly what period of time was meant. According to Numbers 28:4 the daily burnt offering called for the sacrifice of one lamb in the morning and of another "in the evening." According to Exodus 12:6 the passover lambs were to be killed "in the evening" of the fourteenth day of the first month, and Leviticus 23:5 gives the same date for "the Lord's passover." In all three passages the Hebrew is literally "between the two evenings" (ASV margin), although in the first two cases the Septuagint translates simply πρὸς ἑσπέραν, "towards evening," and only in the Leviticus passage renders ἀνὰ μέσον τῶν ἑσπερινῶν, "between the evenings." The Mishnah[19] states that the daily evening burnt offering was slaughtered at eight and a half hours, that is two-thirty o'clock, and offered at nine and a half hours, that is three-thirty o'clock. If it was the eve of passover it was slaughtered at seven and a half hours, one-thirty o'clock, and offered at eight and a half hours, two-thirty o'clock, whether on a weekday or the sabbath; if it was the eve of passover and this fell on the eve of a sabbath, that is on a Friday, it was slaughtered at six and a half hours, twelve-thirty o'clock, and offered at seven and a half hours, one-thirty o'clock; and then the passover offering was slaughtered after that.

Explaining this procedure the accompanying Gemara[20] states that "between the evenings" means "from the time that the sun commences to decline in the west," and that the "two evenings" give "two and a half hours before and two and a half hours after and one hour for preparation" of the sacrifice. This means that "evening" begins as soon as the sun passes its midday zenith, and that the "two evenings" are from twelve to two-thirty o'clock, and from three-thirty until six o'clock respectively. Thus the daily evening burnt offering is ordinarily sacrificed in the hour between these two evenings, but when the passover must also be sacrificed the same afternoon then the daily sacrifice is moved ahead. In another passage the Mishnah[21] deals with the requirement of Exodus 34:25 that the passover sacrifice not be offered with leaven, and states that everything leavened must be burned at the beginning of the sixth hour, that is at twelve o'clock noon. As the accompanying discussion in the Gemara[22] shows,

---

[19] *Pesaḥim.* v, 1; DM p.141. [20] *Pesaḥim.* 58a; SBT pp.287f.
[21] *Pesaḥim.* I, 4; DM p.137. [22] *Pesaḥim.* 5a; SBT p.17.

this indicates that the sacrificing could begin immediately after noon. According to Josephus[23] the passover sacrifices were conducted from the ninth to the eleventh hour, that is from three to five o'clock in the afternoon, and this was presumably the standard practice in the first century A.D.

According to the foregoing passages, then, the "evening" was substantially equivalent to the entire afternoon. In Deuteronomy 16:6, however, it is said that the passover sacrifice is to be offered "in the evening at the going down of the sun." The Talmudic explanation of this was that the evening meant the afternoon and was the time when the passover was to be slaughtered, and that the sunset was the time when it was to be eaten.[24] The Sadducees and the Samaritans, however, held that the slaughtering of the lamb itself was to take place between sunset and darkness.[25] The Book of Jubilees seems to agree with this when it says about the passover lamb: "It is not permissible to slay it during any period of the light, but during the period bordering on the evening, and let them eat it at the time of the evening until the third part of the night" (49:12).[26] The Targum of Onkelos also rendered "between the two evenings" in Exodus 12:6 as "between the two suns,"[27] and this was then explained as meaning the time between sunset and the coming out of the stars.[28]

In either case, however, whether it meant the afternoon time up until sunset, or the time from sunset until the stars became visible, the "evening" in the sense and in the regard just discussed evidently belonged to the closing part of the day, and it was only with the sunset or the appearing of the stars that the next day began.

THE WEEK

A sequence of seven days forms a week. Since the ancient Babylonians recognized seven winds, as may be seen in the Creation Epic where Marduk "sent forth the winds he had brought forth, the seven of them,"[29] it has been surmised that originally one day was dedicated to each of the winds and thus a week of seven days was

---

[23] *War.* VI, ix, 3.   [24] *Berakoth.* 9a; SBT pp.46f.
[25] Emil G. Hirsch in JE IX, p.553.   [26] CAP II, p.80.
[27] J. W. Etheridge, ed., *The Targums of Onkelos and Jonathan ben Uzziel on the Pentateuch; With the Fragments of the Jerusalem Targum from the Chaldee.* 2 vols. 1862-65, I, p.370.
[28] S. R. Driver, *The Book of Exodus* (The Cambridge Bible for Schools and Colleges). 1911, p.89 n.
[29] ANET p.66.

formed.[30] In the Bible the days are simply numbered and the seventh day is also named the sabbath (שבת, *shabbat*; σάββατον). In addition to this, the day before the sabbath was called the day of Preparation,[31] and by the Christians the first day of the week was called the Lord's day (Revelation 1:10). The name of the entire week was derived from the sabbath day and the week was called שבע (*shebua'*) in Hebrew (Genesis 29:27, etc.), σάββατον in Greek (Luke 18:12, etc.).

The custom of naming the seven days of the week after the seven planets is attested in the first century B.C. when Tibullus (d. 19 B.C.) mentions the day of Saturn, and in the first century A.D. when Greek and Latin wall inscriptions at Pompeii (A.D. 79) list "the days of the gods," namely of Saturn, the sun, the moon, Mars, Mercury, Jupiter, and Venus.[32] Dio Cassius[33] (d. A.D. c.235) says this custom was instituted by the Egyptians and was in his own time found among all mankind. Dio's remark in this connection, that the Jews dedicate to their God "the day called the day of Saturn," is of course correct as far as Jewish observance of Saturday or the sabbath is concerned, but they would hardly have designated the day by the name which the pagan writer uses. In an apocryphal rabbinic work, however, the *Pirqe de Rabbi Eliezer*, the final edition of which probably dates in the ninth century A.D., the planets which rule the week are named. For each day a pair is given, the first being the ruler of the nighttime and the second the regent of the following daytime: "The planets serve . . . as the regents of the seven days of the week, to wit: On the first day, Mercury and the Sun; on the second, Jupiter and the Moon; on the third, Venus and Mars; on the fourth, Saturn and Mercury; on the fifth, the Sun and Jupiter; on the sixth, the Moon and Venus; on the seventh, Mars and Saturn."[34]

[30] Hildegard and Julius Lewy in HUCA 17 (1942-43), pp.6-25.

[31] παρασκευή, Josephus, *Ant.* XVI, vi, 2; Matthew 27:62; Luke 23:54; John 19:31, 42; προσάββατον, Mark 15:42.

[32]

Θεων ημερας	(dies)	(the day of)	
Κρονου	Saturni	Saturn	Saturday
Ηλιου	Solis	the Sun	Sunday
Σεληνης	Lunae	the Moon	Monday
Αρεως	Martis	Mars	Tuesday (Tiw's day)
Ε[ρ]μου	(Mercurii)	**Mercury**	Wednesday (Woden's day)
Διος	Jovis	Jupiter	Thursday (Thor's day)
[Αφρο]δειτης	Veneris	Venus	Friday (Frigg's day)

Emil Schürer in ZNW 6 (1905), pp.25, 27.

[33] *Roman History.* XXXVII, xvii-xix.

[34] VI, 13b. *Pirkê de Rabbi Eliezer (The Chapters of Rabbi Eliezer the Great)* according to the Text of the Manuscript belonging to Abraham Epstein of Vienna. ed.

THE MONTH

If the day and the week were connected first of all with climatic conditions and only later with astronomical objects it could be that something similar was true of the month. In fact, when the Israelite calendar is discussed below, it will be seen that the Gezer Calendar relates the months to the tasks to be performed in the successive phases of agricultural work, and that the old month names in the Old Testament describe their respective periods of time in terms of agricultural and climatic conditions.

Etymologically, however, the word "month" shows the connection between this time unit and the moon. In Hebrew the word ירח (*yerah*) means both "moon" and "month," as may be seen for example in Deuteronomy 33:14 where the alternative translations are, "the precious things of the growth of the moons" (ASV), and "the rich yield of the months" (RSV). Likewise the term חדש (*hodesh*), which originally meant "the shining, glittering new moon," was later used as the designation of the festival of the day of the new moon, and also as the name of the entire month which is, as it were, the lifetime of the newly born moon. In Genesis 29:14, for example, this word clearly means "month," in I Samuel 20:5 and other passages it means the "new moon" day.[35] Likewise in Greek the word μήνη means "moon" and μήν means "month." In the Septuagint μήν is the translation of both ירח (Deuteronomy 33:14, etc.) and חדש (Genesis 29:14). In the New Testament μήν regularly means "month" (Luke 1:24, etc.), but in one case (Galatians 4:10) probably refers to the new moon festival.

In so far as the month was related to the moon, the determination of its length depended upon observation of the phases of the moon. In Egypt, where the day probably began at dawn, it is thought that the month probably began with a lunar phenomenon which could be observed at that time of day. As the moon wanes, the old crescent is finally just visible in the eastern sky before sunrise one morning and on the next morning it is invisible. It may have been, therefore, on the morning when the old crescent could no longer be seen that the Egyptian lunar month began.[36] In Mesopotamia, on the other hand,

---

Gerald Friedlander. 1916, p.32; Solomon Gandz in *Proceedings of the American Academy for Jewish Research.* 18 (1948-49), p.230. See also F. H. Colson, *The Week.* 1926.

[35] Solomon Gandz in JQR 39 (1948-49), pp.259f.

[36] PCAE pp.9-23.

the day began in the evening, and the month began when the crescent of the new moon was first visible in the western sky at sunset.[37]

In modern astronomy the time from one new moon to the next, which is known as the synodic or ordinary month, is determined as 29.530588 days, or 29 days, 12 hours, 44 minutes, 2.8 seconds.[38] This means that on the average the new moon will be seen approximately every twenty-nine and one-half days, and that the full moon will come approximately fourteen and three-quarter days after the appearing of the new moon, that is on the fifteenth day of the lunar month, with the day reckoned from evening to evening.[39]

After the accumulation of data by observation, the month could have been calculated in advance. Likewise it could have been established as a standard unit, say of thirty days, rather than left variable as it must be to agree with the observed phases of the moon.

THE YEAR

The ordinary Hebrew word for "year" is שָׁנָה (shanah). It is etymologically connected with the idea of "change" or "repeated action," and thus describes a "revolution of time." In the Septuagint it is translated both by ἐνιαυτός (Genesis 1:14, etc.), properly a "cycle of time," and more frequently by ἔτος (Genesis 5:3, etc.), and both Greek words are used for "year" in the New Testament (John 11:49, etc.; Luke 3:1, etc.).

Climatic and agricultural factors doubtless first called attention to the cycle of time that is the year. In Egypt the annual inundation of the Nile was an unusually prominent reminder of the return of the cycle, and was regularly followed by the season of sowing. In Palestine the climate was marked by the "early rain" or "autumn rain" which came in October/November, and the "later rain" or "spring rain" which came in March/April (Deuteronomy 11:14; Jeremiah 5:24),[40] as well as by the recurrence of summer and winter (Zechariah 14:8, etc.), and the agricultural seasons likewise returned regularly with the ripening of the olives in the fall (September/October-October/November), for example, and the shooting into ear of the barley in the spring (March/April).[41]

The autumn and spring seasons, to which attention was thus par-

[37] PDBC p.1.
[38] The American Ephemeris and Nautical Almanac for the Year 1958. 1956, p.xvi.
[39] Julian Morgenstern in HUCA 10 (1935), p.25.
[40] E. Hull in HDB IV, p.195.
[41] W. F. Albright in BASOR 92 (Dec. 1943), pp.22f. n.30 and n.37.

ticularly drawn by climatic and agricultural events, were also marked by the equality in length of day and night which occurs everywhere when the sun crosses the equator in each season. These points are now called the equinoxes, and by our reckoning the autumnal equinox falls about September 23, the vernal equinox about March 21. Likewise the summer and winter were marked respectively by the times when the day was at its greatest length and at its shortest length, or the times when the sun seems to stand still in its northward movement and again in its southward movement. These points are called the summer solstice and the winter solstice, and come by our reckoning about June 21 and December 22. When these several points were recognized they provided definite markers in the course of the year, and it was no doubt possible to establish them with precision by observation of the length of day and night and by measurement of the shadow of the sun.[42]

When such a mark as the vernal equinox is established, the length of the year from that point through a "revolution of time" and back to the same point can be measured. In Egypt, as will be noted in discussing the Egyptian calendar below, the length of the year was probably recognized as early as the third millennium B.C. as being 365 days, and with more exact measurements it was later found to be about 365¼ days. Among the Jews, Mar Samuel (A.D. c.165-c.250), who directed a school at Nehardea in Babylonia and was said to be as familiar with the paths of heaven as with the streets of his own city,[43] reckoned the year at 365 days and 6 hours, while his contemporary, Rab Adda, made it 365 days, 5 hours, 55 minutes, 25 and a fraction seconds.[44] In modern astronomy the length of the ordinary, tropical, or solar year, as it is called, is given as 365.24219879 days, or 365 days, 5 hours, 48 minutes, 45.975 seconds.[45]

When the four points of the vernal and autumnal equinoxes and the summer and winter solstices are taken, the year is readily divisible into four parts. Such a division of the solar year is found in the Talmud,[46] where the word תקופה (*tequfah*) is used as the name of each of the four periods. The word means "cycle" or "season," and a related form was found as "circuit" in the Manual of Discipline (see above p.294).

[42] Russell, Dugan, and Stewart, *Astronomy*, I, p.151.
[43] *Berakoth*. 58b; SBT p.365.
[44] JE III, p.500.
[45] *The American Ephemeris and Nautical Almanac for the Year 1958*, p.xvi.
[46] *Sanhedrin*. 11b; GBT VII, pp.36f.

In the course of the year the sun also seems to trace a path east-ward against the background of the stars. This path is known as the zodiac. In a month the sun travels approximately one-twelfth of the way around this circle, and perhaps for this reason, the zodiac was divided into twelve sections.[47] Using the sexagesimal system of ancient Mesopotamia, the entire circle of the zodiac comprises 360 degrees, each of the twelve sections, 30 degrees. These divisions of the zodiac are designated according to the constellations of stars which they contain. Already in the Babylonian epic of creation we read of the work of Marduk:

> He constructed stations for the great gods,
> Fixing their astral likenesses as constellations.
> He determined the year by designating the zones:
> He set up three constellations for each of the
> twelve months.[48]

Later a single constellation was taken as the sign of each of the twelve parts of the zodiac. In the tractate Berakoth[49] of the Talmud, the "Sovereign of the Universe" says: "Twelve constellations have I created in the firmament, and for each constellation I have created thirty hosts, and for each host I have created thirty legions, and for each legion I have created thirty cohorts, and for each cohort I have created thirty maniples,[50] and for each maniple I have created thirty camps, and to each camp I have attached three hundred and sixty-five thousands of myriads of stars, corresponding to the days of the solar year." In the Sefer Yeṣirah, a Jewish work of unknown antiquity, the names of the constellations are given as follows:[51] Taleh, Shor, Te'omin, Sarṭan, Aryeh, Betulah, Moznayim, 'Aqrab, Qeshet, Gedi, Deli, and Dagim. The Greek names, as found in Hipparchus, were as follows, the Latin forms and the meanings also being given:

1. ὁ Κριός, Aries, the Ram
2. ὁ Ταῦρος, Taurus, the Bull
3. οἱ Δίδυμοι, Gemini, the Twins
4. ὁ Καρκίνος, Cancer, the Crab
5. ὁ Λέων, Leo, the Lion
6. ἡ Παρθένος, Virgo, the Virgin

[47] F. von Oefele in HERE XII, p.51.
[48] ANET p.67.   [49] 32b; SBT p.201.
[50] Like the other terms, a subdivision of the Roman military organization.
[51] JE XII, p.688.

7. αἱ Χηλαί, Libra, the Balance
8. ὁ Σκορπίος, Scorpio, the Scorpion
9. ὁ Τοξότης, Sagittarius, the Archer
10. ὁ Ἀιγόκερως, Capricornus, the Goat
11. ὁ Ὑδροχόος, Aquarius, the Water Carrier
12. οἱ Ἰχθύες, Pisces, the Fishes

Since most of these were animals, from the word ζῴδιον, "a little animal," the entire zone was called ὁ ζῳδιακὸς κύκλος,[52] the zodiacal circle, or zodiac.

2. THE EGYPTIAN CALENDAR

IN ANCIENT Egypt the year was divided into three seasons. The first was called Akhet or "Inundation" and was the time when the Nile rose and overflowed the fields. The second was Peroyet or "Coming-Forth" when the fields emerged again from the flood waters and seeding, tilling, growth, and harvest took place. The third was Shomu or "Deficiency" and was the season of low water which came after the harvest and before the next inundation.[1] The recognition of these seasons, based upon climatic and agricultural factors, was undoubtedly very old.

It was also recognized that each season comprised approximately four lunar months. The year probably started with the lunar month which began after the river began to rise. The rise of the river normally begins at Aswan in late May or early June, and is about ten days later at Memphis. In addition to the observation of the moon there was another astronomical phenomenon which attracted attention in Egypt at an early time. This was the annual heliacal rising or first reappearance at dawn of the star Sirius, known as Sothis in the Greek spelling of its Egyptian name. In the fifth and fourth millenniums B.C. this rising was taking place at about the same time as the inundation and was probably recognized as the harbinger of the flood. As such it provided a precise point for the beginning of the year. Thus an inscription of the First Dynasty probably reads: "Sothis, the opener of the year; the inundation."[2]

Since the year was composed of lunar months this may be called

[52] Hipparchus I, vi, 4. ed. Manitius, p.56.
[1] Frankfort, *Kingship and the Gods*, p.367 n.3; PCAE p.32.
[2] PCAE pp.32, 34, 74 n.22.

a lunar calendar; since the beginning of the year was fixed by reference to a star, it may be described more specifically as a lunistellar calendar. A year composed of twelve lunar months, ordinarily alternating between twenty-nine and thirty days in length, makes 354 days, which is approximately eleven days short of the solar year. To keep the calendar year beginning in the spring in general and at the time of the heliacal rising of Sothis in particular, it must have been necessary to insert an additional month every three years or so. It seems that when this occurred, the intercalary month was put at the head of the new lunar year. This, it is believed, was the original lunar calendar of Egypt, and it was probably still in use in the Protodynastic period.[3]

Whether it was by averaging a series of these lunar years or by counting the days between successive heliacal risings of Sothis, it was also established that the true length of the year to the nearest number of days was 365. The disadvantages of a year composed now of twelve and again of thirteen lunar months must have been evident, and with the recognition of the year's length as 365 days the possibility of a new system emerged. After the analogy of the lunar system the year was still divided into three seasons and twelve months, but for the sake of simplicity and regularity each month was made thirty days in length. This left a shortage of only five days and, after the example of the intercalated month at the beginning of the lunar year, five epagomenal days were inserted before the new year. Since the months were no longer kept in relationship to the real moon but were fixed units in the solar year instead, this may be recognized as essentially a solar calendar, and since the units have an artificial regularity it may be called a "schematic" calendar. This system was introduced, there is reason to believe, between c.2937 and c.2821 B.C. and from then on served as the standard civil calendar of Egypt.[4]

The civil calendar of 365 days was still, however, not in exact agreement with the solar year since the latter is actually closer to 365¼ days in length. At the outset, it may be assumed, the first day of the civil year coincided with the heliacal rising of Sothis. After four years it would begin on the day before the rising of Sothis,

---

[3] PCAE pp.30-50, 53.

[4] PCAE p.53. This Egyptian calendar consisting of twelve months of thirty days each and five additional days at the end of each year has been called by Neugebauer (*The Exact Sciences in Antiquity*, p.81) "the only intelligent calendar which ever existed in human history."

after eight years, two days before, and so on. Only after 1,460 years, therefore, would the beginning of the civil year have moved all the way around the cycle to coincide once again with the rising of Sothis. Since the original lunar calendar was periodically corrected to keep its beginning point in connection with the heliacal rising of Sothis, the civil calendar gradually diverged more and more from the lunar calendar. It is assumed that this divergence would have become apparent by say 2500 B.C., and that around that time a second lunar calendar was introduced which was thereafter maintained in substantial harmony with the civil year. Thus from that time on, Egypt actually had no less than three calendars and three calendar years, and all of these continued in use throughout the remainder of ancient Egyptian history.[5]

3. THE MESOPOTAMIAN CALENDAR

IN MESOPOTAMIA also there was a lunar, or more strictly a lunisolar calendar. The moon-god was very prominent in Mesopotamia,[1] and observation of the moon no doubt began very early. As based upon the sighting of the new moon, the months were usually alternately twenty-nine and thirty days in length, although sometimes months of the same length in days would come in sequence, and occasionally there seems even to have been a month of twenty-eight days, which is explained on the supposition that two months of twenty-nine days had come together but bad visibility had prevented the seeing of the crescent and the first month had been erroneously assigned thirty days. Whether the months were eventually determined by calculation instead of visual observation is not known.[2]

Twelve lunar months constituted the year, and the year began in the spring. The following list gives the months in order together with their approximate equivalents in our calendar:[3]

---

[5] PCAE pp.54, 56.

[1] The moon-god was known as Nanna to the Sumerians (ANET p.38), and as Sin to the Akkadians (ANET p.88). Sin was the son of the air-god Enlil, the husband of the goddess Ningal, and they were the parents of the sun-god Shamash (ANET p.164 n.10; p.400 n.3). Sin was called "the lamp of heaven and earth" (ANET p.390), and he was worshiped specially at the temple of Egishnugal in Ur (ANET p.164). The crescent which is his symbol is familiar in Mesopotamian art (ANEP Nos.453, 518, etc.), and the god himself may be represented on the cylinder seal of an official of King Ur-Nammu of Ur (Hugo Gressmann, *Altorientalische Bilder zum Alten Testament*, 2d ed. [1927], Fig. 323).

[2] PDBC p.3.   [3] PDBC p.26.

1.	Nisanu	March/April
2.	Aiaru	April/May
3.	Simanu	May/June
4.	Duzu	June/July
5.	Abu	July/August
6.	Ululu	August/September
7.	Tashritu	September/October
8.	Arahsamnu	October/November
9.	Kislimu	November/December
10.	Tebetu	December/January
11.	Shabatu	January/February
12.	Addaru	February/March

Twelve lunar months fell of course approximately eleven days short of the solar year. At first the rectification of this discrepancy may have been made by simply taking the month which began nearest the vernal equinox as the first month of the new year. Later the method of intercalating an additional month as necessary was employed. This system was developed by the Sumerians and Babylonians and was adopted by the Assyrians probably by the time of Tiglath-pileser I (c.1114-c.1076 B.C.).[4]

By the eighth century B.C. there is evidence that it was recognized in Babylonia that the insertion of seven additional lunar months within a nineteen-year period would closely approximate the additional time needed to stabilize the calendar. By the fourth century B.C. fixed points were established for these seven intercalations, and the nineteen-year cycle was fully standardized. The months added were a second Ululu, the sixth month, or a second Addaru, the twelfth month.[5]

Since new-moon dates can be calculated astronomically for ancient Babylonia, and since the system of intercalation has been reconstructed on the basis of intercalary months actually mentioned in cuneiform texts, it is possible to construct tables which represent the Babylonian calendar with a high degree of probable accuracy.[6]

The achievement of the ancient Babylonian astronomers in devising the nineteen year cycle with its seven intercalated months was indeed remarkable. It has been noted above that one solar year equals 365.24219879 days while one lunar month equals 29.530588

---

[4] P. van der Meer, *The Ancient Chronology of Western Asia and Egypt.* 1947, pp.1f.

[5] PDBC pp.1f.   [6] PDBC p.25.

days. Nineteen solar years, therefore, equals 6939.601777 days. In 19 12-month years there are 228 months; adding 7 more months makes a total of 235 months. Two hundred thirty-five lunar months equals 6939.688180 days. Thus, the difference between 235 lunar months and 19 solar years is only .086403 day or 2 hours, 4 minutes, 25.22 seconds. This is how close the ancient Babylonian system came to solving the problem of the relationship between the lunar year and the solar year.[7]

How the system worked in actual practice may be seen in the accompanying tabulation (p.569). This shows the first nineteen years of the reign of Nebuchadnezzar II (604-562 B.C.). The years are numbered and their equivalents in terms of B.C. are given; leap years are indicated by italicizing the last figure of the year when first given. The month names are abbreviated; U II and A II mean a second Ululu and a second Addaru respectively where these are intercalated. From the source table,[8] which shows the first day of each month in terms of our Julian calendar, the number of days in each month is counted and it is this figure which is shown for each month. The total number of days for the nineteen years is 6940; this is the nearest full number to the exact figure already noted above of 6939.-601777 days.

In Egypt we saw that the complexity of the original lunar calendar led to the introduction of a simplified civil calendar with twelve months of thirty days each plus five additional days prior to the new year. In Mesopotamia, too, there was a second calendar of exactly this same sort which was used alongside the real lunar calendar. Since its twelve months of thirty days each, running on in regular sequence regardless of the real moon, were really standardized divisions of the solar year, this was a solar calendar or a "schematic calendar." In Babylonian documents many dates have been found which are evidently given in this schematic calendar, and in some cases it is not possible to prove whether it is the schematic calendar or the real lunar calendar which is intended. But whereas the schematic calendar became the generally used civil calendar in Egypt, in Babylonia it seems to have been the lunar calendar which remained in most general usage, and Mesopotamia has properly been called "the classical country of the strictly lunar calendar."[9]

---

[7] Small as the difference is, it is precisely this discrepancy of 2 hours, 4 minutes, 25.22 seconds which provides the greatest complication in computing a perpetually fixed lunisolar calendar. cf. Siegfried H. Horn in JBL 76 (1957), pp.169f.

[8] PDBC pp.27f.   [9] O. Neugebauer in JNES 1 (1942), pp.398-401.

NEBUCHADNEZZAR II (FIRST NINETEEN YEARS OF REIGN)

Yr.	B.C.	Nis	Aia	Sim	Duz	Abu	Ulu	U II	Tas	Ara	Kis	B.C.	Teb	B.C.	Sha	Add	A II	Number of Days in Year
1	604	29	29	30	29	30	30		29	30	30		30	603	29	29		354
2	603	30	29	29	29	30	30	30	29	30	30	602	29		30	29		384
3	602	30	29	29	30	29	30		30	29	30	601	29		30	30		355
4	601	29	30	29	29	30	29		30	30	30		30	600	29	30		354
5	600	29	30	29	30	29	30	28	30	30	29	599	29		29	30		383
6	599	30	30	29	30	30	29		30	29	30		30	598	29	30		355
7	598	29	30	29	30	30	30	29	30	29	29	597	30		29	29		383
8	597	30	29	30	30	30	30		29	29	29	596	29		30	29		355
9	596	29	30	29	30	30	30	30	29	29	30	595	29		30	29		384
10	595	29	30	29	29	30	29		30	30	30	594	30		29	30		355
11	594	29	29	30	29	30	30		29	30	29	593	30		30	29	30	384
12	593	30	29	30	30	29	29		30	29	29	592	30		30	29		354
13	592	30	30	29	29	29	30		29	29	30	591	30		30	29		354
14	591	30	29	30	29	30	29		30	29	29		30	590	30	30	30	384
15	590	30	29	30	29	30	29		30	29	29	589	29		29	29		354
16	589	30	29	30	29	30	30		29	30	29	588	30	587	29	29		354
17	588	30	29	30	29	30	30		30	29	30		29		30	29	29	384
18	587	30	29	30	29	30	30		30	29	30	586	29		30	29		355
19	586	29	30	29	29	30	30		30	30	29	585	30		29	30		355

Total 6940

4. THE ISRAELITE CALENDAR

THE GEZER Calendar, which we have already described (p.182) as a small limestone tablet of around 925 B.C., written perhaps as a schoolboy's exercise, contains a list of months and therewith an outline of the year as it was evidently reckoned at that time in Palestine. The word used for "month" is ירח and the months are grouped and designated according to the type of agricultural work done at the time. Since the agricultural seasons in Palestine are well known (cf. above p. 561), including the ripening of the olive crop in September/October-October/November, the shooting into ear of the barley in March/April, and the subsequent barley harvest in April/May,[1] it is possible to tabulate the sequence of months in the Gezer Calendar together with their equivalents as follows:

1.	2 months '	olive harvest	September/October
2.			October/November
3.	2 months	planting grain	November/December
4.			December/January
5.	2 months	late planting	January/February
6.			February/March
7.	1 month	hoeing flax	March/April
8.	1 month	harvest of barley	April/May
9.	1 month	harvest and festivity	May/June
10.	2 months	vine tending	June/July
11.			July/August
12.	1 month	summer fruit	August/September

We see, therefore, that at this time in Palestine the year was reckoned as beginning in the fall, and that it contained twelve months which were related to agriculture.

Turning to the Old Testament we find first a group of month names which are connected with agriculture and climate. There are four of these as follows: (1) The month Abib.[2] This word means a "fresh ear" of grain, as in Leviticus 2:14, and is used of barley when it is "in the ear," as in Exodus 9:31; hence used as a month name and with the article, "the Abib," it refers to the period when the barley shoots into ear. (2) The month Ziv.[3] This term signifies

---

[1] The harvest of barley begins in the Jordan Valley about the middle of April and in the highlands up to a month later. J. W. Paterson in HDB I, p.49.

[2] חדש האביב, Exodus 13:4; 23:15; 34:18; Deuteronomy 16:1.

[3] חדש זו, I Kings 6:1; ירח זו, I Kings 6:37.

"splendor" and is used of the "beauty of flowers"; hence the month name refers to the time of flowers. (3) The month Ethanim.[4] Coming from a word which means "permanent," this term is used in the plural and with the article as a month name which refers to "the permanent streams." (4) The month Bul.[5] The word probably refers to a period of "rain." Of these words both Ethanim and Bul have also been found as month names in North Semitic inscriptions,[6] hence these names, and probably others like them for other months, were no doubt common property among various Semitic peoples in this part of the world. We may call them the Canaanite month names.

Since Abib is, by the etymology of the name, the month when the barley shoots into the ear, we know that it must have been approximately equivalent to March/April (cf. above p.561), and it may therefore be equated with the seventh month in the list of the Gezer Calendar. According to Deuteronomy 16:1 Abib is the month of the passover, and according to Exodus 12:2f. the passover is held in the first month. This manner of reference makes Abib the first month rather than the seventh, and must simply represent a time when the year was reckoned as beginning in the spring rather than the fall and when the months were numbered from the spring. Similarly Ziv, the month of flowers, must be a spring month, and in I Kings 6:1 its name is followed by the explanation, "which is the second month." Likewise Bul, the month of rain, must be the month of "early rain" or October/November (cf. above p.561), and it is called the eighth month in I Kings 6:38. Ethanim, too, is named as the seventh month in I Kings 8:2. Showing, then, the months numbered both from the fall and from the spring, the Canaanite month names fit into the calendar as follows:

1	7	Ethanim	September/October
2	8	Bul	October/November
3	9		November/December
4	10		December/January
5	11		January/February
6	12		February/March
7	1	Abib	March/April

[4] ירח האתנים, I Kings 8:2.
[5] ירח בול, I Kings 6:38.
[6] Mark Lidzbarski, *Handbuch der nordsemitischen Epigraphik nebst ausgewählten Inschriften.* I (1898), pp.231, 236, 412.

8	2	Ziv	April/May
9	3		May/June
10	4		June/July
11	5		July/August
12	6		August/September

It is perhaps not without significance that it is precisely the first
two months of the fall and the first two of the spring of which the
names are preserved in the Old Testament. These are not only times
of special importance in Palestinian agriculture but also the times
of the two equinoxes. It will also be remembered (p.553) that in the
early period the day was probably reckoned from the morning. These
facts suggest that the orientation of this calendar was primarily toward the sun: the rising of the sun began the day; the equinoxes
were the turning points of the year. If this was the case then, in the
lack of other evidence, the guess may be hazarded that the months
were not tied closely to the phases of the moon but were units of
the solar year, probably thirty days in length, as in the "schematic"
calendars of Egypt and Mesopotamia, and that the resultant shortage of about five days was simply made up by the insertion of additional days at the end of the year.[7]

The supposition is, therefore, that the Israelite calendar was originally agricultural and that as it was harmonized more accurately
with the movements of the celestial bodies it was primarily the relationship to the sun that was kept in view. In this period both Egyptian and Phoenician influences were strong in Israel, and both would
be expected to have contributed to the solar emphasis. As far as
Egypt is concerned, this was the great power which cast its shadow
over Palestine until the defeat of Pharaoh Necho by Nebuchadnezzar
in 605 B.C. (pp.130, 220). In Egypt the sun was very prominent, as
evidenced by the numerous sun deities in the pantheon, and a schematic solar calendar was the standard civil calendar (p.565).

As far as Phoenicia is concerned, we know that Solomon, who
reigned shortly before the time ascribed to the Gezer Calendar, entered into close relationships with Hiram, King of Tyre, particularly
for help in the building of the temple at Jerusalem (I Kings 5, etc.).
According to Josephus,[8] Hiram built new temples to Astarte and

[7] In his study of intercalation and the Hebrew calendar (in vt 7 [1957], pp.250-
307), J. B. Segal adduces evidence to show that intercalation was already practiced
in Israel in the early days of the monarchy (*ibid.*, p.259).

[8] *Against Apion.* i, 18; *Ant.* viii, v, 3.

Herakles, which suggests interest in the celestial bodies particularly including the sun, since Astarte was generally associated with the planet Venus or with the moon, and Herakles was connected with the sun especially in Phoenicia. According to Porphyry (A.D. 233-c.304) who was born in Phoenicia, probably at Tyre, the Phoenicians gave the name of Herakles to the sun and considered the twelve labors of Herakles to represent the passage of the sun through the twelve signs of the zodiac.[9]

At Jerusalem the temple which Hiram helped Solomon to build may have been so constructed that the sun shone directly in through its eastern gate on the two equinoctial days of the year,[10] and we find that later Josiah "removed the horses that the kings of Judah had dedicated to the sun, at the entrance to the house of the Lord" and "burned the chariots of the sun with fire" (II Kings 23:11), and that again in Ezekiel's time men stood at the door of the temple, "with their backs to the temple of the Lord, and their faces toward the east, worshiping the sun toward the east" (Ezekiel 8:16). Therefore it seems entirely likely that at least from the time of Solomon and under the influence of Egypt and Phoenicia the calendar of Israel was a schematic solar calendar.[11]

5. THE BABYLONIAN CALENDAR IN PALESTINE

It has been noted in the preceding section that the month names Abib, Ziv, Ethanim, and Bul appear in the Old Testament, that these are probably the old Canaanite designations, and that in some instances the occurrence of the names is followed by an explanatory statement indicating, for example, that Ziv is the second month, Ethanim the seventh month, and so on. These numerical equivalents look as if they were added to the records at a time when the old names were no longer so commonly employed and when a different system had come into use, namely a designation of the months by number alone. Such a system is actually found elsewhere in Kings (I 12:32, etc.), Jeremiah (1:3, etc.), Ezekiel (1:1, etc.), and many other books of the Old Testament, and all of the months from the

---

[9] Quoted by Eusebius, *Praeparatio Evangelica.* III, xi, 25. ed. Karl Mras in GCS, Eusebius VIII, 1 (1954), pp.139f. cf. Charles Anthon, *A Classical Dictionary.* 1843, p.599.

[10] Julian Morgenstern in HUCA 6 (1929), pp.16-19.

[11] Julian Morgenstern in VT 5 (1955), pp.67-69.

first to the twelfth are so designated. Likewise in the majority of the apocryphal and pseudepigraphical writings the same system of indicating the months by number is followed.[1]

It has also been noted that in the earlier system the months were listed from the fall, but in the new system where the months are designated by number the numbering begins in the spring. In addition to evidence already cited, there is a plain example of the latter usage when Jeremiah 36:9 mentions the ninth month and the following verse 22 indicates that it was in the winter: counting from the fall, the ninth month would be in the summer; counting from the spring, the ninth month would be in the winter.

The beginning of the year in the spring is in accordance with what we have seen was the usage in Mesopotamia, and it is therefore a reasonable surmise that the new calendrical system was derived from that source. The latest contemporary use of the old Canaanite names is probably in Deuteronomy 16:1.[2] The book of Deuteronomy is commonly supposed to have been edited in connection with the reformation of Josiah and found in the temple in 621 B.C. (II Kings 22:8).[3] The earliest citation in terms of the new system is probably that of the ninth month in the fifth year of Jehoiakim (604/603 B.C.) in Jeremiah 36:9. According to this evidence, the new system was introduced in Judah between 621 and 604 B.C. In 605 B.C., as we have already seen (pp.130, 220), Nebuchadnezzar defeated Necho, and Palestine passed from the sway of Egypt to the domination of Babylon. It may be concluded, accordingly, that it was at that time that the Babylonian way of reckoning was officially established in Palestine.[4]

That the new system of months numbered from a point of beginning in the spring was really the Babylonian system is shown by the fact that the Babylonian names for the months are also found later in the Old Testament. In a number of passages in Esther and Zechariah the month is cited first by number and then by name. The months which so appear are: "the first month, which is the month of Nisan" (Esther 3:7); "the third month, which is the month of Sivan" (Esther 8:9); "the ninth month, which is Chislev" (Zechariah 7:1); "the tenth month, which is the month of Tebeth" (Esther 2:16); "the eleventh month, which is the month of Shebat" (Zechariah

[1] Julian Morgenstern in HUCA 1 (1924), p.19.
[2] Morgenstern in HUCA 1 (1924), p.18.
[3] Pfeiffer, Introduction to the Old Testament, p.181.
[4] Elias Auerbach in VT 2 (1952), p.336.

1:7); and "the twelfth month, which is the month of Adar" (Esther 3:7, etc.). In Ezra and Nehemiah the month is sometimes referred to by number (Ezra 7:8, etc.; Nehemiah 7:73, etc.), but in the following cases is cited by name alone: Nisan (Nehemiah 2:1), Elul (Nehemiah 6:15), Chislev (Nehemiah 1:1); Adar (Ezra 6:15). The sources just cited are generally considered to be among the latest books in the Old Testament, and thus the use of these month names must have begun relatively late, perhaps from the fourth century B.C. on.[5] The first work in which only the Babylonian names are employed is probably Megillat Ta'anit, the "Scroll of Fasting." This is essentially a list, written probably just after the beginning of the first century A.D., of thirty-six Jewish festivals. The book is divided into twelve chapters, corresponding to the twelve months. The first chapter treats the memorial days of the first month, Nisan, and so on to the twelfth chapter which deals with those of the twelfth month, Adar.[6]

The fact that the numbering of the months according to the Babylonian system came into use among the Jews before the actual month names were adopted may indicate a complex evolution,[7] but would seem to be explicable most simply on the grounds that the numbers did not carry the associations of pagan religion which some of the names did. Thus the month Tammuz (Babylonian Duzu) bore the name of the famous dying god of Mesopotamia, the weeping for whom of the women of Jerusalem was such an abomination in the eyes of Ezekiel (8:14) (cf. above p.533 n.22); and the month Elul may have meant "shouting for joy" in the celebration of the restoration to life of the same deity.[8]

As a result of the development just sketched, then, the list of months in use among the Jews at the end of the Old Testament period was as shown in the following table where the number, Babylonian name, Hebrew name, and approximate equivalent in our months are given:[9]

---

[5] Morgenstern in HUCA 1 (1924), p.20.
[6] Hans Lichtenstein in HUCA 8-9 (1931-32), pp.257-351; J. Z. Lauterbach in JE VIII, pp.427f.
[7] Morgenstern in HUCA 1 (1924), p.21.
[8] I. Abrahams in HDB IV, p.765.
[9] PDBC p.24.

Number	Babylonian Name	Hebrew Name	Approximate Equivalent
1	Nisanu	Nisan	March/April
2	Aiaru	Iyyar	April/May
3	Simanu	Sivan	May/June
4	Duzu	Tammuz	June/July
5	Abu	Ab	July/August
6	Ululu	Elul	August/September
7	Tashritu	Tishri	September/October
8	Arahsamnu	Marheshvan or, Heshvan	October/November
9	Kislimu	Kislev or, Chislev	November/December
10	Tebetu	Tebeth	December/January
11	Shabatu	Shebat	January/February
12	Addaru	Adar	February/March

The Babylonian calendar was, as we have seen, essentially luni-solar. The months began with the first appearing of the crescent of the new moon in the evening sky, and the intercalation of seven months in nineteen years kept the year of lunar months in close approximation to the solar year. The question which now arises is whether along with the Babylonian order and names of the months, the full Babylonian system of strictly lunar months and of the intercalation of months was also adopted? The sources which will next be cited show that in general this is what was done, but that there were some variations in Jewish practice from Babylonian.

In Palestine it was the responsibility of the Sanhedrin in Jerusalem to determine matters connected with the calendar, and in practice this was done by a council of three men.

As in Babylonia, the month began when the new moon was first seen in the evening, but since the new moon was visible at Jerusalem thirty-seven minutes before it was visible at Babylon, it was possible that upon occasion the new month would begin a day earlier than in Babylonia.[10] The determination that the new moon had actually appeared and the declaration that the new month had thereby begun had to be made by the council just referred to, and the rules according to which this was done are presented and discussed in the Tal-

[10] PDBC pp.23f.

mud in the tractate Rosh Hashanah.[11] The testimony of at least two witnesses was required to establish that the new moon had been seen. So important were the observations of these witnesses that for the fixing of the new moons of Nisan and Tishri, the pivotal points of the year in the spring and fall, they might even exceed the travel limit of two thousand cubits on the sabbath day to bring their report to Jerusalem.[12] In Jerusalem there was a special courtyard where the witnesses were examined and entertained. In earlier time if they came on the sabbath they could not leave this place the whole day, because they had doubtless already used up their allowed travel distance, but Rabbi Gamaliel the Elder ruled that they could go two thousand cubits from it.[13] In the examination of the witnesses they were interrogated with such questions as whether the moon had been seen to the north or to the south of the sun. The point of this question lay in the fact that the new moon always appears due west; hence in the summer when the sun sets in the northwest the new moon is south of the sun, in the winter it is north of the sun.[14] Rabbi Gamaliel II even had a diagram of the phases of the moon on a tablet hung on the wall of his upper chamber, and used this in questioning the witnesses.[15]

When it was determined that the new moon had been seen, the beginning of the new month was proclaimed. On the scriptural warrant of Leviticus 23:44 where "Moses declared . . . the appointed feasts of the Lord," this was done by the solemn declaration of the head of the Sanhedrin that the new moon was "sanctified."[16] Also a trumpet was sounded,[17] as it is said in Psalm 81:3, "Blow the trumpet at the new moon." At one time flares were lighted too to signal the new month, but when the Samaritans introduced confusion by lighting misleading flares, messengers were sent out instead.[18]

While it was considered "a religious duty to sanctify [the new moon] on the strength of actual observation,"[19] it was also recognized that conditions might be such that the actual visual sighting could not be made and in this case it was established that one month would

[11] i, 3-iii, 1; 18a-25b; sbt pp.73-115; cf. *Sanhedrin*. i, 2; dm p.382.
[12] *Rosh Hashanah*. 19b; sbt p.81 n.4.
[13] *Rosh Hashanah*. ii, 5; 23b; sbt p.101.
[14] *Rosh Hashanah*. ii, 6; 23b-24a; sbt pp.102f.
[15] *Rosh Hashanah*. ii, 8; 24a; sbt p.105.
[16] *Rosh Hashanah*. ii, 7; 24a; sbt p.104.
[17] *Rosh Hashanah*. iii, 3; 26a; sbt p.115.
[18] *Rosh Hashanah*. ii, 2-4; 22b-23b; sbt pp.96-100.
[19] *Rosh Hashanah*. 20a; sbt p.81.

have thirty days and the next twenty-nine. The month with twenty-nine days was considered "deficient" by half a day, the month with thirty days was "full," being half a day over the true lunar period. It was agreed that the year should not have less than five nor more than seven "full" months. At least in post-Talmudic times Nisan, Sivan, Ab, Tishri, Kislev, and Shebat had thirty days, and Iyyar, Tammuz, Elul, Heshvan, Tebeth, and Adar had twenty-nine. The science by which these determinations were made was known as the "fixing of the month" or as the "sanctification of the new moon."[20]

In his work entitled *Sanctification of the New Moon*, Maimonides (A.D. 1135-1204) gives in Chapters I-V a description of the way in which the calendar was anciently regulated by the Sanhedrin, and in his description of the manner of determining the new moon he shows that calculation as well as observation was employed. Maimonides writes:[21]

"Just as the astronomers who discern the positions and motions of the stars engage in calculation, so the Jewish court, too, used to study and investigate and perform mathematical operations, in order to find out whether or not it would be possible for the new crescent to be visible in its 'proper time,' which is the night of the 30th day. If the members of the court found that the new moon might be visible, they were obliged to be in attendance at the court house for the whole 30th day and be on the watch for the arrival of witnesses. If witnesses did arrive, they were duly examined and tested, and if their testimony appeared trustworthy, this day was sanctified as New Moon Day. If the new crescent did not appear and no witnesses arrived, this day was counted as the 30th day of the old month, which thus became an embolismic[22] month."

It was also necessary for the same council of the Sanhedrin to determine when an intercalary month should be added to the year. There is a discussion of "the intercalating of the year" in the tractate Sanhedrin.[23] Here in addition to mention of the council of three it is also stated that "A year cannot be intercalated unless the Nasi sanctions it."[24] The Nasi was the "prince" or chief of the Sanhedrin, and it would appear that he might or might not be a member of the council of three. An example is given where "Rabban Gamaliel

---

[20] JE III, pp.499f. (Cyrus Adler); 502f. (M. Friedländer).

[21] *The Code of Maimonides, Book Three, Treatise Eight, Sanctification of the New Moon*, tr. by Solomon Gandz, with introduction by Julian Obermann, and astronomical commentary by Otto Neugebauer (Yale Judaica Series, 11). 1956, pp.4f. (I, 6).

[22] That is, a month containing an added day.

[23] I, 2; DM p.382; 10b-13b; SBT pp.42-61.

[24] 11a; SBT p.47.

was away obtaining permission from the Governor of Syria,[25] and, as his return was delayed, the year was intercalated subject to Rabban Gamaliel's later approval."[26]

The rabbis taught, it is stated, that "a year may be intercalated on three grounds: on account of the premature state of the corn crops; or that of the fruit trees; or on account of the lateness of the Tequfah. Any two of these reasons can justify intercalation, but not one alone."[27] The minute calculations involved are referred to, and an example is given where the rabbis did not finish their calculation until the last day of the month preceding the month to be intercalated.[28] In Babylonia, as we saw, either a second Ululu or a second Addaru might be inserted in the year, but here it is stated flatly that "only an Adar can be intercalated."[29] When the intercalation took place the added month was called the Second Adar.[30] The length of the added month was left to the judgment of the council, and it might be either twenty-nine or thirty days in length.[31]

In the same tractate letters are quoted which were sent out by Rabbi Simeon ben Gamaliel and Rabban Gamaliel II. Simeon, son of Gamaliel I and head of the Sanhedrin in the two decades before the destruction of the Temple, wrote as follows: "We beg to inform you that the doves are still tender and the lambs still young, and the grain has not yet ripened. I have considered the matter and thought it advisable to add thirty days to the year." The letter of Gamaliel II differs only in that he, more modestly as the Talmud observes, associates his "colleagues" with himself in the decision of intercalation.[32]

In agreement with the foregoing, Maimonides[33] also gives a lucid account of the process of intercalation as conducted under the Sanhedrin. Noting that the solar year exceeds the lunar year by approximately eleven days, he says that whenever this excess accumulates to about thirty days, or a little more or less, one month is added and the particular year is made to consist of thirteen months. The extra

[25] Probably to obtain confirmation of his appointment as Nasi rather than to secure permission for intercalating the year, since it seems unlikely that the latter would have been required.

[26] 11a; SBT p.47. [27] 11b; SBT p.49. [28] 12b; SBT p.57.

[29] 12b; SBT p.55.

[30] The book of Esther was specified to be read in the month Adar, and in Megillah I, 4 (DM p.202) it is discussed whether, if the book has already been read in the First Adar and the year is subsequently intercalated, it must be read again in the Second Adar.

[31] 11a; SBT p.48. [32] 11a-11b; SBT pp.47-49.

[33] Sanctification of the New Moon, I, 2; IV, 1-17. ed. Gandz, pp.4, 16-22.

month is never anything other than an added Adar, and hence an intercalated year has a First Adar and a Second Adar. This added month may consist of either twenty-nine or thirty days. The decision is made by the Council of Intercalation, with a minimum membership of three; if the Nasi or chief of the supreme court was not one of them his assent was also necessary. Continuing with his own exposition of the mathematics involved, Maimonides states that each group of nineteen years contains seven intercalated years and twelve ordinary years.[34] Therefore, in spite of the fact that the Jewish system used only added Adars, the result was the same as in the Babylonian system and seven months were intercalated in each nineteen years.

Both the tractate Sanhedrin and Maimonides[35] also show that the solar year was divided likewise into four seasons or *tequfoth* and into twelve signs of the zodiac (cf. above pp. 562-564). On the basis of a year of 365¼ days, one Tequfah was reckoned at 91 days, 7½ hours. The four Tequfoth were: the Tequfah of Nisan which began at the vernal equinox when the sun enters the constellation of Aries; the Tequfah of Tammuz at the summer solstice when the sun enters Cancer; the Tequfah of Tishri at the autumnal equinox when the sun enters Libra; and the Tequfah of Tebeth at the winter solstice when the sun enters Capricorn.[36]

6. THE CALENDAR OF JUBILEES

IN THE discussion of the Dead Sea Scrolls it was established (pp.293-297) that the Qumran community was zealous in its observance of what it held to be correct times and seasons, that these were different from what other Jews adhered to, that in this connection the community cited and possessed the book of Jubilees, and that in

[34] *Sanctification of the New Moon*, vi, 10. ed. Gandz, p.29.

[35] *Sanhedrin*. 11b; SBT p.49 and n.5; Maimonides, *Sanctification of the New Moon*, IX, 2-3. ed. Gandz, pp.36f.

[36] On the evolution of the calendar see also Hildegard and Julius Lewy in HUCA 17 (1942-43), pp.1-152C; Julian Morgenstern in HUCA 1 (1924), pp.13-78; 10 (1935), pp.1-148; 20 (1947), pp.1-136; 21 (1948), pp.365-496; and in *Occident and Orient, Gaster Anniversary Volume*, ed. Bruno Schindler. 1936, pp.439-456; P. J. Heawood in JQR 36 (1945-46), pp.393-401; Solomon Zeitlin in JQR 36 (1945-46), pp.403-414; Solomon Gandz in JQR 39 (1948-49), pp.259-280; 40 (1949-50), pp.157-172, 251-277; 43 (1952-53), pp.177-192, 249-270; and in *Proceedings of the American Academy for Jewish Research*. 17 (1947-48), pp.9-17; 18 (1948-49), pp.213-254. On chronology see also A. Hermann, F. Schmidtke, and L. Koep in KRAC III, cols. 30-60.

fragments of an actual calendar found in Cave 4 at Qumran historical dates are cited in Babylonian month names but liturgical dates are given in a system in which days of the week are fixed points as well as days of the month. The date of passover, for example, is fixed by Old Testament law (Exodus 12:6) as the evening of the fourteenth day of the first month of the year. It is evident that this date can readily be ascertained in terms of the Babylonian calendar, but that in this calendar the date will fall on different days of the week in different years. The Qumran liturgical calendar, however, also identifies the passover date as the evening of Tuesday, hence this was a calendar in which the days of the week remained constant in relation to the days of the month. Since the clue is available that the community referred to the book of Jubilees in the reckoning of time, it is necessary to ascertain if the calendar of Jubilees satisfies the condition just mentioned and to establish the nature of this calendar.

The book of Jubilees was probably written in the original Hebrew between 135 and 105 B.C., and is preserved in Ethiopic manuscripts and Latin and Greek fragments as well as the two Hebrew fragments which have now been found in Cave 1 at Qumran. Essentially a rewriting of the book of Genesis in the form of a communication from "the angel of the presence" to Moses on Mount Sinai, Jubilees places the biblical narrative within a chronological framework of years, weeks of years, and jubilees, and lays much emphasis upon the institution and proper observance of the festivals of the religious year.[1]

The passage in this book which tells most about the calendar is Jubilees 6:23-32:[2]

"And on the new moon of the first month, and on the new moon of the fourth month, and on the new moon of the seventh month, and on the new moon of the tenth month are the days of remembrance, and the days of the seasons in the four divisions of the year. These are written and ordained as a testimony for ever. And Noah ordained them for himself as feasts for the generations for ever, so that they have become thereby a memorial unto him. And on the new moon of the first month he was bidden to make for himself an ark, and on that (day) the earth became dry and he opened (the ark) and saw the earth. And on the new moon of the fourth month the mouths of the depths of the abyss beneath were closed. And on the new moon of the seventh month all the mouths of the abysses of the earth were opened, and the waters began to descend into them. And on the new moon of the tenth month the tops of the mountains were seen, and Noah was glad. And on this account he ordained them for him-

[1] CAP II, pp.1-10; A. C. Headlam in HDB II, p.791.
[2] CAP II, pp.22f.

self as feasts for a memorial for ever, and thus are they ordained. And they placed them on the heavenly tablets, each had thirteen weeks; from one to another (passed) their memorial, from the first to the second, and from the second to the third, and from the third to the fourth. And all the days of the commandment will be two and fifty weeks of days, and (these will make) the entire year complete. Thus it is engraven and ordained on the heavenly tablets. And there is no neglecting (this comandment) for a single year or from year to year. And command thou the children of Israel that they observe the years according to this reckoning—three hundred and sixty-four days, and (these) will constitute a complete year, and they will not disturb its time from its days and from its feasts; for everything will fall out in them according to their testimony, and they will not leave out any day nor disturb any feasts."

From this we learn that the year was divided into four periods or seasons. The beginning of each of the four successive periods was marked by the "new moon," which probably means simply the "first day," of the first month, the fourth month, the seventh month, and the tenth month, in other words each period comprised three months. Each period also contained thirteen weeks. Since this equals 91 days, there must have been two months of 30 days each and one month of 31 days in each group of three months. The complete year was composed, therefore, as it is also explicitly stated, of 52 weeks or of 364 days.

The nature of the calendar just outlined will be discussed further in a moment but first it is necessary to indicate that what seems to be the same system of reckoning is found in the book of Enoch. The book of Enoch[3] is a large and composite work preserved in a number of Ethiopic manuscripts and Greek and Latin fragments. Of the 108 chapters into which it is customarily divided, chapters 72-82 are called the "Book of the Heavenly Luminaries" and constitute a treatise on the laws of the celestial bodies. This part, and at least much of the rest of the book, was probably written originally in Hebrew. This section must be referred to in Jubilees 4:17 where it is said that Enoch "wrote down the signs of heaven according to the order of their months in a book, that men might know the seasons of the years according to the order of their separate months." This citation indicates a date earlier than Jubilees for the "Book of the Heavenly Luminaries," say not later than 110 B.C., and also shows that the

---

[3] Also known as I Enoch or the (Ethiopic) book of Enoch. On the book see CAP II, pp.163-187; R. H. Charles in HDB I, pp.705-708. For a date for all the principal sections of I Enoch in the reign or shortly after the death of Antiochus Epiphanes see H. H. Rowley, *Jewish Apocalyptic and the Dead Sea Scrolls.* 1957, pp.8f.

author of Jubilees held it in high regard, therefore presumably agreed with it as to calendar.

In the "Book of the Heavenly Luminaries" the motion of the sun is described (I Enoch 72) in relation to twelve "portals" which must be the equivalent of the signs of the zodiac. Beginning at what must be the vernal equinox, the sun rises, it is said, in the fourth of the six eastern portals. It comes forth through that portal thirty mornings in succession, during which time the day grows daily longer and the night nightly shorter. Moving into the fifth portal, the sun rises for thirty mornings; moving on into the sixth portal, it rises for thirty-one mornings. The relative lengths of day and night continue to change, and by this time the day reaches its maximum duration and the night its minimum, in other words it is the summer solstice. Then "the sun mounts up to make the day shorter and the night longer" (v. 15), and after thirty, thirty, and thirty-one mornings the day and night are of equal length, in other words the autumnal equinox is reached. The corresponding sequence is followed on through the second half of the year until at last again day and night are of equal length and the cycle has been completed at the vernal equinox. So, it is concluded, "the year is exactly as to its days three hundred and sixty-four" (v. 32).

This certainly appears to be the same calendar as in Jubilees, and is of special importance because it answers a question on which specific information was not provided in Jubilees, namely which month in each series of three months has the added day to make it thirty-one days in length. Here we learn that in each group of three months their respective lengths are thirty days, thirty days, and thirty-one days.

We may, accordingly, outline a series of three months in the calendar of Jubilees and I Enoch as follows:[4]

I.IV.VII.X.	II.V.VIII.XI.	III.VI.IX.XII.	
1 8 15 22 29	6 13 20 27	4 11 18 25	Wednesday
2 9 16 23 30	7 14 21 28	5 12 19 26	Thursday
3 10 17 24	1 8 15 22 29	6 13 20 27	Friday
4 11 18 25	2 9 16 23 30	7 14 21 28	Saturday
5 12 19 26	3 10 17 24	1 8 15 22 29	Sunday
6 13 20 27	4 11 18 25	2 9 16 23 30	Monday
7 14 21 28	5 12 19 26	3 10 17 24 31	Tuesday

[4] A. Jaubert in vt 7 (1957), p.35.

Since thirteen weeks are thus filled out exactly, it is evident that this same tabulation can represent not only the first three-month period of the year but also the second, third, and fourth groups of months as well. In other words, the first month is identical with the fourth, seventh, and tenth months; the second month is identical with the fifth, eighth, and eleventh months; and the third month is identical with the sixth, ninth, and twelfth months. Thus the one tabulation suffices to represent the entire year.

From I Enoch we also learn that the calendar year must have been considered as beginning at the vernal equinox, since the description there starts at the point where the days are first beginning to grow longer than the nights.

It is also necessary to ask on what day of the week the calendar begins. A clue is found in *The Chronology of Ancient Nations* by the Muslim author al-Biruni (A.D. 973-1048). As a source concerning Jewish sects al-Biruni uses the Kitab al-Maqalat, a manual of the history of religions written by Abu 'Isa al-Warraq in the ninth century. In this work this author speaks, says al-Biruni, "of a Jewish sect called the Maghribis, who maintain that the feasts are not legal unless the moon rises in Palestine as a full moon in the night of Wednesday, which follows after the day of Tuesday, at the time of sunset. Such is their New Year's Day. From this point the days and months are counted, and here begins the rotation of the annual festivals. For God created the two great lights on a Wednesday. Likewise they do not allow Passover to fall on any other day except on Wednesday. And the obligations and rites prescribed for Passover they do not hold to be necessary, except for those who dwell in the country of the Israelites. All this stands in opposition to the custom of the majority of the Jews, and to the prescriptions of the Torah."[5]

The Maghribis were a "cave sect," and there is reason to believe that they may have been the Qumran group or others connected with them.[6] Since it is stated that Wednesday is their New Year's Day, the calendar should probably begin with that day, and the days of the week should fall as shown in the tabulation above. The theological reason given for this beginning point is that on a Wednesday God created the two great lights. This is an obvious reference to Genesis 1:14-19 where God made the sun, moon, and stars on the

[5] *The Chronology of Ancient Nations*, ed. C. Edward Sachau. 1879, p.278.
[6] R. de Vaux in RB 57 (1950), pp.422f.; Rowley, *The Zadokite Fragments and the Dead Sea Scrolls*, pp.23f.; cf. Ernst Bammel in ZNW 49 (1958), pp.77-88.

"fourth day," and ordained that these "lights in the firmament" should be "for signs and for seasons and for days and years." It is evident that though the year begins with Wednesday, as far as numbering the days of the week is concerned Wednesday is still the fourth day, Saturday or the sabbath is the seventh, and so on. That the beginning of the year is also marked by the rise of the full moon can hardly be taken as anything other than an ideal statement, since even if in a given year Wednesday was full moon day it would not be so regularly.

While in the calendar that is arranged as we have just indicated, the days of the week and the days of the month cannot possibly remain in a fixed relationship to the phases of the moon, it is plain that the days of the week do remain in a fixed relation with the days of the month. Therefore it is possible to identify the position of festivals or other dates in terms of both the day of the month and the day of the week. Thus if the passover sacrifice is slain on the fourteenth day of the first month (Exodus 12:6) and the fifteenth day is the first day of passover,[7] it is Tuesday which is the eve of passover and Wednesday which is the passover day, and this is the case in every year. This agrees with the date of passover as given in the calendar fragments from Qumran Cave 4, and the other festival dates as given there (see above p.297) are also in exact agreement with what may be ascertained in our present tabulation, falling regularly on Wednesday, Friday, and Sunday.

The fixed relationship of the days of the month with the days of the week is of course precisely what is not found in a calendar of lunar months. As we have stated, in the Babylonian lunisolar calendar the fourteenth day of the first month falls upon different days of the week in different years. The point at issue here was evidently of much importance to those who used the calendar of Jubilees. By the observance of this calendar, it was said, as we have seen, "they will not disturb its time from its days and from its feasts . . . and they will not leave out any day nor disturb any feasts." Together with this positive affirmation concerning its own calendar, the book of Jubilees speaks strongly of the harm that is done by the use of a different calendar (6:36f.):

"For there will be those who will assuredly make observations of the moon—how (it) disturbs the seasons and comes in from year to year ten days too soon. For this reason the years will come upon them when they

[7] JE III, p.505.

will disturb (the order), and make an abominable (day) the day of testimony, and an unclean day a feast day, and they will confound all the
days, the holy with the unclean, and the unclean day with the holy; for
they will go wrong as to the months and sabbaths and feasts and jubilees."

That the calendar to which Jubilees objects is a lunar calendar is
shown by the statement that it is based upon "observations of the
moon," and also that it makes the year come in annually "ten days
too soon." According to Jubilees, "three hundred and sixty-four days
. . . constitute a complete year"; in the Babylonian calendar, twelve
lunar months of alternately twenty-nine and thirty days each make a
year of three hundred and fifty-four days.

If Jubilees objects to lunar reckoning, its own system is presumably
essentially solar. That this is indeed its basis is made explicit by the
mention of "the rule of the sun" in Jubilees 4:21, and the fuller
statement in Jubilees 2:9: "And God appointed the sun to be a great
sign on the earth for days and for sabbaths and for months and for
feasts and for years and for sabbaths of years and for jubilees and for
all seasons of the years." As a solar calendar, then, it evidently began
the year with the vernal equinox, and it divided the year into four
solar periods, twelve solar months, fifty-two weeks, and three hundred and sixty-four days as has already been outlined.

While the calendar is thus based upon the solar year and actually
corresponds with it quite closely and subdivides it quite symmetri-
cally, its total of three hundred and sixty-four days is still actually
about one and one-quarter days short of the true solar year of about
365¼ days. With the passage of time this annual shortage would have
accumulated into an obvious discrepancy with the seasons and would
have required rectification. How the rectification was accomplished
is not indicated in the sources with which we have just been dealing,
but there is a possible clue in the Pirqe de Rabbi Eliezer where it
is stated: "The great cycle of the sun is 28 years."[8] In twenty-eight
years an annual shortage of one and one-quarter days would amount
to thirty-five days. Thus if there were some system for intercalating
five weeks in each 28-year cycle, the calendar would be kept in ad-
justment. Since a nineteen-year cycle of intercalation was derived
from the Babylonian calendar, this 28-year cycle must have had some

[8] vi; ed. Friedlander, p.34. This work, already cited above (p.559), treats of the
creation and at this point has reached the fourth day (vi-viii), therefore discusses
the course of the planets, the sun, and the moon.

other origin and it would at any rate have fitted perfectly with the calendar of Jubilees.[9]

The calendar of Jubilees seems, therefore, to have been the calendar of the Qumran community. The community was willing to use the Babylonian calendar for matters of everyday life, but for dating the all-important festivals of the religious year it adhered to this other calendar which did "not leave out any day nor disturb any feasts." The Babylonian calendar was no doubt in general and official use at this time, but the community of the covenant evidently did not feel that it did justice to the requirements of the religious year. The calendar to which the community adhered was presumably, therefore, an older one which was believed to be connected with the proper arrangement of the festivals from some authoritative antiquity. Since this was a solar calendar, in distinction from the lunisolar Babylonian calendar, and since, as we have seen reason to believe, the ancient Israelite calendar developed in a solar form, it seems likely that the community believed itself to be maintaining the traditions of an immemorial past.

In the poem on times and seasons in the Manual of Discipline, we found (pp. 294f.) the acrostic Aleph, Mem, Nun, forming the word Amen. The numerical values of these letters of the Hebrew alphabet are 1, 40, and 50, making a total of 91,[10] exactly the number of days in each of the four divisions of the calendar. Thus, to the initiated ear, the liturgical response of the community in its prayers was a solemn affirmation of the divine wisdom so marvelously shown forth in the stately movement of the sun through the four 91-day seasons of the solar year, a movement which set the splendid pattern within which the divine Being was rightly to be worshiped.

[9] For the calendar of Jubilees see Julian Morgenstern in VT 5 (1955), pp.34-76; A. Jaubert in VT 3 (1953), pp.250-264; 7 (1957), pp.35-61; Joseph M. Baumgarten in JBL 77 (1958), pp.355-360. For other suggestions as to the method of intercalation in the calendar of Jubilees see E. R. Leach in VT 7 (1957), pp.392-397.

[10] The numerical values of the letters of the Hebrew alphabet are: Aleph א, 1; Beth (ב), 2; Gimel (ג), 3; Daleth (ד), 4; He (ה), 5; Waw (ו), 6; Zayin (ז), 7; Heth (ח), 8; Teth (ט), 9; Yodh (י), 10; Kaph (כ), 20; Lamedh (ל), 30; Mem (מ), 40; Nun (נ), 50; Samekh (ס), 60; Ayin (ע), 70; Pe (פ), 80; Tsadhe (צ), 90; Qoph (ק), 100; Resh (ר), 200; S(h)in (ש), 300; Taw (ת), 400. For this interpretation of the acrostic see D. Barthélemy in RB 59 (1952), p.200.

7. PROBLEMS OF BIBLICAL CHRONOLOGY

THE application of the calendrical principles worked out above to the solution of problems in biblical chronology is not always easy. It is at once evident that one question that arises in the interpretation of biblical dates is when the year was considered as beginning. In the early Israelite calendar, as we have seen, the year began in the autumn, while in the Babylonian calendar it began in the spring. From the tractate Rosh Hashana[1] we learn that a year beginning in the fall and specifically on the first of Tishri, the seventh month, continued in use for a long time, and also a year beginning in the spring and specifically on the first of Nisan, the first month. "On the first of Tishri is New Year for years, for release and jubilee years, for plantation and for vegetables," it is stated; and, "On the first of Nisan is New Year for kings and for festivals."

But in Bible dates it is not always easy to determine which manner of reckoning is used. Thus from I Kings 6:1, 37, 38 Edwin R. Thiele[2] deduces that the regnal year in the time of Solomon was counted from the first of Tishri in the fall, although the year beginning the first of Nisan was used for reckoning ordinary and ecclesiastical dates; but Julian Morgenstern finds that the same passages indicate a regnal year beginning with Nisan.[3] Again, when Nehemiah 1:1 and 2:1 refer to the month Kislev and the following Nisan, both in the twentieth year of Artaxerxes, Morgenstern[4] thinks Nehemiah was using a year beginning in Tishri, but Hayim Tadmor[5] suggests that Nehemiah simply carried over "the twentieth year" by mistake when the month of Nisan was actually the beginning of the twenty-first year or, alternatively, that the text should read "the twenty-fifth year" as in Josephus,[6] although the latter mistakenly changes the ruler to Xerxes. Thiele[7] thinks that the regnal year was counted from Tishri in Judah but from Nisan in Northern Israel; moreover that while the books of Kings and Jeremiah use a regnal year beginning in Tishri for the kings of Judah, in references to Babylonian or Persian kings the writers of Kings, Jeremiah, Haggai, and Zechariah use a year reckoned from Nisan, as Ezekiel also does in giving the years of the captivity of Jehoiachin; but W. F. Albright[8] finds this

---

[1] I, 1; DM p.188; 2a; SBT p.1.   [2] TMN p.31.
[3] *Occident and Orient, Gaster Anniversary Volume*, p.446.
[4] *op.cit.*, p.441.   [5] In JNES 15 (1956), p.227 n.10.   [6] *Ant.*, XI, v, 7.
[7] TMN pp.32f., 157.   [8] In BASOR 100 (Dec. 1945), pp.17f.

system too elaborate. At all events, whether the year was reckoned from fall or spring, in referring to the months by number the Old Testament always counts from Nisan as the first month.[9]

Another question which arises is as to when the regnal year of a king was considered to begin. The system which prevailed in Babylonia, Assyria, and Persia was that the balance of the calendar year in which a king came to the throne was counted as his accession year, and the first full year of his reign was reckoned as beginning with the next New Year's day. Thus, for example (cf. above p.208), Shalmaneser V died in the tenth month, Tebetu, of his fifth year of reign, and on the twelfth day of the same month, about the last of December, 722 B.C., his successor, Sargon II, ascended the throne. This calendar year was accordingly both the last year of Shalmaneser and the accession year of Sargon. Only with the following Nisan 1 did the first full regnal year of the new king begin. An event dated in the first year of Sargon II would fall, therefore, in 721 B.C. Since the year began in the spring rather than on our January 1, this date would be more precisely indicated as Nisan 721 to Nisan 720, or as 721/720 B.C.

In the alternative nonaccession-year system the year in which the king comes to the throne is counted as his first year of reign. If the reign of Sargon II were referred to according to this system, his first year of reign would be 722/721.

Again in the interpretation of biblical dates it is important to determine if possible which system is followed. Thiele[10] thinks that the kings of Judah followed the accession-year system from Rehoboam to Jehoshaphat, the nonaccession-year system from Jehoram to Joash, and the accession-year system again from Amaziah to Zedekiah; and that the kings of Israel followed the nonaccession-year system from Jeroboam I to Jehoahaz, and the accession-year system from Jehoash to Hoshea. If this is correct, then in the later period of the two monarchies both were using the accession-year system, and at the same time the biblical writers would presumably have used the accession-year system in their references to Babylonian or Persian kings.

Now for concrete illustration of the attempt to apply these principles to the establishment of Old Testament dates we may turn to the closing period in the history of the kingdom of Judah, the rele-

[9] TMN p.31.   [10] TMN pp.157, 281f.

vant archeological materials for which have already been presented in the chapter on Egypt (pp.129ff.) and the section on New Babylonia (pp.220ff.). There it was established from the Babylonian chronicle that the crucial battle of Carchemish took place approximately in Simanu (May/June), 605 B.C. The contemporary prophet Jeremiah equates the date of the battle of Carchemish with the fourth year of King Jehoiakim of Judah (Jeremiah 46:2).[11] We dated the death of Josiah at Megiddo shortly before Duzu (June /July), 609 B.C. The three months of reign of his successor, Jehoahaz (II Kings 23:31), were therefore Tammuz (Babylonian Duzu), Ab (July/August), and Elul (August/September). The accession of the next king, Jehoiakim, was then in Tishri (September/October), 609 B.C. Assuming the accession-year system and a regnal year beginning with Nisan, the first full year of Jehoiakim's reign began on Nisan 1, 608, and his fourth year began on Nisan 1, 605. Since the battle of Carchemish took place in the following summer, this is in agreement with the correlation attested by Jeremiah.[12]

According to II Kings 23:36 and II Chronicles 36:5 Jehoiakim reigned eleven years. If his fourth regnal year was 605/604 B.C., his eleventh year was 598/597.

From the Babylonian chronicle we have learned that it was in his seventh year (598/597 B.C.) and in the month Kislimu that Nebuchadnezzar marched to the Hatti-land and besieged Jerusalem, and that it was on the second day of Addaru, March 16, 597 B.C., that he seized the city.

The reign of Jehoiachin was three months in length (II Kings 24:8) or, more exactly, three months and ten days (II Chronicles 36:9). If it was counted as extending to the day of the fall of the city, Addaru 2, 597 B.C., three months and ten days before that was the twenty-second day of Arahsamnu, December 9, 598 B.C.[13] It will be noted below that Jehoiachin may not actually have been carried away from Jerusalem into exile until a few weeks after the capture of the city, perhaps on the tenth day of the following Nisan, April 22, 597. If his reign was counted as extending to that point, three

---

[11] cf. Josephus, *Ant.* x, vi, 1. In Jeremiah 25:1, according to the usual translation, the fourth year of Jehoiakim is equated with the first year of Nebuchadnezzar, but the Hebrew phrase used here is unique in the Old Testament and may perhaps be held to designate or at least include the accession year.

[12] Hayim Tadmor in JNES 15 (1956), pp.226f.; Edwin R. Thiele in BASOR 143 (Oct. 1956), p.24.

[13] WCCK p.33 equates the twenty-second of Arahsamnu with December 6/7.

months and ten days before would have been the first day of Tebeth, January 16, 597 B.C. It was in the immediately preceding month, Kislimu, that Nebuchadnezzar marched to the Hatti-land and besieged Jerusalem, hence the change in rulers must have come very close to the time of the inauguration of the siege. II Kings 24:8, 10 may even give the impression that Jehoiachin had already come to the throne at the time the siege was started, and Jeremiah 22:18f.; 36:30 may be interpreted as suggesting that Jehoiakim was killed in a court uprising which might have had the purpose of replacing him with the presumably more pro-Babylonian Jehoiachin in a last-minute effort to avert the attack of Nebuchadnezzar;[14] but II Chronicles 36:6 says that Nebuchadnezzar put Jehoiakim in fetters, and Josephus[15] states that it was the Babylonian king who killed him and ordered him cast out unburied before the walls.

Jeremiah 52:28-30 gives the number of people carried away captive by Nebuchadrezzar on three different occasions. The first item is: "in the seventh year, three thousand and twenty-three Jews." Josephus doubtless follows this source when he says[16] that Nebuchadnezzar carried three thousand captives to Babylon. Since Jeremiah here specifies the seventh year of Nebuchadnezzar this seems to be in agreement with the Babylonian chronicle which says that Nebuchadnezzar marched to the Hatti-land and took Jerusalem in his seventh year.

In II Kings 24:12-16, however, it is stated that it was in the eighth year of the king of Babylon that Jehoiachin was taken prisoner and he and "all Jerusalem" carried away to Babylon. Also the total number of those deported is given as ten thousand. The apparent discrepancy may doubtless be explained most simply by supposing that Jeremiah 52:28 is using the Babylonian system in counting the years of Nebuchadnezzar's reign, hence states the date exactly as the Babylonian chronicle does; but that II Kings 24:12 uses the nonaccession-year system, hence calls this Nebuchadnezzar's eighth year; or that II Kings 24:12 uses a year beginning with the preceding Tishri, hence by such reckoning this was already the eighth year. The fact that Jeremiah 52:28-30 is omitted in the LXX might be explained in line with this interpretation as due to the fact that the Babylonian system of dating was not understood in the West.

[14] W. F. Albright in JBL 51 (1932), p.91.
[15] *Ant.* x, vi, 3.
[16] *Ant.* x, vi, 3.

It must be noted on the other hand that the date of the capture of Jerusalem on the second day of Addaru in the seventh year of Nebuchadnezzar means that the city was taken within the very last month of that regnal year of the Babylonian king, and that with the first day of the ensuing month Nisan his eighth year began. If II Kings 24:14 is correct that the total number of persons selected for deportation was ten thousand, and if much booty was taken and prepared for transport, even to the cutting in pieces of the vessels of gold in the temple as II Kings 24:13 states, then it may readily be supposed that the assembling of the captives and goods took several weeks and that the final caravan did not depart until Nebuchadnezzar's eighth year had begun. If some three thousand captives[17] were taken off before the end of Addaru and the balance only after the beginning of Nisan, then both the seventh and the eighth years of Nebuchadnezzar were involved and both Jeremiah and II Kings could be using the accession-year system of reckoning.

That the final deportation took place as a new year was beginning is probably confirmed by II Chronicles 36:10 which gives the time as "in the spring of the year" according to the translation of the Revised Standard Version, but more literally "at the return of the year" (ASV) or "at the turn of the year," which must signify the month Nisan. Likewise Ezekiel 40:1 speaks of what seems to be an exact anniversary ("that very day") of the inauguration of the exile and dates it "at the beginning of the year, on the tenth day of the month." This must mean the tenth day of Nisan, and would date the final deportation on April 22, 597 B.C., a little more than a month after the fall of the city on March 16.

Upon the capture and deportation of Jehoiachin, Zedekiah was put on the throne at Jerusalem (II Kings 24:17; II Chronicles 36:10), and was king there when the city was taken for the second and last time by Nebuchadnezzar. Jeremiah 52:29 states that "in the eighteenth year of Nebuchadrezzar he carried away captive from Jerusalem eight hundred and thirty-two persons." II Kings 25:8 and Jeremiah 52:12 specify the seventh and tenth days of the fifth month in the nineteenth year of King Nebuchadnezzar for the final destruction of Jerusalem.

[17] Since the 3,023 persons are called "Jews" in Jeremiah 52:28 while the deportees mentioned in the next verse are specifically said to have been "from Jerusalem," it has even been suggested (A. Malamat in IEJ 6 [1956], p.253) that the first group were people captured in other towns of Judea and deported forthwith while the siege of Jerusalem was still in progress.

As previously we had given the seventh and the eighth years, so here we have the eighteenth and the nineteenth. Again the simplest explanation is probably that Jeremiah 52:29 uses the Babylonian system, but II Kings 25:8 and Jeremiah 52:12 use either a nonaccession-year system or a year beginning in Tishri, hence designate as the nineteenth year what in the Babylonian system is the eighteenth. The eighteenth year of Nebuchadnezzar was 587/586 B.C., and the seventh and tenth days of the fifth month were August 26 and August 29, 587 B.C.

There is, however, once more another possibility to be considered. The number of 832 persons taken captive from Jerusalem seems very small to represent the final fall of that city, particularly when it is remembered, for example, that Sargon claims 27,290 captives in the capture of Samaria,[18] hence Jeremiah 52:29 may simply record a preliminary deportation of a group of captives apprehended while the siege of Jerusalem was still in progress. II Kings 25:8 and Jeremiah 52:12 might then also use the Babylonian system of reckoning, and in this case the seventh and tenth days of the fifth month in the nineteenth year of Nebuchadnezzar would mean August 15 and 18, 586 B.C.

The fall of Jerusalem is also dated in terms of the reign of Zedekiah. In the ninth year of his reign, in the tenth month, on the tenth day of the month, the siege began (II Kings 25:1).[19] In the tenth year of Zedekiah which was the eighteenth year of Nebuchadrezzar, the siege was in progress and Jeremiah was in custody (Jeremiah 32:1).[20] In the eleventh year of Zedekiah, in the fourth month, on the ninth day, the walls of the city were breached (II Kings 25:2-4; Jeremiah 39:2). In the fifth month, on the seventh or the tenth day, which was in the nineteenth year of Nebuchadnezzar, Nebuzaradan came and destroyed the city (II Kings 25:8; Jeremiah 52:12).

[18] See above p.209 and cf. Thiele in BASOR 143 (Oct. 1956), p.25. The 745 persons carried captive in the twenty-third year of Nebuchadrezzar (582/581), according to Jeremiah 52:30, must have been prisoners taken in some minor uprising subsequent to the fall of Jerusalem, such as the revolt in which Gedaliah was slain (II Kings 25:25). Since this figure is nearly as large as the figure of 832 persons it supports the idea that that number also represented only a minor group and not the total number of prisoners upon the final fall of the capital of Judah.

[19] Jeremiah 39:1 gives the same date lacking the specification of the day.

[20] Since Jeremiah 37:4f. states that the threat of the army of Egypt which caused the Babylonians to lift the siege of Jerusalem temporarily came before Jeremiah was put in prison, that event (cf. above p.131) may have taken place at the end of the ninth or in the early part of the tenth year of Zedekiah.

If the dates in the reign of Zedekiah are stated in terms of the Babylonian system, and his eleventh year coincided with the nineteenth year of Nebuchadnezzar (586/585 B.C.), then his first year would have been the ninth year of Nebuchadnezzar (596/595), and his accession year the eighth year of Nebuchadnezzar (597/596). According to a possible reckoning worked out above, it was in this year on the tenth day of Nisan, April 22, 597 B.C., that Jehoiachin was carried away into exile. Therefore it is quite possible that it was at this time that Zedekiah was installed and that this year, 597/596 B.C., was considered his accession year. On the supposition that 597/596 was the accession year of Zedekiah then his ninth year was 588/587 and the tenth day of the tenth month when the siege began was January 4, 587; his tenth year when Jeremiah was in prison was 587/586; and in his eleventh year (586/585) the ninth day of the fourth month when the walls were breached was July 19, 586, while the seventh and tenth days of the fifth month when the city was finally destroyed were August 15 and 18, 586.

If the second fall of Jerusalem was in the eighteenth year of Nebuchadnezzar rather than the nineteenth, that is in 587 instead of 586, then the accession of Zedekiah could be presumed to have been counted as taking place in 598/597, the seventh year of Nebuchadnezzar, when at almost the end of the year the city and Jehoiachin fell into the hands of the Babylonian king. In this case Zedekiah's ninth year was 589/588 and the siege began on January 15, 588; his tenth year was 588/587; and his eleventh year was 587/586, the walls being breached on July 29, 587, and the destruction coming on August 26 and 29, 587. In this case, however, the tenth and eleventh years of Zedekiah would not correspond with the eighteenth and nineteenth years of Nebuchadnezzar, hence this system seems less likely.

According to II Kings 25:27 Jehoiachin was brought up out of his prison in Babylon in the thirty-seventh year of his exile, the twelfth month, and the twenty-seventh day, which was in the year that Evil-merodach began to reign. Jeremiah 52:31 gives the same date except that the twenty-fifth day of the month is specified, and also says that this was the year that Evil-merodach became king. Evil-merodach is the Babylonian king Amel-Marduk who acceded to the throne in succession to Nebuchadnezzar in 562/561 B.C. If the accession year of Amel-Marduk was the thirty-seventh year of Jehoiachin's exile, the first year of that exile was 598/597, the year in which on the second day of Addaru, March 16, 597 B.C., Jerusalem was captured. It is possible and even probable, however, that the words in II Kings 25:27 and Jeremiah 52:31 concerning Evil-merodach should be translated "in the first year of his reign" (Moffatt Translation).[21] Amel-Marduk's first full year of reign was 561/560, and counting back thirty-seven years from this Jehoiachin's first year of exile would have been 597/596. This would correspond with his going into captivity on the tenth day of Nisan, April 22, 597 B.C., as we have seen reason to believe was the case.

Ezekiel 1:2 refers to the fifth year of the exile of King Jehoiachin, and there follows in the same book a series of dates (8:1; 20:1; 24:1; 26:1; 29:1, 17; 30:21; 31:1; 32:1, 17; 33:21; 40:1) which are evidently stated likewise in terms of the years of Jehoiachin's exile. It must have been a number of months before Jehoiachin actually arrived in Babylon on the long journey from Jerusalem, even as later it took Ezra a full four months to make the reverse trip from Babylon to Jerusalem (Ezra 7:9). Writing from the point of view of Babylon, therefore, it may well be that Ezekiel considered the balance of 597/596 as what we might call the "inception year" of the exile, just as the same year was the accession year of Zedekiah in Jerusalem, and if this was the basis of reckoning then the first full year of Jehoiachin's exile was 596/595, even as it was the first full regnal year of Zedekiah. Such a basis of reckoning seems required by Ezekiel 24:1 where the beginning of the final siege of Jerusalem is dated, presumably with reference to the years of the exile, in the ninth year, tenth month, and tenth day, exactly as in II Kings 25:1 (cf. Jeremiah 39:1) the same event is dated in the ninth year, tenth month, and tenth day of the reign of Zedekiah (January 4, 587 B.C.). If Ezekiel had also given the date of the fall of the city it would then presumably have been the same as that in II Kings 25:8 and Jeremiah 52:12, the seventh-tenth day of the fifth month of the eleventh year, probably August 15-18, 586 B.C. What Ezekiel does give is the date (33: 21) when a fugitive from Jerusalem reached Babylon with the first news that the city had fallen. This was on the fifth day of the tenth month in what is given as the twelfth year in the usual text, but as the eleventh year in a number of Hebrew, Greek, and Syriac manu-

---

[21] cf. W. F. Albright in JBL 51 (1932), pp.101f.

scripts.[22] Accepting the latter reading, this date in the eleventh year was January 8, 585, which allows the fugitive slightly less than five months to come from Jerusalem to Babylon, a reasonable length of time compared with the journey of Ezra noted above.

Ezekiel 40:1 speaks of an exact anniversary ("that very day") of the inauguration of the exile on the tenth day of the month at the beginning of the year, that is Nisan 10. This anniversary was in the twenty-fifth year of the exile, that is 572/571. This was also, it is stated, the fourteenth year after the city was conquered. If the city was conquered in the year 586/585, the fourteenth year *after* that was 572/571.

Turning to the New Testament we may note the problem of the date of the Last Supper of Jesus with his disciples. According to the Synoptic Gospels Jesus ate the passover with his disciples before he died (Mark 14:12 = Matthew 26:17 = Luke 22:8f.). According to the Fourth Gospel the crucifixion itself took place on the day of Preparation, that is the day on which the lambs were slain in preparation for the passover meal which followed that night; and this day was itself immediately prior to the sabbath, a sabbath which was a "high day," no doubt meaning that it was at the same time the first day of passover (John 19:31). The representation in the Fourth Gospel is supported by I Corinthians 5:7, "Christ, our paschal lamb has been sacrificed"; and by the tractate Sanhedrin, "On the eve of Passover Yeshu was hanged."[23]

One suggestion for reconciliation of the difference between the Synoptic and the Johannine accounts is based upon the calendar with which we have become acquainted at Qumran. If by any chance Jesus and the disciples had had reason to follow this calendar they would have eaten their passover already on the preceding Tuesday evening, for by that calendar that was the appointed time for it and Wednesday was the first day of passover in this year as in every year. While the Gospel records are usually held to place the Last Supper on Thursday evening and the crucifixion immediately thereafter on Friday, it may be that all the events of the taking into custody of Jesus and the holding of his trials before Jewish and Roman authorities would fit better within the longer period from Tuesday evening until Fri-

[22] Rudolf Kittel, ed., *Biblia Hebraica*, 1937, p.866 n.21a. Herbert G. May in IB 6, p.247; Albright in JBL 51 (1932), p.96; Julius A. Bewer in ZAW 54 (1936), p.114.
[23] 43a. GBT VII, p.181; SBT p.281.

day. Interestingly enough, in the early Christian work known as the Didascalia[24] the apostles are quoted as saying that it was on Tuesday evening that they ate the passover with Jesus, and on Wednesday that he was taken captive and held in custody in the house of Caiaphas.[25]

Another suggestion is that Jesus and the disciples, perhaps in conformity with Galilean usage, followed the ancient practice of reckoning the day from morning to morning rather than from evening to evening (cf. above p.553) and that this could account for their eating their passover one day earlier than official Judaism, that is on Thursday evening rather than on Friday evening.[26]

Again it always remains possible that it was simply by deliberate choice and in view of the ominous developments of those days that Jesus moved his observance of the passover ahead one day.[27]

Whether it was on account of calendrical variations or individual choice, it seems likely that the Last Supper was a passover meal held ahead of the official observance and that, as John represents, Jesus died on the day when the passover lambs were slain. According to Jewish law (Exodus 12:6) this date was Nisan 14; according to the sequence of days in the Gospels it was a Friday. According to the Babylonian calendar, in A.D. 30 Nisan 1 fell on March 25 and Nisan 14 came on April 7, a Friday. Again in A.D. 33, supposing only that the Jews did not intercalate a Second Adar at the end of the preceding year (as was probably done in Babylonia), Nisan 1 fell on March 21 and Nisan 14 on April 3, a Friday.[28]

[24] The Didascalia is preserved in Syriac but was probably written originally in Greek, perhaps in the third or second century B.C.; it is now incorporated as the first six books in the *Apostolical Constitutions,* a work of the fourth or fifth century (CAP I, p.613). It is edited by F. X. Funk, *Didascalia et Constitutiones Apostolorum.* 2 vols. 1905.

[25] *Didascalia.* XXI = v, 4-6; ed. Funk. I, p.272. See A. Jaubert in RHR 146 (1954), pp.140-173; and *La date de la cene.* 1957; cf. E. Vogt in *Biblica.* 39 (1958), pp.72-77; BML p.83; James A. Walther in JBL 77 (1958), pp.116-122.

[26] Morgenstern in VT 5 (1955), p.64 n.2. cf. Sherman E. Johnson in IB 7, p.572; and *Jesus in His Homeland,* p.19.

[27] Official practice was to sacrifice the lambs in the temple, according to Deuteronomy 16:2,5-7, which Jesus and the disciples could hardly have done if they diverged from the official dating, and there is in fact no mention of the passover lamb in the Gospel accounts.

[28] PDBC p.46. See A. T. Olmstead in ATR 24 (1942), pp.1-26; *Jesus in the Light of History.* 1942, pp.279-281; T. J. Meek in JNES 2 (1943), pp.124f.; Carl H. Kraeling in ATR 24 (1942), pp.336f.; J. K. Fotheringham in JTS 35 (1934), pp.146-162; Ogg, *The Chronology of the Public Ministry of Jesus,* pp.276f.

In such chronological calculations as we have adduced in regard to both Old Testament and New Testament dates it is evident that the factors involved are complex, and therefore such results as we have indicated must be regarded as provisional. At least the discussion will have shown the sort of materials now available for the study of chronological problems, and it may be hoped that further discoveries will be made in the future which will cast further light upon the framework of days and years in which the biblical events are set.

Index of Scriptural References

General Index

All references are to pages, except where Figures, Maps, or Plans are specifically indicated.